ECONOMETRICS

ECONOMETRICS

Theory and Applications

SUKESH K. GHOSH

Professor of Economics
University of Waterloo, Ontario

Prentice Hall, Englewood Cliffs, New Jersey 07632

Library of Congress Cataloging-in-Publication Data

GHOSH, SUKESH K.,
Econometrics : theory and applications / Sukesh K. Ghosh.
p. cm.
Includes bibliographical references and index.
ISBN 0-13-223785-7
1. Econometrics. I. Title.
HB139.G48 1991
330'.01'5195—dc20 90-49024
CIP

Cover design: Patricia Kelly
Manufacturing buyer: Trudy Pisciotti/Bob Anderson

Printed in the United States of America

10 9 8 7 6 5 4 3 2 1

ISBN 0-13-223785-7

Prentice-Hall International (UK) Limited, *London*
Prentice-Hall of Australia Pty. Limited, *Sydney*
Prentice-Hall Canada Inc., *Toronto*
Prentice-Hall Hispanoamericana, S.A., *Mexico*
Prentice-Hall of India Private Limited, *New Delhi*
Prentice-Hall of Japan, Inc., *Tokyo*
Simon & Schuster Asia Pte. Ltd., *Singapore*
Editora Prentice-Hall do Brasil, Ltda., *Rio de Janeiro*

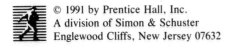

TO: Mā
SEJOMAMA
MAMIMA
NANDITA
MIMI ANANYA
SIDDIQER RAHAMAN

Contents

Preface *xvii*

1

Econometrics, Its Meaning, and the Objective of the Book *1*

1.1 INTRODUCTION *1*
1.1.1 The Meaning of Economics and Economic Models *1*
1.1.2 A Model *1*
1.1.3 A Simple Income Determination Model *2*
1.1.4 Criticism of the Model *3*
1.1.5 Baffling Problems Underlying Economic Model Formulation *4*
1.2 THE MEANING OF ECONOMETRICS *5*
1.2.1 An Example from the Micro Consumption Function *5*
1.3 OBJECTIVE OF THE BOOK *11*
1.4 CONCLUSION *13*

2

The Simple Linear Model in Two Variables and Its Extensions *14*

2.1 INTRODUCTION *14*
2.1.1 Assumptions about the Distribution of ϵs *17*

2.2 THE ORDINARY LEAST-SQUARES (OLS) TECHNIQUE *18*
2.3 THE GOODNESS OF FIT TEST *22*
2.3.1 Decomposition of the Total Sum of Squares *22*
2.3.2 The Coefficient of Correlation and the Coefficient of Multiple Determination *24*
2.4 TESTS OF SIGNIFICANCE OF REGRESSION COEFFICIENTS *26*
2.4.1 The Mean and Variance of OLS Estimates *26*
2.4.2 The Estimated Variance of the Error Variable *30*
2.4.3 The Estimated Standard Error of Estimate *31*
2.5 THE GAUSS–MARKOV THEOREM *32*
2.6 THE STUDENT *t* TEST AND STATISTICAL INFERENCE *33*
2.7 ANALYSIS OF VARIANCE *37*
2.8 PREDICTION *39*
2.9 AN APPLIED STUDY OF A TWO-VARIABLE REGRESSION *43*
2.10 AN EXTENSION TO THREE VARIABLES AND AN INTRODUCTION TO MULTIPLE REGRESSION *43*
2.11 AN APPLIED THREE-VARIABLE REGRESSION MODEL *49*
2.12 EXTENSION TO NONLINEAR RELATIONS AND TRANSFORMATIONS TO LINEARITY *49*
PROBLEMS *52*

3

Linear Algebra *59*

3.1 INTRODUCTION *59*
3.2 VECTORS AND MATRICES *60*
3.2.1 Matrix Operations *61*
3.2.2 Transposition and Trace of a Matrix *63*
3.2.3 Partitioned Matrices *65*
3.3 DETERMINANTS *68*
3.4 LINEAR DEPENDENCE (INDEPENDENCE) AND RANK OF A MATRIX *70*
3.5 SOLUTION OF SIMULTANEOUS HOMOGENEOUS EQUATIONS *71*
3.6 THE INVERSE AND ORTHOGONAL MATRICES *72*
3.7 SOLUTION OF SYSTEMS OF LINEAR EQUATIONS: CRAMER'S RULE *75*
3.8 LINEAR TRANSFORMATIONS, EIGENVECTORS, AND EIGENVALUES *76*
3.9 QUADRATIC FORMS AND DEFINITE MATRICES *79*
3.10 VECTOR AND MATRIX DERIVATIVES AND DETERMINATION OF EXTREMA *81*
3.11 UNCONSTRAINED AND CONSTRAINED EXTREMA *83*
3.12 SUGGESTED READING *86*
PROBLEMS *86*

4

Statistics *89*

4.1 INTRODUCTION *89*
4.2 FREQUENCY AND PROBABILITY DISTRIBUTION *90*
4.2.1 Bivariate Distribution *91*
4.3 SOME DESCRIPTIVE STATISTICS MEASURES OF FREQUENCY DISTRIBUTIONS *94*

4.4 RANDOM VARIABLES AND PROBABILITY DISTRIBUTIONS *97*

4.4.1 Probability Distributions of Functions of Random Variables *100*

4.5 THE EXPECTATION LOGIC *101*

4.6 SAMPLING METHODS, LIKELIHOOD FUNCTIONS, AND SAMPLING DISTRIBUTIONS *106*

4.6.1 Some Important Measures of Sampling Distributions *107*

4.6.2 Some Properties of the Sample Mean *107*

4.6.3 Some Properties of the Sample Variance *108*

4.7 NORMAL, x^2, F, AND t DISTRIBUTIONS *109*

4.7.1 Univariate Normal *109*

4.7.2 Multivariate Normal *111*

4.7.3 The Special Case of the Bivariate Normal *112*

4.7.4 The Marginal and Conditional Distributions *113*

4.7.5 Derivatives of the Normal Distribution *115*

4.8 DISTRIBUTION OF LINEAR AND QUADRATIC FORMS *115*

4.9 ASYMPTOTIC THEORY *117*

4.10 THE CENTRAL LIMIT THEOREM AND CONVERGENCE IN DISTRIBUTION *120*

4.11 PROPERTIES OF ESTIMATORS *121*

4.11.1 Small Sample (or General) Properties *121*

4.11.2 Large Sample (or Asymptotic) Properties *122*

4.12 MAXIMUM LIKELIHOOD ESTIMATORS 123

4.12.1 Properties of Maximum Likelihood Estimators *124*

4.13 SUGGESTED READINGS *129*

PROBLEMS *129*

5

The Linear Model and Ordinary Least Squares (OLS) Method *134*

5.1 INTRODUCTION: AN APPLIED OLS PROBLEM ON INTERNATIONAL PRODUCTION DUE TO DOUGLAS (1948) *134*

5.2 THE GENERAL LINEAR MODEL *135*

5.3 ESTIMATION BY OLS *137*

5.4 STATISTICAL INFERENCE IN THE LINEAR MODEL *139*

5.4.1 Analysis of Variance and the F Test *140*

5.4.2 Goodness of Fit *142*

5.4.3 Tests of Hypotheses *143*

5.4.4 Problem 1 *145*

5.5 FORECASTING *147*

5.5.1 Forecasting the Mean Value of Future Observations on Y *147*

5.5.2 Forecasting One Single Future Observation on Y *148*

5.5.3 Forecasting Accuracy and Theil's U Coefficient *149*

5.6 FURTHER APPLIED STUDIES ON OLS *151*

5.6.1 The Henry Schultz Study on U.S. Agriculture (1938) *151*

5.6.2 Allen and Bowley Study on U. K. Engel's Curve (1935) *152*

5.6.3 The Feige (1964) Study on Demand for Liquid Assets *153*

5.6.4 Latane (1954) on Cash Demand *153*

5.6.5 Weiss (1974) on Industrial Organization *154*

PROBLEMS *154*

6

The General Linear Model and Some Problems *164*

6.1 MULTICOLLINEARITY (M/C) *164*
- 6.1.1 An Applied Study Due to Bordo and Choudhri (1982) *164*
- 6.1.2 The Effect of Imperfect M/C on Tests and Errors *165*
- 6.1.3 Detection of M/C—The Condition Number *166*
- 6.1.4 Remedy of M/C *168*
- 6.1.5 Ridge Regression *170*
- 6.1.6 Conditional Omitted Variable Estimator *171*

6.2 FUNCTIONAL FORMS AND EXTENSIONS OF LINEAR REGRESSION *174*
- 6.2.1 Cobb-Douglas Production Function *174*
- 6.2.2 Polynomial and Reciprocal Type Functions *175*
- 6.2.3 Demand for Money Function *177*
- 6.2.4 Exponential Functions and Log–Normal Errors *177*

6.3 CONSTRAINED LEAST SQUARES *179*
- 6.3.1 Structural Changes *181*

6.4 DUMMY VARIABLES *183*
- 6.4.1 The Comanor and Wilson (1971) Applied Study *183*
- 6.4.2 Theoretical Aspects of the Dummy Variable Method *184*
- 6.4.3 Qualitative Classification of Data *187*
- 6.4.4 An Applied Study Due to Auld, Christofides, Swidinsky and Wilton (1979) *189*
- 6.4.5 Two-Way Classification and Interaction *190*
- 6.4.6 A Further Applied Study: Horst (1972) on the Decision to Invest Abroad: Its Firm and Industry Determinants *191*
- 6.4.7 Variation of Dummy Variable Representation: The Spline Functions *193*

6.5 SPECIFICATION ERROR *196*
- 6.5.1 Its Origin *196*
- 6.5.2 Omitted Relevant Variables *197*
- 6.5.3 Some Irrelevant Variables Included *199*
- 6.5.4 An Applied Study: Bays' (1980) Hospital Cost Function *200*

PROBLEMS *200*

7

The Generalized Linear Regression Model *210*

7.1 CIRCUMSTANCES REQUIRING A REVIEW OF THE OLS ASSUMPTIONS: THE PHILLIPS CURVE AND OTHER APPLIED STUDIES *210*

7.2 THE HETEROSCEDASTIC ERROR STRUCTURE *212*
- 7.2.1 The Savings or Family Budget Studies *212*
- 7.2.2 Tests of Heteroscedasticity *213*
- 7.2.3 Application of a Heteroscedasticity Test: Ravencraft (1983) *214*

7.3 AUTOCORRELATED ERROR STRUCTURE *215*
- 7.3.1 Its Origin: Wage Negotiations of Labor Unions *215*
- 7.3.2 AR (1), AR (2), and AR (3) Processes *216*

7.3.3 MA (s) Process *217*
7.3.4 Relation Between AR and MA Processes *218*
7.3.5 Durbin-Watson Test of Autocorrelation *218*
7.3.6 Estimation with Autocorrelation: The Cochrane and Orcutt Method *224*
7.3.7 An Applied Study: Laumas and Spencer (1980) on Shifting Demand for Money *226*
7.3.8 Durbin's Two-Step Estimator, Klein's Nonlinear Method and Monte Carlo Results *226*
7.3.9 The Maximum Likelihood Method *227*
7.3.10 The Generalized Least Squares Estimation *229*
7.3.11 Zellner's SURE Method *230*
7.3.12 Further Empirical Illustrations *232*
7.3.13 The Autoregressive Conditional Heteroscedasticity (or ARCH) Process and Its Applications *236*

7.4 QUALITATIVE AND LIMITED DEPENDENT VARIABLES *238*
7.4.1 Linear Probability Rule *238*
7.4.2 Logit Analysis *239*
7.4.3 Probit Analysis *242*
7.4.4 Logit and Probit Analyses *243*
7.4.5 Multinomial Logit *244*
7.4.6 Multinomial Probit *245*
7.4.7 Limited Dependent Variables and the Tobit Method *246*
7.4.8 The Heckman Two-Step Estimator *247*
7.4.9 Empirical Studies Using Logit Analysis *248*
7.4.10 Empirical Study Using Linear Probability and Probit Model: The Maddala and Trost (1982) South Carolina Mortgage Loan Study *251*
7.4.11 Empirical Analysis Using Tobit Method *252*

PROBLEMS *254*

8

Stochastic Regression and Lag Models *261*

8.1 INTRODUCTION: LINEARIZING NONLINEAR SITUATIONS AND USING LARGE SAMPLE OR ASYMPTOTIC RESULTS *261*
8.2 PROBABILITY LIMITS AND SLUTSKY'S THEOREM *262*
8.3 X AND ϵ PROCESSES INDEPENDENT, AND CONSISTENCY OF OLS ESTIMATES *263*
8.4 X AND ϵ NOT INDEPENDENT AND THE INSTRUMENTAL VARIABLE (IV) METHOD *264*
8.5 ERRORS IN VARIABLES *265*
8.6 AN APPLIED STUDY DUE TO BERHMAN *267*
8.7 LAG MODELS *269*
8.7.1 Distributed Lags in an Independent Variable—Koyck's Model *270*
8.7.2 Lags in Dependent Variable—Partial Adjustment Model *272*
8.7.3 Estimation *273*
8.7.4 Applied Studies: Partial Adjustment and Expectation Models *278*
8.7.5 Almon Distributed Lags *280*
8.7.6 Applied Studies on Almon Lags *287*
8.7.7 Lagged Model Estimation Using Time Series Methods *289*
8.7.8 Analysis of Stationary Stochastic Processes *290*
8.7.9 Autoregressive Processes: ARMA and ARIMA Schemes and Their Estimation *291*
8.7.10 Prewhitening Mechanism *296*

8.7.11 Diagnostic Check on Normality of Residuals: The Box-Pierce Q Statistic Test *297*
8.7.12 Causality Analysis *298*
8.7.13 An Applied Study on Double Prewhitening and Causality: Frenkel (1977) on German Hyper-Inflation *300*
PROBLEMS *303*

9

Further Studies in Consumption, Production, and Investment Functions, and Other Studies *312*

9.1 INTRODUCTION *312*
9.2 CONSUMPTION FUNCTION *312*
9.3 RELATIVE INCOME, LIFE CYCLE, AND PERMANENT INCOME HYPOTHESES *313*
9.4 SYSTEMS OF DEMAND EQUATIONS *319*
9.4.1 The Linear Expenditure System: Engel's Curve *319*
9.4.2 The Goldberger and Gamaletsos (1970) Study *320*
9.5 EVIDENCE ON INTERTEMPORAL ELASTICITIES *321*
9.6 PRODUCTION FUNCTION *326*
9.7 NONCONSTANT RETURNS TO SCALE CES FUNCTION AND AN APPLICATION *328*
9.8 THE BURLEY (1973) STUDY ON AUSTRALIAN MANUFACTURING AND REINHARDT (1972) STUDY ON U.S. PHYSICIANS' SERVICES *328*
9.9 GENERALIZATIONS OF THE COBB-DOUGLAS AND CES FUNCTIONS: THE TRANSLOG FUNCTIONS *331*
9.9.1 The Translog Cost Function: An Application Due to Pindyck (1979) *333*
9.9.2 The CES–Translog Cost Function Due to Pollak and Others (1984) *337*
9.10 TECHNICAL PROGRESS: THE BECKMAN AND SATO (1969) STUDY *339*
9.11 INVESTMENT *344*
9.12 THE ACCELERATOR MODELS *345*
9.13 DISTRIBUTED LAG MODELS *346*
9.13.1 The Error Terms and Autocorrelated Residuals *347*
9.14 AN APPLICATION BY BEAN (1979) WITH PARAMETER CONSTRAINTS *348*
9.15 ADDITIONAL VARIABLES AND EXPLICIT OPTIMIZING RATIONALE FOR INVESTMENT *350*
9.16 OTHER INVESTMENT FUNCTIONS *351*
9.16.1 The Boatwright and Eaton (1972) Model of U.K. Investment *351*
9.16.2 The Jorgenson and Stephenson (1967) Model of U.S. Investment *353*
9.17 CONCLUSION *355*
9.18 MISCELLANEOUS APPLIED STUDIES *355*
9.18.1 Studies by Rosen (1974 and 1986) *355*
9.18.2 Studies by Griliches (1980, 1977, and 1986) *356*
9.18.3 Studies by Fama (1976) and Fama and Stewart (1977) *360*
9.18.4 Studies by Hausman (1979 and 1980) *361*
9.18.5 Study by Flavin (1981) *361*
9.18.6 Study by Levine and Mitchell (1988) *362*
9.18.7 Study by Wales and Woodland (1977) *362*
PROBLEMS *363*

10

Variation of Classical Themes and Other Approaches to Inference *365*

10.1 INTRODUCTION *365*
10.2 ECONOMETRIC TESTS: THE CASE OF THE NULL VERSUS ALTERNATIVE HYPOTHESES *366*
10.2.1 Some Basic Ideas *366*
10.2.2 Some Statistical Prerequisite *367*
10.3 THE WALD, LIKELIHOOD RATIO, AND LAGRANGE MULTIPLIER TESTS *368*
10.3.1 Some Examples *370*
10.4 SAMPLE SELECTIVITY BIAS *373*
10.5 A SIMPLE MODEL OF SELECTION BIAS *373*
10.5.1 The Heckman Estimator Assuming Normal Errors and Its Properties *375*
10.6 PROBLEMS ARISING FROM UNOBSERVABLE VARIABLES *377*
10.6.1 The Problem of Latent Variables *379*
10.6.2 Application of the MIMIC Model Due to Robins and West (1977) *382*
10.7 POOLED TIME SERIES AND CROSSSECTION DATA AND VARIABLE COEFFICIENT MODELS *383*
10.7.1 The Error Components Model *385*
10.7.2 A Fixed Effects Model Applied: Sadan and Tropp (1973) *389*
10.8 VARIABLE COEFFICIENT MODELS *392*
10.8.1 Switching Regimes *392*
10.8.2 Random Coefficient Models *394*
10.8.3 The Swamy Model *396*
10.8.4 An Application by Gordon and Hynes (1970) *399*
10.8.5 Another Application: Cooley and Prescott (1973) *400*
10.9 BAYESIAN INFERENCE *401*
10.10 BAYESIAN APPROACH TO A SIMPLE LINEAR REGRESSION MODEL *403*
PROBLEMS *406*

11

Simultaneous Equation Systems *410*

11.1 INTRODUCTION: THE SYSTEM'S SPECIAL FEATURES ILLUSTRATED FROM APPLIED STUDIES *410*
11.2 THE GENERAL SIMULTANEOUS EQUATION SYSTEM: ITS GENERAL FEATURES AND IDENTIFICATION *415*
11.3 STATISTICAL SPECIFICATIONS *416*
11.4 THE IDENTIFICATION PROBLEM *418*
11.4.1 General Linear Restrictions on Structural Parameters *419*
11.4.2 Further Specifications Helping Identifications *424*
11.5 ESTIMATION METHODS FOR SIMULTANEOUS EQUATIONS *425*
11.5.1 Indirect Least Squares *427*
11.5.2 Two-Stage Least Squares Method *430*

11.5.3 Equivalence of 2SLS and IV Estimates: Consistency of 2SLS Estimates *436*
11.5.4 Some Extensions: Nonlinearity in Variables; Number of Variables and Observations; Principal Components of Variables; Instrumental Variables and Economy-Wide Models *437*
11.5.5 Three Stage Least Squares Method *441*
11.5.6 Full Information Maximum Likelihood (FIML) Method *448*
11.5.7 Small Sample Properties of Estimators: Some Monte Carlo Experiment Results *451*
PROBLEMS *454*

12

Some Applied Macroeconometric Models and Models of Rational Expectations *462*

12.1 INTRODUCTION *462*
12.2 THE KLEIN AND GOLDBERGER (1955) MODEL *463*
12.3 THE WHARTON GROUP OF MODELS *464*
12.4 THE BROOKINGS QUARTERLY ECONOMETRIC MODEL OF THE UNITED STATES *466*
12.5 FEDERAL RESERVE BANK OF ST. LOUIS (FRB ST. LOUIS) MODEL *469*
12.5.1 Evaluation of the Model *469*
12.6 THE LIU AND HWA (1974) MONTHLY MODEL 470
12.6.1 Performance of the Model *471*
12.7 THE TORONTO ANNUAL CANADIAN ECONOMETRIC MODEL OR THE TRACE MODEL *472*
12.7.1 Notation and the Flow Chart of the Simplified Version *473*
12.7.2 Disaggregation *475*
12.7.3 Forecasts *476*
12.8 THE RDX2 MODEL OF THE CANADIAN ECONOMY *477*
12.8.1 Private Aggregate Demand *478*
12.8.2 Private Sector Employment and Wages, Prices, and Income Distribution *480*
12.8.3 Operations of the Government *481*
12.8.4 The Financial Sector *481*
12.8.5 International Capital Flows and Foreign Exchange Market *481*
12.8.6 Recent Revisions in the RDX2 Model *482*
12.9 POLICY APPRAISAL BY ECONOMETRIC MODELS *483*
12.10 THE LUCAS CRITIQUE OF ECONOMETRIC POLICY APPRAISAL *483*
12.11 RATIONAL EXPECTATIONS MODELS AND SOME ECONOMETRIC ISSUES AND IMPLICATIONS *485*
12.11.1 Expectations in Macroeconomics *485*
12.11.2 Rational Expectations *486*
12.12 RATIONAL EXPECTATIONS AND SOME ECONOMETRIC ISSUES *488*
12.13 DIRECT TESTS OF THE RATIONAL EXPECTATIONS HYPOTHESIS (REH) *488*
12.13.1 Equating Rationally Expected Variable Values to Their Actual Values *490*
12.13.2 Test of Restrictions Imposed by Rational Expectations *492*
12.14 AN APPLICATION à la BARRO (1977) *494*
12.15 STRUCTURAL NEUTRALITY *497*
12.16 OUTPUT AND INFLATION TRADE-OFFS OF LUCAS' (1973) AND BARRO'S (1977) EFFECT OF UNANTICIPATED MONETARY GROWTH ON REAL OUTPUT AND UNEMPLOYMENT *497*

12.17 POSTSCRIPTS ON LUCAS AND BARRO MODELS: THEIR FURTHER ASSESSMENT *498*
12.17.1 Measurement Error and Process Misspecification *499*
12.18 EXTENSIONS OF THE LUCAS AND BARRO TESTS *500*
PROBLEMS *502*

13

Some Special Problems: Disequilibrium Models, Model Selection, Specification Testing, and Unit Root Models 505

13.1 INTRODUCTION *505*
13.2 MODELS OF DISEQUILIBRIUM *506*
13.2.1 An Early Disequilibrium Model Due to Quandt *506*
13.2.2 The Fair and Jaffee Model *507*
13.2.3 The Fair and Jaffee Model and Crude Price Level Variation *507*
13.2.4 The Fair and Jaffee Model and Exact Price Level Variation *508*
13.3 TESTS OF EQUILIBRIUM *509*
13.4 MODEL SELECTION *510*
13.5 NESTED MODELS *510*
13.6 NONNESTED MODELS *512*
13.7 AN APPLIED STUDY DUE TO McALEER AND OTHERS (1982) *514*
13.8 MIZON AND RICHARD'S ENCOMPASSING PRINCIPLE *516*
13.9 CRITERIA USED IN THE GENERAL SELECTION OF THE REGRESSORS AND THE MODEL *517*
13.10 LEAMER'S POSTERIOR ODDS CRITERION AND THE CRITICAL F RATIO *520*
13.11 CROSS-VALIDATION AND PREDICTED AND STUDENTIZED RESIDUALS *522*
13.11.1 "Predicted Errors" and "Studentized Errors" *523*
13.12 MODEL WITH REGRESSORS INDEPENDENT OF ERRORS: HAUSMAN'S TEST *524*
13.13 THE UNIT ROOT MODELS *526*
13.13.1 The Deseasonalizing Mechanisms *526*
13.13.2 The Detrending Mechanisms *529*
13.14 THE STOCHASTIC TREND AND ITS ELIMINATION *530*
13.15 SOME ECONOMETRIC ISSUES WITH STOCHASTIC TRENDS AND THE UNIT ROOT INVESTIGATION *532*
13.15.1 Spurious Regressions *532*
13.15.2 The Cointegrated Vector *535*
13.15.3 The Cointegrated Vector and Error Correction Representation *536*
PROBLEMS *537*

Appendix A

Additional Methods and Results 544

A.1 THE PRAIS-WINSTON METHOD *544*
A.2 THE GAUSS-MARKOV THEOREM IN THE GENERALIZED MODEL *546*
A.3 MEAN VALUE OF THE VARIABLE IN THE TOBIT MODEL (OR, DERIVATION OF (7.120) OF CHAPTER 7) *547*

A.4 THE MARGINAL POSTERIOR PROBABILITY DENSITY FUNCTION FOR REGRESSION COEFFICIENTS IN THE SIMPLE REGRESSION MODEL (OR, DERIVATION OF EQUATION (10.171) OF CHAPTER 10) *548*
A.5 METHOD OF PRINCIPAL COMPONENTS *549*
A.6 THE MAXIMUM LIKELIHOOD ESTIMATION OF SIMULTANEOUS EQUATIONS WITH VECTOR AUTOREGRESSIVE RESIDUALS *553*

Appendix B

Statistical Tables *555*

Bibliography *569*

Index *595*

Preface

This book grew out of a desire, first, to motivate students into a study of econometrics and, then, to educate them in the subject, an approach that is rarely, if at all, found in existing textbooks. Evidence of this objective is clear in the introduction to almost every chapter of this book. An economic problem is discussed both for its substantive or theory content and for its implications for statistical estimation, two essential ingredients of a problem in applied econometrics. This sort of orientation of the problem should then motivate the students to learn more about econometric principles. After this, additional problems taken from diverse areas in applied econometrics (published up to the current year) are cited and discussed. The intention is to make students relatively knowledgeable about the applications end of the principles that they have just learned.

Until recently, textbooks were available only on econometric techniques or methods covering them with varying degrees of sophistication. Very recently, a limited tendency toward applications has been evident. Unfortunately, in some textbooks, methods have been kept separate from applications, creating a wedge between the two that, needless to say, creates an unnecessary hardship for students. Besides, methods have often been compromised to make room for the structural aspects of applied projects. In others, even though an attempt to integrate both is evident, some techniques are not shown as applied to real world problems. In other words, the proper balance between methods and real applications is lacking. Above all, in most of these books, the task of systematically motivating the reader seems strikingly absent.

This book is intended as a text for a one-year course in econometrics at the senior undergraduate and junior graduate levels. Its theoretical concern is with problems of estimating and testing socioeconomic relationships, arising both in single and simultaneous equations. Initially, assumptions of the classical type are used, which are subsequently relaxed to make them more realistic. Its applications are drawn from the conventional domains of consumption, production, and investment functions and in these and other respects they can be classified as problems of such diverse areas as industrial organization, labor, education, public finance, international trade, money, financial economics, etc. Of course, problem areas are chosen often at random and the degree of emphasis within and between areas is intended to be without a pattern, unless it would be otherwise due perhaps to the author's own biases. The consequential structure of the book should also make it worthwhile as a reference book for applied socioeconomic study and research.

As for prerequisites, some linear algebra and statistical concepts and results are necessary ingredients for an understanding of the methods portion of this book. A comprehensive review of these is included in two early chapters, one on matrix algebra and the other on statistics and probability. Students with some knowledge in these areas would do well to glean through them; others, less fortunate, should master them first before moving on to the more mundane matters of the text.

It must be mentioned that problems of limitations of space and prerequisites for the book do not allow us to dwell on the intricate mathematical and statistical aspects of some of the methods and/or applied studies. Often, when the theoretical arguments seem too complex, a verbal summary of the steps of the analysis is attempted and presented in either the text or footnotes depending on the level of abstraction. In applied studies, sometimes what is presented is no more than a very brief introduction to the structure of the study followed immediately by its major conclusions, skipping the data descriptions, their sources, and the concrete statistical results derived. This may have resulted in some unintended injustice to both these areas. But, on the positive side, a reader is informed and made sufficiently motivated to look for more details if necessary, from the references cited in those contexts.

It is a pleasure to acknowledge the debt owed to various people (without implicating them) in the preparation of this book. For my training in statistics, I am deeply indebted to especially Prof. A. Bhattacharyya of Presidency College, Calcutta and Prof. H. K. Nandi of the University of Calcutta, India, and, for my training in econometrics, I am similarly indebted to especially Prof. Arnold Zellner of the University of Chicago, U.S.A., and Prof. Arthur Goldberger of the University of Wisconsin-Madison, U.S.A. To somebody who knows, traces of their teachings must be noticeable throughout the book. He or she may also see traces of my bias in international economics as evident in a great number of applied examples drawn from this area, and that interest, I am happy to acknowledge, was largely enkindled by Prof. Robert Mundell of Columbia University, U.S.A.

Some of the questions of the end-of-chapter problem sets have been kindly provided by friends and colleagues: Arnold Zellner, Charles Beach, and Badi Baltagi. I am deeply indebted to them for their help. A few questions have been obtained from the Oxford University Press and the Royal Statistical Society. I thank them for permission to use them. The text and Appendix B contain extensive sets of econometric and statistical tables and I make grateful acknowledgment to their sources for permission to republish them.

My sincere thanks are due to many people who directly or indirectly helped in the preparation, editing, and improvement of this manuscript: Prof. John Kane of the State University of New York at Oswego, Prof. David Wilton, Benjamin Kwok, Fadl Naqib, and Glen Stirling of the University of Waterloo, Ontario, two sets of three anonymous reviewers, and some of my past students. While I am grateful to Prentice-Hall for the contract for this book generally, I would like to single out one of its members, Bill Webber, Executive Editor in economics, for special thanks for his apt counseling and encouragement at a time when I needed them most.

I am grateful to Ann Wendt, Karen Musselman, Paul Pilon, Sylvia Roberts, Chrysoula Hovis, and Sharon Pickering for their painstaking efforts in typing what is unquestionably difficult material. Last but not least, I acknowledge with thanks the modest publication assistance received under a General Research Grant from the Social Sciences and Humanities Research Council of Canada.

S. K. Ghosh

1

Econometrics, Its Meaning, and the Objective of the Book

1.1 INTRODUCTION

1.1.1 The Meaning of Economics and Economic Models

As an introduction to the meaning of the word econometrics, we should perhaps explain the meaning of the word economics. However, the principles of econometrics need not be related to or constrained by economics alone; they are of general relevance in the social sciences, to which economics belongs.

Simply stated, economics is what economists do about the economy. This consists of their efforts to understand it, to appreciate how it works, to make predictions about its future evolution, to make policy evaluations, and, above all, to test economic theories in terms of their relevance to the real world. But to do all this they should have a model. What is a model?

1.1.2 A Model

A model is a representation of an actual phenomenon such as that embodied in the real world. It seeks to strike a balance between reality and manageability, because the real world may be extremely complex, if not at times impossible, to model and solve under a given technological setting. A model may involve macro and/or micro considerations. Examples of macro considerations are the national income, the employment level, and the general price level of the United States; an example of micro considerations is the price of fluid milk in Wisconsin.

Whether the model is on macro aggregates or micro variables, it will almost always include behavioral equations and technological constraints. The former should be included because economic agents behave and act in different ways; the latter should be included because there may be some limitations on such things as resource and product availability imposed by the existing state of technology. Besides, there may typically be some identities or truisms in an economic model, such as the sum total of aggregate consumption, investment, and government expenditure being equal to the gross national product, or the total income of an economy being the sum total of income earned by its entrepreneurs and workers.

1.1.3 A Simple Income Determination Model

As will be discussed in much greater detail in Chapter 11, let us consider a three-equation model of a national economy as follows:

$$C_t = \mathrm{f}(Y_t) \tag{1.1}$$

$$= \beta_0 + \beta_1 Y_t \qquad \beta_0, \beta_1 > 0 \tag{1.2}$$

$$I_t = I_0 \tag{1.3}$$

$$Y_t = C_t + I_t \tag{1.4}$$

Equation (1.1) is the aggregate consumption function of the economy relating consumption C_t to national income Y_t using a general functional form f( ). In (1.2), a particular functional form, that which is a simple linear form, to be exact, is used. This form is based on the underlying assumptions that the marginal propensity to consume out of income, β_1, is positive and can almost be unity, and that the autonomous or exogenous consumption (unrelated to income), β_0, is also positive.

Equation (1.3) is an identity. It equates aggregate investment I_t to a fixed or an exogenously determined level I_0. Similarly, equation (1.4) is an identity. It generates Y_t, the national income, by summing up aggregate consumption C_t and investment I_t. Notice that the model does not recognize either the government or the external sector, which means that the entire national income generated is also available as disposable income (there being no taxes), which determines how much will be spent on consumption. The remainder of the national income goes into investment expenditure, there being no expenditure on account of the government, nor on account of net exports.

The model has three equations, including one identity, and three variables, C, I, and Y; therefore, their values are determinate. These values are obtained after the original equations, (1.2)–(1.4), called the structural equations, are cast into their reduced forms by the method of repeated substitution and elimination of variables:[1]

$$C_t = \frac{\beta_0}{(1 - \beta_1)} + \frac{\beta_1}{(1 - \beta_1)} I_0 \qquad (1.5)$$

$$Y_t = \frac{\beta_0}{(1 - \beta_1)} + \frac{1}{(1 - \beta_1)} I_0 \qquad (1.6)$$

$$I_t = I_0 \qquad (1.7)$$

Since I_0 is assumed known, all three variables are directly solvable. Note that the reduced form equations are equations for the currently determined or endogenous variables, C_t and Y_t, expressed exclusively in terms of variables that are exogenous; that is, those whose values are determined outside the model. In our model, we have only one such exogenous variable, namely I_t (investment).

1.1.4 Criticism of the Model

The economic theory leading to this model consists primarily of a postulated behavioral relation in consumption only, specifying its explanatory variables and the signs of its parameters. But both the theory and the model are, at best, an oversimplification of how a real-world economy functions. The theory does not explain how investment expenditure is determined, nor what is meant by consumption expenditure. Is it actual consumption expenditure, or is it the value of the flow of services from the stock of consumption goods? The theory also does not explain the government and the foreign trade sectors and thus there is no provision kept for such important variables as the tax rate, interest rate, and exchange rate, and how they influence the course of the economy. Nor does the theory address the questions of micro disaggregations and micro foundations of macroeconomic activities, such as aggregate consumption and investment, which might generate innumerable other variables (and relations), creating further problems of variable definition or measurement. Similarly, it does not take into consideration the use of a distributed lag with which some variables (such as capital appropriations) work upon others (such as investment expenditures). The lag structure is especially important when we think of the dynamic adjustment of the system to the instruments of change. Also, the process of adjustment may be different depending on whether it is a long-period change taking place over short-

[1] Notice that we have reproduced a structural equation as a reduced form equation because of the way investment expenditures have been assumed in the model. Had such expenditures been assumed to be a function of, for instance, the interest rate, each of equations (1.5)–(1.7) would have included an additional term involving the interest rate.

period sequences or over longer-period sequences. Unfortunately, our theory is silent on all these points.

There are other important considerations that have been left out. We have used, for instance, a linear functional form for the consumption function. However, economic theory could postulate a state of saturation in consumption with increases in income beyond a certain level. This might give rise to a nonlinear functional form for the consumption function described appropriately by a curve known as the logistic curve.[2] Or, there might be other functional forms possible about which economic theory might shed no light at all. That would lead economists to experiment, and the consequences would, at best, be uncertain.

Another consideration is the neglect of competing explanations for economic behavior. For example, we have taken aggregate consumption expenditure to depend on actual income. What if a competing theory were to suggest, as has happened in recent times, that consumption expenditure depends on the rationally expected[3] values of some variables, such as permanent or expected income. This sort of expectation will have important implications for government policy. If the government were, for instance, stimulating the economy, one way to do so would be to increase its expenditure. The increase in government expenditure would lead to an increase in actual national income, which would in turn cause further expansion in aggregate consumption expenditures, by the Keynesian multiplier theory. But this result would hold only if actual rather than permanent income determined consumption. However, if government expenditure will not influence consumers' expected income, but the latter is thought to be important for their consumption decision, the proposed government policy will not produce the desired effect.

1.1.5 Baffling Problems Underlying Economic Model Formulation

While formulating and modeling economic theory an economist often runs into several problems. These include a choice between competing theories, an urge to build a good micro foundation of a macro theoretic model, an attempt to unfold the dynamic adjustment of the economic system to instruments of change and the underlying lag structure in variables (affecting other variables), and the choice of appropriate functional forms. One may add to this list the problem of variable definition and measurement. While these problems are problems which an econometrician should address as much as a general economist does, he or she *almost* exclusively addresses the last problem (i.e. variable definition and measurement), and *exclusively* addresses still another problem. This is the problem of statistical specifications, along with the associated problems of estimation and testing, of

[2] See Chapter 7 for definition of this curve in connection with the logit model.

[3] See Chapter 12, Section 12.11.1, for more on rational expectation models.

an economic model. With this introduction to what an econometrician may do, let us formally ask what is econometrics?

1.2 THE MEANING OF ECONOMETRICS

Econometrics is economic theory in relation to mathematics and statistics. Mathematics is needed as a language or as a method of deduction or induction. Statistics may be classified as sample surveys[4] or probability theory and inference, each of which may, at the same time, contain an element of descriptive statistics. The relation to sample surveys is based primarily on three needs: measuring, collecting, and summarizing data to construct generalizations. These generalizations are basic to the theory and may lead to testable conclusions. Often these conclusions are uncertain in their directions and thus nonunique. More importantly, they indicate whether what the theory predicts is right or wrong compared to real-world results.

The relation to statistics as probability theory and inference helps make economic predictions probabilistic, rather than definitive or unique. This is important because chance predictions go well with an uncertain socioeconomic environment, something that is not available from a nonprobabilistic treatment of economic theory. Thus, statistics is extremely useful in economics. In fact, statistics provides a scientific orientation to economics.

1.2.1 An Example from the Micro Consumption Function

Take a very simple example. Theory may suggest that consumption (Y) of a consumer depends on his income (X) according to the relation $Y = \mathrm{f}(X)$, where f stands for the functional form. This may be represented as a linear relation:

$$Y = \beta_0 + \beta_1 X$$

where β_0 is the intercept, and β_1 the slope of the line portraying the function. We have assumed that β_0 and β_1 are constant and that the function is linear. Other forms of this function are possible, but suppose we make this linear function our starting point. Then the mathematical equation describes exactly what the theory wants us to believe; that is, for every income, there is a certain consumption expenditure, and this expenditure increases as the income increases. Don't we commonly find a rich person spending more on consumption goods and services than a poor person? Mathematics is here a language by which the particular economic theory is described.

[4] We do not wish to convey the wrong idea that sample surveys are devoid of probability theory. But, for our present purposes that aspect is not essentially important.

Mathematics is also used as a tool of deduction. For instance, one may ask what the marginal propensity to consume (MPC) is. The answer will be β_1, which is the slope of the function, or, in other words, dY/dX, the first derivative of Y with respect to X. It can also be deduced mathematically that the average propensity to consume Y/X is larger than the marginal propensity to consume dY/dX in the short run, but equal to the MPC in the long run. These deductions are indeed very simple. There may be more complex deductions that are possible using mathematics but we choose not to pursue them at the moment.

The above example shows the connection of economic theory with mathematics. The connection with statistics may be seen in the following way.

Suppose there are five individuals in a very small locality with the following data, however chosen and measured, for their income and consumption expenditures:

	Individual				
	1	2	3	4	5
Income	\$5,000	\$10,000	\$15,000	\$20,000	\$25,000
Consumption	\$2,500	\$ 5,000	\$ 7,500	\$10,000	\$12,500

The data show that for every consumer of a certain income there is a definite consumption and that as the income changes, so does the consumption. However, in respect to all the consumers, there is a definite relation between income and consumption. Exactly half of every dollar earned goes to consumption. This relationship is valid no matter how one constructs it: one may relate total consumption to total income, where division of the former by the latter gives the measure of the average propensity to consume (APC), or relate marginal consumption to marginal income, where similar division gives the measure of the marginal propensity to consume (MPC). Both measures work out, in this example, to the value of $\frac{1}{2}$, as we have already noted.

Now the questions may be how the consumption and income of the average consumer relate to each other and what the spread (or dispersion) of individual consumers is around the average. The answers to these questions may depend on the methods of descriptive statistics, such as central tendency and dispersion. We would say, using the arithmetic average as a measure of central tendency, that an average consumer with an income of \$15,000 has the consumption of \$7,500 with APC $= \frac{1}{2}$. Further, if we use range as a measure of dispersion, then individual consumers are scattered around the average to the extent of \$2,500 for consumption for an income of \$5,000 with APC $= \frac{1}{2}$ on the low side, compared to \$12,500 for consumption for an income of \$25,000 with APC $= \frac{1}{2}$ on the high side. In other words, the range is zero for the average propensity to consume for individual consumers around the average. And since APC $=$ MPC throughout all incomes in this simple numerical example, the range is simply zero for the marginal propensity to consume.

One offshoot of this analysis is the determinacy of the theory: Provided one knows what the income of the consumer is, his consumption expenditure is definitely determined using the unambiguous and unique ratio of $\frac{1}{2}$ of consumption to income. But theory does not always produce this determinacy. Two consumers with the same income may often have two different consumption expenditures. This is just one example of the problem of indeterminacy of the theory and the problem may become more formidable as the economic environment changes. What can we do? The answer is: do anything but panic. There is the theory of statistics to save us from and legitimize the indeterminacy of economic theory, for statistics gives us the theory of indeterminateness or probability with the associated theory of errors. This point is now explained further.

The part of the theory of consumer behavior that says that, for every consumer, the marginal propensity to consume is $\frac{1}{2}$ and so consumption expenditure at the margin is $\frac{1}{2}$ of the consumer's income is an example of the partial equilibrium theory. This theory, as everyone should perhaps know, assumes a host of other factors to be constant and studies the partial effect of the change of a variable, for instance, income, on another variable, such as consumption. In this form, we see economic theory operating in an ivory tower. However, when we bring it out into the real world, it needs some adaptation to be real. For instance, it should capture the effect of variables other than income on consumption, e.g. location, occupation, education, age, and ethnic background of the consumer in a cross-section context and his pre- and postwar situation as well in a time series context. Thus, when different consumers with the same income are found to differ in their consumption expenditures, the reason for the difference is to be found in how each one is endowed with various factors other than income, or how each one is located spatially or dynamically from the others.

Thus, if there are two consumers with the same income, for example \$15,000, their consumption expenditures may be \$7,400 and \$7,600 obtained from their consumption functions. Let us put these expenditures into the equation for the consumption function. Thus, we have

$$7{,}400 = Y = \beta_1 X_1 + \beta_2 X_2 + \beta_3 X_3 \tag{1.8}$$

for the first consumer, and

$$7{,}600 = Y = \beta_1 X_1 + \beta_2 X_2 + \beta_3 X_3 \tag{1.9}$$

for the second consumer. In (1.8) and (1.9), X_1 is income and for both the consumers is the same, \$15,000. X_2 and X_3 are other variables that identify each consumer, such as occupation and education suitably defined qualitatively and/or quantitatively. β_1, β_2, and β_3, which are assumed to be fixed, are the marginal effects of the X_is on Y. That is,

$$\beta_i = \frac{\partial Y}{\partial X_i} \qquad i = 1, 2, 3$$

In other words, taking, for instance, $i = 2$ for occupation, β_2 is equal to the change in consumption when a consumer changes, at the margin, to the next occupation. The other βs have similar meanings.

Thus, simply because two consumers have each an income of \$15,000 does not mean that they have the same consumption expenditure (\$7,500). One has more, and the other less than that expenditure, but the average expenditure comes to \$7,500. This is the same as saying that the expenditure of the average consumer is \$7,500. This hypothetical average consumer has the same income as each one of the "real" consumers, but his endowment of occupation and education is an average of that of the two. Thus, we can make an average statement:

$$\mathrm{E}\,(Y/X_1 = \$15{,}000) = \$7{,}500 = \beta_1 X_1 \tag{1.10}$$

which may be stated as follows: the expected or the average consumption expenditure for an income X_1 of \$15,000, denoted by the symbol $\mathrm{E}(Y/X_1 = \$15{,}000)$, is \$7,500. This is obtained by averaging over the two consumers' occupation and educational identifications. Thus, (1.10) is an average of

$$Y = \beta_1 X_1 + \epsilon_1' \tag{1.11}$$

and

$$Y = \beta_1 X_1 + \epsilon_2' \tag{1.12}$$

of the first and second consumer's consumption functions, respectively, in which

$$\epsilon_1' = \beta_2 X_2 + \beta_3 X_3 \tag{1.13}$$

and

$$\epsilon_2' = \beta_2 X_2 + \beta_3 X_3 \tag{1.14}$$

These are the effects of the two new explanatory variables X_2 and X_3 with different values for the first and the second consumer, respectively. For instance, the first consumer may be a skilled laborer ($=X_2$) with a basic elementary education ($=X_3$), while the second consumer is an unskilled laborer ($=X_2$) with a high school degree ($=X_3$); the former's consumption expenditure is \$100 below ($\epsilon_1' = -\$100$), while the latter's is \$100 above ($\epsilon_2' = +\$100$) the average consumption expenditure of \$7,500.

The procedure of presenting the conditional value of Y for a given value of X_1, i.e. $\mathrm{E}(Y/X_1)$ for an average individual, rather than for each individual separately, is to economize expressions. Such conditional average values lie on what is commonly known as the regression function of Y on X_1, or the function of the dependence of Y on X_1. Naturally, the specification of X_1 is important in the sense that the conditional average value of Y may change as X_1 changes. The discussion that we have had with the fixed value of $X_1 = \$15{,}000$ will then be repeated with the other values. Thus, generally

$$\mathrm{E}\;Y/X_1 = \beta_1 X_1 \tag{1.15}$$

with

$$Y_1 = \beta_1 X_1 + \epsilon_1' \tag{1.16}$$

and

$$Y_2 = \beta_1 X_1 + \epsilon_2' \tag{1.17}$$

where Y_1 and Y_2 are the values of the dependent variable Y, each of which varies with X_1, the independent variable. They are the consumption expenditures of the two consumers.

Instead of the fixed income of \$15,000, one may consider income over a certain range, for instance, \$10,000–\$20,000, and study the consumption expenditures of all consumers with income in that range. It is quite possible that the number of such consumers will be larger than two. Even then the previous discussion of the conditional average consumption expenditure and the vanishing error term as well as the individual consumption expenditure and the nonvanishing error term will be relevant. The only difference now will be that the error of the average function, for instance, will vanish because of some new considerations as well. These relate to the individual deviations from the average consumption expenditure brought about by the range in income. Even then some consumers will have above-average and others below-average consumption expenditures such that the average error will cancel out in the final analysis. The case of the individual expenditures and the nonvanishing error term can be similarly argued.

A model identified by (1.15) is said to have the associated errors ϵ_i' ($i = 1, 2$), which are due to the neglect of the two independent variables X_2 and X_3 of which they are made. These are called specification errors. We have assumed that X_2 and X_3 are the only other independent variables possible. This need not be so. There may be many other causal variables with effects on consumption expenditures. Some of these, e.g. $X_3, X_4, \ldots, X_m$, may have been conceived of and included in the equation. This will extend the regression equation to

$$E(Y/X_1, X_2, \ldots, X_m) = \beta_1 X_1 + \beta_2 X_2 + \cdots + \beta_m X_m \tag{1.18}$$

with

$$Y_1 = \beta_1 X_1 + \beta_2 X_2 + \cdots + \beta_m X_m + \epsilon_1' \tag{1.19}$$

and

$$Y_2 = \beta_1 X_1 + \beta_2 X_2 + \cdots + \beta_m X_m + \epsilon_2' \tag{1.20}$$

The three equations are the prototypes of (1.15)–(1.17) except that they include more X variables. Still, there may be other variables that have not been included in the regression equation for various reasons that are too important to be totally neglected. Thus, they must be implicitly included somewhere in the model. Let ϵ', called the error variable, represent the effects of all such left-out variables as a group. This appears in the consumption function of each consumer, but disappears in the conditional expectation function of the average consumer, the assumption being

$$E(\epsilon'/X_1, X_2, \ldots, X_m) = 0 \tag{1.21}$$

That is, the imaginary average consumer's consumption expenditure goes through the line of zero error. On either side of this line are located individual consumers with errors in expenditures, positive or negative, but of such magnitudes and so frequent (or with such probabilities) that the average error becomes zero.

Equation (1.18) defines the line of multiple regression of Y on $X_1, X_2, \ldots, X_m$. Two consumers with identical values of the independent variables, $X_1, X_2, \ldots, X_m$, might still experience different consumption expenditures as a result of influences of unaccounted for variables (subsumed in) ϵ_1' and ϵ_2' of (1.19) and (1.20). These error variables may have two components, one that is fixed and common to all the consumers regardless of the values of the explanatory variables actually accounted for, and another that is statistical or stochastic, defined by a set of outcomes, and thus probabilistic. The first component becomes the intercept of the regression equation. This, in the consumption function example, may represent the effects of, for instance, biological necessities as well as a state of readiness for such impending events as war and inflation. The second component is specific to the individual regardless of the values of the variables X actually used to explain his behavior and, therefore, it changes in value only when the individual changes. But even for the same individual there is a probability distribution of the values of this component depending on the way the left-out variables tend to be distributed in the bigger aggregate or the population. Thus, algebraically,

$$\left.\begin{aligned} \epsilon_i' &= \beta_0 + \epsilon_i \\ E(Y_i/X_1, \ldots, X_m) &= \beta_0 + \sum_{j=1}^{m} \beta_j X_{ij} \\ Y_i &= \beta_0 + \sum_{j=1}^{m} \beta_j X_{ij} + \epsilon_i \end{aligned}\right\} \quad i = 1, 2, \ldots, 5$$

These equations are theoretical relations among true variables. In practice, they are estimated using sample observations on these variables. Depending on the way observations are measured, there may be errors of various kinds. We assume that these errors are included in the ϵs. Thus, ϵs may consist of two types of errors, specification errors (including measurement errors) and sampling errors, and the two together are assumed to generate a random variable with the characteristics of zero means and identical variances.

1.3 OBJECTIVE OF THE BOOK

The basic features of the regression model constitute the features of the single-equation classical (or ordinary) linear regression model. This model is discussed in Chapters 2 and 5. Chapter 2 deals with simple regression (one variable), while Chapter 5 deals with multiple regression (two or more variables). Chapter 3 briefly discusses matrix or linear algebra, and Chapter 4 discusses statistical distribution and inference. These are helpful in solving special problems associated with two or more variables and in smoothing the transition from the simple to the multiple regression model.

Some of these problems (Chapter 6) will include the mutual dependence among explanatory variables, a feature known as *multicollinearity*. Others (Chapter 6) will include (1) nonlinear functional forms, especially those that can be transformed back to linear forms; (2) structural changes in the model handled by the method of constrained least squares; (3) unconventional nonlinearities of the model tackled by the method of dummy variables; and (4) specification errors. Still other problems are caused by the nonidentical variances of the error variables at different times or places, called *heteroscedasticity,* or the correlation among these error variables, called *autocorrelation of residuals*. These will be discussed in Chapter 7 as problems of the generalized linear model.

Chapter 7 will then go on to analyze the problem of the qualitative and limited dependent variables. This problem is included in this chapter primarily because there is an element of generalized error variance at its base. Logit, probit and Tobit methods will be discussed here in succession to deal with the special problems of such models.

However, the variations of the classical theme contained in Chapters 6 and 7 are not without one fundamental classical assumption regarding the explanatory variables. That is, these variables are fixed in repeated samples. This assumption will be relaxed in Chapter 8, and, accordingly, we will have the stochastic linear regression models. Of special importance here will be the errors in variable models and lag models that will be dealt with in depth. The others are the stationary stochastic processes, the autoregressive-moving average (ARMA) and autoregressive-integrated-moving average (ARIMA) schemes and their associated transfer function estimation and prewhitening mechanism or causality analysis that will be dealt with only briefly.

At this point we should perhaps emphasize an important aspect of this book, that of applications. This aspect is confined not merely to illustrating the various econometric methods by hypothetical data and computations. It extends into some real-world applied econometric studies. These are covered in various degrees in the various chapters.

Chapter 9 is devoted to a good number of other applied studies not covered in the previous chapters. These deal with studies from both the classical and modern periods based exclusively on single equation models. They are divided into four general areas: the consumption function, the production function, the investment function, and others. These others include topics from such diverse areas as industrial organization, education, economic growth, international economics, financial economics, and labor economics.

On the methods side, there are a number of items which represent further variations of the classical procedures, or which indicate entirely different approaches. Among the first are those that represent novel test procedures. Examples are the Wald test, the Lagrange Multiplier test and the Likelihood Ratio test. The essence of these test procedures is to attach different emphasis to the null and the alternative hypotheses. Also there may be situations when the strict method of random sampling may have to be compromised in favor of some kind of selective sampling. This may very well be the source of a new bias called the sample selectivity bias. In addition, the investigator may sometimes be confronted with errors which arise from pooled time series and cross section data structures, or he may be dealing with a regression model in which the parameters of the model are not fixed but random. Besides, there may be some entirely new approaches to analysis, for instance the approach of Bayesian econometrics. This approach is rooted in the distinction between prior and posterior hypotheses. It is also based on the conviction that the distribution of a parameter or parameters, the objective of the prior hypothesis, can be just as good a "fact" as the distribution of sample observations given the unobservable parameters, the classicist's mainstay of analysis. All of these items are treated in Chapter 10. That treatment is generally brief for all items; however, for some it is even more brief than others.

In most of the next two chapters, we change the frame of reference from one single equation to simultaneous equations. The role of the simultaneous equation models in economics or social science need not be emphasized. They are so useful. Chapter 11 addresses questions of both identification and estimation of such models. However, in matters of estimation it follows both the single equation and the systems method of estimation. Chapter 12 then briefly draws on some small to large size comprehensive macroeconometric models of both the United States and Canada only to refer, at the end, to Lucas' critique on the usefulness of such models for evaluating the effects of policy changes. But all this comprises only about half of this chapter. The other half is devoted to a discussion of a widely debated model of the eighties, that of rational expectations. Since this model has been primarily in relation to the analysis of macroeconomic problems, we have decided to put this topic in this chapter. Our emphasis will be, however, on the econometric issues raised by these models and their implications and to put the position of their proponents and opponents in proper perspective.

The last chapter (Chapter 13) is devoted to a number of special problems which have gained prominence in recent times. One is the problem of economic disequilibrium models, testing of which leads to another general problem, the problem of model selection. In model selection, two major specification problems are discussed, the problem of nested and that of nonnested hypotheses corresponding to whether one model is or is not a special case of the other model. The last problem deals with the periodic ups and downs, termed "business cycles", of an economic time series. Since these cycles are interpreted as deviations from growth trends, their determination is linked to that of trends. Special problems will, however, arise from the fact that trends can be stochastic, just as they can be deterministic. Under stochastic trends, the possibility of "spurious regressions" becomes important, leading to the need for a theoretical rationale developed for it. This rationale is formalized in terms of models with unit roots. Such models with their underlying characteristics are dealt with at the end of this chapter.

1.4 CONCLUSION

In conclusion, we would like to comment on the scope of this book. Our view is that the scope of econometrics defined in this book is, at best, limited. This scope defines the relation of econometrics to mathematics and statistics with which we started the Introduction. That relation may easily lead us to much more difficult areas of both mathematics and statistics than we can appropriately deal with in this book, even though these might be desirable econometrically for many reasons. For example, one area of econometric research which has grown in popularity in recent times is in approximating the distributions of econometric estimators and test statistics. Another is in time series and spectral methods. Still others are in dynamic specifications, continuous time stochastic models, analysis of panel data, and latent variable models. We may have touched upon some of these in a very rudimentary way in this book, far from the level at which these should be pitched for an adequate understanding of these subjects. But that would call for a much more formidable prerequisite on the part of the students beyond what has been assumed in this book. Therefore, for better or worse, a full treatment of these topics is left out of this book.

2

The Simple Linear Model in Two Variables and Its Extensions

2.1 INTRODUCTION

Let us begin by using a commodity demand schedule (or curve) as an example of a two-variable linear model. As we know from economic theory, there exists a negative relationship between the quantity demanded of a commodity and its price, given that all other things remain constant. In other words, when the price of a commodity rises, its quantity demanded falls and vice versa.

Clearly, quantity demanded becomes the dependent and price the independent variable. The linear relationship between the two variables can be expressed as

$$Y = \beta_0 + \beta_1 X \tag{2.1}$$

where

$$Y = \text{quantity demanded}$$

$$X = \text{price of the product}$$

$$\beta_0, \beta_1 = \text{coefficients}$$

The coefficients β_0 and β_1 are important as a description of the demand phenomenon. For instance, β_0 is the constant amount of the commodity demanded regardless of price considerations, and β_1 is related to the price elasticity of demand η for the commodity in the following way:

$$\eta = \beta_1 \frac{\overline{X}}{\overline{Y}}$$

Figure 2.1

where $\overline{X}$ and $\overline{Y}$ are the mean values of X and Y over the sample period. For inelastic commodities, $\eta < 1$, and given $\overline{X}$ and $\overline{Y}$, β_1 should adjust to these values. Similar adjustments should be made to β_1 for elastic commodities for which $\eta >$ 1.

The demand relationship (2.1) is exact or deterministic. That is, the data on price and quantity, if plotted on a two-dimensional plane, would lie on a straight line. But, as indicated in Chapter 1, such a relationship is hardly so. In fact, the relationship is only an inexact one and might look like a straight line. This line is obtained as a best fit of the scatter of points drawn from the observations on Y and X as shown in Figure 2.1.

In Chapter 1 we explained some of the factors that give rise to the indeterminacy in a functional relationship or in the scatter of points when it is graphed. In the particular context of the demand relationship, we can list these factors as follows: the omission of variables, random elements in human behavior, inappropriate functional form or model, and errors of aggregation and measurement.

Among variables omitted from a demand formulation, prices of other commodities, tastes, ethnic background, income, and asset position of consumers might be important. The caprices of human behavior are too common to need any special explanation. As to functional forms, often a nonlinear relationship should be used when a linear form is used instead. Sometimes, the model formulation is not appropriate. For instance, the demand for a given commodity, say housing, may be embedded in a network of demand and supply relationships of other commodities, all of which should be simultaneously considered. In other words, the single equation illustrated here might be imperfect, and should be replaced by a simultaneous equation. Lastly, errors arising from the aggregation of dissimilar behavior patterns or from measurement errors associated with the collection of data and processing of statistical information are too common and obvious to require any elaborate explanation.

To account for the errors mentioned above, the usual econometric practice is to allow for a random disturbance term ϵ into the functional form. Thus, the equation of the model inclusive of the random error term becomes

$$Y_i = \beta_0 + \beta_1 X_i + \epsilon_i \tag{2.2}$$

where the subscript i refers to the ith sample observation. Once again ϵ accounts

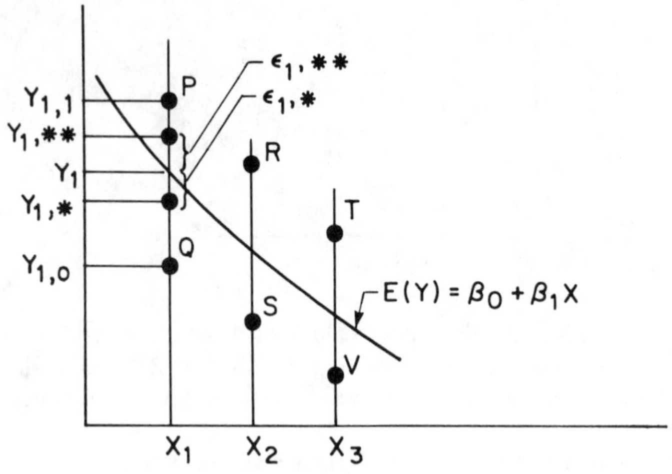

Figure 2.2

for the effects of other variables not explicitly included in the model, as well as the errors of various other sorts indicated above.

Another way of looking at (2.2) is as follows. At a given value of X there may be numerous values of Y. These values are caused by various (positive or negative) values of ϵ pertaining to individual observations at that value of X. This is depicted in Figure 2.2. Assume that the price of butter is X_1; at this price, there may be several individuals for whom the value of Y may lie anywhere between $Y_{1,0}$ and $Y_{1,1}$. If, for example, the demand for margarine goes up when some essential nutrients are added to its production, which impacts negatively on the demand for butter (showing the working of chance events), the quantity of butter will not be Y_1 as equation (2.1) indicates but a lesser quantity, $Y_{1,*}$. This is because of the extra competition from margarine which generates a negative value $\epsilon_{1,*}$ for the error term. On the other hand, suppose word gets around that there is going to be an increase in income for residents in the area. This will cause a consumer of butter of that area to buy more butter at a given price. This means that at price X_1 the quantity demanded of butter will be a larger quantity $Y_{1,**}$ as a result of the change in anticipation generating a higher value $\epsilon_{1,**}$ for the error term.

This argument can be repeated with any other price $X_2, X_3, \ldots,$ with the incidental spread RS, TV, . . . , in the quantity demanded, comparable to the spread PQ based on the price X_1.

The estimation of the coefficients β_0 and β_1 has to be based on observations on X, Y, and ϵ. But, unlike the other variables, ϵ is unobservable, which means that we should guess the values of ϵ. In other words, we should make some assumptions about the distribution of each ϵ in terms of its mean, variance, and covariance with other ϵs.

2.1.1 Assumptions about the Distribution of ϵs

Since ϵs capture the effects of unaccounted for and unmeasurable variables, they tend to push the values of Y up or down. Otherwise, they are not expected to have a bias or a pattern on the average of any kind. Thus, we assume that the sum total of the positive and negative values of ϵ cancel out, or, that its mean or expected value is zero:

$$E(\epsilon_i) = 0 \qquad \text{for any } i \tag{2.3}$$

The second assumption about ϵ is that the variance of ϵ_i is constant:

$$V(\epsilon_i) = \sigma^2 \qquad \text{for any } i \tag{2.4}$$

This means that, for all X, the ϵs will exhibit the same dispersion around their mean. This is shown in Figure 2.2 by taking equal spreads, $PQ = RS = TV \ldots$, in the values of ϵ around its mean $E(\epsilon) = 0$ (lying on the line $E(Y) = \beta_0 + \beta_1 X$). These values correspond to different values of X, such as $X_1, X_2, X_3, \ldots$. In the figure, equal spreads or ranges express the fact that the dispersions are equal, even though in a practical situation this need not be the case.

The third assumption is that any two ϵs, say ϵ_i and ϵ_j, $i \neq j = 1, 2, \ldots, n$, are statistically independent. In symbols, this is written as

$$E(\epsilon_i \epsilon_j) = 0 \qquad i \neq j = 1, 2, \ldots, n \tag{2.5}$$

In other words, the covariances of any ϵ_i with any other ϵ_j are zero. This means that the value of the stochastic disturbance term in any one period is not influenced by its value in any other period. Again, in a practical situation, this assumption may be hard to defend. For one thing, economic and other policies may be supposed to affect the values of all variables including the disturbance term, and the way these will affect the disturbance term in any one period is expected to be the same as in any other period, causing a common effect or covariance between them.

The fourth assumption is that ϵ_i is independent of the explanatory variable X. In other words, all covariances of ϵ and X are zero. This assumption will follow automatically in the basic linear regression model, because whereas in this model we assume ϵs to be stochastic or random, we assume the Xs to be nonstochastic. That is, the Xs are a set of fixed values in the hypothetical sense of repeated sampling, which is indeed the presumption of the basic linear regression model. For instance, we may choose the same set of market prices, $X_1, X_2, \ldots$, for a commodity each day, their corresponding Y values being $Y_1, Y_2, \ldots$. The Xs of one day are still the same Xs on any other day; but the Ys of one day are not the same as the Ys of another. These will be subject to random variations.

The fifth assumption is that the ϵs, which are random, are conceived of as being drawn independently from a normal distribution, whose identifying symbol

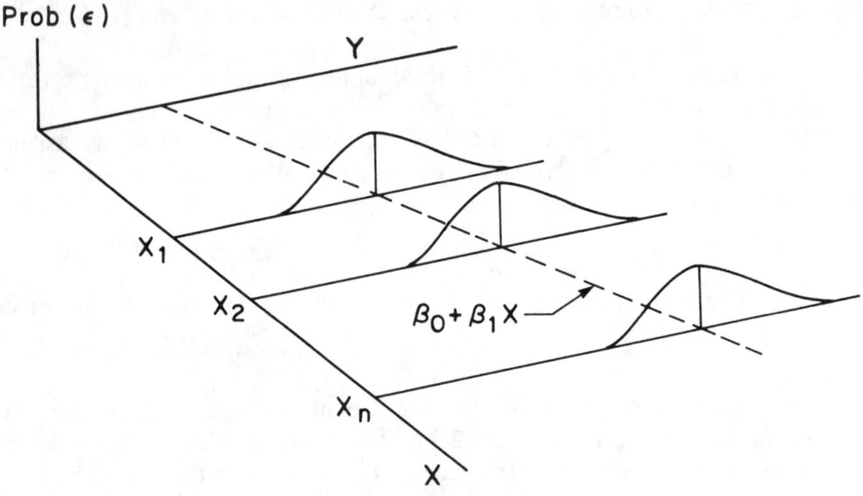

Figure 2.3

is N. Along with assumptions 1 and 2, this assumption is represented in the expression:

$$\epsilon \sim N(0, \sigma^2) \tag{2.6a}$$

In other words, ϵ is distributed normally, with zero mean and variance σ^2. This distribution is portrayed in Figure 2.3 as a bell-shaped curve at each value of $X = X_1, X_2, \ldots, X_n$.

The assumption that the ϵs constitute independent drawings from a normal distribution $N(0, \sigma^2)$ is sometimes expressed as

$$\epsilon \sim NID(0, \sigma^2) \tag{2.6b}$$

where NID means normally and independently distributed.

2.2 THE ORDINARY LEAST-SQUARES (OLS) TECHNIQUE

Our initial position is to conceive of a relation (2.2) that holds for the population of observations on Y, X, and ϵ. However, the population concept is not very feasible. That is why we take recourse to the concept of sample observations. Any straight line drawn through the scatter of sample observations can be imagined to be an estimate of the relationship given in (2.2). Suppose one such line is represented by

$$\hat{Y}_i = \beta_0 + \beta_1 X_i \tag{2.7}$$

where $\hat{Y}_i$ is given by the vertical distance of the fitted line at a given value X_i of X. It is also the estimate of Y that follows from the estimate $\hat{\beta}_0$ and $\hat{\beta}_1$ of the

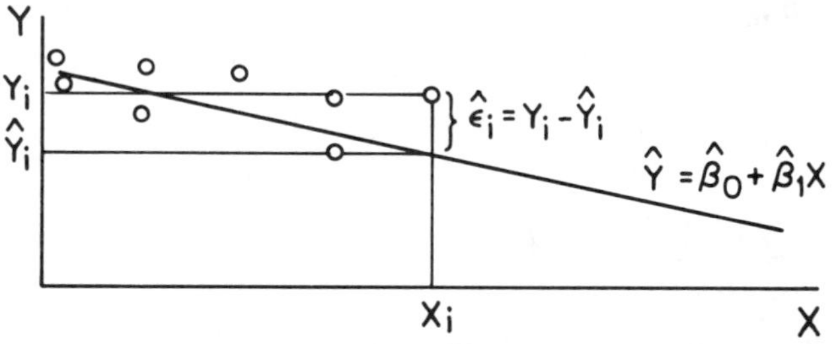

Figure 2.4

coefficients imputed into (2.2). After (2.7) is passed through the scatter of points, there will be some points above and others below that line, as shown in Figure 2.4. Define the error of using (2.7) as the estimated line by

$$\hat{\epsilon}_i = Y_i - \hat{Y}_i \qquad i = 1, 2, \ldots, n \tag{2.8}$$

This particular error is shown in Figure 2.4 at $X = X_i$. Similarly there will be other errors corresponding to other sample observations. These errors or the deviations of the observations from the fitted line will depend on the estimated values $\hat{\beta}_0$ and $\hat{\beta}_1$ of the coefficients. There are as many techniques of fitting the line as there are such lines, with as many sets of errors. Under the principle of least squares, we choose the line from among all possible lines that produces the smallest value for the sum of squares of the residuals from that line.[1]

Taking the residuals as $\hat{\epsilon}_i$, substituting for $\hat{Y}$ from (2.7) and (2.8), and squaring and adding, we obtain the sum of squares due to residuals:

$$\Sigma \hat{\epsilon}_i^2 = \sum_1^n (Y_i - \hat{\beta}_0 - \hat{\beta}_1 X_i)^2 \tag{2.9}$$

This is a function of $\hat{\beta}_0$ and $\hat{\beta}_1$. Denote this by $f(\hat{\beta}_0, \hat{\beta}_1)$. The first-order (or necessary) conditions for the minimum of $f(\hat{\beta}_0, \hat{\beta}_1)$ are

$$\frac{\partial}{\partial \beta_i} f(\hat{\beta}_0, \hat{\beta}_1) = 0 \qquad i = 0, 1$$

With reference to (2.9), these conditions reduce to[2]

$$\Sigma Y_i = n\hat{\beta}_0 + \hat{\beta}_1 \Sigma X_i \tag{2.10}$$

$$\Sigma X_i Y_i = \hat{\beta}_0 \Sigma X_i + \hat{\beta}_1 \Sigma X_i^2 \tag{2.11}$$

[1] The alternative would be to choose a line for which not the sum of squares but the simple algebraic sum of residuals becomes zero. Such a line would be given by the equation $Y = \beta_0 + \beta_1 X$. That is, the values of β_0 and β_1 should be so chosen that the line passes through the point (X, Y). In fact, such a line might have any slope whatsoever, and this indeterminacy makes the criterion impracticable.

[2] From $(\partial/\partial\hat{\beta}_0)f = 0$, we get $-2\Sigma(Y_i - \hat{\beta}_0 - \hat{\beta}_1 X_i) = 0$ or, simplifying, $\Sigma Y_i = n\hat{\beta}_0 + \hat{\beta}_1 \Sigma X_i$, or equation (2.10); from $(\partial/\partial\hat{\beta}_1)f = 0$, we get $-2\Sigma X_i(Y_i - \hat{\beta}_0 - \hat{\beta}_1 X_i) = 0$, from which we get $\Sigma X_i Y_i = \hat{\beta}_0 \Sigma X_i + \hat{\beta}_1 \Sigma X_i Y_i$, or equation (2.11).

These are called normal equations. Solving these equations, we obtain the OLS estimates (the subscripts have been suppressed):

$$\hat{\beta}_0 = \frac{\Sigma X^2 \Sigma Y - \Sigma X \Sigma XY}{n\Sigma X^2 - (\Sigma X)^2} \tag{2.12}$$

$$\hat{\beta}_1 = \frac{n\Sigma XY - \Sigma X \Sigma Y}{n\Sigma X^2 - (\Sigma X)^2} \tag{2.13}$$

We can alternatively derive the same formulas more simply based on the deviations of the variables from their means. Using lowercase letters for such deviations, we have

$$x_i = X_i - \overline{X} \qquad y_i = Y_i - \overline{Y}$$

Since[3] (again suppressing subscripts for the sake of clarity)

$$\Sigma x_i^2 = \frac{n\Sigma X^2 - (\Sigma X)^2}{n} \tag{2.14}$$

$$\Sigma x_i y_i = \frac{n\Sigma XY - \Sigma X \Sigma Y}{n} \tag{2.15}$$

then

$$\hat{\beta}_1 = \frac{\Sigma x_i y_i}{\Sigma x_i^2} = \frac{n\Sigma XY - \Sigma X \Sigma Y}{n\Sigma X^2 - (\Sigma X)^2} \tag{2.16}$$

Dividing (2.10) by n, we have

$$\frac{\Sigma Y_i}{n} = \hat{\beta}_0 + \hat{\beta}_1 \frac{\Sigma X_i}{n}$$

or

$$\overline{Y} = \beta_0 + \beta_1 \overline{X} \tag{2.17}$$

This shows that the regression line passes through the means $\overline{X}$, $\overline{Y}$ of the variables. Using (2.16) for an expression for $\hat{\beta}_1$ in terms of x_i and y_i put into (2.17), one obtains the same expression for $\hat{\beta}_0$ as in (2.12).

[3] $$\Sigma x_i^2 = \Sigma(X_i - \overline{X})^2 = \Sigma X_i^2 - 2\overline{X}\Sigma X_i + n\overline{X}^2 = \Sigma X_i^2 - 2n\overline{X}^2 + n\overline{X}^2$$
$$= \Sigma X_i^2 - n\overline{X}^2 = \Sigma X_i^2 - \frac{(\Sigma X_i)^2}{n} = \frac{n\Sigma X_i^2 - (\Sigma X_i)^2}{n}$$

$\overline{X}$ being $\Sigma X_i / n$. Similarly,

$$\Sigma x_i y_i = \Sigma(X_i - \overline{X})(Y_i - \overline{Y}) = \Sigma X_i Y_i - \overline{X}\Sigma Y_i - \overline{Y}\Sigma X_i + n\overline{X}\overline{Y}$$
$$= \Sigma X_i Y_i - n\overline{X}\overline{Y} - n\overline{X}\overline{Y} + n\overline{X}\overline{Y} = \Sigma X_i Y_i - n\overline{X}\overline{Y}$$
$$= \Sigma X_i Y_i - \frac{\Sigma X_i \Sigma Y_i}{n} = \frac{n\Sigma XY - \Sigma X \Sigma Y}{n}$$

Example. Suppose 11 pairs of data on X and Y be such that the following results are computed:

$$\Sigma X = 5{,}711 \qquad \Sigma X^2 = 3{,}134{,}543$$

$$\Sigma Y = 2{,}396 \qquad \Sigma XY = 1{,}296{,}836 \qquad \Sigma Y^2 = 5{,}000{,}000$$

For this problem n is 11. Then from (2.12)

$$\begin{aligned}\hat{\beta}_0 &= \frac{\Sigma X^2 \Sigma Y - \Sigma X \Sigma XY}{n\Sigma X^2 - (\Sigma X)^2}\\ &= \frac{(3{,}134{,}543)(2{,}396) - (5{,}711)(1{,}296{,}836)}{11(3{,}134{,}543) - (5{,}711)^2}\\ &= \frac{7.5104 \times 10^9 - 7.4062 \times 10^9}{3.4480 \times 10^7 - 3.2616 \times 10^7}\\ &= \frac{0.1042 \times 10^9}{0.1864 \times 10^7} = 55.9013\end{aligned}$$

and from (2.13)

$$\begin{aligned}\hat{\beta}_1 &= \frac{n\Sigma XY - \Sigma X \Sigma Y}{n\Sigma X^2 - (\Sigma X)^2}\\ &= \frac{11(1{,}296{,}836) - (5{,}711)(2{,}396)}{11(3{,}134{,}543) - (5{,}711)^2}\\ &= \frac{1.4265 \times 10^7 - 1.3684 \times 10^7}{3.4480 \times 10^7 - 3.2616 \times 10^7}\\ &\approx \frac{0.0581 \times 10^7}{0.1864 \times 10^7} = 0.3117\end{aligned}$$

These calculations have been based on original sample observations. But using formulas (2.16) and (2.17) based on the deviations of variables from their means we obtain the same values for $\hat{\beta}_0$ and $\hat{\beta}_1$ (except for rounding up errors or differences):

$$\hat{\beta}_1 = \frac{\Sigma xy}{\Sigma x^2} \approx \frac{5.2876 \times 10^4}{16.9495 \times 10^4} = 0.3119$$

$$\begin{aligned}\hat{\beta}_0 &= \overline{Y} - \hat{\beta}_1 \overline{X} = 217.8182 - (0.3119)\frac{5{,}711}{11}\\ &= 217.8182 - 161.9328 = 55.8845\end{aligned}$$

The fitted function is

$$\hat{Y} = 55.8845 + 0.3119X$$

If the intercept β_0 of the regression line is zero, and equation (2.2) is modified to

$$Y_i = \beta_1 X_i + \epsilon_i \tag{2.18}$$

$\hat{\beta}_1$ will be given by

$$\hat{\beta}_1 = \frac{\Sigma XY}{\Sigma X^2} \tag{2.19}$$

This will easily follow from the normal equations (2.10) and (2.11) by suppressing β_0. Comparing (2.19) with (2.16), we find that when the intercept is zero, the absolute values of the variables (equation (2.19)) and variables expressed in terms of deviations from their means (equation (2.16)) make no difference in the computed value for $\hat{\beta}_1$.

2.3 THE GOODNESS OF FIT TEST

Once the regression line has been fitted, we would like to know how good the fit is; in other words, we would like to measure the discrepancy of actual observations (Y, X) from the fitted line. This is important since the closer the data to the line, the better the fit or, in other words, the better the explanation of variation of the dependent variable provided by the independent variables.

A usual measure of the goodness of fit is the square of the correlation coefficient, r^2. This is the proportion of the total variation of the dependent variable caused by the independent variable. In other words,

$$r^2 = \frac{\text{Regression sum of squares}}{\text{Total sum of squares}} \tag{2.20}$$

An explanation of the various sums of squares appearing in equation (2.20) will be evident in the following decomposition of the total sum of squares.

2.3.1 Decomposition of the Total Sum of Squares

The total variation of Y around its mean is made up of the variation accounted for by the linear regression and the variation unaccounted for by linear regression. As before, let

$$x = X - \overline{X} \qquad y = Y - \overline{Y} \qquad \hat{y} = \hat{Y} - \overline{\hat{Y}} \tag{2.21}$$

where $\overline{\hat{Y}}$ is the mean of $\hat{Y}$s. Note that[4] $\overline{\hat{Y}} = \overline{Y}$ and $\hat{\epsilon}(= Y - \hat{Y})$ and X are orthogonal[5] to each other, their product sum being zero: $\Sigma\hat{\epsilon}_i X_i = 0$.

[4] Since $\hat{Y}_i = \hat{\beta}_0 + \hat{\beta}_1 X_i$, we have, by summing over i from $i = 1$ to $i = n$ and dividing by n,

$$\overline{\hat{Y}} = \hat{\beta}_0 + \hat{\beta}_1 \overline{X} \tag{a}$$

But from the first normal equation (2.10), after dividing both sides by n, we have

$$\overline{Y} = \hat{\beta}_0 + \hat{\beta}_1 \overline{X} \tag{b}$$

Since the right-hand sides of (a) and (b) are equal, $\overline{\hat{Y}} = \overline{Y}$.

Then

$$Y_i = y_i + \overline{Y}$$

$$\hat{Y}_i = \hat{y}_i + \overline{Y}$$

and subtracting we get

$$Y_i - \hat{Y}_i = y_i - \hat{y}_i \tag{2.22}$$

which can be expressed as

$$\hat{\epsilon}_i = y_i - \hat{y}_i \tag{2.23}$$

or

$$y_i = \hat{y}_i + \hat{\epsilon}_i$$

Squaring and summing over all observations, we get

$$\begin{aligned} \Sigma y_i^2 &= \Sigma \hat{y}_i^2 + \Sigma \hat{\epsilon}_i^2 + 2\Sigma \hat{y}_i \hat{\epsilon}_i \\ &= \Sigma \hat{y}_i^2 + \Sigma \hat{\epsilon}_i^2 + 2\hat{\beta}_1 \Sigma x_i \hat{\epsilon}_i \\ &= \Sigma \hat{y}_i^2 + \Sigma \hat{\epsilon}_i^2 \\ &= \hat{\beta}_1^2 \Sigma x_i^2 + \Sigma \hat{\epsilon}_i^2 \end{aligned} \tag{2.24}$$

We have used $\Sigma x_i \hat{\epsilon}_i = 0$; by the orthogonality of X and $\hat{\epsilon}$:

$$\begin{aligned} \Sigma x_i \hat{\epsilon}_i &= \Sigma (X_i - \overline{X}) \hat{\epsilon}_i \\ &= \Sigma X_i \hat{\epsilon}_i - \frac{1}{n} \Sigma X_i \hat{\epsilon}_i \\ &= 0 - \frac{1}{n} \times 0 \\ &= 0 \end{aligned}$$

Equation (2.24) shows that the total sum of squares (TSS), $\Sigma y_i^2 = \Sigma (Y - \overline{Y})^2$, is decomposed into the regression sum of squares (RSS), $\Sigma \hat{y}_i^2 = \Sigma (\hat{Y}_i - \overline{Y})^2$, and the unexplained, residual, or error sum of squares (ESS), $\Sigma \hat{\epsilon}_i^2$. The regression sum of squares can be expressed as

$$\text{RSS} = \Sigma \hat{y}^2 = \hat{\beta}_1^2 \Sigma x^2 = \hat{\beta}_1 \Sigma xy = \frac{(\Sigma xy)^2}{\Sigma x^2} \tag{2.25}$$

---

[5] Next,

$$Y = \hat{Y} + \hat{\epsilon} \quad \text{or} \quad \hat{\epsilon} = (Y - \hat{Y})$$

Thus,

$$\Sigma \hat{\epsilon}_i X_i = \Sigma X_i Y_i - \Sigma X_i \hat{Y}_i = \Sigma X_i Y_i - \hat{\beta}_0 \Sigma X_i - \hat{\beta}_1 \Sigma X_i^2 = 0$$

after substituting for $\hat{Y}$ $(= \hat{\beta}_0 + \hat{\beta}_1 X)$ and from the difference of the two sides of the second normal equation (2.11).

using equation (2.16). Alternatively, since $\Sigma y^2 = \Sigma \hat{y}^2 + \Sigma \hat{\epsilon}^2$, ESS $= \Sigma y^2 - \Sigma \hat{y}^2$ = TSS − RSS. r^2 is then the ratio of RSS to TSS; that is, r^2 is the proportion of the total variation of Y explained by the variable X.

Example. Continuing with the regression problem of Section 2.2, we have

$$\text{RSS} = \hat{\beta}_1 \, \Sigma xy \approx 0.3117\,(5.2876 \times 10^4)$$

$$\approx 16{,}481.4491$$

$$\text{ESS} = \Sigma y^2 - \text{RSS} = \Sigma Y^2 - \frac{(\Sigma Y)^2}{n} - \text{RSS}$$

$$\approx 5{,}000{,}000 - 521{,}892.36 - 16{,}481.45$$

$$\approx 4\,{,}461{,}626.19$$

Thus,

$$r^2 = \frac{\text{RSS}}{\text{TSS}} = \frac{16{,}481.4491}{4{,}478{,}107.64} = 0.0037$$

This measure is also called the coefficient of determination. The computed value for r^2 of 0.0037 is very low and it means that the fitted line explains only 0.37% of the total variation of the Ys around their mean. The remaining 99.63% is explained by errors, or factors unaccounted for in the model. Thus, judging by this measure, the model turns out to be poor.

2.3.2 The Coefficient of Correlation and the Coefficient of Multiple Determination

The product moment correlation coefficient between the variables Y and X is defined as

$$r = \frac{\text{cov}(X, Y)}{[\text{V}(X)\text{V}(Y)]^{1/2}} \tag{2.26}$$

where cov(X, Y) is the covariance between X and Y given by

$$\text{cov}(X, Y) = \frac{\Sigma xy}{n} = \frac{\Sigma XY - (\Sigma X \Sigma Y)/n}{n}$$

and V(X) and V(Y) are the variances of X and Y:

$$\text{V}(X) = \frac{\Sigma x^2}{n} = \frac{\Sigma X^2 - (\Sigma X)^2/n}{n}$$

$$\text{V}(Y) = \frac{\Sigma y^2}{n} = \frac{\Sigma Y^2 - (\Sigma Y)^2/n}{n}$$

Thus,

$$r = \frac{\Sigma xy}{(\Sigma x^2 \Sigma y^2)^{1/2}} = \frac{\Sigma XY - (\Sigma X \Sigma Y)/n}{[\Sigma X^2 - (\Sigma X)^2/n]^{1/2}[\Sigma Y^2 - (\Sigma Y)^2/n]^{1/2}} \tag{2.27}$$

It follows that

$$\begin{aligned} r^2 &= \frac{(\Sigma xy)^2}{\Sigma x^2 \Sigma y^2} \\ &= \hat{\beta}_1 \frac{\Sigma xy}{\Sigma y^2} \qquad \left(\text{using } \hat{\beta}_1 = \frac{\Sigma xy}{\Sigma x^2}\right) \qquad (2.28) \\ &= \frac{\text{RSS}}{\text{TSS}} \\ &= 1 - \frac{\text{ESS}}{\text{TSS}} \\ &= 1 - \frac{\Sigma \hat{\epsilon}^2/n}{\Sigma y^2/n} \qquad (2.29) \end{aligned}$$

Thus, in this simple linear model, the coefficient of multiple determination is also the square of the simple correlation coefficient. From the last expression of r^2 given above, it follows that r varies between -1 and $+1$. It is 0 if $\Sigma \hat{\epsilon}^2 = \Sigma y^2$; that is, the chosen regressor accounts for none of the variation of Y and everything is due to the unaccounted for factors or errors of the model. It is 1 if $\Sigma \hat{\epsilon}^2 = 0$, which is possible if every residual $\hat{\epsilon}$ is zero, that is if the scatter of observations falls exactly on the fitted line. This is the case of the perfect fit that occurs when the regressor fully explains the variation in Y.

Notice that r is a measure of the strength of association between Y and X when the relation is linear. In the case of a nonlinear relationship, this measure may not be appropriate. For example, for a symmetric nonlinear mathematical function $Y = f(X)$, shown in Figure 2.5, the value of r can be shown to be zero as though there is no relationship between Y and X. But there is a relationship, as is clear from the diagram itself!

Equation (2.28) also gives an important relationship between the correlation

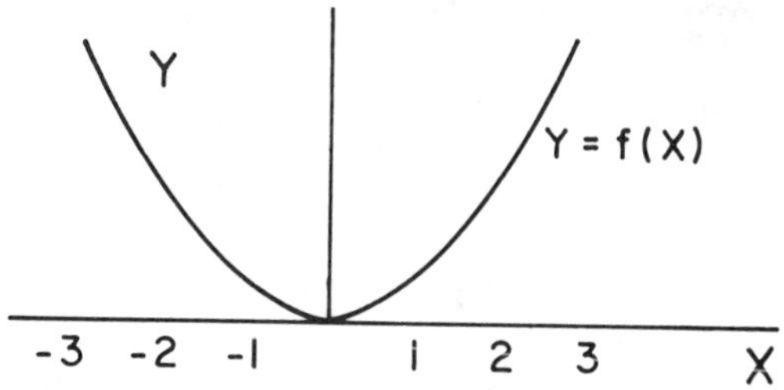

Figure 2.5

coefficient and the regression coefficient. That is,

$$r^2 = \hat{\beta}_1 \frac{\Sigma xy}{\Sigma y^2}$$

But

$$r = \frac{\Sigma xy}{(\Sigma x^2 \Sigma y^2)^{1/2}}$$

so

$$\hat{\beta}_1 = r\sqrt{\frac{\Sigma y^2}{\Sigma x^2}} = r\frac{S_y}{S_x} \tag{2.30}$$

where S_y^2 is the sample variance of Y:

$$S_y^2 = \frac{1}{n}\Sigma x^2 \tag{2.31}$$

and S_x^2 is the sample variance of X:

$$S_x^2 = \frac{1}{n}\Sigma x^2 \tag{2.32}$$

2.4 TESTS OF SIGNIFICANCE OF REGRESSION COEFFICIENTS

After the goodness of fit test, one would like to know whether the OLS estimates of coefficients of the regression line are statistically reliable. The underlying test procedure is based on the concept of sampling distributions of the parameter estimates and their properties. Among these properties, the means and variances of estimates are important. In what follows we show how the mean and variance of the OLS estimates are computed. Then we explain the Student t test for deciding on the statistical significance of the estimates. Finally we discuss the construction of confidence intervals for coefficient estimates.

2.4.1 The Mean and Variance of OLS Estimates

Basically, the following results will be derived:

1. Mean of $\hat{\beta}_0$ and $\hat{\beta}_1$:

$$E(\hat{\beta}_0) = \beta_0 \tag{2.33}$$

$$E(\hat{\beta}_1) = \beta_1 \tag{2.34}$$

2. Variance of $\hat{\beta}_0$ and $\hat{\beta}_1$ and covariance of $\hat{\beta}_0$ and $\hat{\beta}_1$:

$$V(\hat{\beta}_0) = \sigma^2 \frac{\Sigma X_i^2}{n\Sigma x_i^2} \tag{2.35}$$

$$V(\hat{\beta}_1) = \sigma^2 \frac{1}{\Sigma x_i^2} \tag{2.36}$$

$$\text{cov}(\hat{\beta}_0, \hat{\beta}_1) = \sigma^2 \frac{-\overline{X}}{\Sigma x_i^2} \tag{2.37}$$

3. Estimated variance of ϵ:

$$\hat{\sigma}^2 = \frac{\Sigma \hat{\epsilon}_i^2}{n - 2} \tag{2.38}$$

The mean of $\hat{\beta}_1$. We have established before that

$$\hat{\beta}_1 = \frac{\Sigma x_i y_i}{\Sigma x_i^2}$$

Since $\Sigma x_i = 0$, then

$$\hat{\beta}_1 = \frac{\Sigma x_i(Y_i - \overline{Y})}{\Sigma x_i^2} = \frac{\Sigma x_i Y_i}{\Sigma x_i^2}$$

One of our assumptions has been that the Xs are fixed in repeated samples. Thus, λ_i, defined as

$$\lambda_i = \frac{x_i}{\Sigma x_i^2}$$

is fixed in repeated samples. Then

$$\hat{\beta}_1 = \Sigma \lambda_i Y_i \tag{2.39}$$

But from (2.2)

$$Y_i = \beta_0 + \beta_1 X_i + \epsilon_i$$

Substituting, we get

$$\hat{\beta}_1 = \beta_0 \Sigma \lambda_i + \beta_1 \Sigma X_i \lambda_i + \Sigma \lambda_i \epsilon_i$$

But

$$\Sigma \lambda_i = \frac{\Sigma x_i}{\Sigma x_i^2} = 0 \qquad \Sigma X_i \lambda_i = \frac{\Sigma X_i(X_i - \overline{X})}{\Sigma x_i^2} = \frac{\Sigma X_i^2 - (\Sigma X_i)^2/n}{\Sigma X_i^2 - (\Sigma X_i)^2/n} = 1$$

So

$$\hat{\beta}_1 = \beta_1 + \Sigma \lambda_i \epsilon_i$$

Taking expectations gives us

$$E(\hat{\beta}_1) = \beta_1 + \Sigma\lambda_i E(\epsilon_i) = \beta_1 \quad (2.34)$$

since the expectation of a constant (β_1) is the constant itself and, by assumption, $E(\epsilon_i) = 0$, for any i.

The mean of $\hat{\beta}_0$. We have established before that

$$\beta_0 = \overline{Y} - \hat{\beta}_1\overline{X}$$

After substituting for β_1 from (2.39), this becomes

$$\hat{\beta}_0 = \overline{Y} - \overline{X}\Sigma\lambda_i Y_i = \Sigma\frac{Y_i}{n} - \overline{X}\Sigma\lambda_i Y_i = \Sigma\left(\frac{1}{n} - \overline{X}\lambda_i\right) Y_i \quad (2.40)$$

Taking expectations and substituting $\beta_0 + \beta_1 X_i$ for $E(Y_i)$ yields

$$\begin{aligned} E(\hat{\beta}_0) &= \Sigma\left(\frac{1}{n} - \overline{X}\lambda_i\right) E(Y_i) \\ &= \Sigma\left(\frac{1}{n} - \overline{X}\lambda_i\right)(\beta_0 + \beta_1 X_i) \quad (2.33) \\ &= \beta_0 + \beta_1\overline{X} - \beta_1\overline{X} \\ &= \beta_0 \end{aligned}$$

since $\Sigma\lambda_i = 0$ and $\Sigma\lambda_i X_i = 1$.

Results (2.33) and (2.34) show that β_0 and β_1 are unbiased for $\hat{\beta}_0$ and $\hat{\beta}_1$, respectively, since their means (or expected values) are the same as the respective parameters.

The variance of $\hat{\beta}_1$. Since

$$\hat{\beta}_1 = \Sigma\lambda_i Y_i = \Sigma\lambda_i(\beta_0 + \beta_1 X_i + \epsilon_i) = \beta_1 + \Sigma\lambda_i\epsilon_i$$

and

$$E(\hat{\beta}_1) = \beta_1$$

then

$$V(\hat{\beta}_1) = E(\hat{\beta}_1 - \beta_1)^2 = E(\Sigma\lambda_i\epsilon_i)^2$$

But

$$(\Sigma\lambda_i\epsilon_i)^2 = \Sigma\lambda_i^2\epsilon_i^2 + 2\sum_{i<j}\lambda_i\lambda_j\epsilon_i\epsilon_j$$

Taking expectations and using the assumption of independence of ϵ_i and ϵ_j for $i \neq j$, we have

$$\begin{aligned} V(\hat{\beta}_1) &= \sigma^2 \Sigma \lambda_i^2 \\ &= \sigma^2 \frac{1}{\Sigma x_i^2} \end{aligned} \tag{2.36}$$

since

$$\Sigma \lambda_i^2 = \Sigma \frac{x_i^2}{(\Sigma x_i^2)^2} = \frac{1}{\Sigma x_i^2}$$

The variance of $\hat{\beta}_0$. We have

$$V(\hat{\beta}_0) = E(\hat{\beta}_0 - \beta_0)^2$$

Now, since

$$\begin{aligned} \hat{\beta}_0 &= \overline{Y} - \hat{\beta}_1 \overline{X} \\ &= \beta_0 + \beta_1 \overline{X} + \overline{\epsilon} - \hat{\beta}_1 \overline{X} \\ &= \beta_0 - (\hat{\beta}_1 - \beta_1)\overline{X} + \overline{\epsilon} \end{aligned}$$

from which

$$\hat{\beta}_0 - \beta_0 = -(\hat{\beta}_1 - \beta_1)\overline{X} + \overline{\epsilon}$$

then

$$\begin{aligned} V(\hat{\beta}_0) &= E[-(\hat{\beta}_1 - \beta_1)\overline{X} + \overline{\epsilon}]^2 \\ &= \overline{X}^2 E(\hat{\beta}_1 - \beta_1)^2 + E(\overline{\epsilon})^2 - 2\overline{X}E(\hat{\beta}_1 - \beta_1)\overline{\epsilon} \end{aligned}$$

But

$$E(\overline{\epsilon})^2 = \frac{\sigma^2}{n} \qquad \text{(see (4.68) of Chapter 4)}$$

since $\overline{\epsilon}$ is the mean of a random sample of n observations drawn from the population of ϵs which have zero mean and variance σ^2. And

$$\begin{aligned} E(\hat{\beta}_1 - \beta_1)\overline{\epsilon} &= E(\Sigma \lambda_i \epsilon_i)\left(\frac{1}{n}\Sigma \epsilon_i\right) \\ &= E\frac{1}{n}\left[\Sigma \lambda_i \epsilon_i^2 + \sum_{i \neq j} (\lambda_i + \lambda_j)\epsilon_i \epsilon_j\right] \\ &= 0 \end{aligned}$$

Thus, finally

$$\begin{aligned} V(\hat{\beta}_0) &= \overline{X}^2 \frac{\sigma^2}{\Sigma x_i^2} + \frac{\sigma^2}{n} \\ &= \sigma^2 \left(\frac{1}{n} + \frac{\overline{X}^2}{\Sigma x_i^2} \right) \qquad (2.35) \\ &= \sigma^2 \frac{\Sigma X_i^2}{n \Sigma x_i^2} \end{aligned}$$

The covariance between β_0 and β_1. For the calculation of the covariance between the two estimated coefficients, we go through the following steps:

$$\begin{aligned} \text{cov}(\hat{\beta}_0, \hat{\beta}_1) &= E[(\hat{\beta}_0 - \beta_1)(\hat{\beta}_1 - \beta_1)] \\ &= E[\overline{\epsilon} - (\hat{\beta}_1 - \beta_1)\overline{X}](\hat{\beta}_1 - \beta_1) \\ &= -\overline{X}E(\hat{\beta}_1 - \beta_1)^2 \qquad (2.37) \\ &= -\frac{\overline{X}\sigma^2}{\Sigma x_i^2} \end{aligned}$$

since $E(\hat{\beta}_1 - \beta_1)\overline{\epsilon}$ was shown to be zero.

2.4.2 The Estimated Variance of the Error Variable

Recall that

$$\hat{\epsilon}_i = Y_i - \hat{Y}_i$$

which can be reduced to

$$\begin{aligned} \hat{\epsilon}_i &= (\beta_0 + \beta_1 X_i + \epsilon_i) - (\hat{\beta}_0 + \hat{\beta}_1 X_i) \\ &= \epsilon_i - (\hat{\beta}_0 - \beta_0) - (\hat{\beta}_1 - \beta_1) X_i \end{aligned}$$

Looking back into the derivation of (2.37), observe that we have used $\hat{\beta}_0 - \beta_0$ equal to $\overline{\epsilon} - (\hat{\beta}_1 - \beta_1)\overline{X}_i$. Use this again in the expression for $\hat{\epsilon}_i$ above to get

$$\hat{\epsilon}_i = (\epsilon_i - \overline{\epsilon}) - (\hat{\beta}_1 - \beta_1) x_i$$

Squaring and summing we get

$$\begin{aligned} \Sigma \hat{\epsilon}_i^2 &= \Sigma(\epsilon_i - \overline{\epsilon})^2 + (\hat{\beta}_1 - \beta_1)^2 \Sigma x_i^2 - 2(\hat{\beta}_1 - \beta_1)\Sigma x_i(\epsilon_i - \overline{\epsilon}) \\ &= \Sigma \epsilon_i^2 - n\overline{\epsilon}^2 + (\hat{\beta}_1 - \beta_1)^2 \Sigma x_i^2 - 2(\hat{\beta}_1 - \beta_1)\Sigma x_i \epsilon_i \end{aligned}$$

Our purpose is to calculate the expectation of the above equation. The expectations of parts of the right-hand side are now shown, which by combining we will obtain an expression for $E\Sigma \hat{\epsilon}_i^2$:

$$E\Sigma\epsilon_i^2 = n\sigma^2$$

$$E\bar{\epsilon}^2 = E(\bar{\epsilon} - E\bar{\epsilon})^2 = V(\bar{\epsilon}) = \frac{\sigma^2}{n} \qquad (\text{since } E\bar{\epsilon} = 0)$$

$$E(\hat{\beta}_1 - \beta_1)^2 = \frac{\sigma^2}{\Sigma x_i^2}$$

$$\begin{aligned} E(\hat{\beta}_1 - \beta_1)\Sigma x_i\epsilon_i &= E(\Sigma\lambda_i\epsilon_i)(\Sigma x_i\epsilon_i) \\ &= \sigma^2\Sigma\lambda_i x_i \\ &= \sigma^2 \qquad (\text{since } \Sigma\lambda_i x_i = 1) \end{aligned}$$

Thus

$$\begin{aligned} E\Sigma\hat{\epsilon}_i^2 &= n\sigma^2 - \sigma^2 + \sigma^2 - 2\sigma^2 \\ &= (n - 2)\sigma^2 \end{aligned}$$

which leads to

$$E\left(\frac{\Sigma\hat{\epsilon}_i^2}{n - 2}\right) = \sigma^2$$

or

$$E(\hat{\sigma}^2) = E(S^2) = \sigma^2$$

where

$$S^2 = \frac{\Sigma\hat{\epsilon}_i^2}{n - 2} \tag{2.41}$$

In other words, S^2 is an unbiased estimator of σ^2. S^2 will soon be seen to be the mean sum of squares due to error or residuals. It is the ESS divided by $n - 2$ for its degree of freedom. The degree of freedom gets smaller by 2 due to the two coefficients estimated in this simple linear regression model.

For the two-variable problem example of Section 2.3.1 the ESS was found to be 4,461,626.19. Dividing this by 9 ($= n - 2$), we get S^2 equal to 495,736.24, which is an unbiased estimate of σ^2.

2.4.3 The Estimated Standard Error of Estimate

When σ^2 is not known and has to be estimated by S^2, the estimated values of $V(\hat{\beta}_1)$ and $V(\hat{\beta}_0)$ become

$$\hat{V}(\hat{\beta}_1) = \frac{S^2}{\Sigma x_i^2}$$

$$\hat{V}(\hat{\beta}_0) = S^2\left[\frac{1}{n} + \frac{\bar{X}^2}{\Sigma x_i^2}\right]$$

where a caret is used to indicate the estimates. Taking square roots, we obtain the expressions for standard error of coefficient estimates. Using the numerical examples of Section 2.4.1, we have

$$\hat{V}(\hat{\beta}_1) \approx \frac{495{,}736.24}{16.9495 \times 10^4}$$

$$\approx 2.9248$$

$$\hat{V}(\hat{\beta}_0) \approx 495{,}736.24 \frac{1}{11} + \frac{269{,}549.7413}{16.9495 \times 10^4}$$

$$\approx 0.83343 \times 10^6$$

2.5 THE GAUSS–MARKOV THEOREM

The Gauss–Markov theorem states that the OLS estimators have the minimum variance among linear unbiased estimators. We show below that this is true for the slope coefficient estimator.[6] The proof for the intercept estimator follows very similarly and is therefore left out.

We have seen that $\hat{\beta}_1$ is an unbiased (see (2.34)) and a linear estimator. Linearity follows from the fact that the Xs are fixed, and therefore $\lambda_i = x_i/\Sigma x_i^2$ is fixed. So

$$\hat{\beta}_1 = \frac{\Sigma x_i Y_i}{\Sigma x_i^2} = \Sigma \lambda_i Y_i$$

is a linear function of the variable Y, its coefficients being fixed. This, in turn, is a linear combination of the random variable ϵ, as is clear from the model: $Y = X\beta + \epsilon$. If, however, $\hat{\beta}_1$ $(=\Sigma \lambda Y_i)$, which is the OLS estimator, does not have the minimum variance, let us consider another estimator that does: $\beta_1^* = \Sigma l_i Y_i$ based on some set of weights l_i $(i = 1, 2, \ldots, n)$ different from the λs. Using the equation for Y_i from (2.2), we have

$$\beta_1^* = \Sigma l_i(\beta_0 + \beta_1 X_i + \epsilon_i)$$

$$= \beta_0 \Sigma l_i + \beta_1 \Sigma l_i X_i + \Sigma l_i \epsilon_i$$

For β_1^* to be an unbiased estimator for β_1, we must have $E(\beta_1^*) = \beta_1$. This imposes some conditions on the weights l_i of the form

$$\Sigma l_i = 0$$
$$\Sigma l_i X_i = \Sigma l_i x_i = 1 \tag{2.42}$$

Thus,

$$V(\beta_1^*) = E(\beta_1^* - \beta_1)^2 = \sigma^2 \Sigma l_i^2 \tag{2.43}$$

[6] See the proof of this theorem in the case of the general linear model in Chapter 5.

How is Σl_i^2 compared to $\Sigma \lambda_i^2$ so we can compare the variance of β_1^* with that of $\hat{\beta}_1$? Write

$$\begin{aligned}\Sigma l_i^2 &= \Sigma [\lambda_i + l_i - \lambda_i]^2 \\ &= \Sigma \lambda_i^2 + \Sigma (l_i - \lambda_i)^2 + 2\Sigma \lambda_i (l_i - \lambda_i)\end{aligned}$$

Now

$$\Sigma \lambda_i l_i = \frac{\Sigma x_i l_i}{\Sigma x_i^2} = \frac{1}{\Sigma x_i^2} \qquad \text{(using (2.42))}$$

and since

$$\Sigma \lambda_i^2 = \frac{1}{\Sigma x_i^2}$$

we have

$$\Sigma \lambda_i (l_i - \lambda_i) = 0$$

Therefore

$$\begin{aligned}\sigma^2 \Sigma l_i^2 &= \sigma^2 \Sigma \lambda_i^2 + \sigma^2 \Sigma (l_i - \lambda_i)^2 \\ &= V(\hat{\beta}_1) + \sigma^2 \Sigma (l_i - \lambda_i)^2\end{aligned}$$

In other words, since $\sigma^2 \Sigma (l_i - \lambda_i)^2 \geqq 0$, using (2.43), we have

$$V(\beta_1^*) \geqq V(\hat{\beta}_1)$$

The sign of equality occurs only if $l_i = \lambda_i$, that is the alternative estimator is the same as the OLS estimator. Otherwise,

$$V(\beta_1^*) > V(\hat{\beta}_1) \tag{2.44}$$

This is the essence of the Gauss–Markov theorem: The OLS estimates are the best in the sense of minimum variance among linear unbiased estimates. A simpler way to put it is to call the OLS estimates BLUE (best linear unbiased estimates). These properties make the OLS estimates very popular.

2.6 THE STUDENT t TEST AND STATISTICAL INFERENCE

Since

$$\begin{aligned}\hat{\beta}_0 &= \Sigma \left(\frac{1}{n} - \overline{X}\lambda_i\right) (\beta_0 + \beta_1 X_i + \epsilon_i) \\ \hat{\beta}_1 &= \beta_1 + \Sigma \lambda_i \epsilon_i\end{aligned}$$

each of these estimates is a linear combination of the random variable ϵ, given that X_i and $\lambda_i (= x_i/\Sigma x_i^2)$ are fixed in repeated samples, and β_0 and β_1 are constants. In addition, if we assume that the ϵs are normal variables, then since the linear combination of normal variables is a normal variable, $\hat{\beta}_0$ and $\hat{\beta}_1$ will be distributed normally as follows:

$$\hat{\beta}_0 \sim N\left[\beta_0, \sigma^2\left(\frac{1}{n} + \frac{\overline{X}^2}{\Sigma x_i^2}\right)\right] \tag{2.45}$$

$$\hat{\beta}_1 \sim N\left[\beta_1, \frac{\sigma^2}{\Sigma x_i^2}\right] \tag{2.46}$$

The mean and variance of each of these estimates are the same as those calculated before.

To facilitate the test of statistical significance of these estimates, we use the following two results, which are developed in Chapter 4 and used elaborately in Chapter 5:

1. $\Sigma\hat{\epsilon}_i^2/\sigma^2$ is distributed as χ^2 with $n - 2$ degrees of freedom (df).
2. $\Sigma\hat{\epsilon}^2$ is distributed independently of $\hat{\beta}_0$ and $\hat{\beta}_1$.

Another result, which is also used in Chapter 4 in the same context, states how the Student t distribution is obtained from the ratio of a standard normal variate to the square root of a χ^2 per df. Using this result together with results 1 and 2 listed above, we have the following derived with regard to $\hat{\beta}_1$:

$$\frac{\hat{\beta}_1 - \beta_1}{\sigma/(\Sigma x_i^2)^{1/2}} \sim N(0, 1)$$

and

$$\begin{aligned} t &= \frac{(\hat{\beta}_1 - \beta_1)\sqrt{\Sigma x_i^2}}{\sigma} \Bigg/ \sqrt{\frac{\dfrac{\Sigma\hat{\epsilon}_i^2}{\sigma^2}}{n - 2}} \\ &= \frac{\hat{\beta}_1 - \beta_1}{S/(\Sigma x_i^2)^{1/2}} \end{aligned} \tag{2.47}$$

which is Student t with $n - 2$ df.

Similarly, with regard to $\hat{\beta}_0$, the derived results are

$$\frac{\hat{\beta}_0 - \beta_0}{\sigma/(1/n + \overline{X}^2/\Sigma x_i^2)^{1/2}} \sim N(0, 1)$$

and

$$\begin{aligned} t &= \frac{(\hat{\beta}_0 - \beta_0)}{\sigma} \sqrt{\frac{1}{n} + \frac{\overline{X}^2}{\Sigma x_i^2}} \Bigg/ \sqrt{\frac{\Sigma\hat{\epsilon}_i^2/\sigma^2}{n - 2}} \\ &= \frac{\hat{\beta}_0 - \beta_0}{S(1/n + \overline{X}^2/\Sigma x_i^2)^{1/2}} \end{aligned} \tag{2.48}$$

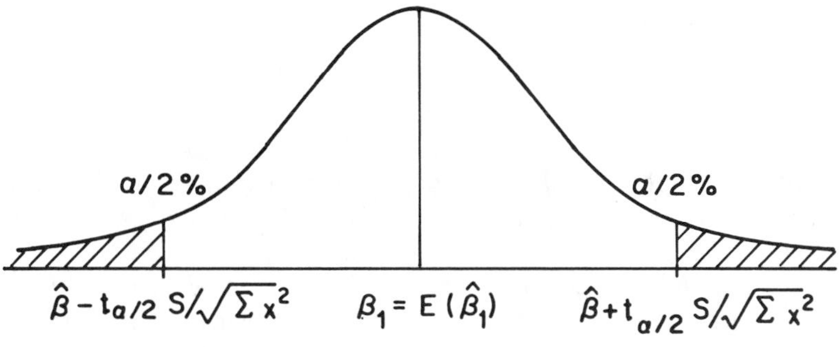

Figure 2.6

which is Student t with $n - 2$ df.

Conventional inference procedures based on formulas (2.47) and (2.48) are as follows. A $100(1 - \alpha)$ percent confidence interval for β_1 is

$$\hat{\beta}_1 \pm \frac{t_{\alpha/2} S}{(\Sigma x^2)^{1/2}} \tag{2.49}$$

where $t_{\alpha/2}$ is read off as the $\alpha/2$ percent point of the t distribution with $n - 2$ df (see Figure 2.6).

Similarly, a $100(1 - \alpha)$ percent confidence interval for β_0 is given by

$$\hat{\beta}_0 \pm t_{\alpha/2}\, S \sqrt{\frac{1}{n} + \frac{\overline{X}^2}{\Sigma x_i^2}} \tag{2.50}$$

In each case, the confidence interval is said to contain the parameter in $100(1 - \alpha)$ percent of the cases. Taking $\alpha = 0.05$, $(1 - \alpha)$, called the confidence coefficient, will be 0.95, and $t_{\alpha/2}$ will correspond to a $2\frac{1}{2}\%$ one-tailed point of the t distribution.

For the test of a specific value of a coefficient, say,

$$H_0\colon \beta_1 = \beta_1^\circ$$

the test statistic is

$$t = \frac{\hat{\beta}_1 - \beta_1^\circ}{S/(\Sigma x_i^2)^{1/2}} \tag{2.51}$$

which is Student t with $n - 2$ df. If the calculated value of t happens to be larger (smaller) than its theoretical or tabulated value at a certain probability level of significance, say α percent, then the null hypothesis $\beta_1 = \beta_1^\circ$ is rejected (accepted) at that probability level of significance. Similarly, for testing the null hypothesis about the intercept term

$$H_0\colon \beta_0 = \beta_0^\circ$$

the test statistic is

$$t = (\hat{\beta}_0 - \beta_0^\circ)/S\sqrt{\frac{1}{n} + \frac{\overline{X}^2}{\Sigma x_i^2}} \tag{2.52}$$

which is Student t with $n - 2$ df. The test procedure and interval estimation are straightforward in this case.

Example. Consider the ongoing numerical problem (Section 2.4.3) for which we assemble the following computed results for $n = 11$:

(1) $\hat{\beta}_0 \approx 55.8845,\ \hat{\beta}_1 \approx 0.3119$

(2) $\sqrt{\hat{V}(\hat{\beta}_0)} = \sqrt{S^2\left(\frac{1}{n} + \frac{\overline{X}^2}{\Sigma x_i^2}\right)} \approx \sqrt{0.83343 \times 10^6} \approx 912.9239$

(3) $\sqrt{\hat{V}(\hat{\beta}_1)} = \sqrt{\frac{S^2}{\Sigma x_i^2}} \approx \sqrt{2.9248} \approx 1.7102$

Using (2.50) and (2) above, the confidence interval for β_0 for $\alpha = 0.05$ is

$$55.8845 \pm t_{0.025}(912.9239)$$

which, since $t_{0.025} = 2.262$ based on $n - 2 = 9$ df, works out to the following:

$$-2009.1494 \text{ to } 2120.9184$$

Using (2.49) and (3) above, the confidence interval for β_1 for $\alpha = 0.05$ is

$$0.3119 \pm 2.262 \times 1.7102$$

or

$$-3.5565 \text{ to } 4.1803$$

Both intervals are so wide that the estimates overwhelmingly lack precision.

For tests of significance, assume that the null hypothesis for testing β_0 is H_0: $\beta_0 = \beta_0^\circ = 0$, and that for testing β_1 is H_0: $\beta_1 = \beta_1^\circ = 0$. Then, using (2.52) and (1) and (2),

$$t \approx \frac{55.8845 - 0}{912.923} \approx 0.0612$$

which is much less than $t_{0.025} = 2.262$ at 9 df, indicating that the test does not refute the zero value for the intercept under the null hypothesis at 5% probability level of significance.

Similarly using (2.51) and (1) and (3), we have

$$t \approx \frac{0.3119 - 0}{1.7102} \approx 0.1824$$

which is again less than $t_{0.025} = 2.262$ at 9 df, implying that the test is unable to refute the zero value of the slope coefficient under the null hypothesis at the 5% probability level of significance.

2.7 ANALYSIS OF VARIANCE

The decomposition of the total sum of squares that was done in connection with the test of the goodness of fit may be presented in a formal way in what is known as the analysis of variance or ANOVA, as in Table 2.1. Notice that items in columns ii and iii are additive. Other details of the items in column iii can be appreciated from (2.25) and the paragraph preceding it. The items of column iv are obtained by dividing the sum of squares of a particular description by its degree of freedom. Briefly, degrees of freedom indicate the number of freely floating values. The degrees of freedom of the total sum of squares is one less than the total number n of Y values: Y can go on assuming any of its n values such that the mean $\bar{Y}$ is always respected. This constraint costs the TSS one degree of freedom. Similarly, the degree of freedom of the regression sum of squares is one because of its reliance on only one free parameter β_1, the other parameter β_0 being constrained by Y and β_1. The degrees of freedom of the error sum of squares are $n - 2$, since, of the total number n of estimated residuals $\hat{\epsilon}$s, two degrees of freedom are lost by two constraints imposed by the least-squares method:[7,8]

$$\Sigma\hat{\epsilon} = 0 \quad \text{and} \quad \Sigma X\hat{\epsilon} = 0$$

In column v, we have shown the F statistic calculated as the ratio of MSR to MSE. Since the latter is an indicator of the effect of other factors, the X effect is detectable only if it rises above the level of the other factors. This motivates

TABLE 2.1 THE ANALYSIS OF VARIANCE TABLE

Source of Variation (i)	Degrees of Freedom (ii)	Sum of Squares (iii)	Mean Sum of Squares (iv)	F Calculated (v)	F Theoretical At 5% (vi)	At 1% (vii)
Regression	1	$\text{RSS} = \hat{\beta}_1\Sigma xy$	$\text{MSR} = \frac{\text{RSS}}{1}$	$\frac{\text{MSR}}{\text{MSE}}$	$F_{0.95}$	$F_{0.99}$
Residual (Error)	$n - 2$	$\text{ESS} = \Sigma y^2 - \hat{\beta}_1\Sigma xy$	$\text{MSE} = \frac{\text{ESS}}{n-2}$			
Total	$n - 1$	$\text{TSS} = \Sigma y^2$				

[7] We have shown in footnote 1 that $\bar{\hat{Y}} = \bar{Y}$, which leads to $\bar{\hat{\epsilon}} = \Sigma\hat{\epsilon}/n = 0$ since $\hat{\epsilon} = Y - \hat{Y}$.

[8] This follows from the orthogonality of X and $\hat{\epsilon}$, see footnote 2.

the inference of the significance of the X effect if only the calculated F (= MSR/MSE) exceeds the critical value of F at a given probability level of significance (5%, 1%, etc.). This probability level, in the case of the F statistic, is read off at the upper end of its distribution. The degrees of freedom of F are 1 and $n - 2$, corresponding to the degrees of freedom of its numerator and denominator sum of squares, respectively.

Example. For the numerical problem described in Sections 2.2 to 2.3.1 and 2.4.3, the ANOVA table works out to Table 2.2. As this table shows, the calculated F of 0.3324 is much smaller than the theoretical F of 5.12 and 10.56 at the 5 and 1% probability levels of significance, respectively. This supports the null hypothesis that $\beta_1 = 0$. That is, the regressor is ineffective.

The degrees of freedom for F, which generally are 1 and $n - 2$, are 1 and 9 for this numerical problem. There is a relation between F and Student t when the numerator degree of freedom of F is 1:

$$F_{(1,n-2)} = t^2_{(n-2)}$$

where the numbers in the parenthesis are the degrees of freedom. Thus,

$$t = \sqrt{F}$$

which gives rise to two formulas, one in terms of β_1 and its test, and the other in terms of the correlation coefficient r (between Y and X) and its test. For the first formula, note that using $\hat{\beta}_1 \Sigma xy = \hat{\beta}_1^2 \Sigma x^2$ from (2.25)

$$t = \sqrt{F} = \sqrt{\frac{\hat{\beta}_1^2 \Sigma x^2}{S^2}} = \frac{\hat{\beta}_1}{S/(\Sigma x^2)^{1/2}}$$

Consequently, a test of F for the overall regression leads to a test of t for $\beta_1 = \beta_1^\circ = 0$ under the null hypothesis. Indeed, the significance of the regression amounts to the significance of the regressor since there is only one free regressor in this simple regression model. (*Warning:* This would not be the case in the multiple regression model, where there will be more than one free regressor.)

TABLE 2.2 THE ANOVA TABLE FOR THE NUMERICAL PROBLEM

Source of Variation	df	SS	MSS	F: Calculated	F: $F_{0.95}$	F: $F_{0.99}$
Regression	1	16 481.4491	16 481.4491	0.3324	5.12	10.56
Residual (Error)	9	4 461 626.19	495 736.2433			
Total	10	4 478 107.64				

For the second formula, note that

$$t = \sqrt{F} = \sqrt{\text{RSS/ESS}/(n - 2)}$$

$$= \sqrt{\frac{r^2(n - 2)}{1 - r^2}}$$

$$= \frac{r\sqrt{n - 2}}{(1 - r^2)^{1/2}}$$

since

$$r^2 = \frac{\text{RSS}}{\text{TSS}} \qquad 1 - r^2 = \frac{\text{ESS}}{\text{TSS}}$$

This formula tests whether the correlation coefficient between Y and X is significant or not. The degrees of freedom of t in both formulas are $n - 2$.

Applying these formulas to the numerical problem at hand, we have

$$t = \frac{\hat{\beta}_1}{S/(\Sigma x^2)^{1/2}} \approx \frac{0.3117}{1.7102} \approx 0.18$$

$$t = \frac{r\sqrt{9}}{(1 - r^2)^{1/2}} \approx \frac{0.0608 \times 3}{0.9981} \approx 0.18$$

The t values are the same and statistically insignificant, and therefore should lead to the same inference, even though in terms of different criteria.

2.8 PREDICTION

Prediction, in the context of the regression model, is the general name given to the determination of a yet unobserved future value of Y, or a value, as yet undetermined, that arises within the sample time period under investigation. This is the time period that has turned out observations Y_i, X_i for the two variables at time points $i = 1, 2, \ldots, n$ and that has led to the estimated regression line $\hat{Y}_i = \hat{\beta}_0 + \hat{\beta}_1 X_i$ based on the OLS method. As a prediction for the future, one uses a predicted value of X, say X_e, however obtained, as the basis for the predicted value Y_e of Y. As a prediction within the sample period, one essentially chooses a known value of X, say X_e, not necessarily equaling the observations $X_1, \ldots, X_n$ within the sample period, to test how the predicted value of Y agrees with its actual value at X_e.

But otherwise the assumption is that the relationship that is capable of generating the sample observations Y_i, X_i $(i = 1, \ldots, n)$ also generates the observable yet undetermined observation within the sample and the strictly unseen observation (Y_e, X_e) outside the sample. To illustrate the prediction problems, assume that we have data on the quantity of milk consumed (Y) and price per unit of milk (X) in Wisconsin available over the period 1970 to 1985 at 5-year intervals to which we have fitted a least-squares line. Y_e, X_e may refer to the future year 1995, or the year 1982 that was a year within the chosen sample period *and within* a 5-year interval. Any existing or assumed value of X in 1982 may be tested for its effect on Y using the estimated regression model.

As with estimates of a parameter, prediction of an observation on Y may entail both a point and an interval concept. For a point prediction, let us consider $\hat{Y}_e$ corresponding to X_e given by

$$\hat{Y}_e = \hat{\beta}_0 + \hat{\beta}_1 X_e$$

Compare it with the actual value Y_e given from the model as

$$Y_e = \beta_0 + \beta_1 X_e + \epsilon_e$$

in which ϵ_e is the observation on the residual term at the point in time e. The forecast error is

$$\begin{aligned} f_e &= Y_e - \hat{Y}_e \\ &= \epsilon_e - (\hat{\beta}_0 - \beta_0) - (\hat{\beta}_1 - \beta_1)X_e \end{aligned} \tag{2.53}$$

It is easy to see that f_e has a mean value 0 and variance

$$\sigma^2 \left[1 + \frac{1}{n} + \frac{(X_e - \overline{X})^2}{\Sigma x_i^2} \right]$$

because

$$E(f_e) = 0$$

due to $E(\epsilon_e) = 0$; $\hat{\beta}_0$ and $\hat{\beta}_1$ are unbiased for β_0 and β_1, and

$$\begin{aligned} V(f_e) &= V(\epsilon_e) + V(\hat{\beta}_0) + V(\hat{\beta}_1)X_e^2 + 2\,\mathrm{cov}(\hat{\beta}_0, \hat{\beta}_1)X_e \\ &= \sigma^2 \left[1 + \frac{1}{n} + \frac{\overline{X}^2}{\Sigma x_i^2} + \frac{X_e^2}{\Sigma x_i^2} - \frac{2X_e\overline{X}}{\Sigma x_i^2} \right] \\ &= \sigma^2 \left[1 + \frac{1}{n} + \frac{(X_e - \overline{X})^2}{\Sigma x_i^2} \right] \end{aligned} \tag{2.54}$$

using the results (2.35) to (2.37). It is evident from (2.53) that $\hat{\epsilon}_e$ is a linear combination of normal variables. Its distribution will be normal, as expressed in

$$\frac{f_e}{\sigma \sqrt{1 + \dfrac{1}{n} + \dfrac{(X_e - \overline{X})^2}{\Sigma x^2}}} \sim N(0, 1)$$

Also, from (2.54), should σ^2 be unknown and be replaced by $S^2 = \Sigma\hat{\epsilon}^2/(n - 2)$, then, as in the case of the test of a regression coefficient described in Section

2.6, we have

$$(Y_e - \hat{Y}_e)/S\sqrt{1 + \frac{1}{n} + \frac{(X_e - \overline{X})^2}{\Sigma x_i^2}} \sim t_{(n-2)} \qquad (2.55)$$

In other words, it is a Student t with $n - 2$ degrees of freedom. The 99% confidence interval for Y_e, using (2.55), is derived as

$$\hat{Y}_e \pm t_{0.005}S\sqrt{1 + \frac{1}{n} + \frac{(X_e - \overline{X})^2}{\Sigma x_i^2}} \qquad (2.56)$$

where $\hat{Y}_e$ equals $\hat{\beta}_0 + \hat{\beta}_1 X_e$.

In some contexts, one may be interested in forecasting the mean value of Y at a future date, say $E(Y_e)$, rather than predict one individual future observation Y_e, which may not be easy to identify. As Figure 2.7 shows, there are multiple values of Y_e: $Y_e^1, Y_e^2, \ldots, Y_e^l$ with the mean value $E(Y_e)$ in the population corresponding to X_e. The forecast error for the mean is then:

$$\begin{aligned} f_e &= E(Y_e) - \hat{Y}_e \\ &= -(\hat{\beta}_0 - \beta_0) - (\hat{\beta}_1 - \beta_1)X_e \end{aligned}$$

f_e is distributed normally with zero mean and variance:

$$\begin{aligned} V(f_e) &= V(\hat{\beta}_0) + X_e^2 V(\hat{\beta}_1) + 2X_e \operatorname{cov}(\hat{\beta}_0, \hat{\beta}_1) \\ &= \sigma^2\left(\frac{1}{n} + \frac{\overline{X}^2}{\Sigma x_i^2} + \frac{X_e^2}{\Sigma x_i^2} - \frac{2X_e\overline{X}}{\Sigma x_i^2}\right) \\ &= \sigma^2\left[\frac{1}{n} + \frac{(X_e - \overline{X})^2}{\Sigma x_i^2}\right] \end{aligned}$$

Like before, we have

$$\frac{E(Y_e) - \hat{Y}_e}{S[1/n + (X_e - \overline{X})^2/\Sigma x_i^2]^{1/2}} \sim t_{(n-2)} \qquad (2.57)$$

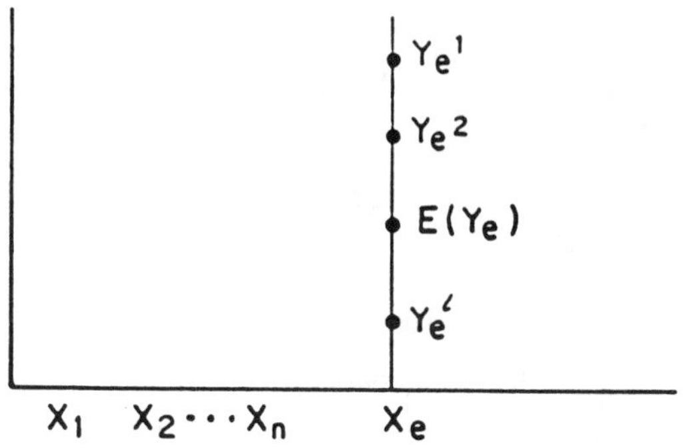

Figure 2.7

and a 99% confidence interval for $E(Y_e)$ is

$$\hat{Y}_e \pm t_{0.005} S \sqrt{\frac{1}{n} + \frac{(X_e - \overline{X})^2}{\Sigma x_i^2}} \tag{2.58}$$

For confidence intervals with different confidence coefficients, the critical value of t will change, its degree of freedom $n - 2$ remaining the same. For instance, for the confidence coefficient of 100(1 − 0.05) or 95%, the critical value of t will be denoted by $t_{0.025}$.

Example. We want to illustrate the problem of prediction with the previous numerical example of this chapter. The relevant information is

$$\hat{Y} = 55.8845 + 0.3119X$$

$$X = 519.1818$$

$$S^2 = \frac{\Sigma \hat{\epsilon}^2}{n - 2} = 495{,}736.24$$

$$\Sigma x_i^2 = 16.9495 \times 10^4$$

$$n = 11$$

Let X_e be 600.00. Then a 99% confidence interval for Y_e is

$$55.8845 + 0.3119(600.00) \pm 3.250 \times 704.0854 \sqrt{1 + \frac{1}{11} + \frac{(600.00 - 519.18)^2}{16.9495 \times 10^4}}$$

or

$$243.0245 \pm 2431.9783$$

or

$$-2188.9538 \text{ to } 2675.0028$$

Similarly, a 99% confidence interval for $E(Y_e)$ is

$$243.0245 \pm 3.250 \times 704.0854 \sqrt{\frac{1}{11} + \frac{(600.00 - 519.18)^2}{16.9495 \times 10^4}}$$

or

$$243.0245 \pm 823.3222$$

or

$$-580.2977 \text{ to } 1066.3467$$

Both intervals are too wide, in keeping with what we have already observed in the context of confidence intervals, for a regression coefficient in this numerical problem. Large intervals imply little or no importance of the sample forecast in locating a single future observation or the mean (expected) observation on the dependent variable in the population. Small intervals do just the opposite.

2.9 AN APPLIED STUDY OF A TWO-VARIABLE REGRESSION

Mayes (1981) uses annual data for the United Kingdom over the period 1949 to 1975 to derive the following consumption function for that country by the OLS method:

$$C = \underset{(312)}{4{,}141} + \underset{(0.01)}{0.78}\, Y \qquad R^2 = 99.6\%$$

where C is aggregate consumption, Y aggregate income, and both are measured in 1970 prices. The figures within parentheses are standard errors of coefficients. The marginal propensity to consume ($= dC/dY$) is 0.78, the coefficient of Y. The fit is quite good on the basis of a very high value of R^2. Both the intercept and slope coefficients are significantly different from zero by the t test (having values of 13.3 and 74.3, respectively) and these coefficients have the expected signs and values.

2.10 AN EXTENSION TO THREE VARIABLES AND AN INTRODUCTION TO MULTIPLE REGRESSION

Here we very briefly consider the three-variable regression

$$Y_i = \beta_0 + \beta_1 X_{i1} + \beta_2 X_{i2} + \epsilon_i \qquad i = 1, 2, \ldots, n$$

where X_1 and X_2 are the two independent variables, Y is the dependent variable, the βs are the coefficients, and ϵ is the random component. If X_1 is the price of a commodity, say coffee, X_2 is consumer income, and Y is the demand for that commodity, then we expect β_1 to be negative but β_2 to be positive. The latter follows from the fact that for normal commodities such as coffee the quantity demanded moves in the same direction as income.

As before, the estimates of the βs are derived by minimizing the sum of squared residuals

$$\text{ESS} = \sum_1^n \hat{\epsilon}_i^2 = \sum_1^n (Y_i - \hat{Y}_i)^2 = \sum_1^n (Y_i - \hat{\beta}_0 - \hat{\beta}_1 X_{i1} - \hat{\beta}_2 X_{i2})^2 \qquad (2.59)$$

where

$$\hat{Y}_i = \hat{\beta}_0 + \hat{\beta}_1 X_{i1} + \hat{\beta}_2 X_{i2}$$

is the ith observation ($i = 1, 2, \ldots, n$) on the OLS estimated Y, and $\hat{\beta}_0$, $\hat{\beta}_1$, and

$\hat{\beta}_2$ are the OLS estimated values of the parameters β_0, β_1, and β_2. The ESS is a function of $\hat{\beta}_0$, $\hat{\beta}_1$, and $\hat{\beta}_2$. Thus, the necessary condition for a minimum of ESS is

$$\frac{\partial \text{ESS}}{\partial \hat{\beta}_0} = \frac{\partial \text{ESS}}{\partial \hat{\beta}_1} = \frac{\partial \text{ESS}}{\partial \hat{\beta}_2} = 0$$

These lead to three normal equations:

$$\Sigma Y = n\hat{\beta}_0 + \hat{\beta}_1 \Sigma X_1 + \hat{\beta}_2 \Sigma X_2$$

$$\Sigma X_1 Y = \hat{\beta}_0 \Sigma X_1 + \hat{\beta}_1 \Sigma X_1^2 + \hat{\beta}_2 \Sigma X_1 X_2$$

$$\Sigma X_2 Y = \hat{\beta}_0 \Sigma X_2 + \hat{\beta}_1 \Sigma X_1 X_2 + \hat{\beta}_2 \Sigma X_2^2$$

The summations are over the n sample observations of the variables. These three equations are derived in the same way as the two normal equations in the two-variable case, as shown in footnote 2. Solution of these equations will follow a very lengthy process of elimination of variables, which can very simply be handled with matrix algebra (Chapter 3), as will indeed be used in Chapter 5 in connection with the general multiple regression model. That model includes the three-variable model as a special case.

As in the two-variable case, solution of the normal equations can be facilitated by expressing the variables as deviations from their means. As before, we use lowercase letters for such deviations:

$$y_i = Y_i - \overline{Y} \qquad x_{i1} = X_{i1} - \overline{X}_1 \qquad x_{i2} = X_{i2} - \overline{X}_2$$

where $\overline{Y}$, $\overline{X}_1$, and $\overline{X}_2$ are the means of the Ys, X_1s, and X_2s. From the first normal equation, dividing both sides by n we get

$$\overline{Y} = \hat{\beta}_0 + \hat{\beta}_1 \overline{X}_1 + \hat{\beta}_2 \overline{X}_2 \tag{2.60}$$

And since

$$\hat{Y} = \hat{\beta}_0 + \hat{\beta}_1 X_1 + \hat{\beta}_2 X_2$$

summing this over all observations and dividing by n, we get

$$\overline{\hat{Y}} = \hat{\beta}_0 + \hat{\beta}_1 \overline{X}_1 + \hat{\beta}_2 \overline{X}_2 \tag{2.61}$$

where $\overline{\hat{Y}}$ is the mean of $\hat{Y}$s. If the right-hand sides of (2.60) and (2.61) are equal, then $\overline{Y}$ and $\overline{\hat{Y}}$ are equal. Thus,

$$\hat{\epsilon}_i = y_i - \hat{y}_i$$

where

$$\hat{y}_i = \hat{Y}_i - \overline{Y} = \hat{\beta}_1 x_{i1} + \hat{\beta}_2 x_{i2}$$

The sum of squared residuals is

$$\text{ESS} = \Sigma \hat{\epsilon}_i^2 = \Sigma (y_i - \hat{y}_i)^2 = \Sigma (y_i - \hat{\beta}_1 x_{i1} - \hat{\beta}_2 x_{i2})^2 \tag{2.62}$$

Minimizing this with respect to $\hat{\beta}_1$ and $\hat{\beta}_2$, that is setting $\partial \Sigma \hat{\epsilon}_i^2 / \partial \hat{\beta}_i = 0$ for $i = 1$, 2, we get (after often suppressing the subscript for sample observations)

$$\begin{aligned} \Sigma x_1 y &= \hat{\beta}_1 \Sigma x_1^2 + \hat{\beta}_2 \Sigma x_1 x_2 \\ \Sigma x_2 y &= \hat{\beta}_1 \Sigma x_1 x_2 + \hat{\beta}_2 \Sigma x_2^2 \end{aligned} \tag{2.63}$$

Solving, we get

$$\begin{aligned} \hat{\beta}_1 &= \frac{\Sigma x_1 y \Sigma x_2^2 - \Sigma x_2 y \Sigma x_1 x_2}{\Sigma x_1^2 \Sigma x_2^2 - (\Sigma x_1 x_2)^2} \\ \hat{\beta}_2 &= \frac{\Sigma x_2 y\, \Sigma x_1^2 - \Sigma x_1 y \Sigma x_1 x_2}{\Sigma x_1^2 \Sigma x_2^2 - (\Sigma x_1 x_2)^2} \end{aligned} \tag{2.64}$$

and therefore

$$\hat{\beta}_0 = \overline{Y} - \hat{\beta}_1 \overline{X}_1 - \hat{\beta}_2 \overline{X}_2 \tag{2.65}$$

For the calculation of the coefficient of multiple determination denoted now as R^2, we still use the formula

$$R^2 = \frac{\Sigma \hat{y}^2}{\Sigma y^2} = \frac{\text{Regression Sum of Squares}}{\text{Total Sum of Squares}} \tag{2.66}$$

which equivalently can be expressed as

$$R^2 = 1 - \frac{\Sigma \hat{\epsilon}^2}{\Sigma y^2} = 1 - \frac{\text{ESS}}{\text{TSS}} \tag{2.67}$$

Now

$$\begin{aligned} \Sigma \hat{\epsilon}_i^2 &= \Sigma \hat{\epsilon}_i (y_i - \hat{y}_i) \\ &= \Sigma \hat{\epsilon}_i (y_i - \hat{\beta}_1 x_{i1} - \hat{\beta}_2 x_{i2}) \\ &= \Sigma \hat{\epsilon}_i y_i - \hat{\beta}_1 \Sigma \hat{\epsilon}_i x_{i1} - \hat{\beta}_2 \Sigma x_{i2} \hat{\epsilon}_i \end{aligned}$$

But, we can show from $\partial \text{ESS} / \partial \hat{\beta}_1 = 0$ and $\partial \text{ESS} / \partial \hat{\beta}_2 = 0$ that

$$\Sigma \hat{\epsilon}_i x_{i1} = 0 \qquad \Sigma \hat{\epsilon}_i x_{i2} = 0$$

Thus,

$$\begin{aligned} \Sigma \hat{\epsilon}_i^2 &= \Sigma \hat{\epsilon}_i y_i \\ &= \Sigma (y_i - \hat{y}_i) y_i \\ &= \Sigma y_i^2 - \hat{\beta}_1 \Sigma y x_1 - \hat{\beta}_2 \Sigma y x_2 \end{aligned} \tag{2.68}$$

Therefore,

$$R^2 = 1 - \frac{\Sigma \hat{\epsilon}^2}{\Sigma y^2} = \frac{\hat{\beta}_1 \Sigma x_1 y + \hat{\beta}_2 \Sigma x_2 y}{\Sigma y^2} \tag{2.69}$$

On the other hand, the regression sum of squares is

$$\begin{aligned} \text{RSS} &= \Sigma\hat{y}^2 \\ &= \Sigma\hat{y}(\hat{\beta}_1 x_1 + \hat{\beta}_2 x_2) \qquad (2.70) \\ &= \hat{\beta}_1 \Sigma x_1 y + \hat{\beta}_2 \Sigma x_2 y \end{aligned}$$

Thus, R^2, from (2.70), is RSS/TSS.

2.10.1 Partial Correlation

Incidentally, in the context of two or more independent variables the concept of the *partial* correlation coefficient becomes important. This measures the correlation between any two variables, when all other variables are kept constant, in other words when we have eliminated the effect of other variables from these two variables. It can be shown that

$$r_{yx_1 \cdot x_2} = \frac{r_{yx_1} - r_{yx_2} r_{x_1x_2}}{(1 - r_{yx_2}^2)^{1/2}(1 - r_{x_1x_2}^2)^{1/2}}$$

where

$r_{yx_1 \cdot x_2}$ = the partial correlation coefficient between Y and X_1, net of the influence of X_2

r_{yx_1}, r_{yx_2} = the simple correlation coefficient between Y and X_1, between Y and X_2

$r_{x_1x_2}$ = the simple correlation coefficient between X_1 and X_2

For a numerical example, if

$$r_{yx_1} = 0.3 \qquad r_{yx_2} = 0.5 \qquad r_{x_1x_2} = 0.4$$

then

$$\begin{aligned} r_{yx_1 \cdot x_2} &= \frac{0.3 - (0.5)(0.4)}{(1 - 0.25)^{1/2}(1 - 0.16)^{1/2}} \\ &\approx \frac{0.1}{0.7937} \\ &\approx 0.126 \end{aligned}$$

Notice that there can be another partial correlation coefficient, namely $r_{yx_2 \cdot x_1}$, which is the partial correlation coefficient between Y and X_2, net of the effect of X_1. This is expressed as

$$r_{yx_2 \cdot x_1} = \frac{r_{yx_2} - r_{yx_1} r_{x_1x_2}}{(1 - r_{yx_1}^2)^{1/2}(1 - r_{x_1x_2}^2)^{1/2}}$$

Notice also that any such partial correlation coefficient between two variables can be looked at or obtained from the correlation coefficient between the residuals remaining in each variable after the linear effect of other regressors has been eliminated. For instance $r_{yx_1 \cdot x_2}$ is the correlation coefficient between $y - \beta_{y2}x_2$ and $x_1 - \beta_{12}x_2$: The first is the residual from a regression of Y on X_2 alone, with β_{y2} the associated regression coefficient, and the second the residual from a regression of X_1 on X_2 alone, the so-called auxiliary regression, with β_{12} the associated regression coefficient. The residuals are a way of removing the effect of the variable or variables held fixed while defining the partial correlation coefficient. The residuals have been defined here in terms of variables Y, X_1, and X_2 expressed as deviations y, x_1, and x_2 from their means so that the intercept terms of the regressions have been netted out. Similarly, $r_{yx_2 \cdot x_1}$ is the partial correlation coefficient obtained by correlating the residuals $y - \beta_{y1}x_1$ and $x_2 - \beta_{21}x_1$.

The concept of partial correlation coefficients can be extended to models based on a larger number of explanatory variables in a straightforward fashion.[9] Going back to the OLS estimates of the βs, there are other inference properties of them that we have not discussed yet. Indeed, we do not like to examine these properties in the context of the three-variable case; they are discussed in a more general setting in Chapter 5. We now illustrate the calculation of the estimates in a three-variable case, present an actual applied study, and discuss some simple extensions to nonlinear situations.

Example. An estimated three-variable model. Take the following variables in a hypothetical regression problem:

Y = percent Republican vote in a county

X_1 = median family income in thousands of dollars

X_2 = median number of school years completed by voters

Using data from 60 counties of a state in the presidential election of a past year, the following results are used to fit the following model:

$$Y = \beta_0 + \beta_1 X_1 + \beta_2 X_2 + \epsilon$$

$$\Sigma X_1 = 1{,}878.0 \qquad \Sigma X_1^2 = 65{,}300.0 \qquad \Sigma X_1 Y = 98{,}354.2$$

$$\Sigma X_2 = 484.9 \qquad \Sigma X_2^2 = 4{,}038.89 \qquad \Sigma X_2 Y = 26{,}242.93$$

$$\Sigma Y = 3{,}266.3 \qquad \Sigma Y^2 = 191{,}766.56 \qquad \Sigma X_1 X_2 = 15{,}171.7$$

Expressed in deviations from the means of variables, the following results are computed:

$$\Sigma x_1^2 = 6{,}518.6 \qquad \Sigma x_1 y = -3{,}882.0$$

$$\Sigma x_2^2 = 120.09 \qquad \Sigma x_2 y = -154.22$$

$$\Sigma y^2 = 13{,}955.00 \qquad \Sigma x_1 x_2 = -5.7$$

[9] For definition and proof of these concepts and results, see a second-year statistics text, e.g. Mood and Graybill (1965).

Using (2.64), we have

$$\hat{\beta}_1 = \frac{(-3{,}882.0)(120.09) - (-154.22)(-5.7)}{6{,}518.6 \times 120.09 - (-5.7)^2}$$

$$= \frac{-466{,}189.35 - 8{,}790.54}{782{,}818.67 - 32.49}$$

$$= \frac{-474{,}979.92}{782{,}786.18} = -0.61$$

$$\hat{\beta}_2 = \frac{(-154.22)6{,}518.6 - (-3{,}882.0)(-5.7)}{6{,}518.6 \times 120.09 - (-5.7)^2}$$

$$= \frac{-1{,}005{,}298.5 - 22{,}127.4}{782{,}786.18}$$

$$= \frac{-1{,}027{,}425.9}{782{,}786.18} = -1.03$$

Thus,

$$\hat{\beta}_0 = \overline{Y} - \hat{\beta}_1\overline{X}_1 - \hat{\beta}_2\overline{X}_2$$

$$= \frac{1}{60}[3{,}266.3 - (-0.61) \times 1{,}878.0 - (-1.03)484.9]$$

$$= \frac{1}{60}[4{,}911.33] = 81.85$$

Therefore,

$$\hat{Y} = 81.85 - 0.61X_1 - 1.03X_2$$

This line indicates that voter preference for the Republican party did not go hand in hand with family income ($\beta_1 < 0$). The same is true with voter education ($\beta_2 < 0$). It also reveals an autonomous voter preference for this party of much more than 50% ($\beta_0 = 81.85$), regardless of their income and education levels.

The coefficient of multiple determination R^2 is computed as

$$R^2 = \frac{\beta_1 \Sigma x_1 y + \beta_2 \Sigma x_2 y}{\Sigma y^2}$$

$$= \frac{2{,}368.02 + 158.85}{13{,}955.00}$$

$$= \frac{2{,}526.87}{13{,}955.00}$$

$$= 0.18$$

The fit is poor, as is evident from the value of R^2, which is as low as 18%.

2.11 AN APPLIED THREE-VARIABLE REGRESSION MODEL

We refer to the "life-cycle" theory of consumption propounded by Ando and Modigliani (1963). According to this, a consumer's current consumption is a function of the expected value of his future (lifetime) stream of income. To test this theory, the authors use the following formulation of the consumption function:

$$C_t = \beta_0 + \beta_1 Y_{dt} + \beta_2 A_{t-1} + \epsilon_t$$

where C_t is consumption, Y_{dt} is current disposable labor income (used as a proxy for expected income from labor services), A_{t-1} is the last period's net worth of consumers, used to measure expected nonlabor property income, and ϵ_t is the disturbance term. Annual data over the period 1929 to 1959 are used (excluding the war years, 1941 to 1945). These are in billions of current dollars. The estimated function, based on 25 observations, is obtained as

$$\underset{}{C_t} = \underset{(1.46)}{5.33} + \underset{(0.047)}{0.767}\, Y_{dt} + \underset{(0.010)}{0.047}\, A_{t-1} \qquad R^2 = 0.999$$

The figures underneath the coefficients are their estimated standard errors.

All the coefficients come out positive, as expected. The marginal propensity to consume from the disposable labor income (the coefficient of Y_{dt}) is between zero and unity; but that of last year's rental or interest income (the coefficient of A_{t-1}) is significantly smaller. The t test results indicate that the coefficients are statistically significant at both the 5 and 1% probability levels of significance. The fit is quite good, going by the very high value of R^2.

Even then, we should perhaps remember one important thing. However favorable the statistical support is for a particular theory such as the "life-cycle" hypothesis, the evidence should not be taken to mean that that is the only theory and that there cannot be other theories of consumption possible or acceptable. What growing empirical evidence may offer is only reasonable grounds, and we may use them to discriminate between competing theories to be able ultimately to choose the "best" theory.

2.12 EXTENSION TO NONLINEAR RELATIONS AND TRANSFORMATIONS TO LINEARITY

For many economic problems, the linear relationship between the dependent and independent variables may be untenable. Indeed, nonlinear relations may be the rule rather than the exception in a complex world such as ours.

Some frequently occurring nonlinear relationships are represented by polynomials in the Xs as in

$$Y = \beta_0 + \beta_1 X + \beta_2 X^2 + \cdots + \epsilon \tag{2.71}$$

or by a constant elasticity formula:

$$Y = \beta_0 X_1^{\beta_1} X_2^{\beta_2} \epsilon \tag{2.72}$$

where

$$\beta_1 = \text{the elasticity of } Y \text{ with respect to } X_1$$

$$\beta_2 = \text{the elasticity of } Y \text{ with respect to } X_2$$

For instance, a U-shaped average cost curve may follow from a total cost curve, which is fairly adequately expressed by a polynomial of the third degree in output:

$$Y = \beta_0 + \beta_1 X - \beta_2 X^2 + \beta_3 X^3 + \epsilon$$

where Y stands for total cost and X is output. Dividing both sides by X, we get the U-shaped average cost curve:

$$\frac{Y}{X} = \frac{\beta_0}{X} + \beta_1 - \beta_2 X + \beta_3 X^2$$

except for the error term.

A constant elasticity formula (2.72) is exemplified by a demand equation with constant price and income elasticities. Here X_1 stands for the price of a commodity, X_2 is consumers' disposable income, and Y is the quantity demanded of the commodity. Then

$$\beta_1 = \eta_{x1} = \frac{dY}{dX_1}\frac{X_1}{Y} = \frac{d \ln Y}{d \ln X_1}$$

is the price elasticity of demand, and

$$\beta_2 = \eta_{x2} = \frac{dY}{dX_2}\frac{X_2}{Y} = \frac{d \ln Y}{d \ln X_2}$$

is the income elasticity of demand.

Direct estimation of nonlinear relations may involve very complicated computations. However, estimation can still be performed by suitable transformations so that the relations become linear as a result and the OLS method can be applied. Take, for instance, the two nonlinear examples already cited.

For the polynomial relation

$$Y = \beta_0 + \beta_1 X + \beta_2 X^2 + \cdots + \epsilon \tag{2.73}$$

the transformation used is to equate old to new variables:

$$\begin{aligned} X &= X_1 \\ X^2 &= X_2 \\ &\cdots \end{aligned} \tag{2.74}$$

so that in terms of the new variables $X_1, X_2, \ldots$ the relationship is linear:

$$Y = \beta_0 + \beta_1 X_1 + \beta_2 X_2 + \cdots + \epsilon \tag{2.75}$$

Therefore, the OLS method is immediately applicable to such a linear function. Similarly, the constant elasticity function can be linearized by the logarithmic transformation:

$$\begin{aligned} \ln Y &= y \\ \ln X &= x_1 \\ \ln X_2 &= x_2 \\ \ln \epsilon &= u \end{aligned} \tag{2.76}$$

The transformed function is

$$y = \beta_0 + \beta_1 x_1 + \beta_2 x_2 + u \tag{2.77}$$

which is linear. Therefore, it can be fitted by the OLS method.[10]

This transformation is simply called the log–log or double-log transformation. Another transformation of the logarithmic variety is called the semilog transformation. This is applied to an equation of the following type:

$$Y = \exp(\beta_0 + \beta_1 X + \epsilon) \tag{2.78}$$

After transformation it becomes

$$\ln Y = \beta_0 + \beta_1 X + \epsilon \tag{2.79}$$

It follows that

$$\frac{1}{Y}\frac{dY}{dX} = \beta_1$$

In other words, β_1 is the proportionate rate of change of Y for one unit change in X. A model such as (2.79) is extensively employed in problems of human capital. There Y represents earnings and X years of school. For more details, see Mincer (1974).

Substituting

$$\ln Y = y \qquad X = x \qquad \epsilon = \epsilon \tag{2.80}$$

we have

$$y = \beta_0 + \beta_1 x + \epsilon \tag{2.81}$$

which is linear and can be fitted by the OLS method.

There are other transformations applicable to other model situations, or more complicated aspects of a transformation already considered. All of these will be

[10] In Chapter 6 we point out and address some special problems that arise with logarithmic transformations.

taken up in Chapter 6, only after the general multiple regression model has been presented and discussed.

PROBLEMS

2-1. Consider a simple linear regression model specified by

$$Y_i = \beta_0 + \beta_1 X_i + \epsilon_i$$

with OLS assumptions. $\overline{\beta}_1$ is a ratio estimator defined as

$$\overline{\beta}_1 = \frac{1}{n-1} \sum_{i=2}^{n} \frac{Y_i - Y_{i-1}}{X_i - X_{i-1}}$$

(a) How do you interpret this estimator to be a slope estimator?

(b) Writing

$$E(Y_i) = \beta_1 X_i$$

$$E(Y_{i-1}) = \beta_1 X_{i-1}$$

show that $\overline{\beta}_1$ is unbiased for β_1.

(c) Using the method of Section 2.4, compute $V(\overline{\beta}_1)$. Compare this variance with the variance of the OLS estimator $\hat{\beta}_1$. Which is smaller and which is higher? Why?

2-2. In a consumption function study involving five families, suppose the following are the data on their income and consumption expenditure:

Family	Income Y (\$)	Consumption expenditure C (\$)
1	32,000	28,000
2	44,000	36,000
3	36,000	31,000
4	24,000	21,000
5	25,000	23,000

(a) Fit and plot the line of regression of consumption expenditure C on income Y.

(b) What is the special significance of the intercept term of this relation?

2-3. To arrive at a demand schedule for watermelons, an investigator observes that the price of watermelons drops significantly during periods of abundant supply and special sales, and rises appreciably during periods of scarcity. Suppose the following are the data on quantity of watermelons sold (Y) and price (X) in 8 weeks during the summer collected from a local grocery store:

Watermelons sold $Y\ (\times 10^3)$	Price per watermelon X (\$)
10	3
9	4
8	5
7	$5\frac{1}{2}$
6	6
5	$6\frac{1}{2}$
4	7
2	$7\frac{1}{2}$

Assume that all the watermelons sold are of equal weights.

(a) Fit a demand equation to the above data given by

$$Y = \beta_0 + \beta_1 X + \epsilon$$

(b) What is the 95% confidence interval for the quantity of watermelons sold in week 9 when the price per watermelon is \$8 in that week?

(c) What are the problems associated with the interpretation of the fitted demand equation of (a) to be a genuine demand relationship that is an inverse relationship between quantity and price (of watermelons)?

2-4. The objective is to construct a regression line using salary Y (in thousands of dollars) as the dependent variable and years of experience X (defined as years since receiving Ph.D) as the independent variable. Suppose you are particularly interested in analyzing the salary structure of economists hired by your local university. Assume that the following data are released to you by that university on condition that you will use them for no other purpose than preparing a term paper for an introductory econometrics course.

Y	X	Y	X	Y	X
85.5	42	45.5	23	49.2	8
80.7	39	42.2	22	38.2	8
82.9	36	40.1	16	45.6	8
75.6	32	35.6	9	30.2	3
73.2	30	33.2	6	44.6	5
69.9	28	39.7	8	40.2	3
65.4	26	30.5	4		
63.2	29	29.9	3		
61.9	30	41.2	14		
49.2	20	49.7	21		
58.7	27	46.2	19		
49.9	22	50.3	20		

(a) Estimate the linear regression of Y on X: $Y = \alpha + \beta X + \epsilon$.

(b) What are the standard errors of estimates $\hat{\alpha}$ and $\hat{\beta}$ of α and β, respectively? What are their estimates? What are the values of t and F statistics and the value of R^2?

(c) As you perhaps have realized, the relationship between salary and years of experience may have been seriously influenced by other neglected variables such as achievements in research and teaching. Under the circumstances, does the fitted regression do adequate justice to the influence of years of experience alone? Write an essay on such and other neglected factors based on the pattern derived from the calculated residuals.

2-5. The following table gives data on corporate profits (after taxes) and sales of U.S. manufacturing companies during the period 1958–1987 collected from the *Economic Report of the President,* 1989 (Table B-90, p. 412).

Year	Profits (Billion $)	Sales (Billion $)	Year	Profits (Billion $)	Sales (Billion $)
1958	12.7	305.3	1971	31.0	751.1
1959	16.3	338.0	1972	36.5	849.5
1960	15.2	345.7	1973	48.1	1,017.2
1961	15.3	356.4	1974	58.7	1,060.6
1962	17.7	389.4	1975	49.1	1,065.2
1963	19.5	412.7	1976	64.5	1,203.2
1964	23.2	443.1	1977	70.4	1,328.1
1965	27.5	492.2	1978	81.1	1,496.4
1966	30.9	554.2	1979	98.7	1,741.8
1967	29.0	575.4	1980	92.6	1,912.8
1968	32.1	631.9	1981	101.3	2,144.7
1969	33.2	694.6	1982	70.9	2,039.4
1970	28.6	708.8	1983	85.8	2,114.3
			1984	107.6	2,335.0
			1985	87.6	2,331.4
			1986	83.1	2,220.9
			1987	115.6	2,378.2

(a) Apply the OLS method to estimate

$$Y_t = \beta_0 + \beta_1 X_t + \epsilon_t$$

where Y is profits, X is sales, ϵ the error term, and β_0 and β_1 are the coefficients.

(b) Calculate R^2 and the estimated standard error of the estimates of the coefficients.

(c) Carry out the tests of hypothesis: $\beta_0 = 0$, and separately, $\beta_1 = 0$ at appropriate levels of significance.

(d) Assume that the extrapolated sales in the year 1991 is 2700 billions of U.S. dollars. What is the forecast for profit for that year? What are its standard error and confidence interval?

(e) Just as profits may depend on sales, so also may sales depend on profits. What will be the estimated regression line if you were to regress sales on profits? Find out, for this line, the value of R^2, estimated standard errors of coefficient estimates, and the t and F statistics. Is the line statistically significant?

(f) Write a comparative report on the estimated lines of (a) and (e) bringing out their salient economic and statistical aspects.

2-6. Consider the following data on unemployment rate of all workers and average hourly earnings of total private nonagricultural workers of the United States over the period 1970–1987:

DATA ON UNEMPLOYMENT RATES AND AVERAGE HOURLY EARNINGS IN NONAGRICULTURAL INDUSTRIES IN THE UNITED STATES, 1970–1987

Year	Unemployment rate of all workers	Average hourly earnings in total private nonagricultural industries
1970	4.8	3.23
1971	5.8	3.45
1972	5.5	3.70
1973	4.8	3.94
1974	5.5	4.24
1975	8.3	4.53
1976	7.6	4.86
1977	6.9	5.25
1978	6.0	5.69
1979	5.8	6.16
1980	7.0	6.66
1981	7.5	7.25
1982	9.5	7.68
1983	9.5	8.02
1984	7.4	8.32
1985	7.1	8.57
1986	6.9	8.76
1987	6.1	8.96

Source: Economic Report of the President, 1989, Tables B-39 and B-44.

(a) Convert the data on average hourly earnings into year-to-year percentage changes in average hourly earnings. In so doing, you lose the figure for one year. Which year is that?

(b) Suppose Y is the percentage change in average hourly earnings in total private nonagricultural industries and X is the unemployment rate of all workers. Estimate the relationship

$$Y = \alpha + \beta X + \epsilon$$

where ϵ is the error term.

(c) Construct a scatter diagram by plotting estimated Y against X. Is the fit a good one? What is the value of R^2? What did you expect the fit to be like?

(d) What is the estimated standard error of the residuals? Estimate the standard errors of $\hat{\alpha}$ and $\hat{\beta}$.

(e) Apply t tests to test $\alpha = 0$ and, separately, $\beta = 0$, choosing an appropriate probability level of significance in each case.

(f) As you know, the Phillips' curve depicts an inverse relationship between percentage change in prices (or wages) and the unemployment rate. With this in mind, how do you view the relationship obtained in (b) above? Discuss.

2-7. The research department of a large fertilizer company stipulates that the company's sale of fertilizer has been growing at a constant rate r according to the formula

$$Y_t = A(1 + r)^t$$

where A is a constant and t is time. Suppose it derives the following estimated line using the OLS method:

$$Y_t = 6.3870 + 0.0389t$$

(a) What is the estimated growth rate of the sale of fertilizer of this company?

(b) What do you predict to be the sale of this company 10 years from now?

(c) Under what circumstances could the growth rate r change?

2-8. An infinite price elasticity of demand is exhibited from a demand curve shown in Figure 2.8, where AB is the demand curve, and P and Q are the price and quantity of a commodity. Yet when you look at the demand curve AB, it appears to be a line of regression of P on Q in which P is constant and does not depend on Q at all. How do you reconcile this property with the infinite price elasticity of demand for this commodity?

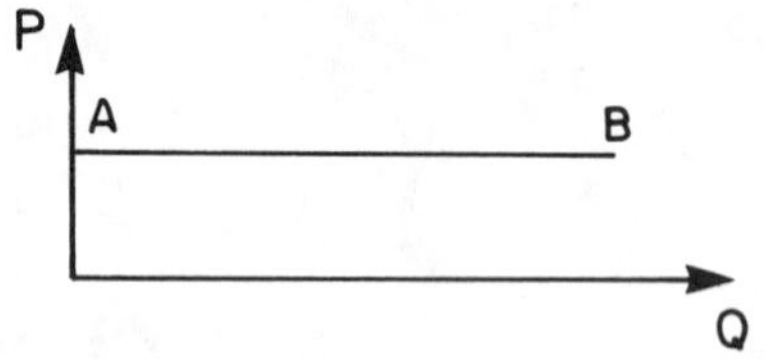

Figure 2.8

2-9. What are the assumptions made in a two-variable regression model regarding the disturbance term? Explain as clearly as possible what is meant by

$$E(\epsilon_1) = E(\epsilon_2) = \cdots = E(\epsilon_n) = 0$$

or

$$V(\epsilon_1) = V(\epsilon_2) = \cdots = V(\epsilon_n)$$

where ϵ is the error term and $1, 2, \ldots, n$ are the n time dates. Under what conditions would these assumptions not hold good? Illustrate.

2-10. Suppose you want to find out the effect of the exchange rate on the aggregate volume of exports in the United States. Would you find this effect from observations on aggregate exports and exchange rates when the latter are fluctuating wildly, or when they are being kept relatively constant by appropriate monetary policy followed by the Federal Reserve System? Explain why.

2-11. Based on data on the consumption of beer (BEERCONS) in Ontario measured in thousands of gallons over the period 1970–1983, a student estimated the following linear relations by the OLS method:

$$\text{BEERCONS} = 134{,}471.0 - 10{,}586.5 * \text{BEERPRIC}$$
$$+ 7.90119 * \text{DISPINC} \qquad R^2 = 0.826242$$

$$\text{BEERCONS} = 85{,}014.6 + 3.6719 * \text{SPIRITS}$$
$$+ 1.28862 * \text{WINE} \qquad R^2 = 0.922146$$

$$\text{BEERCONS} = -227{,}964.0 - 2{,}083.28 * \text{BEERPRIC}$$
$$-1.42979 * \text{DISPINC} + 48.1421 * \text{ONTPOP} \qquad R^2 = 0.930919$$

where BEERPRIC is beer price ($), DISPINC is disposable income ($), and SPIRITS and WINE are spirits and wine in thousands of gallons.

(a) Calculate the F statistics and test each model for overall goodness of fit at a 5% probability level of significance.
(*Hint:* Use $F = (R^2/k - 1)/[(1 - R^2)/n - k]$ where k is the total number of regressors including the intercept term.)

(b) Which model seems to be the best and why?

(c) Write an essay on the comparative functions and results of the three models. Suggest what other variables could have been profitably included in the models.

2-12. Show that if Z_1 are independent quantities from the same population, with variance σ^2, then the sampling variance of

$$b = \sum_{i=1}^{n} a_i z_i$$

is $\sigma^2 \sum_{i=1}^{n} a_i^2$. Observations Y_i are related to fixed quantities X_i and the quantities z_i above by the relations $Y_i = \alpha + \beta X_i + z_i$ $(i = 1, \ldots, n)$. If the values of X_i are

X_1	X_2	X_3	X_4	X_5	X_6
1	2	3	4	5	6

an alternative estimate of β is

$$\tfrac{1}{8}(Y_6 + Y_5 - Y_2 - Y_1)$$

Deduce the sampling variance of this estimate and compare it with the sampling variance of the least-squares estimate.

(Reprinted with permission of Oxford University, 1958)

2-13. An investigator is interested in the two following series:

	1935	1936	1937	1938	1939	1940	1941	1942	1943	1944	1945	1946
X, deaths of children under 1 year (thousands)	60	62	61	55	53	60	63	53	52	48	49	43
Y, consumption of beer (bulk barrels)	23	23	25	25	26	26	29	30	30	32	33	31

(a) Calculate the coefficient of correlation between X and Y.

(b) A linear time trend may be fitted to X (or Y) by calculating an OLS regression of X (or Y) on time t. This requires choosing an origin and a unit of measurement for time. For example, if the origin is set at mid-1935 and the unit of measurement is 1 year, then the year 1942 corresponds to $t = 7$. If the origin is set at end-1940 (beginning of 1941) and the unit of measurement is 6 months, then 1937 corresponds to $t = -7$. Show that any computed trend value $\hat{X}_1 = \alpha + bt$ is unaffected by the choice of origin and the unit of measurement.

(c) Let $\tilde{X}$ be X with any time trend removed; that is, $\tilde{X}_t = X_t - \hat{X}_t$. Calculate the correlation between $\tilde{X}$ and Y, and between $\tilde{X}$ and $\tilde{Y}$. Compare these values with that obtained in part (a), and comment on the difference.

(Reprinted with permission of the Royal Statistical Society Certificate, 1954)

(*Note:* The definition of the coefficient of correlation between X and Y is

$$\text{corr}(Y, X) = r_{YX} = \frac{1/n\,[\Sigma_1^n X_iY_i - (\Sigma_1^n X_i\,\Sigma_1^n Y_i)\,/n]}{\{1/n\,[\Sigma_1^n X_i^2 - (\Sigma_1^n X_i)^2\,/n]\;1/n\,[\Sigma_1^n Y_i^2 - (\Sigma_1^n Y_i)^2\,/n]\}^{1/2}}$$

3
Linear Algebra

3.1 INTRODUCTION

The two-variable linear regression model and its associated computations were rather simple in structure. The model's step-by-step extension to many variables could be excessively strenuous and difficult. An economical way out would be to use the methods of matrix or linear algebra. To illustrate the preliminary use of vectors and matrices, let us take a preview of the $m + 1$ variable regression model with its ith observation given by

$$Y_i = \beta_0 + \sum_{j=1}^{m} \beta_j X_{ij} + \epsilon_i \qquad i = 1, 2, \ldots, n \tag{3.1}$$

In compact notation, the above is given by

$$\mathbf{Y} = X\boldsymbol{\beta} + \boldsymbol{\epsilon} \tag{3.2}$$

where

$$\mathbf{Y} = \begin{bmatrix} Y_1 \\ Y_2 \\ \vdots \\ Y_n \end{bmatrix} \qquad X = \begin{bmatrix} 1 & X_{11} & \cdots & X_{1m} \\ 1 & X_{21} & & X_{2m} \\ \vdots & \vdots & & \vdots \\ 1 & X_{n1} & & X_{nm} \end{bmatrix} \qquad \boldsymbol{\beta} = \begin{bmatrix} \beta_0 \\ \beta_1 \\ \vdots \\ \beta_m \end{bmatrix} \qquad \boldsymbol{\epsilon} = \begin{bmatrix} \epsilon_1 \\ \epsilon_2 \\ \vdots \\ \epsilon_n \end{bmatrix}$$

$\mathbf{Y}$, $\boldsymbol{\beta}$, and $\boldsymbol{\epsilon}$ are column vectors of n, $m + 1$, and n elements, respectively, and X is a matrix with n rows and $m + 1$ columns. The matrix X is rectangular since its number of rows n differs from its number of columns $m + 1$; for n equal to $m + 1$, it would be square.

The matrix X can be looked at as a collection of rows or a collection of columns. Thus,

$$X = \begin{bmatrix} \mathbf{R}_1 \\ \mathbf{R}_2 \\ \vdots \\ \mathbf{R}_n \end{bmatrix}$$

or

$$X = [\mathbf{C}_1 \quad \mathbf{C}_2 \cdots \mathbf{C}_m]$$

where

$$\begin{aligned} \mathbf{R}_1 &= [1 \quad X_{11} \cdots X_{1m}] \\ \mathbf{R}_2 &= [1 \quad X_{21} \cdots X_{2m}] \\ &\vdots \\ \mathbf{R}_n &= [1 \quad X_{n1} \cdots X_{nm}] \end{aligned}$$

are a set of row vectors, each of $m + 1$ elements, and

$$\mathbf{C}_1 = \begin{bmatrix} 1 \\ 1 \\ \vdots \\ 1 \end{bmatrix} \quad \mathbf{C}_2 = \begin{bmatrix} X_{11} \\ X_{21} \\ \vdots \\ X_{n1} \end{bmatrix} \quad \cdots \quad \mathbf{C}_\mathrm{m} = \begin{bmatrix} X_{1m} \\ X_{2m} \\ \vdots \\ X_{nm} \end{bmatrix}$$

are a set of column vectors, each of n elements.

The representation of (3.1) by (3.2) in an equivalent way, or, for that matter, other aspects of any one of them presupposes a knowledge of operations involving vectors and matrices as well as their properties. It is to these operations and properties that we now turn in a systematic way.

3.2 VECTORS AND MATRICES

To present the notions more formally, let us define an $m \times n$ matrix as arranged in m rows and n columns:

$$A = \begin{bmatrix} a_{11} & a_{12} & \cdots & a_{1n} \\ a_{21} & a_{22} & & a_{2n} \\ \vdots & & & \vdots \\ a_{m1} & a_{m2} & \cdots & a_{mn} \end{bmatrix} \tag{3.3}$$

with a_{ij} ($i = 1, \ldots, m; j = 1, 2, \ldots, n$) as its elements. Sometimes A is written as (a_{ij}), implying that A is the matrix whose representative element is a_{ij}. If $m = n = 1$, the matrix becomes a scalar, which is a real number. For m or n equal to 1, the matrix becomes a vector, which is either a row vector of dimension $1 \times n$ for $m = 1$, or a column vector of size $m \times 1$ for $n = 1$. For $m = n$, which implies an equal number of rows and columns, the matrix is square. In such a case, the elements for $i = j$ are elements on the principal diagonal. These begin at the upper left corner with the first row and first column, the (1, 1) element, and then go down to the lower right corner up to the (m, n) element.

Some examples of vectors and matrices from the linear regression model have already been cited. A further example concerns the variance–covariance matrix $\boldsymbol{\Sigma}$ of the error term $\boldsymbol{\epsilon}$:

$$\boldsymbol{\Sigma} = \begin{bmatrix} \sigma_{11} & \sigma_{12} & \cdots & \sigma_{1n} \\ \sigma_{21} & \sigma_{22} & \cdots & \sigma_{2n} \\ \vdots & \vdots & & \vdots \\ \sigma_{n1} & \sigma_{n2} & \cdots & \sigma_{nn} \end{bmatrix} \tag{3.4}$$

This matrix contains the elements σ_{ii} for $i = 1, 2, \ldots, n$, which are the variances, and σ_{ij} for $i \neq j = 1, \ldots, n$, which are the covariances.

Note that two matrices $\boldsymbol{A} = (a_{ij})$ and $\boldsymbol{B} = (b_{ij})$ are equal if and only if they are equal for every corresponding element. That is,

$$\boldsymbol{A} = \boldsymbol{B}$$

if and only if

$$a_{ij} = b_{ij} \qquad i = 1, 2, \ldots, m \quad j = 1, 2, \ldots, n$$

3.2.1 Matrix Operations

Two matrices, each of the same order as the other, are added by adding their elements, element for element; for example,

$$\boldsymbol{A} + \boldsymbol{B} = [\boldsymbol{A} + \boldsymbol{B}] \tag{3.5}$$

if and only if

$$a_{ij} + b_{ij} = c_{ij} \qquad i = 1, \ldots, m \quad j = 1, \ldots, n$$

where c_{ij} is a representative element of $[\boldsymbol{A} + \boldsymbol{B}]$. One minor operation is to multiply a matrix by a scalar. This will result in each of its elements being multiplied by that scalar:

$$\boldsymbol{A} = c\boldsymbol{B} \tag{3.6}$$

if and only if

$$a_{ij} = cb_{ij}$$

for all permissible values of i and j. The two foregoing operations can be used to define a linear combination of a number of matrices:

$$\boldsymbol{A} = c_1\boldsymbol{B}^{(1)} + c_2\boldsymbol{B}^{(2)} + \cdots + c_r\boldsymbol{B}^{(r)} \tag{3.7}$$

if and only if

$$a_{ij} = c_1 b_{ij}^{(1)} + c_2 b_{ij}^{(2)} + \cdots + c_r b_{ij}^{(r)} \qquad \begin{matrix} i = 1, \ldots, m \\ j = 1, \ldots, n \end{matrix}$$

in which $b_{ij}^{(r)}$ is the i, jth element of the rth $m \times n$ matrix $\boldsymbol{B}^{(r)}$. This can be illustrated by

$$4\begin{bmatrix} 2 & -1 \\ 3 & 4 \\ 6 & 0 \end{bmatrix} + 3\begin{bmatrix} 1 & 4 \\ -3 & 2 \\ 2 & 2 \end{bmatrix} = \begin{bmatrix} 8 & -4 \\ 12 & 16 \\ 24 & 0 \end{bmatrix} + \begin{bmatrix} 3 & 12 \\ -9 & 6 \\ 6 & 6 \end{bmatrix} = \begin{bmatrix} 11 & 8 \\ 3 & 22 \\ 30 & 6 \end{bmatrix}$$

The following results are immediate:

$$\begin{aligned} \boldsymbol{A} + \boldsymbol{B} &= \boldsymbol{B} + \boldsymbol{A} \\ (\boldsymbol{A} + \boldsymbol{B}) + \boldsymbol{C} &= \boldsymbol{A} + (\boldsymbol{B} + \boldsymbol{C}) = \boldsymbol{A} + \boldsymbol{B} + \boldsymbol{C} \\ c(\boldsymbol{A} + \boldsymbol{B}) &= c\boldsymbol{A} + c\boldsymbol{B} \\ (c + d)\boldsymbol{A} &= c\boldsymbol{A} + d\boldsymbol{A} \\ cd\boldsymbol{A} &= dc\boldsymbol{A} = c(d\boldsymbol{A}) = d(c\boldsymbol{A}) \end{aligned} \tag{3.8}$$

To multiply two matrices, the number of columns of the matrix to the left and the number of rows of the matrix to the right must be identical. Elements of the product are obtained by multiplying the elements of a row of the left matrix by the corresponding elements of a column of the right matrix and summing these products:

$$\boldsymbol{C}_{m \times p} = \boldsymbol{A}_{m \times n}\boldsymbol{B}_{n \times p} \tag{3.9}$$

if and only if

$$c_{ij} = \sum_{l=1}^{n} a_{il}b_{lj} \qquad i = 1, \ldots, m \quad j = 1, \ldots, p$$

Examples are

$$\underset{2 \times 2}{\begin{bmatrix} a_{11} & a_{12} \\ a_{21} & a_{22} \end{bmatrix}} \underset{2 \times 1}{\begin{bmatrix} b_{11} \\ b_{21} \end{bmatrix}} = \underset{2 \times 1}{\begin{bmatrix} a_{11}b_{11} + a_{12}b_{21} \\ a_{21}b_{11} + a_{22}b_{21} \end{bmatrix}}$$

$$\underset{3 \times 4}{\begin{bmatrix} 0 & 1 & 3 & 1 \\ 2 & -1 & 0 & 2 \\ 1 & 3 & 2 & 2 \end{bmatrix}} \underset{4 \times 2}{\begin{bmatrix} 1 & 2 \\ 3 & 2 \\ 4 & 3 \\ 2 & 1 \end{bmatrix}} = \underset{3 \times 2}{\begin{bmatrix} 0 \times 1 + 1 \times 3 + 3 \times 4 + 1 \times 2 & 0 \times 2 + 1 \times 2 + 3 \times 3 + 1 \times 1 \\ 2 \times 1 + (-1) \times 3 + 0 \times 4 + 2 \times 2 & 2 \times 2 + (-1) \times 2 + 0 \times 3 + 2 \times 1 \\ 1 \times 1 + 3 \times 3 + 2 \times 4 + 2 \times 2 & 1 \times 2 + 3 \times 2 + 2 \times 3 + 2 \times 1 \end{bmatrix}}$$

$$= \underset{3 \times 2}{\begin{bmatrix} 17 & 12 \\ -3 & 4 \\ 22 & 16 \end{bmatrix}}$$

It is important that for the product $\boldsymbol{C} = \boldsymbol{AB}$ to be defined, the number of columns of $\boldsymbol{A}$ must agree with the number of rows of $\boldsymbol{B}$, and then the number of rows and columns of $\boldsymbol{C}$ will conform with those of $\boldsymbol{A}$ and $\boldsymbol{B}$, respectively. In general $\boldsymbol{AB}$ is not the same as $\boldsymbol{BA}$, which means that matrix multiplications are not commutative. This necessitates stating the intended order of multiplications as in *premultiplication,* or multiplication on the left, and *postmultiplication,* or multiplication on the right. For an example, $\boldsymbol{A}$ is said to be postmultiplied by $\boldsymbol{B}$, or $\boldsymbol{B}$ is said to be premultiplied by $\boldsymbol{A}$ in the product $\boldsymbol{AB}$.

The following results of matrix multiplications are straightforward:

$$
\begin{aligned}
(\boldsymbol{AB})\boldsymbol{C} &= \boldsymbol{A}(\boldsymbol{BC}) = \boldsymbol{ABC} \\
\boldsymbol{A}(\boldsymbol{B} + \boldsymbol{C}) &= \boldsymbol{AB} + \boldsymbol{AC} \\
(\boldsymbol{A} + \boldsymbol{B})\boldsymbol{C} &= \boldsymbol{AC} + \boldsymbol{BC} \\
c(\boldsymbol{AB}) &= \boldsymbol{A}c\boldsymbol{B} \\
\boldsymbol{AO} &= \boldsymbol{OA} = \boldsymbol{O} \\
\boldsymbol{AI} &= \boldsymbol{IA} = \boldsymbol{A} \\
\boldsymbol{II} &= \boldsymbol{I} \\
\boldsymbol{OO} &= \boldsymbol{O}
\end{aligned}
\tag{3.10}
$$

In (3.10), $\boldsymbol{O}$ of whatever order is a zero matrix of that order in which all elements are $\boldsymbol{O}$, and $\boldsymbol{I}$, a square matrix of a particular order, is an identity matrix of that order, with unities along its diagonal and zero in off-diagonal positions. Some examples of the $\boldsymbol{O}$ and $\boldsymbol{I}$ matrices of order, say 2×3 and 3×3, respectively, are

$$
\boldsymbol{O} = \begin{bmatrix} 0 & 0 & 0 \\ 0 & 0 & 0 \end{bmatrix} \qquad \boldsymbol{I} = \begin{bmatrix} 1 & 0 & 0 \\ 0 & 1 & 0 \\ 0 & 0 & 1 \end{bmatrix}
$$

3.2.2 Transposition and Trace of a Matrix

An operation known as matrix transposition is usually indicated by a prime on the matrix symbol. Transposition is done by interchanging the rows of a matrix into columns, and vice versa. Accordingly, the $\boldsymbol{A}$ matrix of size $m \times n$, when transposed, becomes the $\boldsymbol{A}'$ matrix of size $n \times m$:

$$
\boldsymbol{A}' = \begin{bmatrix} a_{11} & a_{21} & \cdots & a_{m1} \\ a_{12} & a_{22} & & a_{m2} \\ \vdots & & & \vdots \\ a_{1n} & a_{2n} & \cdots & a_{mn} \end{bmatrix} \tag{3.11}
$$

The following relations derive from the definition of matrix operations and properties of real numbers:

$$(A')' = A$$
$$(A + B)' = A' + B' \tag{3.12}$$
$$(AB)' = B'A'$$

Thus, double transposition revives the original matrix, transposition of a sum of matrices is the sum of the transposition of each matrix, and transposition of a product of two matrices is the product of transpositions of individual matrices *in reverse order*.

Among square matrices, there is one called the idempotent matrix, which is especially important in regression analysis. This is a square symmetric matrix, which means, taking A to be the matrix,

$$A = A'$$

For A to be idempotent, we require

$$A = A^2 = A^3 = \cdots \tag{3.13}$$

In other words, multiplication of the matrix by itself as many times as one pleases does not change the original matrix. An example of A is

$$A = \frac{3}{2}\begin{bmatrix} \frac{1}{3} & -\frac{1}{3} \\ -\frac{1}{3} & \frac{1}{3} \end{bmatrix}$$

It is easily verified that

$$AA = \frac{3}{2}\begin{bmatrix} \frac{1}{3} & -\frac{1}{3} \\ -\frac{1}{3} & \frac{1}{3} \end{bmatrix}\frac{3}{2}\begin{bmatrix} \frac{1}{3} & -\frac{1}{3} \\ -\frac{1}{3} & \frac{1}{3} \end{bmatrix} = \frac{3}{2}\begin{bmatrix} \frac{1}{3} & -\frac{1}{3} \\ -\frac{1}{3} & \frac{1}{3} \end{bmatrix}$$
$$= A$$

Thus A is idempotent.

The trace of a *square* matrix A of order $n \times n$ is the sum of its diagonal entries:

$$\text{Tr}(A) = a_{11} + a_{22} + \cdots + a_{nn} = \sum_{i=1}^{n} a_{ii} \tag{3.14}$$

The following results are immediate:

$$\begin{aligned} \text{Tr}(A + B) &= \text{Tr}(A) + \text{Tr}(B) \\ \text{Tr}(A') &= \text{Tr}(A) \\ \text{Tr}(cA) &= c\text{Tr}(A) \\ \text{Tr}(AB) &= \text{Tr}(BA) = \sum_{i=1}^{n}\sum_{j=1}^{n} a_{ij}b_{ji}, \\ &\quad \text{if } AB \text{ and } BA \text{ are well defined} \\ \text{Tr}(I_{n\times n}) &= n \end{aligned} \tag{3.15}$$

3.2.3 Partitioned Matrices

In many contexts, it is possible to think of submatrices of a matrix obtained by partitioning according to its columns or rows. These are respectively shown in A and B below:

$$A = [A_1 \;\vdots\; A_2] \quad \text{or} \quad B = \begin{bmatrix} B_1 \\ \cdots \\ B_2 \end{bmatrix} \tag{3.16}$$

where A_1 is of size $m \times n_1$ and A_2 of size $m \times n_2$, $n_1 + n_2$ being n, and B_1 is of size $m_1 \times n$ and B_2 $m_2 \times n$, $m_1 + m_2$ being m. Examples are

$$A = [A_1 \;\vdots\; A_2] = \begin{bmatrix} 2 & 3 & \vdots & 4 & 0 \\ -3 & 2 & \vdots & 1 & 4 \\ 0 & 4 & \vdots & 2 & 1 \end{bmatrix} \qquad B = \begin{bmatrix} B_1 \\ \cdots \\ B_2 \end{bmatrix} = \begin{bmatrix} 1 & 2 \\ -1 & 2 \\ \cdots & \cdots \\ 2 & 3 \\ 3 & 0 \end{bmatrix}$$

The transpose of a partitioned matrix is the transpose of its submatrices. More importantly, what was partitioning by columns becomes, after transposition, partitioning by rows, and vice versa,

$$A' = [A_1 \;\vdots\; A_2]' = \begin{bmatrix} A_1' \\ \cdots \\ A_2' \end{bmatrix} \qquad B' = \begin{bmatrix} B_1 \\ \cdots \\ B_2 \end{bmatrix}' = [B_1' \;\vdots\; B_2'] \tag{3.17}$$

or, for the numerical matrices above

$$A' = \begin{bmatrix} 2 & -3 & 0 \\ 3 & 2 & 4 \\ \cdots & \cdots & \cdots \\ 4 & 1 & 2 \\ 0 & 4 & 1 \end{bmatrix} \qquad B' = \begin{bmatrix} 1 & -1 & \vdots & 2 & 3 \\ 2 & 2 & \vdots & 3 & 0 \end{bmatrix}$$

It must have been evident in the above equations how the submatrices have been treated like scalars. This will be even more evident in the matrix multiplications below:

$$C = AB = [A_1 \;\vdots\; A_2] \begin{bmatrix} B_1 \\ \cdots \\ B_2 \end{bmatrix} = [A_1B_1 + A_2B_2] \tag{3.18}$$

provided the orders of A_1 and B_1 (so also of A_2 and B_2) are conformable for matrix multiplications. In the numerical examples of $\boldsymbol{A}$ and $\boldsymbol{B}$ matrices above, $\boldsymbol{C}$ becomes

$$\begin{aligned}
\boldsymbol{C} &= [\boldsymbol{A_1B_1} + \boldsymbol{A_2B_2}] \\
&= \begin{bmatrix} 2 & 3 \\ -3 & 2 \\ 0 & 4 \end{bmatrix} \begin{bmatrix} 1 & 2 \\ -1 & 2 \end{bmatrix} + \begin{bmatrix} 4 & 0 \\ 1 & 4 \\ 2 & 1 \end{bmatrix} \begin{bmatrix} 2 & 3 \\ 3 & 0 \end{bmatrix} \\
&= \begin{bmatrix} -1 & 10 \\ -5 & -2 \\ -4 & 8 \end{bmatrix} + \begin{bmatrix} 8 & 12 \\ 14 & 3 \\ 7 & 6 \end{bmatrix} \\
&= \begin{bmatrix} 7 & 22 \\ 9 & 1 \\ 3 & 14 \end{bmatrix}
\end{aligned}$$

This last result would also have been obtained by direct multiplication of $\boldsymbol{A}$ and $\boldsymbol{B}$ without first partitioning them.

As an extension, each matrix may be partitioned by both columns and rows, and then each may be transposed and each multiplied with the other. (Always check for conformability of submatrix orders before multiplication.) For instance, let

$$\boldsymbol{A} = \begin{bmatrix} \boldsymbol{A_{11}} & : & \boldsymbol{A_{12}} \\ (m_1 \times n_1) & : & (m_1 \times n_2) \\ \cdots\cdots & & \cdots\cdots \\ \boldsymbol{A_{21}} & : & \boldsymbol{A_{22}} \\ (m_2 \times n_1) & : & (m_2 \times n_2) \end{bmatrix} \qquad \boldsymbol{B} = \begin{bmatrix} \boldsymbol{B_{11}} & : & \boldsymbol{B_{12}} \\ (n_1 \times l_1) & : & (n_1 \times l_2) \\ \cdots\cdots & & \cdots\cdots \\ \boldsymbol{B_{21}} & : & \boldsymbol{B_{22}} \\ (n_2 \times l_1) & : & (n_2 \times l_2) \end{bmatrix}$$

where the orders of the submatrices are written below their symbols. Observe that $m_1 + m_2 = m$, $n_1 + n_2 = n$, and $l_1 + l_2 = l$. Then, for example, the transpose of $\boldsymbol{A}$ is

$$\boldsymbol{A}' = \begin{bmatrix} \boldsymbol{A_{11}} & : & \boldsymbol{A_{12}} \\ \cdots\cdots & & \cdots\cdots \\ \boldsymbol{A_{21}} & : & \boldsymbol{A_{22}} \end{bmatrix}' = \begin{bmatrix} \boldsymbol{A'_{11}} & : & \boldsymbol{A'_{21}} \\ \cdots\cdots & & \cdots\cdots \\ \boldsymbol{A'_{12}} & : & \boldsymbol{A'_{22}} \end{bmatrix}$$

and the product $\boldsymbol{C} = \boldsymbol{AB}$ is

$$\begin{aligned}
\boldsymbol{C} &= \begin{bmatrix} \boldsymbol{C_{11}} & : & \boldsymbol{C_{12}} \\ (m_1 \times l_1) & : & (m_1 \times l_2) \\ \cdots\cdots & & \cdots\cdots \\ \boldsymbol{C_{21}} & : & \boldsymbol{C_{22}} \\ (m_2 \times l_1) & : & (m_2 \times l_2) \end{bmatrix} \\
&= \begin{bmatrix} \boldsymbol{A_{11}B_{11}} + \boldsymbol{A_{12}B_{21}} & : & \boldsymbol{A_{11}B_{12}} + \boldsymbol{A_{12}B_{22}} \\ \cdots\cdots & & \cdots\cdots \\ \boldsymbol{A_{21}B_{11}} + \boldsymbol{A_{22}B_{21}} & : & \boldsymbol{A_{21}B_{12}} + \boldsymbol{A_{22}B_{22}} \end{bmatrix}
\end{aligned} \tag{3.19}$$

Taking A and B partitioned as follows

$$A = \begin{bmatrix} A_{11} & \vdots & A_{12} \\ \cdots & \cdots & \cdots \\ A_{21} & \vdots & A_{22} \end{bmatrix} = \begin{bmatrix} 1 & 0 & \vdots & 1 & 2 \\ 0 & -1 & \vdots & 2 & 1 \\ \cdots & \cdots & \cdots & \cdots & \cdots \\ 2 & 3 & \vdots & 3 & 2 \end{bmatrix}$$

$$B = \begin{bmatrix} B_{11} & \vdots & B_{12} \\ \cdots & \cdots & \cdots \\ B_{21} & \vdots & B_{22} \end{bmatrix} = \begin{bmatrix} 0 & \vdots & 2 \\ 1 & \vdots & -1 \\ \cdots & \cdots & \cdots \\ 2 & \vdots & 0 \\ 1 & \vdots & 2 \end{bmatrix}$$

the transpose of A is

$$A' = \begin{bmatrix} A'_{11} & \vdots & A'_{21} \\ \cdots & \cdots & \cdots \\ A'_{12} & \vdots & A'_{22} \end{bmatrix} = \begin{bmatrix} 1 & 0 & \vdots & 2 \\ 0 & -1 & \vdots & 3 \\ \cdots & \cdots & \cdots & \cdots \\ 1 & 2 & \vdots & 3 \\ 2 & 1 & \vdots & 2 \end{bmatrix}$$

and the product $C = AB$ is

$$C = \begin{bmatrix} A_{11}B_{11} + A_{12}B_{21} & \vdots & A_{11}B_{12} + A_{12}B_{22} \\ \cdots & \cdots & \cdots \\ A_{21}B_{11} + A_{22}B_{21} & \vdots & A_{21}B_{12} + A_{22}B_{22} \end{bmatrix}$$

$$= \begin{bmatrix} \begin{bmatrix} 0 \\ -1 \end{bmatrix} + \begin{bmatrix} 4 \\ 5 \end{bmatrix} & \vdots & \begin{bmatrix} 2 \\ 1 \end{bmatrix} + \begin{bmatrix} 4 \\ 2 \end{bmatrix} \\ \cdots & \cdots & \cdots \\ 3 + 8 & \vdots & 1 + 4 \end{bmatrix}$$

$$= \begin{bmatrix} 4 & \vdots & 6 \\ 4 & \vdots & 3 \\ \cdots & \cdots & \cdots \\ 11 & \vdots & 5 \end{bmatrix}$$

In matrix multiplication, a concept called the *Kronecker product* is often used. This is defined as follows. Let A be an $m \times n$ matrix and B a $p \times q$ matrix. Then the direct (or Kronecker)) product of A and B, symbolized as $A \otimes B$, is the $mp \times nq$ matrix C:

$$C = A \otimes B = \begin{bmatrix} a_{11}B & \cdots & a_{1n}B \\ \cdots & \cdots & \cdots \\ a_{m1}B & \cdots & a_{mn}B \end{bmatrix} \tag{3.20}$$

Some of the properties of the Kronecker product of two matrices are

$$\begin{aligned}(A + B) \otimes C &= A \otimes C + B \otimes C \\ A \otimes (B + C) &= A \otimes B + A \otimes C \\ A \otimes (B \otimes C) &= (A \otimes B) \otimes C \\ (A \otimes B)' &= A' \otimes B' \\ (A \otimes B)(C \otimes D) &= AC \otimes BD \\ \mathrm{Tr}(A \otimes B) &= \mathrm{Tr}(A)\,\mathrm{Tr}(B)\end{aligned} \tag{3.21}$$

3.3 DETERMINANTS

The determinant of the matrix A is a scalar, denoted by the symbol $|A|$. The size, say, $n \times n$, of the matrix becomes the order n of the associated determinant. The value of an $n \times n$ determinant $|A|$ is obtained by expansion according to the elements of any row or column of the matrix A in the following way:

$$|A| = \sum_{j=1}^{n} a_{ij}c_{ij} \qquad \text{for any } i = 1, \ldots, n \tag{3.22}$$

where a_{ij} are the elements of the matrix A and c_{ij} their associated cofactors. The cofactor c_{ij} of the element a_{ij} is its "signed" minor: $c_{ij} = (-1)^{i+j}m_{ij}$, where m_{ij}, called the minor of the element a_{ij}, is the determinant of the $(n - 1) \times (n - 1)$ order submatrix of A remaining after its ith row and jth column are deleted. Observe that a first-order determinant is simply the single element a_{11} of its matrix. Next to that is the second-order determinant. This is given by the difference in the product of the diagonal elements of the 2×2 matrix, the downward sloping diagonal being counted first, and the upward rising diagonal counted next. The difference is $a_{11}a_{22} - a_{12}a_{21}$. The value of a higher-order determinant obtained by the expansion method is ultimately reducible to these second-order determinants. This is shown below from a numerical example based on a determinant of order 3:

$$A = \begin{bmatrix} 1 & 2 & 1 \\ 3 & 0 & 2 \\ 2 & -1 & 1 \end{bmatrix}$$

The "signed" minors or the cofactors c_{11}, c_{12}, and c_{13} of the elements of the first row of A are

$$(-1)^{1+1}\begin{vmatrix} 0 & 2 \\ -1 & 1 \end{vmatrix} \qquad (-1)^{1+2}\begin{vmatrix} 3 & 2 \\ 2 & 1 \end{vmatrix} \qquad (-1)^{1+3}\begin{vmatrix} 3 & 0 \\ 2 & -1 \end{vmatrix}$$

which simplify to

$$(-1)^2\{(0 \times 1) - [2 \times (-1)]\} \qquad (-1)^3[(3 \times 1) - (2 \times 2)] \qquad (-1)^4\{[3 \times (-1)] - (0 \times 2)\}$$

or

$$2, \quad 1, \quad -3$$

Expressing the determinant $|A|$ by elements of the first row of A gives

$$|A| = a_{11}c_{11} + a_{12}c_{12} + a_{13}c_{13} = (1 \times 2) + (2 \times 1) + [1 \times (-3)] = 1$$

If we expand the value of a determinant by the elements of a given row (column) and cofactors of elements of a different or "alien" row (column), it becomes immediately clear that the determinant becomes zero. For an $n \times n$ matrix A, this can be expressed as

$$\sum_{j=1}^{n} a_{ij}c_{kj} = 0 \qquad i \neq k \quad i, k = 1, \ldots, n \tag{3.23}$$

The following additional relations would be extremely useful:

(1) A λ multiple of a row (column) of a matrix makes a λ multiple of its determinant. By natural extension, if all the elements of a matrix are multiplied by λ, the determinant will be multiplied only λ times.

(2) $|A| = |A'|$.

(3) $|AB| = |A||B|$.

(4) If A is a diagonal matrix with $a_{ij} = 0$ for $i \neq j$, or a triangular matrix where all entries above or, separately, below the principal diagonal are zero, then $|A| = a_{11}a_{22}\cdots a_{nn}$.

(5) If B is constructed from A by interchanging any two rows (columns) of A, then $|B| = -|A|$.

(6) For identical rows (columns) of a matrix, its determinant is zero.

(7) If a matrix B is constructed from A by adding a multiple of one row (column) to another row (column), then the value of the determinant remains unchanged, that is $|B| = |A|$.

(8) $|-A| = (-1)^n|A|$.

(9) A is singular if $|A| = 0$, and nonsingular if $|A| \neq 0$; the former happens if the rows (columns) of A are linearly dependent, the latter happens when they are independent, as defined in (10).

(10) *Independence of vectors*. If the n column vectors $\mathbf{A_1}, \ldots, \mathbf{A_n}$ of the matrix

A are linearly independent, then their linear combination,

$$c_1\mathbf{A_1} + c_2\mathbf{A_2} + \cdots + c_n\mathbf{A_n} = 0 \tag{3.24}$$

in which $c_1, \ldots, c_n$ are scalars, is true iff *all* such cs are zeros; otherwise, they are linearly dependent.

3.4 LINEAR DEPENDENCE (INDEPENDENCE) AND RANK OF A MATRIX

It must have been evident from the above definition of linear dependence that the columns of A should be amenable to a *nontrivial* linear combination; that is, for values of cs, not *all* of which are zero, $\sum_1^n c_i\mathbf{A_i}$ will be zero. Otherwise, these values are linearly independent. We illustrate these concepts with some examples.

Consider:

$$A = [\mathbf{A_1} \quad \mathbf{A_2} \quad \mathbf{A_3}] = \begin{bmatrix} 2 & 1 & 5 \\ -1 & 0 & -2 \\ 2 & 3 & 7 \end{bmatrix}$$

It is clear that

$$2\mathbf{A_1} + \mathbf{A_2} - \mathbf{A_3} = 0$$

which shows that the matrix A has three linearly dependent column vectors. Compare this to the property of the matrix B, defined as

$$B = [\mathbf{B_1} \quad \mathbf{B_2} \quad \mathbf{B_3}] = \begin{bmatrix} 1 & 0 & 0 \\ 0 & 1 & 0 \\ 0 & 0 & 1 \end{bmatrix}$$

The linear combination of $\mathbf{B}$s is

$$C_1\mathbf{B_1} + C_2\mathbf{B_2} + C_3\mathbf{B_3} = \begin{bmatrix} C_1 \\ C_2 \\ C_3 \end{bmatrix}$$

which can be zero iff $C_1 = C_2 = C_3 = 0$. Thus, B is made up of three linearly independent column vectors.

The idea of linear independence (dependence) can be exploited to define the rank of a matrix. To be general, consider the matrix A of size $m \times n$ consisting of n $m \times 1$ column vectors $\mathbf{A_i}$, $i = 1, \ldots, n$. Then the rank of A, denoted as $\mathrm{R}(A)$, is the largest number of linearly independent vectors in the set of vectors $\mathbf{A_1}, \ldots, \mathbf{A_n}$. For instance, with the numerical example of the matrix A of this subsection, $\mathrm{R}(A)$ is 2, not 3, because the three column vectors as a whole were seen to be linearly dependent, but the set of vectors $\mathbf{A_1}$ and $\mathbf{A_2}$ is linearly independent. On general considerations and very straightforward manipulations, we may observe the following properties to be true:

(1) For a matrix A of size $m \times n$, $R(A) \leqq$ minimum $\{m, n\}$.
(2) $R(A) = R(A')$.
(3) $R(\mathbf{0}) = 0$.
(4) If A is a diagonal matrix, then $R(A)$ is the number of nonzero diagonal entries of A.
(5) $R(I_{n \times n}) = n$, where $I_{n \times n}$ is an identity matrix of size $n \times n$.
(6) $R(A + B) \leqq R(A) + R(B)$, if A and B are of the same size.
(7) $R(AB) \leqq$ minimum $\{R(A), R(B)\}$.
(8) For an $n \times n$ matrix A, $R(A)$ is n iff A is nonsingular; for singular A, $R(A) < n$.
(9) The rank of a matrix is not altered if one row (column) is multiplied by a nonzero scalar, or when this resultant row (column) is added to another row (column).
(10) $R(A \otimes B) = R(A)R(B)$, if both A and B are square.

We shall revert to a few more results on ranks shortly.

3.5 SOLUTION OF SIMULTANEOUS HOMOGENEOUS EQUATIONS

One of the uses of the concept of rank is in the determination of existence and uniqueness of solutions of a set of, for instance, m homogeneous linear equations in n unknowns. These are comparable to the normal equations that arise in the multiple or even simple linear regression contexts for special values of m and n:

$$\begin{array}{c} a_{11}X_1 + \cdots + a_{1n}X_n = 0 \\ \cdots\cdots\cdots\cdots\cdots\cdots\cdots\cdots \\ a_{m1}X_1 + \cdots + a_{mn}X_n = 0 \end{array} \tag{3.25}$$

An equivalent matrix and vector representation of this set of equations is

$$\mathbf{A} \quad \mathbf{X} = \mathbf{0}$$

where

$$\mathbf{A} = \begin{bmatrix} a_{11} & \cdots & a_{1n} \\ \cdots & \cdots & \cdots \\ a_{m1} & \cdots & a_{mn} \end{bmatrix} \qquad \mathbf{X} = \begin{bmatrix} X_1 \\ \vdots \\ X_n \end{bmatrix} \qquad \mathbf{0} = \begin{bmatrix} 0 \\ \vdots \\ 0 \end{bmatrix} \tag{3.27}$$

Without going into the proof, the necessary and sufficient condition for $\mathbf{AX} = \mathbf{0}$ to possess a nontrivial solution is

$$R(A) < n \tag{3.28}$$

There is a more precise condition, however, in case we are interested in solutions that are unique up to a factor of proportionality. This means solutions of variables in relative or ratio (rather than absolute) forms where some variable serves as the *numeraire* or denominator. Then the condition is

$$R(A) = n - 1 \tag{3.29}$$

3.6 THE INVERSE AND ORTHOGONAL MATRICES

Suppose A is square $n \times n$ and nonsingular, implying $R(A)$ is n. Then the inverse of A, denoted by A^{-1}, is such that

$$A^{-1}A = AA^{-1} = I.$$

For the sake of computation of A^{-1}, the formula used is

$$A^{-1} = \frac{\text{Adj}(A)}{|A|} \tag{3.30}$$

where Adj(A) is the adjoint matrix of A of size $n \times n$. This is a transposed matrix of cofactors of A. That is, the (i, j)th element of Adj(A) is C_{ji}, the cofactor of the element a_{ji} of the matrix A.

To illustrate the calculations, go back to the 3×3 numerical matrix A, following (3.21). Its matrix of cofactors is

$$\begin{bmatrix} \begin{vmatrix} 0 & 2 \\ -1 & 1 \end{vmatrix} & -\begin{vmatrix} 3 & 2 \\ 2 & 1 \end{vmatrix} & \begin{vmatrix} 3 & 0 \\ 2 & 1 \end{vmatrix} \\ -\begin{vmatrix} 2 & 1 \\ -1 & 1 \end{vmatrix} & \begin{vmatrix} 1 & 1 \\ 2 & 1 \end{vmatrix} & -\begin{vmatrix} 1 & 2 \\ 2 & -1 \end{vmatrix} \\ \begin{vmatrix} 2 & 1 \\ 0 & 2 \end{vmatrix} & -\begin{vmatrix} 1 & 1 \\ 3 & 2 \end{vmatrix} & \begin{vmatrix} 1 & 2 \\ 3 & 0 \end{vmatrix} \end{bmatrix}$$

which simplifies to

$$\begin{bmatrix} 2 & 1 & -3 \\ -3 & -1 & 5 \\ 4 & 1 & -6 \end{bmatrix}$$

and whose transpose is

$$\begin{bmatrix} 2 & -3 & 4 \\ 1 & -1 & 1 \\ -3 & 5 & -6 \end{bmatrix}$$

Divide this by $|A|$, which was found to be 1. Thus,

$$A^{-1} = \frac{\text{Adj}(A)}{|A|} = \begin{bmatrix} 2 & -3 & 4 \\ 1 & -1 & 1 \\ -3 & 5 & -6 \end{bmatrix}$$

The following properties of an inverse matrix are easily verifiable:

(1) $(A^{-1})^{-1} = A$; $(A')^{-1} = (A^{-1})'$.
(2) $(AB)^{-1} = B^{-1}A^{-1}$, if A and B are nonsingular.
(3) $|A^{-1}| = 1/|A|$.
(4) The inverse of an upper (lower) triangular matrix is similarly an upper (lower) triangular matrix.

Explanation. We can illustrate this point with a 3×3 lower triangular matrix A:

$$A = \begin{bmatrix} a_{11} & 0 & 0 \\ a_{21} & a_{22} & 0 \\ a_{31} & a_{32} & a_{33} \end{bmatrix} \tag{3.31}$$

Notice that three cofactors of this matrix are zero, namely C_{21}, C_{31}, and C_{32}. Thus,

$$A^{-1} = \begin{bmatrix} C_{11} & 0 & 0 \\ C_{12} & C_{22} & 0 \\ C_{13} & C_{23} & C_{33} \end{bmatrix} / |A| \tag{3.32}$$

which is evidently lower triangular. Similarly, the upper triangular case can be established.

(5) (Without proof) The inverse of a partitioned matrix

$$A = \begin{bmatrix} A_{11} & \vdots & A_{12} \\ \cdots & & \cdots \\ A_{21} & \vdots & A_{22} \end{bmatrix}$$

where A_{11} and A_{22} are square and nonsingular matrices is given by

$$A^{-1} = \begin{bmatrix} B_{11} & -B_{11}A_{12}A_{22}^{-1} \\ -A_{22}^{-1}A_{21}B_{11} & A_{22}^{-1} + A_{22}^{-1}A_{21}B_{11}A_{12}A_{22}^{-1} \end{bmatrix} \tag{3.33}$$

given that $B_{11} = (A_{11} - A_{12}A_{22}^{-1}A_{21})^{-1}$, or, alternatively,

$$A^{-1} = \begin{bmatrix} A_{11}^{-1} + A_{11}^{-1}A_{12}B_{22}A_{21}A_{11}^{-1} & -A_{11}^{-1}A_{12}B_{22} \\ -B_{22}A_{21}A_{11}^{-1} & B_{22} \end{bmatrix} \tag{3.34}$$

given that $B_{22} = (A_{22} - A_{21}A_{11}^{-1}A_{12})^{-1}$.

(6) The inverse matrix A^{-1} for the block diagonal matrix A given by

$$A = \begin{bmatrix} A_{11} & 0 \\ 0 & A_{22} \end{bmatrix} \tag{3.35}$$

in which A_{11}, A_{22}, and A are all square matrices, is obtained by simply inverting the diagonal block matrices:

$$A^{-1} = \begin{bmatrix} A_{11}^{-1} & 0 \\ 0 & A_{22}^{-1} \end{bmatrix} \tag{3.36}$$

(This can be easily seen by checking that $AA^{-1} = I$.) An immediate special case is the inverse of a diagonal matrix. Letting $A = [a_{ii}]$, $i = 1, \ldots, n$ be a diagonal matrix, we have

$$A^{-1} = \begin{bmatrix} a_{11}^{-1} & 0 & \cdots 0 \\ 0 & a_{22}^{-1} & \cdots 0 \\ 0 & & \cdots a_{nn}^{-1} \end{bmatrix} \tag{3.37}$$

(7)
$$(A \otimes B)^{-1} = A^{-1} \otimes B^{-1} \tag{3.38}$$

if A and B are square and nonsingular.

The following relation is on the rank of a matrix obtained by pre- and post-multiplication of a matrix by a nonsingular matrix, and involves inverse matrices for its proof.

(8) If A is $m \times n$, P is $m \times m$ and nonsingular, and Q is $n \times n$ and nonsingular, $\mathrm{R}(PAQ) = \mathrm{R}(A)$

Proof: We know $\mathrm{R}(PA) \leqq \mathrm{R}(A)$. Put $PA = C$. Then $A = P^{-1}C$ and so $\mathrm{R}(A) \leqq \mathrm{R}(C) = \mathrm{R}(PA)$. But $\mathrm{R}(A)$ was greater than or equal to $\mathrm{R}(PA)$. Thus, $\mathrm{R}(A) = \mathrm{R}(C)$. Now put $CQ = D$ from which $C = DQ^{-1}$. From the first equality, we have $\mathrm{R}(D) \leqq \mathrm{R}(C)$, while from the second, $\mathrm{R}(C) \leqq \mathrm{R}(D)$. Thus $\mathrm{R}(C) = \mathrm{R}(D)$. But $\mathrm{R}(C) = \mathrm{R}(A)$ found before. So, $\mathrm{R}(A) = \mathrm{R}(C) = \mathrm{R}(D) = \mathrm{R}(PAQ)$.

(9) Any matrix of the form:

$$I - X(X'X)^{-1}X' \tag{3.39}$$

is idempotent. I, in general, is an $n \times n$ identity matrix, and X is, in general, an $n \times k$ matrix, and rank of X is $k \leqq n$.

(10) *The orthogonal matrix, its properties, and its diagonalization.* The main result here involves diagonalization of an orthogonal matrix C by means of a square symmetric matrix A, each of size $n \times n$. But, first, let us define C and lay down some of its properties.

A matrix C of size $n \times n$ is orthogonal if

$$C'C = I$$

That is,

$$\mathbf{C_i'C_j} = 1 \qquad \text{if } i = j$$
$$= 0 \qquad \text{of } i \neq j$$

where $\mathbf{C_i}$ and $\mathbf{C_j}$ are the ith and jth rows of C; $i, j = 1, 2, \ldots, n$. An identity matrix I is an example of an orthogonal matrix.

Taking the determinant of both sides of $C'C = I$, we have $|C'C| = |C|^2 = 1$; that is, $|C| = \pm 1$.

As for the diagonalization of C by A, we have

$$C'AC = \Lambda = \begin{vmatrix} \Lambda_1 & 0 & \cdots & 0 \\ 0 & \Lambda_2 & 0 & 0 \\ 0 & \cdots & & \Lambda_n \end{vmatrix}$$

where the Λ_is are the diagonal elements of Λ.

It follows that the rank of Λ is the number of its nonzero diagonal elements. Also it follows that

$$|C'AC| = |C'||A||C| = |A|$$

and since $|C'AC|$ is the determinant of a diagonal matrix which is the product of its diagonal elements Λ_i, then $|A|$ is also the same product.

3.7 SOLUTION OF SYSTEMS OF LINEAR EQUATIONS: CRAMER'S RULE

Consider a system of m linear equations in n unknowns:

$$\begin{aligned} a_{11}X_1 + a_{12}X_2 + \cdots + a_{1n}X_n &= b_1 \\ \cdots\cdots\cdots\cdots\cdots\cdots\cdots\cdots\cdots\cdots \\ a_{m1}X_1 + a_{m2}X_2 + \cdots + a_{mn}X_n &= b_m \end{aligned} \tag{3.40}$$

or, in matrix notation:

$$\underset{m\times n}{\mathbf{A}}\ \underset{n\times 1}{\mathbf{X}} = \underset{m\times 1}{\mathbf{b}} \tag{3.41}$$

The sizes of the vectors and matrix are written underneath their symbols and the bs are constants. For instance:

$$3X_1 + 2X_2 = 4$$
$$2X_1 + 3X_2 = 3$$

or

$$\begin{bmatrix} 3 & 2 \\ 2 & 3 \end{bmatrix} \begin{bmatrix} X_1 \\ X_2 \end{bmatrix} = \begin{bmatrix} 4 \\ 3 \end{bmatrix}$$

is a system of two equations in two unknowns. For the existence of solution of a system of equations we must have

$$R(A) = R(A:\mathbf{b}) = s \tag{3.42}$$

and for the solution to be unique, if it exists, we must have

$$s = n \tag{3.43}$$

If a solution exists, but $s < n$, $n - s$ of the unknowns have to be arbitrarily determined, and then the rest of the unknowns will be solved for uniquely.

If the coefficient matrix A is square and nonsingular so that its rank equals the number of its rows m and columns n, that is, $m = n = R(A)$, then the solution of the equations is unique, and given by

$$\mathbf{X} = A^{-I}\mathbf{b} \tag{3.44}$$

In the numerical example above

$$\begin{bmatrix} X_1 \\ X_2 \end{bmatrix} = \begin{bmatrix} 3 & 2 \\ 2 & 3 \end{bmatrix}^{-1} \begin{bmatrix} 4 \\ 3 \end{bmatrix} = \frac{1}{5} \begin{bmatrix} 3 & -2 \\ -2 & 3 \end{bmatrix} \begin{bmatrix} 4 \\ 3 \end{bmatrix} = \begin{bmatrix} 1\frac{1}{5} \\ \frac{1}{5} \end{bmatrix}$$

Alternatively, Cramer's rule gives the same solution. For (3.39), the solution is

$$X_i = \frac{|A_i|}{|A|} \qquad i = 1, 2, \ldots, n \tag{3.45}$$

where A_i has the ith column of A replaced by $\mathbf{b}$. For the numerical example above, the solutions are

$$X_1 = \begin{vmatrix} 4 & 2 \\ 3 & 3 \end{vmatrix} \Big/ \begin{vmatrix} 3 & 2 \\ 2 & 3 \end{vmatrix} = 1\tfrac{1}{5}$$

$$X_2 = \begin{vmatrix} 3 & 4 \\ 2 & 3 \end{vmatrix} \Big/ \begin{vmatrix} 3 & 2 \\ 2 & 3 \end{vmatrix} = \tfrac{1}{5}$$

which are the same solutions obtained by the method of inverse matrix.

3.8 LINEAR TRANSFORMATIONS, EIGENVECTORS, AND EIGENVALUES

Any vector $\mathbf{X}$ belonging to E^n, denoted as $\mathbf{X} \in E^n$, where E^n is a Euclidean n space, can be linearly transformed to a unique vector $\mathbf{Y} \in E^m$, where E^m is a Euclidean m space, by means of a transformation matrix A of size $m \times n$ such that

$$\mathbf{Y} = A\mathbf{X} = A(\mathbf{X}) \tag{3.46}$$

This transformation is linear, which means

$$\begin{aligned} A(\mathbf{X}^1 + \mathbf{X}^2) &= A\mathbf{X}^1 + A\mathbf{X}^2 \\ A(\lambda \mathbf{X}^1) &= \lambda A(\mathbf{X}^1) \end{aligned} \tag{3.47}$$

where $\mathbf{X}^1$ and $\mathbf{X}^2$ are vectors in E^n and λ is a scalar. Taking $\lambda = 0$, it follows that

$$A(\mathbf{0}) = \mathbf{0}$$

Extending the argument, we arrive at what is known as an eigenvector or characteristic vector.

An eigenvector for a square matrix A is a nonzero vector, which when (pre-) operated on by A produces the same vector except for a scalar multiplier:

$$A\mathbf{X} = \lambda \mathbf{X} \tag{3.48}$$

The multiplier λ is the eigenvalue or the characteristic (or latent) root of A. Thus, λ is an eigenvalue of A, if and only if, for some $\mathbf{X} \neq \mathbf{0}$, $A\mathbf{X} = \lambda \mathbf{X}$. In other words,

$$(A - \lambda I)\mathbf{X} = \mathbf{0} \tag{3.49}$$

Now, the above is a system of n homogeneous linear equations in n unknowns, which will have a nontrivial solution iff

$$|A - \lambda I| = 0 \tag{3.50}$$

The eigenvalues of A are the n roots, not necessarily distinguishable, of the equation $|A - \lambda I| = 0$. This equation is called the characteristic equation, which is an nth-order polynomial equation in λ as long as the matrix A is of size $n \times n$:

$$|A - \lambda I| = a_0 + a_1\lambda + \cdots + a_n\lambda^n = 0 \tag{3.51}$$

where $a_0, a_1, \ldots,$ are the coefficients of this characteristic polynomial.

Example. Let

$$A = \begin{bmatrix} 3 & 2 \\ 2 & 0 \end{bmatrix}$$

Then

$$(A - \lambda I) = \begin{bmatrix} 3 - \lambda & 2 \\ 2 & -\lambda \end{bmatrix}$$

Its characteristic equation is

$$\lambda^2 - 3\lambda - 4 = 0$$

Its roots are

$$\lambda_1 = 4 \quad \text{and} \quad \lambda_2 = -1$$

To find the characteristic vector for $\lambda_1 = 4$, set up an equation as in (3.49):

$$\begin{bmatrix} -1 & 2 \\ 2 & -4 \end{bmatrix} \begin{bmatrix} x_1 \\ x_2 \end{bmatrix} = 0$$

This yields

$$x_1 = 2x_2$$

To solve absolutely for x_1 and x_2, we follow the convention of equating the length of this eigenvector to unity; that is,

$$x_1^2 + x_2^2 = 1$$

This gives

$$4x_2^2 + x_2^2 = 1 \quad \text{or} \quad x_2 = 1/\sqrt{5}$$

Thus,

$$x_1 = 2x_2 = 2/\sqrt{5}$$

which, along with $x_2 = 1/\sqrt{5}$, gives the vector

$$\mathbf{X_1} = \begin{bmatrix} 2/\sqrt{5} \\ 1/\sqrt{5} \end{bmatrix}$$

For the other root: $\lambda_2 = -1$, the vector is

$$\mathbf{X_2} = \begin{bmatrix} -\sqrt{5}/4 \\ \sqrt{5}/2 \end{bmatrix}$$

These eigenvectors are orthogonal because $\mathbf{X}_1'\mathbf{X}_2 = 0$. Thus, the full set of eigenvectors for the symmetric matrix of this problem defines the orthogonal matrix

$$\boldsymbol{X} = [\mathbf{X_1X_2}] = \begin{bmatrix} 2/\sqrt{5} & -\sqrt{5}/4 \\ 1/\sqrt{5} & \sqrt{5}/2 \end{bmatrix}$$

with $\boldsymbol{X}'\boldsymbol{X} = \boldsymbol{I}$, where $\boldsymbol{I}$ is an identity matrix of size 2. Some properties of the characteristic roots and vectors of any square matrix $\boldsymbol{A}$ follow. Most proofs are left out.

(1) $\lambda_1 + \lambda_2 + \cdots + \lambda_n = \text{Tr}(\boldsymbol{A})$.

(2) $\lambda_1\lambda_2 \cdots \lambda_n = |\boldsymbol{A}|$.

(3) $\lambda_j = \Lambda_j$ if $\boldsymbol{A}$ is the diagonal matrix with the jth diagonal entry Λ_j.

(4) $\lambda_j = \pm 1$, if $\boldsymbol{A}$ is orthogonal.

(5) If $\boldsymbol{A}$ is an idempotent matrix, (a) $\lambda_j = 1$ or 0, (b) $\boldsymbol{C}'\boldsymbol{A}\boldsymbol{C}$ is a diagonal matrix where $\boldsymbol{C}$ is an orthogonal matrix of the same size as $\boldsymbol{A}$, (see result (10) of Section 3.6), and (c) $\text{R}(\boldsymbol{A}) = \text{Tr}(\boldsymbol{A})$. This means that $\boldsymbol{C}'\boldsymbol{A}\boldsymbol{C}$ has the same number of diagonal elements (that are unities) as $\text{R}(\boldsymbol{C}'\boldsymbol{A}\boldsymbol{C})$ or $\text{R}(\boldsymbol{A})$.

Proof. Since $\mathbf{AX} = \lambda\mathbf{X}$ corresponds to the matrix $\boldsymbol{A}$, we must have $\boldsymbol{A}\boldsymbol{A}\mathbf{X} = \lambda\boldsymbol{A}\mathbf{X}$, which is the same as $\boldsymbol{A}^2\mathbf{X} = \boldsymbol{A}\mathbf{X} = \lambda\mathbf{X} = \lambda^2\mathbf{X}$ since $\boldsymbol{A}^2 = \boldsymbol{A}$. From this, we must have $\lambda = \lambda^2$, which may occur if $\lambda = 1$ or 0. This is the first part of the result. For the second part, take $\boldsymbol{C}$ to be an orthogonal matrix. Then $\boldsymbol{\Lambda} = \boldsymbol{C}'\boldsymbol{A}\boldsymbol{C}$ is a diagonal matrix. Thus, $\mathrm{R}(\boldsymbol{\Lambda}) = \mathrm{R}(\boldsymbol{A}) = \mathrm{Tr}(\boldsymbol{\Lambda}) = r$, where r is the number of nonvanishing characteristic roots (i.e. 1) of $\boldsymbol{\Lambda}$, which are the same as the characteristic roots of the matrix $\boldsymbol{A}$.

(6) If $\boldsymbol{A}$ is raised to the power r, then λ_j^r are the characteristic roots of $\boldsymbol{A}^r$ if λ_j are the (nonzero) characteristic roots of $\boldsymbol{A}$, and r is any positive integer (or, for that matter, any integer as long as $\boldsymbol{A}$ is nonsingular).

If, in addition, the matrix $\boldsymbol{A}$ is symmetric, the properties of its characteristic roots $\lambda_1, \ldots, \lambda_n$ include the following:

(a) $\mathrm{R}(\boldsymbol{A})$ is the number of nonzero characteristic roots.
(b) $\lambda_1, \ldots, \lambda_n$ are all real.
(c) Characteristic vectors pertaining to distinct characteristic roots are pairwise orthogonal. That is, if $\mathbf{X_i}$ and $\mathbf{X_j}$ are vectors corresponding to distinct roots λ_i and λ_j, then $\mathbf{X_i}$ and $\mathbf{X_j}$ are orthogonal implying $\mathbf{X_i}'\mathbf{X_j} = 0$. It follows that if a characteristic root is repeated r times, there will be r orthogonal vectors pertaining to this root.
(d) If $\mathbf{X}_i$ is the characteristic vector of $\boldsymbol{A}$ pertaining to the characteristic root λ_i, then $\mathbf{X}_i'\mathbf{X}_i = \lambda_i$.

3.9 QUADRATIC FORMS AND DEFINITE MATRICES

For an $n \times n$ square symmetric matrix $\boldsymbol{A}$ and an n-element column vector $\mathbf{X}$, the quadratic form of $\boldsymbol{A}$ is

$$\begin{aligned} \mathrm{Q}_A(\mathbf{X}) &= \mathbf{X}'\boldsymbol{A}\mathbf{X} \\ &= \sum_{i=1}^{n}\sum_{j=1}^{n} a_{ij}x_ix_j \end{aligned} \tag{3.52}$$

which after expansion, can be presented as

$$\begin{aligned} \mathrm{Q}_A(\mathbf{X}) = a_{11}x_1^2 &+ 2a_{12}x_1x_2 + 2a_{13}x_1x_3 + \cdots + 2a_{1n}x_1x_n \\ &+ a_{22}x_2^2 \quad + 2a_{23}x_2x_3 + \cdots + 2a_{2n}x_2x_n \\ &\qquad\qquad + a_{33}x_3^2 \quad + \cdots + 2a_{3n}x_3x_n \\ &\qquad\qquad\ \vdots \\ &\qquad\qquad\qquad\qquad\qquad + a_{nn}x_n^2 \end{aligned}$$

To illustrate, if we take

$$A = \begin{bmatrix} 3 & 2 \\ 2 & 1 \end{bmatrix}$$

then $Q_A(\mathbf{X})$ becomes

$$3x_1^2 + 4x_1x_2 + x_2^2$$

whereas, if we take A to be the diagonal matrix

$$D = \begin{bmatrix} 3 & 0 \\ 0 & 1 \end{bmatrix}$$

then $Q_D(\mathbf{X})$ becomes the weighted sum of squares:

$$3x_1^2 + x_2^2$$

in which the cross-product terms disappear.

If $Q_A(\mathbf{X}) > 0$ for all $\mathbf{X} \neq 0$, the quadratic form is called positive definite and the intervening matrix A is called a positive definite matrix. If $Q_A(\mathbf{X}) \geqq 0$ for all $\mathbf{X} \neq 0$, the quadratic form and its associated matrix are called positive semidefinite. By reversing the inequality sign, we will have negative definite and negative semidefinite forms and matrices.[1]

The following properties involving definite matrices will be useful.

(1) A is positive definite iff all its characteristic roots are positive, or, equivalently, iff the determinant of every principal submatrix be positive.

As a matter of definition, the principal submatrices of A are a set of n submatrices presented most generally as

$$\underset{(1 \times 1)}{a_{ll}}, \quad \underset{(2 \times 2)}{\begin{bmatrix} a_{ll} & a_{lm} \\ a_{ml} & a_{mm} \end{bmatrix}}, \quad \underset{(3 \times 3)}{\begin{bmatrix} a_{ll} & a_{lm} & a_{ln} \\ a_{ml} & a_{mm} & a_{mn} \\ a_{nl} & a_{nm} & a_{nn} \end{bmatrix}}, \quad \ldots, \quad \underset{(n \times n)}{A}$$

where the sizes of the matrices are written below their structures. By taking $l = 1$, $m = 2$, $n = 3$, . . . , principal submatrices become the upper submatrices, A_1, A_2, . . . , A_n, where

$$A_1 = [a_{11}], \; A_2 = \begin{bmatrix} a_{11} & a_{12} \\ a_{21} & a_{22} \end{bmatrix}, \; \ldots, \; A_n = A$$

(2) If A is positive (negative) definite, then A is nonsingular so that A^{-1} exists and A^{-1} is positive (negative) definite. Also, $R(A) = R(A^{-1}) = n$, if A is $n \times n$.

[1] If the quadratic form is positive for some $\mathbf{X}$ vectors and negative for others, it is called an indefinite quadratic form.

(3) If A is positive (semipositive) definite and the matrix Q is nonsingular, then $Q'AQ$ is positive (semipositive) definite.
(4) If the order of A is $m \times n$ and $R(A) = n < m$, then $A'A$ is positive definite but AA' is positive semidefinite.
(5) If A is positive definite, there exists a nonsingular matrix Q such that $QAQ' = I$ and $Q'Q = A^{-1}$.

3.10 VECTOR AND MATRIX DERIVATIVES AND DETERMINATION OF EXTREMA

We now show how to derive matrices or to derive with respect to matrices.

If we differentiate a vector or matrix with respect to a scalar, we get a vector or matrix of derivatives. These are evident in the following, in which the symbol K is used for a scalar:

(1) Let $\mathbf{Y} = (Y_1 \quad Y_2 \cdots Y_n)'$; then

$$\frac{d\mathbf{Y}}{dK} = \left[\frac{dY_1}{dK} \quad \frac{dY_2}{dK} \cdots \frac{dY_n}{dK}\right]'$$

(2) Let $A = (a_{ij})$, where $i = 1, \ldots, n$ and $j = 1, \ldots, n$, be an $n \times n$ matrix. Then,

$$\frac{dA}{dK} = \left(\frac{da_{ij}}{dK}\right)$$

(3)
$$\frac{dAB}{dK} = A\frac{dB}{dK} + \frac{dA}{dK}B$$

(4)
$$\frac{dA^{-1}}{dK} = -A^{-1}\frac{dA}{dK}A^{-1} \tag{3.53}$$

If we differentiate a scalar with regard to a column (row) vector, we obtain a row (column) vector. This is evident below.

(5) Let $\mathbf{Y} = f(\mathbf{X})$, $\mathbf{X}$ being $(X_1 \quad X_2 \cdots X_n)'$. Then

$$\frac{\partial \mathbf{Y}}{\partial \mathbf{X}} = \left[\frac{\partial f}{\partial X_1} \quad \frac{\partial f}{\partial X_2} \cdots \frac{\partial f}{\partial X_n}\right]$$

This is called the gradient vector $\partial f(\mathbf{X})/\partial \mathbf{X}$.

(6) Suppose $\mathbf{a}'\mathbf{X}$ is a linear form, that is $\mathbf{a}'\mathbf{X} = a_1X_1 + a_2X_2 + \cdots + a_nX_n$. Then

$$\frac{\partial \mathbf{a}'\mathbf{X}}{\partial \mathbf{X}} = \mathbf{a} = [a_1 \quad a_2 \cdots a_n]' \tag{3.54}$$

(7) If $Q_A(\mathbf{X}) = \mathbf{X}'A\mathbf{X}$ is a quadratic form, then

$$Q_A(\mathbf{X}) = a_{11}X_1^2 + 2a_{12}X_1X_2 + \cdots + 2a_{n-1,n}X_{n-1}X_n + a_{nn}X_n^2.$$

Thus,

$$\frac{\partial Q_A(\mathbf{X})}{\partial \mathbf{X}} = 2\begin{bmatrix} \sum_1^n a_{1j}X_j \\ \sum_1^n a_{2j}X_j \\ \vdots \\ \sum_1^n a_{nj}X_j \end{bmatrix} = 2\begin{bmatrix} \mathbf{a}_1\mathbf{X} \\ \mathbf{a}_2\mathbf{X} \\ \vdots \\ \mathbf{a}_n\mathbf{X} \end{bmatrix} = 2A\mathbf{X} \qquad (3.55)$$

where $\mathbf{a_j} = [a_{1j} \quad a_{2j} \cdots a_{nj}]'$; $j = 1, 2, \ldots, n$.

If we differentiate a scalar with regard to an $m \times n$ matrix, the result is an $n \times m$ matrix. This is evident below.

(8) Let $Q_A(\mathbf{X})$ be the quadratic form defined before. Then

$$\frac{\partial Q_A(\mathbf{X})}{\partial A} = \mathbf{XX}' \qquad (3.56)$$

(9) If Tr(A) is trace of A, then

$$\frac{\partial \operatorname{Tr}(A)}{\partial A} = I \qquad (3.57)$$

(10) Let $|A|$ be the determinant of A. Then

$$\frac{\partial |A|}{\partial A} = |A| A^{-1} \qquad (3.58)$$

$$\frac{\partial \ln |A|}{\partial A} = A^{-1} \quad \text{(if } A \text{ is nonsingular)} \qquad (3.59)$$

More results, of use in econometrics, are presented below. These involve the derivative of a vector with respect to a vector, the result being a matrix.

(11) $$\partial A\mathbf{X}/\partial \mathbf{X} = A \qquad (3.60)$$

(12) For the gradient vector ($\partial f/\partial \mathbf{X}$),

$$\frac{\partial}{\partial \mathbf{X}}\left(\frac{\partial f}{\partial \mathbf{X}}\right) = \left(\frac{\partial^2 f}{\partial X_i\, \partial X_j}\right) \qquad (3.61)$$

This is called the *Hessian matrix*.

(13) If $\mathbf{x} = (x_1, x_2, \ldots, x_n)$, and $\mathbf{h} = \mathbf{h}(\mathbf{x}) = [h_1(x) \quad h_2(x) \ldots h_m(x)]$, then the Jacobian matrix of transformation is the derivative of $\mathbf{h}(\mathbf{x})$ with regard to $\mathbf{x}$, that is

$$\frac{\partial \mathbf{h}(\mathbf{x})}{\partial \mathbf{x}} = \left(\frac{\partial g_i}{\partial x_j}\right) \tag{3.62}$$

3.11 UNCONSTRAINED AND CONSTRAINED EXTREMA

Suppose Y is a scalar variable that is a function of n independent variables $\mathbf{x}$: x_1, $x_2, \ldots, x_n$ as follows:

$$\begin{aligned} Y &= f(\mathbf{x}) \\ &= f(x_1, x_2, \ldots, x_n) \end{aligned}$$

If $\mathbf{x}$ belongs to the set X in Euclidean n space E^n, then the first-order necessary condition for $\mathbf{x}^0$ to maximize (minimize) $f(\mathbf{x})$ over $\mathbf{x}$ is to have the gradient vector become zero. That is,

$$\left.\frac{\partial f(\mathbf{x})}{\partial \mathbf{x}}\right|_{\mathbf{x}=\mathbf{x}^0} = \begin{bmatrix} f_1 \\ f_2 \\ \vdots \\ f_n \end{bmatrix}_{|\mathbf{x}=\mathbf{x}^0} = \mathbf{0}$$

where $| \, \mathbf{x} = \mathbf{x}^0$ implies that the derivative has been evaluated at $\mathbf{x} = \mathbf{x}^0$, and $f_j = \partial f / \partial x_j$, $j = 1, 2, \ldots, n$.

A second-order condition, which is also said to be the *sufficient* condition, for a maximum (minimum) is that the Hessian matrix, evaluated at the point $\mathbf{x} = \mathbf{x}^0$; that is,

$$\left.\frac{\partial^2 f(\mathbf{x})}{\partial \mathbf{x}^2}\right|_{\mathbf{x}=\mathbf{x}^0} = \begin{bmatrix} f_{11} & f_{12} \cdots & f_{1n} \\ f_{21} & f_{22} \cdots & f_{2n} \\ \cdots & \cdots & \cdots \\ f_{n1} & f_{n2} \cdots & f_{nn} \end{bmatrix}_{|\mathbf{x}=\mathbf{x}^0}$$

be negative definite (positive definite), where

$$f_{ij} = f_{ji} = \frac{\partial^2 f}{\partial x_i \, \partial x_j} \qquad \text{for } i, j = 1, 2, \ldots, n$$

Example. Let us apply the optimizing technique to the problem of minimizing the sum of squares due to error, where the error ϵ appears in (3.2). Specifically, the problem is as follows:

Minimize, for suitable choice of β,

$$S = \sum_{i=1}^{n} \epsilon_i^2 = (\mathbf{Y} - X\boldsymbol{\beta})'(\mathbf{Y} - X\boldsymbol{\beta}) = \mathbf{Y}'\mathbf{Y} - 2\boldsymbol{\beta}'X'\mathbf{Y} + \boldsymbol{\beta}'X'X\boldsymbol{\beta} \tag{3.63}$$

From the first-order conditions, we have

$$\frac{\partial S}{\partial \boldsymbol{\beta}} = -2X'\mathbf{Y} + 2X'X\boldsymbol{\beta} = 0$$

That is, provided $X'X$ is nonsingular, the minimizing solution $\hat{\boldsymbol{\beta}}$ for $\boldsymbol{\beta}$ comes out as

$$\hat{\boldsymbol{\beta}} = (X'X)^{-1}X'\mathbf{Y} \tag{3.64}$$

The second-order conditions are fulfilled because assuming that $\mathbf{X}$ is of full rank ($= m + 1$), $X'X$ is positive definite, and therefore,

$$\frac{\partial^2 S}{\partial \boldsymbol{\beta}^2} = 2(X'X) \tag{3.65}$$

is positive definite.

Let us now move to the case of constrained optimization. Assume that there are k constraints, where the number n of independent variables exceeds k:

$$g_i(\mathbf{x}) = 0 \qquad i = 1, 2, \ldots, k \quad n > k \tag{3.66}$$

where

$$\mathbf{x} = (x_1 \quad x_2 \cdots x_n)$$

Therefore, our problem is to maximize (minimize):

$$f(\mathbf{x}) \text{ subject to } g(\mathbf{x}) = 0, \tag{3.67}$$

where

$$g(\mathbf{x}) = \begin{bmatrix} g_1(\mathbf{x}) \\ \vdots \\ g_k(\mathbf{x}) \end{bmatrix}$$

By the method of Lagrange multipliers, devise k new variables

$$\boldsymbol{\lambda} = \begin{bmatrix} \lambda_1 \\ \lambda_2 \\ \vdots \\ \lambda_k \end{bmatrix}$$

for the k constraints. These are called the Lagrange multipliers. With their help, define the Lagrange function:

$$L(\mathbf{x}, \boldsymbol{\lambda}) = f(\mathbf{x}) - \boldsymbol{\lambda}'g(\mathbf{x}) \tag{3.68}$$

Evidently L is scalar, being a function of $n + k$ variables $\mathbf{x}$ and $\boldsymbol{\lambda}$. The first-order conditions for a maximum (minimum) of L is that all $n + k$ first-order partial derivatives should be equal to zero; that is,

$$\begin{bmatrix} \dfrac{\partial L}{\partial \mathbf{x}} \\ \\ \dfrac{\partial L}{\partial \boldsymbol{\lambda}} \end{bmatrix} = \begin{bmatrix} \dfrac{\partial f}{\partial \mathbf{x}} - \dfrac{\partial}{\partial \mathbf{x}}(\boldsymbol{\lambda}' g(\mathbf{x})) \\ \\ -g(\mathbf{x}) \end{bmatrix} = \mathit{0} \tag{3.69}$$

Therefore, the constraints $g(\mathbf{x}^0) = 0$ are met at the solution $\mathbf{x}^0$, and furthermore,

$$\left.\frac{\partial f}{\partial \mathbf{x}}\right|_{\mathbf{x}=\mathbf{x}^0} = \lambda \left.\frac{\partial g}{\partial \mathbf{x}}\right|_{\mathbf{x}=\mathbf{x}^0}$$

To illustrate, suppose our objective is to minimize the sum of squares due to error S, subject to k linear constraints:

$$\boldsymbol{R\beta} = \mathbf{r} \tag{3.70}$$

in which $\boldsymbol{R}$ is of size $k \times (m + 1)$ and is of rank $(m + 1)$ and $\mathbf{r}$ is a prespecified $k \times 1$ vector. The Lagrangean function for this constrained least-squares problem is

$$L = \mathbf{Y}'\mathbf{Y} - 2\boldsymbol{\beta}'X'\mathbf{Y} + \boldsymbol{\beta}'X'X\boldsymbol{\beta} - \boldsymbol{\lambda}'(\mathbf{r} - \boldsymbol{R\beta}) \tag{3.71}$$

From the first-order conditions,

$$\frac{\partial L}{\partial \boldsymbol{\beta}} = -2X'\mathbf{Y} + 2X'X\boldsymbol{\beta} + \boldsymbol{R}'\boldsymbol{\lambda} = 0 \tag{3.72}$$

$$\frac{\partial L}{\partial \boldsymbol{\lambda}} = -\mathbf{r} + \boldsymbol{R\beta} = 0 \tag{3.73}$$

Thus, from (3.72),

$$\widehat{\boldsymbol{\beta}} = (X'X)^{-1}(X'\mathbf{Y} - \tfrac{1}{2}\boldsymbol{R}'\boldsymbol{\lambda}) \tag{3.74}$$

And, using the constraint, we have

$$\boldsymbol{R}(X'X)^{-1}X'\mathbf{Y} - \tfrac{1}{2}\boldsymbol{R}(X'X)^{-1}\boldsymbol{R}'\boldsymbol{\lambda} = \mathbf{r} \tag{3.75}$$

From this $\boldsymbol{\lambda}$ is solved as

$$\boldsymbol{\lambda} = 2[\boldsymbol{R}(X'X)^{-1}\boldsymbol{R}']^{-1}[\boldsymbol{R}(X'X)^{-1}X'\mathbf{Y} - \mathbf{r}] \tag{3.76}$$

Using this in (3.74) above, we obtain

$$\widehat{\hat{\boldsymbol{\beta}}} = \hat{\boldsymbol{\beta}} - (X'X)^{-1}\boldsymbol{R}'[\boldsymbol{R}(X'X)^{-1}\boldsymbol{R}']^{-1}[\boldsymbol{R}\hat{\boldsymbol{\beta}} - \mathbf{r}] \tag{3.77}$$

where $\hat{\boldsymbol{\beta}}$ is the unconstrained least-squares estimator used before.

3.12 SUGGESTED READING

For a more detailed treatment of linear algebra, consult Hadley (1961), for instance.

PROBLEMS

3-1. Show that if A is an $n \times n$ symmetric matrix and B is an $n \times m$ matrix, then $B'AB$ is symmetric. (*Hint:* Transpose $B'AB$ to derive the required result.)

3-2. Let

$$A = \begin{bmatrix} 2 & 0 & 4 \\ 4 & 5 & 5 \\ 3 & 2 & 0 \end{bmatrix}$$

$$B = \begin{bmatrix} 4 & 1 \\ 2 & 3 \\ -2 & 0 \end{bmatrix}$$

$$C = [4 \quad 5 \quad 9]$$

Calculate $(CA)'$, $A'C'$, $(AB)'$ and $B'A'$. What is $(AB)'C'$? Is this equal to CAB?

3-3. Show that the product of two symmetric matrices is not, in general, symmetric.

3-4. Find the inverse of the matrix

$$\begin{bmatrix} 1 & 3 & 2 \\ 2 & 6 & 9 \\ 7 & 6 & 1 \end{bmatrix}$$

3-5. Let

$$A = \begin{bmatrix} 2 & 0 & 4 \\ 0 & 5 & 2 \\ 4 & 2 & 6 \end{bmatrix}$$

$$B = \begin{bmatrix} 1 & 3 & 2 \\ 3 & 2 & 4 \\ 2 & 4 & -1 \end{bmatrix}$$

Prove that $\text{Tr}AB = \text{Tr}BA$

3-6. Let A, B, C, and D be $n \times n$ matrices. If $DA = I$, and $\text{Tr}(CB) = \theta$, what is $\text{Tr}(ABCD)$?

3-7. **(a)** Prove that

$$\begin{vmatrix} 1 & \alpha & \alpha^2 \\ 1 & \beta & \beta^2 \\ 1 & \gamma & \gamma^2 \end{vmatrix} = (\gamma - \alpha)(\beta - \gamma)(\alpha - \beta)$$

(b) What would be the value if the determinant instead were

$$\begin{vmatrix} 1 & 1 & 1 \\ \alpha & \beta & \gamma \\ \alpha^2 & \beta^2 & \gamma^2 \end{vmatrix}$$

3-8. Show that if B is diagonal of size $n \times n$, then $\text{Tr}B = \mathbf{i}'B\mathbf{i}$ where

$$\mathbf{i} = \begin{bmatrix} 1 \\ 1 \\ 1 \\ \vdots \\ 1 \end{bmatrix}$$

is the $n \times 1$ unit vector.

3-9. Show that if $\mathbf{Z}^{(1)}$, $\mathbf{Z}^{(2)}$, and $\mathbf{Z}^{(3)}$ are each an $m \times 1$ vector, and $\mathbf{X} = a\mathbf{Z}^{(1)} + b\mathbf{Z}^{(2)} + c\mathbf{Z}^{(3)}$, then $\{\mathbf{X}, \mathbf{Z}^{(1)}, \mathbf{Z}^{(2)}, \mathbf{Z}^{(3)}\}$ is a linearly dependent set.

3-10. If X is of size $n \times m$, $P = X(X'X)^{-1}X'$, and $Q = I - P$, what are

(a) PP?

(b) PX?

(c) QQ?

(d) QP?

(e) QX?

3-11. If ϵ_is are random variables with

$$\text{E}(\boldsymbol{\epsilon}) = \mathbf{0}$$
$$\text{V}(\boldsymbol{\epsilon}) = \sigma^2 I$$

where

$$\boldsymbol{\epsilon} = \begin{bmatrix} \epsilon_1 \\ \epsilon_2 \\ \epsilon_3 \\ \vdots \\ \epsilon_n \end{bmatrix}$$

and I is the identity matrix, prove that

$$\text{E}\boldsymbol{\epsilon}' M \boldsymbol{\epsilon} = \sigma^2 \, \text{Tr}M$$

where M is an $n \times n$ matrix.

3-12. Using the specifications of problem 3-11, and if

$$M = I - X(X'X)^{-1}X'$$

where X is a matrix of size $n \times (m + 1)$ show that

$$\text{E}\boldsymbol{\epsilon}' M \boldsymbol{\epsilon}$$

simplifies further to

$$\sigma^2(n - m - 1)$$

What specific properties of the matrix M did you use?

3-13. Suppose

$$X = \begin{bmatrix} 1 & 2 \\ 0 & -1 \\ 3 & 1 \end{bmatrix}$$

Evaluate $M = [I - X(X'X)^{-1}X']$ where I is an identity matrix of size 3×3. Prove that M is idempotent and find its trace and rank. What are the characteristic roots and the characteristic vectors of M? Can you obtain the orthogonal matrix (based on those characteristic vectors) that will diagonalize the matrix M? Show how.

3-14. Show that if A is a symmetric, positive definite matrix and X is a matrix with full column rank, then $X'AX$ is also positive definite.

3-15. If

$$\begin{bmatrix} \alpha & \beta \\ r & \delta \end{bmatrix} \begin{bmatrix} 2 & 4 \\ 2 & 1 \end{bmatrix} = \begin{bmatrix} 1 & 0 \\ 0 & 2 \end{bmatrix}$$

find, α, β, r, δ without evaluating the inverse of a matrix.

3-16. Show that if

$$A = I - \left(\frac{1}{n}\right) \mathbf{ii}'$$

is an $n \times n$ matrix, where I is an $n \times n$ identity matrix, and $\mathbf{i}$ is a column vector of ones, then

$$\mathbf{X}'A\mathbf{X} = 0$$

where $\mathbf{X}$ is an n-element column vector of constants.

3-17. **(a)** Show that an idempotent matrix is nonnegative definite.

(b) Let X be $n \times m$ and $P = X(X'X)^{-1}X'$. What is (are) the necessary condition(s) on X such that P is defined? Show that P is positive semidefinite. Using the result, for instance, $\text{Tr}AB = \text{Tr}BA$, find the rank of P.

4

Statistics

4.1 INTRODUCTION

Econometrics is basically concerned with the statistical inference of an economic system. With this in mind we review the basic principles of statistical inference in this chapter. The inferential results will be of repetitive use later when we establish and discuss properties and tests concerning various econometric estimators.

Consider an example. The volume of international trade of a country can be posited to be a function of the total world financial reserves. If it is known with certainty that an increase in one will lead to the increase in the other variable, such a positive result will become the output of a fully deterministic theory. However, a theory can often become indeterminate or probabilistic. In that case any one outcome of the theory may have associated with it an error, and the error corresponding to all the outcomes will have a probability distribution of its own. Then we can make statements such as the following: the probability is 1/4 that the volume of international trade of a country, according to theory, is larger than the *actual* volume of its trade by a third; in other words, the error between the theoretical and actual volume of trade is 1/3 in units of volume of trade and this value occurs in just one out of four cases.

This example is used to illustrate the need for a knowledge of the probability distribution of a variable or variables and its properties before statistical inference can be made. We now turn to this problem.

4.2 FREQUENCY AND PROBABILITY DISTRIBUTION

Consider a univariate frequency distribution. This is available from, say, N observations on a variable x grouped into $L \leqq N$ different values of the variable, a typical value x_l appearing with a relative frequency of $f(x_l)$, $l = 1, 2, \ldots, L$. It follows that the relative frequencies sum to one:

$$\sum_{l=1}^{L} f(x_l) = 1 \tag{4.1}$$

This is because the $f(x_l)$s are relative frequencies, and so it is with *certainty* that one must find *any* observation on the variable to arise in *all* the L different groups of its observations.

If L is large, the usual practice is to have a grouped frequency distribution. This includes having the values of the variable x split into a number of nonoverlapping classes and observing the relative frequency of its value occurring in each class. Consider the hypothetical example of the (relative frequency) distribution of income in Table 4.1.

TABLE 4.1 A HYPOTHETICAL FREQUENCY DISTRIBUTION OF INCOME

x	$f(x)$
$-\infty$–5,000	0.080
5,000–10,000	0.343
10,000–∞	0.577

Note that $\Sigma\, f(x)$ for this problem is equal to unity.

In the area of the frequency function, another notion that is useful in statistical analysis is that of cumulative distribution or simply the distribution function. This is usually denoted by the symbol $F(x)$ and gives, for a particular value x_l of x, the relative frequency of observations with x less than or equal x_l. The distribution function corresponding to the hypothetical example of Table 4.1 is shown in Table 4.2.

TABLE 4.2 A DISTRIBUTION FUNCTION OF INCOME

x	$F(x)$
$-\infty$	0
5,000	0.080
10,000	0.423
∞	1.000

TABLE 4.3 A HYPOTHETICAL BIVARIATE FREQUENCY DISTRIBUTION

	y				
x	0–0.25	0.25–0.50	0.50–1.00	$f(x)$:subtotal	$\sum_x f(x)$
$-\infty$–5,000	0.072	0.005	0.003	0.080	
5,000–10,000	0.020	0.073	0.250	0.343	
10,000–∞	0.015	0.230	0.332	0.577	
$f(y)$: subtotal	0.107	0.308	0.585		
$\sum_y f(y)$					1.00

4.2.1 Bivariate Distribution

Suppose now we consider two variables, x and y. There are N observations on each variable which (observations) can be grouped into $L \leqq N$ different values of x and $M \leqq N$ different values of y among the observations. The paired observation (x_l, y_m) occurs with a relative frequency or probability[1] of $f(x_l, y_m)$, $l = 1, 2, \ldots, L$, and $m = 1, 2, \ldots, M$, $L \leqq N$, $M \leqq N$. The sum total of the (relative) frequency over all possible values of the indices l and m must be 1; that is,

$$\sum_{l=1}^{L} \sum_{m=1}^{M} f(x_l, y_m) = 1 \tag{4.2}$$

This is a prototype of the univariate condition (4.1).

When L and M are large, the usual practice is to have a grouped bivariate frequency distribution. This is done by dividing the entire range of values of x and y into a number of nonoverlapping cells and recording the relative frequencies of pairs of values of x and y for those cells. For instance, consider the hypothetical example for income–savings ratio distribution given in Table 4.3. For example, the proportion of people with income in the range \$5,000 to \$10,000 who have their savings ratio between 0.50 and 1.00 is 0.250. Note that at the margin of the rows and columns of this table we have shown what are referred to as the marginal frequencies. $f(x)$, for instance, is the marginal frequency of x. It gives for each value of $x = x_l$, say, the probability $f(x_l)$ of its occurrence, no matter what value of y it is associated with, and similarly $f(y)$. This definition implies the following results:

$$f(x_l) = \sum_{m=1}^{M} f(x_l, y_m) \qquad l = 1, 2, \ldots, L \tag{4.3}$$

[1] There is a fine distinction between relative frequency and probability, but for practical purposes that may be ignored.

TABLE 4.4 THE MARGINAL DISTRIBUTIONS OF x AND y

$f(x)$: Marginal Distribution of x		$f(y)$: Marginal Distribution of y	
x	$f(x)$	y	$f(y)$
$-\infty$–5,000	0.080	0–0.25	0.107
5,000–10,000	0.343	0.25–0.50	0.308
10,000–∞	0.577	0.50–1.00	0.585

$$f(y_m) = \sum_{l=1}^{L} f(x_l, y_m) \qquad m = 1, 2, \ldots, M \tag{4.4}$$

With reference to the bivariate table, we have derived the univariate marginal distributions $f(x)$ and $f(y)$ in Table 4.4. Accordingly, the marginal distributions satisfy the following properties of a univariate probability distribution:

$$f(x) \geqq 0 \qquad \Sigma_x f(x) = 1 \tag{4.5}$$

$$f(y) \geqq 0 \qquad \Sigma_y f(y) = 1 \tag{4.6}$$

Σ_x and Σ_y imply that the summation is over all possible values of x and y, respectively. In the bivariate table, these sums (=1.00) have been shown at the crossroads of the far right column and far bottom row.

A fairly important concept in the context of the bivariate distribution is that of conditional distribution. This is a univariate distribution of one of the two variables depending on given values of the other variable. In the notation of this section, the two conditional distributions may be generally represented by the symbols $f(x \mid y)$ and $f(y \mid x)$, the first being the conditional frequency of x for given values of y, and the second the conditional frequency of y for given values of x. A typical member of the $f(x \mid y)$ family may be $f(x_l \mid y_m)$. This is the relative frequency of $x = x_l$ in the class of cases with $y = y_m$. From the theorem on compound probability, a conditional probability is the ratio of a joint probability to a marginal probability. Thus, we have

$$\begin{aligned} f(x_l \mid y_m) &= \frac{f(x_l, y_m)}{f(y_m)} \qquad \text{provided } f(y_m) \neq 0 \\ f(y_m \mid x_l) &= \frac{f(x_l, y_m)}{f(x_l)} \qquad \text{provided } f(x_l) \neq 0 \end{aligned} \tag{4.7}$$

Or, generally,

$$\begin{aligned} f(x \mid y) &= \frac{f(x, y)}{f(y)} \qquad \text{for } f(y) \neq 0 \\ f(y \mid x) &= \frac{f(x, y)}{f(x)} \qquad \text{for } f(x) \neq 0 \end{aligned} \tag{4.8}$$

TABLE 4.5 CONDITIONAL PROBABILITY DISTRIBUTIONS

(a) $f(x|y)$: x for given y

	y		
x	0–0.25	0.25–0.50	0.50–1.00
$-\infty$–5,000	0.673	0.016	0.005
5,000–10,000	0.187	0.237	0.427
10,000–∞	0.140	0.747	0.568
$\sum_x f(x\|y)$	1.000	1.000	1.000

(b) $f(y|x)$: y for given x

	y			
x	0–0.25	0.25–0.50	0.50–1.00	$\sum_x f(y\|x)$
$-\infty$–5,000	0.900	0.062	0.038	1.000
5,000–10,000	0.058	0.213	0.729	1.000
10,000–∞	0.026	0.399	0.575	1.000

Each one of the conditional frequency functions satisfies the conditions of a probability function, namely

$$f(x \mid y) \geqq 0 \qquad \Sigma_x f(x \mid y) = 1 \tag{4.9}$$ [2]

$$f(y \mid x) \geqq 0 \qquad \Sigma_y f(y \mid x) = 1 \tag{4.10}$$ [3]

The calculations for $f(x \mid y)$ and $f(y \mid x)$ for the data in Table 4.3 are shown in Table 4.5.

To illustrate the calculations of these tables, we refer back to Table 4.3. For a value of y lying over its first range, 0–0.25, $f(x \mid y)$ is obtained by dividing $f(x, y)$ by $f(y)$ for that range of values of y. For instance, if $5{,}000 < x < 10{,}000$ and $0 < y < 0.25$, then $f(x \mid y)$ is 0.020 (which is $f(x, y)$ for those values of x and y) divided by 0.107 (which is $f(y)$ for that value of y). Similarly, if $5{,}000 < x < 10{,}000$ and $0 < y < 0.25$, then $f(y \mid x)$ is 0.020 (which is, once again, $f(x, y)$ for those values of x and y) divided by 0.343 (which is $f(x)$ for that value of x). In the same way, we can repeat this method of calculation by switching to different values of x for a fixed value of y, thus generating a column of Table 4.5(a), or

[2,3] We will show one result. The other will follow in a straightforward fashion.

$$\sum_x f(x \mid y) = \sum_{l=1}^{L} f(x_l \mid y) = \sum_{l=1}^{L} \frac{f(x_l, y)}{f(y)} = \frac{\sum_{l=1}^{L} f(x_l, y)}{f(y)}$$

$$= \frac{f(y)}{f(y)} = 1$$

Notice that y may be fixed at any level, say $y = y_m$, $m = 1, 2, \ldots, M$.

different values of y for a given value of x, thus generating a row. Finally, we can change y itself (Table 4.5(a)) or x itself (Table 4.5(b)) until all of their columns or rows are calculated.

Observe that $\Sigma_x f(x \mid y)$ is actually calculated to be 1 for each value of y, shown in the last line of Table 4.5(a). Similarly $\Sigma_y f(y \mid x)$ is calculated to be 1 for each value of x as shown in the last column of Table 4.5(b).

If the dependence of x on y is not relevant such that $f(x \mid y)$ will be equal to $f(x)$ we will have x statistically independent of y. In that case

$$f(x) = f(x \mid y) = \frac{f(x, y)}{f(y)} \tag{4.11}$$

from which it follows that

$$f(x, y) = f(x)f(y) \tag{4.12}$$

Due to the symmetry of $f(x, y)$ with regard to x and y, this must mean that the statistical independence of x on y implies the same for y on x. That is,

$$f(y \mid x) = \frac{f(x, y)}{f(x)}$$

$$f(y \mid x) = f(y) \tag{4.13}$$

$$f(x, y) = f(y)f(x) = f(x)f(y)$$

With reference to Table 4.3, a simple application of the above rules would indicate the lack of statistical independence between income and the savings ratio. For one example, the value of $f(x, y)$ is 0.072 for values of x and y in their first class. For the same class, $f(x)$ is 0.080 and $f(y)$ 0.107. The product of $f(x)$ and $f(y)$ is therefore 0.0086, which is not equal to 0.072, the value for $f(x, y)$. We find that the law of statistical independence fails here. One can repeat this test for other classes of values of x and y with generally the same conclusion. Thus, income and savings ratio are not statistically independent in this hypothetical example.

When we consider more than two variables, $x, y, \ldots, w$, we find that they are statistically independent if

$$f(x, y, \ldots, w) = f(x)\, f(y) \cdots f(w) \tag{4.14}$$

where $f(x, y, \ldots, w)$ is their joint frequency function and $f(x), f(y), \ldots, f(w)$ are their individual frequency functions.

4.3 SOME DESCRIPTIVE STATISTICS MEASURES OF FREQUENCY DISTRIBUTIONS

Measures of central tendency and dispersion of a frequency distribution are often used to discriminate between distributions. For the central tendency, we use the arithmetic average or mean, and for dispersion we use the variance. The latter measures the strength of variation of individual observations around their mean.

If a univariate frequency distribution is $f(x)$ for x, then its mean μ and variance σ^2 are defined as

$$\mu = \sum_{l=1}^{L} x_l f(x_l) = \sum_x x f(x) \tag{4.15}$$

$$\sigma^2 = \sum_{l=1}^{L} (x_l - \mu)^2 f(x_l) = \sum_x x^2 f(x) - \mu^2 \qquad (4.16)^4$$

To illustrate, go back to the example of Table 4.1 and assume that the representative incomes of the three classes are \$2,500, \$7,500 and \$12,500. Then

$$\mu = 2{,}500 \times 0.080 + 7{,}500 \times 0.343 + 12{,}500 \times 0.577 = 9{,}985$$

$$\begin{aligned}\sigma^2 &= 25^2 \times 104 \times 0.080 + 75^2 \times 10^4 \times 0.343 + 125^2 \\ &\quad \times 10^4 \times 0.577 - 9{,}985^2 \\ &= 10^4\,(500 + 1{,}929.375 + 9{,}015.625) - 99{,}700{,}225 \\ &= 10^6\,(114.45 - 99.70) = 10^6 \times 14.75\end{aligned}$$

With bivariate frequency functions, the definition of means and variances is straightforward with respect to the marginal and conditional distributions, since each is a univariate distribution. Starting from the joint frequency function $f(x, y)$, the means and variances of the marginal and conditional distributions are defined and calculated in Table 4.6 for the numerical example of Table 4.3. Notice that, as in the case of x shown before, we have assumed some representative values of y. These are 0.125, 0.375, and 0.750 for its three classes.

In the bivariate context, an important concept is that of covariance of the variables. When x and y are taken to be these variables, their covariance is defined as and simplified to

$$\begin{aligned}\text{cov}(x, y) &= \sum_{l=1}^{L} \sum_{m=1}^{M} (x_l - \mu_x)(y_m - \mu_y)\, f(x_l, y_m) \\ &= \sum_l \sum_m x_l y_m f(x_l, y_m) - \mu_x \mu_y\end{aligned} \tag{4.17}$$

[4]

$$\begin{aligned}\sum_1^L (x_l - \mu)^2 f(x_l) &= \sum_1^L x_l^2 f(x_l) - 2\mu \sum_1^L x_l f(x_l) + \mu^2 \sum_1^L f(x_l) \\ &= \sum_1^L x_l^2 f(x_l) - 2\mu \cdot \mu + \mu^2 \cdot 1 \\ &= \sum_1^L x_l^2 f(x_l) - \mu^2 = \sum_x x^2 f(x) - \mu^2\end{aligned}$$

Since $\sum_1^L x_l f(x_l) = \mu$ and $\sum_1^L f(x_l) = 1$.

TABLE 4.6 MEANS AND VARIANCES OF MARGINAL AND CONDITIONAL DISTRIBUTIONS

	Marginal x			Marginal y	
Means					
	$\mu_x = \sum_x x f(x)$			$\mu_y = \sum_y y f(y)$	
	$= 99.85 \times 10^2$			$= 0.568$	
Variance					
	$\sigma_x^2 = \sum (x - \mu_x)^2 f(x)$			$\sigma_y^2 = \sum (y - \mu_y)^2 f(y)$	
	$= 14.75 \times 10^6$			$= 0.051$	
	Conditional x/y			Conditional y/x	
	y			x	
0–0.25	0.25–0.50	0.50–1.00	$-\infty$–5,000	5,000–10,000	10,000–∞
Means					
$\mu_{x\|y_m} = \sum_x x f(x\|y_m);\ m = 1, \ldots, M$			$\mu_{y\|x_l} = \sum_y y f(y\|x_l);\ l = 1, \ldots, L$		
48.35×10^2	111.55×10^2	103.15×10^2	0.164	0.634	0.584
Variances					
$\sigma_{x\|y_m}^2 = \sum_x (x - \mu_{x\|y_m})^2 f(x\|y_m);\ m = 1, \ldots, M$			$\sigma_{y\|x_l}^2 = \sum_y (y - \mu_{y\|x_l})^2 f(y\|x_l);\ l = 1, \ldots, L$		
13.23×10^6	5.72×10^6	6.40×10^6	0.0869	0.0390	0.0389

where the simplification follows from the same logic as in the case of variance. Taking the same representative values of x and y in their three respective classes as before, and $f(x_l, y_m)$ as in Table 4.3, $\Sigma\Sigma x_l y_m f(x_l, y_m)$ works out to a value 58.772×10^2. From this, we subtract $\mu_x \mu_y$ ($=99.85 \times 10^2 \times 0.568$, from Table 4.6) which is 56.715×10^2. The result is 2.057×10^2. This then is the covariance between x and y in this numerical example.

Before we go to the next section, we would like to point out that mean, variance, covariance, and so on are special-order moments of a distribution. For instance, define μ_r' and μ_r to be the rth-order raw and corrected moments, respectively, of x with frequency function $f(x)$ and mean μ_x:

$$\mu_r' = \sum_{l=1}^{L} x^r f(x_l) \tag{4.18}$$

$$\mu_r = \sum_{l=1}^{L} (x - \mu_x)^r f(x_l) \tag{4.19}$$

μ_x is seen to be the first-order raw or uncorrected moment μ_1' (from 4.18)), σ_x^2 or variance to be the second-order corrected moment μ_2 (from (4.19)) of x, and μ_3 and μ_4 the third- and fourth-order (corrected) moments of x. More generally, for the joint frequency function $f(x, y)$, the (r, s)th-order corrected moment of the distribution of x and y is defined as

$$\mu_{r,s} = \sum_{l=1}^{L} \sum_{m=1}^{M} (x - \mu_x)^r (y - \mu_y)^s f(x_l, y_m) \tag{4.20}$$

Evidently the covariance cov(x, y) between x and y introduced before is $\mu_{1,1}$ or, in other words, the (1, 1)th order corrected moment of x and y.

While defining moments, we have been talking about a certain correction. The only correction we have considered so far has been with respect to the mean of a distribution. This is a standard procedure, but it need not be the only one. Correction can be made with respect to any other value, say the median, harmonic mean, or any specific value, say the value 10 of a variable. Given this change, the formula for the moment of a specific order should be corrected accordingly.

4.4 RANDOM VARIABLES AND PROBABILITY DISTRIBUTIONS

We begin by considering a discrete random variable x. Suppose that this variable assumes the values $x_1, \ldots, x_L$ with (nonnegative) relative frequencies or probabilities $p_1, \ldots, p_L$ such that

$$\sum_{l=1}^{L} p_l = 1 \tag{4.21}$$

An example of this may be the realization of heads and tails from the tossing of a coin. These give rise to the values 1 and 0, respectively, of what is known to be the *Bernoullian* or *binomial* random variable, an example of a finite random variable. A random variable may also have a countably infinite number of values. An example may be the national income of a country. The values of this variable may be all the positive integers, constituting a countably infinite set.

A random variable may also be continuous. This is when the values assumed by the random variable are from a continuum of points on the real line.

For a random variable X, the distribution function $F(x)$ is defined as

$$F(x) = \text{Probability } \{-\infty < X \leqq x\} \tag{4.22}$$

In other words, it is the total probability that X assumes any values less than or equal to x. For the Bernoulli distribution from a coin tossing we may write

$$\begin{aligned} F(x) &= 0 && \text{for } x < 0 \\ &= \tfrac{1}{2} && \text{for } 0 \leqq x < 1 \\ &= 1 && \text{for } x \leqq 1 \end{aligned} \tag{4.23}$$

Notice that $F(x)$ satisfies

$$0 \leqq F(x) \leqq 1 \qquad \text{for all } x \tag{4.24}$$

for it is a probability. The limiting values of $F(x)$ at $x \to -\infty$ or $x \to +\infty$ are 0 and 1, respectively. Also, $F(x)$ must satisfy the property of nondiminishing values for nondecreasing values of x:

$$F(x_1) \geqq F(x_2) \qquad \text{for } x_1 \geqq x_2 \tag{4.25}$$

Assuming $F(x)$ to be differentiable, since

$$\lim_{\Delta x \to 0} \frac{F(x + \Delta x) - F(x)}{\Delta x} = \frac{\mathrm{d}F(x)}{\mathrm{d}x} = f(x) \tag{4.26}$$

(4.25) must imply

$$f(x) \geqq 0 \qquad -\infty \leqq x \leqq \infty \tag{4.27}$$

$f(x)$ is said to be the probability density function corresponding to the distribution function $F(x)$. Clearly the probability element over the infinitesimal range of values of the variable x is $\mathrm{d}F(x)$, which is equal to the probability density function (pdf) $f(x)$ defined as

$$\mathrm{d}F(x) = f(x)\, dx = \text{Probability } \{x < X < x + dx\} \tag{4.28}$$

The probability that X occurs over the interval x_1 to x_2, $x_1 < x_2$, will then be

$$\begin{aligned}\int_{x_1}^{x_2} \mathrm{d}F(x) &= \int_{x_1}^{x_2} f(x)\, \mathrm{d}x = F(x_2) - F(x_1) \\ &= \text{Probability } (x_1 < X \leqq x_2)\end{aligned} \tag{4.29}$$

Thus, a definite integral of the pdf is the probability of the variable. Therefore,

$$\int_{-\infty}^{\infty} \mathrm{d}F(x) = \int_{-\infty}^{\infty} f(x)\, dx = 1 \tag{4.30}$$

In other words, it is with certainty that the variable x must assume a value over its entire range $-\infty$ to ∞.

Frequently we are confronted with the bivariate random vector:

$$\mathbf{X} = \begin{bmatrix} x_1 \\ x_2 \end{bmatrix} \tag{4.31}$$

Its pdf $f(x)$ is written as $f(x_1, x_2)$. This satisfies the two properties of the probability function:

$$\begin{aligned} &f(x_1, x_2) \geqq 0 \\ &\sum_{x_1} \sum_{x_2} f(x_1, x_2) = 1 \qquad \text{in the discrete case} \\ &\int_{-\infty}^{\infty} \int_{-\infty}^{\infty} f(x_1, x_2)\, dx_1\, dx_2 = 1 \qquad \text{in the continuous case} \end{aligned} \tag{4.32}$$

Given the joint pdf, the marginal pdf is obtained for each variable by summing, in the discrete case, or integrating in the continuous case, over the entire range of values of the other variable. Consequently, the marginal pdf for x_1 is

$$\begin{aligned} \sum_{x_2} f(x_1, x_2) &= f(x_1) \qquad \text{in the discrete case} \\ \int_{-\infty}^{\infty} f(x_1, x_2)\, dx_2 &= f(x_1) \qquad \text{in the continuous case} \end{aligned} \tag{4.33}$$

and that for x_2 is

$$\begin{aligned} \sum_{x_1} f(x_1, x_2) &= f(x_2) \qquad \text{in the discrete case} \\ \int_{-\infty}^{\infty} f(x_1, x_2)\, dx_1 &= f(x_2) \qquad \text{in the continuous case} \end{aligned} \tag{4.34}$$

It is very easy to show that

$$\begin{aligned} f(x_i) &\geqq 0 \qquad \text{i} = 1, 2 \\ \sum_{x_i} f(x_i) &= 1 \qquad i = 1, 2 \qquad \text{in the discrete case} \\ \int_{-\infty}^{\infty} f(x_i)\, dx_i &= 1 \qquad \text{i} = 1, 2 \qquad \text{in the continuous case} \end{aligned} \tag{4.35}$$

A conditional pdf for x_2 for given values of x_1 is

$$f(x_2 \mid x_1) = \frac{f(x_1, x_2)}{f(x_1)} \qquad f(x_1) \neq 0 \tag{4.36}$$

Similarly, a conditional pdf of x_1 given x_2 is

$$f(x_1 \mid x_2) = \frac{f(x_1, x_2)}{f(x_2)} \qquad f(x_2) \neq 0 \tag{4.37}$$

Again, since each conditional pdf is a univariate pdf, it should satisfy the two properties of a probability function such as (4.35) in both discrete and continuous cases.

The above procedure can be generalized to the multivariate case where the random vector

$$\mathbf{X} = \begin{bmatrix} x_1 \\ x_2 \\ \vdots \\ x_n \end{bmatrix} \tag{4.38}$$

contains n elements. Its joint pdf is written as $f(x_1, \ldots, x_n)$ from which the marginal pdf of any subset of $\mathbf{X}$, or, for that matter, the conditional pdf for one subset of variables for given values of the rest of the variables of $\mathbf{X}$ can be obtained.

For example, the marginal pdf for $x_1, \ldots, x_p$ is obtained by integrating $f(x_1, \ldots, x_n)$ over $x_{p+1}, \ldots, x_n$:

$$f(x_1, \ldots, x_p) = \int_{-\infty}^{\infty} \cdots \int_{-\infty}^{\infty} f(x_1, \ldots, x_n)\, dx_{p+1}, \ldots, dx_n \qquad (4.39)$$

The conditional pdf of $x_1, \ldots, x_p$ for given values of $x_{p+1}, \ldots, x_n$ is

$$f(x_1, \ldots, x_p \mid x_{p+1}, \ldots, x_n) = f(x_1, \ldots, x_n) \mid f(x_{p+1}, \ldots, x_n) \qquad (4.40)$$

provided that $f(x_{p+1}, \ldots, x_n) \neq 0$. If the distribution is discrete, then replace integrals, wherever they appear, by summations.[5]

4.4.1 Probability Distributions of Functions of Random Variables

Consider $\psi = \psi(\mathbf{X})$ to be a single-valued function of a random vector $\mathbf{X}$ whose pdf is $f(\mathbf{X})$. ψ will therefore be a random vector and its elements will be determined by the same experiment that determined $\mathbf{X}$. Consequently, there will be a one-to-one relationship in the assignment of probabilities to $\mathbf{X}$ and $\psi(\mathbf{X})$, because the events defined by the elements of one are also the ones defined by the elements of the other. It follows that under general conditions the probability $h(\psi^*)$ that ψ takes on the value ψ^* is derived by summing or integrating $f(\mathbf{X})$ over those $\mathbf{X}$s for which $\psi(\mathbf{X}) = \psi^*$ holds.

Example 1. Let

$$\begin{aligned} f(x) &= \tfrac{3}{4} \qquad \text{for } x = 0 \\ &= \tfrac{1}{4} \qquad \text{for } x = 1 \end{aligned}$$

and let

$$\psi = x^2$$

Then

$$\begin{aligned} h(\psi) = f(x) &= \tfrac{3}{4} \qquad \text{for } \psi = x = 0 \\ &= \tfrac{1}{4} \qquad \text{for } \psi = x = 1 \end{aligned}$$

Example 2. For a continuous random vector $\mathbf{X}$, $\psi = \psi(\mathbf{X})$ may be a discontinuous random vector. For instance, for a continuous random variable x with pdf $f(x)$, let

$$\begin{aligned} \psi &= 0 \qquad \text{for } x \leqq 10 \\ &= 1 \qquad \text{for } x > 10 \end{aligned}$$

[5] The two properties of probability functions, namely, nonnegative values of pdfs and the value 1 for integrations or summations of pdfs over the entire ranges of values of the variables should apply to these multivariate marginal and conditional pdfs as well.

Naturally ψ, which takes on the values 0 or 1, is a discrete random variable, and its probability is

$$\begin{aligned} h(\psi) &= \int_{-\infty}^{10} f(x)\, dx = F(10) \qquad \text{for } \psi = 0 \\ &= \int_{10}^{\infty} f(x)\, dx = 1 - F(10) \qquad \text{for } \psi = 1 \end{aligned} \tag{4.41}$$

where, as introduced before, $F(x)$ is the (cumulative) distribution function corresponding to the pdf $f(x)$.

Similarly examples can be constructed to show that if $\mathbf{X}$ is a continuous random vector, $\boldsymbol{\psi} = \boldsymbol{\psi}(\mathbf{X})$ becomes a continuous vector function.

4.5 THE EXPECTATION LOGIC

We defined the concept of moments of a variable before. That may not be difficult to calculate at all. But moments of a function of a random vector expressed in terms of moments of that random vector itself can be quite difficult. To handle the situation, we get help from a well-developed theory called the *expectation theory*. In what follows we will present this theory starting with the univariate case and building up to the multivariate situation, often emphasizing continuous situations.

Let x be a random variable with mass function or pdf $f(x)$ and let $\psi = \psi(x)$ be a single-valued function of x. Then the expectation of ψ denoted by $\mathrm{E}\psi$ or $\mathrm{E}(\psi)$ is the product sum of $\psi(x)$ and its associated probability, this probability being equal to $\mathrm{f}(x)$[6] for all values of x in the discrete case. In the continuous case, $\mathrm{E}\psi$ is equal to the integral of $\psi(x)\mathrm{f}(x)\, dx$ over the entire range of values of x, that is, $-\infty$ to $+\infty$. In symbols, these are

$$\begin{aligned} \mathrm{E}\psi &= \sum_x \psi(x) f(x) \qquad \text{in the discrete case} \\ \mathrm{E}\psi &= \int_{-\infty}^{\infty} \psi(x) f(x)\, dx \qquad \text{in the continuous case} \end{aligned} \tag{4.42}$$

It should be clear from the above that by taking $\psi(x) = x$, $\mathrm{E}(\psi)$ is $\mathrm{E}(x)$, which is the mean of x, μ_x; and by taking $\psi(x) = (x - \mu_x)^2$, $\mathrm{E}(\psi)$ is $\mathrm{E}(x - \mu_x)^2$ or the variance of x, σ_x^2. Similarly, by taking $\psi = x^r$, $\mathrm{E}(\psi)$ becomes the rth raw moment of x, and by equating ψ to $(x - \mu_x)^r$, $\mathrm{E}(\psi)$ becomes the rth corrected moment of x.

To generalize to the multivariate case, let us take

$$\mathbf{X} = \begin{bmatrix} x_1 \\ \vdots \\ x_n \end{bmatrix}$$

[6] We established in Section 4.4.1 that the probability of a function of a random variable is the same as the probability of that random variable itself.

to be a random vector with mass or density function $f(\mathbf{X})$. Let $\psi = \psi(\mathbf{X})$ be scalar and a single valued function of $\mathbf{X}$. Then

$$\begin{aligned} E(\psi) &= \sum_x \psi(\mathbf{X}) f(\mathbf{X}) && \text{in the discrete case} \\ &= \int_x \psi(\mathbf{X}) f(\mathbf{X})\, d\mathbf{X} && \text{in the continuous case} \end{aligned} \tag{4.43}$$

To illustrate the principle, take a two-element vector

$$\mathbf{X} = \begin{bmatrix} x_1 \\ x_2 \end{bmatrix}$$

Then, for

$$\psi = (x_1 - \mu_{x1})(x_2 - \mu_{x2}) \tag{4.44}$$

we find

$$\begin{aligned} E(\psi) &= E(x_1 - \mu_{x1})(x_2 - \mu_{x2}) \\ &= \sum_{x1}\sum_{x2} (x_1 - \mu_{x1})(x_2 - \mu_{x2}) \\ &= \sigma_{12} \end{aligned} \tag{4.45}$$

which is the covariance of x_1 and x_2 in the discrete case. In the continuous case, replace the summation with an integral.

Notice two minor results involving a random vector or matrix. First, if

$$\mathbf{X} = \begin{bmatrix} x_1 \\ \vdots \\ x_n \end{bmatrix}$$

then

$$E(\mathbf{X}) = \begin{bmatrix} E(x_1) \\ \vdots \\ E(x_n) \end{bmatrix} = \begin{bmatrix} \mu_{x1} \\ \vdots \\ \mu_{xn} \end{bmatrix} = \boldsymbol{\mu} \tag{4.46}$$

Second, if

$$\mathbf{X} = \begin{bmatrix} X_{11} & \cdots & X_{1n} \\ \vdots & & \vdots \\ X_{l1} & \cdots & X_{ln} \end{bmatrix}$$

then

$$E(\mathbf{X}) = \begin{bmatrix} Ex_{11} & \cdots\cdots & Ex_{1n} \\ \vdots & & \vdots \\ Ex_{l1} & \cdots\cdots & Ex_{ln} \end{bmatrix} \tag{4.47}$$

Result 1. If $\mathbf{X}$ is a random vector of n elements and $\boldsymbol{\mu}$ its expected value, then the variance–covariance matrix of $\mathbf{X}$ is given by

$$\sum = \mathrm{E}\,(\mathbf{X} - \boldsymbol{\mu})(\mathbf{X} - \boldsymbol{\mu})' \qquad (4.48)$$

Proof.

$$\sum = \mathrm{E}(\mathbf{X} - \boldsymbol{\mu})(\mathbf{X} - \boldsymbol{\mu})'$$

$$= \mathrm{E}\begin{bmatrix}(x_1 - \mu_{x1}) \\ \vdots \\ (x_n - \mu_{xn})\end{bmatrix}[(x_1 - \mu_{x1}) \cdots (x_n - \mu_{xn})]$$

$$= \begin{bmatrix}\mathrm{E}(x_1 - \mu_{x1})^2 & \mathrm{E}(x_1 - \mu_{x1})(x_2 - \mu_{x2}) \cdots \mathrm{E}(x_1 - \mu_{x1})(x_n - \mu_{xn}) \\ \vdots & \\ \mathrm{E}(x_n - \mu_{xn})\,(x_1 - \mu_{x1}) & \mathrm{E}(x_n - \mu_{xn})(x_2 - \mu_{x2}) \cdots \mathrm{E}(x_n - \mu_{xn})^2\end{bmatrix}$$

$$= \begin{bmatrix}\sigma_{11} & \sigma_{12} \cdots \sigma_{1n} \\ \vdots & \vdots \\ \sigma_{n1} & \sigma_{n2} \cdots \sigma_{nn}\end{bmatrix}$$

QED

Note that for a constant c, its probability is 1 and therefore E(c) = c. This implies that E(cx) = cE(x) where x is the random variable. Also, if there are two random variables x and y,

$$\mathrm{E}(x + y) = \mathrm{E}x + \mathrm{E}y \qquad (4.49)$$

This is because

$$\mathrm{E}(x + y) = \int_{-\infty}^{\infty}\int_{-\infty}^{\infty}(x + y)\,f(x, y)\,dx\,dy$$

$$= \int_{-\infty}^{\infty} x\left[\int_{-\infty}^{\infty} f(x, y)\,dy\right]dx + \int_{-\infty}^{\infty} y\left[\int_{-\infty}^{\infty} f(x, y)\,dx\right]dy$$

$$= \int_{-\infty}^{\infty} x\,f(x)\,dx + \int_{-\infty}^{\infty} y\,f(y)\,dy$$

$$= \mathrm{E}x + \mathrm{E}y$$

QED

In the discrete case, replace integrals by summations. It follows that taking c_1 and c_2 to be constants $\mathrm{E}(c_1\,x + c_2\,y) = c_1\,\mathrm{E}(x) + c_2\,\mathrm{E}(y)$, and therefore we have the following general result.

Result 2. For $x_1, x_2, \ldots, x_n$, which are random variables, and $c_0, c_1, \ldots, c_n$, which are constants,

$$\mathrm{E}(c_0 + c_1x_1 + \cdots + c_nx_n) = c_0 + c_1\,\mathrm{E}(x_1) + \cdots + c_n\,\mathrm{E}(x_n) \qquad (4.50)$$

It is easy to see that the variance is a form of expectations, since

$$\begin{aligned} V(x) &= E(x - Ex)^2 \\ &= Ex^2 - (Ex)^2 \end{aligned} \tag{4.51}$$[7]

Similarly, the covariance of x and y can be expressed in terms of expectations

$$\operatorname{cov}(x, y) = E(x - Ex)(y - Ey) = E(xy) - ExEy \tag{4.52}$$

Since when x and y are independent, their covariance must be zero, we have, using (4.52),

$$E(xy) = ExEy \tag{4.53}$$

That is, the expectation of the product of x and y is the product of their expectations when x and y are independent.

For a constant c, V(c) = 0. This, together with a random variable x, leads to

$$\begin{aligned} V(cx) &= E(cx - cEx)^2 \\ &= c^2\, E(x - Ex)^2 \\ &= c^2\, V(x) \end{aligned} \tag{4.54}$$

Another interesting result is

$$V(x \pm y) = V(x) \pm 2 \operatorname{cov}(x, y) + V(y) \tag{4.55}$$

Generalizing and assuming $c_0, c_1, \ldots, c_n$ to be constants and $x_1, \ldots, x_n$ to be random variables, we obtain the following result.

Result 3.

$$V(c_0 + c_1x_1 + \cdots + c_nx_n) = \sum_{i=1}^{n} c_i^2\, V(x_i) + \sum_{\substack{i=1 \\ i \neq j}}^{n} \sum_{j=1}^{n} c_ic_j \operatorname{cov}(x_i, x_j) \tag{4.56}$$

Note that if $x_1, \ldots, x_n$ are independent, their covariances $\operatorname{cov}(x_i, x_j)$, $i \neq j = 1, \ldots, n$ must vanish. Then

$$V(c_0 + c_1x_1 + \cdots + c_nx_n) = \sum_{i=1}^{n} c_i^2\, V(x_i) \tag{4.57}$$

[7] This is because

$$\begin{aligned} E(x - Ex)^2 &= E[x^2 - 2xEx + (Ex)^2] = Ex^2 - 2ExEx + (Ex)^2 \\ &= Ex^2 - 2(Ex)^2 + (Ex)^2 = Ex^2 - (Ex)^2 \end{aligned}$$

Notice that $E(Ex)^2 = (Ex)^2$ has been used in view of $(Ex)^2$ being a constant, and the expectation of a constant is the constant itself.

Similar other generalizations are possible. For instance, for a constant matrix C, $E(C) = C$. If, in addition, X is a random matrix, then $E(CX) = C\,E(X)$. Further, if Y is a random matrix, and X and Y are independent, then $E(XY) = E(X)\,E(Y)$. The next result follows as a simple deduction.

Result 4. If $\mathbf{X}$ is a random vector with $E(\mathbf{X}) = \boldsymbol{\mu}$, and $E(\mathbf{X} - \boldsymbol{\mu})(\mathbf{X} - \boldsymbol{\mu})' = \boldsymbol{\Sigma}$ and $Y = C\mathbf{X}$ where C is a constant matrix, then

$$E(Y) = C\boldsymbol{\mu} \tag{4.58}$$

$$V(Y) = E(Y - EY)(Y - EY)' = C\boldsymbol{\Sigma}C' \tag{4.59}$$

Result 5. Another important result is concerned with the property of semipositive definiteness of the variance–covariance matrix, say $\boldsymbol{\Sigma}$, of a random vector, say $\mathbf{X}$. However, if the elements of $\mathbf{X}$ are strictly linearly independent, then $\boldsymbol{\Sigma}$ will be positive definite.

Proof. Since $\boldsymbol{\Sigma}$ is a variance–covariance matrix and $\sigma_{ij} = \sigma_{ji}$, $i \neq j = 1, \ldots, n$, it is symmetric. Let us now examine whether it is semipositive definite. Devise a constant vector $\mathbf{C}$ of size $n \times 1$. Then

$$\begin{aligned}\mathbf{C}'\boldsymbol{\Sigma}\mathbf{C} &= \mathbf{C}'\,E[(\mathbf{X} - \boldsymbol{\mu})(\mathbf{X} - \boldsymbol{\mu})']\mathbf{C} \\ &= E[\mathbf{C}'(\mathbf{X} - \boldsymbol{\mu})(\mathbf{X} - \boldsymbol{\mu})'\mathbf{C}] \\ &= E\{\mathbf{C}'(\mathbf{X} - \boldsymbol{\mu})[\mathbf{C}'(\mathbf{X} - \boldsymbol{\mu})]'\} \\ &= E[\mathbf{C}'(\mathbf{X} - \boldsymbol{\mu})]^2 \\ &\geqq 0\end{aligned}$$

since $\mathbf{C}'(\mathbf{X} - \boldsymbol{\mu})$ is a scalar, and $E[\mathbf{C}'(\mathbf{X} - \boldsymbol{\mu})]^2$ is the variance of $\mathbf{C}'(\mathbf{X} - \boldsymbol{\mu})$ and thus nonnegative. This establishes $\boldsymbol{\Sigma}$ as a semipositive definite matrix. However, if $\mathbf{C}'(\mathbf{X} - \boldsymbol{\mu}) \neq 0$ unless all elements of $\mathbf{C}$ are identically zero, $\mathbf{C}'\boldsymbol{\Sigma}\mathbf{C}$ will be greater than zero. In this case, $\boldsymbol{\Sigma}$ will be positive definite. In some instances, as we shall see later, we shall assume that the variance–covariance matrix of a random vector is positive definite. This assumption will be especially necessary if $\boldsymbol{\Sigma}$ is required to be inverted and, as is well known, one can only invert a positive definite (which is a nonsingular) matrix.

Without further elaboration let us note that the expectation calculus can be applied analogously to conditional mass or pdfs. As an example, take a bivariate pdf $f(x, y)$. Then

$$Ex = EE(x \mid y) \tag{4.60}$$

where $E(x \mid y)$, to be calculated first, is the conditional expectation of x for fixed values of y, and the second expectation operator to its left is to be activated next to allow for variations in y.

4.6 SAMPLING METHODS, LIKELIHOOD FUNCTIONS, AND SAMPLING DISTRIBUTIONS

We would often be involved in random sampling from a population identified by a variable, say x, with its associated mass or probability density function $f(x)$. One way of doing this is to take an observation from this population, record its outcome, and then repeat the experiment $(n - 1)$ times, each time independently of the others, until n outcomes denoted as $x_1, \ldots, x_n$ for a sample of size n are obtained. Alternatively, these n observations can be viewed as one observation on a vector of n variables $x_1, \ldots, x_n$ with their probability mass or density function given by $f(x_1, \ldots, x_n)$. This joint pdf will, by the argument of independent drawings, be the product of probability masses or densities of individual observations such as

$$f(x_1, \ldots, x_n) = f(x_1) \cdots f(x_n) = \prod_{l=1}^{n} f(x_l)$$

The above is called a likelihood function $L(x_1, x_2, \ldots, x_n)$.

Example 1. Consider a random sample of size 5 drawn from a Bernoulli population B(1/4) where the probability of a success ($x = 1$) is 1/4 and that of a failure ($x = 0$) is 3/4. Then the likelihood of the random sample (1, 0, 0, 1, 1) is the variance–covariance of any two such observations:

$$L(1, 0, 0, 1, 1) = 1/4 \times 3/4 \times 3/4 \times 1/4 \times 1/4 = 9/1024$$

It is possible that a probability mass or pdf may contain a set of identifying parameters $\theta_1, \ldots, \theta_p$. Then the pdf is written as $f(x \mid \theta_1, \ldots, \theta_p)$. The relation between the likelihood function and the pdfs takes the form

$$\begin{aligned} L(x_1, &\ldots, x_n \mid \theta_1, \ldots, \theta_p) \\ &= f(x_1, \ldots, x_n \mid \theta_1, \ldots, \theta_p) \\ &= f(x_1 \mid \theta_1, \ldots, \theta_p) \cdots f(x_n \mid \theta_1, \ldots, \theta_p) \\ &= \prod_{l=1}^{p} f(x_l \mid \theta_1, \ldots, \theta_p) \end{aligned} \tag{4.61}$$

Example 2. Assume that the random variable x follows the normal distribution: $N(\mu, \sigma^2)$, where N stands for normality, and μ and σ^2 are the mean and variance of the distribution:

$$f(x \mid \mu, \sigma^2) = 1/(\sqrt{2\pi}\sigma) \exp\left[-\frac{1}{2}\frac{(x - \mu)^2}{\sigma^2}\right] \qquad -\infty \leqq x \leqq \infty \tag{4.62}$$

Then the likelihood function of a random sample $(-1, 0, 1)$ is

$$L(-1, 0, 1) = f(-1 \mid \mu, \sigma^2)\, f(0 \mid \mu, \sigma^2)\, f(1 \mid \mu, \sigma^2)$$

$$= \left(\frac{1}{\sqrt{2\pi}\sigma}\right)^3 \exp\left[-\frac{1}{2}\left(\frac{1+\mu}{\sigma}\right)^2\right]$$

$$\times \exp\left[-\frac{1}{2}\left(\frac{\mu}{\sigma}\right)^2\right] \exp\left[-\frac{1}{2}\left(\frac{1-\mu}{\sigma}\right)^2\right]$$

$$= \left(\frac{1}{\sqrt{2\pi}\sigma}\right)^3 \exp\left[-\frac{1}{2\sigma^2}(3\mu^2 + 2)\right]$$

Example 3. The likelihood function for a random sample of n observations drawn from $B(\mu)$ where k observations are successes ($x = 1$) and $n - k$ observations are failures ($x = 0$) is given by

$$L(1, 1, \ldots, 1; 0, \ldots 0 \mid \mu) = \mu^k(1 - \mu)^{n-k} \tag{4.63}$$

Notice that we have assumed a particular order in which successes and failures occurred. If the order was unspecified, then

$$L(1, \ldots, 1; 0, \ldots, 0 \mid \mu) = C_k^n \mu^k(1 - \mu)^{n-k} \tag{4.64}$$

where C_k^n stands for the combination of n things taken k at a time.

4.6.1 Some Important Measures of Sampling Distributions

For a random sample of size n: $x_1, \ldots, x_n$, drawn from any population represented by the random variable x with mean μ_x and variance σ_x^2, we have the following basic results about the population mean of a sample observation and the variance–covariance of any two such observations:

$$E(x_l) = \mu_x \qquad \text{for all } l = 1, \ldots, n \tag{4.65}$$

$$\begin{aligned} E(x_l - \mu_x)(x_{l'} - \mu_x) &= \sigma_x^2 \qquad \text{for } l = l' = 1, \ldots, n \\ &= 0 \qquad \text{for } l \neq l' = 1, \ldots, n \end{aligned} \tag{4.66}$$

The above results follow because every x_l has the mean μ_x and variance σ_x^2, and due to the independence of observations in random sampling, the covariance of any two observations should be zero.

4.6.2 Some Properties of the Sample Mean

For a random sample of size n with observations $x_1, \ldots, x_n$, the sample mean $\bar{x}$ is

$$\bar{x} = \frac{1}{n}\sum_{l=1}^{n} x_l$$

Then

$$E\bar{x} = \frac{1}{n}\sum_{1}^{n} E(x_l) = \frac{1}{n} n\mu_x = \mu_x \tag{4.67}$$

and

$$\begin{aligned}
V(\bar{x}) &= E(\bar{x} - \mu_x)^2 \\
&= E\left\{\frac{1}{n^2}\left[\sum_{l=1}^{n} (x_l - \mu_x)\right]^2\right\} \\
&= \frac{1}{n^2}\left[\sum_{l=1}^{n} E(x_l - \mu_x)^2 + \sum_{\substack{l=1 \\ l \neq l'}}^{n}\sum_{l'=1}^{n} E(x_l - \mu_x)(x_{l'} - \mu_x)\right] \\
&= \frac{1}{n^2}\left(\sum_{l=1}^{n} \sigma_x^2 + 0\right) \\
&= \frac{1}{n^2} n\sigma_x^2 \\
&= \frac{\sigma_x^2}{n}
\end{aligned} \tag{4.68}$$

Combining these results, we observe that the sample mean of observations drawn randomly from any population with mean μ_x and variance σ_x^2 is distributed with the same mean μ_x but variance σ_x^2/n.

4.6.3 Some Properties of the Sample Variance

Suppose the sample variance is

$$S^2 = \frac{1}{n}\sum_{1}^{n} (x_l - \bar{x})^2 \tag{4.69}$$

$\Sigma(x_l - \bar{x})^2$ can be simplified as

$$\begin{aligned}
\sum_{1}^{n} (x_l - \bar{x})^2 &= \sum_{1}^{n} [x_l - \mu_x - (\bar{x} - \mu_x)]^2 \\
&= \sum (x_l - \mu_x)^2 + \sum_{1}^{n} (\bar{x} - \mu_x)^2 - 2(\bar{x} - \mu_x)\sum_{1}^{n} (x_l - \mu_x) \\
&= \sum (x_l - \mu_x)^2 + n(\bar{x} - \mu_x)^2 - 2n(\bar{x} - \mu_x)^2 \\
&= \sum (x_l - \mu_x)^2 - n(\bar{x} - \mu_x)^2
\end{aligned}$$

Thus,

$$S^2 = \frac{1}{n}\sum_{1}^{n}(x_l - \mu_x)^2 - (\bar{x} - \mu_x)^2 \tag{4.70}$$

from which we have, using (4.66) for $l = l'$, and (4.68),

$$\begin{aligned} E(S^2) &= \frac{1}{n}\sum_{1}^{n}\sigma_x^2 - \frac{\sigma_x^2}{n} \\ &= \left(1 - \frac{1}{n}\right)\sigma_x^2 \end{aligned} \tag{4.71}$$

Similarly, we can find, after tedious but straightforward algebraic manipulations, the variance of S^2 as

$$\begin{aligned} V(S^2) &= E(S^2 - ES^2)^2 \\ &= 1/n(\mu_4 - \sigma_x^4) - 2\left[\frac{1}{n^2(\mu_4 - 2\sigma_x^4)}\right] + \frac{1}{n^3(\mu_4 - 3\sigma_x^4)} \end{aligned} \tag{4.72}$$

where μ_4 is the fourth (corrected) moment of x. Notice that if x follows a normal distribution $\mu_4 = 3\sigma_x^4$, in which case $V(S^2)$ reduces to

$$V(S^2) = 2\left(1 - \frac{1}{n}\right)\frac{\sigma_x^4}{n} \tag{4.73}$$

4.7 NORMAL, χ^2, F, AND t DISTRIBUTIONS

4.7.1 Univariate Normal

As introduced in (4.62), for a random variable x to be distributed normally its pdf is

$$f(x) = \frac{1}{(2\pi)^{1/2}\sigma}\exp\left[-\frac{(x - \mu_x)^2}{2\sigma_x^2}\right]$$

with its two parameters μ_x and $V(x)$

$$E(x) = \mu_x$$

$$V(x) = \sigma_x^2$$

This is designated by the identifying symbol $N(\mu_x, \sigma_x^2)$, where N stands for normality, and μ_x and σ_x^2 are the mean and variance of the distribution. This is a continuous distribution extending over the range $(-\infty, \infty)$ and is symmetric. This is why all odd-order moments of this distribution vanish; that is,

$$\mu_r = 0 \qquad \text{for } r = 1, 3, 5, \ldots \tag{4.74}$$

When instead the order is even, we make use of a standard result in statistics to compute an even-order moment:

$$\mu_{2r} = \frac{(2r)!}{2(r!)^2}\,\mu_2^r \qquad \text{for } r = 1, 2, 3, \ldots \tag{4.75}$$

In particular for $r = 2$, we have

$$\begin{aligned} \mu_4 &= \frac{4!}{2(2!)^2}\,\mu_2^2 \\ &= 3\mu_2^2 \\ &= 3\sigma_x^4 \end{aligned} \tag{4.76}$$

a result that was used in the preceding subsection. Note that we have used $\mu_2 = \sigma_x^2$ in (4.76). Another result, which we shall use without proof, is very important. It is about a linear function of a normal variable, which is a normal variable. Specifically, if x is $N(\mu_x, \sigma_x^2)$ and if

$$Y = C(x - x_0) \tag{4.77}$$

where $C \neq 0$ and x_0 are constants, then

$$Y \sim N(C(\mu_x - x_0), C^2\,\sigma_x^2) \tag{4.78}$$

We can readily establish the mean and variance of Y. For the mean, observe that

$$\begin{aligned} E(y) &= CE(x - x_0) \\ &= C(\mu_x - x_0) \end{aligned} \tag{4.79}$$

and, for the variance,

$$\begin{aligned} V(y) &= E(y - Ey)^2 \\ &= E[C(x - x_0 - \mu_x - x_0)]^2 \\ &= C^2\,E(x - \mu_x)^2 \\ &= C^2\sigma_x^2 \end{aligned} \tag{4.80}$$

Indeed, these expressions appear in (4.78).

Taking $C = 1/\sigma_x$ and $x_0 = \mu_x$, we have, using (4.79) and (4.80), y reduced to a variable $Z = (x - \mu_x)/\sigma_x$ whose distribution is

$$Z \sim N(0, 1) \tag{4.81}$$

This is said to be a standard normal variable. It is a normal variable for which the mean is zero and the variance is unity.

Thus, it follows that

$$\int_{x_1}^{x_2} f(x)\, dx = \int_{z_1}^{z_2} f(z)\, dz \qquad (4.82)$$

where z_i is $(x_i - \mu_x)/\sigma_x$ and the second integral measures the area under the standard normal curve between the specified points z_1 and z_2. This area is tabulated in Appendix B, Table B.1.

4.7.2 Multivariate Normal

Consider an n-element random column vector

$$\mathbf{X} = \begin{bmatrix} x_1 \\ \vdots \\ x_n \end{bmatrix}$$

to be distributed multivariate normally. Its pdf is given by

$$f(\mathbf{X}) = \frac{1}{(\sqrt{2\pi})^n} \left(\frac{1}{2} \frac{1}{|\boldsymbol{\Sigma}|^{\frac{1}{2}}} \right) \exp \left[-\frac{1}{2} (\mathbf{X} - \boldsymbol{\mu})' \boldsymbol{\Sigma}^{-1} (\mathbf{X} - \boldsymbol{\mu}) \right] \qquad (4.83)$$

Here, the mean vector is

$$\boldsymbol{\mu} = \begin{bmatrix} \mu_1 \\ \vdots \\ \mu_n \end{bmatrix} = \begin{bmatrix} \mathrm{E}(x_1) \\ \vdots \\ \mathrm{E}(x_n) \end{bmatrix} \qquad (4.84)$$

and the variance–covariance matrix of $\mathbf{X}$ is

$$\boldsymbol{\Sigma} = \begin{bmatrix} \sigma_{11} & \cdots & \sigma_{1n} \\ \vdots & & \vdots \\ \sigma_{n1} & \cdots & \sigma_{nn} \end{bmatrix} = \begin{bmatrix} \mathrm{E}(x_1 - \mu_1)^2 & \cdots & \mathrm{E}(x_1 - \mu_1)(x_n - \mu_n) \\ \vdots & & \vdots \\ \mathrm{E}(x_1 - \mu_1)(\mathrm{x}_n - \mu_n) & \cdots & \mathrm{E}(\mathrm{x}_n - \mu_n)^2 \end{bmatrix} \qquad (4.85)$$

and $|\boldsymbol{\Sigma}|$ is the determinant of $\boldsymbol{\Sigma}$. $\boldsymbol{\mu}$ and $\boldsymbol{\Sigma}$ then are the parameters of the multivariate normal distribution. The shorthand notation for this distribution is

$$\mathbf{X} \sim \mathrm{N}(\boldsymbol{\mu}, \boldsymbol{\Sigma}) \qquad (4.86)$$

Two simpler forms of this distribution become effective when $\boldsymbol{\mu} = \mathbf{0}$ and $\boldsymbol{\Sigma} = \sigma^2\boldsymbol{I}$, and when $\boldsymbol{\mu} = \mathbf{0}$ and $\boldsymbol{\Sigma} = \boldsymbol{I}$. In the first case we have $\mathbf{X} \sim \mathrm{N}(\mathbf{0}, \sigma^2\boldsymbol{I})$ where $\mathbf{X}$ is said to be spherically normally distributed, or which is the same thing as saying that $\mathbf{X}$ is a spherical normal vector. In the second case, we have $\mathbf{X} \sim \mathrm{N}(\mathbf{0}, \boldsymbol{I})$ where $\mathbf{X}$ is a standard normal vector. The special forms of $f(\mathbf{X})$ in the two cases are

$$f(\mathbf{X}) = \frac{1}{(\sqrt{2\pi}\,\sigma)^n} \exp\left(-\frac{1}{2\sigma^2} \mathbf{X}'\mathbf{X} \right) \qquad (4.87)$$

and

$$f(\mathbf{X}) = \frac{1}{(\sqrt{2\pi})^n} \exp\left(-\frac{1}{2}\mathbf{X}'\mathbf{X}\right) \tag{4.88}$$

Let us now consider the multivariate equivalent of a fairly important univariate result. This is about the linear combination of a multivariate normal vector, which, like its univariate counterpart, will be distributed normally. In particular, suppose the $n \times 1$ vector $\mathbf{X}$ is $\mathrm{N}(\boldsymbol{\mu}, \boldsymbol{\Sigma})$ and if

$$\mathbf{Y} = C(\mathbf{X} - \mathbf{X_0}) \tag{4.89}$$

where C is a $K \times n$ matrix of rank K and $\mathbf{X_0}$ is an $n \times 1$ vector and C and $\mathbf{X_0}$ are constant, then

$$\mathbf{Y} \sim \mathrm{N}(C(\boldsymbol{\mu} - \mathbf{X_0}), C\boldsymbol{\Sigma}C') \tag{4.90}$$

We skip the proof that establishes the normality of the distribution. However, the forms of the parameters of this distribution follow very simply. For,

$$\begin{aligned} \mathrm{E}\,\mathbf{Y} &= C\,\mathrm{E}(\mathbf{X} - \mathbf{X_0}) \\ &= C(\boldsymbol{\mu} - \mathbf{X_0}) \end{aligned} \tag{4.91}$$

and

$$\begin{aligned} \mathrm{V}\,\mathbf{Y} &= \mathrm{E}(\mathbf{Y} - \mathrm{E}\mathbf{Y})(\mathbf{Y} - \mathrm{E}\mathbf{Y})' \\ &= C\,\mathrm{E}(\mathbf{X} - \mathrm{E}\mathbf{X})(\mathbf{X} - \mathrm{E}\mathbf{X})'\,C' \\ &= C\,\boldsymbol{\Sigma}\,C' \end{aligned} \tag{4.92}$$

As a corollary to (4.90), we can deduce that by choosing $\mathbf{X_0}$ equal to $\boldsymbol{\mu}$ and C such that $C'C = \boldsymbol{\Sigma}^{-1}$, $\mathbf{Y}$ reduces to $\mathbf{Z}$ where

$$\mathbf{Z} \sim \mathrm{N}(\mathbf{0}, I) \tag{4.93}$$

The fact that $\mathrm{E}(\mathbf{Z}) = \mathbf{0}$ is no mystery. However,

$$\mathrm{V}(\mathbf{Z}) = C(C'C)^{-1}C' = CC^{-1}(C')^{-1}C' = I \tag{4.94}$$

since $C'C = \boldsymbol{\Sigma}^{-1}$. This is the multivariate equivalent of the standard normal distribution.

4.7.3 The Special Case of the Bivariate Normal

In the special case of $n = 2$, the multivariate normal reduces to a bivariate normal. Its pdf has the following form:

$$\begin{aligned} f(x_1, x_2) = [(\sqrt{2\pi})^2\sigma_1\sigma_2\sqrt{1-\rho^2}]^{-1} \exp\left\{-\frac{1}{2(1-\rho)^2}\left[\left(\frac{x_1-\mu_1}{\sigma_1}\right)^2\right.\right. \\ \left.\left. - 2\rho\left(\frac{x_1-\mu_1}{\sigma_1}\right)\left(\frac{x_2-\mu_2}{\sigma_2}\right) + \left(\frac{x_2-\mu_2}{\sigma_2}\right)^2\right]\right\} \end{aligned} \tag{4.95}$$

This is because

$$|\boldsymbol{\Sigma}|^{-1/2} = \begin{vmatrix} \sigma_1^2 & \rho\sigma_1\sigma_2 \\ \rho\sigma_1\sigma_2 & \sigma_2^2 \end{vmatrix}^{-1/2} = \sqrt{\sigma_1^2\sigma_2^2(1-\rho^2)} = \sigma_1\sigma_2\sqrt{1-\rho^2} \tag{4.96}$$

where $\text{cov}(x_1, x_2) = \rho\sigma_1\sigma_2$ and $V(x_i) = \sigma_i^2$, $i = 1, 2$, ρ being the correlation coefficient between x_1 and x_2, and

$$\boldsymbol{\Sigma}^{-1} = \frac{1}{\sigma_1^2\sigma_2^2(1-\rho^2)} \begin{bmatrix} \sigma_2^2 & -\rho\sigma_1\sigma_2 \\ -\rho\sigma_1\sigma_2 & \sigma_1^2 \end{bmatrix} \tag{4.97}$$

and $(\mathbf{X} - \boldsymbol{\mu})' \boldsymbol{\Sigma}^{-1} (\mathbf{X} - \boldsymbol{\mu})$ reduces to the power of the exponent as shown in (4.95).

4.7.4 The Marginal and Conditional Distributions

Let

$$\mathbf{X} = \begin{bmatrix} \mathbf{X}_1 \\ \cdots \\ \mathbf{X}_2 \end{bmatrix} \sim N(\boldsymbol{\mu}, \boldsymbol{\Sigma}) \tag{4.98}$$

where $\mathbf{X}$ is partitioned as

$$\mathbf{X_1} = \begin{bmatrix} x_1 \\ x_2 \\ \vdots \\ x_p \end{bmatrix} \qquad \mathbf{X_2} = \begin{bmatrix} x_{p+1} \\ \vdots \\ \vdots \\ x_{p+q} \end{bmatrix} \tag{4.99}$$

where $p + q = n$, and $\boldsymbol{\mu}$ and $\boldsymbol{\Sigma}$ are similarly partitioned into

$$\begin{bmatrix} \boldsymbol{\mu}_1 \\ \cdots \\ \boldsymbol{\mu}_2 \end{bmatrix} \quad \text{and} \quad \begin{bmatrix} \Sigma_{11} & \vdots & \Sigma_{12} \\ \cdots\cdots & \vdots & \cdots\cdots \\ \Sigma_{21} & \vdots & \Sigma_{22} \end{bmatrix} \tag{4.100}$$

It can be shown that

$$\mathbf{X_1} \sim N(\boldsymbol{\mu}_1, \boldsymbol{\Sigma}_{11}) \tag{4.101}$$

$$\mathbf{X_2} \sim N(\boldsymbol{\mu}_2, \boldsymbol{\Sigma}_{22}) \tag{4.102}$$

These are the marginal distributions. For conditional distributions, it can be shown, for instance, that the distribution of $\mathbf{X_2}$ for given $\mathbf{X_1}$, and that of $\mathbf{X_1}$ for given $\mathbf{X_2}$ are

$$\mathbf{X_2} \mid \mathbf{X_1} \sim N(\boldsymbol{\mu}_2 + \boldsymbol{\Sigma}_{21}\boldsymbol{\Sigma}_{11}^{-1}(\mathbf{X_1} - \boldsymbol{\mu}_1); \boldsymbol{\Sigma}_{22} - \boldsymbol{\Sigma}_{21}\boldsymbol{\Sigma}_{11}^{-1}\boldsymbol{\Sigma}_{12}) \tag{4.103}$$

$$\mathbf{X_1} \mid \mathbf{X_2} \sim N(\boldsymbol{\mu}_1 + \boldsymbol{\Sigma}_{12}\boldsymbol{\Sigma}_{22}^{-1}(\mathbf{X_2} - \boldsymbol{\mu}_2); \boldsymbol{\Sigma}_{11} - \boldsymbol{\Sigma}_{12}\boldsymbol{\Sigma}_{22}^{-1}\boldsymbol{\Sigma}_{21}) \tag{4.104}$$

The above formulas become greatly simplified should they originate from the bivariate normal distributon. Let

$$\mathbf{X} = \begin{bmatrix} x_1 \\ x_2 \end{bmatrix} \qquad \boldsymbol{\mu} = \begin{bmatrix} \mu_1 \\ \mu_2 \end{bmatrix} \qquad \boldsymbol{\Sigma} = \begin{bmatrix} \sigma_1^2 & \rho\sigma_1\sigma_2 \\ \rho\sigma_1\sigma_2 & \sigma_2^2 \end{bmatrix} \tag{4.105}$$

It follows from (4.101) and (4.102) that the marginals are univariate normal:

$$x_1 \sim \mathrm{N}(\mu_1, \sigma_1^2) \tag{4.106}$$

$$x_2 \sim \mathrm{N}(\mu_2, \sigma_2^2) \tag{4.107}$$

Also, the conditionals, following (4.103) and (4.104), are univariate normal:

$$x_2 \mid x_1 \sim \mathrm{N}\left[\mu_2 + \rho\frac{\sigma_2}{\sigma_1}(x_1 - \mu_1),\ \sigma_2^2(1 - \rho^2)\right] \tag{4.108}$$

$$x_1 \mid x_2 \sim \mathrm{N}\left[\mu_1 + \rho\frac{\sigma_1}{\sigma_2}(x_2 - \mu_2),\ \sigma_1^2(1 - \rho^2)\right] \tag{4.109}$$

From the first argument of N(–, –) in (4.108) and (4.109), notice that x_2 (x_1) is not mean independent of x_1 (x_2) because the mean involves x_1 (x_2), but is variance independent because the variance does not involve x_1 (x_2). In each case, the conditional mean lies on a line and that line is the regression line itself. We will review this aspect on the basis of the conditional distribution of x_2, given x_1. The same can be done with the other conditional distribution.

For x_2 given x_1, the conditional mean can be expressed as

$$\begin{aligned} \mathrm{E}(x_2 \mid x_1) &= \mu_2 + \rho\frac{\sigma_2}{\sigma_1}(x_1 - \mu_1) \\ &= \left(\mu_2 - \rho\frac{\sigma_2}{\sigma_1}\mu_1\right) + \rho\frac{\sigma_2}{\sigma_1}x_1 \\ &= \alpha + \beta x_1 \end{aligned} \tag{4.110}$$

This is the equation of a straight line, and it is the line of regression of x_2 on x_1. Notice that the intercept of this line is α, which is $\mu_2 - \beta\mu_1$, whereas the slope of the line is denoted by β ($= \rho\sigma_2/\sigma_1$). The line involves x_1, which reveals the mean dependence of x_2 on x_1.

One can very simply show that in case the normal variable vector has a diagonal variance–covariance matrix, all the elements of this vector are statistically independent. The joint pdf can then be reduced to the product of individual pdfs:

$$f(\mathbf{X}) = \frac{1}{(\sqrt{2\pi})^n\, \sigma_1\, \sigma_2 \cdots \sigma_n} \exp\left[-\frac{1}{2}\sum\left(\frac{x_i - \mu_i}{\sigma_i}\right)^2\right] \tag{4.111}$$

$$= f(x_1)\, f(x_2) \cdots f(x_n) \tag{4.112}$$

Notice that we have used

$$\begin{aligned} \sigma_{ii} &= \sigma_i^2 \qquad & i &= 1, \ldots, n \\ \sigma_{ij} &= \sigma_{ji} = 0 \qquad & i \neq j &= 1, \ldots, n \end{aligned} \tag{4.113}$$

4.7.5 Derivatives of the Normal Distribution

Three distributions, of special use in econometrics in some form or other, are derived from the normal distribution. These will be stated as they are, without any formal proof.

The Chi-Square (χ^2) distribution. The sum of squares of S independent standard normal variables is distributed as χ^2 with S degrees of freedom. It is an asymmetric distribution confined between 0 and ∞ for values of the variable, and the mean and variance of the distribution are S and $2S$, respectively.

The student *t* distribution. Suppose x is an N(0, 1) variable that has a chi-square distribution with S degrees of freedom and x and χ^2 are statistically independent. Then the ratio of x to the square root of χ^2 per degree of freedom is defined to be the t distribution with as many degrees of freedom. In this situation, the mean and variance of t are 0 and $S/(S - 2)$ and as $S \to \infty$, $t \to$ N(0, 1). t is a symmetric distribution extending over the $(-\infty, \infty)$ range.

The *F* distribution. Let χ_1^2 and χ_2^2 be two independent chi-square distributions based on S_1 and S_2 degrees of freedom. Then, Snedecor's F is the ratio of χ_1^2/S_1 to χ_2^2/S_2, and F has the numerator df S_1 and denominator df S_2. This distribution, like the chi-square distribution, is asymmetric, confined between 0 and ∞ for its values. It has its mean value $S_2/(S_2 - 2)$. Particularly, when $S_1 = 1$ and $S_2 = S$, we have the F with $(1, S)$ degrees of freedom obtained just as well from squaring a t distribution based on S df.

4.8 DISTRIBUTION OF LINEAR AND QUADRATIC FORMS

First, we state that orthogonal linear functions of independent normal variables with identical variance are also independent normal variables with the same variance. To see this, suppose $\mathbf{X}$ is an $n \times 1$ vector distributed as $N(\boldsymbol{\mu}, \sigma^2 \boldsymbol{I})$. Let a new $n \times 1$ vector $\mathbf{Z}$ be derived from an orthogonal transformation of $\mathbf{X}$:

$$\mathbf{Z} = \boldsymbol{C}'\mathbf{X} \tag{4.114}$$

where $\boldsymbol{C}'$ is an orthogonal matrix of size $n \times n$. Then

$$\mathrm{E}(\mathbf{Z}) = \boldsymbol{C}'\mathrm{E}(\mathbf{X}) = \boldsymbol{C}'\boldsymbol{\mu}$$

$$\mathrm{V}(\mathbf{Z}) = \boldsymbol{C}'\mathrm{V}(\mathbf{X})\boldsymbol{C} = \sigma^2\boldsymbol{C}'\boldsymbol{I}\boldsymbol{C} = \sigma^2\boldsymbol{I}$$

since, by the orthogonality of C, $C'IC = I$. Thus

$$\mathbf{Z} \sim \mathrm{N}(C'\boldsymbol{\mu}, \sigma^2 I) \tag{4.115}$$

In case $\boldsymbol{\mu}$ is $\mathbf{0}$, $\mathbf{X}$ is a set of spherical normal variables. Then $\mathbf{Z}$ will also be a set of spherical normal variables. If, in addition, $\sigma^2 = 1$, then just as $\mathbf{X}$ is a set of independent standard normal variables, so is $\mathbf{Z}$ a set of independent standard normal variables.

Second, consider an idempotent quadratic form obtained from a standard normal vector. This is a form algebraically expressed as, say, $\mathbf{X}'Q\mathbf{X}$, where Q is an idempotent matrix (Section 3.2.2, Chapter 3) of rank r, and $\mathbf{X}$ an $n \times 1$ vector distributed as $\mathrm{N}(\mathbf{0}, I)$. Then $\mathbf{X}'Q\mathbf{X}$ is a chi-square variable with r degrees of freedom.

To see this, observe that an orthogonal matrix C diagonalizes an idempotent matrix Q (see result 5 of Section 3.8, Chapter 3):

$$C'QC = \Delta = \begin{bmatrix} I & 0 \\ 0 & \mathbf{0} \end{bmatrix} \tag{4.116}$$

Now suppose $\mathbf{Z}$ is as defined in (4.114) and is partitioned into

$$\mathbf{Z} = \begin{bmatrix} \mathbf{Z}_1 \\ \cdots \\ \mathbf{Z}_2 \end{bmatrix} = \begin{bmatrix} z_1 \\ z_2 \\ \vdots \\ z_r \\ \cdots \\ z_{r+1} \\ \vdots \\ z_n \end{bmatrix} \tag{4.117}$$

By a previous result $\mathbf{Z}$ is a set of standard normal variables given that $\mathbf{X}$ is $\mathrm{N}(\mathbf{0}, I)$. Now, since

$$\begin{aligned} \mathbf{X}'Q\mathbf{X} &= \mathbf{X}'(CC')\,Q\,(CC')\mathbf{X} = \mathbf{X}'C(C'QC)C'\mathbf{X} \\ &= \mathbf{Z}'\Delta\mathbf{Z} = [\mathbf{Z}_1\mathbf{Z}_2]\begin{bmatrix} I & 0 \\ 0 & \mathbf{0} \end{bmatrix}\begin{bmatrix} \mathbf{Z}_1 \\ \mathbf{Z}_2 \end{bmatrix} = \mathbf{Z}_1'\mathbf{Z}_1 \end{aligned} \tag{4.118}$$

$\mathbf{X}'Q\mathbf{X}$ will be a chi-square variable with r df, since it reduces to $\mathbf{Z}_1'\mathbf{Z}_1$ which is the sum of squares of r standard normal variables.

If $\mathbf{X} \sim \mathrm{N}(\mathbf{0}, \sigma^2 I)$, that is, if the $\mathbf{X}$s are a set of spherical normal variables, then

$$\frac{\mathbf{X}}{\sigma} \sim N(\mathbf{0}, I)$$

and thus

$$\frac{\mathbf{X}'}{\sigma} Q \frac{\mathbf{X}}{\sigma} = \mathbf{Z}_1'\mathbf{Z}_1 = \chi^2$$

or

$$X'QX = \sigma^2\chi^2 \tag{4.119}$$

That is, an idempotent quadratic form of rank r in spherical normal variables with a common variance σ^2 is distributed as $\sigma^2\chi^2$ with r degrees of freedom.

The next two results, stated without proof, will be of great use in some contexts. First, we lay down the requirement for a linear form $\boldsymbol{P}\mathbf{X}$ to be distributed independently of a quadratic form $\mathbf{X}'\boldsymbol{Q}\mathbf{X}$, where $\boldsymbol{P}$ is an $s \times n$ matrix, $\boldsymbol{Q}$ an idempotent matrix of rank r and $\mathbf{X}$ is $N(\mathbf{0}, \boldsymbol{I})$. For independence of the two forms, we require

$$PQ = 0 \tag{4.120}$$

Notice that even if $\mathbf{X}$ comes from $N(\mathbf{0}, \sigma^2\boldsymbol{I})$, all other aspects remaining unchanged, $\boldsymbol{PQ} = \boldsymbol{0}$ will still determine the independence of the two forms. Second, for independence of two quadratic forms, we similarly require the product of the two intervening matrices to vanish. Specifically, if $\mathbf{X}$ is $n \times 1 \sim N(\mathbf{0}, \boldsymbol{I})$, $\boldsymbol{P}$ is an idempotent matrix of rank m, and $\boldsymbol{Q}$ is an idempotent matrix of rank k, then for the quadratic form $\mathbf{X}'\boldsymbol{P}\mathbf{X}$ to be distributed independently of the quadratic form $\mathbf{X}'\boldsymbol{Q}\mathbf{X}$ we require

$$PQ = 0 \tag{4.121}$$

By now it should be clear that this condition would not change even if $\mathbf{X}$ were distributed as $N(\mathbf{0}, \sigma^2\boldsymbol{I})$.

4.9 ASYMPTOTIC THEORY

This theory attempts to find the tendency of the sampling distribution of a random variable as the sample size increases indefinitely. For example, consider that the random variable is the sample mean $\bar{x}_n$ of sample observations $x_1, \ldots, x_n$ drawn randomly from some population with the identifying variable x, its mean μ, and its variance σ^2. A standard relation in samplings of this kind is that

$$E(\bar{x}_n) = \mu \qquad \text{for any } n$$

which establishes that the sample mean is unbiased for the population mean and also that

$$nV(\bar{x}_n) = E[\sqrt{n}\,(\bar{x}_n - \mu)]^2 = \sigma^2$$

The particular form of the last relation is utilized rather than simply $V(\bar{x}_n)$ to prevent the distribution of $\bar{x}_n$ from concentrating at the point μ in the limit, for as $n \to \infty$, $V(\bar{x}_n) \to 0$, which would mean that all x_ns would converge at μ. That is, the limiting distribution of $\bar{x}_n$ would become degenerate. But since $nV(\bar{x}_n) = \sigma^2 \neq 0$, that possibility is averted. These two results are the basis of the intuition that the sample mean converges to the population mean more closely as the sample size increases indefinitely. One way of expressing this tendency is to write the probability statement:

$$\text{Prob}\{\mu - \lambda < \bar{x}_n < \mu + \lambda\} = \text{Prob}\{\,|\,\bar{x}_n - \mu\,|\, < \lambda\} > 1 - \delta \qquad (4.122)$$

where both λ and δ are preassigned small quantities ($|\,\delta\,| < 1$). These quantities are taken to depend on the sample size n, especially a large enough value n_0 of n such that whenever $n > n_0$, λ becomes increasingly small, $V(\bar{x}_n)$ becomes as close to zero as possible, and correspondingly δ approaches zero. In the limit as $n \to \infty$,

$$\text{Prob}\{\,|\,\bar{x}_n - \mu\,|\, < \lambda\} \to 1 \qquad (4.123)$$

This means that with a probability as high as unity the sample mean converges to the population mean at a large enough value for the sample size. This is the substance of a probability limit statement in asymptotic theory. More briefly, such a statement is expressed as

$$\text{plim } \bar{x}_n = \mu \qquad (4.124)$$

In fact, a probability limit or, in short, a plim statement can be written for any random variable. The attempt can be justified by, if nothing else, Tchebycheff's theorem. Let us review this theorem now.

Suppose x is a random variable with $E(x) = \mu$ and $V(x) = \sigma^2$. Then, for any $\epsilon > 0$, Tchebycheff's theorem requires that

$$\text{Prob}\{\,|\,x - \sigma\mu\,|\, > \epsilon\,\sigma\} < \frac{1}{\epsilon^2} \qquad (4.125)$$

As an example, if x_n is such that

$$E(x_n) = \mu + \frac{C_1}{n} + \frac{C_2}{n^2} + \cdots$$

that is, $E(x_n)$ is a power series in $n^0, n^{-1}, n^{-2}, \ldots$ where $C_1, C_2, \ldots$ are constants, then

$$\text{Prob}\left\{\left|\, x_n - \left(\mu + \frac{C_1}{n} + \frac{C_2}{n^2} + \cdots\right)\right| > \epsilon\sqrt{V(x_n)}\right\} < \frac{1}{\epsilon^2}$$

Equating $\epsilon\sqrt{V(x_n)}$ with λ, we have

$$\text{Prob}\left\{\left|\, x_n - \left(\mu + \frac{C_1}{n} + \frac{C_2}{n^2} + \cdots\right)\right| > \lambda\right\} < \frac{V(x_n)}{\lambda^2}$$

Assume now that as $n \to \infty$, $V(x_n) \to 0$. Then

$$\lim n \to \infty \qquad \text{Prob}\{\,|\,x_n - \mu\,|\, > \lambda\} \to 0$$

In the case where $x_n = \bar{x}_n$, this coincides with the previous plim statement for the sample mean. In fact, the sample mean is unbiased for the population mean for *all* sample sizes, small or large.

The plim statement, which is the basis of the property of large sample or asymptotic unbiasedness, is used synonymously with the property of consistency of an estimator. Conversely, consistency does not necessarily guarantee asymptotic unbiasedness, as Sewell (1969) has shown with estimators from a simultaneous equation model.[8]

A very useful property of probability limits pertains to a continuous function of a random variable. This property is due to Slutsky. According to it, the probability limit of a continuous function of a random variable is the function of the probability limit of the variable. Thus, if

$$\text{plim } x = x^*$$

and if $\psi(x)$ is a continuous function of x, then[9]

$$\text{plim } \psi(x) = \psi(x^*) \tag{4.126}$$

Examples of this are

$$\begin{aligned} \text{plim}(x^p) &= (\text{plim } x)^p \\ \text{plim}(x^{-q}) &= (\text{plim } x)^{-q} \\ \text{plim}\left(\frac{x}{z}\right) &= \frac{\text{plim } x}{\text{plim } z} \\ \text{plim}(xz) &= (\text{plim } x)\,(\text{plim } z) \end{aligned} \tag{4.127}$$

Extensions of these plim results to vectors and matrices are straightforward. Taking $\boldsymbol{A}$ and $\boldsymbol{B}$ to be matrices, since the elements of the product of two matrices are continuous functions of the elements of these matrices, and similarly, the elements of an inverse matrix are continuous functions of the elements of the original matrix, we have

$$\begin{aligned} \text{plim}(\boldsymbol{AB}) &= (\text{plim } \boldsymbol{A})(\text{plim } \boldsymbol{B}) \\ \text{plim } \boldsymbol{A}^{-1} &= (\text{plim } \boldsymbol{A})^{-1} \end{aligned} \tag{4.128}$$

An important result in probability limits is based on the observation that the asymptotic variance of the sequence[10] $\{x^{(n)}\}$ is the product of $1/n$ and the asymptotic expectation of the sequence $\{[\sqrt{n}\,(x^{(n)} - \text{E}x^{(n)})]^2\}$. Extending this result to vectors and matrices, we have the following straightforward result:

If

$$\text{plim}[\sqrt{n}\,(\mathbf{X}^{(n)} - \text{E}\mathbf{X}^{(n)})][\sqrt{n}\,(\mathbf{X}^{(n)} - \text{E}\mathbf{X}^{(n)})]' = \boldsymbol{\Omega} \tag{4.129}$$

[8] An estimator is consistent for a population parameter if it is asymptotically unbiased and its variance is asymptotically zero.

[9] The proof of this theorem is given in Wilks (1962). Notice that this theorem will not generally hold in terms of expectations replacing plim statements.

[10] A sequence $\{x^n\}$ is $x^{(1)}, \ldots, x^{(n)}, \ldots$. Asymptotic expectation of this sequence is $\lim_{n\to\infty} \{\text{E}(x^{(n)})\} \triangleq \overline{\text{E}}x^{(n)} = \mu$ since $\lim_{n\to\infty} \text{E}(x^{(n)}) = \mu$, where μ is finite and constant.

where $\mathbf{X}$ is a vector and $\boldsymbol{\Omega}$ a matrix, then

$$\overline{\mathrm{E}}(\mathbf{X} - \overline{\mathrm{E}}\mathbf{X})(\mathbf{X} - \overline{\mathrm{E}}\mathbf{X})' = n^{-1}\boldsymbol{\Omega} \tag{4.130}$$

where $\overline{\mathrm{E}}$ denotes the asymptotic expectation of the sequence $\{\mathbf{X}^{(n)}\}$.

4.10 THE CENTRAL LIMIT THEOREM AND CONVERGENCE IN DISTRIBUTION

We have already observed that in random sampling from a normal population identified by $X \sim \mathrm{N}(\mu, \sigma^2)$ the sample mean $\bar{x}_n$, based on sample size n, has a normal probability density function as implied in

$$\bar{x}_n \sim \mathrm{N}\left(\mu, \frac{\sigma^2}{n}\right)$$

This is true for any value of n. Since, however, as $n \to \infty$, $\mathrm{V}(\bar{x}_n)$ $(=\sigma^2/n)$ tends to zero, the whole probability mass of the distribution of $\bar{x}_n$ falls on the central point μ. This is a sign of a degenerate distribution. One can avoid this tendency by effecting a transformation of $\bar{x}_n$ to y_n defined as

$$y_n = \sqrt{n}(\bar{x}_n - \mu)$$

It is easy to show that the new variable is normal

$$y_n \sim \mathrm{N}(0, \sigma^2)$$

regardless of n, which means that both the finite sample and the asymptotic distributions of y_n are one and the same.

This is just one example of many possible situations. The important use of an example like this is the conjecture that we can take advantage of a known limiting distribution as an approximation to the finite sample distribution of a statistic, when the latter distribution is either not known or not tractable. This will be clear in the context of an important theorem, known as the central limit theorem (CLT), to be stated next.

Assume that the variable X has mean μ and variance σ^2, but otherwise its distribution is unknown. The CLT, under general conditions, states that the limiting distribution of $y = \sqrt{n}(\bar{x}_n - \mu)$ is $\mathrm{N}(0, \sigma^2)$.[11]

The general conditions center around the requirement that the variance of none of the components x_i, $i = 1, 2, \ldots, n$ of the mean $\bar{x}_n$ overpowers the variance of the mean. It is this theorem that has given the normal distribution the central role in mathematical statistics; even though individual variable distributions are not necessarily normal, the sum or the mean of a large number of these variables will tend to be normal.

[11] The CLT, under the same general conditions, also has the sum $\sum_1^n x_i - n\mu$ converge to $\mathrm{N}(0, n\sigma^2)$ in the limit. For proof of this theorem, see Wilks (1962).

There are other ways of expressing the CLT result. These are

$$y_n \xrightarrow{D} N(0, \sigma^2) \tag{4.131}$$

which is the same thing as saying that y_n converges in distribution to $N(0, \sigma^2)$. For x_n, we say

$$\bar{x}_n \approx \text{AN}\left(\mu, \frac{\sigma^2}{n}\right) \tag{4.132}$$

where AN stands for asymptotic normal, and σ^2/n is conventionally defined to be the asymptotic variance (asy var) of $\bar{x}_n$:

$$\text{asy var}(\bar{x}_n) = n^{-1} \lim_{n\to\infty} E[\sqrt{n}\,(\bar{x}_n - \mu)]^2 = \frac{\sigma^2}{n} \tag{4.133}$$

We mentioned before that the asymptotic distribution of $\bar{x}_n$ is degenerate. However, there is a practical use made of the conventional asymptotic normal distribution assigned to this variable. When, for small sample sizes, the distribution of the sample mean cannot be determined, we can still approximately take its asymptotic distribution to be normal. Such a result will have one of its greatest uses in the multiple regression model, the central theme of this book. That is when the residual terms of the model are random but not normal. Generalizations of the CLT to other multivariate situations are quite straightforward.

4.11 PROPERTIES OF ESTIMATORS

4.11.1 Small Sample (or General) Properties

Throughout this book, we will be referring to some desirable properties of sample estimators while estimating a population parameter or parameters. Some of these properties are small sample properties, even though they could apply equally well to all sizes of samples; others are basically large sample or asymptotic properties.

First we will present the "small" sample properties. Reference is made here to an estimator $\hat{\theta}$ or $\bar{\theta}$ constructed from a random sample of size n: $x_1, \ldots, x_n$ trying to estimate the population parameter θ.

(1) $\hat{\theta}$ is unbiased for θ if

$$E(\hat{\theta}) = \theta \tag{4.134}$$

(2) $\hat{\theta}$ is the minimum variance estimator of θ if

$$E(\hat{\theta} - E\hat{\theta})^2 \leqq E(\bar{\theta} - E\bar{\theta})^2 \tag{4.135}$$

where $\bar{\theta}$ is any other estimator of θ.

(3) $\hat{\theta}$ is minimum variance unbiased (MVU) or best unbiased (or efficient) for θ if

$$E(\hat{\theta} - \theta)^2 \leqq E(\bar{\theta} - \theta)^2 \tag{4.136}$$

where $\bar{\theta}$ is any other unbiased estimator of θ.

(4) $\hat{\theta}$ is the minimum mean square error estimator of θ if

$$E(\hat{\theta} - \theta)^2 \leqq E(\bar{\theta} - \theta)^2 \tag{4.137}$$

where $\bar{\theta}$ is any other estimator of θ.

From property (1), the bias of the estimator $\hat{\theta}$ can be expressed as

$$B(\hat{\theta}) = E(\hat{\theta}) - \theta \tag{4.138}$$

Thus, the mean squared error becomes the sum of the variance and the square of the bias:

$$\begin{aligned} E(\hat{\theta} - \theta)^2 &= E(\hat{\theta} - E\hat{\theta} + E\hat{\theta} - \theta)^2 \\ &= E(\hat{\theta} - E\hat{\theta})^2 + [E\hat{\theta} - \theta]^2 \\ &= V(\hat{\theta}) + [B(\theta)]^2 \end{aligned} \tag{4.139}$$

(5) $\hat{\theta}$ is a best linear unbiased estimator (BLUE) of θ if it is a linear, unbiased, and minimum variance estimator of θ among linear estimators.

4.11.2 Large Sample (or Asymptotic) Properties

Applying the convention that $\bar{E}$ stands for asymptotic expectation, and $\hat{\theta}$, $\bar{\theta}$, and θ are as defined in the preceding section, the following asymptotic properties of estimators can be used as a guide for desirable estimators.

(6) $\hat{\theta}$ is asymptotically unbiased for θ if

$$\bar{E}(\hat{\theta}) = \theta \tag{4.140}$$

(7) $\hat{\theta}$ is consistent for θ if

$$\text{plim } \hat{\theta} = \theta \tag{4.141}$$

(8) $\hat{\theta}$ is asymptotically efficient for θ if

$$\bar{E}(\hat{\theta} - \theta)^2 \leqq \bar{E}(\bar{\theta} - \theta)^2 \tag{4.142}$$

where $\bar{\theta}$ is any other consistent estimator of θ.

(9) If $\hat{\theta}$ is a consistent estimator of θ, and $g = g(\theta)$ is a continuous function of θ, then

$$\hat{g} = g(\hat{\theta}) \tag{4.143}$$

That is, a consistent estimator of the function of the parameter is the function of the consistent estimator of the parameter.

These properties can be easily generalized to multiparameter cases, where $\hat{\boldsymbol{\theta}}$ is now a vector estimator, and $E(\hat{\boldsymbol{\theta}} - E\hat{\boldsymbol{\theta}})(\hat{\boldsymbol{\theta}} - E\hat{\boldsymbol{\theta}})'$, and $E(\hat{\boldsymbol{\theta}} - \boldsymbol{\theta})(\hat{\boldsymbol{\theta}} - \boldsymbol{\theta})'$ are the variance–covariance matrix and the matrix for mean squared errors, respectively, for the vector estimator $\hat{\boldsymbol{\theta}}$, and similarly for other estimators, such as $\bar{\boldsymbol{\theta}}$, both for small (or general) and large sample situations.

4.12 MAXIMUM LIKELIHOOD ESTIMATORS

The desirable properties of estimators listed above will be shown to apply to least-squares estimators of coefficients of a multiple regression model, the major preoccupation of this book. For some versions of this model, the least-squares estimators will have those properties for samples of any size, small or large; for other versions, such estimates will have only large sample or asymptotic properties.

There is still another class of estimates, called the maximum likelihood estimates (MLEs) that under fairly general conditions can be shown to have desirable asymptotic properties, if nothing else. We shall come back to these properties later, but first we introduce the method itself.

The likelihood function for a random sample of size n with observations x_1, $x_2, \ldots x_n$ drawn from a population with parameters $\theta_1, \ldots, \theta_p$ is denoted as

$$L(x_1, \ldots, x_n \mid \theta_1, \ldots, \theta_p)$$

In short, it is written as

$$L(\mathbf{x} \mid \boldsymbol{\theta}) = L$$

where $\mathbf{x}$ and $\boldsymbol{\theta}$ are vectors.

The maximum likelihood estimator of $\boldsymbol{\theta}$ is the vector $\hat{\boldsymbol{\theta}}$, based on those sample observations, which makes that likelihood the largest. That is, it is that value $\hat{\boldsymbol{\theta}}$ of $\boldsymbol{\theta}$ which makes the observed sample to have most likely originated from the population with parameter θ. Algebraically, the method requires

$$L(\mathbf{x} \mid \hat{\boldsymbol{\theta}}) \geqq L(\mathbf{x} \mid \bar{\boldsymbol{\theta}})$$

where $\bar{\boldsymbol{\theta}}$ is any other value for $\boldsymbol{\theta}$.

Since the sample is random, observations are independent and so

$$\begin{aligned} L(\mathbf{x} \mid \boldsymbol{\theta}) &= f(x_1 \mid \boldsymbol{\theta})\, f(x_2 \mid \boldsymbol{\theta}) \cdots f(x_n \mid \boldsymbol{\theta}) \\ &= \prod_{t=1}^{n} f(x_t \mid \boldsymbol{\theta}) \end{aligned} \tag{4.144}$$

where $f(x_t \mid \boldsymbol{\theta})$ represents the likelihood or probability of the tth observation being drawn. Noting that the logarithm of a function increases monotonically with the function itself, it follows that the maximum of log L will occur whenever the maximum of L does. Add to this the simplicity of results derived from using the logarithms of pdfs. For instance, many pdfs have powers of exponentials that are eliminated by logarithmic operations and, also, the logarithm of the product of likelihoods is the sum of the logarithms of individual likelihoods. For these reasons we will most often illustrate the method using log L or ln L, where ln is the natural logarithm.

4.12.1 Properties of Maximum Likelihood Estimators

(1) Under fairly general conditions[12] an MLE is asymptotically unbiased, consistent, and asymptotically efficient.

(2) Under fairly general conditions,[13] the asymptotic variance–covariance matrix of MLE $\hat{\boldsymbol{\theta}}$ is given by

$$\boldsymbol{\Sigma} = \left(- \frac{\partial^2 \log \mathrm{L}}{\partial \boldsymbol{\theta}^2} \right)^{-1} \tag{4.145}$$

where the derivatives are computed at $\boldsymbol{\theta} = \hat{\boldsymbol{\theta}}$, and

$$\hat{\boldsymbol{\theta}} \xrightarrow{\mathrm{D}} \mathrm{N}(\boldsymbol{\theta}, \boldsymbol{\Sigma}) \tag{4.146}$$

(3) The MLE are MVB (minimum variance bound) estimators if the latter exist.

This property follows from what is referred to in the statistical literature as the Cramer–Rao inequality. It assigns a minimum value to the variance of an unbiased estimator in a more general class than merely the linear. Note that situations may arise where the minimum variance bound (MVB) does not exist, but still an MVU (minimum variance unbiased) estimator may be available with a larger variance than indicated by the MVB estimator.

To illustrate the MVB concept, we start from the likelihood in a general situation:

$$\mathrm{L}(\mathbf{Y} \mid \theta) = \prod_{t=1}^{n} f(Y_i \mid \theta)$$

where θ is a single parameter, the parent pdf is $f(Y \mid \theta)$, and a random sample of size n is drawn from this population. Denoting by $\hat{\theta}$ an unbiased estimator for θ, the Cramer–Rao inequality stands as

$$\mathrm{V}(\hat{\theta}) \geqq \left[\mathrm{E} \left(\frac{\partial \ln \mathrm{L}^2}{\partial \theta} \right) \right]^{-1} = - \left[\frac{\mathrm{E}\partial^2 \ln \mathrm{L}}{\partial \theta^2} \right]^{-1} \tag{4.147}$$

The MVB is then any one of the two right-hand expressions.

[12] See Wilks (1962; pp. 358–363, 379–381), and Kendall and Stuart (1961; pp. 35–46, 51–60).

[13] Ibid.

We can generalize the bound to a multiparameter, say a p-parameter, situation. Take $\boldsymbol{\theta}$ to be an unbiased vector of estimates, its variance–covariance matrix being denoted by $\mathbf{V}(\boldsymbol{\theta})$. Then, denoting by $\boldsymbol{I}(\boldsymbol{\theta})$ the denominator, with sign changed, of the extreme right-hand expression of the Cramer–Rao inequality in the p-parameter situation, we have

$$\boldsymbol{I}(\boldsymbol{\theta}) = -\left(\frac{E(\partial^2 \ln L)}{\partial\boldsymbol{\theta}\partial\boldsymbol{\theta}'}\right) \tag{4.148}$$

The diagonal elements of this $\boldsymbol{I}(\boldsymbol{\theta})$ matrix, sometimes referred to as the information matrix, are $\frac{\partial^2 \ln L}{\partial\theta_1^2}, \ldots, \frac{\partial^2 \ln L}{\partial\theta_p^2}$. Its off-diagonal elements are $\partial^2 \ln L/\partial\theta_i\partial\theta_j$ where $i \neq j = 1, 2, \ldots, p$. For instance for $i = 1, j = 2, \ldots, p$, the off-diagonal elements in the first row are $\partial^2 \ln L/\partial\theta_1\partial\theta_2, \ldots, \partial^2 \ln L/\partial\theta_1\partial\theta_p$, and, similarly, the off-diagonal elements in the second to the pth row, that is, when $i = 2, \ldots, p$.

Thus the multiparameter version of the Cramer–Rao inequality[14] becomes $\mathbf{V}(\boldsymbol{\theta}) - \boldsymbol{I}^{-1}(\boldsymbol{\theta})$ which is a nonnegative definite matrix.

(4) *Invariance Property of MLE* If $\hat{\boldsymbol{\theta}}$ is the MLE for $\boldsymbol{\theta}$ and if $\mathbf{g} = \mathbf{g}(\boldsymbol{\theta})$ is a vector of single valued functions of $\boldsymbol{\theta}$, then $\hat{\mathbf{g}} = \mathbf{g}(\hat{\boldsymbol{\theta}})$ is the MLE for $\mathbf{g}$.

Example 1. Sampling from a Bernoulli population. Let us consider the problem of estimating the mean proportion of success p in random sampling (of size n) from a Bernoulli population with the probability of success p. In particular, assume that the number of successes is r and the number of failures is $n - r$, all of which occurred in a particular order. Then the log-likelihood function is

$$\log L(\mathbf{x} \mid p) = \log[p^r(1 - p)^{n-r}] = r \log p + (n - r) \log(1 - p)$$

The first-order condition for the maximum of log L is

$$0 = \frac{\partial \log L}{\partial p} = \frac{r}{p} - \frac{n - r}{1 - p}$$

from which

$$\hat{p} = \frac{r}{n}$$

is obtained. But r/n is the proportion of success in the sample. Thus, the sample proportion is the MLE of the population proportion of success. We will now

[14] A number of sources can be consulted for the derivation of the Cramer–Rao inequality, e.g. Kendall and Stuart (1961, Chapter 17).

compute the asymptotic variance of the MLE $\hat{p}$. Since

$$\left[\frac{\partial^2 \log L}{\partial p^2}\right]_{p=\hat{p}} = \left[\frac{-r}{p^2} - \frac{n-r}{(1-p)^2}\right]_{p=\hat{p}} = -\frac{n}{\hat{p}(1-\hat{p})}$$

the asymptotic variance of $\hat{p}$ is

$$-\left[\frac{\partial^2 \log L}{\partial p^2}\right]^{-1}_{p=\hat{p}} = \frac{\hat{p}(1-\hat{p})}{n}$$

Example 2. Sampling from normal population. Suppose we take a random sample of size n from a $N(\mu, \sigma^2)$ population. We are concerned with the MLE of μ and σ^2. The likelihood function for this sample is

$$L(\mathbf{x} \mid \mu, \sigma^2) = \left(\frac{1}{\sqrt{2\pi}\sigma}\right)^n \exp\left[-\frac{1}{2\sigma^2}\sum_{t=1}^{n}(x_t - \mu)^2\right]$$

Since

$$\log L = -\frac{n}{2}\log \sigma^2 - \frac{1}{2\sigma^2}\sum_{t=1}^{n}(x_t - \mu)^2$$

where the constant term $-(n/2) \log 2\pi$ has been suppressed, we have

$$\mathbf{0} = \begin{bmatrix} \dfrac{\partial \log L}{\partial \mu} \\ \\ \dfrac{\partial \log L}{\partial \sigma^2} \end{bmatrix} = \begin{bmatrix} \dfrac{\Sigma(x_t - \mu)}{\sigma^2} \\ \\ -\dfrac{n}{(2\sigma^2)} + \dfrac{\Sigma(x_t - \mu)^2}{2\sigma^4} \end{bmatrix}$$

The solutions of the two equations give

$$\hat{\mu} = \frac{\Sigma x_t}{n} = \bar{x}$$

$$\hat{\sigma}^2 = \frac{\Sigma(x_t - \hat{\mu})^2}{n} = \frac{\Sigma(x_t - \bar{x})^2}{n} = S^2$$

This means that in random sampling from a normal population, the sample mean and the sample variance are the MLEs of the corresponding population mean and variance.

A simple exercise will show that the asymptotic variance–covariance matrix of $[\hat{\mu}\ \sigma^2]'$ will be

$$\mathbf{\Sigma} = -\left[\frac{\partial^2 \log L}{\partial \boldsymbol{\theta}^2}\right]^{-1}_{\boldsymbol{\theta}=\hat{\boldsymbol{\theta}}} = \begin{bmatrix} \dfrac{\hat{\sigma}^2}{n} & 0 \\ 0 & \dfrac{2\hat{\sigma}^4}{n} \end{bmatrix}$$

From the structure of $\boldsymbol{\Sigma}$, particularly zero off-diagonal elements, we immediately infer that $\bar{x}$ and S^2 are asymptotically independent in random sampling from a normal population. Indeed, in sampling from this population, $\bar{x}$ and S^2 are independent for *any sample size*.

Example 3. The multiple regression model and MLE. We will now illustrate the maximum likelihood method taking the multiple regression model

$$\mathbf{Y} = X\boldsymbol{\beta} + \boldsymbol{\epsilon}$$

where $\mathbf{Y}$ and $\boldsymbol{\epsilon}$ are each an $n \times 1$ vector and X is an $n \times (m + 1)$ matrix and $\boldsymbol{\beta}$ an $(m + 1) \times 1$ vector. This model is soon to become the centrepiece of study in this book.

To proceed to the likelihood, we transform $\boldsymbol{\epsilon}$ to $\mathbf{Y}$ in probability using the Jacobian $\mathrm{J} = \dfrac{\partial(\epsilon_1 \ldots . \epsilon_n)}{\partial(\mathrm{Y}_1 \ldots . \mathrm{Y}_n)} = |\,I\,| = 1$ (I being the identity matrix):

$$\mathrm{Prob}\{\mathbf{Y}\} = \mathrm{J}\ \mathrm{Prob}\{\boldsymbol{\epsilon}\} = \mathrm{Prob}\{\boldsymbol{\epsilon}\}$$

Now since

$$\mathrm{Prob}\{\boldsymbol{\epsilon}\} = \frac{1}{(\sqrt{2\pi}\ \sigma)^n} \exp\left(-\frac{1}{2\sigma^2}\boldsymbol{\epsilon}'\,\boldsymbol{\epsilon}\right)$$

therefore,

$$\mathrm{Prob}\{\mathbf{Y}\} = \frac{1}{(\sqrt{2\pi}\sigma)^n} \exp\left[-\frac{1}{2\sigma^2}(\mathbf{Y} - X\boldsymbol{\beta})'(\mathbf{Y} - X\boldsymbol{\beta})\right]$$

This last expression is $\mathrm{L}(\mathbf{Y}/\sigma^2, \boldsymbol{\beta})$. Then

$$\ln \mathrm{L}(\mathbf{Y} \mid \sigma^2, \boldsymbol{\beta}) = \frac{-n}{2}\ln 2\pi - \frac{n}{2}\ln \sigma^2 - \frac{1}{2\sigma^2}(\mathbf{Y} - X\boldsymbol{\beta})'(\mathbf{Y} - X\boldsymbol{\beta})$$

Thus, the MLE of σ^2 and $\boldsymbol{\beta}$ are derived by solving

$$\frac{\partial \ln \mathrm{L}}{\partial\sigma^2} = -\frac{n}{2\sigma^2} + \frac{1}{2\sigma^4}(\mathbf{Y} - X\hat{\boldsymbol{\beta}})'(\mathbf{Y} - X\hat{\boldsymbol{\beta}}) = 0$$

$$\frac{\partial \ln \mathrm{L}}{\partial\boldsymbol{\beta}} = -\frac{1}{2\sigma^2}(-2X'\mathbf{Y} + 2X'X\hat{\boldsymbol{\beta}}) = \mathbf{0}$$

These estimates are

$$\hat{\boldsymbol{\beta}} = (X'X)^{-1}X'\mathbf{Y} \tag{4.149}$$

$$\hat{\sigma}^2 = \frac{\hat{\boldsymbol{\epsilon}}'\hat{\boldsymbol{\epsilon}}}{n} \tag{4.150}$$

where

$$\hat{\boldsymbol{\epsilon}} = \mathbf{Y} - X\hat{\boldsymbol{\beta}}$$

Later we will show that the MLE of $\boldsymbol{\beta}$ are the same as their least-squares estimates. For σ^2, since[15]

$$\mathrm{E}(\hat{\sigma}^2) = \frac{(n - m - 1)\sigma^2}{n} \neq \sigma^2 \tag{4.151}$$

the MLE $\hat{\sigma}^2$ can therefore be biased for σ^2. However, the MLE $\hat{\boldsymbol{\beta}}$ are unbiased for $\boldsymbol{\beta}$, since

$$\mathrm{E}(\hat{\boldsymbol{\beta}}) = (X'X)^{-1}X'X\boldsymbol{\beta} + E(\boldsymbol{\epsilon}) = \boldsymbol{\beta}$$

$\mathrm{E}(\boldsymbol{\epsilon})$ being zero by assumption.

An illustration of the MVB property of MLE from the multiple regression model seems to be in order. Observe that

$$\frac{\partial^2 \ln \mathrm{L}}{\partial\boldsymbol{\beta}\partial\boldsymbol{\beta}'} = -\frac{1}{\sigma^2}X'X$$

$$\frac{\partial^2 \ln \mathrm{L}}{\partial\boldsymbol{\beta}\partial\sigma^2} = -\frac{1}{2\sigma^4}(X'\mathrm{Y} - X'X\boldsymbol{\beta})$$

$$\frac{\partial^2 \ln \mathrm{L}}{\partial\sigma^2} = \frac{n}{2\sigma^4} - \frac{(\mathrm{Y} - X\boldsymbol{\beta})'(\mathrm{Y} - X\boldsymbol{\beta})}{\sigma^6}$$

and their expectations, with the sign changed, are

$$-\mathrm{E}\frac{\partial^2 \ln \mathrm{L}}{\partial\boldsymbol{\beta}\partial\boldsymbol{\beta}'} = \frac{1}{\sigma^2}X'X$$

$$-\mathrm{E}\frac{\partial 2 \ln \mathrm{L}}{\partial\boldsymbol{\beta}\partial\sigma^2} = \frac{1}{2\sigma^4}\mathrm{E}[X'(\mathrm{Y} - X\boldsymbol{\beta})] = \frac{\mathrm{E}X'\boldsymbol{\epsilon}}{2\sigma^4} = \mathbf{0}$$

$$-\mathrm{E}\frac{\partial^2 \ln \mathrm{L}}{\partial\sigma^2} = -\frac{n}{2\sigma^4} + \frac{\mathrm{E}\boldsymbol{\epsilon}'\boldsymbol{\epsilon}}{\sigma^6} = -\frac{n}{2\sigma^4} + \frac{n\sigma^2}{\sigma^6} = \frac{n}{2\sigma^4}$$

In the middle result above, we have used $\mathrm{E}X'\boldsymbol{\epsilon} = X'\mathrm{E}(\boldsymbol{\epsilon}) = \mathbf{0}$, since we have assumed $\mathrm{E}(\epsilon) = \mathbf{0}$. In the last result, we have used $\mathrm{E}\boldsymbol{\epsilon}'\boldsymbol{\epsilon} = \mathrm{E}\Sigma\epsilon_i^2 = n\sigma^2$ since the ϵs have been assumed to have equal variances. Using these last three results and inverting, we have

$$I^{-1}\begin{bmatrix}\boldsymbol{\beta}\\ \sigma^2\end{bmatrix} = \begin{bmatrix}\sigma^2(X'X)^{-1} & \mathbf{0}\\ \mathbf{0} & \dfrac{2\sigma^4}{n}\end{bmatrix} \tag{4.152}$$

We shall show later, from the property of the least-squares estimator of $\boldsymbol{\beta}$, that $\mathrm{V}(\hat{\boldsymbol{\beta}}) = \sigma^2(X'X)^{-1}$, where $\hat{\boldsymbol{\beta}}$ is the ordinary least-squares estimator, the same as the MLE. Thus, for present purposes, the MLE of $\boldsymbol{\beta}$ is also the MVB estimator.

[15] For the time being, assume $\mathrm{E}(\hat{\boldsymbol{\epsilon}}'\hat{\boldsymbol{\epsilon}}) = (n - m - 1)\,\sigma^2$. We shall prove this result when we apply the ordinary least-squares method to the regression model.

Unfortunately, the same cannot be said about the MLE of σ^2. Now we can show[16] that

$$V(\hat{\sigma}^2) = \frac{2(n - m - 1)\sigma^4}{n^2}$$

But the MVB(σ^2) available from the second row, second column entry of the $\boldsymbol{I}^{-1}$ matrix above is $2\sigma^4/n$, which is unequal to (indeed larger than) $V(\hat{\sigma}^2)$.

To illustrate the invariance property of MLE, let us observe that the MLE of σ^2 found before; that is,

$$\hat{\sigma}^2 = \frac{\sum_1^n \hat{\epsilon}_t^2}{n}$$

would imply from

$$g = \sigma = \sqrt{\sigma^2} = g(\sigma^2)$$

that σ will have its MLE:

$$\sqrt{\hat{\sigma}^2} = g(\hat{\sigma}^2)$$

which confirms the invariance property.

4.13 SUGGESTED READINGS

For a more detailed treatment of the various topics of this chapter, the following sources may be consulted: Ezekiel and Fox (1959), Hoel (1962), Graybill (1961), Mood and Graybill (1965), Scheffe (1959), Anderson (1958), and Kendall and Stuart (1961).

PROBLEMS

4-1. Show that, in the context of probability density functions, if $f(y/x) = f(y)$, then $f(x/y) = f(x)$.

4-2. Suppose

$$\mathbf{X} = \begin{bmatrix} X_1 \\ X_2 \\ \vdots \\ X_n \end{bmatrix}$$

[16] Briefly, $\hat{\sigma}^2 = \hat{\boldsymbol{\epsilon}}'\hat{\boldsymbol{\epsilon}}/n = \boldsymbol{\epsilon}'\boldsymbol{M}\boldsymbol{\epsilon}/n$, where $\boldsymbol{M} = \boldsymbol{I} - \boldsymbol{X}(\boldsymbol{X}'\boldsymbol{X})^{-1}\boldsymbol{X}'$ is an idempotent matrix with rank n − m − 1. See Chapter 5, especially 5.4.3. There we show $\hat{\boldsymbol{\epsilon}}'\hat{\boldsymbol{\epsilon}}/\sigma^2$ is distributed as χ^2 with $n - m - 1$ df. Therefore, since $V(\chi^2)$ is twice its degree of freedom ($= n - m - 1$), $V(\hat{\sigma}^2) = \sigma^4 V(\chi^2)/n^2 = [2(n - m - 1)/n^2]\,\sigma^4$. This is less than MVB($\sigma^2$) $= 2\sigma^4/n$.

with $E(\mathbf{X}) = \boldsymbol{\mu}$ and $V(\mathbf{X}) = \boldsymbol{\Sigma}$. If $\mathbf{Z} = \boldsymbol{B}\mathbf{X}$ where $\boldsymbol{B}$ is a nonrandom matrix of size $k \times n$, what is:

(a) $E(\mathbf{Z})$?

(b) $V(\mathbf{Z})$?

4-3. Let **X** be a random vector with

$$E(\mathbf{X}) = \mathbf{0}$$

$$V(\mathbf{X}) = \boldsymbol{I}$$

where $\mathbf{0}$ and $\boldsymbol{I}$ are the null vector and identity matrix, respectively. Let $\mathbf{i} = (1\ 1 \ldots 1)'$ of size $n \times 1$. What are the mean and variance of $\mathbf{i}'\mathbf{X}/n$?

4-4. Let X be a random variable with pdf

$$f(X) = \frac{3X^2}{8} \qquad 0 < X < 2$$

$$= 0 \qquad \text{otherwise}$$

Find:

(a) Probability $(0 < X < \frac{1}{2})$

(b) Probability $(1 < X < 2)$

(c) Probability $(0 < X < \frac{1}{2}$, or, $1 < X < 2)$

(*Hint:* Use the formula: $\int_a^b X^n\, dx = \left.\frac{X^{n+1}}{n+1}\right]_a^b = \frac{b^{n+1} - a^{n+1}}{n+1}$.)

4-5. Consider the following hypothetical data on the joint distribution $f(X, Y)$ of per capita disposable income X (in thousands of dollars) and savings ratio Y, where $f(X, Y)$ are given in proportions and X and Y represent the midpoints of intervals:

Y/X	1.5	2.5	3.5	4.5	5.5	6.5	7.5	8.5	9.5
0.50	.012	.007	.006	.005	.005	.008	.009	.014	.004
.40	.003	.006	.007	.010	.007	.008	.009	.008	.007
.30	.008	.004	.007	.010	.011	.020	.019	.013	.006
.20	.011	.009	.012	.016	.020	.042	.054	.024	.020
.10	.033	.033	.031	.041	.029	.047	.039	.042	.007
0	.026	.000	.002	.001	.000	.000	.000	.000	.000
−.10	.013	.011	.005	.012	.016	.017	.014	.004	.003
−.20	.010	.010	.006	.009	.008	.008	.008	.006	.002
−.30	.018	.093	.006	.009	.007	.005	.003	.002	.003

(a) Calculate

(1) $f(X)$, $f(Y)$, $E(X)$, $E(Y)$, $V(X)$, and $V(Y)$.

(2) $f(Y \mid X)$ for different values of X.

(3) $E(Y \mid X)$. Plot these data.

(4) $V(Y \mid X)$. Plot these data.

(b) Confirm that

$$EY = \sum_X E(Y \mid X)\, f(X)$$

(c) Confirm that

$$V(Y) = \sum_X V(Y \mid X)f(X) + \sum_X [E(Y \mid X) - E(Y)]^2 f(X)$$

4-6. Consider the distribution

$$f(X, Y) = \frac{9}{2} X^{1/2} Y^{1/2} \qquad \text{for } 0 \leqq Y < X < 1$$

$$= 0 \qquad \text{elsewhere}$$

For this distribution:

(a) Confirm that it fulfills the basic requirements for a bivariate probability distribution.

(*Hint:* prove that $f(X, Y) \geqq 0 \quad \int_{-\infty}^{\infty} \int_{-\infty}^{\infty} f(X, Y)\, dX\, dY = 1.$)

(b) What is the chance that:

$$X = 1/3 \qquad \text{and } Y = 1/4?$$

$$X \leqq 1/3 \qquad \text{and } Y \leqq 1/4?$$

(*Hint:* The first is the probability at a point, and the second has the limits for Y and X as $\int_0^{1/4}$ for Y and $\int_{1/4}^{1/3}$ for X.)

(c) Find the marginal pdfs $f(X)$ and $f(Y)$ and confirm that they satisfy the basic conditions of probability distributions.

(*Hint:* For $f(X)$, integrate $f(X, Y)$ over Y from 0 to X, and for $f(Y)$, integrate $f(X, Y)$ over X from Y to 1.)

(d) What is the probability that:

$$X = 1/3?$$

$$1/4 \leqq Y \leqq 3/4?$$

(e) Find the conditional pdfs $f(Y \mid X)$ and $f(X \mid Y)$.

(*Hint:* $f(Y \mid X) = f(X, Y)/f(X)$; similarly the other.)

4-7. In problem 4-5 above, find:

(a) $E(X)$ and $E(Y)$.

(*Hint:* Use $0 < X < 1$ and $0 < Y < 1$ in the first and second case.)

(b) $E(X \mid Y)$ and $E(Y \mid X)$.

(*Hint:* Use $Y < X < 1$ in the first and $0 \leqq Y < X$ in the second case.)

(c) $V(X)$ and $V(Y)$.

(d) $V(X \mid Y)$ and $V(Y \mid X)$.

(e) What is the value of $E(Y \mid X)$ and $V(Y \mid X)$ when $X = 0.60$?

(f) Is Y mean and variance independent of X? Is X mean and variance independent of Y? Why or why not?

4-8. Suppose the vector $\mathbf{X} = (X_1 X_2 \ldots X_n)'$ is the vector of random sample observations from a N(0, 1) population, and $\underline{\mathbf{i}} = [1\ 1 \cdots 1]'$. Show that

(a) $\mathbf{i}'\mathbf{X}/n$ is the sample mean: $\overline{\mathbf{X}} = \Sigma_1^n \mathbf{X}_i/n$.

(b) $\mathbf{X}'A\mathbf{X}/(n - 1)$ is the sample variance:

$$S^2 = \frac{1}{n - 1}\Sigma(\mathbf{X}_i - \overline{\mathbf{X}})^2$$

where $A = I - \mathbf{i}(\mathbf{i}'\mathbf{i})^{-1}\mathbf{i}'$.

(*Note:* A is an idempotent matrix with rank $n - 1$. Verify this.)

(c) $\overline{X} \sim \mathrm{N}(0, 1/n)$.

(d) $\mathrm{E}(S^2) = 1$.

(e) $\overline{X}/\sqrt{(S^2/n)} \sim t_{(n-1)}$ where $t_{(n-1)}$ is Student t with $n - 1$ df.

4-9. Show that if **X** is spherical normal with zero mean and variance σ^2, then the quantity $\mathbf{X}'A\mathbf{X}/\sigma^2$ will be distributed as chi square, where A is an idempotent matrix. Explain how you determine the degrees of freedom of the chi square distribution.

4-10.

(a) Given the random sample

$$\mathbf{X}' = [4 \quad -2 \quad -6 \quad 8]'$$

drawn from a normal population with mean μ and variance σ^2, test the following hypotheses:

$$H_0\colon \mu = 0$$

$$H_1\colon \mu \neq 0$$

(b) How would the test change in (a) if you were given to understand that σ was 1.3? Carry out the test for the same null hypothesis against the alternative hypothesis of (a) under this new knowledge.

4-11.

(a) [4, 3, 6] is a random sample of size 3 on the random variable x. Given that x is normally distributed with unknown mean μ and variance 3, what is the likelihood of the sample?

(b) $\begin{bmatrix} 4 \\ 3 \\ 6 \end{bmatrix}$ is a sample of size 1 on the 3×1 random vector **x**. Given that **x** is normally distributed with unknown mean vector $\boldsymbol{\mu}$ and covariance matrix $3\boldsymbol{I}$ ($\boldsymbol{I}$ being the identity matrix), what is the likelihood of the sample?

4-12. Let us consider a probability density function:

$$f(x) = 5(1 + \alpha)\,x^{4+5\alpha} \quad \text{for } 0 < x < 1, \quad \alpha > 0$$
$$= 0 \quad \text{otherwise}$$

(a) What are $\mathrm{E}(x)$, $\mathrm{E}(x^2)$, and $\mathrm{V}(x)$?

(b) What is the maximum likelihood estimator $\hat{\alpha}$ of α from the random sample of size $n : x_1, x_2, \ldots, x_n$?

(*Hint:* Show that the maximum likelihood estimator is

$$\hat{\alpha} = -1 - \frac{1}{\left\{5\left(\sum_{1}^{n} \ln x_i\right) \Big/ n\right\}}. \quad)$$

(c) What is the asymptotic variance of $\hat{\alpha}$?

(d) By means of the invariance property of maximum likelihood estimators, obtain the maximum likelihood estimator of $\mu = E(x)$.

5

The Linear Model and Ordinary Least Squares (OLS) Method

5.1 INTRODUCTION: AN APPLIED OLS PROBLEM ON INTERNATIONAL PRODUCTION DUE TO DOUGLAS (1948)

We begin by referring to a very important piece of work done by Douglas on a production function of the simple Cobb–Douglas (1928) type. Even though the function is applied to the aggregate economies of the United States, Australia (Victoria and New South Wales) and New Zealand, for present purposes we report on the United States only in order to focus on the central theme of this chapter. Douglas gets four estimates of the United States, all based on different data although for the same period: 1899–1922. The first data set, marked I, includes the inputs L and K, where L stands for the average number of employed wage earners, and K for the value of plants, buildings, tools and machinery (adjusted for investment deflated by a price index averaged over the prices of metals, building materials, and labor). It also includes output V, where V is the original Day index of production. The second data set (II) has the labor input L which includes clerical and salaried staff, and the output V which is the Day–Thomas index of production. The third data set (III) allows for changes in the length of the standard work week to capture more accurately the number of man hours worked. The last data set (IV) has all the three time-series used in the second data set, but each is free of trends.[1] The production function is:

$$Y = AL^{\alpha}K^{\beta}; \qquad \alpha + \beta = 1$$

[1] Douglas believes that production data, based on materials used, perhaps underestimates production in view of the trend of a bias towards more manufactured goods, and the fact that new products only slowly enter into the index. There is a bit of detail concerning the construction of output ratios that go into the Day's index as well as the revised Day–Thomas index. For the first index, see Day and Persons (1920), and Day (1923); for the second, see Day and Thomas (1928).

TABLE 5.1*

		A	α	β	$\alpha + \beta$	N
U.S. I	1899–1922	0.84	0.81 (0.15)	0.23 (0.06)	1.04	24
U.S. II	1899–1922	1.38	0.78 (0.14)	0.15 (0.08)	0.93	24
U.S. III	1899–1922	1.12	0.73 (0.12)	0.25 (0.05)	0.98	24
U.S. IV	1899–1922	1.35	0.63 (0.15)	0.30 (0.05)	0.93	24

* Used with permission. P. Douglas, Table 1, *American Economic Review,* Vol. 38, 1948, p. 12.

which is transformed to a linear relation by logarithmic transformation:

$$\log Y = \log A + \alpha \log L + \beta \log K$$

The OLS estimated coefficients A, α, and β, and N the sample number of observations for the United States are presented in Table 5.1 (figures in parentheses below the coefficients are their estimated standard errors: see (5.35) to appear later). One of Douglas' conclusions from the results in Table 5.1 is that production is subject to constant returns to scale as evident from $\alpha + \beta$ clustering around the value 1. Another is the constancy of the wage share of total income (found to be around 60%, something we have not reported in Table 5.1). And both conclusions are in the spirit of perfect competition.[2]

There are two points of the above analysis that should be carefully noted: (1) A nonlinear functional form (introduced in Section 2.12 of Chapter 2) is transformed to linearity; thus linear functions, by themselves, and as a result of transformation, become an important area for study, and (2) the method of OLS is available for parameter estimation in general (not just simple) linear situations. We shall discuss nonlinear situations extensively later; at the moment we focus on the OLS method including its assumptions, operations, and statistical properties. The model used is a multiple linear regression model.

5.2 THE GENERAL LINEAR MODEL

Let us reconsider the linear multiple regression model of Chapter 1. This has the dependent variable Y, m independent variables, X and β the associated coefficients, and ϵ the error term, n being the number of sample observations:

$$Y_i = \beta_0 + \sum_{j=1}^{m} \beta_j X_{ij} + \epsilon_i \qquad i = 1, 2, \ldots, n \tag{5.1}$$

[2] However, these startling results are more an outcome of poor data than anything else. See Bridge (1971), pp. 354–355, for an explanation of the way the formation of data could provide the deduced empirical results.

This, in matrix notation, becomes

$$\mathbf{Y} = X\boldsymbol{\beta} + \boldsymbol{\epsilon} \tag{5.2}$$

where $\boldsymbol{\epsilon}$, as before, is assumed random, and

$$\mathbf{Y} = \begin{bmatrix} Y_1 \\ Y_2 \\ \vdots \\ Y_n \end{bmatrix} \quad X = \begin{bmatrix} 1 & X_{11} & \cdots & X_{1m} \\ 1 & X_{21} & \cdots & X_{2m} \\ \vdots & \vdots & & \vdots \\ 1 & X_{n1} & \cdots & X_{nm} \end{bmatrix} \quad \boldsymbol{\beta} = \begin{bmatrix} \beta_0 \\ \beta_1 \\ \vdots \\ \beta_m \end{bmatrix} \quad \boldsymbol{\epsilon} = \begin{bmatrix} \epsilon_1 \\ \epsilon_2 \\ \vdots \\ \epsilon_n \end{bmatrix} \tag{5.3}$$

Unless otherwise specified, we shall use 4 sample observations ($n = 4$) and 2 (i.e. $m = 2$) independent variables X_1 and X_2 in addition to the intercept term 1 which gives rise to the column of 1's in the matrix X above. This will considerably simplify the initial exposition.

The coefficients β and parameters of the error (ϵ) distribution are generally unknown and are to be estimated. The simplest assumptions of the estimating model in matrix notation are:

$$\mathrm{E}(\boldsymbol{\epsilon}) = \mathbf{0} \tag{5.4a}$$

$$\mathrm{E}(\boldsymbol{\epsilon\epsilon}') = \sigma^2 \boldsymbol{I_4} \tag{5.4b}$$

$$X : \text{non-stochastic, fixed in repeated samples} \tag{5.4c}$$

$$\mathrm{R}(X) = m + 1 = 3 < n = 4 \tag{5.4d}$$

Assumption (5.4a) has each ϵ_i, $i = 1, 2, 3, 4$, average out to zero, as explained in Chapters 1 and 2. To comprehend (5.4b), write

$$\mathrm{E}(\boldsymbol{\epsilon\epsilon}') = \mathrm{E}\begin{bmatrix} \epsilon_1 \\ \vdots \\ \epsilon_4 \end{bmatrix} [\epsilon_1 \cdots \epsilon_4] = \begin{bmatrix} \mathrm{E}(\epsilon_1^2) & \mathrm{E}(\epsilon_1\epsilon_2) & \cdots & \mathrm{E}(\epsilon_1\epsilon_4) \\ \mathrm{E}(\epsilon_2\epsilon_1) & \mathrm{E}(\epsilon_2^2) & \cdots & \mathrm{E}(\epsilon_2\epsilon_4) \\ \vdots & \vdots & \cdots & \vdots \\ \mathrm{E}(\epsilon_4\epsilon_1) & \mathrm{E}(\epsilon_4\epsilon_2) & \cdots & \mathrm{E}(\epsilon_4^2) \end{bmatrix}$$

$$= \begin{bmatrix} \sigma^2 & 0 & \cdots & 0 \\ 0 & \sigma^2 & \cdots & 0 \\ \vdots & & \cdots & \vdots \\ 0 & 0 & \cdots & \sigma^2 \end{bmatrix} = \sigma^2 \boldsymbol{I_4} \tag{5.5}$$

where $\boldsymbol{I_4}$ is a (4×4) identity matrix. Since the diagonal entries of $\mathrm{E}(\boldsymbol{\epsilon\epsilon}')$ are $\mathrm{E}(\epsilon_i^2)$, $i = 1, 2, 3, 4$, these represent the variances of ϵ_i, all of which are identical to σ^2 and hence the name homoscedasticity. Again since the off-diagonal entries denote the covariances of ϵ_i and ϵ_j, $i, j = 1, 2, 3, 4$, and these are all zeros, the error ϵs are pairwise uncorrelated.

Some general properties of the distribution of the error term were discussed in Chapter 2. These should be reviewed once again. At the risk of repetition, let us reinterpret two of its important properties in the form of answers to the following questions: What do the assumptions of homoscedasticity and independence of errors mean in economic terms, for instance? These mean (1) the distribution of the neglected effects of the model (which together constitute the error) is so stable period after period that its dispersion measured by its variance is invariant through time, and (2) the actions of economic agents with respect to the neglected variables do not carry over from one period to the next, thus generating no overlapping effects through time. Therefore they remain fairly independent period after period. Anyway, these assumptions might be violated in an environment of instability, or common policies followed by economic agents through time.

The next assumption (5.4c) has X fixed. This might arise in controlled experiments. Still it is used at this stage to simplify matters, to be relaxed in Chapter 8. The immediate implication of this is that $\mathbf{Y}$ varies randomly due solely to $\boldsymbol{\epsilon}$, X being fixed. The last assumption (5.4d) is really two-pronged. First it requires that the matrix X has full rank ($= m + 1 = 3$) and, second, the number of observations n ($= 4$, for instance) should be larger than the number of parameters ($m + 1 = 3$, for instance) to be estimated. The full rank of X is required (see results (2) and (4) of Section 3.9 of Chapter 3) because, then, the matrix $X'X$ will have full rank too, in which case it will be invertible. As will follow soon, the parameter estimates will involve $(X'X)^{-1}$. If X, and so $X'X$, has any rank less than the full rank, the column (row) vectors of Xs will be linearly dependent, that is at least one column (row) of this matrix could be obtained as a constant multiple of one other column (row) or by a linear combination of at least two other columns (rows) (see Section 3.4 of Chapter 3). In that case, $X'X$ will not be invertible and thus attempts at estimating the parameters will be unsuccessful.

5.3 ESTIMATION BY OLS

Suppose (5.2) is estimated with $\hat{\boldsymbol{\beta}}$ and $\hat{\boldsymbol{\epsilon}}$ ($= \mathbf{Y} - X\hat{\boldsymbol{\beta}}$) the estimated values of coefficients $\boldsymbol{\beta}$ and residuals $\boldsymbol{\epsilon}$. The estimated form of (5.2) can then be written as

$$\mathbf{Y} = X\hat{\boldsymbol{\beta}} + \hat{\boldsymbol{\epsilon}} \tag{5.6}$$

Thus,

$$\sum_{1}^{4} \hat{\epsilon}_i^2 = \hat{\boldsymbol{\epsilon}}'\hat{\boldsymbol{\epsilon}} = (\mathbf{Y} - X\hat{\boldsymbol{\beta}})'(\mathbf{Y} - X\hat{\boldsymbol{\beta}}) = \mathbf{Y}'\mathbf{Y} - 2\hat{\boldsymbol{\beta}}'X'\mathbf{Y} + \hat{\boldsymbol{\beta}}'X'X\hat{\boldsymbol{\beta}} \qquad (5.7)^3$$

Since the $\hat{\boldsymbol{\beta}}$ are the least-squares estimated solutions, these can be obtained from the solutions of equations $\frac{\partial}{\partial \boldsymbol{\beta}} \hat{\boldsymbol{\epsilon}}'\hat{\boldsymbol{\epsilon}} = \mathbf{0}$, which lead to the normal equations[4]

$$X'X\hat{\boldsymbol{\beta}} = X'\mathbf{Y} \tag{5.8}$$

[3] This follows since $\hat{\boldsymbol{\beta}}'X'\mathbf{Y}$ is equal to its transpose $\mathbf{Y}'X\hat{\boldsymbol{\beta}}$, each being a scalar.

[4] One step before this equation is: $\frac{\partial}{\partial \boldsymbol{\beta}}(\hat{\boldsymbol{\epsilon}}'\hat{\boldsymbol{\epsilon}}) = -2X'\mathbf{Y} + 2X'X\hat{\boldsymbol{\beta}} = \mathbf{0}$ (using results (6) and (7) of Section 3.10 of Chapter 3), which after rearrangement leads to (5.8).

Thus, assuming that $(X'X)^{-1}$ exists, and premultiplying both sides of (5.8) by this, we have the ordinary least squares (OLS) solution for $\boldsymbol{\beta}$ derived as

$$\hat{\boldsymbol{\beta}} = (X'X)^{-1}X'\mathbf{Y} \tag{5.9}$$

To simplify and illustrate the computation, let us take recourse to the two-independent variable case. Then (5.8) reduces to the following:

$$\begin{bmatrix} 4 & \sum X_1 & \sum X_2 \\ \sum X_1 & \sum X_1^2 & \sum X_1X_2 \\ \sum X_2 & \sum X_1X_2 & \sum X_2^2 \end{bmatrix} \begin{bmatrix} \hat{\beta}_0 \\ \hat{\beta}_1 \\ \hat{\beta}_2 \end{bmatrix} = \begin{bmatrix} \sum Y \\ \sum X_1 Y \\ \sum X_2 Y \end{bmatrix}$$

From this, we derive the three normal equations for solving the three coefficients $\hat{\beta}_0$, $\hat{\beta}_1$, and $\hat{\beta}_2$:

$$\sum Y = 4\hat{\beta}_0 + \hat{\beta}_1 \sum X_1 + \hat{\beta}_2 \sum X_2$$

$$\sum X_1 Y = \hat{\beta}_0 \sum X_1 + \hat{\beta}_1 \sum X_1^2 + \hat{\beta}_2 \sum X_1X_2$$

$$\sum X_2 Y = \hat{\beta}_0 \sum X_2 + \hat{\beta}_1 \sum X_1X_2 + \hat{\beta}_2 \sum X_2^2$$

This is the same equation set as (2.61) of Chapter 2.

Change of base. A great deal of simplification in the derivation of the OLS estimates of coefficients can be obtained by making a change in the measurement of variables. We illustrate one such change, called the base change, in which all variables are measured as deviations from their means. With that end in view, we slightly change our notation. We use lower case letters for deviations, namely

$$y_i = Y_i - \overline{Y} \qquad x_{ij} = X_{ij} - \overline{X}_j \qquad i = 1, 2, \ldots, n \qquad j = 1, 2, \ldots, m$$

where $\overline{Y}$ is the sample mean of Y and $\overline{X}_j$ is the sample mean of X_{ij}s ($j = 1, 2, \ldots, m$). The effect of this base change will be to change the model given by (5.1), that is

$$Y_i = \beta_0 + \beta_1 X_{i1} + \cdots + \beta_m X_{im} \tag{5.1}$$

changes to

$$y_i = \beta_1 x_{i1} + \cdots + \beta_m x_{im} \tag{5.10}$$

when the subscript i is for the ith observation. To show this, let us sum and divide by n both sides of the equation (5.1) to get

$$\overline{Y} = \beta_0 + \beta_1 \overline{X}_1 + \cdots + \beta_m \overline{X}_m \tag{5.11}$$

Subtract this from (5.1), side for side, to get:

$$y_i = Y_i - \overline{Y} = \beta_1(X_{i1} - \overline{X}_1) + \cdots + \beta_m(X_{im} - \overline{X}_m)$$

$$= \beta_1 x_{i1} + \cdots + \beta_m x_{im}$$

This is exactly equation (5.10) shown above in the deviation form of the variables. Notice that this equation has all the βs except β_0.

Changing the model equation from the absolute to the deviation form of the variables would naturally change the normal equations given in (5.8) to the following:

$$\mathbf{x}'\mathbf{x}\hat{\boldsymbol{\beta}} = \mathbf{x}'\mathbf{y} \tag{5.12}$$

This is an important transformation of (5.8). In the new form we have eliminated the intercept term of the regression equation which, therefore, will lead to some gain in computational efficiency. However, once the $\hat{\boldsymbol{\beta}}$ are computed by solving (5.12), we can plug them back into (5.11) to recover $\hat{\beta}_0$:

$$\hat{\beta}_0 = \overline{Y} - \hat{\beta}_1\overline{X}_1 - \hat{\beta}_2\overline{X}_2 - \cdots - \hat{\beta}_m\overline{X}_m \tag{5.13}$$

A problem (Problem 1). Suppose that $\sum x_1^2 = 50.5$, $\sum x_2^2 = 967.1$, $\sum x_1x_2 = -66.2$ and $\sum x_1y = 36.8$, $\sum x_2y = 39.1$, and $\overline{X}_1 = 5.8$, $\overline{X}_2 = 5.9$, and $\overline{Y} = 3.9$. These are the results derived from a cost study of 98 firms where Y is cost and X_1 and X_2 are the rate of output and rate of absenteeism, respectively, and the lower case letters y, x_j for $j = 1$ and 2 are the same variables as these but in their deviation form. That is

$$y = Y - \overline{Y}$$
$$x_j = X_j - \overline{X}_j \qquad j = 1 \text{ and } 2$$

Then from (5.12) and (5.13) we have the following solution of the coefficients of the regression of Y on X_1 and X_2:

$$\hat{\beta}_0 = \overline{Y} - \hat{\beta}_1\overline{X}_1 - \hat{\beta}_2\overline{X}_2 = 5.92 \tag{5.14}$$

$$\begin{bmatrix}\hat{\beta}_1\\ \hat{\beta}_2\end{bmatrix} = \frac{\begin{bmatrix}\sum x_2^2 & -\sum x_1x_2\\ -\sum x_1x_2 & \sum x_1^2\end{bmatrix}\begin{bmatrix}\sum x_1y\\ \sum x_2y\end{bmatrix}}{\sum x_1^2\sum x_2^2 - (\sum x_1x_2)^2} = \begin{bmatrix}0.859\\ 0.099\end{bmatrix}$$

We will revert to this problem later in connection with the statistical properties of estimates.

5.4 STATISTICAL INFERENCE IN THE LINEAR MODEL

Two desirable properties of a linear estimator are that it is unbiased and that it is the best in the sense of its having the minimum variance or maximum efficiency among alternative estimators. To show that the OLS estimate is unbiased, write

$$\hat{\boldsymbol{\beta}} = (X'X)^{-1}X'(X\boldsymbol{\beta} + \boldsymbol{\epsilon}) = \boldsymbol{\beta} + (X'X)^{-1}X'\boldsymbol{\epsilon} \tag{5.15}$$[5]

[5] The complicated looking expression for $\hat{\boldsymbol{\beta}}$ should not obscure the fact that it is a linear estimator. This is so because the coefficient of $\mathbf{Y}$, that is $(X'X)^{-1}X'$, is nonstochastic which would make $\hat{\boldsymbol{\beta}}$ a linear function of the random variable $\mathbf{Y}$. Later on (in Chapter 8), as X also becomes stochastic, the least-squares estimate will be a nonlinear function of random variables.

after substituting $X\boldsymbol{\beta} + \boldsymbol{\epsilon}$ for $\mathbf{Y}$ in the right-hand side of (5.8). Then since X and $\boldsymbol{\beta}$ are fixed, and $E(\boldsymbol{\epsilon}) = \mathbf{0}$, we have

$$E(\hat{\boldsymbol{\beta}}) = \boldsymbol{\beta} + (X'X)^{-1}E(\boldsymbol{\epsilon}) = \boldsymbol{\beta} \tag{5.16}$$

This proves that $\hat{\boldsymbol{\beta}}$ is unbiased. To prove that it is the best (which is essentially the Gauss–Markov theorem), find out its variance and covariance matrix. Using (5.15), this matrix is

$$\begin{aligned} V(\hat{\boldsymbol{\beta}}) &= E(\hat{\boldsymbol{\beta}} - \boldsymbol{\beta})(\hat{\boldsymbol{\beta}} - \boldsymbol{\beta})' = E(X'X)^{-1}X'\boldsymbol{\epsilon\epsilon}'X(X'X)^{-1} \\ &= (X'X)^{-1}X'E(\boldsymbol{\epsilon\epsilon}')X(X'X)^{-1} = \sigma^2(X'X)^{-1} \end{aligned} \tag{5.17}$$

where we have noted that $E(\boldsymbol{\epsilon\epsilon}') = \sigma^2 I$ and, further, the expectation operator E is effective on the random variable $\boldsymbol{\epsilon\epsilon}'$ only, since X is fixed.

Consider a new linear estimator $\hat{\hat{\boldsymbol{\beta}}}$ constructed from $\boldsymbol{\beta}$ through the augmented term $P'\mathbf{Y}$, where P', a fixed matrix, is of size $(m + 1) \times n$:

$$\hat{\hat{\boldsymbol{\beta}}} = \{(X'X)^{-1}X' + P'\}\mathbf{Y} = \hat{\boldsymbol{\beta}} + P'\mathbf{Y} \tag{5.18}$$

The middle expression clearly shows an augmentation in the coefficient of $\mathbf{Y}$. For $\hat{\hat{\boldsymbol{\beta}}}$ to be unbiased, we must have $P'X = \mathbf{0}$.[6] Thus, the variance-covariance matrix of $\hat{\hat{\boldsymbol{\beta}}}$ is

$$\begin{aligned} V(\hat{\hat{\boldsymbol{\beta}}}) &= \sigma^2\{[(X'X)^{-1}X' + P'][(X'X)^{-1}X' + P']'\} \\ &= \sigma^2[(X'X)^{-1} + P'P] = V(\hat{\boldsymbol{\beta}}) + \sigma^2 P'P \end{aligned} \tag{5.19}$$

The second line of the expression above is greatly simplified because two of its other terms become zero from their vanishing multiplicative factors $P'X$ and $X'P$. Since $P'P$ in (5.19) is a semipositive definite matrix,[7] so will be $V(\hat{\hat{\boldsymbol{\beta}}}) - V(\hat{\boldsymbol{\beta}})$; and since $\hat{\hat{\boldsymbol{\beta}}}$ is *any other* rival estimator it will have at least as large a variance as $\hat{\boldsymbol{\beta}}$. In other words, $\hat{\boldsymbol{\beta}}$ is the best or minimum variance estimator of $\boldsymbol{\beta}$. This is the essence of the Gauss–Markov theorem applied to the classical model.

Thus the least-squares estimator $\hat{\boldsymbol{\beta}}$ is the best linear unbiased estimate (BLUE).

5.4.1 Analysis of Variance and the F Test

Based on the least squares estimate $\hat{\boldsymbol{\beta}}$, the estimated or calculated value of $\mathbf{Y}$, denoted as $\hat{\mathbf{Y}}$, is given by

$$\hat{\mathbf{Y}} = X\hat{\boldsymbol{\beta}} \tag{5.20}$$

This gives the estimated error $\hat{\boldsymbol{\epsilon}}$ as

$$\hat{\boldsymbol{\epsilon}} = \mathbf{Y} - \hat{\mathbf{Y}} \tag{5.21}$$

[6] Since $E(\hat{\hat{\boldsymbol{\beta}}}) = E(\hat{\boldsymbol{\beta}}) + P'E(X\boldsymbol{\beta} + \boldsymbol{\epsilon}) = \boldsymbol{\beta} + P'X\boldsymbol{\beta} + \mathbf{0} = \boldsymbol{\beta} \Rightarrow P'X = \mathbf{0}$.

[7] See result (4), Section 3.9, Chapter 3. Equate P' to the matrix A used in that result, and make appropriate changes in the size of A in line with that of P'.

TABLE 5.2

Variation due to	Degrees of Freedom	Sum of Squares	Mean Sum of Squares	F Calculated
Regression	m	$\sum(\hat{Y}_i - \overline{Y})^2$	$\text{MSR} = \sum(\hat{Y}_i - \overline{Y})^2/m$	$\dfrac{\text{MSR}}{\text{MSE}}$
Error	$n - m - 1$	$\sum(Y_i - \hat{Y}_i)^2$	$\text{MSE} = \sum(Y_i - \hat{Y}_i)^2/n - m - 1$	
Total	$n - 1$	$\sum(Y_i - \overline{Y})^2$		

Since the means of $\hat{\mathbf{Y}}$ and $\mathbf{Y}$, denoted by $\overline{\hat{Y}}$ and $\overline{Y}$, respectively, are identical,[8] and X and $\hat{\boldsymbol{\epsilon}}$ are orthogonal,[9] we can decompose the total sum of squares (TSS) into the sum of squares due to regression (RSS) and sum of squares due to error (ESS) as follows

$$\sum (Y_i - \overline{Y})^2 = \sum (Y_i - \hat{Y}_i)^2 + \sum (\hat{Y}_i - \overline{Y})^2 \tag{5.22}$$

(that is TSS = RSS + ESS). In (5.22) the crossproduct term $2 \sum (Y_i - \hat{Y}_i)(\hat{Y}_i - \overline{Y})$ vanishes because, using (5.21), $\overline{Y} = \overline{\hat{Y}}$ from footnote 8, and so $\sum_i \hat{\epsilon}_i = 0$, we have

$$\begin{aligned} 2 \sum (Y_i - \hat{Y}_i)(\hat{Y}_i - \overline{Y}) &= 2 \sum \hat{\epsilon}_i(\hat{Y}_i - \overline{\hat{Y}}) \\ &= 2 \sum_j \beta_j \sum_i \hat{\epsilon}_i X_{ij} - \overline{\hat{Y}} \sum_i \hat{\epsilon}_i \\ &= 0 \end{aligned}$$

the term involving $\sum_i \hat{\epsilon}_i X_{ij}$ vanishing in view of the orthogonality of X and $\hat{\boldsymbol{\epsilon}}$.

Thus the analysis of variance table, following the conceptual introduction of Section 2.7 of Chapter 2, becomes that of Table 5.2.

In Table 5.2 MSR and MSE are the mean sum of squares due to regression and error, respectively. Division of MSR by MSE yields the calculated value of the F-statistic. It has two kinds of degrees of freedom, for example m and $n - m - 1$, the former due to its numerator, or the regression (arising from the m regressors excepting the intercept), and the latter due to its denominator, or the

[8] This is so because the first normal equation gives $\mathbf{X}_0' X\hat{\boldsymbol{\beta}} = \mathbf{X}_0'\mathbf{Y}$, where $\mathbf{X}_0$ is the first column vector of the observation matrix X. Using this and also premultiplying both sides of $\hat{\mathbf{Y}} = X\hat{\boldsymbol{\beta}}$ by $\mathbf{X}_0'$, we get

$$\mathbf{X}_0'\hat{\mathbf{Y}} = \mathbf{X}_0' X\hat{\boldsymbol{\beta}} = \mathbf{X}_0'\mathbf{Y}$$

Since $\mathbf{X}_0' = [1 \quad 1 \ldots 1]$, the above yields $\sum \hat{Y}_i = \sum Y_i$, from which, dividing both sides by n, we have $\overline{\hat{Y}} = \overline{Y}$.

[9] Premultiplying $\hat{\boldsymbol{\epsilon}} = \mathbf{Y} - \hat{\mathbf{Y}}$ by X', we get $X'\hat{\boldsymbol{\epsilon}} = X'\hat{\mathbf{Y}} - X'\mathbf{Y} = X'\mathbf{Y} - X'X\hat{\boldsymbol{\beta}} = \mathbf{0}$ following from the normal equations $X'X\hat{\boldsymbol{\beta}} - X'\mathbf{Y} = \mathbf{0}$. Thus X and $\hat{\boldsymbol{\epsilon}}$ are orthogonal.

error sum of squares. The usual procedure is to compare this value with the tabulated or theoretical value of F at a given probability level (say 5%, 1%, etc.) of significance (see Appendix B, Table B.4). If the calculated value of F is less (greater) than its theoretical value, the null hypothesis of insignificant regression cannot be refuted (accepted) at that probability level of significance.

For computational efficiency, expressions for the two sums of squares can be simplified as follows. Since $\hat{\mathbf{Y}} = X\hat{\boldsymbol{\beta}}$ and $\overline{Y} = \overline{\hat{Y}} = \overline{\mathbf{X}}\hat{\boldsymbol{\beta}}$, where $\overline{\mathbf{X}} = [\overline{\mathrm{X}}_0 \ \overline{\mathrm{X}}_1 \cdots \overline{\mathrm{X}}_m]'$, so

$$\sum (\hat{Y}_i - \overline{Y})^2 = (\hat{\mathbf{Y}} - \overline{\hat{\mathbf{Y}}})'(\hat{\mathbf{Y}} - \overline{\hat{\mathbf{Y}}}) = \hat{\boldsymbol{\beta}}'(X - \overline{X})(X - \overline{X})'\hat{\boldsymbol{\beta}}$$

$$= \hat{\boldsymbol{\beta}}'\mathbf{x}'\mathbf{y} = \sum_{j=1}^{m} \hat{\beta}_j \sum_{i=1}^{n} x_{ij} y_i \qquad (5.23)$$

Above, we have used variables in their deviation form:

$$x_{ij} = X_{ij} - \overline{X}_j, \qquad y_i = Y_i - \overline{Y} \qquad i = 1, \ldots, n \quad j = 1, \ldots, m$$

And normal equations are expressed in the deviation form of the variables:[10]

$$\mathbf{x}'\mathbf{x}\hat{\boldsymbol{\beta}} = \mathbf{x}'\mathbf{y}$$

Thus the ESS is:

$$\mathrm{ESS} = \sum (Y - \hat{Y})^2 = \sum y_i^2 - \sum_{j=1}^{m} \hat{\beta}_j \sum_{i=1}^{n} x_{ij} y_i \qquad (5.24)$$

5.4.2 Goodness of Fit

One may be curious to know how good the least-squares fit is. With that end in view, we compute, as we did in Chapter 1, what is known as the coefficient of multiple determination R^2, a measure of descriptive statistics, defined as:

$$R^2 = \frac{\mathrm{RSS}}{\mathrm{TSS}} = \frac{\sum (\hat{Y} - \overline{Y})^2}{\sum (Y - \overline{Y})^2} \qquad (5.25a)$$

$$= 1 - \frac{\mathrm{ESS}}{\mathrm{TSS}} = 1 - \frac{\sum (Y - \hat{Y})^2}{\sum (Y - \overline{Y})^2} \qquad (5.25b)$$

From the above, it should be clear that R^2 varies between 0 and 1. It is zero when $\hat{Y} = \overline{Y}$ (equation (5.25a)), that is the regression line is a perfectly flat line without any slope whatsoever. It is one when $Y = \hat{Y}$ (equation (5.25b)), that is every actual observation on Y coincides with its corresponding observation on the regression line. In other words, the fit is perfect.

Looking at (5.25) it is clear that R^2 does not address the question of degrees

[10] See equation (5.12) derived before.

of freedom and that there is room for adjusting the value of R^2 based on the respective degrees of freedom of the RSS and ESS. Suppose that this adjustment has been made. Then we would end up with the following definition of what is known as the adjusted coefficient of multiple determinations, $\bar{R}^2$:

$$\bar{R}^2 = 1 - \frac{\text{ESS}/n - m - 1}{\text{RSS}/n - 1} = 1 - \frac{n - 1}{n - m - 1}(1 - R^2) \tag{5.26}$$

The effect of the degrees of freedom on $\bar{R}^2$ is as follows. As m goes up $n - 1/(n - m - 1)$ (suppose we call this the degree of freedom factor) goes up too, but $1 - R^2$ (the information factor) falls, provided the new variable proves to be informative about Y. From the opposite nature of these two factors it follows that when the information factor is falling, it has to fall enough to offset the rise in value of the degree of freedom factor (and so m) before $\bar{R}^2$ would rise. This implies one should sparingly increase m; in other words, one should be scrupulous about the choice of regressors. Too many of these regressors may be too expensive in the sense of lost information paradoxically caused by them. Thus the $\bar{R}^2$ coefficient has associated with it a penalty for any irresponsible enlargement of the number of regressors.

5.4.3 Tests of Hypotheses

Just as the information from the analysis of variance table may be used to ascertain whether the entire regression is meaningful for Y, so also information from piecemeal tests may be used to infer about a part, or parts, of that regression. For instance, we may inquire whether one particular β coefficient, or more than one β coefficient for that matter, is significantly different from zero. The test of one coefficient will be covered below, that involving more than one coefficient will be taken up in the course of tests of constraints on coefficients to be discussed later. Notice, however, that (unless otherwise stated) for the following tests and predictions, we will not only assume that the ϵ are random, but also they are normal with zero mean and variance σ^2.

A test of this sort is performed by means of a statistic, say $\hat{\beta}_i$, the OLS estimate of the ith parameter β_i. Should σ be known, the criterion $[\hat{\beta}_i - \beta_i]/\sigma\sqrt{s^{ii}}$, where s^{ii} is the $(i + 1, i + 1)$ element of the $(X'X)^{-1}$ matrix, would be distributed as a standard normal[11] variable given that, as already mentioned, ϵ is not only random but also a normal variable. However, if σ be not known, it is to be estimated from the sample. In that case it can be shown that $(\hat{\beta}_i -$

[11] Since $\hat{\beta}_i - \beta_i \leftarrow (X'X)^{-1}X'\boldsymbol{\epsilon}$, $E(\hat{\beta}_i - \beta_i) = 0$ in view of $E(\boldsymbol{\epsilon}) = \mathbf{0}$ and X being fixed. Also, since $\sqrt{V(\hat{\beta}_i)} = \sigma\sqrt{s^{ii}}$ using (5.17) and $\hat{\beta}_i - \beta_i$ is a linear combination of normal variables ϵ_i with $E(\epsilon_i) = 0$ and $V(\epsilon_i) = \sigma^2$ for all i $(i = 1, \ldots, n)$, $(\hat{\beta}_i - \beta)/\sigma\sqrt{s^{ii}}$ is a standard normal variable, that is a normal variable with mean zero and variance unity. For this and other results following, the reader should review Section 2.4, 2.6 and 2.8 of Chapter 2 and Sections 4.7 and 4.8 of Chapter 4.

$\beta_i)/\hat{\sigma}\sqrt{s^{ii}}$, where $\hat{\sigma}$ is the estimate[12] of σ, is distributed as Student t with $n - m - 1$ df, the same as that of the MSE. Notice that $\hat{\sigma}$ is defined here equal to the square root of the MSE, where MSE is the mean sum of squares due to error used in the preceding analysis of variance table. In what follows we will develop the arguments step-by-step for the use of the t test.

Estimate of σ^2. From (5.21), (5.20), (5.2) and (5.9),

$$\begin{aligned}\hat{\boldsymbol{\epsilon}} &= \mathbf{Y} - \hat{\mathbf{Y}} = \mathbf{Y} - X\hat{\boldsymbol{\beta}} = X\boldsymbol{\beta} + \boldsymbol{\epsilon} - X(X'X)^{-1}X'(X\boldsymbol{\beta} + \boldsymbol{\epsilon}) \\ &= \boldsymbol{\epsilon} - X(X'X)^{-1}X'\boldsymbol{\epsilon} = [I_n - X(X'X)^{-1}X']\boldsymbol{\epsilon} = M\boldsymbol{\epsilon}\end{aligned} \tag{5.27}$$

where M is an idempotent matrix: $I_n - X(X'X)^{-1}X'$ and I_n an identity matrix of size n. The sum of squares due to error, given by $\sum(Y_i - \hat{Y}_i)^2$ or $\sum \hat{\epsilon}_i^2$ can be expressed as:

$$\sum \hat{\epsilon}_i^2 = \hat{\boldsymbol{\epsilon}}'\hat{\boldsymbol{\epsilon}} = \boldsymbol{\epsilon}'M'M\boldsymbol{\epsilon} = \boldsymbol{\epsilon}'M\boldsymbol{\epsilon} \tag{5.28}$$

Thus,

$$\begin{aligned}\mathrm{E}(\textstyle\sum \hat{\epsilon}_i^2) &= \mathrm{E}(\boldsymbol{\epsilon}'M\boldsymbol{\epsilon}) = \mathrm{E}\ \mathrm{Tr}(\boldsymbol{\epsilon}'M\boldsymbol{\epsilon}) = \mathrm{E}\ \mathrm{Tr}\ M\boldsymbol{\epsilon}\boldsymbol{\epsilon}' = \mathrm{Tr}\ \mathrm{E}(M\boldsymbol{\epsilon}\boldsymbol{\epsilon}') \\ &= \mathrm{Tr}\ M\mathrm{E}(\boldsymbol{\epsilon}\boldsymbol{\epsilon}') = \mathrm{Tr}\ M\sigma^2 I_n = \sigma^2\ \mathrm{Tr}\ M\end{aligned} \tag{5.29}$$

In the above we have used a few considerations. First, $\boldsymbol{\epsilon}'M\boldsymbol{\epsilon}$ being a scalar, its trace is equal to itself. Second, from (3.15) of Chapter 3, Tr (AB) = Tr (BA), where A and B are any well defined matrices. Third, trace being a linear function, E Tr( ) = Tr E( ); and last, M being nonstochastic, it is not affected by the operator E. Now it can be shown that[13]

$$\mathrm{Tr}\ M = n - (m + 1)$$

Thus,

$$\mathrm{E} \sum \hat{\epsilon}_i^2 = \sigma^2(n - m - 1) \tag{5.30}$$

which leads to

$$\mathrm{E}\ \frac{\sum \hat{\epsilon}_i^2}{n - m - 1} = \mathrm{E(MSE)} = \sigma^2 \tag{5.31}$$

Therefore the MSE is unbiased for σ^2. Hence $\hat{\sigma} = \sqrt{\mathrm{MSE}}$ where $\sigma^2 = \sum \hat{\epsilon}_i^2/n - m - 1$, something we have hinted at before.

Distribution of $\hat{\sigma}^2$ or the MSE. Assuming that $\boldsymbol{\epsilon}$ is $N(\mathbf{0}, \sigma^2 I_n)$, it follows from (4.119) of Chapter 4 that $\sum \hat{\epsilon}_i^2$ which, from (5.28), is $\boldsymbol{\epsilon}'M\boldsymbol{\epsilon}$ is distributed as

[12] Notice that we are using $\hat{\sigma}$ in place of S of Chapter 2. This is in order not to mix up S with s of s^{ii} of this chapter. However, as we have done in other chapters, S is generally used for the square root of the MSE.

[13] $\mathrm{Tr}\ M = \mathrm{Tr}(I_n) - \mathrm{Tr}\ X(X'X)^{-1}X' = \mathrm{Tr}(I_n) - \mathrm{Tr}[X'X(X'X)^{-1}] = \mathrm{Tr}\ I_n - \mathrm{Tr}\ I_{m+1} = n - (m + 1)$, since $\mathrm{Tr}(I_n) = n$ and $\mathrm{Tr}(I_{m+1}) = m + 1$. For the definition and properties of an idempotent matrix, see Section 3.2.2 of Chapter 3.

$\chi^2\sigma^2$ with degrees of freedom equal to the rank of the intervening idempotent matrix $\boldsymbol{M}$. We have already seen this rank to be $n - m - 1$. Thus, $\sum \hat{\epsilon}_i^2/\sigma^2(n - m - 1)$ is distributed as $\chi^2/(n - m - 1)$.

The t test for single coefficients. We have also seen that $(\hat{\beta}_i - \beta_i)/\sigma\sqrt{s^{ii}}$ is N(0, 1). Now since the Student t is defined fundamentally (see Section 4.7.5 of Chapter 4) as the ratio of a standard normal variable to the square root of χ^2 per degree of freedom, that is

$$t = \frac{\mathrm{N}(0, 1)}{\sqrt{\chi^2/\mathrm{df}}} \tag{5.32}$$

where df is the degree of freedom of χ^2, the expression for t used to test a given value of β_i becomes

$$t = \frac{\hat{\beta}_i - \beta_i}{\sigma\sqrt{s^{ii}}}\left[\frac{\sum \hat{\epsilon}_i^2}{\sigma^2(n - m - 1)}\right]^{-\frac{1}{2}} = \frac{\hat{\beta}_i - \beta_i}{\hat{\sigma}\sqrt{s^{ii}}} \tag{5.33}$$

where $\hat{\sigma}^2 = \sum \hat{\epsilon}_i^2/(n - m - 1)$. It is based on $n - m - 1$ df. The above expression can be further simplified to:

$$t = (\hat{\beta}_i - \beta_i)/\hat{\sigma}_{\hat{\beta}_i} \tag{5.34}$$

where $\hat{\sigma}_{\hat{\beta}_i}$ is the estimated standard error of estimate $\hat{\beta}_i$ given by:

$$\hat{\sigma}^2_{\hat{\beta}_i} = \hat{\sigma}^2 s^{ii} \tag{5.35}$$

In Table 5.1, the figures in brackets given below the estimated coefficients are their estimated standard error $\hat{\sigma}^2_{\hat{\beta}_i}$.

In future tests of hypothesis involving βs or linear functions of βs, we shall make straightforward applications of the t test given in (5.33), provided that its basic conditions are fulfilled.

5.4.4 *Problem 1* (Continued)

We will now illustrate the calculation underlying the various formulas derived above with respect to the data of Problem 1, introduced before. Suppose that:

$$\sum (Y_i - \overline{Y})^2 = \sum y_i^2 = 113.6.$$

Then the analysis of variance is calculated as in Table 5.3. Since the calculated

TABLE 5.3

Source	Sum of Squares	df	Mean Sum of Squares	F Calculated	Theoretical 1%
Regression	35.48	2	17.74	21.63	4.9
Error	78.12	95	.84		
Total	113.60	97			

F is greater than its theoretical value at a probability level of 1% (one-tailed test), the overall regression is significant at that level. How are the partial effects of X_1 and X_2? For these, we perform the t test. Its ingredients are:

$$\hat{\sigma} = \sqrt{\text{MSE}} = 0.9055$$

$$(s^{ii}) = \begin{pmatrix} s^{11} & s^{12} \\ s^{21} & s^{22} \end{pmatrix} = (X'X)^{-1} = \begin{pmatrix} 0.021754 & 0.001489 \\ 0.001489 & 0.001136 \end{pmatrix}$$

$$s^{11} = 0.021754$$

$$s^{22} = 0.001136$$

$$\hat{\sigma}_{\hat{\beta}_1} = \sqrt{\hat{\sigma}^2 s^{11}} = 0.13356$$

$$\hat{\sigma}_{\hat{\beta}_2} = \sqrt{\hat{\sigma}^2 s^{22}} = 0.03052 \qquad \text{(from (5.35))}$$

(Incidentally, the estimated covariance between $\hat{\beta}_1$ and $\hat{\beta}_2$ is $\hat{\sigma} s^{12} = 0.82 \times 0.001489 = 0.00122$.) Thus:

For hypothesis[14]:

$$\beta_1 = 0$$

$$t = \frac{\hat{\beta}_1 - 0}{\hat{\sigma}\sqrt{s^{11}}} = 6.43 \qquad \text{(significant at 1 and 5 percent levels)}$$

For hypothesis:

$$\beta_2 = 0$$

$$t = \frac{\hat{\beta}_2 - 0}{\hat{\sigma}\sqrt{s^{22}}} = 3.24 \qquad \text{(significant at both levels)}$$

The 5% confidence interval for β_i (i = 1 and 2) is:

$$\text{Probability } \{\hat{\beta}_i - t_{0.025}\, \hat{\sigma}\sqrt{s^{11}} < \beta_i < \hat{\beta}_i + t_{0.025}\, \hat{\sigma}\sqrt{s^{ii}}\} = 0.95$$

For β_1, these limits are 0.597 and 1.121 and, for β_2, they are -0.163 and 0.361 based on a two-tailed 5% probability point of t at 95 df (equal to approximately 1.99). It is interesting to note that, in some examples such as the present one, the rate of absenteeism X_2 could have a negative effect (indicated by a negative value of β_2) on cost Y. Clearly it would mean that at some level of output, labor, which generally is indispensable, would start to become dispensable and at that level, the greater the absenteeism, the greater the saving in costs.

[14] Even though we are testing $\beta = 0$, this need not always be the case. We may test any value of β for that matter.

5.5 FORECASTING

The multiple regression model is an excellent base from which to make predictions for future values of Y. Depending on what one does, one may be predicting either the mean of observations, or just one observation on Y at a future date. These two problems will be dealt with now.

5.5.1 Forecasting The Mean Value of Future Observations on Y

For predicting the mean at time,[15] say T, which lies beyond the time point n, consider the observation (row) vector at that point to be

$$\mathbf{X}_\mathbf{T}' = [1, X_{T1}, X_{T2}, \ldots, X_{Tm}] \tag{5.36}$$

Then, the value of Y at time T is related to $\mathbf{X}_\mathbf{T}$ through error ϵ_T as

$$Y_T = \mathbf{X}_\mathbf{T}'\boldsymbol{\beta} + \epsilon_T \tag{5.37}$$

whose mean is $\mathrm{E}(Y_T) = \mathbf{X}_\mathbf{T}'\boldsymbol{\beta}$.

Since the unbiased minimum variance estimate[16] of $\mathrm{E}(Y_T)$ is $\hat{Y}_T$ where

$$\hat{Y}_T = \mathbf{X}_\mathbf{T}'\hat{\boldsymbol{\beta}} = \hat{\beta}_0 + \hat{\beta}_1\mathrm{X}_{T,1} + \cdots + \hat{\beta}_m\mathrm{X}_{T,m} \tag{5.38}$$

$\hat{Y}_T$ is suggested as the forecast of $\mathrm{E}(Y_T)$. For testing the significance of values of the mean, we need to compute the mean and variance of $\hat{Y}_T$:

$$\mathrm{E}(\hat{Y}_T) = \mathbf{X}_\mathbf{T}'\boldsymbol{\beta} = \mathrm{E}(Y_T) \tag{5.39}$$

$$\mathrm{V}(\hat{Y}_T) = \sigma^2\mathbf{X}_\mathbf{T}'(X'X)^{-1}\mathbf{X}_\mathbf{T} \tag{5.40}$$

Given the usual normality assumption for ϵ, we have seen

$$\hat{\beta}_i \sim \mathrm{N}(\beta_i, \sigma^2 s^{ii}) \tag{5.41}$$

Thus a linear combination of $\hat{\beta}_i$ such as $\hat{Y}_T(= \mathbf{X}_\mathbf{T}'\hat{\boldsymbol{\beta}})$ is normally distributed:

$$\hat{Y}_T \sim \mathrm{N}(\mathbf{X}_\mathbf{T}'\boldsymbol{\beta}, \sigma^2\mathbf{X}_\mathbf{T}'(X'X)^{-1}\mathbf{X}_\mathbf{T}) \tag{5.42}$$

from which, in recognition of the arguments underlying (5.33), it follows that

$$t = \frac{\mathbf{X}_\mathbf{T}'\boldsymbol{\beta} - \mathbf{X}_\mathbf{T}'\hat{\boldsymbol{\beta}}}{\hat{\sigma}\sqrt{\mathbf{X}_\mathbf{T}'(X'X)^{-1}\mathbf{X}_\mathbf{T}}} \qquad \mathrm{df} = n - m - 1 \tag{5.43}$$

where

$$\hat{\sigma} = \sqrt{\mathrm{MSE}} \tag{5.44}$$

[15] We have used the symbol e for T in Chapter 2.

[16] It can be shown, using the unbiased and minimum variance property of least-squares estimates, that any linear combination of such estimates will retain these properties with respect to the corresponding linear combination of parameters.

Problem 1 (continued): t Test. Suppose that $\mathbf{X}'_\mathbf{T} = (1, 5.1, 3.5)$ which becomes $\mathbf{x}'_\mathbf{T} = (-0.7, 0.6)$ after the variables are corrected for their means, that is they are expressed as deviations from their means. Then, assuming that $\mathbf{X}'_\mathbf{T}\boldsymbol{\beta}$, under the null hypothesis, is equal to 1, t becomes

$$t = \frac{1.000 + 0.5419}{0.9055\sqrt{0.0981766}} = \frac{1.5419}{(0.9055)(0.313)} = \frac{1.5419}{0.283693} = 5.44 \qquad (\text{df} = 95)$$

Here we have used the deviation form of the variables in the matrix $(X'X)^{-1}$ and its value as calculated in Section 5.4.4. The calculated numerical value of t is clearly significant at both the 1% and 5% probability levels of significance. This means that the statistical evidence is at variance with the hypothetical value of $E(Y_T)$ to be equal to 1.

A confidence interval for $E(Y_T)$ with, say, 0.95 confidence coefficient is

$$\mathbf{X}'_\mathbf{T}\hat{\boldsymbol{\beta}} \pm t_{0.025}\hat{\sigma}[\mathbf{X}'_\mathbf{T}(X'X)^{-1}\mathbf{X}_\mathbf{T}]^{\frac{1}{2}} \tag{5.45}$$

Problem 1 (continued): Confidence interval. For this problem, these limits are $-0.5419 \pm 1.99(0.2836)$, or -1.1063 and $+0.0224$, which means that the actual future mean value of Y will be covered by this confidence interval 95% of the times.

In the case of one regressor, the confidence interval reduces[17] to:

$$[\hat{\beta}_0 + \hat{\beta}_1 X_T] \pm t_{0.005}\hat{\sigma}\left[\frac{1}{n} + \frac{(X_T - \overline{X})^2}{\sum (X_i - \overline{X})^2}\right]^{1/2} \tag{5.46}$$

This is the same as (2.58) in Chapter 2 equating $\hat{\sigma}$ to S, T to e, and $\hat{Y}_e$ to $\hat{\beta}_0 + \hat{\beta}_1 X_T$ (see footnotes 12 and 15).

5.5.2 Forecasting One Single Future Observation on Y

On the other hand, for predicting one individual value Y_T at time T, we actually observe

$$Y_T = \mathbf{X}'_\mathbf{T}\boldsymbol{\beta} + \epsilon_T \tag{5.47}$$

[17] For, with the model

$$Y_i = \beta_0 + \beta_1 X_i + \epsilon_i$$

$$(X'X) = \begin{bmatrix} n & \sum X_i \\ \sum X_i & \sum X_i^2 \end{bmatrix} \qquad \mathbf{X}'_\mathbf{T} = [1 \quad X_T]$$

so

$$\mathbf{X}'_\mathbf{T}(X'X)^{-1}\mathbf{X}_\mathbf{T} = \frac{\sum X_i^2 - 2X_T \sum X + nX_T^2}{\sum (X_i - \overline{X})^2} = \frac{1}{n} + \frac{(X_T - \overline{X})^2}{\sum (X_i - \overline{X})^2}$$

The rest of the computation is simple and straightforward.

and the forecast $\hat{Y}_T$ would generate the forecast error e as the difference between $\hat{Y}_T$ and Y_T:

$$e = Y_T - \hat{Y}_T = -\mathbf{X}_\mathbf{T}'(\hat{\boldsymbol{\beta}} + \boldsymbol{\beta}) - \epsilon_T \tag{5.48}$$

Since

$$\mathrm{E}(e) = 0 \; (\mathrm{E}(\hat{\boldsymbol{\beta}}) = \boldsymbol{\beta} \quad \text{and} \quad \mathrm{E}(\boldsymbol{\epsilon}) = \mathbf{0})$$

and

$$\begin{aligned} \mathrm{E}(\epsilon_i\epsilon_j) &= 0; \qquad i \neq j = 1, 2, \ldots, n \\ \mathrm{V}(e) &= \sigma^2(1 + \mathbf{X}_\mathbf{T}'(X'X)^{-1}\mathbf{X}_\mathbf{T}) \end{aligned} \tag{5.49}$$

it follows that

$$e \sim \mathrm{N}(0, \sigma[1 + \mathbf{X}_\mathbf{T}'(X'X)^{-1}\mathbf{X}_\mathbf{T})]^{1/2} \tag{5.50}$$

Consequently, t is given by

$$t = \frac{Y_T - \hat{Y}_T}{\hat{\sigma}[1 + \mathbf{X}_\mathbf{T}'(X'X)^{-1}\mathbf{X}_\mathbf{T}]^{1/2}} \tag{5.51}$$

and the 95% confidence interval for Y_T is

$$\mathbf{X}_\mathbf{T}'\hat{\boldsymbol{\beta}} \pm t_{0.025}\hat{\sigma}[1 + \mathbf{X}_\mathbf{T}'(X'X)^{-1}\mathbf{X}_\mathbf{T}]^{1/2} \tag{5.52}$$

Remember that $\hat{\sigma} = \sqrt{\text{MSE}}$.

Problem 1 (continued): Confidence interval. Continuing with our Problem 1 specifications, the confidence limits become

$$-0.5419 \pm (1.99)0.9055(1 + 0.0981766)^{1/2}$$

or, equivalently,

$$-0.5419 \pm 1.8884$$

That is, the interval from -2.4293 to 1.3465 will cover the actual future individual value of Y 95% of the times.

5.5.3 Forecasting Accuracy and Theil's U Coefficient

A measure of the accuracy of various forecasts is available in what is known as Theil's U inequality coefficient.[18] This is given by the expression

$$U_T = \frac{\left[(1/n)\sum_1^n (F_{Ti} - A_{Ti})^2\right]^{1/2}}{\left[(1/n)\sum_{i=1}^n A_{Ti}^2\right]^{1/2}} \tag{5.53}$$

[18] See Theil (1961) and (1966).

where

F_{Ti}, A_{Ti} = forecasted, actual change in the dependent variable for period i,

$$i = 1, 2, \ldots, n \tag{5.54}$$

The numerator of the coefficient is the root mean square error of the forecast and the denominator is also the same except that the forecasted change is now assumed zero. Perfect forecasts would imply $F_{Ti} = A_{Ti}$, which would make $U_T = 0$. When $F_{Ti} = 0$, U_T would equal 1. This is the case when the model predicts no change in the value of the variable. If $U_T > 1$, the forecasting power of the model is worse than that of the status quo forecasts.

To trace through the origins of inaccuracy, it is convenient to show the square of the coefficient as decomposed into three parts, as follows. The square of the numerator is written as

$$1/n \sum^{n} [(F_{Ti} - \overline{F}) - (A_{Ti} - \overline{A}) + (\overline{F} - \overline{A})]^2 \tag{5.55}$$

in which $\overline{F}$ and $\overline{A}$ are the average forecasted and actual percentage changes, respectively. However, simplifying the squared bracketed terms, we get

$$U_T^2 = [(\overline{F} - \overline{A})^2 + (S_F - S_A)^2 + 2(1 - r)S_F S_A]/\{(1/n) \sum A_{Ti}^2\} \tag{5.56}$$

where S_F and S_A are the standard deviations of productions annd realizations, respectively, and r is the correlation coefficient of predicted and realized changes. U_T^2 is thus split into three terms. The first shows the squared difference in the means, referred to as the *bias component* of the inequality coefficient. The second term shows the squared difference between standard deviations, referred to as the *variance component* of the inequality coefficient. The third term involves the correlation coefficient and is therefore called the *covariance component* of the inequality coefficient. The first two terms and the last term express systematic errors and nonsystematic (or random) error, respectively. While the first two errors should be avoided, the last should be minimized.

An example. The hypothetical data in Table 5.4 give the predicted changes F_{Ti} from a linear regression of the consumption of a country and the realized changes of consumption A_{ti} both in appropriate units. Then the inequality coefficient is calculated as:

$$U_T = \sqrt{\frac{1/n \sum (F_{Ti} - A_{Ti})^2}{1/n \sum A_{Ti}^2}} = \sqrt{\frac{9.3}{16.7}} = 0.7462$$

U_T being less than 1, the predictive performance of the estimated consumption function is only fairly good. After decomposing the forecast error, we get the following calculated quantities:

TABLE 5.4

Forecast Period	Predicted Change in Consumption	Actual Change in Consumption	F_{Ti}^2	A_{Ti}^2	$F_{Ti}A_{Ti}$	$F_{Ti} - A_{Ti}$	$(F_{Ti} - A_{Ti})^2$
1978	+6	+9	36	81	54	−3	9
1979	+3	+3	9	9	9	0	0
1980	−3	−5	9	25	15	2	4
1981	−1	+2	1	4	−2	−3	9
1982	0	+3	0	9	0	−3	9
1983	+2	+4	4	16	8	−2	4
1984	+5	+3	25	9	15	2	4
1985	+4	−3	16	9	−12	7	49
1986	−3	−2	9	4	6	−1	1
1987	−3	−1	9	1	3	−2	4
Subtotal	10	13	118	167	96		93

$$\overline{F} = 1 \qquad \overline{A} = 1.3 \qquad S_F^2 = 11.00 \qquad S_F = 3.32$$

$$S_A^2 = 15.01 \qquad S_A = 3.87 \qquad r = 0.646$$

$$(\overline{F} - \overline{A})^2 = 0.09 \qquad (S_F - S_A)^2 = 0.3025$$

$$2(1 - r)S_F S_A \approx 9.0967 \qquad 1/n \sum A_{Ti}^2 = 16.7$$

The numerator of U_T^2 is decomposed as follows:

$$9.3 \approx 0.09 + 0.3025 + 9.0967$$

The first two terms on the right-hand side are small but the third term is large compared to the left-hand side. This means that the high correlation between F_{Ti} and A_{Ti} is the principal factor behind the error in the forecast. However, nothing much can be done to improve the predictive power of the regression model.

5.6 FURTHER APPLIED STUDIES ON OLS

5.6.1 The Henry Schultz Study on U.S. Agriculture (1938)

We would like to conclude this chapter by drawing on a few examples to show the use of the OLS technique. One study, made as far back as 1938, is concerned with the demand for the U.S. agricultural products for the period 1896–1914. Its author is Henry Schultz. In this study*, the per capita demand equation for, for

* Reprinted material from Henry Schultz, *The Theory and Measurement of Demand,* 1938 obtained from the University of Chicago Press and the author.

TABLE 5.5 PRICE ELASTICITIES OF DEMAND FOR THE UNITED STATES, 1915–1929 (EXCLUDING 1917–1921)

Commodity	Price Elasticity of Demand
Wheat	−0.0809 (0.0401)
Sugar	−0.3388 (0.1130)
Potatoes	−0.3171 (0.0832)
Barley	−0.53 (0.4171)
Corn	−0.4844 (0.2003)
Oats	−0.6003 (0.5519)
Hay	−0.4639 (0.2741)

instance, sugar, is estimated, following OLS, to be (the symbol for estimates is suppressed):

$$Y_i = 92.9 - \underset{(1.01)}{3.34p_i} + \underset{(0.15)}{0.92t} \tag{5.57}$$

where

$$\begin{aligned} Y_i &= \text{demand for sugar in year } i \\ p_i &= \text{price of sugar in year } i \\ t &= \text{the time trend (figures in parentheses below the coefficients are, once again, their standard errors)} \end{aligned} \tag{5.58}$$

The price elasticity of demand, calculated at the mean value for price and quantity, is estimated using the formula

$$\eta = \frac{\partial Y \bar{p}}{\partial p \bar{Y}} = -3.34 \frac{\bar{p}}{\bar{Y}} \tag{5.59}$$

in which the mean values of prices and quantities are $\bar{p}$ and $\bar{Y}$, respectively. This value being less, in absolute terms, than unity implies an inelastic demand for sugar. The same can be said about the price elasticity of demand of farm commodities in general for the next time period: 1915–1929 (excluding the war years) for which the author has the estimated elasticities. These figures are reproduced in Table 5.5 (with standard errors shown in parentheses).

5.6.2 Allen and Bowley Study on U.K. Engel's Curve (1935)

The demand function (5.49) does not include the income variable. We now refer to an early study, due to Allen and Bowley, which does include this variable. Thus we have an Engel curve fitted by the OLS method to the crosssection data pertaining to 112 British urban families during 1926:

$$Y = 0.47I + 62.66 \tag{5.60}$$

Y above stands for total expenditure. The expenditure elasticity of demand for these items is calculated by using the formula: $\partial Y/\partial I(\bar{I}/\bar{Y})$ where $\bar{I}$ and $\bar{Y}$ are the means of I and Y. This comes to 0.8 for these families. This value, being less than 1, implies that consumers in British urban society tend to be conservative in their expenditure pattern going by the experience of the year 1926.

5.6.3 The Feige (1964) Study on Demand For Liquid Assets

The next example includes a special item: demand deposits at commercial banks in the United States during 1949–1959. The demand function for such deposits is estimated by the OLS method by Feige. Part of the estimated function is:

$$Y = 0.365X_1 + 535X_2 - 35X_3 + 53X_4 \qquad \bar{R}^2 = 0.978 \tag{5.61}$$

where

$$\begin{aligned} Y &= \text{per capita commercial bank demand deposits} \\ X_1 &= \text{permanent}^{19} \text{ per capita personal income} \\ X_2 &= \text{service charge on demand deposits (negative)} \\ X_3 &= \text{interest rate on commercial bank time deposits} \\ X_4 &= \text{interest rate on savings and loan association shares} \end{aligned} \tag{5.62}$$

Income elasticity of demand for commercial bank demand deposits is calculated at the mean values of the X variables. Various values of the elasticity are obtained: the one with respect to X_2 and another with respect to X_4 are calculated at -0.30 and -0.31, respectively, that with respect to X_3 is calculated at 0.10, and still another with respect to X_1 at 0.92. From the values, signs and statistical significance of the coefficients, Feige's conclusions are that income elasticity for bank deposits could be equated to 1, that a rise in service charges would negatively affect demand deposits, and that demand deposits and commercial bank time deposits could be taken as weak substitutes, whereas demand deposits and savings and loan association shares could be taken as complements. For a complete knowledge of the analysis, see Feige (1964) or Zellner (1969).

5.6.4 Latane (1954) on Cash Demand

Let us continue illustrating the demand for money. We refer now to a study by Latane, who fits a relation between the velocity of money V and the long-term rate of interest r_L. The country to which it is fitted is the United States and the

[19] Permanent income is the long-term projected income of income earners, free of transitory ups and downs. It is usually obtained from an exponentially weighted array of present and past levels of income.

years are 1919–1952, save and except for the years 1932, 1933, 1942, 1946, and 1947, which are left out because they are deemed to be unrepresentative (due to bank failures, excessive war demands, etc.). The estimated relation, following OLS, comes out as:

$$M/Y = \frac{1}{V} = 0.00743\left(\frac{1}{r_L}\right) + 0.019 \qquad R^2 = 0.911 \tag{5.63}$$

This relation shows, as expected, an inverse relation between the demand for money and the interest rate.

5.6.5 Weiss (1974) on Industrial Organization

The last example is from industrial organization. Here we refer to a study by Weiss concerning profits of 399 United States' industries in 1973. The profit function is fitted to be (using OLS):

$$\underset{}{\pi} = \underset{(0.010)}{0.193} + \underset{(0.0002)}{0.0011\text{CR}} - \underset{(0.0001)}{0.0003\text{GD}} + \underset{(0.0002)}{0.0009\text{K/O}} \qquad \text{R}^2 = 0.20 \tag{5.64}$$

where

$$\begin{aligned} \pi &= \text{price–cost margin, being the value of shipments less the cost} \\ &\quad\ \text{of materials and payroll, all divided by the value of shipments} \\ \text{CR} &= \text{four-firm concentration ratio} \\ \text{GD} &= \text{geographic dispersion index} \\ \text{K/O} &= \text{fixed capital shipment ratio} \end{aligned} \tag{5.65}$$

The coefficients for both CR and K/O are statistically significant. For CR the coefficient is positive, implying positive effect of concentration ratio on profit margin in particularly 'normal', or inflation-free years. This is just in line with the result obtained from many other econometric studies.

PROBLEMS

5-1. Consider the following 8 observations on three variables, x_1, x_2, and y:

x_1	−3	−5	3	4	6	−6	0	1
x_2	−2	3	0	6	8	−8	−3	−4
y	−7	9	3	8	10	−12	−8	−3

Note that the means of all variables are zero, which implies that the raw sums of squares and products involving these variables are also their corrected sums of squares and products. As a result, all the regression slopes can be derived from them without explicitly allowing for the intercept term.

(a) Calculate the sums of squares and sums of products:

$$\begin{array}{ccc} \sum x_1^2 & \sum x_1x_2 & \sum x_1y \\ & \sum x_2^2 & \sum x_2y \\ & & \sum y^2 \end{array}$$

(b) Consider the multiple regression of y on both x_1 and x_2; let the OLS-estimated slopes be represented by $\hat{\beta}_{.1}$ and $\hat{\beta}_{.2}$

(c) Consider the regression of y on x_1 alone and calculate the residuals from this regression. Let the slope be $\hat{\beta}_1$ and the residuals be $y_{.1}$

(d) Take the regression of x_2 on x_1 and calculate the residuals from this regression. Let the slope be $\hat{\beta}_{21}$ and the residuals be $x_{2.1}$

(e) Regress y on $x_{2.1}$ to get the slope $\hat{\beta}_{(\cdot 2 \cdot 1)}$

(f) Regress $y_{.1}$ on $x_{2.1}$ to get the slope $\hat{\beta}_{(.1)(2.1)}$

(g) Regress y on x_2 alone to get the slope $\hat{\beta}_2$

(h) It can be shown (no theoretical proof needed) that

$$\hat{\beta}_2 \neq \hat{\beta}_{.2.1} = \hat{\beta}_{(.1)(2.1)} = \hat{\beta}_{.2}$$

Confirm this result using the data of this problem.

(i) Show that

$$\hat{\beta}_1 = \hat{\beta}_{.1} + \hat{\beta}_{21}\hat{\beta}_{.2}$$

Confirm this result using the data of this problem.

5-2. Suppose the model is

$$\mathbf{Y} = \boldsymbol{X_l\beta_1} + \boldsymbol{X_2\beta_2} + \mathbf{u}$$

where $\boldsymbol{X_l}$ and $\boldsymbol{X_2}$ are fixed in repeated samples and have full column ranks; $E(\mathbf{u}) = \mathbf{0}$ and $E(\mathbf{uu}') = \sigma^2\boldsymbol{I}$. Suppose also that we got a gift, from some source, of an unbiased estimator $\hat{\boldsymbol{\beta}}_1$ for the $m_1 \times 1$ vector $\boldsymbol{\beta}_1$. Assume that this estimator has a variance–covariance matrix $\boldsymbol{\Omega_l}$ and $\hat{\boldsymbol{\beta}}_1$ is uncorrelated with $\mathbf{u}$.

(a) Regress $(Y - X_l\hat{\beta}_l)$ on $\boldsymbol{X_2}$ to obtain the conditional regression estimate of $\boldsymbol{\beta}_2$.

(b) How do you show that the conditional estimator $\hat{\boldsymbol{\beta}}_2$ of $\boldsymbol{\beta}_2$ derived in (a) above is an unbiased estimator of $\boldsymbol{\beta}_2$?

5-3. In terms of the multiple regression model of this chapter, let two estimates of the population error variance σ^2 be:

$$\sigma^2 = \hat{\boldsymbol{\epsilon}}'\hat{\boldsymbol{\epsilon}}/\{n - (m + 1)\}$$

and

$$\hat{\sigma}_u^2 = \hat{\boldsymbol{\epsilon}}'\hat{\boldsymbol{\epsilon}}/n$$

where $\hat{\boldsymbol{\epsilon}}$ is the OLS-estimated residual vector. What is the bias of each one of them?

What is the variance of each one of them? Using the criterion of mean squared error, which of these estimators would you prefer?

(*Hint*: For calculating variance, use properties of the distribution of $\hat{\sigma}^2$ or the mean sum of squares due to error, S^2, given in Section 5.4.2 and the property of the chi-square distribution, especially its variance, given in Section 4.7.5.)

5-4. Given a linear regression model

$$\mathbf{Y} = X\boldsymbol{\beta} + \boldsymbol{\epsilon}$$

satisfying all standard assumptions

(a) derive the best linear unbiased estimator $\hat{\pi}$ for

$$\pi = \beta_0 + \beta_1 + \beta_2 + \cdots + \beta_m$$

(b) What is the variance of $\hat{\pi}$?

5-5. Suppose that the true model is

$$\mathbf{Y} = X\boldsymbol{\beta} + \boldsymbol{\epsilon}$$

where there are $m + 1$ regressors including the intercept term, but a researcher has, through oversight, augmented the set of explanatory variables by K extra nonrandom regressors, the observations on which are the elements of an $n \times K$ matrix $\boldsymbol{W}$.

(a) What is the expression for the least squares estimator of $\boldsymbol{\beta}$ from this augmented model (of regressing $\mathbf{Y}$ on $(X\ \boldsymbol{W})$) and what is its bias?

(b) If $\hat{\boldsymbol{\epsilon}}$ is the residual vector of this regression, show that

$$\hat{\sigma}^2 = \hat{\boldsymbol{\epsilon}}'\hat{\boldsymbol{\epsilon}}/\{n - K - (m + 1)\}$$

is unbiased for σ^2.

5-6. Let the linear regression be:

$$Y_t = \beta_1 + \beta_2 X_{t2} + \beta_3 X_{t3} + u_t$$

(a) How would you estimate

$$\gamma = 2\beta_2 + 3\beta_3$$

without re-running the regression?

(b) Show that your estimator of γ is unbiased.

(c) Explain two ways to estimate the standard error of your estimate of γ.

(*Hint*: One method has the regression to be re-run in a different form utilizing, for instance, $\beta_2 = (\gamma - 3\beta_3)/2$ obtained from (a) and plugged into the regression equation, and the other method does the estimation directly.)

5-7. In the linear regression model $\mathbf{Y} = X\boldsymbol{\beta} + \boldsymbol{\epsilon}$ let us partition X into $X = [\mathbf{X}_1 \vdots X_2]$, where $\mathbf{X}_1$ is an $n \times 1$ vector and X_2 is an $n \times m$ matrix, and perform a corresponding partitioning of the coefficient vector $\boldsymbol{\beta}$ into $\boldsymbol{\beta}' = [\beta_1 \vdots \boldsymbol{\beta}_2]$, where β_1 is a scalar and $\boldsymbol{\beta}_2$ is $m \times 1$.

(a) Find the OLS estimator of $\boldsymbol{\beta}_2$ by performing partitioned inversion on

$$\hat{\boldsymbol{\beta}} = (X'X)^{-1}X'\mathbf{Y}$$

(*Hint*: Consult Sections 3.2.3 and 3.6 for partitioning of matrices and inverse matrices.)

(b) Now consider a special case of your result in (a) when $\mathbf{X}_1$ is a vector of 1s, that is the model contains an intercept term. What will be the special expression for $\hat{\boldsymbol{\beta}}$?

(c) Suppose

$$A = I - (1/n)\mathbf{ii}'$$

where I is an identity matrix of size $n \times n$, and $\mathbf{i}$ is a column vector of unities. Thus AX_2 is an $n \times m$ matrix (of X_2 expressed in deviations from mean) and $A\mathbf{Y}$ is $\mathbf{Y}$ expressed in deviations from mean. Perform least squares regression on the model:

$$A\mathbf{Y} = AX_2\boldsymbol{\beta}_2 + \boldsymbol{\nu}$$

to obtain the OLS estimator for $\boldsymbol{\beta}_2$. Compare this result with the one from (b) and review your findings.

5-8. Table 5.6 gives annual data for the United States over the period 1968–1987. The table headings stand for the following variables.

CONS(C_t) Real consumption expenditure in billions of 1982 dollars

GNP(Y_t) Real gross national product in billions of 1982 dollars

TABLE 5.6 YEARLY U.S. DATA ON CONSUMPTION, GNP, WAGE BILL AND PRICES

Year	CONS	GNP	WAGES	PRIDFL
1968	1405.9	2365.6	524.7	39.3
1969	1456.7	2423.3	578.4	41.0
1970	1492.0	2416.2	618.3	42.9
1971	1538.8	2484.8	659.4	44.9
1972	1621.9	2608.5	726.2	46.7
1973	1689.6	2744.1	812.8	49.6
1974	1674.0	2729.3	891.3	54.8
1975	1711.9	2695.0	948.7	59.2
1976	1803.9	2826.7	1057.9	62.6
1977	1883.8	2958.6	1167.6	66.7
1978	1961.0	3115.2	1329.2	71.6
1979	2004.4	3192.4	1491.4	78.2
1980	2000.4	3187.1	1638.2	86.6
1981	2024.2	3248.8	1807.4	94.6
1982	2050.7	3166.0	1907.0	100.0
1983	2146.0	3279.1	2020.7	104.1
1984	2249.3	3501.4	2213.9	108.1
1985	2354.8	3618.7	2367.5	111.6
1986	2455.2	3721.7	2507.1	114.3
1987	2521.0	3847.0	2683.4	119.5

Source: Economic Report of the President, 1989, Table B-2 (p. 310), B-3 (p. 312), and B-24 (p. 334).

WAGES Total compensation of employees (wages, salaries, and supplements) in billions of current dollars

PRIDFL Implicit price deflator for consumption, 1982 = 100 (consider this to be the price index of consumer goods)

Both CONS and GNP are in real terms, not WAGES. To obtain the wage bill in real term, divide WAGES by PRIDFL and multiply by 100. This is the real wage bill denoted by the symbol W_t. Next calculate the profit earner's income by subtracting W_t from Y_t. Call that P_t.

(a) Find the OLS-estimated line showing the regression of real consumption expenditure on real wage bill and (real) profit income.
(b) Calculate R^2 and $\overline{R}^2$ for this problem.
(c) Draw up the associated analysis of variance table, and carry out the F test for the overall regression.
(d) Is the real wage bill significant in its impact on real consumption expenditure at a given probability level of significance? Show all the work.
(e) Is the profit earners' income significant in its effect on consumption expenditure at a given probability level of significance? Show all the work.

5-9. For problem 5-8 above,
(a) Calculate a 95% confidence interval for the marginal propensity to consume out of wage-earners' income.
(b) Calculate a 95% confidence interval for the marginal propensity to consume out of profit-earners' income.
(c) Would the intervals in (a) and (b) be narrower or wider if the confidence coefficient were 0.90? Give all the details of numerical calculations.

5-10. Continuing with problem 5-8, suppose your objective is to use the estimated line for prediction purposes. With that end in view, if you are told that the extrapolated data (using 1982 = 100) for the year 2000 on the various explanatory variables are:

Year	GNP	WAGES	PRIDFL
2000	5529.6	4443.4	179.3

(a) What would be your forecast for the U.S. aggregate real consumption expenditure in the year 2000?
(b) Test for the significance of the forecasted (real) consumption expenditure obtained in (a) at a suitable probability level of significance.
(c) Set up a 90% confidence interval for the actual (real) consumption expenditure for the year 2000.
(d) In Section 5.5, the text discusses the problem of forecasting the mean value of future observations and forecasting one single future observation on the dependent variable. Which of these did you use in (a)–(c) above? Explain why.

5-11. Referring back to problem 5-8, suppose you are involved in forecasting over the future period 1988–1995 the aggregate real consumption expenditure of the United

States based on the estimated line of problem 5-8 and the following extrapolated data, however obtained:

Years	CONS	GNP	WAGES	PRIDFL
1988	2590.0	3967.3	2812.7	129.8
1989	2630.4	4100.2	2900.2	138.7
1990	2658.9	4325.7	3019.7	143.6
1991	2700.1	4390.8	3420.5	152.7
1992	2740.3	4720.1	3550.2	158.9
1993	2758.9	4800.2	3690.0	162.8
1994	2812.2	4879.9	3881.1	188.2
1995	2889.6	4999.9	3923.3	194.5

(a) Obtain the forecast estimate of real aggregate consumption expenditure of the United States over the period 1988–1995.

(b) How do you infer on the accuracy of your forecasts based on Theil's U coefficient?

(c) Write a report on the forecast accuracy of this problem based on the bias, the variance and the covariance components of the inequality coefficient.

5-12. Answer *True* (T) or *False* (F) each of the following questions and briefly justify why:

(a) In the usual notation

$$S^2 = \hat{\boldsymbol{\epsilon}}'\hat{\boldsymbol{\epsilon}}/\{n - (m + 1)\}$$

is the best linear unbiased estimator of σ^2.

(b) A necessary condition for the OLS-estimator of $\boldsymbol{\beta}$ in the linear regression model to be unbiased is that the error term has zero mean.

(c) Adding a variable to a regression containing an intercept always increases R^2 and $\bar{R}^2$.

(d) If $\boldsymbol{X}$ is the matrix of regressors, $\boldsymbol{\beta}$ the coefficient vector, $\hat{\boldsymbol{\beta}}$ its OLS-estimate and $\hat{\boldsymbol{\epsilon}}$ the OLS-estimated residual vector, then $\boldsymbol{X}'\hat{\boldsymbol{\epsilon}} = \boldsymbol{X}'\boldsymbol{X}(\hat{\boldsymbol{\beta}} - \boldsymbol{\beta})$.

(e) If $R^2 = 0$, all parameters (except the intercept coefficient) in the linear regression model must be zero in value.

(f) The sum of the OLS-estimated regression residuals is zero.

(g) If $\boldsymbol{M} = \boldsymbol{I} - \boldsymbol{X}(\boldsymbol{X}'\boldsymbol{X})^{-1}\boldsymbol{X}'$, and $\boldsymbol{X}$ has full rank $m + 1$, then $\boldsymbol{X}$ is nonsingular and so $\boldsymbol{M} = \boldsymbol{0}$ in this case.

(h) If $\hat{\beta}_1$ and $\hat{\beta}_2$ are the first two elements of the OLS-estimator of $\boldsymbol{\beta}$ in the model $\mathbf{Y} = \boldsymbol{X\beta} + \boldsymbol{\epsilon}$, where *all* of the usual OLS-assumptions about $\boldsymbol{X}$ and $\boldsymbol{\epsilon}$ are fulfilled, $\hat{\beta}_1$ and $\hat{\beta}_2$ are independently distributed with means β_1 and β_2, respectively.

5-13. An investigator was assigned the problem of determining the factors that caused work stoppages in Canada during the period 1977–1985. He applied some form of a step-wise OLS method to fit a linear regression between the dependent variable (called STRIKE) and independent variables of the following descriptions:

STRIKE The number of work days lost due to stoppages per 1000 people employed [data obtained from "Strike and Lockout in Canada", Statistics Canada, 1985]

UNEMP The unemployment rate [data obtained from "Labour Force Annual Averages", Statistics Canada, 1985]

DENSIT The labor union density [data obtained from "Directory of Labour Organization in Canada", Statistics Canada, 1985]

WAGES Money wages [data obtained from "The Labour Force", Statistics Canada, 1985]

PRNDX Price index [data obtained from "The Consumer Price Index", Statistics Canada, 1985]

TIME Time trend

CONTROL A (dummy) variable taking the value 1 during each of the years 1976, 1977, and 1978 [when the government of Canada implemented a policy of wage increase of a given percentage amount (the so-called "Six and Five" rule)] and zero for other years.

Five alternative model results including estimated coefficients and associated statistics are given below (the figures in parentheses underneath coefficient estimates are their standard errors):

Variable	Model I	Model II	Model III	Model IV	Model V	Model VI
CONST	1301.27	−3144.66	1269.22	1345.43	1302.36	−5994.4
	(277.797)	(6101.94)	(207.451)	(222.451)	(212.864)	(6428.0)
UNEMP	−84.665		−118.511	−116.615	−124.379	−109.95
	(29.3676)		(25.553)	(29.438)	(26.609)	(65.31)
DENSIT		118.83				244.52
		(198.172)				(212.4)
PRNDX(−1)*			48.983		33.399	
			(19.052)		(25.518)	
WAGES(−2)*				0.2864	0.1489	
				(0.128)	(0.160)	
TIME						9.586
						(63.42)
CONTROL						−247.97
						(196.46)
$\bar{R}^2$	0.4774	−0.0871	0.709	0.667	0.703	0.534

(* These are the variables with lags of 1 and 2 periods)

(a) What could be the rationale for each model? What signs of coefficients could you have expected for the variables included in Model VI a priori? What agreements and disagreements do you notice between your expected signs and the signs appearing in the results of the investigator? How do you reconcile the disagreements, if any?

(b) In each model, apply the F test to conclude about the efficacy of the model. (*Hint*: Use the relation between $\overline{R}^2$, R^2, and F.)

(c) Apply the t test to determine whether each coefficient in each model is significant.

(d) Which of the six models do you find to be the most appropriate for explaining the incidence of work stoppages due to labor strikes in Canada during the period 1977–1985? What are your reasons?

5-15. Based on data collected for the period 1960–1980 from various publications of the governments of Pakistan and India and of the United Nations, a researcher tries to explain what determines public expenditure in Pakistan. Total public expenditure in Pakistan (in short, E) is divided into development expenditure (DEV), nondevelopment expenditure (NDEV), defence expenditure (DEF), and nondefence expenditure (NDEF). The researcher then sets up a function with each one of these as the dependent variable. The independent variables in the functions for the different dependent variables are variously chosen from the following set:

GNP	GNP of Pakistan
EL	Lagged public expenditure of Pakistan
GNPI	GNP of India
EI	Public expenditure of India
DEVI	Development expenditure of India
DEFI	Defence expenditure of India

The following are the estimated results, together with the values of related statistics, for the various linear regressions fitted to the data (figures in parentheses are the values of the t statistics):

$$\text{(I)} \quad \underset{}{E} = \underset{(-0.745)}{-696.66} + \underset{(2.93)}{0.21\text{GNP}} + \underset{(1.31)}{0.31\text{EL}} + \underset{(0.551)}{0.04\text{DEFI}} + \underset{(0.645)}{0.03\text{DEVI}} - \underset{(-0.952)}{0.04\text{EI}} - \underset{(-0.537)}{0.002\text{GNPI}} \qquad \overline{R}^2 = 0.997$$

$$\text{(II)} \quad \text{DEV} = \underset{(0.251)}{315.13} + \underset{(2.064)}{0.381\text{E}} - \underset{(-1.878)}{0.08\text{DEVI}} + \underset{(2.103)}{0.06\text{EI}} - \underset{(-0.294)}{0.02\text{DEFI}} \qquad \overline{R}^2 = 0.98$$

$$\text{(III)} \quad \text{NDEV} = \underset{(-0.251)}{-315.13} + \underset{(3.312)}{0.62\text{E}} + \underset{(1.878)}{0.08\text{DEVI}} - \underset{(-2.103)}{0.06\text{EI}} + \underset{(0.29)}{0.02\text{DEFI}} \qquad \overline{R}^2 = 0.92$$

$$\text{(IV)} \quad \text{DEF} = \underset{(3.115)}{2036.23} + \underset{(0.607)}{0.04\text{E}} + \underset{(6.49)}{0.08\text{DEVI}} - \underset{(-6.96)}{0.06\text{EI}} - \underset{(-1.833)}{0.03\text{DEFI}} \qquad \overline{R}^2 = 0.94$$

$$\text{(V)} \quad \text{NDEF} = \underset{(-0.108)}{-184.83} + \underset{(2.606)}{0.71\text{E}} - \underset{(-0.128)}{0.01\text{DEVI}} + \underset{(0.26)}{0.02\text{EI}} - \underset{(-0.219)}{0.03\text{DEFI}}$$

$$\bar{R}^2 = 0.79$$

(a) Based on these 5 different estimated model results, write an articulate (statistical and economic) report on the factors affecting total public expenditure in Pakistan. How do these factors change as you try to explain various components into which the total Pakistan public expenditure is divided.

(b) According to Wagner's law, the elasticity $(\Delta E/\Delta GNP)$ (GNP/E) should be greater than 1, where E and GNP were defined before. To see whether this law is valid in Pakistan, the investigator uses the following estimated line:

$$\text{E} = \underset{(-0.827)}{-347.856} + \underset{(21.16)}{0.25\text{GNP}} \qquad \bar{R}^2 = 0.957$$

Given that the data on GNP and E for Pakistan are the following over the period of 1971–1980 (in millions of rupees in 1959–1960 prices):

Year	E	GNP
1971	7549.93	32883.0
1972	7679.96	35360.0
1973	8622.93	38085.0
1974	10251.4	39651.0
1975	10648.6	41410.0
1976	10484.9	43022.0
1977	10818.0	47480.0
1978	12511.0	49953.0
1979	13343.3	53292.0
1980	12625.2	56237.0

What conclusion do you draw about the validity of Wagner's law as applied to Pakistan total public expenditure?

5-15. The percentage of fat X and the percentage of nonfat solids Y are measured on milk samples of a number of dairy cows in two herds. A summary of the data is set out below. Calculate the linear regression of Y on X for each herd, and test whether the two lines differ in slope.

Herd A, number of cows = 16:

$$\sum X = 51.13, \quad \sum Y = 117.25, \quad \sum x^2 = 1.27, \quad \sum y^2 = 4.78, \quad \sum xy = 1.84$$

Herd B, number of cows = 10:

$$\sum X = 37.20, \quad \sum Y = 78.75, \quad \sum x^2 = 1.03, \quad \sum y^2 = 2.48, \quad \sum xy = 1.10$$

(Reprinted with permission of R.S.S. Certificate, 1956)

(*Hint*: Assuming normality of errors in the two regressions, and, in particular, $\hat{\beta}_1$

$\sim$ N(β_1, $\sigma_1^2/\sum x_1^2$), $\hat{\beta}_2 \sim$ N(β_2, $\sigma_2^2/\sum x_2^2$) where β_1 and β_2 are the regression coefficients, $\hat{\beta}_1$ and $\hat{\beta}_2$ their OLS-estimates, and σ_1^2 and σ_2^2 are the variances of errors from the two herds (note that we have used x_1 and x_2 for x for the two herds), we have, assuming σ_1^2 and σ_2^2 to be unknown and the null hypothesis to be: $\beta_1 - \beta_2 = 0$, that

$$t = \frac{\hat{\beta}_1 - \hat{\beta}_2}{[\hat{V}(\hat{\beta}_1) + \hat{V}(\hat{\beta}_2) - 2\,\mathrm{cov}(\hat{\beta}_1, \hat{\beta}_2)]^{1/2}}$$

Note that $V(\hat{\beta}_i) = \sigma_i^2/\sum x_i^2$, $i = 1, 2$, $\mathrm{cov}(\hat{\beta}_1, \hat{\beta}_2) = 0$ (assuming that $\hat{\beta}_1$ and $\hat{\beta}_2$ are independent), and $\hat{V}$ implies that the variance is estimated from the sample. For instance, $\hat{V}(\hat{\beta}_1) = S_1^2/\sum x_1^2$, where S_1^2 is the mean sum of squares due to error in the first sample. The df for t is 22 (confirm it). The same technique can be used to test for the significance of the difference in two regression coefficients from the same regression equation.)

6

The General Linear Model and Some Problems

6.1 MULTICOLLINEARITY (M/C)

6.1.1 An Applied Study Due to Bordo and Choudhri (1982)

We refer to a study on the demand for money and currency substitution by Bordo and Choudhri (1982) who reject an earlier result derived by Miles (1978) on significant currency substitution. Bordo and Choudhri argue that the reason why Miles finds a significant currency substitution between the Canadian and United States currencies is because he does not include an additional important variable, namely the Canadian interest rate, in his demand for money equation. As soon as that variable is included, currency substitution becomes insignificant. Ghosh (1989) later argues that such a refutal of Miles' result is unwarranted unless the added variable is uncorrelated with one of the old variables. Indeed this is not the case, for the added variable, Canadian interest rate, is correlated or collinear with the old variable, the American and Canadian interest rate differential.

This sort of collinearity, or rather multicollinearity, may be a real problem in regression models. Simply stated, it means that the X variables are not independent of each other as the basic model assumes.

Depending on its strength, multicollinearity may be perfect or imperfect. Under perfect M/C, the rank of the X matrix is less than the full rank $m + 1$; thus the rank of the $X'X$ matrix is less than its full rank $m + 1$. As a result $|X'X|$ is equal to zero, which means $X'X$ cannot be inverted and so $\hat{\boldsymbol{\beta}}$, which involves $(X'X)^{-1}$, is indeterminate.[1]

[1] See Sections 3.3–3.4 and Section 3.9: Results 2 and 3 of Chapter 3 and Section 5.2 of Chapter 5 for more on rank and linear dependence or independence.

6.1.2 The Effect of Imperfect M/C on Tests and Errors

Under imperfect M/C, $|X'X|$ is as close to zero as possible depending on the strength of multicollinearity. Thus $X'X$ can still be inverted and $\hat{\boldsymbol{\beta}}$ determined by the OLS method. In the process, errors ($= \hat{\boldsymbol{\beta}} - \boldsymbol{\beta}$) of estimates will arise that will vary directly or inversely with multicollinearity depending on the coefficient. On the other hand, the elements of the $(X'X)^{-1}$ matrix will tend to be large, $|X'X|$ being small. Since the diagonal elements of this matrix are a part of the standard errors of coefficient estimates (see Section 5.4.3 of Chapter 5) and the standard errors go into the denominator of the t statistics, the t statistics will be small. This will tend to make a coefficient statistically insignificant as a result of multicollinearity.

To appreciate these points, consider a two-variable model in the deviation form of the variables.[2] In this model y, x_1 and x_2 are the variables, $\bar{\epsilon}$ is the sample mean of the error variable ϵ and the βs are the coefficients:

$$y = \beta_0 + \beta_1 x_1 + \beta_2 x_2 + (\epsilon - \bar{\epsilon}) \qquad \Sigma x_1 = \Sigma x_2 = 0 \tag{6.1}$$

Let x_2 be collinear with x_1 as evident from the relation:

$$x_2 = \theta x_1 + \nu \tag{6.2}$$

and let, for the sake of simplicity, x_2 and x_1 be so chosen that

$$\Sigma x_2^2 = \Sigma x_3^2 = 1, \qquad \Sigma \nu = 0, \qquad \Sigma x_1 \nu = 0 \tag{6.3}$$

Then, the correlation coefficient[3] between X_1 and X_2 is θ. In other words, θ stands for the measure of multicollinearity. Also,

$$(X'X) = \begin{bmatrix} 1 & \theta \\ \theta & 1 \end{bmatrix} \qquad (X'X)^{-1} = \frac{1}{1-\theta^2}\begin{bmatrix} 1 & -\theta \\ -\theta & 1 \end{bmatrix} \tag{6.4}$$

Thus, the variance–covariance of OLS estimate $\hat{\beta}$, in matrix form, is:

$$\mathrm{V}(\hat{\boldsymbol{\beta}}) = \sigma^2 (X'X)^{-1} = \frac{\sigma^2}{1-\theta^2}\begin{bmatrix} 1 & -\theta \\ -\theta & 1 \end{bmatrix} \tag{6.5}$$

which implies

$$\mathrm{V}(\hat{\beta}_1) = \mathrm{V}(\hat{\beta}_2) = \frac{\sigma^2}{1-\theta^2} \qquad \mathrm{cov}(\hat{\beta}_1, \hat{\beta}_2) = -\frac{\theta}{1-\theta^2}\sigma^2 \tag{6.6}$$

Therefore, as θ increases, so does $\mathrm{V}(\hat{\beta}_i)$, a point indicated before. But

[2] Remember that the upper case letters are for variables in their absolute form, while the lower case letters are for the same variables but in their deviation form. As before, Y is the dependent and X_1 and X_2 the explanatory variables. And $y = Y - \bar{Y}$, and $x_j = X_j - \bar{X}_j$, $j = 1, 2$, where $\bar{Y}$, $\bar{X}_1$ and $\bar{X}_2$ are the means of Y, X_1 and X_2, respectively.

[3] Since correlation coefficient $(X_1, X_2) = \Sigma x_1 x_2 / (\Sigma x_1^2 \, \Sigma x_2^2)^{1/2} = \theta \Sigma x_1^2 / (\Sigma x_1^2 \, \Sigma x_2^2)^{1/2} = \theta$.

$\text{cov}(\hat{\beta}_1, \hat{\beta}_2)$ decreases. This can be appreciated by exploring the effect of M/C on the errors of estimates.

For the errors of estimate, since

$$\hat{\boldsymbol{\beta}} - \boldsymbol{\beta} = (X'X)^{-1} X'\boldsymbol{\epsilon}$$

so, using $(X'X)^{-1}$ from (6.4), we get[4]

$$\hat{\beta}_1 - \beta_1 = \Sigma \epsilon x_1 - \frac{\theta}{1 - \theta^2} \Sigma \epsilon v \tag{6.7}$$

$$\hat{\beta}_2 - \beta_2 = \frac{1}{1 - \theta^2} \Sigma \epsilon v \tag{6.8}$$

From the last two expressions it is clear that the two errors, while being large and opposite under multicollinearity (something that we have indicated at the beginning), depend on θ in such a way that while $\hat{\beta}_1$ underestimates β_1, $\hat{\beta}_2$ overestimates β_2. This is how $\text{cov}(\hat{\beta}_1, \hat{\beta}_2)$ comes to be negative.

What about $\hat{\sigma}^2$ which is the estimated value of σ^2? Without any proof, we like to observe[5] that there does not seem to be any a priori reason why multicollinearity[6] should seriously bias the estimate of σ^2.

The moot point is that, when multicollinearity is present, the t test will indicate that an effect is either less significant or even insignificant. This is a natural outcome, since the standard error of the estimate (which is the denominator of the t ratio) increases under multicollinearity. This is why the previously obtained significant effect of the Canada–United States interest rate differential on the demand for money in Canada becomes insignificant as soon as the collinear variable of Canadian interest rate is introduced into the equation by Bordo and Choudhri, a point made early on in the discussion.

6.1.3 Detection of M/C—The Condition Number

How can we detect multicollinearity? And how can we be sure that its effect, to the large extent that it is known to exist, is really not very serious? In terms of

[4] We also use $X = [\mathbf{x}_1\ \mathbf{x}_2]$, where x_i is the ith column of X and the lower case letter implies the deviation form of the variable. For instance:

$$X'\boldsymbol{\epsilon} = \begin{bmatrix} \mathbf{x}_1'\boldsymbol{\epsilon} \\ \mathbf{x}_2'\boldsymbol{\epsilon} \end{bmatrix} = \begin{bmatrix} \Sigma x_1 \epsilon \\ \Sigma x_2 \epsilon \end{bmatrix},$$

which when premultiplied by $(X'X)^{-1}$ gives the right-hand side of (6.7).

[5] This can be seen by examining the effect of θ on $S^2 = \Sigma \hat{\epsilon}^2/(n - 3)$ which, one may recall from (5.31) of Chapter 5, is the estimate of σ^2. The underlying algebra is a little cumbersome and will be left out ($\hat{\epsilon}$ is the OLS estimated value of the residual ϵ).

[6] We should point out that a test of whether multicollinearity is present in the population is provided by Farrar and Glauber (1967). It is a familiar F test to test the significance of relations among the Xs. But the snag here is that multicollinearity is essentially a sample phenomenon, not a population one, and thus testing its existence in the population does not seem to serve much useful purpose.

the determinant of a $(m + 1) \times (m + 1)$ matrix $X'X$, we naturally suspect that it has a very small value, and since this determinant is the product of its eigenvalues (see Section 3.8, Chapter 3) λs, that is $|X'X| = \lambda_0\lambda_1 \ldots \lambda_m\lambda_m$, we similarly suspect very small values of possibly a large number of such λs. Also, an important question is: how do we ascertain the effects of collinearity on different coefficients?

One way, of course, is to compute and rank $R^2_{X_i} \mid \dot{X}_i$, $i = 0, 1, \ldots, m$, where $R^2_{X_i} \mid \dot{X}_i$ is the square of the coefficient of multiple determination while regressing X_i on all the rest of the regressors denoted together as $\dot{X}_i$. It is even better, from the point of view of a magnified scale, to use the relation:[7]

$$V(\hat{\beta}_{X_i} \mid \dot{X}_i)/V(\hat{\beta}_{X_i} \perp \dot{X}_i) = 1/(1 - R^2_{X_i} \mid \dot{X}_i) \tag{6.9}$$

where V is variance, the subscript $X_i \mid \dot{X}_i$ has the same meaning as in $R^2_{X_i} \mid \dot{X}_i$, and the subscript $X_i \perp \dot{X}_i$ has also the same interpretation, except that now X_i is thoroughly unrelated or orthogonal ($\perp$) to the other Xs. The ratio of the two variances therefore would indicate the effect of collinearity arising from the ith coefficient.

Some computer programs, notably TROLL, make use of a phrase "condition number" of the X matrix to denote the collinearity of coefficients. This is borrowed from the work of Belsley, Kuh, and Welsch (1980, Chapter 3), and is defined as:

$$\kappa(X) = \sqrt{\lambda_L}/\sqrt{\lambda_S}$$

where λ_L and λ_S are respectively the largest and smallest eigenvalues of the matrix $X'X$. With the lengths of the columns of X adjusted to unity, $\kappa(X)$ becomes equal to one for orthogonal X columns and larger than one for collinear Xs. The value of κ lying between 20 and 30 is taken to indicate, based on real and experimental data, severe multicollinearity. Each eigenvalue will have a definite value of the condition number, the smallest eigenvalue producing the number 1 and the largest producing any number.

A closely related method is to split the variance of a regression coefficient according to the eigenvalues in the following way. Given that X is of size $n \times (m + 1)$ for an orthogonal matrix c that diagonalizes $X'X$ (result 10 of Section 3.6, Chapter 3) we have:

$$c'(X'X)c = \Lambda \tag{6.10}$$

in which Λ is the diagonal matrix. Since $(c')^{-1} = c$,

$$(c')^{-1}c'(X'X)c = (c')^{-1}\Lambda$$

or

$$(X'X)c = c\Lambda \tag{6.11}$$

[7] We can show that $V(\hat{\beta}_{X_i} \mid \dot{X}_i) = \sigma^2/\text{ESS}_i = \sigma^2/\text{TSS}_i\,(1 - R^2_{X_i} \mid \dot{X}_i)$ where TSS_i and ESS_i are total and error sum of squares, respectively, in a regression of X_i on all the rest of Xs. And since for $X_i \perp \dot{X}_i$, $R^2_{X_i} \mid \dot{X}_i = 0$, $V(\hat{\beta}_{X_i} \perp \dot{X}_i) = \sigma^2/\text{TSS}_i$. Thus, taking the ratio of the two variances, (6.9) follows.

Thus,

$$V(\hat{\boldsymbol{\beta}}) = \sigma^2(X'X)^{-1} = \sigma^2 \boldsymbol{c}\,\Lambda^{-1}\boldsymbol{c}' \tag{6.12}$$

and

$$V(\hat{\beta}_i) = \sigma^2\left(\frac{c_{i0}^2}{\lambda_0} + \frac{c_{i1}^2}{\lambda_1} + \cdots + \frac{c_{im}^2}{\lambda_m}\right) \qquad i = 0, 1, \ldots, m \tag{6.13}$$

Obviously $c_{i0}, \ldots, c_{im}$ are the ith row elements of $\boldsymbol{c}$. This formula is the source of $V(\hat{\beta}_i)$ split according to λs. The overall procedure then consists of calculating λs, ascertaining those λs registering "dangerous" values (say, beyond the 20 to 30 range) of the condition number, calculating the proportion of $V(\hat{\beta}_i)$ due to a selected eigenvalue and trying to see if that proportion exceeds a benchmark value of, say, 0.50 to conclude if the coefficient has been seriously handicapped by multicollinearity.

6.1.4 Remedy of M/C

This section will be concluded with a few suggestions for reduction or elimination of multicollinearity.

Use controlled experiments. First, in some cases one may take recourse to controlled experiments and arrange the X data in such a way that multicollinearity may be removed. For instance, in a production function experiment, the following rearrangement of the labor (L) and capital (K) data:

L	K
1	1
1	2
1	3
2	1
2	2
2	3
3	1
3	2
3	3

can be shown to generate a correlation coefficient between L and K equal to zero, which otherwise would have been nonzero should such data originally arise in a different pattern (not shown) than this.

Revise the model. Second, at times the best way out of M/C may be to revise the entire model because multicollinearity will simply not disappear. For instance, fitting a consumption function to "permanent" and last period's income is doomed to failure if the economy is continuously prospering. For, in such an environment, both the regressors will move harmoniously and their effects will be indistinguishable from each other.

Use prior economic theory and/or empirical results. Third, often the investigator has the benefit of prior economic theory or empirical results. Take two examples. In an inflationary growth period of an economy the attempt to fit consumption (C_t) to price (P_t) and income (Y_t) of the following type:

$$E(C_t) = \beta_0 + \beta_1 P_t + \beta_2 Y_t$$

may be highly questionable in view of a strong correlation existing between the latter variables. One may still separate out these variables as follows. Fit consumption to price using crosssection data and derive $\hat{\beta}_1$, as the OLS estimate of β_1; then fit, using time series data, C_t^* to Y_t, where $C_t^* = C_t - \hat{\beta}_1 P_t$, and $E(C_t^*) = \beta_0 + \beta_2 Y_t$. Thus the feuding variables are kept apart, eliminating the multicollinearity problem.[8]

In one of the theoretical growth models, especially the one propounded by Nicholas Kaldor (1955–1956), aggregate consumption C_t is taken to depend on profit-earners' income P_t and wage-earners' income W_t. However, when inflation is fuelled by harmonious wage and price relationships, effects of P_t and W_t are almost impossible to disentangle. In a situation like this, prior empirical results may be of help. For instance if it is known that the marginal propensity to consume from out of capitalists' income is a known fraction, say, half of that out of labourers' income, this knowledge will provide a way of aggregating the two variables P_t and W_t and eliminating the M/C problem as follows. Since $\beta_1 = 1/2\ \beta_2$, so $\beta_1 P_t + \beta_2 W_t (= \beta_1 P_t + 2\beta_1 W_t)$ is $\beta_1 P_t^*$ where $P_t^* = P_t + 2W_t$. Now fit the function to only one independent variable P_t^*, rather than two:

$$E(C_t) = \beta_0 + \beta_1 P_t^*$$

Obviously, we do not have any M/C problem in this relationship.

Use the method of deflation of variables and combine coefficients for test purposes. Two other situations should be briefly mentioned. In one, multicollinearity is reduced or removed by the method of deflating; in the other the same objectives are achieved by setting up the hypothesis test in a combinatorial way.

Take, for instance, consumption as a function of price of a commodity P_t and prices P_t' of all other commodities. Since P_t and P_t' may sometimes be correlated, the function may instead be formulated with $P_t/\overline{P}$ as the independent variable, where $\overline{P}$ is the general price level. Any common effect between P_t and

[8] One should remember that while the M/C problem may have been overcome or lessened, the problem of pooled crosssection and time series error may have been introduced, which may adversely affect the efficiency of estimates. This problem will be analyzed later in Chapter 10.

$\overline{P}$ will be eliminated or reduced as the regressor is put in the ratio form. Still the aspect of the general equilibrium formulation of the demand function is retained in the revised equation.

Secondly, in many contexts one may be interested in testing not just one effect but a combination of effects. The net effect of the combination will be to reduce or eliminate multicollinearity. For instance, taking β_1 and β_2 as the two partial effects and the "^" on top of a symbol to indicate its estimate, since $V(\hat{\beta}_1 \pm \hat{\beta}_2) = V(\hat{\beta}_1) + V(\hat{\beta}_2) \pm 2\,\text{cov}(\hat{\beta}_1, \hat{\beta}_2)$, it is possible that the effect of multicollinearity on $V(\hat{\beta}_1 \pm \hat{\beta}_2)$ through $V(\hat{\beta}_i)$, $i = 1, 2$ will be lessened due to the offsetting influence through $\text{cov}(\hat{\beta}_1, \hat{\beta}_2)$. Remember that the test of a hypothesis, say, $\beta_1 \pm \beta_2 = 0$ may be performed by the t ratio in which the denominator[9] is $\sqrt{\hat{V}(\hat{\beta}_1 \pm \hat{\beta}_2)}$.

A practical example of a combinatorial hypothesis is available from macrointernational economics. For instance, one may be interested to know whether fiscal or monetary policies are the more effective devices to promote aggregate income of an open economy under either flexible or fixed exchange rates. This sort of a hypothesis under a given exchange rate regime may be set up in the form of $\beta_1 - \beta_2 = C$, where C is a constant whose value will be set according to the belief of the investigator, and β_1 and β_2 are the slope coefficients of the two policies in the equation for national income. For instance, economic theory tells us that, assuming perfect capital mobility, monetary policy is more effective in a regime of flexible exchange rates, whereas fiscal policy is more effective in a regime of fixed exchange rates for a small open economy (see Mundell (1968)). These theories can be tested using a hypothesis such as: $\beta_1 - \beta_2 = C$ by appropriately assigning β_1 or β_2 to either a given monetary or fiscal policy for a given exchange rate system. This kind of combination of coefficients may reduce collinearity.

6.1.5 Ridge Regression

A mechanical and largely numerical technique of coping with multicollinearity is the technique of ridge regression.[10] The ridge regression estimate of β is an augmented OLS estimate that can be presented as follows:

$$\hat{\boldsymbol{\beta}}_{RR} = (X'X + \lambda I)^{-1}X'Y \tag{6.14}$$

with λ an arbitrary scalar. This has the effect of inflating the diagonal elements but leaving unaffected the off-diagonal elements of the $X'X$ matrix. It follows that

$$E(\hat{\boldsymbol{\beta}}_{RR}) = (X'X + \lambda I)^{-1}X'X\boldsymbol{\beta} \tag{6.15}$$

$$V(\hat{\boldsymbol{\beta}}_{RR}) = \sigma^2(X'X + \lambda I)^{-1}X'X(X'X + \lambda I)^{-1} \tag{6.16}$$

[9] Notice that in $\hat{V}(\hat{\beta}_1 \pm \hat{\beta}_2)$ we will merely replace the population variance of the residual term by its estimate from the sample. This estimate is the usual mean sum of squares due to error.

[10] See Hoerl and Kennard (1970), pp. 55–68, 69–82.

The augmented estimates are biased. However, as Schmidt (1976) has shown, they have smaller variances than the OLS estimates. Combining the two properties, could we say that the ridge estimates have smaller mean square error (MSE)? Choice of the proper numerical value of the constant λ would of course have great influence on the answer to this question. But even if we would try to determine λ by a method such as minimization of the total MSE with respect to the various ridge estimators as Schmidt (1976) has done, the terminal condition would be seriously limited by unknown parameters. Trying to estimate these parameters from samples drawn for this purpose would necessitate a knowledge of their sampling distribution properties which are essentially unknown, and therefore the interpretation of the estimates would be hazardous.[11]

6.1.6 Conditional Omitted Variable Estimator

We would now discuss another method called the conditional omitted variable, or, in short, the COV estimator of β. This has been developed by Feldstein (1973). It is an attempt to improve the MSE by dropping one or more explanatory variables so that the MSE of the rest of the variables may improve.

To begin with, let the multiple regression model expressed in the deviation form of the variables be:

$$y = \beta_{yL.K}l + \beta_{yK.L}k + (\epsilon - \bar{\epsilon}) \tag{6.17}$$

where $l = L - \bar{L}$ and $k = K - \bar{K}$ are the labor and capital variables, and y (= $Y - \bar{Y}$) is output. Another version of the same model that includes only the labor input as the explanatory variable would produce a simple regression model.

Suppose both the versions have been estimated by OLS. From the normal equation of the multiple regression involving the sum of products of y and l:

$$\Sigma yl = \hat{\beta}_{yL.K}\Sigma l^2 + \hat{\beta}_{yK.L}\Sigma lk \tag{6.18}$$

and dividing both sides by Σl^2, we get

$$\Sigma yl/\Sigma l^2 = \hat{\beta}_{yL.K} + \hat{\beta}_{yK.L}b_{LK} \tag{6.19}$$

where

$$b_{LK} = \Sigma lk/\Sigma l^2 \tag{6.20}$$

And from the normal equation of the simple regression

$$\Sigma yl = \hat{\beta}_L \Sigma l^2 \tag{6.21}$$

by dividing both sides by Σl^2, we get

$$(\Sigma yl/\Sigma l^2) = \hat{\beta}_L \tag{6.22}$$

[11] In this context, the series of papers that appear in the *Journal of the American Statistical Association* (1980), pp. 74–103, would be very useful.

where

$$\hat{\beta}_L = \Sigma yl/\Sigma l^2 \tag{6.23}$$

Thus from (6.22) and (6.19),

$$\hat{\beta}_L = \hat{\beta}_{yL.K} + \hat{\beta}_{yK.L}\, b_{LK} \tag{6.24}$$

Taking expectations and using the unbiasedness property of the OLS estimates we have

$$\beta_L = \beta_{yL.K} + \beta_{yK.L}\, b_{LK} \tag{6.25}$$

Therefore $\hat{\beta}_L$ is a biased estimator of $\beta_{yL.K}$, unless b_{LK} equals zero, that is, L and K are orthogonal. However, the interesting thing is that the former has a lower sampling variance than the latter as can be simply shown as follows.

From the simple regression,

$$V(\hat{\beta}_L) = \sigma^2/\Sigma l^2 \tag{6.26}$$

and from the multiple regression

$$V(\hat{\beta}_{yL.K}) = \sigma^2 \bigg/ \left\{\Sigma l^2\left(1 - \frac{(\Sigma lk)^2}{\Sigma l^2 \Sigma k^2}\right)\right\} = \frac{\sigma^2}{\Sigma l^2(1 - \gamma_{LK}^2)} \tag{6.27}$$

where γ_{LK} is the simple correlation coefficient[12] between L and K. For $0 < \gamma_{LK}^2 < 1$, $1 - \gamma_{LK}^2$ is a fraction, which makes $1/(1 - \gamma_{LK}^2)$ ordinarily greater than 1. Thus, $V(\hat{\beta}_{yL.K}) > V(\hat{\beta}_L)$, or $V(\hat{\beta}_L) < V(\hat{\beta}_{yL.K})$. This opens up trade-off possibilities between the bias and variance of the $\hat{\beta}_L$ estimator. Combining the two, could we find situations in which $MSE(\hat{\beta}_L) < MSE(\hat{\beta}_{yL.K})$?

Employing the relation between MSE, variance, and bias, that is

$$MSE = \text{Variance} + (\text{bias})^2 \tag{6.28}$$

we have

$$MSE(\hat{\beta}_L) = \sigma^2/\Sigma l^2 + \beta_{yK.L}^2\, b_{LK}^2 \tag{6.29}$$

and since $\hat{\beta}_{yL.K}$ is unbiased for $\beta_{yL.K}$,

$$MSE(\hat{\beta}_{yL.K}) = V(\hat{\beta}_{yL.K}) = \frac{\sigma^2}{\Sigma l^2(1 - \gamma_{LK}^2)} \tag{6.30}$$

Thus,

$$MSE(\hat{\beta}_L)/MSE(\hat{\beta}_{yL.K}) = 1 + \gamma_{LK}^2(\theta^2 - 1) \tag{6.31}$$

in which

$$\theta^2 = \beta_{yK.L}^2 \bigg/ \left\{\frac{\sigma^2}{\Sigma k^2(1 - \gamma_{LK}^2)}\right\} = \frac{\beta_{yK.L}^2}{V(\hat{\beta}_{yK.L})} \tag{6.32}$$

[12] This correlation coefficient is: $\gamma_{LK} = \Sigma lk/\sqrt{(\Sigma l^2\, \Sigma k^2)}$

Should $\theta^2 < 1$, we will have $\text{MSE}(\hat{\beta}_L) < \text{MSE}(\hat{\beta}_{yL.K})$, which might justify dropping the K-input from the production function and make it dependent on L only. But for $\theta^2 > 1$, there are cases where the $\text{MSE}(\hat{\beta}_L)$ might be many times $\text{MSE}(\hat{\beta}_{yL.K})$, in which case dropping K would be erroneous.

The condition that $\theta < 1$ boils down to the following, after using S^2 as an unbiased estimate of σ^2:

$$\frac{\hat{\beta}^2_{yK.L}}{S^2/(\Sigma k^2(1 - \gamma^2_{LK}))} = t^2 = F < 1 \tag{6.33}$$

(t and F are the usual test statistics[13]). This value of F is considered insignificant for practical purposes. Such a value would discard the associated variable K from the regression. This leads to the COV estimator of β_L as $\hat{\beta}_L$, if $F < 1$, or $\hat{\beta}_{yL.K}$, if otherwise.

In view of (6.31), Feldstein computes the ratio of the two MSEs for different values of γ_{KL} and θ, and for various critical values of F. He shows that for $|\theta| > 1$, one could still obtain $F < 1$ due to sampling error and therefore the COV estimators (such as $\hat{\beta}_L$) could be worse than the OLS estimators (such as $\hat{\beta}_{yL.K}$) in the MSE sense. In general, unless there are strong reasons to believe that $\theta < 1$, the OLS is better than the COV estimators, according to Feldstein.

How about combining $\hat{\beta}_L$ and $\hat{\beta}_{yL.K}$ linearly for deriving a weighted (WTD) estimator? Feldstein does that too. He takes the following weighted estimator:

$$\hat{\beta}_{\text{WTD}} = \phi\hat{\beta}_{yL.K} + (1 - \phi)\hat{\beta}_L \tag{6.34}$$

He shows that the ϕ that minimizes $\text{MSE}(\hat{\beta}_{\text{WTD}})$ is related to θ as follows:

$$\phi^0 = \theta^2/1 + \theta^2 \tag{6.35}$$

Since θ^2 is unknown, one way out would be to equate θ^2 to t^2 of (6.33) and use this value to compute ϕ^0 before substituting for ϕ in (6.34). Due to the nature of the underlying combination, $\hat{\beta}_{\text{WTD}}$ is found by Feldstein to be generally better than the COV estimator in his simulation study, but is still worse than the OLS estimator for $|\theta| > 1.5$.

The moral of the investigation is as follows. Use OLS and include, for instance, both L and K in the production function model even when the explanatory variables are highly correlated, unless the second variable, say K, has to be dropped. This is because its associated regression coefficient is considered to be less than its standard error. But this moral would perhaps not apply unless it is the first variable, L in this example, that would be the preferred variable.

Extensions to larger numbers of explanatory variables have been tackled by various authors. See Toro-Vizcarrondo and Wallace (1968), Wallace and Toro-Vizcarrondo (1969), Wallace (1972), and Goodnight and Wallace (1972). Some of

[13] As is stated in Section 4.7.5 of Chapter 4, a t^2 with, say, S degrees of freedom is an F with the numerator degree of freedom 1 and the denominator degrees of freedom S.

these are theoretically complicated, involving noncentral[14] F distributions and their graduation. But as with Feldstein's COV methods, they rely on a priori significance tests. Whether or not these tests are valid will essentially depend upon future sample results. Also, deleting variables for the sake of improved precision in the MSE sense may, as with the COV methods, introduce bias of misspecification. Thus ultimately the solution of the problem will depend on the relative weights given by the investigator to improved precision and reduced bias.

6.2 FUNCTIONAL FORMS AND EXTENSIONS OF LINEAR REGRESSION

6.2.1 Cobb–Douglas Production Function

At the beginning of Chapter 5 an example is cited on linear multiple regression. However, the example is originally for a Cobb–Douglas production function of a usual nonlinear type:

$$V = AL^{\alpha}K^{\beta}$$

This is then changed, after logarithmic transformation of variables, to a linear form:

$$\ln V = \ln \mathrm{A} + \alpha \ln L + \beta \ln K$$

Recall that V is output, L and K inputs of labor and capital, α and β are parameters, and ln stands for natural logarithm.

Examples of this sort are quite widespread in economics and other social sciences, and the transformation helps linearize (what basically is) a nonlinear function. This does not mean that nonlinearities are always conventional or free of analytical complications. Indeed sometimes they are not. We shall address these problems later but first we like to give another example of a linearizable nonlinear function.

The CES production function. This example is taken from a different class of production functions, called the constant elasticity of substitution production functions (the CES production functions) invented by Arrow and others (1961). The equation for such a function is given below:

$$Y = A[\delta K^{-\rho} + (1 - \delta)L^{-\rho}]^{-1/\rho} \tag{6.36}$$

[14] A noncentral F is the ratio of a noncentral χ^2 and a central χ^2, each divided by its degree of freedom. A central χ^2 is the usual χ^2 where the mean value of the originating normal population is zero in the null hypothesis. When this is not so, a noncentral χ^2 results.

where

$$\begin{aligned} Y &= \text{output} \\ L, K &= \text{labor and capital inputs} \\ A &= \text{efficiency parameter, } A > 0 \\ \delta &= \text{distribution parameter, } 0 < \delta < 1 \\ \rho &= \text{extent of substitution between labor and capital, related to} \\ &\quad \sigma\text{, the elasticity of substitution: } \rho = 1/\sigma - 1;\ \rho \geq -1 \end{aligned} \tag{6.37}$$

Now we discuss the estimation of the elasticity parameter of this function, reverting to estimation of other parameters in other chapters.

Using the profit maximization condition (that is, marginal product of labor equal to real wage rate), we have

$$\frac{\partial Y}{\partial L} = A' \left(\frac{Y}{L}\right)^{1+\rho} = \frac{W}{P} \tag{6.38}$$

where A′ is a constant, and W/P is the real wage rate. This yields a solution of Y/L as:

$$Y/L = A''(W/P)^{1/1+\rho} \tag{6.39}$$

Taking natural logarithms and equating σ to $1/1 + \rho$, we have:

$$\ln \frac{Y}{L} = A_0 + \frac{1}{1+\rho} \ln \frac{W}{P} = A_0 + \sigma \ln \frac{W}{P} \qquad A_0 = \ln A'' \tag{6.40}$$

Arrow and others indeed reverse the roles of Y/L and W/P and estimate σ from the equation:

$$\ln W/P = A_0' + (1 + \rho) \ln Y/L \tag{6.41}$$

They use crosssection data on selected industries from 19 countries over the period 1950–1956 and assume additive disturbances. Their least squares estimate of σ comes predominantly to below unity. Indeed 10 out of 24 industries turn out an estimate significantly different from and below unity. This indicates that the production function of these industries is not of the Cobb–Douglas type. For had this been so, the elasticity of substitution would have been equal to unity.

Two aspects of the above example are particularly important: (1) the transformation to linearize, and (2) the status of the error term. One or both of these aspects will be discussed below as more examples are covered. (We do not discuss a third aspect relating to linearity obtained by invoking special conditions such as optimizing producers' behavior, because that rather belongs to economic theory.)

6.2.2 Polynomial and Reciprocal Type Functions

The law of diminishing returns or the law of diminishing utilities, two important laws of microeconomic theory, cannot be described properly by a linear function

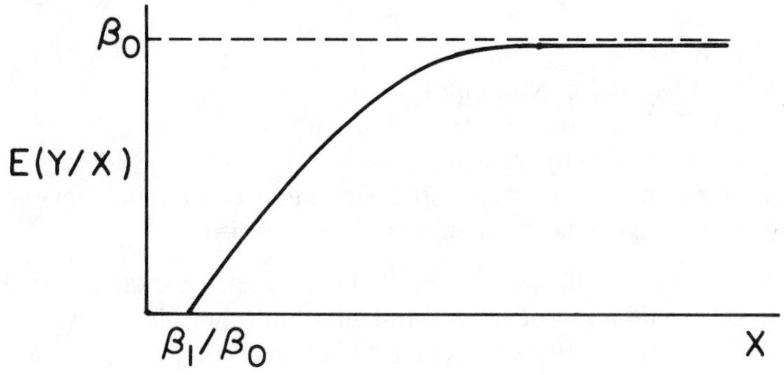

Figure 6.1

of (the quantity of) input used or output consumed. A second powered term in these variables with negative coefficients may be required. Still higher powered terms may be necessary if theory will stipulate the effects of higher order changes in them.

These problems appear difficult but they are not so in reality, because nonlinearities like these can be transformed back to linearity by equating the second and the higher powered terms to new variables that can be treated as linear components in the regression equation. For instance, the nonlinear function of X

$$E(Y \mid X) = \beta_0 + \beta_1 X + \beta_2 X^2$$

can be transformed into a linear function, such as

$$E(y \mid x_1, x_2) = \beta_0 + \beta_1 x_1 + \beta_2 x_2$$

in which the new variables, y and xs, are related to the old variables, Y and Xs through relations

$$y = Y \qquad x_1 = X \qquad x_2 = X^2$$

Similarly, consider a reciprocal function such as

$$E(Y \mid X) = \beta_0 + \beta_1/X \qquad \beta_0 > 0, \beta_1 < 0$$

which is graphed as in Figure 6.1. This may be illustrated by the Engel's curve in consumer economics equating Y and X to expenditure on a commodity and consumer income, respectively. This nonlinear function can be transformed to a linear function

$$E(y \mid x) = \beta_0 + \beta_1 x$$

by the definitional identities

$$y = Y \qquad x = 1/X$$

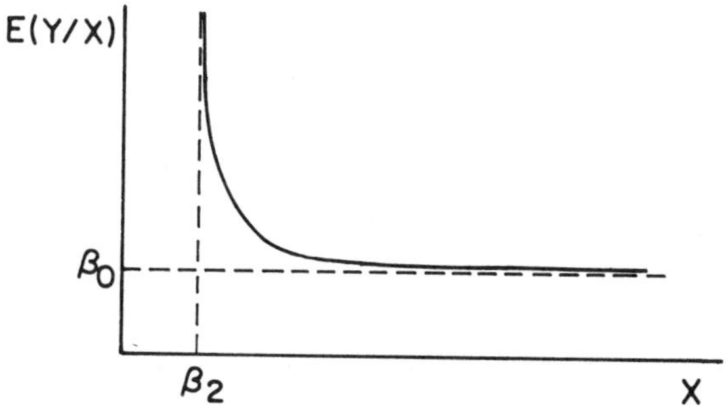

Figure 6.2

6.2.3 Demand for Money Function

However, linear transformations of this sort should not be applied blindly. For, assume a relation:

$$E(Y \mid X) = \beta_0 + \beta_1/(X - \beta_2) \qquad \beta_0, \beta_1, \beta_2 > 0$$

which can be graphed as in Figure 6.2.

An example of this graph may be the liquidity preference schedule in monetary economics. There, Y is the interest rate, X is cash, β_0 the liquidity trap value of interest rate, and β_2 the transaction demand for cash. A transformation such as $y = Y$, and $x = 1/(X - \beta_2)$ to change $E(Y \mid X)$ to an apparently linear form $E(y/x) = \beta_0 + \beta_1 x$ will not really make $E(y \mid x)$ linear. The reason is simple. The substitution of x for $1/(X - \beta_2)$ is of course logical, but not operational, since the latter includes an unknown parameter β_2. This makes the functional form, even after transformation, nonlinear. Thus the properties of the Ordinary Least Squares method for linear relations will not carry over to this function.[15]

6.2.4 Exponential Functions and Log–Normal Errors

Next we discuss an exponential function which is converted to a linear form by a double log transformation. The coefficients of this linear function have a simple interpretation. They are called elasticity. This kind of transformation is quite popular in econometric work.

Let the exponential relation be given by

$$Y = \beta_0^* X^{\beta_1} \tag{6.42}$$

[15] One can of course apply the method of least squares of an iterative type. For this an initial value of β_2 has to be assumed. At this value, an application of ordinary least squares will lead to the estimated residuals and sum of squares due to residuals. This procedure would be repeated with revised values of β_2 each time checking to see if the residual sum of squares decreases. Iteration will stop when no further reduction in the residual sum of squares will take place. Evidently this routine is that of nonlinear least squares.

whose linear form is:

$$y = \beta_0^{**} + \beta_1 x \tag{6.43}$$

where

$$y = \ln Y, \qquad \beta_0^{**} = \ln \beta_0^*, \qquad \text{and } x = \ln X \tag{6.44}$$

To be able to estimate and especially apply the OLS method to this function, we require that the error ϵ^* appear multiplicatively in the equation. In particular, we assume $E(\epsilon^*) = 1$, $V(\epsilon^*) = \sigma_*^2$, and ϵ^* independent of the Xs. Then we can show that

$$V(Y \mid X) = E(Y - E(Y \mid X))^2 = [E(Y \mid X)]^2 \sigma_*^2 \tag{6.45}$$

That is, the conditional variance of Y for given X varies systematically with the square of the conditional mean, which in turn varies with X.

If we make transformations:

$$y = \ln Y, \qquad x = \ln X, \qquad \beta_0^{**} = \ln \beta_0^*, \qquad \epsilon^{**} = \ln \epsilon^* \tag{6.46}$$

the model equation changes to:

$$y = \beta_0^{**} + \beta_1 x + \epsilon^{**} \tag{6.47}$$

Still the OLS technique is not applicable since[16]

$$E(\epsilon^{**}) = E(\ln \epsilon^*) < \ln E(\epsilon^*) = 0 \tag{6.48}$$

Letting

$$E(\epsilon^{**}) = \mu, \qquad \epsilon = \epsilon^{**} - \mu \qquad \text{and } \beta_0 = \beta^{**} + \mu \tag{6.49}$$

we have

$$y = \beta_0 + \beta_1 x + \epsilon \tag{6.50}$$

Now the OLS technique is readily applicable to this equation since $E(\epsilon) = 0$, $V(\epsilon) = \sigma^2$, and the ϵs are independent of X.

In this model, $\hat{\beta}_0$ and $\hat{\beta}_1$ are BLUE for β_0 and β_1. But what can be said about the estimate of β_0^*?

We can not say much unless an additional assumption is made. Recall that $\beta_0 = \ln \beta_0^* + \mu$ from which we have $\beta_0^* = e^{\beta_0} \cdot e^{-\mu}$. If ϵ^*, the error of the original model, is distributed log normally with $E(\epsilon^*) = 1$, and $V(\epsilon^*) = \sigma_*^2$, then we can show[17] that

$$\beta_0^* = e^{\beta_0} e^{\sigma^2/2}$$

[16] This result follows from an established theorem: If Z is a random variable with mean $E(Z)$, then it must imply $E(\ln Z) \leq \ln E(Z)$. The equality sign holds if $V(Z) = 0$.

[17] To give some background on a log–normal distribution, observe that the logarithm of a log–

This can be estimated by

$$e^{\hat{\beta}_0} e^{S^2/2} \tag{6.51}$$

where S^2 is the sum of squares[18] due to error divided by its degrees of freedom $n - 2$.

Example. Suppose Y is the end of the year U.S. money supply in billions of current dollars, and X is U.S. GNP in billions of current dollars. Let the data on both Y and X for 13 years, namely 1953–1965 be presented as follows:

Y = 173 181 185 188 193 206 209 214 228 245 265 286 314

X = 365 365 398 419 441 447 484 504 520 560 589 629 676

(Data Source: *Economic Report of the President*, 1966, pp. 263 and 209.) Assume that the relation between Y and X is the same as of this section, and ϵ^* log-normally distributed with $E(\epsilon^*) = 1$, and $V(\epsilon^*) = \sigma^2_*$. We can easily compute: $\hat{\beta}_1 = 0.9117$, $\hat{\beta}_0 = -0.2480$, SST $= 0.4177$, SSR $= \hat{\beta}_1[\Sigma XY - \Sigma X \Sigma Y] = 0.3990$, SSE $=$ SST $-$ SSR $= 0.0187$; $S^2 =$ SSE/11 $= 0.0017$. Thus, $\hat{\beta}_0^* = e^{-0.2480 + 0.0017/2} = e^{-0.2472}$, or $\log_e \hat{\beta}_0^* = -0.2472$, so $\hat{\beta}_0^*$ is the antilog of -0.2472, which is 0.781. Therefore, $\hat{\beta}_0^* = 0.785$.

6.3 CONSTRAINED LEAST SQUARES

Let the model $\mathbf{Y} = X\boldsymbol{\beta} + \boldsymbol{\epsilon}$ be subject to $l(\leq m + 1)$ independent linear restrictions on the $\boldsymbol{\beta}$ parameters:

$$\mathbf{r} = R\boldsymbol{\beta} \tag{6.52}$$

where $\mathbf{r}$ is a $l \times 1$ known vector and R is a $l \times (m + 1)$ known matrix of rank $l < m + 1$. Two short examples are: (1) $\beta_2 = \beta_2^*$ (all other βs being unrestricted) implying: $r = \beta_2^*$ and $R = (0010 \ldots 0)$, which ultimately boils down to the familiar single coefficient test case, and (2) a linear sum of βs equal to one, namely $\Sigma_0^m \beta_i = 1$, equating r to 1 and R to the vector $(1 \quad 1 \ldots 1)$. This reduces to the test

---

normally distributed variable, say ϵ^*, is normally distributed. That is, $\log \epsilon^*$ is $N(\mu, \sigma^2)$. Then it follows from one of the standard properties of log-normal and normal distributions:

$$E(\epsilon^*) = \exp\left(\mu + \frac{\sigma^2}{2}\right)$$

And since we assume $E(\epsilon^*) = 1$ it follows that $e^{\mu + (\sigma^2/2)} = e^0$, from which $\mu = -\sigma^2/2$. Thus $\beta_0^* = e^{\beta_0} e^{-\mu} = e^{\beta_0} e^{\sigma^2/2}$.

[18] This estimator will be unbiased in large samples, even though it may be biased in small samples.

of constant returns to scale, when both output and inputs of the production function are in logarithms, and the βs are the coefficients in the resulting linear relation.

For the general problem we follow the method of restricted least squares. Minimize

$$L = (\mathbf{Y} - X\boldsymbol{\beta})'(\mathbf{Y} - X\boldsymbol{\beta}) - 2\boldsymbol{\mu}'(R\boldsymbol{\beta} - \mathbf{r}) \tag{6.53}$$

where $\boldsymbol{\mu}$ is a $l \times 1$ vector of Lagrangean multipliers.

The first order conditions of minimization yield

$$\frac{\partial L}{\partial \boldsymbol{\beta}} = -2X'\mathbf{Y} + 2X'X\hat{\boldsymbol{\beta}}^* - 2R'\boldsymbol{\mu} = \mathbf{0} \tag{6.54}$$

$$\frac{\partial L}{\partial \boldsymbol{\mu}} = -2(R\hat{\boldsymbol{\beta}}^* - \mathbf{r}) = \mathbf{0} \tag{6.55}$$

Solutions of $\hat{\boldsymbol{\beta}}^*$ are, using the OLS estimator $\hat{\boldsymbol{\beta}} = (X'X)^{-1}X'\mathbf{Y}$,

$$\hat{\boldsymbol{\beta}}^* = \hat{\boldsymbol{\beta}} + (X'X)^{-1} R'\boldsymbol{\mu} \tag{6.56}$$

To solve for $\boldsymbol{\mu}$, premultiply the above by R:

$$R\hat{\boldsymbol{\beta}}^* = R\hat{\boldsymbol{\beta}} + R(X'X)^{-1} R'\boldsymbol{\mu} \tag{6.57}$$

in which substitution of the restriction $R\hat{\boldsymbol{\beta}}^* = \mathbf{r}$ yields

$$\mathbf{r} = R\hat{\boldsymbol{\beta}}^* = R\hat{\boldsymbol{\beta}} + R(X'X)^{-1} R'\boldsymbol{\mu} \tag{6.58}$$

A rearrangement of this gives

$$\boldsymbol{\mu} = [R(X'X)^{-1}R']^{-1} (\mathbf{r} - R\hat{\boldsymbol{\beta}}) \tag{6.59}$$

Thus, finally,

$$\hat{\boldsymbol{\beta}}^* = \hat{\boldsymbol{\beta}} + R(X'X)^{-1}R'[R(X'X)^{-1}R']^{-1}(\mathbf{r} - R\hat{\boldsymbol{\beta}}) \tag{6.60}$$

To develop a test procedure for the linear parametric restrictions, proceed as follows. The error vector for the $\hat{\boldsymbol{\beta}}^*$ estimates are:

$$\hat{\boldsymbol{\epsilon}}^* = \mathbf{Y} - X\hat{\boldsymbol{\beta}}^* \tag{6.61}$$

This can be expressed as

$$\begin{aligned}\hat{\boldsymbol{\epsilon}}^* &= \mathbf{Y} - X\hat{\boldsymbol{\beta}} - X(\hat{\boldsymbol{\beta}}^* - \hat{\boldsymbol{\beta}}) \\ &= \hat{\boldsymbol{\epsilon}} - X(\hat{\boldsymbol{\beta}}^* - \hat{\boldsymbol{\beta}})\end{aligned} \tag{6.62}$$

where $\hat{\boldsymbol{\epsilon}}$ is the OLS estimated error vector. The sum of squares due to the (restricted) residuals is

$$\hat{\boldsymbol{\epsilon}}^{*\prime}\hat{\boldsymbol{\epsilon}} = \hat{\boldsymbol{\epsilon}}'\hat{\boldsymbol{\epsilon}} + (\hat{\boldsymbol{\beta}}^* - \hat{\boldsymbol{\beta}})'X'X(\hat{\boldsymbol{\beta}}^* - \hat{\boldsymbol{\beta}}) \tag{6.63}$$

which using (6.60) can be rearranged as:

$$\hat{\boldsymbol{\epsilon}}^{*\prime}\hat{\boldsymbol{\epsilon}}^* - \hat{\boldsymbol{\epsilon}}'\hat{\boldsymbol{\epsilon}} = (\mathbf{r} - R\hat{\boldsymbol{\beta}})'[R(X'X)^{-1}R']^{-1}(\mathbf{r} - R\hat{\boldsymbol{\beta}}) \tag{6.64}$$

It can be easily proved[19] that this criterion is distributed as χ^2 with l df. Since earlier we have seen that $\hat{\boldsymbol{\epsilon}}'\hat{\boldsymbol{\epsilon}}/\sigma^2$ is χ^2 with $n - m - 1$ df, therefore the hypothesis H_0: $\boldsymbol{R\beta} = \mathbf{r}$ can be tested by the F statistic defined as:

$$F = \frac{(\mathbf{r} - \boldsymbol{R\hat{\beta}})'[\boldsymbol{R}(X'X)^{-1}\boldsymbol{R}']^{-1}(\mathbf{r} - \boldsymbol{R\hat{\beta}})/l}{\hat{\boldsymbol{\epsilon}}'\hat{\boldsymbol{\epsilon}}/(n - m - 1)} \tag{6.65}$$

with l and $(n - m - 1)$ df. One can of course derive alternative expressions for F depending on whether

$$(\hat{\boldsymbol{\beta}}^* - \hat{\boldsymbol{\beta}})'X'X(\hat{\boldsymbol{\beta}}^* - \hat{\boldsymbol{\beta}})/l \qquad \text{or } (\hat{\boldsymbol{\epsilon}}^{*\prime}\hat{\boldsymbol{\epsilon}}^* - \hat{\boldsymbol{\epsilon}}'\hat{\boldsymbol{\epsilon}})/l$$

is the form of the numerator of F in which it is computed, the denominator remaining the same as in (6.65).

6.3.1 Structural Changes

This technique can be used to test structural changes as evident in changes in the behavioral characteristics of individuals. Typically the changes may involve different values of the intercept term, or the slope coefficients, or both the intercept and slope coefficients of the regression equation in two different time periods. These problems can be equally or perhaps more efficiently solved by following the method of dummy variables as will be clear in the next section.

A generalized extension of structural changes may involve m variables and t time periods. For instance, an investigator may like to know whether the demand for money underwent any structural changes from the pre-World War I, through the interwar, down to the post-World War II periods. Similarly, a relationship can be tested for its stability across countries, industries, interest groups, and so on.

The model and computational formats may be described in three types of hypothesis tests as follows:

Common intercept and common slopes in all t periods:

$$\begin{bmatrix} \mathbf{Y}_1 \\ \vdots \\ \mathbf{Y}_t \end{bmatrix} = \begin{bmatrix} \mathbf{i}_1 & X_1^c \\ \mathbf{i}_2 & X_2^c \\ \vdots & \vdots \\ \mathbf{i}_t & X_t^c \end{bmatrix} \begin{bmatrix} \boldsymbol{\beta}_0 \\ \boldsymbol{\beta}^c \end{bmatrix} + \boldsymbol{\epsilon} \qquad \text{Model I}$$

Intercepts different but slopes common in t periods:

$$\begin{bmatrix} \mathbf{Y}_1 \\ \mathbf{Y}_2 \\ \vdots \\ \mathbf{Y}_t \end{bmatrix} = \begin{bmatrix} \mathbf{i}_1 & \mathbf{0} & \cdots & \mathbf{0} & X_1^c \\ \mathbf{0} & \mathbf{i}_2 & \cdots & \mathbf{0} & X_2^c \\ \cdots & \cdots & \cdots & \cdots & \cdots \\ \mathbf{0} & \mathbf{0} & & \mathbf{i}_t & X_t^c \end{bmatrix} \begin{bmatrix} \boldsymbol{\beta}_0^1 \\ \boldsymbol{\beta}_0^2 \\ \vdots \\ \boldsymbol{\beta}_0^t \\ \boldsymbol{\beta}^c \end{bmatrix} + \boldsymbol{\epsilon} \qquad \text{Model II}$$

[19] Since $\hat{\boldsymbol{\beta}}$ is multivariate normal, $\boldsymbol{R\hat{\beta}} \sim \mathrm{N}(\boldsymbol{R\beta}, \sigma^2\boldsymbol{R}(X'X)^{-1}\boldsymbol{R}')$, $\boldsymbol{R}(\hat{\boldsymbol{\beta}} - \boldsymbol{\beta}) = \boldsymbol{R\hat{\beta}} - \mathbf{r} \sim \mathrm{N}(\mathbf{0}, \sigma^2\boldsymbol{R}(X'X)^{-1}\boldsymbol{R}')$. Therefore, $(\boldsymbol{R\hat{\beta}} - \mathbf{r})[\sigma^2\boldsymbol{R}(X'X)^{-1}\boldsymbol{R}']^{-1}(\boldsymbol{R\hat{\beta}} - \mathbf{r}) \sim \chi^2$ with l df.

Intercepts different, slopes different in all t periods:

$$\begin{bmatrix} \mathbf{Y}_1 \\ \mathbf{Y}_2 \\ \vdots \\ \mathbf{Y}_t \end{bmatrix} = \begin{bmatrix} \mathbf{i}_1 & \mathbf{0} & \cdots & \mathbf{0} & X_1^c & 0 & \cdots & 0 \\ \mathbf{0} & \mathbf{i}_2 & \cdots & \mathbf{0} & 0 & X_2^c & \cdots & 0 \\ \cdots & & & & & & & \cdots \\ \mathbf{0} & \mathbf{0} & \cdots & \mathbf{i}_t & 0 & 0 & \cdots & X_t^c \end{bmatrix} \begin{bmatrix} \boldsymbol{\beta}_0^1 \\ \boldsymbol{\beta}_0^2 \\ \vdots \\ \boldsymbol{\beta}_0^t \\ \boldsymbol{\beta}_1^c \\ \boldsymbol{\beta}_2^c \\ \vdots \\ \boldsymbol{\beta}_t^c \end{bmatrix} + \boldsymbol{\epsilon} \qquad \text{Model III}$$

In the above, $\mathbf{i}_j$ is a column vector of n_j elements ($j = 1, 2, \ldots, t$) and X_j^c is an $n_j \times (m + 1)$ matrix of observations on the explanatory variables in class j ($j = 1, 2, \ldots, t$). In models I, II, and III, the degrees of freedom for the error sums of squares are $n - m - 1$, $n - t - m$, and $n - t(m + 1)$, respectively, where $n = \Sigma_{j=1}^{t} n_j$. Denoting the three error sums of squares as ESS_1, ESS_2, and ESS_3, and following the general procedure discussed in the preceding section, the following tests are recommended:

$$\text{(a)} \qquad F = \frac{(\text{ESS}_2 - \text{ESS}_3)/m(t - 1)}{\text{ESS}_3/\{n - t(m + 1)\}} \tag{6.66}$$

to test for a common slope of the regression with $m(t - 1)$ and $n - t(m + 1)$ df.

$$\text{(b)} \qquad F = \frac{(\text{ESS}_1 - \text{ESS}_2)/(t - 1)}{\text{ESS}_2/(n - t - m)} \tag{6.67}$$

to test for common intercepts given that a common regression slope exists, at $t - 1$ and $n - t - m$ df.

$$\text{(c)} \qquad F = \frac{(\text{ESS}_1 - \text{ESS}_3)/(m + 1)(t - 1)}{\text{ESS}_3/\{n - t(m + 1)\}} \tag{6.68}$$

to test for the homogeneity of regressions across the various periods, with $(m + 1)(t - 1)$ and $n - t(m + 1)$ df. When $t = 2$ and $n_2 \leqq m + 1$, we can show that (6.68) reduces to the equivalent Chow (1960) and Fisher (1970) test statistics used to test whether the second n_2 observations belong to the same structure as the first n_1 observations. In that case, the numerator degrees of freedom become n_2, and the denominator degrees of freedom become $n_1 - (m + 1)$. As usual, n_1 is larger than $m + 1$.

To conclude, we should point out that the structural shift analysis of this section presupposes a strong belief as to when or where changes took place. If the switch points are unknown, the analysis becomes substantially more difficult. It then belongs to the area of variable parameter models, a topic to be discussed later. Also, the analysis would be very complicated if a transition phase or phases had to exist between regimes.

Above we have presented methods to cope with only a few classes of cases.

As we have indicated before, the same analysis could be performed by the method of dummy variables for the same as well as different classes of cases. With that end in view we will skip computational illustrations of the structural shift analysis of this section so we can immediately proceed to the dummy variable analysis. This follows.

6.4 DUMMY VARIABLES

6.4.1 The Comanor and Wilson (1971) Applied Study

Let us begin by showing how a dummy variable approach is used by drawing an example from, say, industrial organization. Comanor and Wilson (1971) fit advertising to concentration for 41 U.S. consumer goods industries for the period 1954–1957. Their equation is:

$$\underset{}{A/S} = \underset{(0.02825)}{-\,0.00565} + \underset{(0.0086)}{0.0118 \ln CR} + \underset{(0.0132)}{0.0204 \ln G} - \underset{(0.0105)}{0.0178D} - \underset{(0.0133)}{0.0154T}$$

$$R^2 = 0.17$$

In the above, A/S is advertising to sales ratio, CR is the four-farm concentration ratio, G the growth rate of sales, D a durable goods industry dummy variable, and T a high-technical-barrier dummy variable. D is equal to 1 for the durable goods industry, 0 otherwise. The negative coefficient of this variable means that the durable goods industries tend to cut down on advertising expenditure (this is a standard belief or result with this kind of an industry—it might be quite different with a consumer goods one). Even the concentration ratio does not seem to significantly affect A/S, even though the effect is positive. On the whole, the poor performance indicated by the coefficient of multiple determination implies that the regression is unreliable. There must be other variables, left out in the equation, which ought to explain advertising expenditures better.

A better relation is fitted by Comanor and Wilson showing the effects of advertising and concentration on profit for the same sample of 41 consumer goods industries:

$$\pi = \underset{(0.0119)}{0.0375} + \underset{(0.147)}{0.318\ A/S} - \underset{(0.000406)}{0.000065\ CR} + \underset{(0.0062)}{0.0107 \ln KR}$$

$$+ \underset{(0.0151)}{0.0269 \ln G} + \underset{(0.0180)}{0.0258\ L} \qquad R^2 = 0.52$$

In the above, π stands for profit rate on stockholders' equity, A/S, CR, and G have been defined before, KR is capital requirement, being the amount of capital necessary for entry at the single efficient plant scale, and L is a dummy variable, with the value 1 for local industries, but the value 0 otherwise. This variable has a positive effect on profit rate, even though not statistically significant. For related results, see Comanor and Wilson (1967) and Sherman and Tollison (1971).

It is time we discussed the theoretical aspects of the dummy variable method to appreciate how it worked. This we do now.

6.4.2 Theoretical Aspects of the Dummy Variable Method

Suppose consumption expenditure Y depends on income X. But different levels of income produce different values of the marginal propensity to consume. An example might be the following:

$$\begin{aligned} E(Y \mid X) &= \beta_1, \text{ if } X < \$1000 \text{ (called Group 1)} \\ &= \beta_2, \text{ if } \$1000 \leq X < \$5000 \text{ (called Group 2)} \\ &= \beta_3, \text{ if } X \geq \$5000 \text{ (called Group 3)} \end{aligned} \tag{6.69}$$

This nonlinear formulation can be put in a linear form such as:

$$E(Y \mid x) = \beta_1 x_1 + \beta_2 x_2 + \beta_3 x_3 \tag{6.70}$$

where the xs are the dummy or binary coded variables defined as $x_1 = 1$, if $X <$ \$1000, or 0, if otherwise; $x_2 = 1$ if $\$1000 \leq X < \$5000$, or 0, if otherwise; and $x_3 = 1$, if $X \geq \$5000$, or 0, if otherwise.

The two formulations have equivalent implications. For instance, for Group 1, $x_2 = 1$, but $x_2 = x_3 = 0$ which means $E(Y \mid \text{Group 1}) = \beta_1$, the same as in the nonlinear formulation. Hence $E(Y \mid \text{Group } i) = \beta_i$, $i = 1, 2, 3$.

For the OLS estimation of the βs, take n_i observations. Each of these observations has $x_i = 1$ and $x_j\ (j \neq i) = 0$; $i, j = 1, 2, 3$. Let $n = \Sigma_1^3 n_i$. Then $X'X$ is a 3×3 diagonal matrix with diagonal entries n_i $(i = 1, 2, 3)$, and $(X'X)^{-1}$ a similar matrix[20] with entries $1/n_i$; $(i = 1, 2, 3)$. Thus

$$\hat{\beta} = \begin{bmatrix} \hat{\beta}_1 \\ \hat{\beta}_2 \\ \hat{\beta}_3 \end{bmatrix} = (X'X)^{-1}X'\mathbf{Y} = \begin{bmatrix} 1/n_1 & 0 & 0 \\ 0 & 1/n_2 & 0 \\ 0 & 0 & 1/n_3 \end{bmatrix} \begin{bmatrix} \Sigma^1 Y_i \\ \Sigma^2 Y_i \\ \Sigma^3 Y_i \end{bmatrix} = \begin{bmatrix} \overline{Y}_1 \\ \overline{Y}_2 \\ \overline{Y}_3 \end{bmatrix} \tag{6.71}$$

$\Sigma^1 Y_i$, for instance, implies the sum of Y observations for the first (n_1) set of observations, and $\overline{Y}_1$ is the mean of such observations and, similarly, $\Sigma^2 Y_i$ and $\Sigma^3 Y_i$, and $\overline{Y}_2$ and $\overline{Y}_3$. Thus the estimated regression coefficient for a group is the same as its mean of Ys. This is a very simple result arising because of the simplicity of the observation matrix structure.

Since

$$\hat{Y} = \hat{\beta}_1 x_1 + \hat{\beta}_2 x_2 + \hat{\beta}_3 x_3 = \sum_1^3 \overline{Y}_i x_i \tag{6.72}$$

we have

$$\hat{Y}_1 = \overline{Y}_1, \qquad \hat{Y}_2 = \overline{Y}_2, \qquad \hat{Y}_3 = \overline{Y}_3 \tag{6.73}$$

[20] See (3.37) of Chapter 3 for this result.

Thus the following ANOVA table results:

Variation Due To	Sum of Squares	DF	Mean Sum Squares
Between Groups	$SSR = \sum_{i=1}^{3} n_i(\overline{Y}_i - \overline{Y})^2$	3	$MSR = \frac{SSR}{3}$
Within Groups	$SSE = \sum_{1}^{n_1} (Y_i - \overline{Y}_1)^2 + \sum_{n_1+1}^{n_1+n_2} (Y_i - \overline{Y}_2)^2$	$n - 4$	$MSE = \frac{SSE}{n - 4}$
	$+ \sum_{n_1+n_2+1}^{n} (Y_i - \overline{Y}_3)^2$		
Total	$SST = \sum^{n} (Y - \overline{Y})^2$	$n - 1$	

The rest of the table can be computed in the usual way and is not shown. Under the null hypothesis, all βs are identical. Thus a significant F (= MSR/MSE) would only reject that hypothesis in favor of the alternative: $\beta_1 \neq \beta_2 \neq \beta_3$.

Example. If $n_1 = n_2 = n_3 = 3$, and $\mathbf{Y}' = [3\ 4\ 5\ 8\ 10\ 12\ 13\ 14\ 18]$ we have: $\hat{\beta}_1 = \overline{Y}_1 = 4$, $\hat{\beta}_2 = \overline{Y}_2 = 10$, and $\hat{\beta}_3 = \overline{Y}_3 = 15$. Also, $\hat{Y}_1 = 4$, $\hat{Y}_2 = 10$, and $\hat{Y}_3 = 15$. Further, $SST = \Sigma Y^2 - (\Sigma Y)^2/9 = 1047 - 841 = 206$; $SSR = 3[(5\ 2/3)^2 + (1/3)^2 + (5\ 1/3)^2] = 182$, and $SSE = SST - SSR = 24$. Thus, $F = MSR/MSE = 182/3\ /\ 24/5 = 12.64$. This is larger than F at both 5% and 1% probability levels of significance (the values being 5.41 and 12.06, respectively). Therefore, we would be unable to accept the null hypothesis $\beta_1 = \beta_2 = \beta_3$ at these probability levels of significance.

Intercept term and reformulation. What would happen if we kept an intercept term in the preceding model? We would then run into the problem of perfect multicollinearity. Calling x_0 the intercept variable, all the observations on which are equal to 1, it can be easily seen that $\mathbf{x}_0 = \mathbf{x}_1 + \mathbf{x}_2 + \mathbf{x}_3$ in vector notation. This implies linear dependence among the xs and consequently a singular (and an uninvertible) matrix $(X'X)$ would result. Thus the coefficients βs cannot be estimated.

A way out would be to redefine the variables xs. Let us switch to the new variables χ with representative observations in the 3 different groups defined as follows (along with observations on the Ys):

Group	χ_1	χ_2	χ_3	Y
Group 1	1	0	0	Y_{i1}
Group 2	1	1	0	Y_{j2}
Group 3	1	0	1	Y_{k3}

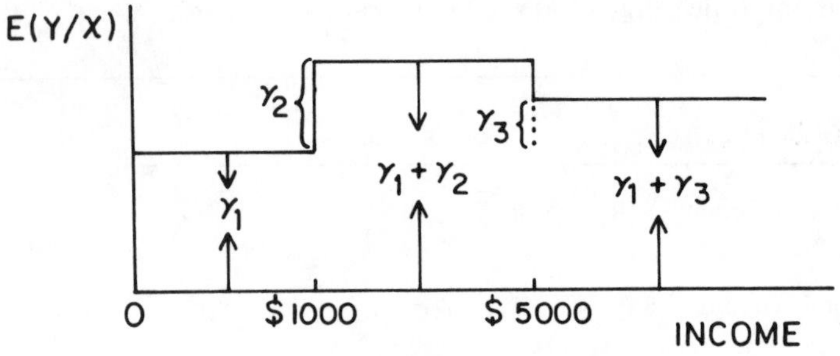

Figure 6.3

That is, χ_1 equals 1 for observations in all groups, and χ_2 and χ_3 each equals 1 for observations in Group 2 and Group 3 respectively, being 0 outside its respective group. Then the model is:

$$E(Y \mid X) = \gamma_1\chi_1 + \gamma_2\chi_2 + \gamma_3\chi_3 \tag{6.74}$$

From the above, the mean values of Y in the groups are:

$$E(Y \mid \text{Group 1}) = \gamma_1; \qquad E(Y \mid \text{Group 2}) = \gamma_1 + \gamma_2;$$
$$E(Y \mid \text{Group 3}) = \gamma_1 + \gamma_3 \tag{6.75}$$

This is a clear indication of the fact that the first group mean is lumped up with the second, and separately with the third group mean, and therefore the first group can be looked upon as a benchmark group against which other group effects are measured. Graphically, the position looks like Figure 6.3.

In the graph the specific effects of group 2 and 3 have been shown to be γ_2 and γ_3 respectively.

The estimated values of the new coefficients $\hat{\gamma}$s are found as before. Since the new observation matrix $\boldsymbol{X}$ is derived from the old observation matrix $\boldsymbol{X}$ through the transformation matrix $\boldsymbol{T}$, that is $\boldsymbol{X} = \boldsymbol{XT}$, where

$$\boldsymbol{T} = \begin{bmatrix} 1 & 0 & 0 \\ 1 & 1 & 0 \\ 1 & 0 & 1 \end{bmatrix}$$

there is an immediate relation between the new coefficient estimates and the old ones as follows:

$$\hat{\gamma} = (\boldsymbol{X'X})^{-1}\boldsymbol{X'}\mathbf{Y} = (\boldsymbol{T'X'XT})^{-1}\boldsymbol{T'X'}\mathbf{Y} = \boldsymbol{P}^{-1}\hat{\boldsymbol{\beta}} \tag{6.76}$$

Thus

$$\begin{bmatrix} \hat{\gamma}_1 \\ \hat{\gamma}_2 \\ \hat{\gamma}_3 \end{bmatrix} = \begin{bmatrix} 1 & 0 & 0 \\ -1 & 1 & 0 \\ -1 & 0 & 1 \end{bmatrix} \begin{bmatrix} \overline{Y}_1 \\ \overline{Y}_2 \\ \overline{Y}_3 \end{bmatrix} = \begin{bmatrix} \overline{Y}_1 \\ \overline{Y}_2 - \overline{Y}_1 \\ \overline{Y}_3 - \overline{Y}_1 \end{bmatrix} = \begin{bmatrix} \hat{\beta}_1 \\ \hat{\beta}_2 - \hat{\beta}_1 \\ \hat{\beta}_3 - \hat{\beta}_1 \end{bmatrix} \tag{6.77}$$

And since $\hat{Y} = \Sigma\hat{\gamma}_i\chi_i$, it follows that

$$\hat{Y}_1 = \hat{\gamma}_1 = \overline{Y}_1; \qquad \hat{Y}_2 = \hat{\gamma}_1 + \hat{\gamma}_2 = \overline{Y}_2; \qquad \hat{Y}_3 = \hat{\gamma}_1 + \hat{\gamma}_3 = \overline{Y}_3 \qquad (6.78)$$

Thus the estimates of E(Y | Group i) are $\hat{Y}_i = \overline{Y}_i$, $i = 1, 2, 3$, the same as those obtained in the original formulation. Consequently the SSR, SSE, and the other features, including the statistical tests, of the ANOVA table will remain the same as before. The only difference is in the interpretation of the effects of the groups: the Group 2 and 3 effects are linked with the effect of Group 1 which, when subtracted out, will yield the specific group effects as before.

It should be borne in mind that both the original formulation and the reformulation can be easily generalized to any number of groups, and the choice of the benchmark group in the latter case is dictated precisely by need. Both the formulations can of course be criticized on the grounds that they are expensive in terms of the degrees of freedom: to test the function in one group, one needs to consider the number of observations (the df) coming from that group only, which may be too few, whereas in the fitting of ordinary smooth functions, tests are based on the degrees of freedom or the number of observations coming from all the groups. While this point may be important in some cases, economists or social scientists may refute it by saying that the setting up of a step function itself depends on theory and data and that may substitute for the loss of information due to a lesser degree of freedom.

6.4.3 Qualitative Classification of Data

In studies of, for instance, income functions, one interesting classification of income earners might be by broad occupations, namely, whether income earners are entrepreneurs, professionals, laborers, etc. Fitting a smooth function in such a case would treat equally the marginal differences between the first and the second occupation group of earners with those between the second and the third group of earners, and so on. A dummy variable approach, by contrast, would maintain the specificity (in the sense of conditional mean income) of earners in each and every occupation group as different from that in every other occupation group.

Other examples might be cited. A country may be under free trade or restricted trade, an industry may be subsidized or not, a country may be in peace or war time conditions, etc. Continuing with this last (war–peace) example, there might be different hypotheses set up for testing purposes. With a consumption function, for instance, a hypothesis might be whether the intercept of the function (representing the autonomous or exogenous part of consumption) shifted, or its slope (representing, for example, the marginal propensity to consume) shifted, or both its intercept and slope shifted when the economy was involved in the war.

As for the intercept alone, the test would be for the null hypothesis $\beta_2 =$

0. For this the following formulation of the consumption function would be relevant:

$$Y = \beta_0 + \beta_1 X + \beta_2 W + \epsilon \tag{6.79}$$

Above, Y = consumption, X = income, W = 1 for 1939–1945 (the war period), and W = 0 otherwise, and ϵ is the well-behaved error term. Evidently,

$$E(Y \mid \text{peace}) = \beta_0 + \beta_1 X \tag{6.80}$$

whereas

$$E(Y \mid \text{war}) = \beta_0 + \beta_1 X + \beta_2 = (\beta_0 + \beta_2) + \beta_1 X \tag{6.81}$$

The comparison of (6.81) with (6.80) shows that the intercept has jumped by β_2 during the war period. To test for the significance of the slope, on the other hand, one should set up the null hypothesis $\gamma_2 = 0$ in the following reformulation of the function

$$Y = \gamma_0 + \gamma_1 X + \gamma_2 \zeta + \epsilon \tag{6.82}$$

where Y and X are the same as before, γs are the new coefficients, and $\zeta = WX$, W being equal to 1 during 1939–1945, 0 otherwise. Lastly, to test whether both the intercept term and the slope coefficient shifted, the basic model is rewritten as

$$Y = \delta_0 + \delta_1 W + \delta_2 X + \delta_3 \zeta + \epsilon \tag{6.83}$$

A little calculation would show that there will be a joint null hypothesis $\delta_1 = 0$ and $\delta_3 = 0$ that has to be tested for the above purposes.

Example. Suppose the following hypothetical data are on a country's military expenditure and GNP over the years 1935–1948 of which 1940–1945 are some of the World War II years:

Year	1935	1936	1937	1938	1939	1940	1941	1942	1943	1944	1945	1946	1947	1948
Military Expenditure (Y)	3.6	3.7	3.8	4.1	4.4	7.1	8.0	8.9	9.7	10.2	10.1	7.9	8.7	9.1
GNP (X)	3.1	3.4	3.9	4.0	4.2	5.1	6.3	8.1	8.8	9.6	9.7	9.6	10.4	12

On these data, we first run two separate regressions, one for each of the peace and the war time periods—without the use of dummy variables whatsoever—and see how the intercept term shifts from the peace to the wartime period. These OLS-estimated regression lines are

$$\textit{Peacetime:} \quad \hat{Y} = 1.47 + 0.66\,X$$

$$\textit{Wartime:} \quad \hat{Y} = 3.74 + 0.66\,X$$

Comparing the intercepts between the two periods, autonomous military expenditure seems to have risen by 3.74 − 1.47, that is, 2.27 units in the war period.

Second, we run 2 new regressions: (1) using a dummy variable for the intercept shift alone—the W variable, and (2) using a dummy variable for the slope coefficient shift alone—the ζ variable. Taking $W = 1$ for 1940–1945, and $W = 0$ for other years, we obtain the regression line as:

$$\hat{Y} = 1.472 + 0.6630\, X + 2.2722\, W$$

The coefficient for W is 2.27. This represents the war effect. This is also the effect that we obtained previously by running two separate regressions for the two periods and comparing their estimated intercept terms.

On the other hand, using the ζ variable, the regression line is estimated to be:

$$\hat{Y} = 1.76 + 0.63\, X + 0.27\, \zeta$$

where $\zeta = WX$, and $W = 1$ for war years and 0 for other years. The coefficient of 0.27 for ζ shows how the war affected the country's military expenditure at the margin in response to GNP.

In conclusion, one should be careful about the use of dummy variables in case heterogeneities between the subperiods are too many and too different. In that case it may be advisable to consider distinctly different subperiods within an historical time period and run a separate regression in each subperiod, rather than piece all the subperiods together and run one regression for the entire period. The point is that when changes are frequent, the different subperiods may be subject to different errors. To pool the pieces together into one series believing as though the same error persisted through the entire period may be highly erroneous.

6.4.4 An Applied Study Due to Auld, Christofides, Swidinsky and Wilton (1979)

An application of the intercept shift and/or slope coefficient shift is illustrated in an actual study due to Auld, Christofides, Swidinsky and Wilton (1979). This is on the effect of the 1975 Anti-Inflation Board (AIB) guidelines on negotiated wage settlements in Canada. This study includes both the private and public sectors. For both sectors, the coefficient of a single intercept-shift dummy variable comes out highly significant. Particularly, wage settlements are roughly 2 to $2\frac{1}{2}\%$ lower in the 1975IV–1977III period of voluntary wage control than what would have resulted had there been no such control. On the basis of the slope coefficient dummies, on the other hand, the authors find that the price expectations coefficients are remarkably higher and price catch-up coefficients lower in the AIB period than other periods. On the whole, the conclusion confirms that the AIB is able to cause an impressive change in the structure of the Canadian wage inflation compared to when it is not in existence.

For structural shift arising from the Canada–United States Automotive Agreement, see Wilton (1975).

6.4.5 Two-Way Classification and Interaction

Sometimes, individuals or subjects are classified according to more than one qualitative characteristic, for example occupation and education. If, for instance, two kinds of occupation ("laborers" and "professionals") and three levels of education ("elementary", "secondary" and "postsecondary") are considered, subjects can be placed in any of 2 × 3 or 6 categories according to their affiliation or attachment to the 6 different (occupation–education) classes. In this case 6 dummy variables can be devised such that the first variable x_1 will be equal to 1 if the subject belongs to the category identified by laborers with no more than elementary level of education, and 0, otherwise; and similarly the other dummy variables x_2 through x_6.

An alternative model is one with a benchmark variable. It is represented by a dummy variable x_0 acting as the intercept term. The other variables of the model are: x_1 for the occupation variable, x_2 and x_3 for the education variables, and ϵ for the error term. The model equation is:

$$Y = \beta_0 x_0 + \beta_1 x_1 + \beta_2 x_2 + \beta_3 x_3 + \epsilon \tag{6.84}$$

These regressors take on values according to the format of Table 6.1 suggested by the occupation and education levels. The group expected incomes can be classified by occupation and education levels as follows:

	Education		
	E	S	PS
Occupation L	β_0	$\beta_0 + \beta_2$	$\beta_0 + \beta_3$
P	$\beta_0 + \beta_1$	$\beta_0 + \beta_1 + \beta_2$	$\beta_0 + \beta_1 + \beta_3$

A simple check would show that the differential impact on income between a professional and a laborer is β_1 regardless of the education level, but the differential impacts as between a secondary and a postsecondary education level (relative to elementary) are β_2 and β_3, respectively, regardless of occupation in

TABLE 6.1

Occupation*	Education**	x_0	x_1	x_2	x_3
L	E	1	0	0	0
L	S	1	0	1	0
L	PS	1	0	0	1
P	E	1	1	0	0
P	S	1	1	1	0
P	PS	1	1	0	1

* L = Laborers, P = Professionals

** E = Elementary, S = Secondary, PS = Postsecondary

each case. This clearly means that the effects of the two ways of classifying the income earners are independent of such classifications. But this need not always be the case, for there may be interaction between them.

We can indeed add, in Table 6.1, two more dummy variables: x_4 and x_5 with typical values (against the previous occupation and the education levels) such as: [0 0 0 0 1 0] and [0 0 0 0 0 1]. Each set of these numbers is to be arranged along a column, not a row. The X_4 and X_5 columns have been obtained by multiplying x_2 by x_1 and x_3 by x_1, respectively. With these changes the group mean incomes can be tabulated as:

	Education		
	E	S	PS
Occupation L	β_0	$\beta_0 + \beta_2$	$\beta_0 + \beta_3$
P	$\beta_0 + \beta_1$	$\beta_0 + \beta_1 + \beta_2 + \beta_4$	$\beta_0 + \beta_1 + \beta_3 + \beta_5$

After inspection, we find that the effect of occupation depends on the level of education and vice versa. For instance, the differential impact on income between a professional and a laborer is β_1 when each has elementary education, but a different value $\beta_1 + \beta_4$, when each has secondary education, and still a different value $\beta_1 + \beta_5$, when each has postsecondary education.

On the whole, equations like (6.84) can be estimated in the usual way.

This marks the end of this section. However, before we leave this section, we would like to point out that in many socioeconomic contexts it is the dependent variable, and not just the independent variables, that may act like dummy variables. An example may be a couple deciding to have a child or not, or to buy a house or not, which in turn may depend on its income, occupation, asset, age, etc. Problems like this can be tackled by some specialized statistical techniques but, since we may run into the problems of generalized error variances, we would rather postpone the discussion of this topic until after the general linear model has been extended to include generalized residual variances.

6.4.6 A Further Applied Study: Horst (1972) on The Decision to Invest Abroad: Its Firm and Industry Determinants*

We now present a dummy variable formulation in a general setting. This is illustrated by the empirical work of Horst (1972) and concerns the firm and industry determinants of the decision to invest abroad.

Horst takes two sets of data, one consisting of 1191 U.S. manufacturing

* Used with permission. T. Horst, "Firm and Industry Determinants to Invest Abroad: An Empirical Study," *Review of Economics and Statistics*, (1972), 44, p 263–64. Harvard University and the author.

companies (of which 576 own majority interest in a Canadian subsidiary in 1967), and the other their subset of 500 largest[21] corporations. Of these, 187 are multinational companies, as designated by the Harvard Business School.

Various distinctions are made in the structure and conduct of the firm and the industry: (1) firms investing in Canada and not so, (2) multinationals and nonmultinationals, and (3) multinationals investing in Canada and those investing in 6 other countries.

The author attempts a synthesis of industry and firm approaches by jointly allowing for, yet discriminating, industry-specific and firm-specific considerations. One of his objectives is to explain why some firms invest abroad while others do not, using features general to all firms in an industry rather than to firms investing abroad. The other is to derive a relationship between foreign direct investment and seller concentration in foreign industries. For this, he uses data on the value of an industry's foreign investment and the number of firms in that industry investing outside the country.

He defines the following variables:

C:	percentage of firms in an industry investing abroad
R & D:	research and development expenditure
Resource:	a dummy variable taking on the value 1 for 5 industries: wood, paper, petroleum, nonmetallurgic minerals, and base metals; 0 otherwise
Resource × Concentration:	resource defined above, and concentration[22] measured by the share of a U.S. industry's assets controlled by firms with assets of more than 250 million dollars
Cansize:	an estimate of minimal efficient plant size
Foreign:	share of the Canadian industry's sales going to foreign controlled firms

Three sets of regression results are presented now (with the t values in parentheses and an asterisk indicating statistical significance):

Multinational firms investing in Canada.

$$C = 0.13 + \underset{(2.1)}{4.95^*}\ \text{R\&D} + \underset{(0.5)}{0.5}\ \text{Resource} - \underset{(-2.0)}{0.0058}\ \text{Cansize}^*;$$

$$R^2 = 0.50 \qquad df = 16$$

$$C = 0.13 + \underset{(2.1)}{4.99^*}\ \text{R\&D} + \underset{(.38)}{0.09}\ \text{Resource} \times \text{Concentration}$$

$$- \underset{(-1.5)}{0.0075}\ \text{Cansize}; \quad R^2 = 0.49 \qquad df = 16$$

[21] As selected by *Fortune*.

[22] A high seller concentration implies a stimulus to invest abroad in resource intensive industries.

Firms investing in Canada.

$$C = 0.11 + \underset{(4.9)}{10.1^*}\ R\&D + \underset{(1.7)}{0.17^*}\ \text{Resource} - \underset{(-2.4)}{0.0076^*}\ \text{Cansize};$$

$$R^2 = .68 \qquad df = 16$$

$$C = 0.11 + \underset{(5.4)}{10.4^*}\ R\&D + \underset{(2.4)}{0.45^*}\ \text{Resource} \times \text{Concentration}$$

$$- \underset{(-2.9)}{0.0120^*}\ \text{Cansize};\ R^2 = 0.72 \qquad df = 16$$

Foreign investment and seller concentration.

$$\text{Foreign} = 0.11 + \underset{(4.7)}{13.9^*}\ R\&D - \underset{(-1.7)}{0.38^*}\ \text{Resource} \times \text{Concentration}$$

$$+ \underset{(4.2)}{0.02^*}\ \text{Cansize}; \qquad R^2 = 0.72 \qquad df = 16$$

The results indicate that R&D significantly affects the decision to invest abroad for all firms. Further, for most firms the economy of scale consideration, ordinarily favorable for large firm sizes in the United States, tends to make foreign investing more difficult (as evident from the negative coefficient of the Cansize variable in all but the last regression) due to the limited size of the Canadian markets. On the other hand, industries in which the economy of scale consideration is important tend to have a larger share (indicated by the positive coefficient of the Cansize variable in the last regression) of the Canadian industry's sales controlled by foreign firms with a larger efficient plant size.

The first 4 regressions show a positive effect of resource intensity, and/or resource cum asset size of U.S. industries on the decision to invest abroad. But the effect is insignificant if it originates with multinational firms and significant if it originates with firms investing in Canada. In contrast, this effect is negative on the share of the Canadian industry's sales going to the foreign-controlled firms.

On the whole, one of the author's important conclusions is that industries which rely on economy of size tend to have fewer foreign investing firms that control a greater percentage of the foreign market. This clearly reveals a tendency towards concentration in the foreign control of Canadian industries.

6.4.7 Variation of Dummy Variable Representation: The Spline Functions

A variation of the dummy variable method is the subject matter of the Poirier and Garber (1974) or Poirier (1974) study. This is on the profit rate of the aerospace industry of the United States during the 1951–1971 period. The total period is

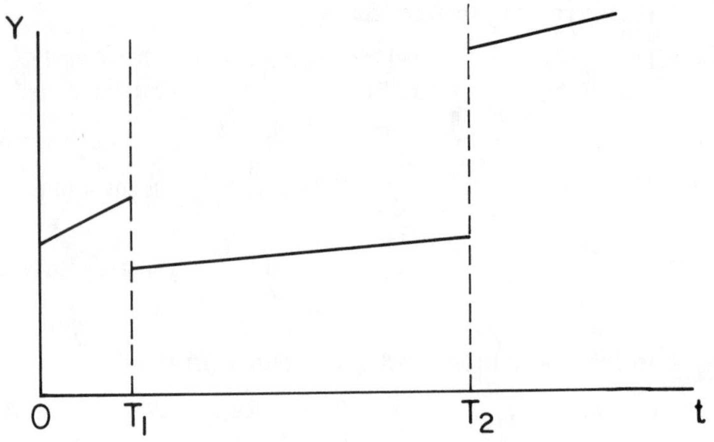

Figure 6.4

divided into three subperiods: 1951–54, the Korean War period; 1954–65, the Peace period; and 1965–71, the Vietnam War period. The authors study the linear effect of time on profit rate, abstracting from the effects of eleven other explanatory variables. They set up a spline function model illustrated as follows:

$$\begin{aligned} Y_t &= \beta_{0,1} + \beta_{1,1}t + \epsilon_t \qquad t \le T_1: \qquad \text{Korean War period} \\ Y_t &= \beta_{0,2} + \beta_{1,2}t + \epsilon_t \qquad T_1 < t \le T_2: \qquad \text{Peace period} \\ Y_t &= \beta_{0,3} + \beta_{1,3}t + \epsilon_t \qquad T_2 < t: \qquad \text{Vietnam War period} \end{aligned} \tag{6.85}$$

With 1950 as the origin or zero, $T_1 = 4$, and $T_2 = 15$. Data over the three different time periods could be used to fit functions which would generally appear like the *disjointed* trend lines shown in Figure 6.4. On the other hand, Figure 6.5 shows a linear spline function without discontinuities at the join points or knots at $t = T_1$ and $t = T_2$.

There are two ways in which (6.85) can be estimated. One is the method of unrestricted least squares and the other that of restricted least squares. For the first method, we introduce the w variables as follows:

$$\begin{aligned} w_{1t} &= t \\ w_{2t} &= \begin{cases} 0 & \text{if } t \le T_1 \\ t - T_1 & \text{if } t > T_1 \end{cases} \\ w_{3t} &= \begin{cases} 0 & \text{if } t \le T_2 \\ t - T_2 & \text{if } t > T_2 \end{cases} \end{aligned} \tag{6.86}$$

By means of these variables, the reparameterized form of (6.85) becomes

$$Y_t = \beta_{0,1} + \gamma_1 w_{1t} + \gamma_2 w_{2t} + \gamma_3 w_{3t} + \epsilon_t \tag{6.87}$$

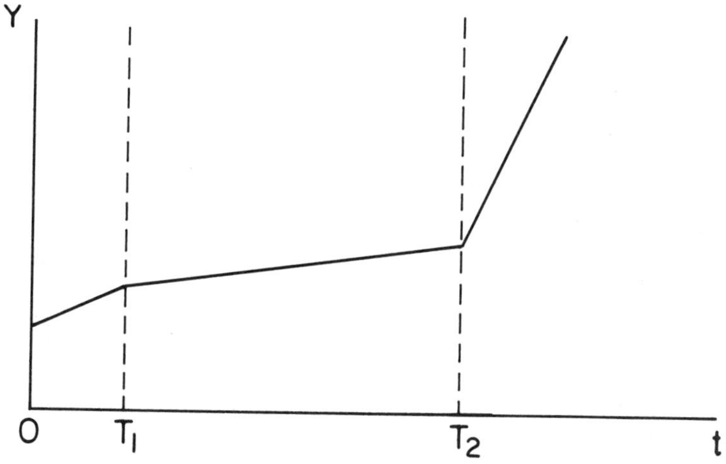

Figure 6.5

in which the parameter relations, in view of (6.85) and (6.86), are

$$\begin{aligned} \beta_{1,1} &= \gamma_1 \\ \beta_{1,2} &= \gamma_1 + \gamma_2 \qquad \beta_{0,2} = \beta_{0,1} - \gamma_2 T_1 \\ \beta_{1,3} &= \gamma_1 + \gamma_2 + \gamma_3 \qquad \beta_{0,3} = \beta_{0,2} - \gamma_3 T_2 \end{aligned} \tag{6.88}$$

One can apply OLS to (6.87) to derive the estimated spline function, obtain the estimates of the old parameters β from the new ones γ using (6.88), and ultimately test for βs from the tests of γs. For instance, the test for γ_1 will provide a test of $\beta_{1,1}$ in the sense of whether the Korean War period has a positive or a negative trend. Similarly, the test of γ_2 is a test of $\beta_{1,2} - \beta_{1,1}$ and will confirm whether the slope of the function during the Peace period is any different from that in the Korean War period. Likewise, the test of γ_3 will confirm whether the slope in the Vietnam War period differs significantly from that in the Peace period.

It should be clear from the preceding discussion that if $\gamma_2 = \gamma_3 = 0$, the old and the new parameters should be the same, which means that the functional relation is given by a single trend line as, for instance,

$$Y_t = \beta_{0,1} + \gamma_1 w_{1t} + \epsilon_t \tag{6.89}$$

This then becomes the restricted relation, the spline function being the unrestricted one. Therefore, as developed in Section 6.3, the F test can be used to test for the validity of the restrictions.

The other method is that of the restricted least squares. Here the first step of the work is to set up restrictions to make the join points coincide, for example

$$\begin{aligned} \beta_{0,1} + \beta_{1,1}T_1 &= \beta_{0,2} + \beta_{1,2}T_1 \\ \beta_{0,2} + \beta_{1,2}T_2 &= \beta_{0,3} + \beta_{1,3}T_2 \end{aligned} \tag{6.90}$$

This can be alternatively set up in the matrix form of restrictions: $\mathbf{r} = \boldsymbol{R\beta}$, where

$$\mathbf{r} = \begin{bmatrix} 0 \\ 0 \end{bmatrix}; \quad \boldsymbol{R} = \begin{bmatrix} 1 & T_1 & -1 & -T_1 & 0 & 0 \\ 0 & 0 & 1 & T_2 & -1 & -T_2 \end{bmatrix} \tag{6.91}$$

$$\boldsymbol{\beta}' = [\beta_{0,1}\ \beta_{1,1}\ \beta_{0,2}\ \beta_{1,2}\ \beta_{0,3}\ \beta_{1,3}]'$$

These restrictions are operative on the model whose equation is:

$$\begin{bmatrix} Y_1 \\ \vdots \\ Y_{T_1} \\ Y_{T_1+1} \\ \vdots \\ Y_{T_1+T_2} \\ Y_{T_1+T_2+1} \\ \vdots \\ Y_n \end{bmatrix} = \begin{bmatrix} 1 & 1 & & & & \\ 1 & 2 & & & & \\ \cdots & \cdots & & & & \\ 1 & T_1 & & & & \\ & & 1 & T_1+1 & & \\ & & 1 & T_1+2 & & \\ & & \cdots & \cdots & & \\ & & 1 & T_1+T_2 & & \\ & & & & 1 & T_1+T_2+1 \\ & & & & 1 & T_1+T_2+2 \\ & & & & \cdots & \cdots \\ & & & & 1 & n \end{bmatrix} \begin{bmatrix} \beta_{0,1} \\ \beta_{1,1} \\ \beta_{0,2} \\ \beta_{1,2} \\ \beta_{0,3} \\ \beta_{1,3} \end{bmatrix} + \begin{bmatrix} \epsilon_1 \\ \epsilon_2 \\ \vdots \\ \epsilon_n \end{bmatrix} \tag{6.92}$$

the empty blocks containing zero elements. The results of the restricted OLS as shown in (6.60) should be used here for parameter estimates, which incidentally should be identical to those derived in (6.87).

This sort of a spline function is very general and need not apply to time alone. Other explanatory variables can equally well be treated by it. The interesting point is when it is a linear spline, the function itself is continuous but not its slope or the first derivative. For the latter to be continuous as well, one should use a second degree spline function. But now the second derivative of the function will be discontinuous, and to overcome this, a third degree spline function should be used. Estimation in these extended cases involves a bit more algebra; otherwise the procedure is straightforward. The interested reader should consult Buse and Lim (1977).[23]

6.5 SPECIFICATION ERROR

6.5.1 Its Origin

Representation of economic theory often presents problems of specification error both in terms of the underlying functional form and the data matrix $\boldsymbol{X}$ used. The first may be illustrated by the theory of diminishing marginal return for which a minimum of a second degree polynomial for the production function may have

[23] The spline function may involve 2 explanatory variables at the same time in which case it is called a bilinear spline. For applications of this, see Poirier (1974).

to be provided. Using a linear production function instead would be erroneous in the sense of specification error. The second may be illustrated by the data matrix containing either too few or too many variables or, even if there is the right number of variables, errors are made in that some variables are difficult to measure and therefore have to be replaced by their measurable proxies.[24] Too few or too many variables are cases of relevant variables excluded or irrelevant variables included. For instance, a consumption function having excluded the ethnic identity of the consumer may have dropped an important variable, and a supply function having included consumer's income as a variable may have unnecessarily included it. In addition, unmeasurable variables are illustrated by the variable, say income, which usually is found overreported by low income earners and underreported by high income earners. The practice in such cases may be to use the proxy of total consumption expenditure which, even though reasonably free of reporting errors, may differ from income itself.

In what follows we shall discuss specification errors caused by the inclusion of irrelevant variables or omission of relevant variables. The considerations of errors arising due to the wrong functional forms chosen are dependent so much on economic theory that we should at best leave them out here. The topic of measurement errors will be covered in Chapter 8.

6.5.2 Omitted Relevant Variables

Let the data matrix X be partitioned into $[X_I \vdots X_E]$ where

$$X_I = [\mathbf{X}_1\ \mathbf{X}_2 \cdots \mathbf{X}_p] \tag{6.93}$$

is the part, consisting of pXs, that is included in, and

$$X_E = [\mathbf{X}_{p+1} \cdots \mathbf{X}_m] \tag{6.94}$$

is the part, consisting of $(m - p)$ Xs, that is excluded from a given equation. Suppose that economic theory wants us to believe that these last variables are relevant. What are the effects of this exclusion on the estimate and test of the coefficients?

Since the specified model is

$$\mathbf{Y} = X_I\boldsymbol{\beta} + \boldsymbol{\epsilon} \tag{6.95}$$

the estimated coefficients, designated as

$$\hat{\boldsymbol{\beta}}_{\mathbf{I}} = (X_I' X_I)^{-1} X_I'\mathbf{Y} \tag{6.96}$$

[24] See, for instance, an Australian study which uses technical, to be precise, horsepower energy rather than monetary measures of capital: Burley (1973). The interesting finding is that linear and time trend shifts from true capital series need not necessarily bias the estimated elasticity of substitution and that there might be a systematic relation between the horsepower measure and true capital.

But **Y** indeed is truly represented by

$$\mathbf{Y} = X\boldsymbol{\beta} + \boldsymbol{\epsilon} = (X_I : X_E)\boldsymbol{\beta} + \boldsymbol{\epsilon} \tag{6.97}$$

Substituting this in (6.96), we have:

$$\begin{aligned}\hat{\boldsymbol{\beta}}_I &= (X_I'X_I)^{-1}[X_I'X_I : X_I'X_E]\boldsymbol{\beta} + (X_I'X_I)^{-1}\boldsymbol{\epsilon} \\ &= [I_p : (X_I'X_I)^{-1}X_I'X_E]\boldsymbol{\beta} + (X_I'X_I)^{-1}X_I'\boldsymbol{\epsilon}\end{aligned} \tag{6.98}$$

Taking the expectation, we have:

$$\mathrm{E}(\hat{\boldsymbol{\beta}}_I) = [I_p : (X_I'X_I)^{-1}X_I'X_E]\boldsymbol{\beta} \tag{6.99}$$

Thus, for a single element, say $\hat{\beta}_{Ii}$, of $\hat{\boldsymbol{\beta}}_I$

$$\mathrm{E}(\hat{\beta}_{Ii}) = \beta_i + b_{i,p+1}\,\beta_{p+1} + \cdots + b_{im}\beta_m \tag{6.100}$$

where $b_{i,p+1}, \ldots, b_{i,m}$ define the ith row of $(X_I'X_I)^{-1}X_I'X_E$. These elements denote the OLS estimated coefficients obtained by regressing each of the $(m - p)$ Xs excluded from the model on the ith included X variable, $i = 1, 2, \ldots, p$. Since $\mathrm{E}(\hat{\beta}_{Ii}) \neq \beta_i$, the difference, which from (6.100) is a linear function of the true coefficients of the excluded variables, constitutes the bias in the OLS estimate when important variables are excluded.

By following Riddell and Buse (1980), it can be shown that

$$\mathrm{E}\left(\frac{\mathrm{ESS}}{n - p}\right) = \sigma^2 + \frac{1}{n - p}\,\boldsymbol{\beta}_E'X_E'\,M_IX_E\boldsymbol{\beta}_E \tag{6.101}$$

where

$$\begin{aligned}\sigma^2 &= \text{variance of } \boldsymbol{\epsilon} \\ \mathrm{ESS} &= \text{error sum of squares} = \mathbf{Y}'M_I\mathbf{Y} \\ M_I &= I - X_I(X_I'X_I)^{-1}X_I'\end{aligned} \tag{6.102}$$

and

$$\boldsymbol{\beta} = \begin{bmatrix}\boldsymbol{\beta}_I \\ \cdots \\ \boldsymbol{\beta}_E\end{bmatrix}$$

Since $\boldsymbol{\beta}_E'X_E'M_IX_E\boldsymbol{\beta}_E$ is a variance–covariance matrix of the error variables from the regressions of X_E on X_I, it can only be positive semidefinite. Thus $\mathrm{ESS}/(n - p)$ will generally overestimate the true error variance σ^2, and this property will carry over even when X_E and X_I are orthogonal to each other, which will reduce the bias from misspecification to zero.

As Kinal and Lahiri (1983) have pointed out, stochastic regressors (Chapter 8) would increase the error variance, hence the variance of estimates, more than in the present nonstochastic type of omitted variable models.

6.5.3 Some Irrelevant Variables Included

Let the included data matrix be denoted as before by X_I. Partition this into relevant and irrelevant subdata sets indicated by the subscripts R and .R:

$$\underset{n \times p}{X_I} = [\underset{n \times m}{X_R} \quad \underset{n \times (p-m)}{X_{.R}}] \tag{6.103}$$

In (6.103), we have shown the matrix sizes below their symbols. Evidently, X and X_R are identical and X_I is the misspecified data set. We have

$$(X_I'X_I)^{-1}X_I'X = \begin{bmatrix} I_m \\ 0 \end{bmatrix} \tag{6.104}$$

This follows from the fact that when each true variable in X_R is regressed on the set of relevant and irrelevant data set $[X_R \; X_{.R}]$, the OLS estimated regression coefficients of relevant variables will be unity but those of the *irrelevant* variables will be zero. Thus,

$$\begin{aligned} E(\hat{\beta}_{1i}) &= \beta_{1i} \qquad i = 1, 2, \ldots, m \\ &= 0 \qquad i = m + 1, \ldots, p \end{aligned} \tag{6.105}$$

It can be proved[25] that the mean sum of squares due to error is unbiased, that is

$$E\left(\frac{\text{ESS}}{n - p}\right) = \sigma^2 \tag{6.106}$$

where p is the number of X variables actually included in the model, and ESS is the error sum of squares given by

$$\text{ESS} = \boldsymbol{\epsilon}'M\boldsymbol{\epsilon} \tag{6.107}$$

where

$$M = I - X_I(X_I'X_I)^{-1}X_I' \tag{6.108}$$

The unbiasedness of the OLS estimated coefficients and that of the sample error variance when the model misspecification is due to the inclusion of irrelevant variables might render this sort of misspecification less serious than in the other kind of misspecification model, in which both the estimates and the sample error variance turn out to be biased. However, one should remember that the larger the number of variables included, regardless of their relevance, the larger the imprecision of estimates possible. Also, with a large number, the variables might be collinear, which would cause imprecision of estimates in the first place.

[25] See Riddell and Buse (1980).

6.5.4 An Applied Study: Bays' (1980) Hospital Cost Function

We will conclude this chapter by referring to an applied study dealing with the neglect of a relevant variable in the estimation of hospital cost functions. The study is by Bays (1980). The question analyzed is whether ignoring the admitting physician input—as has been the practice in previous studies—biases the estimates of the economies of scale. Taking the average cost function to include such variables as the number of beds, case flow (defined as the number of cases per bed per year), and a vector of case-mix proportions (defined equivalent to a measure of aggregation of the proportions of cases admitted in each of 19 broad International Classification of Diseases Amended (ICDA) diagnostic categories), the author finds somewhat like Feldstein (1968) for British hospitals that the decrease in the average costs up to the moderate sizes of hospitals reflects the failure to include the input of admitting physicians. The clear implication is that, had this input been duly provided for, there would be no strong evidence for economies of scale in U.S. hospitals, as in the case of the British hospitals.

PROBLEMS

6-1. Let

$$n = 20$$

$$\mathbf{Y}'X = [1 \quad 4 \quad 3 \quad 1]$$

$$(X'X)^{-1} = \begin{bmatrix} 4 & 1 & 1 & 3 \\ 1 & 2 & 1 & 2 \\ 1 & 1 & 3 & 2 \\ 1 & 2 & 2 & 4 \end{bmatrix}$$

(a) What are the least squares estimators of β_0 and β_3 from the model

$$Y_i = \beta_0 X_0 + \beta_1 X_1 + \cdots + \beta_3 X_3 + \epsilon_i; \qquad (i = 1, 2, \ldots, n)?$$

(b) Suppose that ϵ is distributed normally and let the sum of squared residuals be 16. Test the null hypothesis

$$H_0 : \beta_3/\beta_0 = 2$$

against the alternative:

$$H_1 : \beta_3/\beta_0 \neq 2$$

at the 1% probability level of significance.

(c) Test the hypothesis:

$$\beta_0 = \beta_3 = 0.$$

6-2. Let the linear regression model be

$$Y_t = \beta_1 + \beta_2 X_{2t} + \beta_3 X_{3t} + \epsilon_t \qquad t = 1, 2, \ldots, n$$

A researcher takes 37 random sample observations to estimate this function. The relevant data are given below:

$$X'X = \begin{bmatrix} 37 & 99 & 88 \\ 99 & 317 & 205 \\ 88 & 205 & 394 \end{bmatrix}, \qquad X'Y = \begin{bmatrix} 51 \\ 197 \\ 211 \end{bmatrix}, \qquad Y'Y = 261$$

(a) Find the OLS estimators of β_1, β_2 and β_3.
(b) Test the hypothesis : $\beta_2 = 1$
(c) Test the hypothesis: $1.5\beta_2 = \beta_3$
(d) Obtain the sum of squares due to error and the R^2 for the regression.

6-3. Let the model be:

$$Y_t = \beta_0 + [\beta_1/(X_t - \beta_2)] + u_t$$

with

$$E(u_t) = 0, \qquad V(u_t) = \sigma^2$$

$$E(u_t u_{t'}) = 0, \qquad t \neq t'$$

$$t = 1, 2, \ldots, n; \qquad t' = 1, 2, \ldots, n$$

and X_t, for $t = 1, 2, \ldots, n$, are fixed in repeated samples with $\Sigma(X_t - \overline{X})^2 \neq 0$, $\overline{X}$ being the mean of the Xs.

(a) Define

$$E = \sum_{t=1}^{n} \left[Y_t - \beta_0 - \frac{\beta_1}{X_t - \beta_2} \right]^2$$

Obtain the normal equations for least squares estimation by differentiating E with respect to the parameters β_0, β_1, and β_2 and equating the results to zero. Indicate what might be a procedure for solving these equations.

(*Hint:* Use the principles of iterative least squares.)

(b) Suppose that the u_ts are normally distributed. What is the likelihood function for the u_ts? Show why the maximum likelihood estimates of the parameters in this case are equivalent to their least squares estimates.

(*Hint:* Use Section 4.12 for maximum likelihood estimation.)

6-4. Let a nonlinear model be given by

$$Y_t = \beta_0^* X_t^{\beta_1} + u_t; \qquad t = 1, 2, \ldots, n$$

with

$$E(u_t) = 0$$

$$V(u_t) = \sigma^2$$

$$E(u_t u_{t'}) = 0, \qquad t \neq t'$$

$$t, t' = 1, 2, \ldots, n$$

where X_t, $t = 1, 2, \ldots, n$, are fixed in repeated samples with $\Sigma(X_t - \overline{X})^2 \neq 0$, $\overline{X}$ being the mean of Xs.

(a) Define

$$E = \Sigma[Y_t - \beta_0^* X_t^{\beta_1}]^2$$

Obtain the normal equations for least squares estimation by differentiating E with respect to the parameters β_0^* and β_1 and equating the results to zero. Indicate how you could solve these equations.

(*Hint:* Use the principles of iterative least squares.)

(b) Assuming that the us are normally distributed, show the likelihood function and indicate why the maximum likelihood estimates of the parameters in this case are equivalent to their least squares estimates.

6-5. The following data are on U.S. money stocks M2, where M2 is the sum of currency, demand deposits, checks and other checkable deposits, and overnight RP's and Eurodollars, MMMF balances, MMDA's and savings, and small time deposits. These are averages of daily figures expressed in billions of current dollars, seasonally adjusted. Call these stocks Y. The other data are on U.S. GNP in billions of current dollars. Call these X. The period for which these data are taken and reported below is 1975–1987.

U.S. MONEY STOCK AND GNP

Year	Y	X
1975	1023.2	1598.4
1976	1163.7	1782.8
1977	1286.7	1990.5
1978	1389.0	2249.7
1979	1500.2	2508.2
1980	1633.1	2732.0
1981	1795.5	3052.6
1982	1954.0	3166.0
1983	2185.2	3405.7
1984	2363.6	3772.2
1985	2562.6	4014.9
1986	2807.7	4240.3
1987	2901.0	4526.7

Source: *Economic Report of the President*, 1989; Table B-1 (p. 308) and Table B-67 (p. 385).

Assume that the data are a sample of observations from a money demand function of the following type:

$$Y_t = \beta_0^* X_t^{\beta_1} u_t^*$$

where u_t^* is log–normally distributed with $E(u_t^*) = 1$, $V(u_t^*) = \sigma_*^2$ for $t = 1, 2, \ldots, n$, and u_t^*, $u_{t'}^*$ are independent for $t \neq t'$; and $X_1, \ldots, X_n$ are fixed in repeated samples with $\Sigma(X_t - \overline{X})^2 \neq 0$, $\overline{X}$ being the mean of the Xs.

This model can be transformed to the following by logarithmic transformation:

$$y_t = \beta_0 + \beta_1 x_t + u_t$$

where

$$y_t = \ln Y_t$$

$$x_t = \ln X_t$$

$$u_t = \ln u_t^* + \sigma^2/2$$

$$\beta_0 = \ln \beta_0^* - \sigma^2/2$$

$$\sigma^2 = \ln (1 + \sigma_*^2)$$

(a) This transformation makes the model suitable for estimation by the OLS method. Explain why. What are the assumptions used?

(b) Regress y on x to obtain $\hat{\beta}_0$, $\hat{\beta}_1$ and S^2 as the estimates of β_0, β_1 and σ^2. What does S^2 stand for?

(c) How do you estimate β_0^*?

(d) Estimate the conditional mean of money stock (Y) when the value of GNP(X) is 5 trillion dollars.

6-6. Let the standard linear regression model be:

$$Y_t = \beta_0 + \beta_1 X_{t1} + \beta_2 X_{t2} + u_t$$

where

$$u_t \sim \text{NID}(0, \sigma^2)$$

Suppose you are interested in testing the hypothesis:

$$\beta_2 = -\beta_1$$

(a) Explain how you would perform a standard t test for this hypothesis.

(*Hint:* Write $\beta_2 + \beta_1 = \theta$ in the regression equation to have $Y_t = \beta_0 + \beta_1 (X_{t1} - X_{t2}) + \theta X_{t2} + u_t$ and apply a t test for θ.)

(b) Using a general formula for testing linear restrictions in terms of sum of squared residuals ($\Sigma \hat{\epsilon}_t^2$), explain how you would test this hypothesis by an F test.

(c) Using an alternative general formula for testing linear restriction (of the form $\boldsymbol{R\beta} = \mathbf{r}$):

$$F = \frac{(\boldsymbol{R\hat{\beta}} - \mathbf{r})' [\boldsymbol{R}(\boldsymbol{X'X})^{-1}\boldsymbol{R}']^{-1} (\boldsymbol{R\hat{\beta}} - \mathbf{r})}{\hat{\boldsymbol{\epsilon}}'\hat{\boldsymbol{\epsilon}}/\{n - (m + 1)\}}$$

explain how you would perform a test of the same hypothesis. (Note that the total number of regressors is $m + 1$ which is 3 in the problem above.)

(d) How are these different tests related?

6-7. **(a)** What is a Chow test for structural change? Explain exactly the underlying assumptions of the test and what hypothesis the test addresses.

(*Hint:* You can, if you want, consult Chow (1960) for preparing for this question. Otherwise Section 6.3.1, especially the modified equation (6.68), will be good enough.)

(b) Attempt a dummy variable implementation of the Chow test. What is the test criterion in the new set-up?

(c) Assume that not only the regression structure but also the error structure have changed between regimes. Explain how you would test this new hypothesis.

6-8. The following table presents the indexes of food consumption(Y), food price(P) and consumer income(I) in the United States over the period 1930–1960 excluding the years 1942–1947.

Year	Food Consumption Per Capita[a]	Food Price[b]	Consumer Income[c]
1930	88.7	90.9	56.3
1931	88.0	82.3	52.7
1932	85.9	76.3	44.4
1933	86.0	78.3	43.8
1934	87.1	84.3	47.8
1935	85.4	88.1	52.1
1936	88.5	88.0	58.0
1937	88.4	88.4	59.8
1938	88.6	83.5	55.9
1939	91.7	82.4	60.3
1940	93.3	83.0	64.1
1941	95.1	86.2	73.7
1948	96.7	105.3	82.1
1949	96.7	102.0	83.1
1950	98.0	102.4	88.6
1951	96.1	105.4	88.3
1952	98.1	105.0	89.1
1953	99.1	102.6	92.1
1954	99.1	101.9	91.7
1955	99.8	100.8	96.5
1956	101.5	100.0	99.8
1957	99.9	99.8	99.9
1958	99.1	101.2	98.4
1959	101.0	98.8	101.8
1960	100.7	98.4	101.8

[a] 1957–1959 = 100.

[b] Retail prices of Bureau Labor Statistics, deflated by dividing by Consumer Price Index.

[c] Per capita disposable income, deflated by dividing by Consumer Price Index.

Source: Data on Y and I generated from and Consumer Price Index taken from various tables of *Economic Report of the President*, 1984, 1968.

Consider the model:

$$\ln Y_t = \beta_0 + \beta_1 \ln P_t + \beta_2 \ln I_t + \epsilon_t$$

Supposing that the assumptions of the OLS model apply to this model equation, estimate the βs, estimate σ^2, where σ^2 is the variance of the disturbance term, estimate $V(\hat{\beta}_i)$ for $i = 0, 1, 2$, and calculate the t statistics to find out whether each regression coefficient is statistically significant or not. Also carry out the F test for the overall regression. Use data over the period 1948–1960, not the entire period. Briefly discuss the effect on the parameter estimates of ignoring the data of the other years.

6-9. Refer back to problem 6-7, its data and its equation.

(a) Apply a Chow test for structural changes by running separate regressions over the subperiods 1930–1941 and 1948–1960, then a joint regression over the entire period, and calculating the suitable test statistic.

(b) Alternatively, apply the Chow test over the same periods using suitably defined dummy variables. How does the result compare with that obtained in 6-9(a). Interpret the results.

6-10. Assume that you are to test the hypothesis that $\beta_2 = -\beta_1$ in the model of problem 6-8 over the entire historical period 1930–1960 excluding the years 1942–1947. State what might motivate an objective like this.

(a) Carry out the standard t test for this hypothesis.

(b) Using the general F test for testing linear restrictions

$$F = \frac{(\hat{\boldsymbol{\epsilon}}^{*\prime}\hat{\boldsymbol{\epsilon}}^{*} - \hat{\boldsymbol{\epsilon}}'\hat{\boldsymbol{\epsilon}})/l}{\hat{\boldsymbol{\epsilon}}'\hat{\boldsymbol{\epsilon}}/(n - m - 1)}$$

do an equivalent test of the hypothesis.

(c) Using the alternative general F test for testing linear restrictions

$$F = \frac{(\boldsymbol{R}\hat{\boldsymbol{\beta}} - \mathbf{r})' [\boldsymbol{R}(X'X)^{-1}\boldsymbol{R}']^{-1} (\boldsymbol{R}\hat{\boldsymbol{\beta}} - \mathbf{r})/l}{\hat{\boldsymbol{\epsilon}}'\hat{\boldsymbol{\epsilon}}/(n - m - 1)}$$

do yet another test of the hypothesis.

(d) How are these different tests related?

6-11. For the ith firm in a sample of n firms, let V_i = output/year, L_i = labor input/year, and K_i = capital service input/year and assume a Cobb–Douglas production function with a multiplicative error term, that is

$$V_i = AL_i^{\beta_2} K_i^{\beta_3} e^{u_i}, \qquad i = 1, 2, \ldots, n$$

where A, β_2, and β_3 are unknown parameters and u_i is an error term. If $y_i = \ln V_i$, $x_{i2} = \ln L_i$ and $x_{i3} = \ln K_i$, we can write the production function as

$$y_i = \beta_1 + \beta_2 x_{i2} + \beta_3 x_{i3} + u_i, \qquad i = 1, 2, \ldots, n \qquad \text{with } \beta_1 = \ln A$$

(a) Interpret the following assumptions in terms of properties of firms' production activities:

(1) $Eu_i = 0, \quad i = 1, 2, \ldots, n$

(2) $Eu_i^2 = \sigma^2, \quad i = 1, 2, \ldots, n$

(3) $Eu_iu_j = 0, \quad i \neq j$

(4) x_{i2} and x_{i3} are distributed independently of the u_is.

(b) Derive explicit expressions of the least squares estimators for β_1, β_2 and β_3 and comment on their properties.

(c) How do you estimate the returns to scale parameter, $\eta = \beta_2 + \beta_3$? What are the properties of your estimator for η? In particular with the u_is assuming NID(0, σ^2), what is the pdf for your estimator for η given the xs? Derive its mean and variance.

(d) If in the original production function (that is, before its logarithmic transformation), u_i is N(0, σ^2), what is the mathematical expectation of V_i given L_i and K_i?

6-12. If a term $\beta_4 X_{i4}$ reflecting managerial input should appear in the equation relating y_i to x_{i2}, x_{i3}, and u_i of problem 6-11 but is left out, how will the least squares estimators of β_1, β_2, and β_3 be affected? That is, what are the expectations of the least squares estimators of β_1, β_2, and β_3 when the variable x_{i4} is omitted?

6-13. An investigator follows the specifications of a step-wise regression as given below:

$$Y_i = \beta_0 + \beta_1 X_i + \epsilon_i$$

$$Y_i = \gamma_0 + \gamma_1 X_i + \gamma_2 Z_i + \nu_i$$

Supposing that a "hat" over a symbol indicates its estimate, state how you would justify the following results:

(a)

(1) $\hat{\beta}_1 = \hat{\gamma}_1$

(2) $\Sigma \hat{\epsilon}_i^2 \geqq \Sigma \hat{\nu}_i^2$

(3) $\hat{\beta}_1$ is statistically significant (at the 5% level), yet $\hat{\gamma}_1$ is not.

(4) $\hat{\beta}_1$ is not statistically significant (at the 5% level), yet $\hat{\gamma}_1$ is.

(b) Would you expect any change in the results of (3)–(4) of (a) above had you to change the level of significance from 5% to 1%?

6-14. If you run an OLS regression of $\mathbf{Y}$ on X, an $n \times m$ matrix of rank m, with no column of ones (that is, no intercept term), show that $\mathbf{i}'\hat{\boldsymbol{\epsilon}} = \mathbf{i}'(\mathbf{Y} - X\hat{\boldsymbol{\beta}}) \neq 0$, where $\mathbf{i}' = [1 \;\; 1 \;\; 1 \; .\,.\,.\,.\; 1]$, $\hat{\boldsymbol{\beta}}$ OLS estimates of $\boldsymbol{\beta}$ and $\hat{\boldsymbol{\epsilon}}$ OLS estimated residuals, and that $R^2 = 1 - [(\hat{\boldsymbol{\epsilon}}'\hat{\boldsymbol{\epsilon}})/\{(\mathbf{Y} - \mathbf{i}\bar{\mathbf{Y}})'(\mathbf{Y} - \mathbf{i}\bar{\mathbf{Y}})\}]$ need not satisfy $0 \leqq R^2 \leqq 1$. Can you suggest a goodness of fit measure for this case, say R_c^2, which satisfies $0 \leqq R_c^2 \leqq 1$?

(*Hint:* Follow a method of constrained least squares with $\beta_0 = 0$ where β_0 is the coefficient of X_0, the 0th column of X with unities as its elements, its (that is, Xs) 1st, 2nd, and mth columns being $\mathbf{X}_1, \mathbf{X}_2, \ldots, \mathbf{X}_m$, respectively, and then conform to the requirements of the problem.)

6-15. In a study on sectoral reallocation in the Canadian labor market a research investigator obtained the following estimated equation based on Canadian data over the period 1965–1983 (the figures in parentheses underneath the coefficients are their standard errors):

$$\underset{}{\text{SIG}} = \underset{(0.000931)}{0.022143} + \underset{(0.001312)}{0.006781}\,{*}\text{CHUR} + \underset{(0.0031)}{0.004082}\,{*}\text{DUMOIL}$$

$$+ \underset{(0.005676)}{0.001801}\,{*}\text{DUMREC}; \qquad R^2 = 0.794198, \qquad n = 21$$

where

SIG = Index of friction in the Canadian economy indicating labor market reallocation using D. M. Lilien's index [See D. M. Lilien, "Sectoral Shifts and Cyclical Unemployment," *Journal of Political Economy*, Vol. 90, Aug. 82, pp. 777–793]

CHUR = Change in unemployment rate

DUMOIL = Dummy variable for oil price shocks (1973 and 1979)

DUMREC = Dummy variable for recession (1981)

(a) Since the computed R^2 is not high enough, you might think that the model could be improved. Perform a test of the above model for its overall goodness of fit.
(b) Carry out t tests of all the regression coefficients separately at the 5% probability level of significance. What are your inferences?
(c) Should you add other variables to the model? What are they? What effect would these new variables have on the statistical properties (for example, unbiasedness, BLUE, and suitability of tests) of the above estimates?
(d) The research investigator referred to before, being unhappy with the above results, remodelled sectoral labor market reallocation differently. The following is the result of that remodelling:

$$\underset{}{\text{SIG}} = \underset{(0.003388)}{0.025465} + \underset{(0.001325)}{0.003557^{*}\text{CHUR}} - \underset{(0.000425)}{0.001043^{*}\text{CHGDP}}$$

$$+ \underset{(0.087247);}{0.079494^{*}\text{EARN};} \qquad R^2 = 0.830784, \qquad n = 21$$

where the new variables are:

CHGDP = Percentage change in Canadian gross domestic product (a variant of GNP emphasizing the domestic content of aggregate output)

EARN = Index of earning differentials between sectors.

Are there reasons to believe that the second model is better than the first? Why or why not?

6-16. Continue with the second estimated model of problem 6-15. In case you would like to test the hypothesis that the numerical effect of change in unemployment rate (CHUR) is the same as that of percentage change in gross domestic product (CHGDP) on the Canadian labor market reallocation, explain how each of the three methods specified in problem 6-6 on testing a linear combination of coefficients would be employed to test this hypothesis.

6-17. **(a)** Continue with the first estimated model of problem 6-15. As you must have seen, the t statistic for the variable DUMREC is very low, which might lead you to eliminate this variable from the model. What might be the nature of the specification error as a result of this elimination? What will be its effect on the unbiasedness of coefficient estimates?
(b) Continue with the second estimated model of problem 6-15. Do you notice any

possible multicollinearity effect on the CHUR and EARN variables of the model? If so, what do you propose to do about it?

6-18. **(a)** Explain what you understand by the word multicollinearity. What are its possible effects on coefficient tests and estimates?

(b) How would you propose to reduce the effect of multicollinearity in typical circumstances?

(c) Explain the methods of ridge regression and conditional omitted variable regression. What are their purposes?

6-19. Based on the 1981 Census data for the provinces of Manitoba and Saskatchewan a research investigator conducted an inquiry into the male/female differentials in income viewed as differential returns to education and age. She took 4 levels of education, namely, public school, high school, college, and university undergraduate, and two age groups, namely, 25–34 years and 35–44 years of the income earners. Using the logarithm of earnings as the dependent variable, she fitted two equations, one for females and the other for males as follows:

$$\begin{aligned}\ln \text{FINC} = {} & \underset{(222.05)}{8.5483^*(E_0A_1)} + \underset{(9.0061)}{0.4903^*(E_1)} + \underset{(11.5231)}{0.6274^*(E_2)} + \underset{(17.9225)}{0.9760^*(E_3)} \\ & + \underset{(5.0214)}{0.2734^*(A_2)} - \underset{(-2.7995)}{0.2155^*(E_1A_2)} - \underset{(-4.1967)}{0.3231^*(E_2A_2)} - \underset{(-1.7018)}{0.1310^*(E_3A_2)};\end{aligned}$$

$$n = 16, \quad R^2 = 0.9868, \quad F = 85.58$$

$$\begin{aligned}\ln \text{MINC} = {} & \underset{(383.19)}{9.3591^*(E_0A_1)} + \underset{(10.8439)}{0.3746^*(E_1)} + \underset{(12.8293)}{0.4431^*(E_2)} + \underset{(16.0744)}{0.5552^*(E_3)} \\ & + \underset{(5.5085)}{0.1903^*(A_2)} + \underset{(1.5788)}{0.0771^*(E_1A_2)} - \underset{(-0.6992)}{0.0342^*(E_2A_2)} + \underset{(3.8368)}{0.1874^*(E_3A_2)};\end{aligned}$$

$$n = 16, \quad R^2 = 0.9918, \quad F = 138.119$$

where:

FINC = Female income

MINC = Male income

E_0A_1 = 1 for all observations

$$E_1 = \begin{cases} 1 & \text{if education level is high school} \\ 0 & \text{otherwise} \end{cases}$$

$$E_2 = \begin{cases} 1 & \text{if education level is college} \\ 0 & \text{otherwise} \end{cases}$$

$$E_3 = \begin{cases} 1 & \text{if education level is university undergraduate} \\ 0 & \text{otherwise} \end{cases}$$

A_2 = 1 for all observations

$$E_1A_2 = \begin{cases} 1 & \text{if education level is high school and age group is 2} \\ 0 & \text{otherwise} \end{cases}$$

$$E_2A_2 = \begin{cases} 1 & \text{if education level is college and age group is 2} \\ 0 & \text{otherwise} \end{cases}$$

$$E_3A_2 = \begin{cases} 1 & \text{if education level is university undergraduate and age group 2} \\ 0 & \text{otherwise} \end{cases}$$

(a) Draw up two tables to show the theoretical group expected values of ln FINC and ln MINC as classified between education levels on the one hand and age groups on the other.

(b) Write a report on the estimated model results for both females and males, especially emphasizing earnings differentials between the genders that cannot be explained by education and/or age of the earners.

(c) You would perhaps argue in favor of disaggregation of data in terms of industries where people work, or in terms of some additional variables being included in the model such as ability, experience (quite apart from age), etc. If these were done or included, how do you think the model results would have changed? Explain.

6-20. Response rates at various levels of ratable values:

Range of ratable value	A	B	C	D	E	F	G	H	I	J
Assumed central X, £/annum	3	7	12	17	25	35	45	55	70	120
Response rate Y, percent	86	79	76	69	65	62	52	51	51	48

The data relate to a survey recently conducted in England. Estimate the constants in the regression equation

$$100/(100 - Y) = \text{a} + (\text{b}/X)$$

(Oxford University, 1955)

7

The Generalized Linear Regression Model

The basic linear regression model of Chapter 5 is not without technical problems. One such problem is that of multicollinearity and it is discussed in Chapter 6. There are three other major problems, each with fairly important variations: heteroscedasticity (with or without autocorrelation of residuals), qualitative dependent variables (with dummy variable roles for *dependent* variables), and stochastic regressors (including lagged variables, and errors in variables). Stochastic regressors will be discussed in the next chapter. In this chapter we discuss heteroscedasticity and autocorrelation of residuals, and qualitative dependent variables.

7.1 CIRCUMSTANCES REQUIRING A REVIEW OF THE OLS ASSUMPTIONS: THE PHILLIPS CURVE AND OTHER APPLIED STUDIES

To begin with, consider an example. The Phillips curve phenomenon in economics has been an important phenomenon for quite sometime. This is concerned with an inverse relationship between rates of increases in prices (and wages) and unemployment. Empirically, the curve has been fitted to data of many economies by the OLS method based on ordinary assumptions. However, Rowley and Wilton (1973) criticize the use of the OLS method on the ground that the error structure in the case of two economies, the United States and Canada, based as they are on quarterly data is anything but homoscedastic. By the application of the Generalized Least Squares (GLS) method, which allows for heteroscedastic error structures, they are able to show that the inverse Phillips curve relation is not significantly important in any of these economies.

A second example consists of Ando and Modigliani's (1963) aggregate consumption function based on the life cycle hypothesis. This function is fitted to annual U.S. data over the period 1929–1959. It has the following specification:

$$C_t = \alpha_1' Y_{L_t} + \alpha_2' Y_{L_t}^e + \alpha_3' A_{t-1}$$

where

$$\begin{aligned} C_t &= \text{aggregate consumption at period } t \\ Y_{L_t} &= \text{income earned by the labor force } L_t \\ Y_{L_t}^e &= \text{expected } Y_{L_t} \\ A_{t-1} &= \text{asset position last period} \end{aligned}$$

The authors hypothesize that $Y_{L_t}^e = \beta Y_{L_t}$ where $\beta \simeq 1$.

By equating α_1 approximately to $\alpha_1' + \alpha_2'$ and α_3' to α_3, they reduce the consumption function to

$$C_t = \alpha_1 Y_{L_t} + \alpha_3 A_{t-1}$$

The OLS estimated results are

α_1	α_3	R^2	DW
0.56	0.081	0.997	0.33
(0.09)	(0.015)		

The results from the same method applied to the first difference of the variables are

α_1	α_3	R^2	DW
0.52	0.072	0.929	1.85
(0.11)	(0.018)		

DW is the Durbin–Watson measure of autocorrelation of the residuals.

As we shall see later, the results based on (the first difference) transformation of the variables provide the best or most efficient results and in this form the residuals become free of autocorrelation. This is not so when the variables are in their absolute forms, generating autocorrelation of errors and rendering the OLS method inefficient.

We stop short of presenting examples of results from qualitative dependent variable models. The reason is these involve some very intricate methodological problems. Consequently, an illustration of these results should follow the presentation of the methods on which they are based. We will come back to it later, but now we will present the methods.

7.2 THE HETEROSCEDASTIC ERROR STRUCTURE

7.2.1 The Savings or Family Budget Studies

If we inquire into the saving behavior of income earners, we inevitably will find that there is a larger variation in this behavior among high-income than low-income families. The reason is simple. The low-income families are left with such a low level of saving (or no saving at all) that at that level, nothing but a uniform saving behavior results. In contrast, the behavior of the high-income families varies all the way between that of the extremely miserly tycoons who virtually save all their incomes, and that of those who recently became rich. These people have to spend a lot, and save almost nothing, perhaps to display their wealth. Accordingly, a saving income relation of the form

$$Y = \beta_0 + \beta_1 X + \epsilon$$

where Y is saving and X income might be hypothesized to have the variance of the error term to depend in some way on income, for example

$$\mathrm{V}(\epsilon_i) = \sigma^2 X_i^2 \qquad i = 1, \ldots, n$$

Obviously, the ϵs are no longer homoscedastic.

For another example, refer to the following Lancaster (1968) study. He takes 200 observations of dividends D and profits P for 20 manufacturing companies and classifies them into 20 classes. Then he calculates the variance of dividends and average profit $\overline{P}$ in each class and estimates the relationship:

$$\mathrm{V}(D_i) = \alpha \overline{P}_i^{\beta}$$

or

$$\ln \mathrm{V}(D_i) = \ln \alpha + \beta \ln \overline{P}_i$$

which yields

$$\hat{\beta} = 1.47 \qquad R^2 = 0.88$$

Taking investment or saving to be a function of profit income and error, and considering error to be the sum total of neglected effects which could very well be measured by dividends, it is clear that dividends or error do depend on mean profits. This result indeed shows the invalidity of the homoscedasticity assumption of the error term.

In any case, the OLS estimated coefficients in models of this kind will produce inefficient results, even though their linearity and unbiasedness will remain unaffected. Also, the estimates of the variance of such coefficient estimates will not be unbiased which is why all the tests of hypotheses, based on the t or F statistics, will be suspect.

7.2.2 Tests of Heteroscedasticity

Thus efforts must be made to test for homoscedasticity of errors and to correct it when it is present. One particular test, the one proposed by Goldfeld and Quandt (1965), is as follows. Assume that $E(\epsilon_i^2) = \sigma^2 X_{ij}^2$. Arrange observations on all variables in an increasing order of magnitude of one variable X_j on which $E(\epsilon_i^2)$ depends. Choose arbitrarily the number c of middle observations to be omitted and divide the sample into two subsamples in an arranged sequence, where $n_1 = (n - c)/2$ is the size of the subsample of the first $(n - c)/2$ observations and $n_2 = (n - c)/2$ is that of the second $(n - c)/2$ observations.

Apply OLS to n_1 and n_2 observations separately. Calculate the residuals $(\hat{\epsilon}_i)_1$ and $(\hat{\epsilon}_i)_2$ from the two subsamples and construct $\Sigma(\hat{\epsilon}_i)_1^2$ and $\Sigma(\hat{\epsilon}_i)_2^2$. Then assuming that errors are distributed normally, it has been shown that

$$G = \sum_{i=1}^{n_2} (\hat{\epsilon}_i)_2^2 \Big/ \sum_{i=1}^{n_1} (\hat{\epsilon}_i)_1^2$$

is distributed as F with $(n_1 - K, n_2 - K)$ df, where K is the number of parameters. Heteroscedasticity of errors would be indicated by a significant F test.[1]

Another test, due to Breusch and Pagan (1979), is developed to test a general form of heteroscedasticity centering around the OLS errors. Consider, for instance, the general linear model:

$$\mathbf{Y} = X\boldsymbol{\beta} + \boldsymbol{\epsilon}$$

where the errors ϵ_i are specified to be normally and independently distributed with variances

$$\sigma_i^2 = f(\mathbf{C}_i'\boldsymbol{\theta})$$

where f stands for the functional form, $\mathbf{C}_i$, related to heteroscedasticity, is a $l \times 1$ vector of variables, its first element being unity and other elements wholly or partly depending on the Xs, and $\boldsymbol{\theta}$ is a $l \times 1$ vector of coefficients, unrelated to the βs. Thus, when $\theta_2, \theta_3, \ldots, \theta_l$ are all equal to zero it means $\sigma_i^2 = f(\theta_1)$ for all i; in other words, it means homoscedasticity. The asymptotic test of Breusch and Pagan consists of computing the OLS residuals, the $\hat{\epsilon}$s, the estimated variance $\hat{\sigma}^2 = \Sigma_{i=1}^n \hat{\epsilon}_i^2/n$, and the sequence $\{\phi_i\} = \{\hat{\epsilon}_i^2/\hat{\sigma}^2\}$, $i = 1, 2, \ldots, n$. Then, regressing ϕ_i on $\mathbf{C}_i'$ and computing the regression sum of squares (RSS), they show that the quantity RSS/2 is, under the null hypothesis $\theta_2 = \theta_3 = \cdots = \theta_l = 0$, asymptotically

[1] See an alternative test of homogeneity provided by M. S. Bartlett (see Goldfeld and Quandt (1965) for reference). This test is disfavored by econometricians in view of the requirement that we divide the total sample into a certain number of independent subsamples.

The power of the test will depend, among other things, on whether the values of c are too small or too large. A crude rule is to take $c = 1/3\ n$; see Harvey and Phillips (1973).

distributed as χ^2 with $l - 1$ degrees of freedom. Significance of this test at a given probability level of significance would indicate the lack of homoscedasticity of disturbances at that level.

The last test to be discussed is, like the Goldfeld and Quandt test, developed for simple situations. According to it, the heteroscedasticity is taken to depend on a particular variable C, which could, in turn, be related to one of the X variables. The author of the test, Glesjer (1969), regresses the absolute value of the OLS estimated error $\hat{\epsilon}_i$ on C_i^p:

$$|\hat{\epsilon}_i| = \gamma_0 + \gamma_1 C_i^p + \text{error}$$

where p is some power of C_i, and γ_0, and γ_1 are the coefficients. He tries $p = 1, -1$ and $1/2$, and obtains in each case the estimate of γ_1. Using this estimate, he then performs the usual test of the hypotheses $\gamma_1 = 0$ for homoscedasticity[2].

7.2.3 Application of a Heteroscedasticity Test: Ravencraft (1983)

An interesting application of Glejser's test appears in Ravencraft (1983). This is a study of the relationship between concentration ratio and profit at business lines and industry levels. He uses the absolute value of the residuals from the OLS estimated equations to regress upon all the independent variables, along with the levels of assets and sales in various functional forms. Variables that are found insignificant at the 10% level are eliminated by a step-wise routine. The predicted errors from this regression are then used to purge the equations of heteroscedasticity.

In the line of business regressions with the variable of market share included there is no positive relationship found between profitability and concentration, quite like earlier results. The industry regression results, however, do find some positive relationships, but these results are, by no means, unambiguous. The difference with the business line results might be due to the omission of market share from the regressions. This concludes our discussion of Ravencraft's test results.

Going back to the general problem of this section, a correction of heteroscedasticity is made by the deflation of variables. In the saving/income example, deflating by income transforms the relation to

$$Y/X = \beta_0/X + \beta_1 + \epsilon/X$$

from which, given that $1/X$ and ϵ/X are uncorrelated and the new fact that V(ϵ/

[2] Halbert White (1980) has devised a test of heteroscedasticity asymptotically equated to chi-square with df one less than the number of regressors in the equation. His is a very useful method since it requires no specification of the type of heteroscedasticity; yet, one can make inferences on OLS estimators applied to a heteroscedastic situation.

$X) = \sigma^2$, we would be back to the assumption of homoscedasticity with its associated simplicity. There will be more about this when the generalized least squares method is discussed.

7.3 AUTOCORRELATED ERROR STRUCTURE

7.3.1 Its Origin: Wage Negotiations of Labor Unions

An autocorrelated error structure relates to the phenomenon of correlation of errors over time or space. Consider, for example, an industry employing workers with affiliations to two unions. Assume that the wage renewals of these two types of workers come due in the two halves of the year, the first half for one, and the second half for the other type of workers. A researcher is trying to study the relationship between wage rate change and unemployment for workers in this industry. Accordingly he collects semiannual data, which are used for the computation of, for instance, wage rate changes in the form $(w_i - w_{i-2})/w_{i-2}$, where w_i is the measure of wage in a given half-yearly period i. Since $w_i - w_{i-2} = (w_i - w_{i-1}) + (w_{i-1} - w_{i-2})$; that is, total wage change is made up of two component (period to period) wage changes in which both groups of workers might be involved, the disturbance term ϵ_i of the wage equation would be[3] the arithmetic average of the two semiannual disturbances ν_i and ν_{i-1}:

$$\epsilon_i = 1/2\,(\nu_i + \nu_{i-1}) \tag{7.1}$$

Assume that

$$\mathrm{E}(\boldsymbol{\nu}) = \mathbf{0} \qquad \text{and} \quad \mathrm{E}(\boldsymbol{\nu\nu}') = \sigma_\nu^2 \boldsymbol{I} \tag{7.2}$$

Then, the following results are immediate:

$$\begin{aligned} \mathrm{E}(\epsilon_i^2) &= 1/2\,\sigma_\nu^2 \\ \mathrm{E}(\epsilon_i\epsilon_{i-1}) &= 1/4\,\sigma_\nu^2 \\ \mathrm{E}(\epsilon_i\epsilon_{i-j}) &= 0 \qquad \text{for } j \geq 2 \end{aligned} \tag{7.3}$$

These results imply a pattern in the variance–covariance matrix of the disturbance terms of the wage equation. This pattern is

$$\mathrm{E}(\boldsymbol{\epsilon\epsilon}') = \begin{bmatrix} 1 & 1/2 & 0 & \cdots & 0 \\ 1/2 & 1 & 1/2 & \cdots & 0 \\ \cdots & \cdots & \cdots & \cdots & \cdots \\ \cdots & \cdots & \cdots & 1/2 & 1 \end{bmatrix} \tag{7.4}$$

[3] Assuming an equal distribution of the two groups of workers over the two halves of the year.

in which each element is measured in units of 1/4 σ_ν^2. Clearly, the nonvanishing off-diagonal entries of this matrix indicate autocorrelation. However, the strength of the autocorrelation is not too great and does not extend even beyond the adjacent semiannual periods on either side of a given period.

7.3.2 AR(1), AR(2), and AR(3) Processes

When autocorrelation is present, the diagonal entries of the variance–covariance matrix of the model disturbances will be generally nonzero. In the wage determination models for instance, abnormal wage settlements this period might influence settlements next period, and this, as explained already, might be the source of autocorrelation in the error terms. Generally speaking, the pattern of autocorrelation may simply follow what is known as the first order autoregressive process, denoted as AR(1). It is the most commonly used autoregressive model. Its equation is

$$\epsilon_i = \rho\epsilon_{i-1} + \nu_i \qquad \text{for all i} \qquad |\rho| < 1 \tag{7.5}$$

where ν_is have means zero, variances all equal ($= \sigma_\nu^2$), and covariances zero. For this model, we can show that:[4]

$$E(\boldsymbol{\epsilon\epsilon}') = \sigma^2 \begin{bmatrix} 1 & \rho & \rho^2 & \cdots \rho^{n-2} & \rho^{n-1} \\ \rho & 1 & \rho & \cdots \rho^{n-3} & \rho^{n-2} \\ \cdots & \cdots & \cdots & \cdots & \cdots \\ \rho^{n-1} & \rho^{n-2} & \rho^{n-3} & \cdots \rho & 1 \end{bmatrix} \tag{7.6}$$

Since $|\rho| < 1$, for positive ρ autocorrelations will decay over time exponentially, but, for negative ρ, they will alternate in sign.

In this book, we will be dealing primarily with the AR(1) process. However,

[4] Proceed as follows. We can express ϵ_i as:

$$\epsilon_i = \rho\epsilon_{i-1} + \nu_i = \rho(\rho\epsilon_{i-2} + \nu_{i-1}) + \nu_i$$

$$= \nu_i + \rho\nu_{i-1} + \rho^2\nu_{i-2} + \cdots = \sum_{j=0}^{\infty} \rho^j \nu_{i-j}$$

Therefore $E(\epsilon_i) = 0$ since $E(\nu_i) = 0$ for all i. Thus

$$\sigma^2 = E(\epsilon_i^2) = E(\nu_i^2) + \rho^2 E(\nu_{i-1}^2) + \rho^4 E(\nu_{i-2}^2) + \cdots$$

$$= (1 + \rho^2 + \rho^4 + \cdots + \text{ad. inf.})\sigma_\nu^2 = \sigma_\nu^2/(1 - \rho^2) \qquad \text{for all } i$$

For covariances of consecutive ϵs, we have:

$$E(\epsilon_i\epsilon_{i-1}) = E[(\nu_i + \rho\nu_{i-1} + \rho^2\nu_{i-2} + \cdots)(\nu_{i-1} + \rho\nu_{i-2} + \rho^2\nu_{i-3} + \cdots)]$$

$$= E\{\nu_i + \rho(\nu_{i-1} + \rho\nu_{i-2} + \cdots)\}(\nu_{i-1} + \rho\nu_{i-2} + \cdots)$$

$$= \rho E(\nu_{i-1} + \rho\nu_{i-2} + \cdots)^2 = \rho\sigma^2$$

Similarly, $E(\epsilon_i\epsilon_{i-2}) = \rho^2\sigma^2$. In general $E(\epsilon_i\epsilon_{i\pm s}) = \rho^s\sigma^2$. These calculations go into the structure of $E(\boldsymbol{\epsilon\epsilon}')$.

it will be useful to introduce higher order or more general forms of the AR process, and show their relation to another kind of a time series process called the moving average or, briefly, the MA process.

An AR(2) process is given by:

$$\epsilon_i = \rho_1\epsilon_{i-1} + \rho_2\epsilon_{i-2} + \nu_i \tag{7.7}$$

with the conditions of stationarity:[5]

$$|\rho_2| < 1 \qquad \rho_2 + \rho_1 < 1 \qquad \rho_2 - \rho_1 < 1 \tag{7.8}$$

The autocorrelations of this AR process are obtained by taking the expectation of $\epsilon_i\epsilon_{i-j}$ using (7.7), for $j > 0$, and dividing through by its variance to have

$$R_j = \rho_1 R_{j-1} + \rho_2 R_{j-2} \tag{7.9}$$

Putting $j = 1$, and noting that $R_0 = 1$, and $R_{-1} = R_1$, we have

$$R_1 = \rho_1/(1 - \rho_2) \tag{7.10}$$

Putting $j = 2$ and using the above equation, yields

$$R_2 = \rho_2 + \rho_1^2/(1 - \rho_2) \tag{7.11}$$

Using further the equations for R_1 and R_2, and that for R_j above will give expressions for $R_3, R_4, \ldots$ in terms of the ρs. To derive the variance of the ϵ series, take the expectation of the square of equation (7.7) and substitute for R_1 from (7.10) to obtain

$$\sigma^2 = (1 - \rho_2)\sigma_\nu^2/\{(1 + \rho_2)\,[(1 - \rho_2)^2 - \rho_1^2]\} \tag{7.12}$$

Generalizing, an autoregressive process of order r, AR(r), is given by

$$\epsilon_i = \rho_1\epsilon_{i-1} + \rho_2\epsilon_{i-2} + \cdots + \rho_r\epsilon_{i-r} + \nu_i \tag{7.13}$$

where the $\{\nu\}$ process is independently, randomly distributed with zero means, and $\rho_1, \rho_2, \ldots, \rho_r$, which are the autocorrelations of various orders, are subject to stationary conditions.

7.3.3 MA(s) Process

On the other hand, a moving average process of order s, MA(s), is specified as

$$\epsilon_i = \nu_i + \theta_1\nu_{i-1} + \theta_2\nu_{i-2} + \cdots + \theta_s\nu_{i-s} \tag{7.14}$$

We have seen an example of this kind of a process but for order 2 in equation (7.1). For an MA(1), which is given by:

$$\epsilon_i = \nu_i + \theta\nu_{i-1}$$

we can obtain

$$R_1 = \theta/(1 + \theta^2) \tag{7.15}$$

[5] See Box and Jenkins (1976), p. 58.

and show that $R_2, R_3, \ldots$ are all zero, that is all autocorrelation coefficients of order higher than the order of the MA process are zero. This can be verified from (7.4) in the case of the MA(2) process. There, the autocorrelations with time lags (or leads) larger than 2 were all zero.

7.3.4 Relation Between AR and MA Processes

An interesting property of AR and MR processes is that a finite order of each process can be transformed into an infinite order of the other process, and vice versa. Finally, a combined AR and MA process of order r and s, respectively, denoted as ARMA (r, s) is given by

$$\epsilon_i = \rho_1\epsilon_{i-1} + \cdots + \rho_r\epsilon_{i-r} + \nu_i + \theta_1\nu_{i-1} + \cdots + \theta_s\nu_{i-s} \tag{7.16}$$

or, alternatively, as

$$\rho(\delta)\epsilon_i = \theta(\delta)\nu_i \tag{7.17}$$

where

$$\rho(\delta) = 1 - \rho_1\delta - \rho_2\delta^2 - \cdots - \rho_r\delta^r \tag{7.18}$$

and

$$\theta(\delta) = 1 + \theta_1\delta + \theta_2\delta^2 + \cdots + \theta_s\delta^s \tag{7.19}$$

δ standing for the lag operator, that is $\delta\epsilon_i = \epsilon_{i-1}$, $\delta^2\epsilon_i = \epsilon_{i-2}, \ldots$, and so on. We shall talk more later about an ARMA or the related autoregressive integrated moving average (ARIMA) process.

7.3.5 Durbin–Watson Test of Autocorrelation

The preceding sections assumed that ρ was nonzero. However, before proceeding any further, we should perhaps test to see if indeed $\rho \neq 0$. With this in view, we use the Durbin–Watson (DW) (1950 and 1951) test statistic d, where d depends on the autocorrelation coefficient ρ as follows:[6,7]

$$d = \sum_2^n (\hat{\epsilon}_i - \hat{\epsilon}_{i-1})^2 \Big/ \sum_1^n \hat{\epsilon}_i^2 \simeq 2(1 - \hat{\rho}) \tag{7.20}$$

[6] This will follow by observing that

$$\sum_2^n \hat{\epsilon}_i^2 \simeq \sum_2^n \hat{\epsilon}_{i-1}^2 \simeq \sum_1^n \hat{\epsilon}_i^2$$

It may be remarked that the DW statistic is closely related to another important statistic, called the von Neumann ratio δ^2/s^2 according to $d = (\delta^2/s^2)(n - 1)/n$, where

$$\delta^2 = \sum_2^n (\hat{\epsilon}_i - \hat{\epsilon}_{i-1})^2/(n - 1) \quad \text{and} \quad s^2 = \sum_1^n \hat{\epsilon}_i^2/n.$$

in which the $\hat{\epsilon}$s are the OLS estimated residuals in relation to the equation $\mathbf{Y} = X\boldsymbol{\beta} + \boldsymbol{\epsilon}$, and $\hat{\rho} = \Sigma_2^n \hat{\epsilon}_i\hat{\epsilon}_{i-1}/\Sigma_1^n \hat{\epsilon}_i^2$ is the estimated value of ρ.

For positive values of $\hat{\rho}$, d will be less than 2, whereas for negative values of $\hat{\rho}$ it will be greater than 2. For $\hat{\rho}$ equal to zero, d is 2. These values give a first impression about the possible strength of autocorrelation in the population.

The test procedure involving the d statistic includes the following considerations. Tables have been computed about 2 types of values of d, called the lower and upper bound values d_L and d_U representing the significance levels of d for a given sample size n, and a given number of coefficients to be calculated $m + 1$. For instance, for $n = 20$, and $m + 1 = 5$, $d_L = 0.90$ and $d_U = 1.83$ at the 5% probability level. If the calculated value of d from a sample is such that $d < d_L$, then the inference is to reject the null hypothesis $\rho = 0$; if, on the other hand, $d > d_U$, one accepts the null hypothesis and, if $d_L < d < d_U$, the test is inconclusive. The intuitive explanation for, for instance, the case of the rejection of the null hypothesis is that since d is roughly equal to $2(1 - \hat{\rho})$, as $\hat{\rho}$ moves significantly above 0, d moves significantly below 2. A value lower than the tabulated lower limit value is taken to indicate a value of $\hat{\rho}$ significantly above 0. In all these cases, the alternative hypothesis is $\rho > 0$. If instead $\rho < 0$, then since $4 - d = 4 - 2[1 - (-\hat{\rho})] = 2(1 - \hat{\rho})$ inferences drawn on the basis of this statistic, that is, $4 - d$ in which $\rho < 0$, are just equivalent to those under d in which $\rho > 0$. Thus for the alternative hypothesis $\rho < 0$, the trick consists of computing the statistic $4 - d$ instead of d but then conducting the test as though it were a test based on d. For instance, if $\hat{\rho} = -0.7$, compute $4 - d$, where $4 - d = 2(1 - 0.7) = 0.6$. Now if $n = 20$ and $m + 1 = 5$, since $d_L = 0.90$ and $d_U = 1.83$, and $4 - d = 0.6 < d_L = 0.90$, reject the null hypothesis $\rho = 0$ against the alternative $\rho < 0$.

Incidentally the original table of critical values worked out by Durbin and

---

For large n, δ^2/s^2 is distributed as $N(2n/(n - 1), 4n^2(n - 2)/\{(n + 1)(n - 1)^3\})$. An exact test against the autocorrelation coefficient is available by comparing the computed value of δ^2/s^2 with the significant points of the ratio—see Hart (1942) for these critical points. But Hart's calculation assumes that the expected value of the series under review is some unknown fixed value. But our $\hat{\epsilon}$s are supposed to have the mean value zero. Using this presumption, we may refer to the significant points for the von Neumann ratio that Press and Brooks (1969) have computed under a comparable condition. For these significant points, see Appendix B. The von Neumann ratio test may give results that do not have the inconclusive zone that the Durbin–Watson test has; on this latter point, see the text below.

[7] King (1981) considers an alternative test statistic called d' defined as

$$d' = d + (\hat{\epsilon}_1^2 + \hat{\epsilon}_n^2) \Big/ \sum_1^n \hat{\epsilon}_i^2$$

and compares its theoretical and empirical properties with those of the DW test based on d. He establishes that d is locally best invariant while d' approximately best invariant. However, d' comes out to be more powerful (i.e. with lesser probability for the error of the second kind; in other words, accepting the null hypothesis incorrectly) than d against negative values of the autocorrelation and for low values of this coefficient against its positive values. He also calculates a table showing the selected bounds for the significance points of d'.

Watson had sample sizes between 15 and 100 and the maximum number of regressors 5. This table has now been extended by Savin and White, with $6 \leq n \leq 200$, and the maximum number of regressors 15 (see Appendix B for 5% and 1% points).

There are three aspects of the DW test which have come under careful scrutiny recently. The first is about its dependence on the X matrix assumed to be nonstochastic. Indeed if some of the regressors include lagged dependent variables, they would no longer be nonstochastic. As Nerlove and Wallis (1966) have shown, the DW test will have an upward bias in such a case with inappropriate test implications. For a possible corrective test, refer to Durbin's development of the h statistics, to appear later.

The intercept term and the DW test. The second aspect of the DW test is its use of the intercept term in the regression. If the intercept term is absent, Farebrother (1980) has modified the DW test range as: $d_M \leq d \leq d_U$, where d_U is the upper bound in the usual DW test, and d_M replaces DW's lower bound d_L. The author has tabulated both lower and upper 1% and 5% significance points for d_M.

Inconclusive DW test: the Theil and Nagar modification. The third aspect is the inconclusive nature of the test procedure itself. There are exact and approximate procedures that have been proposed to solve this problem. Theil and Nagar's (1961) procedure depends on certain critical conditions. Assuming that the first and second differences of the explanatory variables are small in absolute values relative to the ranges of these variables, they show that the test would have true critical values established very near the DW upper bound d_U. According to them, for $d \leq d_U$, reject the null hypothesis $\rho = 0$ (against alternatives $\rho > 0$) but, for $d > d_U$, accept it.

DW's $a + b\, d_U$ procedure and Jeong's (1985) procedure. Durbin and Watson's (1971) $a + b\, d_U$ procedure uses an approximation given by

$$d_\alpha(\mathrm{U}) = \mathrm{E}(d) - b\{\mathrm{E}(d_U) - d_{U_\alpha}\} \tag{7.21}$$

where d_U and d are already defined, and d's critical point is d_{U_α} and $b = \sqrt{\{\mathrm{V}(d)/\mathrm{V}(d_U)\}}$. The reason for the approximation is that the shape of the distribution of d might be better represented by that of d_U. If instead it would be better approximated by the distribution of d_L, then the following more suitable approximation becomes imperative:

$$d_\alpha(\mathrm{L}) = \mathrm{E}(d) - b\{\mathrm{E}(d_L) - d_{L_\alpha}\} \tag{7.22}$$

Jeong (1985) combines the $d_\alpha(\mathrm{U})$ and $d_\alpha(\mathrm{L})$ procedures and proposes a weighted average of these as

$$\begin{aligned} d_\alpha(\mathrm{J}) &= w d_\alpha(\mathrm{U}) + (1 - w) d_\alpha(\mathrm{L}) \\ &= \mathrm{E}(d) - b\{\mathrm{E}(d) - \bar{d}_\alpha\} \end{aligned} \tag{7.23}$$

the weight w being

$$w = \{E(d) - E(d_L)\}/\{E(d_U) - E(d_L)\} \tag{7.24}$$

and the quantity

$$\bar{d}_\alpha = wd_{U_\alpha} + (1 - w)d_{L_\alpha} \tag{7.25}$$

Jeong establishes that his d_α(J) procedure gives more reliable performance than Durbin and Watson's d_α(U) procedure with almost the same burden of calculation. The important point to remember is that, for best performances, the amount of calculation becomes virtually prohibitive.[8]

Tests for higher and general order autocorrelation; presence of lagged dependent variables. Wallis (1972) argues that since many empirical models are quarterly, such models should rather contain fourth-order autocorrelation in their error terms, as, for instance, given by

$$\epsilon_i = \rho_4 \epsilon_{i-4} + \nu_i$$

Thus, the null hypothesis for such autocorrelation models should be

$$H_0: \rho_4 = 0$$

He proposes a test statistic for such a hypothesis which very much resembles the Durbin–Watson statistic:

$$d_4 = \sum_{i=5}^{n} (\hat{\epsilon}_i - \hat{\epsilon}_{i-4})^2 \bigg/ \sum_{i=1}^{n} \hat{\epsilon}_i^2$$

in which the $\hat{\epsilon}_i$s are the OLS estimated residuals. The upper and lower limits for d_4 have been computed by Wallis for nonstochastic Xs. These are 5% points (see Appendix B). Additional points at 0.5%, 1.0% and 2.5% have been calculated by Giles and King (1978).[9]

Before we proceed to the case of the general order autocorrelation, we will present Durbin's (1970) test through his h statistic where the regression model contains lagged dependent variables among its regressors.

Let the model be given by:

$$Y_i = \beta_1 Y_{i-1} + \cdots + \beta_p Y_{i-p} + \beta_{p+1} X_{1i} + \cdots + \beta_{p+q} X_{qi} + \epsilon_i \tag{7.26}$$

[8] King (1981) has shown that the size of the inconclusive region may be reduced by reducing the uncertainty of the X matrix such as that available from the use of some common regressors, for example seasonal dummy variables and linear trends. He also gives tabulated bounds for 3 classes of linear regression models: (1) regression with a full set of quarterly dummy variables, (2) regression with the intercept and linear trend variables, and (3) regression with both.

[9] See King and Giles (1977) for testing $\rho_4 = 0$ against alternatives $\rho_4 < 0$, where, among other things, the authors establish $4 - d_4$ as the correct test statistic with $4 - d_{4U}$ and $4 - d_{4L}$ as the 5 percent values as available from Wallis.

with

$$\epsilon_i = \rho\epsilon_{i-1} + \nu_i \qquad \text{and} \qquad \boldsymbol{\nu} \sim \mathrm{N}(\mathbf{0}, \sigma_\nu^2 \boldsymbol{I}) \tag{7.27}$$

Durbin has shown that under H_0: $\rho = 0$, the statistic

$$h = r\sqrt{\{n/[1 - n\hat{\mathrm{V}}(b_1)]\}} \tag{7.28}$$

will be asymptotically normally distributed with zero mean and variance unity, where n is the sample size, and $\hat{\mathrm{V}}(b_1)$ is the estimated sampling variance of the coefficient of Y_{i-1} in the OLS regression of (7.26) above, and r,[10] equal to $\hat{\rho}$ defined in connection with (7.20), is the estimate of ρ from the OLS regression of $\hat{\epsilon}_i$ on $\hat{\epsilon}_{i-1}$, the $\hat{\epsilon}$s being the OLS estimated residuals from (7.26).[11,12]

There has been some criticism of Durbin's h test applied to samples of small sizes. Several Monte Carlo studies[13] have indicated weaknesses in the test, especially in regions of the parameter space where the power of the test is poor and its computational difficulty extremely high. In such situations, McNown and Hunter (1980) have suggested an alternative test (free of those problems) from multiple regression routines, which they have shown to be asymptotically normally distributed.

Let us start from the following multiple regression equation for Y_i without the intercept term:

$$Y_i = \beta_1 X_i + \beta_2 Y_{i-1} + \epsilon_i \tag{7.29}$$

Then we multiply by ρ the lagged value of Y_i, namely Y_{i-1} obtained from (7.29) after lagging. Next subtract ρY_{i-1} from (7.29), and rearrange to have

$$\begin{aligned} Y_i &= \beta_1 X_i - \beta_1 \rho X_{i-1} + (\beta_2 + \rho) Y_{i-1} - \beta_2 \rho Y_{i-2} + \nu_i \\ &= a_0 X_i + a_1 X_{i-1} + d_1 Y_{i-1} + d_2 Y_{i-2} + \nu_i \end{aligned} \tag{7.30}$$

where

$$\nu_i = \epsilon_i - \rho\epsilon_{i-1} \tag{7.31}$$

and the as and ds are related to the βs and ρ. Suppose that equation (7.30) is fitted by OLS, and a symbol with a "^" on top implies an OLS estimate. Since $\rho = -a_1/a_0$ with $a_0 \neq 0$, a_1 is zero if ρ is zero. This suggests a test for $\rho = 0$

[10] If d has already been computed, find r from the approximate relation: $r \simeq 1 - d/2$ instead of working it out directly.

[11] This test can be analogously performed for negative autocorrelation situations. Notice that the test breaks down when $\hat{\mathrm{V}}(b_1) \geq 1$. Durbin finds that an asymptotically equivalent test is obtained by regressing, by OLS, $\hat{\epsilon}_i$ on $\hat{\epsilon}_{i-1}$, $Y_{i-1}, \ldots, X_{qi}$ and testing for the coefficient of $\hat{\epsilon}_{i-1}$.

[12] For a generalization of the Durbin significance test, especially in its relation to dynamic specification, see Sargan and Mehta (1983).

[13] For instance, Kenkel (1974) has found some instances typified by a small value of b_1, a small number of observations ($n = 20$) and/or a large residual variance ($\sigma^2 = 40$) where the h test is inapplicable. More concretely, in his experiment with $b_1 = 0.1$, $\rho = 0.00$, $n = 20$, and $\sigma^2 = 40$, 411 inapplicable h-test statistics are experienced before the requisite 200 successful tests could be carried out. Kenkel also finds a low power for the h test confirming the results of an earlier Monte Carlo study by Maddala and Rao (1973).

in terms of the coefficient of X_{i-1}. Thus under the null hypothesis $a_1 = 0$, $\sqrt{n}\,\hat{a}_1$, the OLS estimate of $\sqrt{n}\,a_1$, will be asymptotically normal if:

(1) both the roots of the polynomial equation

$$\lambda^2 - d_1\lambda - d_2 = 0$$

have absolute values less than unity.

(2) For $s = 0, 1, 2$, each 2×2 matrix whose (j, k)th element $(j = 1, 2; k = 1, 2)$ is

$$(n - 1 - s)^{-1} \sum_{i=2}^{n-s} X_{i-j+1}X_{i-k+s+1}$$

converges to a finite matrix Λ_s as $n \to \infty$, and the matrix Λ_0 is positive definite.

(3) The presample values Y_0, Y_{-1}, Y_{-2} are constants.

(4) The residuals ν_i are independently and identically distributed random variables with mean zero, variance constant, and higher-order moments finite.

Thus, for $a_0 \neq 0$ and assuming (1)–(4) to be valid, the hypothesis H_0: $\rho = 0$ may be tested in terms of the ratio of $\hat{a}_1$ and its estimated standard error distributed as a normal variate. A one-tailed test covers a critical region in the lower tail end area of the standard normal distribution.

Some Monte Carlo experiments are conducted to compare the proposed test with Durbin's h test. The power of both the tests is found to be just comparable as long as the model is not marred by severe multicollinearity.[14]

General order autocorrelation. Let us now consider a general order autocorrelation model of the following form:

$$\epsilon_i = \rho_1\epsilon_{i-1} + \rho_2\epsilon_{i-2} + \cdots + \rho_r\epsilon_{i-r} + \nu_i \tag{7.32}$$

This model is an rth order autocorrelation model and a d test that tests only for values of the first order autocorrelation coefficient does justice neither to ρ_1, which is now a part of the whole model, nor, for that matter, to $\rho_2, \rho_3, \ldots$, and ρ_r, the other (higher order) correlation coefficients that are left out in the test. Fortunately, Godfrey (1978) and Breusch (1978) have come up with a general test for this problem. For the usual linear model of this chapter but with the possibility that X may include lagged dependent variables, their assumption about the form of the distribution of the disturbance term ν, under the null hypothesis, is that these are independently distributed standard normal variables identified as follows:

$$\boldsymbol{\nu} \sim \mathrm{N}(\mathbf{0}, \sigma_\nu^2 \boldsymbol{I})$$

[14] Indeed, the proposed test has a lower power than the DW test but here the results are vitiated by the much larger Type 1 error of the latter test.

where $V(\nu_i) = \sigma_\nu^2$, for all i, and $\boldsymbol{I}$ is the identity matrix. The alternative hypotheses considered are the AR(r) and MA(r) processes given respectively by

$$\epsilon_i + \phi_1\epsilon_{i-1} + \cdots + \phi_r\epsilon_{i-r} = \nu_i \tag{7.33}$$

and

$$\epsilon_i = \nu_i + \phi_1\nu_{i-1} + \cdots + \phi_r\nu_{i-r} \tag{7.34}$$

in which the ν_is are conventional random variables. Based on the OLS estimated residuals $\hat{\epsilon}_i$, the test is aimed at the joint significance of their first r autocorrelations. However, this does not depend on which alternative hypothesis it is against which the null hypothesis is compared. Given that

$$\begin{aligned} \hat{\boldsymbol{\epsilon}} &= \mathbf{Y} - X\hat{\boldsymbol{\beta}} \\ \hat{\sigma}^2 &= \hat{\boldsymbol{\epsilon}}'\hat{\boldsymbol{\epsilon}}/n \; (= \text{the ML estimate of } \sigma^2) \end{aligned} \tag{7.35}$$

$$\tilde{\boldsymbol{\varepsilon}} = [\tilde{\boldsymbol{\epsilon}}_1, \tilde{\boldsymbol{\epsilon}}_2, \ldots, \tilde{\boldsymbol{\epsilon}}_r] = \begin{bmatrix} 0 & 0 & \cdots 0 \\ \hat{\epsilon}_1 & 0 & \cdots 0 \\ \hat{\epsilon}_2 & \hat{\epsilon}_1 & \cdots 0 \\ \cdots\cdots & \cdots\cdots & \cdots\cdots \\ \cdots & \cdots & \cdots\;\cdots \\ \vdots & \vdots & \cdots \hat{\epsilon}_1 \\ & & \vdots \\ \hat{\epsilon}_{n-1} & \hat{\epsilon}_{n-2} & \cdots \hat{\epsilon}_{n-r} \end{bmatrix}$$

the Godfrey–Breusch test statistic is given by:

$$\tilde{d} = \hat{\boldsymbol{\epsilon}}'\tilde{\boldsymbol{\varepsilon}}[\tilde{\boldsymbol{\varepsilon}}'\tilde{\boldsymbol{\varepsilon}} - \tilde{\boldsymbol{\varepsilon}}'X(X'X)^{-1}X'\tilde{\boldsymbol{\varepsilon}}]^{-1}\tilde{\boldsymbol{\varepsilon}}'\hat{\boldsymbol{\epsilon}}/\hat{\sigma}^2 \tag{7.36}$$

Alternatively, after regressing $\hat{\boldsymbol{\epsilon}}$ on $[\tilde{\boldsymbol{\varepsilon}}\ X]$ and computing the error sum of squares therefrom, it can be shown that R^2, the coefficient of multiple determination, is the error sum of squares divided by $\hat{\boldsymbol{\epsilon}}'\hat{\boldsymbol{\epsilon}}$, and that $\tilde{d} = nR^2$. This provides a much simpler computational expression for $\tilde{d}$ than the one presented in (7.36). Either way, $\tilde{d}$ is asymptotically distributed as χ^2 with r degrees of freedom. A significantly large value of $\tilde{d}$ would indicate the existence of a general order autocorrelation, even though its exact form would be ambiguous.[15]

7.3.6 Estimation With Autocorrelation: The Cochrane and Orcutt Method

Assume that autocorrelation is present. The question is: What can we do about it? One answer is: Revise the model so that the new variables introduced do not

[15] Godfrey has shown that in case X includes all exogenous variables, $\tilde{d} = n(\hat{\rho}_1^2 + \hat{\rho}_2^2 + \cdots + \hat{\rho}_r^2)$, where

$$\hat{\rho}_j = \sum_{i=j+1}^{n} \hat{\epsilon}_i\hat{\epsilon}_{i-j} \Big/ \sum_{i=1}^{n} \hat{\epsilon}_i^2 \qquad j = 1, 2, \ldots,$$

is the jth order autocorrelation coefficient of the $\hat{\epsilon}_i$s.

give out signs of autocorrelation and the OLS method would therefore be safe. If that does not help, follow the Cochrane and Orcutt (1949) (the C–O) iterative routine.[16]

This routine has the model cast into a new form. This involves the "ρ-differencing" transformation of the original variables. Assume, for simplicity, that the model includes only one explanatory variable X. Then the initial manipulations of the C–O routine are as follows:

Original Equation:

$$Y_i = \beta_0 + \beta_1 X_i + \epsilon_i \qquad i = 1, \ldots n \tag{7.37}$$

Error:

$$\epsilon_i = \rho\epsilon_{i-1} + \nu_i \tag{7.38}$$

ρ Times Original Equation Lagged One Period:

$$\rho Y_{i-1} = \beta_0\rho + \beta_1\rho X_{i-1} + \rho\epsilon_{i-1} \tag{7.39}$$

This Subtracted from Original:

$$Y_i - \rho Y_{i-1} = \beta_0(1 - \rho) + \beta_1(X_i - \rho X_{i-1}) + \nu_i \tag{7.40}$$

Suppose the initial value of ρ is $\hat{\rho}_1$. Then, the sum of squares due to errors is

$$\Sigma\hat{\nu}_i^2 = \Sigma[(Y_i - \hat{\rho}_1 Y_{i-1}) - \beta_0(1 - \hat{\rho}_1) - \beta_1(X_i - \hat{\rho}_1 X_{i-1})]^2 \tag{7.41}$$

This is a nonlinear equation in the parameters. Differentiate this with respect to β_0 and β_1 to obtain their solutions $\hat{\beta}_{0,1}$ and $\hat{\beta}_{1,1}$. Plug these solutions in $\Sigma\hat{\nu}_i^2$, but now pose as though ρ is unknown. Naturally $\Sigma\hat{\nu}_i^2$ will be a function of this unknown. Solve out the unknown from an equation that represents the first order condition of the minimum of this function. Let this solution value be $\hat{\rho}_2$. Repeat the procedure as in the preceding round, calculate $\Sigma\hat{\nu}_i^2$ with a new set of solutions for parameters, and check to see if the sum of squares due to error has declined. If so, then go through several such iterations until finally $\Sigma\hat{\nu}_i^2$ does not decline any more. The solution of parameters in the immediately preceding iteration then constitutes the optimum solution.[17] (See problem 7-4 for an alternative method called Hildreth–Lu or HILU method.)

[16] It ρ is known, an OLS method involving the Y and X differences, that is $Y_i - \rho Y_{i-1}$ and $X_i - \rho X_{i-1}$ would directly generate estimates of β_0 and β_1. This is the simple Orcutt method.

[17] Two questions seem important in this connection, one concerning the convergence of iterations and the other concerning the possibility of local versus global minimum and multiple minima. J. D. Sargan and his associates have some interesting inputs on these questions. They suggest that the C–O iterations would always converge to a stationary solution. This is because we are minimizing a quadratic function which is essentially a bounded decreasing function, and therefore would have a limit. There could, of course, be several local minima possible and convergence to one of them would be dependent on the initial point. However, their particular empirical investigations find no evidence of multiple minima. See Sargan (1964).

7.3.7 An Applied Study: Laumas and Spencer (1980) on Shifting Demand for Money

To illustrate the application of the technique, refer to Laumas and Spencer (1980). The authors explore the question, raised by some economists, of the shifting nature of the demand for money—the "missing money" phenomenon—during the post-1973 period of the United States. With this end in view, they use the estimated results from the period 1954II to 1973IV as the reference results against which the extrapolated results from the subsequent period, 1974I to 1979IV, are compared. The results for the benchmark period are presented below (absolute values of t given in parentheses):

$$\begin{aligned}\ln M_t = \underset{(5.869)}{-0.2832} + \underset{(5.422)}{0.0562} \ln Y_{pt} - \underset{(5.412)}{0.0171} \ln \mathrm{RCP}_t + \underset{(26.572)}{0.9141} \ln M_{t-1}\\ R^2 = 0.9940, \qquad \mathrm{DW} = 1.8140 \qquad (7.42)\end{aligned}$$

In (7.42), M_t is actual stock of real M1 money, Y_{pt} real permanent income, and RCP_t rate on 4–6 month prime commercial paper. The extrapolated results (not reported here) show an improvement in the forecast error over (especially) Goldfeld (1976). This is ascribed to the use of permanent income,[18] rather than Goldfeld's use of measured income, in the demand for money function particularly in periods of uncertainty, such as the post-1973 period, when the two measures of income differ considerably and the former is a superior measure.[19]

However, the "missing money" puzzle is not solved. In view of results signifying over-predictions for the post-sample period, even though the forecast errors are less than Goldfeld's, the authors conclude that a shift in the demand for money function might not have been, if anything, as much as is commonly believed.

7.3.8 Durbin's Two-Step Estimator, Klein's Nonlinear Method and Monte Carlo Results

There is another method, called Durbin's (1960) method, which uses a two-step procedure. In this, the ρ-transformed equation is rewritten as

$$Y_i = \beta_0(1 - \rho) + \rho Y_{i-1} + \beta_1 X_i - \beta_1 \rho X_{i-1} + v_i \qquad (7.43)$$

The first step then consists of getting the OLS estimate $\hat{\rho}$ of ρ by regressing Y_i

[18] A level of income projected to the current period from a long-term expected income profile of an earner during his earning span. See Friedman (1957).

[19] It should be pointed out that the authors also apply a still superior estimation technique (with lesser forecast errors) due to Hatanaka (1976) in recognition of the fact that the estimating equation has a lagged dependent variable and a serially correlated disturbance term, under which the Cochrane–Orcutt method would neither be consistent nor efficient. See later discussions on estimation of models with such variables.

on Y_{i-1}. In the second step, $\hat{\rho}$ is plugged into $(Y_i - \rho Y_{i-1})$ and $(X_i - \rho X_{i-1})$, and the former is regressed on the latter to obtain the estimate $\hat{\beta}_1$ of β_1. β_0 is estimated last from the intercept term, given that $\rho = \hat{\rho}$ is known.

We now refer to some Monte Carlo study results assembled by Griliches and Rao (1969). This is a way of comparing the merits of the three estimation procedures in the presence of autocorrelated errors: the OLS, Cochrane–Orcutt, and Durbin's two-step. Add to these a fourth estimator, Klein's nonlinear estimator used in relation to Durbin's equation (7.43) which, except for the intercept term, can be rewritten as:

$$Y_i = \rho Y_{i-1} + \beta X_i - \beta\rho X_{i-1} + \nu_i \tag{7.44}$$

This equation contains an over-identifying restriction in that any independent estimates of ρ and β have to satisfy the estimate of $-\beta\rho$ (the coefficient of the third term above), that is $-\widehat{\beta\rho} = -\hat{\beta}\hat{\rho}$. This is obviously a nonlinear restriction and a least-squares routine that satisfies it will evidently be nonlinear.

The conclusions of the Monte Carlo experiments are as follows. The OLS method is less efficient than the other methods for sizes of samples of 20: this is especially true for values of $|\rho| > 0.3$. For lower values, the OLS may perform better. Also, the Durbin estimator is probably better than others and the nonlinear method is no better than the simpler two-stage method.

The above conclusions are valid according to Griliches and Rao also when the group of four estimators is extended to include another. This is called the Prais and Winston (1954) estimator. For details on this estimator, see Appendix A.1.

7.3.9 The Maximum Likelihood Method

It is well known (see (4.149) and (5.8)) that the methods of least squares and maximum likelihood applied to the classical (ordinary) linear model produce equivalent implications when the errors are distributed normally. What would happen if the errors arose from an AR(1) process? For this reconsider the model

$$\mathbf{Y} = X\boldsymbol{\beta} + \boldsymbol{\epsilon}$$

with the disturbance $\boldsymbol{\epsilon}$ arising from the AR(1) process as follows:

$$\epsilon_i = \rho\epsilon_{i-1} + \nu_i \qquad \boldsymbol{\nu} \equiv \mathrm{N}(\mathbf{0}, \sigma_\nu^2 I)$$

It can be shown[20,21] that the log-likelihood function of ϵs is

$$\ln L(\boldsymbol{\epsilon}) = \text{constant} - n/2 \ln \sigma_\nu^2 + 1/2 \ln (1 - \rho^2) - \{1/2\sigma_\nu^2\} (\Sigma \nu_i^2) \tag{7.45}$$

[20] See Beach and MacKinnon (1978a). The same authors also treat the case of second order autocorrelation in a different article—see Beach and MacKinnon (1978b).

[21] For more complicated treatments of the error term such as MA and ARMA, see Harvey (1981), Chapter 6, and Harvey and McAvinchey (1979).

which implies that by minimizing $\Sigma \nu_i^2$ one would not automatically achieve[22] the full maximization of the likelihood. This is because the attempt ignores the term involving $1 - \rho^2$. In the Beach and MacKinnon (1978) method, full maximization of the likelihood, recognizing the term in $1 - \rho^2$, is essentially an iterative method. This is used by White (1978) in his SHAZAM computer package and in the updated versions of the time series processor TSP. The interesting aspect of their study is the results of some Monte Carlo experiments conducted by them. These show that their ML method might yield better estimates than other methods, such as the iterative Cochrane–Orcutt method, and that their method is computationally superior.[23]

Using the same ML method but in relation to the ρ-differencing form of the equation (7.40) as reproduced below:

$$Y_i - \rho Y_{i-1} = \beta_0(1 - \rho) + \beta_1(X_i - \rho X_{i-1}) + \nu_i \tag{7.40}$$

with ϵ following an AR(1):

$$\nu_i = \epsilon_i - \rho\epsilon_i$$

we can derive[24] the following expressions for asymptotic variance for the ML estimated coefficients β_0, β_1, and the parameter ρ:

$$\text{asy Var}\begin{pmatrix}\hat{\beta}_0\\ \hat{\beta}_1\end{pmatrix} = \sigma_\nu^2\,(X_*'X_*)^{-1} \tag{7.46}$$

$$\text{asy Var}(\hat{\rho}) = (1 - \rho^2)/(n - 1) \tag{7.47}$$

where X_*, the ρ-differenced form of X, is:

$$X_*' = \begin{bmatrix} 1 & -\rho & 1 & -\rho & \cdots & 1 & -\rho \\ X_2 & -\rho X_1 & X_3 & -\rho X_2 & \cdots & X_n & -\rho X_{n-1}\end{bmatrix} \tag{7.48}$$

These are the same asymptotic variance expressions that would have been obtained by following instead the method of least $\Sigma \nu_i^2$ from (7.40) above.

[22] It may be of some interest to observe, following Carroll and Ruppert (1982), that in a model with normally distributed but heteroscedastic errors, small misspecifications in the dependence of the error term on the regression parameters can easily make the GLS estimates preferable to MLE.

[23] For more comparative results from experimental methods, especially when the auto correlation model includes trended data, see Park and Mitchell (1980).

[24] Some clues seem to be in order. Taking

$$\ln L = -\{(n - 1)/2\} \ln 2 - \{(n - 1)/2\} \ln \sigma_\nu^2 - \{1/(2\sigma_\nu^2)\} \sum_{i=1}^{n} \nu_i^2$$

compute expressions for the first order and second order derivatives of $\ln L$ with respect to β_0, β_1, ρ, and σ_ν^2. The negative of the expectations of the matrix of second order derivatives is the information matrix. This will be found to be block diagonal showing the estimated coefficients $\hat{\beta}_1$ to be independent of $\hat{\rho}$ and separately $\hat{\sigma}_\nu^2$. The inverse of the block due to $\hat{\beta}_0$ and $\hat{\beta}_1$ gives (7.46), and that due to $\hat{\rho}$ gives (7.47).

7.3.10 The Generalized Least Squares Estimation

The model is:

$$\mathbf{Y} = X\boldsymbol{\beta} + \boldsymbol{\epsilon} \qquad E(\boldsymbol{\epsilon}) = \mathbf{0} \qquad E(\boldsymbol{\epsilon\epsilon}') = \sigma^2\boldsymbol{\Omega} \tag{7.49}$$

In (7.49), $\boldsymbol{\Omega}$ is known, symmetric and positive definite of order n. As an example, when $n = 2$,

$$\sigma^2\boldsymbol{\Omega} = \begin{bmatrix} \sigma_{11} & \sigma_{12} \\ \sigma_{21} & \sigma_{22} \end{bmatrix} \qquad \sigma_{11} > 0 \qquad \sigma_{22} > 0 \qquad \sigma_{11}\sigma_{22} - \sigma_{12}^2 > 0 \tag{7.50}$$

But $\sigma_{11}\sigma_{22} - \sigma_{12}^2 = \sigma_{11}\sigma_{12}(1 - \rho_{12}^2)$ which implies $|\rho_{12}| < 1$. Extending this result, one can see that one of the requirements of the $\boldsymbol{\Omega}$ matrix would turn on correlation coefficients of various orders being numerically less than 1.

Before estimation, we want to lay down a few basic results on variable transformations. First, if $\boldsymbol{\Omega} = \boldsymbol{TT}'$ where $\boldsymbol{T}$ is a nonsingular matrix, then pre- and postmultiplying both sides by $\boldsymbol{T}^{-1}$ and $(\boldsymbol{T}')^{-1}$, we have

$$\boldsymbol{T}^{-1}\boldsymbol{\Omega}(\boldsymbol{T}')^{-1} = \boldsymbol{T}^{-1}\boldsymbol{TT}'(\boldsymbol{T}')^{-1}$$

or,

$$\boldsymbol{T}^{-1}\boldsymbol{\Omega}(\boldsymbol{T}')^{-1} = \boldsymbol{I} \tag{7.51}$$

Second, since $\boldsymbol{\Omega}$ is positive definite, by inverting it we have

$$\boldsymbol{\Omega}^{-1} = (\boldsymbol{T}')^{-1}\boldsymbol{T}^{-1} \tag{7.52}$$

Now premultiply the model equation by $\boldsymbol{T}^{-1}$ to get

$$\mathbf{Y}_* = X_*\boldsymbol{\beta} + \boldsymbol{\epsilon}_* \tag{7.53}$$

where

$$\mathbf{Y}_* = \boldsymbol{T}^{-1}\mathbf{Y} \qquad X_* = \boldsymbol{T}^{-1}X \qquad \boldsymbol{\epsilon}_* = \boldsymbol{T}^{-1}\boldsymbol{\epsilon} \tag{7.54}$$

The interesting aspect of the transformed model is that its error $\boldsymbol{\epsilon}_*$ has the variance–covariance matrix

$$E(\boldsymbol{\epsilon}_*\boldsymbol{\epsilon}_*') = E(\boldsymbol{T}^{-1}\,\boldsymbol{\epsilon\epsilon}'\,\boldsymbol{T}'^{-1}) = \sigma^2\boldsymbol{T}^{-1}\boldsymbol{\Omega}\boldsymbol{T}'^{-1} = \sigma^2\boldsymbol{I} \tag{7.55}$$

using the first result. Its structure is the same as that of the basic model including homoscedastic and unautocorrelated errors. The other useful aspect is that the restrictions applicable to X are also applicable to X_*. These validate the use of OLS in the transformed model. Thus, the following estimates and their properties become immediate:

$$\hat{\boldsymbol{\beta}} = (X_*'X_*)\,X_*'Y_* = (X'\boldsymbol{\Omega}^{-1}X)^{-1}X'\boldsymbol{\Omega}^{-1}\,Y \tag{7.56}$$

$$V(\hat{\boldsymbol{\beta}}) = \sigma^2\,(X_*'X_*)^{-1} = \sigma^2(X'\boldsymbol{\Omega}^{-1}X)^{-1} \tag{7.57}$$

$$
\begin{aligned}
\hat{\sigma}^2 &= \{1/(n - m - 1)\}\,(\mathbf{Y}_* - X_*\hat{\boldsymbol{\beta}})'(\mathbf{Y}_* - X_*\hat{\boldsymbol{\beta}}) \\
&= \{1/(n - m - 1)\}\,(\mathbf{Y} - X\hat{\boldsymbol{\beta}})'\boldsymbol{\Omega}^{-1}(\mathbf{Y} - X\hat{\boldsymbol{\beta}}) \\
&= \{1/(n - m - 1)\}\,\hat{\boldsymbol{\epsilon}}'\boldsymbol{\Omega}^{-1}\hat{\boldsymbol{\epsilon}}
\end{aligned} \tag{7.58}
$$

By the Gauss–Markov theorem, as explained in Appendix A.2, the $\hat{\boldsymbol{\beta}}$, which are the Generalized Least Squares (GLS) estimates, are BLUE. A simple deduction reveals that $\hat{\sigma}^2$, which is the estimate of σ^2, is unbiased.

Moreover, if $\boldsymbol{\epsilon}$ is normally distributed, $\boldsymbol{\epsilon}_*$ is also normally distributed. In that case $\hat{\boldsymbol{\beta}}$ will also be maximum likelihood estimates with minimum variance in the class of unbiased estimates.

An example of heteroscedastic but unautocorrelated disturbances would have $\boldsymbol{\Omega}$ given by a diagonal matrix with diagonal entries, say, $\sigma_1^2, \sigma_2^2, \ldots, \sigma_n^2$ and off-diagonal entries zero. In that case, since $\boldsymbol{\Omega}^{-1} = (\boldsymbol{T}'\boldsymbol{T})^{-1}$, we must have $\boldsymbol{T}^{-1}$ equal to a diagonal matrix with diagonal entries $1/\sigma_1, 1/\sigma_2, \ldots, 1/\sigma_n$. Thus the transformations $\mathbf{Y}_* = \boldsymbol{T}^{-1}\mathbf{Y}$ and $X_* = \boldsymbol{T}^{-1}X$ will lead to the typical element of $\mathbf{Y}_*$ and X_* equal to Y_i/σ_i and X_i/σ_i, respectively; $i = 1, 2, \ldots, n$. Such a transformation could be used in connection with the savings–income relationship of Section 7.2.1.

An example of autocorrelation with homoscedasticity was already cited and discussed. Additionally observe that since $\boldsymbol{\Omega} = \boldsymbol{TT}'$ and $\boldsymbol{\Omega}$ is known, $\boldsymbol{T}^{-1}$ of size $(n - 1) \times n$ will work out to:

$$
\boldsymbol{T}^{-1} = \begin{bmatrix} -\rho & 1 & 0 \cdots & 0 & 0 \\ 0 & -\rho & 1 \cdots & 0 & 0 \\ & & & & \\ 0 & 0 & 0 \cdots & -\rho & 1 \end{bmatrix} \tag{7.59}
$$

The ρ-differencing method of estimation involves calculating $\boldsymbol{T}^{-1}\mathbf{Y} = \mathbf{Y}_*$ and $\boldsymbol{T}^{-1}X = X_*$ before the OLS method is applied to the $\mathbf{Y}_*$ and X_* relationship. The rest of the method and its implication are discussed in Sections 7.3.6 and 7.3.8.

7.3.11 Zellner's SURE Method

We will conclude this section by briefly referring to Zellner's (1962) seemingly unrelated regression or, in short, SURE technique. We do so because it falls within the area of generalized regression. Take an example. An industry (for instance, General Electric Co.) investment may be posited to depend on expected profit, retained earnings, capital stock, and interest rate. However, variables like the interest rate also apply to several other companies (for instance, Westinghouse) in correlated industries. Therefore one industry's function will be correlated with similar other industries' functions. Also the disturbance terms of various industry functions, which may be influenced by the common underlying factors of the economy not specific to an industry, will be correlated. This generally will give rise to the phenomenon of contemporaneous autocovariance of disturbances. Under this phenomenon, the OLS method will be inefficient and Zellner's SURE technique, which is an example of the GLS technique, will produce efficient results.

To demonstrate it, consider only two industries, their regression functions being given by:

$$\mathbf{Y} = X\boldsymbol{\beta} + \boldsymbol{\epsilon}$$

that is

$$\underset{(2n \times 1)}{\begin{bmatrix} \mathbf{Y}_1 \\ \cdots \\ \mathbf{Y}_2 \end{bmatrix}} = \underset{(2n \times \overline{2m + 2})}{\begin{bmatrix} X_1 & 0 \\ & \\ 0 & X_2 \end{bmatrix}} \underset{(\overline{2m + 2} \times 1)}{\begin{bmatrix} \boldsymbol{\beta}_1 \\ \cdots \\ \boldsymbol{\beta}_2 \end{bmatrix}} + \underset{(2n \times 1)}{\begin{bmatrix} \boldsymbol{\epsilon}_1 \\ \cdots \\ \boldsymbol{\epsilon}_2 \end{bmatrix}} \tag{7.60}$$

the dimensions of the vectors and matrices written underneath their symbols in parentheses.

Then denoting by $\sigma^2\boldsymbol{\Omega}$ the variance–covariance matrix of $\boldsymbol{\epsilon}$, and its inverse as

$$(\sigma^2\boldsymbol{\Omega})^{-1} = \begin{bmatrix} V(\epsilon_1) & \text{cov}(\epsilon_1, \epsilon_2) \\ \text{cov}(\epsilon_1\epsilon_2) & V(\epsilon_2) \end{bmatrix}^{-1} = \begin{bmatrix} \sigma^{11}\boldsymbol{I} & \sigma^{12}\boldsymbol{I} \\ \sigma^{21}\boldsymbol{I} & \sigma^{22}\boldsymbol{I} \end{bmatrix} \tag{7.61}$$

where $\sigma^{ij}\boldsymbol{I}$ is the (i, j)th element of $(\sigma^2\boldsymbol{\Omega})^{-1}$, $i, j = 1, 2$, the estimated coefficients[25] are given by:

$$\begin{bmatrix} \hat{\boldsymbol{\beta}}_1 \\ \hat{\boldsymbol{\beta}}_2 \end{bmatrix} = \left\{ \begin{bmatrix} X_1' & 0 \\ 0 & X_2' \end{bmatrix} \boldsymbol{\Omega}^{-1} \begin{bmatrix} X_1 & 0 \\ 0 & X_2 \end{bmatrix} \right\}^{-1} \begin{bmatrix} X_1' & 0 \\ 0 & X_2' \end{bmatrix} \boldsymbol{\Omega}^{-1} \begin{bmatrix} \mathbf{Y}_1 \\ \cdots \\ \mathbf{Y}_2 \end{bmatrix} \tag{7.62}$$

These estimates, often called the SURE estimates, are BLUE. These will be equivalent to the OLS estimates if the disturbances are uncorrelated between equations and all equations have unchanged Xs. If not, the GLS estimators would be asymptotically more efficient than the OLS estimators. Indeed many industry equations are taken to be unrelated (seemingly unrelated) in terms of their disturbances and, because of this, the OLS method is applied to each equation. If the seemingly unrelated relations are, in fact, faulty, and correlations are present, the GLS procedure should be applied instead.

[25] This can be easily generalized to any number of coefficients. The form of the variance of the estimated coefficients is the same as in the GLS situation. Zellner has suggested a way of estimating the elements of the $(\sigma^2\boldsymbol{\Omega})^{-1}$ matrix. This is by estimating the OLS residuals for each industry and then taking the mean sums of squares and products of these residuals for the diagonal (and off-diagonal) entries of that matrix. The effect on the relative efficiency of the GLS over OLS estimates for very small disturbance covariances in small sample situations is investigated by Kmenta and Gilbert (1968).

7.3.12 Further Empirical Illustrations

We will now illustrate a few other empirical studies. First, consider Barten (1964). This study is concerned with the derivation of the Netherlands' consumer demand function for commodities. It assumes that consumer preferences for these commodities are almost additive,[26] and the stochastic disturbances of the functions are subject to extraneous constraints. Based on these, it derives the posterior estimates of coefficients.

The data series are 14 in number for 14 groups of commodities. The time periods chosen are 1921–1939 and 1948–1958.

We do not intend to report on all the phases of this work except to focus on some unconventional specification aspect of the stochastic term. Taking u to be the error and i and t the equation and time, respectively, he assumes

$$
\begin{aligned}
\mathrm{E}u_i(t) &= 0 && \text{for all } i \text{ and } t \\
\mathrm{E}u_i(t)\, u_j\,(t') &= 0 && \text{if } t \neq t' \\
&= \sigma_{ij} && \text{if } t = t' \leq 1939 \\
&= 1/2\ \sigma_{ij} && \text{if } t = t' \geq 1948
\end{aligned} \tag{7.63}
$$

Evidently the specifications provide for interequation correlation but not intertemporal autocorrelation. Also, the post-war variances are assumed equal to half of the pre-war variances of the disturbance terms, an indication of a higher reliability of the former time period.

This is an example of the use of generalized variance of the error term which would call for the use of the GLS procedure for estimation. Barten ultimately provides estimates of income elasticities, direct price elasticities and interaction (or cross) price elasticities. All his results indicate that the estimates using the prior information on errors produce gains in efficiency of estimates.

Next, we like to refer to the work of Denny and others (1978) on the demand for energy in Canadian manufacturing. The study is meant to be an introduction to or a dialogue for an energy policy in Canada. The basis of the work is four demand functions: for labour, capital, energy, and materials, all of the nonhomothetic[27] generalized Leontief cost function type.

[26] This means that the matrix of the double (own and cross) derivatives of utilities of the commodities would be almost diagonal, but not exactly so. For a more elaborate definition, see the original source.

[27] A nonhomothetic function is obviously the opposite of a homothetic function. A homothetic function is a monotonic transformation of a homogeneous function. Thus it remains invariant under a radial expansion, just as the homogeneous function does. That is, the slopes of the isoquant curves derived from the homothetic (or homogeneous) functions are the same along each point of a given ray drawn out of the origin.

A generalized Leontief cost function, derived by Diewert (1971), is presented below:

$$C = \sum_i \sum_j \beta_{ij}\,(p_i/p_j)^{1/2}\ \mathrm{h}(Q)$$

The general findings of the study are as follows. The own price elasticity of energy is small but its substitution possibilities with other inputs are immense. Also, any argument in favor of homotheticity is rejected. Some simulation studies are made that show only small effects of large energy price increases on costs of production.

However, the most interesting aspect of the study is that the errors of the input demand functions are assumed to have generalized variance–covariance matrices. For the purpose of coefficient estimation, these matrices are first estimated and then the data are transformed on the basis of these estimates before a GLS-type technique is applied.

The last study we refer to is the one by Gillen and Guccione (1970). This is concerned with the estimation of the post-war regional consumption functions in Canada. The regions taken in this study are the Maritimes, Quebec, Ontario, the Prairies, and British Columbia (including Yukon and the North-West Territories) and the exact period is 1947–1966.

The consumption function for region r is postulated to be

$$[\mathbf{C}]_r = [Y]_{rr}\,[\boldsymbol{\beta}]_r + [\boldsymbol{\epsilon}]_r \qquad r = 1, 2, \ldots, 5 \tag{7.64}$$

where

$$[\mathbf{C}] = \begin{bmatrix} C_{r1} \\ \vdots \\ C_{r7} \end{bmatrix}; \qquad [Y]_r = \begin{bmatrix} 1 & Y_{r1} \\ \vdots & \vdots \\ 1 & Y_{r7} \end{bmatrix}; \qquad [\boldsymbol{\beta}]_r = \begin{bmatrix} \beta_{r0} \\ \beta_{r1} \end{bmatrix}; \qquad [\boldsymbol{\epsilon}]_r = \begin{bmatrix} \epsilon_{r1} \\ \vdots \\ \epsilon_{r7} \end{bmatrix} \tag{7.65}$$

The first 7 observations above correspond to the years 1948, 1953, 1955, 1957, 1959, 1962, and 1964. The last 13 observations are on the national consumption function and corresponded to 1947 to 1966 excluding the first 7 observations.

Thus

$$[\mathbf{C}_6] = [Y]_{61}[\boldsymbol{\beta}]_1 + [Y]_{62}[\boldsymbol{\beta}]_2 + \cdots + [Y]_{65}[\boldsymbol{\beta}]_5 + [\boldsymbol{\epsilon}]_6 \tag{7.66}$$

---

where C is total cost, p_i is the price of factor i (similarly j), Q, assumed linear homogeneous, is the level of gross output, and h(Q) is a homothetic function. To illustrate switching to a simple nonhomothetic function, replace h(Q) by Q, and observe that $\beta_{ij} = C_{ij} + C_{i0}Q^{-1}$, for $i = j$, but $\beta_{ij} = C_{ij}$ for $i \neq j$. Then the demand equation for factor X_i can be shown to reduce to:

$$X_i = C_{i0} + C_{ii}\,\mathrm{Q} + \sum_{j=1} (p_j/p_i)^{1/2}\,Q \qquad i \neq j$$

C_{i0} is the preconceived expenditure on input i. If the C_{i0}s are zero, the input demand or cost function is linear homogeneous in this example, otherwise it is nonhomothetic. That is, if prices of inputs increase by, say, a factor λ so that $(\lambda p_j/\lambda p_i)^{1/2} = (p_j/p_i)$, then the factor involving input price ratio remains unchanged. Moreover, if the quantities of inputs decrease by a factor λ, then, by the property of linear homogeneity, Q decreases by the same factor λ. But X_i, due to the presence of C_{i0}, will decrease by less than λ. This is indicative of the non-homotheticity of X_i. This formulation is used by Denny and others.

where

$$[\mathrm{C}_6] = \begin{bmatrix} \mathrm{C}_8 \\ \vdots \\ \mathrm{C}_{20} \end{bmatrix}; \qquad [Y]_{6r} = \begin{bmatrix} 1 & Y_{r8} \\ \vdots & \vdots \\ 1 & Y_{r20} \end{bmatrix}; \qquad [\boldsymbol{\epsilon}]_6 = \begin{bmatrix} \epsilon_8 \\ \vdots \\ \epsilon_{20} \end{bmatrix}$$

Combining (7.64) and (7.66), we obtain

$$\mathbf{C} = Y\boldsymbol{\beta} + \boldsymbol{\epsilon} \tag{7.67}$$

from which

$$\hat{\boldsymbol{\beta}} = [Y'\boldsymbol{\Omega}^{-1}Y]^{-1}Y'\boldsymbol{\Omega}^{-1}\mathbf{C} \tag{7.68}$$

In above $\boldsymbol{\Omega}$ is a 48 × 48 variance-covariance matrix, assumed serially independent across regions but homoscedastic in each region. Specifically

$$\boldsymbol{\Omega} = \begin{bmatrix} \sigma_1^2 \boldsymbol{I}_7 & \boldsymbol{0} & \cdots & \boldsymbol{0} \\ \boldsymbol{0} & \sigma_2^2 \boldsymbol{I}_7 & & \boldsymbol{0} \\ \cdots & \cdots & \cdots & \cdots \\ \boldsymbol{0} & \cdots & \sigma_5^2 \boldsymbol{I}_7 & \boldsymbol{0} \\ \boldsymbol{0} & \cdots & \cdots & \sigma^2 \boldsymbol{I}_{13} \end{bmatrix} \tag{7.69}$$

where

$$\sigma_r^2 = \text{variance from equation (7.64) in region } r$$

$$\sigma^2 = \text{variance from equation (7.66)}$$

$$\boldsymbol{I}_n = \text{identity matrix of size } n \times n$$

For the estimation of the unknown $\boldsymbol{\Omega}$, the following procedure is used. The 7 observations for each region's consumption and the 20 observations on the national consumption are treated as separate samples. These give rise to the initial estimates of the diagonal elements of $\boldsymbol{\Omega}$, which are used in the first approximation calculations for $\boldsymbol{\Omega}^{-1}$. These last results are then used to estimate $\hat{\boldsymbol{\beta}}$ from equation (7.68). The second approximations are obtained by putting $\hat{\boldsymbol{\beta}}$ in equation (7.67), then reestimating $\boldsymbol{\Omega}^{-1}$ and at last reestimating $\hat{\boldsymbol{\beta}}$ from (7.68).

The following consumption functions are derived*:

Maritimes:

$$C_{1t} = \underset{(231.82)}{72.87} + \underset{(0.174)}{0.994}\, Y_{1t} \qquad R^2 = 0.85$$

Quebec:

$$C_{2t} = \underset{(219.85)}{-120.36} + \underset{(0.047)}{0.974}\, Y_{2t} \qquad R^2 = 0.99$$

* These are used with the permission of W. J. Gillen and A. Guccione, "The Estimation of Post-War Regional Consumption," *Canadian Journal of Economics*, University of Toronto Press (1970) 13, p. 283.

Ontario:

$$\underset{}{C_{3t}} = \underset{(396.43)}{60.67} + \underset{(0.056)}{0.909}\, Y_{3t} \qquad R^2 = 0.97 \tag{7.70}$$

Prairies:

$$C_{4t} = \underset{(451.12)}{95.29} + \underset{(0.139)}{0.917}\, Y_{4t} \qquad R^2 = 0.89$$

British Columbia:

$$C_{5t} = \underset{(153.81)}{-12.93} + \underset{(0.080)}{0.901}\, Y_{5t} \qquad R^2 = 0.96$$

From these, no significant differences are noticeable among the different regional consumption functions. Also there is a general tendency for estimates of regional MPCs to rank in the same order as regional per capita income, except for Quebec and the Maritime region, where the estimated MPCs are rather high.

The regional consumption functions are found to be quite consistent with the national consumption function. This is given by:

$$C_t = \underset{(285.59)}{-27.55} + \underset{(0.016)}{0.940}\, Y_t \tag{7.71}$$

One of the most successful uses of the GLS technique has been in the investigation of the suitability of what is known as the Phillips curve or its variants to various economies. Without any claim to completeness in our references to the literature, let us only observe that the study by Rowley and Wilton (1973) is perhaps one of the first early attempts to cast doubts on this. These doubts are on the statistical validity of a number[28] of important articles in this area, published during the late fifties through to early seventies. Their study focusses on the implications of an aggregative procedure employed, making possible the use of a "four-quarter overlapping change" representation of the dependent variable in a quarterly analysis of the wage variable, and the use of moving averages for explanatory variables. These are rigorously shown to give rise to the problem of serial correlation in the error term. In particular, if all explanatory variables have the same moving average patterns as assumed in many empirical studies, then the aggregate error must also have the same (moving average) pattern. These would therefore give rise to biases, using the traditional formulas for standard errors and test statistics. The amount of the bias though would vary from one empirical situation to another.

To show the consequence of the bias, the authors choose three earlier studies and recalculate their tests using the GLS procedure based on correction for autocorrelations. Certain variables considered earlier to be of major significance in the wage determination process are immediately reduced to doubtful significance. For instance, eight equations, based on the GLS calculations, show each of the

[28] See Rowley and Wilton for reference to these articles.

unemployment and price change variables to be significant at the 5% level only twice, compared to seven and eight times (respectively) based on results of the classical OLS method. Thus the Phillips curve representations of aggregate wage changes attempted by the earlier economists in the United States come to receive a severe blow.[29] A year later, the same authors (Rowley and Wilton (1974)) seriously question the empirical foundation of a Canadian Phillips curve.[30]

7.3.13 The Autoregressive Conditional Heteroscedasticity (or ARCH) Process and Its Applications

This concept has been introduced by Engle (1982). Its explanation, following Engle, is as follows. Suppose we have a random variable Y_t that is drawn from the conditional pdf $f(Y_t/Y_{t-1})$. That is, we predict this year's Y_t on the basis of past year's Y_{t-1} through $E(Y_t/Y_{t-1})$, given that all assumptions used are standard. Let us denote the one-period forecast variance by $V(Y_t/Y_{t-1})$. Evidently, this conditional variance is random having to depend on the past information, contrary to how it is treated in the conventional models. This novelty will be the cornerstone of the concept called the autoregressive conditional heteroscedasticity process.

Let us begin with an AR(1) process given by

$$Y_t = \rho Y_{t-1} + \nu_t \qquad \nu_t \sim N(0, \sigma_\nu^2)$$

Then the conditional mean and variance of Y_t, given Y_{t-1}, are

$$E(Y_t/Y_{t-1}) = \rho Y_{t-1} \qquad V(Y_t/Y_{t-1}) = \sigma_\nu^2/1 - \rho^2$$

But, the unconditional mean and variance are

$$E(Y_t) = 0 \qquad V(Y_t) = \sigma_\nu^2$$

On the basis of both the mean and the variance, the forecasts will improve when

[29] In a more recent study, Nichols (1983) establishes the complete collapse of the Phillips curve type equations. He finds no links at all between the disaggregated unemployment changes and the disaggregated wage changes in a restricted section of the wage earners, namely the white-collar occupation. The method used is the GLS one.

[30] It is interesting to mention that traditional wage analyses based on aggregative approaches lack in the correct institutional specifications of the labor market, such as multiyear contracts, deferred increments and the variable nature of the bargaining calendar. Use of microdata (before aggregation) corrects these specificational errors. In particular, this type of data helps separate expected inflation from price catch-ups and facilitates the study of their separate effects on the wage determination process. In the Canadian context, see two outstanding studies, one by Christofides, Swidinsky and Wilton (1980) devoted to the private sector, and the other by Auld, Christofides, Swidinsky and Wilton (1986) addressed to the public sector. In the private sector, both price expectations and price catch-up are found to be significant determinants of wage changes, whereas unemployment rate is found to be a poor, if perverse, performer. Other important variables are job vacancies or help wanted, and the 1971 Unemployment Insurance Act (UIA) revision. In the public sector, both price movements and labor market conditions are found to affect the base wage rates in a way not much unlike that in the private sector.

the influence of the past information is used through their conditional measures, rather than their unconditional ones.

In the usual models of heteroscedasticity, we devise an exogenous variable X_t on which the variance of Y_t depends. This relation may be given by

$$Y_t = \nu_t X_{t-1}$$

Then,

$$\mathrm{V}(Y_t) = \sigma_\nu^2 X_{t-1}^2$$

This means that the development of the exogenous variable will influence the forecast interval. This may be useful as a concept. But to make it fully satisfactory, we should try to lay down the *causes* as to why the variance changes. This is not an easy matter in time series analysis.

Consider the following model which can remedy the above problem:

$$\begin{aligned} Y_t &= \nu_t l_t^{1/2} \\ l_t &= \delta_0 + \delta_1 Y_{t-1}^2 \end{aligned} \tag{7.72}$$

ν_t is now standardized to have $\mathrm{V}(\nu_t) = 1$. This example is used to illustrate an ARCH model. Suppose we assume normality for Y_t and use ϕ_t to denote the information available at time t. Then,

$$\begin{aligned} f(Y_t/\phi_{t-1}) &\approx \mathrm{N}(0, l_t) \\ l_t &= \delta_0 + \delta_1 Y_{t-1}^2 \end{aligned} \tag{7.73}$$

For an rth order ARCH process, l_t depends on $Y_{t-1}, \ldots, Y_{t-r}$

$$l_t = l(Y_{t-1}, Y_{t-2}, \ldots, Y_{t-r}, \boldsymbol{\delta}) \tag{7.74}$$

where $\boldsymbol{\delta}$ is a vector of coefficients. In the ARCH regression model, we assume that

$$\mathrm{E}(Y_t/\phi_{t-1}) = \mathbf{X}_t\boldsymbol{\beta} \tag{7.75}$$

We can generalize the variance function l_t to include the present and past observations on Xs. Then l_t becomes

$$l_t = l(\epsilon_{t-1}, \ldots, \epsilon_{t-r}, X_t, X_{t-1}, \ldots, X_{t-r}, \boldsymbol{\delta}) \tag{7.76}$$

One particular form of the above is obtained when the X and the ϵ components are separable, that is

$$l_t = l_\epsilon(\epsilon_{t-1}, \ldots, \epsilon_{t-r}, \boldsymbol{\delta})\, l_x(X_t, \ldots, X_{t-r}) \tag{7.77}$$

This would require, for example, making a correction for the X-type of heteroscedasticity first and then applying the ARCH regression model to the purified data.

Engle uses both the Maximum Likelihood and OLS methods for estimation, even though he claims that the former method is more efficient. The ARCH model is then used to calculate the means and variances of inflation in the United Kingdom. The ARCH effect comes out significant for a fourth-order linear ARCH process. Also, the estimated variances of inflation are found to increase considerably during the inflationary period of the seventies.

A multivariate generalization of the ARCH process appears in Bollerslev and others (1988). The generalization is applied to a capital asset premia model in which the expected returns to bills, bonds, and stocks are taken to be proportional to the conditional variance of each return, given that there is a fully diversified or market portfolio. It is found that the conditional covariances of asset returns vary over time. These covariances are taken to be a strong determinant of the time-varying risk pricing of assets. Among the other explanatory variables, the authors suggest innovations in consumption to be an important item of the investors' information set influencing the conditional distribution of returns.

7.4 QUALITATIVE AND LIMITED DEPENDENT VARIABLES

Consider that a family faces an option (Y) of buying (with $Y = 1$) or not buying (with $Y = 0$) a house. This will depend on a number of variables (X), such as income, number of dependants, asset position and so on. One way of formulating the problem is by a linear probability rule.

7.4.1 Linear Probability Rule

This rule is such that it includes $\boldsymbol{\epsilon}$ for the error term and $\boldsymbol{\beta}$ the coefficient of $\mathbf{X}$ as in the following:

$$\mathbf{Y} = X\boldsymbol{\beta} + \boldsymbol{\epsilon} \tag{7.78}$$

in which Y is a binomial variable. Thus, $E(\mathbf{Y} \mid X)$ or the mean proportion of houses bought will represent the probability that the house is or is not bought and $\hat{\mathbf{Y}}$ will be its estimated chance.

For the estimation of this relation, one should use the GLS procedure since ϵ is not homoscedastic.[31] However, the problem remains that $E(Y_i/X_{i1}, X_{i2}, \ldots, X_{im})$, which is equal to an unbounded linear function, could fall outside the range of 0 to 1. This is bad for $E(Y_i/X_{i1}, X_{i2}, \ldots, X_{im})$, because the latter is a probability, and probability cannot lie outside that range. Thus, a modification of this approach seems desirable.

[31] To see this, write $\epsilon_i = Y_i - X_i\beta$ assuming, without any loss of generality, that there is only one regressor X. Then ϵ_i can be either $1 - X_i\beta$ or $0 - X_i\beta$ depending on $Y_i = 1$ or 0. With probabilities $X_i\beta$ and $1 - X_i\beta$, respectively (remember $E(Y_i/X)$ = probability of $Y_i = 1$). Thus $E(\epsilon_i) = (1 - X_i\beta)X_i\beta + (-X_i\beta)(1 - X_i\beta) = 0$. And $V(\epsilon_i) = E(\epsilon_i^2) = (-X_i\beta)^2(1 - X_i\beta) + (1 - X_i\beta)^2 X_i\beta = X_i\beta(1 - X_i\beta) = EY_i(1 - EY_i)$ which is proportional to Y_i or X_i showing the absence of homoscedasticity.

Two modifications of this approach are available. The first is the logit analysis and the second the probit analysis.

7.4.2 Logit Analysis

In logit analysis, the regression is fitted in a modified form:

$$\ln \mathrm{E}Y/(1 - \mathrm{E}Y) = X\boldsymbol{\beta} \tag{7.79}$$

where $\boldsymbol{\beta}$ represents the set of modified coefficients, and $\mathrm{E}Y$ = probability (Y = 1). Then, simplifying, we obtain EY related to $X\boldsymbol{\beta}$ as:

$$\mathrm{E}Y = e^{X\boldsymbol{\beta}}/(1 + e^{X\boldsymbol{\beta}}) = 1/(1 + e^{-X\boldsymbol{\beta}}) \tag{7.80}$$

For estimated values $\hat{\boldsymbol{\beta}}$ of $\boldsymbol{\beta}$ (from (7.79)) and forecasted values $\hat{X}$ of X, the forecast $\hat{Y}$ is:

$$\hat{Y} = 1/(1 + e^{-\hat{X}\hat{\boldsymbol{\beta}}}) \tag{7.81}$$

It is a simple exercise to show[32,33] that $\hat{Y}$ (the estimated probability) varies between 0 and 1, regardless of the values of $\hat{X}\hat{\boldsymbol{\beta}}$.

[32] In fact $\hat{Y}$ represents an S-shaped logistic curve, usually fitted to population growth. $\hat{Y}$, lying above the horizontal axis, never goes beyond the limit of 1.

In an empirical context, $\hat{\mathrm{E}}Y$ has to be construed as the sample proportion of those families which buy a house. Then from (7.79), $\hat{\boldsymbol{\beta}}$ has to be computed by relating $\{\hat{\mathrm{E}}Y/(1 - \hat{\mathrm{E}}Y)\}$ to X, where X is, say, family income, and so on. Taking $\mathrm{E}(Y)$ equal to P, where P is probability of $Y = 1$, we can also equate $\hat{\mathrm{E}}(Y)$ to p, the sample proportion of success.

[33] In the linear model based on binary response data (see Manski (1986)) to which the logit model belongs, a relatively new estimation method called the maximum score estimation method, due to Manski (1975), has come to command the attention of some econometricians. The method is based on the idea of a "threshold" level of binary response when an observable indicator Y^* and a latent scalar variable Y are such that:

$$\begin{aligned} Y^* &= 1 \qquad \text{if } Y \geqq 0 \\ &= -1 \qquad \text{if } Y < 0 \end{aligned}$$

Y, of course, is a function of an observable random variable X and an unobservable random variable ϵ as follows

$$Y = X\boldsymbol{\beta} + \boldsymbol{\epsilon}$$

where $\boldsymbol{\beta}$ is the parameter vector. The next steps in the method are to compute conditional response probabilities, relate these to $\boldsymbol{\beta}$, and the distribution of $\boldsymbol{\epsilon}$, given X and its prespecified quantities or percentage points. Manski (1975) has shown that $\boldsymbol{\beta}$ can be estimated by the method of maximum score consistently under weak distributional assumptions.

Very briefly stated, the method of maximum score estimation originates from a *stochastic* utility theory of choice. A certain θ-utility index, based on material attributes, is assigned to every pair of decision maker and good, which then leads to a ranking of alternatives. At this point, sample scores S are assigned to a set of real numbers W into which those rankings are mapped. Thus S is a function of W, θ, and T, where T is the number of decision makers. According to the maximum score estimation method, $\hat{\theta}$ is the maximum score if: $S(W, \hat{\theta}, T) \geqq S(W, \theta, T)$ for all θ belonging to the parameter space.

For the estimation of a logit model, we distinguish between two cases: the cases of the unreplicated and replicated observations. The method we use in the first case is the maximum likelihood and in the second case the generalized least squares or the minimum chi-square method. We assume below that there is only one regressor X, and β_0, β_1 are the coefficients.

In the case of unreplicated observations, suppose the observations are Y_is, where each Y_i may have the value of 1 with probability P_i and the value of 0 with probability $(1 - P_i)$. For n independent observations, their log-likelihood function becomes:

$$\log L = \sum_{i=1}^{n} \{Y_i \log P_i + (1 - Y_i) \log(1 - P_i)\} \tag{7.82}$$

For a typical observation, say the ith, we will have $E(Y_i)$ related to X_i through (7.82) above, except that Y and X will now be replaced by Y_i and X_i respectively. And $E(Y_i)$ is really P_i. Thus $\log L$ reduces to:

$$\log L = \sum_{i} \{Y_i(\beta_0 + \beta_1 X_i) - \log[1 + \exp(\beta_0 + \beta_1 X_i)]\} \tag{7.83}$$

Maximization of $\log L$ will be based on the following two conditions:

$$\begin{aligned} \partial \log L/\partial\beta_0 &= \sum_{i} (Y_i - \hat{P}_i) = 0 \\ \partial \log L/\partial\beta_1 &= \sum_{i} (Y_i - \hat{P}_i) X_i = 0 \end{aligned} \tag{7.84}$$

But, using (7.80) and (7.81),

$$\hat{P}_i = \frac{\exp(\hat{\beta}_0 + \hat{\beta}_1 X_i)}{1 + \exp(\hat{\beta}_0 + \hat{\beta}_1 X_i)} \tag{7.85}$$

Therefore, (7.84) will lead to the maximum likelihood estimates of β_0 and β_1.

In the case of replicated observations, on the other hand, suppose that the values of X represented as X_i are available in I classes or groups, $i = 1, \ldots, I$, and the corresponding values of Y are Y_{ij}, $i = 1, 2, \ldots, I$, and $j = 1, 2, \ldots, n_i$. Using p_i (the estimate of P_i) as the sample proportion of success, we have

$$p_i = (1/n_i) \sum_{j=1}^{n_i} Y_{ij} \tag{7.86}$$

Since in the case of the Bernoulli distribution the sample proportion of success is unbiased (regardless of the size of the sample) for the population proportion of success, we can use this information to very simply derive the generalized least square estimates of the parameters. This is done as follows. Let

$$p_i - P_i = e_i \tag{7.87}$$

then[34]

$$\log\left(\frac{p_i}{1 - p_i}\right) = \log[(P_i + e_i)/(1 - P_i - e_i)]$$
$$= \log\left(\frac{P_i}{1 - P_i}\right) + \log(1 + e_i/P_i) - \log\left(1 - \frac{e_i}{1 - P_i}\right) \tag{7.88}$$

which can be approximated to

$$\beta_0 + \beta_1 X_i + e_i/P_i + \frac{e_i}{1 - P_i} \tag{7.89}$$

$$= \beta_0 + \beta_1 X_i + [e_i/\{P_i(1 - P_i)\}] \tag{7.90}$$

using expansion of the $\log(1 + z)$ series [35] and ignoring higher order terms, which become negligible anyway as n_i becomes large. Since the variance of $e_i/\{P_i(1 - P_i)\}$ can be simplified to

$$V_i = V[e_i/\{P_i(1 - P_i)\}] = V[p_i/\{P_i(1 - P_i)\}]$$
$$= [1/\{P_i(1 - P_i)\}^2]\,[P_i(1 - P_i)/n_i] \tag{7.91}$$
$$= 1/\{n_i P_i(1 - P_i)\}$$

a consistent estimator of this variance is $\hat{V}_i$, where $\hat{V}_i$ is given by

$$\hat{V}_i = 1/\{np_i(1 - p_i)\} \tag{7.92}$$

This suggests that the OLS method can be applied to the model corrected for the heteroscedasticity of its disturbance term. The corrected model becomes

$$(1/\hat{V}_i)\log(p_i/1 - p_i) = \{(\beta_0 + \beta_1 X_i)/\hat{V}_i\} + \epsilon_i \tag{7.93}$$

where ϵ_i is the transformed error term which will be homoscedastic. The estimates $\hat{\beta}$ are the least-squares estimates, free of the problem of error due to heteroscedasticity.

Amemiya (1976) has suggested an alternative method to obtain parameter estimates in the case of replicated observations. This is based on the following asymptotic results:

$$p_i \sim N(P_i, [P_i(1 - P_i)/n_i]) \tag{7.94}$$

$$[(p_i - P_i)\sqrt{n_i}/\sqrt{\{P_i(1 - P_i)\}}] \sim N(0, 1) \tag{7.95}$$

[34] $\log[(P_i + e_i)/(1 - P_i - e_i)]$ is indeed $\log[(P_i/(1 - P_i)]\,[(1 + e_i/P_i)/(1 - e_i/(1 - P_i))]$ from which the end result follows.

[35] $\log(1 \mp z) = z \pm z^2/2 + z^3/3 \pm z^4/4 + \cdots$. In the expansions that follow, equate z to e_i/P_i and, separately, to $e_i/(1 - P_i)$.

Thus

$$\sum_{i=1}^{I} [(n_i(p_i - P_i)^2)/(P_i(1 - P_i))] \sim \chi_I^2 \tag{7.96}$$

The last result suggests minimizing χ^2 to generate estimates of β_0 and β_1. Given that P_i is a nonlinear function of the parameters, the minimum χ^2 method will amount to a weighted nonlinear least squares method.

To summarize, we apply the maximum likelihood method for estimation of parameters of the logit model when observations are unreplicated. But if observations are replicated, we can apply either the least-squares method corrected for heteroscedasticity, or the minimum chi-square method. The important point to note is that all the three methods provide estimates that have desirable asymptotic properties.

7.4.3 Probit Analysis

Probit analysis, on the other hand, is somewhat complicated and is based on the concept of cumulative normal distribution. Here, for instance, the ith person with a high value of an index ($= I^N$), assumed to be distributed normally, decides to buy a house (with $Y = 1$) only if his capabilities measured by variables such as income ($= X$) be so high that $I_i = \mathbf{X}_i'\boldsymbol{\beta} \geq I_i^N$; reverse otherwise. That is, he does not decide to buy a house (with $Y = 0$) if $I_i < I_i^N$. Note that the βs are the regression coefficients.

Taking $F(Z)$ to be a standard cumulative normal distribution, we have the following probabilities for $Y = 1$ or 0:

$$\text{Prob}\{Y = 1/I\} = \text{Prob}\{I^N \leq I/I\} = F(I) \tag{7.97}$$

$$\text{Prob}\{Y = 0/I\} = \text{Prob}\{I^N > I/I\} = 1 - F(I) \tag{7.98}$$

By definition, I is a function of the βs. Therefore, $F(I)$ is a function of β, since it is a function of I. This gives rise to the idea that the βs can be estimated from $F(I)$.

To estimate the βs, take a sample of size n of which g observations turn out $Y = 1$ and the remaining $n - g$ observations turn out $Y = 0$. Then the method of maximum likelihood will be based on maximizing the following (logarithmic) likelihood function:

$$\begin{aligned} L &= \ln[\{F(I_1) \ldots F(I_g)\} \{(1 - F(I_{g+1})) \ldots (1 - F(I_n))\}] \\ &= \sum_{1}^{g} \ln F(I_i) + \sum_{g+1}^{n} \ln(1 - F(I_i)) \end{aligned} \tag{7.99}$$

in which $F(I_i)$ is given by

$$F(I_i) = (1/\sqrt{2\pi}) \int_{-\infty}^{\mathbf{X}_i'\boldsymbol{\beta}} e^{-t^2/2}\, dt \tag{7.100}$$

That is, the solutions $\hat{\beta}$ will arise from the equations $\partial L/\partial\beta = 0$. These equations are nonlinear. Consequently a nonlinear solution routine will be required. Now given that the expected proportion $E(Y_i/I_i)$ is equal[36] to $F(I_i)$, and the latter is an ordinate of the cumulative normal distribution, its estimate $\hat{Y}_i$ will be $F(\hat{I}_i)$. This is equal to $F(\mathbf{X}_i'\hat{\boldsymbol{\beta}})$, an ordinate of a cumulative normal distribution. Therefore $\hat{Y}_i$ will lie over the range 0 to 1 and there is no danger of the mean proportion or its estimate ever turning out negative or larger than 1.[37]

7.4.4 Logit and Probit Analyses

We will now review the estimates of β obtained using the logit and the probit models. Comparing ϵ_i of (7.79) with I_i^N as defined in the lead paragraph of Section 7.4.3, we have $\epsilon_i = -I_i^N$, and

$$\begin{aligned} P_i &= \text{Prob}\{Y_i = 1\} = \text{Prob}\{I_i - I_i^N > 0\} \\ &= \text{Prob}\{\epsilon_i > \mathbf{X}_i'\boldsymbol{\beta}\} = 1 - f(\mathbf{X}_i'\boldsymbol{\beta}) \end{aligned} \tag{7.101}$$

Assuming that the distribution of ϵ is symmetric so that $1 - F(-Z) = F(Z)$, (7.101) reduces to the following, using (7.80):

$$\begin{aligned} P_i &= \text{Prob}\{Z_i \leqq \mathbf{X}_i'\boldsymbol{\beta}\} = F(\mathbf{X}_i'\boldsymbol{\beta}) = Y = e^{\mathbf{X}_i'\boldsymbol{\beta}}/(1 + e^{\mathbf{X}_i'\boldsymbol{\beta}}) \\ &= e^{Z_i}/(1 + e^{Z_i}) \end{aligned} \tag{7.102}$$

Thus the pdf of Z_i is

$$f(Z_i) = \frac{e^{Z_i}}{(1 + e^{Z_i})^2} \tag{7.103}$$

which is called the logistic distribution.

On the other hand, equation (7.100), reproduced below, defines the distribution of errors of the probit model:

$$F(Z_i) = F(I_i) = (1/\sqrt{2\pi}) \int_{-\infty}^{\mathbf{X}_i'\boldsymbol{\beta}} e^{-t^2/2}\, dt \tag{7.100}$$

equating Z_i to I_i. This is the distribution function of a standard normal variable with variance equal to unity.

We can show that the variance of the logistic distribution is $\pi^2/3$ which implies that the estimates of β_i from the logit model have to be multiplied by $\sqrt{3}/\pi$ before these are compared with the estimates from the probit model.

Amemiya (1981) has shown that a multiplier equal to 1/1.6 (=0.625), rather than $\sqrt{3}/\pi$, should be used to effect a closer agreement between the logistic and standard normal distribution. He also finds a relationship between the estimated β coefficients of the linear probability model (say, the $\hat{\beta}_{LP}$s) and those of the logit

[36] Since $E(Y_i(I_i)) = \text{Prob}\{Y_i = 1/I_i\} = F(I_i)$.

[37] See Tobin (1955) for an empirical example.

model (say, the $\hat{\beta}_L$s). That relationship is

$$\hat{\beta}_{Lp} \approx 0.25\ \hat{\beta}_L \tag{7.104}$$

But the above should be modified by the relation

$$\hat{\beta}_{Lp} \approx 0.25\ \hat{\beta}_L + 0.5 \tag{7.105}$$

in the case of the intercept term. In other words, using $\hat{\beta}_p$ to represent the estimated coefficients from the probit model, we will have

$$2.5\ \hat{\beta}_{Lp} \approx 0.625\hat{\beta}_L \approx \hat{\beta}_p \tag{7.106}$$

For the intercept term, the relationship will be instead

$$2.5\ \hat{\beta}_{Lp} - 1.25 \approx 0.625\ \hat{\beta}_L \approx \hat{\beta}_p \tag{7.107}$$

7.4.5 Multinomial Logit

So far we have characterized the dependent variable to be a dichotomous choice variable. However there are times when this variable need not be dichotomous. That is, it can take more than two alternative values. When a logit model is based on a variable of this type with multiple possible values, we call the model a multinomial logit model.

Let the value 1 for the variable Y_{ij} represent the ith individual's choice of an alternative j, otherwise the value is zero; $j = 1, 2, 3, \ldots$. For example, let $j = 1$ imply the individual's wanting to have 1 child, $j = 2$ imply wanting to have 2 children, and so on. Using P_{ij} for the probability that $Y_{ij} = 1$, we have:

$$P_{i1} + P_{i2} + P_{i3} + \cdots = 1 \tag{7.108}$$

Thus the multinomial logit model is expressed by a combination of the following rules (assuming, for the sake of simplicity, zero intercept coefficients and using (7.80) adapted to the present case):

$$\begin{aligned} \log(P_{i2}/P_{i1}) &= \beta_2 X_i \\ \log(P_{i3}/P_{i2}) &= \beta_3 X_i \\ \ldots\ldots & \quad \ldots\ldots\ldots \\ P_{i1} = 1 - P_{i2} &- P_{i3} - \cdots \end{aligned} \tag{7.109}$$

Assuming that there are K alternative choices possible, we have, by following a method similar to that of (7.80),

$$P_{ij} = e^{\beta_j X_i} \Big/ \left\{ 1 + \sum_{j \neq 1 = 2}^{K} e^{\beta_j X_i} \right\} \tag{7.110}$$

In above we have used the normalization rule $\beta_1 = 0$ based on the use of the first alternative as the reference point for comparative purposes. For estimation of the parameters of this model, we simply follow the method of maximizing the log-likelihood function

$$\log L = \sum_{i=1}^{n} \sum_{j=1}^{K} Y_{ij} \log P_{ij} \tag{7.111}$$

with respect to these parameters.

One aspect of the multinomial logit model relates to its weakness and that has been subjected to rigorous specification tests. Recall that the model allows for a choice between two options, assuming that this choice can be made quite independently of the other options. This assumption is popularly known as "independence of irrelevant alternatives". But the problem is that these "other" alternatives may not be irrelevant in the determination of odds of choosing between the "first" two alternatives. Is it not true that the choices of selecting, for instance, a car rather than a red bus may differ in respect of whether the third mode of transportation is a train or a blue bus?

Analysts do realize that there is a problem but sometimes they suggest a solution to it by offering to group together these alternatives when these are strong substitutes. Still the problem may not be completely eliminated when the alternatives are not strong substitutes since in this case their merger is not appropriate. Or, even if they were close substitutes, their separate recognition might still be necessary to make any sense. In any case, tests of "independence of irrelevant alternatives" seem to be quite important an issue in multinomial logit type models.[38]

7.4.6 Multinomial Probit

In a multinomial probit model, a multivariate normal distribution is the source of its probabilities. As is clear from Hausman and Wise (1978), its estimation is both difficult and expensive. However, if choice options can be ordered, the calculations become less difficult. Below we will sketch the method of maximum likelihood to derive estimates of parameters of an ordered probit model.

As before, let the basic, unobservable variable I exist and be represented by

$$\mathbf{I} = X\boldsymbol{\beta} + \boldsymbol{\epsilon} \tag{7.112}$$

where ϵ is a standard normal variable, and any two different observations on the error variable, ϵ_i and ϵ_j, $i \neq j$, are independent, and the Xs are the explanatory variables. The relationship among the index variable I^N, decision variable Y, and

[38] Specification tests of this kind have been made in an article by Hausman and McFadden (1984), pp. 1219–40.

the basic variable I (and its explanatory variables X) for their ith observation indicated by the subscript i is expressed as follows:

$$\begin{aligned} Y_i &= 1 \qquad \text{if } I_i^N < 0 \\ &= 2 \qquad \text{if } 0 \leqq I_i^N < I_{i,1} \\ &= 3 \qquad \text{if } I_{i,1} \leqq I_i^N < I_{i,2} \\ &\ldots \qquad \ldots \\ &\ldots \qquad \ldots \\ &= m \qquad \text{if } I_{i,m-2} \leqq I_i^N \end{aligned} \tag{7.113}$$

The corresponding probabilities become:

$$\begin{aligned} \text{Prob}(Y_i = 1) &= F(-\mathbf{X}_i'\boldsymbol{\beta}) \\ \text{Prob}(Y_i = 2) &= F(I_{i,1} - \mathbf{X}_i'\boldsymbol{\beta}) - F(-\mathbf{X}_i'\boldsymbol{\beta}) \\ \text{Prob}(Y_i = 3) &= F(I_{i,2} - \mathbf{X}_i'\boldsymbol{\beta}) - F(\mathrm{I}_{i,1} - \mathbf{X}_i'\boldsymbol{\beta}) \\ &\ldots \qquad \ldots \\ &\ldots \qquad \ldots \\ \text{Prob}(Y_i = m) &= 1 - F(I_{i,m-2} - \mathbf{X}_i'\boldsymbol{\beta}) \end{aligned} \tag{7.114}$$

As before, F(·) stands for the cumulative probability of a standard normal deviate. The maximum likelihood estimates of parameters β and I_i will be based on these cumulative probabilities and follow the same procedure as described in connection with (7.99).

7.4.7 Limited Dependent Variables and the Tobit Method

One of the major weaknesses of the previous method is analytic. It does not tackle the question of how many of the houses that are indeed bought ($Y = 1$) are of high, or low quality (or prices). All it does is to analyze whether or not they were bought. The other problem is the questionable value of the linear regression technique, because it is possible that there would be a crowding of nonbuyers ($Y = 0$) among the sample observations. This together with the habitual absence of negative values of Y would serve to pull down the estimated value of the probability of house purchases. However, there is a method called the Tobit method, so named because it combines both Probit and Tobin's methods, that can be profitably used to correct these problems. It is to this method that we turn next.

Let the index I be defined such that $I_i = \mathbf{X}_i'\boldsymbol{\beta}$; that is, I depends on the Xs.

However, individual household behavior is determined from the following values of Y:

$$Y_i = 0, \quad \text{if } I_i < I_i^N, \text{ that is those } Y\text{s for which the critical values of } I^N \text{ are so high that the index } I_i \text{ falls short of } I_i^N$$
$$= I_i - I_i^N \quad \text{if } I_i \geq I_i^N \tag{7.115}$$

The last value of Y can be appreciated as follows. Families behave differently with respect to Y. This cannot be accounted for by just Xs alone or the fact that $Y = 0$. The extra factors can be taken as random and reflected in the error term $(= I_i^N)$, assumed distributed normally with zero mean and variance σ^2.

Define $F(Z)$ as a standard normal cumulative distribution. Then the probability of $Y = 0$ and $Y > Y^* \geq 0$ becomes

$$\text{Prob}\{Y = 0/I\} = \text{Prob}\{I^N > I/I\} = 1 - \text{F}(I/\sigma) \tag{7.116}$$

$$\text{Prob}\{Y > Y^N \geq 0/I\} = \text{Prob}\{Y = I - I^N > Y^N \geq 0/I\} \tag{7.117}$$
$$= \text{Prob}\{I^N < I - Y^N/I\} = F((I - Y^N)/\sigma)$$

From the above it is clear that I and the various probabilities are functions of β and σ. Therefore they can be estimated by, say, the maximum likelihood method.

As in the probit method, divide a sample of n observations into the first g observations that have $Y = 0$ and the remaining $n - g$ observations that have $Y > 0$. Accordingly, the likelihood function is

$$L = \sum_{1}^{g} \ln[1 - F(I_i/\sigma)] - (n - g) \ln \sigma + \sum_{g+1}^{n} \ln f\{(I_i - Y_i)/\sigma\} \tag{7.118}$$

in which $f(Z)$ is the value of a standard normal *density* function. Nonlinear normal equations are obtained from $\partial L/\partial\beta = 0$ and $\partial L/\partial\sigma = 0$. It can be shown that

$$\text{E}(Y_i/I_i) = I_i F(I_i/\sigma) + \sigma f(I_i/\sigma) \tag{7.119}$$

which is estimated by:

$$\hat{Y}_i = \hat{I}_i F(\hat{I}_i/\hat{\sigma}) + \hat{\sigma} f(\hat{I}_i/\hat{\sigma}) \tag{7.120}$$

The likelihood function L as well as $\text{E}(Y_i/I_i)$ and $\hat{Y}$ based on Tobin's formulations, are developed in Appendix A.3.

7.4.8 The Heckman Two-Step Estimator

Heckman (1976) comes up with a two-step estimator in connection with the Tobit model. This estimator is shown to be consistent and its asymptotic distribution is derived by Amemiya (1985).[39] We shall present below only a short description of the estimation method.

Suppose we take only the positive observation of Y_i in equation (7.80). Then

$$E(Y_i/Y_i > 0) = \mathbf{X}_i'\boldsymbol{\beta} - E(I_i^N/I_i^N < \mathbf{X}_i'\boldsymbol{\beta}) \tag{7.121}$$

The second term on the right-hand side of (7.121) is nonzero without any loss of generality, indicating the fact that OLS estimates of β based on only positive observations on Y_i will be biased. In keeping with the Tobit model, if I_i^N is assumed to be normally distributed, it can be shown by simple integration that[40]

$$E(Y_i/Y_i > 0) = \mathbf{X}_i'\boldsymbol{\beta} - \sigma\,\psi\,(\mathbf{X}_i'\boldsymbol{\beta}/\sigma) \tag{7.122}$$

where $\psi(z) = f(z)/F(z)$. Rewrite (7.122) as

$$Y_i = \mathbf{X}_i'\boldsymbol{\beta} - \sigma\,\psi\,(\mathbf{X}_i'\boldsymbol{\gamma}) + \epsilon_i \tag{7.123}$$

where $\boldsymbol{\gamma} \equiv \boldsymbol{\beta}/\sigma$, and $\epsilon_i = Y_i - E(Y_i/Y_i > 0)$. From this, it follows that

$$E(\epsilon_i) = 0$$

The variance of ϵ_i can be shown to reduce to:

$$V(\epsilon_i) = \sigma^2 - \sigma^2\,\mathbf{X}_i'\boldsymbol{\gamma}\,\psi\,(\mathbf{X}_i'\boldsymbol{\gamma}) - \sigma^2\,[\psi(\mathbf{X}_i'\boldsymbol{\gamma})]^2 \tag{7.124}$$

Thus ϵ_i is heteroscedastic, which means that (7.123) is a heteroscedastic nonlinear regression model. Heckman proposes the following two steps to estimate the model:

Step 1 Use probit MLE for the estimation of γ. Let the estimate be $\hat{\gamma}$.

Step 2 Using strictly positive values for Y_i, regress Y_i on X_i and $\psi(\mathbf{X}_i'\hat{\gamma})$ using OLS to get estimated values of β_i and σ^2.

7.4.9 Empirical Studies Using Logit Analysis

Rubinfeld* (1977) applies logit analysis to voting in a local school election in the United States. He sets the desired level of educational expenditure per pupil between the amounts E_0 and E_p. In addition he assumes that a critical level of expenditure E_i' could be found such that a point would be reached at which the gap between the desired and actual expenditure would be large enough to generate a "yes" vote. It is assumed that E_i' varies randomly, that is $E_i' = E' + \nu_i$, where ν_i is random and $E_0 < E' < E_p$.

[39] As Amemiya (1985) acknowledges (p. 369), The asymptotic distribution of Heckman's two-step estimator follows as a special case of Heckman's derivation in a different context. See Heckman (1979).

[40] One can use the method of Appendix A.3 to establish this result.

* Reprinted with permission of Daniel L. Rubinfeld, "Voting in a Local School Election—A Micro Analysis," *Review of Economics and Statistics*, 49 (1977) p. 33, North Holland Publishing Co.

The voting rule is defined as follows:

$$\begin{array}{ll} \text{Vote ``yes''} & \text{if } E_i^* \geq E_i' \\ \text{Vote ``no''} & \text{if } E_i^* < E_i' \end{array} \tag{7.125}$$

As in (7.79), it can be shown that:

$$\ln \text{Prob}(\text{``Yes''})/(1 - \text{Prob}(\text{``Yes''})) = \mathbf{Z\beta} \tag{7.126}$$

where Z are the variables on which the probability of the "Yes" vote depends and β are their coefficients. The particular Z variables used in the study are defined as follows:

SEX = 1 if female; 0 if male

MAR = 1 if married with spouse; 0 otherwise

OTHER = 1 if separated, divorced or widow; 0 otherwise

A_{35-49} = 1 if aged 35–49 years; 0 otherwise

A_{50-64} = 1 if aged 50–64 years; 0 otherwise

A_{65+} = 1 if aged 65 or more; 0 otherwise

PUBi = 1 if i children go to public school, 0 otherwise ($i = 1, 2, \ldots, 5$)

PRIV = 1 if a family has 1 or more children in private school; 0 otherwise

YEARS = number of years living in Troy, Michigan

SCHOOL = 1 if an individual is employed as a teacher (in private or public school); 0 otherwise

ln (INC) = logarithm of annual household income ($)

ln (PRICE) = logarithm of price of public schooling in $ (7.127)

The right-hand side of the logit equation is:

$$\begin{array}{l} -\underset{(3.84)}{23.15^*} + \underset{(0.24)}{0.24}\ \text{SEX} + \underset{(1.13)}{1.13}\ \text{MAR} + \underset{(1.47)}{1.09}\ \text{OTHER} + \underset{(0.30)}{0.08}\ A_{35-49} \\ + \underset{(0.41)}{0.61}\ A_{50-64} + \underset{(0.79)}{1.04}\ A_{65+} + \underset{(0.34)}{1.44^*}\ \text{PUB1} + \underset{(0.35)}{1.38^*}\ \text{PUB2} + \underset{(0.42)}{1.30^*}\ \text{PUB3} \\ + \underset{(0.58)}{2.00^*}\ \text{PUB4} + \underset{(0.79)}{2.16^*}\ \text{PUB5} - \underset{(0.42)}{0.56}\ \text{PRIV} - \underset{(0.01)}{0.02^*}\ \text{YEARS} \\ + \underset{(0.84)}{3.07^*}\ \text{SCHOOL} + \underset{(0.37)}{2.14^*}\ \ln \text{INC} - \underset{(0.44)}{1.21^*}\ \ln \text{PRICE} \\ \text{df} = 408 \qquad \chi^2 = 156.2^* \end{array} \tag{7.128}$$

In (7.128), asymptotic standard errors are in parentheses and * denotes significance at 5% level; the method of estimation is maximum likelihood as developed by Forrest Nelson of the U.S. National Bureau of Economic Research.

The sex dummy is insignificant for the May election, but significant for the June election (not reported here). Marital status is insignificant but has the expected sign. While it is insignificant, the coefficient of the OTHER (dummy) variable, by its quantitative value, implies that it is almost equally likely that those married without their spouses present would favorably vote in the election as those married with their spouses present. In terms of the computed results (not reported here), the age of the voter does not seem to have any significant effect on voting which is a little unexpected. It is believed that older people with a lesser probability of having school going children would be voting "No".

All other variables show significant effects, as is expected.

We will now briefly discuss two other applications involving multinomial (rather than the usual binomial) logit type methods: Goldberg and Nold (1980), and Hill (1983). The first concerns an empirical analysis of risk and return, and attempts to answer such questions as to whether reporting deters burglars. The second concerns female labor force participation in developing and developed countries. It examines the question of whether individual women regard the decision to engage in family work as identical to the decision to work as an employee.

The first study has for its dependent variable the probabilities of each of six categories of loots: \$0, \$1–\$25, \$26–\$75, \$76–\$250, \$251–\$500, over \$500, and for explanatory variables income (divided into several classes: \$0–\$3,000, . . . , over \$25,000), race (black and others), number of adult family members (2 or more), rent (as an indicator of multiunit structure), length of residence, and irregular housing structures (trailers, single units, etc., that are being more easily accessible). The study concludes that the more likely the household is to report crimes, the more are burglars deterred.

The second study considers women's work in the informal sector, defined as follows. Women could be producing goods at home for market sale, or working on the family farm, or, for that matter, working in a small family business. The maximum likelihood logit estimates of this trichotomous labor force participation model serves to confirm that individual women do not regard the decision to engage in family work as identical to the decision to work as an employee. This implies that aggregation of these two choices might obscure the underlying individual behavior. This is evident in the case of Japanese women in the previously estimated negative wage effect on women's decision to work, which is possibly a result of aggregation.[41]

[41] A recent theoretical development in the area of multinomial logit models is concerned with the tests for omitted variables or functional misspecifications in such models. McFadden (1987) suggests testing the significance of auxiliary regressions of residuals on variables that are both included and excluded. Specific test procedures, as in Lagrange multipliers (see our Chapter 10) and the Hangman–McFadden test (see McFadden (1987)) of the property of independence from irrelevant alter-

7.4.10 *Empirical Study Using Linear Probability and Probit Model: The Maddala and Trost (1982) South Carolina Mortgage Loan Study*

This study uses 750 mortgage loan applications in the metropolitan area of Columbia, South Carolina. Of these applications, 500 become successful and 250 are rejected. The variable y is defined as:

$$y = \begin{cases} 1, & \text{if the loan application is accepted} \\ 0, & \text{if the loan application is not accepted} \end{cases}$$

The explanatory variables used are:

AI = applicant's and coapplicant's income ('000 dollars)
XMD = debt minus mortgage payment ('000 dollars)
DF = dummy variable with the value 1 for female, and 0 for male
DR = dummy variable with the value 1 for nonwhite and 0 for white
DS = dummy variable with the value 1 for single and 0 otherwise
DA = age of house ('00 years)
NNWP = percent nonwhite in the neighborhood ($\times 10^3$)
NMFI = neighborhood mean family income ('00000 dollars)
NA = neighborhood average age of homes ('00 years)

The regression results appear in Table 7-1.

As explained before, to make results comparable with the probit model, all estimated coefficients of the linear probability model are multiplied by 2.5 except for the constant term for which an extra deduction of 1.25 is made.

---

natives of multinomial logit models, can be applied by utilizing appropriately defined excluded variables. These procedures help in two respects:

(a) to test against various sources of misspecifications, and
(b) to indicate the nature of deviations from the multinomial logit models.

Incidentally, the assumption or property of independence of irrelevant alternatives of multinomial logit models has been relaxed in an article by Hausman (1978). This suggests a computationally feasible procedure to estimate parameters when the model is not constrained by the independence restriction. It provides for correlation among random components of consumer preferences, especially consumer tastes for specific characteristics of alternative qualitative choices. The particular problem to which the author applies his method is the three-alternative-travel-mode-choice problem of commuters who commute to the central business district of Washington D.C. He finds considerable differences in results between using and not using the independence property.

TABLE 7.1 REGRESSION RESULTS USING LINEAR PROBABILITY AND PROBIT MODELS: SOUTH CAROLINA LOAN APPLICATIONS DATA[a*]

Variable	Linear Probability Model	Probit Model
AI	1.489(4.69)	2.030(4.73)
XMD	−1.505(5.74)	−1.773(5.67)
DF	0.140(0.78)	0.206(0.95)
DR	−0.265(1.84)	−0.279(1.66)
DS	−0.238(1.75)	−0.274(1.70)
DA	−1.422(3.52)	−1.570(3.29)
NNWP	−1.758(0.74)	−2.360(0.85)
NMFI	0.150(0.23)	0.194(0.25)
NA	−0.393(1.34)	−0.425(1.26)
Constant	0.503	0.488

[a] Figures in parentheses are the t ratios.

* Used with permission of G. S. Maddala and R. P. Trost, "On Measuring Discrimination in Loan Markets," *Housing Finance Review*, (1982) Table 3, p. 245–68.

As is clear from the table, some of the estimated coefficients compare favorably while a few others compare unfavorably between the two models.[42]

7.4.11 Empirical Analysis Using Tobit Method

Last, let us illustrate the Tobit model. To that effect, we draw first on the Tobin (1958) study itself.* Let x_1 be age with a value of 1 for those 18–24 years old, . . . , and the value of 6 for those over 65 years old; x_2 be the initial ratio of liquid assets to disposable income, and y be the ratio of durable expenditures to disposable income. Then the estimated index is calculated to be:

$$\hat{I} = 0.1669 - 0.028\, x_1 + 0.004\, x_2 \tag{7.129}$$

[42] This example illustrates a question that may be asked regarding how the data should be analyzed when the number of observations in one of the classes is considerably smaller than that in the other class. In the Columbia, South Carolina loan applications case, there are as high as 4600 applications in the successful class but only 250 applications in the unsuccessful class. In other examples, such as with the analysis of bank insolvency, the number of insolvent banks may be much less than the number of solvent banks. In such cases, the suggestion may be to sample the two classes at two different rates, using a much higher rate for the class with a much lesser number of observations. This procedure though will not require using any weighted linear probability or probit (or logit) rule as is the case with error heteroscedasticity even though the constant term of the logit model may have to be adjusted. See Maddala (1983), pp. 90–91.

* Reprinted with permission of J. Tobin, "Estimation of Relationship for Limited Dependent Variables," *Econometrica*, 50 (1958) p. 32 and 34.

and $\hat{\sigma}$ is 0.124657. The calculation of $\hat{Y}$ is shown in the following table assuming $x_1 = 1, 2, 4$ and $x_2 = 0$:

x_1	$\hat{I}$	$F(\hat{I}/\hat{\sigma})$	$\hat{Y}$
1	0.14	0.867	0.147
2	0.11	0.813	0.123
4	0.06	0.670	0.082

The second study shows the application of the Tobit method in addition to the Probit and OLS methods. This is by Roy (1981) on the "tariff and non-tariff barriers to trade in the U.S. and abroad". The independent variables included are: constant, industry concentration, economy of scale, skill intensity, labor intensity, product heterogeneity, U.S. simple tariff, foreign simple tariff, U.S. import proxy, U.S. export proxy, capital intensity, U.S. non-tariff barrier proxy, foreign non-tariff barrier proxy, etc. The dependent variables together with the methods, shown in parentheses, used to fit the relationships are: U.S. simple tariff (OLS), foreign simple tariff (OLS), U.S. non-tariff barriers to trade index (Tobit), dummy variables for U.S. non-tariff barriers to trade (Probit), foreign weighted non-tariff barriers to trade index (Tobit), and dummy variable for foreign non-tariff barriers to trade (Probit). Observations included are for 225 four-digit manufacturing industries in the United States in 1970.

Without referring to the figures, we shall only indicate here three of Roy's main results. First, there is no empirical evidence to show whether restrictions have any associated effects on the structure of U.S. imports. If anything, these (restrictions) mean well for U.S. exports. Second, among the more heavily protected industries, non-tariff barriers serve to reinforce tariff protection. Third, U.S. retaliations against non-tariff barriers are by non-tariff barriers.[43]

[43] Since the probit and Tobit models often involve complex mathematical formulations, we have cited only very limited empirical examples from both these models. Indeed we have not cited any applied example from multinomial probit models per se. To complete the cycle, let us refer to one study: McElroy (1985). This study makes use of a trinomial probit model, the trichotomy coming from consumption, household membership, and market work of young men in the United States, the subject of the study.

It uses a Nash bargaining model. This is a game theory model involving, in this case, a two-person (youth versus parents) non-zero-sum game. The idea is that family members act jointly as if to maximize a Nash objective function subject to family budget constraints. This objective function is monotonically increasing in the young men's and parents' utility levels but monotonically decreasing in the "threat point" (that is, points based on penalty measures associated with the nonfulfillment of objectives) of each.

The author finds that the ML-estimates of the parameters of the model are very different from those derived when both market work and household membership are exogenous. Using data from the National Longitudinal Surveys relating to white male youth, the study finds support for the belief that parents insure their sons against bad market prospects.

PROBLEMS

7-1. The following is an example of a Monte Carlo experiment involving linear regression models with heteroscedastic errors. Assume that here is only one explanatory variable X which is fixed in repeated samples and which can assume values 0 and ± 3 as shown in the following table. The values of ϵ, the residual or disturbance term, are the results of random experiments with the tossing of two coins the rules of which are appropriately defined. There are 10 sets of values of ϵ obtained from the random experiment repeated 10 times such that $E(\epsilon_t) = 0$ for all t, and $E(\epsilon_t^2) = 1/2$ for $t = 1, 3, 5$, but $E(\epsilon_t^2) = 2$ for $t = 2, 4, 6$, and $E(\epsilon_t \epsilon_{t'}) = 0$ for $t \neq t'$; $t, t' = 1, 2, \ldots, 6$. The values of the dependent variable Y are obtained from the equation:

$$Y_t = 1 + 3.5X_t + \epsilon_t \qquad t = 1, 2, \ldots, 6$$

						ϵ						
t	X	(1)	(2)	(3)	(4)	(5)	(6)	(7)	(8)	(9)	(10)	Y
1	3	1	−1	0	−1	1	−1	1	0	−1	1	
2	3	2	0	2	2	−2	−2	2	2	0	1	
3	0	1	−1	−1	1	1	1	−1	0	−1	2	
4	0	0	−2	2	−2	−2	2	2	0	0	−1	
5	−3	−1	1	−1	0	1	1	0	1	0	−1	
6	−3	−2	2	0	−2	0	2	2	0	−2	0	

(a) Complete the 10 columns of values under Y.

(b) Set up the regression equation:

$$\mathbf{Y} = X\boldsymbol{\beta} + \boldsymbol{\epsilon}$$

by specifying X and $\boldsymbol{\beta}$, given that $\boldsymbol{\epsilon}$ appears in the table above in the 10 different columns marked (1)–(10), and you have computed $\mathbf{Y}$ and placed its values in the next 10 different columns.

(c) Is X fixed? What is the rank of the matrix X?

(d) What is the variance–covariance matrix (written as $\sigma^2 \boldsymbol{\Omega}$, where σ^2 is constant) of $\boldsymbol{\epsilon}$? Set it up in a form such as to satisfy the convention that

$$T_r \boldsymbol{\Omega} = n, \; (n = 6 \text{ in this example})$$

What is σ^2? What are K_t if $E(\epsilon_t^2)$ is written as $\sigma^2 K_t$?

(e) Calculate the OLS estimator $\hat{\beta}$ of the slope (ignoring the problem of heteroscedasticity).

(f) Calculate the GLS estimator $\tilde{\beta}$ of the slope (which takes account of the heteroscedasticity).

(g) What are the expected values of $\hat{\beta}$ and $\tilde{\beta}$ in numerical terms? Why?

(h) Calculate the variance of $\hat{\beta}$ and $\tilde{\beta}$. Which one is the larger and why?

7-2. The following is an example of a Monte Carlo experiment involving a linear regression model with autocorrelated errors and is a modification of specifications of problem 7-1. While t and X are the same as before, the values of ϵ are generated in a different way explained as follows. Suppose, in the first stage, there is a random variable ν whose values are determined randomly by the tossing of two independent coins according to some well-defined rules. There are 10 sets of values of ν obtained from the random experiment repeated 10 times such that $E(\nu_t) = 0$ and $E(\nu_t^2) = 1/2$ for $t = 0, 1, 2, \ldots, 6$, and $E(\nu_t \nu_{t'}) = 0$, for $t \neq t'$; $t, t' = 0, 1, 2, \ldots, 6$. Suppose, in the second stage, the ϵs which are the disturbance terms of the linear model are generated by the very simple rule:

$$\epsilon_t = \nu_{t-1} + \nu_t$$

For example $\epsilon_1 = \nu_0 + \nu_1$; $\epsilon_2 = \nu_1 + \nu_2$, etc.

		ν											
t	X	(1)	(2)	(3)	(4)	(5)	(6)	(7)	(8)	(9)	(10)	ϵ	Y
0	—												
1	3	1	−1	0	−1	−1	1	1	−1	−1	0		
2	3	1	0	0	−1	0	0	−1	−1	1	0		
3	0	0	−1	0	1	0	1	−1	0	1	1		
4	0	−1	−1	1	0	1	0	1	0	1	−1		
5	−2	−1	1	1	0	1	1	0	0	0	−1		
6	−2	−1	1	−1	0	1	0	0	1	0	1		

(a) Compute the 10 columns of values under ϵ from the assumed relationship between ϵ and ν.

(b) Taking the model to be

$$Y_t = 1 + 3.5X_t + \epsilon_t; \qquad t = 1, 2, \ldots, 6$$

Compute 10 new columns under Y.

(c) Compute the OLS estimator $\hat{\beta}$ of the regression slope (ignoring the problem of autocorrelation of residuals).

(d) Setting up the model in the form

$$\mathbf{Y} = X\boldsymbol{\beta} + \boldsymbol{\epsilon}$$

after appropriately defining X and $\boldsymbol{\beta}$ (define these) in addition to $\mathbf{Y}$ and $\boldsymbol{\epsilon}$ (values of which you have already computed in (a) and (b) above), find out $E(\boldsymbol{\epsilon}\boldsymbol{\epsilon}')$ and put it in the form:

$$E(\boldsymbol{\epsilon}\boldsymbol{\epsilon}') = \sigma^2 \boldsymbol{\Omega}$$

where σ^2 is a constant. What is the numerical value of σ^2 and what are the elements of the $\boldsymbol{\Omega}$ matrix?

(e) Calculate the GLS estimator $\tilde{\beta}$ of the slope (which recognizes autocorrelation among the residuals).

(f) What are the values of $E(\hat{\beta})$ and $E(\tilde{\beta})$ in numerical terms?
(g) What is the variance of $\hat{\beta}$?
(h) What is the variance of $\tilde{\beta}$?
(i) How do the two variances compare?

7-3. Refer back to the data of problem 5-8 and its solution. To recapitulate, you fitted the data on annual real consumption expenditure (CONS) to those on real compensation of employees (WAGES) and total real profits (call it PROFT) for the U.S. economy over the period 1968–1987.

(a) Obtain for this model the value of the Durbin–Watson statistic d. Test the model for zero first order autocorrelation against a suitably defined alternative hypothesis. What are your inferences? Explain. What are the properties of your estimates and their associated statistics? Are you sure about the validity of the tests of hypothesis? Explain.
(b) Explain how you would apply the Cochrane–Orcutt method to estimate the parameters of the above model. What can you say about the statistical properties of these estimates?
(c) Estimate the model by the Cochrane–Orcutt (or CORC) method.

7-4. An alternative to the CORC method is the Hildreth–Lu (HILU) search method (see Hildreth and Lu (1960)). According to this method, you follow the same steps as in the CORC method up to equation (7.41) of the text, but now suppose equations (7.40) and (7.41) are derived or expressed more generally to include more than one explanatory variable. Suppose $\Sigma \hat{\nu}_i^2$ of (7.41) is calculated for an initial value ρ_1 of ρ using OLS as explained in footnote 16 and is denoted as ESS(ρ_1). For a different value of $\rho = \rho_2$, repeat all your previous calculations and obtain ESS(ρ_2), and so on, until you get ESS(ρ) for all values of ρ lying between -1 and $+1$, where ρ is increased at intervals of 0.05 or 0.01. Select that ρ at which ESS(ρ) becomes minimum. At this value of ρ, estimate by OLS the equation like (7.40) extended to include more than one regressor.

(a) Apply the HILU method to reestimate the regression equation of problem 5-8.
(b) Do the CORC method applied in part (c) of problem 7-3 and HILU method above give equivalent or similar results?
(c) Combining the estimates and their associated statistics of problems 7-3 with those of 7-4, what would you say about the relevance of the results?

7-5. Estimate the model in problem 6-10 with the maintained assumption that $\beta_2 = -\beta_1$ by GLS on the assumption that

$$\epsilon_t = 0.3\,\epsilon_{t-1} + \nu_t$$

where $E(\boldsymbol{\nu\nu}') = \sigma^2 \boldsymbol{I}$, with σ^2 and $\boldsymbol{I}$ having their usual meaning. Disregard the first observation in your transformation.

7-6. Let us undertake to estimate the simple regression model:

$$Y_t = \beta X_t + \epsilon_t$$

where $E(\epsilon_t) = 0$, $V(\epsilon_t) = \sigma^2 X_t^4$, and $\text{cov}(\epsilon_t, \epsilon_{t'}) = 0$; $t, t' = 1, \ldots, n$ $(t \neq t')$.

Suppose we are given the following data set:

t	X_t	Y_t
1	2	3
2	3	1
3	3	3
4	2	4
5	5	6
6	7	5
7	4	2
8	7	5

(a) Calculate the OLS estimate of β based on these data.

(b) Given that X is nonstochastic, what will be the BLUE of β based on the above observations?

7-7. Suppose that in $\mathbf{Y} = X\boldsymbol{\beta} + \boldsymbol{\epsilon}$, with X a given $n \times (m + 1)$ matrix of rank $m + 1$, we have $E(\boldsymbol{\epsilon}) = \mathbf{0}$ and $E(\boldsymbol{\epsilon}\boldsymbol{\epsilon}') = \boldsymbol{D}$, an $n \times n$ diagonal matrix with diagonal elements $0 < \sigma_{ii} < \infty$, $i = 1, 2, \ldots, n$. Derive properties of the estimators

$$\hat{\boldsymbol{\beta}} = (X'X)^{-1} X'\mathbf{Y}$$

$$S^2 = (\mathbf{Y} - X\hat{\boldsymbol{\beta}})'(\mathbf{Y} - X\hat{\boldsymbol{\beta}})/(n - m - 1)$$

7-8. If the matrix $\boldsymbol{D}$ in problem 7-7 has elements whose values are known, explain how this information can be utilized to construct an estimator for $\boldsymbol{\beta}$ say $\tilde{\boldsymbol{\beta}}$, whose elements have variances smaller than those of the corresponding elements of $\hat{\boldsymbol{\beta}} = (X'X)^{-1} X'\mathbf{Y}$. Provide expressions for $E(\tilde{\boldsymbol{\beta}})$ and $E(\tilde{\boldsymbol{\beta}} - E\tilde{\boldsymbol{\beta}})(\tilde{\boldsymbol{\beta}} - E\tilde{\boldsymbol{\beta}})'$.

7-9. In problem 7-7, assume $E(\boldsymbol{\epsilon}) = \mathbf{0}$ and $E(\boldsymbol{\epsilon}\boldsymbol{\epsilon}') = \boldsymbol{\Sigma}$, an $n \times n$ positive definite symmetric matrix. Establish properties of $\hat{\boldsymbol{\beta}} = (X'X)^{-1} X'\mathbf{Y}$ in this case. If the elements of $\boldsymbol{\Sigma}$ have known values, provide an estimator for $\boldsymbol{\beta}$ which exploits this information and establish its properties.

7-10. Assume that the disturbance terms in a usual linear multiple regression model $\mathbf{Y} = X\boldsymbol{\beta} + \boldsymbol{\epsilon}$ are generated by a stationary first order autoregressive process

$$\epsilon_t = \rho\epsilon_{t-1} + \nu_t \qquad |\rho| < 1$$

where ν_t satisfies $E(\nu_t) = 0$ and $E(\nu_t^2) = \sigma^2$, for all t, and $E(\nu_t \nu_{t'}) = 0$ for all t and t' such that $t \neq t'$.

(a) Define the term "stationary" and indicate what condition the parameter ρ must satisfy for ϵ_t to be a stationary process.

(b) Given that ϵ_t is stationary, compute the variance, $E(\epsilon_t^2)$, of ϵ_t.

(c) Evaluate the following expectations, $E(\epsilon_t \epsilon_{t-\theta})$ for $\theta = 1, 2, 3 \ldots$, and then use these results to provide an expression for $E(\boldsymbol{\epsilon}\boldsymbol{\epsilon}')$, the covariance matrix for $\boldsymbol{\epsilon}$.

7-11. For problem 7-10, evaluate $E(\hat{\beta})$ and $V(\hat{\beta}) = E(\hat{\beta} - \beta)(\hat{\beta} - \beta)'$ where $\hat{\beta} = (X'X)^{-1} X'\mathbf{Y}$. Is the least squares estimator minimum variance linear unbiased estimator for β? How would you estimate $V(\hat{\beta})$?

7-12. Show how the model in problem 7-10 can be expressed as

$$\mathbf{Y} - \rho\mathbf{Y}_{-1} = (X - \rho X_{-1})\beta + \boldsymbol{\nu}$$

or

$$\mathbf{Y} - X\beta = \rho(\mathbf{Y}_{-1} - X_{-1}\beta) + \boldsymbol{\nu}$$

where

$$\mathbf{Y}' = [Y_1\ Y_2 \ldots .\ Y_n], \qquad \mathbf{Y}'_{-1} = [Y_0\ Y_1 \ldots .\ Y_n]$$

$$\boldsymbol{\nu}' = [\nu_1\ \nu_2 \ldots .\ \nu_n]$$

X is a $n \times (m + 1)$ matrix with the tth row $\mathbf{X}'_t$, a $1 \times (m + 1)$ vector and X_{-1} is a $n \times (m + 1)$ matrix with the tth row $\mathbf{X}'_{t-1}$, $t = 1, 2, \ldots, n$.

(a) If ρ in the first equation above (that is, involving $\mathbf{Y} - \rho\mathbf{Y}_{-1}$) has a known value, say $\rho = \rho_0$, indicate how you would estimate β and derive properties of your estimator.

(b) Compare properties of your estimator in (a) with those obtained in problem 7-11.

(c) With ρ's value unknown, explain a convenient computational procedure for finding values of β and ρ that minimize the sum of squared errors, $\boldsymbol{\nu}'\boldsymbol{\nu}$.

7-13. If instead of $\epsilon_t = \rho\epsilon_{t-1} + \nu_t$ (see problem 7-10), the ϵs satisfy:

$$\epsilon_t = \nu_t + \lambda_1 \nu_{t-1} + \lambda_2 \nu_{t-2}$$

a second order moving average process with the ν_ts having zero means, constant common variance, and being nonautocorrelated, derive the variance and serial covariances of the ϵ_ts. Compare the correlograms (define) for the process in the first order autocorrelated residuals with the process in the second order moving average of residuals. Can elements of the residual vector $\hat{\boldsymbol{\epsilon}} = \mathbf{Y} - X\hat{\beta}$, where $\hat{\beta} = (X'X)^{-1} X'\mathbf{Y}$ be used to estimate the correlogram? How?

(*Note:* A correlogram is a plot of the correlation coefficient between ϵ_t and ϵ_{t-s} for values of s from 0 to $t - 1$. The autocorrelation function is defined as: $\rho(s) = \text{Corr}(\epsilon_t, \epsilon_{t-s}) = E(\epsilon_t\, \epsilon_{t-s})/E(\epsilon_t^2)$.)

7-14. The Durbin–Watson test statistic

$$d = \sum_{t=2}^{n} (\hat{\epsilon}_t - \hat{\epsilon}_{t-1})^2 \Big/ \sum_{t=1}^{n} \hat{\epsilon}_t^2$$

where the $\hat{\epsilon}_t$s are least-squares residuals in the usual multiple regression model, is often used to test the hypothesis that the ϵ_ts are nonautocorrelated. Explain the nature and properties of this test and then indicate when you would use d in a "one-tailed" rather than a "two-tailed" test.

7-15. If in the simple regression model, $Y_i = \beta_0 + \beta_1 X_i + \epsilon_i$, $i = 1, 2, \ldots, n$, the ϵ_is are mutually uncorrelated with zero means and variances $E(\epsilon_i^2) = z_i^2\sigma^2$, $i = 1, 2, \ldots, n$, where the z_is have known values (say, measures of size), explain and justify how you would estimate β_0, β_1, and σ^2 and test hypotheses about these parameters.

If instead of $E(\epsilon_i^2) = z_i^2\, \sigma^2$, we have $E(\epsilon_i^2) = \sigma^2 f(z_i, \alpha)$ where f has a known functional form and α is a parameter with unknown value, provide a method of computing maximum likelihood estimates for parameters given that the ϵ_is are assumed normally distributed.

7-16. Consider the following problems in connection with the multiple regression model. For each, describe how you would detect its presence, its consequences for a usual least-squares analysis, and available remedies: (a) multicollinearity, (b) heteroscedasticity, and (c) left out variables.

7-17. In a study of factors influencing a female's decision to study engineering at a university, an investigator conducted a survey among 29 female students and obtained the following equation fitted by the method of maximum likelihood using probit analysis (the figures in parentheses are standard errors and those in [ ] brackets are t ratios):

$$\begin{aligned}
Y = &\underset{\substack{(54.390)\\[-0.1652]}}{-8.9874} - \underset{\substack{(1.9925)\\[-2.0294]}}{4.0437}*\text{BCITY} - \underset{\substack{(1.6163)\\[-1.4833]}}{2.3975}*\text{MCITY} + \underset{\substack{(54.372)\\[0.1365]}}{7.4193}*\text{PVT}\\
&+ \underset{\substack{(54.358)\\[0.1219]}}{6.6248}*\text{COL} + \underset{\substack{(0.4708)\\[2.1889]}}{1.0305}*\text{MS} + \underset{\substack{(0.8546)\\[1.2929]}}{1.1049}*\text{MPJOB} + \underset{\substack{(0.9951)\\[0.6400]}}{0.6368}*\text{MNJOB}\\
&- \underset{\substack{(0.8344)\\[-1.9566]}}{1.6326}*\text{FPJOB} + \underset{\substack{(0.7554)\\[0.9464]}}{0.7149}*\text{GUID}; \qquad R^2 = 0.54
\end{aligned}$$

where

$$\text{Y} = \begin{cases} 1 & \text{if the female intends to study engineering} \\ 0 & \text{otherwise} \end{cases}$$

$$\text{BCITY} = \begin{cases} 1 & \text{if the female came from a large city (with population greater than 250,000)} \\ 0 & \text{otherwise} \end{cases}$$

$$\text{MCITY} = \begin{cases} 1 & \text{if the female came from a medium city (population less than 250,000)} \\ 0 & \text{otherwise} \end{cases}$$

$$\text{PVT} = \begin{cases} 1 & \text{if the female attended a private high school} \\ 0 & \text{otherwise} \end{cases}$$

$$\text{COL} = \begin{cases} 1 & \text{if the female attended a collegiate high school} \\ 0 & \text{otherwise} \end{cases}$$

MS the number of mathematics and science courses taken in grade 12

$$\text{MPJOB} = \begin{cases} 1 & \text{if the mother has a professional job} \\ 0 & \text{otherwise} \end{cases}$$

$$\text{MNPJOB} = \begin{cases} 1 & \text{if the mother has a trade job} \\ 0 & \text{otherwise} \end{cases}$$

$$\text{FPJOB} = \begin{cases} 1 & \text{if the female has a professional job} \\ 0 & \text{otherwise} \end{cases}$$

$$\text{GUID} = \begin{cases} 1 & \text{if the female thought the guidance she had received was helpful} \\ 0 & \text{otherwise} \end{cases}$$

(a) Write a critique on the estimated model results.

(b) What do you think are the reasons underlying the low value of R^2? How could the model formulation be improved to increase this value?
(*Hint:* Think especially of income variables that are missing from the current formulation.)

(c) "In addition to the low value of R^2, the likelihood ratio test approximated to by chi-square produced a low value, namely 15.67, at 9 degrees of freedom", said the investigator. How do you account for those degrees of freedom and how do you justify that the value of chi-square is indeed low at the 1% probability level of significance?
(*Hint:* See Section 10.3 of Chapter 10 for help on the likelihood ratio test.)

7-18. Rubinfeld (1977) applies logit analysis to voting in a local school election in the United States.

(a) How does he relate voting behavior of the electorate to expenditure?

(b) How does he formulate the logit model? Specify the dependent and the independent variables.

(c) Briefly comment on the main result derived by him.

(d) In Rubinfeld's computation, age did not seem to make any significant effect on voting. Does this appear a little unexpected to you? Why or why not?

7-19. **(a)** Explain the specifications of a multinomial logit model.

(b) For estimation of parameters of this model, the method of maximum likelihood has been found to be useful. Provide all the steps of the analysis until you show how the log-likelihood function is formulated.

(c) Discuss one weakness of this method that is related to "independence of irrelevant alternatives".

(d) Discuss Goldberg and Nold (1980) and Hill (1983) to show whether reporting on burglaries deters burglars (the Goldberg and Nold study) and whether individual women think that the decision to engage in family work is identical to the decision to work as an employee (the Hill study).
(*Hint:* See the section on applied studies relating to multinomial logit models.)

7-20. **(a)** Discuss the study due to Maddala and Trost (1982) which shows, among other things, how linear probability and probit models are used to explain the factors responsible for the success of mortgage loan applications in South Carolina.

(b) Discuss the study by Roy (1981) on the "tariff and non-tariff barriers to trade in the U.S. and abroad" showing how the OLS, probit and Tobit models are applied to problems of trade restrictions in the United States and abroad.

7-21. **(a)** You are given two seemingly unrelated regression equations with an *equal* number of observations. Show that the BLUE estimator is the OLS estimator if $\boldsymbol{\Sigma}$, the variance–covariance matrix of the disturbances, is diagonal.

(b) Does this result still necessarily hold for two seemingly unrelated regression equations with an *unequal* number of observations?

8

Stochastic Regression and Lag Models

8.1 INTRODUCTION: LINEARIZING NONLINEAR SITUATIONS AND USING LARGE SAMPLE OR ASYMPTOTIC RESULTS

In this section we give a cursory treatment of stochastic regressors to provide a general understanding of the estimation problems of stochastic regression models based on them.

Now why are regressors stochastic? Let us discuss this question in the context of an example, say, a consumption function. Consider that consumption depends on past consumption, current income, past income, and other factors such as wealth, and aggregate price level. If current consumption is stochastic following from the random nature of the disturbance term of the consumption function, there is no reason why past consumption will not be the same either. Variables like past consumption indicate inertia on the part of consumers, and the inertia factor might have a probability distribution of its own rather than have fixed values in repeated samples. Similarly, current income, past income, and other factors might show statistical or probabilistic variations. All this implies that the included regressors of the model are stochastic just as excluded regressors (summed up in the disturbance term) are, at least by assumption. We could similarly use other examples, say, an investment function in which the investment expenditure depends on the level of output, profit, capital stock, both current and past, and the interest ıate. The argument as to why these explanatory variables might be stochastic or random would still be the same as in the case of the consumption function. Similarly examples from other areas can be cited and the argument for the probability distribution of the regressors would still be the same.

One characteristic of the stochastic models is the emergence of a nonlinear[1] structure of the regression coefficient estimates due to the random nature of both the regressand and regressors. Nonlinear structures are difficult to handle. This necessitates the use of some simplifying treatments for them. There are essentially two simplifications available: linearizing a nonlinear situation, and using large sample approximations. For linearizing purposes, Taylor series expansions[2] are used, while for large sample approximations asymptotic distribution theory is used.

The statistical underpinnings of the Taylor series expansion can be quite extensive and should be studied from a statistics textbook. The basic implications of the asymptotic theory are presented below.

8.2 PROBABILITY LIMITS AND SLUTSKY'S THEOREM

If $\hat{\beta}$, based on sample size n, is an estimate of β, then the bias of the estimate as well as its variance will go down as the sample size n is increased. Then for arbitrarily small η and δ, we can write the following probability statement of $\hat{\beta}$ with the increase in the sample size n:

$$\text{Prob}\{\,|\,\hat{\beta}^{(n)} - \beta\,| < \eta\} > 1 - \delta \qquad \text{for all } n > n_1 \tag{8.1}$$

where $\hat{\beta}^{(n)}$ shows that $\hat{\beta}$ depends on n, and n_1 is the initial size of n. Alternatively, we say

$$\lim_{n\to\infty} \text{Prob}\{\,|\,\hat{\beta}^{(n)} - \beta\,| < \eta\} = 1 \tag{8.2}$$

or

$$\text{plim } \hat{\beta}^{(n)} = \beta \tag{8.3}$$

where plim stands for probability limit. This limit statement makes the estimator

[1] Using OLS, we have $\hat{\boldsymbol{\beta}} = \boldsymbol{\beta} + (X'X)^{-1}X'\boldsymbol{\epsilon}$, which will be a nonlinear estimate since its arguments X and $\boldsymbol{\epsilon}$ both are random and they appear in a multiplicative and hence nonlinear way. This was not so when $\boldsymbol{\epsilon}$ only was *random*, $(X'X)^{-1}X'$ was just a *fixed* set of constants, and therefore $\boldsymbol{\beta}$ was an estimate *linear* in $\boldsymbol{\epsilon}$. The reader is urged to go through Sections 4.9, 4.10, 4.12, etc. of Chapter 4 before going ahead into this chapter.

[2] A Taylor series expansion of $Y = f(\underline{X})$ might be:

$$Y = f(E(\underline{X})) + f_X^*(\underline{X} - E(\underline{X})) + 1/2!\, f_{XX}^*(\underline{X} - E(\underline{X}))^2 + 1/3!\, f_{XXX}^*(\underline{X} - E(\underline{X}))^3 + \cdots$$

in which, for instance, f_{XX}^* is the second derivative of $f(\underline{X})$ with respect to $\underline{X}$ and all derivatives are evaluated at the point of mean of $\underline{X}$, that is, $E(\underline{X})$. $\underline{X}$ may include more than one variable X.

$\hat{\beta}$ a consistent estimator for β or, generally speaking, an asymptotically unbiased[3] estimator for β.

There is an invariance theorem in probability limits called Slutsky's theorem after its inventor. According to it, if plim $\hat{\beta} = \beta$ and $f(\hat{\beta})$ is a continuous function of $\hat{\beta}$, then

$$\text{plim } f(\hat{\beta}) = f(\beta) \tag{8.4}$$

Some examples are:

$$\text{plim } (\hat{\beta}^K) = (\text{plim } \hat{\beta})^K \tag{8.5}$$

$$\text{plim } (\hat{\beta}^{-K}) = (\text{plim } \hat{\beta})^{-K} \tag{8.6}$$

In multiparameter cases,

$$\begin{aligned} &\text{plim } \hat{\boldsymbol{\beta}} = \boldsymbol{\beta}, \text{ plim } XZ = \text{plim } (X) \text{ plim } (Z) \\ &\text{plim } X^{-I} = (\text{plim } X)^{-1}, \text{ plim } (1/n\, X'X)^{-1} = (\text{plim } 1/n\, X'X)^{-1} \end{aligned} \tag{8.7}$$

8.3 X AND ϵ PROCESSES INDEPENDENT, AND CONSISTENCY OF OLS ESTIMATES

Let us now go back to our regression model

$$\mathbf{Y} = X\boldsymbol{\beta} + \boldsymbol{\epsilon}$$

where X is stochastic but independent of $\boldsymbol{\epsilon}$ in the sense that each row of X is independent of the corresponding elements of $\boldsymbol{\epsilon}$ and the following implications apply as a result of $E(\boldsymbol{\epsilon} \mid X) = E(\boldsymbol{\epsilon}) = 0$:

$$\begin{aligned} &E(\mathbf{Y} \mid X) = X\boldsymbol{\beta} + E(\boldsymbol{\epsilon} \mid X) = X\boldsymbol{\beta} \\ &E(\boldsymbol{\epsilon}\boldsymbol{\epsilon}' \mid X) = \sigma^2 \boldsymbol{I} \\ &\text{plim } (1/n\, \boldsymbol{\epsilon}'\boldsymbol{\epsilon}) = \sigma^2 \\ &\text{plim } (1/n\, X'X) = \boldsymbol{\Sigma}_{XX} \\ &\text{plim } (1/n\, X'\boldsymbol{\epsilon}) = \mathbf{0} \end{aligned} \tag{8.8}$$

The OLS estimator $\hat{\boldsymbol{\beta}}$ given by $\boldsymbol{\beta} + (X'X)^{-1}X'\boldsymbol{\epsilon}$ is asymptotically unbiased since

$$\text{plim } \hat{\boldsymbol{\beta}} = \boldsymbol{\beta} + \text{plim } (1/n\, X'X)^{-1} \text{ plim } (1/n\, X'\boldsymbol{\epsilon}) = \boldsymbol{\beta} + \boldsymbol{\Sigma}_{XX}^{-1} \cdot \mathbf{0} = \boldsymbol{\beta} \tag{8.9}$$

[3] However, as Sewell (1969) has shown, in some cases plim and asymptotic expectation may not be identical, especially with some simultaneous equation estimators.

The variance–covariance matrix of $\hat{\beta}$ is given by $\sigma^2 E(X'X)^{-1}$. This can be seen as follows:

$$\begin{aligned} V(\hat{\beta}) &= n^{-1} \lim_{n\to\infty} E \sqrt{n}\,(\hat{\beta} - \beta) \sqrt{n}\,(\hat{\beta} - \beta)' \\ &= n^{-1} \lim_{n\to\infty} nE\{E(X'X)^{-1}X'\epsilon\epsilon'X(X'X)^{-1} \mid X\} \qquad (8.10)^4 \\ &= n^{-1}\sigma^2 \lim E(1/n\, X'X)^{-1} = n^{-1}\sigma^2 \Sigma_{XX}^{-1} \end{aligned}$$

It will follow simply that $V(\hat{\beta})$ is estimated consistently by

$$n^{-1} S^2 (1/n\, X'X)^{-1} \tag{8.11}$$

where S^2 is the mean sum of squares due to the estimated residuals $\hat{\epsilon}$:

$$S^2 = \hat{\epsilon}'\hat{\epsilon}/(n - m - 1) \tag{8.12}$$

and

$$\text{plim } S^2 = \sigma^2$$

8.4 X AND ϵ NOT INDEPENDENT AND THE INSTRUMENTAL VARIABLE (IV) METHOD

If the assumption that

$$\text{plim } (1/n\, X'\epsilon) = \mathbf{0} \tag{8.13}$$

is not tenable, then the OLS estimate will be biased in even large samples. Because, then,

$$\begin{aligned} \text{plim } \hat{\beta} &= \beta\, \Sigma_{XX}^{-1} \text{ plim } (1/n\, X'\epsilon) \\ &\neq \beta \end{aligned} \tag{8.14}$$

In such cases, the alternative method, called the Instrumental Variable (IV) method, consists of suggesting the proxy or instrumental variables Z for X with the following properties:

$$\begin{aligned} &\text{plim } 1/n\, Z'\epsilon = \mathbf{0}: \text{(Z and } \epsilon \text{ uncorrelated)} \\ &\text{plim } 1/n\, Z'X = \Sigma_{ZX}: \text{(limit exists and } \Sigma_{ZX} \text{ nonsingular)} \\ &\text{plim } 1/n\, Z'Z = \Sigma_{ZZ}: \text{(limit exists)} \end{aligned} \tag{8.15}$$

Then the Instrumental Variable estimator $\hat{\beta}_Z$ is defined as

$$\hat{\beta}_Z = (Z'X)^{-1}Z'Y \tag{8.16}$$

[4] Since plim $\underline{X'X}/n\,(= \Sigma_{XX})$ exists, so $\lim_{n\to\infty} E(1/n\, X'X)^{-1}$ exists and is equal to Σ_{XX}^{-1}.

It can be easily established that

$$\text{plim } \hat{\boldsymbol{\beta}}_Z = \boldsymbol{\beta} \tag{8.17}$$

$$n^{-1} \lim_{n\to\infty} n\text{E}(\hat{\boldsymbol{\beta}}_Z - \boldsymbol{\beta})(\hat{\boldsymbol{\beta}}_Z - \boldsymbol{\beta})' = n^{-1} \sigma^2 \boldsymbol{\Sigma}_{ZX}^{-1} \boldsymbol{\Sigma}_{ZZ} \boldsymbol{\Sigma}_{XZ}^{-1} \tag{8.18}$$

The first result implies that the IV estimator $\hat{\boldsymbol{\beta}}_Z$ is consistent for $\boldsymbol{\beta}$. The second result gives the asymptotic variance of $\hat{\boldsymbol{\beta}}_Z$. This asymptotic variance is estimated by

$$S^2(Z'X)^{-1}(Z'Z)(X'Z)^{-1} \tag{8.19}$$

where S^2 is the usual mean sum of squares due to error.

The above is not to imply that the choice of Z is simple or straightforward. The difficulty lies in the fact that $\boldsymbol{\epsilon}$ is unobservable. In addition, Z is required to be as little correlated with $\boldsymbol{\epsilon}$ as possible. A few examples will be discussed below to shed more light on these problems.[5]

8.5 ERRORS IN VARIABLES

Let the measured X be related to the true X (= X^*) through the relation

$$X = X^* + \boldsymbol{\varepsilon}_X \tag{8.20}$$

where $\boldsymbol{\varepsilon}_X$ are the measurement errors in X. Then the regression relation

$$\mathbf{Y} = X^*\boldsymbol{\beta} + \boldsymbol{\epsilon}_Y \tag{8.21}$$

becomes

$$\mathbf{Y} = X\boldsymbol{\beta} + (\boldsymbol{\epsilon}_Y - \boldsymbol{\varepsilon}_X\boldsymbol{\beta}) \tag{8.22}$$

The OLS estimate of $\boldsymbol{\beta}$ is

$$\hat{\boldsymbol{\beta}} = \boldsymbol{\beta} + (X'X)^{-1}X'(\boldsymbol{\epsilon}_Y - \boldsymbol{\varepsilon}_X\boldsymbol{\beta}) \tag{8.23}$$

Should the asymptotic expectation of $\hat{\boldsymbol{\beta}}$ be $\boldsymbol{\beta}$, we must have

$$\text{plim } 1/n\, X'(\boldsymbol{\epsilon}_Y - \boldsymbol{\varepsilon}_X\boldsymbol{\beta}) = 0 \tag{8.24}$$

But (8.24) is not true. This can be seen as follows. Since

$$\text{plim } 1/n\, X^{*\prime}\boldsymbol{\varepsilon}_X = \mathit{0}; \qquad \text{plim } 1/n\, X^{*\prime}\boldsymbol{\epsilon}_Y = \mathbf{0}, \qquad \text{plim } \boldsymbol{\varepsilon}_X'\boldsymbol{\epsilon}_Y = \mathbf{0} \tag{8.25}$$

[5] The analysis shown here establishes the consistency property of the IV estimators. But there are cases when such estimators may be inconsistent. For example, empirical relationships may be formulated and IV estimators used in which the instruments or proxies are, without the knowledge of the investigator, correlated with the equation errors. Hendry (1979) sets up a linear, stationary, and dynamic simultaneous equation system (see our Chapter 11 for an introduction to simultaneous equation models) with autoregressive errors to explore the inconsistency properties of IV estimators with the above feature.

that is, measurement errors in one variable are in the limit uncorrelated with measurement errors in the other variable, and measurement errors in both variables are uncorrelated with their true values, we have

$$\begin{aligned} \text{plim } 1/n\, \boldsymbol{X}'(\boldsymbol{\epsilon}_Y - \boldsymbol{\varepsilon}_X\boldsymbol{\beta}) &= \text{plim } 1/n\, \boldsymbol{X}'\boldsymbol{\epsilon}_Y - \text{plim } 1/n\, \boldsymbol{X}'\boldsymbol{\varepsilon}_X\boldsymbol{\beta} \\ &= -\{\text{plim } 1/n\, \boldsymbol{X}^{*\prime}\boldsymbol{\varepsilon}_X + \text{plim } 1/n\, \boldsymbol{\varepsilon}_X'\boldsymbol{\varepsilon}_X\}\boldsymbol{\beta} \qquad (8.26) \\ &= -\text{plim } (1/n\, \boldsymbol{\varepsilon}_X'\boldsymbol{\varepsilon}_X)\boldsymbol{\beta} \neq \mathbf{0} \end{aligned}$$

because plim $1/n\, \boldsymbol{\varepsilon}_X'\boldsymbol{\varepsilon}_X$ is not zero. Thus,

$$\text{plim } \hat{\boldsymbol{\beta}} \neq \boldsymbol{\beta}$$

In other words, the OLS estimator $\hat{\boldsymbol{\beta}}$ is inconsistent for $\boldsymbol{\beta}$.

With a two variable (Y and X) regression without the intercept term the expression of plim $\hat{\beta}$ simplifies[6] to

$$\beta/(1 + \sigma^2_{\epsilon X}/\sigma^2_{X^*}) \qquad (8.27)$$

where $\sigma^2_{\epsilon X}$ and $\sigma^2_{X^*}$ are variances of ϵ_X and X^* respectively. The larger the $\sigma_{\epsilon X}$ or the smaller the σ_{X^*}, the larger the underestimation through $\hat{\beta}$, and conversely.

In order to rectify the problem in the general case, devise an instrumental variable $\boldsymbol{Z}$ for $\boldsymbol{X}$, taken to be independent, in the probability limit sense, of $\boldsymbol{\varepsilon}_X$ and $\boldsymbol{\epsilon}_Y$. Then $\hat{\boldsymbol{\beta}}_Z$ will be given by

$$\hat{\boldsymbol{\beta}}_Z = (\boldsymbol{Z}'\boldsymbol{X})^{-1}\boldsymbol{Z}'\mathbf{Y} \qquad (8.28)$$

It will be a consistent estimator of $\boldsymbol{\beta}$ with its asymptotic variance equal to

$$n^{-1} \lim_{n\to\infty} n\text{V}(\hat{\boldsymbol{\beta}}_Z) = n^{-1}\sigma^2 \text{ plim}(1/n\, \boldsymbol{Z}'\boldsymbol{X})^{-1} \text{ plim}(1/n\, \boldsymbol{Z}'\mathbf{Z})\cdot\text{plim}(1/n\, \boldsymbol{X}'\mathbf{Z})^{-1} \qquad (8.29)$$

In the two-variable (Y, X) situation, Wald (1940) has proposed an instrumental variable $\boldsymbol{Z}$ for $\boldsymbol{X}$, where

$$\boldsymbol{Z}' = \begin{bmatrix} 1 & 1 & 1 \cdots & 1 \\ -1 & -1 & +1 \cdots & -1 \end{bmatrix} \quad \boldsymbol{X}' = \begin{bmatrix} 1 & 1 & \cdots 1 \\ X_1 & X_2 & \cdots X_n \end{bmatrix} \qquad (8.30)$$

in which the second row of $\boldsymbol{Z}'$ has elements Z = +1 or −1 depending on whether X is above or below the median X, and the second row of $\boldsymbol{X}'$ has $X_1\ X_2, \ldots,$

[6] This is because

$$\begin{aligned} \text{plim } \hat{\beta} &= \beta - \text{plim}(1/n\, \mathbf{X}'\mathbf{X})^{-1} \text{ plim}(1/n\, \boldsymbol{\epsilon}_X'\boldsymbol{\epsilon}_X)\beta = \beta - \sigma_{X^2}^{-1}\sigma^2_{\epsilon X}\beta \\ &= \beta(1 - \sigma^2_{\epsilon X}/\sigma^2_X) = \beta\, \sigma^2_{X^*}/\sigma^2_X = \beta/(1 + \sigma^2_{\epsilon X}/\sigma^2_{X^*}) \end{aligned}$$

where σ^2_X is the variance of X.

X_n for the observations on X. By plugging these in (8.28) and simplifying, $\hat{\beta}$ is calculated as:

$$\hat{\beta}_Z = \left[\frac{\overline{Y}}{(\overline{Y}_2 - \overline{Y}_1)/(\overline{X}_2 - \overline{X}_1)}\right] \tag{8.31}$$

where $\overline{X}_2$ and $\overline{X}_1$ are the means of X above and below the median X, respectively, and similarly $\overline{Y}_2$ and $\overline{Y}_1$; $\overline{Y}$ is the grand mean of the Ys. This estimator looks naive but is consistent even though its sampling variance may be large.

The foregoing assumes an even value for n. Should n be odd, the suggestion is to ignore the central observation and carry on the estimation posing as though n were even.

Durbin (1954) has modified Wald's method by ranking the X observations with the numbers 1, 2, . . . , n and assigning these to an instrumental variable. He has shown[7] that, for large samples, the Wald type of estimator is only 96% as efficient as the OLS estimator, and for samples of size 20 the efficiency may hover around 86%.

8.6 AN APPLIED STUDY DUE TO BERHMAN

Berhman (1972) does actually use an errors-in-variable submodel while estimating a CES production function for real sector value added. The author assumes that technological change is factor augmenting (see Section 9.10, Chapter 9 for definition). The objective is to verify the charges of inflexibility of factor substitution in the production function of developing countries. Presumably this rigidity is taken to be the cause of unemployment and underemployment there. The particular country taken is Chile and nine of its production sectors are tested.

He starts from a CES production function (with the degree of homogeneity equal to one) defined as follows:

$$CV = [(E_L L)^{-\rho} + (E_K K)^{-\rho}]^{-1/\rho} \tag{8.32}$$

where CV is capacity value added, L is the quantity of labor from the trend line, K is capital stock, E_L is efficiency level of labor (equal to $be^{\gamma t}$), E_K is efficiency level of capital (equal to $b'e^{\gamma' t}$), t is a time trend, and b, b$'$, γ and γ' are constants.

Due to data availability problems associated with the above equation, the

[7] Durbin's original estimator does not provide for an intercept term. However, as in Wald's estimator, an intercept term can easily be included. In that case, the slope coefficient will be:

$$\hat{\beta}_Z \left(= \sum_1^n iy_i \Big/ \sum_1^n ix_i \right)$$

and intercept equal to $\overline{Y} - \hat{\beta}_Z\overline{X}$, where x, y are deviations of X, Y from their means.

following estimable equation is derived based on the equality of marginal value product and nominal wage of labor:

$$\ln CV/L = \{1/(1 + \rho)\} \ln W/P + \{\rho/(1 + \rho)\} \gamma t + \{\rho/(1 + \rho)\} \ln \mathrm{b} \tag{8.33}$$

In (8.33), W is nominal wage, and P is nominal gross product price. This equation is assumed to represent the desired level of $\ln(CV/L)$ towards which the actual level of $\ln(CV/L)$ gravitates in a Koyck–Cagan–Nerlove adjustment process. Accordingly a new equation is derived which is then estimated by the OLS method:

$$\ln CV/L = (1 - \lambda) \ln(CV/L)_{-1} + \lambda\sigma \ln W/P + \lambda\sigma\rho\gamma t + \lambda\sigma\rho \ln \mathrm{b} \tag{8.34}$$

in which $\sigma = 1/(1 + \rho)$ is the elasticity of substitution between capital and labor, and λ is the coefficient of adjustment.

The important point here is the emphasis given on the long-run structure rather than on the short-run tendencies. Thus the capacity of real value added is used rather than current real value added; also the wage to price ratio is the weighted[8] average of such ratios with lags of one to five years rather than just the current wage price ratio. The long run adjustment mechanism underlying the equation can be appreciated as follows.

Let the true structural relation be relation (8.35) below (with $\gamma = 0$), but the current values of $\ln V/L$ and $\ln W/P$ are as in (8.36) and (8.37) further below:

$$\ln (V/L)^* = \sigma \ln (W/P)^* + \text{constant} \tag{8.35}$$

In (8.35), $(V/L)^*$ and $(W/P)^*$ are the true long-run value added per worker and wage–price ratio, respectively;

$$\begin{aligned} \ln V/L &= \ln (V/L)^* + v \\ \ln W/P &= \ln (W/P)^* + u \end{aligned} \tag{8.36}$$

in which V/L and W/P are the currently observed value added per worker and real wage rate respectively, and u and v are the transitory parts of these relations; and

$$\ln (V/L) = \sigma \ln (W/P) + \text{constant} + w \tag{8.37}$$

where

$$w = v - \sigma u \tag{8.38}$$

As is evident from (8.36), $\ln W/P$ and w will be correlated. As a result, OLS estimated σ will be biased even asymptotically. This has prompted the author to use close approximations for $\ln (V/L)^*$ and $\ln (W/P)^*$ in place of these variables, rather than their current values. We quote here in Table 8.1 the results from two of the nine sectors, namely agriculture and manufacturing, for the sake of illustration.

[8] The weights used for the various lagged quantities are estimated for each sector with a maximum-likelihood scanning procedure. For more on this see the original source.

TABLE 8.1*

Sector	$\ln(CV/L)_{-1}$	$\ln E(W/P)$	Time	Constant	$\bar{R}^2$	σ (Long Run)
Agriculture	0.58	0.13		1.38	0.89	0.31
	(3.58)	(2.26)		(2.63)		
Manufacturing	0.74	0.21	0.004	1.53	0.99	0.76
	(6.82)	(3.03)	(1.53)	(1.93)		

(Figures in parentheses are *t* values. All *t* values are significant at the 5% level except for the coefficient of time which is significant at the 10% level.)

* Reprinted with permission of J. R. Behrman, "Sectional Elasticity of Substitution," *Econometrica* 40: Table 1 (1972) p. 316.

However, we will report here the conclusions drawn by the author comprising all the sectors. First, all the model equations come out reasonably alright by the F tests at least at the 1% level. Second, there is nonzero technical change for only four sectors, namely mining, manufacturing, services and transportation. Third, there are some sectoral differences in the way the adjustment of actual levels to desired levels occurs, the sectors with adjustment coefficients in order of magnitude being: government, housing services, manufacturing, construction, agriculture, transportation. It is a bit odd to find the adjustment in industry to be slower than that in agriculture, mining, and transportation. For adjustment coefficients in terms of real wages, the slowest adjusting sector is found to be government and manufacturing. Lastly, the values of σ indicate limited substitution possibilities. This means that the fast growing primary sector would decrease its (primary) factor share. The relatively high σ in the manufacturing sector means that there is room for dynamic flexibility. This would probably call for government help in labor retraining, etc., programs associated with the growth of this sector.[9]

8.7 LAG MODELS

Not all dependent variables react to independent variables instantaneously. Technical, institutional or psychological factors cause a lag or a pattern of lags in their response to them. The time requirement of a production run or the durability of capital goods are well-known examples of technical factors. The former causes lagged price effects and the latter causes lagged investment (decision) effects on

[9] As Griliches and Hausman (1986) indicate, there are problems of availability of extraneous information by means of which errors-in-variables models may be identified. However, they show how one can do without the use of external instruments to identify and estimate, for instance, panel data, even though this example seems to be too simplistic. That example is on the estimation of labor demand relationships giving rise to the so called "short run increasing returns" puzzle.

outputs. Adjustment of institutional (government or industry) contracts or payment schedules to changes in external circumstances also takes time. Lastly, inertia and habits, two of the most fundamental psychological elements in human behavior, take a toll on time and they express themselves in a lag between stimulus and response.

However, it is not always true that lags arise in only the independent variables. Sometimes the dynamics of individuals' behavior, as in partial stock adjustment or adaptive expectations models, reflects itself in lags in the dependent variables. Or, lags in the explanatory variables are imparted to lags in dependent variables, as in Koyck's models. We shall endeavour to discuss such models in some details below.

8.7.1 Distributed Lags in an Independent Variable—Koyck's Model

Take a linear distributed lag model given by:

$$Y_t = \beta_0 X_t + \beta_1 X_{t-1} + \cdots + \epsilon_t \tag{8.39}$$

with only one independent variable recorded at current time t, and an infinite number of past time points $t - 1, t - 2, \ldots$ The model stipulates that the βs decline in importance as we move back into the past until, in the limit, they assume a zero value, but the sum total of all the βs is finite.

Before we go on to discuss the Koyck model, we would like to explain some preliminary mechanisms based on the lag operator δ and the concept of the mean and the median lag. These follow.

The lag operator and the mean and median lag. Let the lag operator δ be defined as $\delta^r X_t = X_{t-r}$, $r = 1, 2, \ldots, n$. For example, $\delta X_t = X_{t-1}$. When the lag structure is finite as represented in (8.39), which, apart from the error term, can be represented as $Y_t = D(\delta)X_t$, where $D(\delta)$ is $\beta_0 + \beta_1\delta + \cdots + \beta_r\delta^r$, it can be seen that $\beta_0, \beta_1, \ldots, \beta_r$ are the impact multipliers $\Delta Y_t/\Delta X_t$ at periods $t, t - 1, \ldots, t - r$, respectively. Since $D(1)$ is $\beta_0 + \beta_1 + \cdots + \beta_r$, $D(1)$ implies the total effect on Y_t attained from ΔX_t both currently and in the allowable past. Therefore

$$\beta_i \Big/ \sum_0^r \beta_i$$

denotes the proportional effect in period $t - i$; $i = 0, 1, \ldots, r$. Two useful concepts in this context are the median and mean lags. A median lag is the number of periods by which exactly 50% of the total effect occurs. A mean lag is, assuming all the βs to be positive, given by

$$\sum_{i=0}^r i\beta_i \Big/ \sum_{i=0}^r \beta_i = (\beta_1 + 2\beta_2 + \cdots + r\beta_r)/(\beta_0 + \beta_1 + \beta_2 + \cdots + \beta_r)$$

Since the first derivative of $D(\delta)$ with respect to δ is $D'(\delta)$, which is $\beta_1 + 2\beta_2\delta + \cdots + r\beta_r\delta^{r-1}$, and $D'(1)$ is $\beta_1 + 2\beta_2 + \cdots + r\beta_r$, therefore the mean lag is $D'(1)/D(1)$. For the median lag, take a simple four-period example in which the proportional effects

$$\beta_i \Big/ \sum_0^3 \beta_i$$

are, say, 0.20, 0.25, 0.45, and 0.10 at the end of the four different periods. The cumulative effects from these in the successive periods are 0.20, (0.20 + 0.25 =)0.45, (0.20 + 0.25 + 0.45 =)0.90, and (0.20 + 0.25 + 0.45 + 0.10 =)1.00. Thus the median lag occurs between period 1 and 2, and is calculated at:

$$1 + (0.50 - 0.45)/(0.90 - 0.45) = 1.11 \text{ periods.}$$

The Koyck model. Without loss of generality, we can write β_j of (8.39) as follows, where β is a constant:

$$w_j = \beta_j/\beta \tag{8.40}$$

Define as before the operator δ as

$$\delta X_t = X_{t-1} \tag{8.41}$$

and remember that $\Sigma w_j = 1$. Then Koyck's (1954) weight system is given by:

$$w_i = (1 - \mu)\mu^i \qquad 0 < \mu < 1 \tag{8.42}$$

Then

$$\begin{aligned} Y_t &= \beta_0 X_t + \beta_1 X_{t-1} + \cdots + \epsilon_t \\ &= \beta(w_0 + w_1\delta + w_2\delta^2 + \cdots)X_t + \epsilon_t \\ &= \beta[(1 - \mu)/(1 - \mu\delta)]X_t + \epsilon_t \end{aligned} \tag{8.43}$$

since,

$$\begin{aligned} w_0 + w_1\delta + w_2\delta^2 + \cdots &= (1 - \mu)\,(1 + \mu\delta + \mu^2\delta^2 + \cdots) \\ &= (1 - \mu)/(1 - \mu\delta) \end{aligned} \tag{8.44}$$

It therefore follows that

$$Y_t = \beta(1 - \mu)X_t + \mu Y_{t-1} + (\epsilon_t - \mu\epsilon_{t-1}) \tag{8.45}$$

This is a clear example of the basic model with lags in the independent variable[10] X. This also illustrates the fact that such lags are transmitted to the dependent variable Y in a special way since the final model equation involves a term in Y_{t-1}.

[10] The point must be made that there might be the distributed lag effect of not just one, but more than one explanatory variable on the dependent variable. To give an example with two explan-

8.7.2 Lags in Dependent Variable—Partial Adjustment Model

An example of the Koyck's distributed lag is the stock adjustment or the partial adjustment model. The model is partial because of several reasons. One may be the lack of complete knowledge, another may be the inertia of not making change, and still another may be the cost associated with change.

Define by Y_t^d the desired Y which depends on X_t according to

$$Y_t^d = \beta_0 + \beta_1 X_t \tag{8.46}$$

Examples of Y_t^d and X_t could be optimal expenditure and disposable income, or optimal production rate and sales. The partial adjustment equation is

$$Y_t - Y_{t-1} = \theta(Y_t^d - Y_{t-1}) + \epsilon_t \qquad 0 < \theta < 1 \tag{8.47}$$

In other words, the actual year-to-year change in *actual* Y is postulated to be a fraction θ of the discrepancy between *desired* Y this period and *actual* Y last period, subject to some adjustment made due to errors of judgement or anticipation.

Combining the two equations, we have[11]

$$Y_t = \beta_0\theta + \beta_1\theta X_t + (1 - \theta)Y_{t-1} + \epsilon_t \tag{8.48}$$

---

atory variables, that is, X with the lag structure identified by parameters β and μ already considered, and Z, with the lag structure with parameters γ and ν, similar manipulations will yield:

$$Y_t = \{\beta(1 - \mu)/(1 - \mu\delta)\}X_t + \{\gamma(1 - \nu)/(1 - \nu\delta)\}Z_t + \epsilon_t$$

that is

$$Y_t = (\mu + \nu)Y_{t-1} - \mu\nu Y_{t-2} + \beta(1 - \mu)(X_t - \nu X_{t-1})$$
$$+ \gamma(1 - \nu)(Z_t - \mu Z_{t-1}) + \epsilon_t - (\mu + \nu)\epsilon_{t-1} + \mu\nu\epsilon_{t-2}$$

Here the error structure is more complex and there are more lagged endogenous and exogenous variables appearing than before.

[11] In some contexts, the form of stock adjustment may look quite different from this. For example, Hodgson and Holmes (1977) analyze structural stability of international capital movement or, more concretely, movement in short-term Canada and U.S. bank claims in terms of changes in the values of determinants of such movements. They use a stock adjustment hypothesis in which changes in the stock of a given security are taken to be a function of the risk-free rate of return on it, risks for it, other variables that affect portfolio composition, and a scale variable. Risk-free rates of return are proxied by covered interest rate differentials, risks by uncovered interest rate differentials, other variables by interest rate in a third country or countries (meaning to measure the opportunity cost of holding wealth in the securities of the two primary countries), and the scale variable by the total size of the portfolio. As should be clear, there is no explicit room for desired stock in the formulation unlike equation (8.47). Yet desired stock is implicit because that has been replaced by the variables that determine it, as in equation (8.48).

To introduce the reader quickly to one of the main results of this analysis, let us point to the conclusion of the study. Capital mobility between the United States and Canada, according to the study, might have *declined* slightly between the years 1969 and 1974.

The intercept term and the error term are not like those in the Koyck's model, but the other terms are.

A criticism of the stock adjustment model is in its relating desired Y to current X. However, the latter may change so much year after year that it may be difficult to pin down the relation. In such cases, it may be better to relate Y_t to the currently expected level of X. One implication of this would be to have a sense of the desired Y to arise out of the projected stream of X.

What we have described so far is the essential ingredient of an expectation hypothesis. In symbols, we have

$$Y_t = \beta_0 + \beta_1 X_t^e + \epsilon_t \tag{8.49}$$

where X_t^e is the expected level of X at time t. However, the important question now is: how do we expect X? For that, consider the following rule:

$$X_t^e - X_{t-1}^e = \Psi(X_t - X_{t-1}^e) \qquad 0 \leq \Psi \leq 1 \tag{8.50}$$

that is, expectations are revised this period over the last by a fraction of the amount by which actual X this period exceeds its expected value last period.

From (8.50), using the lag operator δ, we have

$$X_t^e - (1 - \Psi)X_{t-1}^e = \Psi X_t$$

or

$$(1 - (1 - \Psi)\delta)X_t^e = \Psi X_t \tag{8.51}$$

Substituting this in (8.49), we have

$$Y_t = \beta_0 + \beta_1\{\Psi/(1 - (1 - \Psi)\delta)\}X_t + \epsilon_t \tag{8.52}$$

which can be expressed in the form

$$Y_t = \beta_0\Psi + \beta_1\Psi X_t + (1 - \Psi)Y_{t-1} + \{\epsilon_t - (1 - \Psi)\epsilon_{t-1}\} \tag{8.53}$$

This is analogous to the stock adjustment equation except for the error term. However, it is similar to Koyck's model except for the intercept term.[12]

8.7.3 Estimation

The three models that we have discussed so far have their general equation reduced ultimately to

$$Y_t = \beta_0 + \beta_1 Y_{t-1} + \beta_2 X_t + u_t \tag{8.54}$$

[12] It is possible that both the partial adjustment model and expectations hypothesis may arise simultaneously in the model. One example is when "permanent" consumption is related to "permanent" income, the former being explained by partial adjustment and the latter by adaptive expectation—see Friedman (1957). The final estimating equation can be similarly deduced.

where u_t is the error term. The estimation of this model will depend on the specific assumption made about u_t. Consider the following assumptions:

(1) the us are normally and independently distributed with mean 0 and variance σ_u^2.

(2) $u_t = \epsilon_t - \theta\,\epsilon_{t-1}$, $0 < \theta < 1$, in which the ϵs are normally and independently distributed with either (a) 0 mean and variance σ^2, or (b) $\epsilon_t = \rho\epsilon_{t-1} + \nu_t$; $|\rho| < 1$, ν_ts being distributed independently normally with 0 mean and variance σ_ν^2.

(3) $u_t = \rho u_{t-1} + \nu_t$; $|\rho| < 1$, ν_ts being distributed independently normally with 0 mean and variance σ_ν^2.

Under assumption (1) the aspect that $E(Y_{t+s}u_t) \neq 0$[13] for $s \geq 0$, for all t, would imply that OLS estimates will be biased in small samples. To illustrate it, we refer to White's (1961) study. He takes a simple model: $Y_t = \beta Y_{t-1} + u_t$, with $|\beta| < 1$ and u_t serially uncorrelated. The OLS estimator of β is

$$\hat{\beta} = \sum_2^n Y_t Y_{t-1} \Big/ \sum_2^n Y_{t-1}^2 \tag{8.55}$$

retaining terms of order up to n^{-1}. The bias is calculated to be

$$E(\hat{\beta}) - \beta \approx -2\beta/n \tag{8.56}$$

This implies that the bias would disappear as n is increased indefinitely.[14]

Refer back to equation (8.54). By including the intercept term and the term involving X_t, the equation can be expressed in matrix notation as:

$$\mathbf{Y} = \mathbf{Z}\boldsymbol{\beta} + \mathbf{u} \tag{8.57}$$

the notation $\mathbf{Z}$, not just X alone, being used to imply that it contains both X and $\mathbf{Y}$ elements as follows:

$$\mathbf{Z} = \begin{bmatrix} 1 & Y_0 & X_1 \\ 1 & Y_1 & X_2 \\ \vdots & \vdots & \vdots \\ 1 & Y_n & X_n \end{bmatrix} \tag{8.58}$$

Clearly we are assuming that X_t and Y_{t-1} are statistically independent of u_t, for all t. We add to this the condition that $\text{plim}(1/n\ \mathbf{Z}'\mathbf{Z}) = \boldsymbol{\Sigma}_{ZZ}$ is a symmetric positive definite matrix. This is required for two reasons. The first is to secure

[13] This is so because $Y_t = \beta_0 + \beta_1 Y_{t-1} + \beta_2 X_t + u_t$ which shows $E(Y_t u_t) \neq 0$. Also, $Y_{t+s} = \beta_0 + \beta_1 Y_{t+s-1} + \beta_2 X_{t+s-1} + u_{t+s-1}$ which implies $E(Y_{t+s}u_{t+s-1}) \neq 0$ for $s \geq 0$, for all t. So, combining $E(Y_t u_t) \neq 0$ and $E(Y_{t+s}u_{t+s-1}) \neq 0$, we have $E(Y_{t+s}u_t) \neq 0$ for $s \geq 0$, for all t.

[14] The reader is referred to the studies by Marriott and Pope (1954) and Copas (1966) for some interesting alternative estimators and their efficiency in Monte Carlo experiments.

those values of $\boldsymbol{\beta}$ that will guarantee the stability of the model, and the second is to have bounded values for the second order moments of $\boldsymbol{X}$.[15]

Now the OLS estimator of $\boldsymbol{\beta}$ is

$$\hat{\boldsymbol{\beta}} = (\mathbf{Z}'\mathbf{Z})^{-1}\mathbf{Z}'\mathbf{Y} = \boldsymbol{\beta} + (\mathbf{Z}'\mathbf{Z})^{-1}\mathbf{Z}'\mathbf{u} \tag{8.59}$$

However, by virtue of the Mann and Wald (1943) results:

$$\text{plim } 1/n\ \mathbf{Z}'\mathbf{u} = 0 \tag{8.60}$$

and

$$(1/\sqrt{n})\mathbf{Z}'\mathbf{u} \sim \text{N}(0, \sigma_u^2\ \boldsymbol{\Sigma}_{ZZ}) \tag{8.61}$$

and the general results in (4.129), (4.130) and Section 4.10 of Chapter 4,[16] we have:

$$\sqrt{n}\ (\hat{\boldsymbol{\beta}} - \boldsymbol{\beta}) = (1/n\ \mathbf{Z}'\mathbf{Z})^{-1}\ (1/\sqrt{n})\mathbf{Z}'\mathbf{u} \tag{8.62}$$

distributed as asymptotic normal. In other words, $\hat{\boldsymbol{\beta}}$ is asymptotic normal with mean $\boldsymbol{\beta}$ and variance–covariance matrix $(1/n)\ \sigma_u^2\ \boldsymbol{\Sigma}_{ZZ}^{-1}$. Such estimates are also equivalent to the ML estimates and efficient (see Section 4.12 of Chapter 4).

The above result assumes the us to be distributed normally, but this need not be the case. Only random us will guarantee this result.

Under assumption (2), we have an MA(1) process, rather than an AR(1) process, for the error variable. Both Koyck's and adaptive expectations models are found to give rise to this kind of error structure. Let us rewrite the model equation for these cases as

$$Y_t = \beta_0 + \theta Y_{t-1} + \beta_2 X_t + (\epsilon_t - \theta\epsilon_{t-1}) \qquad |\,\theta\,| < 1 \tag{8.63}$$

where θ, the parameter of the MA(1) process, is, at the same time, the coefficient of the lagged dependent variable Y_{t-1}. Note that ϵ here is assumed to be normally independently distributed: $\text{N}(\mathbf{0}, \sigma^2\boldsymbol{I})$.

Writing Y_t^* for $Y_t - \epsilon_t$, and by repeated substitution for Y_t^*, (8.63) can be written as:

$$Y_t^* = \beta_0(1 + \theta + \theta^2 + \cdots + \theta^{t-1}) + \beta_2(X_t + \theta X_{t-1} + \cdots + \theta^{t-1}X_1) + Y_0^*\theta^t \tag{8.64}$$

or,

$$Y_t = \beta_0(1 + \theta + \theta^2 + \cdots + \theta^{t-1}) + \beta_2 X_t^* + Y_0^*\theta^t + \epsilon_t \tag{8.65}$$

where

$$X_t^* = X_t + \theta X_{t-1} + \cdots + \theta^{t-1}X_1 = X_t + \theta X_{t-1}^* \tag{8.66}$$

given that $X_1^* = X_1$.

[15] See Malinvaud (1970), p. 540 for detailed explanations.

[16] That is, if $\sqrt{n}\ (\hat{\boldsymbol{\beta}} - \boldsymbol{\beta}) \rightarrow \text{N}(0, \sigma_u^2\ \boldsymbol{\Sigma}^{-1})$, then $\hat{\boldsymbol{\beta}}$ is asymptotically normal: $\text{AN}(\boldsymbol{\beta}, 1/n\ \sigma_u^2\boldsymbol{\Sigma}^{-1})$.

Since ϵ_t is a normal variable, (8.65) can be treated by both OLS and ML procedures. The data matrix for the OLS procedure is

$$X(\boldsymbol{\theta}) = \begin{bmatrix} 1 & X_1^* & \theta \\ 1+\theta & X_2^* & \theta^2 \\ 1+\theta+\theta^2 & X_3^* & \theta^3 \\ \cdots & \cdots & \cdots \\ 1+\theta+\cdots+\theta^{n-1} & X_n^* & \theta^n \end{bmatrix} \tag{8.67}$$

Following the method of grid search for values of θ over the interval $0 < \theta \leq 1$, $X(\boldsymbol{\theta})$ is calculated each time for a specific value of θ. This goes into the OLS estimation of (8.65) and the parameter estimates are used to calculate the error sum of squares. The method is repeated until finally the error sum of squares does not decrease any more. The parameter estimates at this stage are the optimum estimates.

For the asymptotic standard errors, we follow the method of ML and derivation of the information matrix as usual. The log likelihood of (8.65) is

$$\ln L = -(n/2)\ln(2\pi) - (n/2)\sigma^2 - \{1/(2\sigma^2)\}\Sigma\epsilon_t^2 \tag{8.68}$$

where

$$\epsilon_t = Y_t - \beta_0 V_t - \beta_2 X_t^* - Y_0^*\,\theta^t \tag{8.69}$$

and

$$V_t = 1 + \theta + \cdots + \theta^{t-1} \tag{8.70}$$

The parameters to be estimated[17] are β_0, β_2, θ, Y_0^*, and σ^2. However, the information matrix (see equations (4.148) and (4.152) of Chapter 4) containing the expectation of the second order partial derivatives with regard to these parameters shows that σ^2 has nothing to do with the other parameters. The ML estimate of σ^2 is $\Sigma\hat{\epsilon}_t^2/n$ and its asymptotic standard error $\sqrt{2\sigma^4/n}$. For the other parameters, the information matrix $\boldsymbol{I}$ is:

$$\boldsymbol{I}\begin{bmatrix} \beta_0 \\ \beta_2 \\ \theta \\ Y_0^* \end{bmatrix} = 1/\sigma^2 \begin{bmatrix} \Sigma V_t^2 & \Sigma V_t X_t^* & \Sigma V_t V_t^* & \Sigma V_t \theta^t \\ & \Sigma X_t^{*2} & \Sigma X_t^* V_t^* & \Sigma X_t^* \theta^t \\ & & \Sigma V_t^{*2} & \Sigma V_t^* \theta^t \\ & & & \Sigma \theta^{2t} \end{bmatrix} \tag{8.71}$$

[17] We will not discuss the details of the ML method to derive the estimates since we have already indicated how to derive the equivalent OLS estimates. However, the ML estimates are also possible. These are obtained by solving the normal equations which are the first derivatives of (8.68) with respect to β_0, β_2, Y_0^*, and σ^2, each equated to zero. However, these are equations nonlinear in parameters for the solution of which some simple numerical routines are available. These consist of iterative techniques in which an initial estimate of the parameters is used, to begin with, and then a new, (hopefully) improved estimate is obtained by following what is known as the descent or the maximum gradient method—see Harvey (1981), p. 119–43 for details. A similar solution procedure relating to a nonlinear equation is illustrated toward the end of Section 8.7.9.

where V_t^*, as yet unexplained, is:

$$V_t^* = -\partial\epsilon_t/\partial\theta = \beta_0[1 + 2\theta + \cdots + (t-1)\theta^{t-2})] + \beta_2[X_{t-1} + 2\theta X_{t-2} + \cdots + (t-1)\theta^{t-2}X_1] + tY_0^*\theta^{t-1} \tag{8.72}$$

Under assumption (3), which involves lagged dependent and autocorrelated error variables, a general result is immediate. This follows from the correlation between u_{t-1} and Y_{t-1}, u_{t-1} and u_t, and finally u_t and Y_{t-1}. That is, OLS estimates would be biased in large samples, let alone small samples. As Griliches (1961) has shown from a model:

$$Y_t = \beta Y_{t-1} + u_t \qquad u_t = \rho u_{t-1} + \epsilon_t$$

$$\hat{\beta} = \sum_2^n Y_t Y_{t-1} \bigg/ \sum_2^n Y_{t-1}^2 \tag{8.73}$$

$$\text{plim } \hat{\beta} - \beta = \rho(1 - \beta^2)/(1 + \beta\rho) \tag{8.74}$$

The above shows that the asymptotic bias of the OLS estimates can be large for small values of β and large values of ρ. As $\rho \rightarrow 1$, this bias tends to $1 - \beta$.

Generally, a way out is to use the IV method. Accordingly one usually selects X_{t-1} as the instrument for Y_{t-1}. This of course will eliminate the possibility of the correlation between the lagged dependent and residual variables. But still the problem of autocorrelation of the residuals would remain, which might ruin the property of consistency and asymptotic normality of the IV estimator available from the usual random residual situation.[18]

Under assumption (2)—(a) and (b) specifically—there are some estimation routines suggested by Zellner and Geisel (1968). These involve search procedures, which can be computationally very heavy, even though they are theoretically impeccable. The reader is referred to the original source for more details.

Under assumption (3), we can show that the variance–covariance matrix of us is:

$$E(\mathbf{uu}') = \sigma_v^2\boldsymbol{\Omega} = \sigma_v^2 \begin{bmatrix} 1 & \rho & \rho^2 & \cdots \rho^{n-2} & \rho^{n-1} \\ \cdots & \cdots & \cdots & \cdots\cdots & \cdots \\ \rho^{n-1} & \rho^{n-2} & \rho^{n-3} & \cdots \rho & 1 \end{bmatrix} \tag{8.75}$$

The GLS estimator of $\boldsymbol{\beta}$ is then $\hat{\boldsymbol{\beta}}$, where

$$\hat{\boldsymbol{\beta}} = (X'\boldsymbol{\Omega}^{-1}X)^{-1}X'\boldsymbol{\Omega}^{-1}\mathbf{Y} \tag{8.76}$$

As we have seen in the section on autocorrelation, the alternative is to use the

[18] The possibility will arise for the invalidity of the DW test when the model includes a lagged dependent variable as one of the explanatory variables. See Nerlove and Wallis (1966) for a precise extent of the asymptotic bias in the DW statistic in this case.

ρ-difference transformation of the original model and then apply the OLS technique on the transformed variables.[19]

If ρ is known, estimation is simple. If it is not known, one can apply an iterative routine like that of the Cochrane–Orcutt method. However, search and iterative procedures can be very costly. That is why various short cuts have been suggested in the literature. One such is to use a two-step procedure: in the first step estimate ρ (as $\hat{\rho}$) as negative of the ratio of the coefficient of X_{t-1} to that of X_t; in the second step, apply the OLS technique to the $\hat{\rho}$-difference-transformed variables to estimate all the remaining parameters.[20]

The above iterative Cochrane–Orcutt method, convenient as it may seem for practical purposes, has come under criticism on theoretical grounds. Betancourt and Kelejian (1981) have shown that the Cochrane–Orcutt estimators will inevitably converge to a fixed point, but that may indicate a local, rather than a global, minimum of the sum of squares of the residuals. Consequently, the probability limit of the estimators will not be identical with the parameter vector. For consistency of the iterative estimates, one should start with a consistent estimator for ρ that should rule out its zero value. (A zero value of ρ makes the OLS estimates of coefficients of the untransformed equation inconsistent.) Alternatively, a fine grid search method for values of ρ over the interval $(-1, 1)$ that discriminates the global from the local minimum might be used.

8.7.4 Applied Studies: Partial Adjustment and Expectation Models

A perfect example of the partial stock adjustment model appears in Blomqvist and Haessel (1978). This study is about the disaggregated demand functions for cars by size and age class. Its primary object is to ascertain the effect of gasoline price on the composition of demand. Data relate to the Canadian provinces over the period 1971–1975. Stocks of cars of a certain age and class are taken to change in accordance with a certain fraction of the discrepancy between the desired stock and the lagged stock, besides the error of such adjustment. Without reporting on any of the study's quantitative results, let us only mention that it finds the demand composition of cars to substantially change with relative car prices. However, the effect of the gasoline prices on such composition is essentially inconclusive.

A combination of the partial stock adjustment and the expectation hypothesis is empirically provided by Hickman (1965). He uses annual data over the period 1949–1960 to explain why the U.S. economy has operated, since 1957, below its

[19] The transformed model would be:

$$(Y_t - \rho Y_{t-1}) = \beta_0(1 - \rho) + \beta_1(Y_{t-1} - \rho Y_{t-2}) + \beta_2(X_t - \rho X_{t-1}) + v_t$$

The Y transformed variable is $Y_t - \rho Y_{t-1}$, similarly the other transformed variables. The method would then consist of regressing the transformed Y on the other transformed variables.

[20] An alternative simplified technique is described by Liviatan (1963).

potential and then conjectures if it would do the same in the rest of the sixties. In what follows we would merely illustrate the practical working of the two hypotheses without trying to attend to the other aspects of the article.

For the capital stock adjustment model the author takes the desired stock to be a function of the expected or normal profit, the expected or normal prices, and the level of technology. Normal output and prices are determined by the weighted average of the recent quantities, the weights being decided by the data. Technology is determined from a smooth trend. Thus:

$$K^* = a_1 Y_t^{*a_2} P^{*a_3} e^{a_4 T} \tag{8.77}$$

where

K^* = desired capital stock
Y^* = normal output
P^* = normal relative price of capital
T = trend

Equation (8.77) in logarithmic form is

$$\ln K^* = \ln a_1 + a_2 \ln Y_t^* + a_3 \ln P^* + a_4 T \tag{8.78}$$

The normal output Y_t^* and price P^*, being geometric means of this and last year's quantities, are determined from

$$a_2 \ln Y_t^* = a_{21} \ln Y_t + a_{22} \ln Y_{t-1} \tag{8.79}$$

$$a_3 \ln P_t^* = a_{31} \ln P_t + a_{32} \ln P_{t-1} \tag{8.80}$$

The Koyck's adjustment equation is

$$K_t/K_{t-1} = (K_t^*/K_{t-1})^b \tag{8.81}$$

which reduces to:

$$\ln K_t - \ln K_{t-1} = b \ln a_1 + ba_{21} \ln Y_t + ba_{22} \ln Y_{t-1} + ba_{31} \ln P_t + ba_{32} \ln P_{t-1} + ba_4 T - b \ln K_{t-1} \tag{8.82}$$

where

$$\begin{aligned} b &= \text{adjustment coefficient} \\ a_{21} + a_{22} &= \text{long run elasticity of capital stock with respect to output} \end{aligned} \tag{8.83}$$

Since the inherent production function has constant returns to scale, the elasticity, $a_{21} + a_{22}$, has to be equal to 1, even though this is violated in some of his calculations. To guarantee this value, he rather estimates the following equation:

$$\ln K_t - \ln K_{t-1} = \ln c_1 + c_2(\ln Y_t - \ln K_{t-1}) + c_3(\ln Y_{t-1} - \ln K_{t-1}) + c_4 T \tag{8.84}$$

This equation, applied to all the industries and separately the manufacturing sector, leads to the following results (based on the OLS method):*

All industries.

$$\ln K_t - \ln K_{t-1} = \underset{(0.0018)}{0.0337} + \underset{(0.0142)}{0.1236}(\ln Y_t - \ln K_{t-1}) + \underset{(0.0157)}{0.1141}(\ln Y_{t-1} - \ln K_{t-1}) - \underset{(0.0001)}{0.0018}T$$

$$\overline{R}^2 = 0.969 \qquad \text{DW} = 2.48 \tag{8.85}$$

Manufacturing.

$$\ln K_t - \ln K_{t-1} = \underset{(0.0043)}{-0.0265} + \underset{(0.0238)}{0.1529}(\ln Y_t - \ln K_{t-1}) + \underset{(0.0291)}{0.2173}(\ln Y_{t-1} - \ln K_{t-1}) + \underset{(0.0008)}{0.0007}T - \underset{(0.0001)}{0.0002}T^2$$

$$\overline{R}^2 = 0.954 \qquad \text{DW} = 2.72 \tag{8.86}$$

These results come off well by the standard tests. He comments that the trend coefficients might reflect not only the technological progress but other effects also, such as scale effects, price effects, and interindustry shifts. Notice that there is a term involving T^2 appearing in the manufacturing equation. The idea is to use it as an indicator of change in the rate of growth of the industry. It comes out significant as well.

8.7.5 Almon Distributed Lags

The next study we discuss is Almon (1965). Apart from its empirical underpinnings, the study seems to be important for a theoretical reason. It makes use of a flexible form distributed lag or a finite length polynomial lag, compared to the infinite length lag of the Koyck lag structure.

Almon's objective is to predict quarterly capital expenditures in manufacturing industries from present and past capital appropriations. Since the importance of past appropriations is provided for by a pattern of weights, the problem is one of distributed lags. She uses varying periods of lags and then chooses the one that is the best among them, decided upon by some objective criterion.

Lagrangean polynomial. Almon's distributed lag model is given by

$$Y_t = \sum_{i=0}^{n-1} w(i) X_{t-i} \tag{8.87}$$

* Reprinted with permission of B. G. Hickman, "Investment Demand and U.S. Economic Growth" (1965) The Brookings Institution, Table 3, p. 50.

where Y and X are the dependent and independent variables, and $w(i)$ are the weights of the Xs. These weights, depending on a few parameters, are determined from the following equation:

$$w(i) = \sum_{j=0}^{q+1} \phi\,(i)b_j \qquad (i = 0, 1, \ldots, n-1) \tag{8.88}$$

where $w(x)$, a polynomial of degree $q + 1$, $q < n$, is determined from $q + 2$ known parametric points, $b_0, b_1, \ldots, b_{q+1}$:

$$w(x_0) = \mathrm{b}_0, \qquad w(\mathrm{x}_1) = b_1, \ldots, \qquad w(x_{q+1}) = b_{q+1} \tag{8.89}$$

Any value of $w(x)$ for $x \neq x_0, x_1, \ldots, x_{q+1}$ is obtained from the Lagrangean polynomial interpolation formula:

$$\begin{aligned} \phi_0(x) &= \frac{(x - x_1)(x - x_2)\cdots(x - x_{q+1})}{(x_0 - x_1)(x_0 - x_2)\cdots(x_0 - x_{q+1})} \\ \phi_1(x) &= \frac{(x - x_0)(x - x_2)\cdots(x - x_{q+1})}{(x_1 - x_0)(x_1 - x_2)\cdots(x_1 - x_{q+1})} \\ \phi_{q+1}(x) &= \frac{(x - x_0)(x - x_1)\cdots(x - x_q)}{(x_{q+1} - x_0)(x_{q+1} - x_1)\cdots(x_{q+1} - x_q)} \end{aligned} \tag{8.90}$$

Since $\phi_j(x_j) = 1; j = 0, 1, \ldots, q + 1$, and $\phi_j(x_k) = 0, j \neq k, j = 0, 1, \ldots, q + 1; k = 0, 1, \ldots, q + 1$, it follows that

$$w(x) = \sum_{j=0}^{q+1} \phi_j(i)b_j \tag{8.91}$$

Thus $w(x)$ is a polynomial of degree $q + 1$ with b_js its values corresponding to the points x_js. This justifies the use of the form (8.88) for $w(x)$.

The final form of $w(i)$ can be obtained by noting and using the following:

$w(-1) = w(n) = 0$ (that is, weights before time 0 and after time $n - 1$ are zero)[21]

Hence,

$$x_0 = -1, \qquad x_{q+1} = n, \qquad b_0 = b_{q+1} = 0 \tag{8.92}$$

Thus,

$$w(i) = \sum_{j=1}^{q} \phi_j(i)b_j \tag{8.93}$$

[21] As Dhrymes (1971) and Schmidt and Waud (1973) have indicated, impositions of these kinds of restrictions imply, via the relation between ws and bs, restrictions on the way $X_t, X_{t-1}, \ldots, X_{t-(n-1)}$ affect Y_t, and there do not seem to be any great theoretical reasons for including them.

Substituting (8.93) into (8.87), we get an expression for Y_t as:

$$Y_t = \sum_{i=0}^{n-1} \left(\sum_{j=1}^{q} \phi_j(i) b_j \right) X_{t-i} = \sum_{j=1}^{q} b_j \sum_{i=0}^{n-1} \phi_j(i) X_{t-i} \tag{8.94}$$

The above implies that the b_js can be estimated by regressing Y_t on the Z_{tj}s where:

$$Z_{tj} = \sum_{i=0}^{n-1} \phi_j(i) X_{t-i}; \qquad j = 1, 2, \ldots, q \tag{8.95}$$

By plugging these estimated b_js into (8.93), the $w(i)$s are estimated.[22]

Let us briefly look at Almon's empirical model and results. First of all, how does she choose the values of n and q? For n, she calculates the correlation coefficient between expenditure Y and successive lagged values of capital appropriations X. That quarterly lag for which appropriations correlate with expenditures as well as those without any lag at all is chosen as the middle point of a range of ns. For instance, for the chemical industries, such correlations are 0.08, 0.45, 0.68, 0.82, 0.86, 0.77, 0.56, 0.36, and 0.09 corresponding to 0 quarter lag down to 1, 2, . . . , 7 and 8 quarter lags. She also uses the first differences in expenditures. Using these, she finds erratically positive correlations until the nine-quarter-lag mark at which point the correlation is slightly negative. Thus, she takes nine quarters to be the optimal length of lag. Accordingly, the range for which this would be the central lag would be from 6 to 12 quarters (that is (6 + 12)/2 = 9).

The idea is to go as far back in time as to obtain very feeble or no correlation at all between current investment expenditure and past capital appropriations just the same as one would expect to get between such expenditure and *current* appropriations.

The purpose of using 6 to 12 quarter lags is to try a number of lags of various lengths and then choose the one that produces the best estimation results. "Best" is in the sense of having the minimum value of the sum of squares due to error.

The other parameter q is limited by the number of observations available. However, there appears to be no other theoretical basis discussed for the choice of q. In her case, she chooses q to be 3; that is, she chooses a (3 + 1, or) fourth degree polynomial for $w(x)$.

Her central equation is

$$E_t = a_1 s_1 + a_2 s_2 + a_3 s_3 + \sum_{j=1}^{3} b_j \sum_{i=0}^{n-1} \phi_j(i) A_{t-i} + u_t \tag{8.96}$$

[22] It requires very simple calculations to show that when the ws are not given exactly by the Lagrangean polynomial formula (8.90), the Almon estimates may be biased in finite samples and even be inconsistent. However, these problems would disappear if the ws lie exactly on that polynomial.

where

$$
\begin{aligned}
E &= \text{expenditure} \\
s_1, s_2, s_3 &= \text{seasonal dummies} \\
A &= \text{capital appropriations} \\
n &= 6, 7, \ldots, 11, 12
\end{aligned}
\tag{8.97}
$$

This function is fitted to all U.S. manufacturing industries, to durable and non-durable goods industries separately, and to their 15 constituent industries.

Broadly speaking, her results on the goodness of fit are as follows. For 12 out of 15 industries, $\bar{R}^2$ is greater than 0.8; for the aggregate industries including all manufacturing and durable and nondurable industries, it is larger than 0.9. Therefore the results, on the whole, are good.

Ordinary polynomials. The analysis so far has been useful in many respects, but it has not indicated a criterion by following which the degree of the polynomial can be determined. In what follows, we present a method of constrained least squares applied to a simpler polynomial (than the Lagranean polynomial) for the purpose of determining its degree. To this end, we start from the regression equation (8.87) modified as:

$$
Y_t = \alpha + \beta_0 X_t + \beta_1 X_{t-1} + \cdots + \beta_n X_{t-n} + \epsilon_t \tag{8.98}
$$

where Y and X are the dependent and independent variables, α is the intercept term, the βs are the weights of the current and lagged values of X, and ϵ is the residual term. According to the Almon scheme, we assume that the weights β can be approximated by some function $\beta_i \approx f(l)$. Assuming, for example, that $f(l)$ is a third degree polynomial:

$$
f(l) = \gamma_0 + \gamma_1 l + \gamma_2 l^2 + \gamma_3 l^3
$$

We have roughly:

$$
\begin{aligned}
\beta_0 &= f(0) = \gamma_0 \\
\beta_1 &= f(1) = \gamma_0 + \gamma_1 + \gamma_2 + \gamma_3 \\
\beta_2 &= f(2) = \gamma_0 + 2\gamma_1 + 4\gamma_2 + 8\gamma_3 \\
\beta_3 &= f(3) = \gamma_0 + 3\gamma_1 + 9\gamma_2 + 27\gamma_3 \\
\cdot\cdot \;\; & \cdots\cdot \;\; \cdot\cdot \;\; \cdots \;\; \cdots \;\; \cdots\cdot \\
\beta_n &= f(n) = \gamma_0 + n\gamma_1 + n^2\gamma_2 + n^3\gamma_3
\end{aligned}
\tag{8.99}
$$

Putting (8.99) in (8.98) and simplifying, we obtain

$$\begin{aligned} Y_t = \alpha &+ \gamma_0(X_t + X_{t-1} + \cdots + X_{t-n}) \\ &+ \gamma_1(X_{t-1} + 2X_{t-2} + 3X_{t-3} + \cdots + nX_{t-n}) \\ &+ \gamma_2(X_{t-1} + 4X_{t-2} + 9X_{t-3} + \cdots + n^2X_{t-n}) \\ &+ \gamma_3(X_{t-1} + 8X_{t-2} + 27X_{t-3} + \cdots + n^3X_{t-n}) \end{aligned} \tag{8.100}$$

Equating Zs to the linear combinations of Xs:

$$\begin{aligned} Z_0 &= X_t + X_{t-1} + \cdots + X_{t-n} \\ Z_1 &= X_{t-1} + 2X_{t-2} + \cdots + nX_{t-n} \\ Z_2 &= X_{t-1} + 4X_{t-2} + \cdots + n^2X_{t-n} \\ Z_3 &= X_{t-1} + 8X_{t-2} + \cdots + n^3X_{t-n} \end{aligned} \tag{8.101}$$

we have (8.100) reproduced as

$$Y_t = \alpha + \gamma_0 Z_0 + \gamma_1 Z_1 + \gamma_2 Z_2 + \gamma_3 Z_3 \tag{8.102}$$

Clearly the Zs are the regressors. Regressing Y on the Zs will yield estimates of α and the γs. The estimated γs will then yield the estimated βs via (8.99).

For statistical inference, the sampling variances (covariances) of the $\hat{\beta}$s can be obtained from those of the $\hat{\gamma}$s ("^" indicating estimates). Let us define the matrix V_3 corresponding to the matrix of coefficients of (8.99):

$$V_3 = \begin{bmatrix} 1 & 0 & 0 & 0 \\ 1 & 1 & 1 & 1 \\ 1 & 2 & 4 & 8 \\ 1 & 3 & 9 & 27 \\ \cdots & \cdots & \cdots & \cdots \\ 1 & n & n^2 & n^3 \end{bmatrix}$$

(8.99), in matrix form, becomes:

$$\boldsymbol{\beta} = V_3\, \boldsymbol{\gamma} \tag{8.103}$$

where $\boldsymbol{\beta}$ is an $(n + 1)$ element and $\boldsymbol{\gamma}$ a three-element column vector. From (8.103), it is clear that

$$\hat{\boldsymbol{\beta}} = V_3\, \hat{\boldsymbol{\gamma}}$$

Our initial equation (8.98) is recast, using (8.103), in vector and matrix notation as follows, where $\mathrm{i} = [1\ 1\ \cdots\ 1]'$:

$$\begin{aligned} \mathbf{Y} &= \mathbf{i}\,\alpha + X\,\boldsymbol{\beta} + \boldsymbol{\epsilon} \\ &= \mathbf{i}\,\alpha + X\,V_3\,\boldsymbol{\gamma} + \boldsymbol{\epsilon} \end{aligned} \tag{8.104}$$

Regressing $\mathbf{Y}$ on $[\mathbf{i}\ X\ V_3]$, where $X\ V_3$ are the $\mathbf{Z}$-regressors shown in (8.101), we obtain the OLS estimated coefficients:

$$\begin{bmatrix} \hat{\alpha} \\ \hat{\boldsymbol{\gamma}} \end{bmatrix} = \begin{bmatrix} \mathbf{i}'\mathbf{i} & \mathbf{i}'XV_3 \\ V_3'X'\mathbf{i} & V_3'X'XV_3 \end{bmatrix}^{-1} \begin{bmatrix} \mathbf{i}'\mathbf{Y} \\ V_3'X'\mathbf{Y} \end{bmatrix} \tag{8.105}$$

The variance–covariance matrix of $\hat{\boldsymbol{\gamma}}$ is

$$\mathrm{V}(\hat{\boldsymbol{\gamma}}) = \sigma_\epsilon^2 \, [V_3'X'XV_3 - (1/T)V_3'X'\mathbf{i}\mathbf{i}'XV_3]^{-1} \tag{8.106}$$

where we have used σ_ϵ^2 for the variance of $\boldsymbol{\epsilon}$, and temporarily used T for the sample size. From $\hat{\boldsymbol{\beta}} = V_3\, \hat{\boldsymbol{\gamma}}$, we have

$$\mathrm{E}(\hat{\boldsymbol{\beta}}) = V_3\mathrm{E}(\hat{\boldsymbol{\gamma}}) = V_3\boldsymbol{\gamma} = \boldsymbol{\beta}$$

and

$$\mathrm{V}(\hat{\boldsymbol{\beta}}) = V_3\, \mathrm{V}(\hat{\boldsymbol{\gamma}})\, V_3' \tag{8.107}$$

(8.107) is determined using $\mathrm{V}(\hat{\boldsymbol{\gamma}})$ from (8.106).

The scheme presented above may be used to determine the degree of the polynomial $f(l)$, given that we know the maximum period of the lag. But any procedure based on it will be computationally very difficult and lengthy. A simpler and less lengthy approach involves testing the constraints on the coefficients of the approximating polynomial. This method follows.

Suppose that we have obtained the unconstrained OLS estimates of (8.98) for a given value of n. Once the degree of the polynomial has been decided upon, the Almon estimators are then derived by the method of constrained least squares (see Chapter 6). Let us begin again with a third-degree polynomial approximation of β_i:

$$\beta_i = \gamma_0 + \gamma_1 l + \gamma_2 l^2 + \gamma_3 l^3$$

Since this is a third-degree polynomial, differencing it once will lead to a second-degree polynomial, differencing it twice and three times will lead to a first-degree polynomial and zero-degree polynomial (which is a constant), respectively. Thus, differencing it four times will lead to a zero value. That is

$$\Delta^4\, \beta_i = 0 \tag{8.108}$$

where Δ is the sign of difference. Now,

$$\begin{aligned} \Delta\beta_i &= \beta_i - \beta_{i-1} \\ \Delta^2\beta_i &= \Delta(\Delta\beta_i) \\ &= \Delta\beta_i - \Delta\beta_{i-1} \\ &= \beta_i - 2\beta_{i-1} + \beta_{i-2} \end{aligned}$$

Similarly,

$$\begin{aligned}\Delta^3\beta_i &= \beta_i - 3\beta_{i-1} + 3\beta_{i-2} - \beta_{i-3} \\ \Delta^4\beta_i &= \beta_i - 4\beta_{i-1} + 6\beta_{i-2} - 4\beta_{i-3} + \beta_{i-4}\end{aligned} \tag{8.109}$$

(8.109), using (8.108), becomes

$$\Delta^4\beta_i = \beta_i - 4\beta_{i-1} + 6\beta_{i-2} - 4\beta_{i-3} + \beta_{i-4} = 0 \qquad (i = 4, 5, 6, \ldots, n) \tag{8.110}$$

These are the restrictions on the polynomial coefficients. However, α is free of any restriction. Thus, the constraints represented by (8.110) are expressed in a compact form as:

$$\boldsymbol{R_3}\begin{bmatrix}\alpha \\ \boldsymbol{\beta}\end{bmatrix} = 0 \tag{8.111}$$

where α is a scalar and $\boldsymbol{\beta}$ a vector, and $\boldsymbol{R_3}$ is:

$$\boldsymbol{R_3} = \begin{bmatrix} 0 & 1 & -4 & 6 & -4 & 1 & 0 & \cdot\cdot & 0 \\ 0 & 0 & 1 & -4 & 6 & -4 & 1 & \cdot\cdot & 0 \\ \vdots & \vdots & \vdots & \vdots & \vdots & \vdots & \vdots & \vdots\,\vdots & \vdots \\ \vdots & \vdots & \vdots & \vdots & \vdots & \vdots & \vdots & \vdots\,\vdots & \vdots \\ 0 & 0 & 0 & 0 & 0 & 0 & 0 & \cdot\cdot & 1 \end{bmatrix} \tag{8.112}$$

$\boldsymbol{R_3}$ is of size $(n - 3) \times (n + 2)$. It can be easily seen that when the approximating polynomial is of degree 2, there will be $n - 2$ linear constraints:

$$\boldsymbol{R_2}\begin{bmatrix}\alpha \\ \boldsymbol{\beta}\end{bmatrix} = 0 \tag{8.113}$$

where the restriction matrix $\boldsymbol{R_2}$ of size $(n - 2) \times (n + 2)$ is

$$\boldsymbol{R_2} = \begin{bmatrix} 0 & -1 & 3 & -3 & 1 & 0 & \cdot\cdot & 0 \\ 0 & 0 & -1 & 3 & -3 & 1 & \cdot\cdot & 0 \\ \vdots & \vdots & \vdots & \vdots & \vdots & \vdots & \vdots\,\vdots & \vdots \\ \vdots & \vdots & \vdots & \vdots & \vdots & \vdots & \vdots\,\vdots & \vdots \\ 0 & \cdot\cdot & \cdot\cdot & \cdot\cdot & \cdot\cdot & \cdot\cdot & \cdot\cdot & 1 \end{bmatrix} \tag{8.114}$$

There is a simple rule to construct the nonzero elements of the rows of the $\boldsymbol{R}$ matrix. In a general case when the degree of the polynomial is s, the nonzero elements of a row of $\boldsymbol{R_s}$ are given by the coefficients of the increasing powers of δ in the expansion of the polynomial $(1 - \delta)^{s+1}$.

To summarize, start initially with a fairly large degree, for example, the fourth. Set up the corresponding $\boldsymbol{R_4}$ matrix and test the null hypothesis:

$$\boldsymbol{R_4}\begin{bmatrix}\alpha \\ \boldsymbol{\beta}\end{bmatrix} = 0$$

For this, use the F statistic given in equation (6.64) of Chapter 6 on the basis of the results of the unconstrained OLS applied to (8.98). The degrees of freedom of F will be $(n - s, T - n - 2)$, in which s is the degree of the polynomial used. In case the null hypothesis cannot be accepted, try a higher degree of the polynomial; if, on the other hand, it is accepted, try a lower degree. Reset the linear restriction anew and keep repeating the procedure until the null hypothesis has to be rejected at a certain degree. The next higher degree is then the appropriate degree for the approximating polynomial.[23]

8.7.6 Applied Studies on Almon Lags

There have been innumerable applications of Almon's lag technique to economic problems, too many to mention, let alone, discuss here. Still we would like to mention, very briefly, a sample of four studies: Agarwala and Drinkwater (1972), Cargill and Meyer (1978), Christofides, Swidinsky, and Wilton (1980a), and Christofides and Wilton (1983) to show how extensive and intensive these applications may be.

The Agarwala and Drinkwater study captures the influence on consumption of changing population composition measured by shift parameters. Out of the several socioeconomic factors causing the shift, married female participation in the work force is singled out for special effect. In particular, this effect is visible in the following formulation of the marginal propensity to consume:

$$\mathrm{MPC}_{jt} = \alpha_j + \beta_j \,\mathrm{M}_t\, \mathrm{POP_{FAM}/POP} = \alpha_j \cdot \mathrm{AD}_{jt} \tag{8.115}$$

where

$$\begin{aligned} \mathrm{MPC}_{jt} &= \text{marginal propensity to consume item } j \text{ at time } t \\ \mathrm{M}_t &= \text{proportion of families with working wives at time } t \\ \mathrm{POP_{FAM}/POP} &= \text{population in families/total population} \\ \mathrm{AD}_{jt} &= (1 + (\beta_j/\alpha_j)\mathrm{M}_t\, \mathrm{POP_{FAM}/POP}) \end{aligned} \tag{8.116}$$

Clearly, the MPC is not constant. It depends on the participation rate of married women and the population in families. Finally the consumption function is formulated as:

$$(\mathrm{C}_j/\mathrm{POP})_t = \delta_j + \alpha_j \sum_{0}^{n_1} w_{ij}(\mathrm{AD}_j\ \mathrm{YD/POP})_{t-\mathrm{i}} + \gamma_j \sum_{0}^{n_2} \lambda_{ij}(P_j/\mathrm{P})_{t-i} \tag{8.117}$$

where:

$$\begin{aligned} \mathrm{C}_j &= \text{time series figures for consumer's expenditure on item } j \\ \mathrm{YD} &= \text{real disposable income} \\ \mathrm{P}_j/\mathrm{P} &= \text{relative price on item } j \end{aligned} \tag{8.118}$$

[23] The procedure for determining the maximum length of the lag might still be the same as discussed before (for the Lagrangean polynomial).

In other words, per capita consumption is taken to be a distributed lag function of female participation rates in the work force (that determine the disposable income), and, separately, relative prices. It is these lags that are estimated by the Almon technique. However, the final results indicate only a small quantitative effect of changes in female participation rates on the MPC. This points to the need for more research on shifting parameters in this kind of study.

The Cargill and Meyer study is on the time varying response of income to changes in monetary and fiscal policy. They use the following multivariate Taylor series expansion (with remainder R_n) version of a continuous parameter variation[24] model $\beta(\tau, t)$ formulated as:

$$\beta(\tau, t) = \sum_{k=0}^{n} \sum_{j=0}^{k} \alpha_{kj}\, \tau^j\, t^{k-j} + R_n \tag{8.119}$$

where the βs are the coefficients of the income determination model taken to be a mix of the Keynesian theory of income and quantity theory of money and the αs are the response weights. This response function naturally contains Almon's lag (as evident from the term involving τ^j) and the no-distributed-lag constant coefficient (the same constant coefficient or fixed parameter case as we have considered so far) models as special cases. The author fits both constant coefficient and selected time varying models for income and other variables such as consumption, investment, and short and long term corporate bond sales. To cut a long story short, the empirical results indicate that the hypothesis of time independent marginal response could not be sustained statistically.

The Christofides and others study develops and tests models of wage spillovers in Canada using a microdata base built from collective bargaining wage contracts signed between 1966 and October 1975 (the beginning of voluntary wage controls in Canada). They use three assumptions as to the way weights are attached to past wage settlements. Of particular significance here is the one that uses time delay polynomial weights. According to this, the following quadratic time polynomial is used to determine these weights:

$$\nu_j = 1 - (\theta_1 d_j + \theta_2 d_j^2) \tag{8.120}$$

in which ν_j is the weight assigned to the jth last wage settlement within the reference group, and d_j the number of months that have elapsed since the jth last settlement.

The time decay polynomial spillover model specifies the following variables:

$$\dot{W}^s = \sum_{j=1}^{J} \nu_j \underline{\dot{W}_j^s}/J = \sum_{j=1}^{J} \underline{\dot{W}_j^s}/J - \theta_1 \sum_{j=1}^{J} \mathrm{d}_j \underline{\dot{W}_j^s}/j - \theta_2 \sum_{j=1}^{J} d_j^2 \underline{\dot{W}_j^s} \tag{8.121}$$

in which $\underline{\dot{W}_j^s}$ is the jth last settlement within the reference set, and J the number

[24] Even though we have not yet dealt with varying coefficient models, this will serve to illustrate such models. See Chapter 10 for such models.

of past settlements which minimizes the regression standard error of estimate. The method is to add, in historical reverse order, past settlements until the regression standard error of estimate starts to go up. At that point, any settlement farther distant in time would not contain any meaningful spillover effects, and therefore could be neglected.

The above equation is a variation of the Almon model in the sense that the lag points are not fixed but are based on variable time intervals.

Without going into the other aspects of this large study, we like to point out that its most important finding is to statistically establish the existence of wage spillovers. However, this depends on the characteristics of the reference group. The one such characteristic that receives the most pronounced statistical support in this study is industry classification. And the "more narrowly defined the industry classification, the sharper the statistical results".

The last study is the one by Christofides and Wilton. This study is concerned with the factors influencing wage-contract length and confirms the already existing theoretical conclusions based on Canadian data that inflation uncertainty and transaction costs are two very important determinants of wage-contract length.

For inflation uncertainty, a proxy is used:

$$\dot{P}_t = b_0 + b_1\dot{P}_{t-1} + b_2\dot{P}_{t-2} + \cdots + b_N\dot{P}_{t-N} + V_t \tag{8.122}$$

where $\dot{P}_t$ is the change in price at time t, similarly the other lagged price change variables, and V_t the error. The Almon method is employed with a lag length of 11 quarters, a polynomial of degree three, and distributed lag weights not constrained to add up to unity. The square of the standard error of estimate from these sliding regressions is used as a measure of the expected inflation in corresponding quarters.

8.7.7 Lagged Model Estimation Using Time Series Methods

We introduced a time series representation of economic models before (see Section 8.7.1). That was given by

$$\begin{aligned} Y_t &= (\beta_0 + \beta_1\delta + \cdots + \beta_r\delta^r)X_t + \epsilon_t \\ &= D(\delta)X_t + \epsilon_t \end{aligned} \tag{8.123}$$

where δ is the lag operator and

$$D(\delta) = \beta_0 + \beta_1\delta + \cdots + \beta_r\delta^r \tag{8.124}$$

But if there are reasons to believe that the distributed lags persist in both the X and Y series of the following kinds:

$$A(\delta) = 1 - \alpha_1\delta - \cdots - \alpha_t\delta^t \tag{8.125}$$

$$C(\delta) = \gamma_0 + \gamma_1\delta + \cdots + \gamma_2\delta^s \tag{8.126}$$

where

$$t + s < r$$

then the fundamental relation between Y and X is

$$A(\delta)Y_t = C(\delta)X_t + \nu_t$$

or,

$$Y_t = [C(\delta)/A(\delta)]X_t + \nu_t/A(\delta) \tag{8.127}$$

In the above, clearly

$$A(\delta)\epsilon_t = \nu_t \tag{8.128}$$

Thus, comparing (8.124) and (8.127),

$$D(\delta) = C(\delta)/A(\delta) \tag{8.129}$$

If in (8.123) we put $Y_t - Y_0$ instead of Y_t alone, where Y_0 is constant, then the resulting equation would be

$$Y_t = Y_0 + \{C(\delta)/A(\delta)\}X_t + \epsilon_t \tag{8.130}$$

This is called a transfer function.

In estimating (8.130) above, there are four characteristics which would make the time series method distinctly different from the conventional methods discussed in Sections (8.7.1–8.7.6). First, both the input X_t and the output Y_t series should be sufficiently differenced before both series would become stationary. Second, empirical data must determine the orders of the polynomials $C(\delta)$ and $A(\delta)$ before deciding on any preassigned paths among their coefficients. Third, the error term should be treated generally, not just as only an AR or an MA process. Fourth, the development of the transfer function approach is still basically a single-input one. Extensions to more inputs, each with its appropriate lags, are still very diverse, and would require a greater consensus among theoreticians than available at present before the results could be effectively used.

In what follows, we will cover these points somewhat elaborately.

8.7.8 Analysis of Stationary Stochastic Processes

Consider a stochastic process defined as a family of random variables $\{\epsilon_t\}$ where $t = \ldots, -2, -1, 0, 1, 2, \ldots$ is the time subscript such that for every finite subset of t, for instance, $t_1, \ldots, t_n$, a joint probability distribution for the random variables $\epsilon_{t_1}, \ldots, \epsilon_{t_n}$ is defined. If, in addition, the joint probability distributions are invariant for translations along the time axis, that is the distribution of the subset over $t_1, \ldots, t_n$: $\epsilon_{t_1}, \ldots, \epsilon_{t_n}$ is the same as the distribution of another subset τ periods hence: $\epsilon_{t_1+\tau}, \ldots, \epsilon_{t_n+\tau}$, for $\tau = \ldots, -2, -1, 0, 1, 2, \ldots,$ then the stochastic process is said to be stationary. If ϵ_t is a white noise: N(0,

σ_ϵ^2), then the mean, variance, covariance, and autocorrelation ρ_r of order r of the ϵ process are:

$$\begin{aligned} E(\epsilon_t) &= 0 \qquad \text{for all } t \\ V(\epsilon_t) &= \sigma_\epsilon^2 \qquad \text{for all } t \\ \text{cov}(\epsilon_t, \epsilon_{t+r}) &= \gamma_r = 0 \qquad \text{for all } t,\ r \neq 0 \\ \rho_r &= \gamma_r/\gamma_0 = \begin{cases} 1 & \text{for } r = 0 \\ 0 & \text{for } r \neq 0 \end{cases} \end{aligned} \tag{8.131}$$

That is, the mean, variance, and covariance (autocorrelation coefficients) are constant, finite, and independent of time. Such a series is weakly stationary because the time subset is narrowly defined. On the other hand, by defining $\{\epsilon_t\}$ over wider but finite time subsets and observing that distributions over such subsets will be multivariate normal, specified fully by the first- and second-order moments, we will have $\{\epsilon_t\}$ strictly stationary.

8.7.9 Autoregressive Processes: ARMA and ARIMA Schemes and Their Estimation

Suppose that the Xs arise from an AR(1) process of the following description:

$$X_t = \theta X_{t-1} + \epsilon_t \qquad \epsilon_t \sim N(0, \sigma_\epsilon^2) \tag{8.132}$$

Equivalently this becomes:

$$(1 - \theta\delta)X_t = \phi(\delta)X_t = \epsilon_t \tag{8.133}$$

That is,

$$X_t = (1 - \theta\delta)^{-1}\epsilon_t = \epsilon_t + \theta\epsilon_{t-1} + \theta^2\epsilon_{t-2} + \dots \tag{8.134}$$

This same form was analyzed before, in Chapter 7, Section 7.3.2. Switching now to the X series, we have its mean, variance and autocorrelation function calculated as

$$\begin{aligned} E(X_t) &= 0 \qquad \text{for all } t \\ V(X_t) &= \sigma_\epsilon^2/(1 - \theta^2) \qquad |\,\theta\,| < 1 \\ \text{corr}(X_t, X_{t-r}) &= \rho^r = \theta^r \end{aligned} \tag{8.135}$$

These results indicate that the AR(1) process of (8.133) is stationary if $|\,\theta\,| < 1$. Since $\phi(\delta) = 1 - \theta\delta$, $|\,\theta\,| < 1$ implies that the root $|\,\delta\,|$ of $\phi(\delta) = 0$ (implying $\delta = 1/\theta$) has to be larger than unity. This is usually referred to as the root of $\phi(\delta)$ lying outside the unit circle.[25]

[25] Obviously for $|\,\theta\,| > 1$, the root of $\phi(\delta) = 0$ would lie outside the unit circle, and the AR process would explode. For $|\,\theta\,| = 1$, we have a random walk: $X_t = X_{t-1} + \epsilon_t$, which implies $V(X_t)$ will be explosive. However, changing this to the first difference in X_t, that is $\Delta X_t = \epsilon_t$, we would be back to a stationary series.

Extending the order of the autoregressive process to 2, we can write

$$X_t = \theta_1 X_{t-1} + \theta_2 X_{t-2} + \epsilon_t \tag{8.136}$$

or, equivalently,

$$\phi(\delta)X_t = \epsilon_t \qquad \phi(\delta) = 1 - \theta_1\delta - \theta_2\delta^2 \tag{8.137}$$

from which, after some algebraic manipulations, it will follow that:

$$X_t = l(\epsilon_t + f_1\epsilon_{t-1} + f_1^2\epsilon_{t-2} + \ldots) + (1 - l)(\epsilon_t + f_2\epsilon_{t-1} + f_2^2\epsilon_{t-2} + \ldots) \tag{8.138}$$

where

$$\begin{aligned} \phi(\delta) &= (1 - f_1\delta)(1 - f_2\delta); \\ 1/\{(1 - f_1\delta)(1 - f_2\delta)\} &= l/(1 - f_1\delta) + (1 - l)/(1 - f_2\delta) \end{aligned} \tag{8.139}$$

As before, we can show that $V(X_t)$ will be finite and constant, provided $| f_1 | <$ 1 and $| f_2 | < 1$, that is the roots of $\phi(\delta) = 0$ lie outside the unit circle. In terms of θ_1 and θ_2, this means:[26]

$$| \theta_2 | < 1$$

$$\theta_2 + \theta_1 < 1$$

$$\theta_2 - \theta_1 < 1$$

Further extensions of the above derivations are possible. First, $\phi(\delta)$ may be a polynomial of order t. Second, depending on the number, say r, of unit roots of $\phi(\delta) = 0$ the X_t series may have to be differenced as many times for the sake of stationarity. Third, it is possible that in a general situation ϵ_t, like the X_t series, may be subject to a generating process. The usual process assigned to disturbances is the moving average process. Assume that this process, denoted symbolically as MA(s), has an order s. All three considerations are exhibited in the following generalized version of equation (8.139):

$$\phi(\delta)(1 - \delta)^d X_t = \psi(\delta)\epsilon_t \tag{8.140}$$

where $\phi(\delta)$ defined before is of order p, $(1 - \delta)X_t$ is ΔX_t meaning $(1 - \delta)^d X_t$ is $\Delta^d X_t$, that is, X_t is differenced d times. This implies further that the differenced series has to be summed or integrated to reproduce the original series. Note also that $\psi(\delta)$ is a finite MA operator given by:

$$\psi(\delta) = 1 - \psi_1\delta - \psi_2\delta^2 - \cdots - \psi_q\delta^q \tag{8.141}$$

so that $\psi(\delta)\epsilon_t$ is stationary.[27] Because of these characteristics, the scheme goes

[26] For a simple case, by taking $\theta_1 = \theta_2 = 1$ and producing the random walk $X_t = X_{t-1} + X_{t-2} + \epsilon_t$, we can figure out that second differencing the random walk series generates a stationary series, whereas the original series is not stationary.

[27] We did not model ϵ_t before because our underlying assumption was that ϵ_t was already stationary.

by the name of autoregressive, integrated, moving average, in short, ARIMA (p, d, q) schemes, with p, d, and q the order of the autoregressive polynomial, the degree of differencing, and the order of the MA polynomial respectively. A time series that becomes stationary after differencing it r times is sometimes called homogeneous nonstationary of degree r. Such a series is not explosive, but may exhibit drift or short-run growth tendencies, with irregular oscillations. An ARIMA (p, d, q) in terms of X_t is an ARMA (p, q) in terms of the x_t series,[28] where x_t is $(1 - \delta)^d X_t$.

While identifying an ARIMA model, it is specified for the data generating process based on the estimated autocorrelations and partial autocorrelations. Possible work in this area may be divided into four classes:

(1) If autocorrelations do not die out completely, even though they taper off, this is a sign of nonstationarity and differencing (in most cases not more than once or twice) is required. An ARMA model of the differenced series is thus identified.

(2) To determine the order of the MA process, if autocorrelations of order k become zero, for all $k > q$, and the partial autocorrelations taper off, then the underlying MA process is an MA(q).

(3) For an AR process, if partial autocorrelations of order k become zero, for $k > t$, and the autocorrelations taper off, then we have an AR(p) process before us.

(4) If the cut-off points (that is, zero values) of neither the autocorrelations nor the partial autocorrelations are available, still an ARMA model may be appropriate. The degrees of the AR and MA processes have to be ascertained from the underlying autocorrelation and partial autocorrelation patterns.

After identification, comes the problem of estimation. In the Box–Jenkins estimation method, initial estimates of the θ and ψ parameters are obtained, which are then fed into the subsequent iterations of a nonlinear iterative estimation technique. Then the fitted model is subjected to a number of diagnostic checks.

Let us return to the problem of the transfer function estimation in which the

[28] Extensive use of ARIMA and ARMA models in monetary economic contexts has been made by Makin (1982), pp. 126–134, and pp. 374–384. These models basically show the measurements of money surprises and go on to lead to some outstanding conclusions. From one of these we learn that in the presence of anticipated money, unanticipated money has no additional explanatory power in equations describing the growth of employment and real output.

For more complicated use of ARIMA models, see Riddell and Smith (1982). They use ARIMA $[(p, d, q)\ (P, D, Q)_s]$ defined as:

$$(1 - \delta)^d(1 - \delta^s)^D(1 - \phi_1\theta - \phi_2\theta^2 - \cdots - \phi_p\theta^p)(1 - \Phi_1\theta^s - \cdots - \Phi_p\theta^{PS})\text{CPI}_t$$
$$= (1 - \psi_1\theta - \cdots - \psi_q\theta^q)(1 - \Psi_1\theta^S - \cdots - \Psi_Q\theta^{QS})\epsilon_t$$

where CPI is consumer price index, and ϵ_t is white noise with variance σ^2. This device is used to measure Canadian inflationary expectation based on realistic assumptions about the information available to those forming expectations. This estimate is then used to study the factors determining wage changes in Canada during the 1967–1981 period.

univariate time series modeling method just now described may be applied to advantage. Assume that the Y and X series have been appropriately differenced to bring about stationarity in each series and that the new series are represented by their lower case letters y and x. Also assume that there is a delay in the amount of $b \geq 0$ in the propagation of any effect from x to y. Thus, the transfer function (8.130) may be restated as

$$A(\delta)y_t = C(\delta)x_{t-b} + v_t$$

or

$$y_t = D(\delta)x_{t-b} + \epsilon_t \tag{8.142}$$

This transfer function is of order (t, s, b). Therefore its estimation involves the determination of orders t, s, and b, and the parameters αs and γs or βs.

In the Box–Jenkins method, we begin with the computation of covariances between x and y and the covariances of the x series. These lead to a set of simultaneous equations, the solutions of which provide estimates of the βs. At this point, we study the relationship between the pattern of the estimated β coefficients and the theoretical patterns of these coefficients for various values of t, s, and b. From this, initial guestimates of these orders are made. The βs would also lead to some rough values of the α and the γ coefficients, before a full fledged iterative estimation is to be performed. Concurrently, we monitor the relation between the estimation of the transfer function parameters and the representation of the error term by an ARIMA model. The reason is that any differencing needed generally might produce a very complex, if not intractable, transformed error if the original error is complex. With white noise errors to begin with, we know we would end up with MA errors after differencing. But this represents only a simple example of a tractable kind. More frequently we have examples of intractable kinds.

Example: An ARMA(1,1) estimation. Assume that $\Delta^d Y_t = Z_t$, where Z_t is stationary. In addition, take an ARMA(1,1) process which has an AR(1) as well as an MA(1) process underlying it. Then (8.140)) will first change to

$$\phi(\delta)\Delta^d Y_t = \phi(\delta)Z_t = \psi(\delta)\epsilon_t$$

which will then reduce to

$$\epsilon_t = \frac{1 - \theta_1\delta}{1 - \psi_1\delta} Z_t \tag{8.143}$$

where θ_1 and ψ_1 are the only parameters of the AR(1) and MA(1) process respectively. Clearly, (8.143) will be nonlinear in ψ_1. However, we can use a Taylor series expansion to approximate it around some initial guesses $\overline{\theta}_1$ and $\overline{\psi}_1$ of θ_1 and ψ_1, respectively. This is done by first computing and evaluating the first derivatives of ϵ_t with respect to θ_1 and ψ_1 at that initial point:

$$\dot{\epsilon}_{1t} = \left.\frac{\partial \epsilon_t}{\partial \theta_1}\right|_{\bar{\theta}_1, \bar{\psi}_1} = -\frac{\delta}{1 - \overline{\psi}_1\delta} Z_t \tag{8.144}$$

$$\dot{\epsilon}_{2t} = \left.\frac{\partial \epsilon_t}{\partial \theta_1}\right|_{\bar{\theta}_1, \bar{\psi}_1} = -\frac{\delta(1 - \bar{\theta}_1 \delta)}{(1 - \bar{\psi}_1 \delta)^2} Z_t \tag{8.145}$$

Since δ is the lag operator, we have from (8.144) and (8.145)

$$\dot{\epsilon}_{1t} = \bar{\psi}_1 \, \dot{\epsilon}_{1(t-1)} - Z_{t-1} \tag{8.146}$$

$$\dot{\epsilon}_{2t} = 2\bar{\psi}_1 \, \dot{\epsilon}_{2(t-1)} - \bar{\psi}_1^2 \, \dot{\epsilon}_{2(t-2)} + Z_{t-1} - \bar{\theta}_1 \, Z_{t-2} \tag{8.147}$$

We can use (8.146) and (8.147) to construct two numerical time series for $\dot{\epsilon}_{1t}$ and $\dot{\epsilon}_{2t}$ over $t = 1$ to $t = n$ (these can be used as data packages for linear regressions). With respect to $\dot{\epsilon}_{1t}$, assume $Z_0 = \dot{\epsilon}_{10} = 0$. Then solve (8.146) sequentially to obtain the time series observations for $\dot{\epsilon}_{1t}$. For instance, the first, second, third, . . . values of $\dot{\epsilon}_{1t}$ are

$$\begin{aligned} \dot{\epsilon}_{11} &= 0 \\ \dot{\epsilon}_{12} &= -Z_1 \\ \dot{\epsilon}_{13} &= \bar{\psi}_1 \, Z_1 - Z_2 \end{aligned} \tag{8.148}$$

Similarly, with respect to (8.147), set

$$\dot{\epsilon}_{21} = \dot{\epsilon}_{20} = Z_0 = Z_{-1} = 0 \tag{8.149}$$

Then the first, second, third, . . . values of $\dot{\epsilon}_{2t}$ will be

$$\begin{aligned} \dot{\epsilon}_{21} &= 0 \\ \dot{\epsilon}_{22} &= Z_1 \\ \dot{\epsilon}_{23} &= 2\bar{\psi}_1 \, Z_1 + Z_2 - \bar{\theta}_1 \, Z_1 \\ \vdots \quad & \quad \vdots \quad \vdots \qquad \vdots \qquad \vdots \quad \vdots \end{aligned} \tag{8.150}$$

Also, we require a series of ϵ_{0t}, $t = 1, 2, \ldots, n$, where ϵ_{0t} is determined by Z_t according to

$$\epsilon_{0t} = \frac{1 - \bar{\theta}_1 \delta}{1 - \bar{\psi}_1 \delta} Z_t \tag{8.151}$$

The other factors that influence the values of ϵ_{0t}, which is a series of residuals, are the initial values $\bar{\theta}_1$ and $\bar{\psi}_1$ of θ_1 and ψ_1, respectively.

Assembling (8.151), (8.144), and (8.145), we have the following Taylor expansion of (8.143), where (8.143) gives a function, say $f(\theta_1, \psi_1)$, of 2 variables θ_1 and ψ_1:

$$\begin{aligned} \epsilon_t &\approx f(\theta_1, \psi_1) \\ &\approx f(\theta_1, \psi_1)\Big|_{\bar{\theta}_1, \bar{\psi}_1} + (\theta_1 - \bar{\theta}_1) \left.\frac{\delta f}{\delta \theta_1}\right|_{\bar{\theta}_1, \bar{\psi}_1} + (\psi_1 - \bar{\psi}_1) \left.\frac{\delta f}{\delta \psi_1}\right|_{\bar{\theta}_1, \bar{\psi}_1} \\ &\approx \epsilon_{0t} + (\theta_1 - \bar{\theta}_1) \, \dot{\epsilon}_{1t} + (\psi_1 - \bar{\psi}_1) \, \dot{\epsilon}_{2t} \end{aligned} \tag{8.152}$$

The above is an approximate representation since we have ignored terms involving higher than the first derivatives of f ($= f(\theta_1, \psi_1)$) with respect to θ_1 and ψ_1. Thus, (8.152) is rewritten as

$$\epsilon_{0t} - \bar{\theta}_1 \dot{\epsilon}_{1t} - \bar{\psi}_1 \dot{\epsilon}_{2t} = -\theta_1 \epsilon_{1t} - \psi_1 \epsilon_{2t} + \epsilon_t \tag{8.153}$$

This equation is a linear regression equation and OLS applied to it will yield the estimates of θ_1 and ψ_1. If these estimates are different from their initial guesses $\bar{\theta}_1$ and $\bar{\psi}_1$, then they are used as new first estimates and the previous procedure is repeated to derive new second estimates of θ_1 and ψ_1, and so on. It is possible that the process will converge in a finite number of iterations. But there is no guarantee that it will do so, nor is it sure that convergence will ever take place. Should convergence falter, it may be worthwhile to start all over again with a radically different initial guess of the parameters.

8.7.10 Prewhitening Mechanism

For the sake of higher efficiency, the Box–Jenkins method recommends what is known as the prewhitening of the input series, or the prewhitening of both the input and output series. Let us describe the method of single prewhitening, before going on to the method of double prewhitening.

Let us fit an ARIMA model to the x_t series, the scheme being

$$\Phi_x(\delta)x_t = \zeta_x(\delta)\xi_t \tag{8.154}$$

where ξ_t is an approximate white noise series. The method of prewhitening consists of changing the x_t of the model

$$y_t = D(\delta)x_t + \epsilon_t \tag{8.155}$$

to the approximate white noise ξ_t without changing its coefficient $D(\delta)$. This suggests multiplying this model throughout by the factor $\zeta_x^{-1}(\delta)\Phi_x(\delta)$ to get

$$y_t^* = D(\delta)\xi_t + \nu_t \tag{8.156}$$

where

$$y_t^* = \zeta_x^{-1}(\delta)\Phi_x(\delta)y_t; \qquad \nu_t = \zeta_x^{-1}(\delta)\Phi_x(\delta)\epsilon_t \tag{8.157}$$

The fact that x_t of the original equation is replaced by ξ_t of the transformed equation makes the task of estimating the βs of $D(\delta)$ simpler because the ξs have approximately zero autocovariances. This leads to a set of roughly unrelated equations, rather than simultaneous equations, to be solved which is obviously easier. The operator $\zeta_x^{-1}(\delta)\Phi_x(\delta)$ is called a filter, and, in this example, the same filter "purifies" both the input and output series.

For double prewhitening, consider fitting a separate ARMA model to each series given by

$$\hat{\Phi}_y(\delta)y_t = \hat{\zeta}_y(\delta)\hat{\xi}_{yt}$$

and (8.158)

$$\hat{\Phi}_x(\delta)x_t = \hat{\zeta}_x(\delta)\hat{\xi}_{xt}$$

where the estimated residuals $\hat{\xi}_{yt}$ and $\hat{\xi}_{xt}$ are approximate white noise series. The filter for y_t is $\hat{\zeta}_y^{-1}(\delta)\hat{\Phi}_y(\delta)$ leading to $\hat{\xi}_{yt}$, and that for x_t is $\hat{\zeta}_x^{-1}(\delta)\hat{\Phi}_x(\delta)$ leading to $\hat{\xi}_{xt}$.

The method may be used to indicate the direction of causation between the y and x series: y to x, *or* x to y, or y to x, *and* vice versa. This is done by a study of cross correlations between the two residual series, $\hat{\xi}_{yt}$ and $\hat{\xi}_{xt}$, with positive and negative lags. Assuming, for instance, x affects y, a transfer function model of the following form may be postulated:

$$\hat{\xi}_{yt} = \Delta(\delta)\hat{\xi}_{xt} + \text{error} \tag{8.159}$$

in which $\Delta(\delta)$, obviously different from $D(\delta)$ of the original transfer function model between y and x, is given by

$$\Delta(\delta) = \tau_0 + \tau_1\delta + \tau_2\delta^2 + \ldots \tag{8.160}$$

Thus, by substituting in (8.159) for $\hat{\xi}_{yt}$ and $\hat{\xi}_{xt}$ from (8.158) and recasting (8.159) in the form of a transfer function relation between y and x, we get:

$$y_t = [\hat{\zeta}_y(\delta)\hat{\Phi}_y^{-1}(\delta)\Delta(\delta)\hat{\zeta}_x^{-1}(\delta)\hat{\Phi}_x(\delta)]x_t + \text{error} \tag{8.161}$$

Evidently the term within the square brackets on the right hand side of the above equation can be equated to $D(\delta)$ in keeping with the transfer function model for y and x, and then the solution of the structural coefficients β is obtained.

8.7.11 Diagnostic Check on Normality of Residuals: The Box-Pierce Q Statistic Test

After an ARMA model of the kind ARMA(p, q) has been estimated, a diagnostic check may be applied to see if the residuals are roughly random. With this end in view, the main test statistic used is the Box–Pierce Q statistic. This is defined as

$$Q = n \sum_{t=1}^{T} r_t^2 \tag{8.162}$$

In (8.162), r_t is the tth order sample autocorrelation[29] in the residuals, the max-

[29] Just as the first order autocorrelation of residuals is obtained by correlating consecutive residuals, a tth order autocorrelation is obtained by correlating a residual now and a residual t periods hence over the entire period of the residuals.

imum order used being T, and n is the number of sample observations. Box and Pierce (1970) have shown that Q is approximately distributed as χ^2 with $T - p - q$ degrees of freedom under a correct specification of the model. If Q is large, the test will reject the claim that the specification is correct. In that case, we go through a new cycle of identification, estimation and diagnostic checking, until the last result will indicate that the model specification is correct and we stop.

8.7.12 Causality Analysis

There is an alternative to the foregoing approach of the prewhitening of both series to assess the pattern of causality between two variables. Indeed an economic time series analysis is often performed in the spirit of the discovery of a cause and effect relationship. Given that this relationship is unidirectional, it is then important to investigate whether the relationship really exists. As we of course are familiar by now, our usual course of action is to regress the effect variable on the causal one, and test for the significance of this regression coefficient. But what does a 'significant' coefficient mean? Does it mean that the relationship exists? One cannot be sure, because the significance might be caused by the spurious configuration of the data. In fact, even though a certain dynamic structure is superimposed on the relationship in the sense that the effect variable is influenced by the current and past values of the causal variable, and not the other way round, there is no guarantee that data alone would confirm this relationship. What the data show might just be a statistical accident without a substantive or philosophical truth. The evidence is rather for *predictability* than for the stronger concept called causality.

Even though there is a history for this concept, Granger (1969) is one of the earliest in recent times to have made a formal application of it.

Granger's causality. First there is a strict rule of causality generally used by econometricians. This rule does not allow the future to predict the past or the present. It is the past that can predict the present or the future. Second, and this definition is especially due to Granger, taking X to cause Y, the past values of X will improve the prediction for Y. Granger bases his forecasts on unbiased least squares predictions, and has the accuracy of predictions determined by the variance of the one-step-ahead prediction error. In this he takes note of the special effect of a given information set. More formally, Granger's definition is expressed as follows.

Suppose I is an information set that includes all present and past information, and $\bar{I}$ includes all but the present information. Let I_x represent all present and past information on the variable X, that is $X = X_i$, for all $i \leqq t$, and let $\bar{I}_x$ be I_x excluding the present information on X, that is $X = X_i$, $i < t$. Then the variable X is supposed to cause Y, if the one-step-ahead predictor of Y, $\tilde{Y}$, which is based on *all* past information, has a lesser mean squared error than the predictor of Y

based on all past information excluding X. In symbols, $X \rightarrow Y$, that is X causes Y, if

$$\text{MSE}\ (\tilde{Y}/\bar{I}) < \text{MSE}\ \{\tilde{Y}/(\bar{I} - \bar{I}_x)\} \tag{8.163}$$

By the same token, $X \rightarrow Y$, that is X causes Y instantaneously, if

$$\text{MSE}\ (\tilde{Y}/I) < \text{MSE}\ \{\tilde{Y}/(I - I_x)\} \tag{8.164}$$

There may be an aspect of nonoperationality in the Granger concept in that I stands for *all* available information. However, this position may be improved by taking I to include all *relevant* information. Obviously, economic theory will play a major role in generating this information and, therefore, choice of information does not appear to be a big problem.

Causality tests. Suppose $[X_t, Y_t]$ is a bivariate time series. It is linear, covariance stationary (see Section 8.7.8) and purely probabilistic. A typical autoregressive representation of such a process is

$$\begin{bmatrix} \gamma_{11}(\delta) & \gamma_{21}(\delta) \\ \gamma_{12}(\delta) & \gamma_{22}(\delta) \end{bmatrix} \begin{bmatrix} Y_t \\ X_t \end{bmatrix} = \begin{bmatrix} u_t \\ v_t \end{bmatrix} \tag{8.165}$$

where $[u_t\ v_t]'$ is a bivariate white noise process with zero mean and covariance matrix $\mathbf{\Sigma}$, and the coefficient matrix involving the $\gamma(\delta)$s is a 2×2 polynomial in the lag operator δ. The system of (8.165) will indicate the direction of causality from X to Y if $\gamma_{21}(\delta) = 0$, if, of course, the relationship between the two variables exists.

The following tests are the tests of the hypothesis that Y does not affect X, regardless of the nature of the effect of X on Y, instantaneous or not.

Granger's test. In order that the second line of (8.165) gives an equation primarily in X_t, we require that the leading terms in $\gamma_{21}(\delta)$ and $\gamma_{22}(\delta)$ are zero and one, respectively. Thus, this equation will express, after rearrangement, X_t as a linear combination of past Xs and Ys. In this set up, the question of whether or not Y causes X can be tested by regressing X_t on $Y_{t-1}, \ldots, Y_{t-m}, X_{t-1}, \ldots, X_{t-n}$, and then isolating out the joint effect of the Ys. Having $\gamma_{12}(\delta) = 0$ would, however, rub out any effect of the Ys on X_t.

This test would fundamentally depend on the value of m and n so that the associated error term is indeed a white noise. More importantly, though, it would depend on the value of n because as n becomes smaller, that is the lesser the number of relevant past values of X, the more the influence of the past values of Y. In other words, the test would show an inflated effect of Y on X.

Sims' test. This test is an extension of Granger's test of causality. Suppose Y and X are given by an autoregressive representation such that a distributed lag function of current and past values of X determines Y subject to an error which is uncorrelated with the history, the current status, as well as the future of X. Then it must mean that Y does not cause X in Granger's sense. This implies that in the regression equation

$$Y_t = \sum_{i=n}^{-m} \alpha_i X_{t-i} + \epsilon_t \tag{8.166}$$

the fact that X is not caused by Y would be tested by the hypothesis: H_0: $\alpha_{-1} = \alpha_{-2} = \cdots = \alpha_{-m} = 0$. But one problem might arise if the error term is having a serial correlation, for then the F test would not be appropriate. Sims (1972) corrects for this possibility by assuming an AR(2) process for the residual term with $\rho_1 = 1.5$ and $\rho_2 = 0.5626$.[30]

According to this, variables are transformed by their multiplication by the operator $1 - 1.5\delta + 0.5625\delta^2$ where δ is the lag operator. This type of ad hoc filtering could of course be replaced by a nonparametric approach whereby the residual term could be treated by an autoregressive model of an arbitrarily high order. The advantage of this approach would be the generation of a white noise disturbance term, which would not even be approximately possible with the ad hoc type of filtering.

Sims applies this method to the study of the relationship between (the logarithm of) GNP and money supply based on the U.S. data over the period 1947 to 1949. The specific values of n and m tried are 8 and 4. Two definitions of money supply are used: (1) currency plus reserves corrected for changes in reserve requirements, and (2) currency plus demand deposits. Sims' findings are that regressing GNP (Y) on the future values of money supply (X) produces insignificant effects, whereas regressing money supply on GNP produces significant effects.[31] Thus the conclusion is that the GNP does not cause money supply, but money supply does cause GNP. The direction of causation—money supply to GNP—is thus clearly brought out in the Sims study based on the U.S. post-war data.

8.7.13 An Applied Study on Double Prewhitening and Causality: Frenkel (1977) on German Hyper-Inflation

An interesting application of the prewhitening of both the input and output series is made by Frenkel (1977). This is a study of expectations and the demand for money in Germany during its hyper-inflationary period. In particular, it examines the existence, the direction of causality, and the interdependence between money and (two indices of) prices. The price indices are computed in two ways, one by the Box–Jenkins time series analysis regarding the direction of causality, and the

[30] These are values of the autocorrelation coefficients of the residuals of the first and second orders.

[31] By the F statistic at the 5% level.

Table 8.2 FITTED TIME SERIES—ARIMA (1, 1, 1) DATA FROM FEBRUARY 1921–AUGUST 1923 BY MONTHS*

Variable	Constant	AR_1	MA_1
$\log M$	0.027	0.984	−0.660
	(0.060)	(0.048)	(0.421)
$\log P_w$	0.206	0.522	−0.898
	(0.121)	(0.188)	(0.74)
$\log P_c$	0.031	0.974	−0.521
	(0.058)	(0.059)	(0.176)

* Reprinted with permission of J. A. Frenkel, "The Forward Exchange Rate, Expectations, and the Demand for Money," *American Economic Review* 67 (1977) Table 4 and 5 p. 665–66.

other by the Christopher Sims' technique regarding the interdependence. As for the Box–Jenkins method, the first differences of the logarithm of money, and the two price indices give stationarity of each series. Based on the values of the sample autocorrelation functions for the three processes, he identifies the models on ARIMA (1, 1, 1). These processes are then estimated by the maximum likelihood method. The parameter estimates are reproduced in Table 8.2, with values of standard errors of coefficients shown below the coefficients. To test for the significance of the serial correlations of the residuals with lags of periods 1 through T the Box–Pierce $Q(T)$ statistic is computed, whose approximate distribution is χ^2 with $(T - p - q)$ degrees of freedom, where p and q are the orders of the autoregressive and the moving average processes, respectively. The test results (not reported here) indicate that the residuals are not serially correlated and therefore the transformation has converted the observed data into white noise.

In the next stage of the analysis crosscorrelations between the residuals from the fitted series for prices (the prewhitened price series) and the residuals from the fitted series for money (the prewhitened money series) are computed. These correlations appear in Table 8.3.

Based on these results it is clear that money and prices are not independent. For both the price series, prices are correlated with future money one month ahead indicating that prices cause money in the Granger (1969) sense. For the interdependence hypothesis in the Sims (see Section 8.7.12) sense, Frenkel tests two hypotheses. The first is that there is no feedback from current inflation to future rates of money creation. This necessitates regressing current inflation on past and on current and future rates of money creation. The second hypothesis is that there is no feedback from current rates of money expansion to future rates of inflation. This requires regressing current monetary expansion on past, current and future rates of inflation. The test results (again not reported here) confirm that there *is* a feedback from current inflation to future rates of monetary expansion, and that, for the reverse hypothesis, there is *no* feedback from current rates

TABLE 8.3 CROSSCORRELATIONS OF PREWHITENED MONEY SERIES ($n + k$) WITH PREWHITENED PRICE SERIES (n)

log$M$	Lag:													St.
and	−6	−5	−4	−3	−2	−1	0	+1	+2	+3	+4	+5	+6	Error
logP_c	−0.02	−0.04	−0.13	−0.28	0.27	−0.04	0.49*	0.43*	−0.34	0.03	−0.12	0.06	−0.07	0.18
logP_w	−0.21	0.24	−0.27	−0.17	0.07	0.40*	0.13	0.50*	−0.02	−0.24	0.18	−0.14	0.01	0.18

Note: Significant crosscorrelations, exceeding twice the standard error, are indicated by an (*) sign. Residuals are taken from the previous table.

of money expansion to future rates of inflation. Thus prices cause money, not the other way around, accounting for the endogeneity of the money supply.

As yet there do not seem to be widespread applications made of both the single and double prewhitening methods to socioeconomic problems. Some empirical evidence often points to the lack of relations among economic variables, even in those cases where the variables are perceived to be strongly related.[32] Even the directions of causations, which are found to be of one kind by some authors, might easily be reversed or differently established by others for the same problems.[33] When all this evidence points to the need for discretion or judgement to be used by time series practitioners, as is done by conventional econometricians, it is still early to comment on the practical efficacy of such methods in relation to socioeconomic problems.

PROBLEMS

8-1. Suppose that the housing market adjusts instantaneously to changes in demand. Then $H_t = H_t^*$, where H_t is the observed stock of housing and H_t^* the desired stock of housing for all individuals in an economy. When desires are not fulfilled, housing stock adjustment goes on according to the equation

$$H_t - H_{t-1} = \gamma(H_t^* - H_{t-1}) \qquad 0 < \gamma < 1$$

in which the additive random disturbance term u_t, not shown, can also be considered. Since the desired level of housing is unobserved, we may like to determine it as a function of the different variables that affect housing demand:

$$H_t^* = \alpha_0 + \alpha_1 X_{1,t-1} + \alpha_2 X_{2,t-1} + \cdots\cdots$$

where the $X_{i,t-1}$s are the lagged explanatory variables. Two examples of $X_{i,t-l}$ are price of housing and mortgage rate of interest. Suppose these are the only two X variables considered in what follows.

(a) Formulate an econometric model that theoretically can be utilized to estimate γ, α_0, α_1, and α_2.

(b) Suppose $E(u_t) = 0$, for $t = 1, 2, \ldots, n$ and $E(\mathbf{u}\,\mathbf{u}') = I$, where $\mathbf{u} = [u_1\ u_2 \cdots u_n]'$. Let H_{t-1} and the $X_{i,t-1}$s be uncorrelated with u_t. Explain whether the OLS estimates are (i) unbiased, (ii) consistent.

(c) If you have reasons to believe that

$$u_t = \rho u_{t-1} + v_t$$

where v_ts have properties just like u_ts in (b), explain whether the OLS estimates would be (i) unbiased, (ii) consistent.

[32] See, for instance, Pierce (1977) for the relationship between money and interest rates.

[33] See, for example, Haugh and Box (1977) for the feedback effect between unemployment rate and GNP of the U.K.

8-2. Now suppose that the description of the initial conditions of problem 8-1 serves as the background for the problem to be explained below. A research investigator uses quarterly Canadian data over the period from 1964 quarter 1 to 1984 quarter 4 and obtains the following estimated equation using the method of maximum likelihood (to avoid the problem of nonlinearity of equations):

$$\Delta H_t = \underset{(5.5824)}{0.0012}\ \big(\underset{(-1.1528)}{-3.3399} + \underset{(2.2780)}{1.5750}\ Y^p_{t-1} - \underset{(-6.0600)}{4.6033}\ P_{t-1}$$

$$- \underset{(-1.7252)}{0.0450}\ MR_{t-1} + \underset{(1.1671)}{18.656}\ H_{t-1}\big) \qquad \overline{R}^2 = 0.46, \qquad DW = 0.724$$

where

ΔH_t	$H_t - H_{t-1}$ (measured by the number of single family and multiple family dwelling starts)
Y^p_{t-1}	permanent income at time $t - 1$ (obtained by subtracting data on real transitory income from data on real disposable income)
P_{t-1}	price of housing last period (measured by implicit price index for residential construction)
MR_{t-1}	average mortgage interest rate last period (measured by the average interest rate on National Housing Act and conventional mortgages)

Note that the figures in parentheses are the estimated standard errors of coefficient estimates.

(a) Explain how the form of the equation can be justified based on the theory underlying problem 8-1.

(b) Test the equation for first order autocorrelation among residuals at the 1% level using a suitably devised alternative hypothesis for this problem.

(c) Based on your inference from (b), are the maximum likelihood estimates unbiased? Are these consistent? What are your reasons?

(d) Write a critique on the estimated results and the model structure.

(e) Calculate the income elasticity of demand for housing according to

$$(\partial \Delta H/\partial Y^p)(Y^p/\Delta H) = \gamma\, \alpha_1 (Y^p/\Delta H)$$

and the price elasticity of demand according to

$$(\partial \Delta H/\partial P)(P/\Delta H) = \gamma\, \alpha_2 (P/\Delta H)$$

at the mean value of ΔH equal to 0.002236, that of P_t equal to 0.4764, and that of Y^p equal to 1.8760.

8-3. Consider the Table 8.4 which gives annual data on the gross national product (GNP), money supply (M), government expenditure (X) of the United States over the period 1960–1987. As you can see, most data are in constant 1982 dollars except government expenditure (GE) and receipts and money supply. These have to be expressed in constant 1982 dollars as well: for GE and receipts, use the implicit price deflator for these items, and for money supply use the implicit price deflator for the GNP. All the questions to be asked now presuppose that these conversions (into constant 1982 dollars) have been made.

TABLE 8.4 DATA ON U.S. GNP, GOVERNMENT EXPENDITURE AND RECEIPTS, EXPORTS OF GOODS AND SERVICES, AND IMPLICIT PRICE DEFLATORS, 1960–1987

Year	Gross National Product (in billions of constant 1982 $)	Implicit Price Deflator for GNP (1982 = 100)	Government Expenditure (Billions of current $)	Government Receipts (Billions of current $)	Implicit Price Deflator for Government Expenditure and Receipts (1982 = 100)	Exports of Goods and Services (Billions of 1982 $)	Money[a] Supply (Billions of current $)
1960	1665.3	30.9	137.3	140.4	24.9	98.4	315.3
1961	1708.7	31.2	150.1	145.9	25.4	100.7	341.1
1962	1799.4	31.9	161.6	157.9	26.3	106.9	371.5
1963	1873.3	32.4	169.1	169.8	26.9	114.7	406.1
1964	1973.3	32.9	177.8	175.6	27.6	128.8	442.5
1965	2087.6	33.8	189.6	190.2	28.5	132.0	482.3
1966	2208.3	35.0	215.6	214.4	29.8	138.4	505.1
1967	2271.4	35.9	245.0	230.8	31.2	143.6	557.1
1968	2365.6	37.7	272.2	266.2	33.1	155.7	606.3
1969	2423.3	39.8	290.2	300.1	35.1	165.0	615.1
1970	2416.2	42.0	317.4	306.8	38.1	178.3	677.4
1971	2484.8	44.4	346.8	327.3	41.0	179.2	776.2
1972	2608.5	46.5	377.3	374.0	43.8	195.2	886.1
1973	2744.1	49.5	411.7	419.6	47.1	242.3	985.1
1974	2729.3	54.0	467.4	463.1	52.2	269.1	1070.4
1975	2695.0	59.3	544.9	480.0	57.7	259.7	1172.2
1976	2826.7	63.1	587.5	549.1	61.5	274.4	1311.9
1977	2958.6	67.3	635.7	616.6	65.8	281.6	1472.8
1978	3115.2	72.2	694.8	694.4	70.4	312.6	1646.9
1979	3192.4	78.6	768.3	779.8	76.8	356.8	1806.6
1980	3187.1	85.7	889.6	855.1	85.5	388.9	1990.8
1981	3248.8	94.0	1006.9	977.2	93.4	392.7	2236.5
1982	3166.0	100.0	1111.6	1000.8	100.0	361.9	2443.2
1983	3279.1	103.9	1189.9	1061.3	104.0	348.1	2693.2
1984	3501.4	107.7	1277.9	1172.9	108.6	371.8	2978.3
1985	3618.7	110.9	1402.6	1270.8	112.3	367.2	3196.4
1986	3721.7	113.9	1489.0	1344.6	114.6	378.4	3490.8
1987	3847.0	117.7	1574.4	1496.5	118.5	427.8	3664.1

Source: *Economic Report of the President*, 1989, various tables.

[a] This consists of the M3 money aggregate.

We are going to posit that the GNP of the United States (GNP_t) depends on such policy and other variables as money supply (M_t), GE (G_t), taxes (T_t), and exports (X_t).

(a) Based on the data of this problem, use OLS to estimate the equation

$$\text{GNP}_t = \beta_0 + \beta_1 G_t + \beta_2 T_t + \beta_3 X_t + \beta_4 M_t + \epsilon_t$$

(b) Interpret the estimated results in terms of your prior notions about the likely results. If any discrepancies arise, how do you rationalize them?

(c) Do you sense any (first order) autocorrelations among the model's residuals? Test whether the first order autocorrelation exists using the DW test.

(d) Discuss how you would apply the CORC procedure to obtain corrections for autocorrelation among the residuals.

8-4. Refer to problem 8-3 and answer the following questions:

(a) Using lags of up to 3 years in all variables except the GNP, fit a new model by the OLS method. Do the $\overline{R}^2$ and the F statistics improve for this over the model of problem 8-3?

(b) Do you sense any multicollinearity problem from the way you have reformulated the model?

(c) Is serial correlation a problem? Test if this is present and, if it is present, apply the CORC method to derive new estimates. Do you see merits in these estimates?

(d) Now apply the Almon lag procedure to reset and reestimate the model. You may use a polynomial of degree 2 and contrast the new results with those obtained in (a) above.

(e) As you see, we have used annual rather than quarterly data. Had we to use quarterly data instead, would we expect much difference in results from the ones obtained above? Why or why not?

8-5. A research investigator set out to analyze the consumption pattern of Pakistan. With that end in view, he collected annual data on the real per capita private consumption, C_t, and the real per capita disposable income, Y_t, of Pakistan both measured in constant 1959 rupees over the years 1959–1984. The OLS-estimated line came out as follows:

$$C_t = \underset{(3.388)}{31.851} + \underset{(42.93)}{0.853Y_t} \qquad R^2 = 0.987 \qquad DW = 1.001$$

The figures in parentheses are values of the t statistic.

(a) Test if the first order autocorrelation is present at the 1% probability level of significance. What is your alternative hypothesis? Explain your choice.

(b) Depending on the above test result, comment on the properties of the OLS estimates stressing their unbiasedness, consistency, and appropriateness of tests of hypotheses.

The investigator thought of reformulating the model based on the habit persistence behavior of consumption and its adjustment in terms of the year to year changes in disposable income. However, he found that the effect of lagged (disposable) income was appreciably insignificant. Thus he ended up with the following estimated line:

$$C_t = \underset{(2.11)}{40.4} + \underset{(6.51)}{0.78Y_t} + \underset{(0.43)}{0.06C_{t-1}} \qquad R^2 = 0.98 \qquad DW = 1.66$$

The figures in parentheses are, as before, the values of the t statistic.

(c) Test if the first-order autocorrelation is present or not. What are the null and alternative hypotheses?

(d) Using the above test result, what can you say about the unbiasedness and consistency of the OLS estimates?

(e) If autocorrelation was present, how (indicate only) do you get rid of it? Would the correction of the autocorrelation generate estimates with more desirable properties? Explain.

8-6. Troubled by the incidence of high inflation in Guatemala, a Guatemalan researcher sets up a project to explain Guatemalan inflation by structural, monetary, and a combination of structural and monetary variables. He applies the OLS technique to Guatemalan data collected over the period 1952–1982.

The three estimated lines are presented below (with the values of the t statistic shown in parentheses):

Structuralist Model

$$\underset{}{\dot{P}_t} = \underset{(1.77)}{213.675} - \underset{(-0.01)}{0.003^*\dot{P}_{t-1}} - \underset{(1.33)}{0.040^*Y_t} + \underset{(-0.24)}{11.651^*Z_t}$$

$$R^2 = 0.995 \qquad DW = 2.073$$

Monetarist Model

$$\dot{P}_t = \underset{(19.32)}{90.538} - \underset{(-0.31)}{0.097^*\dot{P}_{t-1}} + \underset{(3.77)}{0.154^*M_t} + \underset{(4.76)}{0.222^*M_{t-1}}$$

$$R^2 = 0.995 \qquad DW = 1.356$$

Structuralist/Monetarist Model

$$\dot{P}_t = \underset{(16.07)}{124.825} + \underset{(0.15)}{0.033^*\dot{P}_{t-1}} + \underset{(7.15)}{0.217^*M_t} + \underset{(8.07)}{0.239^*M_{t-1}} - \underset{(-4.76)}{0.025^*Y_t} - \underset{(-1.19)}{43.782^*Z_t}$$

$$R^2 = 0.998 \qquad DW = 2.134$$

The variables appearing in these equations are:

$\dot{P}_t$ inflation in period t : annual percentage change of the consumer price index (base 1946 = 100) [similarly $\dot{P}_{t-1}$]

M_t money supply in period t : sum of currency, demand deposits and term deposits [similarly M_{t-1}]

Y_t real income in period t : annual gross domestic product (GDP) in constant 1958 quetzales

Z_t openness of the economy : proportion of the sum of exports and imports relative to the domestic product

Write an essay on inflation in Guatemala as explained by the three kinds of model formulations. In the process, you may dwell on the properties of the OLS-estimated coefficients, serial correlation among residuals, and the adjustment mechanism of inflation to different types of variables selected by the researcher. At the end, you may point out how the model or models could be improved.

8-7. Irving Fisher postulated the following relationship between nominal and real rate of interest and the rate of (price) inflation:

$$i_t = r_t^e + \beta\, \dot{p}_t^e$$

where i_t is the nominal interest rate; r_t^e (assumed constant) is the expected real rate of interest, and $\dot{p}_t^e$ is the rate of inflation. If nominal interest rates move one-for-one with inflation expectations, one would be interested in testing the hypothesis "$\beta = 1$". Suppose that the OLS estimated $\dot{p}_t^e$ is given by

$$\dot{p}_t^e = \hat{\gamma}_1 \dot{p}_{t-1} + \hat{\gamma}_2 \dot{p}_{t-2}$$

where $\dot{p}_{t-1}$ and $\dot{p}_{t-2}$ are, respectively, actual inflation rates last period and two periods before, and $\hat{\gamma}_1$ and $\hat{\gamma}_2$ are estimated coefficients. By means of data collected over a period of twenty years from, say, *Economic Report of the President* (latest issue), test whether $\beta = 1$, and whether Fisher's equation is valid in terms of the U.S. data. Write a critical report on your results commenting on the possible effects on interest rate of income taxes and economic activity for a better empirical realism of Fisher's equation in relation to the U.S. data.

(*Hint:* If, for instance, taxes at the marginal rate of T_t are imposed on interest rates, then the nominal interest rate required to leave the lender the same as in the preinflationary situation, assuming neither money nor fiscal illusion, would be: $i_t = [r_t + (\dot{p}_t^e/1 - T_t)]$. Also, if one introduces business cycles into the model, the expected real rate of interest assumed constant and equal to the natural rate of interest will indeed depart from the natural rate according to the following relation:

$$r_t^e = r_t^N + \theta(u - \bar{u})_t; \qquad 0 < \theta < 1$$

where r_t^N is the natural rate of interest and $(u - \bar{u})_t$ is one measure of economic activity which is the excess of the current, actual level u over the equilibrium level of activity $\bar{u}$, both measured at the time point t.)

8-8. Assume that the aggregate investment demand in an economy is given by

$$I_t = \beta_0 + \beta_1 Y_t^* + \beta_2 i_t$$

where I_t is aggregate real investment expenditure, Y_t^* is expected real aggregate income and i_t is the interest rate at time t. Y_t^* is made up from an adaptive expectation hypothesis: $Y_t^* = \theta Y_{t-1} + (1 - \theta) Y_{t-1}^* + \epsilon_t$, $0 < \theta < 1$. Suppose you are given data on I_t, Y_t, and i_t but Y_t^* is unobservable and has to be estimated from the adaptive expectation rule.

(a) How can you estimate the parameters β_0, β_1, β_2, and θ?

(b) Assume that $E(\epsilon_t) = 0$, $E(\epsilon_t^2) = \sigma^2$, $E(\epsilon_t \epsilon_{t'}) = 0$ for $t \neq t'$, and Y_{t-1}, i_t, I_{t-1}, and i_{t-1} are uncorrelated with ϵ_t. Would the OLS estimates be (i) unbiased, and (ii) consistent? Explain your reasons.

(c) If, instead, $\epsilon_t = \rho\epsilon_{t-1} + \nu_t$, where the ν_ts are independent random variables with zero means and equal variances at all time points, would the OLS estimates be (i) unbiased, and (ii) consistent? Justify your answer.

8-9. Show that the infinite distributed lag model

(a) $Y_t = \delta \sum_{i=0}^{\infty} \lambda^i X_{t-1} + \epsilon_t \qquad 0 < \lambda < 1$

can be written as

(b) $Y_t = \lambda Y_{t-1} + \delta X_t + \epsilon_t - \lambda\epsilon_{t-1} \qquad \epsilon_t \sim N(0, \sigma^2)$

Describe two consistent methods of estimating the parameters δ and λ.

8-10. Consider the model:

$$Y_t = \beta_0 X_t + \beta_1 Z_t + v_t \qquad v_t = \epsilon_t + Z_t u_t$$

where Z_t is a random variable with distribution defined by

Z_t	probability (Z_t)
1	1/2
0	1/2

X is nonstochastic and $E(Z_t\, u_t) = 0$ and $E(Z_t\, \epsilon_t) = 0$. What can you say about the consistency of $\hat{\beta}_1$, which is the OLS estimate of β_1?

8-11. Suppose a model is formulated as:

$$Y_{1t} = X_{1t}\beta_{11} + X_{2t}\beta_{21} + Y_{2t}^*\gamma_{11} + \epsilon_{1t}$$

where Y_{1t} is an endogenous variable, X_{1t} and X_{2t} are exogenous variables, Y_{2t}^* is the expected (unobservable) value of Y_{2t} which, in turn, is an observable endogenous variable, and ϵ_{1t}, the disturbance term, is distributed as $N(0, \sigma^2)$.

If Y_{2t}^* is determined by an adaptive expectation rule, complete the specification of the model. What will be the likelihood function for this model? Why is the function interesting and how can you maximize it?

8-12. Given a translog production function with 2 inputs X_i, $i = 1, 2$, cost minimization may result in a set of equations representing the share of each input in the cost of production of the form:

$$S_{it} = \alpha_i + \sum_{j=1}^{2} \beta_{ij} \ln X_{jt} + \epsilon_{it} \qquad i = 1, 2 \qquad t = 1, \ldots, n$$

where S_{it} is observation t on the share of input i in production cost, X_{jt} is observation t on the quantity of input j used, and ϵ_{it} is an independent, normal disturbance term with mean zero and variance σ_{ii}.

Describe how you can obtain consistent and asymptotically efficient estimators of the parameters assuming that "$\beta_{ij} = \beta_{ji}$" holds good.

8-13. Consider that the demand for inventories is given by

$$\Delta H_t = \gamma(\beta S_t^e - H_{t-1}) + \epsilon_t$$

$$S_t^e = \sum_{i=1}^{m} \alpha_i S_{t-i}$$

where

H_t = stock of inventories at end of period t

S_t^e = expected sales in period t

S_t = actual sales in period t

ϵ_t = error term in period t

(a) Show how this relationship follows from a stock adjustment model. What is the rationale for this approach?

(b) What are the conditions under which the Almon technique would be useful for estimating the coefficients α_i ($i = 1, 2, \ldots, m$)? Explain how this technique could be applied to this case.

(c) What do you think the properties of the OLS estimator would be assuming (i) ϵ_ts to be unautocorrelated, and (ii) ϵ_ts to be autocorrelated?

8-14. Consider a distributed lag function of the type

$$Y_t = \sum_{k=1}^{\infty} p_k X_{t-k} + \epsilon_t$$

where ϵ_t is a disturbance term, and $\sum_{k=1}^{\infty} |p_k| < \infty$. Assume that the sequence $\{p_k\}$ of coefficients has a rational generating function

$$P(s) = p_0 + p_1 s + p_2 s^2 + \ldots.$$

and

$$P(s) = U(s)/V(s)$$

Then the equation involving Y_t can be expressed as

$$\begin{aligned} Y_t &= p_0 X_t + p_1 X_{t-1} + p_2 X_{t-2} + \ldots \\ &= p_0 X_t + p_1 L X_t + p_2 L^2 X_t + \ldots \\ &= P(L) X_t \\ &= \{U(L)/V(L)\} X_t, \end{aligned}$$

where L is the lag operator such that $LX_t = X_{t-1}$, $L^2 X_t = X_{t-2}$, etc.

(a) Show that if $U(L) = 1 - \lambda$, and $V(L) = 1 - \lambda L$ then $Y_t = \{U(L)/V(L)\}X_t$ gives the Koyck distributed lag.

(b) What estimation procedure would you employ for the Koyck distributed lag? Consider both when the ϵ_ts are not autocorrelated and are autocorrelated.

8-15. We present now a flexible accelerator (developed by Chenery) generalized to:

$$I_t = \theta(s)\,(K_t^E - K_{t-1}^E) + \delta K_{t-1} + \epsilon_t$$

where

I_t is investment in year t

K_t^E is expected capital stock in year t

$\theta(s)$ is a "reaction coefficient" and may be expressed by the lag operator s as: $\theta(s) = \theta_0 + \theta_1 s + \theta_2 s^2 + \cdots = f(s)/g(s)$

ϵ_t is a disturbance term

Consider now a production function of the Cobb–Douglas type:

$$X = A\, L^{\alpha}\, K^{\beta}$$

where X is output and L is labor input. Then the marginal productivity of capital will be given by:

$$(\partial X/\partial K) = \beta(X/K) = (c/p)$$

where c is the rate of return on capital and p is the price of output X. Then the expected capital stock is

$$K^E = \beta(pX/c)$$

Substituting we obtain

$$I_t = \beta\ \theta(s)[(px/c)_t - (px/c)_{t-1}] + \delta K_{t-1} + \epsilon_t$$

Let us take

$$f(s) = \gamma_1 s + \gamma_2 s^2 + \gamma_3 s^3$$

$$g(s) = 1 + \delta_1 s$$

where s is the lag operator.

(a) What is $\theta(s)$ using these particular forms of $f(s)$ and $g(s)$?

(b) Using $\theta(s)$ in the equation for I_t, derive a new equation for estimation purposes.

(c) This equation is nonlinear in parameters; for instance, terms like $\beta\gamma_1$ will be involved. Describe a method of estimating the equation.

(*Note:* Part (c) may be a little difficult and should be treated as optional. Outside references may be consulted, if necessary.)

8-16. **(a)** Describe a procedure for estimation of an ARMA(1, 1) process.

(b) What is a prewhitening mechanism? Explain it carefully by using the Frenkel (1977) study on German hyper-inflation as a brief illustration.

8-17. **(a)** What does a causality analysis try to do? What do you mean by Granger's causality?

(b) Explain the procedures of a general causality test and the causality tests proposed by Granger and Sims.

9

Further Studies in Consumption, Production, and Investment Functions, and Other Studies

9.1 INTRODUCTION

In the course of practical illustrations of the single equation econometric technique made in the previous chapters, we have already dwelt upon various applied studies. Still so many other studies exist. In this chapter we group some of these others under four broad headings: consumption (including demand), production (including costs), investment, and miscellaneous. Each topic or area is vast in terms of its underlying mathematical formulations and statistical ramifications, and our space is limited. Therefore we can only afford an introductory and cursory treatment of each of these topics. The details that are reluctantly left out may be picked up from the original sources.

9.2 CONSUMPTION FUNCTION

Two early studies on demand are by Wold and Jureen (1953) and Stone (1954). These studies have proved to be seminal through the passage of time. The first relates to Sweden and the second to the United Kingdom. Both use interwar data from the 1920s and 1930s, and estimate various commodity demand relationships. The special parameters estimated are the price and income elasticities of demand and these are utilized to predict the future course of demand of commodities once the wartime regulations are withdrawn. The interesting thing is that these predictions have worked well both in terms of forecast accuracy and their implications for government policy, for these predictions have been instrumental in the eventual lifting of commodity rationing by both countries' governments.

In the following sections, we briefly dwell on the development of relative income, life cycle, and permanent income hypotheses, we discuss estimation of systems of demand equations and the linear expenditure system, and finally we review the evidence on intertemporal elasticities, a development of the 1980s.

9.3 RELATIVE INCOME, LIFE CYCLE, AND PERMANENT INCOME HYPOTHESES

Any history of the consumption function is incomplete without a mention of the early development of the function. This development is best described in terms of three hypotheses: relative income, life cycle, and permanent income.

Duesenberry (1949) postulates that one consumer's utility is affected by or dependent upon the consumption of others. This leads to the solution of an individual's consumption C, relative to other people's consumption C'. This solution comes out in the form of a function the arguments of which are: the consumer's current income and assets, Y_1 and A_1; his future incomes and assets $Y_2, \ldots, Y_n$ and $A_2, \ldots, A_n$; his current and expected future interest rates r_1 and $r_2, \ldots, r_n$; and other people's current consumption C':

$$\frac{C}{C'} = F\left(\frac{Y_1}{C'}, \ldots, \frac{Y_n}{C'}; \frac{A_1}{C'}, \ldots, \frac{A_n}{C'}; r_1, r_2, \ldots, r_n\right) \tag{9.1}$$

Duesenberry makes two important conclusions from the above formulation. The first is that the savings ratio is independent of the level of income. This is because of the following argument. If all present and future incomes, and consequently all assets change by a constant percentage, then an individual will change his consumption by the same percentage. The immediate implication is that the aggregate savings ratio, defined as savings over income, will be the same, in spite of the aggregate income going up. The second conclusion is that rich people tend to save more than the poor in relation to the respective people's income.

The above results are established using positions at equilibrium. For cyclical changes in the savings ratio, he considers people with different incomes. The rich, in periods of depression, undergo a fall in current income, even though their expected income does not suffer a setback. This plus the effect of inertia of habits and standards of living leads them to cut consumption not as much as income. In short, in recession and depression, the last peak level of income influences their consumption and this effect is maintained for a few years depending on their past accumulated savings. However, this will not be the case with the poor people or people in and out of employment. For them, the influence on current consumption of their last peak level of income or consumption will be very little.

Thus Duesenberry concludes in favor of the special effect of income or consumption of the last cyclical peak on consumption at a given (lower than the peak) level of income. Based on data for the United States over the period 1929–1940, he calculates the following regression

$$\frac{S}{Y} = 0.196 + 0.25\,\frac{Y}{Y_0} \tag{9.2}$$

in which S stands for aggregate real per capita savings, Y for aggregate real per capita income, and Y_0 the last highest real per capita income.

This savings function can directly be used to support Kuznets' (1942) finding. This relates to the constancy of the long-term savings propensity of the U.S. economy for the period 1880–1930. Assuming that the U.S. income grew at 3%, that is Y_t/Y_{t-1} equals 1.03, S/Y becomes 0.06 from the Duesenberry function. This is a little less than 10% obtained by Kuznets.

The next phase of the development of the consumption function is based on the life cycle hypothesis, propounded by Modigliani and Brumberg (1954) and Ando and Modigliani (1963). According to this formulation, suppose a consumer has a life span of L periods, where L is $N + M$, N being the number of earning periods and M the number of retirement periods. Then, assuming perfect knowledge of his future income, he distributes his income throughout his life such as to derive the following utility from consumption during his life span:

$$U = U(C_t, C_{t+1}, \ldots, C_L) \tag{9.3}$$

C_t, in (9.3), is consumption, excluding durables, in the tth year of his earning span. The problem for him is to choose C_i for $i = t, t + 1, \ldots, L$, subject to the budget constraint:

$$a_{t-1} + y_t + \sum_{\tau=t+1}^{N} \frac{y_\tau^e}{(1 + r)^{\tau - t}} = \sum_{\tau=t}^{L} \frac{C_\tau}{(1 + r)^{\tau - t}} \tag{9.4}$$

assuming that the rate of interest r is not to change. In (9.4), the following definitions apply

a_{t-1} = value of the consumer's assets at the beginning of the tth period

y_t = nonproperty income in period t

y_τ^e = nonproperty income expected in period τ

C_τ = consumption in period τ

Assume now that the utility function is such as to make the consumer's optimal consumption through the year the same, independent of the level of his income. Then, aggregating over all individuals aged t years, the optimal aggregate consumption C_t^* equal to $\sum c_t^*$, where c_t^* is the optimal consumption in period t of a consumer's earning, becomes

$$C_t^* = \sum c_t^* = \alpha A_{t-1} + \beta Y_{tL} + \delta(N - T)Y_{tL}^e \tag{9.5}$$

TABLE 9.1 COEFFICIENTS OF THE LIFE CYCLE CONSUMPTION FUNCTION UNDER CERTAIN ASSUMPTIONS*

Yield on Assets (%)	0	0	0	3	5	5	5
Annual Rate of Growth of Income (%)	0	3	4	0	0	3	4
$\alpha_1 + \alpha_2$	0.61	0.64	—	0.69	0.73	—	—
α_3	0.08	0.07	0.07	0.11	0.13	0.12	0.12

* Reprinted with permission A. Ando and F. Modigliani, "The Life Cycle Hypothesis of Saving," *American Economic Review* 53(1963) Table 1, p. 60.

In (9.5) we have

Y_{tL} = aggregate non-property income of individuals aged t
A_{t-1} = aggregate net worth of individuals aged t
Y^e_{tL} = aggregate nonproperty income expected of individuals aged t
α, β, δ = constants

Aggregating over C^*_t over all ages, the total aggregate consumption for all ages is obtained. However, it is possible that assets and income are correlated with age. Thus aggregation has its problem. But if α, β, and δ, the age structure, and the distribution of income do not change through time[1], then

$$C = \alpha'_1 Y_{Lt} + \alpha'_2 Y^e_{Lt} + \alpha'_3 A_{t-1} \tag{9.6}$$

where

C = aggregate optimal consumption
A_{t-1} = net worth
Y_L = aggregate nonproperty income
Y^e_L = aggregate expected nonproperty income
$\alpha'_1, \alpha'_2, \alpha'_3$ = constants

Ando and Modigliani go on to estimate the parameters as follows. They set out some prior estimates of the above coefficients for the purpose of judging the 'reasonableness' of their estimates. They use three assumptions about α'_1, α'_2, and α'_3 insofar as they are functions (see Table 9.1) of the yield on assets and the annual rate of growth of income. These assumptions tend to make these parameters relatively insensitive to changes in the values of the (yield and growth) variables.

Next, two hypotheses are set up to cope with the measurement of Y^e. In hypothesis I, $Y^e_{Lt} = \beta Y_{Lt}$, with $\beta = 1$. In hypothesis II, an allowance is made

[1] α, β, and δ can be shown to be the weighted average of quantities $\sum_{\tau=t}^{L} \frac{K_{\tau-t}}{(1+r)^{\tau-t}}$, where, for instance, the Ks are defined from: $C^*_{t+1} = K_1 C^*_t$, $C_{t+2} = K_2 C^*_t$, etc., with weights as a_{t-1}, y_t and y^e_t, respectively.

for different income expectations of employed and unemployed people. Assuming that an average employed person expects an income of $\beta_1 Y_{Lt}/E_t$, where E_t is the number employed, L_t the total labour force, and $\beta_1 \approx 1$; that is, the expected income is almost the present average wage, and the unemployed expect a much lesser income, that is $\beta_2 Y_{Lt}/E_t$, with $\beta_2 < 1$. The total expected income of the two groups of people is the weighted sum of the two expected incomes:

$$\begin{aligned} Y^e &= E_t\beta_1 \frac{Y_{L_t}}{E_t} + (L_t - E_t)\beta_2 \frac{Y_{L_t}}{E_t} \\ &= (\beta_1 - \beta_2)Y_{L_t} + \beta_2 \frac{L_t}{E_t} Y_t \end{aligned} \tag{9.7}$$

Thus, using hypothesis I, C_t becomes

$$C_t = \alpha_1 Y_{L_t} + \alpha_3 A_{t-1} \qquad (\alpha_1 \approx \alpha_1' + \alpha_2') \tag{9.8}$$

and using hypothesis II, C_t becomes

$$C_t = \alpha_1 Y_{L_t} + \alpha_2 \frac{L_t}{E_t} Y_{L_t} + \alpha_3 A_{t-1} \tag{9.9}$$

In the above,

$$\alpha_1 = \alpha_1' + \alpha_2'(\beta_1 - \beta_2) \qquad \alpha_2 = \alpha_2'\beta_2 \qquad \alpha_3 = \alpha_3' \tag{9.10}$$

and

$$\alpha_1 + \alpha_2 \approx \alpha_1' + \alpha_2' \tag{9.11}$$

The coefficient estimates along with the values of R^2 and DW under hypothesis I based on the absolute values of the variables as well as their first differences are presented in Section 1 of Chapter 7. Transformation has eliminated a great deal of the autocorrelation of residuals and the trend influence in the variables. The latter has helped to ultimately lessen multicollinearity. Hypothesis II results originally have shown a great deal of autocorrelation which is removed after transformation. The transformed results are shown below (with standard errors given underneath the coefficient estimates):

α_1	α_2	α_3	R^2	DW
0.44 (0.12)	0.24 (0.15)	0.049 (0.022)	0.936	1.74

It is clear that the coefficients of both Y and A are lower under Hypothesis II than Hypothesis I. Ando and Modigliani suggest this could have been due to the correlation between changes in $Y_{L_t}L_t/E_t$ (which is an income variable) and A_{t-1}, being themselves cyclically stable. While this, by and large, proves the basic hypothesis concerning the influence of assets, problems of segregating the effects of wealth, income, and expected income remain. Also, the possibility of simultaneous equation bias[2] exists.

The third in the development of the consumption function theory is the permanent income hypothesis invented by Friedman (1957). Assuming a homogeneous utility function, and a constant quantity of resources, he finds permanent consumption to be a constant fraction of (the quantity of) resources:

$$C_p = K(u, i)iW = K(u, i)Y_p \tag{9.12}$$

in which

C_p = permanent consumption

W = level of resources

i = rate of interest

u = a variable dependent on age and family composition of individuals

Y_p = permanent income

The variables C_p and Y_p are nonmeasurable. For the sake of their measurement, one can use identity $Y = Y_p + \eta$ and $C = C_p + \epsilon$, where Y and C are measured (or current) income and consumption, and η and ϵ are transitory (or windfall) income and transitory consumption. It is assumed that η and ϵ are uncorrelated.

Assuming that permanent income Y_p depends upon past and present income according to the relation:

$$Y_p = W_0 Y_t + W_1 Y_{t-1} + \dots \qquad 0 \leqq W_i \leqq 1 \qquad \sum W_i = 1 \dots \tag{9.13}$$

and further assuming, like Friedman, that the weights decline geometrically, the consumption function reduces to

$$C_t = (1 - \lambda)KY_t + \lambda C_{t-1} + \epsilon_t - \lambda \epsilon_{t-1} \tag{9.14}$$

This turns out to be exactly like the distributed lag model in independent variables. The problems of estimation of such a model were discussed in Chapter 8, Section 7.1. Taking $\hat{\beta}_0$ and $\hat{\beta}_1$ to be the least squares estimates of the intercept and slope coefficients in the regression of consumption on income, and using a plim method similar to the measurement error model of Chapter 8, the following results emerge:

$$\begin{aligned} \hat{\beta}_1 &= K\frac{\sum (Y_p - \overline{Y}_p)^2}{\sum (Y - \overline{Y})^2} = Kf \text{ (say)} \\ \hat{\beta}_0 &= \overline{C} - Kf\overline{\eta} + K(1 - f)\overline{Y}_p \end{aligned} \tag{9.15}$$

The slope coefficient estimate indicates that a group of consumers with the possibility of speculative income, like farmers, would have a smaller value of $\hat{\beta}_1$ than consumers with no such income, like fixed income earners.

[2] See Chapter 11, Section 1 for an explanation for this sort of bias.

TABLE 9.2* THREE CONSUMPTION FUNCTIONS OF THE UNITED STATES: REGRESSIONS OF CONSUMPTION ON CURRENT AND PAST INCOMES, 1905 THROUGH 1951, WAR PERIODS EXCLUDED[a]

Regression	Ratio of Permanent Consumption to Permanent Income (k)	Weight Attached, in Computing Permanent Income, to				Square of Multiple Correlation Coefficient (R^2)	Standard Error of Estimate as a Percentage of Average Value of Measured Consumption
		Highest Previous Income	Current Income	Preceding Year's Income	All Prior Years Combined		
Highest Previous Income[b]	0.88	0.45	0.55			0.98	2.8
Preceding Year's Income[b]	0.90		0.64	0.36		0.94	5.0
Expected Income[c]	0.88		0.33	0.22	0.45	0.96	4.0

[a] Years 1917–1918, 1942–1945 excluded.

[b] In spite of 1942–1945 being the war years, 1945 was used as the year of the highest preceding income and as the preceding year's income for the 1946 current income observation, the year 1941 being far out of line. For World War I, the years 1917–1918 were omitted for other variables as well.

[c] The weights for 17 individual years, current to backward, are: 0.330, 0.221, 0.148, 0.099, 0.067, 0.045, 0.030, 0.020, 0.013, 0.009, 0.006, 0.004, 0.003, 0.002, 0.001, 0.001 and 0.001.

N.B. Consumption is real consumption per capita, and income is real disposable income per capita.

* Reprinted with permission M. Friedman, *A Theory of Consumption Function* (1957), Princeton University Press, Table 15, p. 147.

Friedman computes three regressions based on Goldsmith's (1955) data. For the calculation of expected income, geometrically declining weights as in (9.13) are taken. All specifications seem to be good but, based on the goodness of fit results, the highest previous income seems to be the best (see Table 9.2).

9.4 SYSTEMS OF DEMAND EQUATIONS

We now turn to the problem of estimation of demand equations. Some empirical examples of simple demand equations including Engel's curve were given while discussing their methods of estimation. Consequently, we present below (empirical) problems of estimation of *systems* of demand equations. Observe the following system:

$$Y_j = Y_j(p_1, p_2, \ldots, p_n, I, \epsilon_j) \qquad j = 1, 2, \ldots, n \tag{9.16}$$

Two particular functional forms of the above are represented by a linear system and a log-linear (or constant elasticity) system. These are respectively as follows:

$$\begin{aligned} Y_j &= a_j + \sum_K b_{jK} p_K + c_j I + \epsilon_j \qquad j = 1, 2, \ldots, n \\ \ln Y_j &= a_j' + \sum_K b_{jK}' \ln p_K + C_j' \ln I + \epsilon_j' \qquad j = 1, 2, \ldots, n \end{aligned} \tag{9.17}$$

In the above $Y_1, \ldots, Y_n$ are the quantities consumed of n goods. These are taken to be the endogenous variables. Then there are the variables $p_1, \ldots, p_n$, which are their prices and the variable I which is consumer income. These are treated as the exogenous variables. ϵ is the error term. A budget equation completes the system. This system enables one to derive the interdependence among the goods, which, among other things, is reflected in changes in prices of some goods leading to changes in quantities demanded of other goods.

9.4.1. The Linear Expenditure System: Engel's Curve

However, an important functional form which is perhaps the most widely used form is the linear expenditure system given by

$$p_j Y_j = p_j Y_j^0 + \beta_j \left(I - \sum_{K=1}^{n} p_K Y_K^0 \right) \qquad j = 1, 2, \ldots, n \tag{9.18}$$

with

$$Y_j - Y_j^0 > 0 \qquad 0 < \beta_j < 1 \qquad \sum \beta_j = 1 \tag{9.19}$$

This means there is as though an expenditure on a base amount Y_j^0 of good j, which the consumer must make for minimal subsistence. In addition there is a component of total expenditure equal to a fraction β_j of the so called "supernumerary income", being the income above the subsistence level of income $\sum p_K Y_K^0$ (which buys the base quantities). The two components therefore imply committed and discretionary expenditures on good j.

Dividing (9.18) by p_j, and writing the variables I and p_K for $K \neq j$ with a bar on top implying that they are held constant, we get the equation for the jth good's demand curve:

$$Y_j = Y_j^0(1 - \beta_j) + \beta_j(\bar{I} - \sum_{K \neq j} \bar{p}_K Y_K^0)p_j^{-1} \tag{9.20}$$

Multiplying throughout by $\bar{p}_j$, where p_j now is held constant, we get the Engel's curve:

$$X_j = \bar{p}_j Y_j = (\bar{p}_j Y_j^0 - \beta_j \sum \bar{p}_K Y_K^0) + \beta_j I \tag{9.21}$$

This shows a linear relationship between expenditure X_j and income I, hence the name linear expenditure system.

The derivation and interpretation of the system are simple. However, its estimation is not quite without problems. For one thing, it is linear in variables but nonlinear in parameters. For instance in (9.20) and (9.21) the product of parameters β_j and Y_K^0 is involved making the term nonlinear in parameters.

There are a few ways of estimating the parameters. According to one, have Y_K^0 estimated from extraneous information or a priori judgments. Then, from (9.21), the linear regression of $p_j Y_j - p_j Y_j^0$ on supernumerary income would provide the single equation estimate of parameters β_j. In another approach, get the budget shares β_js determined from similar sources (or from Engel's curve (9.21)). Then estimate the Y_K^0s by regressing $p_j x_j - \beta_j I$ on all prices so as to minimize the sum of squared errors. In the third approach, an iterative one, combine the method of the first two approaches. Here use estimates of β_j subject to Y_K^0 of the first approach and the estimates of Y_K^0 subject to β_j of the second approach, and iterate until the sum of squared errors is minimized. Then β_j based on the last estimated Y_K^0, and Y_K^0 based on the last estimated β_j will be the retained estimated values of β_j and Y_K^0. The fourth and the last approach is as follows. Choose β_j and Y_j^0 at the same time by constructing a grid of $2n - 1$ possible[3] parameter values and locate at a point on the grid which minimizes the sum of squared errors over all goods and observations.

9.4.2 The Goldberger and Gamaletsos (1970) Study

Table 9.3 reports on the results of the linear expenditure system for three countries, the United States, Canada and the United Kingdom, drawn from the study by Goldberger and Gamaletsos (1970). The table gives data on estimated base quantities, in domestic currency, of expenditures per capita Y_j^0 and estimated

[3] The constraint $\sum \beta_j = 1$ reduces the number by one.

TABLE 9.3 LINEAR EXPENDITURE SYSTEM ESTIMATES FOR THE UNITED STATES, CANADA AND THE UNITED KINGDOM, 1950–1961[a]

	Country					
	United States		Canada		United Kingdom	
Commodity Group	Y_j^0	β_j	Y_j^0	β_j	Y_j^0	β_j
1. Food	0.33	0.081	0.20	0.177	0.074	0.172
2. Clothing	0.14	0.055	0.10	0.029	0.027	0.130
3. Rent	0.14	0.190	0.06	0.279	0.020	0.052
4. Durables	0.15	0.096	0.07	0.133	0.022	0.269
5. Other	0.52	0.578	0.32	0.382	0.106	0.377

Source: Reprinted with permission A. S. Goldberger and T. Gamaletsos, "A Cross-Country Comparison of Consumer Expenditure Patterns," Elsevier Science Publishers, *European Economic Review* (1970) 1, Table 2, p. 372.

[a] Units of measurements: thousands of dollars; exchange rates of 1961 used: 98.73 U.S. cents per Canadian \$, and 280.27 U.S. cents per U.K. £.

marginal budget shares β_j ($\sum \beta_j = 1$). For instance, in terms of units of measurement of thousands of dollars, base quantities are \$190 worth of food per capita, \$90 of clothing, and so on. The figures for budget shares indicate that 17.7% of income over supernumerary levels is claimed by food, 2.9% by clothing, etc. It is interesting to note that for all countries the base quantities, while being similar in the case of items, namely, clothing, rent and durables, are much lower for these than in the case of food.

9.5 EVIDENCE ON INTERTEMPORAL ELASTICITIES

It is very difficult to survey or review the remaining literature on consumer behavior or consumption function because it is so vast. Still, a modest review of its development insofar as it relates to evidence on intertemporal elasticities can be made, especially because this relates to the most recent decade, the 1980s.

This evidence is mixed mainly because of the model, rather than the data used. The position described is in the spirit of evaluating, rather than estimating the life cycle model, biased as it has been towards micro-data bases. Inherent in it has been the lack of regard for time separability and interaction of goods with labour supply decisions, and too much stress made on, first, the liquidity constraints and, second, the extreme sensitivity of consumption to current disposable income.

We refer here especially to thirteen studies: Hall and Mishkin (1982), Hayashi (1982, 1985a and b), Blinder and Deaton (1985), Deaton (1985), Altonji and Siow (1985), Altonji and others (1986), Muelbauer and Bover (1986), McCurdy (1986), Mariger (1987a and b), and Campbell and Deaton (1987). These are based on both aggregate and individual level data sources. However, all these studies agree on one point: that is, time separable models of the following type:

$$\Delta \ln C_t = \rho \Delta \ln \alpha_t + \rho(\ln \tau_t - \Delta \ln b_t) + \epsilon_t$$

where

$$C_t = \text{consumption at time } t$$

$$\ln \tau_t - \Delta \ln b_t \approx \text{real interest rate}$$

$$\alpha_t, \beta = \text{intertemporal parameters in the indirect utility function given by}$$

$$V_t = \alpha_t(Y_t^\tau)^\beta/\beta; \quad (\beta < 1)$$

$$Y_t^\tau = \text{real supernumerary expenditure}$$

b_t = price index for supernumerary consumption approximated to by the retail price index

$$\rho = 1/(\beta - 1)$$

$$\epsilon_t = \text{error}$$

do not lend themselves to a satisfactory characterization of intertemporal behavior. This is true for at least a significant class of consumers. The reason for this sort of result, or how stable this result is, is hard to pin down. In general, liquidity constraints may explain why consumption remains extremely sensitive to current income changes but habits, as evident in lagged consumption, tend to smooth out that effect. Even then for at least the group of young or unemployed, liquidity constraints are found to be rather compelling, as is consumers' habit persistence for some goods.

In the context of evaluation rather than estimation of the basic consumption model, Campbell and Deaton (1987) strongly believe that the joint process of both consumption and income would be quite effective. This kind of analysis may be performed by panel data, but one may not lose sight of the possible contaminating effects of measurement errors in dynamic panel data models.[4] More particularly, the data used are weekly expenditures on food computed from yearly average figures and the commodity breakdown of these expenditures is not shown. In spite of this, the tests proposed seem to be well conceived and reasonable.

Hall and Mishkin (1982) assume constant real return on assets and work through the following model equations. First, they take consumption expenditure to be given by the real interest earnings on real life cycle wealth as expected in time t:

$$C_t = r^* W_t^* \tag{9.22}$$

[4] See Altonji and Siow (1985) for a similar observation. This is also true for the expenditure data in the Michigan PSID panel used by Hall and Mishkin (1982).

where

$$\begin{aligned} C_t &= \text{consumption expenditure} \\ r^* &= \text{real interest rate} \\ W^* &= \text{real life cycle wealth as expected in time } t \end{aligned} \tag{9.23}$$

Then, revisions to real consumption are taken as

$$C_{t+1} - C_t = r^* \sum_{s=t}^{\infty} (\mathrm{E}_{t+1} - \mathrm{E}_t)\mu_s \tag{9.24}$$

where

$$\begin{aligned} \mu &= \text{real (discounted) income} \\ \mathrm{E}_t &= \text{symbol of expectation conditional on information available at time } t \end{aligned} \tag{9.25}$$

A simple deduction is available if we assume μ_s to follow a random walk such as

$$(1 + r^*)\mu_s = \mu_{s-1} + \epsilon_s \tag{9.26}$$

where ϵ_s is the random innovation term. Then $C_{t+1} - C_t$ reduces to ϵ_t; that is, consumption adjusts to the latest innovation in real income. However, Hall and Mishkin assume that

$$\mu_s = \mu_t^L + \mu_t^s \tag{9.27}$$

that is, nondeterministic income μ_s is made up of two types of innovation in real income, μ_t^L, which indicates variations in lifetime prospects, and μ_t^s which captures transitory effects. The first is assumed to follow a random walk and the second a moving average of past transitory effects. Under the life cycle hypothesis, these two effects jointly can be interpreted to be the annuity value of incremental wealth following from a unit unexpected income. This added wealth is at the same time the real interest rate in the infinite horizon model. Consequently, by testing the coefficient of this variable in $C_{t+1} - C_t$ it is possible to come up with a test of the life cycle hypothesis. Notice that the innovation error process contains a part that is due to transitory effects. This will help the test of hypotheses.

In fact, if C_t is real consumption net of the effects of deterministic components such as age, demographic factors, etc. then, for a quadratic utility function and for real interest rates, marginal utility becomes a linear function of C_t. From these, one can show that[5]

$$\Delta C_t = \epsilon_t + \beta_t \eta_t \tag{9.28}$$

[5] This kind of framework is particularly useful in models of rational expectations as would be evident in what follows.

where

$$\eta_t = \text{transitory income}$$
$$\beta_t = \text{annuity value described above} \tag{9.29}$$
$$\epsilon_t = \text{innovation in } \mu_t^L$$

Using (9.27), we obtain

$$\Delta\mu_t = \epsilon_t + (\eta_t - \eta_{t-1}) \tag{9.30}$$

where $\Delta\mu_t^L$ is equal to ϵ_t, and μ_t^s, equal to η_s, is serially uncorrelated. It follows that

$$V(\Delta\mu_t) = \sigma_\epsilon^2 + 2\sigma_\eta^2$$
$$\text{cov}(\Delta\mu_t, \Delta\mu_{t-1}) = -\sigma_\eta^2 \tag{9.31}$$

where $V(\epsilon_t)$ is σ_ϵ^2 and $V(\eta_t)$ is σ_η^2. Rewrite (9.28) as

$$\Delta C_t = \alpha\epsilon_t + \alpha\beta\eta_t \tag{9.32}$$

where

$$\alpha = \text{marginal propensity to consume food out of permanent income} \tag{9.33}$$
$$\beta_t = \beta\text{: assumed constant over } t \text{ by Hall and Mishkin}$$

Combine (9.30) and (9.32) to get

$$\begin{aligned}\text{cov}(\Delta C_t, \Delta\mu_t) &= \alpha\sigma_\epsilon^2 + \alpha\beta\sigma_\eta^2 \\ &= C_0 \text{ (say)}\end{aligned} \tag{9.34}$$

Let

$$C_1 = \text{cov}(\Delta C_t, \Delta\mu_{t+1}) = -\alpha\beta\sigma_\eta^2$$

Then

$$\alpha = \frac{(C_0 + C_1)}{\sigma_\epsilon^2} \tag{9.35}$$

$$\beta = \alpha\sigma_\eta^2 \tag{9.36}$$

Hall and Mishkin use (9.35) and (9.36) to estimate α and β. They provide for measurement error in consumption, a more general process for the development of transitory income, and utilize advance information on income. Their estimates are

$$\alpha \approx 0.11$$
$$\beta \approx 0.29 \tag{9.37}$$

Since the average propensity to consume food is roughly 0.19, the estimated value of α is not far off. But given that β is interpreted to be the annuity value of added wealth from a unit unexpected income, β seems high, but not as high ($\beta = 1$) as it would be in the completely liquidity constrained case where current income and consumption are equal. The authors also study the effect of $\Delta \mu_{t-1}$ on ΔC_t. This effect should be zero in the life cycle model but significant in the liquidity constrained case. Hall and Mishkin find a small but significant negative effect.

They reformulate the model to allow for a proportion δ (estimated to be 0.2) of consumption[6] registering a value of $\beta = 1$. Then the value of β for the rest of the consumption is estimated to be 0.174, which makes more sense. In both cases, the value of α is kept fixed at 0.1. They conclude that in about 20% of consumption the simple life cycle hypothesis is not applicable. Therefore, that much consumption is subject to binding liquidity constraints. This sort of conclusion is supported by Hayashi (1985a) based on evidence from panel data on Japanese household expenditures.

One should reflect on the policy implications of the above results. When liquidity constraints are binding, both consumption and borrowing will be affected, which would result in too high a level of saving. This would imply that the efficiency loss of income tax relative to consumption tax will go down since consumers with binding liquidity constraints would tend not to engage in intertemporal substitution. So whether liquidity constraints or the life cycle hypothesis are valid for consumption will have important policy implications. Perhaps this explains why there have been a number of important follow-up studies since the Hall and Mishkin study appeared.

However, there is the tendency on the part of these studies to locate on either the current income constrained or the life cycle tracks, the two extreme positions conceivable. The exception to this is Mariger (1987) who is concerned with a continuum of liquidity constrained positions in which the current income constrained position is the extreme.

In conclusion, we would like to analyze the problem of robustness of the foregoing results in the presence of measurement errors which, even though smaller in groups or aggregate data, are still present in panel data. In this context, the findings of Altonji and Siow (1985) and Altonji and others (1986) seem to be important. They draw data from the same source as Hall and Mishkin and obtain estimates for the coefficients on the right-hand side of equation (9.32) using ad-

[6] This type of constrained consumption extends to studies which allow for expenditure on one or more goods to be zero for a high percentage of a random variable—see Wales and Woodland (1987). They use the Amemiya (1972) and Tobin (1958) type of model that is in keeping with the conventional approach to estimation of systems of demand equations and make special use of the property of truncated distribution of random disturbances. Their models are estimated by the maximum likelihood method applied to data on Australian meat consumption.

ditional determinants of income such as wage rates, employment, and other labor market characteristics. Using the consistently estimated values of β, they estimate the underlying discount factor for consumers with infinite horizon. This factor lies between -0.04 and 1.60 compared to Hall and Mishkin's value of 0.77.

Mariger (1987b), like King (1986), uses a model with a built-in value of the minimum net worth below which households cannot borrow. His finding from two crosssections of survey data is that only a small proportion of families faces one period horizons in which the extreme current income liquidity constraint of the Hall and Mishkin (1982) and Hayashi (1985b) type becomes important. Rather, the horizons of many households are much smaller than their remaining lifetime. Still they seem to take part in some intertemporal substitution. The end result of all this is to create a dispersion in the estimated discount factor. Anyway, the problem seems to be sufficiently important to deserve more attention by researchers in the future.

9.6 PRODUCTION FUNCTION

A production function is a relation between the inputs in a production process and its output. This relation can be based on both micro (or desegregated) and macro (or aggregated) considerations as in the case of a production function relating to a firm and to an industrial sector, respectively. One of the simplest kinds of production functions is due to Leontief (1951). It has inputs related in a fixed proportion to output as in the following:

$$X_j/Y = a_j \tag{9.38}$$

where a_j is the input–output coefficient for the jth factor of production and is constant for all time points, X_j is the amount of the jth factor, and Y the level of output. This is an overly simple and rigid description of the productive process of an economy for, once a certain level of output for the economy as a whole is conceived of or planned, the input requirement for that level is determined by a very simple manipulation. In this system, inputs are the same as outputs, current production is the source of inputs, outputs are used as inputs and they use inputs, and these go on backwards through the system until an infinite sequence is generated. This sequence is convergent and its total input requirements are determinate, if the sum total of produced inputs is smaller than the value of each industrial output.

The 'neoclassical' theory of the production function does not depend on the above formulation except as a very special case. Here two factors of production are used, usually labor L and capital K, and the output (Y) function is formulated as

$$Y = f(L, K) \tag{9.39}$$

subject to:

$$\partial Y/\partial L, \qquad \partial Y/\partial K > 0 \qquad (9.40)$$
$$\partial^2 Y/\partial L^2, \qquad \partial^2 Y/\partial K^2 < 0$$

The second set of conditions implies that production obeys the law of diminishing return to each factor as the quantity of that factor is increased.

We have already introduced production functions of two other kinds. These are the Cobb–Douglas (C–D) and CES (constant elasticity of substitution) production functions by means of which we illustrated the OLS estimation procedure and nonlinear functional form, respectively.[7] For present purposes, we write these functions, except for the error terms, as follows:

$$Y = \alpha L^{\beta_1} K^{\beta_2} \quad \text{Cobb–Douglas production function} \qquad (9.41)$$

$$Y = A[\delta L^{-\rho} + (1 - \delta)K^{-\rho}]^{-1/\rho} \quad \text{CES production function.} \qquad (9.42)$$

In these equations, Y is output, α, β_1, β_2, A, ρ, and δ are parameters, and L and K are labor and capital inputs. $\beta_1 + \beta_2$ is the scale factor with the Cobb–Douglas production function. This will imply constant, increasing, or decreasing returns to scale depending on whether $\beta_1 + \beta_2$ is equal to, greater than, or less than unity. With the CES function, δ is the parameter of distribution between the L and K inputs; A, like α in the C–D function, reflects the scale of operation, and ρ, equal to $\{(1/\sigma) - 1)\}$, is a substitution parameter and is the elasticity of substitution between labor and capital.[8,9]

With this introduction, we will cover the following aspects and applications of production functions: nonconstant returns to scale CES function with application by Ferguson (1965), other applications by Burley (1973) on Australian manufacturing industries, and Reinhardt (1972) on production function of U.S. physicians' services, the transcendental function due to Zellner and Revankar (1969), Nerlove (1963), and Ringstad (1967); generalized transcendental functions due to Christensen and others (1973) based on Cobb–Douglas and CES functions, the variable elasticity of substitution (VES) production function due to Revankar (1971), among others; Pindyck (1979) on interfuel substitution and demand for energy using translog production and cost functions; Pollak and others (1984) on CES translog functions; and Beckman and Sato (1969) on technical progress in aggregate production.

[7] See Chapter 5, Section 1 and Chapter 8, Section 6.

[8] This is symbolically defined by

$$\frac{\dfrac{d(L/K)}{L/K}}{\dfrac{d(\partial K/\partial L)}{\partial K/\partial L}}$$

[9] See Arrow and others (1961) for the original practical application of the CES function.

9.7 NONCONSTANT RETURNS TO SCALE CES FUNCTION AND AN APPLICATION

The CES function need not always be constant returns to scale. A nonconstant return (to scale) but homogeneous CES production function is also possible. Such a function will have the following equation

$$Y = A[\delta L^{-\beta} + (1 - \delta)K^{-\beta}]^{-h/\beta}$$

in which h stands for the degree of homogeneity. Clearly, the value of h equal to unity revives the constant return to scale CES function.

Empirically speaking, Ferguson (1965), for one, obtains estimates of σ, the elasticity of substitution, and h, the degree of homogeneity, for 18 U.S. manufacturing industries during the period 1949–1961 based on times series census data. To cite some examples, his estimate of σ (with standard error given in parentheses) is 0.905 (0.067) for lumber and wood, 1.123 (0.045) for furniture and fixtures, 1.104 (0.44) for textile mill products, 1.248 (0.072) for chemicals, and 1.041 (0.04) for nonelectrical machinery. However, some of these results compare favorably, while others strikingly unfavorably with estimates derived by Dhrymes (1965). The latter's comparable σ estimates are 1.109 for lumber and wood, 1.101 for furniture and fixture, and 0.936 for textile mill products. The strikingly different σ estimates are 0.506 for chemicals and 0.050 for nonelectrical machinery.

9.8 THE BURLEY (1973) STUDY ON AUSTRALIAN MANUFACTURING AND REINHARDT (1972) STUDY ON U.S. PHYSICIANS' SERVICES

In what follows, two more applied production functions will be discussed before transcendental production functions and technical progress will be introduced. In one, which is applied to the Australian manufacturing industries, use will be made of an energy (in horsepower units) measure of capital in relation to the CES production function. In another, where production of physicians' services will be studied, the production function will represent some transformation of a Cobb–Douglas function of inputs. These two studies are by Burley (1973) and Reinhardt (1972), respectively.

The Burley study is based on a modification of the Arrow, Chenery, Minhas, and Solow, in short, the ACMS[10] (1961) production function. That function can be shown to translate into

$$\ln \frac{K}{L} = \frac{\sigma}{1 - \sigma} \ln \frac{\delta}{1 - \delta} + (v - u)t + \frac{\sigma}{1 - \sigma} \ln \frac{W}{Y - W} + \frac{\epsilon}{1 - \sigma} \tag{9.43}$$

[10] See footnote 11 for a brief formulation of this function.

where

$$\begin{aligned}
\sigma &= \text{elasticity of substitution between labor } L \text{ and capital } K \\
\delta &= \text{capital intensity of the production process} \\
t &= \text{time trend} \\
W &= \text{wage bill in monetary units} \\
Y &= \text{aggregate output in monetary units} \\
v - u &= \text{bias of technical process} \\
\epsilon &= \text{error term}
\end{aligned} \tag{9.44}$$

In this formulation, the exogenous variables and the error variable are not correlated, unlike in the ACMS formulation.[11] This would obviously eliminate the possibility of bias in least squares coefficient estimates.

Since the capital input K is measured by horsepower, the question of error of misspecification might arise. However, the author has used true capital as a linear and time trend shift of the horsepower measure. Based on this, he has shown that this kind of measurement would not bias σ. To see this, consider the true relation[11]

$$\ln K/L = \sigma \ln \frac{\delta}{1-\delta} + \sigma \ln(w/r) + (1-\sigma)(v-u)t \tag{9.45}$$

which can be written, after appropriate use of symbols, as

$$\ln \text{K/L} = \beta_1 + \beta_2 \ln(w/r) + \beta_3 t \tag{9.46}$$

$$= \beta_1 + \beta_2 \ln\{wK/(Y-W)\} + \beta_3 t \tag{9.47}$$

Using K^* for the horsepower measure of K and assuming, not unreasonably, that the true measure of K might be a linear and time trend shift of K^*, that is $K_t = (a + bt)K_t^*$, a and b being unknowns, (9.47) reduces to

$$\begin{aligned}
\ln \frac{K^*}{L} &= \beta_1 + \beta_2 \ln \frac{wK^*}{Y-W} + (\beta_2 - 1)\ln(a+bt) + \beta_3 t \\
&= \beta_1^* + \beta_2 \ln \frac{wK^*}{Y-W} + \beta_3^* t
\end{aligned} \tag{9.48}$$

This implies that the horsepower specification does not bias β_2, that is, σ.[12]

[11] The ACMS function is formulated as:

$$\ln K/L = \sigma \ln \frac{\delta}{1-\delta} + (1-\sigma)(v-u)t + \sigma \ln \frac{w}{r} + \epsilon$$

where w and r are the wage and the rental rates, the other variables being as defined in (9.43). In this formulation, the errors of measurement in the exogenous variables w and r may depend on those in the endogenous variables K and L. Since ACMS used $w = W/L$ and $r = (Y - W)/K$, it means that r is not independent of K. That is, any error in measurement in K would be transmitted to r. Now the ACMS function has the error ϵ which contains the error of measurement of K/L. However, the 'exogenous' w/r is deduced from K/L and thus the error term ϵ would be correlated with this exogenous variable. Hence, estimates of σ may be biased.

[12] Without knowing the exact values of a and b, nothing precisely can be said about β_1 and β_3.

Empirical determination of the above function is based on the Australian manufacturing industries. Data relating to them extend over the 19 year period from 1949–1950 to 1967–1968. Without going into their details, we will report on the main observations drawn by the author. For all the industries, σ comes out positive but less than one, implying that the CES property is fulfilled. The R^2 values are significantly high. There is very little collinearity between $wK/(Y - W)$ and t. Since $(v - u)$ is strongly positive, all industries could be looked upon as becoming energy intensive over time as evident from a relationship between K and K^*. There is significant substitution of capital for labor taking place whenever the wage and rental ratio becomes high and vice versa, a finding that agrees well with the typical marginal productivity theory.

The second study to report on is by Reinhardt. It makes the important conclusion that the average American physician could profitably use about twice the number of assistants or aides currently being used, and thereby improve his hourly productivity by about 25%. The reason why he does not do so is indicated to be his fee increases which are higher than in other sectors. This sort of fee hikes, according to the study, serves to act as a substitute for increased efficiency.

The production function is specified as (with lower case letters indicating logarithms):[13]

$$q_i = \alpha_0 + \alpha_1 h_i - \beta_1 H_i + \alpha_2 K_i + \sum_{j=1}^{3} \gamma_j L_{ji} - \theta \left[\sum_{1}^{3} L_{ji} \right]^2 + \eta G_i + \sum_{s} \delta_i D_{si} + u_i \tag{9.49}$$

where:

q_i = (logarithm of) physicians rate of output in the ith practice

H = weekly input of physician's time (hours)

K = index of capital usage

L_1, L_2, and L_3 = number of registered nurses, technicians, and aides, respectively

G (= dummy variable) = 1 for specialty group but 0 for sole practitioner

D_s = quantitative indices: physician–population ratio (PPR) of the state in which the physician practices and percentage of hospital (PHV) and home (PHC) visits in total patient visits.

There are two other variables included: F, a physician's customary fee for an initial office visit, and Y, the dummy variable for year, assuming a value of 0 during 1965, the year of medical economics survey, and 1 for the year 1967.

Table 9.4 reports partly on the results obtained. Output shown is measured in three ways: total patient visits, the physician's own office visits, and patient billings (gross sales revenue). This is to cope with the difficulty of measuring the impact of physicians' services on patients' health.

[13] The form of this function seems to be a generalization of the Cobb–Douglas function.

TABLE 9.4 ESTIMATED PRODUCTION FUNCTIONS FOR GENERAL PRACTITIONERS IN PRIVATE PRACTICE*

	Sample Mean	Output Measured By Total Patient Visits		Output Measured By Office Visits		Output Measured By Patient Billings	
		Coefficient	S.E.[c]	Coefficient	S.E.[c]	Coefficient	S.E.[c]
log H[a]	4.06	1.67	0.23	—	—	1.04	0.18
H	60.98	−0.015	0.004	—	—	−0.0086	0.003
log OH[b]	3.53	—	—	0.67	0.04	—	—
log K	4.06	0.04	0.01	0.04	0.01	0.08	0.009
L_1	0.46	0.27	0.03	0.36	0.03	0.28	0.026
L_2	0.26	0.245	0.03	0.31	0.035	0.28	0.028
L_3	1.24	0.240	0.02	0.31	0.028	0.26	0.022
$(\Sigma L)^2$	5.13	−0.024	0.004	−0.035	0.005	−0.026	0.004
G	0.21	0.045	0.02	0.05	0.025	0.055	0.018
PPR	1.31	−0.058	0.03	−0.10	0.031	−0.044	0.024
PHV	0.15	0.217	0.09	—	—	0.222	0.075
PHC	0.04	−0.457	0.23	—	—	−0.514	0.186
log F	1.82	—	—	—	—	0.494	0.126
Year	0.52	—	—	—	—	0.051	0.017
Constant		−1.174	—	2.08	—	−1.403	—
$\overline{R}^2$		0.52		0.50		0.67	

[a] log of total weekly practice hours.

[b] log of total weekly office hours.

[c] All estimates statistically significant at the 1% level.

* Reprinted with permission V. Reinhardt, "A Production Function for Physician Services," *Review of Economics and Statistics* 42 (1972) Table 1, p. 59.

The table shows the sample mean of H to be about 61 hours per week, a very long work week indeed. The mean number of registered nurses, technicians, and aides is 0.46, 0.26, and 1.24, respectively. These numbers are small by any standard. By increasing these numbers, more profitable results should have been obtained. The $\overline{R}^2$ values are small but all coefficients are statistically significant at the 1% probability level.

9.9 GENERALIZATIONS OF THE COBB–DOUGLAS AND CES FUNCTIONS: THE TRANSLOG FUNCTIONS

Just as the CES function is a generalization of the Cobb–Douglas function, there are yet other generalizations possible. One, due to Zellner and Revankar (1969) has the function as:

$$Y \exp(CY) = AL^{\alpha}K^{\beta} \qquad C \geqq 0 \tag{9.50}$$

or,

$$\ln Y + CY = \ln A + \alpha \ln L + \beta \ln K \tag{9.51}$$

This is some kind of a transcendental function involving the outputs in which output and logarithm of output appear on the left-hand side, whereas in the conventional transcendental function inputs and logarithm of inputs appear on the right-hand side (see Halter and others (1957)).

Another generalization due to Nerlove (1963) and Ringstad (1967) has the equation

$$Y^{1+C \ln Y} = AL^{\alpha}K^{\beta} \qquad C \geqq 0 \tag{9.52}$$

or,

$$(1 + C \ln Y) \ln Y = \ln A + \alpha \ln L + \beta \ln K \tag{9.53}$$

in which $\ln Y$ and $(\ln Y)^2$ appear on the left-hand side.

A more generalized transcendental function, developed by Christensen and others (1973), which at the same time can be viewed as a generalization of the C–D function, is called a translog function, with a form such as

$$\ln Y = \ln A + \alpha \ln L + \beta \ln K + \gamma \ln L \ln K + \delta (\ln L)^2 + \epsilon(\ln K)^2 \tag{9.54}$$

It has a nonunitary elasticity of substitution and is therefore capable of describing the general substitution possibilities of diverse production technologies. See Griliches and Ringstad (1971) for similar conclusions drawn from a translog function fitted to the Norwegian manufacturing industry.

Like the C–D function, there are generalizations possible of the CES function. One such is based on input combinations of a given level to form factors at "higher levels" and then convert these into output, every time according to the CES function. This can be illustrated as follows:

$$Y = A\{[\alpha X_1^{-\gamma_1} + (1 - \alpha)X_2^{-\gamma_1}]^{-\gamma/\gamma_1} + [\beta X_3^{-\gamma_2} + (1 - \beta)X_4^{-\gamma_2}]^{\frac{-\gamma}{\gamma_2}}\}^{\frac{-1}{\gamma}} \tag{9.55}$$

In (9.55), the implication is X_1 and X_2 are mixed in a "higher level" factor, whose elasticity of substitution is $(1 + \gamma_1)^{-1}$, while X_3 and X_4 are mixed with an elasticity of substitution of $(1 + \gamma_2)^{-1}$. The "higher level" inputs are then mixed with elasticity $(1 + \gamma)^{-1}$ to produce outputs—see Sato (1967). Still another generalization produces what is called the VES or the variable elasticity of substitution function. Here the factor proportion determines the elasticity of substitution. One way of estimating the function is to regress the logarithm of output per worker on both the real wage and the capital–labor ratio—see Sato and Hoffman (1968), Lee and Fletcher (1968), Revankar (1971), Lovell (1973), and Hildebrand and Liu (1965).

Revankar (1971) applies the VES function to 12 U.S. industries. However, he concludes that in five of these the VES specification is superior to the CES one. Also he finds that the elasticity of substitution tends to be greater the more the industry is labor intensive. This is in keeping with conventional wisdom:

capital intensive technologies admit of lesser substitution possibilities than basic labor intensive ones. Note particularly that along any isoquant in the Revankar model, the elasticity of substitution keeps changing, whereas the elasticity is constant along a ray drawn from the origin in the north-east direction, regardless of the levels of the isoquants.

9.9.1 The Translog Cost Function: An Application Due to Pindyck (1979)

We will now illustrate how translog cost functions are derived. However, this will be done on the basis of an actual applied study, its subject matter being an international comparison of interfuel substitution and industrial demand for energy, Pindyck[14] (1979).

His translog cost function is assumed to be homothetically separable[15] in capital (K), labor (L), and energy (E) aggregates. This makes possible the supposition that expenditure shares for fuels are independent of expenditure shares for capital and labor, and the expenditure shares for fuels are independent of expenditure on total energy.

[14] This study follows a number of related studies—see, for instance, Berndt and Wood (1975), Fuss and Waverman (1975), Halvorsen (1976), Griffin and Gregory (1976), Fuss (1977), and Halvorsen and Ford (1978).

[15] The properties shown by homogeneous functions are shown by all functions that are monotonic increasing transformations of homogeneous functions. Production functions within this general class, including homogeneous functions, are said to be homothetic. If a production function is homothetic, rates of factor substitution will depend on relative rather than absolute amounts of factors.

A production or a cost function is strongly separable in all of its arguments if it can be represented as

$$Z = F\left[\sum_{i=1}^{n} f_i(x_i)\right]$$

where F and f are increasing functions. The function Z is strongly additive if

$$Z = \sum_{i=1}^{n} f_i(x_i)$$

where the f_is are increasing. Separability includes additivity as a special case. The function Z is weakly separable if the variables can be split into two (or more) groups $(x_1, \ldots, x_l)$ and $(x_{l+1}, \ldots, x_n)$ such that

$$Z = f_1(x_1, \ldots, x_l) + f_2(x_{l+1}, \ldots, x_n)$$

It is weakly additive if

$$Z = f_1(x_1, \ldots, x_l) + f_2(x_{l+1}, \ldots, x_n)$$

If the functions F and f_i, as in the case of weak separability and additivity, respectively, are homothetic, Z will exhibit homothetic (weak) separability and (weak) additivity. It will exhibit homothetic (strong) separability if F is homothetic.

A brief discussion of his method is presented first, followed then by an indication of his broad results.

The production function relates output Q to capital (K), labor (L), four kinds of energy (E) inputs F_1, F_2, F_3, and F_4, and materials M according to:

$$\mathrm{Q} = \mathrm{f(K, L, E(F_1, F_2, F_3, F_4), M)} \tag{9.56}$$

From this, a weakly separable[16] cost function of the following kind can be derived:

$$C = C[F(P_K, P_L, P_E(P_{F_1}, P_{F_2}, P_{F_3}, P_{F_4}), Q); P_M, Q] \tag{9.57}$$

where C is cost, F is a functional form, the Ps with appropriate subscripts for inputs represent prices of inputs, P_E is an aggregate price index of energy inputs, based on prices of fuels: P_{F_i}, $i = 1, 2, 3, 4$. This cost function is assumed homothetic.

The translog cost function happens to be a second order approximation to an arbitrary cost function:

$$\ln C = \beta_0 + \beta_Q \ln Q + \sum_i \beta_i \ln P_i + 1/2\, \gamma_{QQ} (\ln Q)^2$$
$$+ 1/2 \sum_i \sum_j \gamma_{ij} \ln P_i \ln P_j + \sum_i \gamma_{Qi} \ln Q \ln P_i \tag{9.58}$$

Using Shephard's Lemma[17], the author then finds derived demand for factors, from which the factor shares S_i are obtained[18]:

$$\begin{aligned} S_i &= \partial \ln C/\partial \ln P_i \\ &= \beta_i + \gamma_{Q_i} \ln Q + \sum_j \gamma_{ij} \ln P_j \qquad (i = 1, 2, \ldots, n) \end{aligned} \tag{9.59}$$

[16] See footnote 15 for its definition.

[17] Shephard's Lemma: Let us minimize expenditures on commodities in order to have a given utility level for a consumer. The solution for the quantity q_i of the ith good provides the compensated demand function for that good. (That is, a situation may be imagined in which some public agency taxes or subsidizes a consumer such that his utility is unaltered after a price change. This is the idea behind the notion of compensated demand.) If the solutions q_is are substituted in the expenditure: $\Sigma p_i q_i$, where p_i is the price per unit of the ith commodity, the expenditure function $X(p_1, \ldots, p_n, U^0)$, defined to be the minimum expenditure for a given utility level U^0, is obtained. Shephard's Lemma states that the partial derivative of X with respect to p_i is the ith compensated demand function, that is

$$\frac{\partial X}{\partial p_i} = q_i(p_1, \ldots, p_n, U^0)$$

[18] The following conditions will be satisfied by a cost function known to be homogeneous of degree 1 in prices, which conditions correspond to those that a well-behaved production function will satisfy $\sum S_i = 1$, $\sum \beta_i = 1$, $\sum \gamma_{Q_i} = 0$, $\gamma_{ij} = \gamma_{ji}$, $i \neq j$: $\sum_i \gamma_{ij} = \sum_j \gamma_{ji} = 0$. For homotheticity, we will require $\gamma_{Q_i} = 0$. See the original article for conditions for other properties of the cost function.

The author next computes the values of Allen's[19] partial elasticity of substitution using Uzawa (1962) simplifications from:

$$Q_{ij} = C(C_{ij}/C_iC_j) \tag{9.60}$$

In terms of the translog cost function, these measures become

$$\begin{aligned} \sigma_{ij} &= (\gamma_{ij} + S_iS_j)/(S_iS_j) \qquad i \neq j \\ \sigma_{ii} &= [\gamma_{ii} + S_i(S_i - 1)]/S_i^2 \end{aligned} \tag{9.61}$$

These lead to the own and cross partial elasticity of substitution η_{ii} and η_{ij} defined as:

$$\eta_{ii} = \sigma_{ii}S_i \tag{9.62}$$

$$\eta_{ij} = \sigma_{ij}S_j \tag{9.63}$$

assuming that the total quantity of energy used is constant.

For the measure of total price elasticity, define

$$\begin{aligned} \eta_{ii}^* &= d \ln X_i/d \ln P_i \\ &= \frac{P_i}{X_i}\left[\frac{\partial X_i}{\partial P_i}\bigg|_{E\,=\,\text{constant}} + \frac{\partial X_i}{\partial E}\frac{\partial E}{\partial P_E}\frac{\partial P_E}{\partial P_i}\right] \end{aligned} \tag{9.64}$$

where E is the total quantity of energy consumed and P_E the price index of energy. Now P_E is assumed to be given by a homothetic translog cost function with constant returns to scale. Therefore,

$$\ln P_E = \beta_0 + \sum_i \beta_i \ln P_i + \sum_i \sum_j \gamma_{ij} \ln P_i \ln P_j \tag{9.65}$$

[19] Allen's partial elasticity of substitution: suppose there are n factors of production and $f(x) = f(x_1, \ldots, x_n)$ is the production function with $x_1, x_2, \ldots, x_n$ the quantities of the n factors used. Assume that production is characterized by constant returns to scale and diminishing marginal rates of substitution. Then Allen's partial elasticity of substitution σ_{ij} between the ith and the jth $(i \neq j)$ factors of production is given by

$$\sigma_{ij} = \frac{x_1f_1 + \cdots + x_nf_n}{x_ix_j}\frac{\Delta_{ij}}{\Delta}$$

where $f_i = \dfrac{\partial f}{\partial x_i}$, $f_{ij} = \dfrac{\partial^2 f}{\partial x_i \partial x_j}$

$$\Delta = \begin{vmatrix} 0 & f_1 & \cdots & f_n \\ f_1 & f_{11} & \cdots & f_{1n} \\ \cdot\cdot & \cdot\cdot & \cdots & \cdot \\ f_n & f_{n1} & \cdots & f_{nn} \end{vmatrix}$$

and Δ_{ij} is the cofactor of the element f_{ij} in the determinant Δ.

In (9.60), C_i and C_j are the first derivatives of C with regard to its ith and jth arguments, and the C_{ij}s are the cross derivatives.

from which the factor shares are derived as

$$S_i = \frac{\partial \ln P_E}{\partial P_i} = \beta_i + \sum_j \gamma_{ij} \ln P_j \tag{9.66}$$

Thus

$$\eta^*_{ii} = \eta_{ii} + \eta_{EE} S_i \tag{9.67}$$

where η_{EE} is the own price elasticity of aggregate energy use. Similarly, for a given fuel,

$$\eta^*_{ij} = \eta_{ij} + \eta_{EE} S_j \tag{9.68}$$

Next, the total output elasticity is defined as

$$\eta^*_{iQ} = \frac{\partial \ln X_i}{\partial \ln Q} = \frac{Q}{X_i} \frac{\partial X_i}{\partial E} \frac{\partial E}{\partial Q} \tag{9.69}$$

Assuming that the energy cost function is homothetic, it follows that

$$\eta^*_{iQ} = \eta_{EQ} \tag{9.70}$$

where η_{EQ} is the elasticity of energy use with respect to output changes, given by

$$\eta_{EQ} = \frac{\gamma_{QE}}{S_E} + \beta_Q + \gamma_{QQ} \ln Q + \sum_{i=K}^{L,E} \gamma_{Qi} \ln P_i \tag{9.71}$$

The author equates β_Q to 1 and γ_{QQ} to 0 to simplify the calculations.

Next, the elasticity of average cost (AC) of production with respect to price of energy is calculated from:

$$\eta_{CE} = \partial \ln AC/\partial \ln P_E \tag{9.72}$$

$$\eta_{Ci} = \partial \ln AC/\partial \ln P_i \tag{9.73}$$

Using the homothetic translog cost function form (9.58), adapting it to provide an expression for average cost, we have

$$\eta_{CE} = \beta_E + \gamma_{EE} \ln P_E + \gamma_{EK} \ln P_K + \gamma_{EL} \ln P_L + \gamma_{QE} \ln Q \tag{9.74}$$

Since the energy cost function is homothetic, it follows that

$$\eta_{Ci} = \eta_{CE}\, S_i \tag{9.75}$$

Pindyck uses the above elasticity formulas and applies them to ten countries: Canada, France, Italy, Japan, Netherlands, Norway, Sweden, the United Kingdom, the United States, and West Germany. Data used relate to the period 1959–1973; however, due to data limitations, a shorter period, 1963–1973, is used for the share equations. We now report his broad results. Reference to some earlier studies for numerical comparison of results appears in footnote 14.

Energy and capital come out as strong complements in the Pindyck study. On the other hand, Fuss and Waverman (1975) obtain mixed results based on energy–capital substitutability and these extend over to some special industries or special forms of cost function used. However, Griffin and Gregory (1976) report strong evidence of capital–energy substitutability and their estimate of Allen elasticity of substitution of 1.01 happens to be not too different from Pindyck's (0.8).

On questions of energy policy, the own price elasticity of aggregate energy use is often deemed to be a useful parameter. The approximate value of −0.8 for this elasticity obtained by both Pindyck and Griffin and Gregory seems to be larger than others' estimates and is much larger than the consensus estimates of −0.2 to −0.3 often used by policy analysts in the United States. However, Pindyck's estimate of output elasticity of energy use of 0.7 to 0.8 seems to be less than most consensus estimates of around 1.0. This may be because of the nonhomotheticity of the estimated aggregate cost functions assumed by these estimates.

Turning to partial and total fuel price elasticities, Pindyck's estimates are −0.08 to −0.16 for partial elasticity for electricity. These compare unfavorably with others' estimates of −0.5 to −1.2, but his estimates of −0.54 to −0.63 for total elasticity for this commodity do not compare too unfavorably with others' estimates of −0.74 (Fuss (1977)) to −0.92 (Halvorsen (1976)).

In addition, the own price elasticity for oil (−0.22 to −1.17) obtained by Pindyck disagrees considerably from Halvorsen's (−2.82) but less so from Fuss's (−1.30). The disagreement is much less though in terms of similar elasticity figures for coal (−1.29 to −2.24) and for natural gas (−0.41 to −2.34) between Pindyck's and others'.

9.9.2 The CES–Translog Cost Function Due to Pollak and Others (1984)

An extension of the n factor translog cost function of the Christensen and others (1973) type to include a CES cost function is developed by Pollak and others (1984). To demonstrate it, we begin by laying down the translog cost function[20] as

$$\ln C(Q, W) = \beta_0 + \beta_Q \ln Q + \sum_K \beta_K \ln W_K + \frac{1}{2}\sum_K \sum_j \beta_{Kj} \ln W_K \ln W_j + \sum_K \gamma_{QK} \ln Q \ln W_K \tag{9.76}$$

[20] A similar application of the translog production and cost function is made to the U.S. trucking industry in a very recent study. See Daughety and Nelson (1988). One of its two broad conclusions is that similarity between early periods of regulation and deregulation of this industry is greater than between early and late periods of regulation. The other is that higher burdens of regulation are borne by those trucking firms that are inflicted with higher costs to start with.

where:

$$Q = \text{output}$$
$$Ws = \text{factor prices}$$
$$\beta_{ij} = \text{coefficients, with } \beta_{ij} = \beta_{ji} \text{ for all } i \text{ and } j$$
$$\sum_K \beta_K = 1$$
$$\sum_K \beta_{Ki} = 0 \text{ for all } i$$
$$\sum_K \gamma_{QK} = 0$$

The extension to the CES–translog format changes the cost function to

$$\ln C(Q, W) = \beta_0 + \beta_Q \ln Q + \ln \left[\sum_K \beta_K W_K^{1-\sigma} \right]^{\frac{1}{1-\sigma}} + \frac{1}{2} \sum_K \sum_j \beta_{Kj} \ln W_K \ln W_j \tag{9.77}$$

with the restrictions on coefficients or parameters remaining unchanged. Using Shephard's Lemma, cost minimizing factor demand functions are derived from which the solution for the share S_i of the ith factor is obtained and simplified to

$$S_i = \frac{\beta_i W_i^{1-\sigma}}{\sum_K \beta_K W_K^{1-\sigma}} + \sum_K \beta_{iK} \ln W_K + \gamma_{Qi} \ln Q \tag{9.78}$$

Also, the cross Allen elasticity of substitution is derived as

$$\sigma_{ij} = \left\{ (\sigma - 1) \left[\frac{\beta_i W_i^{1-\sigma}}{\sum \beta_K W_K^{1-\sigma}} \right] \left[\frac{\beta_j W_j^{1-\sigma}}{\sum \beta_K W_K^{1-\sigma}} \right] + \beta_{ij} + S_i S_j \right\} \bigg/ m_i m_j \tag{9.79}$$

A few simplifications of the above formulas are in order for special values of the parameters. For instance, if the βs and γs are zero, the CES–translog factor demand and cost function reduce to the CES factor demand and cost function. On the other hand, if $\sigma = 1$, the CES–translog factor demand and cost function reduce to the translog factor demand and cost function, respectively.

The authors use eight data sets on labor, capital, and material and four forms of energy: coal, oil, natural gas, and electricity corresponding to U.S. and Dutch manufacturing industries. They assume production to be homothetic, technical progress Harrod neutral,[21] factor prices exogenous, and factor shares to adjust instantaneously to factor price changes. One should look into their numerical and

[21] See the study by Beckman and Sato (1969), reported next, for its definition.

statistical results for a more complete knowledge of this important piece of work. However, we wish to reiterate here their most fundamental observation. That is, the CES–translog function is "superior" to the translog function.[22] This is established using likelihood ratio[23] tests of restrictions and regularity conditions.[24] This concludes our discussion of the work of Pollak and others (1984).

In the context of production costs, derived demand and share systems, we wish to especially note one point. This relates to many applied production studies which center around a deterministic model of the firm as a basis for generating the equations of input demand and share systems. At the end, these studies appear to "embed" the system in a stochastic framework by allowing for linear error terms. One can compare this approach to an approach of general error models (GEMs) initiated by McElroy (1987). In this, the error specifications are taken to arise in various parts of the optimizing model and are then combined into an integrated whole. These models give special statistical meaning to George Stigler's view that analysts' lack of knowledge of the true optimization problem may indeed be the source of some apparent inefficiencies indicated by their analysis.[25]

9.10 TECHNICAL PROGRESS: THE BECKMAN AND SATO (1969) STUDY

The last study is on technical progress. Its authors, Beckman and Sato, maintain that the problem of specification of production function and the form of technical progress are not independent of each other. Some forms of the former preclude some forms of the latter. For example, in the case of a C–D production function, technical change could bring about changes in the production function in more ways than just changing the coefficients of labor and capital. However, if, due to neutrality, these coefficients would not change, the change must enter the function in a multiplicative fashion. In that case, it should either be Hicks neutral or Harrod neutral—to be defined—(or any combination of the two, called factor augmenting technical progress) but any way these could not be separately identifiable. In other cases, it could be shown that certain production functions preclude certain types of technical progress.

Thus the point is made that in choosing the kind of technical progress, one should be confined not only to the Hicks or Harrod neutral form but also to other forms, to be determined empirically, as is done by Beckman and Sato. Their study is concerned with the U.S., Japanese, and German economies.

[22] In fact, the superiority is established in all but one of their cases investigated.

[23] See especially Chapter 10 for details of this test.

[24] These include the conditions that the function is continuous, and at least twice differentiable, among other things.

[25] Indeed McElroy uses additive GEMs. By means of specification tests, she concludes that a translog additive GEM is superior to an ordinary translog model.

For their model, consider the following notation:

Y = output

K = capital

L = labor

$y = Y/K$ = output–capital ratio

$x = L/K$ = labor–capital ratio

$z = Y/L$ = output–labor ratio

$k = K/L = 1/x$ = capital–labor ratio

r = return on capital

w = wage rate

$R = r/y$ = capital's relative share of income

$\beta = 1 - \alpha = w/z$ = labor's share of income

t = time, index of exogenous technical progress

$A(t)$ = technical progress term

Let the production function be defined by

$$Y(t) = F(K(t), L(t), t) \tag{9.80}$$

Assume it to be homogeneous of degree 1 in K and L. Further, assume factor and output markets to be competitive, and technical progress exogenous. Then the following relations can be derived:

$$y(t) = F(1, L/K, t) = f(x, t) \rightarrow r = \partial F/\partial K = f - xf_x = \phi_k \tag{9.81}$$

$$z = F(K/L, 1, t) = \phi(k, t) \rightarrow w = \partial F/\partial L = \phi - k\phi_k = f_x \tag{9.82}$$

That is, the rental and wage rates are equated to the marginal productivity of capital and labor, respectively.

A technical change may consist of not only changes in the variable values such as y, z, k, the marginal productivities, and the marginal rates of substitution (MRS), but also, as often overlooked in the literature, changes in relations concerning these variables. If these relations are to be unchanged, technical changes, if any, would be called neutral. These would be Hicks neutral (HN) when the relation between the MRS and the factor proportion is invariant; they would be called Harrod neutral (HDN) if the relation between the capital–output ratio and the interest rate is invariant; or they would be Solow neutral (SN) when the relation between output per worker and wage rate is unchanged.

The various types of technical progress can be categorized in four classes:

1. Product augmenting

   1.1 Hicks neutrality:

$$Y = A(t)\, F(K, L) \tag{9.83}$$

   Here technical change increases the level of output a constant number of times of the level that would obtain in the absence of such a change.

   1.2 Labor additive:

$$Y = A(t)\, L + F(K, L) \tag{9.84}$$

   Here output expands in proportion to labor used.

   1.3 Capital additive:

$$Y = A(t)\, K + F(K, L) \tag{9.85}$$

   The implication is the same as in 1.2 above, except that the change is in terms of capital.

2. Labor augmenting

   2.1 Harrod neutrality

$$Y = F(K, AL) \tag{9.86}$$

   2.2 Labor combining

$$Y = F(K, A(t)K + L) \tag{9.87}$$

   Here labor augmentation is in terms of capital used.

3. Capital augmenting (similar to 2)

   3.1 Solow neutrality:

$$Y = F(AK, L) \tag{9.88}$$

   3.2 Capital combining

$$Y = F(K + A(t)L, L) \tag{9.89}$$

4. Input decreasing

   4.1 Labor decreasing: The inverse production function has the form:

$$L = G(K, Y) + C(t)Y \qquad dC/dt < 0 \tag{9.90}$$

   This means that L decreases in proportion to Y as time progresses, since dC/dt is negative.

   4.2 Capital decreasing (similar to 4.1)

$$K = H(K, Y) + C(t)Y \qquad dC/dt < 0 \tag{9.91}$$

5. Factor augmenting technical progress

$$Y = F[A(t)K, B(t)L] \tag{9.92}$$

TABLE 9.5 TYPES OF TECHNICAL PROGRESS IMPLIED BY ALTERNATIVE INVARIANT RELATIONSHIPS*

	1 $\frac{\text{output}}{\text{capital}}$ (y)	2 $\frac{\text{output}}{\text{labor}}$ (z)	3 $\frac{\text{labor}}{\text{capital}}$ (x)	4 Interest (r)	5 Wage (w)	6 MRS (R)
4 Interest (r)	Harrod II	Capital combining V	Labor additive IX			
5 Wage (w)	Labor combining IV	Solow III	Capital additive VIII	No progress	No progress	
6 MRS (R)	Labor VI decreasing	Capital decreasing VII	Hicks I	No progress	No progress	
7 Share (β)	Harrod II	Solow III	Hicks I	Harrod II	Solow III	Hicks I

* Reprinted with permission M. Beckman and K. Sato, "Production Function and Technical Progress," *American Economic Review* 59 (1969) Table 1, p. 92.

Evidently this combines Harrod and Hicks neutrality, or Solow and Hicks neutrality. It occurs when the capital–output ratio is a separable function of labor's share and time,

$$Y/K = A(t)\ \phi\ (\text{share}) \tag{9.93}$$

The various relationships are summarized in Table 9-5. The authors perform a regression analysis of time series data relating to the United States, Japan, and Germany (for nonfarm sectors). Linear and nonlinear equations of the type:

$$q(t) = a + bp(t) + u(t) \tag{9.94}$$

$$\log q(t) = a + b \log p(t) + u(t) \tag{9.95}$$

are fitted, when $p(t)$ and $q(t)$ represent economic variables such as R and x for Hicks neutrality. These equations are estimated for the relationships of Table 9.5, rather than the implied production functions. The reason is that the latter involve nonlinearity, which would make estimation very difficult.

For testing the invariance of these relationships with respect to time, a time trend t is also included in the above equations.

Table 9-6 provides values of R^2 and their ranks for various definitions of neutrality in the United States, Japan and Germany. The table shows that both the United States and Germany have Solow neutral technical progress rank first, but Japan has it rank third. Japan, on the other hand, has Harrod neutrality rank first, the United States has it second but Germany has it ranked very low (seventh).

TABLE 9.6 VALUES OF R^2 AND THEIR RANKS IN LOG-LINEAR REGRESSIONS FOR THE UNITED STATES, JAPAN AND GERMANY*

Type		United States		Japan		Germany	
		R^2	Rank	R^2	Rank	R^2	Rank
I	Hicks	0.831	4	0.785	2	0.708	4
II	Harrod	0.933	2	0.855	1	0.422	7
III	Solow	0.944	1	0.758	3	0.980	1
IV	Labor-combining	0.897	3	0.021	8	0.770	3
V	Capital-combining	0.818	5	0.039	7	0.272	9
VI	Labor-decreasing	0.466	8	0.755	4	0.692	5
VII	Capital-decreasing	0.702	7	0.001	9	0.653	6
VIII	Capital-additive	0.779	6	0.473	6	0.950	2
IX	Labor-additive	0.411	9	0.633	5	0.347	8

* Reprinted with permission M. Beckman and K. Sato, "Production Function and Technical Progress," *American Economic Review* 59 (1969) Table 3, p. 95.

For none of the countries Hicks neutrality ranks as high as Solow or Harrod neutrality. It is interesting to note that capital-additive neutrality ranks high (second) in Germany but not as high in either the United States or Japan.

The finding that Solow and Harrod neutrality rank high in these countries is not surprising. It is associated with the log-linear relations leading to production functions of the CES type.

The reproduction of the detailed regression results would be rather lengthy. It would be useful, however, to summarize them in a few points. First, among the unconventional types of technical progress, some do well in one or the other country, but none is outstanding in any country. Examples of technical progress with fair ranks are: *United States* labor-combining and capital-combining: *Japan* labor-decreasing and labor-additive; and *Germany* both labor and capital decreasing and capital additive technology. Second, the conventional types of neutrality (Hicks, Harrod, and Solow) are about as good or better, in all countries, than the unconventional types. Third, the introduction of time as an additional explanatory variable improves only marginally the statistical fit. Thus, general factor augmenting technical progress does not seem to provide a significantly improved explanation of observed phenomenon over limited technical progress (augmenting only one factor). Fourth, regardless of the kind of technical change, the underlying production function turns out to be approximately a C–D or a CES function in each situation.

9.11 INVESTMENT

Investment, by its very nature, is a dynamic phenomenon and thus its determinants arise over various past periods. Such intertemporal relations produce the problems of autocorrelation of errors, because the latter are a part of those determinants.

In terms of most investment function formulations, the dynamics are provided for by lags. But the formulations themselves may vary as between output and relative prices being given a major role in the determination of investment. The first gives rise to a rather ad hoc class of models, called the accelerator models, while the second generates what are called the neoclassical models based on well-defined optimizing techniques (Jorgenson (1971)).

In what follows, we discuss accelerator models, distributed lag models of various descriptions, the status of the error terms and the role of autocorrelated residuals as a convenience, not a nuisance; Bean's (1979) model of U.K. investment showing parameter constraints of the investment equation; the role of additional (financial, etc.) variables and optimizing rationale for investment including Jorgenson's neoclassical approach to it, and an application by Boatwright and Eaton (1972) compared to Jorgenson and Stephenson (1967), etc.

9.12 THE ACCELERATOR MODELS

Investment is a flow concept. But it is related to capital which is a stock concept. Consider the following two relations, the first due to net and the second due to gross investment:

$$I_t^n = K_t - K_{t-1} \tag{9.96}$$

$$I_t^g = I_t^n + \delta_t \tag{9.97}$$

where K_i is the capital stock at the end of period i, $i = t - 1, t$; δ_t is depreciation or capital stock consumed during the period; and I_t^g and I_t^n are gross and net investments. Evidently depreciation is a part of gross investment but it is netted out in the net investment; otherwise it is capital accumulation (decumulation) that determines the flow of investment.

Capital changes with an eye to a desired level of the capital stock, and investment propels the actual capital stock in that direction. In terms of output Y_t and the desired capital stock K_t^*, the fixed relation is

$$Y_t = \alpha\, K_t^*$$

From this, K_t^* is solved out as

$$K_t^* = \gamma\, Y_t \tag{9.98}$$

where γ is the reciprocal of α. Assume for the sake of simplicity that the desired capital stock is always realized at the end of the period. Then, assuming δ_t to be either zero or a fraction θ of last period's capital stock K_{t-1}, we have either

$$I_t^g = \gamma(Y_t - Y_{t-1}) \tag{9.99}$$

or,

$$I_t^g = \gamma\, Y_t - \gamma(1 - \theta)\, Y_{t-1} \tag{9.100}$$

The first describes the very simple accelerator model of investment. Here investment depends not on the simple rate but the growth rate of output, hence the name accelerator model of investment. This principle is also present in the second equation, but is more complete in this equation than the first because of the presence of depreciation. However, the right-hand side of this equation reveals the working of the time lag or, more precisely, the distributed lag of output in its effect on gross investment.

But the assumption that desired capital stocks are realized at the end of every period is hardly defensible. Instead, one can use the model of partial stock adjustment

$$K_t - K_{t-1} = \beta(K_t^* - K_{t-1}) \qquad 0 < \beta < 1 \tag{9.101}$$

into the previous equations to obtain

$$I_t^g = \beta\gamma Y_t - \beta\gamma(1 - \theta)\, Y_{t-1} + (1 - \beta)\, I_{t-1}^g \tag{9.102}$$

Structurally this is the same equation as (9.100) except for the inclusion of a lagged dependent variable on its right-hand side. Also, in (9.102), the variables Y_t and Y_{t-1} have, to a large extent, common coefficients. This could be the source of a collinearity problem in equation estimation.

Still the greater problem, as pointed out by Hines and Catephores (1970) in the context of empirical models of investment for the U.K. economy, seems to be relating desired capital stock to actual rather than desired output. For a change, one could use an adaptive output model. Even then the emerging equation for gross investment would not be too much different from (9.102). More complex models of desire formation would perhaps be better but they would give rise to more complex and extensive patterns of distributed lags in output and investment. This kind of feature runs prominently across the investment function models of, for instance, Eisner (1960), deLeeuw (1962), Almon (1965), and Evans (1969).

9.13 DISTRIBUTED LAG MODELS

A very pioneering form of distributed lags in investment is used by Koyck (1954). According to this, capital stock is simply a distributed lag function of output, where the lags start after the first quarter and the weights of lags proportionally decline with time:

$$K_t = a_0 Y_t + a_1 Y_{t-1} + a_1 b Y_{t-2} + a_1 b^2 Y_{t-3} + \ldots \tag{9.103}$$

From the above pattern, we have

$$bK_{t-1} = a_0 b Y_{t-1} + a_1 \sum_{0}^{\infty} b^{j+1}\, Y_{t-j-2} \tag{9.104}$$

Thus,

$$K_t - bK_{t-1} = a_0 Y_t + (a_1 - a_0 b)\, Y_{t-1} \tag{9.105}$$

and net investment I_t^n, which is $K_t - K_{t-1}$, is

$$\begin{aligned} I_t^n &= K_t - bK_{t-1} + bK_{t-1} - K_{t-1} \\ &= a_0 Y_t + (a_1 - a_0 b)\, Y_{t-1} - (1 - b)\, K_{t-1} \end{aligned} \tag{9.106}$$

We have seen this kind of modeling before (Section 8.7.1 of Chapter 8). One may take issue with whether the geometrically declining weights would be the best possible model of lags in behavior. For instance, delays between output and consequential investment may be caused by not only lags in decision making but also the fact that it may involve several months and sometimes years for the completion of capital projects in equipments and buildings. These kinds of decision and construction lags might imply a deviation from uniformly declining weights of lags: the weights might rise through more distant periods before falling still further back in history. One such pattern might be described by an 'inverted *W*', where there are two peaks. One of these is due to decision lags. This arises prior to the other lag, which is due to construction delays. Such a pattern is used by Evans (1967 and 1969).

With more complex lag patterns, obviously larger numbers of lagged values have to be tried. But that would cause the problems of both lesser numbers of degrees of freedom, and possibly multicollinearity. A way out is to impose constraints on the coefficients of the lag distribution to reduce their number. An example is the Koyck lag structure, which ultimately is reduced to include three coefficients only.[26]

Another way out is illustrated by the Almon (1965) technique. According to this, select the form of the lag distribution, say a polynomial distributed lag in output, estimate the parameters of the polynomial form, and then determine the investment function. This technique is fully discussed in Section 8.7.5.

Two special features should be emphasized while explaining investment expenditures by means of distributed lags: the status of the disturbance terms, and the importance of other variables such as cash flow, long run rate of interest, and so on. These are financial variables which reflect on the firm's internal source of funds, and its ability to raise capital from external sources.

9.13.1 The Error Terms and Autocorrelated Residuals

The error structures and the estimation problems arising from these are discussed in Chapter 8, Section 8.7.3. This section should be reviewed for a better perspective. The only last point on errors we would like to mention is the role usually assigned to autocorrelation of residuals. This is often looked at as a nuisance, but as Hendry and Mizon (1978) point out, this need not be so. Indeed, if there is a dynamic process generating, for instance, the investment data, and if the model can be ultimately shown to reduce to a form that involves an autoregressive error, one can show that autocorrelation is an economical and useful means of describing the dynamic relationship. Since the autocorrelation model represents a constrained form of the dynamic model, it will lead to the lessening of the number of parameters by the number of constraints used, and thus improved statistical efficiency.

Take, for instance, the investment model to be of the form:

$$I_t^g = \beta_1 I_{t-1}^g + \gamma_0 X_t + \gamma_1 X_{t-1} + \epsilon_t \tag{9.107}$$

where X is a relevant economic variable determining investment I^g and ϵ is the residual variable. Assume:

[26] See Chapter 8, Section 8.7.1 for more on this.

$$
\begin{aligned}
|\beta_1| &< 1 \\
E(\epsilon_t) &= 0 \\
V(\epsilon_t) &= \sigma^2, \qquad \text{for all } t \\
\text{cov}(\epsilon_t, \epsilon_s) &= 0, \qquad \text{for } t \neq s \\
L_n I_t^g &= I_{t-n}^g
\end{aligned} \tag{9.108}
$$

Evidently, L is the lag operator. Then

$$(1 - \beta_1 L) I_t^g = (\gamma_0 + \gamma_1 L)\, X_t + \epsilon_t \tag{9.109}$$

Therefore, assuming that

$$\gamma_1 = -\beta_1 \gamma_0 \tag{9.110}$$

and using this constraint in (9.109), and dividing both sides of the resulting equation by the common factor $1 - \beta_1 L$, we have

$$I_t^g = \gamma_0 X_t + u_t \tag{9.111}$$

where

$$u_t = \epsilon_t / (1 - \beta_1 L) \tag{9.112}$$

The ultimate error u_t can be expressed as

$$u_t = \beta_1 u_{t-1} + \epsilon_t \tag{9.113}$$

This has the form of the first-order autoregressive process with the implied autocorrelation coefficient β_1. As we have already seen, this coefficient is the common root of the polynomial in the log operator $1 - \beta_1 L = 0$. Thus, when the original equation is written as a static model with the residual term u_t, the constraint among the parameters of the original model works out a root that is none other than the serial correlation of the first-order autoregressive process u_t. Therefore the autoregressive process is a convenience, not a nuisance. Moreover, equation (9.111) requires 2 parameters (γ_0 and β_1) to be estimated rather than three (γ_0, γ_1, and β_1) of the original equation implying statistical efficiency.

9.14 AN APPLICATION BY BEAN (1979) WITH PARAMETER CONSTRAINTS

Use of constraints on parameters of the investment equation is the special feature of Bean (1979). He takes quarterly data for the United Kingdom for the period 1957 III–1975 IV and relates current investment expenditures to such expenditures as well as output over the last 10 quarters. Otherwise the lag coefficients are unconstrained to begin with. The particular equation used is as follows with the values of coefficients $\hat{\beta}_i$, $\hat{\gamma}_i$, and $\hat{\delta}_i$ shown in (9.114b):

$$\ln I_t^g = \underset{(0.7)}{-1.04} + \sum_{i=1}^{10} \hat{\beta}_i \ln I_{t-i}^g + \sum_{i=0}^{10} \hat{\gamma}_i \ln X_{t-1} + \sum_{i=1}^{3} \hat{\delta}_i S_i - \underset{(1.2)}{0.003t} \quad (9.114a)$$

$$\text{SEE} = 0.046 \qquad \chi_1^2\,(8) = 27.2 \qquad \chi_2^2\,(3) = 3.8$$

In the above, X is output, S is quarterly dummy, t is the time trend, and the variables I^g and X are expressed in seasonally unadjusted values. $\chi_1^2(n_1)$ and $\chi_2^2(n_2)$ are the values of the chi-squared statistics with respective degrees of freedom: the first tests[27] the stability of parameters in future time periods, and the second tests[28] the lack of autocorrelation of higher orders. The t values are given in parentheses.

Bean goes on then to restrict the lag coefficients of I^g and X both separately and jointly. His ultimate estimated equation

i	$\hat{\beta}_i$	$\hat{\gamma}_i$	$\hat{\delta}_i$
0	—	0.3(0.8)	—
1	0.43(3.0)	0.42(0.9)	−0.34(2.2)
2	0.25(1.6)	−0.06(0.1)	−0.24(2.2)
3	0.19(1.2)	0.56(1.2)	−0.36(2.4)
4	0.25(1.6)	−1.04(2.2)	
5	−0.28(1.7)	1.19(2.4)	
6	−0.11(0.7)	−0.29(0.5)	
7	−0.05(0.3)	−0.12(0.2)	
8	0.11(0.7)	−0.7(1.4)	
9	−0.08(0.5)	0.56(1.1)	
10	0.07(0.05)	−0.15(0.4)	

(9.114b)

becomes:

$$\begin{aligned}\Delta_4 \ln I_t^g = {} & \underset{(6.2)}{0.82}\, \Delta_4 \ln X_t + \underset{(8.6)}{1.33}\, \Delta_4 \ln X_{t-5} + \underset{(4.7)}{0.4}\, \Delta_4 \ln \frac{I_t^g}{X_{t-5}} \\ & + \underset{(3.4)}{0.19} \sum_{i=1}^{4} \ln \left(\frac{I_{t-i}^g}{X_{t-i-5}} \right) - \underset{(5.1)}{1.03} \ln \left(\frac{I_{t-4}^g}{X_{t-9}} \right) + \underset{(3.6)}{0.07}\, \Delta_4 D \\ & - \underset{(3.4)}{0.25}\, \Delta \ln R_{t-5}^* - 0.05\, \Delta \ln C_{t-5} - 0.12\, CA_{t-6}\end{aligned} \quad (9.115)$$

$$\text{SEE} = 0.036 \qquad \chi_1^2\,(9) = 6.5 \qquad F(8.38) = 1.96$$

[27] This test is a test of the accuracy of future (one period) forecasts of the dependent variable for each of n_1 periods, every time using the estimated coefficients and the *actual* data on the independent variables of the regression equation.

[28] This test is based on the number n_2, which is the maximum order of autoregression—see Pierce (1971).

The above is only a part of the equation in that it does not show the intercept term nor the seasonal dummies. The new variables in this equation are D, R, C, and CA. D is a dummy variable which has the value 1 in 1968 IV, −1 in 1969 IV, and 0 elsewhere. The purpose is to evaluate how investment was affected as the special bonus on investment grants was eliminated in 1968. R^* is interest on bank loans, a proxy for nominal interest rates; C is the real capital cost; and CA the excess of proportion of firms reporting adequate capacity to meet demand over those having shortfalls in capacity. The Δ_4 differences reflect changes over a four-quarter period. For instance, $\Delta_4 X_t = X_t - X_{t-4}$.

Three special features of Bean's revised equation should be noted. First, investment changes are affected by output changes, unlike the accelerator principle in which output changes are taken to influence the level of investment. Second, changes in the ratio of investment to output happening in past periods (that is periods $t-5$ and $t-9$) affect the current change in investment, indicating a tendency towards the equilibrium ratio of output to investment in the long run. Third, movements in the ratios of investment to output *cumulatively*[29] influence current investment changes.

There are a few criteria that lie behind the selection of the above lag structure. First, the short-run variations have the ripple effect on a certain long-run relation. That relation in Bean's study is given by:

$$\frac{I^g}{X} = \exp(\mathrm{c} + 5.66\, r)$$

where c is a constant, and r the rate of growth of output. Second, the more complete the length of the distribution of lags the better. Lastly, from the forecast statistic $\chi_1^2(n_1)$ we gather that the relation remains stable outside the sample period chosen. Also the autocorrelation statistic $\chi_1^2(n_2)$ indicates the lack of any higher order autocorrelations.

9.15 ADDITIONAL VARIABLES AND EXPLICIT OPTIMIZING RATIONALE FOR INVESTMENT

After the variables of the nominal interest rate and the real cost of capital there are still other variables, for instance prices, which can be included as additional explanatory variables. Also, the relation between investment and output can be established on a more objective basis. For instance, it may be derived from the optimizing behavior of the firms. One such behavior is reflected in the work of Jorgenson and his associates,[30] described in the literature as the neoclassical approach.

[29] As per the term $\sum_{1}^{4} \ln \frac{I^g_{t-i}}{X_{t-i-5}}$

[30] See Jorgenson (1963, 1965, and 1967), Jorgenson and Stephenson (1967), Jorgenson and Siebert (1968), and Jorgenson, Hunter, and Nadiri (1970).

This (neoclassical) approach consists of maximizing the present value of the firm, subject to a given production function. This function is chosen to be a C–D production function. The other constraint of the maximization process is a simple proportionate requirement for the depreciation of capital: depreciation is a constant fraction of the preexisting level of capital stock.

In what follows we dwell on a more recent model that includes both additional explanatory variables, and the Jorgenson type of neoclassical theory of capital accumulation even though based on the CES production function. Later we refer to some of the other Jorgenson models for comparative purposes.

9.16 OTHER INVESTMENT FUNCTIONS

An empirical example of an investment function centering around the U.S. business fixed investment demand fitted to annual data over the period 1949–1960 was discussed before[31] (Hickman (1965)). Below we report on a similar model applied to U.K. manufacturing industries. The model is due to Boatwright and Eaton (1972). The novelty of the work seems to be using the estimated model to evaluate how investment is promoted by three types of investment incentive schemes. This is examined by means of a taxation function derived for this purpose.

9.16.1 The Boatwright and Eaton (1972) Model of U.K. Investment

This model uses two kinds of lags: (1) lags between a change in relevant economic variables and the start of a project, and (2) gestation lags between the start of a project and its completion. Based on these and the Jorgenson type of neoclassical theory of capital accumulation as indicated before, the authors obtain the following equation for net investment I_t:

$$I_t = \sum_{i=0}^{n} w_i \Delta[\alpha^{\gamma}(p/c)^{\gamma} Q]_{t-i} + \delta K_{t-1} \tag{9.116}$$

where

$$\begin{aligned}
K &= \text{capital} \\
\delta &= \text{rate of depreciation or replacement} \\
Q &= \text{output} \\
\alpha &= \text{coefficient of capital in the production function} \\
\gamma &= \text{elasticity of substitution between labor and capital} \\
c &= \text{unit cost of capital}
\end{aligned} \tag{9.117}$$

[31] See Chapter 8, Section 8.7.4.

p = price of output per unit
w_i = proportion of work completed i periods after start
n = number of periods by which a project had to be completed
Δ = sign of first difference

They take the short form of this equation and use an adapted form of Almon lags. The modified form of the equation is

$$I_t = b_1A_1 + b_2A_2 + b_3A_3 + \delta K_{t-1} \tag{9.118}$$

In (9.118) two weights, at the start and end of the period, are assumed to be zero. Also three intermediate weights b_1, b_2, and b_3 are the regression coefficients of the Almon variables A_1, A_2, and A_3. A_i, $i = 1, 2, 3$, is the weighted average of $\Delta[(p/c)^{\gamma}Q]$, in which the weights w_t to w_{t-j} and w_{t-n-1} are zeros just so the first j weights of the lags could be zeros and the distributed lags could be limited to a length of n periods.

The fitted equation and associated results are:[32]

$$\underset{(7.92)}{I_t = 81.97} + \underset{(0.1409)}{0.4572\,A_1} + \underset{(0.1295)}{1.0304\,A_2} + \underset{(0.1733)}{1.2971\,A_3} + 0.0235\,K_{t-1} \tag{9.119}$$

$$\bar{R}^2 = 0.977 \qquad \text{SEE} = 5.3626 \qquad DW = 1.38$$

The remaining interpolated lag coefficients (with standard errors in parentheses) are shown below:

t-2	0.1272	(0.1065)
t-3	0.2520	(0.1454)
t-4	0.3854	(0.1465)
t-5	0.5328	(0.1347)
t-6	0.6942	(0.1268)
t-7	0.8638	(0.1265)
t-8	1.0304	(0.1295)
t-9	1.1772	(0.1343)
t-10	1.3163	(0.1450)
t-11	1.2818	(0.1635)
t-12	1.2437	(0.1808)
t-13	1.0355	(0.1775)
t-14	0.6365	(0.1775)

(9.120)

[32] The authors also try other kinds of distribution weights but due to the unsatisfactory results leave them out of consideration. The figures in parentheses are standard errors of estimates. Reprinted with permission B. D. Boatwright and J. R. Eaton, "The Estimation of Investment Function for Manufacturing Industry in the United Kingdom," *Economica*, 39 (1972) p. 409.

The above distribution seems satisfactory in view of its smoothness and unimodal character. Its peak happens after 10 quarters. In terms of the last equation, the estimated gross investment and actual gross investment agree fairly well.[33] This shows that the attempt is reasonably successful.

9.16.2 The Jorgenson and Stephenson (1967) Model of U.S. Investment

It is interesting to put this investment model side by side with an earlier one formulated by Jorgenson and Stephenson (1967). This model covers 16 industries of the United States and is empirically determined from quarterly data for the period 1949 I to 1960 IV. It has the following general equation:

$$I = a\gamma(\theta)[(px/c)_t - (px/c)_{t-1}] + [1 - w(\theta)]\,[I_t - \delta K_{t-1}] + \beta \qquad (9.121)$$

The symbols above and the underlying mechanism are briefly explained now.

I = net investment

α = elasticity of production with respect to capital

x = output

p = price of unit output

δ = depreciation rate

$$c = q\left[\frac{1-uv}{1-u}\delta + \frac{1-uw}{1-u}r\right] = \text{(interpreted as) implicit rental of capital, assuming no transitory capital gains} \qquad (9.122)$$

q = price of capital good

r = cost of capital

u = tax rate of net income

v = tax allowance on depreciation

β = constant term, interpreted as the sample mean error of the equation

In addition $\gamma(\theta)$ and $w(\theta)$ are two lag distributions. These follow from

$$\mu(\theta) = \mu_0 + \mu_1\theta + \mu_2\theta^2 + \ldots \qquad (9.123)$$

where θ is the lag operator such that $\theta x_t = x_{t-1}$, $\theta^2 x_t = x_{t-2}$, etc. The actual importance of the μs appears in a relation connecting the number of new projects IN_t, IN_{t-1}, etc. initiated in period t, $t - 1$, etc. to the level of investment completions IE_t in period t, that is

$$IE_t = \mu_0 IN_t + \mu_1 IN_{t-1} + \mu_2 IN_{t-2} + \ldots \qquad (9.124)$$

[33] These figures that appear in the article are not reported here.

In other words,

$$IE_t = \mu(\theta)\, IN_t \tag{9.125}$$

However, Jorgenson (1965) maintains that there are intermediate stages between the initiation of projects and the actual investment expenditure made, for instance, the appropriation of funds, letting out of contracts, and issuing of orders. Depending on the sector and the industry, the lags during these stages should be suitably related to the overall lag $\mu(\theta)$, suitability being judged by that form of the distribution that produces the lowest standard error for the regression. Each distributed lag is a rational distributed lag and can be written as the ratio of two distributions, that is $\mu(\theta) = \dfrac{\gamma(\theta)}{w(\theta)}$. In this ratio, $\gamma(\theta)$ and $w(\theta)$ are polynomials in θ, their degree depending on the sector and the industry, and the γs and ws are the coefficients of the powers of the θs. $w(\theta)$ is taken to be of the form $1 + w_1\theta + w_2\theta^2$.

Jorgenson and Stephenson assume certain constraints on the w_is and γ_is. These are

$$-4w_2 \geqq w_1^2 \tag{9.126}$$

and the leading coefficient of $\gamma(\theta)$ is positive, that is

$$\gamma_0 > 0 \tag{9.127}$$

where γ_0 is the leading coefficient in $\gamma(\theta)$:

$$\gamma(\theta) = \gamma_0 + \gamma_1\theta + \gamma_2\theta^2 + \ldots$$

The latter, not the former, constraint is imposed on the distributed lag function. When the OLS estimates do not respect the former, the authors compute $w_2 = -(1/4)w_1^2$ with the OLS estimate of w_1, and reestimate the equations with w_1 and w_2 fixed at these values.

The fitted function for total manufacturing is:

$$\begin{aligned} I = {} & \underset{(0.00077)}{0.00305}\,\alpha\gamma_4 + \underset{(0.00076)}{0.00153}\,\alpha\gamma_5 + \underset{(0.00070)}{0.00190}\,\alpha\gamma_6 \\ & + \underset{(0.00080)}{0.00270}\,\alpha\gamma_7 - 1.20525\, w_1 + 0.36316\, w_2 + \underset{(0.00178)}{0.02084}\,\delta \end{aligned} \tag{9.128}$$

$$R^2 = 0.9644 \qquad DW = 1.9597$$

The use of a C–D production function in the formulation of the investment function is severely criticized by Eisner and Nadiri (1968). However, Jorgenson and Stephenson (1969) reply by saying that the assumption of unitary elasticity of substitution (associated with the C–D function) is reasonably vindicated from data.

9.17 CONCLUSION

We will conclude this section by commenting back on the Boatwright and Eaton model. Its authors stipulate that the U.K. government's planned introduction in 1979 of the systems of investment allowances would have adversely affected investment by 4.5% in 1970, had the allowances been introduced in 1967. Thus the policy would have had an undesirable effect on investment, contrary to what was deemed to be its objective.

9.18 MISCELLANEOUS APPLIED STUDIES

The topics included in this and subsequent sections extend over diverse areas and their exposition is meant to be introductory and illustrative. Our objective is to give a sample idea of the kinds of things investigated by researchers in recent times and the reader may want to supplement the mathematical and statistical aspects of the studies by referring to the original sources. In the reportings below, many important studies are left out due to limitations of space and/or complexity of their underlying theories and techniques. The particular ones that are included are by Rosen, Griliches, Fama, Hausman, Flavin, Levine and Mitchell, and Wales and Woodland.

9.18.1 Studies by Rosen (1974 and 1986)

Rosen (1974) pioneers the concept of hedonic prices and implicit markets in the context of product differentiation not in imperfect but pure competition. Some objectively measured characteristics are made the basis of product differentiation, and product prices and amounts of characteristics pertaining to each good are shown to generate a set of implicit or hedonic prices. These prices are seen as a problem in spatial equilibrium involving locational decisions of both producers and consumers in the characteristics space. Various aspects of the market equilibrium are explored, and implications for hedonic price regressions and index numbers based on such prices are brought out.

The same author (Rosen (1986)) investigates the problem of prizes and incentives in elimination tournaments. In these tournaments, high-ranking prizes usually receive a disproportionate weight; indeed, "a large first-place prize gives survivors something to shoot for, independent of past performances and accomplishments".

This is viewed as a problem of performance incentives in career and related games of survival. Its solution is the same as that of simple game theoretic models. Particularly, the relationship between wages (prizes) and marginal products becomes important. But the latter concept needs to be redefined to include the value to the team of maintaining high incentives and securing the best players at various rungs of the career ladder, not merely the marginal contribution made at each step.

9.18.2 Studies by Griliches (1980, 1977, and 1986)

Switching to Griliches, we consider his 1980 study relating to schooling interruption, work while in school, and the returns from schooling. He uses the Young Men NLS (National Longitudinal Survey) data for the United States for the year 1970, the number of observations being 2136. The dependent variable is the natural logarithm of hourly wages from current or last job as of 1970. The independent variables are: school years completed, IQ test score, length of schooling interruptions (in years), a dummy variable with the value 1 if the respondent has at least one schooling interruption as of 1969, otherwise it has the value zero, and other variables like armed forces services (in years) and so on. Based on the OLS method the fitted regression is found to have a value of R^2 around 0.39. There is some interpretation problem arising from self-selection of (some) data. Otherwise the study does not find any negative effect of interruptions or work while in school on the returns from schooling.

Earlier, Griliches (1977) attempts to estimate the returns to schooling and discuss an econometric problem arising from the neglect of a special variable called ability. Defining y or $\ln Y$ to be the logarithm of income, earnings, or wage rate, G the schooling or grades completed, Z the set of other variables, u the disturbance, and the subscript i the sample observation, he sets up the wage equation as

$$y_i = \ln Y_i = \alpha + \beta G_i + Z_i\gamma + u_i \tag{9.129}$$

In (9.129), α, β, and γ are coefficients. An explanation for this sort of final equation is available from the two equations below with some variables already defined:

$$\begin{aligned} Y &= p_h H e^u \\ H &= e^{\beta s} e^{\nu} \end{aligned} \tag{9.130}$$

where

$$\begin{aligned} p_h &= \text{market or rental price of a unit of human capital} \\ H &= \text{unobserved quantity of human capital} \\ \nu &= \text{other effects including quality of school and differences in ability} \end{aligned} \tag{9.131}$$

The second equation describes an implicit production function of human capital. According to it, human capital depends on time spent in school s and other effects such as ν. The first equation defines the market contribution or value of human capital which expresses itself in such things as the wage rate. Combining these two equations, the following is obtained:

$$y = \ln Y = \ln p_h + \beta s + u + v \tag{9.132}$$

which is comparable to equation (9.129). The term v or $Z_i\gamma$ can be expressed as simply δA where A is ability, excluding other possible effects in order to magnify the role of this special variable. Equating $\ln p_h$ with α, we have (9.132) expressed as

$$y = \alpha + \beta s + \delta A + u \tag{9.133}$$

Taking b_{ys} to be the OLS estimated coefficient of $\ln Y$ on s, and b_{As} that of A on s, Griliches shows that

$$E(b_{ys}) = \beta + \delta b_{As} = \beta + \delta \operatorname{cov}(A,s)/V(s) \tag{9.134}$$

Thus, b_{ys} will be biased upward if (1) ability positively influences earnings ($\delta > 0$), (2) the sample turns out a positive relationship between the excluded variable, ability and the included variable, schooling ($b_{As} > 0$), and (3) ability is the only variable that is unaccounted for and other usual OLS assumptions are valid.

Griliches computes the value of the ability bias to be roughly 0.008 from an equation in which age is held constant, but 0.006 where experience is constant. But the implied estimate of the bias in percentage terms differs by a factor of 4. This indicates that the percentage bias is dependent on the model and is not independent of either the data sets or formulations.[34]

One of the important areas of Griliches' contribution is productivity of research and development (R and D) expenditures at the farm level in the United States. Such expenditures are often divided between basic and applied research as also between privately and federally funded research. The area is important because R and D expenditure in real terms in the United States was at its maximum around 1968, then decreased somewhat in the early 1970s before picking up slightly in the late 1970s. More particularly, such expenditures as a ratio of total sales in industry fell from 4.2% in 1968 to a minimum of 2.6% in 1979 before rising to 3.7% by 1982. When the expenditures are looked at as divided between privately and federally funded programs, the trends are somewhat different. This is because the privately funded R and D, as a ratio of manufacturing sales, remained virtually the same throughout, whereas the federally financed R and D fell from 2.1% in 1967 to as low as 0.7% in 1979 before recovering slightly after that year. During the same period, the U.S. economy went through one of the deepest and extended recessions of the post-war era and a pronounced decline in productivity. Worst

[34] Griliches goes on to formulate a more complete model by including an early test and late test schooling dichotomy, and measured and unmeasured family effects. The reader should pick up its details from the original article. Note that Griliches sorts out ability from work experience by using the model of Mincer (1974) for the latter.

declines occurred in metals, motor vehicles and other heavy, energy-related industries, those that were among the less R and D intensive industries.[35]

Against this background of the trend in R and D expenditures in the U.S. industries, Griliches (1986) fits a production function of the form

$$Y_t = Ae^{\lambda t} k_t^{\alpha} C_t^{\beta} L_t^{1-\beta} \tag{9.135}$$

where

$$\begin{aligned}
Y_t &= \text{output, sales, or value added} \\
C_t &= \text{capital} \\
L_t &= \text{labor} \\
k &= \Sigma \theta_i R_{t-i} = \text{a measure of accumulated and still productive research capital defined to be equal to ``knowledge''} \\
R_t &= \text{real gross investment in research} \\
\theta_i &= \text{weight of past research on current state of knowledge} \\
\lambda &= \text{disembodied external technical change} \\
A, \beta &= \text{parameters}
\end{aligned} \tag{9.136}$$

This function is based on the assumption of constant returns to scale. He tackles the question of one or the other kind of R and D expenditures in promoting productivity growth as follows. He defines

$$\begin{aligned} R^* &= R_1 + (1 + \delta)R_2 \\ &= R(1 + \delta s) \end{aligned} \tag{9.137}$$

where

$$\begin{aligned}
R &= R_1 + R_2, R_1 \text{ and } R_2 \text{ being privately and federally funded, or basic and applied research expenditures} \\
s &= R_2/R = \text{share of } R_2 \text{ in total R and D expenditures, } R_2 \text{ being more weighted than } R_1
\end{aligned} \tag{9.138}$$

It follows that

$$\alpha \ln R^* \approx \alpha \ln R + \alpha\delta s \tag{9.139}$$

It is assumed that R_2, given a δ premium, is weighted more than R_1. Therefore, the sign and importance of s will signify the strength of δ.

For the purpose of growth formulation, Griliches uses lower case letters for growth rates and observes that

$$r = (1 - s)r_1 + sr_2 \tag{9.140}$$

[35] This paragraph is based on Griliches (1986).

while

$$r^* = (1 - s)r_1 + (1 + \delta)sr_2 \tag{9.141}$$

If, as is frequently the case,

$$r_1 \approx r_2 \tag{9.142}$$

then

$$r^* = r(1 + \delta s) \tag{9.143}$$

This implies that the coefficient of s contains some information on the "premium" or "discount" on R_2 since αr^* is approximately equal to

$$\alpha r^* \approx (\alpha + \delta\bar{s})r + (\alpha\bar{r}\delta)s \tag{9.144}$$

$\bar{s}$ and $\bar{r}$ being the typical value of s and r around which the approximations are valid.

Given data peculiarities and imperfections, he chooses to do a level and growth rate analysis for the years 1967, 1972, and 1977, and not a complete annual data analysis. He uses yearly data based on average growth rates for two subperiods: 1957–1965 and 1966–1977 completed from the regressions of logarithm

TABLE 9.7 THE REGRESSION RESULTS IN THE R AND D STUDY*

	Coefficients of				
Dependent Variable and Sample Size	Constant	R and D Capital to Total Fixed Assets Ratio	Basic R and D Ratio	Fraction Private	SEE
GPR 72					
N = 652(a)	0.144	0.088	0.344	0.107	0.262
	(0.049)	(0.012)	(0.144)	(0.048)	
(b)		0.060	0.187	−0.012	0.237
		(0.013)	(0.138)	(0.052)	
N = 491(a)	0.117	0.080	0.514	0.154	0.264
	(0.052)	(0.013)	(0.139)	(0.051)	
(b)		0.061	0.366	0.074	0.227
		(0.015)	(0.138)	(0.057)	
GPR 77					
N = 491(a)	0.341	0.031	0.402	0.033	0.313
	(0.064)	(0.019)	(0.187)	(0.068)	
(b)		0.004	0.261	−0.028	0.292
		(0.022)	(0.187)	(0.077)	

Notes (a) Regressions do not have industry dummies.
(b) Regressions have industry dummies.

* Reprinted with permission Z. Griliches, "Productivity, Research and Development and Basic Research," *American Economic Review*, 76 (1986), Table 5, p. 151.

of relevant variables on time trends, and thus eliminates the missing data problem within each subperiod.

We like to report here on Griliches' results on relative profitability of firms in 1972 and 1977, leaving out his results on crosssectional production functions and growth rates of partial productivity (1966–1977), overall and by industry (see Table 9.7). The dependent variable in the profitability study is GPR, which is the ratio of gross profit (value added minus labor cost and plus R and D) to total gross fixed assets. Independent variables are: the ratio of R and D capital expenditure (undepreciated) to total fixed assets, and the R and D mix variables: the basic research and fraction private ratios.

Interestingly enough, the coefficient of the R and D capital variable comes out positive and most often statistically significant, even though too small. The basic variable coefficient comes out large and significant, perhaps too large. The fraction private ratio has a positive but quantitatively negligible effect after industry differences are allowed for. Given that the ratio of R and D capital to total fixed assets is 0.5 on the average, the coefficient for this variable implies a value of discount rate δ of 30 to 60. As between 1972 and 1977, the results for the latter year are weaker than for the former but the residual variance is significantly larger. However, the importance of basic research is confirmed by the evidence from both these years.

9.18.3 Studies by Fama (1976) and Fama and Stewart (1977)

We now turn to Fama and Stewart (1977) who estimate the relationship between asset returns and inflation to find out to what extent different assets are hedges against expected and unexpected parts of the rate of inflation over the period 1953–1971. That is, how far do the returns set on various assets at a given time take the expected and unexpected components of inflation into account. They establish that U.S. government bonds and bills are a complete hedge against expected inflation and private residential real estate is a complete hedge against both the expected and unexpected inflation. On the other hand, labor income has little to do with inflation, expected or unexpected, and, surprisingly enough, returns on stocks are only negatively affected by expected inflation and perhaps by unexpected inflation too.

Another interesting work relates to forward rates as forecasters of future spot (interest) rates. This work is by Fama (1976) alone. His conclusion is that when forward interest rates are adjusted by expected premium changes through time, these (forward) rates (which are built in Treasury Bill prices) reflect an evaluation of future expected spot rates. This gives roughly as good future rates as those that are obtainable from past spot rates. This result is a confirmation of the efficient market hypothesis: in fixing bill prices, the market correctly utilizes the information available from past spot rates. The author apparently uses the OLS technique for deriving the various results.

9.18.4 Studies by Hausman (1979 and 1980)

As regards the Hausman studies, we briefly present Hausman (1980) and Hausman (1979). The first is on the effect of wages, taxes, etc. on women's labor force participation, and the second on discount rates and their influence on the purchase and utilization of energy-using durables.

In the first study, Hausman takes two programs: AFDC (welfare program for female headed households in the United States) and NIT (negative income tax program), and selects a sample of about 1000 families headed by black females in Gary, Indiana. The income transfer aspect of the AFDC varies according to family size and assumes marginal tax rates on earnings of 67% up to a break-even point. After that point, federal and state taxes are imposed, even though at a much lower rate than 67%. The initial and terminal rates for federal taxes are 14% and 50%, respectively. For the NIT program, four different plans are used together with two income guarantees. The levels of income under these guarantees are 22% and 51% higher than the corresponding AFDC levels, and the marginal tax rates are either 40% or 60%. When earnings exceed break-even point, like the AFDC, they are taxed according to usual federal and state tax rates.

The model used is basically a probit model discriminating between utility when working and utility when not working, and whichever state offers the greater utility is chosen by the woman. There is some nonlinearity in the budget set, but since a probit model is estimated by the maximum likelihood method, that is found to be no big problem.

In the second study, Hausman develops a model of technical substitution and consumer choice in capital stock decision. His objective is to capture the trade-offs between capital costs for more energy-efficient appliances (room air conditioners, in particular) and their operating costs. He sets up a purchase equation based on a discrete choice model,[36] and finds that consumers "do trade-off capital costs and expected operating costs". More importantly, he concludes that the trade-off decision is based on a discount rate of about 20% and this rate falls or rises as income rises or falls.

9.18.5 Study by Flavin (1981)

The next study is by Flavin (1981). She analyzes how consumption adjusts to future income when expectations are changing. As is well known, expectation changes are going to cause changes in permanent income. Flavin proposes an alternative test of the permanent income rational expectations hypothesis of Hall (1978) and Sargent (1978). The implication of this joint hypothesis is the following: if consumption is a fraction of permanent income in each period, and permanent income is the best estimate, given the information presently available, of an in-

[36] He uses the same arguments as of Hausman and Wise (1978) for quantitative choice models.

dividual's total lifetime earnings,[37] then consumption this year may depart from consumption last year by the revision in permanent income taking place since.

Hall (1978) and Sargent (1978) study the relationship between consumption, lagged consumption, and the revision in permanent income, given lagged information sets. But Hall accepts and Sargent rejects the permanent income hypothesis. Flavin, however, corrects "an incorrect definition of permanent income used in Sargent's formulation of restrictions", and after the correction, obtains parameter restrictions identical to those used by Hall. In spite of this sort of reconciliation of the two papers, Flavin rejects the joint rational expectations permanent income hypothesis. This is done by means of a structural econometric model of consumption in which time series analysis is used to measure the revision in permanent income caused by an innovation in current income. For the rest of the details, see Flavin (1981).

9.18.6 Study by Levine and Mitchell (1988)

The Levine and Mitchell (1988) study concerns the U.S. baby boom's effect on relative wages in the twenty first century. Specifically, they estimate the effect in the year 2020 when the present generation will turn out to be the oldest segment of the work force. They use national time series data for the period 1955–1984 and compute demand for workers in eight age–sex groups: 16–19 years, 20–34 years, 35–54 years, and 55 years and over for each sex. The estimated demand coefficients are then used to forecast how relative wages will change in the year 2020. Based on these coefficients, elasticities of age complementarity and factor price elasticities are calculated.

The general results indicate the following. First, except for teens, there is evidence of gender substitutability and age complementarity (for a given gender). In particular, older men are found to be complementary with young men but substitutable with teenage women, whereas older women are substitutable with older men. Secondly, the baby boom is not going to adversely affect wages of prime age workers relative to older workers, the evidence in the case of teenaged workers being inconclusive. However, this general result does not apply to women. Prime age women are expected to lose relative to older workers and, compared to men alone, the evidence is for widening, rather than narrowing wage differentials by sex.

9.18.7 Study by Wales and Woodland (1977)

We will conclude this section by briefly reporting on Wales and Woodland (1977). This study is on the allocation of time between work, leisure, and housework. The study finds that if housework hours are not counted in leisure hours, there are significant differences in labor supply response from a situation that does

[37] This is in essence the rational expectation hypothesis in the present context.

include housework within leisure. But the estimates of the labor supply response are likely to be biased if housework hours are assumed to be exogenous. The reason is that if disturbances influencing leisure and housework hours are correlated, an exogenous treatment of the latter will result in simultaneous equation bias.[38] This problem has been eliminated by keeping and estimating separate equations for hours of housework.

Some special results of the study are as follows. The relative wage rates of the husband and wife in a family is a small contributing factor to the sharing of housework between the two people. For families without children, housework hours go down as income increases and vice versa, whereas for families with children, the two things move together, up and down.

PROBLEMS

9-1. **(a)** How did Duesenberry (1949) formulate the relative income hypothesis? How do you use his estimated savings (ratio) function for the U.S. economy given by (define all the symbols used):

$$S/Y = 0.196 + 0.25\ Y/Y_0$$

to support Kuznets' finding of the constancy of the long-term saving propensity of the U.S. economy over the period 1880–1930?

(b) How did Ando and Modigliani (1963) arrive at a certain consumption function using the life cycle hypothesis? What assumption did Ando and Modigliani use to make the parameters of the consumption function relatively insensitive to yields on assets and annual rate of growth of income?

(c) Develop the form of the consumption function using Friedman's permanent income hypothesis. As you may know, Friedman computed three regressions based on Goldsmith's (1955) data. Which regression produced the best result?

9-2. **(a)** Define a linear expenditure system. Derive the equation of such a system and interpret it. What are the econometric problems in estimating it? Describe three ways of estimating a linear expenditure system.

(b) Discuss the Goldberger and Gamaletsos (1970) study comparing the results on the linear expenditure system for the United States, Canada, and the United Kingdom for five different expenditure groups.

9-3. **(a)** Describe the structural aspects of the Burley (1973) study on Australian manufacturing stressing particularly the production function and measurement of the capital input used. What are the broad conclusions drawn by the author based on his estimated results?

(b) What conclusions are drawn by Reinhardt regarding the productivity of the average American general physician services based on the application of a production function for such services?

[38] See the introductory section of the chapter on simultaneous equations for an explanation of this phenomenon.

9-4. **(a)** How is a translog production function defined? Are substitution possibilities quite general in such a function?

(b) Bring out the salient aspects of the Pindyck (1979) study on interfuel substitution and industrial demand for energy from an international perspective. In the process, you should particularly explain how translog cost functions are derived.

9-5. Discuss the Pollak and others (1984) study on the CES cost function derived as an extension of the n-factor translog cost function of the Christensen and others (1973) type. What general observation is made by this study regarding the comparative efficacy of the CES cost function over a simple translog cost function?

9-6. **(a)** How does the Hendry and Mizon (1978) study conclude that autocorrelation among residuals of, for instance, an investment function need not be a nuisance but may be an economical way of describing the dynamic relationship underlying investment?

(b) **(1)** What variables are included in the initial and the revised version of the investment function for the U.K. economy estimated by Bean (1979)?

(2) Describe three special features of Bean's revised investment equation.

(3) What criteria are used by Bean for selection of the lag structure in this investment model?

(c) Explain the investment equation used by Boatwright and Eaton (1972) for the U.K. economy especially dwelling upon the two kinds of lags used by them. How is that equation modified as a result of adapting to Almon lags?

9-7. Write a critique of the Jorgenson and Stephenson (1967) model of investment estimated from U.S. quarterly data for the period 1949 I to 1960 IV.

9-8. **(a)** Discuss the theoretical model developed by Griliches (1977) to estimate the returns to schooling. How does he cope with the econometric problem arising from the neglect of a special variable, namely, ability? What theoretical and empirical conclusions does he derive about the bias (caused by this special variable) of the OLS-estimated coefficient while regressing wage (or income) on human capital (or time spent in school)?

(b) Write a critique of Griliches (1986) which is a study based on the production function of U.S. industries with R and D expenditures used as a special input.

10

Variation of Classical Themes and Other Approaches to Inference

10.1 INTRODUCTION

This chapter deals with hybrid topics. On the one hand, it allows variations in classical themes, and still remains classical in approach. For instance, it sheds light on *variations* of the alternative hypothesis in relation to the null, rather than considering a unique alternative hypothesis as in the classical test procedure. This becomes the subject matter of a few sections (Sections 10.2–10.3.1) of this chapter. Also, it examines the problem of sample selectivity bias arising when random sampling methods, used in the classical procedure, have to be abandoned in favor of some self-selection rule (Sections 10.4–10.5.1). Then there are the problems arising from unobservable variables, which it addresses in Sections 10.6–10.6.2. In addition, it looks at crosssection and time series data structure, not separately but in an integrated way, to provide different insights into classical inference (Sections 10.7–10.7.2). This is also true when the assumption of nonstochastic parameters of the regression model is relaxed to allow for variable parameters (Sections 10.8–10.8.5).

On the other hand, the chapter will deal with one completely different approach. This is the approach of the Bayesian analysis (Sections 10.9–10.10) which will introduce the concept of posterior hypothesis based on prior beliefs, judgment or information, posing as if these are not inferior to observable facts that the classicists use for each guess of the unknown or unobservable parameters. However, this analysis characteristically uses a level of mathematics and statistics somewhat beyond the scope of this book. Thus this treatment will be merely introductory and illustrative in nature.

10.2 ECONOMETRIC TESTS: THE CASE OF THE NULL VERSUS ALTERNATIVE HYPOTHESES

Economic theories look for empirical support from various fields. The usual procedure is to set up a testable null hypothesis and try to test it against some prespecified alternative hypothesis or hypotheses. In areas of investigation where least squares theory is employed for estimation, tests of estimates are based on least squares properties, and both estimates and tests have worked well for quite some time.

But the increasing statistical complications of many economic models often make the least squares theory somewhat unsuitable; in contrast, the maximum likelihood principle works better. However, even here, the properties of estimates and tests that are available are often only asymptotic properties. Indeed we may have two asymptotically equivalent methods which bear considerably different computational implications and differ in small sample performances. In view of these discrepancies, economists' attention has naturally switched to several other tests.

Three tests, widely used in the literature, that will be discussed here are: the Wald, the Likelihood Ratio (or the LR), and the Lagrangean Multiplier (or the LM) tests. The LM test begins with the null and examines if any transition to the alternative will improve things. The Wald test starts from the alternative and moves back to the null. The LR test weighs one hypothesis against another with prejudice to none.

10.2.1 Some Basic Ideas

Before we cover more on these tests, some basic ideas are presented. These relate to the null and the alternative hypotheses, the critical region, Type I and Type II statistical errors, power of a test, consistency of a test, optimality of a test including asymptotic optimality, etc.

When the value of a test statistic under the null hypothesis lies in a delineated section of the sample space called the critical region, the test recommends that the null hypothesis be rejected. If not, the hypothesis should be accepted. Underlying these decisions, there can be two erroneous conclusions: (1) when the null hypothesis is wrongly rejected in which case Type I error is committed, and (2) when it is falsely accepted in which case Type II error is committed. The probability of Type I error, usually designated as α, stands for the size of the test, and the complement to the probability of Type II error, denoted by the expression $1 - \beta$, is the power of the test. It indicates the probability of rejecting the null when it is false. Among rival tests with the same value of α, that one which has the highest value of $1 - \beta$ is said to be the best.

However, a crucial problem is one of identifying the alternative hypothesis, when, indeed, the test rejects the null hypothesis. For when the null is rejected, the result might still imply another alternative hypothesis, rather than the particular one against which the test was performed, to be the better. Or, one might argue that the sample data finds the null to be untenable, but the chosen alternative to be even more so. This might happen when, for instance, the null and the alternative include, respectively, a zero and a nonzero positive value for the autocorrelation coefficient of the residuals of a linear regression model. Should the test reject the null, the culprit might be either the wrong functional form used or dire misspecification of the model. Having a zero value for the correlation coefficient of residuals might indeed be less offensive than having positive values for the same.

10.2.2 Some Statistical Prerequisite

Let $\mathbf{Y}$ be an $n \times 1$ random vector, its observations coming from the joint pdf $f(\mathbf{Y}, \boldsymbol{\theta})$ where $\boldsymbol{\theta}$ is an $m \times 1$ vector of unknown parameters belonging to the total parameter space ϕ. Let the null hypothesis be: $\boldsymbol{\theta} \in \phi_0 \subset \phi$, and the alternative be: $\boldsymbol{\theta} \in \phi_1 \subset \phi$, and let $\phi_0 \cap$ (intersection) $\phi_1 = 0$, that is ϕ_0 and ϕ_1 do not contain any common elements. Then for a critical region C_n, its size α_n is simply

$$\alpha_n = \text{Prob}\{\mathbf{Y} \in C_n \mid \boldsymbol{\theta} \in \phi_0\} \tag{10.1}$$

and its associated power of the test is

$$P_n(\boldsymbol{\theta}) = \text{Prob}\{\mathbf{Y} \in C_n \mid \boldsymbol{\theta}\} \qquad \text{where } \boldsymbol{\theta} \in \phi_1 \tag{10.2}$$

Sometimes it may be difficult to calculate the size precisely, or calculate it free of its reliance on the actual point within the parameter space. Then the usual practice is to look into the asymptotic tendency of the optimality of a test. What does this tendency mean?

Suppose that C_n is a sequence of critical regions corresponding to, say, a sequence of vectors of statistics T_n $(\mathbf{Y})$ being at least as large as a sequence of constant vectors. The asymptotic size and power of a test are then denoted by

$$\begin{aligned} \alpha &= \lim_{n\to\infty} \alpha_n \\ P(\boldsymbol{\theta}) &= \lim_{n\to\infty} P_n(\boldsymbol{\theta}) \qquad \text{for } \boldsymbol{\theta} \in \phi_1 \end{aligned} \tag{10.3}$$

An extreme case is when $P(\boldsymbol{\theta})$ is 1; in other words, the test *always* rejects the null when it is false. Such a test is said to be consistent.

A problem with asymptotic tests, as in the case of asymptotic properties of estimators, is that most often the tests are consistent as are estimates. Discrimination among them is usually made in terms of their power against alternatives that are in the neighborhood of the null hypothesis. As the sample size grows, the alternative comes closer to the null, and a powerful test should signal this. Thus, the power against such alternatives, where all tests are of equal asymptotic size, will define the asymptotic power of tests.

In a large number of cases, econometric tests are performed on the basis of given values of a few parameters, while others are unrestricted in values. This may be simply illustrated with a two parameter situation, where θ_1 is the parameter whose value the null specifies, and θ_2 is the other parameter that is free:

$$H_0: \theta_1 = \theta_1^0 \qquad \theta_2 \text{ free} \tag{10.4}$$

A sequence of local alternative hypotheses may be

$$\{H_1\} : \theta_1^n = \theta_1^0 + t/n^{1/2} \qquad \theta_2 \text{ free} \tag{10.5}$$

for some number t. Should a test be powerful in all directions t, it will be called an *invariant* test.

Often by the phrase asymptotically optimal test is meant an asymptotically locally most powerful test among invariant tests. Such a property applies to the likelihood ratio test. Two tests with identical critical values are asymptotically equivalent if they perform equally well asymptotically based on the null and local alternatives.

The foregoing characterizations can be easily extended even when $\boldsymbol{\theta}_1$ and $\boldsymbol{\theta}_2$ are each a vector, and the test problem has nonlinear hypotheses such as $\psi(\boldsymbol{\theta}) = 0$. In the latter case, no generality is lost by linearizing the nonlinear hypotheses by Taylor's expansion around local alternatives, and, especially, by considering hypothesized values of a subset of the total parameter vector.

10.3 THE WALD, LIKELIHOOD RATIO, AND LAGRANGE MULTIPLIER TESTS

In the following general formulations of the three tests we assume that the likelihood function admits of the Taylor expansion up to two terms and that integrals and derivatives are mutually interchangeable. Also, the information matrix is nonsingular implying that the parameters are locally identifiable.

Let the joint probability density function for the observations on $\mathbf{Y}$ be $f(\mathbf{Y}, \boldsymbol{\theta})$, which is equal to the likelihood $L = L(\mathbf{Y}, \boldsymbol{\theta})$ and let $\boldsymbol{\theta} = \boldsymbol{\theta}^0$ under the null hypothesis, and $\boldsymbol{\theta} \in R^m$ under the alternative. The first order condition for the maximum of the log-likelihood function is given by

$$\frac{\partial}{\partial \boldsymbol{\theta}} \ln L(\mathbf{Y}, \hat{\boldsymbol{\theta}}) = \mathbf{0} \tag{10.6}$$

where $\hat{\boldsymbol{\theta}}$ is the likelihood maximizing value of $\boldsymbol{\theta}$. For simplicity, let

$$\mathbf{l}(\mathbf{Y}, \boldsymbol{\theta}) = \frac{\partial}{\partial \boldsymbol{\theta}} \ln L(\mathbf{Y}, \boldsymbol{\theta}) \tag{10.7}$$

be defined to be the score. Then the MLE has $\mathbf{l} = \mathbf{0}$. From the property of MLE, the variance $\mathrm{V}(\hat{\boldsymbol{\theta}})$ is given by the inverse of the information matrix $\boldsymbol{I}(\hat{\boldsymbol{\theta}})$:

$$\mathrm{V}(\hat{\boldsymbol{\theta}}) = \frac{I^{-1}(\boldsymbol{\theta})}{n} \tag{10.8}$$

where

$$I(\boldsymbol{\theta}) = -\,\mathrm{E}\,\frac{\partial^2 \ln L(\boldsymbol{\theta})}{\partial\boldsymbol{\theta}\partial\boldsymbol{\theta}'} \bigg/ n \tag{10.9}$$

Given that $\hat{\boldsymbol{\theta}}$ is distributed, in the limit, as a normal distribution, and $I(\hat{\boldsymbol{\theta}})$ is a consistent estimator of $I(\boldsymbol{\theta})$, it can be shown that the criterion:

$$\Omega_w = n(\hat{\boldsymbol{\theta}} - \boldsymbol{\theta}^o)'\, I(\hat{\boldsymbol{\theta}})\, (\hat{\boldsymbol{\theta}} - \boldsymbol{\theta}^o) \tag{10.10}$$

will be distributed[1] asymptotically as a χ^2 with n df under the null hypothesis. This is the essence of the Wald test.

For the likelihood ratio test, the criterion is

$$\Omega_{LR} = -2\,[\ln L(\mathbf{Y}, \boldsymbol{\theta}^0) - \ln L(\mathbf{Y}, \boldsymbol{\theta})] \tag{10.11}$$

which is evidently derived from the difference in the maximum of the likelihood under the null and the alternative hypotheses. It can be shown that Ω_{LR} will have a limiting χ^2 distribution when the null hypothesis is true.

The Lagrange multiplier test is based on the constrained maximization of the log-likelihood, where the constraints are $\boldsymbol{\theta} = \boldsymbol{\theta}^0$. In the process, a set of Lagrange multipliers are obtained which serve as the imputed costs of the constraints. High costs imply that the constraints are untenable with the data and should be disregarded. Let the Lagrangean be S:

$$S = \ln L(\mathbf{Y}, \boldsymbol{\theta}) - \boldsymbol{\lambda}'(\boldsymbol{\theta} - \boldsymbol{\theta}^0) \tag{10.12}$$

Then the first order conditions for the maximum of S are:

$$\frac{\partial S}{\partial \boldsymbol{\theta}} = \mathbf{0} \qquad \boldsymbol{\theta} = \boldsymbol{\theta}_0 \tag{10.13}$$

That is,

$$\boldsymbol{\lambda} = \mathbf{l}(\mathbf{Y}, \boldsymbol{\theta}^0) \tag{10.14}$$

This means that the Lagrange multipliers test is the same as the one on the basis of the score developed by Rao (1948). Whatever the origin, the distribution of the multiplier or the score under the null hypothesis has a mean value of zero and variance $I(\boldsymbol{\theta}^0)\, n$. Assuming that the central limit theorem applies to the scores, it can be shown that the criterion

$$\Omega_{LM} = \mathbf{l}'(\mathbf{Y}, \boldsymbol{\theta}^0)\, I^{-1}(\boldsymbol{\theta}^0)\mathbf{l}(\mathbf{Y}, \boldsymbol{\theta}^0)/n \tag{10.15}$$

will, in the limit, be distributed as χ^2 with m df.

[1] The clue is to adapt the result given in (4.118) of Chapter 4 to the present problem.

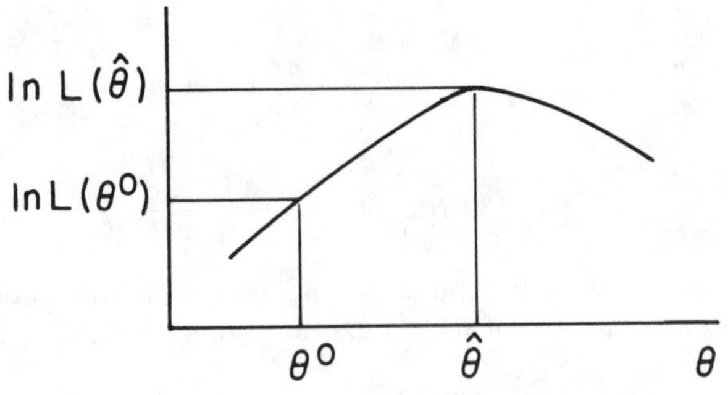

Figure 10.1

To summarize, the three tests are based on criteria that reflect the difference between the null and alternative hypotheses in different ways. This can be simply seen in a geometrical portrayal of the relation between ln $L(\theta)$ and θ, where ln $L(\theta)$ is placed along the vertical axis and θ along the horizontal axis. In this graph, the Wald test reflects the horizontal difference between θ^0 and $\hat{\theta}$, the LR test the difference between ln $L(\theta^\circ)$ and ln $L(\hat{\theta})$ and the LM test the slope of ln $L(\theta)$ at the point $\theta = \theta^0$.

10.3.1 Some Examples

Example 1 The Bernoulli distribution. We have already considered the case of a variable Y, which is a Bernoulli variable, with θ the probability of success ($Y = 1$), and $(1 - \theta)$ the probability of failure ($Y = 0$). Denote the sample mean of Y by

$$\bar{Y} = \sum_{t=1}^{n} \frac{Y_t}{n}$$

Recall

$$\ln L(\mathbf{Y}, \theta) = \sum_t \{Y_t \ln \theta + (1 - Y_t)\ln(1 - \theta)\}$$

Equating $\dfrac{\partial \ln L}{\partial \theta}$ to 0 and solving, we get $\hat{\theta} = \bar{Y}$, where $\hat{\theta}$ is the MLE. The score becomes:

$$l(\mathbf{Y}, \theta) = \frac{1}{\theta(1 - \theta)} \sum_t (Y_t - \theta)$$

The information matrix is

$$\mathrm{I}(\theta) = \mathrm{E}\left(\frac{n\theta(1 - \theta) + (1 - 2\theta)\sum(Y_t - \theta)}{\theta^2(1 - \theta)^2}\right) \Big/ n$$

which clearly is a scalar. We shall now work out the values of Ω_w, Ω_{LR}, and Ω_{LM}:

$$\Omega_w = \left[\frac{\sum(Y_t - \theta^0)}{\theta^0(1 - \theta^0)}\right]^2 \frac{\theta^0(1 - \theta^0)}{n} \tag{10.16}$$

$$\Omega_{LR} = 2n\{\bar{Y}\ln \bar{Y}/\theta^0 + (1 - \bar{Y})\ln(1 - \bar{Y})/(1 - \theta^0)\} \tag{10.17}$$

$$\Omega_{LM} = n(\theta^0 - \bar{Y})^2/\{\theta^0(1 - \theta^0)\} \tag{10.18}$$

It can be easily[2] shown that both the Wald and LM tests have an asymptotic χ^2 distribution with 1 df; the LR test can be shown, only after expansion up to a two-term Taylor series, to have the same distribution under the null hypothesis. For the null hypothesis as well as a local alternative, the additional implication is that both the Wald and LM tests will be asymptotically equivalent. All three tests will reject the null the more often the larger the difference between the sample mean and the value of the parameter under the null hypothesis.

Example 2 The multiple regression model. Let the linear regression based on the error $\mathbf{u}$ be:

$$\mathbf{Y} = X\boldsymbol{\beta} + \mathbf{u}$$

where $\mathbf{Y}$ and $\mathbf{u}$ are each an $n \times 1$ vector, and X is an $n \times (m + 1)$ matrix.

Let

$$\mathbf{Y} \mid X \sim \mathrm{N}(X\boldsymbol{\beta}, \sigma_u^2 I)$$

and

$$\mathbf{r} = R\boldsymbol{\beta}$$

be constraints on the parameters $\boldsymbol{\beta}$, where R is an $m_1 \times (m + 1)$ matrix of constants, of rank m_1, and $\mathbf{r}$ is an $m_1 \times 1$ vector of constants.

For this model, the log-likelihood function is

$$\ln L(\mathbf{Y}; \boldsymbol{\beta}, \sigma_u^2) = \mathrm{c} - \frac{n}{2}\ln \sigma_u^2 - \frac{1}{2\sigma_u^2}(\mathbf{Y} - X\boldsymbol{\beta})'(\mathbf{Y} - X\boldsymbol{\beta})$$

where c is a constant. If σ_u^2 were known, we could show[3] the exact equivalence of the Wald, LR, and LM tests. In that case, the tests would differ in terms of the estimates of σ_u^2 used. For the parameters β, the score is, using $\mathbf{u} = \mathbf{Y} - X\boldsymbol{\beta}$:

$$l(\mathbf{Y}, \boldsymbol{\beta}) = \frac{X'\mathbf{u}}{\sigma_u^2}$$

[2] The clue is that a binomial variable becomes a normal variable in the limit when n is large, and the sum of squares of a set of n standard normal variables is a χ^2 with as many degrees of freedom. The rest follows after algebraic simplifications.

[3] This can be done by using Lemmas 1 and 2 of Engle (1983), p. 782–783.

The information matrix is

$$I_{\beta\beta} = \frac{X'X}{(n\sigma_u^2)}$$

This matrix is block diagonal between the βs and σ_u^2.

The calculation of the three test criteria leads to the following expressions:

$$\Omega_w = (\boldsymbol{\beta}_1^0 - \hat{\boldsymbol{\beta}}_1)'(X_1'X_1 - X_1'X_2(X_2'X_2)^{-1}X_2'X_1)(\boldsymbol{\beta}_1^0 - \hat{\boldsymbol{\beta}}_1)'/\hat{\sigma}_u^2 \qquad (10.19)$$

$$\Omega_{LM} = \tilde{\mathbf{u}}'X_1(X_1'X_1 - X_1'X_2(X_2'X_2)^{-1}X_2'X_1)^{-1}X_1'\tilde{\mathbf{u}}/\tilde{\sigma}_u^2 \qquad (10.20)$$

$$\Omega_{LR} = n\ln(\tilde{\mathbf{u}}'\tilde{\mathbf{u}}/\hat{\mathbf{u}}'\hat{\mathbf{u}}) \qquad (10.21)$$

In the above, we have used:

$$\hat{\mathbf{u}} = \mathbf{Y} - X\hat{\boldsymbol{\beta}} \qquad \tilde{\mathbf{u}} = \mathbf{Y} - X\tilde{\boldsymbol{\beta}} \qquad \hat{\sigma}_u^2 = \hat{\mathbf{u}}'\hat{\mathbf{u}}/n \qquad \tilde{\sigma}^2 = \tilde{\mathbf{u}}'\tilde{\mathbf{u}}/n$$

when $\hat{\boldsymbol{\beta}}$ and $\hat{\mathbf{u}}$ correspond to OLS and $\tilde{\boldsymbol{\beta}}$ and $\tilde{\mathbf{u}}$ to estimates under the null. Also, we have used $\boldsymbol{\beta}_1$ as a subset of the regression coefficients which, under the null hypothesis, will assume the value $\boldsymbol{\beta}_1^0$, and X as partitioned into:

$$X = [X_1X_2]$$

where X_1 conforms to $\boldsymbol{\beta}_1$. These criteria can be further simplified to the following by using the theory of projections:[4]

$$\Omega_w = n[\tilde{\mathbf{u}}'\tilde{\mathbf{u}} - \hat{\mathbf{u}}'\hat{\mathbf{u}}]/\hat{\mathbf{u}}'\hat{\mathbf{u}} \qquad (10.22)$$

$$\Omega_{LM} = n[\tilde{\mathbf{u}}'\tilde{\mathbf{u}} - \hat{\mathbf{u}}'\hat{\mathbf{u}}]/\hat{\mathbf{u}}'\hat{\mathbf{u}} \qquad (10.23)$$

Thus

$$\Omega_{LR} = n\ln(1 + \Omega_w/n) \qquad (10.24)$$

$$\Omega_{LM} = \Omega_w/(1 + \Omega_w/n) \qquad (10.25)$$

From these, we can show that

$$(n - (m + 1))\,\Omega_w/(nm_1) \qquad (10.26)$$

will be distributed as $F_{m_1, n-(m+1)}$ when the null hypothesis is true. In view of the other criteria being monotonic functions of the F statistic, the tests for these criteria will be exact and all the critical regions will be the same. However, if one uses asymptotic distributions as the basis of (calculation of) critical values, some problems may arise. See Savin (1976), Evans and Savin (1982), and Rothenberg (1980) for details.

[4] Since the theory of projections is outside the scope of this book, we want the reader to take these results without proof.

10.4 SAMPLE SELECTIVITY BIAS

There are two ways in which sample selection bias may occur: (1) self-selection by individuals or by data units being explored, and (2) sample selection rules used by investigators or data processors equivalent to self-selection rules.

Some examples will clarify the concept. In matters of supply of labor by women, one finds the market wage for female workers to be higher than that of their family wage at zero hours of work. In the context of migrant–nonmigrant labor, one cannot use the wage of migrant labor as a reliable estimate of what a nonmigrant worker would make had he to migrate. The problem is quite similar in the case of trainee–nontrainee wages. Also, not all potential laborers do indeed supply positive hours of labor. Specifically, women workers whose reservation wage is higher than the market wage will not offer their labor services at all. These examples serve to make one point: wage functions calculated on the basis of selected samples generally would not estimate the population wage functions. There would be a problem of sample selectivity bias arising from the attempt to compare, say, the wage of migrants with that of nonmigrants. The bias would arise because migration is treated as random, whereas actually it is not. Similarly, in the reservation wage problems of women workers, dividing the samples into subsamples of workers and nonworkers will not be a random process. This will give rise to selectivity bias.

Nonrandomness of data might also be a result of the analysts' decision. For instance, with panel data, the tendency to select "intact" observations as required by considerations of stability of the family unit may give rise to this kind of problem. In life cycle fertility and manpower programs, the tendency is to drop the attritions out of considerations to have a complete length of the sample. In all such cases, the effects on coefficient estimates will be the same as in the case of self-selection.

10.5 A SIMPLE MODEL OF SELECTION BIAS

Consider a two equation system, which can easily be generalized to a multiple equation system.

Let n be the number of sample observations. Observation i corresponding to the two equations is given by

$$Y_i = \mathbf{X}_i\boldsymbol{\beta} + \epsilon_i \tag{10.27}$$

$$Z_i = \mathbf{W}_i\boldsymbol{\gamma} + \nu_i \tag{10.28}$$

$\mathbf{X}_i$ is a $1 \times k$, $\mathbf{W}_i$ is a $1 \times l$ vector of exogenous explanatory variables, $\boldsymbol{\beta}$ is a $k \times 1$ and $\boldsymbol{\gamma}$ an $l \times 1$ vector of coefficients, and

$$\begin{aligned} E(\epsilon_i) &= E(\nu_i) = 0 && \text{for all } i \\ E(\epsilon_i \nu_j) &= \sigma_{\epsilon\nu} && \text{for } i = j \\ &= 0 && \text{for } i \neq j \end{aligned} \tag{10.29}$$

Let us denote by $f(\epsilon_i, \nu_i)$ the joint pdf of the ith observation on the two error variables. We assume that the matrices of observations on the explanatory variables are of full rank. This would facilitate using OLS for estimation of the structural coefficients of each equation.

Proceeding to estimate (10.27), suppose we discover that some data on **Y** are missing for which we propose to make certain adjustment. Based, first, on no missing data, we have the population regression function for (10.27) given by:

$$E(Y_i \mid \mathbf{X}_i) = \mathbf{X}_i\boldsymbol{\beta} \qquad i = 1, 2, \ldots, n \tag{10.30}$$

Based, second, on missing data and the subsample of available observations, we have the regression function (10.27) now represented as

$$E(Y_i \mid \mathbf{X}_i, \text{Sample Selection Rule}) = \mathbf{X}_i\boldsymbol{\beta} + E(\epsilon_i \mid \text{Sample Selection rule}) \qquad i = 1, 2, \ldots, n \tag{10.31}$$

where we suppose that the first $n_1 < n$ data are available on Y_i.

The resulting position is as follows. If $E(\epsilon_i \mid \text{Sample Selection Rule})$ in (10.31) is zero, there will be no difference between the subsample and the population regression function. OLS can therefore be used on that subsample for estimating $\boldsymbol{\beta}$, even though at some loss of efficiency. But generally the situation will not be all that simple; there will probably be some dire effects of data unavailability. Consider the following specific sample selection rule and its effect.

Assume that whenever Z_i is zero or positive, data on Y_i are available, not otherwise. Equation (10.31) would now stand as

$$E(\epsilon_i \mid \mathbf{X}_i, \text{Sample Selection Rule}) = E(\epsilon_i \mid \mathbf{X}_i, Z_i \geqq 0) \equiv E(\epsilon_i \mid \mathbf{X}_i, \nu_i \geqq -\mathbf{W}_i\boldsymbol{\gamma}) \tag{10.32}$$

Therefore, the regression function following from the particular sample selection rule will be

$$E(Y_i \mid \mathbf{X}_i, Z_i \geqq 0) = \mathbf{X}_i\beta + E(\epsilon_i \mid \nu_i \geqq -\mathbf{W}_i\boldsymbol{\gamma}) \tag{10.33}$$

Clearly, in estimating (10.27), we would take no note of the second term of (10.33) as regressors. Still this term arises from samples selected nonrandomly and thus would be the source of bias. This is the same kind of bias that arises from omitted variables, and therefore the problem of selected samples resembles that of omitted variables.

10.5.1 The Heckman Estimator Assuming Normal Errors and Its Properties

Suppose $f(\epsilon_i, \nu_i)$ is a bivariate normal pdf. Using the results of Johnson and Kotz (1972), p. 112–113, we have

$$E(\epsilon_i \mid \nu_i \geqq -W_i\gamma) = -\frac{\sigma_{\epsilon\nu}}{(\sigma_{\nu\nu})^{1/2}}\lambda_i \tag{10.34}$$

$$E(\nu_i \mid \nu_i \geqq -W_i\gamma) = \frac{\sigma_{\nu\nu}}{(\sigma_{\nu\nu})^{1/2}}\lambda_i \tag{10.35}$$

where

$$\lambda_i = \frac{\phi(V_i)}{1 - \Phi(V_i)} = \frac{\phi(V_i)}{\Phi(-V_i)} \tag{10.36}$$

ϕ and Φ are pdf and distribution function for the standard normal variable,

$$V_i = \frac{W_i\gamma}{(\sigma_{\nu\nu})^{1/2}}$$

and λ_i is the reciprocal of Mill's ratio. It decreases monotonically $\left(\text{that is } \frac{\partial\lambda_i}{\partial\Phi(-V_i)} < 0\right)$ with the probability $\Phi(-\nu)$ of an observation being selected in the sample. Note that $\Phi(-V_i) = 1 - \Phi(V_i)$. Note also that

$$\lim_{\Phi(-V_i)\to 1} \lambda_i = 0 \qquad \lim_{\Phi(-V_i)\to 0} \lambda_i = \infty \tag{10.37}$$

The regression functions for selected samples are calculated to be:

$$E(Y_i \mid X_i, Z_i \geqq 0) = X_i\beta + \frac{\sigma_{\epsilon\nu}}{(\sigma_{\nu\nu})^{1/2}}\lambda_i \tag{10.38}$$

$$E(Z_i \mid W_i, Z_i \geqq 0) = W_i\gamma + \frac{\sigma_{\nu\nu}}{(\sigma_{\nu\nu})^{1/2}}\lambda_i \tag{10.39}$$

From (10.38) and (10.39), we get individual observations on the regression lines as

$$Y_i = E(Y_i \mid X_i, Z_i \geqq 0) + \tilde{\epsilon}_i \tag{10.40}$$

$$Z_i = E(Z_i \mid W_i, Z_i \geqq 0) + \tilde{\nu}_i \tag{10.41}$$

where

$$E(\tilde{\epsilon}_i \mid X_i, \lambda_i, \nu_i \geqq -W_i\gamma) = 0 \tag{10.42}$$

$$E(\tilde{\nu}_i \mid W_i, \lambda_i, \nu_i \geqq -W_i\gamma) = 0 \tag{10.43}$$

$$E(\tilde{\nu}_i\tilde{\epsilon}_i \mid X_i, W_i, \lambda_i, \nu_i \geqq -W_i\gamma) = 0 \qquad \text{for } i \neq i' \tag{10.44}$$

Also,[5]

$$E(\tilde{\epsilon}_i^2 \mid X_i, \lambda_i, \nu_i \geqq -W_i\gamma) = \sigma_{\epsilon\epsilon}\{(1-\rho^2) + \rho^2(1 + V_i\lambda_i - \lambda_i^2)\} \tag{10.45}$$

$$E(\tilde{\epsilon}_i\tilde{\nu}_i \mid X_i, W_i, \lambda_i, \nu_i \geqq -W_i\gamma) = \sigma_{\epsilon\nu}(1 + V_i\lambda_i - \lambda_i^2) \tag{10.46}$$

$$E(\tilde{\nu}_i^2 \mid W_i, \lambda_i, \nu_i \geqq -W_i\gamma) = \sigma_{\nu\nu}(1 + V_i\lambda_i - \lambda_i^2) \tag{10.47}$$

where

$$\rho^2 = \frac{\sigma_{\epsilon\nu}^2}{\sigma_{\epsilon\epsilon}\sigma_{\nu\nu}}$$

and

$$0 \leqq 1 + \lambda_i V_i - \lambda_i^2 \leqq 1 \tag{10.48}$$

Suppose now that V_i and so λ_i are known. Then from (10.38) it is clear that the data on λ_i (which is a regressor in (10.40)) could be used to estimate (10.40) by OLS to produce unbiased estimates for β and $\frac{\sigma_{\epsilon\nu}}{(\sigma_{\nu\nu})^{1/2}}$. However, since from (10.45) $\tilde{\epsilon}_i$ is heteroscedastic (its variance depends on W_i), the OLS estimates would be inefficient. Inequality (10.48) together with (10.45) and (10.46) would mean that the OLS estimator of $\sigma_{\epsilon\epsilon}$ and $\sigma_{\epsilon\nu}$ will be biased under. Heckman (1976) suggests a standard GLS routine to obtain the standard errors for the estimated coefficients of (10.40).

However, in practice λ_i is usually not known. In cases where Y_i is not known if $Z_i < 0$, but the corresponding W_i are known, Heckman suggests the following step-wise procedure:

1. Use probit analysis for the complete sample to determine the parameters of the probability that $Z_i \geqq 0$ $\left(\text{that is } \frac{\gamma}{(\sigma_{\nu\nu})^{1/2}}\right)$. Suppose the estimated value of the parameters is $\hat{\gamma}$.
2. Using $\hat{\gamma}$, one can estimate V_i and therefore λ_i. These estimators are consistent.
3. Use the estimated value of λ_i for fitting (10.40) from the selected sample. Estimated coefficients β and $\frac{\sigma_{\epsilon\nu}}{(\sigma_{\nu\nu})^{1/2}}$ are consistent.
4. To generate consistent estimate of $\sigma_{\epsilon\epsilon}$, use step 3 to consistently estimate $C = \rho\, \sigma_{\epsilon\epsilon}^{1/2} = \frac{\sigma_{\epsilon\nu}}{\sigma_{\nu\nu}^{1/2}}$. Suppose $\tilde{\epsilon}_i$ stands for the residual from step 3 and $\hat{C}$ for the estimate of C. Then $\hat{\sigma}_{\epsilon\nu}$, the estimate of $\sigma_{\epsilon\nu}$, is

$$\hat{\sigma}_{\epsilon\nu} = \sum_{i=1}^{n_1} \frac{\hat{\epsilon}_i^2}{n_1} - \frac{\hat{C}}{n_1} \sum_{i=1}^{n_1} (\hat{\lambda}_i\hat{V}_i - \hat{\lambda}_i^2)$$

[5] See Johnson and Kotz (1972) for a clue to these results.

$\hat{\lambda}_i$ and $\hat{V}_i$ are the estimated λ_i and V_i obtained from step 2. $\hat{\sigma}_{\epsilon\nu}$ is consistent.

One should consult Heckman (1979) for the limiting distribution of the estimator when λ_i is not known. The caveat is that the formulas for the least squares coefficients are not proper except when zero sample selection bias is provided for (that is $C = 0$).[6]

10.6 PROBLEMS ARISING FROM UNOBSERVABLE VARIABLES

Socioeconomic variables are often unobservable, not merely unmeasurable. The problems arising from the latter variables as captured through measurement errors were discussed before[7] (Section 8.5). We will now discuss variables that are inherently unobservable such as "technical progress", "education", or "skill". Such unobservable variables are of two kinds, those for which proxy variables can be used, and others, called *latent variables*, which are functionally determined by means of some indicators. Among variables of the first kind, we have, for instance, "technical progress" proxied by the time trend, and "education" proxied by years of schooling, and among those of the second kind, we have "skill" or "intelligence" determined by such indicators as IQ, performance in SAT (special aptitute test), GRE (graduate records examination), MCAT (medical college admission test), etc.

Use of proxy variables. To simplify matters, we use a simple linear regression model satisfying all OLS assumptions:

$$Y_i = \beta_0 + \beta_1 X_i + \epsilon_i \tag{10.49}$$

If X is not observable, let us suppose that another closely related variable Z, which is observable can be used as its proxy. Let Z and X be related according to

$$Z_i = \gamma_0 + \gamma_1 X_i + \nu_i \tag{10.50}$$

[6] An interesting article on sample selectivity bias and labor supply function is Wales and Woodland (1980). These authors explore various ways of estimating a labor supply function when several of the individuals in the sample are not working and therefore their wages are unknown. There are a few criteria that determine the choice among these various methods: computational facilities, possible correlation between disturbances in the hours and wage equations, availability of complete or incomplete information about nonworkers, wage equation misspecified or not, and the desire to obtain asymptotic efficiency *as well as* consistency of estimators. They generally establish the superiority of the ML method over others in estimating the labor supply function under sample selectivity bias.

[7] Notice that measurement errors, in principle, can be eliminated and the variables can be made free of such errors. But variables that are unobservable are essentially unmeasurable.

from which:

$$X_i = -\gamma_0/\gamma_1 + Z_i/\gamma_1 - v_i/\gamma_1 \tag{10.51}$$

It is assumed that v is an identically, and independently distributed normal variable with zero mean and variance σ_v^2. It is also assumed that ϵ and v are independent for any and all observations.

Using (10.51) in (10.49), we obtain

$$Y_i = \beta_0^* + \beta_1^* Z_i + \epsilon_i^* \tag{10.52}$$

where

$$\beta_0^* = \beta_0 - (\beta_1\gamma_0/\gamma_1) \tag{10.53}$$

$$\beta_1^* = \beta_1/\gamma_1 \tag{10.54}$$

$$\epsilon_i^* = \epsilon_i - \beta_1(v_i/\gamma_1) \tag{10.55}$$

Notice that Z_i and ϵ_i^* have a constant component that depends on v_i and are therefore correlated. Thus the OLS estimate of β_1^* would be inconsistent. This would not be the case if Z were perfect for X which would mean v, the common component, would be absent. That is, the OLS estimate of β_1^* would be consistent for β_1/γ_1, even though a consistent estimate of β_1 would still be unavailable. That should not deter us from testing if $\beta_1^* = 0$ whenever $\beta_1 = 0$. In other words, the effectiveness of X as a determining variable for Y can be established even when X is unobservable, only if a perfect proxy for it were available.

Let us now suppose that the model includes more than one explanatory variable, one of which is unobservable. A simple case is illustrated in the following formulation:

$$Y_i = \beta_0 + \beta_1 X_{i1} + \beta_2 X_{i2} + \epsilon_i \tag{10.56}$$

where X_2 is not observable. Let its proxy Z be related to it according to

$$Z_i = \gamma_0 + \gamma_1 X_{i2} + v_i \tag{10.57}$$

the error term v_i being the same as before. The OLS estimate of β_1, denoted by $\hat{\beta}_1$, can be derived[8] as

$$\hat{\beta}_1 = \frac{\left[\left(\sum y_i x_{i1} \sum z_i^2\right) - \left(\sum y_i z_i \sum x_{i1} z_i\right)\right]}{\left[\left(\sum x_{i1}^2 \sum z_i^2\right) - \left(\sum x_{i1} z_i\right)^2\right]} \tag{10.58}$$

the lower case letters used above imply that the variables are in the form of

[8] See equation (2.63) of Chapter 2.

deviations from their means. Using the value of Y_i from (10.56) and putting it in (10.58), and taking probability limits, we get

$$\operatorname{plim} \hat{\beta}_1 = \beta_1 + \beta_2 \operatorname{plim} \left[\frac{\left(\sum x_{i1}x_{i2}/n\right)\left(\sum z_i^2/n\right) - \left(\sum z_i x_{i2}/n\right)\left(\sum x_{i1}z_i/n\right)}{\left(\sum x_{i1}^2/n\right)\left(\sum z_i^2/n\right) - \left(\sum x_{i1}z_i/n\right)} \right] \tag{10.59}$$

It is clear from the expression within [ ] brackets that we have the OLS estimated coefficient of X_2 on X_1 obtained from the regression of X_2 on X_1 and Z. It follows that should u be zero (in which case Z would be perfect for X), the plim of the square bracketed expression would vanish and so

$$\operatorname{plim} \hat{\beta}_1 = \beta_1 \tag{10.60}$$

But generally $\hat{\beta}_1$ would be inconsistent. The question that is important, then, would be whether a simpler estimate is available. One such estimate is obtained by eliminating X_2 from the regression. Its resulting expression is:

$$\tilde{\beta}_1 = \left(\sum y_i x_{i1}\right) \Big/ \left(\sum x_{i1}^2\right) \tag{10.61}$$

Thus,

$$\operatorname{plim} \tilde{\beta}_1 = \beta_1 + \beta_2 \operatorname{plim} \left(\frac{\sum x_{i1}x_{i2}/n}{\sum x_{i1}^2/n} \right) \tag{10.62}$$

which shows that $\tilde{\beta}_1$ is inconsistent, as $\hat{\beta}_1$ has been. The ultimate choice of one or the other estimator may be made, as pointed out recently, by the criterion of lesser asymptotic bias or lesser mean squared error. By the first criterion, $\hat{\beta}_1$ is preferred in situations of both stochastic and nonstochastic X variables[9]. By the second criterion, the choice is not unambiguous: still $\hat{\beta}_1$, on the whole, is preferred.[10,11]

10.6.1 The Problem of Latent Variables

We have defined and illustrated such variables before. Further examples include "permanent income", which also illustrates a perhaps extreme form of a theoretical and an unmeasurable concept. The best that can be done in this case is to

[9] These points are developed in McCallum (1972) and Wickens (1972).

[10] Aigner (1974) and Kinal and Lahiri (1983) make these points.

[11] The foregoing results appear to obtain even when the criterion chosen is asymptotic bias used in traditional significance tests—see Ohtani (1985).

represent it by means of measurable indicators such as age of the earner, his earning span, his asset portfolio, his professional status (which, in turn, will include his educational level and occupational identity), and so on. We will discuss below a latent variable model, which is essentially a multiple cause model and discuss its estimation by following the routines suggested by Zellner (1970) and Goldberger (1972). We will follow this up by what is known as a MIMIC or multiple indicator multiple cause model, a more formidable example of a latent variable model.

Let the multiple cause model be

$$Y_i = \beta Z_i + \epsilon_i \tag{10.63}$$

where

$$\begin{aligned} Z_i &= \alpha_1 X_{i1} + \alpha_2 X_{i2} + \cdots + \alpha_k X_{ik} \\ \epsilon_i &: N(0, \sigma_\epsilon^2) \end{aligned} \tag{10.64}$$

and

$$\begin{aligned} Z_i^* &= Z_i + \nu_i \\ \nu_i &: N(0, \sigma_\nu^2) \end{aligned} \tag{10.65}$$

Clearly, the latent variable is Z, which is unobservable, but all other variables, namely Y, Z^*, and the Xs are measurable. In the permanent income example, Z is permanent income and its indicators are $X_1, X_2, \ldots$ being, respectively, age, earning span, ... The disturbance terms ϵ and ν are independently distributed, besides each being normal with parameters as specified above.

As for estimation, Zellner proposes a two-step procedure. Since, in vector and matrix notation,

$$\underset{(n \times 1)}{\mathbf{Y}} = \underset{(n \times 1)}{\mathbf{Z}} \underset{(1 \times 1)}{\boldsymbol{\beta}} + \underset{(n \times 1)}{\boldsymbol{\epsilon}} \tag{10.66}$$

$$\underset{(n \times 1)}{\mathbf{Z}} = \underset{(n \times k)}{\mathbf{X}} \underset{(k \times 1)}{\boldsymbol{\alpha}} \tag{10.67}$$

$$\underset{(n \times 1)}{\mathbf{Z}^*} = \underset{(n \times 1)}{\mathbf{Z}} + \underset{(n \times 1)}{\boldsymbol{\nu}} \tag{10.68}$$

where the sizes of the vectors and matrices are shown below their symbols, combine (10.66) with (10.67) and separately (10.67) with (10.68) to obtain

$$\mathbf{Y} = X\boldsymbol{\gamma} + \boldsymbol{\epsilon} \tag{10.69}$$

$$\mathbf{Z}^* = X\boldsymbol{\alpha} + \boldsymbol{\nu} \tag{10.70}$$

In above we have used the relation

$$\boldsymbol{\gamma} = \boldsymbol{\alpha\beta} \tag{10.71}$$

Now, apply OLS to these equations to get estimates of $\boldsymbol{\gamma}$ and $\boldsymbol{\alpha}$, say $\hat{\boldsymbol{\gamma}}$ and $\hat{\boldsymbol{\alpha}}$, and estimates of σ_ϵ^2 and σ_ν^2, denoted by s_ϵ^2 and s_ν^2. Expressions for s_ϵ^2 and s_ν^2 are as follows:

$$s_\epsilon^2 = \{1/(n - k)\}(\mathbf{Y} - X\hat{\boldsymbol{\gamma}})'(\mathbf{Y} - X\hat{\boldsymbol{\gamma}}) \tag{10.72}$$

$$s_\nu^2 = (1/(n - k))(\mathbf{Z}^* - X\hat{\boldsymbol{\alpha}})'(\mathbf{Z}^* - X\hat{\boldsymbol{\alpha}}) \tag{10.73}$$

The above represents the work in the first step. In the second step, minimize:

$$\begin{aligned} \mathrm{V} = (1/s_\epsilon^2) = (\mathbf{Y} - X\boldsymbol{\alpha\beta})'(\mathbf{Y} - X\boldsymbol{\alpha\beta}) \\ + (1/s_\nu^2)(\mathbf{Z}^* - X\boldsymbol{\alpha})'(\mathbf{Z}^* - X\boldsymbol{\alpha}) \end{aligned} \tag{10.74}$$

with respect to the values of $\boldsymbol{\beta}$ and $\boldsymbol{\alpha}$. The work in the two steps together constitutes Zellner's method.

Goldberger's method on the other hand, is a maximum likelihood method. Rewriting (10.69) as

$$\mathbf{Y} = X\boldsymbol{\alpha\beta} + \boldsymbol{\epsilon} \tag{10.75}$$

it then uses (10.75) and (10.70) to obtain the following log-likelihood function:

$$\begin{aligned} \log L = \text{constant} - (n/2)\log\sigma_\epsilon^2 - \{1/(2\sigma_\epsilon^2)\}(\mathbf{Y} - X\boldsymbol{\alpha\beta})'(\mathbf{Y} - X\boldsymbol{\alpha\beta}) \\ - (n/2)\log\sigma_\nu^2 - \{1/(2\sigma_\nu^2)\}(\mathbf{Z}^* - X\boldsymbol{\alpha})'(\mathbf{Z}^* - X\boldsymbol{\alpha}) \end{aligned} \tag{10.76}$$

and maximizes it with respect to $\boldsymbol{\beta}$, $\boldsymbol{\alpha}$, σ_ϵ^2, and σ_ν^2.

The two methods differ in the way σ_ϵ^2 and σ_ν^2 are treated for their estimates: Zellner's method estimates them first before developing the estimates of other parameters, whereas Goldberger's method estimates them simultaneously with other parameters. But the asymptotic properties of all the estimates from both methods are the same.[12,13]

In the MIMIC model, the latent variable appears as a regressor in various regression equations. Since it is itself unobservable, several causal factors are used to determine it. Consider the following representation of the model:

$$\begin{aligned} Y_{i1} &= \beta_1 Z_i + \epsilon_{i1} \\ Y_{i2} &= \beta_2 Z_i + \epsilon_{i2} \\ \cdots &\quad \cdots\cdot \\ Y_{il} &= \beta_l Z_i + \epsilon_{il} \\ Z_i &= \alpha_i X_{i1} + \alpha_2 X_{i2} + \cdots + \alpha_k X_{ik} + u_i \end{aligned} \tag{10.77}$$

[12] See Pagan (1984) for these results.

[13] Attfield (1983) tackles a specification problem arising from the omission of important explanatory variables from (10.70). He shows that estimates of $\boldsymbol{\alpha}$ will in that case be inconsistent from both methods, but those of $\boldsymbol{\beta}$ will be consistent.

TABLE 10.1 HOME VALUE EQUATIONS BY THREE METHODS OF VALUATION

Equation	Intercept	Slope	$\hat{\sigma}_\epsilon$
Appraised Value	0	1.00	2.415
Owner Estimate	1.257	0.973 (0.119)	2.771
Assessed Value	−5.909	1.339 (0.120)	1.612

The ϵs and u are assumed statistically independent, besides being normal each with zero mean and constant variance. The variables Y play the role of indicators for the latent variable Z. This model has been estimated by Joreskog and Goldberger (1975) using the maximum likelihood method. We now turn to an application of the MIMIC model.

10.6.2 Application of the MIMIC Model Due to Robins and West (1977)

The problem under investigation is estimation of home values in Seattle, Washington, U.S.A. The variable Z represents the actual market value of the home, its three indicator variables being the value appraised by a real estate company, the owner's suggested value, and the value arrived at by county officials. Twelve causal factors are taken. These relate to property features, for example lot size, age of property, and number of rooms in the building. The equation for the real estate appraised value is specified to have a zero intercept term and a slope coefficient equal to one. There are 138 houses selected in the sample and these arise in the Seattle Income Maintenance Experiment of 1971. The (maximum likelihood) coefficient estimates of the home value measurement equations are as in Table 10.1, the estimated standard errors of the coefficients being shown in parentheses. The estimates $\hat{\sigma}_\epsilon$ of σ_ϵ are also shown.

The results show that home owners generally overvalue their home by an average of \$1257. Otherwise, since the slope coefficient is insignificantly different from one, their estimate of the home value is close to the true market value. Also, the degree of accuracy of owner estimate is about the same as in the case of appraised value. This follows from a comparison of the reciprocal of the estimated value of σ_ϵ in the two cases (1/2.771 almost equal to 1/2.415). Notice that the assessed value is considerably off the mark by being less than the true market value by as much as \$5910.[14]

[14] There is a class of structural equation models that includes unobservable variables in the role of both independent and dependent variables. Such models are usually called LISREL (which is the short form for *li*near *s*tructural *rel*ations) models, named after a computer program developed by Joreskog and Sorbom (1981). The interested reader should consult the original source.

10.7 POOLED TIME SERIES AND CROSSSECTION DATA AND VARIABLE COEFFICIENT MODELS

Many economic problems are observed from individuals' behavior distributed over time and space. This is revealed from data arising in time series *and* cross-sections. For example, problems such as how individual households in various parts of the United States make their consumption expenditure decisions[15] through time, or problems such as what determines the unemployment rate in various provinces of Canada over time will require the pooling of time series and cross-section data.

In symbols, the data in a general situation may be represented by Y_{il} and X_{ijl}, $i = 1, 2, \ldots, n, j = 1, 2, \ldots, m$, and $l = 1, 2, \ldots, r$, where Y_{il} is the value of the dependent variable for crosssection unit l in period i depending on m explanatory variables $X_{ijl}; j = 1, 2, \ldots, m$ belonging to the unit l at time i. The linear regression equation connecting Y and X is as follows:

$$Y_{il} = \beta_0 + \sum_{j=1}^{m} \beta_j X_{ijl} + \epsilon_{il} \tag{10.78}$$

in which a common set of coefficients for all units in all time periods is assumed. The data sets including the disturbance vector for this model arranged according to the lth unit are:

$$\mathbf{Y}_l = \begin{bmatrix} Y_{1l} \\ \vdots \\ Y_{nl} \end{bmatrix} \qquad X_l = \begin{bmatrix} 1 & X_{11l} & \cdots & X_{1ml} \\ \vdots & \vdots & & \vdots \\ 1 & X_{n1l} & \cdots & X_{nml} \end{bmatrix} \qquad \boldsymbol{\epsilon}_l = \begin{bmatrix} \epsilon_{1l} \\ \vdots \\ \epsilon_{nl} \end{bmatrix} \tag{10.79}$$

In compact notation these sets become

$$\mathbf{Y} = \begin{bmatrix} \mathbf{Y}_1 \\ \vdots \\ \mathbf{Y}_r \end{bmatrix} \qquad X = \begin{bmatrix} X_1 \\ \vdots \\ X_r \end{bmatrix} \qquad \boldsymbol{\epsilon} = \begin{bmatrix} \boldsymbol{\epsilon}_1 \\ \vdots \\ \boldsymbol{\epsilon}_r \end{bmatrix} \tag{10.80}$$

their sizes being $nr \times 1$, $nr \times m$, and $nr \times 1$, respectively. Thus the compact model becomes:

$$\mathbf{Y} = X\boldsymbol{\beta} + \boldsymbol{\epsilon} \tag{10.81}$$

Notice that various assumptions made about the intercept and slope coefficients as well as the disturbance terms of (10.81) will lead to various models. For two such models, assume that β is the same for all i and l, but one model has $E(\boldsymbol{\epsilon\epsilon}') = \sigma^2 \boldsymbol{I}_{nr}$, where nr is the size of $\boldsymbol{I}$, and the other has $E(\boldsymbol{\epsilon\epsilon}') = \sigma^2 \boldsymbol{\Omega}$. With the errors in one model assumed to be identically and independently distributed, OLS

[15] The usual decision considerations are income, asset positions, family size, ethnic background, etc. of consumers.

estimation will be valid, and with the further assumption that these are normally distributed, usual statistical inferences will apply.

For the other model, various patterns of assumption about the error terms are possible. Suppose an investigator would specify:

$$\begin{aligned} E(\epsilon_{il}^2) &= \sigma_{ll} && \text{for all } i \quad l = 1, \ldots, r \\ E(\epsilon_{il}\epsilon_{il'}) &= \sigma_{ll'} && \text{for all } i \text{ and } l \neq l' \\ E(\epsilon_{il}E_{i'l'}) &= 0 && \text{for all } l,\ l' \text{ and } i \neq i' \end{aligned} \tag{10.82}$$

Here we have heteroscedasticity of errors for different units and nonvanishing contemporaneous covariances of errors of different units; otherwise no lagged autocorrelations of errors within and between units are being postulated. At the cost of elaborate details, GLS estimators of the following kind:

$$\boldsymbol{\beta}_{\text{GLS}} = (X'\Omega^{-1}X)^{-1}X'\Omega^{-1}\mathbf{Y} \tag{10.83}$$

where

$$E(\boldsymbol{\epsilon\epsilon}') = \sigma^2\boldsymbol{\Omega} = \begin{bmatrix} \sigma_{11}I_n & \cdots & \sigma_{1r}I_n \\ \vdots & \vdots & \vdots \\ \sigma_{1r}I_n & \cdots & \sigma_{rr}I_n \end{bmatrix} \tag{10.84}$$

with the σ_{ij}s unknown will, as usual, be the minimum variance unbiased linear estimates. For constructing feasible GLS estimates, one can, of course, substitute OLS estimated residuals for the σ_{ij}s. These estimates have well-known asymptotic properties.

If, in addition, disturbances within each unit are autocorrelated, the amount of algebra will be even more but the problem will still be the same.

Now assume that the intercept varies over the units even though the slope coefficients are common for various time dates and (crosssection) units, but the errors arise from either the fixed effects or random effects. The model equation in the case of fixed effects becomes:

$$\begin{bmatrix} \mathbf{Y}_1 \\ \mathbf{Y}_2 \\ \vdots \\ \mathbf{Y}_r \end{bmatrix} = \begin{bmatrix} \mathbf{i}_k & \mathbf{0}\cdots\mathbf{0} & X_{.1} \\ \vdots & \vdots & X_{.2} \\ \mathbf{0} & \mathbf{i}_k\cdots\mathbf{0} & \vdots \\ \cdot & \cdots & \cdot \\ \mathbf{0} & \cdots\ \mathbf{i}_k & X_{.r} \end{bmatrix} \begin{bmatrix} \beta_{01} \\ \vdots \\ \beta_{0r} \\ \boldsymbol{\beta}_. \end{bmatrix} + \boldsymbol{\epsilon} \tag{10.85}$$

$$\text{or, } \mathbf{Y} = W\boldsymbol{\beta}_0 + X_.\boldsymbol{\beta}_. + \boldsymbol{\epsilon} \tag{10.86}$$

$$\text{where} \quad W = \begin{bmatrix} \mathbf{i}_k & \mathbf{0} \cdots \mathbf{0} \\ \mathbf{0}\ \cdots & \cdots\ \mathbf{0} \\ \vdots & \vdots\ \vdots \\ \mathbf{0} & \mathbf{0} \cdots \mathbf{i}_k \end{bmatrix} \quad \boldsymbol{\beta}_0 = \begin{bmatrix} \beta_{01} \\ \vdots \\ \beta_{0r} \end{bmatrix} \quad X_. = \begin{bmatrix} X_{.1} \\ \vdots \\ X_{.r} \end{bmatrix} \tag{10.87}$$

and $X_{.1}, \ldots, X_{.r}$ are X_l, for $l = 1, 2, \ldots, r$ except that X_l does not include the first column consisting of unities; and $\boldsymbol{\beta}_.$ includes all βs except β_0.

It can be shown that the OLS estimates of $\beta_.$ are given by

$$\hat{\boldsymbol{\beta}}_. = (X_.' R X_.)^{-1} X_.' R \mathbf{Y} \tag{10.88}$$

where

$$R = I_n - \frac{1}{n}\begin{bmatrix} \mathbf{i}_n\mathbf{i}_n' & \cdots & \mathbf{0} & \cdots & \mathbf{0} \\ \cdot & \cdot & \cdot & \cdot & \cdot \\ \mathbf{0} & \cdots & \mathbf{i}_n\mathbf{i}_n' & \cdots & \mathbf{0} \\ \mathbf{0} & \cdots & \mathbf{0} & \cdots & \mathbf{i}_n\mathbf{i}_n' \end{bmatrix} \tag{10.89}$$

I_n is the identity matrix of size n, and $i_k i_k'$ the $k \times k$ matrix of unities. Operating R on $X_.$ and $\mathbf{Y}$ serves to replace the original observation on $X_.$ and $\mathbf{Y}$ by their deviations from their sample averages. By usual reasonings, the estimate of $\boldsymbol{\beta}_0$ becomes

$$\hat{\boldsymbol{\beta}}_0 = (W'W)^{-1}(W'\mathbf{Y} - W'X_.\hat{\boldsymbol{\beta}}_.) \tag{10.90}$$

which, in a particular case, yields

$$\hat{\beta}_{0l} = \overline{Y}_l - \hat{\beta}_{.l}\overline{X}_{1l} - \hat{\beta}_{.2}\overline{X}_{2l} - \cdots\cdots - \hat{\beta}_{.m}\overline{X}_{ml} \tag{10.91}$$

The errors of the model could instead be assumed to be heteroscedastic and, then, GLS estimates would be justified. Be that as it may, the $\hat{\boldsymbol{\beta}}_.$ vector is sometimes called the "within" estimator since it is computed from "within group or within unit" deviations as indicated before.[16]

10.7.1 The Error Components Model

We will now consider the random effects model, which is also called the error components model. This sort of a model has been extensively used by econometricians in recent times. Here the assumption is that the intercepts are the same β_0 for the r groups except for the parts β_{0i}; $i = 1, 2, \ldots, r$, which, being random, are immersed in the error term. That is, the model which is

$$\mathbf{Y} = [\mathbf{i}\; X_.]\begin{bmatrix} \beta_0 \\ \beta_. \end{bmatrix} + \boldsymbol{\epsilon} \tag{10.92}$$

has the error ϵ decomposed as follows:

$$\epsilon_{il} = \beta_{0l} + \nu_{il} \tag{10.93}$$

with

$$\beta_{0l} \sim \mathrm{N}(0, \sigma_\beta^2) \qquad \nu_{il} \sim \mathrm{N}(0, \sigma_\nu^2) \tag{10.94}$$

[16] This is a more organized analysis than the one in connection with the tests of structural change done in a previous chapter.

To develop the variance–covariance matrix of ϵ, proceed as follows. Since

$$\boldsymbol{\epsilon}_l = \beta_{0l}\mathbf{i}_n + \boldsymbol{\nu}_l$$

so

$$E(\boldsymbol{\epsilon}_l\boldsymbol{\epsilon}_l') = \sigma_\beta^2 U_n + \sigma_\nu^2 I_n \qquad l = 1, 2, \ldots, r \tag{10.95}$$

where

$$U_n = i_n i_n' \tag{10.96}$$

Thus

$$E(\boldsymbol{\epsilon}_l\boldsymbol{\epsilon}_l') = \begin{bmatrix} \sigma_\beta^2 + \sigma_\nu^2 & \sigma_\beta^2 & \cdots & \sigma_\beta^2 \\ \sigma_\beta^2 & \sigma_\beta^2 + \sigma_\nu^2 & \cdots & \sigma_\beta^2 \\ \cdots & \cdots & \cdots & \cdots \\ \sigma_\beta^2 & \sigma_\beta^2 & \cdots & \sigma_\beta^2 + \sigma_\nu^2 \end{bmatrix}$$
$$= \sigma_\epsilon^2 \begin{bmatrix} 1 & \theta & \cdots & \theta \\ \theta & 1 & \cdots & \theta \\ \cdot & \cdot & \cdots & \cdot \\ \theta & \theta & \cdots & 1 \end{bmatrix} = \sigma_\epsilon^2 \boldsymbol{\phi} \tag{10.97}$$

using

$$\sigma_\epsilon^2 = \sigma_\beta^2 + \sigma_\nu^2$$
$$\theta = \sigma_\beta^2/\sigma_\epsilon^2 \tag{10.98}$$

Under usual assumptions $E(\boldsymbol{\epsilon}_l\boldsymbol{\epsilon}_{l'}') = \boldsymbol{0}$. Thus

$$V = E(\boldsymbol{\epsilon}\boldsymbol{\epsilon}') = \sigma_\epsilon^2 \begin{bmatrix} \boldsymbol{\phi} & 0 & \cdots & 0 \\ 0 & \boldsymbol{\phi} & \cdots & 0 \\ 0 & 0 & \cdots & \boldsymbol{\phi} \end{bmatrix} = \sigma_\epsilon^2 I_r \boldsymbol{\phi} \tag{10.99}$$

It takes a few simple calculations to show that

$$V^{-1} = \frac{1}{\sigma_\epsilon^2} \begin{bmatrix} \boldsymbol{\phi}^{-1} & 0 & \cdots & 0 \\ 0 & \boldsymbol{\phi}^{-1} & \cdots & 0 \\ 0 & 0 & \cdots & \boldsymbol{\phi}^{-1} \end{bmatrix} \tag{10.100}$$

Use this expression for V^{-1} into the following GLS estimates of parameters:

$$\begin{bmatrix} \hat{\beta}_0 \\ \hat{\boldsymbol{\beta}}_. \end{bmatrix} = \{[\mathbf{i}\ X_.]'\ V^{-1}[\mathbf{i}\ X_.]\}^{-1}\ [\mathbf{i}\ X_.]'\ V^{-1}\mathbf{Y} \tag{10.101}$$

For a computational procedure, it will help to set up the analysis of variance table first. The main focus of this table will be on the expected mean sums of squares. These would provide a basis for using sample computed mean sums of squares for their corresponding expected values, specifically those that go into V^{-1}. As (10.101) shows, V^{-1} is used in the expressions for GLS parameter estimates.

TABLE 10.2 ANALYSIS OF VARIANCE TABLE

Variation Due to	SS	DF	MSS	E(MSS)
Between units	$\sum_{l,i} (\bar{\epsilon}_l - \bar{\bar{\epsilon}})^2$	$r - 1$	$\sum \frac{(\bar{\epsilon}_l - \bar{\bar{\epsilon}})^2}{r - 1}$	$\sigma_\nu^2 + n\sigma_\beta^2$
Within units	$\sum_{l,i} (\epsilon_{il} - \bar{\epsilon}_l)^2$	$r(n - 1)$	$\sum \frac{(\epsilon_{il} - \bar{\epsilon}_l)^2}{r(n - 1)}$	σ_ν^2
Total	$\sum_{l,i} (\epsilon_{il} - \bar{\bar{\epsilon}})^2$	$rn - 1$		

With that end in view, we construct Table 10.2 as an analysis of variance table.[17] Using the ANOVA table, it is possible to provide estimates of $\theta = \sigma_\beta^2/\sigma_\nu^2$ based on the OLS computed residuals. Thus, s_ν^2 taken to be an estimate of σ_ν^2 can be computed from

$$s_\nu^2 = \frac{1}{r(n - 1)} \sum (\hat{\epsilon}_{il} - \bar{\hat{\epsilon}}_l)^2 \tag{10.102}$$

where a symbol with a "^" indicates the OLS estimated residuals, and s_β^2, an estimate of σ_β^2, can be computed from

$$s_\beta^2 = \frac{1}{n}\left(\frac{n}{r - 1} \sum (\bar{\hat{\epsilon}}_l - \bar{\bar{\hat{\epsilon}}})^2 - s_\nu^2\right) \tag{10.103}$$

[17] Some explanations for the items of the ANOVA table are in order. We have $\epsilon_{il} = \beta_{0l} + \nu_{il}$, $\bar{\epsilon}_l = \beta_{0l} + \bar{\nu}_l$, and $\bar{\bar{\epsilon}} = \bar{\beta}_0 + \bar{\bar{\nu}}$ where $\bar{\epsilon}_l$ is the average over i, $\bar{\bar{\epsilon}}$ the average of $\bar{\epsilon}_l$ over l; similarly other symbols with single or double bars. Thus

$$\sum_{i,l} (\epsilon_{il} - \bar{\bar{\epsilon}})^2 = \sum_{i,l} (\epsilon_{il} - \bar{\epsilon}_l)^2 + \sum_{i,l} (\bar{\epsilon}_l - \bar{\bar{\epsilon}})^2$$

which is the central equation for the decomposition of total sum of squares into the sum of squares between and within units. Now since

$$\mathrm{E} \sum_i (\epsilon_{il} - \bar{\epsilon}_l)^2 = (n - 1)\sigma_\nu^2, \qquad \mathrm{E} \sum_i \sum_l (\epsilon_{il} - \bar{\epsilon}_l)^2 = r(n - 1)\sigma_\nu^2$$

we have, for the within unit MSS, the expected value σ_ν^2. Similarly,

$$\mathrm{E} \sum_{l,i} (\bar{\epsilon}_l - \bar{\bar{\epsilon}})^2 = \mathrm{E} \sum_{l,i} (\beta_{0l} - \bar{\beta}_0)^2 + \mathrm{E} \sum_{l,i} (\bar{\nu}_l - \bar{\bar{\nu}})^2,$$

the expectation of the cross-product term vanishing due to the independence of the β and ν components. But the first expectation is equal to $n(r - 1)\sigma_\beta^2$, the second to $n(r - 1)\dfrac{\sigma_\nu^2}{n}$, therefore

$$\mathrm{E} \sum \sum (\bar{\epsilon}_l - \bar{\bar{\epsilon}})^2 = n(r - 1)\sigma_\beta^2 + (r - 1)\epsilon_\nu^2$$

which implies that the expectation of the mean sum of squares due to "between units" is, after division by $(r - 1)$, equal to $\sigma_\nu^2 + n\sigma_\beta^2$.

Since $\sigma_\epsilon^2 = \sigma_\beta^2 + \sigma_\nu^2$, so s_ϵ^2, the estimate of σ_ϵ^2, is $s_\beta^2 + s_\nu^2$. Thus

$$\hat{\theta} = \frac{s_\beta^2}{s_\epsilon^2} \tag{10.104}$$

Using $\hat{\theta}$ and s_ϵ^2, V can be estimated, which then can be plugged into the expression of the GLS estimates (10.101).

There are problems in estimating the variance components by means of the OLS residuals in case X includes lagged Ys. In such a case, since θ lies between 0 and 1, use an iterative ML estimator with search procedures confined to grids over the (0, 1) interval following Balestra and Nerlove (1966) and Maddala (1977). Bear in mind that whether to use fixed effects or random effects models should depend on the context. For instance, if decision units are drawn from some population based on individual unit variations about the average according to some unknown random factors, then a random effects model should be the proper choice.[18]

Among the rest of the models, there is a class (of models) for which the intercept varies over both time and units, the slope coefficients remaining the same throughout. These may arise in the context of either the fixed effects or random effects. In the former context, one should expand equation (10.85) by including a set of dummy variables (one less than the number of time points to avoid multicollinearity), and in the latter context modify equation (10.92) to include a time-specific component of error. The rest of the treatments would be routine and direct. For elaborate treatments, see Maddala (1971), Balestra and Nerlove (1966), Wallace and Hussain (1969), Mundlak (1978), and Ghosh (1976).

The models in which both the intercept and slope coefficients vary across times and units would be the last category of models. Depending on what is assumed about their disturbances terms, one could use the methods of constrained regression or of the 'seemingly unrelated regression'. Also, should the models be of the random effects type, one should suitably modify the error variance matrix before proceeding to the (algebraically heavy) tasks of estimation and tests of hypotheses. We prefer not to go into these problems in this book—see Baltagi (1981) and Anderson and Hsiao (1981).[19]

[18] Some special results can be derived. For example, when $n \to \infty$, the GLS estimator with random effects will reduce to the same estimator with fixed effects. Also as $\sigma_\beta^2/\sigma_\nu^2 \to \infty$, the two effects estimators will be identical. Lastly, as $\sigma_\beta^2 \to 0$, the GLS random effects estimator will converge to the OLS estimator.

[19] This article is interesting because of its emphasis on dynamic models with error components. Different assumptions about initial conditions have been used here: (1) initial state fixed, (2) initial state random, and (3) the unobserved individual effect uncorrelated with the unobserved dynamic process, given a fixed or random initial value. Asymptotic properties of the ML and covariance methods and also a simple consistent estimator, independent of initial conditions, have been established.

10.7.2 A Fixed Effects Model Applied: Sadan and Tropp (1973)

An application in fixed coefficient models will be in order. Let us consider the specific study by Sadan and Tropp (1973). This study uses the error components model technique of Wallace and Hussain (1969), Mundlak (1963), and Hoch (1962). The technique is applied to a consumption function analysis of Israeli "kibbutz" or communal households based on data taken from crosssections and time series. The communal household is an integration of a cooperative and egalitarian commune in which the underlying concept is that of a continual household without a predetermined life span and a life cycle. The study is to determine the consumption–income relation based on the "continuous" nature of a communal household.

This study starts with an equation:

$$C^*_{it} = \alpha + \beta Y^*_{it} \tag{10.105}$$

where

α = constant

β = coefficient

C^*_{it} = consumption allowance of household i for year t

Y^*_{it} = determinant income variable given by:

$(1 - w)Y_{it} + wY_{.t}$

Y_{it} = 'normal' income for household i and year t (10.106)

$Y_{.t} = \frac{1}{m} \sum_{i=1} Y_{it}$ = average standing for standard income of m households in year t

w = 1 for "keeping up with the Joneses"

= 0 for individual experience guiding consumption (identifiable with Friedman's long-term income)

$(1 < w < 0)$

After substitution for variables, the consumption relation becomes

$$C_{it} = a + b_1 Y_{it} + b_2 Y_{.t} + U_{it} \tag{10.107}$$

where

a = estimate of α

b_1 = estimate of $\beta(1 - w)$

$$
\begin{aligned}
b_2 &= \text{estimate of } \beta w \\
C_{it} &= \text{measured consumption expenditure} \\
Y_{it} &= \text{measured income (equated to the 'true' income variable)} \\
U_{it} &= C_{it} - C^*_{it} = \text{random disturbances} \\
&\quad (\mathrm{E}(U) = \mathrm{cov}(C, U) = \mathrm{cov}(Y, U) = 0, \\
&\quad \text{for all households and for all years})
\end{aligned}
\tag{10.108}
$$

A time series analysis of (10.107) yields:

$$C_{.t} = A + BY_{.t} + U_{.t} \tag{10.109}$$

where

$$C_{.t} = \sum_{1}^{m} C_{it}, \text{ etc.}$$

$$A = \hat{\alpha}$$

$$B = \hat{\beta}$$

A crosssectional analysis based on a single period $t = t^*$, for example, leads to:

$$C_{it^*} = A_{t^*} + B_{1t^*} Y_{it^*} + U_{it^*} \tag{10.110}$$

where

$$A_{t^*} = \text{estimate of } (\alpha + \beta w Y_{.t^*})$$

$$B_{1t^*} = \text{estimate of } [\beta(1 - w)]$$

For $0 < w < 1$, B_{1t^*} will be systematically smaller than β and B.

The authors then go on to take z as an instrumental variable for Y such that

$$\hat{B}_{1t} = B_{1t}(z) = \mathrm{cov}_t(C, z)/\mathrm{cov}_t(Y, z) \tag{10.111}$$

For a proper choice of z, we can have

$$\mathrm{E}(B_{1t}(z)) = \beta(1 - w) \tag{10.112}$$

TABLE 10.3 ESTIMATE OF THE CONSUMPTION–INCOME COEFFICIENT, CROSSSECTION AND TIME SERIES OF AVERAGES: THE ESTABLISHED KIBBUTZ, 1936–1968*

The Crosssection of Intrahousehold Averages over time[a]	0.59 (0.093)	0.73 (0.09)
The Time series of Annual Interhousehold Averages[b]	0.86 (0.025)	0.93 (0.025)

[a] the estimated coefficient is $\overline{\mathrm{B}}_1$, equation (10.114)

[b] the estimated coefficient is B, equation (10.109)

* Reprinted with permission E. Sadan and Z. Tropp, "Consumption Function Analysis in a Commercial Household," *Review of Economics and Statistics*, 45 (1973) Table 1, p. 479.

A revised version of (10.110) entails weighted averages of a series of crosssectional estimates, such as

$$C_{it} = A_t + B_{1.}Y_{it} + U_{it} \tag{10.113}$$

$$C_{i.} = \overline{A} + \overline{B}_1 Y_{i.} + U_{i.} \tag{10.114}$$

where

$$\begin{aligned} A_t &= \text{estimate of } \alpha + \beta w Y_{.t} \\ \overline{A} &= \text{estimate of } \alpha + \beta w Y_{..} \text{ with } Y_{..} = \frac{1}{n}\sum_1^n Y_{i.} \\ B_{1.} &= \text{estimate of } \beta(1 - w) \\ C_{i.} &= \frac{1}{n}\sum_1^n C_{it}, \text{ etc.} \end{aligned} \tag{10.115}$$

Using Hoch (1962), Mundlak (1963) and Wallace and Hussain (1969), the authors then obtain:

$$\begin{aligned} B_{1.} &= \sum_{t=1}^{n} \frac{V_t(Y)\, B_{1t}}{\sum_1^n V_t(Y)} = \text{weighted average of } n \text{ crosssection estimates} \\ B_{1.}(z) &= \sum_{t=1}^{n} \frac{\text{cov}_t(C, z)}{\sum_1^n \text{cov}_t(Y, z)} B_{1t}(z) \end{aligned} \tag{10.116}$$

The first set of results, presented in Table 10.3, shows the difference between crosssection and time series methods. The other results, presented in Table 10.4, are weighted averages of crosssection estimates and those obtained by the instrumental variable method. While the other results do not differ widely among

TABLE 10.4 CROSSSECTION ESTIMATES OF THE CONSUMPTION FUNCTION COEFFICIENTS: THE ESTABLISHED KIBBUTZ, 1938–1967*

		Estimates Arrived at Using Instrumental Variables[b]		
Version	Direct Estimate[a]	Income in period $t + 1$	Income in period $t - 1$	Income in period $t - 2$
Linear	0.42	0.49	0.5286	0.53
	(0.0905)	(0.0925)	(0.0938)	(0.09)
Log	0.5738	0.6564	0.6808	0.70
	(0.0136)	(0.0137)	(0.0138)	(0.014)

[a] Estimates of $B_{1.}$, equations (10.110) and (10.115)

[b] Estimates of $B_{1.}(z)$, equations (10.110) and (10.116)

* Reprinted with permission E. Sadan and Z. Tropp, "Consumption Function Analysis in a Commercial Household," *Review of Economics and Statistics*, 45 (1973) Table 2, p. 479.

themselves, the first set of results shows some wide disparity as between the crosssection and time series methods. About a fourth of the disparity, as the authors claim, could be attributed to errors in the measured income variable, the remainder to systematic errors. The authors dwell on an important implication of the results when $w = 1$ (not reported here). This is used to determine the "keeping up with the Joneses" effect. They find decreased savings among constituents with lower than "average" income, but increased savings among constituents with above "average" income.

10.8 VARIABLE COEFFICIENT MODELS

These models signify structural changes associated with variations in parameters of a function. However, unlike some of the cases studied before where structural breaks happened at known points, for example peace and war dichotomy in dummy variable models, parameter variations at known time points in pooled crosssection and time series models, we would now treat these time points as rather unknown. This would be clear from the discussion of two general types of models to appear below, one on (a known but small number of) switching regimes with unknown switching points, and the other relying on the assumption that the parameters vary continuously through time.

10.8.1 Switching Regimes

Take, at the minimum, two different regimes. These are illustrated by wage and price decisions of a trade-sensitive sector in periods of low and high external values of a country's currency. Let the time period t include n sample observations, and, in terms of an unknown time point t_0, let the hypothesis before and after that time point be stated as

$$\begin{aligned} &\text{Regime 1:} \quad Y_t = \beta_{01} + \beta_1 X_t + \epsilon_{1t} \qquad \text{for } t \leqq t_0 \\ &\text{Regime 2:} \quad Y_t = \beta_{02} + \beta_2 X_t + \epsilon_{2t} \qquad \text{for } t > t_0 \end{aligned} \tag{10.117}$$

Assume that the ϵs are normally and independently distributed with zero means and variances σ_1^2 and σ_2^2. Then the logarithm of the likelihood function becomes:

$$\begin{aligned} \ln L = &-\frac{n}{2}\ln 2\pi - \frac{t_0}{2}\sigma_1^2 - \frac{n-t_0}{2}\ln\sigma_2^2 - \frac{1}{2\sigma_1^2}\sum_{t=1}^{t_0}(Y_t - \beta_{01} - \beta_1 X_t)^2 \\ &- \frac{1}{2\sigma_2^2}\sum_{t=t_0+1}^{n}(Y_t - \beta_{02} - \beta_2 X_t)^2 \end{aligned} \tag{10.118}$$

It is well known that, for a problem of the kind under review, the ML and OLS estimates are equivalent.[20] Specifically estimates of β_{0i}, β_i, and σ_i^2 ($i = 1$,

[20] See equation (4.149) of Chapter 4 and equation (5.9) of Chapter 5, which give identical estimates.

2) are the same as their OLS estimates both for periods $t \leqq t_0$, and $t > t_0$. Since $\hat{\sigma}_1^2$ and $\hat{\sigma}^2$ given by

$$\hat{\sigma}_1^2 = \frac{1}{t_0} \sum_{1}^{t_0} (Y_t - \beta_{01} - \beta_1 X_t)^2$$
$$\hat{\sigma}_2^2 = \frac{1}{n - t_0} \sum_{t_0+1}^{n} (Y_t - \beta_{02} - \beta_2 X_t)^2 \tag{10.119}$$

are such estimates of σ_1^2 and σ_2^2, respectively, and since the sum of the last two terms of (10.119) is $-n/2$, therefore

$$\ln L = n/2 \ln 2\pi - t_0/2 \ln \hat{\sigma}_1^2 - (n - t_0)/2 \ln \hat{\sigma}_2^2 - n/2 \tag{10.120}$$

Obviously, ln L being a function of t_0 will be maximized for a given value of t_0, assuming that n is known. With two parameters β_{0i}, and β_i, $(i = 1, 2)$, t_0 will range from $t_0 = 3$ to $t_0 = n - 3$ calling for $n - 5$ pairs of regressions. This may be computationally very strenuous. A way out is suggested by Riddell (1980). His method is the method of recursive residuals as explained now.

In the model $\mathbf{Y} = X\boldsymbol{\beta} + \boldsymbol{\epsilon}$, where $\boldsymbol{\epsilon} \sim N(\mathbf{0}, \sigma^2 I)$ let X, a matrix of size $n \times (m + 1)$, be rewritten as

$$X = [\mathbf{x}_1 \mathbf{x}_2 \ldots \mathbf{x}_n]' \tag{10.121}$$

where $\mathbf{x}_j$ represents the $(m + 1) \times 1$ vector of observations on $(m + 1)$ explanatory variables at time point j. Denote by X_{t-1} the $(t - 1) \times (m + 1)$ matrix obtained from the first $t - 1$ rows of X. Similarly $\mathbf{y}_{t-1}$ is the subvector of $\mathbf{Y}$ obtained from the first $t - 1$ entries of $\mathbf{Y}$. Operating X_{t-1} on $\mathbf{y}_{t-1}$ leads to the estimated coefficient:

$$\hat{\boldsymbol{\beta}}_{t-1} = (X'_{t-1} X_{t-1})^{-1} X'_{t-1} \mathbf{y}_{t-1} \tag{10.122}$$

This may be used for obtaining the forecast Y_t at the time point t based on the vector $\mathbf{x}_t$ of regressors at the same time point. The associated prediction error is

$$Y_t - \mathbf{x}'_t \hat{\boldsymbol{\beta}}_{t-1} \tag{10.123}$$

Its variance, as in equation (5.45) of Chapter 5, is

$$\sigma^2(1 + \mathbf{x}'_t (X'_{t-1} X_{t-1})^{-1} \mathbf{x}_t) \tag{10.124}$$

The standardized recursive residual, distributed as $N(0, \sigma^2)$, is defined as:[21]

$$f_t = \frac{Y_t - \mathbf{x}'_t \hat{\boldsymbol{\beta}}_{t-1}}{\sqrt{\{1 + \mathbf{x}'_t (X'_{t-1} X_{t-1})^{-1} \mathbf{x}_t\}}} \tag{10.125}$$

[21] This is derived by using two relations:

$$(X'_t X_t)^{-1} = (X'_{t-1} X_{t-1})^{-1} - \frac{(X'_{t-1} X_{t-1})^{-1} \mathbf{x}_t \mathbf{x}'_t (X'_{t-1} X_{t-1})^{-1}}{1 + \mathbf{x}'_t (X'_{t-1} X_{t-1})^{-1} \mathbf{x}_t}$$

and

$$\hat{\boldsymbol{\beta}}_t = \hat{\boldsymbol{\beta}}_{t-1} + (X'_t X_t)^{-1} \mathbf{x}_t (Y_t - \mathbf{x}'_t \hat{\boldsymbol{\beta}}_{t-1})$$

It can be shown that

$$\text{ESS}_t = \text{ESS}_{t-1} + f_t^2 \tag{10.126}$$

where ESS_t representing the error sum of squares based on the first t of the X variables is given by:

$$\text{ESS}_t = (\mathbf{y}_t - X_t\hat{\boldsymbol{\beta}}_t)'(\mathbf{y}_t - X_t\hat{\boldsymbol{\beta}}_t) \tag{10.127}$$

From this it follows, using forward residuals $f_3, f_4, \ldots,$ that

$$\text{ESS}_{t_0} = \sum_{t=3}^{t_0} f_t^2 \qquad \hat{\sigma}_1^2(t_0) = \frac{\text{ESS}_{t_0}}{t_0} \tag{10.128}$$

Similarly, it is possible to obtain the estimate $\hat{\sigma}_2^2(t_0)$ using the set of backward recursive residuals. Therefore, these two sets of residuals will produce all the data necessary for maximizing equation (10.118).

To test that there is no switch, we use the following likelihood ratio statistic

$$\lambda = \frac{L(\hat{\omega})}{L(\hat{\Omega})} \tag{10.129}$$

In (10.129), $L(\hat{\Omega})$ is the unrestricted maximum of the likelihood for all parameter values, and $L(\hat{\omega})$ the maximum of the same over a subset ω of Ω over which the parametric restrictions become operative. It can be shown that

$$\lambda = \frac{(\hat{\sigma}_1^2)^{t_0/2}\,(\hat{\sigma}_2^2)^{(n-t_0)/2}}{(\hat{\sigma}^2)^{n/2}} \tag{10.130}$$

Unfortunately, $-2 \ln \lambda$ does not approximate to a χ^2 distribution in the asymptotic case because the likelihood function is based on only integral values of t_0. But, as in Brown and others (1975), one can plot λ against t to study its asymptotic tendency.[22]

10.8.2 Random Coefficient Models

Among the models that admit of continuous parameter variations, the random coefficient models are prime examples. We shall begin with the Hildreth and Houck (1968) specifications of such models. According to these, a random coefficient model is denoted by

$$Y_i = \mathbf{x}_i'\beta + \epsilon_i \qquad i = 1, 2, \ldots, n \tag{10.131}$$

[22] See Goldfeld and Quandt (1976) for switching regimes in other nonstochastic as well as stochastic situations. For disequilibrium model situations, see Fair and Jaffee (1972), Fair and Kelejian (1974), Amemiya (1974), Maddala and Nelson (1974), and Goldfeld and Quandt (1975).

where

$$\mathbf{x}_i' = [1\ X_{i1}X_{i2} \cdots X_{im}]$$
$$\epsilon_i = \mathbf{x}_i'\boldsymbol{\nu}_i \qquad (10.132)$$
$$\boldsymbol{\nu}_i' = [\nu_{i0}\nu_{i1} \cdots \nu_{im}]$$

In other words,

$$Y_i = (\beta_0 + \nu_{i0}) + (\beta_1 + \nu_{i1})X_{i1} + \cdots + (\beta_m + \nu_{im})X_{im} \qquad i = 1, \ldots, n \qquad (10.133)$$

That is, with βs as unknown constants common to all sample observations and νs as statistical variables influencing the slope coefficients in addition to the disturbances, the coefficients are no longer fixed but random. For instance, the effect of income on consumption demand may itself be subject to the influence of unobservable variables such as the attitude of consumers to the nature of consumption.

Assume that the statistical terms ν_is of the model have zero means. Assume also that they are uncorrelated between observation points and between different coefficients for the same observation point. That is,

$$E(\boldsymbol{\nu}_i) = \mathbf{0} \qquad i = 1, \ldots, n$$
$$E(\boldsymbol{\nu}_i\boldsymbol{\nu}_i') = \begin{bmatrix} \gamma_0 & 0 & 0 \\ 0 & \gamma_1 & 0 \\ 0 & 0 & \gamma_m \end{bmatrix} = \boldsymbol{\Gamma} \qquad (10.134)$$
$$E(\boldsymbol{\nu}_i\boldsymbol{\nu}_{i'}') = \boldsymbol{0} \qquad i,i' = 1, \ldots, n \qquad i \neq i'$$

The corresponding properties of the εs are

$$E(\epsilon_i) = 0 \qquad i = 1, 2, \ldots, n$$
$$E(\epsilon_i^2) = E(\mathbf{x}_i'\boldsymbol{\nu}_i\boldsymbol{\nu}_i'\mathbf{x}_i) = \mathbf{x}_i'\boldsymbol{\Gamma}\mathbf{x}_i \qquad i = 1, \ldots, n \qquad (10.135)$$
$$E(\epsilon_i\epsilon_{i'}) = 0 \qquad i, j = 1, \ldots, n; \qquad i \neq j$$

It follows that

$$\sigma_i^2 = E(\epsilon_i^2) = \sum_{j=1}^{m} X_{ij}^2\gamma_j = \mathbf{x}_i^{2'}\boldsymbol{\gamma} \qquad (10.136)$$

where

$$\mathbf{x}_i^{2'} = [1\ X_{i1}^2 \cdots X_{im}^2]$$
$$\boldsymbol{\gamma}' = [\gamma_1\gamma_2 \cdots \gamma_m] \qquad (10.137)$$

Therefore the model (10.131) has heteroscedastic errors. Specifically, their variances are proportional to the squares of the sample X observations. For all the samples together, the variances are collected as:

$$\boldsymbol{\sigma}^2 = [\sigma_1^2 \cdots \sigma_n^2]' = X^2\boldsymbol{\gamma} \tag{10.138}$$

In above, X^2 is the same matrix X except that every element of it is to be squared. The form of (10.138) suggests a way of estimating $\boldsymbol{\gamma}$ by regressing $\boldsymbol{\sigma}^2$ on X^2, should data on $\boldsymbol{\sigma}^2$ be given. From Chapter 5 we know that, for the model $\mathbf{Y} = \boldsymbol{x\beta} + \boldsymbol{\epsilon}$, $\mathrm{E}(\hat{\boldsymbol{\epsilon}}\hat{\boldsymbol{\epsilon}}') = M\,\mathrm{E}(\boldsymbol{\epsilon\epsilon}')\,M$ where the OLS estimated residuals are

$$\hat{\boldsymbol{\epsilon}} = \mathbf{Y} - X\hat{\boldsymbol{\beta}}$$

and

$$M = I - X(X'X)^{-1}X'$$

is an idempodent matrix. Thus,

$$\mathrm{E}(\hat{\boldsymbol{\epsilon}}^2) = \begin{bmatrix} \mathrm{E}\hat{\epsilon}_1^2 \\ \mathrm{E}\hat{\epsilon}_2^2 \\ \vdots \\ \mathrm{E}\hat{\epsilon}_n^2 \end{bmatrix} = M^2\boldsymbol{\sigma}^2 = M^2X^2\boldsymbol{\gamma} \tag{10.139}$$

Summarizing, then, the procedure of obtaining the GLS estimate of $\boldsymbol{\beta}$ consists of, first, fitting OLS to (10.131) and squaring the residuals to generate the vector $\hat{\boldsymbol{\epsilon}}^2$; second, regressing $\hat{\boldsymbol{\epsilon}}^2$ on M^2X^2 for deriving estimates $\hat{\boldsymbol{\gamma}}$ of $\boldsymbol{\gamma}$; third, putting these estimates in (10.138) to generate estimates $\hat{\sigma}_i^2$ of σ_i^2, and, lastly, using these $\hat{\sigma}_i^2$s to obtain the GLS estimate of $\boldsymbol{\beta}$.

There are a few problems with the Hildreth and Houck estimation procedure some of which are pointed out by the authors themselves. One problem is when the $\hat{\gamma}$s are negative in which case the authors suggest replacing them by zeros. They also indicate a few other ways of obtaining consistent estimates of β. But their efficiencies in, especially, small sample situations are unknown.

Consider now a different case. Let the data come from a crosssection cum time series structure. This is different from a structure which produces a sample with one observation per unit, as is the case with the Hildreth–Houck study. The specific model we have in mind is due to Swamy (1974).

10.8.3 The Swamy Model

Its equation is given by

$$\mathbf{Y}_l = X_l(\boldsymbol{\beta} + \boldsymbol{\nu}_l) + \boldsymbol{\epsilon}_l \qquad l = 1, 2, \ldots, r \tag{10.140}$$

As indicated in the introductory pages of Section 10.7, the model has r units, each unit with n observations. The size of X_l is $n \times (m + 1)$ and $\mathrm{R}\,(X_l)$ is $m + 1$. The coefficient vector $\boldsymbol{\beta}$ applies to all units identically. These coefficients are subject to statistical fluctuations that extend over different units. The assumptions of the model are:

$$
\begin{aligned}
&(1)\ \mathrm{E}(\boldsymbol{\epsilon}_l) = \mathbf{0} \qquad \mathrm{E}(\boldsymbol{\epsilon}_l\boldsymbol{\epsilon}_{l'}) = \begin{cases} \sigma_{ll}\boldsymbol{I}_n & \text{if } l = l' \\ \boldsymbol{0} & \text{if } l \neq l' \end{cases} \\
&(2)\ \mathrm{E}(\boldsymbol{\nu}_l) = \mathbf{0} \qquad \mathrm{E}(\boldsymbol{\nu}_l\boldsymbol{\nu}_{l'}) = \begin{cases} \boldsymbol{\Gamma} & \text{for } l = l' \\ \boldsymbol{0} & \text{for } l \neq l' \end{cases} \\
&(3)\ \mathrm{E}(\boldsymbol{\nu}_l\boldsymbol{\epsilon}_{l'}) = \boldsymbol{0}
\end{aligned}
\tag{10.141}
$$

In an elaborate form, the model is expressed as:

$$
\begin{bmatrix} \mathbf{Y}_1 \\ \vdots \\ \mathbf{Y}_r \end{bmatrix} = \begin{bmatrix} X_1 \\ \vdots \\ X_r \end{bmatrix} \boldsymbol{\beta} + \begin{bmatrix} X_1 & \cdot & \cdots & \boldsymbol{0} \\ \boldsymbol{0} & X_2 & \cdots & \boldsymbol{0} \\ \vdots & \vdots & \cdots & \\ \boldsymbol{0} & \boldsymbol{0} & \cdots & X_r \end{bmatrix} \begin{bmatrix} \boldsymbol{\nu}_1 \\ \vdots \\ \boldsymbol{\nu}_r \end{bmatrix} + \begin{bmatrix} \boldsymbol{\epsilon}_1 \\ \vdots \\ \boldsymbol{\epsilon}_r \end{bmatrix}
\tag{10.142}
$$

Naturally the error term is the sum total of the last two terms above. Using assumptions (1)–(3), the variance–covariance matrix of this hybrid error structure becomes:

$$
\boldsymbol{\Omega} = \begin{bmatrix} X_1\boldsymbol{\Gamma}X_1' + \sigma_{11}\boldsymbol{I}_n & \boldsymbol{0} & & \boldsymbol{0} \\ \boldsymbol{0} & X_2\boldsymbol{\Gamma}X_2' + \sigma_{22}\boldsymbol{I}_n & \cdots & \boldsymbol{0} \\ \cdots & \cdots & \cdots & \\ \boldsymbol{0} & \boldsymbol{0} & & X_r\boldsymbol{\Gamma}X_r' + \sigma_{rr}\boldsymbol{I} \end{bmatrix}
\tag{10.143}
$$

The Swamy procedure for obtaining the GLS estimator of $\boldsymbol{\beta}$ can be described in a few steps as follows:

(a) Obtain the OLS coefficient vector for the lth unit ($l = 1, 2, \ldots, r$) as

$$\hat{\boldsymbol{\beta}}_l = (X_l'X_l)^{-1} X_l'\mathbf{Y}_l$$

and the error vector:

$$\hat{\boldsymbol{\epsilon}}_l = \mathbf{Y}_l - X_l\hat{\boldsymbol{\beta}}_l$$

(b) By reasons similar to those used in Chapter 5, an unbiased estimator of σ_{ll} is

$$\hat{\sigma}_{ll} = \hat{\boldsymbol{\epsilon}}_l'\hat{\boldsymbol{\epsilon}}_l/n - (m + 1)$$

(c) It can be shown that an unbiased estimator of $\boldsymbol{\Gamma}$ is

$$\hat{\boldsymbol{\Gamma}} = \frac{\hat{\Sigma}_{\hat{\boldsymbol{\beta}}}}{r - 1} - \frac{1}{r}\sum_{l=1}^{r} \hat{\sigma}_{ll}(X_l'X_l)^{-1}$$

where

$$\hat{\Sigma}_{\hat{\boldsymbol{\beta}}} = \sum_{l=1}^{r} \hat{\boldsymbol{\beta}}_l\hat{\boldsymbol{\beta}}_l' - \frac{1}{r}\sum_{l=1}^{r} \boldsymbol{\beta}_l \sum_{l=1}^{r} \boldsymbol{\beta}_l'$$

(d) Using $\hat{\sigma}_{ll}$ and $\hat{\boldsymbol{\Gamma}}$ from steps (b) and (c) above into $\boldsymbol{\Omega}$ to obtain its estimate $\hat{\boldsymbol{\Omega}}$, we get the GLS estimate $\hat{\boldsymbol{\beta}}^*$ as

$$\hat{\boldsymbol{\beta}}^* = (X'\hat{\boldsymbol{\Omega}}^{-1}X)^{-1}X'\hat{\boldsymbol{\Omega}}^{-1}\mathbf{Y}$$

where $\mathbf{Y} = [Y_1 \cdots Y_r]'$, and $X = [X_1 \cdots X_r]'$, and the estimated variance–covariance matrix of $\hat{\boldsymbol{\beta}}^*$ is

$$\hat{V}(\hat{\boldsymbol{\beta}}^*) = (X'\hat{\boldsymbol{\Omega}}^{-1}X)^{-1}$$

$\hat{\boldsymbol{\beta}}^*$ will have asymptotic test properties.

A test of whether the coefficient vectors differ among units is available as follows. The null hypothesis regarding the $(m + 1) \times 1$ vector of coefficients for the lth unit becomes

$$H_0 : \boldsymbol{\beta}_1 = \boldsymbol{\beta}_2 = \cdots = \boldsymbol{\beta}_r = \boldsymbol{\beta}$$

which equivalently can be put in the form:

$$\boldsymbol{\beta}_1 = \boldsymbol{\beta}_2$$

$$\boldsymbol{\beta}_1 = \boldsymbol{\beta}_3$$

$$\cdots$$

$$\boldsymbol{\beta}_1 = \boldsymbol{\beta}_r$$

Then, one of the ways of setting up the test statistic would be by using the error sums of squares from the restricted and unrestricted model. Under H_0, the restricted model is of the form

$$\begin{bmatrix} \mathbf{Y}_1 \\ \vdots \\ \mathbf{Y}_r \end{bmatrix} = \begin{bmatrix} X_1 \\ \vdots \\ X_r \end{bmatrix} \boldsymbol{\beta} + \begin{bmatrix} \boldsymbol{\epsilon}_1 \\ \vdots \\ \boldsymbol{\epsilon}_r \end{bmatrix} \tag{10.144}$$

and the unrestricted form, as from (10.142) except for the terms in ν, is:

$$\begin{bmatrix} \mathbf{Y}_1 \\ \vdots \\ \mathbf{Y}_r \end{bmatrix} = \begin{bmatrix} X_1 & \cdots & \mathbf{0} \\ \vdots & & \vdots \\ \mathbf{0} & \cdots & X_r \end{bmatrix} \begin{bmatrix} \boldsymbol{\beta}_1 \\ \vdots \\ \boldsymbol{\beta}_r \end{bmatrix} + \begin{bmatrix} \boldsymbol{\epsilon}_1 \\ \vdots \\ \boldsymbol{\epsilon}_r \end{bmatrix} \tag{10.145}$$

We have seen before ((10.141)) that $E(\boldsymbol{\epsilon}_l\boldsymbol{\epsilon}_{l'}) = \sigma_{ll}\boldsymbol{I}_n$ or $\boldsymbol{0}$ depending on $l = l'$, or $l \neq l'$, which imply:

$$E(\boldsymbol{\epsilon\epsilon}') = \begin{bmatrix} \sigma_{11} & \cdots & 0 \\ \vdots & & \vdots \\ 0 & \cdots & \sigma_{rr} \end{bmatrix} \boldsymbol{I}_n \tag{10.146}$$

The heteroscedasticity of the error terms suggests dividing the observations for the lth unit by $\sqrt{\sigma_{ll}}$ $(l = 1, 2, \ldots, r)$ and applying OLS to the transformed variables. The restricted model then has the following error sum of squares, with the summations running over from $l = 1$ to $l = r$:

$$\boldsymbol{\epsilon}^{*\prime}\boldsymbol{\epsilon}^{*} = \sum \frac{\mathbf{Y}_l'\mathbf{Y}_l}{\sigma_{ll}} - \sum \frac{\mathbf{Y}_l'X_l\hat{\boldsymbol{\beta}}^{*}}{\sigma_{ll}} \tag{10.147}$$

where:

$$\hat{\beta}^{*} = \left(\sum \frac{X_l'\mathbf{Y}_l}{\sigma_{ll}}\right)^{-1} \sum \frac{X_l'\mathbf{Y}_l}{\sigma_{ll}} \tag{10.148}$$

On the other hand, from the unrestricted model, the error sum of squares is

$$\boldsymbol{\epsilon}'\boldsymbol{\epsilon} = \sum \frac{\mathbf{Y}_l'\mathbf{Y}_l}{\sigma_{ll}} - \sum \mathbf{Y}_l'X_l\hat{\boldsymbol{\beta}}_l \tag{10.149}$$

in which

$$\hat{\boldsymbol{\beta}}_l = (X_l'X_l)^{-1}X_l'\mathbf{Y}_l$$

The difference in the two error sums of squares is then

$$\hat{\boldsymbol{\epsilon}}^{*\prime}\hat{\boldsymbol{\epsilon}}^{*} - \hat{\boldsymbol{\epsilon}}'\hat{\boldsymbol{\epsilon}} = \sum \frac{(\hat{\boldsymbol{\beta}}_l - \hat{\boldsymbol{\beta}}^{*})'X_l'\mathbf{Y}_l}{\sigma_{ll}} = \frac{(\hat{\boldsymbol{\beta}}_l - \hat{\boldsymbol{\beta}}^{*})'X_l'X_l\hat{\boldsymbol{\beta}}_l}{\sigma_{ll}} \tag{10.150}$$

after using the solutions $\hat{\boldsymbol{\beta}}_l$ from the normal equations.

Assuming further that the ϵs are normally distributed, the test statistic, under H_0, is

$$F = \frac{(\hat{\boldsymbol{\epsilon}}^{*\prime}\hat{\boldsymbol{\epsilon}}^{*} - \hat{\boldsymbol{\epsilon}}'\hat{\boldsymbol{\epsilon}})}{(l - 1)} \tag{10.151}$$

which is distributed as F with $(m + 1)(r - 1)$, $r(n - m - 1)$ degrees of freedom. Replacing the σ_{ll} by $\hat{\sigma}_{ll}$, when the former are unknown, would still give an F test but only asymptotically. Swamy has also extended[23] the model to exclude lagged variables and other structures of the error variable vectors $\boldsymbol{\nu}_i$.

10.8.4 An Application by Gordon and Hynes (1970)

Gordon and Hynes suggest a number of factors that, in their opinion, are responsible for instability in the short run Phillips curve. These are, for instance, imperfect modeling of labor markets, lags in learning, erratic macropolicy shocks, and adjustment costs. One way to account for this instability is to use a random coefficients model of the Phillips curve regression, of the type shown in Section 10.8.2.

They estimate the following regression equation based on annual U.S. data over the period 1930–1966:

$$W_l = \beta_0 + \beta_{1l}u_l + \beta_{2l}m_l + \beta_{3l}p_l \qquad l = 1, 2, \ldots, r$$

[23] See Swamy (1971, 1973, and 1974)

where, for the lth unit

$$W_l = \text{percentage rate of change of money wages}$$
$$u_l = \text{unemployment rate}$$
$$m_l = \text{percentage rate of change of money supply}$$
$$p_l = \text{percentage rate of change of labor productivity}$$

The expected signs for the βs are

$$\beta_{1l} < 0 \qquad \beta_{2l}, \beta_{3l} > 0$$

The (inefficient) OLS estimated version of the equation is

$$\hat{W}_l = \underset{(0.0135)}{0.04033} - \underset{(0.00111)}{0.00201}u_l + \underset{(0.11033)}{0.3533}m_l + \underset{(0.06335)}{0.1284}p_l$$

$$\bar{R}^2 = 0.70 \qquad DW = 1.84 \qquad n = 37$$

the numbers in parentheses being the estimated standard errors of coefficients. Using the GLS estimation method, the equation is estimated as

$$\tilde{W}_l = \underset{(0.0134)}{0.0537} - \underset{(0.00119)}{0.00264}u_l + \underset{(0.06031)}{0.2522}m_l + \underset{(0.0468)}{0.1689}p_l$$

Two implications of the foregoing results immediately present themselves. First, in view of estimates of β_0 and β_1 being higher under the random coefficient than the fixed coefficient approach, the former approach imparts greater elasticity to the wage inflation equation than the latter. Second, the low quantitative magnitude of β_0 implies that once the influence of some important variables such as employment, productivity, and money supply is taken into account, nothing much would remain and the Phillips curve would rather relapse into a long run relation.[24]

10.8.5 Another Application: Cooley and Prescott (1973)

A different kind of random coefficient model develops into an adaptive regression model with typical dynamic evolution of the coefficients. Consider the model set up by Cooley and Prescott (1973a, b, and c). Their adaptive model has the equation

$$\mathbf{Y}_l = \mathbf{X}_l \boldsymbol{\beta}_l^*$$

[24] Raj and Ullah (1981), pp. 114–115 have tested the predictive power of both these approaches. Their conclusion has been that modeling wage inflation with random coefficients provides more accurate forecasts than the same with fixed coefficients. Also, the rather good forecasting ability of the random coefficient approach has been taken to mean that there probably has been no shift taking place in the curve after 1966, the last year of the Gordon and Hynes study—see also Rappoport and Kniesner (1974) on the shift of the curve.

such that $\boldsymbol{\beta}_l^* = \boldsymbol{\beta}_l + \boldsymbol{\nu}_l$ and $\boldsymbol{\beta}_l = \boldsymbol{\beta}_{l-1} + \boldsymbol{\mu}_l$ for $l = 1, 2, \ldots, r$, where $\boldsymbol{\beta}_l$ and $\boldsymbol{\mu}_l$ are normally distributed with zero means and stationary covariance matrices $\boldsymbol{\Sigma}_{\boldsymbol{\nu}}^*$ and $\boldsymbol{\Sigma}_{\boldsymbol{\mu}}^*$, respectively. We will not go into the details of these sorts of models here except to say that the stability test for the coefficients under the adaptive model assumption is a test of the null hypothesis: $\boldsymbol{\Sigma}_{\boldsymbol{\nu}}^* = \boldsymbol{0}$. An exact and computationally well-defined test is available in LaMotte and McWhorter (1976), and an application to the problem of testing of the stability of the demand for money in Canada has been made by Rausser and Laumas (1976). The interested reader is referred to these sources for details.

10.9 BAYESIAN INFERENCE

In the classical approach to inference, we are concerned with drawing conclusions about unobservables β from given facts that include data on observable Y and a conditional probability distribution $f(Y \mid \beta)$, giving the probability of various values of Y for given values of β. In the Bayesian approach, on the contrary, a distinctive feature is to include what is called the "prior" probability function $f(\beta)$ among the facts, and to pose as though $f(\beta)$ is a no lesser "fact" than $f(Y \mid \beta)$. To the classicist, $f(Y \mid \beta)$ is objectively verifiable, whereas $f(\beta)$, being highly subjective, may even be fictitious. Also, Bayesians criticize the procedures of classical inference in that these rely on sampling distributions obtained from the tendency of estimators in repeated sets of samples. But these samples are not actually drawn, except for one and this one is made the sole basis of drawing whatever inference is possible under the circumstances. There is no penalty built into the choice of inference procedures as a result of losses incurred from wrong conclusions drawn.

The Bayesian procedure is perhaps free of these problems, but, on the other hand, has its own problems particularly in practical applications of extensive and theoretically complex, if not intractable, models. The basic theory is of course very simple as can be appreciated from the following illustration.

Let $\mathrm{P}(\mathbf{Y}, \boldsymbol{\beta})$ be the joint pdf for a random observation vector $\mathbf{Y}$ and a random parameter vector $\boldsymbol{\beta}$. Then, from the elementary rules of probability we have

$$\mathrm{P}(\mathbf{Y}, \boldsymbol{\beta}) = \mathrm{P}(\mathbf{Y} \mid \boldsymbol{\beta})\, \mathrm{P}(\boldsymbol{\beta}) \tag{10.152}$$

$$= \mathrm{P}(\boldsymbol{\beta} \mid \mathbf{Y})\, \mathrm{P}(\mathbf{Y}) \tag{10.153}$$

and therefore

$$\mathrm{P}(\boldsymbol{\beta} \mid \mathbf{Y}) = \frac{\mathrm{P}(\boldsymbol{\beta})\, \mathrm{P}(\mathbf{Y} \mid \boldsymbol{\beta})}{\mathrm{P}(\mathbf{Y})} \tag{10.154}$$

with $P(\mathbf{Y}) \neq 0$. In other words,

$$P(\boldsymbol{\beta} \mid \mathbf{Y}) \propto P(\boldsymbol{\beta})\, P(\mathbf{Y} \mid \boldsymbol{\beta}) = \text{prior pdf} \times \text{likelihood function} \tag{10.155}$$

where $\propto$ is the sign of proportionality, $P(\boldsymbol{\beta} \mid \mathbf{Y})$ is the posterior pdf for the parameter vector $\boldsymbol{\beta}$ given the sample observations $\mathbf{Y}$, and $P(\mathbf{Y} \mid \boldsymbol{\beta})$ is the likelihood function.

As an example, assume that we have n observations $\mathbf{Y}' = (Y_1, Y_2, \ldots, Y_n)$ drawn at random from a normal population with (unknown) mean μ and known variance $\sigma^2 = \sigma_0^2$. We want to find out the posterior pdf for μ. Applying (10.155) to the current problem, we have

$$P(\mu \mid \mathbf{Y}, \sigma_0^2) \propto p(\mu)\, P(\mathbf{Y} \mid \mu, \sigma_0^2) \tag{10.156}$$

$P(\mu \mid \mathbf{Y}, \sigma_0^2)$ is the posterior pdf for the assumed known value σ_0^2, $P(\mu)$ is the prior pdf, and $P(\mathbf{Y} \mid \mu, \sigma_0^2)$ is the likelihood function. The likelihood function is, using $\hat{\mu} = \Sigma \dfrac{Y_i}{n}$ for the same mean, and $s^2 = \dfrac{1}{n-1} \Sigma (Y_i - \hat{\mu})^2$ for the sample variance,

$$\begin{aligned} P(\mathbf{Y} \mid \mu, \sigma_0^2) &= \prod_{i=1}^{n} P(Y_i \mid \mu, \sigma_0^2) \\ &= (2\pi\sigma_0^2)^{-n/2} \exp\left[-1/2\sigma^2 \sum_1^n (Y_i - \mu)^2 \right] \qquad (10.157) \\ &\propto \exp\{-(1/2\sigma^2)[(n-1)s^2 + n(\mu - \hat{\mu})^2]\} \qquad (10.158) \end{aligned}$$

The prior pdf may be established using prior theoretical or empirical results, or using beliefs, judgment, or guesses. Let us suppose that $p(\mu)$ is consistent with the likelihood given in (10.158). Then $p(\mu)$ is called a conjugate prior, which in this case is a normal distribution and represented as

$$P(\mu) = (2\pi\sigma_1^2)^{-1/2} \exp\left[-\frac{1}{2\sigma_1^2} (\mu - \mu_1)^2 \right] \tag{10.159}$$

where μ_1 and σ_1^2 are the prior mean and prior variance, respectively, their values being assigned by the investigator based on his prior knowledge. Using (10.158) and (10.159) in (10.154), we get the posterior pdf for μ as

$$\begin{aligned} P(\mu \mid \mathbf{Y}, \sigma_0^2) &\propto p(\mu)\, P(\mathbf{Y} \mid \mu, \sigma_0^2) \\ &\propto \exp\left\{ -\frac{1}{2}\left[\frac{(\mu - \mu_1)^2}{\sigma_1^2} + \frac{n}{\sigma_0^2}(\mu - \hat{\mu})^2 \right] \right\} \qquad (10.160) \\ &\propto \exp\left[-\frac{1}{2} \frac{1}{[(\sigma_0^2/n)^{-1} + (\sigma_1^2)^{-1}]^{-1}} \left(\mu - \frac{\hat{\mu}\sigma_1^2 + \mu_1\sigma_0^2/n}{\sigma_1^2 + \sigma_0^2/n} \right)^2 \right] \end{aligned}$$

The above indicates[25] that the posterior pdf for μ is normal with the following mean and variance

$$\begin{aligned} E(\mu) &= \frac{\hat{\mu}(\sigma_0^2/n)^{-1} + \mu_1(\sigma_1^2)^{-1}}{(\sigma_0^2/n)^{-1} + (\sigma_1^2)^{-1}} \\ V(\mu) &= \frac{1}{(\sigma_0^2/n)^{-1} + (\sigma_1^2)^{-1}} \end{aligned} \tag{10.161}$$

The posterior mean $E(\mu)$ is a weighted average of the sample mean $\hat{\mu}$ and the prior mean μ_1, the weights being the reciprocals of σ_0^2/n and σ_1^2, that is their respective precision factors. More precise prior information makes the prior mean a stronger determinant of the posterior mean; conversely, more precise sample information makes the sample mean a stronger determinant.

10.10 BAYESIAN APPROACH TO A SIMPLE LINEAR REGRESSION MODEL

Let us revise the simple linear regression model of Chapter 2 given by:

$$Y = \beta_0 + \beta_1 X + \epsilon \tag{10.162}$$

involving all its assumptions, especially the one that has the errors ϵ_i, $i = 1, 2, \ldots, n$ distributed normally and independently, each with zero mean and a common variance σ^2. But assume, unlike Chapter 2, that X_i, $i = 1, 2, \ldots, n$ are random variables distributed independently of ϵ_i and its pdf does not involve the parameters β_0, β_1, and σ^2.

The joint pdf for $\mathbf{Y}' = (Y_1 \ldots Y_n)$ and $\mathbf{X}' = (X_1 X_2 \ldots X_n)$ is

$$P(\mathbf{Y}, \mathbf{X} \mid \beta_0, \beta_1, \sigma^2, \phi) = P(\mathbf{Y} \mid \mathbf{X}, \beta_0, \beta_1, \sigma^2)h(\phi) \tag{10.163}$$

where ϕ represents the parameters of the marginal pdf $h(\phi)$ of $\mathbf{X}$. The assumption that $\mathbf{X}$ is independent of β_0, β_1, and σ^2 makes possible the split in the probability densities shown on the right-hand side of (10.163).

For given X, β_0, β_1, and σ^2, Y is normally distributed with its conditional mean given by $\beta_0 + \beta_1 X$ from (10.161) and conditional variance σ^2, and $Y_1, Y_2, \ldots, Y_n$ are independent. Therefore

$$P(\mathbf{Y} \mid \mathbf{X}, \beta_0, \beta_1, \sigma^2) \propto (1/\sigma^n) \exp\left[-\frac{1}{2\sigma^2}\sum (Y_i - \beta_0 - \beta_1 X_i)^2\right] \tag{10.164}$$

[25] This can be appreciated by comparing the above form with the simple form of the normal pdf given by

$$P(Y \mid E(Y), V(Y)) \propto \exp\left\{-\frac{1}{2V(Y)}[Y - E(Y)]^2\right\}$$

the summation being over $i = 1$ to $i = n$. Notice that the above, which is called the likelihood function, would have obtained even if the Xs were fixed in repeated samples, as assumed in Chapter 2.

The posterior distribution of the parameters for a diffuse prior. Let us suppose that the prior pdf for β_0, β_1, and σ (or ln σ, the implication being the same) is

$$P(\beta_0, \beta_1, \sigma) \propto \frac{1}{\sigma}, \qquad -\infty < \beta_0, \qquad \beta_1 < \infty \; 0 < \sigma < \infty \tag{10.165}$$

This follows from the fact that β_0, β_1, and ln σ are assumed uniformly and independently distributed. The posterior pdf is, using (10.164) and (10.165),

$$P(\beta_0, \beta_1, \sigma \mid \mathbf{Y}, \mathbf{X}) \propto \frac{1}{\sigma^{n+1}} \exp[-(1/2\sigma^2)\, \Sigma(Y_i - \beta_0 - \beta_1 X_i)^2] \tag{10.166}$$

This can be simplified[26] to

$$P(\beta_0, \beta_1, \sigma \mid \mathbf{Y}, \mathbf{X}) \propto \frac{1}{\sigma^{n+1}} \exp[-(1/2\sigma^2)[(n-2)s^2 + n(\beta_0 - \hat{\beta}_0)^2 \tag{10.167}$$
$$+ (\beta_1 - \hat{\beta}_1)^2\, \Sigma X_i^2 + 2(\beta_0 - \hat{\beta}_0)(\beta_1 - \hat{\beta}_1)\, \Sigma X_i]]$$

where

$$\begin{aligned} \hat{\beta}_0 &= \overline{Y} - \hat{\beta}_1 \overline{X} \\ \hat{\beta}_1 &= \Sigma(X_i - \overline{X})(Y_i - \overline{Y})/\Sigma(X_i - \overline{X})^2 \\ s^2 &= (n-2)^{-1}\, \Sigma(Y_i - \hat{\beta}_0 - \hat{\beta}_1 X_i)^2 \\ \overline{Y} &= n^{-1}\, \Sigma Y_i \\ \overline{X} &= n^{-1}\, \Sigma X_i \end{aligned} \tag{10.168}$$

Notice that, given σ, the conditional posterior distribution of β_0 and β_1 works out to

$$P(\beta_0, \beta_1 \mid \mathbf{Y}, \mathbf{X}, \sigma) = P(\beta_0, \beta_1, \sigma \mid \mathbf{Y}, \mathbf{X})/P(\sigma \mid \mathbf{Y}, \mathbf{X})$$
$$\propto \frac{1}{\sigma^2} \exp\{-1/2\sigma^2[n(\beta_0 - \hat{\beta}_0)^2 + (\beta_1 - \hat{\beta}_1)^2 \Sigma X_i^2 \tag{10.169}$$
$$+ 2(\beta_0 - \hat{\beta}_0)(\beta_1 - \hat{\beta}_1)\, \Sigma X_i]\}$$

[26] Observe that, since $\hat{Y}_i = \hat{\beta}_0 + \hat{\beta}_1 X_i$,

$$\Sigma(Y_i - \beta_0 - \beta_1 X_i)^2 = \Sigma[Y_i - \hat{Y}_i - (\beta_0 - \hat{\beta}_0) - (\beta_1 - \hat{\beta}_1)X_i]^2$$
$$= \Sigma(Y_i - \hat{Y}_i)^2 + n(\beta_0 - \hat{\beta})^2 + (\beta_1 - \hat{\beta}_1)^2 \Sigma X_i^2 + 2(\beta_0 - \hat{\beta}_0)(\beta_1 - \hat{\beta}_1)\, \Sigma X_i$$

the cross-product terms vanishing since $\Sigma Y_i = \Sigma \hat{Y}_i$ and X and $(Y - \hat{Y})$ are uncorrelated.

This is a bivariate normal distribution with means $\hat{\beta}_0$ and $\hat{\beta}_1$ and variance–covariance[27] matrix

$$\sigma^2 \begin{bmatrix} n & \Sigma X_i \\ \Sigma X_i & \Sigma X_i^2 \end{bmatrix}^{-1} \tag{10.170}$$

Most often σ^2 is unknown. Therefore, it is worthwhile to eliminate this factor. This leads to the concept of the marginal pdf of $\hat{\beta}_0$ and $\hat{\beta}_1$, which[28] is obtained by integrating (10.169) out in respect of σ:

$$\begin{aligned} P(\beta_0, \beta_1 \mid \mathbf{Y}, \mathbf{X}) &= \int_0^\infty P(\beta_0, \beta_1 \mid \mathbf{Y}, \mathbf{X}, \sigma)\, d\sigma \\ &\propto [(\mathrm{n} - 2)s^2 + n(\beta_0 - \hat{\beta}_0)^2 + (\beta_1 - \hat{\beta}_1)^2 \Sigma X_i^2 \\ &\quad + 2(\beta_0 - \hat{\beta}_0)(\beta_1 - \hat{\beta}_1)\Sigma X_i]^{-n/2} \end{aligned} \tag{10.171}$$

This is said to follow the bivariate Student t, from the properties of which the following two univariate results can be obtained:[29]

$$P(\beta_0 \mid \mathbf{Y}, \mathbf{X}) \propto \left[(n-2) + \frac{\Sigma(X_i - \overline{X})^2}{s^2 \Sigma X_i^2/n}(\beta_0 - \hat{\beta}_0)^2\right]^{-\{(n-1)/2\}} \qquad -\infty < \beta_0 < \infty \tag{10.172}$$

$$P(\beta_1 \mid \mathbf{Y}, \mathbf{X}) \propto \left[(n-2) + \frac{\Sigma(X_i - \overline{X})^2}{s^2}(\beta_1 - \hat{\beta}_1)^2\right]^{-\{(n-1)/2\}} \qquad -\infty < \beta_0 < \infty \tag{10.173}$$

More interestingly, the distribution of the following statistics

$$\left[\frac{\Sigma(X_i - \overline{X})^2}{s^2 \Sigma X_i^2/n}\right]^{1/2} (\beta_0 - \hat{\beta}_0) = t \tag{10.174}$$

as well as

$$\frac{(\beta_1 - \hat{\beta}_1)}{\mathrm{s}/[\Sigma(\mathrm{X_i} - \overline{\mathrm{X}})^2]^{1/2}} = t \tag{10.175}$$

is Student t each with $n - 2$ df. After this, standard inference procedures based on the t distribution can be drawn up in a straightforward fashion.

A prototype of (10.171) in the case of the model of the linear multiple regression can be set up as follows:

$$P(\boldsymbol{\beta} \mid \mathbf{Y}, X) \propto [(n - m - 1)s^2 + (\boldsymbol{\beta} - \hat{\boldsymbol{\beta}})\, X'X(\boldsymbol{\beta} - \hat{\boldsymbol{\beta}})]^{-n/2} \tag{10.176}$$

[27] This uses the same principle as the variance–covariance of estimated least squares coefficient estimators, which generally is written as $\sigma^2\,(X'X)^{-1}$

[28] See Appendix A.4 for derivation of (10.171).

[29] For these and the rest of the results using transformations, see Zellner (1971), p. 61.

where $\mathbf{Y}$ is an $n \times 1$ vector of observations on the dependent variable, X an $n \times (m + 1)$ matrix, with rank $(m + 1)$, of observations on $(m + 1)$ independent variables, $\boldsymbol{\beta}$ an $(m + 1) \times 1$ vector of regression coefficients, and $\hat{\boldsymbol{\beta}}$ and s^2 are given by:

$$\hat{\boldsymbol{\beta}} = (X'X)^{-1} X'\mathbf{Y} \tag{10.177}$$
$$s^2 = \frac{(\mathbf{Y} - X\hat{\boldsymbol{\beta}})'(\mathbf{Y} - X\hat{\boldsymbol{\beta}})}{(n - m - 1)}$$

Relation (10.176) gives the pdf of a multivariate Student t.

Before one proceeds further, one should master the properties of this and other more complicated distributions, for instance the Wishart distribution. The knowledge will be necessary if the Bayesian approach is to be used in the multiple regression model containing special properties of the error terms, for example heteroscedastic and correlated residuals, and time series aspects of the model including distributed lags. It will also be necessary if the model includes multivariate or simultaneous equation specifications. See Zellner (1971) for all of these topics, and his and others' more recent[30] contributions to other topics including the important class of estimators known as *M*inimum *E*xpected *Lo*ss or, in short, MELO estimators. On the question of specification searches by following which an investigator is driven to adopt one specification of the model rather than another, or led to the difficult problem of drawing *appropriate* inferences when confronted with ambiguous data-generating mechanisms, see Leamer (1978),[31] among others.

PROBLEMS

10-1. (a) Recent econometric literature relies in some way or other on likelihood ratio, Lagrange multiplier and Wald tests of hypotheses. What are these techniques? What are their similarities and dissimilarities?

[30] See Zellner (1978), Zellner and Park (1979) and Park (1982) on MELO estimators, Zellner (1985) on extended MELO estimators, Mehta and Swamy (1978) on existence of moments of Bayes' estimators in simultaneous equation models, Swamy and Rappoport (1975 and 1978) on efficiencies of Bayes estimators in dynamic models with serially correlated errors, Ohtani (1982) on Bayesian estimation of the switching regression model with autocorrelated errors, Tsurumi and Shiba (1982) on Bayesian treatment of a random coefficient model in a simple Keynesian context, Zellner and Rossi (1984) on Bayesian estimation of dichotomous quintal response models, and Zellner and Hong (1985), Zellner (1986), García-Ferrar et al (1977), Zellner and others (1987), and Zellner (1988) on Bayesian estimation and forecasting, to name only some studies.

[31] Also, see Pesaran (1974) on the general problem of model selection. Zellner (1988) discusses five propositions regarding econometrics and challenges that these propositions face. He also puts Bayesian estimation, prediction, control, and decision procedures in perspective and brings in a number of canonical econometric problems to make a case for the Bayesian approach in econometrics and other scientific areas.

(b) What are Bayesian tests of hypotheses? Compare them with those of (a) above.

In assuming both (a) and (b), indicate the effect of such factors as lack of prior information, small samples, and model misspecification on the various techniques.

(*Hint:* You may consult the book by Leamer (1978) for a good coverage on Bayesian methodology.)

10-2. Let the model be:

$$\mathbf{Y} = X\boldsymbol{\beta} + \mathbf{u} \qquad \mathbf{u} \sim \mathrm{N}(\mathbf{0}, \sigma_u^2 I)$$

Prove that the LR, LM, and W tests for $H_0 : \mathbf{r} = R\boldsymbol{\beta}$ are monotonic functions of the F test. Are these tests equivalent?

10-3. Suppose that the real wage paid to the lth worker at time i, Y_{il}, is a stochastic linear function of that worker's experience at time i, X_{il}, plus two constants: θ_l is a constant over time showing how the level of the wage equation depends on the individual worker's basic skills, ϕ_i is a constant over all workers indicating how the level of the equation depends on the general state of the economy at time i. Suppose you have available n observations on r workers. Discuss how you would obtain consistent, asymptotically efficient estimates of the slope of the equation and its two constants.

(*Hint:* See the last two paragraphs of Section 10.7.1 for clues.)

10-4. From economic theory, it is possible to formulate a suitable model for crosssection data as:

$$C_l = \alpha + \beta Y_l + \gamma X_l + \epsilon_l$$

where l refers to individual families and $\mathrm{E}(\epsilon) = 0$. Also we can get a suitable model for time series data formulated as:

$$C_i = \delta + \beta Y_i + \mu Z_i + \nu_i$$

where i refers to years and $\mathrm{E}(\nu_i) = 0$.

Suppose you have both crosssection and aggregate time series data available. Describe how you would estimate β.

10-5. An econometrically trained finance executive claims that the price of a unit of stock of the lth company in year i ($P_{il} : l = 1, 2, \ldots, r;\ i = 1, 2, \ldots, n$) depends on the corresponding dividend paid (d_{il}), retained earnings (r_{il}), and net assets (K_{il}) according to: (I) $P_{il} = \alpha_i(1 + \gamma_i K_{il})d_{il} + \beta_i r_{il} + \epsilon_{il}$ where α_i, β_i, and γ_i are constants for given i and where (II) $\epsilon_{il} \sim \mathrm{NID}(0, \sigma_{il}^2)$; $\sigma_{il}^2 \propto d_{il}\sigma^2$; $d_{il}, r_{il}, K_{il} > 0$. To be able to use (I) and (II) for forecasting purposes, the executive believes that the hypothesis H_0: $\alpha_i/\beta_i = \theta$, $i = 1, 2, \ldots, n$, is true. Suppose you do not believe in his hypothesis and you have a total of nr observations on r companies for n years. Analyze how you would obtain (a) efficient estimates of α_i, β_i, and γ_i; $i = 1, 2, \ldots, n$, where (I) and (II) hold good but not H_0; (b) an estimate of θ when H_0 is valid; and lastly, (c) do you think assumption (II) is reasonable? Why or why not?

10-6. (a) Define and illustrate sample selectivity bias.

(b) Show that the bias arising from "selected" samples resembles that from omitted variables.

(c) Explain the regression functions for selected samples to which the Heckman estimator technique is applied. Briefly indicate how these functions are estimated by this technique.

10-7. **(a)** What is an error components model and what is its purpose?
(b) Discuss the Sadan and Tropp (1973) analysis of the consumption function of Israel's "kibbutz" based on crosssection and time series data.

10-8. **(a)** What general models do the models on switching regimes belong to?
(b) Suppose you would like to analyze the wage and price decisions of a trade-sensitive sector in periods of high external values of a country's currency. Let the time period t include n sample observations and in terms of an unknown time point t_0 let the hypothesis before and after that time point be:

$$\text{Regime 1: } Y_t = \beta_{01} + \beta_1 X_t + \epsilon_{1t} \qquad \text{for } t \leqq t_0 \text{ (low exchange rates)}$$

$$\text{Regime 2: } Y_t = \beta_{02} + \beta_2 X_t + \epsilon_{2t} \qquad \text{for } t \geqq t_0 \text{ (high exchange rates)}$$

Assume that

$$\epsilon_1 \sim \text{NID}(0, \sigma_1^2) \qquad \epsilon_2 \sim \text{NID}(0, \sigma_2^2)$$

(i) Write the log-likelihood function and simplify it by imputing in it the maximum likelihood estimates of σ_1^2 and σ_2^2.
(ii) Discuss Riddell's (1980) method of forward and backward recursive residuals to maximize the log-likelihood of (i) for deriving estimates of β_{0i} and β_i, $i = 1, 2$.
(iii) How do you test that there is no switch centering around the time point $t = t_0$?

10-9. Briefly discuss Gordon and Hynes (1970) as an example of the application of random coefficient models. What economic problem was investigated by this study and what general empirical conclusions were derived?

10-10. Consider models containing unobservable variables which are determined by proxy variables. Consider in particular the following model:

$$\text{(I)} \quad Y_i = \beta_0 + \beta_1 X_{i1} + \beta_2 X_{i2} + \epsilon_i$$

with classical assumptions applicable regarding the X and the ϵ. Assume that X_{i2} is not observable, but there is a proxy variable Z that will determine it according to

$$\text{(II)} \quad Z_i = \gamma_0 + \gamma_1 X_{i2} + \nu_i$$

ν_i is the classical disturbance assumed independent of ϵ_i. There are two ways of estimating β_1. One consists of replacing X_{i2} of (I) by its expression in terms of Z_i from (II) and then applying OLS to the resulting equation, and the other consists of eliminating X_{i2} from (I) and then estimating β_1 by OLS from the resulting equation. How would the asymptotic bias compare in the two situations? What empirical evidence exists in the literature regarding the desirability of one type of estimator of β_1 over the other on the basis of the criterion of mean squared error?

10-11. Let the model be:

$$y_i = \beta Z_i + \epsilon_i \qquad \epsilon_i \sim \text{N}(0, \sigma_\epsilon^2)$$

where

$$Z_i = \alpha_1 X_{i1}$$

$$Z_i^* = Z_i + \nu_i \qquad \nu_i \sim \mathrm{N}(0, \sigma_\nu^2)$$

That is, we have a "single cause" model to determine the unobservable variable Z. Suppose ϵ and ν are mutually independent and are independent of X.

(a) Discuss Zellner's (1970) and Goldberger's (1972) methods of obtaining consistent estimators of β.

(b) Now suppose that Z_i is given by $Z_i = \alpha_1 X_{i1} + \alpha_2 X_{i2}$, all other specifications remaining the same as before. How do you show that the estimators of β obtained in (a) are again consistent?

11

Simultaneous Equation Systems

11.1 INTRODUCTION: THE SYSTEM'S SPECIAL FEATURES ILLUSTRATED FROM APPLIED STUDIES

We have so far been involved, almost exclusively, with the estimation of single equations in economic variables. However, economic theory hardly arises in single equations. Often it arises in a system of equations. Thus an estimation technique that neglects to build the simultaneous equation aspect into the procedure may very easily be imperfect. As an example, when an equation is embedded in a system, some variables will characteristically be stochastic and, at the same time, be correlated with the disturbance term as a result of the simultaneity of the structural equations. In such cases, as is well known from the previous chapters, the OLS estimates will be inconsistent. The moral of this is simple. We should devise methods which can produce consistent estimates at the very least.

Before we go any further, some examples of a simultaneous equation system are in order. We will give two examples, one on a simple Keynesian model and the other on the Klein (1950) inter-war model.

The simple Keynesian model is a structural equation model of a national economy. It consists of two equations and an identity:

$$C_t = \beta_0 + \beta_1 Y_t + \epsilon_t \quad : \text{consumption function}$$

$$I_t = I_0 \quad : \text{investment function}$$

$$Y_t = C_t + I_t \quad : \text{national income accounting identity}$$

where C = aggregate consumption expenditure
Y = national income
I = investment expenditure, assumed fixed at the level I_0
ϵ = a random disturbance term

For the sake of simplicity, the model does not allow for either the government sector or the external account. As it stands it seeks to determine C and Y given the (fixed) values of I. This gives rise to a possible distinction among the variables. Some variables are endogenous variables because they are being currently determined within the model. C and Y are such variables in this model. Other variables such as I are exogenous; they are not so determined. They are autonomous.

By the method of repeated substitution and elimination of variables, we can arrive at the following reduced form equation set from the above structural equation set:

$$C_t = \frac{\beta_0}{1 - \beta_1} + \frac{\beta_1}{1 - \beta_1} I_0 + e_t$$

$$Y_t = \frac{\beta_0}{1 - \beta_1} + \frac{1}{1 - \beta_1} I_0 + e_t$$

where $e_t = \epsilon_t/(1 - \beta_1)$. e_t is called the reduced form disturbance.

Thus it is obvious that e_t influences Y_t, and since e_t and ϵ_t are related to each other, ϵ_t and Y_t are correlated. This is the source of the simultaneous equation bias often referred to in the literature. In the above structural model, the bias pertains to the consumption function which contains the explanatory variable Y_t and the disturbance ϵ_t. These two have become correlated via the equation (identity) $Y_t = C_t + I_t$, which is another part of the simultaneous equation model.

We can show that

$$\text{plim}(1/n \sum Y_t e_t) = \text{plim } 1/n \sum e_t^2 = \sigma_\epsilon^2/(1 - \beta_1)^2$$

and since $e_t = \epsilon_t/(1 - \beta_1)$, we have

$$\text{plim } 1/n \sum Y_t \epsilon_t = \sigma_\epsilon^2/(1 - \beta_1) \neq 0$$

This result confirms that OLS applied to the estimation of the consumption function will produce inconsistent estimates.

The other model is Klein's inter-war model built along the Keynesian line. It has six endogenous or currently determined variables: output Y, consumption C, investment I, private wages W^*, profit P, and capital stock K; and four exogenous variables, variables that are predetermined or fixed: government nonwage expenditure G, public wages W^{**}, business taxes T, and time trend A.[1]

[1] All variables are measured in billions of dollars in constant 1934 dollars per year, except A which is annual deviation (positive or negative) from 1931.

The estimated model* has the following equations:

$$
\begin{aligned}
C &= 16.78 + 0.80(W^* + W^{**}) + 0.020P + 0.23P_{-1} \\
I &= 17.79 + 0.23P + 0.55P_{-1} - 0.15K_{-1} \\
W^* &= 1.60 + 0.420(Y + T - W^{**}) \\
&\quad + 0.16(Y + T - W^{**})_{-1} + 0.13A \qquad (11.1) \\
Y &= C + I + G \\
P &= Y - W^* - T \\
K &= K_{-1} + I
\end{aligned}
$$

Consumption, as per the equation for C in (11.1), depends on the various components of income differently. This is reflected in a value of 0.80 (the coefficient for $W^* + W^{**}$) for the MPC (that is, the marginal propensity to consume) from out of wage income as compared to the considerably smaller values of 0.020 and 0.23 (the coefficients for P and P_{-1}) from out of current and last periods profit incomes, respectively. Notice the large difference in the MPC between the last period's and current period's profit income, and also notice the absence of lagged wage variables. Investment, as per the equation for I in (11.1), depends on the current and last period's income of the profit earners, in complete exclusion of the income of the wage earners. Capital depreciation in this equation accounts for 15% of replacement investment expenditure (see the coefficient for K_{-1}). The private sector wage bill, as per the equation for W^* in (11.1), is a function of current and lagged income and the time trend. Income, however, includes business taxes and excludes wages paid to public sector employees. The time trend is included in view of technological progress, productivity improvement, increased capacity utilization and the fact that the labor unions have, by and large, been progressively successful in having their demands for higher wages met.

The last three equations are identities. The first of these is the national income accounting identity with income equal to the sum total of consumption, investment and government expenditure. The second defines the profit of the private sector as the difference between the value of the national economy's output and its cost, the latter being the total of private sector wages and taxes. The last defines net investment as the year to year change in capital stock. On the whole, the model is indeed an extended version of the Keynesian income determination model of the simplest kind that we have seen before.

We have seen that the OLS method generates inconsistent estimates of parameters. Another example of this can now be cited. Taking ϵ_1, ϵ_2, and ϵ_3 to be the disturbances of the equations for C, I, and W^*, respectively, and a_1 the coef-

* Reprinted with permission L. Klein, *Economic Fluctuations in the United States*, Monograph No. 11 (1950) p. 68.

ficient of $W^* + W^{**}$ in the consumption function, and C_1 the coefficient of $Y + T - W^{**}$ in the private wage function, it can be shown that

$$\text{cov}(\epsilon_1, P) = \frac{(1 - C_1)V(\epsilon_1) + (1 - C_1)\,\text{cov}(\epsilon_1, \epsilon_2) - (1 - a_1)\,\text{cov}(\epsilon_1, \epsilon_3)}{D} \tag{11.2}$$

where D stands for the determinant of coefficients. Even if $\text{cov}(\epsilon_1, \epsilon_2)$ and $\text{cov}(\epsilon_1, \epsilon_3)$ would not be nonzero, $V(\epsilon_1)$ can hardly be expected to be zero. Therefore $\text{cov}(\epsilon_1, P)$ would not be identically equal to zero.

This shows that one of the regressors of the consumption function is correlated with its disturbance term; similarly others in the same and other functions. The result is obvious: OLS estimates will be inconsistent.

One of the most prominent aspects of the simultaneous equation models is their structure. This involves both endogenous and exogenous variables working, through a network of equations, to produce the interconnected structure of an economic theory. This is evident in the equations of the Klein inter-war model as well. However, for the sake of determining policy implications it is often useful to sort out the endogenous variables from the exogenous or predetermined variables.

When starting from the structural equations each and every endogenous variable is, after transformation, expressed as a function exclusively of the exogenous or predetermined variables, a set of reduced form equations is said to have been derived. We have seen the reduced form equations arising from the simple Keynesian model. The reduced form equations of the Klein interwar model, as estimated by Theil and Boot (1962), are presented below:

$$\mathbf{y} = \mathbf{X}_1\hat{\boldsymbol{\pi}}_I + \mathbf{X}_2\hat{\boldsymbol{\pi}}_2 \tag{11.3}$$

where

$$\mathbf{y} = (P\ Y\ K\ C\ W^*\ I) \tag{11.4}$$

$$\mathbf{X}_1 = y_{-1} = (P\ Y\ K\ C\ W^*\ I)_{-1} \tag{11.5}$$

$$\mathbf{X}_2 = (W^{**}\ T\ G\ A\ W^{**}_{-1}\ T_{-1}) \tag{11.6}$$

$$\hat{\boldsymbol{\pi}}_I = \begin{bmatrix} -0.863 & 1.489 & 0.746 & 0.743 & 0.626 & 0.746 \\ -0.063 & 0.174 & -0.015 & 0.189 & 0.237 & -0.015 \\ -0.164 & -0.283 & 0.816 & -0.098 & -0.119 & -0.184 \\ 0 & 0 & 0 & 0 & 0 & 0 \\ 0 & 0 & 0 & 0 & 0 & 0 \\ 0 & 0 & 0 & 0 & 0 & 0 \end{bmatrix} \tag{11.7*}$$

* Reprinted with permission H. Theil and J. C. Boot, "The Final Form of Econometric Equation Systems," *Review of the International Statistical Institute*, 30 (1962) Table 1, p. 138.

$$\hat{\pi}_2 = \begin{bmatrix} -0.224 & 0.614 & -0.052 & 0.666 & -0.162 & -0.052 \\ -1.281 & -1.484 & -0.296 & -0.188 & -0.204 & -0.296 \\ 1.119 & 1.930 & 0.259 & 0.671 & 0.811 & 0.259 \\ -0.052 & 0.143 & -0.012 & 0.155 & 0.195 & -0.012 \\ 0.063 & -0.174 & 0.015 & -0.189 & -0.237 & 0.015 \\ -0.063 & 0.174 & -0.015 & 0.189 & 0.237 & -0.015 \end{bmatrix} \tag{11.8}$$

We have used a hat '^' over the π_1 and π_2 symbols to indicate that these are estimated. Consider $\hat{\pi}_1$ first. The last three rows of the $\hat{\pi}_1$ matrix have all zero elements. This is because the variables C, W^*, and I with lags are excluded from the model, which is equivalent to putting their coefficients equal to zero. This is the case of zero restriction on coefficients of nonoccurring variables in equations of this kind of models.

Consider now $\hat{\pi}_2$. The coefficients shown in the $\hat{\pi}_2$ matrix have great economic significance. These can be interpreted to be multipliers associated with policy type variables. For instance, a billion dollar hike in business taxes will reduce national income by \$1.484 billion, profit income by \$1.281 billion, consumption by \$0.188 billion, and investment by \$0.296 billion. These are the figures in row 2 of the $\hat{\pi}_2$ matrix. The balanced budget multiplier, where there are offsetting changes in government expenditures and taxes, is $1.930 - 1.484 = 0.446$. As Theil and Boot have calculated, the long run multipliers for T and G are -1.569 and 2.323, respectively, from which the long run balanced budget multiplier works out to $2.323 - 1.569 = 0.754$. Thus the previous balanced budget multiplier of 0.446, which is a portion of 0.754, must have arisen in only the first year, right on impact, and hence its name impact multiplier.[2,3]

The working of these and other aspects of models of this kind cannot be entirely grasped in terms of a numerical model alone. For this a general model is required. In what follows we present some preliminary specifications of such models, along with some of the ways of identifying them. Then, we discuss their estimation techniques. Last, we review some applied studies based on them.

[2] It follows analogously that one can obtain a set of impact multipliers showing the effects of changes in the predetermined variables on the system during the period when these changes take place. Moreover, it is possible to transform the dynamic model into an equilibrium system by discarding the trend terms and time subscripts, and by bringing other changes to bear on the system; that is, in equilibrium, inventories do not change. The multipliers obtained after these changes are called equilibrium multipliers. They are useful for appraising ultimate effects of changes in the exogenous variables.

[3] This kind of analysis illustrated from the model is called structural analysis. The model has been used for forecasting and policy evaluation as well. However, its success as a predictor of postwar results has been very limited at best. It seems that the change in the structure of the U.S. economy was the reason why predictions did not come off well. On the whole the model uses highly aggregated variables and does not seek to explain other important variables such as production, economic growth, and financial factors.

11.2 THE GENERAL SIMULTANEOUS EQUATION SYSTEM: ITS GENERAL FEATURES AND IDENTIFICATION

As indicated before, an economic theory gives rise to a set of simultaneous equations expressing the behavior of individuals, sectors or markets. The structural form of such equations is presented below:

$$\underset{1\times m}{\mathbf{y}'(\mathbf{i})}\ \underset{m\times m}{\boldsymbol{\Gamma}} + \underset{1\times k}{\mathbf{x}'(\mathbf{i})}\ \underset{k\times m}{\boldsymbol{B}} + \underset{1\times m}{\boldsymbol{\epsilon}'(\mathbf{i})} = \mathbf{0} \qquad i = 1, 2, \ldots, n \tag{11.9}$$

$\mathbf{y}(\mathbf{i})$ is the column vector of m endogenous variables, each at its ith observation, $\mathbf{x}(\mathbf{i})$ the column vector of k predetermined (including exogenous or lagged endogenous) variables, each at its ith observation, and $\boldsymbol{\epsilon}(\mathbf{i})$ a column vector of m stochastic error terms, each at its ith observation.[4] i runs from 1 to n where n is the sample size. The coefficient matrices associated with the endogenous and exogenous variables are $\boldsymbol{\Gamma}$ and $\boldsymbol{B}$, respectively, the former of size of $m \times m$, necessarily square and nonsingular, and the latter of size $k \times m$, which can be rectangular. There are m equations jointly determining the m endogenous variables, given that there are k predetermined variables, m stochastic error terms, and $m^2 + mk$ coefficients of the model.

Expanding (11.9) over all observations, we have the entire system defined compactly by:

$$\boldsymbol{Y\Gamma} + \boldsymbol{XB} + \boldsymbol{\varepsilon} = \boldsymbol{0} \tag{11.10}$$

where

$$\underset{n\times m}{\mathbf{Y}} = \begin{bmatrix} \mathbf{y}'(1) \\ \vdots \\ \mathbf{y}'(\mathbf{n}) \end{bmatrix} \qquad \underset{n\times k}{\mathbf{X}} = \begin{bmatrix} \mathbf{x}'(1) \\ \vdots \\ \mathbf{x}'(\mathbf{n}) \end{bmatrix} \qquad \underset{n\times m}{\boldsymbol{\varepsilon}} = \begin{bmatrix} \boldsymbol{\epsilon}'(1) \\ \vdots \\ \boldsymbol{\epsilon}'(\mathbf{n}) \end{bmatrix} \tag{11.11}$$

The ith row of (11.10) is (11.9).

The structural form mixes up the endogenous with the predetermined variables. To separate the former from the latter, we perform the reduced form operation. This involves postmultiplying (11.10) by $\boldsymbol{\Gamma}^{-1}$ and rearranging it to get:

$$\begin{aligned} \mathbf{y}'(\mathbf{i}) &= \mathbf{x}'(\mathbf{i})(-\boldsymbol{B\Gamma}^{-1}) + \boldsymbol{\epsilon}'(\mathbf{i})(-\boldsymbol{\Gamma}^{-1}) \\ &= \mathbf{x}'(\mathbf{i})\boldsymbol{\pi} + \mathbf{e}'(\mathbf{i}) \end{aligned} \tag{11.12}$$

in which

$$\boldsymbol{\pi} = -\boldsymbol{B\Gamma}^{-1} = (\pi_{ij}) \tag{11.13}$$

is a $k \times m$ reduced form coefficient matrix (π_{ij}) $i = 1, \ldots, k; j = 1, \ldots, m$, each of its columns corresponding to a given equation, and

$$\mathbf{e}'(\mathbf{i}) = -\boldsymbol{\epsilon}'(\mathbf{i})\boldsymbol{\Gamma}^{-1} \tag{11.14}$$

[4] The sign of a prime over a variable of (11.9) indicates the mark of transposition of a vector or matrix.

is a $1 \times m$ row vector at the ith observation of the reduced form errors. For the entire system, the compact reduced form is:

$$Y = X\pi + e \tag{11.15}$$

where e of size $n \times m$ is a matrix whose rows are $\mathbf{e}'(\mathbf{1}) = [\mathrm{e}_1(1) \ldots \mathrm{e}_m(1)], \ldots, \mathbf{e}'(\boldsymbol{n}) = [\mathrm{e}_1(n) \ldots \mathrm{e}_m(n)]$ and

$$e = -\epsilon \Gamma^{-1} \tag{11.16}$$

The ith row of (11.15) is (11.12).

It is clear that a reduced form coefficient is a function of the structural coefficients of Γ and a row of B. Similarly, a reduced form error is a linear function of all the contemporary structural errors. Symbolically, a reduced form coefficient[5] is given by

$$\pi_{ij} = -\sum_{j'=1}^{m} \beta_{ij'}\gamma^{j'j} \tag{11.17}$$

and a reduced form disturbance given by

$$e_j(i) = -\sum_{j'=1}^{m} \gamma^{j'j}\epsilon_{j'}(i) \tag{11.18}$$

where the βs are the individual coefficients of the B matrix and $\gamma^{j'j}$ are those of the matrix Γ^{-1}.

11.3 STATISTICAL SPECIFICATIONS

Refer back to the structural form (11.9). Its disturbance term row vectors $\boldsymbol{\epsilon}'(\mathbf{i})$ are assumed to have zero means

$$\mathrm{E}(\boldsymbol{\epsilon}'(\mathbf{i})) = \mathbf{0} \qquad i = 1, 2, \ldots, n \tag{11.19}$$

and a symmetric, nonnegative definite variance-covariance matrix defined as

$$\underset{m \times m}{\boldsymbol{\Sigma}} = \mathrm{E}(\boldsymbol{\epsilon}(\mathbf{i})\boldsymbol{\epsilon}'(\mathbf{i})) \qquad i = 1, 2, \ldots, n \tag{11.20}$$

This last condition implies that the covariance matrix of the errors in different equations is the same for all i, or $\mathrm{E}(\epsilon_j(i)\epsilon_{j'}(i)] = \sigma_{jj'}$ for all i.[6] Further, the error

[5] The reduced form coefficients are also called impact multipliers in some economic contexts. See their definitions and computations in an excellent article by Rhomberg (1964). This develops a model of the Canadian economy under fixed and flexible exchange rates. See also Fleisher and Rhodes (1976) for reduced form coefficient estimates in another economic area, namely the economics of labor.

[6] Also implied is the correlation between stochastic error terms of different equations. This element is the main reason why a simultaneous equation model should be estimated as a system rather than as disjointed single equations.

vector is temporally independent, all lagged covariances between errors in the same or different equations vanish, or $E[\epsilon_j(i)\epsilon_{j'}(i')] = 0$ for all j, j', i, i' with $i \neq i'$.[7,8]

We can work out the statistical properties of the new reduced form disturbances from the linear relationship between these and structural disturbances. Thus we derive that the reduced form disturbances have zero means, since

$$E[\mathbf{e(i)}] = E[-\boldsymbol{\Gamma}'^{-1}\boldsymbol{\epsilon}\mathbf{(i)}] = -\boldsymbol{\Gamma}'^{-1}E(\boldsymbol{\epsilon}\mathbf{(i)}) = 0 \qquad i = 1, \ldots, n \tag{11.21}$$

or,

$$E(\boldsymbol{e}) = \boldsymbol{0} \tag{11.22}$$

and have a square, nonnegative definite contemporaneous variance-covariance matrix relating to different equations:

$$\begin{aligned} E[\mathbf{e(i)e'(i)}] &= E[-\boldsymbol{\Gamma}'^{-1}\boldsymbol{\epsilon}\mathbf{(i)}\boldsymbol{\epsilon}'\mathbf{(i)}(-\boldsymbol{\Gamma}^{-1})] \\ &= \boldsymbol{\Gamma}'^{-1}E[\boldsymbol{\epsilon}\mathbf{(i)}\boldsymbol{\epsilon}'\mathbf{(i)}]\boldsymbol{\Gamma}^{-1} \\ &= \boldsymbol{\Gamma}'^{-1}\boldsymbol{\Sigma}\boldsymbol{\Gamma}^{-1} = \boldsymbol{\Omega} \qquad i = 1, 2, \ldots, n \end{aligned} \tag{11.23}$$

where $\boldsymbol{\varepsilon}$ is an $m \times m$ matrix of contemporaneous reduced form disturbances. The relationship between $\boldsymbol{\Omega}$ and $\boldsymbol{\Sigma}$ can be more simply presented as follows:

$$\boldsymbol{\Sigma} = \boldsymbol{\Gamma}'\boldsymbol{\Omega}\boldsymbol{\Gamma} \tag{11.24}$$

Also $\mathbf{e(i)}$ and $\mathbf{e(i')}$ are uncorrelated, since

$$\begin{aligned} E[\mathbf{e(i)e'(i')}] &= E[(-\boldsymbol{\Gamma}'^{-1})\boldsymbol{\epsilon}\mathbf{(i)}\boldsymbol{\epsilon}'\mathbf{(i')}(-\boldsymbol{\Gamma}^{-1})] \\ &= \boldsymbol{\Gamma}'^{-1}E\{\boldsymbol{\epsilon}\mathbf{(i)}\boldsymbol{\epsilon}'\mathbf{(i')}\}\boldsymbol{\Gamma}^{-1} \\ &= \boldsymbol{0}\ (i, i' = 1, \ldots, n; i \neq i') \end{aligned} \tag{11.25}$$

[7] It should be pointed out that errors in simultaneous equation contexts often arise heteroscedastically. To test for such possibilities, both exact and approximate tests are available—see Harvey and Phillips (1981). This study develops the approximate tests as Lagrangean multiplier tests. It also calculates Type 1 error probabilities of these tests and the powers of both exact and approximate tests using Monte Carlo experiments for simple cases of heteroscedasticity.

[8] In some alternative specification, the practice is to assume that the structural disturbances are created by a stationary multivariate stochastic process, with their means and variance–covariances given by (11.19) and (11.20), but their sample variances and covariances tending in the probability limits to their corresponding population parameters. Also, the predetermined or exogenous variables, which are assumed to be fixed in repeated samples here, might alternatively be assumed to be generated by a stationary multivariate stochastic process with (1) nonsingular contemporaneous covariance matrix, (2) the plim of their sample variance (covariance) matrix tending to their corresponding population variance (covariance) matrix, (3) the process creating the predetermined variables contemporaneously uncorrelated with the process giving rise to the disturbances, and (4) the plim of sample covariances between the predetermined variables and disturbance terms tending to the corresponding population covariances, which are zero. Notice that the general results following from the assumptions of the text and the alternative specifications would be the same. For more on this see Goldberger (1964; p. 3–55, 299–301).

A distinctive aspect of the structural and reduced form equation estimation is appreciated as follows. Let us apply the normalization rule to a structural equation. This is equivalent to taking the coefficient of one jointly dependent variable in that equation as -1. Now let us transfer this variable to the left-hand side and all the other members of the equation to the right-hand side. It is then easy to see that the other jointly dependent variables and the structural errors will be correlated. Thus the OLS estimates of the parameters of this equation will be inconsistent. On the contrary, a reduced form equation for a given endogenous variable is expressed entirely in terms of predetermined variables and reduced form errors, which are obviously uncorrelated. Thus, OLS estimates of reduced form coefficients will be consistent.

The problem is how to generate consistent estimates of structural parameters. One way might be to get reduced form coefficient estimates and then go back to the structural coefficient estimates utilizing the relations between the two kind of coefficients. While this approach may be straightforward and successful in some cases, in others it may not be so at all and then we will face the problem of identification. It is to a discussion of this problem that we turn next.

11.4 THE IDENTIFICATION PROBLEM

The reduced form system gives us the knowledge of the joint distribution of the dependent variables for given values of the predetermined variables. This includes a knowledge of a few things: first, the conditional means of the distribution, identified by the coefficient matrix of the reduced form; second, its conditional variance; and, third, its other higher order moments. The latter two are identified with its other parameters. Conversely, a knowledge of all these parameters identifies the reduced form distribution of the dependent variables for given values of the predetermined variables.

The problem of identification in simultaneous equation models boils down to determining the structural equation parameters from reduced form parameters. This problem can be illustrated by counting the number of "givens" from the reduced form equations and relating it to the number of "unknowns" from the structural equations. For just or exact identifiability these two numbers should be equal. Confining the calculations to no more than the second order moment or variance, there are $m \times k$ elements of $\boldsymbol{\pi}$ and $m(m+1)/2$ elements of $\boldsymbol{\Omega}$, altogether $[mk + m(m+1)/2]$ "givens"; there are m^2 elements of $\boldsymbol{\Gamma}$, mk elements of $\boldsymbol{B}$ and $m(m+1)/2$ elements of $\boldsymbol{\Sigma}$, altogether $m^2 + mk + m(m+1)/2$ structural equation 'unknowns'. Subtract from this the number m, being the number of times a dependent variable has been equated to -1 as a result of the normalization rule. Thus the effective number of unknowns becomes $m^2 + mk + m(m+1)/2 - m$. The difference between the number of "unknowns" and "givens" is $m^2 - m = m(m-1)$, that is, "unknowns" are larger than the "givens". Thus the implication is that, without additional information, determination of parameters of the structural equations from reduced form equations can not be made.

In what follows, we show how the problem of identification is helped by means of general linear restrictions on structural coefficients. These restrictions include zero restrictions as particular cases. Later we briefly discuss remedies by other means.

11.4.1 General Linear Restrictions on Structural Parameters

We assume that out of the three parameter systems $\boldsymbol{\Gamma}$, $\boldsymbol{B}$, and $\boldsymbol{\Sigma}$, $\boldsymbol{\Sigma}$ is unrestricted but the other two are not. The restrictions on $\boldsymbol{\Gamma}$ and $\boldsymbol{B}$ are linear. These include as special cases zero restrictions, and other restrictions, such as equality of coefficients of a dependent and an exogenous variable in the same equation.

We begin with the connection between the reduced form and structural equation parameters:

$$\boldsymbol{\pi} = -\boldsymbol{B}\boldsymbol{\Gamma}^{-1} \tag{11.26}$$

or,

$$\boldsymbol{\pi}\boldsymbol{\Gamma} + \boldsymbol{B} = \boldsymbol{0}$$

or,

$$[\boldsymbol{\pi}\ \boldsymbol{I}_k]\begin{bmatrix}\boldsymbol{\Gamma}\\ \cdots \\ \boldsymbol{B}\end{bmatrix} = \boldsymbol{0}$$

or,

$$\boldsymbol{RS} = \boldsymbol{0} \tag{11.27}$$

where

$$\boldsymbol{R} = [\boldsymbol{\pi}\ \boldsymbol{I}_k] \tag{11.28}$$

and

$$\boldsymbol{S} = \begin{bmatrix}\boldsymbol{\Gamma}\\ \cdots \\ \boldsymbol{B}\end{bmatrix} \tag{11.29}$$

That is, $\boldsymbol{R}$ is the $k \times (m + k)$ matrix, with rank k, of reduced form coefficients augmented by an identity matrix of size k, and $\boldsymbol{S}$ is the $(m + k) \times m$ matrix of structural equation coefficients.

Consider the estimability of an equation, say, the ith equation of $\boldsymbol{RS} = \boldsymbol{0}$, that is

$$\boldsymbol{R}\mathbf{s}_i = \mathbf{0} \tag{11.30}$$

$\mathbf{s_i}$ being the ith column of $\boldsymbol{S}$. Since $\boldsymbol{R}$ may be completely known, or it may be estimated consistently, if unknown, and its rank is k, the above represents a set of k independent equations in $m + k$ (that is, the elements of the $\mathbf{s_i}$ vector) unknowns. Thus $\mathbf{s_i}$ cannot be determined from this equation alone. This fact suggests the use of, say, prior restrictions on coefficients, usually available in the form of additional equations, before it can be fully estimated.

Restrictions of these sorts can be expressed as:

$$\boldsymbol{T}\mathbf{s_i} = \mathbf{0} \tag{11.31}$$

where $\boldsymbol{T}$ has $(m + k)$ columns and as many rows as restrictions. For instance, a row such as $[0 \quad 0 \quad 1 \quad 0 \quad 0 \cdots 0]$ would reduce the third element of the $\mathbf{s_i}$ vector, that is, the element of γ_{3i} to zero through $\boldsymbol{T}\mathbf{s_i} = \mathbf{0}$. Similarly, a row such as $[1 \quad 0 \quad -1 \quad 0 \quad 0 \cdots 0]$ would simply equate γ_{1i} to γ_{3i}, and so on.

$(\boldsymbol{R}\mathbf{s_i} = \mathbf{0})$ and $(\boldsymbol{T}\mathbf{s_i} = \mathbf{0})$ together can be expressed as

$$\begin{bmatrix} \boldsymbol{R} \\ \cdots \\ \boldsymbol{T} \end{bmatrix} \mathbf{s_i} = \mathbf{0} \tag{11.32}$$

Now the $(m + k)$ elements of the $\mathbf{s_i}$ vector will be determined uniquely (and so the ith equation of $\boldsymbol{RS} = \boldsymbol{0}$ will be identified) if two conditions are satisfied: (1) The rank of $\begin{bmatrix} \boldsymbol{R} \\ \cdots \\ \boldsymbol{T} \end{bmatrix}$ be $m + k - 1$; this is called the rank condition for identifiability,[9] and (2) an additional restriction is imposed, such as the normalization rule, which sets one coefficient at minus unity.

Since $\begin{bmatrix} \boldsymbol{R} \\ \cdots \\ \boldsymbol{T} \end{bmatrix}$ has $(k + r)$ rows and $(m + k)$ columns where r is the number of restrictions, it follows that the number of its rows should be at least as large as its rank:

$$k + r \geqq m + k - 1$$

or,

$$r \geqq m - 1 \tag{11.33}$$

In other words, the number of prior restrictions would be at least as large as the number of equations in the model less one. This condition, usually known as the

[9] This will ensure that all solutions to (11.32) would lie on a single ray through the origin. The exact location of the solution point on this ray is determined by the normalization rule that appears in (2) next.

order condition of identifiability, is a necessary condition for guaranteeing that the rank of $\begin{bmatrix} \boldsymbol{R} \\ \cdots \\ \boldsymbol{T} \end{bmatrix}$ be $m + k - 1$. In case the prior restrictions all involve exclusion restrictions, the foregoing result would place the number of variables excluded, at the very minimum, at the number of equations of the model minus one.

This last condition can be put in another form as follows. Let m_0 and k_0 be the number of jointly dependent and predetermined variables included in equation i. The number of variables excluded is therefore

$$r = m - m_0 + k - k_0$$

It follows from (11.33) that the necessary condition would read as

$$m - m_0 + k - k_0 \geqq m - 1$$

which, alternatively, is

$$k - k_0 \geqq m_0 - 1 \tag{11.34}$$

In other words, the number of exogenous variables excluded from the equation has to be at least as large as one less than the number of jointly dependent variables included. This is known as the order condition with regard to the exclusion restrictions.

It can be shown (see Fisher (1966), Chapter 2) that the rank condition for identifiability, that is, rank $\begin{bmatrix} \boldsymbol{R} \\ \cdots \\ \boldsymbol{T} \end{bmatrix} = m + k - 1$, will be automatically met if a simpler condition, namely

$$\mathrm{R}(\boldsymbol{TS}) = m - 1$$

is fulfilled. This condition, which is both necessary and sufficient, is operationally very convenient, and therefore preferable. It follows that

$$\mathrm{R}(\boldsymbol{T}) \geqq m - 1 \tag{11.35}$$

This is because multiplying $\boldsymbol{T}$ by another matrix $\boldsymbol{S}$ will produce a rank for the product lower than or equal to the rank of its components. This is the general order condition and is only a necessary condition for identifiability.

An example. Consider Tintner's (1952) meat market model in the American economy:

$$Y_1 = \gamma_{21} Y_2 + \beta_{11} X_1 + \epsilon_1 \tag{11.36}$$

$$Y_1 = \gamma_{22} Y_2 + \beta_{22} X_2 + \beta_{32} X_3 + \epsilon_2 \tag{11.37}$$

In these, Y_1 and Y_2, the endogenous variables, are meat consumption per capita and meat price, respectively, and X_1, X_2, and X_3, the predetermined variables, are per capita disposable income, unit cost of meat processing, and unit cost of agricultural production, respectively.

Here $m = 2$ and $k = 3$ and

$$S = \begin{bmatrix} \Gamma \\ B \end{bmatrix} = \begin{bmatrix} -1 & \gamma_{12} \\ \gamma_{21} & -1 \\ \cdots & \cdots \\ \beta_{11} & \beta_{12} \\ \beta_{21} & \beta_{22} \\ \beta_{31} & \beta_{32} \end{bmatrix}$$

The prior restrictions are obviously

$$\beta_{12} = \beta_{21} = \beta_{31} = 0$$

For the first equation, T is a matrix consisting of two row vectors

$$\begin{bmatrix} 0 & 0 & 0 & 1 & 0 \\ 0 & 0 & 0 & 0 & 1 \end{bmatrix}$$

Thus

$$TS = \begin{bmatrix} \beta_{21} & \beta_{22} \\ \beta_{31} & \beta_{32} \end{bmatrix} = \begin{bmatrix} 0 & \beta_{22} \\ 0 & \beta_{32} \end{bmatrix}$$

and

$$\mathrm{R}\begin{bmatrix} 0 & \beta_{22} \\ 0 & \beta_{32} \end{bmatrix} = 1 = m - 1 = 2 - 1 = 1$$

Therefore the first equation is identified provided β_{22} and β_{32} do not vanish. Similarly, for the second equation, the restriction is:

$$T = [0 \quad 0 \quad 1 \quad 0 \quad 0]$$

and

$$TS = [\beta_{11} \quad \beta_{12}] = [\beta_{11} \quad 0]$$

Thus

$$\mathrm{R}(TS) = 1 = m - 1 = 2 - 1$$

if $\beta_{11} \neq 0$. So the second equation is identified.

Since the restrictions here are solely exclusion restrictions, equation (11.34), reproduced once again below, should be satisfied:

$$k - k_0 \geqq m_0 - 1$$

For the first equation, the number of predetermined variables excluded is 2 and the number of endogenous variables included less one is 1. Thus the condition is satisfied. For the second equation, corresponding numbers are 1 and 1. The condition is again satisfied. Hence, on the whole, both the rank and order conditions are satisfied for each of Tintner's meat market equations. Therefore his model is identified.

For the sake of curiosity, let us see if the identification of this model can be achieved another way. That is, whether the structural equation parameters can be derived uniquely from the reduced form parameters and the prior restrictions. For this suppose we consider the first equation. Then equation (11.32) for $i = 1$, that is

$$\begin{bmatrix} R \\ \cdots \\ T \end{bmatrix} \mathbf{s}_1 = \mathbf{0}$$

becomes:

$$\begin{bmatrix} \pi_{11} & \pi_{12} & \vdots & 1 & 0 & 0 \\ \pi_{21} & \pi_{22} & \vdots & 0 & 1 & 0 \\ \pi_{31} & \pi_{32} & \vdots & 0 & 0 & 1 \\ \cdots & \cdots & \cdots & \cdots & \cdots & \cdots \\ 0 & 0 & \vdots & 0 & 1 & 0 \\ 0 & 0 & \vdots & 0 & 0 & 1 \end{bmatrix} \begin{bmatrix} -1 \\ \gamma_{21} \\ \cdots \\ \beta_{11} \\ \beta_{21} \\ \beta_{31} \end{bmatrix} = \begin{bmatrix} 0 \\ 0 \\ 0 \\ 0 \\ 0 \\ 0 \end{bmatrix}$$

This leads to the following equations

$$\begin{aligned} -\pi_{11} + \gamma_{21}\pi_{12} + \beta_{11} &= 0 \\ -\pi_{21} + \gamma_{21}\pi_{22} + \beta_{21} &= 0 \\ -\pi_{31} + \gamma_{21}\pi_{32} + \beta_{31} &= 0 \\ \beta_{21} &= 0 \\ \beta_{31} &= 0 \end{aligned}$$

from which

$$\gamma_{21} = \frac{\pi_{21}}{\pi_{22}} = \frac{\pi_{31}}{\pi_{32}}$$

$$\beta_{11} = \pi_{11} - \frac{\pi_{21}\pi_{12}}{\pi_{22}} = \pi_{11} - \frac{\pi_{31}\pi_{12}}{\pi_{32}}$$

Since γ_{21} can be solved from any one of two ratios, π_{21}/π_{22} and π_{31}/π_{32}, the coefficient is over-identified. So is β_{11}. Thus the structural parameters of the first equation are over-identified. Similar computations will show that the second equation is just-identified.

This example illustrates an important distinction of equations in terms of whether they are identified or over-identified. Equations may also be unidentified. Accordingly the following taxonomy and the associated rank conditions would be useful. The equation i is

$$\begin{aligned} \text{just-identified if } R(\boldsymbol{TS}) &= m - 1, \text{ and } R(\boldsymbol{T}) = m - 1 \\ \text{over-identified if } R(\boldsymbol{TS}) &= m - 1, \text{ and } R(\boldsymbol{T}) > m - 1 \\ \text{under-identified if } R(\boldsymbol{TS}) &= m - 1, \text{ and } R(\boldsymbol{T}) < m - 1 \\ \text{unidentified if } R(\boldsymbol{TS}) &= m - 1, \text{ and } R(\boldsymbol{T}) \geqq m - 1 \end{aligned} \tag{11.38}$$

In just identified cases, structural equations can be estimated from ordinary least squares estimates of the reduced form, a technique called indirect least squares. In over-identified situations, there are a number of techniques available, for instance, two stage least squares, and other limited information methods. With under-identified or unidentified equations, one should be cautious. Rather than try to estimate them, one should wait until the equations are respecified for identifiability before any estimation should begin.[10]

11.4.2 Further Specifications Helping Identifications

Apart from zero restrictions or general linear restrictions on coefficients of the $\boldsymbol{\Gamma}$ and $\boldsymbol{B}$ matrices, the following list could be cited as additional means of identifying equations.

1. The Recursive Systems

   Here the jointly dependent variables *and* the structural equations can be so arranged that $\boldsymbol{\Gamma}$ becomes a triangular matrix and $\boldsymbol{\Sigma}$, the variance-covariance matrix of structural disturbances, a diagonal matrix. According to the first set of restrictions, variables appearing in higher-numbered equations will not appear in lower-numbered equations. According to the second set of constraints, disturbances in any two structural equations are statistically uncorrelated.[11]

   It can be easily shown that the above restrictions along with the normalization rules would uniquely determine the structural coefficients as ex-

[10] There is a relationship between the state of identification and the use of exact or asymptotic tests. Maddala (1974) has recommended the use of exact t tests for coefficients in exactly identified, but asymptotic t tests for over-identified equation situations. An applied study making use of this scheme is Fleisher and Rhodes (1976) on "unemployment and the labor force participation of married men and women: a simultaneous model."

[11] This kind of zero covariances between disturbances of two equations may arise in even nonrecursive situations—see the problem of identifying either a demand or supply curve in Leamer (1981). Leamer here also discusses inequality constraints on parameters as a means of partially identifying under-identified systems.

plicit functions of the reduced form coefficients. In other words, these will help identification of the recursive structural equations.

2. Prior Restrictions on the Disturbance Variance Matrix $\boldsymbol{\Sigma}$

   This is more general than has been exemplified in the recursive system above. Restrictions on elements of the $\boldsymbol{\Sigma}$ matrix will improve the identifiability of the structural equations.

   The argument goes on as follows. If an original structure of coefficients is transformed by multiplication by a nonsingular matrix, the new structure will be said to be admissible, if it obeys all prior restrictions on the original variance matrix. Combining the two conditions, it should be clear why specifying particular structures for the disturbance variance matrix will help admissibility and thus identification.

3. Form of Distribution of Structural Disturbances

   Even though normality of distribution is often assumed for structural disturbances, some disturbances may, in fact, deviate from this form. For instance, an equation designated for income may be subject to a nonnormal, say Pareto, distribution for its disturbance. Thus the income equation may be identified.

4. Bounds on Values of Some Structural Coefficients

   For instance, the price–quantity coefficient in a supply equation can be specified to be strictly greater than zero.

5. Relations Between Coefficients of One Structural Equation and Another

   For instance, between a production and a demand function included in the model, economic theory may specify that the coefficient of the wage rate variable be the same. That is, the cost effect on supply and the income effect on demand of wage (price) changes are considered to be of identical magnitude.

6. Known Values of Some Structural Coefficients Other than Zeros

   For instance, "identities" contain known coefficient values equal to unity. Treatment of such identities should be the same as of general linear restrictions on coefficients for the sake of equation identification discussed before.

This is by no means an exhaustive list, but it contains the more important practical items.

11.5 ESTIMATION METHODS FOR SIMULTANEOUS EQUATIONS

Any single structural equation, say the jth, selected out of (11.9), with normalization rule applied to the jth endogenous variable (that is, $\gamma_{jj} = -1$) would lead to the following form:

$$y_j(i) = \mathbf{Y}_j(i)\boldsymbol{\gamma}_\mathbf{j} + \mathbf{X}_j(i)\boldsymbol{\beta}_\mathbf{j} + \epsilon_j(i) \tag{11.39}$$

where $y_j(i)$ is the ith observation on the left-hand side dependent variable y_j, $\mathbf{Y}_j(i)$ is the ith observation on all the other jointly dependent variables included in the equation, $m_j - 1$ in number, $\boldsymbol{\gamma}_j$ is an $(m_j - 1) \times 1$ vector of coefficients of the right-hand side dependent variables, $\mathbf{X}_j(i)$ is the ith observation on the k_j included predetermined variables, and $\boldsymbol{\beta}_j$ is the $k_j \times 1$ vector of coefficients of these variables, and $\epsilon_j(i)$ is the associated error term of this structural equation. The index i runs from 1 to n for the observations.

An example is the demand function of Tintner's meat market model:

$$Y_1 = \gamma_{21} Y_2 + \beta_{11} X_1 + \epsilon_1 \tag{11.40}$$

which is cast in the form of equation (11.39). The complete two-equation model is given by

$$[Y_1 Y_2] \begin{bmatrix} -1 & -1 \\ \gamma_{21} & \gamma_{22} \end{bmatrix} + [X_1 X_2 X_3] \begin{bmatrix} \beta_{11} & 0 \\ 0 & \beta_{22} \\ 0 & \beta_{32} \end{bmatrix} + [\epsilon_1 \epsilon_2] = [0 \quad 0] \tag{11.41}$$

We have already seen that the first equation is over-identified, but the second is just-identified. This kind of state of identification runs through most equations of a simultaneous equation system.

The error $[\epsilon_1 \epsilon_2]$ follows the same statistical specification as in Section (11.3).

As mentioned in the introduction, a naive application of ordinary least squares to an equation, like equation (11.39), of a model will produce biased and inconsistent estimates. This is because the equation includes some current endogenous variables, for instance $Y_j(i)$, which will generally be correlated with the disturbance term $\epsilon_j(i)$ producing the bias even asymptotically.[12] Thus there is not too much to talk about the OLS method as applied to an equation in a simultaneous equation system.

The methods that are generally available in such a situation with some claim to legitimacy can be divided into two groups, (1) those that are limited information, and (2) others that are full information, or systems methods. The limited information methods, as the OLS method, are single equation methods, estimating equations like (11.39), but, unlike it, distinguishing between those variables that are included endogenous (that is the Y_js) and others that are included exogenous (the X_js). Thus they keep track of variables, both endogenous and exogenous, that are excluded from the given equation but are included in the rest of the system. In spite of this, the methods are limited information methods, since they do not exploit the information available about (including identifying restrictions on) the other equations of the system.

[12] It can be shown, however, that in the case of recursive models the OLS method will provide consistent estimates of structural coefficients.

There are two broad groups of methods available that are of the limited information type. One group, with only one method, namely indirect least squares (ILS), is available for exactly identified equations. The other group, with several methods, for example two-stage least squares (2SLS), K-class estimators, and limited information maximum likelihood (LIML) methods, applies to over-identified situations. These methods can be viewed as examples of the instrumental variable (IV) method for specific choices of instruments.

As for the full information or system methods, they are so called because they attempt to estimate all the structural equations (equation (11.9), or equation (11.39) for all values of j) simultaneously. In this they exploit the information from the entire system while estimating each of its structural equations. This information is available in the form of restrictions on its equation coefficients. Note that prior restrictions may arise as general linear relations in, or, in particular, as zero values, of the elements of the $\boldsymbol{\Gamma}$ and/or $\boldsymbol{B}$ and/or $\boldsymbol{\Sigma}$ matrices as indicated in the section on identification.

There are two methods belonging to the family of full information methods: three stage least squares (3SLS), and full information maximum likelihood (FIML) methods.

From this rudimentary discussion of limited information and full information methods it should be clear that the elementary methods underlying the single equation or systems estimation methods involve either the least squares or the maximum likelihood methods. The former methods, used relatively much more, appear in Section 11.5.1–11.5.5, while the latter appears in Section 11.5.6. However, both methods reappear in Section 11.5.7 in the concluding discussion on their comparative properties in small or finite sample situations.

11.5.1 Indirect Least Squares

This method applies to equations that are just-identified. It starts by estimating the reduced form coefficients by the OLS method and then estimating the structural equation parameters from the usual relationships between the structural and reduced form coefficients.

The reduced form coefficient estimates, utilizing the reduced form equations (11.15), that is $\boldsymbol{Y} = \boldsymbol{X}\boldsymbol{\pi} + \boldsymbol{e}$, and the OLS method, are:

$$\underset{k \times m}{\hat{\boldsymbol{\pi}}} = \underset{k \times k}{(\boldsymbol{X}'\boldsymbol{X})^{-1}} \; \underset{k \times n}{\boldsymbol{X}'} \; \underset{n \times m}{\boldsymbol{Y}} \tag{11.42}$$

Since $\hat{\boldsymbol{\pi}}$ has m columns, each column presents the coefficient estimates corresponding to a given dependent variable. For instance, the first column provides estimates pertaining to the first dependent variable y_1; similarly others. Assume that we are estimating, in particular, the structural equation for the dependent variable y_1, that is, take $j = 1$ in (11.39). Then the reduced form (11.15) can be partitioned in variables and coefficients as follows:

$$\underset{n \times 1}{(\mathbf{y_1}} \;\vdots\; \underset{n \times (m_1 - 1)}{Y_I} \;\vdots\; \underset{n \times (m - m_1)}{Y_{.I})}$$

$$= \underset{n \times k_1}{(X_I} \;\vdots\; \underset{n \times (k - k_1)}{X_{.I})} \begin{bmatrix} \hat{\pi}_1^y & \vdots & \hat{\pi}_I^Y & \vdots & \hat{\pi}_I^{Y.} \\ \cdots & & \cdots & & \cdots \\ \hat{\pi}_{.1}^y & \vdots & \hat{\pi}_{.I}^Y & \vdots & \hat{\pi}_{.I}^{Y.} \end{bmatrix} \qquad (11.43)$$

$$+ \underset{n \times 1}{(\mathbf{u}^y} \;\vdots\; \underset{n \times (m_1 - 1)}{u^Y} \;\vdots\; \underset{n \times (m - m_1)}{u^{Y.})}$$

In above, the stochastic error term has been partitioned in the same way as the jointly dependent variable Y, that is, according to the endogenous variable of importance of a given equation, the other $m_1 - 1$ included endogenous variables, and the $m - m_1$ excluded endogenous variables. While the predetermined variables are partitioned into those that are included in that equation and others that are not, the $\boldsymbol{\pi}$ matrix is partitioned according to columns and rows. The columns correspond to the group of y_1, Y_1, and $Y_{.1}$ variables (whose numbers are 1, $m_1 - 1$ and $m - m_1$, respectively), and the rows correspond to $k_1 X_1$s and $k - k_1 X_{.1}$s. Thus, for instance, the size of $\hat{\pi}_{.1}^{Y.}$, its subscript and superscript corresponding to predetermined and dependent variables, is $k - k_1 \times m - m_1$.

In terms of the above partitioning, equations

$$\hat{\boldsymbol{\pi}}\boldsymbol{\Gamma} = -\boldsymbol{B}$$

can be written as

$$\begin{bmatrix} \hat{\pi}_1^y & \vdots & \hat{\pi}_1^Y & \vdots & \hat{\pi}_1^{Y.} \\ \cdots & & \cdots & & \cdots \\ \hat{\pi}_{.1}^y & \vdots & \hat{\pi}_{.1}^Y & \vdots & \hat{\pi}_{.1}^{Y.} \end{bmatrix} \begin{bmatrix} -1 \\ \cdots \\ \boldsymbol{\gamma}_1 \\ \cdots \\ \mathbf{0} \end{bmatrix} = - \begin{bmatrix} \boldsymbol{\beta}_1 \\ \cdots \\ \mathbf{0} \end{bmatrix} \qquad (11.44)$$

That is,

$$-\hat{\pi}_1^y + \hat{\pi}_I^Y \boldsymbol{\gamma}_1 = -\boldsymbol{\beta}_1 \qquad (11.45)$$

$$-\hat{\pi}_{.1}^y + \hat{\pi}_{.I}^Y \boldsymbol{\gamma}_1 = \mathbf{0} \qquad (11.46)$$

$\hat{\pi}_{.I}^Y$ is of size $(k - k_1) \times (m_1 - 1)$. However, $k - k_1$ is equal to $m_1 - 1$ in the case of a just-identified equation. Thus, this matrix is square. Assuming it is nonsingular, from (11.46),

$$\hat{\boldsymbol{\gamma}}_1 = (\hat{\pi}_{.I}^Y)^{-1} \hat{\pi}_{.I}^y \qquad (11.47)$$

Substituting $\hat{\boldsymbol{\gamma}}_1$ for $\boldsymbol{\gamma}_1$ in (11.45), $\boldsymbol{\beta}_1$ is estimated as:

$$\hat{\boldsymbol{\beta}}_1 = \hat{\pi}_I^y - \hat{\pi}_I^Y (\hat{\pi}_{.I}^Y)^{-1} \hat{\pi}_{.I}^y \qquad (11.48)$$

These estimates are unique. They are called indirect least squares estimates, since the structural coefficient estimates are determined indirectly from the OLS estimates of reduced form coefficients. They are consistent estimates, because, taking probability limits of (11.46) and recognizing that $\hat{\pi}$ is consistent, we have,

$$\text{plim}\ \hat{\gamma}_1 = \text{plim}(\hat{\pi}^Y_{.1})^{-1}\ \text{plim}(\hat{\pi}^y_{.1}) = (\pi^Y_{.1})^{-1}\pi^y_{.1} = \gamma_1 \tag{11.49}$$

Similarly, taking probability limits of (11.45)

$$\text{plim}\ \hat{\beta}_1 = \beta_1 \tag{11.50}$$

ILS Computations Illustrated. Consider the supply function of Tintner's meat market model. The matrix of sums of square and sums of products of exogenous and endogenous variables around their means using U.S. annual data over the period 1919–1941 are:

$$\begin{bmatrix} X'X & X'Y \\ & Y'Y \end{bmatrix} = \begin{array}{c} \\ x_1 \\ x_2 \\ x_3 \\ y_1 \\ y_2 \end{array} \begin{bmatrix} x_1 & x_2 & x_3 & y_1 & y_2 \\ 83{,}433.65 & 3{,}611.72 & 12{,}204.77 & 3{,}671.91 & 8{,}354.59 \\ & 2{,}534.80 & 730.78 & -536.48 & 850.33 \\ & & 2{,}626.99 & 983.86 & 1{,}235.76 \\ & & & 1{,}369.54 & -352.44 \\ & & & & 1{,}581.49 \end{bmatrix} \tag{11.51}$$

Using this information, the estimated reduced form coefficient matrix is:

$$\hat{\pi} = (X'X)^{-1}X'Y = \begin{array}{c} \\ x_2 \\ x_3 \\ x_1 \end{array} \begin{bmatrix} y_1 & y_2 \\ -0.344626 & 0.208343 \\ 0.613660 & -0.033902 \\ -0.030839 & 0.096075 \end{bmatrix} \tag{11.52}$$

Proper partitioning of this leads to the following estimates of its submatrices:

$$\hat{\pi}^y_{.1} = -0.030839$$

$$\hat{\pi}^Y_{.1} = 0.096075$$

$$\hat{\pi}^y_1 = \begin{bmatrix} -0.344626 \\ 0.613660 \end{bmatrix}$$

$$\hat{\pi}^Y_1 = \begin{bmatrix} 0.208343 \\ -0.033902 \end{bmatrix}$$

from which:

$$\hat{\gamma}_1 = (\hat{\pi}^Y_{.1})^{-1}\hat{\pi}^y_{.1} = -0.030839/0.096075 = -0.320989 = \gamma_{22} \tag{11.53}$$

$$\hat{\boldsymbol{\beta}}_1 = \hat{\boldsymbol{\pi}}_1^{\mathbf{y}} - \hat{\boldsymbol{\pi}}_1^{\mathbf{Y}}(\hat{\pi}_{.1}^{Y})^{-1}\hat{\pi}_{.1}^{y} = \begin{bmatrix} -0.344626 \\ 0.613660 \end{bmatrix} - \begin{bmatrix} 0.208343 \\ -0.033902 \end{bmatrix} \times (-0.320989)$$

$$= \begin{bmatrix} -0.344626 \\ 0.613660 \end{bmatrix} - \begin{bmatrix} -0.066876 \\ 0.010882 \end{bmatrix} \tag{11.54}$$

$$= \begin{bmatrix} -0.277750 \\ 0.602778 \end{bmatrix} = \begin{bmatrix} \hat{\beta}_{22} \\ \hat{\beta}_{32} \end{bmatrix}$$

Thus, the supply function of Tintner's meat market model is estimated to be

$$Y_1 = -0.32Y_2 - 0.28X_2 + 0.60X_3 \tag{11.55}$$

by the method of indirect least squares.

11.5.2 Two-Stage Least Squares Method

This method applies to both just- and over-identified equations. It was invented by Theil (1953 and 1961) and at the same time by Basmann (1957).

For the sake of convenience, we use the single equation form as given in (11.39), except that we equate j to 1 corresponding to the variable being explained by that equation. With this change the equation becomes

$$\underset{n \times 1}{\mathbf{y}_1} = \underset{n \times (m_1 - 1)}{Y_I} \; \underset{(m_1 - 1) \times 1}{\boldsymbol{\gamma}_1} + \underset{n \times k_1}{X_I} \; \underset{k_1 \times 1}{\boldsymbol{\beta}_1} + \underset{n \times 1}{\boldsymbol{\epsilon}_1} \tag{11.56}$$

where $\mathbf{y}_1$, Y_I, X_I, and $\boldsymbol{\epsilon}_1$ are vectors or matrices involving sample observations or variables.

We have shown in (11.43) the complete set of reduced form equations when the dependent variables (also error variables) are partitioned into three sets: left-hand and right-hand side included and excluded dependent variables (also error variables); predetermined variables split into the included and excluded sets; and the $\boldsymbol{\pi}$ coefficient matrix partitioned column- and row-wise corresponding to (the partitioning of) the dependent and predetermined variables. Under this arrangement, the part of the reduced form equations (11.43) that refers to the right-hand side dependent variables Y_I will be

$$\begin{aligned} \underset{n \times (m_1 - 1)}{Y_I} &= \underset{n \times k_1}{X_I} \; \underset{k_1 \times (m_1 - 1)}{\hat{\boldsymbol{\pi}}_I^Y} \\ &\quad + \underset{n \times (k - k_1)}{X_{.I}} \; \underset{(k - k_1) \times (m_1 - 1)}{\hat{\boldsymbol{\pi}}_{.I}^Y} \\ &\quad + \underset{n \times (m_1 - 1)}{u^Y} = \underset{n \times k}{X} \; \underset{k \times (m - 1)}{\hat{\boldsymbol{\pi}}^Y} + \underset{n \times (m_1 - 1)}{u^Y} \end{aligned} \tag{11.57}$$

where

$$X = [X_I X_{.I}] \qquad \text{and} \qquad \hat{\pi}^Y = \begin{bmatrix} \hat{\pi}_I^Y \\ \hat{\pi}_{.I}^Y \end{bmatrix} \tag{11.58}$$

Inserting Y_I from (11.57) into (11.56) gives

$$\mathbf{y}_1 = X\hat{\pi}^Y \boldsymbol{\gamma}_1 + X_I \boldsymbol{\beta}_1 + (\boldsymbol{\epsilon}_1 + u^Y \boldsymbol{\gamma}_1) \tag{11.59}$$

The predetermined variables and the hybrid error terms above are uncorrelated. Besides we have used the symbol $\hat{\pi}^Y$ to imply that the π^Y coefficients are already estimated. These estimates come from stage 1 of the 2SLS method. More precisely,

$$\hat{\pi}^Y = (X'X)^{-1}X'Y_I \tag{11.60}$$

Let

$$\hat{Y}_I = X\hat{\pi}^Y \tag{11.61}$$

Then in stage 2, we regress $\mathbf{y}_1$ on $\hat{Y}_I$ and X_I to obtain the OLS estimates $\hat{\boldsymbol{\gamma}}_1$ and $\hat{\boldsymbol{\beta}}_1$ of $\boldsymbol{\gamma}_1$ and $\boldsymbol{\beta}_1$, respectively. Thus,

$$\begin{bmatrix} \hat{\boldsymbol{\gamma}}_1 \\ \hat{\boldsymbol{\beta}}_1 \end{bmatrix} = \begin{bmatrix} \hat{Y}_I'\hat{Y}_I & \hat{Y}_I'X_I \\ X_I'\hat{Y}_I & X_I'X_I \end{bmatrix}^{-1} \begin{bmatrix} \hat{Y}_I'\mathbf{y}_1 \\ X_I'\mathbf{y}_1 \end{bmatrix}$$

$$= \begin{bmatrix} Y_I'X(X'X)^{-1}X'Y_I & Y_I'X_I \\ X_I'Y_I & X_I'X_I \end{bmatrix}^{-1} \begin{bmatrix} Y_I'X(X'X)^{-1}X'\mathbf{y}_1 \\ X_I'\mathbf{y}_1 \end{bmatrix} \tag{11.62}$$

Since $m_1 - 1 + k_1$ unknowns are solved out of exactly as many normal equations, the solutions are unique.

To illustrate the 2SLS computations, we refer back to the reestimation of the supply equation of Tintner's meat market model. Using the matrices of computed moments using yearly data, U.S. 1919–1941, as given in (11.51), and the estimated reduced form matrix as in (11.52), we have the following data[13] vectors or matrices extracted (recall, $y_1 = Y_1$, $Y_1 = Y_2$, $X_1 = [X_2 \quad X_3]$, $X = [X_1 \quad X_2 \quad X_3]$):

$$(X'X)^{-1}X'Y_I \qquad Y_I'X \quad [8354.59 \quad 850.33 \quad 1235.76]$$

$$0.096075 \qquad \mathbf{y}_1'X \quad [3671.91 \quad -536.48 \quad 983.86]$$

$$0.208343 \tag{11.63}$$

$$-0.033902 \qquad Y_I'X_I \quad [850.33 \quad 1235.76]$$

$$X_I'X_I \qquad X_I'\mathbf{y}_1$$

$$\begin{bmatrix} 2534.80 & 730.78 \\ & 2628.99 \end{bmatrix} \qquad \begin{bmatrix} -536.48 \\ 983.86 \end{bmatrix}$$

[13] The data are placed below or alongside algebraic symbols. For the equivalence of variables, we show their current notation on the left hand side and the notation of variables of equation (11.37) on the right hand side of equations.

Using these in (11.62), we obtain the following 2SLS estimates

$$\hat{\gamma}_1 = -0.32 \qquad \hat{\beta}_1 = -0.28 \qquad \hat{\beta}_2 = 0.60 \tag{11.64}$$

Comparing these with the ILS estimates derived in (11.55), it is clear that the ILS and 2SLS are equivalent,[14] a result valid only when the equation estimated is just-identified as in the present case.

Some applied studies. We want to illustrate the 2SLS method by referring to the Farber (1981) study of industrial organization. This study explains (the dependent variables of) the number of R & D scientists and engineers per worker (ES/N), advertising sales ratios (A/S), and seller concentration (SCR) of 50 U.S. industries in terms of the following independent variables:

Const = constant
π_{-1} = lagged price–cost margin
BCR = buyer concentration
E = measure of financial and technical entry barriers other than those created by R & D and advertising
KR = financial barrier to entry
CONS = consumer orientation
TO = measure of technological opportunities
GR = industry growth
DUR = index of product durability taking the value 1 if durable product, 0 otherwise
RELWAGE = ratio of average wages of engineers and scientists to average wages of all workers in industry

[14] This result can be established theoretically as well. Very briefly, the argument goes on as follows. Use the middle expression of (11.57) into (11.56), and collect terms to obtain:

$$\mathbf{y}_1 = X_I(\hat{\pi}_I^Y \boldsymbol{\gamma}_1 + \boldsymbol{\beta}_1) + X_{.I}\hat{\pi}_{.I}^Y \boldsymbol{\gamma}_1 + (u^Y \boldsymbol{\gamma}_1 + \boldsymbol{\epsilon}_1)$$

$$= X \begin{bmatrix} \hat{\pi}^Y \boldsymbol{\gamma}_1 + \boldsymbol{\beta}_1 \\ \hat{\pi}_{.I}^Y \boldsymbol{\gamma}_1 \end{bmatrix} + (u^Y \boldsymbol{\gamma}_1 + \boldsymbol{\epsilon}_1)$$

The OLS estimate of the above equation, which, by definition, is the 2SLS estimate, leads to:

$$\begin{bmatrix} \hat{\pi}^Y \hat{\boldsymbol{\gamma}}_1 + \hat{\boldsymbol{\beta}}_1 \\ \hat{\pi}_{.I}^Y \hat{\boldsymbol{\gamma}}_1 \end{bmatrix} = (\boldsymbol{X}'\boldsymbol{X})^{-1}\boldsymbol{X}'\,\mathbf{y}_1 = \begin{bmatrix} \hat{\pi}_I^Y \\ \hat{\pi}_{.I}^Y \end{bmatrix}$$

where $\hat{\boldsymbol{\gamma}}_1$ and $\hat{\boldsymbol{\beta}}_1$ are the 2SLS estimates of $\boldsymbol{\gamma}_1$ and $\boldsymbol{\beta}_1$. For (11.56) to be exactly identified, $\hat{\pi}_{.I}^Y$ will be square. Assuming it to be nonsingular as well, solutions $\hat{\boldsymbol{\gamma}}_1$ and $\hat{\boldsymbol{\beta}}_1$ are derived, which are the same as the ILS estimates given in (11.47) and (11.48), respectively.

$$M = \begin{cases} 1, \text{ if industry fell in a moderately progressive class} \\ 0, \text{ otherwise} \end{cases}$$

$$CE = \begin{cases} 1, \text{ if it is a chemical or technical industry} \\ 0, \text{ otherwise} \end{cases}$$

$$RBFS = \text{measure of monopoly power}$$

The results derived are organized in Table 11-1.

Briefly the results indicate three things. Firstly, when a selling industry is unconcentrated, increased buyer concentration would lead to decreased R & D

TABLE 11.1* 2SLS REGRESSIONS EXPLAINING THE EMPLOYMENT OF SCIENTISTS AND ENGINEERS, ADVERTISING AND SELLER CONCENTRATION, 50 U.S. INDUSTRIES[15]

Variable	ES/N	t	A/S	t	SCR	t
Const	0.0021	1.37^c	-1.6561^c	-1.48	0.0809	2.26^b
π_{-1}	0.4597×10^{-4}	1.86^b	0.0486	1.29	—	—
BCR	-0.0112	-3.52^a	-3.3619	-1.94^b	—	—
SCR	-0.0064	-3.53^a	10.4769	2.33^b	—	—
SCR^2	—	—	-12.814	-2.3^b	—	—
SCRXBCR	0.0382	5.35^a	—	—	—	—
A/S	0.0004	2.54^a	—	—	0.0065	0.58
ES/N	—	—	595.2635	2.54^a	21.8977	1.86^b
MESD20	-0.1285×10^{-7}	-4.31^a	0.1747×10^{-4}	3.26^a	0.7102×10^{-6}	2.04^b
KR	-0.3916×10^{-10}	-4.05^a	0.1073×10^{-7}	0.69	0.3136×10^{-8}	4.07^a
CONS	-0.0016	-3.75^a	1.2231	1.67^c	—	—
SCR-1	—	—	—	—	0.5847	6.70^a
GR	—	—	0.0221^b	1.82	0.0003	0.43
M	0.0001	0.51	—	—	—	—
CE	-0.0008	-1.60^c	—	—	—	—
DUR	—	—	-0.7513	-2.0^b	—	—
RELWAGE	-0.0004	-0.50	—	—	—	—
RBFS	-317.4281	-1.78^b	—	—	—	—
R^2	0.80	—	0.63	—	0.80	—

[a] Implies significance at 1% one tail.

[b] Implies significance at 5% one tail.

[c] Implies significance at 10% one tail.

* Reprinted with permission S. Farber, "Buyer Market Structure and R and D Effort—A Simultaneous Equation Approach," *Review of Economics and Statistics*, 58 (1981) Table 1, p. 342.

[15] There are two nonlinear endogenous variables SCR and SCR × BCR. The author uses the method of Kelejian (1971) to obtain the predicted values for these endogenous variables from a second order polynomial of the reduced form equations. These values are then used to estimate the structural equations. Another variable used MESD20 relates to the minimum efficient scale of plants.

due to its negative effect on appropriability and rates of adoption. Secondly, average advertising expenditure would increase with R & D intensity (this result is particularly brought in by the 2SLS over the OLS method), and, thirdly, R & D intensity would be positively and significantly related to seller concentration.

Another use of 2SLS is illustrated by Saunders (1982). This is a study on the determinants of interindustry variation of foreign ownership in Canadian manufacturing. It is based on a seven equation model of the Canadian economy. We will not report here the details of this study except to say that the determinants that are found important are managerial resources and relative labor costs, and multiplant development in corresponding U.S. industries. It particularly supports the view that the pattern of foreign ownership in the Canadian manufacturing sector is determined in part by the ability of foreign firms to exploit intangible assets, by locating and producing in Canada.

In the Canada–United States context, an interesting problem often is speculation in the forward exchange market. McCallum (1977) tries to test the Stoll–Kesselman–Haas[16] (in short the S–K–H) formulation of foreign market equilibrium. According to it, the forward exchange rate is fixed at a weighted average of the corresponding interest parity forward rate and the expected spot rate, all rates applying to the same period of time in future. In other words,

$$F_t = (1 - \theta)F_t^* + \theta S_{t+3}^e \qquad 0 < \theta < 1 \tag{11.65}$$

where

F_t = 3 period forward rate as of period t

F_t^* = interest-parity 3 period forward rate = $S_t R_t$

S_{t+3}^e = expected spot rate to prevail 3 periods[17] hence

S_t = spot exchange rate (all rates are Canadian $ price of U.S. $)

$R_t = (1 + i_{ct})/(1 + i_{ut})$

i_{ct}, i_{ut} = 90 day interest rate in Canada, United States

Using the rules of rational expectation (see Chapter 12, Sections 12.11.1 and 12.11.2), McCallum sets up the equation

$$S_{t+3}^e = \mathrm{E}(S_{t+3}/\Phi) \tag{11.66}$$

where Φ_t is the information at time t of the random variable S_{t+3}. Separately, he does a number of things. First he uses the rules of excess demand for forward claims made by arbitrageurs and speculators; second, he uses their market clearing

[16] The interested reader should pick up the exact references from McCallum (1977). Notice that the interest parity forward rate F_t^* defined here is such a rate that $F_t^*(1 + i_{ut})$ becomes equal to $S_t(1 + i_{ct})$, where i_u and i_c are the U.S. and Canadian interest rates and S is the spot exchange rate.

[17] 3 periods chosen because of monthly observations used on 90 day forward rates.

TABLE 11.2* ESTIMATES[a] OF THE FORWARD RATE EQUATION BASED ON MONTHLY OBSERVATIONS, JANUARY 1953–NOVEMBER 1960

Explanatory Variables	Parameter Estimates and t ratios			
	Case I	Case II	Case III	Case IV
Constant	0.0037	−0.0245	−0.0221	0.0706
	(0.25)	(1.29)	(1.19)	(1.63)
F_t^*	0.9852	0.9335	0.9364	0.9084
	(54.4)	(33.8)	(35.0)	(22.8)
S_{t+3}	0.0123	0.0930	0.0875	0.0200
	(0.72)	(2.83)	(2.81)	(0.40)
R^2	0.9823	0.9779	0.9785	0.9735
S.E.	0.00175	0.00196	0.00193	0.00106
DW	0.377	0.403	0.402	2.213

[a] Case I: OLS of (11.68)
Case II: Regressor variables in the first stage computation used to generate instrumental variable $\hat{S}_{t+3}$ for S_{t+3} are R_t, F_{t-3}, S_{t-1}, S_{t-2}, and a constant.
Case III: Add R_{t-1} and F_{t-4} to the list of regressor variables of Case II.
Case IV: Assume $\epsilon_t = \rho\epsilon_{t-1} + \xi_t$: $|\rho| < 1$ and use the 2SLS method.

* Reprinted with permission B. T. McCallum, "The Role of Speculation in Canadian Forward Exchange Market," *Review of Economics and Statistics*, 49 (1977) Table 1, p. 149.

condition; third, he linearizes F_t^* $(= S_tR_t \approx S_t + R_t - 1)$, and last he uses the spot market equilibrium condition and the disturbance term to obtain a reduced form equation for F_t^*. This equation is expressed in terms of the predetermined variables R_t, F_{t-3}, and S_{t+3}^e:

$$F_t^* = \pi_0 + \pi_1 R_t + \pi_2 F_{t-3} + \pi_3 S_{t+3}^e + \nu_t \tag{11.67}$$

ν_t is the associated error term. Putting the rational expectations value of S_{t+3}^e, he gets:

$$F_t = \gamma_0 + \gamma_1 F_t^* + \gamma_2 S_{t+3} + \epsilon_t \tag{11.68}$$

where ϵ_t is the new error term. What McCallum does is use $\hat{F}_t^*$ for F_t^* from the reduced form above. This constitutes the first stage of estimation. Then he puts $\hat{F}_t^*$ back into (11.68) at the second stage of the 2SLS estimation. His results are reported in Table 11.2. These are based on (11.68) and four different ways of estimating the equation. Their explanations are given in the footnote to the table. One of his conclusions is that since $\gamma_0 \to 0$ and $\gamma_1 + \gamma_2 \to 1$, the conditions for the S–K–H market equilibrium do not differ substantially from the simpler formulation that the interest parity theory of forward rate implies. Secondly, the supply of arbitrage funds is highly elastic compared to the supply of speculative funds for the Canada–U.S. trades over the period 1953–1962. This follows from the consistently higher estimated coefficients of F_t^* than those of S_{t+3} as the table shows.

11.5.3 Equivalence of 2SLS and IV Estimates: Consistency of 2SLS Estimates

Let us review (11.56) and think that its right-hand side dependent and exogenous variables Y_I and X_I are to be replaced by their instruments $\hat{Y}_I$ and X_I, respectively, where $\hat{Y}_1$ is as in (11.61). The choice of the instruments is valid, since they are uncorrelated, in the probability limit, with the error term $\boldsymbol{\epsilon}_1$:

$$\text{plim } X_I'\boldsymbol{\epsilon}_1/n = \mathbf{0}$$

$$\text{plim } \hat{Y}_I'\boldsymbol{\epsilon}_1/n = \text{plim } \hat{\pi}^{Y\prime}X'\boldsymbol{\epsilon}_1/n = \mathbf{0}^{18}$$

The IV estimator of the coefficients of (11.56) would be obtained from

$$\begin{bmatrix} \hat{Y}_I'Y_I & \hat{Y}_I'X_I \\ X_I'Y_I & X_I'X_I \end{bmatrix} \begin{bmatrix} \hat{\boldsymbol{\gamma}}_1 \\ \hat{\boldsymbol{\beta}}_1 \end{bmatrix} = \begin{bmatrix} \hat{Y}_I'\mathbf{y}_1 \\ X_I'\mathbf{y}_1 \end{bmatrix} \tag{11.69}$$

Now review especially the middle member of the three-member identity (11.62), against (11.67), to see that the following reductions for individual items are possible:

$$\begin{aligned} \hat{Y}_I'\hat{Y}_I &= Y_I'X(X'X)^{-1}X'X(X'X)^{-1}X'Y_I \\ &= Y_I'X(X'X)^{-1}X'Y_I = \hat{Y}_I'Y_I \end{aligned} \tag{11.70}$$

and

$$\begin{aligned} \hat{Y}_I'X_I &= Y_I'X(X'X)^{-1}X'X_I \\ &= Y_I'(X_IX_{.I}) \begin{bmatrix} X_I'X_I & X_I'X_{.I} \\ X_{.I}'X_I & X_{.I}'X_{.I} \end{bmatrix}^{-1} \begin{bmatrix} X_I'X_I \\ X_{.I}'X_I \end{bmatrix} \\ &= Y_I'(X_IX_{.I}) \begin{bmatrix} I \\ 0 \end{bmatrix} = Y_I'X_I \end{aligned} \tag{11.71}$$

Thus we establish that the 2SLS and IV estimates are equivalent. And since the IV estimates have already been proved to be consistent, so are the 2SLS estimates consistent.

By reference to (8.18) of Chapter 8, the asymptotic covariance matrix of the IV–2SLS estimates would be

$$\frac{1}{n}\sigma^2 \left[\text{plim } \frac{1}{n}\begin{pmatrix} \hat{Y}_I'Y_I & \hat{Y}_I'X_I \\ X_I'Y_I & X_I'X_I \end{pmatrix}\right]^{-1} \left[\text{plim } \frac{1}{n}\begin{pmatrix} \hat{Y}_I'\hat{Y}_I & \hat{Y}_I'X_I \\ X_I'\hat{Y}_I & X_I'X_I \end{pmatrix}\right] \left[\text{plim } \frac{1}{n}\begin{pmatrix} Y_I'\hat{Y}_I & Y_I'X_I \\ X_I'\hat{Y}_I & X_I'X_I \end{pmatrix}\right]^{-1} \tag{11.72}$$

[18] It is needless to mention that $\hat{\pi}^Y$ is consistent.

in which $V(\epsilon_1)$ is σ^2. The sample consistent estimate of this covariance matrix is

$$S^2 \begin{pmatrix} \hat{Y}_I'Y_I & \hat{Y}_I'X_I \\ X_I'Y_I & X_I'X_I \end{pmatrix}^{-1} \begin{pmatrix} \hat{Y}_I'\hat{Y}_I & \hat{Y}_I'X_I \\ X_I'\hat{Y}_I & X_I'X_I \end{pmatrix} \begin{pmatrix} Y_I'\hat{Y}_I & Y_I'X_I \\ X_I'\hat{Y}_I & X_I'X_I \end{pmatrix}^{-1} \tag{11.73}$$

in which S^2 is the mean sum of squares due to error.[19,20]

11.5.4 Some Extensions: Nonlinearity in Variables; Number of Variables and Observations; Principal Components of Variables; Instrumental Variables and Economy-Wide Models

As noted in footnote (15), the Farber study, cited to illustrate 2SLS estimated results, involves a few endogenous variables nonlinear in form. An earlier study, the one by Masson and Debrock (1980), has a nonlinear form in exogenous variables. Using Kelejian (1971) and Edgerton (1972), these authors show that under certain conditions consistent estimation of equations can be performed with such nonlinear combinations of variables. Specifically, this study, which deals with structural effects of state regulation of retail fluid milk prices, has a hybrid variable Q defined as $C \times POP$, where C is per capita consumption of whole milk and

[19] K-class estimators: it is interesting to recast (11.67) into the following form, where of course $K = 1$:

$$\begin{bmatrix} \hat{\gamma}_1 \\ \hat{\beta}_1 \end{bmatrix} = \begin{bmatrix} Y_I'Y_I - Ku^{Y'}u^Y & Y_I'X_I \\ X_I'Y_I & X_I'X_I \end{bmatrix}^{-1} \begin{bmatrix} Y_I'y_1 - Ku^{Y'}y_1 \\ X_I' \end{bmatrix}$$

noting that

$$Y_I = \hat{Y}_I + u^Y,\ u^Y = M_IY_I \qquad M_I = (I - X_I(X_I'X_I)^{-1}X_I')$$

$$M_IX_I = 0$$

For $K = 0$, the above is the OLS estimator; for $K = 1$, the above is the IV or 2SLS estimator, and for $K = K$, it is the K-class estimator, K lying between 0 and 1, or beyond. Thus, the 2SLS estimates can also be looked upon as an off-shoot of a more general class of estimates, the so-called K-class estimates.

It can be shown that provided

$$\text{plim } K \to 1$$

the K-class estimators will be consistent. This result may also be used to establish the consistency of the 2SLS estimates.

[20] In the case where the model has error components, the 2SLS estimator of the structural parameters of, say, the first equation will be consistent but asymptotically inefficient. Here the error components two stage least squares (EC 2SLS) estimator may be the alternative asymptotically efficient estimator—see Baltagi (1981). For future reference, the method is extended in a straightforward fashion to the three stage least squares method in which case it is called the EC 3SLS method.

POP population of the market. Q is estimated directly in the first stage and then used in the second stage. However the reduced form has *POP* as an exogenous variable even though this variable does not, by itself, enter into the second stage structural estimation, but enters the composite variable Q. According to Edgerton, reduced forms of hybrid variables are not reduced forms of the structural model but are reduced forms based on instruments that could be used for consistent estimation of the structural form.[21,22]

In applied works it is often a problem when the 2SLS method is applied to large econometric models. In such cases, the number of exogenous (predetermined) variables may be large compared to the number of observations. For instance if, using our symbols, $k = n$, the $\mathbf{X}$ matrix will be square. Assuming nonsingularity of $\mathbf{X}$, it can be shown that $\hat{\mathbf{Y}}_I$ and $\mathbf{Y}_I$ are identical. Therefore, 2SLS would reduce to OLS with the associated property of inconsistency of estimates.

However, when $k > n$, the $\mathbf{X}'\mathbf{X}$ matrix, being of order $k \times k$, and rank k, will be singular. Thus 2SLS estimates will break down. But Fisher and Wadycki (1971) have shown that such estimates may still be available which will be the same as OLS estimates.

Some ways out of the largeness of the number of exogenous variables have been suggested by econometricians. For example, Kloek and Mennes (1960) recommend using a smaller number of principal components $\mathbf{C}$ for $\mathbf{X}_{.I}$ in the first stage of regressions. This means using, for instance,

$$\mathbf{P} = [\mathbf{X}_I \; \mathbf{C}]$$

in place of $\mathbf{X}$ in the extreme right-hand-side expression of (11.62) to generate the 2SLS estimates.[23]

Kloek and Mennes require the number of principal components to be at least as large as the number of included dependent variables, less one, for the sake of identification. This may be alright. But the problem is essentially one of choosing

[21] We are tempted to refer here to the main substantive findings of the Masson and Debrock study. Supporters of state wholesale and retail price regulation claim that such control is required to (1) ensure an adequate supply of milk, (2) to maintain stability in the industry, (3) to guard against monopoly, (4) to guarantee some services, and/or (5) to protect small businessmen. This study shows that incentives and distortions under regulation produce results that should lead to the rejection of the first three objectives. The last two objectives, however, are alright but seem to have high social costs associated with them.

[22] A related nonlinear 2SLS method application appears in Tsurumi (1970). He uses the method of steepest descent, the Marquardt (1962 and 1963) method, to start with, and then switches to linearizing by Taylor's expansion near the point of convergence, the Hartley (1964) and Marquardt (1963) method.

[23] An application of this kind of a method, called the 2SLSPC (two stage least squares principal components) method has been made by Darby (1982). Here he carries out tests of significance of oil price variables in an extended Lucas–Barro real income equation for eight countries, namely the United States, the United Kingdom, Canada, France, Germany, Italy, Japan, and Netherlands. See Appendix A.5 for a general discussion on the method of principal components.

the criterion to select the principal components. One choice may be to have those components that have the largest eigenvalues. This implies that the components so chosen will explain the greatest possible variance of the variables in the $\boldsymbol{X}_{.I}$ package, but then these may be highly collinear with variables of the $\boldsymbol{X}_I$ package. In such a case, there will be obvious computational difficulties trying to invert the $\boldsymbol{P}$ matrix. Besides, no uniform set of principal components may be available to serve the need of all structural equations. This implies tremendous computational burdens with regard to both the choice of instruments and estimation of the equations by their means.

A way out of the problem is to use a part of the principal components of the complete set of exogenous variables in the stage 1 regression of each equation. To give an example, refer to the Klein (1969) study which is essentially one of estimating a modified version of the Klein–Goldberger model. In this he uses the four largest eigenvalues, in one case, and the eight largest, in another of the $\boldsymbol{X}'\boldsymbol{X}$ matrix for principal components for the first stage of the regression. The 2SLS estimates, based on four eigenvalues, of the GNP in the sample period are found to have the best predictive accuracy compared to the ones based on eight eigenvalues, or, for that matter, the OLS and the FIML estimates.[24]

An alternative method of estimation available from economy-wide econometric models as proposed by Fisher (1965) merits particular mention. This involves taking for the right-hand-side variables: $\boldsymbol{Z}_I = [\boldsymbol{Y}_I \quad \boldsymbol{X}_I]$ of (11.56) the instruments $\boldsymbol{Z}_I^* = [\boldsymbol{X}_I^* \quad \boldsymbol{X}_I]$. Here $\boldsymbol{X}_I^*$ represents the matrix of $m_1 - 1$ exogenous variables, missing from the first structural equation, chosen for their determining influences on the structural equations for the $\boldsymbol{Y}_I$ variables, as Fisher explains. Denoting by

$$\boldsymbol{d}_I = (\mathbf{Z}_I^{*\prime}\mathbf{Z}_I)^{-1}\mathbf{Z}_I^{*\prime}\mathbf{y}_1 \tag{11.74}$$

the instrumental variable estimates of the first structural equation coefficients, and repeating this for all other equations, one gets the preliminary consistent estimates of the structural coefficient estimates. From these, the complete reduced form coefficient estimates $\hat{\boldsymbol{\pi}}$ can be obtained from the usual relations between the two types of coefficients. The final IV estimator $\boldsymbol{d}_2$ is

$$\boldsymbol{d}_2 = (\hat{\mathbf{Z}}_I'\mathbf{Z}_I)^{-1}\hat{\mathbf{Z}}_I'\mathbf{y}_1 \tag{11.75}$$

[24] An instrumental variables approach has been formulated by Brundy and Jorgenson (1971) to overcome the problem of substantial computations underlying reduced form coefficients estimation used in $\hat{\boldsymbol{Y}}_I$. This involves obtaining consistent estimates of structural equation coefficients, going back to reduced form coefficients using the relation between the structural and reduced form coefficients, and then using an IV method to reestimate the structural equation coefficients (which can be shown to be equivalent to the regular 2SLS estimates). Unfortunately this type of IV method does in no way seem to reduce the burden of work. Moreover, the task of the repetitive estimation of the structural equation coefficients seems hardly logical.

where

$$\hat{Z}_I = [X\hat{\pi}_I \ \ X_I] \tag{11.76}$$

and Z_I is as explained before.[25]

An applied study in IV2SLS. An instrumental variable 2SLS method of a somewhat different kind has been used by Polachek (1981). This study explores occupational self-selection using a human capital approach to occupational structure.* The 2SLS estimated equation in this study is as follows (with values of t shown underneath the coefficients in parentheses):

$$\underset{}{\delta} = \underset{(4.5)}{-10.08} + \underset{(2.0)}{2.05M} + \underset{(18.5)}{2.64S} + \underset{(1.0)}{0.18E} - \underset{(-1.6)}{0.45\hat{H}} \tag{11.77}$$

where

δ = occupation (explained by a vector of characteristics describing types of human capital)

M = marital status

S = lifetime investment measured as the number of years spent in school

E = labor market experience

$\hat{H}$ = number of years spent out of the labor force, for example to bear and raise children (exogenous)

Of special interest is the variable $\hat{H}$ defined as the number of years spent out of the labor force. This variable, assumed exogenous, is proxied in (11.77) by an instrumental variable, which is its estimate obtained from the following equation:

$$\hat{H} = \underset{(1.7)}{3.44} - \underset{(-3.2)}{0.22S} + \underset{(15.3)}{0.56E} + \underset{(4.3)}{1.96M} + \underset{(2.4)}{1.96C} - \underset{(-1.0)}{0.35U}$$

$$- \underset{(-2.6)}{1.24HL} - \underset{(-1.5)}{0.05A_c} - \underset{(-2.3)}{0.10D} \qquad R^2 = 0.22 \tag{11.78}$$

[25] Another approach to consistently estimate an over-identified structural equation is called the limited information least generalized residual variance approach. This was developed by Anderson and Rubin (1949 and 1950). By a change in the assumption about the distribution of the disturbance term, the method is commonly known as the limited information maximum likelihood (LIML) method. There is yet another way of arriving at these estimators, by following the principle of "least variance ratio", as discovered by Koopmans and Hood (1953), pp. 166–177. For the relation between canonical correlation and LIML methods based on zero restrictions and more general linear restrictions on parameters, see Hannan (1967), Chow and Ray-Chaudhuri (1967), and Ghosh (1972).

However, we have chosen not to dwell specifically on the LIML method due to its relative computational and theoretical difficulties.

with the following additional variables:

C = number of children less than 18 years old

U = an urban area dummy variable defined to have the value 1 for central city, 0 otherwise

HL = good or excellent health dummy variable

A_c = age of youngest child

D = index of labor market demand

As (11.77) indicates, both marital status and schooling positively influence the occupational status; labor market experience, even though influential, has only a small positive effect. The study also relates occupation to the duration of time in and out of occupation for women. It finds a negative relation between occupation δ and home time $\hat{H}$, despite an adjustment for simultaneity. Clearly this acts as a deterrent to women's moving through the occupations.

11.5.5 Three Stage Least Squares Method

All the methods we have described so far are limited information methods. The methods to be discussed in Sections 11.5.5 and 11.5.6 are full information methods. They are so called because, as indicated earlier, they take into account the restrictions on parameters of the complete system while estimating any of its structural equations. They are also called system methods in view of their estimating all the structural equations at the same time. Since the information from the complete system is likely to be greater than from the single equations, the full information system methods may asymptotically be more efficient than the limited information single equation methods.

In what follows we shall briefly describe two major full information methods, the three stage least squares (3SLS) and the full information maximum likelihood (FIML) methods. Replace, for example, the first equation of the system, as given in (11.56), by

$$\underset{n \times 1}{\mathbf{y}_I} = \underset{}{Z_I} \underset{(m_1 - 1 + k_1) \times 1}{\boldsymbol{\delta}_1} + \underset{n \times 1}{\boldsymbol{\epsilon}_1} \tag{11.79}$$

where

$$\underset{n \times (m_1 - 1 + k_1)}{Z_I} = [\underset{n \times (m_1 - 1)}{Y_I} \; \vdots \; \underset{n \times k_1}{X_I}] \tag{11.80}$$

and

$$\boldsymbol{\delta}_1 = \begin{bmatrix} \boldsymbol{\gamma}_1 \\ \cdots \\ \boldsymbol{\beta}_1 \end{bmatrix} \tag{11.81}$$

Premultiply (11.79) by the matrix X, of size $n \times k$, of the predetermined variables to get:

$$X'\mathbf{y}_1 = X'Z_1\boldsymbol{\delta}_1 + X'\boldsymbol{\epsilon}_1 \tag{11.82}$$

This premultiplication superimposes on any structural equation, say the first, the effect of the complete system as measured by the predetermined variables. Indeed these variables may be looked upon as a proxy for the socioeconomic system itself. In this sense operating these on a structural equation is, as it were, the next best thing to operating the entire system on it.

The modified error term is heteroscedastic since

$$\mathrm{E}(X'\boldsymbol{\epsilon}_1\boldsymbol{\epsilon}_1'X) = \sigma^2 X'X \tag{11.83}$$

assuming that $\mathrm{E}(\boldsymbol{\epsilon}_1\boldsymbol{\epsilon}_1') = \sigma^2 I$. This is the reason why we should apply Aitken's GLS method to estimating (11.79). Thus

$$[Z_1'X(X'X)^{-1}X'Z_1]\hat{\boldsymbol{\delta}}_1 = Z_1'X(X'X)^{-1}X'Y_1 \tag{11.84}$$

$\hat{\boldsymbol{\delta}}_1$ being the GLS estimates of $\boldsymbol{\delta}_1$. This is an alternative way of writing the 2SLS estimates of (11.79), as can be seen by partitioning Z_1, multiplying out and referring the resulting estimates to those obtained from (11.84).

For deriving the system method estimates, let us assume that the system excludes under-identified equations, if any, identities, to the extent that they exist, have been exploited to eliminate variables, and, lastly, that structural disturbances are linearly uncorrelated; that is,

$$\boldsymbol{\Sigma} : \text{nonsingular} \tag{11.85}$$

Write a representative structural equation as

$$\mathbf{y}_j = Z_j\boldsymbol{\delta}_j + \boldsymbol{\epsilon}_j, \qquad (j = 1, 2, \ldots, m) \tag{11.86}$$

Above, $\mathbf{y}_j$ is $n \times 1$, being the vector of observations on the left-hand dependent variable, $Z_j = [Y_j : X_j]$, being of size $n \times (m_j - 1 + k_j)$, is the matrix of observations on the right-hand dependent and included predetermined variables, and

$$\boldsymbol{\delta}_j = \begin{bmatrix} \boldsymbol{\gamma}_j \\ \cdots \\ \boldsymbol{\beta}_j \end{bmatrix}$$

of size $(m_j - 1 + k_j) \times 1$, is the coefficient vector of these variables. These equations together can be compactly written as

$$\mathbf{y} = Z\boldsymbol{\delta} + \boldsymbol{\epsilon} \tag{11.87}$$

where

$$\mathbf{y} = \begin{bmatrix} y_1 \\ \vdots \\ y_m \end{bmatrix} \quad Z = \begin{bmatrix} Z_1 & 0 & 0 \\ 0 & Z_2 \cdots & 0 \\ \vdots & & \vdots \\ 0 & \cdots & \cdots Z_m \end{bmatrix} \quad \boldsymbol{\delta} = \begin{bmatrix} \boldsymbol{\delta}_1 \\ \vdots \\ \boldsymbol{\delta}_m \end{bmatrix} \quad \boldsymbol{\epsilon} = \begin{bmatrix} \boldsymbol{\epsilon}_1 \\ \vdots \\ \boldsymbol{\epsilon}_m \end{bmatrix} \tag{11.88}$$

Premultiplying (11.87) by X'_*, we get:

$$X'_*\mathbf{y} = X'_*Z + X'_*\boldsymbol{\epsilon} \tag{11.89}$$

where

$$X'_* = \begin{bmatrix} X' & 0 & \cdots & 0 \\ 0 & X' & \cdots & 0 \\ \cdots & \cdots & \cdots & \cdots \\ 0 & \cdot\cdot & \cdots & X' \end{bmatrix} \tag{11.90}$$

Now the variance–covariance matrix of the new disturbances is

$$E(X'_*\boldsymbol{\epsilon\epsilon}'X_*) = \begin{bmatrix} \sigma_{11}\,X'X & \cdots & \sigma_{1m}\,X'X \\ \cdots\ \cdots & \cdots & \cdots \\ \sigma_{m1}X'X & \cdots & \sigma_{mm}\,X'X \end{bmatrix} = \boldsymbol{\Sigma} \otimes X'X \tag{11.91}$$

in which $\overset{\sigma}{jj'}$ are the elements of $\boldsymbol{\Sigma}$; $j, j' = 1, \ldots, m$, and the inverse of this (variance–covariance) matrix is

$$\begin{bmatrix} \sigma^{11}(X'X)^{-1} & \cdots & \sigma^{1m}(X'X)^{-1} \\ \vdots & & \vdots \\ \vdots & & \vdots \\ \vdots & & \vdots \\ \sigma^{m1}(X'X)^{-1} & \cdots & \sigma^{mm}(X'X)^{-1} \end{bmatrix} = \boldsymbol{\Sigma}^{-1} \otimes (X'X)^{-1} \tag{11.92}$$

of which $\sigma^{jj'}$ $(j,j' = 1, \ldots, m)$ are the elements of $\boldsymbol{\Sigma}^{-1}$. At this stage, we could apply the GLS method to the estimation of $\boldsymbol{\delta}$ in (11.87) by regressing $X'_*\mathbf{y}$ on X'_*Z, but the problem is the $\sigma^{jj'}$ are unknown, which makes the procedure unoperational. However, we could still aim at an operational method by consistently estimating $\boldsymbol{\Sigma}$ in the following way. Taking $\hat{\boldsymbol{\epsilon}}_{\mathbf{j}}$ to be the vector of residuals from the 2SLS estimated jth structural equation, we can form the mean sum of squares due to these residuals $s_{jj'}$ given by

$$s_{jj'} = \hat{\boldsymbol{\epsilon}}'_{\mathbf{j}}\hat{\boldsymbol{\epsilon}}_{\mathbf{j}'}/n \tag{11.93}$$

By varying j and j', each over the range 1 to m, we can fill up the body of the estimated variance matrix $\hat{\boldsymbol{\Sigma}}$. It can be easily shown that it is consistent for $\boldsymbol{\Sigma}$. Thus the 3SLS estimated coefficient vector $\hat{\boldsymbol{\delta}}$ is finally given by

$$\hat{\boldsymbol{\delta}} = \{Z'X_*[\hat{\boldsymbol{\Sigma}}^{-1} \otimes (X'X)^{-1}]X'_*Z\}^{-1}\, Z'X[\hat{\boldsymbol{\Sigma}}^{-1} \otimes (X'X)^{-1}]X'_*\mathbf{y} \tag{11.94}$$

or, elaborately,

$$\begin{bmatrix} \hat{\delta}_1 \\ \vdots \\ \hat{\delta}_m \end{bmatrix} = \begin{bmatrix} s^{11}Z'_1X(X'X)^{-1}X'Z_1 & \cdots & s^{1m}Z'_1X(X'X)^{-1}X'Z_m \\ \vdots & & \vdots \\ s^{m1}Z'_mX(X'X)^{-1}X'Z_1 & \cdots & s^{mm}Z'_mX(X'X)^{-1}X'Z_m \end{bmatrix}^{-1} \begin{bmatrix} s^{11}Z'_1X(X'X)^{-1}X'\mathbf{y_1} + \cdot\cdot + s^{1m}Z'_1X(X'X)^{-1}X'\mathbf{y_m} \\ \vdots \qquad\qquad \vdots \\ s^{m1}Z'_mX(X'X)^{-1}X'\mathbf{y_1} + \cdot\cdot + s^{mm}Z'_mX(X'X)^{-1}X'\mathbf{y_m} \end{bmatrix} \tag{11.95}$$

Obviously, $s^{jj'}$ are the elements of the $\hat{\Sigma}^{-1}$ matrix. To summarize, the calculation for the 3SLS method consists of work at three different stages: stage 1—the complete reduced form system is estimated; stage 2—this is where a selection is made of the part of the complete reduced form matrix that corresponds to the included right-hand-side dependent variables of the equation being estimated and, by its means, the 2SLS estimates of their coefficients; and, lastly, their residuals are computed. These estimated residuals, in turn, are used to compute the $\hat{\Sigma}$ matrix. Stage 3—$\hat{\Sigma}$ is inverted and fed into equation (11.94) or (11.95) for the final 3SLS estimates. Zellner and Theil have computed the asymptotic covariance matrix of 3SLS estimates as

$$1/n \text{ plim}\{1/n\, Z'X_*[\hat{\Sigma}^{-1} \otimes (X'X)^{-1}]X_*'Z\}^{-1} \tag{11.96}$$

which, obviously, is estimated by the same expression with the sign of the plim operator omitted.

We will conclude this subsection by making a few observations on the properties of the 3SLS estimators. These estimates are consistent. They are asymptotically more efficient than the 2SLS estimates should the system be correctly formulated. It is a simple deduction to show that both the 3SLS and 2SLS estimators are identical if the different structural equations possess statistically independent errors. For, then, the Σ and Σ^{-1} matrices would be diagonal; $s^{jj'}$ would be zero ($j \neq j' = 1, 2, \ldots, m$), and, therefore, (11.95) would reduce to (11.62).

Also, the presence of a number of exactly identified equations does not lead, as Zellner and Theil (1962) have shown, to a greater efficiency of coefficient estimates of the other equations that are over-identified. In other words, whether these latter equations are estimated alone or are estimated in association with the former equations does not make any difference in the efficiency of their estimates.[26]

Some applied studies. We refer to a recent study by Greenwood (1980) about U.S. metropolitan growth and the intra-metropolitan location of employment, housing, and labor force to illustrate the application of the 3SLS method. The study provides for the possibility that households might change their location not only due to changes in the workplace, but also due to changes in the conditions of housing supply. Thus it lays down a simultaneous equations model of urban growth and intra-urban location that includes housing, employment, and labor force location within the same model. Three blocks of equations are used to define the model: a housing block, a distribution block, and a location block. Growth over the metropolitan area of the housing stock is ascertained within the housing block. When this growth is spread over to either the central city or the suburban

[26] Zellner and Theil (1962), p. 67 have used this property to suggest a computationally efficient method of generating 3SLS estimates, as follows. First derive the 3SLS estimates of the over-identified equations. Then, to obtain the 3SLS estimates of the just-identified equations, add to their 2SLS estimates a linear function of the 3SLS estimates of the over-identified equations.

ring, it becomes a matter of the distribution block. Here such things as metro-wide growth of employment, civilian labor force (CLF), and income are important variables. The location block determines the suburban relative to central city location of CLF in-migrants, as also the CLF movements between the central city and the suburbs and vice versa.

In what follows, we present a description of the variables, and the tabular statement of the 3SLS estimates of the intra-urban location model for the years 1960–1970. Neither the same estimates for the previous decade, that is 1950–1960, nor the 3SLS estimates of sector-specific employment equations for both the decades that the author reports in the study are reviewed below.

Variables

$\dot{H}$	growth of household stock
$\dot{R}$	growth of labor force residents
$\dot{Y}$	growth of family median income
$NMOV$	net intrametropolitan relocation of CLF members from central city to suburbs
V_{t-10}	vacancy rate at the beginning of the period
$\dot{H}SC$	rate of growth of central city housing stock ($= \dot{H}S/\dot{H}C$)
$\dot{E}SC$	rate of growth of suburban employment relative to the rate of growth of central city employment ($= \dot{E}S/\dot{E}C$)
$\dot{R}SC$	rate of growth of suburban CLF residents relative to rate of growth of central city CLF residents ($= \dot{R}S/\dot{R}C$)
$\dot{Y}SC$	relative rates of suburban and central city income growth ($= \dot{Y}S/\dot{Y}C$)
MCS, MSC	movement from central to suburbs, suburbs to central city
VSC_{t-10}	beginning of period suburban vacancy rates relative to central city vacancy rates
$IMSC$	in-migration of CLF members to the suburbs relative to in-migration to the central city
CRM	crime rate
NW	percentage of population that are nonwhite (start of period)
PD	population density (start of period)

Table 11.3 results are self-explanatory. Of 68 coefficients for the two decades, 56 come out with expected signs and 41 of these are significant at the 1% probability level or a lower level. Some of the selective findings are as follows. In the location blocks, as indicated by the equations for *IMSC* and *MCS*, growth of suburban versus central city housing draws both the in-migrants and previous central city residents to the suburbs. Another important variable is suburban income growth. In the distribution block, during each decade, relatively greater rates of suburban compared to central city CLF growth are caused both by the net movement of CLF members from the central city to the suburbs and by the in-migrant CLF members' location in the suburbs. Referring to the equation of growth of metro housing stock (H), growth of CLF residents (R) is positive and significant in each decade, but the growth of income (Y) is negative for each decade but insignificant for the decade of 1960–1970 only.

In summary, one of the main inferences made by the author is that housing

TABLE 11.3 THREE STAGE LEAST SQUARE ESTIMATES OF INTRA-URBAN LOCATION MODEL, 1960–1970*

	Equation for							
	Housing Block	Location Block			Distribution Block			
Independent Variables	H	MCS	MSC	$IMSC$	$\dot{H}SC$	$\dot{E}CS$	$\dot{R}SC$	$\dot{Y}SC$
$\dot{R}$	0.894[a]	—	—	—	—	—	—	—
$NMOV$(e)	0.013[a]	—	—	—	—	—	0.143[a]	—
$\dot{Y}$	−0.044	—	—	—	—	—	—	—
V_{t-10}	−0.018[b]	—	—	—	—	—	—	—
$\dot{H}SC$(e)	—	2.859[a]	—	1.171[a]	—	—	—	—
$\dot{H}CS$(e)	—	—	1.369[a]	—	—	—	—	—
$\dot{E}SC$(e)	—	0.729[a]	—	0.309[b]	—	—	—	0.034
$\dot{E}CS$(e)	—	—	−0.787[a]	—	—	—	—	—
$\dot{Y}SC$(e)	—	4.892[a]	—	−0.493	−1.407[a]	0.281	—	—
$\dot{Y}CS$(e)	—	—	7.363[a]	—	—	—	—	—
$\dot{R}SC$(e)	—	—	—	—	0.492[a]	0.353[a]	—	−0.002
$IMSC$(e)	—	—	—	—	—	—	0.545[a]	—
RC_{t-10}	—	0.205[a]	—	—	—	—	—	—
RS_{t-10}	—	—	0.101[b]	—	—	—	—	—
$CRMC_{t-10}$	—	−0.067	0.089	−0.011	—	—	—	—
$NWSC_{t-10}$	—	—	0.074	—	—	—	—	—
$NWCS_{t-10}$	—	−0.044	—	−0.088[b]	—	—	—	—
PDC_{t-10}	—	−0.390[a]	−0.365[a]	0.053	—	—	—	—
YSC_{t-10}	—	—	—	—	—	—	—	−0.124[a]
VSC_{t-10}	—	—	—	—	0.083[b]	—	—	—
CON	−0.045	−3.022[a]	0.008	−0.201	0.226[b]	0.264[a]	−0.027	0.072[a]
$OLS\ R^2$	0.955	0.628	0.370	0.363	0.509	0.071	0.622	0.064

Note: e indicates endogenous variable. $SC(CS)$ indicates suburban (central city) relative to central city (suburban) value.

[a] Indicates that the coefficient is significant at the 2.5% level (two-tailed).

[b] Indicates that the coefficient is significant at the 10% level (two-tailed).

* Reprinted with permission M. J. Greenwood, "Metropolitan Growth and the Intra-metropolitan Location," *Review of Economics and Statistics*, 52 (1980) Table 2, p. 496–97.

and locational considerations have been rather more important than employment availability ones in drawing labor force members to the suburbs. Such locational factors in turn have caused the growth of both the suburban housing stock and suburban employment.

Before we proceed to the next estimation method, we want to make brief references to another applied study for two reasons. First, it represents some novelty in its theoretical procedure. Second, it represents an example of sets of equations with restrictions across equations and links between various disturbances. Such characteristics are commonly found in cost share equations that are approximated by translog (transcendental logarithmic) functions. These are used in the computation of input substitution elasticities in areas such as energy economics.[27]

The study is by Berndt and Wood (1975) relating to the U.S. manufacturing sector and the derived demand for energy for the period 1947–1970. It follows the method of instrumental variables insofar as it regresses each regressor on a set of variables taken as exogenous to the U.S. manufacturing sector and uses the fitted values from these "first stage" regressions as instruments, in lieu of regressors in the cost share ("SHARE") equations. After such variable replacements, it goes on to apply an iterative 3SLS method, iterative because it does away with the arbitrariness with which the derived demand equation for capital is dropped for fear of singularity of the variance–covariance matrix of the disturbance terms. Iteration is performed until the estimated coefficients and the residual covariance matrix converge. The iterative 3SLS estimates will be consistent and asymptotically efficient.

The summary findings of this study are: (1) energy demand is price responsive, own price elasticity[28] of energy demand being -0.5, (2) energy and labor are slightly substitutes, the Allen[29] partial elasticity of substitution between labor and energy inputs being 0.65, and (3) energy and capital are complements, the Allen partial elasticity of substitution between such inputs being -3.2.

[27] Related studies of interest are Hudson and Jorgenson (1974), Griffin and Gregory (1976), and Christensen and others (1973).

[28,29] These concepts can be explained with regard to the transcendental logarithmic cost function derived from a constant return to scale production function defined below:

$$Y = Y(K, L, E, M)$$

where Y is output, K capital, L labor, E energy, and M materials input. Taking the input prices P_K, P_L, P_E, and P_M to be exogenous, and assuming a symmetry condition for the second order partial derivatives, the translog cost function is derived to be:

$$\begin{aligned}\ln C = {} & \gamma_0 + \ln Y + \gamma_K \ln P_K + \gamma_L \ln P_L + \gamma_E \ln P_E + \gamma_M \ln P_M + \frac{1}{2}\delta_{KK}(\ln P_K)^2 \\ & + \delta_{KL}(\ln P_K)(\ln P_L) + \delta_{KE}(\ln P_K)(\ln P_E) + \delta_{KM}(\ln P_K)(\ln P_M) + \frac{1}{2}\delta_{LL}(\ln P_L)^2 \\ & + \delta_{LE}(\ln P_L)(\ln P_E) + \delta_{LM}(\ln P_L)(\ln P_M) + \frac{1}{2}\delta_{EE}(\ln P_E)^2 \\ & + \delta_{EM}(\ln P_E)(\ln P_M) + \frac{1}{2}\delta_{MM}(\ln P_M)^2\end{aligned}$$

The cost shares due to inputs K, L, E, and M denoted by θs with input subscripts are obtained by taking the derivative of $\ln C$ with respect to the logarithm of the prices. Thus,

$$\theta_K = \gamma_K + \delta_{KK} \ln P_K + \delta_{KL} \ln P_L + \delta_{KE} \ln P_E + \delta_{KM} \ln P_M$$

11.5.6 Full Information Maximum Likelihood (FIML) Method

This is the other system method we referred to before. In its development, it preceded the 3SLS method and was engineered by Koopmans and others (1950). The method, which is basically a maximum likelihood one, is derived under the specification that the structural disturbances are normally distributed, and that all restrictions on all structural equations are operative. In this sense the estimators are full information and efficient. They are also consistent. However, the chief disadvantage of the method is its computational difficulty and associated costs, arising from estimation of nonlinear equations.

Referring to equations (11.10) and (11.9), we note that $E(\boldsymbol{\epsilon}) = \mathbf{0}$, and $E(\boldsymbol{\epsilon\epsilon}') = \boldsymbol{\Sigma}$. Thus assuming that the errors are distributed multivariate normally[30] and the error vectors are serially uncorrelated, the likelihood of $\mathbf{y}(1), \mathbf{y}(2), \ldots, \mathbf{y}(n)$ is

$$L(\mathbf{y}(1), \ldots, \mathbf{y}(n)) = (2\pi)^{-\frac{nm}{2}} |\boldsymbol{\Gamma}|^{n} |\boldsymbol{\Sigma}|^{-n/2} \exp\left[-\frac{1}{2}\sum_{i=1}^{n} (\mathbf{y}'(i)\boldsymbol{\Gamma} + \mathbf{x}'(i)\boldsymbol{B})\boldsymbol{\Sigma}^{-1}(\mathbf{y}'(i)\boldsymbol{\Gamma} + \mathbf{x}'(i)\boldsymbol{B})'\right] \tag{11.97}$$

$$\theta_L = \gamma_L + \delta_{KL} \ln P_K + \delta_{LL} \ln P_L + \delta_{LE} \ln P_E + \delta_{LM} \ln P_M$$

$$\theta_E = \gamma_E + \delta_{KE} \ln P_K + \delta_{LE} \ln P_L + \delta_{EE} \ln P_E + \delta_{EM} \ln P_M$$

$$\theta_M = \gamma_M + \delta_{KM} \ln P_K + \delta_{LM} \ln P_L + \delta_{EM} \ln P_E + \delta_{MM} \ln P_M$$

From the conditions that the δs sum to zero in each column (and row), and that the shares add up to unity, we have

$$\gamma_K + \gamma_L + \gamma_E + \gamma_M = 1$$

Using the symmetry conditions involving the δs and the summation conditions on the δs and γs will enable estimation of all the coefficients of the cost function. Notice that the estimate of the intercept terms γ_0 will be obtained in the usual way.

The input price elasticities with this kind of translog function are given by:

$$E_{ij} = a_{ij}\theta_j$$

where a_{ij}, the Allen partial elasticities of substitution, are defined as (note the difference with Uzawa's simplification as per (9.60) of Chapter 9):

$$a_{ij} = \frac{\delta_{ij} + \theta_i\theta_j}{\theta_i\theta_j} \qquad i \neq j$$

[30] Current research is replete with other assumptions about the form of distribution of the error vectors, for example Prucha and Kelejian (1984), in which this form is taken to be a multivariate Student t. This study uses the ML method to introduce a new class of estimators.

In above, we have used

$$J\left[\frac{\mathbf{y}(1), \ldots, \mathbf{y}(n)}{\boldsymbol{\epsilon}(1), \ldots, \boldsymbol{\epsilon}(n)}\right] = |\boldsymbol{\Gamma}|$$

Define:

$$\begin{bmatrix}\boldsymbol{\Gamma}\\ \boldsymbol{B}\end{bmatrix} = \boldsymbol{D}$$

$$[Y \quad X] = \begin{bmatrix}\mathbf{y}'(1) & \mathbf{x}'(1)\\ \mathbf{y}'(2) & \mathbf{x}'(2)\\ \cdots & \cdots\\ \cdots & \cdots\\ \mathbf{y}'(n) & \mathbf{x}'(n)\end{bmatrix} = \boldsymbol{\xi} \tag{11.98}$$

and note that the exponent (except for the factor $-1/2$) in the above likelihood can be simplified to an expression as follows:

$$\sum_{i=1}^{n} (\mathbf{y}'(i)\boldsymbol{\Gamma} + \mathbf{x}'(i)\boldsymbol{B})\boldsymbol{\Sigma}^{-1}(\mathbf{y}'(i)\boldsymbol{\Gamma} + \mathbf{x}'(i)\boldsymbol{B})'$$

$$= \operatorname{tr} \boldsymbol{\xi}\boldsymbol{D}\boldsymbol{\Sigma}^{-1}\boldsymbol{D}'\boldsymbol{\xi}' = \operatorname{tr}(\boldsymbol{\Sigma}^{-1}\boldsymbol{D}'\boldsymbol{\xi}'\boldsymbol{\xi}\boldsymbol{D}) \tag{11.99}$$

The logarithm of the likelihood in (11.97) becomes

$$\ln L(\boldsymbol{D}, \boldsymbol{\Sigma}) \propto n \ln|\boldsymbol{\Gamma}| - n/2\,|\boldsymbol{\Sigma}| - n/2 \operatorname{tr}(\boldsymbol{\Sigma}^{-1}\boldsymbol{D}'\boldsymbol{\xi}'\boldsymbol{\xi}\boldsymbol{D}) \tag{11.100}$$

After differentiating $\ln L$ with respect to the elements of $\boldsymbol{D}$ and equating the results to zero, normal equations are derived. The solutions of these equations provide the FIML estimates of $\boldsymbol{D}$ and $\boldsymbol{\Sigma}$. These equations are nonlinear and their solutions are difficult and costly. The asymptotic variances of these estimates are found to be the same as those of the 3SLS estimates. Thus, these estimates are asymptotically efficient. The interested reader should consult Koopmans and others (1950) for details.[31]

From the applications point of view, the FIML or 3SLS methods have been applied mostly to fairly small models. Specifically even though the FIML technique has been developed for more than thirty years, its use in larger nonlinear models has long been considered as impossible. Even for the 3SLS method, the largest nonlinear model to which the method has been used consists of 19 equations (Jorgenson and Laffont (1974)). More recently Parke (1982) has come up with a numerical algorithm for calculating FIML and nonlinear 3SLS coefficient estimates for large nonlinear macroeconometric models. This new algorithm, applied to two versions of the 97 equation Ray Fair model,[32] indicates that it is more

[31] See Appendix A.6 for a discussion of vector autoregressive residuals in simultaneous equation models.

[32] The original Ray Fair model (see Fair (1971 and 1974)) is a quarterly model for the U.S. economy covering the period 1956I–1973II. It has 39 variables, divided into 19 endogenous and 20 exogenous. It has 19 equations of which 14 are stochastic and 5 nonstochastic.

effective than other algorithms applied to large FIML and 3SLS estimation situations.[33]

An applied study. In a study of credit rationing and investment behavior in a developing country like Colombia, Tybout (1983) views investment as depending, for demand expectations, on a linear function of past output levels, and, separately, on distributed lags in earnings as follows:

$$I(t) = \gamma + \beta \sum_{s=1}^{S} \alpha\, w_s\, \Delta Q(t + 1 - s) + \sum_{s=1}^{S} \eta_s\, \Delta\pi(t + 1 - s) + (1 - \beta)\, I(t - 1) \tag{11.101}$$

Above, the following variable definitions are used:

$$\begin{aligned} K(t) &= \text{capital stock at time } t \\ I(t) &= \text{investment at time } t \\ Q(t) &= \text{output at time } t \\ \pi(t) &= \text{earnings at time } t \\ \Delta Q(t) &= Q(t) - Q(t - 1) \\ \Delta\pi(t) &= \pi(t) - \pi(t - 1) \\ I(t - 1) &= K(t - 1) - K(t - 2) \end{aligned} \tag{11.102}$$

He then uses the FIML method to the above function, applied to both large and small firms. The estimated coefficients, along with their standard errors shown in parentheses, are given in Table 11.4. These and other results are based on the likelihood ratio tests of constraints on either the large or small firms. These produce the following four general observations: (1) at least among small firms, generation of internal funds is an important part of the investment process, (2) in-

[33] Recently a number of attempts have been made to estimate a stochastic *differential equation* economic system. This system is particularly relevant in studies of economic growth. This has typically assumed nonlinearities of various forms and kinds. Some of these have been in variables and/or others have been in parameters. Also there have been differences in the degree of the differential equation assumed—see Sargan (1974), Phillips (1972 and 1974), and Wymer (1972 and 1973), among others. Robinson (1976a and b) considers a system of simultaneous linear differential equations involving more than the first degree differentials in both the endogenous and exogenous variables. This system is replaced by a discrete approximation that is more conveniently handled in the frequency domain by Fourier transformations. Also he has used a class of IV estimators in the frequency domain (see our Chapter 10: Section 10.8 for its definition) with computationally preferred properties in some situations.

More recently, Ghosh (1986) has proposed a novel approach to the estimation of a stochastic differential equation system. An algorithm is developed and applied along the lines of Dvoretzky (1956) and engineering practices using discrete point approximations. In it, the probability becomes *exactly one* (rather than *almost* one) that the estimate tends to the true parameter value.

TABLE 11.4 FIML ESTIMATES OF THE INVESTMENT EQUATION FOR LARGE AND SMALL FIRMS*

Coefficients	Large Firms	Small Firms
Constant γ	103.625[c]	−1.825
	(33.89)	(5.606)
$\beta\alpha w_1$	−0.058	−0.057
	(0.046)	(0.036)
$\beta\alpha w_2$	−0.008	0.008
	(0.051)	(0.033)
$\beta\alpha w_3$	0.156[a]	0.009
	(0.083)	(0.020)
η_1	0.060	0.077
	(0.075)	(0.047)
η_2	0.252[a]	0.191[b]
	(0.135)	(0.078)
η_3	0.158	0.161[c]
	(0.182)	(0.058)
β	0.781[c]	0.247
	(0.236)	(0.198)

Note: Estimated standard errors are in parentheses.

[a] significant at the 0.1 level.

[b] significant at the 0.05 level.

[c] significant at the 0.01 level.

* Reprinted with permission J. R. Tybout, "Credit Rationing and Investment Behavior in a Developing Country," *Review of Economics and Statistics*, 55 (1983) Table 1, p. 605.

vestment behavior differs considerably across credit access groups in Colombia, (3) the view of binding liquidity constraint of financial market fragmentation explains Colombian patterns rather well, and (4) earning stocks seem rather important for the small firms than the large ones.

11.5.7 Small Sample Properties of Estimators: Some Monte Carlo Experiment Results

It must have been evident by now that any comparison made of the simultaneous equation estimators, be they single equations or systems estimators, has been in terms of their asymptotic or large sample properties, such as consistency and asymptotic efficiency. However, seldom in practice will a researcher have the good fortune of large samples. In small or finite sample situations, these large sample properties will therefore offer little or no guide in choosing between estimators.

Monte Carlo experiments[34] are a device to study small sample properties of estimators. This device was in frequent use by econometricians during the fifties and the sixties, and the early part of the seventies. However, the frequency of its use has considerably declined in recent times.

Before presenting the evidence from such experiments for all the aforementioned periods it is important that we define the experiment as such and point out its weaknesses so that we are aware of its limitations while applying it to the real world.

In a Monte Carlo experiment, the starting point is a model structure with known values of structural coefficients, a given probability distribution of the disturbances, and known values of the predetermined or exogenous variables. Based on these, a sample of a given size, say 15, of observations on the endogenous variables is obtained. The sample is then used to estimate by the various techniques the structural equation parameters, assuming as though these are not known, and the divergences between the estimates underlying each technique and the actual parameters are noted. The whole process is then replicated a certain number of times for more informed inferences to be drawn in terms of the properties of the sampling distributions of estimates, such as their central tendencies, dispersions, or other characteristics. Such experiments may also be used to study the influence of sample size, multicollinearity, and other aspects on various estimators.

From the above description the "laboratory" or "controlled" nature of the experimental results must have been clear. The important question is whether they would apply to the real world, or whether the "particular" results obtained would also apply "generally". This implies the need for careful testing to be done over extensive samples and revising the model structure whenever that would seem prudent.

Almost all the simultaneous equation techniques have come under the purview of the Monte Carlo experiments. However, their verdicts on these techniques have not been decisive. The reason is any differences among estimates due to techniques are usually confounded with differences in the models used, values of the exogenous variables, and elements of the covariance matrix. In other words, they are confounded with the possible range of the data points and/or specifications. In spite of this, the results offer some valuable indications about the estimators' relative desirability.

Among the limited information methods, the 2SLS estimator has come out

[34] See Cragg (1967) and Smith (1973) for surveys of Monte Carlo experiments. See also Mikhail (1975) for a more recent article.

There are two other approaches that have been tried by econometricians. For one concerning exact sampling distribution of estimators, see Basmann (1961, 1963, and 1974), and Richardson (1968), and for the other, concerning approximate finite sampling distributions of estimators, see Nagar (1959 and 1962), Kadane (1971), Sargan and Mikhail (1971), and Anderson and Sawa (1973).

as the best in terms of bias and mean squared error.[35] It has also been found to be generally robust (compared to other methods) in respect of specification changes. Its computation methods are simple and inexpensive. It has, however, the disadvantage of substantial vulnerability when multicollinearity is present. Summing up all the pros and cons, it appears that the 2SLS method is the most meritorious among the limited information techniques at the present time.

But the full information or system methods, illustrated by the 3SLS and FIML methods, surpass the 2SLS method in bias and mean squared error performances, provided the models and the variables are correctly specified and measured. However, these two methods are greatly sensitive to specification errors. This is because a little error somewhere in the system has the scope of being magnified as it is transmitted through the system. Obviously this scope is very restricted with the limited information methods, which is why methods such as the 2SLS method are relatively insensitive to specification errors. Also the computational complexity (and cost) of FIML and 3SLS methods is greater than in the case of other methods. For one thing, the systems take a much larger number of sample observations than the limited information methods.

The naive OLS method, on the other hand, has been found to have the most bias but generally the least variance among the methods studied. Since the mean squared error is the sum of variance and the square of bias of an estimate[36] and the bias overpowers the variance, this method has also the most mean squared error. Nevertheless its simplicity cannot be overlooked. Thus it receives so much favor from research investigators for preliminary works.

Moreover, for recursive structures this method is theoretically justified.

Could all this evidence be summarized and a single method found to be the best for all situations? We do not think so. For, the above points give only a rough guide. Besides they apply to different situations. We should note, however, that as far as some of the Monte Carlo study results go the asymptotic theory bodes well for the small sample theory in terms of most properties of the estimators.[37]

[35] If $\hat{\beta}$ is the estimator for the parameter β, to recapitulate, the bias is:

$$B = E(\hat{\beta}) - \beta$$

The variance is:

$$V = E(\hat{\beta} - E\hat{\beta})^2$$

and the mean squared error is:

$$M = E(\hat{\beta} - \beta)^2$$

[36] From footnote 35, we can easily establish:

$$M = V + B^2$$

[37] See Basmann (1958) for the basic details.

PROBLEMS

11-1. Consider the following demand and supply model containing price, p_t, and quantity, q_t, both endogenous variables:

$$\text{Demand}: \gamma_{11}p_t + \gamma_{12}q_t = u_{1t}$$

$$t = 1, 2, \ldots, n$$

$$\text{Supply}: \gamma_{21}p_t + \gamma_{22}q_t = u_{2t}$$

where u_{1t} and u_{2t} are random disturbance terms satisfying

$$E(\mathbf{u}_t) = \mathbf{0}, \qquad E\,\mathbf{u}_t\mathbf{u}_t' = \boldsymbol{\Sigma}, \qquad E(\mathbf{u}_t\mathbf{u}_{t-\theta}') = \mathbf{0} \qquad \text{for } \theta \neq 0$$

where $\mathbf{u}_t' = [u_{1t} \quad u_{2t}]$. Under these assumptions show that the γs are not identified. What are several sets of assumptions that will serve to identify the parameters of the demand equation?

11-2. Consider the supply and demand model of problem 11-1 elaborated to incorporate exogenous variables X_{1t} and X_{2t} as follows:

$$\text{Demand}: \gamma_{11}p_t + \gamma_{12}q_t = \beta_{11}X_{1t} + \beta_{12}X_{2t} + u_{1t}$$

$$t = 1, 2, \ldots, n$$

$$\text{Supply}: \gamma_{21}p_t + \gamma_{22}q_t = \beta_{21}X_{1t} + \beta_{22}X_{2t} + u_{2t}$$

Let $\mathbf{u}_t$ be NID($\mathbf{0}$, $\boldsymbol{\Sigma}$), where $\mathbf{u}_t' = [u_{1t} \quad u_{2t}]$. Consider the identification properties of the model under the following conditions:

(a) $\beta_{11} = \beta_{12} = 0$;
(b) $\beta_{11} = \beta_{21} = 0$;
(c) $\beta_{11} = 0$;
(d) $\gamma_{22} = \beta_{21} = 0$;
(e) $\boldsymbol{\Sigma}$ is a diagonal matrix ($\sigma_{12} = \sigma_{21} = 0$);
(f) $\gamma_{21} = 0$ and $\boldsymbol{\Sigma}$ diagonal;
(g) $\beta_{12} = \beta_{21} = 0$;
(h) $\beta_{12} = \beta_{21} = \beta_{22} = 0$.

11-3. Explain carefully how normalizing conditions, for example $\gamma_{11} = 1$ and $\gamma_{22} = 1$, for the model of problem 11-2 are involved, if at all, in determining whether or not an equation's parameters are identified.

11-4. Are the parameters (the α's) of the Cobb–Douglas (CD) production function identified in the following model?

$$Y_{0i} = \alpha_0 + \alpha_1 Y_{1i} + \alpha_2 Y_{2i} + u_{0i}$$

$$Y_{1i} = \beta_1 + Y_{0i} + u_{1i} \qquad i = 1, 2, \ldots, n$$

$$Y_{2i} = \beta_2 + Y_{0i} + u_{2i}$$

where for the ith firm, Y_{0i} = log of output, Y_{1i} = log of labor input, and Y_{2i} = log of capital input, are endogenous variables and the us are disturbance terms. Assume that $E(\mathbf{u}_i\mathbf{u}_j') = \mathbf{0}$, $i \neq j$, $E(\mathbf{u}_i) = \mathbf{0}$ and $E(\mathbf{u}_i\mathbf{u}_i') = \boldsymbol{\Sigma}$, a 3×3 positive definite symmetric matrix, i = 1, 2, . . . , n, where $\mathbf{u}_i' = [u_{0i} \quad u_{1i} \quad u_{2i}]$. If the αs are not identified, does this preclude the computation of least squares estimates of the αs from a regression of Y_{0i} on Y_{1i} and Y_{2i}? How would you interpret these estimates?

11-5. What assumptions about the parameters of the C–D production function model in problem 11-4 can serve to identify the parameters of the production function, that is the αs? Explain the economic implications of the identifying assumption. Prove that in fact the assumptions made are sufficient to identify the αs.

11-6. If the model is given by

$$Y_{1t} + \beta_1 Y_{2t} + \gamma_1 X_t = \epsilon_{1t}$$

$$t = 1, 2, \ldots, n$$

$$\beta_2 Y_{1t} + Y_{2t} + \gamma_2 X_t = \epsilon_{2t}$$

in which the Ys are endogenous variables and X is an exogenous variable,

(a) would you say that the model is identified?

(b) how would the conclusion in (a) be influenced if the condition $\gamma_1 + \gamma_2 = 0$ were imposed?

11-7. A research investigator observes that all the households in a state can be divided into two groups, those which are rented and others that are owned. He then goes on to formulate a model based on the following additional information/assumptions: (a) the expenditure on housing by the tenants, denoted by Y_{1t}, is a stochastic linear function of the exogenous variable called X_{1t}, (b) the expenditure on housing by the owners, denoted by Y_{2t}, is a stochastic linear function of another exogenous variable called X_{2t}, and (c) the incidence of renting or owning is linearly influenced by yet another exogenous variable called X_{3t}.

(a) Reproduce the equations of the model that the investigator might have set up.

(b) Explain how you could obtain consistent (and asymptotically efficient) estimates of the parameters of the model.

11-8. In Section 11.1 of Chapter 11, Klein's inter-war model has been presented in the estimated form. If the model were not in fact estimated, how would you identify its consumption equation using both the rank and order conditions of identifiability?

11-9. Let a three equation model be given by

$$Y_1 = \alpha_1 + \beta_1 Y_2$$

$$Y_2 = \alpha_2 + \beta_2 Y_1 + \gamma_2 X_1 + \delta_2 X_2$$

$$Y_3 = \alpha_3 + \beta_3 Y_2 + \gamma_3 X_1$$

where Y_1, Y_2, Y_3 are endogenous and X_1, X_2 are exogenous variables.

(a) Use the order condition to identify the equations.

(b) What is the degree of recursiveness in the above equation? Is the system fully interdependent?

(c) How would you estimate β_1 using (1) OLS, (2) IV, and (3) 2SLS methods?

11-10. Suppose Y_i $(i = 1, 2, 3)$ is an endogenous variable and X_j $(j = 1, \ldots, 5)$ is an exogenous variable, and let the model be given by:

$$Y_1 = \alpha_{11} X_1 + \alpha_{12} X_2 + u_1$$

$$Y_2 = \alpha_{23} X_3 + \alpha_{24} X_4 + \alpha_{25} X_5 + u_2$$

$$Y_3 = \beta_{31} Y_1 + \beta_{32} Y_2 + \alpha_{32} X_2 + \alpha_{35} X_5 + u_3$$

(a) How do you justify the use of single equation least squares to estimate the coefficients of these equations even after making necessary assumptions?

(b) Assume that u_1, u_2, and u_3 are interdependent. Explain an instrumental variable method of estimating the equation for Y_3. Show that such estimates are consistent. What condition must your method satisfy for its validity?

11-11. Explain what a fully recursive structural econometric model (SEM) is and provide a simple demand and supply model in fully recursive form. Then prove that the normalizing and zero restrictions imposed on the general fully recursive model are sufficient to identify its parameters.

11-12. What happens if the 2SLS method is applied equation by equation to estimate the equations of a fully recursive model?

11-13. For an identified two equation linear simultaneous equation model (SEM), define the 2SLS and 3SLS coefficient estimators. From a comparison of their asymptotic covariance matrices, show in what precise sense 3SLS dominates 2SLS. Under what conditions will their performance be asymptotically equivalent?

11-14. Establish the asymptotic equivalence of FIML and 3SLS estimators.

11-15. We are looking at one single equation from a simultaneous linear equations model (SEM) in which the disturbances are all normally distributed and the predetermined variables are all exogenous.

(a) What will happen to the 2SLS estimator of the parameters of this equation if the order condition for its identifiability fails?

(b) Consider that R_i^2 is the (squared) coefficient of multiple determination from the first stage regression of the ith right-hand side endogenous variable from this equation on the full set of exogenous variables. Consider also that this equation is over-identified. What would happen to 2SLS if

(1) all the R_i^2 approached 1.0?

(2) all the R_i^2 approached 0.0?

(c) In each case of (b) (1) and (2) above, how would the properties of 2SLS compare with those of OLS?

11-16. A Greek economic investigator tried to test some general theories of the consumption function using the Greek data over the period 1960 to 1983. She started with the simplest function which related real private consumption GC to real gross national product GY. Using OLS, her estimated line was:

$$GC = \underset{(9.93)}{87{,}936} + \underset{(67.52)}{0.573GY} \qquad R^2 = 0.995 \qquad DW = 1.09$$

the figures in parentheses being the values of the t statistic.

(a) Apply the first order autocorrelation test at the 5% level to conclude that this autocorrelation was significantly different from zero. What are the null and the alternative hypotheses?

(b) Apply the F test to test the overall regression.

To rid the estimated line of the influence of autocorrelation, she applied the CORC procedure and obtained the following results:

$$GC = \underset{(5.23)}{96.785} + \underset{(33.64)}{0.566GY} \qquad R^2 = 0.996 \qquad DW = 1.618$$

(c) Apply the F test to test the overall regression in the new situation. What are the F's degrees of freedom?

Then she looked at the consumption function as embedded in a simultaneous equation system. She added an identity: $GY = GC + Z$, where Z was expenditure on aggregate real demand items except real private consumption.

(d) Applying the order condition of identifiability show that the consumption function is identified. The estimated reduced from equations and values of associated statistics are given below:

$$GC = \underset{(12.64)}{212{,}500} + \underset{(28.66)}{1.32Z} \qquad R^2 = 0.973 \qquad DW = 1.06$$

$$GY = \underset{(12.64)}{212{,}500} + \underset{(50.38)}{2.32Z} \qquad R^2 = 0.99 \qquad DW = 1.06$$

(e) Using the above results, what will be the estimated coefficients of the consumption function using the method of indirect least squares (ILS)? How do these estimates numerically compare with the previous OLS estimates?

11-17. Let us continue with the specifications and results of problem 11-16. The investigator then changed to disposable income GYD (from total income) and fitted the following equation:

$$GC = \underset{(6.657)}{71{,}769} + \underset{(56.86)}{0.61GYD} \qquad R^2 = 0.993 \qquad DW = 1.009$$

Immediately she looked at this equation as one of the equations of a simultaneous equation system. But the system was now augmented by the inclusion of an additional equation over and above the identity $GY = GC + Z$. This additional equation (identity) was given by: $GY = GYD + T$, where T was the total tax receipt and GYD the real disposable income.

(a) Show, using the order condition of identifiability, that the consumption function was over-identified.

(b) Writing

$$GC_t = D_0 + D_1 GYD_t + u_t$$

$$GY_t = GYD_t + T_t$$

$$GY_t = GC_t + Z_t$$

where t is the time subscript and u_t is the error term, show, using $R_t = Z_t - T_t$, that $GYD_t = E_0 + E_1 R_t + u_t$ where $E_0 = D_0/1 - D_1$ and $E_1 = 1/1 - D_1$.

(c) Suppose you have used the OLS method to estimate GYD_t to be $G\hat{Y}D_t$. Regress GC_t on $G\hat{Y}D_t$ (see data in Table 11.5) to obtain the 2SLS-estimated line. Is this estimated line the same as the one below along with the associated results?

$$GC_t = \underset{(2.82)}{77{,}988} + \underset{(21.948)}{0.603G\hat{Y}D} \qquad R^2 = 0.956 \qquad DW = 0.962$$

(d) Assembling all the results from problem 11-16 and 11-7 so far, write a report on the consumption function for the Greek economy. You may touch on the properties of the coefficient estimators, the overall regression fits, and other

TABLE 11.5

GC
ANNUAL DATA FROM 1960 TO 1983

1960	3.159E + 05	3.351E + 05	3.552E + 05	3.732E + 05
1964	4.122E + 05	4.509E + 05	4.738E + 05	5.045E + 05
1968	5.411E + 05	5.760E + 05	6.267E + 05	6.604E + 05
1972	7.029E + 05	7.522E + 05	7.371E + 05	7.728E + 05
1976	8.150E + 05	8.502E + 05	9.008E + 05	9.042E + 05
1980	8.778E + 05	8.776E + 05	8.962E + 05	8.941E + 05

$G\hat{Y}D$
ANNUAL DATA FROM 1960 TO 1983

1960	3.884E + 05	4.517E + 05	4.761E + 05	5.294E + 05
1964	5.748E + 05	6.276E + 05	6.582E + 05	6.767E + 05
1968	7.240E + 05	8.342E + 05	8.908E + 05	9.965E + 05
1972	1.143E + 06	1.315E + 06	1.077E + 06	1.111E + 06
1976	1.240E + 06	1.273E + 06	1.340E + 06	1.448E + 06
1980	1.356E + 06	1.194E + 06	1.248E + 06	1.202E + 06

variables that could have been added (as signalled by the existence of the autocorrelation among residuals) for an improvement in the model itself.

11-18. An economic analyst is studying the trend of increased labor force participation of women aged 15–44 years in Canada based on data over the period 1966 to 1984. She sets up three equations in which the variables chosen are described below:

L	labor force participation (in proportions) of women aged 15–44 years in Canada
WF	female market wages expressed in 1981 constant dollars
WM	male income expressed in 1981 constant dollars
DIV	divorce rate per 100,000 people
FERT	general fertility rate of women aged 15–49 years (*FERT* shortened to *F* in the interactive factor $F \cdot WM$)
S	proportion of labor force in the service sector
UM	male unemployment rate (a proxy for business trends), seasonally unadjusted
M	proportion of women married
X	sex ratio (in percentage of men) of the population
CONST	constant or intercept term

The dependent variable of the first equation is *FERT*, of the second equation *L*, and of the third equation *M*. Based on OLS and 2SLS, the estimated coefficients along with the values of associated statistics (*t* statistics given in parentheses) are computed and are shown in Table 11.6.

TABLE 11.6 EMPIRICAL RESULTS ON THE DETERMINANTS OF FEMALE LABOR FORCE PARTICIPATION RATE IN CANADA, 1966–1984

REGRESSORS	Equation for *FERT*		Equation for *L*		Equation for *M*	
	OLS	2SLS	OLS	2SLS	OLS	2SLS
CONST	110.22 (15.85)	108.817 (15.29)	184.70 (1.68)	257.9 (1.75)	65.13 (3.76)	32.89 (1.04)
L.WF	−0.0021 (−4.06)	−0.0023 (−4.21)			−0.0006 (−12.6)	−0.0006 (−10.8)
M.WM	−0.0023 (−3.22)	−0.0022 (−2.90)				
M/WF			−16.87 (−1.30)	−30.82 (−1.75)		
F.WM			−0.0029 (−2.58)	−0.0044 (−2.99)	0.00202 (1.186)	−0.000009 (−0.271)
S			−1.8197 (−1.07)	−2.910 (−1.19)		
UM			1.1748 (0.948)	1.761 (1.203)		
DIV			0.1382 (3.204)	0.1537 (2.564)		
X					−2.114 (−0.1141)	33.86 (0.98)
R^2	0.95	0.95	0.96	0.96	0.93	0.91
DW	1.0	0.99	1.6	1.3	1.31	1.6

(a) Draw up the theoretical model and check to see if every equation of the model is identified or over-identified.

(b) Write a report on the estimated results especially interpreting the signs of the coefficients, commenting on the desirability of the estimation methods, and reviewing the suitability of the model itself. The last items should include your suggestion for the model's improvement, if any.

(*Hint:* The article by Winegarden (1984) would be of some help in formulating an articulate answer, but is not essential.)

11-19. A research investigator is in the midst of setting up and estimating a model to determine the demand for natural gas in the commercial market in Ontario. After some amount of theoretical experimentation, he ends up with the following model (call this Model 1) formulation:

$$\text{GASCONC} = \text{DD}^{B_1}[B_2 + P^{B_3} * \text{HHOLD}^{B_4} * Y^{B_5} + B_6 * \text{GASCONC}(-1)/(\text{DD}(-1))^{B_1}]$$

where

GASCONC = gas consumption in commercial sector

TABLE 11.7 FIML PARAMETER ESTIMATES OF THE GAS CONSUMPTION MODELS OF ONTARIO, 1959–1985

Coefficients	Model 1	Model 2	Model 3
B_1 (DD)	0.633	0.633	1.000
	(2.731)	(2.833)	(—)
B_2	−1.9	−1.9	−1.9
	(−6.851)	(−6.85)	(−6.793)
B_3(P)	−0.708	−0.808	−0.805
	(−2.553)	(−2.912)	(−2.904)
B_4(HHOLD)	−2.585	−9.051	−9.045
	(−15.258)	(−45.415)	(−45.381)
B_5(Y)	−2.178	−5.972	−5.97
	(−9.134)	(−23.762)	(−23.753)
B_6	1.052	1.052	1.05
	(91.01)	(102.344)	(89.282)
B_7(PE)		1.417	1.419
		(5.113)	(5.12)
R^2	0.991	0.991	.998
DW	0.922	0.922	1.614

P = a price variable to take advantage of price competitiveness among fuels
HHOLD = number of households, a demographic variable
Y = real personal disposable income per household (in thousands of 1981 dollars)
DD = ratio of degree days to average degree days over the sample period (NOTE: "degree days" is the product of degrees below 18°C and number of days)
GASCONC(−1) = GASCONC lagged one period
DD(−1) = DD lagged one period

Seeing that electricity enjoys a growing market share in Ontario, he also includes the price of electricity, PE, as a special variable in the previous formulation and consequently obtains the following Model 2 formulation:

$$\text{GASCONC} = \text{DD}^{B_1}[B_2 + p^{B_3} * \text{HHOLD}^{B_4} * Y^{B_5} * \text{PE}^{B_7} + B_6 * \text{GASCONC}(-1)/(\text{DD}(-1))^{B_1}]$$

However, he wants to illustrate the effect of temperature variations on the demand for natural gas. Specifically he wants to test the hypothesis that "degree days" does not matter (i.e. $B_1 = 0$) which would imply DD = DD(−1) = 1. With this applied to Model 2, Model 3 formulation results:

$$\text{GASCONC} = [B_2 + P^{B_3} * \text{HHOLD}^{B_4} * Y^{B_5} * \text{PE}^{B_7} + B_6 * \text{GASCONC}(-1)]$$

He uses Ontario data over the period 1959 to 1985 for estimation of the three alternative formulations of the gas consumption model for the province. But each model involves nonlinearities to render the application of the linear regression technique such as OLS inappropriate. Thus he is driven to the full information maximum likelihood (FIML) method for estimation of the equations. He uses Troll's Gremlin Version 2 (7/1/78) of FIML and accordingly the results in Table 11.7 are obtained.

(a) How can you rationalize the equation for Model 1? Give all the steps of your analysis.

(b) Interpret and write a critique on the estimated results from the three models.

(c) Indicate how the FIML method would or would not be a defensible method for estimation of parameters of a model of the type under consideration.

(*Hint:* Read Balestra and Nerlove (1966) and Berndt and Watkins (1977) before answering part (a) of the problem. However, if you are not too keen on part (a), skip that part and go right away to the remaining parts.)

12

Some Applied Macroeconometric Models and Models of Rational Expectations

12.1 INTRODUCTION

We have seen before how econometric techniques are applied to macroeconomic models. One such model is the conventional Keynesian model of income determination in which national income and its components such as consumption and investment are the variables, and the model contains two equations and an identity. We have also seen Klein's inter-war model[1] which represents an extended version of the basic Keynesian model, with some more variables, equations, and identities.

As such models are further extended, a few features become very clear. For instance, extensions may be made to an open economy. Then, exports and imports, and net foreign investment would be important considerations. Or, extensions may include disaggregation of variables. For example, income may be disaggregated into labor income and capital income, and output may be disaggregated by industries. Similarly, aggregate consumption may be split into consumption of goods and that of services, while each such component may be further disaggregated. Consumption of goods may be classified into consumption of durables and nondurables, while that of services into travels, communications, insurance, and so on. Likewise, investment may be broken down into business fixed plant investment, inventory accumulation, and residential construction. Or, there may be other extensions emphasizing certain aspects of the economy, such as the government or the public sector, in connection with the evaluation of social wel-

[1] See Chapter 11, Section 11.1.

fare programs, education programs, etc., and/or emphasizing the external sector in connection with the determination of possible effects of measures such as exchange control and the restriction of capital movement when a country's economy is under sustained speculative attacks in the foreign currency markets.

The objective of this chapter is twofold. First, we briefly summarize the broad points of five "medium" to large size macroeconometric models of the U.S. economy, as well as two large size models of the Canadian economy. We also discuss some policy evaluation aspects and problems using macroeconometric models. The five U.S. models are: the Klein-Goldberger model, the Wharton group of models, the Brookings model, the Federal Reserve Bank of St. Louis (the FRB St. Louis) model, and the Liu-Hwa model. The two Canadian models are: the TRACE model and the RDX2 model. The first is published by a private group of economists of the University of Toronto and the second by the Bank of Canada. Both the U.S. and Canadian groups of models are but a sample of all the models that have been built so far. However, they represent some excellent attempts at model building, in the sense that they provide important inputs into newer and fresher models constructed by investigators even today. Note that some of the models that are reported here may not even be actively used by their producers at the present time.

The second objective is to take note of the econometric issues and implications of a very important new approach to applied economic theory that has both fascinated some economists as well as disenchanted some others in recent times. This is the approach of rational expectations. Even though its appeal and application are quite general, the debate centering around it has been characteristically limited to problems that arise in macroeconomics.

12.2 THE KLEIN AND GOLDBERGER (1955) MODEL

This represents one of the earliest attempts to build a macroeconometric model of the U.S. economy. The period covered is 1929–1952 save and except for some of the war years 1942–1945.[2] It has 20 equations, 15 of which are stochastic and the rest identities. It includes 34 variables, 20 of them being endogenous and the rest exogenous.

> The endogenous variables include: income, consumption, gross private investment, depreciation, corporate saving, corporate surplus, private employees, capital stock, liquid assets, prices, interest rates, and imports.
>
> The exogenous variables include: government expenditure, direct taxes, indirect taxes, population and labor force, hours worked, excess reserves, and import prices.

[2] This is done to avoid the extraordinary features of the war economy.

The model provides for disaggregation much more than the previous smaller models.[3] The result of this is evident in the explicit recognition of five kinds of income, five types of population and labor force, four types of direct taxes, three prices, two liquid assets, and two interest rates.

The other features of the model consist of the use of: (1) lags of up to five years, (2) Koyck's distributed lags, (3) time trends, (4) nonlinear equations, (5) stocks and flows (measured in constant 1939 billions of dollars), and (6) limited information maximum likelihood (LIML) method for estimation.[4]

As one gleans through the various aspects of the model, one encounters a particular Keynesian bias. This may explain why a great deal of emphasis is placed on the elements of consumer demand and not much on production. Although both real and monetary aspects are covered, it is the real phenomenon such as the components of demand in GNP less investments that are very adequately represented. There is, however, some problem with investment in that business fixed investment and inventory investment are not treated separately, and therefore investment cycles can hardly be extracted and analyzed. Also, the monetary aspect of the model, especially that part of it which deals with prices and interest rates, is not covered well,[5] probably because of the limited size of the model.[6]

12.3 THE WHARTON GROUP OF MODELS

The original Wharton model is an intermediate size macromodel of the U.S. economy. It is, in many senses, similar to the Klein–Goldberger model, and, in many others, dissimilar to it and other preceding models. Three major differences between this and the other models are noticeable: (1) it uses quarterly (not annual) data and includes 68 observations: 1948I–1964IV, (2) it is a forecasting type of model focusing on national income and unemployment, and (3) it follows disaggregation and attends to the monetary sector a great deal more than its predecessors.[7] There are 76 equations in the model divided into 47 stochastic equations and 29 identities. These equations are based on 118 variables, 76 of these being endogenous and the remainder exogenous. These variables are shown below, with

[3] Examples of these models are the Klein (1950) inter-war model and the Morishima and Saito (1972) model. The former is presented in Chapter 11.

[4] See Fox (1958) which shows not much difference in estimation results when OLS instead is used.

[5] This point is also indicated in Goldberger (1959).

[6] See Adelman and Adelman (1959) who study the long term behavior of the Klein–Goldberger model as compared to actual trends and cycles of the U.S. economy. They use simulated data from 1952 to 2052 using this model as the base. The results are that the simulated series shows business cycles with length, amplitude, and turning points similar to those actually experienced in the U.S. economy. Also, the assumption of the model that its additive random shocks can properly represent the U.S. economy is found to be carried out.

[7] See Evans and Klein (1967 and 1968), Evans (1969), and Evans and others (1972).

numbers in brackets indicating the extent of disaggregation within a general variable group:

> Endogenous variables: output (5), sales (2), income (4), consumption (5), fixed investment (5), depreciation (4), corporate profits (2), dividends, retained earnings (2), cash flow, inventory valuation adjustment, rent and interest payments, taxes (3), transfer payments, labor force (4), hours worked (2), wage bill (2), unemployment rate (2), capital stocks (6), inventories (3), unfilled orders, index of capacity utilization, prices (10), wage rates (2), interest rates (2), imports (3), exports
>
> Exogenous variables: output (2), income, consumption, anticipations, farm fixed investment, farm inventories, investment anticipations (2), depreciation, government purchases (2), interest payments, social security contributions (2), housing starts, population, labor force (5), wage bill (2), prices (7), discount rate, net free reserves, time dummy variables (6), productivity trend, index of world trade, statistical discrepancy

The special features of the model, in addition to the extent of disaggregation revealed from the variable classifications above, include the following. Production functions are of the Cobb–Douglas variety. Unit labor costs are incorporated to influence prices, and capacity utilization is endogenously treated. Government variables, variables arising from the farm sector, consumption and investment anticipations, population, and a productivity trend all come to play the role of exogenous variables in this model. Add to this list the policy variables such as government expenditures, social security contribution, the discount rate, and net free reserves.

The model uses lags of up to 9 quarters and especially uses Almon's distributed lags for the investment function providing for lags between investment decisions and capital appropriations. Some variables arise in the first difference while others in absolute forms. Some nonlinear functional forms are used out of necessity as in the case of the Phillips curve.

The original Wharton model is used to produce several versions of it made at various times. The first version goes by the name of Wharton Mark III model.[8] There are in this version 201 endogenous and 104 exogenous variables, including 67 equations that are stochastic and 134 that are identities. There is a great deal of emphasis placed on the financial sector and the nonmanufacturing sector. Also distributed lags are very extensively used in investment and other functions, and policy instruments that are used are much larger in number (25) than in the original version (7).

The two other versions are called Wharton Annual and Industry Forecasting model and Wharton Anticipations model. The first provides long-run predictions

[8] See McCarthy (1972) and Duggal and others (1974) for details of this version.

of up to 10 years relating to each industry and the second emphasizes anticipations variables. These variables apply to both consumption and investment. For more details, see Preston (1972 and 1975) and Adams and Duggal (1974).

12.4 THE BROOKINGS QUARTERLY ECONOMETRIC MODEL OF THE UNITED STATES

Its structure consists of a set of interrelated dynamic processes concerning production, income, price and wage, and expenditures on goods and services by households, businesses, and governments. The dynamic aspects include (1) lagged relationships and rates of change in variables, (2) relationships as well as stock variables, where the stocks are cumulative flows endogenously generated within the model, and (3) changing exogenous variables and random shocks.[9]

The system of equations comes to more than 150 equations of which nearly all are genuinely estimated. All the consumption equations are treated as potentially related to disposable income, relative price, real liquid assets, population, and lagged consumption. With durables (cars and others), such variables as asset stocks and consumer attitudes or buying plans are taken as special additional variables. Of these variables, stocks seem to significantly affect nonautomotive expenditures while consumer buying plans and attitudes affect car buying. It is odd that liquid assets and population affect the component of demand due to services more than they do other more ordinary components.

The housing equations are based on housing starts integrated with construction expenditures. These along with the unit dwelling value are explained endogenously.

The inventory investment equations belong to the modified stock adjustment variety. Variables included are price changes and unfilled orders.

The investment functions used are pure lag relationships and therefore can be consistently estimated using the least squares method. The dependent variable is actual investment rather than intended investment allowing for investment realization.

Under national accounting methods, three types of government accounts are kept. Under one, on the expenditure side there are purchases of goods and services. Under another, there are taxes, and under still another there are transfers. Transfers occur from payments out of unemployment and retirement accounts. Receipts for these accounts are considered tax collections.

Equations are provided for tax collections from persons and business, and for receipts for unemployment and social insurance funds. Also, there are equations on the expenditure side for, namely, transfer payments out of social security

[9] See Duesenberry and others (1965 and 1969), Fromm (1971), and Fromm and Klein (1975). For a review of this model, see Basmann (1972).

funds and government expenditures. Other equations are for school construction, highways and local services. Military expenditures appear as a major exogenous variable.

The form of the production function is not very typical. It expresses the labor input as a function of output and the capital stock. Employment is categorized into production workers, overhead workers, and hours of work. From the equations of wage and employment hours, labor's factor income is determined. Other factor incomes are interest, rent, inventory valuation adjustment, and dividend payments. The last arises because profits, which are a residual item, are divided between dividends and corporate savings.

Farm income is the difference between farm receipts and expenses. On the receipts side, equations used for food consumption of crop origin are paired with total food consumption functions with the residual determining the consumption of food livestock products. Then an overall margin is used for all food crops as implied in the price conversion equations. Price conversion is done as follows.

Because of the government's price support programs, crop prices are given and thus exogenous. In the food consumption equation, quantity is the dependent variable. Farm price is exogenous and worked up by using the spread between farm and retail prices. Farm inventory demand is explained using the stock adjustment argument as for nonfarm inventories. Farm investment in buildings and machines is treated exogenously, as also is rental income from farm dwellings.

Two forms of depreciation allowances are taken in the model as a physical measure for replacement investment and as an accounting measure for national income and product identities. The former follows Jorgenson's treatment of estimates of capital stock and replacement investment; the latter makes use of a straight line accounting method, assuming an average twenty year (80 quarter) duration of capital equipment.

To convert prices from the production sector to elements of GNP final demand, a set of regressions of estimated final demand, $[\boldsymbol{I} - \boldsymbol{A}]\mathbf{x} = \mathbf{f}$, on selected elements of the GNP is computed. Here $[\boldsymbol{I} - \boldsymbol{A}]$ is a 7×7 input–output matrix, $\mathbf{x}$ is a column vector of 7 gross sector outputs, and $\mathbf{f}$ is a seven-element vector of final demands. Sequential regression estimates are obtained to meet coefficient constraints. First, coefficients for trade and administered sectors are determined to permit marketing margins. Then, some coefficients are fixed by imposing a constraint on their sums in all the regressions, after which the remaining coefficients are estimated. At this stage, simple least squares estimates, even though biased, are computed. These estimates along with the estimated input–output coefficients are used to determine the matrix of conversions from the implicit price deflators of the production sector to prices of the final demand sector.

In the financial sector, three financial variables are emphasized: short- and long-term rates of interest, and total cash holdings. The short-term rates are from equations from housing construction demand and government interest incomes.

The long-term rate is from the investment functions and business interest income equations; cash holdings are from consumer demand functions. These variables are the essential ingredients of the monetary equations. Monetary equations show the influence of monetary policy on the monetary market variables through the minimum cash reserve coefficients, time deposit maximum rates, and maturity structure of the public debt.

Labor force participation rates are classified by an exhaustive set of age–sex groups: females 14 to 19 years, females 20 years and over, males 14 to 19 years, and males 20 years and over. The participation rate equations contain the unemployment variable which is a measure of long-term unemployment—the number unemployed for 27 weeks or more. No attempt is made to explain the duration of unemployment, however, and also no attempt is made to explain anything other than the participation rates, for example, demographic variables which are taken as exogenous.

An evaluation of the Brookings models has been made by Schink (1975), p. 39 on the basis of its condensed version. This version contains 326 variables of which 200 are endogenous, and includes 68 behavioral equations with 13 extra variables from the input–output sector. A comparison of the within-sample and post-sample simulation experiments of the condensed and the large versions of the Brookings model suggests a significant improvement in the overall model simulation and forecasting performance, along with the advantage of increased details in the larger version.

Further, two expansionary policies of similar dollar values, a government expenditure increase and a personal tax reduction, are compared over a ten year horizon. As ordinarily expected, the government expenditure increase generates a greater expansion over the first three years. Beyond that period, the picture reverses dramatically, with the government expenditure increase producing some perverse longer run effects.

We will conclude by referring to three earlier simulation studies based on the Brookings model for the purpose of determining the impacts of U.S. fiscal and monetary policies. One, by Klein (1969b), is concerned with the income tax act of 1964; another, by Fromm (1969), is concerned with two fiscal policies (government purchase of durables and changes in federal personal income tax rates) and four monetary policies (changes in the discount rate, in the deposit reserve ratio, in the time deposit reserve ratio, and in unborrowed reserves); and, still another, by Fromm and Taubman (1968), is concerned with the excise tax cut of 1965. The general procedure followed by all these studies is to determine the time paths of relevant endogenous variables both before and after a policy change. The two solutions are then compared for measuring the impacts of the policy change on the economy. These studies have been very useful as ex-post studies to ascertain the efficiency of fiscal and monetary policies affecting the course of the U.S. economy.

12.5 FEDERAL RESERVE BANK OF ST. LOUIS (FRB ST. LOUIS) MODEL

This is a model, monetarist in outlook, formulated for the purpose of assisting in the framing and assessment of stabilization policies. It is not designed for exact quarter-to-quarter forecasting. Rather, it is for determining the timing and magnitude of the effects of monetary and fiscal policies. The approach followed is a reduced form approach.[10]

At the root of the monetary outlook of the model is the quantity theory of money. According to it, a change in the stock of money causes the actual and desired holdings of cash to diverge, due to which there will be a shuffling of the wealth portfolio. In the adjustment process, expenditure on goods and services will change.

The model has 8 equations. The first equation is for total spending (nominal GNP) and its quarterly change is specified to depend on current and past changes in the stock of money and current and past changes in high employment federal expenditure. The second equation has the quarterly change in the price level influenced by current and past demand pressures and anticipated price changes. Change in total spending in excess of the increase in output produces demand pressure obtained from the third equation.

The fourth equation is an identity relating total spending to its components. The fifth equation is for the market rate of interest as a function of current changes in the stock of money, current and past changes in output, current price changes, and anticipated price changes. Anticipated price changes depend, according to the next equation, on past price changes.

The seventh equation explains the unemployment rate. This is obtained by a transformation (of "Okun's Law" variety) of the GNP gap, defined in the eighth equation, into something expressing unemployment relative to the labor force.

12.5.1 Evaluation of the Model

This we present in the form of strong points and weak points. The strong points are:

1. The model brings out the short-run as against the long-run effects of stabilization policies on such things as real product, prices, unemployment, and interest rates.
2. It testifies to the determining influence of monetary policy on economic activity.

[10] See Rasche and Shapiro (1968), deLeeuw and Gramlich (1968 and 1969), Ando and Modigliani (1969), Ando and others (1972), and Ando (1974).

3. It demonstrates indirectly the influence of costs of information on stabilization analysis.

This is in support of the notion that changes in total demand are identified first in real product and second in prices. The model makes a path analysis showing a trade-off relationship between inflation and unemployment, which relationship disappears in the long run. These findings support the growing literature on costs of information and search.

The weak points are:

1. It does not produce enough observations by which policy makers will know about the long-run effects of their short-run actions.
2. It fails to record short-run movements in velocity.
3. It is unable to register the price movement during periods of control programs and widespread inflation.
4. It is not completely successful in determining the effects of large variations in government spending and the money stock and anticipated changes in money stock.

12.6 THE LIU AND HWA (1974) MONTHLY MODEL

The consumption functions of the model follow the lines of the classical consumer demand theory. Generally, the explanatory variables are disposable personal income, initial liquid assets, relative prices, and, especially in the case of durable goods, initial stocks. The variable of initial liquid assets is found to be unimportant in the equation for automobiles, and price is unimportant in the equation for nonautomobile consumers' durable goods.

As for business fixed investment, separate functions are kept for plant and for equipment based on the neoclassical user cost approach. That apart, a variable in the ratio of unfilled orders to shipments is kept for capacity utilization, incidentally found significant in the equipment equation.

The inventory equation includes the short-term interest rate in real terms, unlike the Wharton model. In spite of the statistical insignificance of this variable, it is considered to be increasingly important in economic investigations.

The equations for manufacturer's new orders, shipments, and unfilled orders involve complicated functions. The first depends on such variables as the last month's total of gross private domestic investments in business construction, producers' durable equipment, and residential construction, last month's total personal consumption expenditures less expenditures for services, last month's exports of goods and services, stock of nonfarm inventories, and a dummy variable for steel strike. The second depends on such variables as a strike dummy variable, lagged values of manufacturers' new orders and manufacturers' shipments. The last depends on the balance between manufacturers' new orders and shipments, and the lagged values of unfilled orders adjusted by the year to year relative prices of wholesale manufactured goods.

A CES production function provides the estimates of coefficients in the private man-hours function. This is found to be quite good for short period simulations even though not for long period ones. For the latter, their linearization produces better results. The linearized version uses, as a proxy for capacity utilization, the ratio of gross private product to business capital. Wage rate is found to significantly influence the civilian labor force, unlike Wharton models.

In the financial sector, the equation specifications are different from the Wharton models in two respects. First, the Liu–Hwa model provides for currency, demand deposits, savings and time deposits, as well as savings and loan association shares held separately by household, business, and government. Second, inflation measured by rates of change of the consumer price level is considered to be an important factor for household holdings of currency and demand deposits, in spite of its statistical insignificance from the small sample used.

The income type equations and those for GNP right up to disposable personal income are simple and straightforward.

The equation for implicit price deflator for gross private product (GPP) has, as explanatory variables, private unit labor cost and the ratio of gross private product to private business capital. These are also the variables that bring out the cost-push and demand-pull influences on the general price level. There are other price deflators, however. They depend on the GPP deflator and the private wage rate. Manufacturers' wholesale price level is influenced by the GPP deflator and the ratio of unfilled orders to shipments. Private wage rate is adjusted by a modified Phillips curve relationship which, in addition to the rate of unemployment, has changes in the consumer price level and corporate profits for variables. A foreign trade sector ultimately closes the model. In addition, there is a set of identities as in most models of this type.

The consumption functions are based on lag structures of the modified Koyck–Nerlove type as discussed in Liu (1963) and the investment functions are based on a "double" Koyck–Nerlove type of lags. The argument is that investment involves two steps: one involves planning and the other involves implementation of the plan.

12.6.1 Performance of the Model

With root mean square error (RMSE) defined as

$$\text{RMSE} = \frac{1}{T}\sum_{t} (F_t - A_t)^2 \tag{12.1}$$

where F_t and A_t are the estimated and actual values of the ith observation and T the number of observations, this criterion has been used as a measure of the forecasting efficiency of the Liu–Hwa model.[11] However, sometimes some var-

[11] See Liu (1969).

iants of it have been used, for example, ratios of RMSEs of different variables to their means, RMSEs for outside sample periods after correction made for the bias component estimated during the sample period.

The main features of the error statistics are as follows: first, some of the aggregate variables have RMSEs less than their components. Thus, there are mutually canceling or opposing errors of components. Second, in general the RMSEs increase with the prediction period. One reason for this is the cumulative prediction errors of lagged endogenous variables used extensively with the increase in the prediction period.

As for comparative predictive efficiency, it is found that the Wharton Mark III quarterly model possesses distinct predictive advantages in the short term. This is true with respect to the implicit price deflator, the unemployment rate, employee compensations, and consumption expenditure on automobiles in 1958 dollars. But the Liu–Hwa model has predicted better with respect to GNP in current and constant dollars, total consumption expenditures, nonfarm residential investment, plant and equipment investment, corporate profits, Moody's average domestic yield, and the 4–6 month commercial paper rate. Thus the monthly model seems to have better comparative advantage in short-run forecasting. But, fortunately, it may also be relatively accurate in longer term forecasting.[12]

12.7 THE TORONTO ANNUAL CANADIAN ECONOMETRIC MODEL OR THE TRACE MODEL

This is an econometric model of which the authors are Choudhry and others (1972). It utilizes primarily Canadian national accounts (annual) data from 1947 to 1966. The data go back to 1928 in the case of growth equations but then the "control period" 1941–1946 is excluded. The model basically ekes out dynamic paths for variables and relates them to policy variables, and is claimed by its authors to be the first Canadian public model providing ex-ante forecasts.

There are 67 stochastic equations and 120 identities in the model. Fifty-two of these 120 identities are essential, the rest involve intermediate variables. Fourteen equations involving predetermined variables are solved separately, but the remaining 53 equations are solved simultaneously. Thus the degree of simultaneity is high.

The method of estimation is 2SLS except in relation to the export and foreign exchange equations. Generally speaking, principal components of exogenous and endogenous variables are formed at the outset. Then, at the first stage, endogenous variables are regressed on principal components (see Appendix A.5 for definition), and, at the second stage, these are replaced by their calculated values. Exogenous variables that enter the regression in the first stage are not directly included in

[12] This point has been established by the authors of the model in comparison with the accuracies of other models, for example, the Bureau of Economic Analysis Model as reported by Hirsch (1973).

the second stage except, indirectly, through their principal components. The form of most equations is linear, that of others nonlinear. The nonlinear equations are estimated by the Newton and Seidel method.[13]

The large size of the model, in spite of its advantages, apparently obscures its basic structure. However, the model's authors present a relatively simple aggregate macroeconomic version of it in line with their concept of the working of the Canadian economy. While this prototype model is not estimated, it provides a basis for sectoral disaggregation of the actual model.

A great deal of simplification is achieved using a single price index. This is the implicit price of gross national product at market prices used as the deflator for all variables expressed in constant dollars. Other simplifications include aggregation of some expenditure groups, aggregation of all production sectors, neglect of corporate saving, and using a single interest rate and a single tax rate.

The general method is to obtain an aggregate demand and an aggregate supply relation. Prices and many predetermined and control variables are the arguments of the demand as well as the supply functions as obviously, from the identity of short-term demand and supply quantities, solutions for the yearly gross national product, its prices, and the values of other endogenous variables are obtained. Existence of lags in, for instance, the equation for capital formation and exogenous labor force growth causes shifts in both the demand and supply curves generating new output and price data in successive periods.

12.7.1 Notation and the Flow Chart of the Simplified Version

A lower case letter gives a quantity in constant dollars or in physical terms. Upper case letters give quantities in current dollars, price indices, or percentages. The following notation appears in Figure 12.1:

B	index of import prices
C	personal expenditure on consumer goods and services
E	foreign exchange rate
G, g	government expenditure on goods and services
GAP	utilization rate
H	foreign exchange reserves
i	business gross fixed capital formation
J	index of world prices of exports
k	stock of producers' capital goods (including housing) at the end of the year
s	stock of goods in inventories at the end of period

[13] See Evans and Klein (1968), pp. 39–49 for the solution procedure.

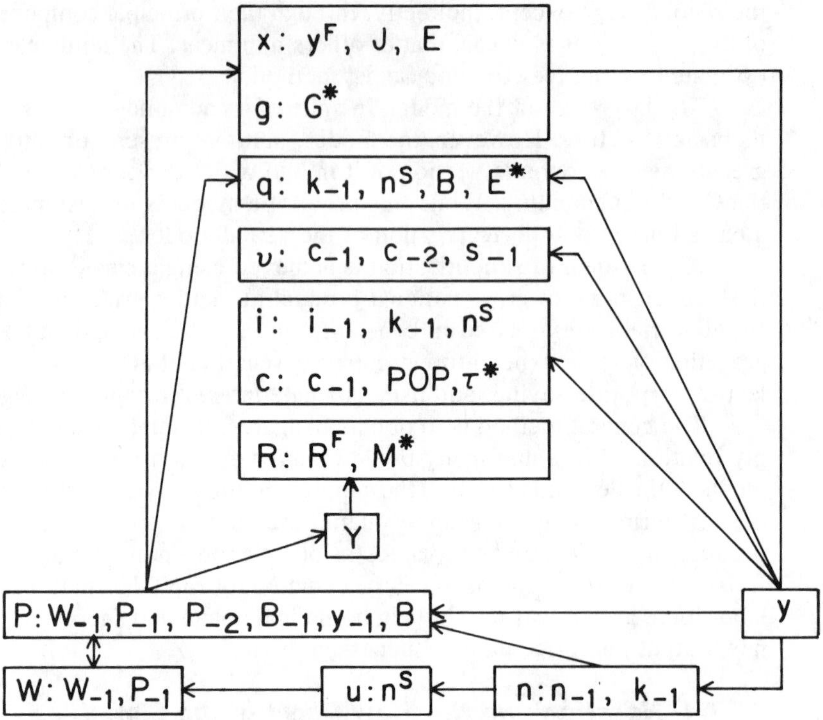

Figure 12.1 Flow chart for the simplified version of the TRACE model.*

M	stock of money at the end of the year
n	employment in man-hours per year
n^s	labor force in man-hours per year
P	implicit price index of gross national product (GNP)
POP	population
q	imports of goods and services
R	rate of interest
R^F	rate of interest in the rest of the world
U	unemployment rate
v	value of the physical change in inventories
W	Wage rate
x	exports of goods and services

* Figures 12.1 and 12.2 reprinted with permission N. K. Choudhry, Y. Kotowitz, J. A. Sawyer and J. W. L. Winder, *The TRACE Econometric Model of the Canadian Economy* (1972) p. 13.

Y, y gross national product (GNP) at market prices

Y^F an index of GNP in the rest of the world

τ rate of taxation

Figure 12.1 brings out the underlying simultaneity of relationships in the simplified version of the TRACE model.

In Figure 12.1 variables to the left of the colon in any box or appearing simply in a box are current endogenous. Starred variables are policy variables, and variables with subscripts are predetermined. All other variables are current endogenous. In the floating exchange rate period of 1950–1961, E takes the place of E^* explained and linked as follows:

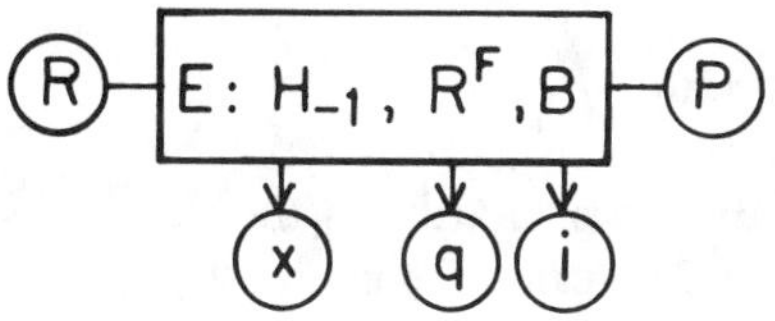

(12.2)

12.7.2 Disaggregation

Within the general philosophy of the simplified version, the level of disaggregation followed is fairly standard. For instance, consumption as well as private fixed investment are split three ways, but, without any apparent reason, there are 24 equations kept for the quantities and prices of exports of goods. The extensive break down of exports, by commodity and destination, implies a disproportionate emphasis on this kind of activity, probably of use to businessmen in export forecasting.

The business sector is structured in a fairly standard fashion. Business output is determined by demand, given the prices. Business employment and investment are set up in the form of differences from their desired levels allowing for distributed lag adjustments. As mentioned before, the desired stock is construed as the ratio of current output to potential output. The latter output is estimated from a Cobb–Douglas production function in which potential employment and actual capital (including the stock of dwellings) are the inputs.[14]

The financial and government sectors are of small scope in the model. The

[14] As Helliwell (1972), p. 462 observes: "It is slightly disturbing that there are several separate production functions for nonagricultural business output". First, there is a Cobb–Douglas function to estimate output directly; second, there is a Cobb–Douglas function implicit in the employment equation; third, there is a similar function underlying the price of business output; and fourth, there are two CES functions behind the business fixed investment equations. These last two functions differ from each other in the elasticities of substitution, which are very small in the first place. Reprinted with permission J. F. Helliwell Book review of *The TRACE Model of the Canadian Economy, Canadian Journal of Economics*, 5(1972).

only financial variables provided for are the Treasury Bill rates and long-term government interest rates, apart from the mortgage rates. The importance of the government sector is reduced by the treatment, as stated already, of all government expenditures as exogenous. But government revenues are accounted for by three tax equations.

In the balance of payments sectors, two long-term capital flow equations, one in U.S. direct investment in Canada and the other in net U.S. portfolio purchases of Canadian securities, and an equation in the exchange rate are tagged on to several equations for trade in goods and services. Changes in official foreign exchange reserves are exogenously determined and thus short-term capital flows are given. Such flows are obtained as the remainder items in the balance of payments identity.[15]

12.7.3 Forecasts

These forecasts appear primarily as the year-by-year solutions (over the period 1957–1966) of different series obtained by substituting actual values of exogenous and lagged endogenous variables of a given year. These solutions are then compared with their actual values yielding the errors. Out of 45 series shown, only 8 forecast badly, some with small and others with large errors. These 8 series are real and current business nonagricultural gross investment in machinery and equipment, real and current business nonagricultural gross investment in nonresidential construction, U.S. direct investment in Canada, net long-term capital movement in securities (including outstanding securities) between Canada and the United States, and real and current business gross fixed capital formation in new nonresidential construction and machinery and equipment. There is also a tendency, common to many models, for errors in the same direction to continue for several years in extended simulations.

Of the years for which forecasts are made, the years 1957, 1960, and 1964 are chosen to capture different cyclical points and exchange rates. For instance, 1957 is the year of low unemployment and flexible exchange rates; 1960 is instead one of high unemployment but flexible exchange rates, whereas 1964 is one of low unemployment but fixed exchange rates. Among the more important variables forecasted, the following receive a closer scrutiny: unemployment rate, implicit price index of gross national expenditure at market price, and real gross national

[15] As Helliwell (1972), p. 462 points out, "This framework is suitable only during the flexible exchange rate regime. From 1961, both the exchange rate and the level of foreign exchange reserves are exogenous policy variables, implying powers verging on the occult for the exchange authorities. In more practical terms, the change in reserves and the exchange rate can only be exogenous in simulations if monetary policy (or some other policy with substantial leverage on trade or capital flows) is made endogenous. TRACE 69 allows any induced deficit in the basic balance to accumulate in the form of private short-term liabilities, without there being any reason for private lenders to perform willingly in this manner."

expenditure at market price and its various components. These components are: real personal expenditure, new residential construction expenditure in constant 1957 dollars, real business gross fixed capital formation in new nonresidential construction (machinery and equipment), real value of physical change in inventories, real total exports of goods and services, and imports of goods and services in constant 1957 dollars.

The forecasts for real GNE at market prices are quite accurate except for the years 1958 and 1962. There is an over-prediction for these years that runs between 2 to 2.5% while, as a result of the U.S. recession, there should have been an under-prediction. Remember that the conversion loan of 1958 causes so much uncertainty that the demand for liquidity increases, but the TRACE model can not reflect that due to weak monetary real linkage. Also, the years 1962–1963 are years of financial crisis and austerity, and there is perhaps no reason for optimistic prediction.

The forecasts for unemployment, implicit price index for GNE and the components of real GNE are quite close in 1957. However, there are substantial but offsetting errors from the GNE components. For instance, real business gross fixed capital formation in new nonresidential construction and imports are underestimated, while new residential construction expenditures are overestimated. The model does not succeed in reflecting prevailing boom conditions in the equations for investment in residential construction and imports. Between 1958 and 1964, there is a varying history of the prediction of the different series.

Regarding turning points for real residential construction and unemployment rate, the turning points in residential construction of 1959, 1961, and 1966 are correctly forecasted. But there is a false signal for a turning point in 1962. For unemployment rate, turning points of 1959, 1960 and 1962 are correctly forecasted, but 1963 produces a false signal.

While the above are ex-post forecasts, there are also some ex-ante forecasts made for only one year, 1970. There have been some great problems due to lack of data, and unusual labor strike conditions in 1969. On the whole, the results indicate mixed performance.

12.8 THE RDX2 MODEL OF THE CANADIAN ECONOMY

This is both a short and a medium term simulation model of the Canadian economy constructed and administered by the Bank of Canada. The original model has gone through several revisions until it recently transformed into what is known as the RDXF model used exclusively for forecasting purposes. These revisions including the RDXF model will be briefly considered later. Below we present the essentials of the original RDX2 model as based on Helliwell and others (1971).

The structure of RDX2 is conspicuously comprehensive with respect to the government and monetary sectors. Also international trade and capital flow relationships are elaborate. For, one of the purposes of the model is to link it with the MPS model[16] of the United States, which is comprehensive in all such respects.

It begins with the building of the supply price of capital as an outgrowth of the measurement of current market values for components of domestic net worth including business capital stock, government debt, dwellings, and consumer durables. This price influences capital expenditure, international capital movement, and savings behavior. Since it is determined both in real and in nominal terms, it provides a way of measuring the expected rate of increase in consumer prices.

Demands, in the model, are structuralized demands for buildings, machinery and equipment, and labor services. A synthetic production function underlies the factor demands, which leads to some new measures of aggregate supply, demand, capacity utilization, and short-term changes in productivity. These measures, in their turn, are important in the equations for prices and foreign trade. The factor demand model also provides a trend measure of efficiency which is a very important consideration for the determination of business real wage.

One distinguishing feature of the model is to specify a model of an expenditure and portfolio allocation which depends upon varying rates of growth of income and wealth. In it, international capital flows are a function of the growth in domestic and foreign portfolios and the level of existing proportions of and rates of returns. This implies that the nonfinancial sector demand for liquid assets is a function of the growth of total portfolio of such assets. Flow of fund accounting is applied as divided into federal, provincial, and municipal government sectors so that here as well the connection between the stock and flow equilibrium is specified. The main wage and price equations are specified such as to allow for reasonable (equilibrium) levels and rates of change in these variables.

Although equilibrium levels are emphasized, they do not sacrifice disequilibrium tendencies. These are provided for through the disequilibrium adjustment mechanisms. The new adjustment process is characterized by a ratio of aggregate demand and supply imbalance, and a measure of credit availability depending on the ratio of chartered bank (earning) liquid assets to total assets. The difference between this last variable and its target value has significant impacts on bank loans, international capital movements, and domestic expenditure.

12.8.1 Private Aggregate Demand

Under this, there are four sectors: consumer expenditure, residential construction, investment and output, and foreign trade. The activities underlying these sectors are reflected in 34 equations and 25 technical relations.

[16] The name MPS stands for *M*IT, *P*ennsylvania, and the *S*ocial Science Research Council. For details of this model, see Rasche and Shapiro (1968), deLeeuw and Gramlich (1968 and 1969), Ando and others (1972), Ando (1974), and Ando and Modigliani (1969).

Sector 1 variables are expected wage income, expected nonwage income, rate of return on savings, and capital gains and losses on equities and government debts. There are two equations in this sector, one for expenditure on motor vehicles and parts, and the other for expenditure on all other consumer durables. These are based on the stock adjustment model with the desired stock set proportional to relative prices, wage income, and nonwage income.

Sector 2 (on residential construction) divides dwellings between single detached and multiple dwellings before these appear in the equations for housing starts and stocks. There is a separate equation for investment in residential construction.

Sector 3 (on business fixed investment) shows a flexible accelerator and cost minimizing behavior, the latter obtained from a production function, vintage measures of capital intensity, expected output, and expected prices of capital and labor services.

Price of capital services depends on tax rates, supply price of capital, and expected price of capital and of capital goods. The production function includes inputs such as stocks of machinery and equipment and nonresidential construction, among other things. Demand for labor is derived from this production function using the assumption of Harrod neutral technical progress (see our Chapter 9).

For the inventory investment equation, three variables defined as follows are important:

UGPPS a measure of current supply of private nonfarm business output

UGPPD a measure of desired output based on labor supply rather than current level of employment

IIB inventory demand

X unintended inventory accumulation or decumulation

Inventory investment is made up of intended and unintended investment. Intended investment is based on expected sales, and unintended investment on the difference between gross private business product (UGPPS) and noninventory investment demand. Viewing X to be the unintended inventory accumulation or decumulation, which is the product of the coefficient of unintended investment in the investment equation and inventory investment, UGPPS may be adjusted for the unintended inventory change as follows:

$$\text{UGPPA} = \text{UGPPS} - \text{X} \tag{12.3}$$

Thus the index of imbalance between aggregate demand and supply defined as UGPPA/UGPPD becomes the driving variable in the equation for business fixed investment.

Sector 4 has 31 equations or relations. Nine of them explain imports and exports disaggregated into commodities and regions, thirteen explain services divided according to the United States and other areas, and nine explain aggregate trade flows. The major explanatory variables taken are economic activity (domestic or foreign), relative prices, capacity utilization rates (domestic and foreign), and qualitative variables for special circumstances. The variable of economic activity is measured by the weighted sum of components of domestic final demand, where weights are the input–output coefficients reflecting import contents suitable for the SITC (Standard Industrial Trade) classification.

12.8.2 Private Sector Employment and Wages, Prices, and Income Distribution

Under this heading, there are four sectors, sector 5 to sector 8. The first gives equations for employment and hours in the private sector, the second gives equations for wages in the same sector, the third gives, in all, 23 price equations, and the last the equations for profits and dividends.

In sector 5, employment in mining, manufacturing, and other businesses is based on a distributed lag adjustment towards desired labor input obtained from the production function. Desired labor input in relation to the actual capital stock leads to output which is the same as demand. Then differences in actual weekly hours and normal hours are determined using differences between actual and desired employment, all of which implies the adjustment mechanism referred to before.

In sector 6, no long-run trade-off between unemployment and rate of increase in business wage rate is provided for. In mining, manufacturing and other businesses, wage rate (in the form of proportionate money wage) is a function of an equilibrium real wage determined by labor efficiency, rate of unemployment (found insignificant in effect), and expected inflation in consumer prices. In construction, wage rate (in the form of percentage change) is a function of unemployment rate and expected rate of increase in consumer prices.

Sector 7 contains equations of prices. Price of investment, considered as currently weighted aggregate deflator, depends on manufacturer's sales tax, labor and material costs, capacity utilization, prices of forest products in export markets, and U.S. prices. U.S. prices especially apply to investment in machinery and equipment because of the high import content of these products and the practice of pricing domestic output to match the landed price of imported substitutes. Price of consumption (based on the weighted aggregate of consumer's price indices) is a function of labor costs, import prices, short-term productivity, capacity utilization, retail sales, and taxes. Import prices depend on foreign price deflators and foreign exchange rates, among other things, and export prices depend on world export prices, U.S. private nonfarm output deflator, and a weighted average of Canadian aggregate demand deflators. The weights of these deflators are the commodity composition of Canadian exports.

12.8.3 Operations of the Government

Sections 9–14 relate to the government activities. In sections 9–13 there are equations for direct taxes, indirect taxes and other government revenues and transfer payments to persons. These are broken down into the three levels of government: federal, provincial, and municipal.

The novelty of the model is to treat certain types of government expenditures as endogenous to find out how much of their variations are dictated by demand for government services.

Section 14 links current expenditures and revenues of the government to changes in foreign exchange reserves, government cash balances, and government debts.

12.8.4 The Financial Sector

Sections 15–18 are concerned with the demand function of liquid asset holdings of the private domestic nonfinancial sector. Nine asset groups are kept including deposits in chartered banks, deposits in nonbank institutions, and government debts. Section 16 especially has equations determining the (earning) liquid asset ratio used in the measure of credit availability. Section 17 has the interest rate equations. One rate is on the short-term Government of Canada bond rate explained by central bank reaction functions. Then there are the rates on deposits, mortgages and three additional maturity classes of government debts. Section 18 jointly determines the value of business capital stock, supply price of capital, and expected annual rate of change in the Consumers Price Index.

12.8.5 International Capital Flows and Foreign Exchange Market

Section 19 has 13 equations for long-term capital. The assumption is that direct investment decisions are taken jointly with decisions to make capital expenditures in the borrowing country. New issues of Canadian bonds sold to U.S. residents depend on borrowing requirement and ease of floating bonds in Canada. All other flows depend primarily on the differentials in interest rates and the composition of the lender's portfolio.

Section 20 has equations that cumulate capital flows into assets and liabilities shown as claims on the Canadian government, and other equations based on industry securities and bonds held by U.S. residents and other foreign residents.

The Canadian holdings of foreign securities are deducted from the balance of payments identity.

Section 21 determines the exchange rate from the market sharing conditions. Here the private demand for foreign exchange is based on the stock adjustment model. According to this, special attention is placed on lagged response to balance of trade and long-term capital flows, the covered interest rate differentials between Canadian net short-term rate and a weighted average of U.S. domestic and Eurodollar interest rates, the accumulated stock of Canadian net short-term liabilities to foreigners, and a special variable representing the speculative pressures on the Canadian dollar in 1968. On the other hand, official demand for foreign exchange is taken to depend on the policy to support the exchange rate between two established support points and a second exchange rate variable. This variable implies greater willingness to sell foreign exchange when the price is above par than to buy it when the price is below par. Other variables include a trading strategy variable and the difference between target and actual reserves at the beginning of the quarter.

In the forward exchange market, the price of forward foreign exchange is taken to depend on the balance of trade and capital flows, interest rate differentials, a speculative variable, and net changes in the forward liabilities of foreign exchange authorities. The remaining equations are for short-term capital flows.

12.8.6 Recent Revisions in the RDX2 Model

In two technical reports, *Bank of Canada Technical Report*, **5** (1976) and **6** (1977), updated data—up to 1972IV—are used to reestimate (Report 5) the RDX2 model. The Canadian federal tax structure is especially modified to reflect federal tax reform and indexing of personal income. Since the economy is under flexible exchange rates at this time, a greater role is assigned to foreign prices and domestic supply constraints as determinants of Canadian imports and prices. In addition, the financial sector is considerably revised. Also partial simulations are undertaken (Report 6) to unfold the sectional dynamics of the Canadian economy on the basis of the revised model. In another technical report, *Bank of Canada Technical Report*, **13** (1978), the response of the revised RDX2 model to a fiscal surprise is studied. That surprise consists of a permanent increase in the level of federal government nonwage expenditure under various monetary and exchange rate scenarios.

But in 1980, as the *Bank of Canada Technical Reports* **25** and **26** indicate, the RDX2 model has lost its specific existence and a new model RDXF has come to take its place even though still "based on the foundations of the Bank's RDX2 model". Its objective is to produce short-term forecasts of the Canadian economy. But perhaps more importantly, it provides an analysis of the dynamic properties of the model equations. In general, the emphasis of the model is on the supply side.

12.9 POLICY APPRAISAL BY ECONOMETRIC MODELS

Economic policy usually addresses a given socioeconomic problem with a view to attaining a stated target or objective. For a given target there may be more than one policy possible. The usual recourse in cases like this is to consider policy alternatives whose effects may be determined within the specifications of an econometric model. These effects are simulated effects, often laying down a series of dynamic paths of important or relevant variables. Each of these paths depends on a given choice of policy. When all such paths are assembled, we come to appreciate not only the possible effects of different policy measures, but also how sensitive the economic system is to these policy alternatives. Measures used for this purpose are usually multipliers and/or elasticities as the Klein (1971) and Eckstein (1976) studies have used trying to forecast and evaluate policies about the U.S. economy based on econometric models. Notice that these simulated results need indicate not only the direct and immediate effects of rival policies, but also, depending on the size and comprehensiveness of the econometric model used, indirect effects in related areas as well as long-term effects.

We have cited numerous applied econometric studies before some of which may be used as examples to illustrate the above points. Note also that in the middle and late 1970s when the price of energy resources was ever shooting up, the simulation of effects of alternative energy policies gained a great deal of momentum. We refer the reader to two particular studies, MacAvoy and Pindyck (1975) and Jorgenson (1976), concerned with problems of this sort. In these and other studies, analysts have almost customarily considered the following policy options: taxes on energy use, trade duties, controls on price and quantity of consumption, and exploring new energy reserves and sources. However, the decade of the 1980s has seen a complete reversal in the energy price trends of the 1970s. Perhaps this has contributed to a decline in the number of simulation studies on energy policies that were so fashionable in the 1970s.

But all this enthusiasm about simulation and forecasting studies used to determine the relative efficacy of alternative policy options gets dampened when we peruse Lucas' critique of policy appraisal. To this we turn next.

12.10 THE LUCAS CRITIQUE OF ECONOMETRIC POLICY APPRAISAL

It is commonly believed that the recommendations of macroeconomic policy advisers have one presumption, that is, the structure or the model of the economy remains constant. In other words they assume that the economic model structure is policy invariant. If so, one can use the same model, however estimated, to evaluate the effects of any number of policy changes.

However, Lucas (1976), for one, believes the opposite. He believes that the assumption of constant structure is seriously flawed. If expectations are rationally made, he argues, the structure of the economy will depend, inter alia, on what policies the authorities follow. Anticipations of any change in policy will lead to the adjustment in actions of rational economic agents. The result will be a new structure of the economy turning up. Thus, the structure of the economy cannot be policy invariant and consequently the normal practice of policy evaluation is seriously in error.

Let us illustrate the problem with an investment model of two equations. In these equations, I_t is investment expenditure at time t, i_t is interest rate at time t, X and W are other explanatory variables, $E_{t-1}i_t$ is the expectation of i done at time $t - 1$ to apply to time t, γs and βs are coefficients and μ_t and ϵ_t are random errors with their means equal to zero:

$$i_t = \gamma_0 + \gamma_1 i_{t-1} + \gamma_2 X_{t-1} + \gamma_3 W_{t-1} + \mu_t \tag{12.4}$$

$$I_t = \beta_0 + \beta_1 \mathrm{E}_{t-1} i_t + \epsilon_t \tag{12.5}$$

An alternative to (12.5) is (12.6), using the value under the rational expectations[17] hypothesis of $\mathrm{E}_{t-1}i_t$ equal to $\gamma_0 + \gamma_1 i_{t-1} + \gamma_2 X_{t-1} + \gamma_3 W_{t-1}$ via (12.4):

$$I_t = \beta_0 + \beta_1\gamma_0 + \beta_1\gamma_1 i_{t-1} + \beta_1\gamma_2 X_{t-1} + \beta_1\gamma_3 W_{t-1} + \epsilon_t \tag{12.6}$$

An econometric analyst, unaware of the structure which leads to (12.6), might incidentally set up an equation with the same variables as of (12.6) in a form such as:

$$I_t = \theta_0 + \theta_1 i_{t-1} + \theta_2 X_{t-1} + \theta_3 W_{t-1} + \epsilon_t \tag{12.7}$$

where the θs are the coefficients, and he might even find a good fit.

Suppose now he would use his estimated equation (12.7) for the evaluation of a policy change. Now (12.7), without rational expectations being used, must mean a nonrational expectations model of investment. Should he use (12.7) as a basis of policy appraisal and recommendation, the nonrational expectations model cannot survive, whereas the rational expectations model will.

The reason is as follows. Suppose the analyst's advice is to change the value of the coefficient γ_2 that links i_t to X_{t-1}. To be specific, suppose that he wants γ_2 to change to γ_4, which, he thinks, will bring about a desirable change in investment. The effect of this is to change θ_2, which is the coefficient of X_{t-1} in his equation (12.7). For θ_2, as far as our rational expectations model theorizes quite beyond his knowledge, is γ_2 times β_1, and if γ_2 will change, $\gamma_2\beta_1$ must change as well. But he assumes that this is not so, and the structure of the economy is still the same as before. But is it? The answer is no!

Examples like the above abound. Lucas' point seems to be very well taken. If the policy regime changes, Lucas says, rationality of economic agents must

[17] See Section 12.11–12.13.1 for more on rational expectations.

mean a reorganization of economic activities. This will mean in turn that what was considered to be a constant structure must change. To ignore this reality in the basis of policy recommendation can possibly lead to seriously flawed policies.

The above critique is a sad commentary on the use of econometric models with unchanged coefficients in the evaluation of alternative policy options or proposals. Some debate has since ensued on its pros and cons but there does not seem to be any profound theoretical position against it. The moral of all this seems to be that one should be really cautious while using econometric models for conventional policy appraisals.

12.11 RATIONAL EXPECTATIONS MODELS AND SOME ECONOMETRIC ISSUES AND IMPLICATIONS

12.11.1 Expectations in Macroeconomics

It is difficult to conceive of a macroeconomic model without some of its relations based on expectation variables. Who has heard about a realistic macroconsumption function, or a macroinvestment function without there being even a slight dependence of the function on expected prices or expected interest rates? Doesn't a recent advance in macromonetary economics center around the contention that changes in the quantity of money influence real output only if they are unexpected? For the expected changes in the quantity of money, according to the proponents of this kind of theory, affect only the level of prices.

One important question about the foregoing is how expectations are formed. Depending on how one answers this question, the nature and implications of the economic system, as amply varied as they are, will be defined. However, we will discuss only one model of expectations and its implications. This model is the model of rational expectations.

But first we will present a few illustrations of expectations in economics. In particular, we consider two examples, one from the post-Keynesian theory of the consumption function based on the permanent income hypothesis, and the other based on the natural rate of unemployment hypothesis, both due to Friedman (1957 and 1968).

In the permanent income hypothesis, the idea is simply that a consumer determines his consumption expenditure based not on his current income but on a long-term view of his earnings expectations. The implication of this is that his current consumption need not be low or high simply because his current income is low or high, but nevertheless it could be high or low because the income projected from his long-run expectation of future earnings, the so-called permanent income stream, is high or low. The expectation variable here is obviously the expected or permanent income. This kind of expectation plays an important role in policy matters. For, if the government wanted to stimulate the economy, one natural way to do so would be to increase its expenditure. The increase in government expenditure would increase actual national income, which would stimulate further expansions in expenditures, by the Keynesian multiplier theory of consumption related to actual income. But all of this would result if and only if actual, rather than permanent, income would affect consumption. However, if this government expenditure will not affect people's expected income, but the latter is important in their consumption decision, this sort of government policy will be ineffective in bringing about the change.

Let us now look into the other example which is about the natural (unemployment) rate hypothesis. The essence of this hypothesis is that workers use as a decision variable not the nominal wage rate, *W*, but the real wage rate, *W/P*, where *P* stands for the general price level. The problem is that while current prices, being readily observable, could be correctly built into current wage demands, the effect of future prices, being themselves unseen and perhaps unpredictable, will be hard to measure and account for. Such effects will depend on the workers' own perceptions or expectations as to how future prices will be. Naturally this will have serious implications for certain government policy initiatives. To appreciate this, consider the following. Suppose there is an increase in the aggregate spending of the government which goes on to increase prices. Firms may then be prompted to expand production for which they need more labor. Suppose also that they stand ready to raise wages. If workers relate the rise in wages to the expected rise in prices, and perceive that the real wage is still going to rise, they will probably be pleased to offer more services. Government's expansionary policy will in this case stimulate employment. But what if they expect that the real wage will either not change, or even fall? They will simply stay put, and employment will not rise at all. In this case, there is an increase in aggregate expenditure, but not an increase in employment! This, once again, shows how the success of a government policy depends crucially on how people expect.

12.11.2 Rational Expectations

Economic agents are usually known or assumed to act rationally. Thus when the question arises as to how to form forecasts on a variable, the sensible course to follow is to utilize all the available information regarding the process which determines that variable.

An example will make the problem clear. Suppose repeated observations on the process leading to the variable *Y* make one believe that last period's *Y*, as well as last period's values of certain other variables, say, *X* and *W*, are enough to determine *Y* presently. That is,

$$Y_t = \beta_0 + \beta_1 Y_{t-1} + \beta_2 X_{t-1} + \beta_3 W_{t-1} + \mu_t \tag{12.8}$$

where t is the time subscript, μ_t is a random error and the βs are the coefficients. It is possible that the values of these coefficients will be completely known through experience. Suppose now that an investigator, while at the period $t - 1$, is interested in obtaining an expectation on Y to apply to the period t. If the basis of his expectation would be the process defined by equation (12.8), then that equation plus all information available on Y, X, and W at the end of period $t - 1$ would be part of his total information set. The expected value of Y, following the principle of rational expectations, will be:

$$\mathrm{E}_{t-1}Y_t = \beta_0 + \beta_1 Y_{t-1} + \beta_2 X_{t-1} + \beta_3 W_{t-1} + \mathrm{E}_{t-1}\,\mu_t \tag{12.9}$$

where $\mathrm{E}_{t-1}Y_t$ and $\mathrm{E}_{t-1}\mu_t$ imply expectations on Y and μ at time period t done on the basis of all information available at the preceding time period. Another way of expressing them would be by the symbols $\mathrm{E}(Y_t/I_{t-1})$ and $\mathrm{E}(\mu_t/I_{t-1})$, where E stands for mathematical expectation, and I_{t-1} is the information set at period $t - 1$. In what follows we shall use both symbolic expressions synonymously.

So far we have been quiet on the random error μ_t. This may be both positive and negative. However, it is customary to believe this to be a variable with a probability distribution of its own whose mean value is zero and which has a finite and constant variance σ^2_μ. The best guess for $\mathrm{E}_{t-1}\mu_t$ that one could use would be the mean value of μ_t, which is zero, based on the information set of period $t - 1$. This is why, we have $E_{t-1}Y_t$ reduced finally to

$$\mathrm{E}_{t-1}Y_t = \beta_0 + \beta_1 Y_{t-1} + \beta_2 X_{t-1} + \beta_3 W_{t-1} \tag{12.10}$$

The difference between (12.8) and (12.10) presents an algebraic expression for the error of expectations:

$$Y_t - \mathrm{E}_{t-1}Y_t = \mu_t \tag{12.11}$$

Before we go on to discuss some econometric issues following from rational expectations, let us note that the concept itself is an equilibrium concept. It is so because expectations are based on processes which occur fairly frequently to have given rise to a trend. Thus, the vehicle of rational expectations may eventually take us to the state of full equilibrium.

There are three prominent characteristics of the errors of rational expectations: (1) their mean value is zero, (2) they do not exhibit any pattern, such as the pattern of serial correlation, and (3) their variance is at least as low as that under any other method of making expectations. Since expectations run through the entire spectrum of macroeconomics, rational expectations will have a great deal of appeal to various problems in this area. This will have obvious implications for government policies which are designed to attack those problems. Whether the method of rational expectations is good or not, it can be tested by its results in comparison with the actual data, and there are various such tests available today on the subject.

12.12 RATIONAL EXPECTATIONS AND SOME ECONOMETRIC ISSUES

Tests of rational expectations are usually tests of restrictions. This is because economic theory, as argued before, is often based on expectations. If rational expectations are used as a model of that expectation, economic theory, on the whole, implies constraints on what we could expect to see in the actual world. Thus the truth of rational expectations can be tested by the validity of those constraints. This explains the origin of many tests of restrictions in the recent literature on rational expectations. And out of these tests has arisen an important issue as to whether the tests themselves are well conceived and designed.

Also, another important issue exists. This concerns the usual practices of building and estimating macroeconomic models and projecting the effects of various economic policies based on them. The problem is that when policies change, the information set changes and therefore a rational expectations hypothesis requires a reworking and reestimation of the macromodel itself. But as is well known, the usual practice is to implicitly assume that the model structure did not change. Thus, the evaluation of alternative or different policies based on a constant and unchanging model structure is likely to give erroneous conclusions.

12.13 DIRECT TESTS OF THE RATIONAL EXPECTATIONS HYPOTHESIS (REH)

We begin by considering test procedures utilizing observations on people's expectations that are available from sample surveys.

Suppose our problem requires data on the future values of exchange rates. Let the spot exchange rates and expected exchange rates be denoted by the symbols e_t and $E_{t-1}e_t$, where data are recorded in quarters such that t is the current quarter, $t - 1$ is the preceding quarter, and so on. Then two basic properties of rational expectations are that the random prediction error μ_t given by the difference between the actual spot and future expected exchange rates

$$e_t - E_{t-1}e_t = \mu_t \tag{12.12}$$

will be serially uncorrelated and will have a mean value of zero. Since μ_t and μ_{t-1}, for example, are uncorrelated, this must mean that μ_t, based on the information set I_{t-1} at time $t - 1$, will not be affected by μ_{t-1}, which is based on the information set I_{t-2} at the preceding time point $t - 2$, and so on for earlier periods.

If $E_{t-1}e_t$ is reasonably observable, as when three month forward exchange rates, for instance, are used as their closest approximations, then it will be possible to estimate a regression relation such as

$$e_t = \beta_0 + \beta_1 E_{t-1}e_t + \epsilon_t \tag{12.13}$$

where the βs are the coefficients, ϵ an error with mean zero, and $E_{t-1}e_t$ is proxied by three month forward rates. A weak test of the rational expectations hypothesis should meet two criteria. First, the joint null hypothesis:

$$H_0: \beta_0 = 0 \qquad \beta_1 = 1$$

should come out insignificant at an acceptable probability level of significance; and, second, the error term ϵ_t should come out serially uncorrelated (by, for example, the Durbin–Watson test). The first criterion is said to define the unbiasedness property of the test.

There is a strong test of the REH, however, based on what is known as the efficiency property of the hypothesis. This derives from the following premise. Under rational expectations, the expected values of a variable are determined by the same process as that of the variable itself and this process should include all of its past history. In symbols, e_t and $E_{t-1}e_t$ are

$$e_t = \gamma_1 e_{t-1} + \gamma_2 e_{t-2} + \cdots + \gamma_l e_{t-l} + \mu_{1t} \tag{12.14}$$

$$E_{t-1}e_t = \delta_1 e_{t-1} + \delta_2 e_{t-2} + \cdots + \gamma_l e_{t-l} + \mu_{2t} \tag{12.15}$$

where we have gone so far as to include l periods into the history of the variable e counting from the present time t, the γs and δs are coefficients, and μ_{1t} and μ_{2t} are the respective random error terms of the relations.

Assume in (12.15) that three month forward exchange rates are used as the closest proxy for the expected exchange rates. Then (12.14) and (12.15) would, between them, produce approximately equal estimated coefficients for the same variable in large samples under rational expectations. A sense of this may be obtained by noting the difference between (12.14) and (12.15), which becomes

$$e_t - E_{t-1}e_t = (\gamma_1 - \delta_1)e_{t-1} + (\gamma_2 - \delta_2)e_{t-2} + \cdots + (\gamma_l - \delta_l)e_{t-l} + \mu_{1t} - \mu_{2t} \tag{12.16}$$

By comparing this with equation (12.12), we see that since the left-hand side of (12.16) should equal an error term, that will come about only if

$$\gamma_i = \delta_i \qquad i = 1, 2, \ldots, l$$

It then becomes obvious that the prediction error $e_t - E_{t-1}e_t$ will not depend on any lagged values of the exchange rate, it will depend on purely random error terms.

Direct tests of the REH are often marred by the relative unavailability of data on the expected variable values. Where such data were available or could be generated reasonably well, some attempts were made to test the REH. Unfortunately, no clear signal has come out of these tests, performed by various authors, for or against the hypothesis.

Turnovsky (1980) tries to test the unbiasedness property of the REH using

U.S. data over the period of 1954 to 1969. These data are collected from a survey of business economists and reflect their predictions[18] of various economic variables. He finds, for instance, for the variable of consumers price index refutation of the REH over the period from 1954 to 1964, but confirmation for the period from 1962 to 1969. Other authors, for example, Pesando (1975), Carlson (1977), Pearce (1979), and Figlewski and Wachtel (1981), also use the same data set, and derive equally mixed inferences.

Friedman (1980) carries out tests using data on interest rate expectations obtained from a group of money market practitioners. The test results, though, do not provide any appreciable support for the REH.

Some economists may, somewhat reasonably, criticize the method of collecting or generating the data on the expected values of variables, before casting doubts on the REH itself. However, one could get around the problem underlying this criticism by taking recourse to what seems to be a very valid alternative approach. This would consist of building the REH into a model and then seeing whether the predictions from it are carried out in the real world. Thus this approach would avoid having to use direct observations on expected variables and would still enable a test of the rationality of expectations from the overall model.

12.13.1 Equating Rationally Expected Variable Values to Their Actual Values

This point can be illustrated by taking a simple example.[19] Suppose that investment expenditure in period t, I_t, depends on what investors in period $t - 1$ expect the interest rate to be in period t, in other words, $E_{t-1}i_t$:

$$I_t = \beta_0 + \beta_1 E_{t-1}i_t + \epsilon_t \tag{12.17}$$

β_0 is the constant of the investment function, β_1 a measure of the marginal sensitivity of investment expenditure to the expected interest rate, and ϵ the disturbance term. Suppose that we want to estimate β_1. By the rationality of expectations, we equate actual interest rate to the expected interest rate plus a random error μ_t:

$$i_t = E_{t-1}i_t + \mu_t \tag{12.18}$$

Substituting for $E_{t-1}i_t$ from (12.18) into (12.17) yields

$$I_t = \beta_0 + \beta_1 i_t + \epsilon_t - \beta_1 \mu_t \tag{12.19}$$

which becomes, after equating $\epsilon_t - \beta_1 \mu_t$ to ν_t:

$$I_t = \beta_0 + \beta_1 i_t + \nu_t \tag{12.20}$$

The problem of estimating β_1 from (12.20) is that i_t, which from (12.18) is cor-

[18] These are six months and one year ahead predictions.

[19] We have already used this example in Section 12.10.

related with μ_t, is correlated with ν_t since ν_t includes μ_t. Thus the OLS estimate of β_1 will be biased for β_1, even asymptotically.

Assume that we have applied the OLS method to the estimation of β_1 of (12.20). Then its estimate $\hat{\beta}_1$ is given by:[20]

$$\hat{\beta}_1 = \beta_1 - \left[\frac{\beta_1 V(\mu)}{V(i)}\right]$$

where $V(\mu)$ and $V(i)$ are the variances of μ and i, respectively. It is clear that $\hat{\beta}_1$ will be equal to β_1 if $V(\mu)$ is zero, which means the actual interest rate is the same as the expected interest rate. On the other hand, if the actual interest rate is perfectly inaccurate for the expected interest rate so that variations in i_t are completely transmitted to variations in μ_t, not to $E_{t-1}e_t$, that is, $V(\mu)$ and $V(i)$ are the same, then $\hat{\beta}_1 = 0$. This range, 0 to β_1, of values of $\hat{\beta}_1$ is caused by the mixed type of the error term of (12.20), and an exact value of β_1 will crucially depend on the values of $V(\mu)$ used, given that the sample will provide an acceptable value for $V(i)$.

Alternatively, one could use an instrumental variable for i_t, which would be uncorrelated with μ_t (and so ν_t) and use the IV method for obtaining an asymptotically unbiased estimate of β_1.

Let us now illustrate the method of building rational expectations into the economic model. This will be done by exploiting the processes that generate the variables and their expectations. We begin by reconsidering the investment function example where interest rate is conceived now of being driven by a process of the form

$$i_t = \gamma_0 + \gamma_1 i_{t-1} + \gamma_2 X_{t-1} + \gamma_3 W_{t-1} + \mu_t \tag{12.21}$$

where X and W are important determining variables for i_t, and the γs are coefficients. For instance, X might stand for the inflation rate, and W for the exchange rate.

Under rational expectations, we have

$$E_{t-1}i_t = \gamma_0 + \gamma_1 i_{t-1} + \gamma_2 X_{t-1} + \gamma_3 W_{t-1} \tag{12.22}$$

Using this in (12.17), we have

$$I_t = \beta_0 + \beta_1\gamma_0 + \beta_1\gamma_1 i_{t-1} + \beta_1\gamma_2 X_{t-1} + \beta_1\gamma_3 W_{t-1} + \epsilon_t \tag{12.23}$$

One way of estimating β_1 of equation (12.17) is to, first, regress i_t on all the regressors of (12.21). This would give the estimated values for the γs. Putting these into (12.22) we will generate an estimate $\hat{E}_{t-1}i_t$ for

$$\hat{E}_{t-1}i_t = \hat{\gamma}_0 + \hat{\gamma}_1 i_{t-1} + \hat{\gamma}_2 X_{t-1} + \hat{\gamma}_3 W_{t-1}$$

At the next stage, obtain the OLS estimates of β_0 and β_1 by replacing $E_{t-1}i_t$ of

[20] $\hat{\beta}_1$ = covariance (I,i)/variance (i), but covariance $(I,i) = \beta_1$ variance $(i) - \beta_1$ covariance (i,μ), and covariance (i,μ) = variance (μ), assuming $E_{t-1}(i_t)$ and μ_t are uncorrelated.

(12.17) by the above $\hat{E}_{t-1}i_t$. This enables us to avoid the problem of correlation between i_t and μ_t—now irrelevant—which was the source of asymptotic bias before.

The form of the investment function developed in equation (12.23) reveals a possible test procedure for the rational expectations hypothesis. By regressing I_t on $\hat{\gamma}_1 i_{t-1}$, $\hat{\gamma}_2 X_{t-1}$, and $\hat{\gamma}_3 W_{t-1}$ where we have imputed the previously determined OLS estimates of γ_1, γ_2, and γ_3, we should be able to get coefficient estimates. These should be exactly identical to each other, because they are the estimates of β_1, which measures the interest rate sensitivity of investment expenditures. If these estimates are not the same, that must mean either (12.17) is wrong or expectations are not rational. If, however, (12.17) is satisfactory, we have to be then concerned with a test procedure that will test the validity of the rational expectations hypothesis.

12.13.2 Test of Restrictions Imposed by Rational Expectations

To illustrate the procedure for testing prior restrictions due to rational expectations, consider the following model:

$$Y_t = \beta_0 + \beta_1 X_t + \beta_2 W_t + \epsilon_t \tag{12.24}$$

where Y is the dependent variable, X and W are independent variables, ϵ is the error term, and the βs are coefficients.

If the effect of rational expectations is to create restrictions such as $\beta_1 - \beta_2 = 0$ in this equation, then building this particular restriction in would produce the new equation

$$Y_t = \beta_0 + \beta_1(X_t + W_t) + \mu_t \tag{12.25}$$

where μ_t is the new error term. In matters of testing the validity of linear restrictions such as $\beta_1 - \beta_2 = 0$, we proceed as follows. We calculate the sum of squared residuals $\sum \hat{\epsilon}_t^2$ and $\sum \hat{\mu}_t^2$ corresponding to equations (12.24) and (12.25), the ˆ over ϵ_t and μ_t indicating that these are OLS estimates.

Assume that ϵ_t and μ_t are normally distributed. Then, as Maddala (1977) has shown, $[(n - m - 1)/l]\,[\sum \hat{\mu}_t^2 - \sum \hat{\epsilon}_t^2]/\sum \hat{\epsilon}_t^2$, is distributed as the F statistic with l and $n - m - 1$ df, where l is the number of restrictions, and $m + 1$ is the number of regressors in (12.24). In the particular test, $l = 1$ and $m = 2$. If the calculated F happens to be larger than the theoretical F at the given degrees of freedom and at a certain probability level of significance, the validity of the restriction will be in doubt.

When restrictions are nonlinear, as in the case of a restriction such as $\beta_1\beta_2$ = constant, the F test would be inappropriate. In such a case, the likelihood ratio (LR) test statistic is available. We can show that the LR test statistic

$$n(\ln \sum \hat{\mu}_t^2 - \ln \sum \hat{\epsilon}_t^2)$$

will, in large samples, be distributed as χ^2 (chi-square) with l df, l being the number of restrictions, and ln standing for the natural logarithm. This test procedure will be found very convenient and appropriate in rational expectations contexts, since restrictions under the REH are often nonlinear and go between equations rather than within.

To illustrate this sort of cross-equation restriction, refer to equations (12.17) and (12.21) reproduced below:

$$I_t = \beta_0 + \beta_1 \mathrm{E}_{t-1} i_t + \epsilon_t \tag{12.17}$$

$$i_t = \gamma_0 + \gamma_1 i_{t-1} + \gamma_2 X_{t-1} + \gamma_3 W_{t-1} + \mu_t \tag{12.21}$$

In equation (12.23) we saw how the effect of rational expectations became visible in cross-equation restrictions on coefficients. That equation is reproduced below:

$$I_t = \beta_0 + \beta_1\gamma_0 + \beta_1\gamma_1 i_{t-1} + \beta_1\gamma_2 X_{t-1} + \beta_1\gamma_3 W_{t-1} + \epsilon_t \tag{12.23}$$

Comparing (12.21) with (12.23), we see that the coefficients of variables of the investment function (12.17) are β_1 times the corresponding coefficient of the interest rate determining equation (12.21). Since the restrictions are essentially nonlinear and cover two equations, we are required to examine the errors of these equations before setting up the LR test statistic. The variance–covariance matrix of errors of equation (12.21) and (12.23) is:

$$\mathrm{E}\begin{bmatrix}\epsilon_t \\ \mu_t\end{bmatrix}[\epsilon_t \quad \mu_t] = \begin{bmatrix}\sigma_\epsilon^2 & \sigma_{\epsilon\mu} \\ \sigma_{\mu\epsilon} & \sigma_\mu^2\end{bmatrix} = \boldsymbol{V_I} \tag{12.26}$$

The generalized variance is the determinant of the matrix $\boldsymbol{V_I}$, i.e. $|\boldsymbol{V_I}| = \sigma_\epsilon^2\sigma_\mu^2 - \sigma_{\epsilon\mu}^2$ where $|\boldsymbol{V_I}|$ is the determinant of $\boldsymbol{V_I}$.

On the other hand, taking (12.21) and (12.23) to be completely free of restrictions, we would have two new equations with two new errors $\bar{\nu}_t$ and $\bar{\mu}_t$:

$$i_t = \delta_0 + \delta_1 i_{t-1} + \delta_2 X_{t-1} + \delta_3 W_{t-1} + \bar{\nu}_t \tag{12.27}$$

$$I_t = \theta_0 + \theta_1 i_{t-1} + \theta_2 X_{t-1} + \theta_3 W_{t-1} + \bar{\mu}_t \tag{12.28}$$

Let their error variance–covariance matrix be

$$\mathrm{E}\begin{bmatrix}\bar{\nu}_t \\ \bar{\mu}_t\end{bmatrix}[\bar{\nu}_t \quad \bar{\mu}_t]) = \boldsymbol{V_2} \tag{12.29}$$

and the generalized variance be $|\boldsymbol{V_2}|$, which is the determinant of $\boldsymbol{V_2}$. Then, for large n, the LR statistic:

$$n[\ln|\hat{\boldsymbol{V}}_{\boldsymbol{I}}| - \ln|\hat{\boldsymbol{V}}_{\boldsymbol{2}}|] \tag{12.30}$$

where '^' is the symbol used to indicate that the quantities under them are estimated, is distributed as χ^2 with l degrees of freedom. l is the number of restrictions used. The sense of the test is that when the restrictions are true, the generalized variances from the unrestricted and restricted equation sets should be about equal, and the test result should be insignificant. This test can be generalized to more than two equations in a straightforward manner.

12.14 AN APPLICATION à la BARRO (1977)

This model is based on the consideration that unexpected changes in aggregate demand will influence real output. Barro takes the quantity of money as the major cause of aggregate demand; thus the former will affect the latter only if the changes in the former are unexpected. If changes in the quantity of money were expected, that would change only the price level leaving unaffected the real output.

Simply represented, Barro's model is

$$Y_t = \beta_0 O_t + \beta_1(\Delta M_t - E_{t-1}\Delta M_t) + \epsilon_t \tag{12.31}$$

where

O_t = variable or variables determining natural level of output
ΔM_t = rate of growth of money at period t
$E_{t-1}\Delta M_t$ = expectation at period $t - 1$ of the rate of growth of money to apply to period t
β_0 = a coefficient or a vector of coefficients
β_1 = a coefficient (>0)
ϵ_t = a random residual with $E(\epsilon_t) = 0$

From (12.31) it is clear that for equal actual and expected growth of money supply, real output will gravitate towards its natural rate. It will, however, exceed or fall short of the natural rate if actual monetary growth exceeds or falls short of expected monetary growth; that is, if unexpected monetary growth is positive or negative. Anyway, equation (12.31) may assume either that expectations are rational, or that they are not. Whatever they are, it is based on the concept of what often is referred to as "structural neutrality". By this is meant a certain lack of independence between expected monetary growth (expectations however made—rationally or otherwise), and real output.

For an application of the REH to the expected money growth variable, consider the following process characteristics of ΔM_t:

$$\Delta M_t = \gamma_1 X_{t-1} + \gamma_2 W_{t-1} + \mu_t \tag{12.32}$$

where X and W are variables whose lagged values offer partial explanations for the money growth variable at the current period, μ_t is the random error term with zero mean, and the γs are the coefficients. Variables X and W could be unemployment rate, inflation rate, exchange rate, and deficit financing requirement, or could stand for any other objective to which monetary policy is tied. Thus

$$E_{t-1}\Delta M_t = \gamma_1 X_{t-1} + \gamma_2 W_{t-1} \tag{12.33}$$

under rational expectations, whereas under nonrational expectations,

$$\Delta M_t^e = \gamma_3 X_{t-1} + \gamma_4 W_{t-1} \tag{12.34}$$

where γ_3 and γ_4 are different from γ_1 and γ_2.

From (12.31), (12.32) and (12.33) we have the rational expectations version of the Barro model as

$$\begin{aligned} \Delta M_t &= \gamma_1 X_{t-1} + \gamma_2 W_{t-1} + \mu_t \\ Y_t &= \beta_0 O_t + \beta_1 \mu_t + \epsilon_t \end{aligned} \tag{12.35}$$

Substituting for μ_t from ΔM_t above into the right-hand side of the equation for Y_t, we have (12.35) reappear as

$$\begin{aligned} \Delta M_t &= \gamma_1 X_{t-1} + \gamma_2 W_{t-1} + \mu_t \\ Y_t &= \beta_0 O_t + \beta_1 \Delta M_t - \beta_1 \gamma_1 X_{t-1} - \beta_1 \gamma_2 W_{t-1} + \epsilon_t \end{aligned} \tag{12.36}$$

Equation (12.36) reveals the restrictions on coefficients of the equations imposed by the rationality of expectations: the coefficients of variables X_{t-1} and W_{t-1} in the equation for Y_t are $-\beta_1$ times the corresponding coefficients of the same variables in the equation for money growth ΔM_t. Note that β_1 is the coefficient of ΔM_t in the equation for Y_t. Should REH be invalid, but everything else of the model satisfactory, no such relation would be forthcoming among the coefficients of the two equations. These coefficients could be any number and would not depend on which equation they came from. Tests of coefficient restrictions can be made using the large sample approximation of the likelihood ratio test that was discussed in the previous subsection, only this time take (12.34) to be the unrestricted expectational model for the variable of interest, the growth of the money supply.

Let us now present the actual results as available from Barro (1977). First he fits an equation like (12.32), where he takes for variables X_{t-1} and W_{t-1} the following concrete variables:

ΔM_{t-1}, ΔM_{t-2}: one and two period lagged values of the money growth variable

$\Delta M_t = \ln M_t - \ln M_{t-1}$: M_t is the annual stock of money in the United States using the definition of M1 for M_t (these variables are used to pick up any lagged adjustment on $E_{t-1}\Delta M_t$ not done by other regressors)

$FEDV_t$: deviation of government expenditure from its normal level, with expected positive effect on $E_{t-1}\Delta M_t$

UN_t: unemployment rate $= \ln U_t/(1 - U_t)$ where U is the yearly unemployment in the work force. UN_t is expected to have a positive effect on $E_{t-1}\Delta M_t$.

His OLS estimates are presented in the following equation:

$$\Delta\hat{M}_t = 0.087 + 0.24\,\Delta M_{t-1} + 0.35\,\Delta M_{t-2} + 0.082\,FEDV_t + 0.027\,UN_{t-1} \qquad R^2 = 90\% \qquad (12.37)$$

where a '^' over a variable indicates its estimate. Particularly, $\Delta\hat{M}_t$ is the estimated value of $E_{t-1}\Delta M_t$, the rationally expected component of ΔM_t. Barro's results show that goodness of fit (by the measure of R^2) is as high as 90% and that there is no pattern of autocorrelation in the residuals as evident from the value of the DW statistic (not reported, even though the use of the DW test is questionable when lagged endogenous variables are present as regressors). One feature of his equation is to presume that all the explanatory variables are known at the end of period $t - 1$; otherwise they cannot forecast ΔM_t at period t. This holds good for all the regressors except $FEDV_t$, the data for which relates to the period t. Barro (1977) seems to have been aware of this problem, but maintains that no sooner will the variable be known than it will affect ΔM_t, being dominated by changes in wartime activity. Pesaran (1982) is, however, uneasy and very critical about this claim.

Barro then calculates unanticipated monetary growth using

$$\Delta\widehat{MR}_t = \Delta M_t - \Delta\hat{M}_t$$

where $\Delta\widehat{MR}_t$ is the residual calculated from the OLS regression (12.37). To carry out the test as to whether the unanticipated part of monetary growth influences real variables, he regresses unemployment on current and lagged $\Delta\widehat{MR}$ and two other variables as is clear from the estimated regression below:

$$\widehat{UN}_t = \underset{(0.15)}{3.07} - \underset{(2.1)}{5.8}\Delta\widehat{MR}_t - \underset{(1.9)}{12.1}\Delta\widehat{MR}_{t-1} - \underset{(1.9)}{4.2}\Delta\widehat{MR}_{t-2} - \underset{(0.08)}{4.7}\,MIL_t + \underset{(0.46)}{0.95}\,MINW_t \qquad R^2 = 0.78 \qquad DW = 1.96 \qquad (12.38)$$

MIL is the ratio of military personnel to male population 15 to 44 years of age in those years in which a selective military draft law is in operation, and *MIL* is zero for other years. The idea for including this variable is that conscription has the effect of lowering the unemployment rate if people are more likely to be drafted into the services if they happen to be out of jobs. The variable *MINW* is used to capture the effect of the minimum wage on the unemployment rate. The estimated standard errors are written below the coefficients.

The t tests indicate that the coefficients of the $\Delta\widehat{MR}$ variables are not zero, thus these ΔMR variables significantly affect the unemployment rate. This is also what economic theory would want us to expect. One of Barro's propositions that unanticipated monetary growth affects a real variable is thus carried out. Observe from the coefficients of the ΔMR variables that the pattern of lags is triangular, as revealed from the modal effect of -12.1 corresponding to a one year lag, after which the effect withers away on either side of it.

Barro also tests whether it is only the unanticipated part of money growth and not also the anticipated part that has any effect on a real variable. With that end in view, he additionally includes three variables, ΔM_t, ΔM_{t-1} and ΔM_{t-2}, into an equation like (12.38), and finds that these variables do not significantly influence the unemployment rate.

In some later papers, Barro (1978) and Barro and Rush (1980), real output rather than unemployment rate is chosen as the testing ground for both unanticipated and anticipated monetary growth variables, and the conclusions are just similar.

One criticism of the above studies is their use of a two-step estimation method conducted in a piecemeal way, and not in a more efficient way of estimating all coefficients jointly with cross-equation restrictions imposed. The latter method is applied in Attfield and others (1981) to the U.K. annual data over the period 1946–1977, and again in a study by the same authors to quarterly U.K. data over the period 1963–1978, each time on unanticipated monetary growth, output, and the price level. As an important item of difference from the first, the second study includes current monetary stock explicitly in the output equation. However, the general conclusion of both studies is that only unanticipated monetary growth affects real output, again vindicating Barro's proposition.

12.15 STRUCTURAL NEUTRALITY

As we have seen before, the structural neutrality hypothesis in Barro's model implies that any monetary growth that is anticipated, howsoever anticipations are made, rationally or not, will not influence any real variable. Leiderman (1980) maintains that Barro's model has two *separate* hypotheses: (1) rational expectations, and (2) structural neutrality. Given rational expectations, it is possible, according to him, to test for structural neutrality. He carries out some test of it using the full information maximum likelihood method but his sample data do not lead to the rejection of either (1) or (2) at some preassigned probability levels of significance. For more details, see Leiderman (1980).

12.16 OUTPUT AND INFLATION TRADE-OFFS OF LUCAS' (1973) AND BARRO'S (1977) EFFECT OF UNANTICIPATED MONETARY GROWTH ON REAL OUTPUT AND UNEMPLOYMENT

In a slightly different context, but still in the area of REH, one can refer to Lucas' 1973 study on output and inflation trade-offs. According to this study, only the unanticipated part of aggregate demand is capable of causing output to depart from its natural rate, *but* the greater its unpredictability, the lesser its effect on real output taken as a difference from its natural rate. A simple statement of the Lucas model would be like the following:

$$O_t = O_t^n + \theta(\sigma_\mu^2, \sigma_\nu^2)\mu_t \tag{12.39}$$

where

O_t: aggregate real output
O_t^n: natural level of output
σ_μ^2: variance of output
σ_ν^2: variance of relative demand shocks
$\theta(\sigma_\mu^2, \sigma_\nu^2)$: a function of σ_μ^2 and σ_ν^2, $\dfrac{\partial\theta}{\partial\sigma_\mu^2} < 0$, and $\dfrac{\partial\theta}{\partial\sigma_\nu^2} > 0$; that is, the larger the value of σ_μ^2, the lower the value of θ, and the larger the value of σ_ν^2, the greater the value of θ, ceteris paribus.

Lucas tests a different, though complex, version of the above hypothesis based on data from 18 countries over the same historical period, 1952 to 1967. It is generally believed that the data used are not highly satisfactory nor that the tests employed are beyond question. Yet his article represents a first major attempt to establish that some of the predictions of the REH are not incompatible with some real-world experience.

There are a few authors who combine the single country Barro model with the multicountry aspect of Lucas' model. Refer particularly to Attfield and Duck (1983) which includes 11 countries: the United States, the Netherlands, Canada, Denmark, Australia, the United Kingdom, Philippines, Colombia, El Salvador, Guatemala, and Argentina. They use annual data over the period from 1951 to 1978. Their overall conclusion is that there is some empirical reason to believe that monetary growth influences real output only if it is unanticipated, but that such an effect decreases with its unpredictability. A broad support to the Attfield and Duck position comes later from a study by Kormendi and Meguire (1984). This study is based on a much larger number of countries, the number being 47.

12.17 POSTSCRIPTS ON LUCAS AND BARRO MODELS: THEIR FURTHER ASSESSMENT

Since the articles of Lucas and Barro, a number of others have been published that have criticized the methodology and central theme of both these authors. The result of these reappraisals has been to seriously weaken the applicability of especially Lucas' test and question whether it is the unanticipated changes in nominal income growth (Lucas' model) or monetary growth (Barro's model) that should predominantly influence output and unemployment. The following is a glimpse into some of the more important studies, even though it should be stressed that the controversy is still not over, nor is it anywhere near resolved.

12.17.1 Measurement Error and Process Misspecification

There are two relative objections made against both the models. One is that the variable called aggregate demand might have been measured with an error, and the second is that the wrong process might have been chosen to explain the behavior of this variable.

We would start with the Lucas model and show the implications of these two objections on his results. The effects on the Barro model and his results would be quite similar.

Let us review Lucas' model as applied to different countries. Refer back to (12.39). Use now the symbol O_t for real output O_t minus the natural level of output O_t^n, and take the rate of growth of aggregate demand or nominal spending ΔX_t to follow a simple process such as

$$\Delta X_t = \pi_0 + \mu_t \tag{12.40}$$

where π_0 is the mean value of ΔX_t over the period, and μ_t is as defined before (equation 12.39). Then a version of the Lucas equation appears:

$$O_t = -\theta_1\pi_0 + \theta_1\Delta X_t + \epsilon_t \tag{12.41}$$

where ϵ_t is the random error term. Suppose now that ΔX_t^* stands for the true ΔX_t relative to measured ΔX_t through

$$\Delta X_t = \Delta X_t^* + \nu_t \tag{12.42}$$

Using ΔX_t^* for ΔX_t, let the true relationship be

$$\text{O}_t = -\theta_2\pi_0 + \theta_1\Delta X_t^* + \eta_t \tag{12.43}$$

which, in terms of measured variables, becomes

$$O_t = -\theta_1\pi_0 + \theta_1\Delta X_t - \theta_1\nu_t + \eta_t \tag{12.44}$$

Clearly (12.44) can be viewed as (12.41) if

$$\epsilon_t = -\theta_1\nu_t + \eta_t \tag{12.45}$$

This kind of hybrid error term is going to produce asymptotic bias for the OLS estimate $\hat{\theta}_1$ of θ_1. It can be shown that

$$\text{plim } \hat{\theta}_1 = \theta_1 \frac{\sigma_*^2}{\sigma_{\Delta X}^2} \tag{12.46}$$

where σ_*^2 is the variance of ΔX_t^* and $\sigma_{\Delta X}^2$ is the variance of ΔX_t. Since $\sigma_{\Delta X}^2 =$

$\sigma_*^2 + \sigma_\nu^2$ where σ_ν^2 is the variance of ν_t, $0 < \sigma_*^2/\sigma_{\Delta X}^2 < 1$. Therefore θ is biased toward zero.

The above implies that for those countries which have a relatively large $\sigma_{\Delta X}^2$ (compared to σ_*^2), estimated values of θ_1 would be small, not due to Lucas' reason but due to the underbias problem. This means that for a country like Chile where there are persistent unstable price movements, one could just as well obtain Lucas' result for a very different reason than his.

The second problem relates to the very simple process taken by Lucas (our equation (12.40)) to determine nominal income growth. Assume that an important variable, say, W_{t-1} is unaccounted for whose inclusion now would modify (12.40) to (12.47):

$$\Delta X_t = \pi_0 + \Gamma_1 W_{t-1} + \mu_t^* \tag{12.47}$$

where Γ_1 is a coefficient, and μ_t^* is the true error term in this equation. Assume also that W_{t-1}, a random variable with zero mean, is known at the point of forecasting ΔX_t. Then we have, from (12.40) and (12.47):

$$\mu_t^* = \mu_t - \Gamma_1 W_{t-1} \tag{12.48}$$

Thus the 'true' equation becomes

$$\begin{aligned} O_t &= \theta_1 \mu_t^* + \eta_t \\ &= -\theta_1 \pi_0 + \theta_1 \Delta X_t - \theta_1 \Gamma_1 W_{t-1} + \eta_t \end{aligned} \tag{12.49}$$

But the Lucas equation was

$$O_t = -\theta_1 \pi_0 + \theta_1 \Delta X_t + \epsilon_t \tag{12.50}$$

With reference to (12.45), one can of course equate ν_t with $\Gamma_1 W_{t-1}$, and then the same inference as that of the "errors in variable" model will appear. That is, those countries that have high variance in W_{t-1}, and consequently ΔX_t, will also be the ones with lower estimated values of θ_1 due to the underbias problem. But now the source of the problem is the misspecification of the Lucas model brought about by the omission of a relevant variable.

A straightforward application of the arguments of "errors in variables" and "omission of relevant variables" can be made to the Barro model to make essentially the same kind of conclusions as in the Lucas model. The new result is that the special real effects that are said to have been due to unanticipated monetary growth might just as well be due to errors in variables or omission of relevant variables.

12.18 EXTENSIONS OF THE LUCAS AND BARRO TESTS

Gordon (1982) extends the Lucas model to the study of the behavior of U.S. nominal income growth—net of the natural growth of output—over the period from 1890 to 1980. The object is to try both the unanticipated and anticipated aggregate demand factors for their effect on nominal income.

In the first stage, he fits the following regression to ΔX_t^f defined as the nominal income growth net of natural growth of output:

$$\Delta X_t^f = \boldsymbol{\alpha}'\mathbf{W_{t-1}} + \mu_t \tag{12.51}$$

where $\mathbf{W_{t-1}}$ is a vector of variables indicating anticipatory factors (with the associated row vector of coefficients $\boldsymbol{\alpha}'$), and μ_t, the unanticipated nominal income growth, is the residual term. Lucas is concerned with only μ_t to affect output; Gordon includes both $\mathbf{W_{t-1}}$ and μ_t (plus other variables) as the explanatory variables in the output equation:

$$O_t = \delta_0 (\boldsymbol{\alpha}'\mathbf{W_{t-1}}) + \delta_1\mu_t + \delta_2 O_{t-1} - \sum \delta_{2+i}\dot{P}_{t-i} + \epsilon_t \tag{12.52}$$

Above the δs are coefficients, O_{t-1} is a term that is also provided for by Lucas to capture the drawn-out effect of aggregate demand shock on output, $\dot{P}_{t-i}$ is the lagged inflation variable recorded at time $t - i$, and ϵ_t the equation random error. The lagged inflation term is included as an additional variable of explanation of output over those used by Lucas. Anyway, if the Lucas model is to be vindicated, δ_0 and δ_{2+i}, for all i, should be zero, and δ_1 and δ_2 should come out positive. But based on the U.S. data from each of two periods, 1929IV–1953IV, and 1954I–1980IV, Gordon's results establish significantly positive and negative values of δ_0 and $\sum_1^n \delta_{2+i}$, respectively, as well as positive values of δ_1 and δ_2. Specifically, effects on output of lagged inflation of up to five years are found to be significantly important. On the whole, Lucas' claim that anticipated changes in aggregate demand have no real effect on the U.S. economy comes to be shattered.

We will now proceed to see how far the Barro claim as to the importance of anticipated monetary policy on real output stands the test of new attacks. Particularly, we will refer to two important studies, both done by Mishkin (1982a and b). He takes lagged terms of up to 20 quarters on anticipated and unanticipated monetary growth and includes them in the output equation in a model of the U.S. economy, 1954 to 1976. He simultaneously fits aggregate demand and output equations and sets up cross-equation restrictions to test for rational expectations separately from the structural neutrality hypothesis. Three measures of the aggregate demand variable are taken: inflation ($\dot{P}$), nominal income growth (ΔX_t), and monetary growth (ΔM_t). For structural neutrality, the unanticipated part of each of these variables is taken.

Based on the likelihood ratio tests of both the rational expectations and structural neutrality hypotheses, Mishkin's conclusion, contrary to Barro, is that anticipated monetary growth does significantly influence output in the United States. More interestingly, the pattern of lags chosen for anticipated money shows the effects of the first ten quarterly terms to be positive while those of the others to be significantly negative. It follows that lags in monetary growth work on output in an elongated and complicated way.

But there seems to be a problem associated with monetary growth as the aggregate demand variable. When this is used, the test shows that the rational expectations hypothesis has to be rejected. If so, the test of the structural neutrality hypothesis should be deemed to be invalid, because the latter hypothesis presupposes the fulfilment of the former.

But this problem does not arise with the two other measures of aggregate demand: nominal income growth and inflation. Using them, the REH is fulfilled but not the structural neutrality hypothesis. The general conclusion is that anticipated changes in aggregate demand do produce nonnegligible effects on real output. The results are very similar when unemployment rather than output is used as the dependent variable.

On a different note, let us look into the econometric practice of the situation. Specifically we will refer to the practice of using generated residuals[21] as regressors as in the case of lagged anticipated or unanticipated variables in Barro's (1977) model. Pagan (1982) observes that the standard error in an OLS routine would generally provide a consistent estimate of the coefficient of an unanticipated variable, but an instrumental variable estimate would not do so. However, this is not the case with Barro's model. Here OLS estimates of the standard errors are inconsistent and there is no recourse available to make them consistent either. Of special interest is Pagan's finding that Barro's result on the neutrality of anticipated monetary policy does not undergo any change even when standard errors are correctly calculated.

As observed before, this is still an unresolved area of investigation, and taking into account the intricacies of the econometric issues involved the debate seems to be far from over.

PROBLEMS

12-1. **(a)** Discuss the econometric problems arising from rational expectations variables contained in economic models.

(b) Let the model be

$$Y_{1t} = \gamma Y_{2t} + X_{1t}\beta_1 + \epsilon_{1t}$$

$$Y_{2t} = \gamma^* Y_{1t}^* + X_{2t}\beta_2 + \epsilon_{2t}$$

where Y_{1t}, Y_{2t} are endogenous, X_{1t}, X_{2t} are exogenous, Y_{1t}^* an expectations variable, and the ϵs are disturbances. Discuss the estimation methods for structural parameters when

(1) Y_{1t}^* is explained by an adaptive expectations scheme

(2) Y_{1t}^* is explained by a rational expectations scheme

[21] See Zellner (1970) and Goldberger (1972) for their work on unobservable variables.

Indicate the restrictions on parameters imposed by the rational expectations hypothesis.

12-2. The following is a rational expectations model:

$$\text{I: } Y_t = \beta_1 X_{1t} + \beta_2 X_{2t} + \lambda \mathrm{E}_{t-1} Y_t + \epsilon_t$$

$$\text{II: } X_{1t} = \rho_1 X_{1t-1} + u_{1t}$$

$$\text{III: } X_{2t} = \rho_2 X_{2t-1} + u_{2t}$$

where Y_t is the dependent variable, the Xs are exogenous variables following the AR(1) processes as given in II and III, E_{t-1} is the expectation of Y_t conditional on the information available at time $t - 1$, the βs and λ are unknown coefficients, $\epsilon_t \sim \mathrm{N}(0, \sigma_\epsilon^2)$, and $u_{it} \sim \mathrm{N}(0, \sigma_i^2)$.

What are the restrictions implied by the rational expectations hypothesis and what could be a test for these restrictions?

12-3. In applied macroeconomics, the following kind of a model is frequently employed:

$$\text{I: } Y_{1t} = \beta_1 Y_{2t}^* + \beta_2 (Y_{2t} - Y_{2t}^*) + \epsilon_{1t}$$
$$\text{II: } Y_{2t} = Y_{2t}^* + \epsilon_{2t} = \mathbf{Z}_t \gamma + \epsilon_{2t}$$

where $(Y_{2t} - Y_{2t}^*)$ is the unanticipated part of Y_{2t} and $\mathbf{Z}_t$ is a $1 \times m$ vector of variables determining Y_{2t}^*. After stating the assumptions (regarding the means, variances and independence of the disturbance terms, etc.), discuss the issues associated with the maximum likelihood and the two-step estimation techniques for the parameters β_1 and β_2.

(*Hint:* The two-step estimation arises from having to estimate Y_2^* from II and then plugging the estimate back into I before β_1 and β_2 can be estimated.)

12-4. Refer to problem 11-11 toward the end of Chapter 11. How would the identification considerations of that problem be modified if expectational endogenous variables appear in equations of the system and use is made of the rational expectations hypothesis? Can a fully recursive system and a non-fully recursive system be observationally equivalent?

12-5. Suppose the model is:

$$Y_{1t} = \beta_1 Y_{2t} + \gamma_1 Y_{2t}^* + \delta_1 X_{1t} + \epsilon_{1t}$$
$$Y_{2t} = \beta_2 Y_{1t} + \delta_2 X_{2t} + \epsilon_{2t}$$

where Y_{2t}^* is the rational expectation of Y_{2t} using information available up to the period $t - 1$, X_{it} are all exogenous, and ϵ_{it} are classical disturbances, distributed normally. Derive the reduced form for Y_{1t} and Y_{2t}. If X_{it}, $i = 1, 2$ follows the AR(1) process, $X_{it} = \rho_i X_{it-1} + u_{it}$, what will be the observable form for the reduced form equations for Y_{1t} and Y_{2t}? Using the reduced form for Y_{2t}, what are the restrictions implied by the rational expectation hypothesis? Propose a test of these restrictions.

12-6. Start from Barro's (1977) output equation in which variables determining the natural level of output, unanticipated change in money supply (anticipation being made according to rational expectations), and a random residual (with zero mean) appear on the right-hand side. Suppose monetary change depends on lagged values of such variables as unemployment rate, inflation rate, exchange rate, etc. (consider only two of these variables), and a random zero mean error term.

(a) What will be the restrictions on coefficients of Barro's output equation implied by the rational expectations hypothesis?
(b) Write a brief commentary on the empirical results obtained by Barro for the above-mentioned model.

12-7. (a) What is the meaning of the structural neutrality hypothesis (used in the context of monetary growth) in its effect on real variables?
(b) What role do measurement error and process misspecification play in the controversy as to whether unanticipated monetary growth materially affects real variables in an economy?

12-8. Let the following 12 equations represent the model of an economy at an aggregative level:

Consumption function: $C_t = \beta_{10} + \beta_{11}(Y_t - T_t) + u_{1t}$
Investment function: $I_t = \beta_{20} + \beta_{21}Y_t + \beta_{22}Y_{t-1} + \beta_{23}i_t + \beta_{24}K_{t-1} + u_{2t}$
Supply (demand) of money: $M_t = \beta_{30} + \beta_{31}Y_t + \beta_{32}i_t + u_{3t}$
Production function: $Y_t = \beta_{40} + \beta_{41}E_t + \beta_{42}K_t + u_{4t}$
Price formation: $\dot{p}_t = \beta_{50} + \beta_{51}\dot{w}_t + \beta_{52}(M_t - M_{t-1}) + u_{5t}$
Wage formation: $\dot{w}_t = \beta_{60} + \beta_{61}U_t + u_{6t}$
National income accounting identity: $Y_t = C_t + I_t + G_t$
Tax receipt: $T_t = \beta_{70} + \beta_{71}Y_t + u_{7t}$
Government expenditure: $G_t = \beta_{80} + \beta_{81}Y_t + u_{8t}$
Balanced budget identity: $G_t = T_t$
Unemployment identity: $U_t = P_t - E_t$
Capital stock identity: $K_t - (1 - \delta)K_{t-1} = I_t$

The variables used above are Y for national income, C for consumption, I for investment, K for capital stock, E for employment, U for unemployment, P for work force, w for wage rate, i for interest rate, p for price level, G for government expenditure, T for tax receipt, and $\dot{p}$ and $\dot{w}$ are changes in prices and wages, respectively. δ is the depreciation rate of capital. The us are the random disturbance terms. As you can appreciate, M and P are exogenous variables.
(a) Construct a flow diagram to portray the interrelationships of the macromodel as implied in its various identities and equations.
(b) If, for whatever reasons, you feel that the model formulation above should be revised, do the revision and show the revised model in a new flow diagram.
(c) In both (a) and (b), present the structural equations of the model in matrix notation.

12-9. Based on the knowledge gathered from the various applied macroeconometric models of Chapter 12, write an essay on the state of macromodel building so far and how you think it can be improved. You may classify your suggestions as to whether they involve statistical (and/or mathematical) methodology or whether they involve new economic theory. You may care to illustrate your points as far as practicable.

13

Some Special Problems: Disequilibrium Models, Model Selection, Specification Testing, and Unit Root Models

13.1 INTRODUCTION

This chapter brings together a number of special problems that have engaged the attention of econometricians in recent times. These are the problems of disequilibrium models, testing of which takes us to another general problem, the problem of model selection. In model selection, two major specification problems are often encountered, those arising from nested and others from nonnested model structures. The former problems arise with, for instance, two models specified in such a way that one model is a special case of the other; the latter problems arise when neither model follows as a special case of the other. The last problem of this chapter deals with the periodic ups and downs of an economic time series. Formally these ups and downs, termed 'business cycles', are interpreted as deviations from the growth trend and therefore their determination is linked to that of the trend. However, special problems arise from the fact that trends can be stochastic, not merely deterministic. Under stochastic trends, empirical problems of "spurious regressions" may frequently arise implying that those relationships are not "real". These problems have led econometricians to explore a theoretical rationale for the empirical "spurious" result. However, the rationale developed is related to the characteristics of models with unit roots. This explains why such models have gained so much prominence in current econometric research.

The discussion that follows is a discussion of the intricacies of these problems presented systematically.

13.2 MODELS OF DISEQUILIBRIUM

The literature on economic theory and econometrics is full of models of market disequilibrium and it is still growing. In what follows, our objective is to present only a brief introduction to the subject.

Simply stated, market equilibria and market clearances are equivalent concepts. When tendencies for excess demand or excess supply, two essential characteristics of a market disequilibrium, develop, the usual correction mechanism consists of the price level moving in the appropriate direction. It rises in periods of excess demand, falls in periods of excess supply, and the rise or fall go on until equilibrium is restored. But in the real world, markets are seldom in equilibrium. Notable examples can be cited from the labor market, where unemployment and vacancies exist side by side indicating that it is not automatic that markets do clear whenever forces of disequilibrium develop.

Let us look into some of the disequilibrium models that have been built to explain the underlying econometric situations.

13.2.1 An Early Disequilibrium Model Due to Quandt[1]

Consider the 'switching regression model' developed by Quandt. It has three equations:

$$Y_t^d = \beta_0^d + \beta_1^d P_t + \gamma_1^d X_{dt} + \epsilon_{dt} \tag{13.1}$$

$$Y_t^s = \beta_0^s + \beta_1^s P_t + \gamma_1^s X_{st} + \epsilon_{st} \tag{13.2}$$

$$D_t = \delta_t Y_t^d + (1 - \delta_t) Y_t^s \tag{13.3}$$

where Y_t^d and Y_t^s are quantities demanded and supplied, D_t is quantity traded, P is price, X_d and X_s are other explanatory variables of particular significance to the demand and supply function respectively, ϵ_d and ϵ_s are the respective equations' disturbance terms with zero means and constant variance, and δ_t is a dummy variable such that

$$\delta_t = \begin{cases} 1 & \text{if } Y_t^d = D_t \\ 0 & \text{if } Y_t^s = D_t \end{cases} \tag{13.4}$$

Note that with P known and Z given exogenously we can use the three equations to solve for the three variables, Y_t^d, Y_t^s, and D_t, uniquely. In particular, when equilibrium occurs, we will have $Y_t^s = Y_t^d = D_t$ and δ_t will be 1 or 0. But there is no mechanism in the model which will ensure that δ_t is known.

Therefore, should δ_t be not known, the values of this variable will be ad-

[1] See Quandt (1958) and Goldfeld and Quandt (1972).

ditional parameters to be determined along with the coefficients of the demand and supply equations. This, in principle, is no problem, since we could use the method of maximum likelihood applied to switching regimes as described in Section 10.7.1 of Chapter 10. In practice, though, there might be a large number of switchings required between the demand and supply equations, giving rise to a large number of switching points. All these would require a great deal of computational work and this could be one reason why the Quandt model has apparently not become popular as a practical model.

13.2.2 The Fair and Jaffee Model[2]

The problem caused by the lack of knowledge about δ_t in the Quandt model is removed in the Fair and Jaffee model. This model is based on the first two equations of the former model, with the following condition substituting for its third equation (that contained δ_t):

$$D_t = \begin{cases} Y_t^d & \text{if } Y_t^d < Y_t^s \\ Y_t^s & \text{if } Y_t^d > Y_t^s \end{cases} \tag{13.5}$$

That is, the quantity *actually* changing hands in the market is the *smaller* of the two quantities, whether these are quantities demanded or supplied. But Y_t^d or Y_t^s are both unobservable, and since price is exogenously determined, the assignment of data to the demand or supply schedule is to be guided by the estimable probability of the event:

$$Y_t^d \leq Y_t^s$$

The interested reader should look into Maddala and Nelson (1974) for the maximum likelihood estimation method applied to this model. Two problems have been especially noted by Maddala (1983) in this connection. One relates to statistical efficiency in that there is not enough prior information usually available to help the assignment of the sample observations to the demand and the supply regimes. The other relates to the values of some parameters. For these values the likelihood function becomes unbounded and therefore its maximization cannot be carried out.

13.2.3 The Fair and Jaffee Model and Crude Price Level Variation

Fair and Jaffee (1972) also specifically include price level variations for the correction of any possible imbalance between the market demand and supply. To see how this may work, let us consider equations (13.1)–(13.3) along with the

[2] See Fair and Jaffee (1972).

following conditional inequalities showing the directions of the price level movement:

$$P_t - P_{t-1} \gtrless 0 \qquad \text{if } Y_t^d \gtrless Y_t^s \tag{13.6}$$

That is, in situations of excess demand (supply), the price level moves up (down). Clearly the price movement is observable and the information obtained will help the assignment of observations to either market demand or supply.

As for estimation, least squares estimates are possible but will be inconsistent since the price level, being correlated with both the demand and supply quantities, will be correlated with the error term of each equation. For maximum likelihood estimates, see Maddala (1983), pp. 305–306 and 308.

13.2.4 The Fair and Jaffee Model and Exact Price Level Variation

The previous model formulation is somewhat crude in the sense that the price movement specifies only the direction; it is not exact. To make it exact, consider (13.1), (13.2), and (13.5) and replace (13.6) by

$$P_t - P_{t-1} = \theta(Y_t^d - Y_t^s) \tag{13.7}$$

For the maximum likelihood estimation of this model, see Maddala (1983), pp. 306–309.

It can be shown that this model and the partial adjustment model have observationally equivalent implications. For, the partial adjustment model can be specified as

$$Y_t^d = \beta_0^d + \beta_1^d P_t^* + \gamma_1^d X_{dt} + \epsilon_{dt} \tag{13.8}$$

$$Y_t^s = \beta_0^s + \beta_1^s P_t^* + \gamma_1^s X_{st} + \epsilon_{st} \tag{13.9}$$

$$Y_t^d = Y_t^s \tag{13.10}$$

$$P_t - P_{t-1} = (1 - \phi)(P_t^* - P_{t-1}) \qquad 0 < \phi < 1 \tag{13.11}$$

where P_t^* is the (unobservable) equilibrium price and ϕ the coefficient of adjustment of actual price to the equilibrium price. Using the market clearing condition and the equilibrium price (obtained from the partial adjustment equation) in the demand and supply equations, we have the actual price solution emerge as a linear function of the variables shown in the functional form

$$P_t = f_1(P_{t-1}, X_{dt}, X_{st}, \bar{\epsilon}_t) \tag{13.12}$$

where

$$\bar{\epsilon}_t = \epsilon_{dt} - \epsilon_{st}$$

Similarly, using (13.1) and (13.2) in the exact price movement equation (13.7), we have P_t emerge as another linear function[3] of the same variables as before:

$$P_t = f_2(P_{t-1}, X_{dt}, X_{st}, \bar{\epsilon}_t) \tag{13.13}$$

Thus the two forms are structurally the same and therefore have equivalent implications.[4]

We can generalize the disequilibrium model based on the price adjustment equation by including a random error term. Consequently, complications including problems of identification will arise. However, the maximum likelihood method will still be available for estimation purposes provided suitable structural changes are incorporated to identify the equations first.[5]

13.3 TESTS OF EQUILIBRIUM

It must be clear by now that equilibrium is a special state of the market that is encompassed by or nested in by its more general state, the state of disequilibrium. The test of equilibrium is, in this sense, the test of a nested hypothesis. Out of all the models of disequilibrium discussed so far, the one that is based on the price adjustment equation (equation (13.7)) admits of testing by the method of nested hypothesis. Since the price level can, according to equation (13.7), be infinitely sensitive to the gap of disequilibrium, that is, θ can be infinity, an equivalent test of this is available from a test of the hypothesis: $1/\theta = 0$. If this hypothesis is tested to be insignificant, it can be taken to be a restatement of the fact that any tendency for a market disequilibrium is instantaneously corrected by the price level moving in the appropriate direction until the equilibrium is restored.

However, the other models of disequilibrium do not have the same advantages as available from the test of nested hypothesis since disequilibria, in these models, are the rule rather than the exception. Consequently, disequilibrium and equilibrium should be viewed as two nonnested hypotheses. But a discussion of tests of such hypotheses is delayed until the more general problem of model selection is discussed. To this we turn next.

[3] The exact coefficients of the two functional forms can be easily derived. The interested reader may try this out as an exercise.

[4] Quandt (1982) p. 6 maintains that the demand and supply equations are distinguishable in the disequilibrium model but not necessarily so in the partial stock adjustment model.

[5] The interested reader may pick up the details of the extensive empirical results of the Fair and Jaffee (1972) model by consulting the original source.

13.4 MODEL SELECTION

The problem of model selection is a problem of choice among competing models. Often economic theory can help in this because it can indicate what explanatory variables should be included in the model. Still there are other aspects of model selection where it may not help enough as in the choice of functional forms, behavioral lags, control (for example, socio–political) and state (for example, policy instrumental) variables, or variable measurements. Typically, the choice of a model follows some preliminary data search. In the case of a regression model, for example, this leads to the specification of regressors that appear to be the most pertinent on prior grounds. Often some regressors occur in one model and reappear in another model giving rise to what are known as nested models; often again neither model, in the context of two models, appears to be a special case of the other model, a feature inherent in nonnested models. In these and other more general cases, the researcher often uses some ad hoc criteria to make a choice of the model. This choice is, at times, refined on the basis of some new searches made, for example hypothesis-testing search, interpretive-testing search, simplification search, and proxy-variable search. Ultimately he or she addresses the question of post-data model construction.

In what follows we will discuss some of the more comprehensive items listed above.

13.5 NESTED MODELS

Consider two rival models with their equations as follows:

$$\underset{(n \times 1)}{\mathbf{Y}} = \underset{(n \times K)}{X}\ \underset{(K \times 1)}{\boldsymbol{\beta}} + \underset{(n \times 1)}{\boldsymbol{\epsilon}} \tag{13.14}$$

$$\underset{(n \times 1)}{\mathbf{Y}} = \underset{(n \times K)}{X}\ \underset{(K \times 1)}{\boldsymbol{\beta}} + \underset{(n \times l)}{Z}\ \underset{(l \times 1)}{\boldsymbol{\gamma}} + \underset{(n \times 1)}{\boldsymbol{\epsilon}} \tag{13.15}$$

in which the sizes of the vectors and matrices are written underneath their symbols. We assume that X and Z are nonstochastic and that classical assumptions apply to the disturbance term $\boldsymbol{\epsilon}$. It is clear that the first model is nested in the second model through the terms involving the X variables. Let us now look into the tests used to decide upon the model that would be acceptable.

(1) The classical F Test:
The null hypothesis is H_0: $\beta = 0$ to be tested against the alternative hypothesis H_1: $\beta \neq 0$. The usual test is the F test defined as:[6]

$$\frac{(S_X^2 - S_{X,Z}^2)/l}{S_{X,Z}^2/(n - K - l)} = F_{l,n-K-l} \tag{13.16}$$

[6] This is based on reasonings similar to those used to obtain (6.67) in Chapter 6.

where S_X^2 and $S_{X,Z}^2$ are the sums of squares due to error from the first and the second models based respectively on the X and the X as well as the Z variables. If H_0 is rejected, the test supports the second model; if not, it supports the first.[7]

(2) The Adjusted Coefficient of Multiple Determination ($\overline{R}^2$) Requirement: Define

$$\overline{R}_X^2 = 1 - \frac{S_X^2/(n - K)}{S_Y^2/(n - 1)} \tag{13.17}$$

and

$$\overline{R}_{X,Z}^2 = 1 - \frac{S_{XZ}^2/(n - K - l)}{S_Y^2/(n - 1)} \tag{13.18}$$

where S_Y^2 $(= \Sigma(Y_i - \overline{Y})^2$, $\overline{Y}$ being the mean of Y) is the total sum of squares. Based on the $\overline{R}^2$s, we choose the first model if

$$\overline{R}^2 > \overline{R}_{XZ}^2 \tag{13.19}$$

and choose the second model otherwise. We can show that this requirement reduces to an *operational* mean square error criterion. The proof follows:

Since $\overline{R}_X^2 > \overline{R}_{XZ}^2$, we have

$$S_{XZ}^2/(n - K - l) > S_X^2/(n - K) \tag{13.20}$$

In other words

$$s_{XZ}^2 > s_X^2 \tag{13.21}$$

where s_{XZ}^2 and s_X^2 are the mean sums of squares due to error from the second and the first model, respectively. That is

$$s_{XZ}^2 = (\mathbf{Y} - X\hat{\boldsymbol{\beta}} - Z\hat{\boldsymbol{\gamma}})'(\mathbf{Y} - X\hat{\boldsymbol{\beta}} - Z\hat{\boldsymbol{\gamma}})/(n - K - l) \tag{13.22}$$

$$s_X^2 = (\mathbf{Y} - X\tilde{\boldsymbol{\beta}})'(\mathbf{Y} - X\tilde{\boldsymbol{\beta}})/(n - K) \tag{13.23}$$

where $\hat{\boldsymbol{\beta}}$ and $\hat{\boldsymbol{\gamma}}$ are the OLS estimates of parameters of the second and $\tilde{\boldsymbol{\beta}}$ the OLS estimates of those of the first model. Since the mean sums of squares are also the estimated error variances, the $\overline{R}^2$ criterion reduces to the criterion in terms of these variances with the inequality reversed. That is, choose the first model if $\overline{R}_X^2 > \overline{R}_{XZ}$, which is the same thing as requiring: $s_X^2 < s_{XZ}^2$. The condition in (13.20) is further reducible in terms of the F statistic. This is shown below. Relation (13.20) can be expressed as

$$S_X^2/(n - K) - \frac{S_{XZ}^2}{n - K - l} < 0$$

[7] It is often the case that X and Z are collinear. Then the power of the F test will be compromised. If the models are nonlinear, recourse should be taken to the likelihood ratio test.

which can be rearranged as:

$$\frac{S_X^2 - S_{XZ}^2}{S_{XZ}^2} \leq [(n - K)/(n - K - l) - 1$$

or

$$\frac{(S_X^2 - S_{XZ}^2)/l}{S_{XZ}^2/(n - K - l)} < 1 \tag{13.24}$$

But from (13.16), the left hand side of the above is F. Thus $F < 1$.[8] On the whole, the $\overline{R}^2$ criterion and the operational mean square error criterion are equivalent.

13.6 NONNESTED MODELS

We will now consider two rival models that are nonnested between themselves. The model equations are:

$$\underset{(n \times 1)}{\mathbf{Y}} = \underset{(n \times K)}{\boldsymbol{X}} \underset{(K \times 1)}{\boldsymbol{\beta}} + \underset{(n \times 1)}{\boldsymbol{\epsilon}} \tag{13.25}$$

$$\underset{(n \times 1)}{\mathbf{Y}} = \underset{(n \times l)}{\mathbf{Z}} \underset{(l \times 1)}{\boldsymbol{\gamma}} + \underset{(n \times 1)}{\boldsymbol{\epsilon}} \tag{13.26}$$

The basic assumptions used for these models are identical to those used for the nested models. In general, however, it is possible that a few variables may be common between the two sets of regressors of the two (nonnested) models.

Consider, for test purposes, the following two hypotheses corresponding to the two models:

$$H_1\text{: E}(\mathbf{Y}) = \boldsymbol{X\beta}$$

$$H_2\text{: E}(\mathbf{Y}) = \mathbf{Z}\boldsymbol{\gamma}$$

A test of H_1 against H_2 is supposed to indicate how far the first model can signal the effectiveness of the second model. Cox[9] (1961) has suggested a test procedure in such a case which is a variant of the likelihood ratio test[10] available for nested models. Such procedures are easily adaptable to nonlinear models.[11]

There are still some other test procedures available that are different from Cox's. One, using the concept of artificial nesting, takes recourse to the F test, but first it sets up a hybrid regression equation of the type

$$\mathbf{Y} = \boldsymbol{X\beta} + \overline{\boldsymbol{Z}}\boldsymbol{\gamma} + \boldsymbol{\epsilon} \tag{13.27}$$

[8] Note that the requirement that $F < 1$ will correspond to a level of significance much larger than the usual 15% or 10%.

[9] See Cox (1961), pp. 239–253.

[10] Cox's method has been extended to non-nested models with variations in their specifications. See McAleer (1985) for a survey of these extensions.

[11] See Pesaran and Deaton (1978) for details of the nonlinear adaptions.

In the above, $\bar{Z}$ is Z except that it does not include those variables that are common to X. The F test used in this case simply tests H_1, which is equivalent to testing: $\boldsymbol{\gamma} = \mathbf{0}$. However, the test is not against the alternative hypothesis H_1, but rather against *some* combination of H_1 and H_2.

Davidson and McKinnon (1981)[12] resolve this problem by setting up a new version of the hybrid equation:

$$\mathbf{Y} = (1 - \alpha)X\boldsymbol{\beta} + \alpha Z\boldsymbol{\gamma} + \boldsymbol{\epsilon} \tag{13.28}$$

The parameter α of this equation regenerates one or the other hypothesis. For instance, $\alpha = 1$ reproduces H_2, and $\alpha = 0$ reproduces H_1. But how should one identify α?

Davidson and McKinnon go on to do that by estimating $\boldsymbol{\gamma}$ by $\hat{\boldsymbol{\gamma}}$, its OLS estimate:

$$\hat{\boldsymbol{\gamma}} = (\mathbf{Z}'\mathbf{Z})^{-1}\mathbf{Z}'\mathbf{Y} \tag{13.29}$$

and then using this estimate in (13.28) to devise a test, called the J test. This test is based on the OLS estimate $\hat{\alpha}$ of the coefficient α of $\mathbf{Z}\hat{\boldsymbol{\gamma}}$. Under H_1, it is shown asymptotically that

$$\hat{\alpha}/s(\hat{\alpha}) \sim N(0, 1)$$

where $s(\hat{\alpha})$ is the estimated standard error of $\hat{\alpha}$.

Fisher and McAleer (1981) modify the J test by proposing, what they call, a JA test. They argue that since, under H_1,

$$\begin{aligned} \text{plim } \hat{\boldsymbol{\gamma}} &= \text{plim}(\mathbf{Z}'\mathbf{Z}/n)^{-1}\mathbf{Z}'\mathbf{Y}/n \\ &= \text{plim}(\mathbf{Z}'\mathbf{Z}/n)^{-1}\mathbf{Z}'(X\boldsymbol{\beta} + \boldsymbol{\epsilon})/n \\ &= \text{plim}(\mathbf{Z}'\mathbf{Z}/n)^{-1}(\mathbf{Z}'X/n)\boldsymbol{\beta} \end{aligned} \tag{13.30}$$

one can find an OLS estimate, say $\hat{\boldsymbol{\beta}}^*$, for $\boldsymbol{\beta}$ obtained as

$$\hat{\boldsymbol{\beta}}^* = (\mathbf{Z}'\mathbf{Z})^{-1}\mathbf{Z}'X\hat{\boldsymbol{\beta}} \tag{13.31}$$

where

$$\hat{\boldsymbol{\beta}} = (X'X)^{-1}X'\mathbf{Y} \tag{13.32}$$

Then the JA test is based on the OLS estimate $\hat{\alpha}^*$ of α, which is the coefficient of $\mathbf{Z}\hat{\boldsymbol{\beta}}^*$ in the model reformulated to

$$\mathbf{Y} = (1 - \alpha)X\boldsymbol{\beta} + \alpha\mathbf{Z}\hat{\boldsymbol{\beta}}^* + \text{error} \tag{13.33}$$

It is shown that

$$\hat{\alpha}^*/s(\hat{\alpha}^*) \sim t \tag{13.34}$$

in small samples if X and $\mathbf{Z}$ are nonstochastic, where $s(\hat{\alpha}^*)$ is the estimated standard

[12] See Davidson and McKinnon (1981) pp. 781–793.

error of $\hat{\alpha}^*$. The interesting point is that both the tests are asymptotically equivalent.

Let us now look into some small sample properties of the two tests available from Monte Carlo experiments that are conducted by Godfrey and Pesaran (1983). The general result from such experiments is that the *J* test, although quite simple, has frequently a very high significance level, for example, 20%. That is, it tends to reject the null hypothesis quite often even though it is correct. On the other hand, the *JA* test has a low probability for the acceptance of the correct alternative hypothesis when $K > 1$. Thus Godfrey and Pesaran conclude that the "*JA* test should only be used if both models being tested" have an identical number of uncommon variables.[13]

We have illustrated the tests of nonnested models on the basis of two hypotheses only. Often a test of H_1 against H_2 that indicates a rejection of H_1 does not necessarily mean that H_2 is the correct hypothesis. It is possible that a third hypothesis connected with a third model might be the correct one and H_2, like H_1, should also be rejected. Or, if both H_1 and H_2 should be accepted, the problem might be one of not being able to choose one over the other hypothesis from the available data. This would call for some amount of "data mining" until perhaps one hypothesis is accepted against conceivable alternative hypotheses. Thus inference based on nonnested models appears to be about as difficult as, if not more difficult than, inference in general.

13.7 AN APPLIED STUDY DUE TO McALEER AND OTHERS (1982)[14]

This study tests several specifications of the demand for money function in the United States fitted over the period 1904–1975. The set of specifications used to define its model (1) has current and lagged permanent income (*YPerm*), current and lagged short-term interest rate (*SRI*), current and lagged price changes ($P(t)$, $P(t - 1), \ldots$), and lagged money (M) demand for the explanatory variables. The set of specifications used in model (2) has all the regressors just mentioned, but the short-term interest rate is uniformly replaced by the long-term interest rate (*LRI*). The specifications of model (3) are rather standard. They include the following explanatory variables: current permanent income, current year long-term interest rate, and money demand lagged one period. All the models come clean in respect of problems of autocorrelation, heteroscedasticity, structural instability, and correlation between the regressors and the disturbance term. Nonnested tests, described in the preceding sections, are applied to the relevant pairs of models.

[13] See Godfrey and Pesaran (1983), pp. 133–154.

[14] See McAleer and others (1982), pp. 572–583.

TABLE 13.1 U.S. LONG-RUN DEMAND FOR MONEY FUNCTIONS, 1904–1975 (dependent variable = ln M2 (*t*))*

Independent Variable[a]	Estimated Regression Models		
	(1)	(2)	(3)
ln *YPerm*(*t*)	0.936 (6.93)	0.904 (5.53)	0.773 (5.30)
ln *YPerm*(*t* − 1)	−1.043 (4.09)	−1.166 (3.83)	
ln *YPerm*(*t* − 2)	0.404 (2.35)	0.359 (1.89)	
ln *SRI*(*t*)	−0.073 (7.85)		
ln *SRI*(*t* − 2)	0.031 (2.27)		
ln *LRI*(*t*)		−0.274 (5.14)	−0.215 (4.00)
ln *LRI*(*t* − 1)		0.265 (5.23)	
Δ ln *P*(*t*)	−0.489 (8.01)	−0.500 (6.83)	
Δ ln *P*(*t* − 1)	0.260 (3.20)	0.305 (3.25)	
Δ ln *P*(*t* − 2)	0.133 (2.13)	0.154 (2.07)	
ln M2(*t* − 1)	1.078 (11.41)	1.214 (12.36)	0.391 (3.40)
ln M2(*t* − 2)	−0.326 (3.95)	−0.291 (2.89)	
R^2	0.998	0.997	0.993
DW[b]	1.94	1.76	2.00
$\hat{\rho}$[c]			0.805 (8.11)

Note: Absolute *t* ratios are shown in parentheses. An intercept term was present in each model.

[a] Money and scale variables are expressed in real per capita form. M2 = the sum of currency, demand deposits, and time deposits at commercial banks. *YPerm* = real permanent income per capita, constructed as a distributed lag of real net national product (*NNP*). *P* = *NNP* deflator with base year 1929. *SRI* = 4–6 month commercial paper rate. *LRI* = 20 year corporate bond rate. Income and price data were supplied by the National Bureau of Economic Research (NBER).

[b] The first elements of the corrected autocorrelation function t statistics of (1) and (2) are 0.33 and 1.48, respectively.

[c] Estimate of the first-order autoregressive parameter.

* Reprinted with permission M. McAleer, G. Fisher, and P. Volker, "Separate Misspecified Regressions and the U.S. Long-Run," *Review of Economics and Statistics*, 64 (1982) Table 1, p. 580.

The authors use a two-tailed test with the associated probability level of significance of no more than 2%. The actual regression results are shown in Table 13.1.

In Table 13.2, the paired comparison A[15] is based on test statistics corresponding to model (1) and model (2). The results indicate the rejection of both models at the 2% level of significance. But since model (1) is rejected less strongly than model (2), the specification of the former model might be favored more, in some sense. The conclusion is that even though both models have good specifications compared to those in the literature, as between themselves neither model is good and hence it is rejected as being false. This is a very important conclusion.

TABLE 13.2 PAIRWISE TESTS OF SEPARATE DEMAND FOR MONEY FUNCTIONS
(dependent variable = ln M2(t))*

Paired Comparison	Tested Model	Test Statistics[a]	
		J	JA
A	(1)	2.47	2.36
	(2)	5.90	5.64
D	(1)	1.73	0.41
	(3)	13.30	3.50

Note: It is clear from the above that (1) is not nested within (2) or (3) and vice versa. However, (2) nests (3). (An intercept was present in each model.)

[a] Each of the test statistics is approximately distributed as N(0,1) in large samples.

* Reprinted with permission M. McAleer, G. Fisher, and P. Volker, "Separate Misspecified Regressions and the U.S. Long-Run," *Review of Economics and Statistics,* 64 (1982) Table 2, p. 581.

13.8 MIZON AND RICHARD'S ENCOMPASSING PRINCIPLE[16]

A review of the tests of the previous sections raises a specific question: are the F test and the J test related to each other? Fortunately, Mizon and Richard (1986) have an answer. This is covered in what they term the encompassing principle.

[15] Similarly, the comparison D corresponds to model (1) and model (3). We report only partly the results from the original source.

[16] See Mizon and Richard (1986), pp. 657–678. See also Fisher (1983) who seems to have been the first to explain not only how all the tests of separate regressions are linked but also how the J and JA tests may be considered as induced tests by decomposition of the F test. For small sample empirical tests of Fisher's argument, see Fijumagari (1986).

They maintain that the "encompassing test" is a general test containing both the F and the J test. The principle underlying this test asks whether one given model can predict the performances of competing models. In terms of the hypotheses H_0 and H_1 corresponding to the nonnested models with equations given in (13.25) and (13.26), suppose that σ_1^2 is the variance of the homoscedastic disturbance term under H_1. If $\hat{\gamma}$ and $\hat{\sigma}_1^2$ are the estimates of γ and σ_1^2 under H_1, a test of H_0 against H_1 would, according to the encompassing principle, require computing, under H_0, the values plim $\hat{\gamma}$ and plim $\hat{\sigma}_1^2$ and comparing them with $\hat{\gamma}$ and $\hat{\sigma}_1^2$, respectively, obtained under H_1. The first comparison falls under the mean encompassing test and the second under the variance encompassing test; accordingly, Mizon and Richard establish that the former gives rise to an F test and the latter to a J test. This explains why the J test has only one degree of freedom regardless of the number of regressors included under any hypothesis.[17]

13.9 CRITERIA USED IN THE GENERAL SELECTION OF THE REGRESSORS AND THE MODEL

We have discussed the use of the F test and $\overline{R}^2$ criterion in the context of selection of models of specific kinds, namely nested and nonnested models. Generally, one confronts a large number of potentially important explanatory variables from which only a subset is finally chosen. The central concept used in this choice is the value of the error sum of squares which, in turn, gives rise to various criteria. These are discussed now.

Suppose there is a model, say the ith, based on K_i regressors giving rise to the error sum of squares ESS_i. Let us now define a measure:

$$\hat{\sigma}_i^2 = \text{ESS}_i/n - K_i \qquad (13.35)$$

to be the estimate of the error variance σ^2 of the ith model. Suppose that $\hat{\sigma}_c^2$ is the estimate of σ^2 where the model includes the complete list of K regressors. Then the following criteria become important:

Theil's $\overline{R}^2$ Criterion
Mallows' C_p Criterion
Hocking's S_p Criterion
Amemiya's PC Criterion
Akaike's IC Criterion

Theil's $\overline{R}^2$ criterion[18] assumes one of the models to be the correct one. If, for

[17] There is a rigorous discussion of what is referred to as a complete encompassing test (CET) formulated as a joint test comparing $\hat{\gamma}$ and $\hat{\sigma}^2$ with their probability limits under H_0. The interested reader should check the original source for this.

[18] See Theil (1961).

instance, the ith model is the true model, then $E(\hat{\sigma}_i^2) = \sigma^2$, but not so if the model were not correctly specified.[19] This means that the correct model chosen will tend to be the one with the minimum value of $\hat{\sigma}^2$, or, equivalently, with the maximum value of $\bar{R}^2$.[20]

But what if the selected model contains not only all the right regressors of the correct model, but also a few more regressors that are irrelevant or nonsensical? Using explanations similar to those of Section 6.5.3 of Chapter 6,[21] we can establish that this will not generate any bias in the estimated error variance. Therefore the criterion of minimum error variance or maximum $\bar{R}^2$ may not lead to the correct model.

All the other criteria are based on a different principle, the principle of minimum mean squared error. This is explained below.

Assume as before that one particular model has K_i regressors compared to the K regressors of the correct model. How do we select the number K_i and the associated variables? For this we use the prediction criterion defined as the minimum value of the mean squared error of prediction: $E(Y_0 - \hat{Y}_p)^2$, where Y_0 is the actual future value of Y, and $\hat{Y}_p$ its forecast. If we make $E(Y_0 - \hat{Y}_p)^2$ dependent on the predicted value X_{pi} of X_i, $i = 1, 2, \ldots, K_i$, then we have the conditional mean squared error (MSE) of prediction; if not, we have the unconditional MSE of prediction.

To derive his PC criterion, Amemiya[22] establishes that

$$\hat{E}(Y_0 - \hat{Y}_p)^2 \simeq \frac{2K_i}{n}\sigma^2 + \frac{\text{ESS}_i}{n} \tag{13.36}$$

where, as before, ESS_i is the error sum of squares based on the model with K_i regressors, and $\hat{E}(\;\;)$ is the estimated MSE of prediction. This result treats the forecasted regressors as stochastic and assumes that the statistical behavior of the regressors, whether they arise in the in-sample period or beyond, makes no difference.

But σ^2 is not known. If this is estimated by $\hat{\sigma}_c^2$, where $\hat{\sigma}_c^2 = \text{ESS}/n - K$ is the mean squared error of the complete model with K regressors, the criterion $\hat{E}(Y_o - \hat{Y}_p)^2$ becomes

$$\hat{E}(Y_0 - \hat{Y}_p)^2 \simeq \frac{2K_i}{n}\hat{\sigma}_c^2 + \frac{\text{ESS}_i}{n} \tag{13.37}$$

Minimizing this is the objective in Mallows' C_p criterion.[23] But if the alternative

[19] The proof of this result can be established by using the techniques of Section 6.5 of Chapter 6 in the estimation of the variance of the disturbance term.

[20] This result will generally follow. For an example, see the inverse relationship established between $\bar{R}^2$ and s^2 in equations (13.19) and (13.21) of this chapter.

[21] Note that one should modify the technique to include the estimation of the variance of the disturbance term in a straightforward fashion.

[22] See Amemiya (1980).

[23] See Mallows (1973).

estimate of σ^2 available in $\hat{\sigma}_i^2$, where $\hat{\sigma}_i^2 = \text{ESS}_i/(n - K_i)$, is used, then $\hat{E}(\ )$ reduces to

$$\hat{E}(Y_0 - \hat{Y}_p)^2 \simeq \frac{n + K_i}{n - K_i} \text{ESS}_i \tag{13.38}$$

Minimization of this leads to Amemiya's *PC* criterion.[24] The interesting point is that, unless the *i*th model is the complete model, $\hat{\sigma}_i^2$ will be biased for σ^2 and in that sense, Amemiya's criteria of model selection will be affected compared to Mallows' C_p criterion.

Notice that one major assumption used so far has been that the X_is are nonstochastic in the sample period. If the X_is are stochastic, no matter where and when they arise, as, for instance, Hocking assumes that they are distributed multivariate normally, the criterion will change. With this special assumption, Hocking derives a criterion called the S_p criterion, defined as:

$$S_p = \text{ESS}_i/\{(n - K_i)(n - K_i - 1)\} \tag{13.39}$$

which results from the minimization of the unconditional MSE of prediction.[25] Note that when the regressors are assumed stochastic throughout, all the three criteria,[26] Amemiya's *PC*, Mallows' C_p, and Hocking's S_p, are equivalent.

The last criterion on our list is Akaike's information criterion (*IC*). It is based on the minimization of

$$-\frac{2 \log L}{n} + \frac{2K_i}{n} \tag{13.40}$$

where K_i parameters are taken to appear in the likelihood function. Applied to the regression models, K_i becomes the number of regressors in the *i*th model and it is shown[27] that the criterion is the same as minimizing $\text{ESS}_i \exp(2K_i/n)$, where ESS_i, as before, is the residual sum of squares of the *i*th model. This criterion is typically used in nonlinear models.

To conclude, we will mention a few points. First, all the five criteria listed before except Hocking's S_p criterion and Akaike's criterion make some use of the existence or notion of the "true" model in the model selection process. The two criteria that are the exceptions to this rule of course do not do so. Second, basically Theil's $\bar{R}^2$ criterion relies on in-sample results, whereas three other criteria, Mallows', Hocking's, and Amemiya's, depend on predictive future results. These three criteria also attach a value to the discriminate use of regressors if that will reduce the MSE of prediction. Third, Akaike's criterion is applicable to any general model whichever will admit of the maximum likelihood method of estimation, and, because of this, the criterion is especially suited for nonlinear

[24] See Amemiya (1980).

[25] See Hocking (1976).

[26] See Kinal and Lahiri (1984) for the derivation of this result.

[27] See Akaike (1973 and 1977) for the derivation of the proof.

models. Last, as we have seen in Section 13.5, a model with a lesser number of regressors (that is, an incomplete model) has a higher value of $\bar{R}^2$ (than in the case of a more complete model) which implies a certain upper limit for the F statistic, that is, $F < 1$. The same can be said about Theil's $\bar{R}^2$ criterion related to the F statistic. By proceeding in an analogous way, and using large sample approximations where appropriate, we can set up corresponding ranges of values of the F statistic for the four other criteria. These are: $F < 2$ for Mallows', $F < 2n/(n + K_i)$ for Amemiya's, $F < 2 + (K - K_i + 1)/(n - K - 1)$ for Hocking's, and $F < (n - K)/(n + K_i)$ for Akaike's criterion.[28] That is, we choose the incomplete model if the F statistic for testing the restrictions (in the sense that $K - K_i$ regressors do not appear in the incomplete model) has values as indicated above in terms of the various criteria. These values carry two significant implications.

The first is that their associated probability levels (of significance) are larger than the usual 5%. The second is that in the case of those criteria for which the upper limit of F depends on the sample size, the significance level generally falls as the sample size rises. The exception to this rule, though, is the Hocking's criterion for which the relationship can be rather ambiguous.[29] In any case, the general lowering of the significance levels with the sample size seems to be only modest compared to the quantitative changes in levels derived by the Bayesian approach. To this approach we turn next.

13.10 LEAMER'S POSTERIOR ODDS CRITERION AND THE CRITICAL F RATIO

In Section 10.9 of Chapter 10, we have seen that the posterior pdf for a parameter vector $\boldsymbol{\beta}$ (given the sample observations $\mathbf{Y}$) is proportional to the product of the prior pdf of the parameter vector (before observing the $\mathbf{Y}$s) and the likelihood function (of sample observations on $\mathbf{Y}$ given the values of $\boldsymbol{\beta}$). Assume, in the context of the problem of choice of regressors, that the parameter vector is instead $\begin{bmatrix} \boldsymbol{\beta} \\ \boldsymbol{\gamma} \end{bmatrix}$ whose values are fixed by two hypotheses, one called the null hypothesis

[28] We do not show the details of the arguments here to save space. We continue to assume that the incomplete model (the ith model) has K_i regressors compared to the K regressors of the complete (or more complete) model. Also, in the case of the Akaike's criterion, the correspondence with the F statistic is based on large sample approximations assuming n to be large relative to K or K_i. Particularly, we will need approximations like: $\exp[K/n] \simeq 1 + (K/n)$, and $\exp[1 + (K_i/n)] \simeq 1 + (K_i/n)$.

[29] For instance, Amemiya's F statistic has a value of less than 2 for small samples but a value close to 2 for large samples. But the situation is rather ambiguous with Hocking's criterion. This is because the value of F is higher than 2 in small samples, but it drops to 2 in large samples.

denoted by H_0 which has $\boldsymbol{\gamma} = \mathbf{0}$, and the other, called the alternative hypothesis denoted by H_1 which has $\boldsymbol{\gamma} \neq \mathbf{0}$.[30] Then using P for probability, we have the posterior odds defined as

$$\frac{\mathrm{P}(\boldsymbol{\beta} / \mathbf{Y})}{\mathrm{P}\left(\begin{bmatrix} \boldsymbol{\beta} \\ \boldsymbol{\gamma} \end{bmatrix} \Big/ \mathbf{Y}\right)} = \frac{\mathrm{P}(\mathbf{Y} / \boldsymbol{\beta})}{\mathrm{P}\left(\mathbf{Y} \Big/ \begin{bmatrix} \boldsymbol{\beta} \\ \boldsymbol{\gamma} \end{bmatrix}\right)} \frac{\mathrm{P}(\boldsymbol{\beta})}{\mathrm{P}\left(\begin{bmatrix} \boldsymbol{\beta} \\ \boldsymbol{\gamma} \end{bmatrix}\right)} \tag{13.41}$$

That is, the posterior odds is the product of the likelihood ratio $\mathrm{P}\left(\mathbf{Y} \Big/ \boldsymbol{\beta}\right) \Big/ \mathrm{P}\left(\mathbf{y} \Big/ \begin{bmatrix} \boldsymbol{\beta} \\ \boldsymbol{\gamma} \end{bmatrix}\right)$ and the prior odds $\mathrm{P}\left(\boldsymbol{\beta}\right) \Big/ \mathrm{P}\left(\begin{bmatrix} \boldsymbol{\beta} \\ \boldsymbol{\gamma} \end{bmatrix}\right)$. The right-hand side of equation (13.41) can be simplified to:

$$\frac{\int L_0 \quad P_0(\boldsymbol{\beta})\, d\boldsymbol{\beta}}{\int L_1\, P_1\left(\begin{bmatrix} \boldsymbol{\beta} \\ \boldsymbol{\gamma} \end{bmatrix}\right) d\begin{bmatrix} \boldsymbol{\beta} \\ \boldsymbol{\gamma} \end{bmatrix}} \frac{P(\boldsymbol{\beta})}{P\left(\begin{bmatrix} \boldsymbol{\beta} \\ \boldsymbol{\gamma} \end{bmatrix}\right)} \tag{13.42}$$

in which L_0 and L_1 are the likelihoods and P_0 and P_1 are the prior distributions of the parameters in the first and the second model, respectively. The first term of (13.42) is often called the *Bayes factor*; let us denote this by the symbol B.

Leamer (1978)[31] has computed an expression for B, which is

$$B = \left(\frac{\mathrm{ESS}_i}{\mathrm{ESS}}\right)^{n/2\, \frac{K_2}{n^2}} \tag{13.43}$$

and used particular forms for P_1 and P_2 under certain conditions, all of which contribute to the posterior odds. K_2 is equal to $n - K_i$, and ESS_i and ESS are as defined in Section 13.9.

According to Leamer, the incomplete model with a lesser number of regressors is acceptable if $B < 1$. This leads to the following values of F, calculated by using equation (13.16):

$$F < \frac{n - K}{K_2} (n^{\frac{K_2}{n}} - 1) \tag{13.44}$$

These values are reproduced in Table 13.3. The figures indicate considerable changes in the values of F with changes in the sample size. Compared to these, the changes in the F ratios of the five criteria listed before[32] are much smaller.

[30] Clearly if the null hypothesis is true, the incomplete model with a lesser number of regressors will be vindicated; if it is not true, then the complete model with a greater number will be vindicated.

[31] See Leamer (1978), p. 114.

[32] See Section 13.9 toward the end.

TABLE 13.3 *F* VALUES CORRESPONDING TO THE BAYESIAN POSTERIOR ODDS CRITERION

	$n - K$	5	10	50	100
$K_2 = 1$	$K = 1$	1.74	2.44	4.01	4.68
	3	1.48	2.18	3.89	4.60
	5	1.29	1.98	3.78	4.53
	10	0.99	1.62	3.53	4.37
	5% point of F	6.60	4.96	4.03	3.94
$K_2 = 3$	$K = 1$	2.42	3.08	4.34	4.90
	3	1.97	2.69	4.20	4.82
	5	1.66	2.40	4.07	4.74
	10	1.20	1.89	3.79	4.56
	5% point of F	5.41	3.71	2.79	2.70
$K_2 = 5$	$K = 1$	3.45	3.95	4.70	5.13
	3	2.67	3.36	4.54	5.05
	5	2.16	2.93	4.40	4.96
	10	1.47	2.23	4.07	4.76
	5% point of F	5.05	3.33	2.40	2.30

Reprinted with permission E. E. Leamer *Specification Searches—An Ad Hoc Inference with Non-Experimental Data,* Wiley, New York (1978), Table 4.1, p. 116. © 1978 Wiley & Sons, Inc.

13.11 CROSS-VALIDATION AND PREDICTED AND STUDENTIZED RESIDUALS

The regressors selected on the basis of a certain criterion to identify the "best" model may still be related to the time period during which the estimation is performed. Should the period change to a prediction period instead during which prediction for future time points is performed, that selection may not remain the best. A procedure often used in such cases is to divide the sample into two parts and utilize one part for estimation and the other for prediction. When the information from the two periods is interchanged in order to arrive at a measure of validity of the model selected, the method is known as cross-validation.

In the sample splitting procedure, we calculate an in-sample and also an out-of-sample set of prediction errors; the former refers to the estimation and the latter to the prediction period. Accordingly, we have the in-sample sum of squares which is the usual error sum of squares, and the out-of-sample prediction sum of squares. A criterion of selection of a model may be based on both of these sums of squares.

In the cross-validation procedure, a cross-validation index is calculated using the formula:

$$I_i = (\mathbf{Y}_1 - X_{i1}\hat{\boldsymbol{\beta}}_{i2})'(\mathbf{Y}_1 - X_{i1}\hat{\boldsymbol{\beta}}_{i2}) + (\mathbf{Y}_2 - X_{i2}\hat{\boldsymbol{\beta}}_{i1})'(\mathbf{Y}_2 - X_{i2}\hat{\boldsymbol{\beta}}_{i1}) \quad (13.45)$$

in which the in-sample and out-of-sample observations are identified by the subscripts 1 and 2, respectively, and the subscript i identifies the ith model, and

$$\hat{\beta}_{ij} = (X'_{ij}X_{ij})^{-1}X'_{ij}Y_j, \qquad (j = 1, 2) \tag{13.46}$$

Using this procedure our criterion consists of selecting that model which has the minimum value for this index. This criterion is the same as minimizing the estimated error variance *and* a penalty for coefficient instability between the estimation and prediction periods.[33] But, as Leamer shows, neither the criterion of (the minimum of the) cross-validation index nor the (minimum of the) sum of squares of "predicted errors" can assure the selection of the true model. In contrast, the $\bar{R}^2$ criterion and the criterion (of minimizing the sum of squares) of "studentized residuals" can, as Leamer further shows,[34] lead to the true model. Below we explain some of these concepts and show how they are calculated.

13.11.1 "Predicted Errors" and "Studentized Errors"

For predicted errors, our n sample observations are split into $n - 1$ observations put in one group and one observation is put in another, the so-called missing observation. The $n - 1$ observations are used to estimate the parameters of the regression line which are then used to predict the last or the missing observation. Suppose the forecast error corresponding to this missing ith observation is denoted as ϵ_i^f given by $\epsilon_i^f = Y_i - \hat{Y}(i)$ where Y_i is the actual and $\hat{Y}(i)$ the estimated Y value, $i = 1, 2, \ldots, n$. The ϵ_i^f are called the "predicted errors". Compared to these, we have the OLS errors denoted as $\hat{\epsilon}_i$ given by $\hat{\epsilon}_i = Y_i - \hat{Y}_i$, where $\hat{Y}_i$ is the OLS estimated ith observation, estimation being based on *all* the n observations, not just the $n - 1$ observations just described.

It can be shown that[35]

$$\epsilon_i^f = \hat{\epsilon}_i/(1 - l_{ii}) \tag{13.47}$$

where

$$l_{ii} = x_i^2/\Sigma x_i^2 \tag{13.48}$$

x_is being the explanatory variables X_i taken as deviations from their sample means. Thus, one could set up a criterion of model selection based on the minimum value of $\Sigma(\epsilon_i^f)^2$, usually called the sum of squares of predicted errors or, in short, PRESS. This is related to the usual error sum of squares ESS, $\Sigma\hat{\epsilon}_i^2$, through (13.47). It can be seen that PRESS will tend to favor a model that predicts outlying observations relatively accurately.

For "studentized errors", we divide the predicted errors by their standard errors. Denoting the sum of squares of "studentized errors" by the abbreviated

[33] The proof of this result is due to Leamer (1983), pp. 320–324.

[34] See Leamer (1983), pp. 285–330.

[35] See Cook and Weisberg (1982) for a proof of this result.

symbol SSSE, we can show[36] that SSSE is a weighted sum of squares of OLS estimated errors $\hat{\epsilon}_i$ as has been the case with the PRESS. Also, as we have seen in the course of (13.21) before, the sum of squares of OLS estimated errors, each divided by its degree of freedom, which equals $\bar{R}^2$, is to be minimized according to the $\bar{R}^2$ criterion of model selection. Going back to the Leamer result introduced before,[37] we see that the $\bar{R}^2$ criterion and the criterion of minimizing the SSSE have each the tendency of identifying the true model[38] more often than not. However, the same cannot be said about the PRESS criterion or the cross-validation criterion.[39]

This result implies that the method of splitting the observation into in- and out-of-sample groups, which constitute the basic premise of any cross-validation criterion, does not measure up to the advantages available from minimizing the SSSE as the criterion of model selection.

13.12 MODEL WITH REGRESSORS INDEPENDENT OF ERRORS: HAUSMAN'S TEST[40]

Suppose that the null hypothesis H_0 stipulates that there is no specification error in the model, and the alternative hypothesis H_1 maintains that there is. In particular, take the model given by

$$\mathbf{Y} = X\boldsymbol{\beta} + \boldsymbol{\epsilon} \tag{13.49}$$

in which the specifications of the two hypotheses are as follows:

$$H_0\text{: } X \text{ and } \boldsymbol{\epsilon} \text{ independent}$$

$$H_1\text{: } X \text{ and } \boldsymbol{\epsilon} \text{ not independent}$$

For the sake of the Hausman test, suppose further that there are two estimators $\hat{\boldsymbol{\beta}}$ and $\tilde{\boldsymbol{\beta}}$ with the properties that $\hat{\boldsymbol{\beta}}$ is both consistent and efficient under H_0 but inconsistent under H_1, whereas $\tilde{\boldsymbol{\beta}}$ is consistent under both H_0 and H_1, but inefficient under H_0. Now consider the difference of the two estimators:

$$\mathbf{d} = \hat{\boldsymbol{\beta}} - \tilde{\boldsymbol{\beta}} \tag{13.50}$$

Assuming H_0, Hausman shows that

$$\text{V}(\mathbf{d}) = \text{V}(\hat{\boldsymbol{\beta}}) - \text{V}(\tilde{\boldsymbol{\beta}}) \tag{13.51}$$

where V stands for variance. Taking $\hat{\text{V}}(\mathbf{d})$ to be a consistent estimator of $\text{V}(\mathbf{d})$,

[36] Use $\sqrt{\text{V}(\epsilon_i^f)} = \sigma/\sqrt{1 - l_{ii}}$, where $\sigma^2 = \text{V}(\epsilon_i)$, for all i, in the expression for studentized error: $\epsilon_i^f/\sqrt{\text{V}(\epsilon_i^f)}$. Then from (13.47) and (13.48), this result will follow.

[37] See the discussion toward the end of Section 13.11.

[38] The criterion that Leamer has used to consistently identify the true model has a lesser expected value for the quantity minimized for the true model than for the alternative models.

[39] See the Leamer result stated toward the end of Section 13.11.

[40] See Hausman (1978).

Hausman shows that the test statistic

$$\mathbf{d}'[\hat{\mathbf{V}}(\mathbf{d})]^{-1}\mathbf{d} \tag{13.52}$$

is asymptotically distributed as χ^2 with m df, where m is the number of $\boldsymbol{X}$ variables involved in the regression. Insignificance of the test statistic will support the null hypothesis that the $\boldsymbol{X}$ and the $\boldsymbol{\epsilon}$ variables are independent.[41]

An alternative way of testing the misspecifications of a model is the differencing test suggested by Plosser and others (1982).[42] This test is meant for time series observations only and is applied to models expressed in the form of both levels and differences. The idea is that in the absence of specification errors, the estimators based on levels and differences would have similar asymptotic properties. However, when such errors are present, the properties would not conform to each other.

An equivalence of the differencing test is the omitted variables test devised by Davidson and others (1985).[43] The omitted variables are the sum totals of the backward and (one period) forward values of the variables.

To illustrate this, let the regression equation be:

$$y_t = \beta_1 X_{t1} + \beta_2 X_{t2} + \epsilon_t \tag{13.53}$$

The differencing test is based on the estimated augmented regression equation

$$y_t = \beta_1 X_{t1} + \beta_2 X_{t2} + \delta_1 w_{t1} + \delta_2 w_{t2} + \epsilon_t \tag{13.54}$$

in which

$$\begin{aligned} w_{t1} &= X_{t+1,1} + X_{t-1,1} \\ w_{t2} &= X_{t+1,2} + X_{t-1,2} \end{aligned} \tag{13.55}$$

The (differencing) test then consists of testing the hypothesis: $\delta_1 = \delta_2$ by the F test.

In the case of a lagged dependent variable appearing as a regressor, the test needs a slight adjustment. For instance, if the model is

$$y_t = \beta_1 y_{t-1} + \beta_2 X_t + \epsilon_t \tag{13.56}$$

and the omitted variables are

$$\begin{aligned} w_{t1} &= y_t + y_{t-2} \\ w_{t2} &= X_{t+1} + X_{t-1} \end{aligned} \tag{13.57}$$

putting w_{t1} and w_{t2} in the expanded regression equation causes a problem of correlation between w_{t1} and ϵ_t because y_t is contained in w_{t1}.[44] But by transferring

[41] This test can be looked upon as a test of the errors in the X variables since X may be related to ϵ through errors in themselves. As in errors in variables models, use of instrumental variables for the Xs will achieve results equivalent to the foregoing results.

[42] See Plosser and others (1982), pp. 535–552.

[43] See Davidson and others (1985), pp. 639–647.

[44] Notice that w_{t2} is free of correlation with ϵ_t.

this to the left-hand side and rearranging the equation we can get around this problem. For example, the augmented equation then becomes

$$(1 - \delta_1)y_t = \beta_1 y_{t-1} + \beta_2 X_t + \delta_1 y_{t-2} + \delta_2 w_{t2} + \epsilon_t \tag{13.58}$$

which leads to

$$y_t = (\beta_1/1 - \delta_1)y_{t-1} + (\beta_2/1 - \delta_1)X_t + (\delta_1/1 - \delta_1)y_{t-2} + (\delta_2/1 - \delta_1)w_{t2} + u_t/1 - \delta_1 \tag{13.59}$$

Thus the differencing test will be to test

$$\frac{\delta_1}{1 - \delta_1} = \frac{\delta_2}{1 - \delta_1} = 0 \tag{13.60}$$

This means that the first omitted variable becomes y_{t-2} and not $y_t + y_{t-2}$, but the second (omitted) variable w_{t2} does not undergo any change. Note that, in case we would like to include higher (than one) order lags in y as explanatory variables in the regression equation, this adaptation will not at all be necessary.

13.13 THE UNIT ROOT MODELS

It is now common experience that there were periodic ups and downs in terms of various macroeconomic aggregates in the United States (as also in other countries) over the past 20 years. Examples of such aggregates are national income, volume of industrial production, investment expenditures, consumer debt, consumption expenditures, and so on. These periodic ups and downs are more formally known as the alternate phases of business cycles. If seasonal swings are excluded, cyclical fluctuations are viewed as the residuals in the economic time series after growth trends are removed from them.

The decomposition of a time series into its trend and cyclical components goes by different names in the literature, for example, secular/cyclical, permanent/transitory, long-run/short-(medium)-run, and permanent/stationary. In what follows, we consider the study of the cyclical component to be basically a study of the trend component of the economic time series, because the detrended series consists of cyclical movements only. This can be appreciated from Figure 13.1, in which t is time, Y is GNP ($= P + S$), P the permanent or trend component, and S the cyclical or stationary component. (If Y, P, and S are in logarithm, then Y is multiplicative in P and S.)

13.13.1 The Deseasonalizing Mechanisms

The seasonal is a smaller period cycle, most frequently found to be an annual cycle. Examples of series with pronounced seasonals are production, sales, personal income and expenditure, government revenue, unemployment rates, and

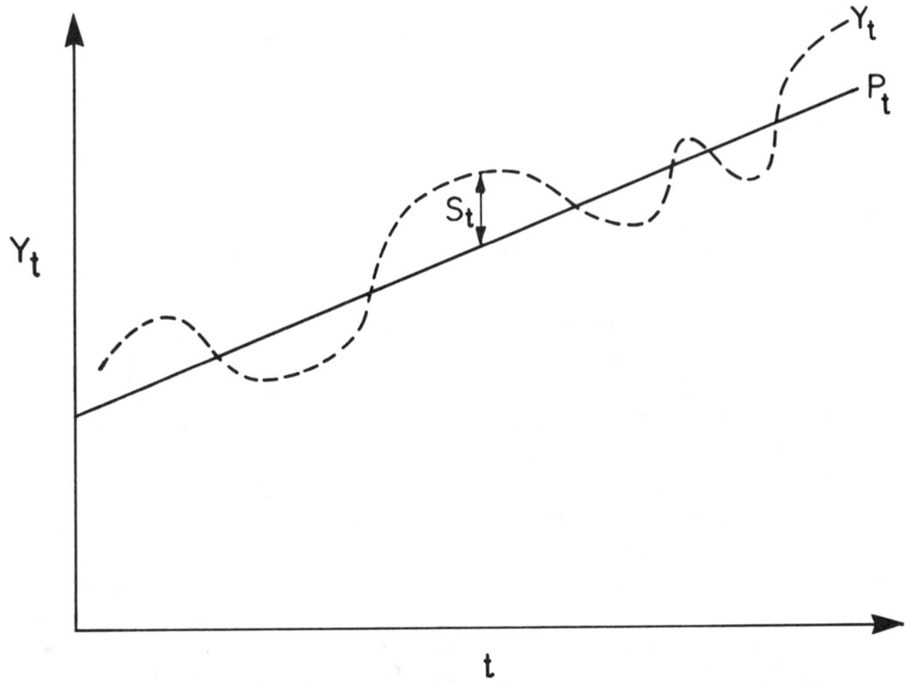

Figure 13.1 GNP broken into trend and cyclical components. [See Stock and Watson (1988), p. 148, for precise graphical depiction of trends and cyclicals in U.S. GNP, consumption, and investment series.]

imports and exports. To illustrate the concept, unemployment rates peak in winter months (the weather effect) due to the winter-time lay-offs of construction workers, retail sales are highest (the holiday or vacation effect) at Christmas and Easter, etc. Similarly the particular timing of the payment of, for instance, corporate dividends, and of the closing of a tax year or an accounting period may cause seasonality in certain other series, such as the income and tax receipt series.

If the seasonal swings were of regular shapes occurring with, say, 12 month intervals, elimination of the seasonal component would be rather easy. One way would be to arrange the data, by months, in a tabular form as in Table 13.4, in which all January figures appear in the first column recorded in higher order of years, similarly the February figures appear in the second column, and lastly the December figures in the last (or twelfth) column. The figures for each month in a column are then averaged. Suppose that these averages are denoted by the symbols $\overline{Y}_J$, $\overline{Y}_F$, . . . , $\overline{Y}_N$, $\overline{Y}_D$ corresponding to the 12 months. The seasonal pattern is then revealed from a plot of these averages (see Figure 13.2). Assuming that the seasonal pattern changes only slightly from one year to the next, the seasonal component is removed from the data by subtracting the column average

TABLE 13.4

	January	February	March	. . .	November	December
Year 1	Y_1	Y_2	Y_3	. . .	Y_{11}	Y_{12}
Year 2	Y_{13}	Y_{14}	Y_{15}	. . .	Y_{23}	Y_{24}
⋮						
Year n	Y_{n-11}	Y_{n-10}	Y_{n-9}	. . .	Y_{n-1}	Y_n
Column Average	$\overline{Y}_J$	$\overline{Y}_F$	$\overline{Y}_M$	. . .	$\overline{Y}_N$	$\overline{Y}_D$

from the data in each column of a table like Table 13.4. The results represent deseasonalized figures.

But if the pattern changes through time, the above method of deseasonalizing the series would not be perfect. A way out of this problem would be to compute monthly averages for a few recent years, say the last three years. With the passage of time, as newer data become available, these can be used to replace older data while computing the averages (see Table 13.5). Suppose that some numerical data called Y_t are recorded by months as in Table 13.5. Of course the data do not seem to reveal any changing seasonal pattern through the years. Still these can be used to illustrate the principle. In January of Year 3, the most recent three January figures are 7, 8, and 11, whose average is 8.7. Therefore the deseasonalized January figure is $11 - 8.7 = 2.3$. Similarly, in the same month in year 4, the most up-to-date January figures are 8, 11, and 9, whose average is 9.3. Thus the de-

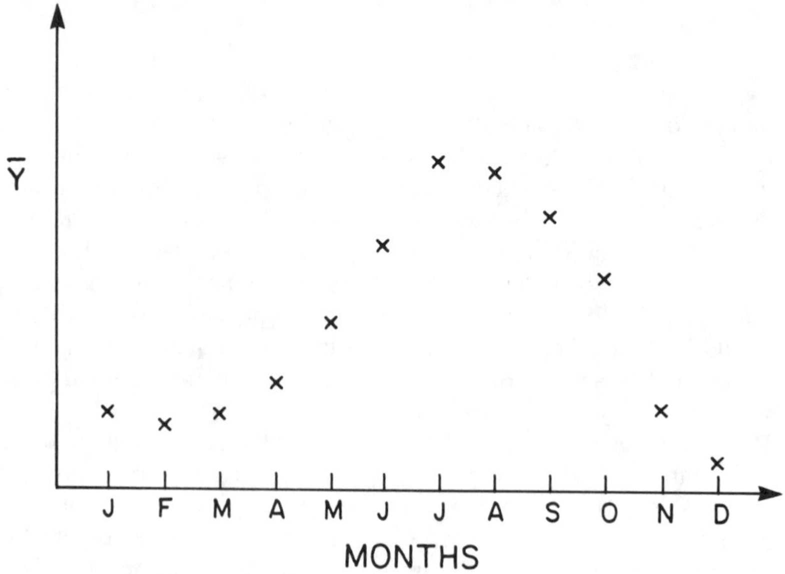

Figure 13.2 Seasonal swing (example: employment rate).

TABLE 13.5

		Year	January	February	March	. . .	November	December
Second Average Period	First Average Period	1	7	4	2	. . .	2	8
		2	8	5	3	. . .	5	7
		3	11	7	2	. . .	4	8
		4	9	6	4	. . .	2	10
Third Year Average			8.7	5.3	2.3	. . .	3.7	7.7
Fourth Year Average			9.3	6.0	3.0	. . .	3.7	8.3

seasonalized figure works out to $9 - 9.3 = -0.3$. In this way, we arrive at the deseasonalized figures in Table 13.6 for all the months corresponding to Year 3 and Year 4.

But if the seasonal is changing, we could consider instead a weighted average of a previous average and a most recent average for a month to construct a current average for that month. The weight used for the most recent average would be the larger the more it is believed that the recent change is the more prominent.[45]

We will conclude this section by observing that most macroseries are published in deseasonalized form by the government. However, the adjustment of the seasonal component can sometimes introduce certain questionable properties in the time series. To a sensitive investigator, this may naturally pose serious model building problems. However, in the subsequent discussions we assume that the time series are free of any seasonal fluctuations.

TABLE 13.6 DESEASONALIZED DATA, RECENT YEARS

Year	January	February	March	. . .	November	December
3	2.3	1.7	−0.3	. . .	0.3	0.3
4	−0.3	0	1.0	. . .	−1.7	1.7

13.13.2 The Detrending Mechanisms

Before we elaborately discuss this item, we should define certain concepts.

Ergodic and Stationary. A series is ergodic if observations sufficiently remote from each other are almost uncorrelated. Observations are stationary if they are essentially generated by the same mechanism through time. Ergodicity implies that averaging a series through time tends to add new and useful information about the economic variable being portrayed. Stationarity implies that as we gather more observations, we gradually increase the knowledge of the data

[45] It is understood that the sum of the weights is equal to unity.

generating mechanism itself. Combining the two concepts, it follows that the historical experiences forming an economic time series should be sufficiently different, yet they should be sufficiently similar. The first requirement will provide additional information on the variable and the second requirement will elucidate the underlying economic structure that generates it.

However, in actual practice it is seldom true that the experiences of, for instance, the 1950s are uncorrelated with those of the 1980s except for a predictable trend. This remark applies to such series as real GNP or, for that matter, its components, such as consumption and investment expenditures. For, the current value of, say, the GNP depends on what happened to it in the past, including the turning points in early 1960s and 1970s. It is possible that these unpredictable changes are very temporary and that they will die out over time. In addition, if trends do not change, the predictions based on the 1950s should not differ from those based on the 1960s. But it is the case that not only are these two predictions different from each other but they are different from the actual values (of GNP) of the 1980s. This gives rise to the suspicion that long-term trends are changing, and that they are changing in a nondeterministic way.

It is thus conceivable that the parts P and S of the time series Y should be assumed random. Any problem in identifying the movement in Y as a movement in P or in S can perhaps be resolved by considering trends as large cyclical swings or viewing cycles as rapidly changing trends.

13.14 THE STOCHASTIC TREND AND ITS ELIMINATION

The method used for a variable trend is a simple extension of that for constant linear time trend. As is well known, the latter predicts a per period constant growth of, say, θ. Thus a variable trend adds an unpredictable random component u_t to θ. In symbols, the constant linear trend comes from a relation such as

$$P_t = \alpha + \theta t \tag{13.61}$$

so that

$$\Delta P_t = \theta \tag{13.62}$$

The variable trend is formulated as

$$\Delta P_t = \theta + u_t \tag{13.63}$$

with

$$\begin{aligned} E(u_t u_s) &= 0 \qquad \text{for all } t \neq s \\ E(u_t) &= 0 \qquad \text{for all } t \end{aligned} \tag{13.64}$$

Since u_t is stochastic, there is no certainty that the series P_t will show any continuous pattern of long-term growth (or decay). The specification of a random trend line is comparable to a "random walk with drift" that is often encountered in the literature on money and finance. What is a "random walk with drift"?

Random walk with drift. A time series Z_t is a random walk if

$$Z_t = Z_{t-1} + u_t \tag{13.65}$$

or,

$$\Delta Z_t = u_t \tag{13.66}$$

where u_t is the identically distributed white noise with zero mean. The same series is a random walk with drift if

$$Z_t = \theta + Z_{t-1} + u_t \tag{13.67}$$

or,

$$\Delta Z_t = \theta + u_t \tag{13.68}$$

Thus it should be clear that ΔP_t given by (13.63) is comparable to ΔZ_t given by (13.68).

It follows that we can rewrite the model as:

$$Y_t = P_t + S_t$$

with

$$\begin{aligned} P_t &= \theta + P_{t-1} + u_t \\ S_t &= \text{ARMA}\,(p, q) \end{aligned} \tag{13.69}$$

where p is the number of autoregressive lags and q the order of the moving average. We assume that S_t is a stationary ARMA process defined as follows.

Stationary time series. A time series is said to be stationary if its distribution remains invariant with respect to time. This is sometimes referred to as strict stationarity. A weak- or covariance-stationary time series has its variances and autocovariances equal to (finite) constants. These constants do not depend upon time. Symbolically, such a series is specified by:

$$\text{cov}(Z_t, Z_{t-s}) = \tau_s \qquad \text{for all } t \text{ and } s \tag{13.70}$$

In Section 8.7.9 of Chapter 8, we have defined an autoregressive integrated moving average process denoted as ARIMA (p, d, q), where p and q are, respectively, the order of the autoregressive and moving average processes and d is the order of differencing of the original series. The order d is necessary for providing stationarity in the series. Since the pathbreaking work of Box and Jenkins (1970) it has been widely recognized that most macrotime series, considered one at a time, could be represented by a stationary ARMA process once the series has been first differenced. That is, the series will follow an ARIMA $(p, 1, q)$ process represented as

$$\Delta Y_t = \rho_1 \Delta Y_{t-1} + \rho_2 \Delta Y_{t-2} + \cdots + \rho_p \Delta Y_{t-p} + \epsilon_t + \gamma_1 \epsilon_{t-1} + \cdots + \gamma_q \epsilon_{t-q} \quad (13.71)$$

where the ρs and γs are the coefficients.[46] In the context of such integrated processes, a certain concept known as unit roots has recently been used in the literature a great deal. We will define the concept now.

An integrated process or variable. A series Z_t without deterministic parts which admits of a stationary invertible ARMA representation of order d is written as

$$Z_t \sim I(d) \quad (13.72)$$

A variable or process that is integrated with $d = 1$ is said to be integrated of order 1 or simply integrated. This can be expressed as

$$Z_t = Z_{t-1} + \zeta_t \quad (13.73)$$

where ζ_t follows an ARMA process. An integrated variable that is at the same time expressed as an autoregressive process:

$$Z_t = \rho Z_{t-1} + \zeta_t \quad (13.74)$$

is said to have unit root; that is, $\rho = 1$.[47]

13.15 SOME ECONOMETRIC ISSUES WITH STOCHASTIC TRENDS AND THE UNIT ROOT INVESTIGATION

13.15.1 Spurious Regressions

Granger and Newbold (1974) in a seminal paper examine the consequences of nonsense or "spurious regressions in econometrics". Their contention is that investigators often place an undue emphasis on a high value of R^2 neglecting the

[46] Note that the innovations u_ts and ϵ_ts which influence the permanent and stationary components of a time series by way of its decomposition shown in (13.70) could be perfectly correlated. This is just an expression of the possibility that business cycle fluctuations could be prompted by growth innovations, or conversely, cyclical variations could prompt variations in long-run growth. To cite some empirical evidence, long-run fluctuations (or, equivalently, changes in the stochastic trend) account for 75 to 93% of the quarterly variations in the per capita real GNP in the United States—see Beveridge and Nelson (1981).

[47] Box and Jenkins (1970) qualify integrated processes as "nonstationary". Conventional though the practice is, it is not without conceptual difficulty. The reason is that all integrated processes are nonstationary, but not all nonstationary processes are integrated. To cite an example, an AR(1) process that has the autocorrelation coefficient $\rho_1 > 1$ is not integrated, even though it is nonstationary.

TABLE 13.7 REGRESSIONS OF A SERIES ON *M* INDEPENDENT "EXPLANATORY" SERIES*

Series either all random walks or all ARIMA (0,1,1) series, or changes in these. $Y_0 = 100$, $Y_t = Y_{t-1} + a_t$, $Y'_t = Y_t + kb_t$; $X_{j,0} = 100$, $X_{j,t} = X_{j,t-1} + a_{j,t}$, $X'_{j,t} = X_{j,t} + kb_{j,t}$; $a_{j,t}$, a_t, b_t, $b_{j,t}$ sets of independent N(0,1) white noises. $k = 0$ gives random walks, $k = 1$ gives ARIMA (0,1,1) series. H_0 = no relationship, is true. Series length = 50, number of simulations = 100, $\bar{R}^2$ = corrected R^2.

		Percent times H_0 rejected[a]	Average Durbin–Watson d	Average $\bar{R}^2$	Percent $\bar{R}^2 > 0.7$
			Random Walks		
Levels	$m = 1$	76	0.32	0.26	5
	$m = 2$	78	0.46	0.34	8
	$m = 3$	93	0.55	0.46	25
	$m = 4$	95	0.74	0.55	34
	$m = 5$	96	0.88	0.59	37
Changes	$m = 1$	8	2.00	0.004	0
	$m = 2$	4	1.99	0.001	0
	$m = 3$	2	1.91	−0.007	0
	$m = 4$	10	2.01	0.006	0
	$m = 5$	6	1.99	0.012	0
			ARIMA (0,1,1)		
Levels	$m = 1$	64	0.73	0.20	3
	$m = 2$	81	0.96	0.30	7
	$m = 3$	82	1.09	0.37	11
	$m = 4$	90	1.14	0.44	9
	$m = 5$	90	1.26	0.45	19
Changes	$m = 1$	8	2.58	0.003	0
	$m = 2$	12	2.57	0.01	0
	$m = 3$	7	2.53	0.005	0
	$m = 4$	9	2.53	0.025	0
	$m = 5$	13	2.54	0.027	0

[a] Test at 5% level, using an overall test on $\bar{R}^2$.

fact that the DW statistic has turned out to be low. Recall that inference procedures in such a case become invalid because autocorrelated errors are present. More particularly, the OLS estimates of standard errors are inconsistent. However, when Granger and Newbold regress one series on m (independent) series, the results indicate not only that particular problem but also other more serious problems. The reason is as follows.

All of their series are of three kinds:

(1) random walks;
(2) ARIMA (0, 1, 1); and
(3) changes in ARIMA (0, 1, 1)

The error terms are taken as standard normal and the ARIMA (0, 1, 1) as a random walk added to an independent white noise.[48] Their simulation results based on "100 replications and series of length 50" are reproduced in Table 13.7.

The table shows that the chances are very high for the null hypothesis H_0 being rejected, that is, the relationship is, in all probability, significant. This is true for $m \geq 3$ when the series on both sides of the relationship are independent random walks. Also, the average coefficient of multiple determination ($\bar{R}^2$) increases with m, as also does the average value of the Durbin–Watson statistic (d). The same is true with the ARIMA (0, 1, 1) process. But when changes in random walks, which produce white noise series, are related, we are back to the efficiency properties of the OLS model since its errors will be distributed as white noise. This is not so, however, with changes in the first order moving average processes ARIMA (0, 1, 1). In such a case, "the null hypothesis is rejected twice as often as it should be".[49]

The immediate conclusion based on such evidence, in the words of the authors, is "*it will be the rule* rather than the exception to find spurious relationships. It is also clear that a high value for . . . $\bar{R}^2$ combined with a low value of d (implying a high autocorrelation) is *no indication of a true relationship*." While this relates precisely to series in level forms, the authors indicate that the first difference of a series (rather than the level form of it) will tend to have small autocorrelation. This means that adding an extra term of the differenced series will, to all intents and purposes, generate new information and will contribute to more efficient estimates. It is not that the incidence of misleading conclusions from efficient estimates will be absent when the series is in the first difference form, but that it will be less than if the series were in the level form.[50]

The Granger and Newbold study has given rise to new efforts to detect unit roots: refer to the Dickey and Fuller (1979) study relating to the simple regression model and subsequent studies as listed in Wasserfallen (1986). But it is only recently that a theoretical rationale for the Granger and Newbold results has been presented (Phillips (1986)).

[48] Refer to (13.71). An ARIMA (0, 1, 1) can be written as:

$$\Delta Y_t = \epsilon_t + \gamma_1 \epsilon_{t-1}$$

that is,

$$Y_t = Y_{t-1} + \epsilon_t + \gamma_1 \epsilon_{t-1}$$

This is the sum total of a random walk and an independent white noise.

[49] This follows from the comparison of the probability, on the average, of rejecting the null hypothesis (for various values of m) of the series (in the relationship) based on changes in random walk with those based on changes in ARIMA (0, 1, 1) processes.

[50] Notice that with the series in level form, the original autocorrelation may be so high that adding an extra term to the relation adds little to that autocorrelation as the new term is highly correlated with the immediate past one. Thus the new term serves to keep the efficiency of estimates low, if it was low to begin with.

Phillips takes the regression model

$$Y_t = \beta_0 + \beta_1 X_t + u_t \qquad t = 1, \ldots, n \tag{13.75}$$

where Y_t and X_t both follow independent random walks

$$\begin{aligned} Y_t &= Y_{t-1} + v_t \\ X_t &= X_{t-1} + w_t \end{aligned} \tag{13.76}$$

He shows that as $n \to \infty$

$$\begin{aligned} &n^{1/2} t_{\beta_1} \Rightarrow \zeta_1 \\ &d \xrightarrow{p} 0 \\ &R^2 \Rightarrow \zeta_2 \end{aligned} \tag{13.77}$$

Above, ζ_1 and ζ_2 are random variables with known distributions, the signs $\Rightarrow$ and $\xrightarrow{p}$ indicate (weak) convergence in distribution and convergence in probability, respectively, t is the Student t statistic, d is the DW statistic and R^2 the coefficient of multiple determination.[51] On the whole, the t statistic for a regression coefficient has a distribution that does not converge to a limiting distribution as the sample size increases (that is, one tends to reject the hypothesis of insignificance); the DW statistic approaches zero in probability and R^2 tends to a nondegenerate limiting distribution. These results imply existence of integrated processes, which can of course be tested by the test of unit roots. The extension of these results to the case of multiple regression is straightforward even when, more importantly, the Ys and Xs are not independent and these are the essential aspects of linear regressions using macrotime series. The exception arises when the Ys and Xs are cointegrated.

13.15.2 The Cointegrated Vector

The components of the vector $\mathbf{X_t}$ are cointegrated of order d and b denoted as

$$\mathbf{X_t} \sim \mathrm{CI}(d, b) \tag{13.78}$$

if: (1) all components of $\mathbf{X_t}$ are integrated of order d; and (2) there is a vector $\boldsymbol{\alpha}$ $(\neq \mathbf{0})$ such that $\mathbf{Z_t} = \boldsymbol{\alpha}'\mathbf{X_t}$ and for which

$$\mathbf{Z_t} \sim \mathrm{I}(d - b) \tag{13.79}$$

for $b > 0$. The vector $\boldsymbol{\alpha}$ is said to be the cointegrating vector.

The foregoing is a very general definition. However, we may often be exploring time series that are integrated (of order 1) and, what is more, there may exist a vector $\boldsymbol{\alpha}$ for which $\boldsymbol{\alpha}'\mathbf{X} \sim \mathrm{I}(0)$. In other words, we may particularly have

[51] Or, (squared) coefficient of simple correlation in the case of the above simple linear regression.

a CI(1, 1) vector which means that the original time series are all nonstationary (integrated) even though their linear combination is stationary. This does not mean that a cointegrating vector such as $\boldsymbol{\alpha}$ always exists. For instance, as Phillips indicates in the case of the U.S. economy, consumption and income series are cointegrated, but the wage and price series are not; short- and long-term interest rates are cointegrated as are the (nominal) GNP and M2 money aggregate, but not the (nominal) GNP and M1 and M3 money aggregates, or aggregate liquid assets.[52]

Note that if the time series are integrated, that is, they have unit roots, we can model their first differences only, not their levels. But if they are cointegrated, we can model their levels. This is further explained as follows.

13.15.3 The Cointegrated Vector and Error Correction Representation

The ensuing discussion is from Engle and Granger (1987). Suppose we take a cointegrated vector CI(1, 1):$\mathbf{Z}_t$. Then under certain conditions, $\mathbf{Z}_t$ can be represented as follows, using B as the back shift operator (that is, $\mathrm{B}\mathbf{Z}_t = \mathbf{Z}_{t-1}$), and a stationary time series in $(1 - \mathrm{B})\mathbf{Z}_t$ with an infinite moving average representation

$$(1 - \mathrm{B})\mathbf{Z}_t = C(\mathrm{B})\boldsymbol{\zeta}_t \tag{13.80}$$

as the initial representation, where $\boldsymbol{\zeta}_t$ is the white noise and $C(\mathrm{B})$ a matrix whose elements are polynomials in B:

$$A(\mathrm{B})\mathbf{Z}_t = \mathrm{d}(\mathrm{B})\boldsymbol{\zeta} \tag{13.81}$$

Above, $A(\mathrm{B})$, like $C(\mathrm{B})$, is a matrix with elements that are polynomials in B, and $\mathrm{d}(\mathrm{B})$ is a scalar lag polynomial.

The error correction representation is

$$A^*(\mathrm{B})(1 - \mathrm{B})\mathbf{Z}_t = -\boldsymbol{\delta}\mathbf{Z}_{t-1} + \mathrm{d}(\mathrm{B})\boldsymbol{\zeta}_t \tag{13.82}$$

where $A^*(\mathrm{B})$, like $C(\mathrm{B})$ and $A(\mathrm{B})$, is a matrix with elements that are polynomials in B, and $\boldsymbol{\delta}$ is a coefficient vector. The coefficients of the polynomials in B that appear variously in $A(\mathrm{B})$, $A^*(\mathrm{B})$, and $C(\mathrm{B})$ are subject to constraints, the details of which can be seen in Engle and Granger (1987).

To conclude, should the time series be integrated, they cannot be analyzed directly, without differencing. But should they be cointegrated of order (1, 1), equation (13.81) and (13.82) can be used for estimation and testing. Engle and Granger use equation (13.82) to these ends. For details, see the original source.[53]

Also, see Sims and others (1986) for those regression equations in which not all variables are integrated. On the whole, problems like this belong to a general

[52] M1, M2, and M3 are the three definitions of cash balances.

[53] Some of the preliminary results of this study reappear in a short form in Stock and Watson (1988).

area in which already a great deal of research is underway and perhaps substantially more is needed.

PROBLEMS

13-1. A different use of the disequilibrium models than discussed in the text leads to what are known as error correction models. These are based on the principle that there frequently is a long-run equilibrium relationship between two variables. An example may be Friedman's permanent income hypothesis in which consumption (Y_t) is directly proportional to "permanent" income (X_t). In general, using a relation $Y_t = AX_t$ and taking logarithms on both sides, we have: $y_t = a + x_t$, where the lower case letters indicate logarithms. Differencing, we get $\Delta y_t = \Delta x_t$, Δ being the sign of difference between time points t and $t - 1$. This leads to a general short-run model given by:

$$\text{I: } y_t = \beta_0 + \beta_1 x_t + \beta_2 x_{t-1} + \gamma_1 y_{t-1} + \epsilon_t$$

(a) What are the conditions under which this short-run model will be compatible with the long-run model?

(*Hint:* Assume $y_t = y_{t-1} = \bar{y}$, $x_t = x_{t-1} = \bar{x}$, and $u_t = 0$ in the long run. Then I reduces to $\bar{y}(1 - \gamma_1) = \beta_0 + (\beta_1 + \beta_2)\bar{x}$. To make this compatible with the long-run model $y_t = a + x_t$, show that $1 - \gamma_1 = \beta_1 + \beta_2$ and $a = \beta_0/(1 - \gamma_1)$.)

(b) Using the parametric conditions required for (a), show that

$$\Delta y_t = \beta_0 + \beta_1 \Delta x_t + \delta(x_{t-1} - y_{t-1}) + u_t$$

where δ is $(1 - \gamma_1)$.

(c) What is the short-run disequilibrium adjustment in (b) above? How do you test the disequilibrium component?

(*Hint:* $\Delta y_t = \Delta x_t$ in the long run. Use this relation to identify the short-run adjustment.)

(d) Suppose you apply a t test for the coefficient δ in (b) and the result indicates δ is statistically insignificant at a given probability level. Set up tests of hypotheses to show that the relation in (b) is indeed a long-run relation.

13-2. According to the quantity theory of money, $M_t V = P_t Y_t$, where M_t is money supply, V is velocity of money, P_t is the price index, and Y_t is output or income in real terms. From this, we get that the long-run rate of monetary growth equals the long-run rate of inflation plus the rate of growth of real income.

(a) Show that the quantity theory of money can be transformed to

$$m_t + v = p_t + y_t$$

where the lower case variables are the logarithms of the upper case ones.

(b) Let the short-run relation be

$$m_t = \beta_0 + \beta_1 m_{t-1} + \beta_2 p_t + \beta_3 p_{t-1} + \beta_4 y_t + \beta_5 y_{t-1} + \epsilon_t$$

Show that in order that this short-run relation be compatible with the long-run relation postulated in the quantity theory, we must have:

$$-v = \beta_0/(1 - \beta_1) \qquad 1 - \beta_1 = \beta_2 + \beta_3 = \beta_4 + \beta_5$$

(c) Set up an error correction model of the change in logarithm of money supply of the kind shown in problem 13-1.

(d) Use the annual data for the United States over the period 1960–1987 as given in problem 8-3. Use especially the data on money supply, M_t, (in billions of current dollars) which should be converted to constant 1982 dollars by dividing these by the GNP implicit price deflators. Use also the data on GNP, Y_t, in billions of constant 1982 dollars and data on the GNP implicit price deflator, P_t, with 1982 as the base year. Based on these data, what will be the estimated error correction model that you set up in (c), and what will be your interpretation of the results?

13-3. You are given two possible models for explaining the same dependent variable:

$$\text{I: } \mathbf{Y} = \boldsymbol{X\beta} + \boldsymbol{\epsilon}$$

$$\text{II: } \mathbf{Y} = \mathbf{Z}\boldsymbol{\gamma} + \mathbf{u}$$

where $\boldsymbol{X}$ and $\mathbf{Z}$ are nonrandom and of full column rank; there are $(m_1 + 1)$ elements in $\boldsymbol{\beta}$ and $(m_2 + 1)$ elements in $\boldsymbol{\gamma}$.

(a) Suppose that you have fitted each model by OLS using n observations on $\mathbf{Y}$ and have available the mean sum of squares due to error, s^2, in each case. How can you show that the choice of the model by the criterion of smaller s^2 will lead to the choice of the "true" model on the average?

(*Hint:* Suppose that I is the "true" model, i.e. $E(\boldsymbol{\epsilon}) = \mathbf{0}$ and $E(\boldsymbol{\epsilon\epsilon}') = \sigma^2\boldsymbol{I}$. Then obtain the average value of s^2 for model II.)

(b) What are the advantages and disadvantages of the rule of model selection as indicated in (a)?

(c) How would the model-selection rule be in terms of $\overline{R}^2$ (coefficient of multiple determination), compared to s^2?

13-4. Suppose our models are given by:

$$H_0: Y = X_1\beta_1 + X_2\beta_2 + \epsilon$$

and

$$H_1: y = X_1\beta_1 + \epsilon$$

where H_0 and H_1 are the null and alternative hypotheses, respectively. Suppose that we have collected data on Y, X_1, and X_2.

(a) How would you test that H_0 is a true model? What are your assumptions and what is the test statistic used?

(b) Suppose now the models are specified to be:

$$H_0: Y = X_1\beta_1 + X_2\beta_2 + \epsilon$$

$$H_1: Y = X_1\beta_1 + Z\gamma + \epsilon$$

where Z is another explanatory variable. Relate the test procedure by which you can discriminate between H_0 and H_1.

13-5. Two equations of the "switching regression" model of Quandt are given by:

$$\text{I: } Y_t^d = \beta_0^d + \beta_1^d P_t + \gamma_1^d X_{dt} + \epsilon_{dt}$$

$$\text{II: } Y_t^s = \beta_0^s + \beta_1^s P_t + \gamma_1^s X_{st} + \epsilon_{st}$$

Add to these the Fair and Jaffee conditions:

$$\text{III: } D_t = \begin{cases} Y_t^d & \text{if } Y_t^d < Y_t^s \\ Y_t^s & \text{if } Y_t^d > Y_t^s \end{cases}$$

$$\text{IV: } P_t - P_{t-1} = \theta(Y_t^d - Y_t^s)$$

An alternative formulation of the disequilibrium model is the partial adjustment model of the following type:

$$Y_t^d = \beta_0^d + \beta_1^d P_t^* + \gamma_1^d X_{dt} + \epsilon_{dt}$$

$$Y_t^s = \beta_0^s + \beta_1^s P_t^* + \gamma_1^s X_{st} + \epsilon_{st}$$

$$Y_t^s = Y_t^d = D_t$$

$$P_t - P_{t-1} = (1 - \phi)(P_t^* - P_{t-1}) \qquad 0 < \phi < 1$$

(a) Show that the disequilibrium model identified by equations I–IV is observationally equivalent to the partial adjustment model.

(b) Conceptually, what is the time run involved in the disequilibrium model of equations I–IV and the error correction model of problem 13-1 part (b)? How do you compare these two types of models?

13-6. Consider two nested models

$$\text{Model I: } \underset{(n \times 1)}{\mathbf{Y}} = \underset{(n \times K)}{X}\ \underset{(K \times 1)}{\boldsymbol{\beta}} + \underset{(n \times 1)}{\boldsymbol{\epsilon}}$$

$$\text{Model II: } \underset{(n \times 1)}{\mathbf{Y}} = \underset{(n \times K)}{X}\ \underset{(K \times 1)}{\boldsymbol{\beta}} + \underset{(n \times l)}{Z}\ \underset{(l \times 1)}{\boldsymbol{\gamma}} + \underset{(n \times 1)}{\boldsymbol{\epsilon}}$$

where the sizes of the vectors and matrices are written below their symbols, and the disturbance term $\boldsymbol{\epsilon}$ has classical properties. Let $\hat{\boldsymbol{\beta}}_1^*$ be the OLS estimator of $\boldsymbol{\beta}$ of Model I and $\hat{\boldsymbol{\beta}}_1$, $\hat{\boldsymbol{\gamma}}$ be the OLS estimators of $\boldsymbol{\beta}$ and $\boldsymbol{\gamma}$ of Model II. Let

$$\hat{\boldsymbol{\beta}} = \begin{bmatrix} \hat{\boldsymbol{\beta}}_1 \\ \hat{\boldsymbol{\gamma}} \end{bmatrix} \qquad \hat{\boldsymbol{\beta}}^* = \begin{bmatrix} \hat{\boldsymbol{\beta}}_1^* \\ \mathbf{0} \end{bmatrix} \qquad W = [X \quad Z]$$

Then, by the criterion of mean square error, you will choose Model I if $E(W\hat{\boldsymbol{\beta}} - W\boldsymbol{\beta})'(W\hat{\boldsymbol{\beta}} - W\boldsymbol{\beta}) - E(W\hat{\boldsymbol{\beta}}^* - W\boldsymbol{\beta})'(W\hat{\boldsymbol{\beta}}^* - W\boldsymbol{\beta}) \geqq 0$. Otherwise you will choose Model II. Show that the above criterion is equivalent to

$$\sigma^2 l - \hat{\boldsymbol{\gamma}}'Z'MZ\hat{\boldsymbol{\gamma}} \geqq 0$$

or

$$l \geqq \frac{(\hat{\boldsymbol{\gamma}}'Z'MZ\hat{\boldsymbol{\gamma}})}{\sigma^2}$$

where

$$E(\epsilon_i^2) = \sigma^2 \qquad i = 1, 2, \ldots, n$$

$$M = I - X(X'X)^{-1}X'$$

13-7. Compute "Studentized errors" for the prediction of GNP (in appropriate units) from the rate (per 1000) of enrollment in higher education (HED) of the following data set:

Country	GNP	HED
Bulgaria	427	478
El Salvador	282	93
Italy	621	380
Jamaica	431	44
Mexico	357	271
New Zealand	1786	881
Nicaragua	206	116
Poland	556	369
Romania	421	237
USSR	736	566
Canada	2689	677
United States	23854	893

Using OLS estimated errors or residuals, examine the problems of outlier and model misspecification. How do these diagnostic findings compare (indicate only, do not be rigorous) with the corresponding results obtained from conventional statistical hypothesis testing?

(*Hint:* Use materials of Section 13.11 and 13.11.1 among others. But remember to use crosssection rather than time series considerations, because the data given are for various countries at a given point in time.)

13-8. **(a)** Explain the general specifications of the three models of the demand for money function in the United States fitted over the period 1904–1975 by McAleer and others (1982). How do you account for the J and JA tests used by the authors in their models?

(b) What general conclusions do the authors make about the relative appropriateness of the first two models as between themselves and as against the conventional models used in the literature? Why?

13-9. Explain the role of the following criteria in the general selection of regressors and the "true" model:

(a) Theil's $\overline{R}^2$ criterion

(b) Mallows' C_p criterion

(c) Hocking's S_p criterion
(d) Amemiya's *PC* criterion
(e) Akaike's *IC* criterion

13-10. The following table presents the estimated coefficients and related statistics for three alternative models on robbery rate (*RB*) in Canada based on data for the period 1962 to 1975 collected from various issues of *Statistics Canada*.

(a) How do you argue that the variables might belong to the model? Are the observed signs of the variables in keeping with your intuition or prior beliefs? If not, how would you rationalize the unexpected signs?

(b) Apply the model selection criteria (which are essentially minimizing various functions of the error sum of squares) listed in problem 13-9 to the present models. Write a review of the three models based on the results of these selection criteria.

(c) You can look at Model II and Model I and separately Model III and Model I as two examples of nested models. How would you decide which model is to be accepted in each case?

(*Hint:* Use the test procedures of Section 13.5.)

ESTIMATED MODELS FOR ROBBERY RATE DATA*

Variable	Model I	Model II	Model III
LDVR(−5)	0.002921	0.002244	0.002866
	(0.001273)	(0.001186)	(0.001257)
RU	−0.181858	−0.191319	−0.59832
	(1.20148)	(1.23776)	(1.09422)
PO	−0.449446	0.052509	
	(0.504199)	(0.312296)	
SP	12.9723		5.55554
	(10.4123)		(6.18822)
AF	−0.926266	−1.04782	−0.868783
	(0.480004)	(0.484187)	(0.470193)
CONST	2.16559	4.25471	2.69303
	(2.7361)	(2.22739)	(2.6407)
$\bar{R}^2$	0.9475	0.9443	0.9487
F	47.9434	56.0993	61.1255
ESS**	0.017496	0.020891	0.019234

* Definition of variables:

RB	robbery rate
LDVR(−5)	divorce rate lagged five years
RU	rate of urbanization
PO	police force intensity
SP	% of the population which is single and nondivorced
AF	average family size
CONST	constant

** ESS is error sum of squares

(d) In models of determination of robbery rates, another variable might be important, namely unemployment rate. Explain what are the technical difficulties of including such a variable in models of the three types considered before.

13-11. The data presented in the table are on murder rates (*MR*) and suicide rates (*SR*) and their various explanatory variables, namely, average family size (*AF*), percentage of the population which is single and nondivorced (*SP*), police force intensity (*PO*), rate of urbanization (*RU*), and divorce rate lagged 5 years ($LDVR(-5)$). These data relate to Canada and are collected from various issues of *Statistics Canada* over the general period 1962 to 1975. As an additional variable, data on unemployment rate (*UE*) are also collected and shown.

DATA ON MURDER RATES AND SUICIDE RATES AND THEIR DETERMINANTS: CANADA, 1962–1975

Year	*MR*	*SR*	*UE**	*LDVR***	*RV*	*SP*	*PO*	*AF*
1975	0.0279	0.1140	7.1	222.0	0.4704	0.2062	2.2	3.54
1974	0.0244	0.1230	5.4	200.6	0.4301	0.2049	2.2	3.58
1973	0.0217	0.1210	5.6	166.1	0.3897	0.2039	2.1	3.62
1972	0.0219	0.1170	6.3	148.4	0.3493	0.2013	2.0	3.66
1971	0.0198	0.1170	6.4	137.6	0.3089	0.1989	1.9	3.70
1970	0.0203	0.1133	5.9	139.8	0.2996	0.1965	1.9	3.74
1969	0.0165	0.1091	4.7	124.2	0.2901	0.1936	1.8	3.78
1968	0.0152	0.0975	4.8	54.8	0.2806	0.1920	1.8	3.82
1967	0.0138	0.0903	4.1	54.8	0.2711	0.1899	1.7	3.86
1966	0.0111	0.0856	3.6	51.2	0.2616	0.1881	1.7	3.90
1965	0.0124	0.0873	3.9	45.7	0.2522	0.1858	1.6	3.90
1964	0.0113	0.0822	4.7	44.7	0.2426	0.1833	1.6	3.90
1963	0.0114	0.0756	5.5	40.6	0.2330	0.1807	1.5	3.90
1962	0.0117	0.0716	5.9	36.4	0.2234	0.1780	1.5	3.90
1961	—	—	—	36.0	—	—	—	—
1960	—	—	—	39.1	—	—	—	—
1959	—	—	—	37.4	—	—	—	—
1958	—	—	—	36.8	—	—	—	—
1957	—	—	—	40.3	—	—	—	—

* In %
** Per 1000

Estimate the models of the three types shown in problem 13-10 and calculate their associated statistics. Then, answer questions (a)–(d) of that problem but related to the new dependent variables:

(a) murder rate; and

(b) suicide rate

For part (d), show what actual problems will be encountered by having to include unemployment rate as an additional variable in Model I trying to explain murder rates and, separately, suicide rates.

13-12. **(a)** Discuss the econometric issues arising from stochastic trends of an economic time series emphasizing the contribution made by Granger and Newbold (1974) on the consequences of nonsense or ''spurious regression in econometrics''.

(b) Describe the main aspects of Phillips' contribution to the development of a theoretical rationale, based on integrated processes or time series with unit roots, for the Granger and Newbold results referred to in (a).

(c) Discuss Engle and Granger's (1987) method of modeling time series in terms of their levels when the series are cointegrated and error correction representation is used.

Appendix A
Additional Methods and Results

A.1 THE PRAIS–WINSTON METHOD

Let us consider the model

$$\mathbf{Y} = X\boldsymbol{\beta} + \boldsymbol{\epsilon}$$

in which

$$\mathrm{E}(\boldsymbol{\epsilon}) = \mathbf{0}$$
$$\mathrm{E}(\boldsymbol{\epsilon\epsilon}') = \sigma^2\boldsymbol{\Omega}$$

In particular, consider a two-variable regression in which $\boldsymbol{\epsilon}$ follows an AR(1) scheme:

$$\begin{aligned} Y_t &= \beta_0 + \beta_1 X_t + \epsilon_t \qquad t = 1, \ldots, n \\ \epsilon_t &= \rho\epsilon_{t-1} + \nu_t \qquad |\rho| < 1 \end{aligned} \tag{A.1.1}$$

the νs are independent random variables with zero means and variances equal to σ_ν^2. In this particular specification of the model, $\boldsymbol{\Omega}$ will be determined as in (7.6) of the text. It can be easily verified (see Kadiyala (1968)) that

$$\boldsymbol{\Omega}^{-1} = \{1/(1 - \rho^2)\} \begin{bmatrix} 1 & -\rho & 0 \cdots & 0 & 0 & 0 \\ -\rho & 1 + \rho^2 & -\rho \cdots & 0 & 0 & 0 \\ \vdots & \vdots & \vdots \; \vdots & \vdots & \vdots & \vdots \\ 0 & 0 & 0 \cdots & -\rho & 1 + \rho^2 & -\rho \\ 0 & 0 & 0 \cdots & 0 & -\rho & 1 \end{bmatrix}$$

Let us now define an $(n - 1) \times n$ transformation matrix $\boldsymbol{T_2}$:

$$\boldsymbol{T_2} = \begin{bmatrix} -\rho & 1 & 0 \cdots & 0 & 0 \\ 0 & -\rho & 1 \cdots & 0 & 0 \\ \vdots & \vdots & \vdots \quad \vdots & \vdots & \vdots \\ 0 & 0 & 0 \cdots & -\rho & 1 \end{bmatrix}$$

From $\boldsymbol{T_2}$, we augment the transformation matrix $\boldsymbol{T_I}$ by merely inserting the first row: $[\sqrt{1 - \rho^2}\ 0\ 0\ \ldots\ 0]$ above $\boldsymbol{T_2}$. Thus,

$$\boldsymbol{T_I} = \begin{bmatrix} \sqrt{1 - \rho^2} & 0 & 0 \cdots & 0 & 0 \\ -\rho & 1 & 0 \cdots & 0 & 0 \\ 0 & -\rho & 1 \cdots & 0 & 0 \\ \vdots & \vdots & \vdots \quad \vdots & \vdots & \vdots \\ 0 & 0 & 0 \cdots & -\rho & 1 \end{bmatrix}$$

Notice that $\boldsymbol{T_I'T_I} = (1 - \rho^2)\boldsymbol{\Omega^{-1}}$. It should be clear that $\boldsymbol{T_I}$ somehow accounts for the first sample observation, whereas $\boldsymbol{T_2}$ does not. Anyway, multiplying equation (A.1.1) throughout by $\boldsymbol{T_2}$, we get the transformed model

$$\begin{bmatrix} Y_2 - \rho Y_1 \\ Y_3 - \rho Y_2 \\ \vdots \\ Y_n - \rho Y_{n-1} \end{bmatrix} = \begin{bmatrix} 1 & X_2 - \rho X_1 \\ 1 & X_3 - \rho X_2 \\ \vdots & \vdots \\ 1 & X_n - \rho X_{n-1} \end{bmatrix} \begin{bmatrix} \beta_0(1 - \rho) \\ \beta_1 \end{bmatrix} + \begin{bmatrix} \nu_2 \\ \nu_3 \\ \vdots \\ \nu_n \end{bmatrix} \qquad \text{(A.1.2)}$$

The above means that an OLS method that is available will estimate the parameters of the equation, which is an equation in the semi-first difference in the variables. The number of observations on these is one less than the full number n. The intercept term in the (A.1.2) formulation is $\beta_0(1 - \rho)$.

If we apply $\boldsymbol{T_I}$ to (A.1.1), we get the transformed model

$$\begin{bmatrix} \sqrt{1 - \rho^2}\, Y_1 \\ Y_2 - \rho Y_1 \\ Y_3 - \rho Y_2 \\ \vdots \\ Y_n - \rho Y_{n-1} \end{bmatrix} = \begin{bmatrix} \sqrt{1 - \rho^2} & \sqrt{1 - \rho^2}\, X_1 \\ 1 - \rho & X_2 - \rho X_1 \\ 1 - \rho & X_3 - \rho X_2 \\ \vdots & \vdots \\ 1 - \rho & X_n - \rho X_{n-1} \end{bmatrix} \begin{bmatrix} \beta_0 \\ \beta_1 \end{bmatrix} + \begin{bmatrix} \sqrt{1 - \rho^2}\, \epsilon_1 \\ \nu_2 \\ \nu_3 \\ \vdots \\ \nu_n \end{bmatrix} \qquad \text{(A.1.3)}$$

Referring back to Section 7.3.6 of Chapter 7, the Cochrane–Orcutt method uses the model of equation (A.1.2) based on the transformation matrix $\boldsymbol{T_2}$.

The Prais–Winston method uses instead equations (A.1.3), based on the transformation matrix $\boldsymbol{T_I}$. In this equation, the first term is directly provided for and may be the cause of increased efficiency of estimates, especially in small sample situations.

A.2 THE GAUSS–MARKOV THEOREM IN THE GENERALIZED MODEL

Let us reproduce (7.56) and (7.57) as follows:

$$\hat{\boldsymbol{\beta}} = (X'\Omega^{-1}X)^{-1}X'\Omega^{-1}\mathbf{Y} \tag{7.56}$$

$$V(\hat{\boldsymbol{\beta}}) = \sigma^2(X'\Omega^{-1}X)^{-1} \tag{7.57}$$

More simply, express:

$$\hat{\boldsymbol{\beta}} = \hat{C}'\mathbf{Y}$$

where

$$\hat{C}' = (X'\Omega^{-1}X)^{-1}X'\Omega^{-1}$$

Then since $\mathbf{Y} = X\boldsymbol{\beta} + \boldsymbol{\epsilon}$, and $\mathrm{E}(\boldsymbol{\epsilon}) = \mathbf{0}$, the fact that $\hat{\boldsymbol{\beta}}$ is unbiased for $\boldsymbol{\beta}$ means

$$\mathrm{E}(\hat{\boldsymbol{\beta}}) = \boldsymbol{\beta}$$

which in turn, means

$$\hat{C}'X = I$$

Let us, without loss of generality, construct another unbiased estimator $\tilde{\boldsymbol{\beta}}$ on the basis of $\hat{\boldsymbol{\beta}}$ such that

$$\tilde{\boldsymbol{\beta}} = \tilde{C}'\mathbf{Y}$$

where

$$\tilde{C}' = \hat{C}' + D'$$

and D' is a $(1 + m) \times n$ nonrandom matrix just as $\hat{C}'$ is. In order that $\tilde{\boldsymbol{\beta}}$ is unbiased for $\boldsymbol{\beta}$, we must have

$$\tilde{C}'X = I$$

But since $\hat{C}'X = I$, it must mean

$$D'X = \mathbf{0}$$

Therefore, the variance–covariance matrix of $\tilde{\boldsymbol{\beta}}$ is

$$\begin{aligned} V(\tilde{\boldsymbol{\beta}}) &= \sigma^2[(\hat{C}' + D')\Omega(\hat{C} + D)] \\ &= \sigma^2[\hat{C}'\Omega\hat{C} + D'\Omega\hat{C} + \hat{C}'\Omega D + D'\Omega D] \\ &= \sigma^2[\hat{C}'\Omega\hat{C} + D'\Omega D] = V(\hat{\boldsymbol{\beta}}) + \sigma^2 D'\Omega D \end{aligned}$$

In above each of the terms $D'\Omega\hat{C}$ and $\hat{C}'\Omega D$ is zero, since

$$\begin{aligned} D'\Omega\hat{C} &= D'\Omega\Omega^{-1}X(X'\Omega^{-1}X)^{-1} \\ &= D'X(X'\Omega^{-1}X)^{-1} \\ &= 0 \end{aligned}$$

because $D'X = 0$. Similarly $\hat{C}'\Omega D = 0$.

Now $D'\Omega D$ is nonnegative definite because Ω is: see result 3 of Section 3.9, Chapter 3. Therefore $\hat{\beta}$ is BLUE for β in this generalized linear regression model. This is the essence of the Gauss–Markov theorem.

A.3 MEAN VALUE OF THE VARIABLE IN THE TOBIT MODEL (OR, DERIVATION OF (7.120) OF CHAPTER 7)

The distribution of $Y - L$, where $L = 0$ is the lower limit of L, is derived from the distribution of $\epsilon = I^N$ as follows:

$$\text{Prob}\{Y = 0/I, L\} = \text{Prob}\{I^N \geqq I/I\} = 1 - F(I/\sigma)$$

$$\text{Prob}\{Y > Y^N \geqq (L = 0)/I\} = \text{Prob}\{I - I^N > Y^N\}$$

$$= \text{Prob}\{I^N < I - Y^N/I\} = F(I - Y^N/\sigma)$$

Thus the cumulative distribution function for Y for given values of I and L ($= 0$, here) is:

$$F(Y^N; I, L) = 0 \text{ (for } Y = Y^N < 0)$$

$$F(Y^N = L = 0; I, L) = 1 - F(I/\sigma) \text{(for } Y = Y^N = 0)$$

$$F(Y^N; I, L) = F\left(\frac{I - Y^N}{\sigma}\right) \text{ (for } Y = Y^N > 0)$$

The maximum likelihood estimates of β and σ are derived from I and the above probability functions, being functions of β and σ. For this a connection between probability density function and cumulative distribution function $F(Y^N; I, L)$ for $Y = Y^N > 0$ has to be established.

Since

$$F(u) = \int_{-\infty}^{u} f(x)\, dx$$

so

$$dF(u) = f(u)du$$

Put $u = \dfrac{I - Y^N}{\sigma}$. Then, $dF\left(\dfrac{I - Y^N}{\sigma}\right)(-1) = f\left(\dfrac{I - Y^N}{\sigma}\right) - dY^N/\sigma$. That is, $dF\left(\dfrac{I - Y^N}{\sigma}\right) = f\left(\dfrac{I - Y^N}{\sigma}\right) dY^N/\sigma$.

The likelihood function of a sample of size n, the first g observations of which have $Y = 1$ and the last $n - g$, $Y > 0$, is:

$$£ = [1 - F(I_1/\sigma)] \ldots [1 - F(I_g/\sigma)]\; 1/\sigma\, f\left(\frac{I_{g+1} - Y_{g+1}}{\sigma}\right) \ldots 1/\sigma\, f\left(\frac{I_n - Y_n}{\sigma}\right)$$

$\ln £ = L$ then becomes expression (7.118) of the text.

Next we find $E(Y/I)$ and $\hat{Y}$:

$$E(Y/I) = \{(Y^N < 0)\ \text{Prob}(Y^N < 0)\} + (Y^N = 0)\ \text{Prob}(Y^N = 0) + (Y^N > 0)\ \text{Prob}(Y^N > 0)$$

$$= 0 + 0 + \int_0^{\infty} Y^N/\sigma\, f\left(\frac{I - Y^N}{\sigma}\right) dY^N$$

Put $\dfrac{I - Y^N}{\sigma} = x$. This implies Y^N varies between 0 and ∞ as x varies between I/σ and $-\infty$. Also $-dY^N/\sigma = dx$, or $dY^N = -\sigma dx$ and $I - \sigma x = Y^N$. Thus,

$$E(Y/I) = \int_0^{\infty} Y^N/\sigma\, f\left(\frac{I - Y^N}{\sigma}\right) dY^N = \int_{-\infty}^{I/\sigma} (I - \sigma x) f(x)\, dx$$

$$= \int_{-\infty}^{I/\sigma} If(x)\, dx + \sigma \int_{-\infty}^{I/\sigma} (-x) f(x)\, dx$$

Now

$$f(x) = (1/\sqrt{2\pi})e^{-x^2/2}$$

so

$$f'(x) = df(x)/dx = -x(1/\sqrt{2\pi})e^{-x^2/2} = -xf(x)$$

Thus

$$\int_{-\infty}^{I/\sigma} -xf(x)\, dx = \int_{-\infty}^{I/\sigma} df(x) = f(I/\sigma)$$

All together, then,

$$E(Y/I) = IF(I/\sigma) + \sigma f(I/\sigma)$$

which is estimated by

$$\hat{Y} = \hat{I}F(\hat{I}/\hat{\sigma}) + \hat{\sigma} f(\hat{I}/\hat{\sigma})$$

where $\hat{I}$ and $\hat{\sigma}$ are the maximum likelihood estimates of I and σ, obtained by solving $\partial L/\partial\sigma = 0$ and $\partial L/\partial\beta = 0$, and using $\mathbf{I} = \mathbf{X}\boldsymbol{\beta}$ adapted to a given sample individual.

A.4 THE MARGINAL POSTERIOR PROBABILITY DENSITY FUNCTION FOR REGRESSION COEFFICIENTS IN THE SIMPLE REGRESSION MODEL (OR, DERIVATION OF EQUATION (10.171) OF CHAPTER 10)

A Standard Gamma function is defined by:

$$\Gamma(p) = \int_0^{\infty} x^{p-1} e^{-x}\, dx \qquad p > 0$$

Then,

$$\int_0^\infty p(\beta_0, \beta_1, \sigma/Y, X)\, d\sigma$$

$$\propto \int_0^\infty (a\sigma^{-2})^{n-2/2} e^{-a\sigma^{-2}}\, d(a\sigma^{-2})$$

$$\propto a^{-n/2} \int_0^\infty (a\sigma^{-2})^{n/2-1} e^{-a\sigma^{-2}}\, d(a\sigma^{-2})$$

$$\propto \Gamma\,(n/2) a^{-n/2}$$

$$\propto a^{-n/2}$$

where

$$a = \tfrac{1}{2}[(n - 2)s^2 + n(\beta_0 - \hat{\beta}_0)^2 + (\beta_1 - \hat{\beta}_1)^2\, \Sigma X_i^2 + 2(\beta_0 - \hat{\beta}_0)(\beta_1 - \hat{\beta}_1)\Sigma X_i]$$

This is equation (10.167) in the text.

A.5 METHOD OF PRINCIPAL COMPONENTS

In econometrics, especially in problems of linear regression, if the number of explanatory variables is large computations become very difficult. Also reliability of coefficient estimates decreases substantially due, firstly, to the loss of degrees of freedom of the residual variance, and secondly, to the possible intercorrelation among the regressors.

The method of principal components is one way of ascertaining the dimensions or the strength of independence among the chosen regressors. Suppose there are p such regressors each producing n sample observations with the mean value zero. These observations are denoted by the various elements of the p columns of the X matrix as presented below:

$$X = \begin{bmatrix} X_{11} & \cdots & X_{1p} \\ \vdots & & \vdots\ \vdots \\ X_{n1} & \cdots & X_{np} \end{bmatrix}$$

The objective of this method is to construct from the p X_js a set of p new variables, W_js, said to be their principal components, which are linear combinations of the X_js as follows:

$$W_j = C_{j1}X_1 + C_{j2}X_2 + \cdots + C_{jp}X_p \qquad j = 1, 2, \ldots, p$$

These W_js are designed to be uncorrelated by pairs. The first principal component W_1 explains the highest possible proportion of the total variation among the Xs, the second principal component W_2 explains the largest of the remaining variation among the Xs (net of the amount already explained by W_1) and so on. Suppose now that $j = 1$. Then

$$\mathbf{W_1} = C_{11}\mathbf{X_1} + C_{12}\mathbf{X_2} + \cdots + C_{1p}\mathbf{X}_p$$
$$= X\mathbf{C_1}$$

where X has been defined before, and $\mathbf{C_1}$ is the column vector whose elements are $C_{11}, \ldots, C_{1p}$. (Notice that a $\mathbf{W_j}$ or an $\mathbf{X_j}$ is a column vector with elements that are the sample observations on each of them, $j = 1, \ldots, p$.) Continuing, the sum of squares due to $\mathbf{W_1}$ is

$$\mathbf{W_1'W_1} = \mathbf{C_1'}X'X\mathbf{C_1} \tag{A.5.1}$$

Our purpose is to maximize this sum of squares for the proper choice of the linearizing coefficients $\mathbf{C_1}$s such that $\mathbf{C_1}$ is of the normalized length secured by the condition

$$\mathbf{C_1'C_1} = 1$$

Accordingly we form the objective function

$$\mathrm{L} = \mathbf{C_1'}X'X\mathbf{C_1} - \lambda_1(\mathbf{C_1'C_1} - 1)$$

in which λ_1 is a Lagrangean multiplier, and set

$$\partial\mathrm{L}/\partial\mathbf{C_1}(= 2X'X\mathbf{C_1} - 2\lambda_1\mathbf{C_1}) = \mathbf{0}$$

The solution of this equation gives

$$X'X\mathbf{C_1} = \lambda_1\mathbf{C_1} \tag{A.5.2}$$

using the normalizing rule. Obviously λ_1 is the characteristic root of $X'X$, and since, from (A.5.1),

$$\mathbf{W_1'W_1} = \mathbf{C_1'}\lambda_1\mathbf{C_1} = \lambda_1\mathbf{C_1'C_1} = \lambda_1$$

maximizing $\mathbf{W_1'W_1}$ would reduce to choosing for λ_1 the maximum characteristic root of $X'X$. If we rule out perfect multicollinearity among the Xs, $X'X$ will be positive definite, and therefore will have positive characteristic roots. This establishes $\mathbf{W_1}$ as the first principal component of X.

For the second principal component $\mathbf{W_2}$, the choice is based on an exactly similar reasoning plus the condition that $\mathbf{W_2}$ would be uncorrelated with $\mathbf{W_1}$. Without much ado, the purpose is to maximize

$$\mathbf{W_2'W_2} = \mathbf{C_2'}X'X\mathbf{C_2}$$

subject to

$$\mathbf{C_2'C_2} = 1$$
$$\mathbf{C_1'C_2} = 0$$

The second condition above is to make the two principal components uncorrelated. Our new objective function is then

$$L = \mathbf{C}_2' X_2' X_2 \mathbf{C}_2 - \lambda_2(\mathbf{C}_2'\mathbf{C}_2 - 1) - \mu \mathbf{C}_1'\mathbf{C}_2$$

λ_2 and μ being Lagrangean multipliers. Maximizing L requires setting

$$\partial L/\partial \mathbf{C}_2 (= 2X'X\mathbf{C}_2 - 2\lambda_2\mathbf{C}_2 - \mu\mathbf{C}_1) = \mathbf{0} \qquad \text{(A.5.3)}$$

from which by premultiplying by $\mathbf{C}_1'$, we derive, by using $\mathbf{C}_1'\mathbf{C}_1 = 1$ and $\mathbf{C}_1'\mathbf{C}_2 = 0$,

$$2\mathbf{C}_1'X'X\mathbf{C}_2 - \mu = 0$$

But from (A.5.2), $(X'X\mathbf{C}_1)' = \mathbf{C}_1'\mathbf{X}'\mathbf{X} = \lambda_1\mathbf{C}_1'$, from which, by post multiplying by $\mathbf{C}_2$, we get

$$\mathbf{C}_1'X'X\mathbf{C}_2 = \lambda_1\mathbf{C}_1'\mathbf{C}_2 = 0$$

Thus

$$\mu = 2\mathbf{C}_1'X'X\mathbf{C}_2 = 2 \times 0 = 0$$

and, from (A.5.3),

$$X'X\mathbf{C}_2 = \lambda_2\mathbf{C}_2$$

After this, all we need to do is choose λ_2 to be the second highest characteristic root of $X'X$. This method can be easily extended to the choice of all the p characteristic roots of the matrix $X'X$: $\lambda_1, \lambda_2, \ldots, \lambda_p$, and formation of the associated characteristic vectors into an orthogonal matrix:

$$C = [\mathbf{C}_1\mathbf{C}_2 \cdots \mathbf{C}_p]$$

The p principal components of X will then come from the $n \times p$ matrix W where

$$W = XC \qquad \text{(A.5.4)}$$

and

$$W'W = C'X'XC = \Lambda = \begin{bmatrix} \lambda_1 & 0 & \cdots & 0 \\ 0 & \lambda_2 & \cdots & 0 \\ \vdots & \vdots & & \vdots \\ 0 & 0 & \cdots & \lambda_p \end{bmatrix} \qquad \text{(A.5.5)}$$

Λ, being a diagonal matrix, indicates that the principal component Ws are uncorrelated by pairs, the off-diagonal elements of Λ being zero, and their sums of squares are the λs, as evident from the diagonal elements of Λ.

We should point out that the rank of X may not be the full rank p. Suppose that that is s, where $s < p$. Then $s - p$ characteristic roots would be zero and necessarily we would use s independent variables to explain the variation in Xs. This remark applies even when the rank of X is full but some of the characteristic roots may be so small that practically a small number of principal components may effectively do the job of explaining the variation in the Xs.

We shall now show how each principal component explains what proportion of the total variation in Xs. To that end, observe that the total variation in X is:

$$\sum X_1^2 + \sum X_2^2 + \cdots + \sum X_p^2 = \text{Trace}(X'X)$$

where each summation is over the n sample observations of a variable. Now since

$$\text{Tr}(C'X'XC) = \text{Tr}(X'XCC') = \text{Tr}(X'X)$$

CC' being an identity matrix, so

$$\sum X_1^2 + \cdots + \sum X_p^2 = \text{Tr}(X'X) = \text{Tr}C'X'XC = \sum_1^p \lambda_j = \sum_1^p W_j'W_j$$

This implies that $\lambda_j/\sum\lambda_j$ will measure the proportionate contribution made by the jth principal component of X towards explaining the total variation in Xs, $j = 1, 2, \ldots, p$.

The foregoing inference can be recast in the form of the proportions of the variation in one X, say X_j, explained by the correlations between this X variable and the various principal components. To see this, consider, for instance, the jth principal component and the X variables. The product $X'\mathbf{W_j}$ gives the product sum of W_j and every X variable, which can be expressed as

$$X'\mathbf{W_j} = X'X\mathbf{C_j} = \lambda_j\mathbf{C_j}$$

This gives rise to the idea that for a specific X, say X_j, and specific W, say W_j, the product moment correlation coefficient is

$$\rho_{jj} = \frac{\lambda_j C_{jj}}{\sqrt{\lambda_j}\sqrt{\sum X_j^2}} = \frac{C_{jj}\sqrt{\lambda_j}}{\sqrt{\sum X_j^2}} \qquad j = 1, 2, \ldots, p$$

where the summation is over all sample observations of X_j, and C_{jj} is the jth element of the vector $\mathbf{C_j}$. On the other hand, correlating X_i and W_j, where i and j can both be the same and different, we have:

$$\rho_{ij} = \frac{C_{ij}\sqrt{\lambda_j}}{\sqrt{\sum X_i^2}} \qquad i, j = 1, \ldots, p$$

Now since, from (A.5.4),

$$W = XC$$

so

$$X' = CW'$$

because C is orthogonal: $(C')^{-1} = C$. Thus

$$X'X = CW'WC' = C\Lambda C'$$

using (A.5.5). Therefore

$$\sum X_j^2 = \sum_{j=1}^p C_{ij}^2\lambda_j \qquad i = 1, \ldots, p$$

from which, dividing throughout by $\sum X_j^2$, we get:

$$1 = \frac{C_{i1}^2\lambda_1}{\sum X_j^2} + \frac{C_{i2}^2\lambda_2}{\sum X_j^2} + \cdots + \frac{C_{ip}^2\lambda_p}{\sum X_j^2}$$

$$= \rho_{i1}^2 + \rho_{i2}^2 + \cdots + \rho_{ip}^2$$

This clearly determines the ρ^2s as the proportions of the variables in X_j ascribed to the different principal components. The lack of zero correlation among the principal components assures that these proportions add up to unity.

A.6 THE MAXIMUM LIKELIHOOD ESTIMATION OF SIMULTANEOUS EQUATIONS WITH VECTOR AUTOREGRESSIVE RESIDUALS

Sargan (1961) takes a simultaneous equation model as

$$\Gamma \mathbf{y}_t + B\mathbf{x}_t = D\mathbf{z}_t = \boldsymbol{\epsilon}_t \qquad t = 1, 2, \ldots, n$$

with the ys endogenous and the xs predetermined variables with coefficients Γ and B, respectively, and

$$\mathbf{z}_t = \begin{bmatrix} \mathbf{y}_t \\ \\ \mathbf{x}_t \end{bmatrix} \qquad D = [\Gamma : B] \qquad |\Gamma| \neq 0$$

The error $\boldsymbol{\epsilon}_t$ is specified to follow a first order autoregressive process of the form

$$\boldsymbol{\epsilon}_t = R\boldsymbol{\epsilon}_{t-1} + \mathbf{u}_t$$

where R represents the matrix of autoregressive parameters (which is the source of the terminology: vector autoregressive residuals), and

$$\mathbf{u}_t \sim \text{NID}(\mathbf{0}, \boldsymbol{\Sigma})$$

NID means independently distributed normal variables. These variables u have zero means and variance–covariance matrix $\boldsymbol{\Sigma}$. Let

$$Z' = [\mathbf{z}_1\mathbf{z}_2 \cdots \mathbf{z}_n]$$

$$\varepsilon' = [\boldsymbol{\epsilon}_1\boldsymbol{\epsilon}_2 \cdots \boldsymbol{\epsilon}_n]$$

and

$$U' = [\mathbf{u}_1\mathbf{u}_2 \cdots \mathbf{u}_n]$$

Then

$$DZ' = \varepsilon' = RDZ'_{-1} + U'$$

Z'_{-1} is the lagged value of the matrix Z'. Thus,

$$DZ' - RDZ'_{-1} = U'$$

The above represents a generalized system of equations which can be estimated by the FIML method based on a specific set of nonlinear constraints on the parameters.

A likelihood ratio test (see Chapter 10, Section 10.3 for basic ideas) of overidentifying restrictions can be made as in the usual FIML method.

The author uses a modified Newton–Raphson nonlinear procedure with the matrix of second derivatives denoted by $V(\boldsymbol{\theta})$: $\hat{\boldsymbol{\theta}}$ will maximize the likelihood if $V(\hat{\boldsymbol{\theta}})$ is positive definite. He uses the method of numerical maximization of the likelihood based on an algorithm that is developed by Powell (1964). See Walsh (1966) on minimization of functions of several variables.

Two articles that make interesting use of Sargan's 1961 work are Hendry (1971) and Hendry and Tremayne (1976) in the context of systems estimation based on vector autoregressive errors.

Appendix B

Statistical Tables

TABLE B.1 THE STANDARD NORMAL DISTRIBUTION

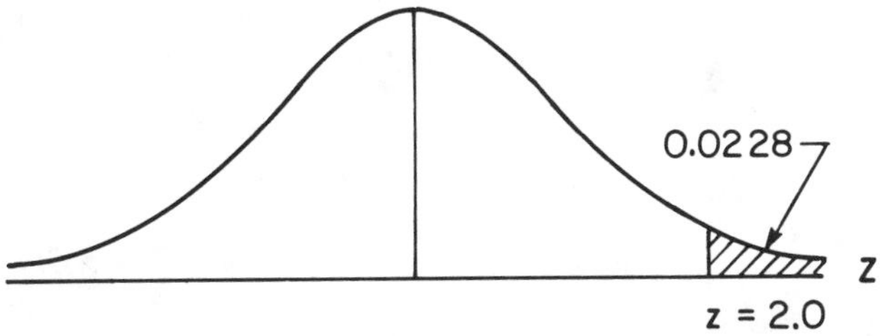

z	0.00	0.01	0.02	0.03	0.04	0.05	0.06	0.07	0.08	0.09
0.0	0.5000	0.4960	0.4920	0.4880	0.4840	0.4801	0.4761	0.4721	0.4681	0.4641
0.1	0.4602	0.4562	0.4522	0.4483	0.4443	0.4404	0.4364	0.4325	0.4286	0.4247
0.2	0.4207	0.4168	0.4129	0.4090	0.4052	0.4013	0.3974	0.3936	0.3897	0.3859
0.3	0.3821	0.3783	0.3745	0.3707	0.3669	0.3632	0.3594	0.3557	0.3520	0.3483
0.4	0.3446	0.3409	0.3372	0.3336	0.3300	0.3264	0.3228	0.3192	0.3156	0.3121
0.5	0.3085	0.3050	0.3015	0.2981	0.2946	0.2912	0.2877	0.2843	0.2810	0.2776
0.6	0.2743	0.2709	0.2676	0.2643	0.2611	0.2578	0.2546	0.2514	0.2483	0.2451
0.7	0.2420	0.2389	0.2358	0.2327	0.2296	0.2266	0.2236	0.2206	0.2177	0.2148
0.8	0.2119	0.2090	0.2061	0.2033	0.2005	0.1977	0.1949	0.1922	0.1894	0.1867
0.9	0.1841	0.1814	0.1788	0.1762	0.1736	0.1711	0.1685	0.1660	0.1635	0.1611
1.0	0.1587	0.1562	0.1539	0.1515	0.1492	0.1469	0.1446	0.1423	0.1401	0.1379
1.1	0.1357	0.1335	0.1314	0.1292	0.1271	0.1251	0.1230	0.1210	0.1190	0.1170
1.2	0.1151	0.1131	0.1112	0.1093	0.1075	0.1056	0.1038	0.1020	0.1003	0.0985
1.3	0.0968	0.0951	0.0934	0.0918	0.0901	0.0885	0.0869	0.0853	0.0838	0.0823
1.4	0.0808	0.0793	0.0778	0.0764	0.0749	0.0735	0.0721	0.0708	0.0694	0.0681
1.5	0.0668	0.0655	0.0643	0.0630	0.0618	0.0606	0.0594	0.0582	0.0571	0.0559
1.6	0.0548	0.0537	0.0526	0.0516	0.0505	0.0495	0.0485	0.0475	0.0465	0.0455
1.7	0.0446	0.0436	0.0427	0.0418	0.0409	0.0401	0.0392	0.0384	0.0375	0.0367
1.8	0.0359	0.0351	0.0344	0.0336	0.0329	0.0322	0.0314	0.0307	0.0301	0.0294
1.9	0.0287	0.0281	0.0274	0.0268	0.0262	0.0256	0.0250	0.0244	0.0239	0.0233
2.0	0.0228	0.0222	0.0217	0.0212	0.0207	0.0202	0.0197	0.0192	0.0188	0.0183
2.1	0.0179	0.0174	0.0170	0.0166	0.0162	0.0158	0.0154	0.0150	0.0146	0.0143
2.2	0.0139	0.0136	0.0132	0.0129	0.0125	0.0122	0.0119	0.0116	0.0113	0.0110
2.3	0.0107	0.0104	0.0102	0.0099	0.0096	0.0094	0.0091	0.0089	0.0087	0.0084
2.4	0.0082	0.0080	0.0078	0.0075	0.0073	0.0071	0.0069	0.0068	0.0066	0.0064
2.5	0.0062	0.0060	0.0059	0.0057	0.0055	0.0054	0.0052	0.0051	0.0049	0.0048
2.6	0.0047	0.0045	0.0044	0.0043	0.0041	0.0040	0.0039	0.0038	0.0037	0.0036
2.7	0.0035	0.0034	0.0033	0.0032	0.0031	0.0030	0.0029	0.0028	0.0027	0.0026
2.8	0.0026	0.0025	0.0024	0.0023	0.0023	0.0022	0.0021	0.0021	0.0020	0.0019
2.9	0.0019	0.0018	0.0018	0.0017	0.0016	0.0016	0.0015	0.0015	0.0014	0.0014
3.0	0.0013	0.0013	0.0013	0.0012	0.0012	0.0011	0.0011	0.0011	0.0010	0.0010

NOTE The table plots the cumulative probability $Z \geq z$.

Source Based on *Biometrika Tables for Statisticians*, Vol. 1, 3rd ed. (1966), with the permission of the *Biometrika* trustees.

TABLE B.2 The χ^2 Distribution

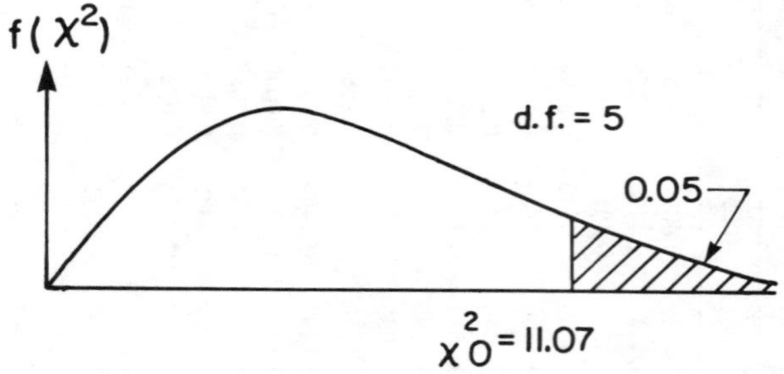

Degrees of freedom	P = 0.99	0.98	0.95	0.90	0.80	0.70	0.50	0.30	0.20	0.10	0.05	0.02	0.01
1	0.000157	0.000628	0.00393	0.0158	0.0642	0.148	0.455	1.074	1.642	2.706	3.841	5.412	6.635
2	0.0201	0.0404	0.103	0.211	0.446	0.713	1.386	2.408	3.219	4.605	5.991	7.824	9.210
3	0.115	0.185	0.352	0.584	1.005	1.424	2.366	3.665	4.642	6.251	7.815	9.837	11.341
4	0.297	0.429	0.711	1.064	1.649	2.195	3.357	4.878	5.989	7.779	9.488	11.668	13.277
5	0.554	0.752	1.145	1.610	2.343	3.000	4.351	6.064	7.289	9.236	11.070	13.388	15.086
6	0.872	1.134	1.635	2.204	3.070	3.828	5.348	7.231	8.558	10.645	12.592	15.033	16.812
7	1.239	1.564	2.167	2.833	3.822	4.671	6.346	8.383	9.803	12.017	14.067	16.622	18.475
8	1.646	2.032	2.733	3.490	4.594	5.527	7.344	9.524	11.030	13.362	15.507	18.168	20.090
9	2.088	2.532	3.325	4.168	5.380	6.393	8.343	10.656	12.242	14.684	16.919	19.679	21.666

10	2.558	3.059	3.940	4.865	6.179	7.267	9.342	11.781	13.442	15.987	18.307	21.161	23.209
11	3.053	3.609	4.575	5.578	6.989	8.148	10.341	12.899	14.631	17.275	19.675	22.618	24.725
12	3.571	4.178	5.226	6.304	7.807	9.034	11.340	14.011	15.812	18.549	21.026	24.054	26.217
13	4.107	4.765	5.892	7.042	8.634	9.926	12.340	15.119	16.985	19.812	22.362	25.472	27.688
14	4.660	5.368	6.571	7.790	9.467	10.821	13.339	16.222	18.151	21.064	23.685	26.073	29.141
15	5.229	5.985	7.261	8.547	10.307	11.721	14.339	17.322	19.311	22.307	24.996	28.259	30.578
16	5.812	6.614	7.962	9.312	11.152	12.624	15.338	18.418	20.465	23.542	26.296	29.633	32.000
17	6.408	7.255	8.672	10.085	12.002	13.531	16.338	19.511	21.615	24.769	27.587	30.995	33.409
18	7.015	7.906	8.390	10.865	12.857	14.440	17.338	20.601	22.760	25.989	28.869	32.346	34.805
19	7.633	8.567	10.117	11.651	13.716	15.352	18.338	21.689	23.900	27.204	30.144	33.687	36.191
20	8.260	9.237	10.851	12.443	14.578	16.266	19.337	22.775	25.038	28.412	31.410	35.020	37.566
21	8.897	9.915	11.591	13.240	15.445	17.182	20.337	23.858	26.171	29.615	32.671	36.343	38.932
22	9.542	10.600	12.338	14.041	16.314	18.101	21.337	24.939	27.301	30.813	33.924	37.659	40.289
23	10.196	11.293	13.091	14.848	17.187	19.021	22.337	26.018	28.429	32.007	35.172	38.968	41.638
24	10.856	11.992	13.848	15.659	18.062	19.943	23.337	27.096	29.553	33.196	36.415	40.270	42.980
25	11.524	12.697	14.611	16.473	18.940	20.867	24.337	28.172	30.675	34.382	37.652	41.566	44.314
26	12.198	13.409	15.379	17.292	19.820	21.792	25.336	29.246	31.795	35.563	38.885	42.856	45.642
27	12.879	14.125	16.151	18.114	20.703	22.719	26.336	30.319	32.912	36.741	40.113	44.140	46.963
28	13.565	14.847	16.928	18.939	21.588	23.647	27.336	31.391	34.027	37.916	41.337	45.419	48.278
29	14.256	15.574	17.708	19.768	22.475	24.577	28.336	32.461	35.139	39.087	42.557	46.693	49.588
30	14.953	16.306	18.493	20.599	23.364	25.508	29.336	33.530	36.250	40.256	43.773	47.962	50.892

For degrees of freedom greater than 30, the expression $\sqrt{2\chi^2} - \sqrt{2n - 1}$ may be used as normal deviate with unit variance, where n is the number of degrees of freedom.

Reprinted from Sir Ronald A. Fisher, *Statistical Methods for Research Workers*, 14th ed., with permission of Hafner Press, a Division of Macmillan Publishing Company. Copyright © 1970 University of Adelaide.

TABLE B.3 THE (STUDENT) *t* DISTRIBUTION

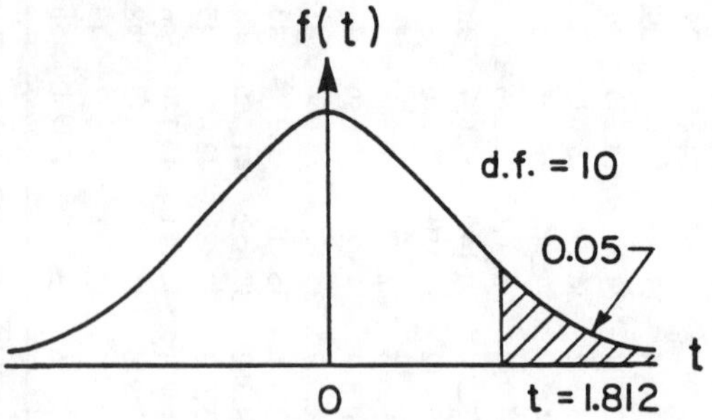

Degree of freedom	Probability of a value at least as large as the table entry					
	0.15	0.1	0.05	0.025	0.01	0.005
1	1.963	3.078	6.314	12.706	31.821	63.657
2	1.386	1.886	2.920	4.303	6.965	9.925
3	1.250	1.638	2.353	3.182	4.541	5.841
4	1.190	1.533	2.132	2.776	3.747	4.604
5	1.156	1.476	2.015	2.571	3.365	4.032
6	1.134	1.440	1.943	2.447	3.143	3.707
7	1.119	1.415	1.895	2.365	2.998	3.499
8	1.108	1.397	1.860	2.306	2.896	3.355
9	1.100	1.383	1.833	2.262	2.821	3.250
10	1.093	1.372	1.812	2.228	2.764	3.169
11	1.088	1.363	1.796	2.201	2.718	3.106
12	1.083	1.356	1.782	2.179	2.681	3.055
13	1.079	1.350	1.771	2.160	2.650	3.012
14	1.076	1.345	1.761	2.145	2.624	2.977
15	1.074	1.341	1.753	2.131	2.602	2.947
16	1.071	1.337	1.746	2.120	2.583	2.921
17	1.069	1.333	1.740	2.110	2.567	2.898
18	1.067	1.330	1.734	2.101	2.552	2.878
19	1.066	1.328	1.729	2.093	2.539	2.861
20	1.064	1.325	1.725	2.086	2.528	2.845
21	1.063	1.323	1.721	2.080	2.518	2.831
22	1.061	1.321	1.717	2.074	2.508	2.819
23	1.060	1.319	1.714	2.069	2.500	2.807
24	1.059	1.318	1.711	2.064	2.492	2.797
25	1.058	1.316	1.708	2.060	2.485	2.787
26	1.058	1.315	1.706	2.056	2.479	2.779
27	1.057	1.314	1.703	2.052	2.473	2.771
28	1.056	1.313	1.701	2.048	2.467	2.763
29	1.055	1.311	1.699	2.045	2.462	2.756
30	1.055	1.310	1.697	2.042	2.457	2.750
(Normal) ∞	1.036	1.282	1.645	1.960	2.326	2.576

Source Reprinted from Table IV in Sir Ronald A. Fisher, *Statistical Methods for Research Workers*, 14th ed. with permission of Hafner Press, a Division of Macmillan Publishing Company. Copyright © 1970 University of Adelaide.

TABLE B.4 THE *F* DISTRIBUTION—5% (ROMAN TYPE) AND 1% (ITALIC TYPE) POINTS OF THE *F* DISTRIBUTION

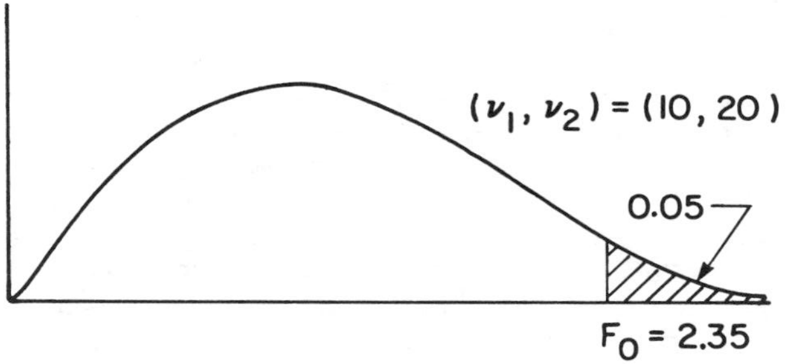

Probability $\{F_{(10,20)} > (F_0 = 2.35)\} = 0.05$

Degrees of freedom for denominator (ν_2)	Degrees of freedom for numerator (ν_1)																							
	1	2	3	4	5	6	7	8	9	10	11	12	14	16	20	24	30	40	50	75	100	200	500	∞
1	161	200	216	225	230	234	237	239	241	242	243	244	245	246	248	249	250	251	252	253	253	254	254	254
	4052	*4999*	*5403*	*5625*	*5764*	*5859*	*5928*	*5981*	*6022*	*6056*	*6082*	*6106*	*6142*	*6169*	*6208*	*6234*	*6258*	*6286*	*6302*	*6323*	*6334*	*6352*	*6361*	*6366*
2	18.51	19.00	19.16	19.25	19.30	19.33	19.36	19.37	19.38	19.39	19.40	19.41	19.42	19.43	19.44	19.45	19.46	19.47	19.47	19.48	19.49	19.49	19.50	19.50
	98.49	*99.01*	*99.17*	*99.25*	*99.30*	*99.33*	*99.34*	*99.36*	*99.38*	*99.40*	*99.41*	*99.42*	*99.43*	*99.44*	*99.45*	*99.46*	*99.47*	*99.48*	*99.48*	*99.49*	*99.49*	*99.49*	*99.50*	*99.50*
3	10.13	9.55	9.28	9.12	9.01	8.94	8.88	8.84	8.81	8.78	8.76	8.74	8.71	8.69	8.66	8.64	8.62	8.60	8.58	8.57	8.56	8.54	8.54	8.53
	34.12	*30.81*	*29.46*	*28.71*	*28.24*	*27.91*	*27.67*	*27.49*	*27.34*	*27.23*	*27.13*	*27.05*	*26.92*	*26.83*	*26.69*	*26.60*	*26.50*	*26.41*	*26.30*	*26.27*	*26.23*	*26.18*	*26.14*	*26.12*
4	7.71	6.94	6.59	6.39	6.26	6.16	6.09	6.04	6.00	5.96	5.93	5.91	5.87	5.84	5.80	5.77	5.74	5.71	5.70	5.68	5.66	5.65	5.64	5.63
	21.20	*18.00*	*16.69*	*15.98*	*15.52*	*15.21*	*14.98*	*14.80*	*14.66*	*14.54*	*14.45*	*14.37*	*14.24*	*14.15*	*14.02*	*13.93*	*13.83*	*13.74*	*13.69*	*13.61*	*13.57*	*13.52*	*13.48*	*13.46*
5	6.61	5.79	5.41	5.19	5.05	4.95	4.88	4.82	4.78	4.74	4.70	4.68	4.64	4.60	4.56	4.53	4.50	4.46	4.44	4.42	4.40	4.38	4.37	4.36
	16.26	*13.27*	*12.06*	*11.39*	*10.97*	*10.67*	*10.45*	*10.27*	*10.15*	*10.05*	*9.96*	*9.89*	*9.77*	*9.68*	*9.55*	*9.47*	*9.38*	*9.29*	*9.24*	*9.17*	*9.13*	*9.07*	*9.04*	*9.02*
6	5.99	5.14	4.76	4.53	4.39	4.28	4.21	4.15	4.10	4.06	4.03	4.00	3.96	3.92	3.87	3.84	3.81	3.77	3.75	3.72	3.71	3.69	3.68	3.67
	13.74	*10.92*	*9.78*	*9.15*	*8.75*	*8.47*	*8.26*	*8.10*	*7.98*	*7.87*	*7.79*	*7.72*	*7.60*	*7.52*	*7.39*	*7.31*	*7.23*	*7.14*	*7.09*	*7.02*	*6.99*	*6.94*	*6.90*	*6.88*
7	5.59	4.74	4.35	4.12	3.97	3.87	3.79	3.73	3.68	3.63	3.60	3.57	3.52	3.49	3.44	3.41	3.38	3.34	3.32	3.29	3.28	3.25	3.24	3.23
	12.25	*9.55*	*8.45*	*7.85*	*7.46*	*7.19*	*7.00*	*6.84*	*6.71*	*6.62*	*6.54*	*6.47*	*6.35*	*6.27*	*6.15*	*6.07*	*5.98*	*5.90*	*5.85*	*5.78*	*5.75*	*5.70*	*5.67*	*5.65*

TABLE B.4 *(continued)*

Degrees of freedom for denominator (ν_2)	Degrees of freedom for numerator (ν_1) 1	2	3	4	5	6	7	8	9	10	11	12	14	16	20	24	30	40	50	75	100	200	500	∞
8	5.32	4.46	4.07	3.84	3.69	3.58	3.50	3.44	3.39	3.34	3.31	3.28	3.23	3.20	3.15	3.12	3.08	3.05	3.03	3.00	2.98	2.96	2.94	2.93
	11.26	*8.65*	*7.59*	*7.01*	*6.63*	*6.37*	*6.19*	*6.03*	*5.91*	*5.82*	*5.74*	*5.67*	*5.56*	*5.48*	*5.36*	*5.28*	*5.20*	*5.11*	*5.06*	*5.00*	*4.96*	*4.91*	*4.88*	*4.86*
9	5.12	4.26	3.86	3.63	3.48	3.37	3.29	3.23	3.18	3.13	3.10	3.07	3.02	2.98	2.93	2.90	2.86	2.82	2.80	2.77	2.76	2.73	2.72	2.71
	10.56	*8.02*	*6.99*	*6.42*	*6.06*	*5.80*	*5.62*	*5.47*	*5.35*	*5.26*	*5.18*	*5.11*	*5.00*	*4.92*	*4.80*	*4.73*	*4.64*	*4.56*	*4.51*	*4.45*	*4.41*	*4.36*	*4.33*	*4.31*
10	4.96	4.10	3.71	3.48	3.33	3.22	3.14	3.07	3.02	2.97	2.94	2.91	2.86	2.82	2.77	2.74	2.70	2.67	2.64	2.61	2.59	2.56	2.55	2.54
	10.04	*7.56*	*6.55*	*5.99*	*5.64*	*5.39*	*5.21*	*5.06*	*4.95*	*4.85*	*4.78*	*4.71*	*4.60*	*4.52*	*4.41*	*4.33*	*4.25*	*4.17*	*4.12*	*4.05*	*4.01*	*3.96*	*3.93*	*3.91*
11	4.84	3.98	3.59	3.36	3.20	3.09	3.01	2.95	2.90	2.96	2.82	2.79	2.74	2.70	2.65	2.61	2.57	2.53	2.50	2.47	2.45	2.42	2.41	2.40
	9.65	*7.20*	*6.22*	*5.67*	*5.32*	*5.07*	*4.88*	*4.74*	*4.63*	*4.54*	*4.46*	*4.40*	*4.29*	*4.21*	*4.10*	*4.02*	*3.94*	*3.86*	*3.80*	*3.74*	*3.70*	*3.66*	*3.62*	*3.60*
12	4.75	3.88	3.49	3.26	3.11	3.00	2.92	2.85	2.80	2.76	2.72	2.69	2.64	2.60	2.54	2.50	2.46	2.42	2.40	2.36	2.35	2.32	2.31	2.30
	9.33	*6.93*	*5.95*	*5.41*	*5.06*	*4.82*	*4.65*	*4.50*	*4.39*	*4.30*	*4.22*	*4.16*	*4.05*	*3.98*	*3.86*	*3.78*	*3.70*	*3.61*	*3.56*	*3.49*	*3.46*	*3.41*	*3.38*	*3.36*
13	4.67	3.80	3.41	3.18	3.02	2.92	2.84	2.77	2.72	2.67	2.63	2.60	2.55	2.51	2.46	2.42	2.38	2.34	2.32	2.28	2.26	2.24	2.22	2.21
	9.07	*6.70*	*5.74*	*5.20*	*4.86*	*4.62*	*4.44*	*4.30*	*4.19*	*4.10*	*4.02*	*3.96*	*3.85*	*3.78*	*3.67*	*3.59*	*3.51*	*3.42*	*3.37*	*3.30*	*3.27*	*3.21*	*3.18*	*3.16*
14	4.60	3.74	3.34	3.11	2.96	2.85	2.77	2.70	2.65	2.60	2.56	2.53	2.48	2.44	2.39	2.35	2.31	2.27	2.24	2.21	2.19	2.16	2.14	2.13
	8.86	*6.51*	*5.56*	*5.03*	*4.69*	*4.46*	*4.28*	*4.14*	*4.03*	*3.94*	*3.86*	*3.80*	*3.70*	*3.62*	*3.51*	*3.43*	*3.34*	*3.26*	*3.21*	*3.14*	*3.11*	*3.06*	*3.02*	*3.00*
15	4.54	3.68	3.29	3.06	2.90	2.79	2.70	2.64	2.59	2.55	2.51	2.48	2.43	2.39	2.33	2.29	2.25	2.21	2.18	2.15	2.12	2.10	2.08	2.07
	8.68	*6.36*	*5.42*	*4.89*	*4.56*	*4.32*	*4.14*	*4.00*	*3.89*	*3.80*	*3.73*	*3.67*	*3.56*	*3.48*	*3.36*	*2.39*	*3.20*	*3.12*	*3.07*	*3.00*	*2.97*	*2.92*	*2.89*	*2.87*
16	4.49	3.63	3.24	3.01	2.85	2.74	2.66	2.59	2.54	2.49	2.45	2.42	2.37	2.33	2.28	2.24	2.20	2.16	2.13	2.09	2.07	2.04	2.02	2.01
	8.53	*6.23*	*5.29*	*4.77*	*4.44*	*4.20*	*4.03*	*3.89*	*3.78*	*3.69*	*3.61*	*3.55*	*3.45*	*3.37*	*3.25*	*3.18*	*3.10*	*3.01*	*2.96*	*2.89*	*2.86*	*2.80*	*2.77*	*2.75*
17	4.45	3.59	3.20	2.96	2.81	2.70	2.62	2.55	2.50	2.45	2.41	2.38	2.33	2.29	2.23	2.19	2.15	2.11	2.08	2.04	2.02	1.99	1.97	1.96
	8.40	*6.11*	*5.18*	*4.67*	*4.34*	*4.10*	*3.93*	*3.79*	*3.68*	*3.59*	*3.52*	*3.45*	*3.35*	*3.27*	*3.16*	*3.08*	*3.00*	*2.92*	*2.86*	*2.79*	*2.76*	*2.70*	*2.67*	*2.65*
18	4.41	3.55	3.16	2.93	2.77	2.66	2.58	2.51	2.46	2.41	2.37	2.34	2.29	2.25	2.19	2.15	2.11	2.07	2.04	2.00	1.98	1.95	1.93	1.92
	8.28	*6.01*	*5.09*	*4.58*	*4.25*	*4.01*	*3.85*	*3.71*	*3.60*	*3.51*	*3.44*	*3.37*	*3.27*	*3.19*	*3.07*	*3.00*	*2.91*	*2.83*	*2.78*	*2.71*	*2.68*	*2.62*	*2.59*	*2.57*
19	4.38	3.52	3.13	2.90	2.74	2.63	2.55	2.48	2.43	2.38	2.34	2.31	2.26	2.21	2.15	2.11	2.07	2.02	2.00	1.96	1.94	1.91	1.90	1.88
	8.18	*5.93*	*5.01*	*4.50*	*4.17*	*3.94*	*3.77*	*3.63*	*3.52*	*3.43*	*3.36*	*3.30*	*3.19*	*3.12*	*3.00*	*2.29*	*2.84*	*2.76*	*2.70*	*2.63*	*2.60*	*2.54*	*2.51*	*2.49*
20	4.35	3.49	3.10	2.87	2.71	2.60	2.52	2.45	2.40	2.35	2.31	2.28	2.23	2.18	2.12	2.08	2.04	1.99	1.96	1.92	1.90	1.87	1.85	1.84
	8.10	*5.85*	*4.94*	*4.43*	*4.10*	*3.87*	*3.71*	*3.56*	*3.45*	*3.37*	*3.30*	*3.23*	*3.13*	*3.05*	*2.94*	*2.86*	*2.77*	*2.69*	*2.63*	*2.56*	*2.53*	*2.47*	*2.44*	*2.42*
21	4.32	3.47	3.07	2.84	2.68	2.57	2.49	2.42	2.37	2.32	2.28	2.25	2.20	2.15	2.09	2.05	2.00	1.96	1.93	1.89	1.87	1.84	1.82	1.81
	8.02	*5.78*	*4.87*	*4.37*	*4.04*	*3.81*	*3.65*	*3.51*	*3.40*	*3.31*	*3.24*	*3.17*	*3.07*	*2.99*	*2.88*	*2.80*	*2.72*	*2.63*	*2.58*	*2.51*	*2.47*	*2.42*	*2.38*	*2.36*

22	4.30	3.44	3.05	2.82	2.66	2.55	2.47	2.40	2.35	2.30	2.26	2.23	2.18	2.13	2.07	2.03	1.98	1.93	1.91	1.87	1.84	1.81	1.80	1.78
	7.94	5.72	4.82	4.31	3.99	3.76	3.59	3.45	3.35	3.26	3.18	3.12	3.02	2.94	2.83	2.75	2.67	2.58	2.53	2.46	2.42	2.37	2.33	2.31
23	4.28	3.42	3.03	2.80	2.64	2.53	2.45	2.38	2.32	2.28	2.24	2.20	2.14	2.10	2.04	2.00	1.96	1.91	1.88	1.84	1.82	1.79	1.77	1.76
	7.88	5.66	4.76	4.26	3.94	3.71	3.54	3.41	3.30	3.21	3.14	3.07	2.97	2.89	2.78	2.70	2.62	2.53	2.48	2.41	2.37	2.32	2.28	2.26
24	4.26	3.40	3.01	2.78	2.62	2.51	2.43	2.36	2.30	2.26	2.22	2.18	2.13	2.09	2.02	1.98	1.94	1.89	1.86	1.82	1.80	1.76	1.74	1.73
	7.82	5.61	4.72	4.22	3.90	3.67	3.50	3.36	3.25	3.17	3.09	3.03	2.93	2.85	2.74	2.66	2.58	2.49	2.44	2.36	2.33	2.27	2.23	2.21
25	4.24	3.38	2.99	2.76	2.60	2.49	2.41	2.34	2.28	2.24	2.20	2.16	2.11	2.06	2.00	1.96	1.92	1.87	1.84	1.80	1.77	1.74	1.72	1.71
	7.77	5.57	4.68	4.18	3.86	3.63	3.46	3.32	3.21	3.13	3.05	2.99	2.89	2.81	2.70	2.62	2.54	2.45	2.40	2.32	2.29	2.23	2.19	2.17
26	4.22	3.37	2.89	2.74	2.59	2.47	2.39	2.32	2.27	2.22	2.18	2.15	2.10	2.05	1.99	1.95	1.90	1.85	1.82	1.78	1.76	1.72	1.70	1.69
	7.72	5.53	4.64	4.14	3.82	3.59	3.42	3.29	3.17	3.09	3.02	2.96	2.86	2.77	2.66	2.58	2.50	2.41	2.36	2.28	2.25	2.19	2.15	2.13
27	4.21	3.35	2.96	2.73	2.57	2.46	2.37	2.30	2.25	2.20	2.16	2.13	2.08	2.03	1.97	1.93	1.88	1.84	1.80	1.76	1.74	1.71	1.68	1.67
	7.68	5.49	4.60	4.11	3.79	3.56	3.39	3.26	3.14	3.06	2.98	2.93	2.83	2.74	2.63	2.55	2.47	2.38	2.33	2.25	2.21	2.16	2.12	2.10
28	4.20	3.34	2.95	2.71	2.56	2.44	2.36	2.29	3.24	2.19	2.15	2.12	2.06	2.02	1.96	1.91	1.87	1.81	1.78	1.75	1.72	1.69	1.67	1.65
	7.64	5.45	4.57	4.07	3.76	3.53	3.36	3.23	3.11	3.03	2.95	2.90	2.80	2.71	2.60	2.52	2.44	2.35	2.30	2.22	2.18	2.13	2.09	2.06
29	4.18	3.33	2.93	2.70	2.54	2.43	2.35	2.28	2.22	2.18	2.14	2.10	2.05	2.00	1.94	1.90	1.85	1.80	1.77	1.73	1.71	1.68	1.65	1.64
	7.60	5.52	4.54	4.04	3.73	3.50	3.33	3.20	3.08	3.00	2.92	2.87	2.77	2.68	2.57	2.49	2.41	2.32	2.27	2.19	2.15	2.10	2.06	2.03
30	4.17	3.32	2.92	2.69	2.53	2.42	2.34	2.27	2.21	2.16	2.12	2.09	2.04	1.99	1.93	1.89	1.84	1.79	1.76	1.72	1.69	1.66	1.64	1.62
	7.56	5.39	4.51	4.02	3.70	3.47	3.30	3.17	3.06	2.98	2.90	2.84	2.74	2.66	2.55	2.47	2.38	2.29	2.24	2.16	2.13	2.07	2.03	2.01
32	4.15	3.30	2.90	2.67	2.51	2.40	2.32	2.25	2.19	2.14	2.10	2.07	2.02	1.97	1.91	1.86	1.82	1.76	1.74	1.69	1.67	1.64	1.61	1.59
	7.50	5.34	4.46	3.97	3.66	3.42	3.25	3.12	3.01	2.94	2.86	2.80	2.70	2.62	2.51	2.42	2.34	2.25	2.20	2.12	2.08	2.02	1.98	1.96
34	4.13	3.28	2.88	2.65	2.49	2.38	2.30	2.23	2.17	2.12	2.08	2.05	2.00	1.95	1.89	1.84	1.80	1.74	1.71	1.67	1.64	1.61	1.59	1.57
	7.44	5.29	4.42	3.93	3.61	3.38	3.21	3.08	2.97	2.89	2.82	2.76	2.66	2.58	2.47	2.38	2.30	2.21	2.15	2.08	2.04	1.98	1.94	1.91
36	4.11	3.26	2.86	2.63	2.48	2.36	2.28	2.21	2.15	2.10	2.06	2.03	1.89	1.93	1.87	1.82	1.78	1.72	1.69	1.65	1.62	1.59	1.56	1.55
	7.39	5.25	4.38	3.89	3.58	3.35	3.18	3.04	2.94	2.86	2.78	2.72	2.62	2.54	2.43	2.35	2.26	2.17	2.12	2.04	2.00	1.94	1.90	1.87
38	4.10	3.25	2.85	2.62	2.46	2.35	2.26	2.19	2.14	2.09	2.05	2.02	1.96	1.92	1.85	1.80	1.76	1.71	1.67	1.63	1.60	1.57	1.54	1.53
	7.35	5.21	4.34	3.86	3.54	3.32	3.15	3.02	2.91	2.82	2.75	2.69	2.59	2.51	2.30	2.32	2.22	2.14	2.08	2.00	1.97	1.90	1.86	1.84
40	4.08	3.23	2.84	2.61	2.45	2.34	2.25	2.18	2.12	2.07	2.04	2.00	1.95	1.90	1.84	1.79	1.74	1.69	1.66	1.61	1.59	1.55	1.53	1.51
	7.31	5.18	4.31	3.83	3.51	3.29	3.12	2.99	2.88	2.80	2.73	2.66	2.56	2.49	2.37	2.29	2.20	2.11	2.05	1.97	1.94	1.88	1.84	1.81
42	4.07	3.22	2.83	2.59	2.44	2.32	2.24	2.17	2.11	2.06	2.02	1.99	1.94	1.89	1.82	1.78	1.73	1.68	1.64	1.60	1.57	1.54	1.51	1.49
	7.27	5.15	4.29	3.80	3.49	3.26	3.10	2.96	2.86	2.77	2.70	2.64	2.54	2.46	2.35	2.26	2.17	2.08	2.02	1.94	1.91	1.85	1.80	1.78
44	4.06	3.21	2.82	2.58	2.43	2.31	2.23	2.16	2.10	2.05	2.01	1.98	1.92	1.88	1.81	1.76	1.72	1.66	1.63	1.58	1.56	1.52	1.50	1.48
	7.24	5.12	4.26	3.78	3.46	3.24	3.07	2.94	2.84	2.75	2.68	2.62	2.52	2.44	2.32	2.24	2.15	2.06	2.00	1.92	1.88	1.82	1.78	1.75
46	4.05	3.20	2.81	2.57	2.42	2.30	2.22	2.14	2.09	2.04	2.00	1.97	1.91	1.87	1.80	1.75	1.71	1.65	1.62	1.57	1.54	1.51	1.48	1.46
	7.21	5.10	4.24	3.76	3.44	3.22	3.05	2.92	2.82	2.73	2.66	2.60	2.50	2.42	2.40	2.22	2.13	2.04	1.98	1.90	1.86	1.80	1.76	1.72
48	4.04	3.19	2.80	2.56	2.41	2.30	2.21	2.14	2.08	2.03	1.99	1.96	1.90	1.86	1.79	1.74	1.70	1.64	1.61	1.56	1.53	1.50	1.47	1.45
	7.19	5.08	4.22	3.74	3.42	3.20	3.04	2.90	2.80	2.71	2.64	2.58	2.48	2.40	2.28	2.20	2.11	2.02	1.96	1.88	1.84	1.78	1.73	1.70

TABLE B.4 (*continued*)

Degrees of freedom for denominator (ν_2)	Degrees of freedom for numerator (ν_1) 1	2	3	4	5	6	7	8	9	10	11	12	14	16	20	24	30	40	50	75	100	200	500	∞
50	4.03	3.18	2.79	2.56	2.40	2.29	2.20	2.13	2.07	2.02	1.98	1.95	1.90	1.85	1.78	1.74	1.69	1.63	1.60	1.55	1.52	1.48	1.46	1.44
	7.17	*5.06*	*4.20*	*3.72*	*3.41*	*3.18*	*3.02*	*2.88*	*2.78*	*2.70*	*2.62*	*2.56*	*2.46*	*2.39*	*2.26*	*2.18*	*2.10*	*2.00*	*1.94*	*1.86*	*1.82*	*1.76*	*1.71*	*1.68*
55	4.02	3.17	2.78	2.54	2.38	2.27	2.18	2.11	2.05	2.00	1.97	1.93	1.88	1.83	1.76	1.72	1.67	1.61	1.58	1.52	1.50	1.46	1.43	1.41
	7.12	*5.01*	*4.16*	*3.68*	*3.37*	*3.15*	*2.98*	*2.85*	*2.75*	*2.66*	*2.59*	*2.53*	*2.43*	*2.35*	*2.23*	*2.15*	*2.06*	*1.96*	*1.90*	*1.82*	*1.78*	*1.71*	*1.66*	*1.64*
60	4.00	3.15	2.76	2.52	2.37	2.25	2.17	2.10	2.04	1.99	1.95	1.92	1.86	1.81	1.75	1.70	1.65	1.59	1.56	1.50	1.48	1.44	1.41	1.39
	7.08	*4.98*	*4.13*	*3.65*	*3.34*	*3.12*	*2.95*	*2.82*	*2.72*	*2.63*	*2.56*	*2.50*	*2.40*	*2.32*	*2.20*	*2.12*	*2.03*	*1.93*	*1.87*	*1.79*	*1.74*	*1.68*	*1.63*	*1.60*
65	3.99	3.14	2.75	2.51	2.36	2.24	2.15	2.08	2.02	1.98	1.94	1.90	1.85	1.80	1.73	1.68	1.63	1.57	1.54	1.49	1.46	1.42	1.39	1.37
	7.04	*4.95*	*4.10*	*3.62*	*3.31*	*3.09*	*2.93*	*2.79*	*2.70*	*2.61*	*2.54*	*2.47*	*2.30*	*2.37*	*2.18*	*2.09*	*2.00*	*1.90*	*1.84*	*1.76*	*1.71*	*1.64*	*1.60*	*1.56*
70	3.98	3.13	2.74	2.50	2.35	2.32	2.14	2.07	2.01	1.97	1.93	1.89	1.84	1.79	1.72	1.67	1.62	1.56	1.53	1.47	1.45	1.40	1.37	1.35
	7.01	*4.92*	*4.08*	*3.60*	*3.29*	*3.07*	*2.91*	*2.77*	*2.67*	*2.59*	*2.51*	*2.45*	*2.35*	*2.28*	*2.15*	*2.07*	*1.98*	*1.88*	*1.82*	*1.74*	*1.69*	*1.63*	*1.56*	*1.53*
80	3.96	3.11	2.72	2.48	2.33	2.21	2.12	2.05	1.99	1.95	1.91	1.88	1.82	1.77	1.70	1.65	1.60	1.54	1.51	1.45	1.42	1.38	1.35	1.32
	6.96	*4.88*	*4.04*	*3.56*	*3.25*	*3.04*	*2.87*	*2.74*	*2.64*	*2.55*	*2.48*	*2.41*	*2.32*	*2.24*	*2.11*	*2.03*	*1.94*	*1.84*	*1.78*	*1.70*	*1.65*	*1.57*	*1.52*	*1.49*
100	3.94	3.09	2.70	2.46	2.30	2.19	2.10	2.03	1.97	1.92	1.88	1.85	1.79	1.75	1.68	1.63	1.57	1.51	1.48	1.42	1.39	1.34	1.30	1.28
	6.90	*4.82*	*3.98*	*3.51*	*3.20*	*2.99*	*2.82*	*2.69*	*2.59*	*2.51*	*2.43*	*2.36*	*2.26*	*2.19*	*2.06*	*1.98*	*1.89*	*1.79*	*1.73*	*1.64*	*1.59*	*1.51*	*1.46*	*1.43*
125	3.92	3.07	2.68	2.44	2.29	2.17	2.08	2.01	1.95	1.90	1.86	1.83	1.77	1.72	1.65	1.60	1.55	1.49	1.45	1.39	1.36	1.31	1.27	1.25
	6.84	*4.78*	*3.94*	*3.47*	*3.17*	*2.95*	*2.79*	*2.65*	*2.56*	*2.47*	*2.40*	*2.33*	*2.23*	*2.15*	*2.03*	*1.94*	*1.85*	*1.75*	*1.68*	*1.59*	*1.54*	*1.46*	*1.40*	*1.37*
150	3.91	3.06	2.67	2.43	2.27	2.16	2.07	2.00	1.94	1.89	1.85	1.82	1.76	1.71	1.64	1.59	1.54	1.47	1.44	1.37	1.34	1.29	1.25	1.22
	6.81	*4.75*	*3.91*	*3.44*	*3.13*	*2.92*	*2.76*	*2.62*	*2.53*	*2.44*	*2.37*	*2.30*	*2.20*	*2.12*	*2.00*	*1.91*	*1.83*	*1.72*	*1.66*	*1.56*	*1.51*	*1.43*	*1.37*	*1.33*
200	3.89	3.04	2.65	2.41	2.26	2.14	2.05	1.98	1.92	1.87	1.83	1.80	1.74	1.69	1.62	1.57	1.52	1.45	1.42	1.35	1.32	1.26	1.22	1.19
	6.76	*4.71*	*3.88*	*3.41*	*3.11*	*2.90*	*2.73*	*2.60*	*2.50*	*2.41*	*2.34*	*2.28*	*2.17*	*2.09*	*1.97*	*1.88*	*1.79*	*1.69*	*1.62*	*1.53*	*1.48*	*1.39*	*1.33*	*1.28*
400	3.86	3.02	2.62	2.39	2.23	2.12	2.03	1.96	1.90	1.85	1.81	1.78	1.72	1.67	1.60	1.54	1.49	1.42	1.38	1.32	1.28	1.22	1.16	1.13
	6.70	*4.66*	*3.83*	*3.36*	*3.06*	*2.85*	*2.69*	*2.55*	*2.46*	*2.37*	*2.29*	*2.23*	*2.12*	*2.04*	*1.92*	*1.84*	*1.74*	*1.64*	*1.57*	*1.47*	*1.42*	*1.32*	*1.24*	*1.19*
1000	3.85	3.00	2.61	2.38	2.22	2.10	2.02	1.95	1.89	1.84	1.80	1.76	1.70	1.65	1.58	1.53	1.47	1.41	1.36	1.30	1.26	1.19	1.13	1.08
	6.66	*4.62*	*3.80*	*3.34*	*3.04*	*2.82*	*2.66*	*2.53*	*2.43*	*2.34*	*2.26*	*2.20*	*2.09*	*2.01*	*1.89*	*1.81*	*1.71*	*1.61*	*1.54*	*1.44*	*1.38*	*1.28*	*1.19*	*1.11*
∞	3.84	2.99	2.60	2.37	2.21	2.09	2.01	1.94	1.88	1.83	1.79	1.75	1.69	1.64	1.57	1.52	1.46	1.40	1.35	1.28	1.24	1.17	1.11	1.00
	6.64	*4.60*	*3.78*	*3.32*	*3.02*	*2.80*	*2.64*	*2.51*	*2.41*	*2.32*	*2.24*	*2.18*	*2.07*	*1.99*	*1.87*	*1.79*	*1.69*	*1.59*	*1.52*	*1.41*	*1.36*	*1.25*	*1.15*	*1.00*

Reprinted by permission from *Statistical Methods* by George W. Snedecor and William G. Cochran, Seventh Edition, © 1980 by The Iowa State University Press, Ames, Iowa.

TABLE B.5 THE DURBIN–WATSON TEST STATISTIC (SAVIN–WHITE RESULTS)
1% SIGNIFICANCE POINTS OF d_L AND d_U[a]

	$k' = 1$		$k' = 2$		$k' = 3$		$k' = 4$		$k' = 5$		$k' = 6$		$k' = 7$		$k' = 8$		$k' = 9$		$k' = 10$	
n	d_L	d_U	d_L	d_U	d_L	d_U	d_L	d_U	d_L	d_U	d_L	d_U	d_L	d_U	d_L	d_U	d_L	d_U	d_L	d_U
6	0.390	1.142	—	—	—	—	—	—	—	—	—	—	—	—	—	—	—	—	—	—
7	0.435	1.036	0.294	1.676	—	—	—	—	—	—	—	—	—	—	—	—	—	—	—	—
8	0.497	1.003	0.345	1.489	0.229	2.102	—	—	—	—	—	—	—	—	—	—	—	—	—	—
9	0.554	0.998	0.408	1.389	0.279	1.875	0.183	2.433	—	—	—	—	—	—	—	—	—	—	—	—
10	0.604	1.001	0.466	1.333	0.340	1.733	0.230	2.193	0.150	2.690	—	—	—	—	—	—	—	—	—	—
11	0.653	1.010	0.519	1.297	0.396	1.640	0.286	2.030	0.193	2.453	0.124	2.892	—	—	—	—	—	—	—	—
12	0.697	1.023	0.569	1.274	0.449	1.575	0.339	1.913	0.244	2.280	0.164	2.665	0.105	3.053	—	—	—	—	—	—
13	0.738	1.038	0.616	1.261	0.499	1.526	0.391	1.826	0.294	2.150	0.211	2.490	0.140	2.838	0.090	3.182	—	—	—	—
14	0.776	1.054	0.660	1.254	0.547	1.490	0.441	1.757	0.343	2.049	0.257	2.354	0.183	2.667	0.122	2.981	0.078	3.287	—	—
15	0.811	1.070	0.700	1.252	0.591	1.464	0.488	1.704	0.391	1.967	0.303	2.244	0.226	2.530	0.161	2.817	0.107	3.101	0.068	3.374
16	0.844	1.086	0.737	1.252	0.633	1.446	0.532	1.663	0.437	1.900	0.349	2.153	0.269	2.416	0.200	2.681	0.142	2.944	0.094	3.201
17	0.874	1.102	0.772	1.255	0.672	1.432	0.574	1.630	0.480	1.847	0.393	2.078	0.313	2.319	0.241	2.566	0.179	2.811	0.127	3.053
18	0.902	1.118	0.805	1.259	0.708	1.422	0.613	1.604	0.522	1.803	0.435	2.015	0.355	2.238	0.282	2.467	0.216	2.697	0.160	2.925
19	0.928	1.132	0.835	1.265	0.742	1.415	0.650	1.584	0.561	1.767	0.476	1.963	0.396	2.169	0.322	2.381	0.255	2.597	0.196	2.813
20	0.952	1.147	0.863	1.271	0.773	1.411	0.685	1.567	0.598	1.737	0.515	1.918	0.436	2.110	0.362	2.308	0.294	2.510	0.232	2.714
21	0.975	1.161	0.890	1.277	0.803	1.408	0.718	1.554	0.633	1.712	0.552	1.881	0.474	2.059	0.400	2.244	0.331	2.434	0.268	2.625
22	0.997	1.174	0.914	1.284	0.831	1.407	0.748	1.543	0.667	1.691	0.587	1.849	0.510	2.015	0.437	2.188	0.368	2.367	0.304	2.548
23	1.018	1.187	0.938	1.291	0.858	1.407	0.777	1.534	0.698	1.673	0.620	1.821	0.545	1.977	0.473	2.140	0.404	2.308	0.340	2.479
24	1.037	1.199	0.960	1.298	0.882	1.407	0.805	1.528	0.728	1.658	0.652	1.797	0.578	1.944	0.507	2.097	0.439	2.255	0.375	2.417
25	1.055	1.211	0.981	1.305	0.906	1.409	0.831	1.523	0.756	1.645	0.682	1.766	0.610	1.915	0.540	2.059	0.473	2.209	0.409	2.362
26	1.072	1.222	1.001	1.312	0.928	1.411	0.855	1.518	0.783	1.635	0.711	1.759	0.640	1.889	0.572	2.026	0.505	2.168	0.441	2.313
27	1.089	1.233	1.019	1.319	0.949	1.413	0.878	1.515	0.808	1.626	0.738	1.743	0.669	1.867	0.602	1.997	0.536	2.131	0.473	2.269
28	1.104	1.244	1.037	1.325	0.969	1.415	0.900	1.513	0.832	1.618	0.764	1.729	0.696	1.847	0.630	1.970	0.566	2.098	0.504	2.229
29	1.119	1.254	1.054	1.332	0.988	1.418	0.921	1.512	0.855	1.611	0.788	1.718	0.723	1.830	0.658	1.947	0.595	2.068	0.533	2.193
30	1.133	1.263	1.070	1.339	1.006	1.421	0.941	1.511	0.877	1.606	0.812	1.707	0.748	1.814	0.684	1.925	0.622	2.041	0.562	2.160
31	1.147	1.273	1.085	1.345	1.023	1.425	0.960	1.510	0.897	1.601	0.834	1.698	0.772	1.800	0.710	1.906	0.649	2.017	0.589	2.131
32	1.160	1.282	1.100	1.352	1.040	1.428	0.979	1.510	0.917	1.597	0.856	1.690	0.794	1.788	0.734	1.889	0.674	1.995	0.615	2.104
33	1.172	1.291	1.114	1.358	1.055	1.432	0.996	1.510	0.936	1.594	0.876	1.683	0.816	1.776	0.757	1.874	0.698	1.975	0.641	2.080
34	1.184	1.299	1.128	1.364	1.070	1.435	1.012	1.511	0.954	1.591	0.896	1.677	0.837	1.766	0.779	1.860	0.722	1.957	0.665	2.057
35	1.195	1.307	1.140	1.370	1.085	1.439	1.028	1.512	0.971	1.589	0.914	1.671	0.857	1.757	0.800	1.847	0.744	1.940	0.689	2.037
36	1.206	1.315	1.153	1.376	1.098	1.442	1.043	1.513	0.988	1.588	0.932	1.666	0.877	1.749	0.821	1.836	0.766	1.925	0.711	2.018
37	1.217	1.323	1.165	1.382	1.112	1.446	1.058	1.514	1.004	1.586	0.950	1.662	0.895	1.742	0.841	1.825	0.787	1.911	0.733	2.001
38	1.227	1.330	1.176	1.388	1.124	1.449	1.072	1.515	1.019	1.585	0.966	1.658	0.913	1.735	0.860	1.816	0.807	1.899	0.754	1.985
39	1.237	1.337	1.187	1.393	1.137	1.453	1.085	1.517	1.034	1.584	0.982	1.655	0.930	1.729	0.878	1.807	0.826	1.887	0.774	1.970
40	1.246	1.344	1.198	1.398	1.148	1.457	1.098	1.518	1.048	1.584	0.997	1.652	0.946	1.724	0.895	1.799	0.844	1.876	0.789	1.956
45	1.288	1.376	1.245	1.423	1.201	1.474	1.156	1.528	1.111	1.584	1.065	1.643	1.019	1.704	0.974	1.768	0.927	1.834	0.881	1.902
50	1.324	1.403	1.285	1.446	1.245	1.491	1.205	1.538	1.164	1.587	1.123	1.639	1.081	1.692	1.039	1.748	0.997	1.805	0.955	1.864
55	1.356	1.427	1.320	1.466	1.284	1.506	1.247	1.548	1.209	1.592	1.172	1.638	1.134	1.685	1.095	1.734	1.057	1.785	1.018	1.837
60	1.383	1.449	1.350	1.484	1.317	1.520	1.283	1.558	1.249	1.598	1.214	1.639	1.179	1.682	1.144	1.726	1.108	1.771	1.072	1.817
65	1.407	1.468	1.377	1.500	1.346	1.534	1.315	1.568	1.283	1.604	1.251	1.642	1.218	1.680	1.186	1.720	1.153	1.761	1.120	1.802
70	1.429	1.485	1.400	1.515	1.372	1.546	1.343	1.578	1.313	1.611	1.283	1.645	1.253	1.680	1.223	1.716	1.192	1.754	1.162	1.792
75	1.448	1.501	1.422	1.529	1.395	1.557	1.368	1.587	1.340	1.617	1.313	1.646	1.284	1.682	1.256	1.716	1.227	1.746	1.199	1.785
80	1.466	1.515	1.441	1.541	1.416	1.568	1.390	1.595	1.364	1.624	1.338	1.653	1.312	1.683	1.285	1.714	1.259	1.745	1.232	1.777
85	1.482	1.528	1.458	1.553	1.435	1.578	1.411	1.603	1.386	1.630	1.362	1.657	1.337	1.685	1.312	1.714	1.287	1.743	1.262	1.773
90	1.496	1.540	1.474	1.563	1.452	1.587	1.429	1.611	1.406	1.636	1.383	1.661	1.360	1.687	1.336	1.714	1.312	1.741	1.288	1.769
95	1.510	1.552	1.489	1.573	1.468	1.596	1.446	1.618	1.425	1.642	1.403	1.666	1.381	1.690	1.358	1.715	1.336	1.741	1.313	1.767
100	1.522	1.562	1.503	1.583	1.482	1.604	1.462	1.625	1.441	1.647	1.421	1.670	1.400	1.693	1.378	1.717	1.357	1.741	1.335	1.765
150	1.611	1.637	1.598	1.651	1.584	1.665	1.571	1.679	1.557	1.693	1.543	1.708	1.530	1.722	1.515	1.737	1.501	1.752	1.486	1.767
200	1.664	1.684	1.653	1.693	1.643	1.704	1.633	1.715	1.623	1.725	1.613	1.735	1.603	1.746	1.592	1.757	1.582	1.768	1.571	1.779

TABLE B.5 *(continued)*

	$k' = 11$		$k' = 12$		$k' = 13$		$k' = 14$		$k' = 15$		$k' = 16$		$k' = 17$		$k' = 18$		$k' = 19$		$k' = 20$	
n	d_L	d_U	d_L	d_U	d_L	d_U	d_L	d_U	d_L	d_U	d_L	d_U	d_L	d_U	d_L	d_U	d_L	d_U	d_L	d_U
16	0.060	3.446	—	—	—	—	—	—	—	—	—	—	—	—	—	—	—	—	—	—
17	0.084	3.286	0.053	3.506	—	—	—	—	—	—	—	—	—	—	—	—	—	—	—	—
18	0.113	3.146	0.075	3.358	0.047	3.557	—	—	—	—	—	—	—	—	—	—	—	—	—	—
19	0.145	3.023	0.102	3.227	0.067	3.420	0.043	3.601	—	—	—	—	—	—	—	—	—	—	—	—
20	0.178	2.914	0.131	3.109	0.092	3.297	0.061	3.474	0.038	3.639	—	—	—	—	—	—	—	—	—	—
21	0.212	2.817	0.162	3.004	0.119	3.185	0.084	3.358	0.055	3.521	0.035	3.671	—	—	—	—	—	—	—	—
22	0.246	2.729	0.194	2.909	0.148	3.084	0.109	3.252	0.077	3.412	0.050	3.562	0.032	3.700	—	—	—	—	—	—
23	0.281	2.651	0.227	2.822	0.178	2.991	0.136	3.155	0.100	3.311	0.070	3.459	0.046	3.597	0.029	3.725	—	—	—	—
24	0.315	2.580	0.260	2.744	0.209	2.906	0.165	3.065	0.125	3.218	0.092	3.363	0.065	3.501	0.043	3.629	0.027	3.747	—	—
25	0.348	2.517	0.292	2.674	0.240	2.829	0.194	2.982	0.152	3.131	0.116	3.274	0.085	3.410	0.060	3.538	0.039	3.657	0.025	3.766
26	0.381	2.460	0.324	2.610	0.272	2.758	0.224	2.906	0.180	3.050	0.141	3.191	0.107	3.325	0.079	3.452	0.055	3.572	0.036	3.682
27	0.413	2.409	0.356	2.552	0.303	2.694	0.253	2.836	0.208	2.976	0.167	3.113	0.131	3.245	0.100	3.371	0.073	3.490	0.051	3.602
28	0.444	2.363	0.387	2.499	0.333	2.635	0.283	2.772	0.237	2.907	0.194	3.040	0.156	3.169	0.122	3.294	0.093	3.412	0.068	3.524
29	0.474	2.321	0.417	2.451	0.363	2.582	0.313	2.713	0.266	2.843	0.222	2.972	0.182	3.098	0.146	3.220	0.114	3.338	0.087	3.450
30	0.503	2.283	0.447	2.407	0.393	2.533	0.342	2.659	0.294	2.785	0.249	2.909	0.208	3.032	0.171	3.152	0.137	3.267	0.107	3.379
31	0.531	2.248	0.475	2.367	0.422	2.487	0.371	2.609	0.322	2.730	0.277	2.851	0.234	2.970	0.196	3.087	0.160	3.201	0.128	3.311
32	0.558	2.216	0.503	2.330	0.450	2.446	0.399	2.563	0.350	2.680	0.304	2.797	0.261	2.912	0.221	3.026	0.184	3.137	0.151	3.246
33	0.585	2.187	0.530	2.296	0.477	2.408	0.426	2.520	0.377	2.633	0.331	2.746	0.287	2.858	0.246	2.969	0.209	3.078	0.174	3.184
34	0.610	2.160	0.556	2.266	0.503	2.373	0.452	2.481	0.404	2.590	0.357	2.699	0.313	2.808	0.272	2.915	0.233	3.022	0.197	3.126
35	0.634	2.136	0.581	2.237	0.529	2.340	0.478	2.444	0.430	2.550	0.383	2.655	0.339	2.761	0.297	2.865	0.257	2.969	0.221	3.071
36	0.658	2.113	0.605	2.210	0.554	2.310	0.504	2.410	0.455	2.512	0.409	2.614	0.364	2.717	0.322	2.818	0.282	2.919	0.244	3.019
37	0.680	2.092	0.628	2.186	0.578	2.282	0.528	2.379	0.480	2.477	0.434	2.576	0.389	2.675	0.347	2.774	0.306	2.872	0.268	2.969
38	0.702	2.073	0.651	2.164	0.601	2.256	0.552	2.350	0.504	2.445	0.458	2.540	0.414	2.637	0.371	2.733	0.330	2.828	0.291	2.923
39	0.723	2.055	0.673	2.143	0.623	2.232	0.575	2.323	0.528	2.414	0.482	2.507	0.438	2.600	0.395	2.694	0.354	2.787	0.315	2.879
40	0.744	2.039	0.694	2.123	0.645	2.210	0.597	2.297	0.551	2.386	0.505	2.476	0.461	2.566	0.418	2.657	0.377	2.748	0.338	2.838
45	0.835	1.972	0.790	2.044	0.744	2.118	0.700	2.193	0.655	2.269	0.612	2.346	0.570	2.424	0.528	2.503	0.488	2.582	0.448	2.661
50	0.913	1.925	0.871	1.987	0.829	2.051	0.787	2.116	0.746	2.182	0.705	2.250	0.665	2.318	0.625	2.387	0.586	2.456	0.548	2.526
55	0.979	1.891	0.940	1.945	0.902	2.002	0.863	2.059	0.825	2.177	0.786	2.176	0.748	2.237	0.711	2.298	0.674	2.359	0.637	2.421
60	1.037	1.865	1.001	1.914	0.965	1.964	0.929	2.015	0.893	2.067	0.857	2.120	0.822	2.173	0.786	2.227	0.751	2.283	0.716	2.338
65	1.087	1.845	1.053	1.889	1.020	1.934	0.986	1.980	0.953	2.027	0.919	2.075	0.886	2.123	0.852	2.172	0.819	2.221	0.786	2.272
70	1.131	1.831	1.099	1.870	1.068	1.911	1.037	1.953	1.005	1.995	0.974	2.038	0.943	2.082	0.911	2.127	0.880	2.172	0.849	2.217
75	1.170	1.819	1.141	1.856	1.111	1.893	1.082	1.931	1.052	1.970	1.023	2.009	0.993	2.049	0.964	2.090	0.934	2.131	0.905	2.172
80	1.205	1.810	1.777	1.844	1.150	1.878	1.122	1.913	1.094	1.949	1.066	1.984	1.039	2.022	1.011	2.057	0.983	2.097	0.955	2.135
85	1.236	1.803	1.210	1.834	1.184	1.866	1.158	1.898	1.132	1.931	1.106	1.965	1.080	1.999	1.053	2.033	1.027	2.068	1.000	2.104
90	1.264	1.798	1.240	1.827	1.215	1.856	1.191	1.886	1.166	1.917	1.141	1.948	1.116	1.979	1.091	2.012	1.066	2.044	1.041	2.077
95	1.290	1.793	1.267	1.821	1.244	1.848	1.221	1.876	1.197	1.905	1.174	1.934	1.150	1.963	1.126	1.993	1.102	2.023	1.079	2.054
100	1.314	1.790	1.292	1.816	1.270	1.841	1.248	1.868	1.225	1.895	1.203	1.922	1.181	1.949	1.158	1.977	1.136	2.006	1.113	2.034
150	1.473	1.783	1.458	1.799	1.444	1.814	1.429	1.830	1.414	1.847	1.400	1.863	1.385	1.880	1.370	1.897	1.355	1.913	1.340	1.931
200	1.561	1.791	1.550	1.801	1.539	1.813	1.528	1.824	1.518	1.836	1.507	1.847	1.495	1.860	1.484	1.871	1.474	1.883	1.462	1.896

n	$k' = 1$		$k' = 2$		$k' = 3$		$k' = 4$		$k' = 5$		$k' = 6$		$k' = 7$		$k' = 8$		$k' = 9$		$k' = 10$	
	d_L	d_U	d_L	d_U	d_L	d_U	d_L	d_U	d_L	d_U	d_L	d_U	d_L	d_U	d_L	d_U	d_L	d_U	d_L	d_U
6	0.610	1.400	—	—	—	—	—	—	—	—	—	—	—	—	—	—	—	—	—	—
7	0.700	1.356	0.467	1.896	—	—	—	—	—	—	—	—	—	—	—	—	—	—	—	—
8	0.763	1.332	0.559	1.777	0.368	2.287	—	—	—	—	—	—	—	—	—	—	—	—	—	—
9	0.824	1.320	0.629	1.699	0.455	2.128	0.296	2.588	—	—	—	—	—	—	—	—	—	—	—	—
10	0.879	1.320	0.697	1.641	0.525	2.016	0.376	2.414	0.243	2.822	—	—	—	—	—	—	—	—	—	—
11	0.927	1.324	0.758	1.604	0.595	1.928	0.444	2.283	0.316	2.645	0.203	3.005	—	—	—	—	—	—	—	—
12	0.971	1.331	0.812	1.579	0.658	1.864	0.512	2.177	0.379	2.506	0.268	2.832	0.171	3.149	—	—	—	—	—	—
13	1.010	1.340	0.861	1.562	0.715	1.816	0.574	2.094	0.445	2.390	0.328	2.692	0.230	2.985	0.147	3.266	—	—	—	—
14	1.045	1.350	0.905	1.551	0.767	1.779	0.632	2.030	0.505	2.296	0.389	2.572	0.286	2.848	0.200	3.111	0.127	3.360	—	—
15	1.077	1.361	0.946	1.543	0.814	1.750	0.685	1.977	0.562	2.220	0.447	2.472	0.343	2.727	0.251	2.979	0.175	3.216	0.111	3.438
16	1.106	1.371	0.982	1.539	0.857	1.728	0.734	1.935	0.615	2.157	0.502	2.388	0.398	2.624	0.304	2.860	0.222	3.090	0.155	3.304
17	1.133	1.381	1.015	1.536	0.897	1.710	0.779	1.900	0.664	2.104	0.554	2.310	0.451	2.537	0.356	2.757	0.272	2.975	0.198	3.184
18	1.158	1.391	1.046	1.535	0.933	1.696	0.820	1.872	0.710	2.060	0.603	2.257	0.502	2.461	0.407	2.667	0.321	2.873	0.244	3.073
19	1.180	1.401	1.074	1.536	0.967	1.685	0.859	1.848	0.752	2.023	0.649	2.206	0.459	2.396	0.456	2.589	0.369	2.783	0.290	2.974
20	1.201	1.411	1.100	1.537	0.998	1.676	0.894	1.828	0.792	1.991	0.692	2.162	0.595	2.339	0.502	2.521	0.416	2.704	0.336	2.885
21	1.221	1.420	1.125	1.538	1.026	1.669	0.927	1.812	0.829	1.964	0.732	2.124	0.637	2.290	0.547	2.460	0.461	2.633	0.380	2.806
22	1.239	1.429	1.147	1.541	1.053	1.664	0.958	1.797	0.863	1.940	0.769	2.090	0.677	2.246	0.588	2.407	0.504	2.571	0.424	2.734
23	1.257	1.437	1.168	1.543	1.078	1.660	0.986	1.785	0.895	1.920	0.804	2.061	0.715	2.208	0.628	2.360	0.545	2.514	0.465	2.670
24	1.273	1.446	1.188	1.546	1.101	1.656	1.013	1.775	0.925	1.902	0.837	2.035	0.751	2.174	0.666	2.318	0.584	2.464	0.506	2.613
25	1.288	1.454	1.206	1.550	1.123	1.654	1.038	1.767	0.953	1.886	0.868	2.012	0.784	2.144	0.702	2.280	0.621	2.419	0.544	2.560
26	1.302	1.461	1.224	1.553	1.143	1.652	1.062	1.759	0.979	1.873	0.897	1.992	0.816	2.117	0.735	2.246	0.657	2.379	0.581	2.513
27	1.316	1.469	1.240	1.556	1.162	1.651	1.084	1.753	1.004	1.861	0.925	1.974	0.845	2.093	0.767	2.216	0.691	2.342	0.616	2.470
28	1.328	1.476	1.255	1.560	1.181	1.650	1.104	1.747	1.028	1.850	0.951	1.958	0.874	2.071	0.798	2.188	0.723	2.309	0.650	2.431
29	1.341	1.483	1.270	1.563	1.198	1.650	1.124	1.743	1.050	1.841	0.975	1.944	0.900	2.052	0.826	2.164	0.753	2.278	0.682	2.396
30	1.352	1.489	1.284	1.567	1.214	1.650	1.143	1.739	1.071	1.833	0.998	1.931	0.926	2.034	0.854	2.141	0.782	2.251	0.712	2.363
31	1.363	1.496	1.297	1.570	1.229	1.650	1.160	1.735	1.090	1.825	1.020	1.920	0.950	2.018	0.879	2.120	0.810	2.226	0.741	2.333
32	1.373	1.502	1.309	1.574	1.244	1.650	1.177	1.732	1.109	1.819	1.041	1.909	0.972	2.004	0.904	2.102	0.836	2.203	0.769	2.306
33	1.383	1.508	1.321	1.577	1.258	1.651	1.193	1.730	1.127	1.813	1.061	1.900	0.994	1.991	0.927	2.085	0.861	2.181	0.795	2.281
34	1.393	1.514	1.333	1.580	1.271	1.652	1.208	1.728	1.144	1.808	1.080	1.891	1.015	1.979	0.950	2.069	0.885	2.162	0.821	2.257
35	1.402	1.519	1.343	1.584	1.283	1.653	1.222	1.726	1.160	1.803	1.097	1.884	1.034	1.967	0.971	2.054	0.908	2.144	0.845	2.236
36	1.411	1.525	1.354	1.587	1.295	1.654	1.236	1.724	1.175	1.799	1.114	1.877	1.053	1.957	0.991	2.041	0.930	2.127	0.868	2.216
37	1.419	1.530	1.364	1.590	1.307	1.655	1.249	1.723	1.190	1.795	1.131	1.870	1.071	1.948	1.011	2.029	0.951	2.112	0.891	2.198
38	1.427	1.535	1.373	1.594	1.318	1.656	1.261	1.722	1.204	1.792	1.146	1.864	1.088	1.939	1.029	2.017	0.970	2.098	0.912	2.180
39	1.435	1.540	1.382	1.597	1.328	1.658	1.273	1.722	1.218	1.789	1.161	1.859	1.104	1.932	1.047	2.007	0.990	2.085	0.932	2.164
40	1.442	1.544	1.391	1.600	1.338	1.659	1.285	1.721	1.230	1.786	1.175	1.854	1.120	1.924	1.064	1.997	1.008	2.072	0.945	2.149
45	1.475	1.566	1.430	1.615	1.383	1.666	1.336	1.720	1.287	1.776	1.238	1.835	1.189	1.895	1.139	1.958	1.089	2.002	1.038	2.088
50	1.503	1.585	1.462	1.628	1.421	1.674	1.378	1.721	1.335	1.771	1.291	1.822	1.246	1.875	1.201	1.930	1.156	1.986	1.110	2.044
55	1.528	1.601	1.490	1.641	1.452	1.681	1.414	1.724	1.374	1.768	1.334	1.814	1.294	1.861	1.253	1.909	1.212	1.959	1.170	2.010
60	1.549	1.616	1.514	1.652	1.480	1.689	1.444	1.727	1.408	1.767	1.372	1.808	1.335	1.850	1.298	1.894	1.260	1.939	1.222	1.984
65	1.567	1.629	1.536	1.662	1.503	1.696	1.471	1.731	1.438	1.767	1.404	1.805	1.370	1.843	1.336	1.882	1.301	1.923	1.266	1.964
70	1.583	1.641	1.554	1.672	1.525	1.703	1.494	1.735	1.464	1.768	1.433	1.802	1.401	1.837	1.369	1.873	1.337	1.910	1.305	1.948
75	1.598	1.652	1.571	1.680	1.543	1.709	1.515	1.739	1.487	1.770	1.458	1.801	1.428	1.834	1.399	1.867	1.369	1.901	1.339	1.935
80	1.611	1.662	1.586	1.688	1.560	1.715	1.534	1.743	1.507	1.772	1.480	1.801	1.453	1.831	1.425	1.861	1.397	1.893	1.369	1.925
85	1.624	1.671	1.600	1.696	1.575	1.721	1.550	1.747	1.525	1.774	1.500	1.801	1.474	1.829	1.448	1.857	1.422	1.886	1.396	1.916
90	1.635	1.679	1.612	1.703	1.589	1.726	1.566	1.751	1.542	1.776	1.518	1.801	1.494	1.827	1.469	1.854	1.445	1.881	1.420	1.909
95	1.645	1.687	1.623	1.709	1.602	1.732	1.579	1.755	1.557	1.778	1.535	1.802	1.512	1.827	1.489	1.852	1.465	1.877	1.442	1.903
100	1.654	1.694	1.634	1.715	1.613	1.736	1.592	1.758	1.571	1.780	1.550	1.803	1.528	1.826	1.506	1.850	1.484	1.874	1.462	1.898
150	1.720	1.746	1.706	1.760	1.693	1.774	1.679	1.788	1.665	1.802	1.651	1.817	1.637	1.832	1.622	1.847	1.608	1.862	1.594	1.877
200	1.758	1.778	1.748	1.789	1.738	1.799	1.728	1.810	1.718	1.820	1.707	1.831	1.697	1.841	1.686	1.852	1.675	1.863	1.665	1.874

TABLE B.5 *(continued)*

	$k' = 11$		$k' = 12$		$k' = 13$		$k' = 14$		$k' = 15$		$k' = 16$		$k' = 17$		$k' = 18$		$k' = 19$		$k' = 20$	
n	d_L	d_U	d_L	d_U	d_L	d_U	d_L	d_U	d_L	d_U	d_L	d_U	d_L	d_U	d_L	d_U	d_L	d_U	d_L	d_U
16	0.098	3.503	—	—	—	—	—	—	—	—	—	—	—	—	—	—	—	—	—	—
17	0.138	3.378	0.087	3.557	—	—	—	—	—	—	—	—	—	—	—	—	—	—	—	—
18	0.177	3.265	0.123	3.441	0.078	3.603	—	—	—	—	—	—	—	—	—	—	—	—	—	—
19	0.220	3.159	0.160	3.335	0.111	3.496	0.070	3.642	—	—	—	—	—	—	—	—	—	—	—	—
20	0.263	3.063	0.200	3.234	0.145	3.395	0.100	3.542	0.063	3.676	—	—	—	—	—	—	—	—	—	—
21	0.307	2.976	0.240	3.141	0.182	3.300	0.132	3.448	0.091	3.583	0.058	3.705	—	—	—	—	—	—	—	—
22	0.349	2.897	0.281	3.057	0.220	3.211	0.166	3.358	0.120	3.495	0.083	3.619	0.052	3.731	—	—	—	—	—	—
23	0.391	2.826	0.322	2.979	0.259	3.128	0.202	3.272	0.153	3.409	0.110	3.535	0.076	3.650	0.048	3.753	—	—	—	—
24	0.431	2.761	0.362	2.908	0.297	3.053	0.239	3.193	0.186	3.327	0.141	3.454	0.101	3.572	0.070	3.678	0.044	3.773	—	—
25	0.470	2.702	0.400	2.844	0.335	2.983	0.275	3.119	0.221	3.251	0.172	3.376	0.130	3.494	0.094	3.604	0.065	3.702	0.041	3.790
26	0.508	2.649	0.438	2.784	0.373	2.919	0.312	3.051	0.256	3.179	0.205	3.303	0.160	3.420	0.120	3.531	0.087	3.632	0.060	3.724
27	0.544	2.600	0.475	2.730	0.409	2.859	0.348	2.987	0.291	3.112	0.238	3.233	0.191	3.349	0.149	3.460	0.112	3.563	0.081	3.650
28	0.578	2.555	0.510	2.680	0.445	2.805	0.383	2.928	0.325	3.050	0.271	3.168	0.222	3.283	0.178	3.392	0.138	3.495	0.104	3.592
29	0.612	2.515	0.544	2.634	0.479	2.755	0.418	2.874	0.359	2.992	0.305	3.107	0.254	3.219	0.208	3.327	0.166	3.431	0.129	3.528
30	0.643	2.477	0.577	2.592	0.512	2.708	0.451	2.823	0.392	2.937	0.337	3.050	0.286	3.160	0.238	3.266	0.195	3.368	0.156	3.465
31	0.674	2.443	0.608	2.553	0.545	2.665	0.484	2.776	0.425	2.987	0.370	2.996	0.317	3.103	0.269	3.208	0.224	3.309	0.183	3.406
32	0.703	2.411	0.638	2.517	0.576	2.625	0.515	2.733	0.457	2.840	0.401	2.946	0.349	3.050	0.299	3.153	0.253	3.252	0.211	3.348
33	0.731	2.388	0.668	2.484	0.606	2.588	0.546	2.692	0.488	2.796	0.432	2.899	0.379	3.000	0.329	3.100	0.283	3.198	0.239	3.293
34	0.758	2.355	0.695	2.454	0.634	2.554	0.575	2.654	0.518	2.754	0.462	2.854	0.409	2.954	0.359	3.051	0.312	3.147	0.267	3.240
35	0.783	2.330	0.722	2.425	0.662	2.521	0.604	2.619	0.547	2.716	0.492	2.813	0.439	2.910	0.388	3.005	0.340	3.099	0.295	3.190
36	0.808	2.306	0.748	2.398	0.689	2.492	0.631	2.586	0.575	2.680	0.520	2.774	0.467	2.868	0.417	2.961	0.369	3.053	0.323	3.142
37	0.831	2.285	0.772	2.374	0.714	2.464	0.657	2.555	0.602	2.646	0.548	2.738	0.495	2.829	0.445	2.920	0.397	3.009	0.351	3.097
38	0.854	2.265	0.796	2.351	0.739	2.438	0.683	2.526	0.628	2.614	0.575	2.703	0.522	2.792	0.472	2.880	0.424	2.968	0.378	3.054
39	0.875	2.246	0.819	2.329	0.763	2.413	0.707	2.499	0.653	2.585	0.600	2.671	0.549	2.757	0.499	2.843	0.451	2.929	0.404	3.013
40	0.896	2.228	0.840	2.309	0.785	2.391	0.731	2.473	0.678	2.557	0.626	2.641	0.575	2.724	0.525	2.808	0.477	2.892	0.430	2.974
45	0.988	2.156	0.938	2.225	0.887	2.296	0.838	2.367	0.788	2.439	0.740	2.512	0.692	2.586	0.644	2.659	0.598	2.733	0.553	2.807
50	1.064	2.103	1.019	2.163	0.973	2.225	0.927	2.287	0.882	2.350	0.836	2.414	0.792	2.479	0.747	2.544	0.703	2.610	0.660	2.675
55	1.129	2.062	1.087	2.116	1.045	2.170	1.003	2.225	0.961	2.281	0.919	2.338	0.877	2.396	0.836	2.454	0.795	2.512	0.754	2.571
60	1.184	2.031	1.145	2.079	1.106	2.127	1.068	2.177	1.029	2.227	0.990	2.278	0.951	2.330	0.913	2.382	0.874	2.434	0.836	2.487
65	1.231	2.006	1.195	2.049	1.160	2.093	1.124	2.138	1.088	2.183	1.052	2.229	1.016	2.276	0.980	2.323	0.944	2.371	0.908	2.419
70	1.272	1.986	1.239	2.026	1.206	2.066	1.172	2.106	1.139	2.148	1.105	2.189	1.072	2.232	1.038	2.275	1.005	2.318	0.971	2.362
75	1.308	1.970	1.277	2.006	1.247	2.043	1.215	2.080	1.184	2.118	1.153	2.156	1.121	2.195	1.090	2.235	1.058	2.275	1.027	2.315
80	1.340	1.957	1.311	1.991	1.283	2.024	1.253	2.059	1.224	2.093	1.195	2.129	1.165	2.165	1.136	2.201	1.106	2.238	1.076	2.275
85	1.369	1.946	1.342	1.977	1.315	2.009	1.287	2.040	1.260	2.073	1.232	2.105	1.205	2.139	1.177	2.172	1.149	2.206	1.121	2.241
90	1.395	1.937	1.369	1.966	1.344	1.995	1.318	2.025	1.292	2.055	1.266	2.085	1.240	2.116	1.213	2.148	1.187	2.179	1.160	2.211
95	1.418	1.929	1.394	1.956	1.370	1.984	1.345	2.012	1.321	2.040	1.296	2.068	1.271	2.097	1.247	2.126	1.222	2.156	1.197	2.186
100	1.434	1.923	1.416	1.948	1.393	1.974	1.371	2.000	1.347	2.026	1.324	2.053	1.301	2.080	1.277	2.108	1.253	2.135	1.229	2.164
150	1.579	1.892	1.564	1.908	1.550	1.924	1.535	1.940	1.519	1.956	1.504	1.972	1.489	1.989	1.474	2.006	1.458	2.023	1.443	2.040
200	1.654	1.885	1.643	1.896	1.632	1.908	1.621	1.919	1.610	1.931	1.599	1.943	1.588	1.955	1.576	1.967	1.565	1.979	1.554	1.991

[a] k' is the number of regressors excluding the intercept.

Reprinted by permission from *Econometrica*, vol. 45, no. 8, 1977, pp. 1992–1995.

TABLE B.6 THE WALLIS STATISTIC FOR FOURTH ORDER AUTOCORRELATION 5% SIGNIFICANCE POINTS FOR $d_{4,L}$ AND $d_{4,U}$ IN REGRESSIONS EXCLUDING QUARTERLY DUMMY VARIABLES ($m = k'$)

	$k' = 1$		$k' = 2$		$k' = 3$		$k' = 4$		$k' = 5$	
n	$d_{4,L}$	$d_{4,U}$	$d_{4,L}$	$d_{4,U}$	$d_{4,L}$	$d_{4,U}$	$d_{4,L}$	$d_{4,U}$	$d_{4,L}$	$d_{4,U}$
16	0.774	0.982	0.662	1.109	0.549	1.275	0.435	1.381	0.350	1.532
20	0.924	1.102	0.827	1.203	0.728	1.327	0.626	1.428	0.544	1.556
24	1.036	1.189	0.953	1.273	0.867	1.371	0.779	1.459	0.702	1.565
28	1.123	1.257	1.050	1.328	0.975	1.410	0.898	1.487	0.828	1.576
32	1.192	1.311	1.127	1.373	1.061	1.443	0.993	1.511	0.929	1.587
36	1.248	1.355	1.191	1.410	1.131	1.471	1.070	1.532	1.013	1.598
40	1.295	1.392	1.243	1.442	1.190	1.496	1.135	1.550	1.082	1.609
44	1.335	1.423	1.288	1.469	1.239	1.518	1.189	1.567	1.141	1.620
48	1.369	1.451	1.326	1.493	1.281	1.537	1.236	1.582	1.191	1.630
52	1.399	1.475	1.359	1.513	1.318	1.554	1.276	1.595	1.235	1.639
56	1.426	1.496	1.389	1.532	1.351	1.569	1.312	1.608	1.273	1.648
60	1.449	1.515	1.415	1.548	1.379	1.583	1.343	1.619	1.307	1.656
64	1.470	1.532	1.438	1.563	1.405	1.596	1.371	1.629	1.337	1.664
68	1.489	1.548	1.459	1.577	1.427	1.608	1.396	1.639	1.364	1.671
72	1.507	1.562	1.478	1.589	1.448	1.618	1.418	1.648	1.388	1.678
76	1.522	1.574	1.495	1.601	1.467	1.628	1.439	1.656	1.411	1.685
80	1.537	1.586	1.511	1.611	1.484	1.637	1.457	1.663	1.431	1.691
84	1.550	1.597	1.525	1.621	1.500	1.646	1.475	1.671	1.449	1.696
88	1.562	1.607	1.539	1.630	1.515	1.654	1.490	1.677	1.466	1.702
92	1.574	1.617	1.551	1.639	1.528	1.661	1.505	1.684	1.482	1.707
96	1.584	1.626	1.563	1.647	1.541	1.668	1.519	1.690	1.496	1.712
100	1.594	1.634	1.573	1.654	1.552	1.674	1.531	1.695	1.510	1.717

5% significance points of $d_{4,L}$ and $d_{4,U}$ for regressions including a constant term and quarterly dummy variables ($m = k'' + 3$)

	$k'' = 1$		$k'' = 2$		$k'' = 3$		$k'' = 4$		$k'' = 5$	
n	$d_{4,L}$	$d_{4,U}$	$d_{4,L}$	$d_{4,U}$	$d_{4,L}$	$d_{4,U}$	$d_{4,L}$	$d_{4,U}$	$d_{4,L}$	$d_{4,U}$
16	1.156	1.381	1.031	1.532	0.902	1.776	0.777	2.191	0.693	2.238
20	1.228	1.428	1.123	1.556	1.013	1.726	0.899	1.954	0.806	2.042
24	1.287	1.459	1.199	1.565	1.107	1.694	1.011	1.856	0.928	1.949
28	1.337	1.487	1.261	1.576	1.181	1.679	1.099	1.803	1.025	1.889
32	1.379	1.511	1.312	1.587	1.243	1.673	1.171	1.773	1.104	1.850
36	1.414	1.532	1.355	1.598	1.293	1.672	1.230	1.755	1.170	1.824
40	1.445	1.550	1.391	1.609	1.336	1.674	1.279	1.745	1.225	1.807
44	1.471	1.567	1.422	1.620	1.373	1.677	1.321	1.739	1.272	1.795
48	1.494	1.582	1.450	1.630	1.404	1.681	1.357	1.737	1.312	1.788
52	1.514	1.595	1.474	1.639	1.432	1.686	1.389	1.736	1.347	1.782
56	1.533	1.608	1.495	1.648	1.456	1.691	1.416	1.736	1.377	1.779
60	1.549	1.619	1.514	1.656	1.478	1.696	1.441	1.737	1.404	1.777
64	1.564	1.629	1.531	1.664	1.497	1.700	1.463	1.739	1.429	1.776
68	1.577	1.639	1.546	1.671	1.515	1.705	1.482	1.741	1.450	1.775
72	1.590	1.648	1.560	1.678	1.531	1.710	1.500	1.743	1.470	1.776
76	1.601	1.656	1.573	1.685	1.545	1.714	1.517	1.746	1.488	1.776
80	1.611	1.663	1.585	1.691	1.559	1.719	1.531	1.748	1.504	1.777
84	1.621	1.671	1.596	1.696	1.571	1.723	1.545	1.751	1.519	1.778
88	1.630	1.677	1.607	1.702	1.582	1.727	1.558	1.753	1.533	1.779
92	1.639	1.684	1.616	1.707	1.593	1.731	1.570	1.756	1.546	1.781
96	1.647	1.690	1.625	1.712	1.603	1.735	1.580	1.759	1.558	1.782
100	1.654	1.695	1.633	1.717	1.612	1.739	1.591	1.761	1.569	1.784

Reprinted by permission from K. F. Wallis, "Testing for Fourth Order Autocorrelation in Quarterly Regression Equations," *Econometrica*, vol. 40, no. 0, (1972) pp. 623–24.

TABLE B.7 THE von NEUMANN RATIO (MODIFIED VERSION)
ITS 5%, 1%, AND 0.1% POINTS

Degrees of Freedom	5%	1%	0.1%	5%	1%	0.1%	Degrees of Freedom	5%	1%	0.1%	5%	1%	0.1%
	One-tailed test against positive autocorrelation			One-tailed test against negative autocorrelation				One-tailed test against positive autocorrelation			One-tailed test against negative autocorrelation		
							31	1.410	1.186	.955	2.595	2.826	3.066
2	.025	.001	.000	3.975	3.999	4.000	32	1.419	1.198	.970	2.585	2.813	3.051
3	.252	.052	.005	4.142	4.427	4.493	33	1.428	1.209	.984	2.576	2.801	3.036
4	.474	.170	.037	3.827	4.295	4.496	34	1.437	1.221	.997	2.567	2.789	3.021
5	.598	.292	.095	3.571	4.076	4.378	35	1.445	1.231	1.010	2.559	2.778	3.007
6	.701	.386	.163	3.413	3.881	4.233	36	1.452	1.241	1.022	2.551	2.767	2.994
7	.790	.464	.228	3.299	3.731	4.095	37	1.460	1.251	1.034	2.544	2.757	2.982
8	.861	.537	.285	3.206	3.618	3.973	38	1.467	1.261	1.045	2.536	2.747	2.969
9	.922	.601	.339	3.131	3.524	3.871	39	1.474	1.270	1.057	2.529	2.738	2.957
10	.975	.657	.390	3.069	3.445	3.784	40	1.480	1.279	1.067	2.522	2.729	2.946
11	1.020	.708	.438	3.016	3.378	3.710	41	1.487	1.287	1.078	2.516	2.720	2.935
12	1.060	.753	.482	2.970	3.319	3.645	42	1.493	1.295	1.088	2.510	2.711	2.925
13	1.096	.795	.523	2.930	3.268	3.587	43	1.499	1.303	1.097	2.504	2.703	2.914
14	1.128	.832	.561	2.895	3.222	3.535	44	1.504	1.311	1.107	2.498	2.695	2.904
15	1.157	.866	.597	2.863	3.181	3.488	45	1.510	1.318	1.116	2.492	2.687	2.895
16	1.183	.898	.630	2.835	3.144	3.445	46	1.515	1.325	1.125	2.487	2.680	2.885
17	1.207	.927	.661	2.809	3.110	3.406	47	1.520	1.332	1.133	2.482	2.673	2.876
18	1.228	.954	.691	2.785	3.079	3.370	48	1.525	1.339	1.142	2.477	2.666	2.868
19	1.249	.979	.718	2.764	3.051	3.337	49	1.530	1.346	1.150	2.472	2.659	2.859
20	1.267	1.003	.744	2.744	3.025	3.306	50	1.535	1.352	1.158	2.467	2.653	2.851
21	1.285	1.024	.769	2.725	3.000	3.277	51	1.540	1.358	1.165	2.462	2.646	2.843
22	1.301	1.045	.792	2.708	2.978	3.250	52	1.544	1.364	1.173	2.458	2.640	2.835
23	1.316	1.064	.814	2.692	2.957	3.225	53	1.548	1.370	1.180	2.453	2.634	2.828
24	1.330	1.082	.834	2.677	2.937	3.201	54	1.552	1.376	1.187	2.449	2.628	2.820
25	1.344	1.100	.854	2.663	2.918	3.179	55	1.557	1.381	1.194	2.445	2.623	2.813
26	1.356	1.116	.873	2.650	2.901	3.157	56	1.561	1.387	1.201	2.441	2.617	2.806
27	1.368	1.131	.891	2.638	2.884	3.137	57	1.564	1.392	1.207	2.437	2.612	2.799
28	1.380	1.146	.908	2.626	2.868	3.118	58	1.568	1.397	1.214	2.433	2.606	2.793
29	1.390	1.160	.925	2.615	2.854	3.100	59	1.572	1.402	1.220	2.429	2.601	2.786
30	1.400	1.173	.940	2.605	2.839	3.083	60	1.575	1.407	1.226	2.426	2.596	2.780

Reprinted by permission of S. J. Press and R. B. Brooks from "Testing for Serial Correlation in Regression," Report No. 6911, Center for Mathematical Studies in Business and Economics. University of Chicago. Chicago, 1969.

Bibliography

ADAMS, F. G., and V. G. DUGGAL (1974), "Anticipations Variables in Econometric Model: The Anticipations Version of Wharton Mark IV", *International Economic Review,* 15:267–284.

ADELMAN, E., and F. ADELMAN (1959), "The Dynamic Properties of the Klein–Goldberger Model", *Econometrica,* 27:596–625.

AGARWALA, R., and J. DRINKWATER (1972), "Consumption Functions with Shifting Parameters Due to Socio-Economic Factors", *Review of Economics and Statistics,* 44:89–96.

AIGNER, D. J. (1974), "MSE Dominance of Least Squares with Errors-of-Observations", *Journal of Econometrics,* 2:365–372.

AKAIKE, H. (1973), "Information Theory and An Extension of the Maximum Likelihood Principle", in B. N. PETROV and F. CSAKI (eds.), *Second International Symposium On Information Theory*. Budapest: Akademiai Kiado.

AKAIKE, H. (1977), "On Entropy Maximization Principle", in P. R. KRISHNAIAH (ed.), *Applications of Statistics*. Amsterdam: North Holland.

ALLEN, R. G. D., and A. L. BOWLEY (1935), *Family Expenditures*. London: P. S. King.

ALMON, S. (1965), "Distributed Lag Between Capital Appropriations and Expenditures", *Econometrica,* 33:178–196.

ALTONJI, J. G., and A. SIOW (1985), "Testing the Response of Consumption of Income Changes with (Noisy) Panel Data", IRS Working Paper No. 186, Princeton University, Princeton, NJ.

ALTONJI, J. G., A. P. MARTENS, and A. SIOW (1986), "Dynamic Factor Models of Consumption, Hours and Income", Mimeo, Northwestern University, Evanston, IL.

AMEMIYA, T. (1973), "Regression Analysis When the Dependent Variable is a Truncated Normal," *Econometrica,* 41:1193–1205.

AMEMIYA, T. (1974), "A Note on a Fair and Jaffee Model", *Econometrica,* 42:759–762.

AMEMIYA, T. (1976), "The Maximum Likelihood, the Minimum Chi-Square and the Non-Linear Weighted Least Squares in the General Qualitative Response Model", *Journal of the American Statistical Association,* 71:347–351.

AMEMIYA, T. (1980), "Selection of Regressors", *International Economic Review,* 21:331–354.

AMEMIYA, T. (1981), "Qualitative Response Model: A Survey", *Journal of Economic Literature,* 19:1483–1536.

AMEMIYA, T. (1985), *Advanced Econometrics*. Cambridge, MA: Harvard University Press.

ANDERSON, T. W. (1958), *An Introduction to Multivariate Statistical Analysis*. New York: Wiley.

ANDERSON, T. W., and C. HSIAO (1981), "Estimation of Dynamic Models with Error Components", *Journal of the American Statistical Association, Theory and Methods,* 76:598–606.

ANDERSON, T. W., and H. RUBIN (1949), "Estimation of the Parameters of a Single Equation in a Complete System of Stochastic Equations", *Annals of Mathematical Statistics,* 21:46–63.

ANDERSON, T. W., and H. RUBIN (1950), "The Asymptotic Properties of Estimates of the Parameters of a Single Equation in a Complete System of Stochastic Equations", *Annals of Mathematical Statistics,* 21:151–163.

ANDERSON, T. W., and T. SAWA (1973), "Distribution of Estimates of Coefficients of a Single Equation in a Simultaneous System and their Asymptotic Expansions", *Econometrica,* 41:683–714.

ANDO, A. (1974), "Some Aspects of Stabilization Policies, the Monetarist Controversy and the MPS Model", *International Economic Review,* 15:541–571.

ANDO, A., and F. MODIGLIANI (1963), "The 'Life Cycle' Hypothesis of Saving: Aggregate Implications and Tests", *American Economic Review,* 53:55–84.

ANDO, A., and F. MODIGLIANI (1969), "Econometric Analysis of Stabilization Policies", *American Economic Review,* 59:296–314.

ANDO, A., F. MODIGLIANI, and R. RASCHE (1972), "Equations and Definitions of Variables for the FRB–MIT–Penn Econometric Model" in B. G. HICKMAN (ed.), *Econometric Models of Cyclical Behavior*. National Bureau of Economic Research. New York: Columbia University Press.

ARROW, K. J., H. B. CHENERY, B. S. MINHAS, and R. M. SOLOW (1961), "Capital Labor Substitution and Economic Efficiency", *Review of Economics and Statistics,* 43:225–235.

ATTFIELD, C. L. F. (1983), "Consistent Estimation of Certain Parameters in the Unobservable Variable Model When there is Specification Error", *Review of Economics and Statistics,* 65:164–167.

ATTFIELD, C. L. F., D. DEMERY, and N. W. DUCK (1981), "Unanticipated Monetary Growth, Output and the Price Level: U. K. 1946–1977", *European Economic Review,* 16:367–385.

ATTFIELD, C. L. F., and N. W. DUCK (1983), "The Influence of Unanticipated Money Growth on Real Output: Some Cross Country Estimates", *Journal of Money, Credit and Banking,* 15:442–454.

AULD, D. A. L., L. N. CHRISTOFIDES, R. SWIDINSKY, and D. A. WILTON (1979), "The Impact of the AIB on Negotiated Wage Settlements", *Canadian Journal of Economics,* 12:195–213.

AULD, D. A. L., L. N. CHRISTOFIDES, R. SWIDINSKY, and D. A. WILTON (1986), "A Micro Economic Analysis of Wage Determination in the Canadian Public Sector", *Journal of Public Economics,* 13:369–387.

BALESTRA, P., and M. NERLOVE (1966), "Pooling Cross-Section and Time Series Data in the Estimation of a Dynamic Model: The Demand for Natural Gas", *Econometrica,* 34:585–612.

BALTAGI, B. H. (1981a), "An Experimental Study of Alternative Testing and Estimation Procedures in a Two-way Error Component Model", *Journal of Econometrics,* 17:21–49.

BALTAGI, B. H. (1981b), "Simultaneous Equations with Error Components", *Journal of Econometrics,* 17:189–200.

BANK OF CANADA (1976), *Technical Report,* No. 5, Ottawa.

BANK OF CANADA (1977), *Technical Report,* No. 6, Ottawa.

BANK OF CANADA (1978), *Technical Report,* No. 13, Ottawa.

BANK OF CANADA (1980a), *Technical Report,* No. 25, Ottawa.

BANK OF CANADA (1980b), *Technical Report,* No. 26, Ottawa.

BARRO, R. J. (1977), "Unanticipated Money Growth and Unemployment in the U.S.", *American Economic Review,* 67:101–115.

BARRO, R. J. (1978), "Unanticipated Money, Output and the Price Level in the U.S.", *Journal of Political Economy,* 86:549–580.

BARRO, R. J., and M. RUSH (1980), "Unanticipated Money and Economic Activity", in S. FISCHER (ed.), *Rational Expectations and Economic Policy.* Chicago: University of Chicago Press.

BARTEN, A. P. (1964), "Consumer Demand Functions Under Conditions of Almost Additive Preferences", *Econometrica,* 32:1–38.

BASMANN, R. L. (1957), "A Generalized Classical Method of Linear Estimation of Coefficients in a Structural Equation", *Econometrica,* 25:77–83.

BASMANN, R. L. (1958). *An Experimental Investigation of Some Small Sample Properties of (GCL) Estimators of Structural Equations: Some Preliminary Results.* Richland, WA: General Electric Co.

BASMANN, R. L. (1961), "A Note on the Exact Finite Sample Frequency Functions of Generalized Classical Linear Estimators in Two Leading Over-Identified Cases", *Journal of the American Statistical Association,* 56:619–636.

BASMANN, R. L. (1963), "A Note on the Exact Finite Sample Frequency Functions of Generalized Classical Linear Estimators in a Leading 3-equation Case", *Journal of the American Statistical Association,* 68:161–171.

BASMANN, R. L. (1972), "The Brookings Quarterly Econometric Model: Science or Number Mysticism?" in K. BRUNNER (ed.), *Problems and Issues in Current Econometric Practice.* Columbus, OH: Ohio State University.

BASMANN, R. L. (1974), "Exact Finite Sample Distributions for Some Econometric Estimators and Test Statistics: A Survey and Appraisal", in M. D. INTRILIGATOR and D.

A. Kendrick (eds.), *Frontiers of Quantitative Economics,* Vol. 2. Amsterdam: North Holland.

Bays, C. W. (1980), "Specification Error in the Estimation of Hospital Cost Functions", *Review of Economics and Statistics,* 52:302–305.

Beach, C. M., and J. G. MacKinnon (1978a), "Full Maximum Likelihood Estimation of Second Order Autoregressive Error Model", *Journal of Econometrics,* 7:187–198.

Beach, C. M., and J. G. MacKinnon (1978b), "A Maximum Likelihood Procedure for Regression with Autocorrelated Errors", *Econometrica,* 46:51–58.

Bean, C. R. (1979), "An Econometric Model of Manufacturing Investment in the U.K.", Government Economic Service, Working Paper No. 29.

Beckman, M., and K. Sato (1969), "Production Function and Technical Progress", *American Economic Review,* 59:88–101.

Belsley, D. A., E. Kuh, and R. E. Welsch (1980), *Regression Diagnostics, Identifying Influential Data and Sources of Collinearity.* New York: Wiley.

Berhman, J. R. (1972), "Sectoral Elasticity of Substitution Between Capital and Labor in a Developing Economy: Time Series Analysis in the Case of Postwar Chile", *Econometrica,* 40:311–326.

Berndt, E. R., and G. C. Watkins (1977), "Demand for Natural Gas: Residential and Commercial Markets in Ontario and British Columbia", *Canadian Journal of Economics,* 10:97–111.

Berndt, E. R., and D. O. Wood (1975), "Technology, Prices and the Derived Demand for Energy", *Review of Economics and Statistics,* 57:259–268.

Betancourt, B., and H. Kelejian (1981), "Lagged Endogenous Variables and the Cochrane–Orcutt Procedure", *Econometrica,* 49:1073–1078.

Beveridge, S., and C. R. Nelson (1981), "A New Approach to Decomposition of Economic Time Series into Permanent and Transitory Components with Particular Attention to Measurement of the 'Business Cycle'", *Journal of Monetary Economics,* 7:151–174.

Blinder, A. S., and A. S. Deaton (1985), *Time Series Consumption Function Revisited,* Brookings Papers on Economic Activity, Vol. 2, pp. 465–521.

Blomqvist, A. G., and W. Haessel (1978), "Small Cars, Large Cars and the Price of Gasoline", *Canadian Journal of Economics,* 11:471–489.

Boatwright, B. D., and J. R. Eaton (1972), "The Estimation of Investment Functions for Manufacturing Industry in the United Kingdom", *Economica,* 39:403–418.

Bollerslev, T., R. F. Engle, and J. M. Woolridge (1988), "A Capital Asset Pricing Model with Time-varying Covariances", *Journal of Political Economy,* 96:116–131.

Bordo, M., and E. U. Choudhry (1982), "Currency Substitution and the Demand for Money: Some Evidence for Canada", *Journal of Money, Credit and Banking,* 14:48–57.

Box, G. E. P., and G. M. Jenkins (1970), *Time Series Analysis, Forecasting and Control.* San Francisco: Holden Day.

Box, G. E. P., and G. M. Jenkins (1976), *Time Series Analysis, Forecasting and Control,* (rev. ed.). San Francisco: Holden Day.

Box, G. E. P., and D. A. Pierce (1970), "Distribution of Residual Autocorrelations in

Autoregressive Integrated Moving Average Time Series Models", *Journal of the American Statistical Association,* 65:1509–1526.

BREUSCH, T. S. (1978), "Testing for Autocorrelation in Dynamic Linear Models", *Australian Economic Papers,* 17:334–355.

BREUSCH, T. S., and A. R. PAGAN (1979), "A Simple Test for Heteroscedasticity and Random Coefficient Variation", *Econometrica,* 47:1287–1294.

BRIDGE, J. L. (1971), *Applied Econometrics.* Amsterdam: North Holland.

BROWN, R. L., J. DURBIN, and J. M. EVANS (1975), "Techniques for Testing the Constancy of Regression Relationships Over Time", *Journal of the Royal Statistical Society, Series B,* 37:149–192.

BRUNDY, J. M., and D. W. JORGENSON (1971), "Efficient Estimation of Simultaneous Equations by Instrumental Variables", *Review of Economics and Statistics,* 53:207–224.

BURLEY, H. T. (1973), "Production Functions for Australian Manufacturing Industries", *Review of Economics and Statistics,* 45:118–122.

BUSE, A., and L. LIM (1977), "Cubic Splines as a Special Case of Restricted Least Squares", *Journal of the American Statistical Association,* 72:64–72.

CAMPBELL, J. Y., and A. S. DEATON (1987), *Is Consumption too Smooth?* Mimeo, National Bureau of Economic Research.

CARGILL, T. F., and R. A. MEYER (1978), "The Time-varying Response of Income to Changes in Monetary and Fiscal Policy", *Review of Economics and Statistics,* 50:1–7.

CARLSON, J. A. (1977), "A Study of Price Forecasts", *Annals of Economic and Social Measurement,* 6:27–56.

CARROLL, R. J., and D. RUPPERT (1982), "A Comparison Between Maximum Likelihood and GLS in a Heteroscedastic Linear Model", *Journal of the American Statistical Association,* 77:878–882.

CHOUDHRY, N. K., Y. KOTOWITZ, J. A. SAWYER, and J. W. L. WINDER (1972), *The TRACE Econometric Model of the Canadian Economy.* Toronto: University of Toronto Press.

CHOW, G. C. (1960), "Tests of Equality Between Sets of Coefficients in Two Linear Regressions", *Econometrica,* 28:591–605.

CHOW, G. C., and D. K. RAY-CHAUDHURI (1967), "An Alternative Proof of Hannan's Theorem on Canonical Correlation and Multiple Equation Systems", *Econometrica,* 35:139–142.

CHRISTENSEN, L. R., D. W. JORGENSON, and L. J. LAU (1973), "Transcendental Logarithmic Production Frontiers", *Review of Economics and Statistics,* 55:28–45.

CHRISTOFIDES, L. N., and D. A. WILTON (1983), "The Determination of Contract Length—An Empirical Analysis Based on Canadian Micro Data", *Journal of Monetary Economics,* 9:309–319.

CHRISTOFIDES, L. N., R. SWIDINSKY, and D. A. WILTON (1980a), "A Micro-Econometric Analysis of Spillovers Within the Canadian Wage Determination Process", *Review of Economics and Statistics,* 52:213–221.

CHRISTOFIDES, L. N., R. SWIDINSKY, and D. A. WILTON (1980b), "A Micro-Econometric Analysis of the Canadian Wage Determination Process", *Economica,* 47:165–178.

COBB, C. W., and P. H. DOUGLAS (1928), "A Theory of Production", *American Economic Review,* 18 (Suppl.):139–165.

COCHRANE, D., and G. H. ORCUTT (1949), "Application of Least Squares Regressions to Relationships Containing Autocorrelated Error Terms", *Journal of the American Statistical Association,* 44:32–61.

COMANOR, W. S., and T. A. WILSON (1967), "Advertising, Market Structure and Performance", *Review of Economics and Statistics,* 39:423–440.

COMANOR, W. S., and T. A. WILSON (1971), "On Advertising and Profitability", *Review of Economics and Statistics,* 53:408–410.

COOK, R. D., and S. WEISBERG (1982), *Residuals and Influence in Regression.* London: Chapman and Hall.

COOLEY, T. F., and E. C. PRESCOTT (1973a), "An Adaptive Regression Model", *International Economic Review,* 14:464–471.

COOLEY, T. F., and E. C. PRESCOTT (1973b), "Tests of An Adaptive Regression Model", *Review of Economics and Statistics,* 55:248–256.

COOLEY, T. F., and E. C. PRESCOTT (1973c), "Systematic (Non-Random) Variation Models: Varying Parameter Regression A Theory and Some Applications", *Annals of Economic and Social Measurement,* 2:463–474.

COPAS, J. B. (1966), "Monte Carlo Results for Estimation in a Stable Markov Time Series", *Journal of the Royal Statistical Society, Series A,* 129:110–116.

COX, D. R. (1961), "Tests of Separate Families of Hypotheses", in *Proceedings of the Fourth Berkeley Symposium on Mathematical Statistics and Probability.* Berkeley: University of California Press.

CRAGG, J. (1967), "On the Relative Small Sample Properties of Several Structural Equation Estimates", *Econometrica,* 35:89–110.

DARBY, M. (1982), "The Price of Oil and World Inflation and Recession", *American Economic Review,* 72:738–751.

DAUGHETY, A. F., and F. D. NELSON (1988), "An Econometric Analysis of Changes in the Cost and Production Structure of the Trucking Industry, 1953–82", *Review of Economics and Statistics,* 60:67–75.

DAVIDSON, R., and J. MACKINNON (1981), "Several Tests for Model Specification in the Presence of Alternative Hypotheses", *Econometrica,* 49:781–793.

DAVIDSON, R., L. G. GODFREY, and J. G. MACKINNON (1985), "A Simplified Version of the Differencing Test", *International Economic Review,* 26:639–647.

DAY, E. E. (1923), "The Physical Volume of Production for the United States for 1922", *Review of Economics and Statistics,* 6:196–211.

DAY, E. E., and W. M. PERSONS (1920), "An Index of the Physical Volume of Production", *Review of Economics and Statistics,* 2:328–329.

DAY, E. E., and W. THOMAS (1928), *The Growth of Manufactures, 1899–1923, Study of Index of Increase in the Volume of Manufactured Products.* Census Monograph 8.

DEATON, A. (1985), "Life Cycle Models of Consumption: Is the Evidence Consistent with Theory?", Invited paper to the Fifth World Congress of the Econometric Society, Cambridge, MA., National Bureau of Economic Research, Working Paper No. 1910.

DELEEUW, F. (1962), "The Demand for Capital Goods by Manufactures: A Study of Quarterly Time Series", *Econometrica,* 30:407–423.

deLeeuw, F., and E. M. Gramlich (1968), "The Federal Reserve–MIT Econometric Model", *The Federal Reserve Bulletin,* 54:11–40.

deLeeuw, F., and E. M. Gramlich (1969), "The Channels of Monetary Policy", *The Federal Reserve Bulletin,* 55:472–491.

Denny, M., J. D. May, and G. Pinto (1978), "The Demand for Energy in Canadian Manufacturing: Prologue to an Energy Policy", *Canadian Journal of Economics,* 11:300–313.

Dhrymes, P. J. (1965), "Some Extensions and Tests for the CES Class of Production Functions", *Review of Economics and Statistics,* 47:357–366.

Dhrymes, P. J. (1971), *Distributed Lags: Problems of Estimation and Formulation.* San Francisco: Holden Day.

Dickey, D. A., and W. A. Fuller (1979), "Distribution of the Estimators for Autoregressive Time Series with a Unit Root", *Journal of the American Statistical Association,* 74:427–431.

Diewert, W. E. (1971), "An Application of the Shephard Duality Theorem: A Generalized Leontief Production Function", *Journal of Political Economy,* 79:481–507.

Douglas, P. (1948), "Are There Laws of Production?" *American Economic Review,* 38:1–41.

Duesenberry, J. S. (1949), *Income, Savings, and the Theory of Consumer Behavior.* Cambridge, MA: Harvard University Press.

Duesenberry, J. S., G. Fromm, L. R. Klein, and E. Kuh (eds.) (1965), *The Brookings Quarterly Econometric Model of the United States.* Chicago: Rand McNally.

Duesenberry, J. S., G. Fromm, L. R. Klein, and E. Kuh (eds.) (1969), *The Brookings Model: Some Further Results.* Chicago: Rand McNally.

Duggal, V. G., L. Klein, and M. D. McCarthy (1974), "The Wharton Model, Mark III: A Modern IS–LM Construct", *International Economic Review,* 15:572–594.

Durbin, J. (1954), "Errors in Variables", *Review of the International Statistical Institute,* 22:23–32.

Durbin, J. (1960), "Estimation of Parameters in Time Series Regression Models", *Journal of the Royal Statistical Society, Series B,* 22:139–153.

Durbin, J. (1970), "Testing for Serial Correlation in Least Squares Regression When Some of the Regressors are Lagged Dependent Variables", *Econometrica,* 38:410–421.

Durbin J., and G. S. Watson (1950), "Testing for Serial Correlation in Least Squares Regression I", *Biometrika,* 37:409–428.

Durbin, J. and G. S. Watson (1951), "Testing for Serial Correlation in Least Squares Regression II", *Biometrika,* 38:159–178.

Durbin, J., and G. S. Watson (1971), "Testing for Serial Correlation in Least Squares Regression III", *Biometrika,* 58:1–19.

Dvoretzky, A. (1956), "On Stochastic Approximations", in *Proceedings of the Third Berkeley Symposium on Mathematical Statistics and Probability, Vol. 1.* Berkeley: University of California Press.

Eckstein, O. (ed.) (1976), *Parameters and Policies in the U.S. Economy.* Amsterdam: North Holland.

EDGERTON, D. L. (1972), "Some Properties of Two Stage Least Squares as Applied to Nonlinear Models", *International Economic Review,* 13:26–32.

EISNER, R. (1960), "A Distributed Lag Investment Function", *Econometrica,* 28:1–30.

EISNER, R., and M. I. NADIRI (1968), "Investment Behavior and Neo-Classical Theory", *Review of Economics and Statistics,* 50:369–382.

ENGLE, R. F. (1982), "Autoregressive Conditional Heteroscedasticity With Estimates of the Variance of United Kingdom Inflations", *Econometrica,* 50:987–1008.

ENGLE, R. F. (1984), "Wald, Likelihood Ratio and Lagrange Multiplier Tests in Econometrics", Chapter 13 in Z. GRILICHES and M. INTRILIGATOR (eds.), *Handbook of Econometrics, Vol. 2.* Amsterdam: North Holland.

ENGLE, R. F., and C. GRANGER (1987), "Co-integration and Error Correction Representation, Estimation and Testing", *Econometrica,* 66:251–276.

EVANS, M. K. (1967), "A Study of Industry Investment Decisions", *Review of Economics and Statistics,* 49:151–164.

EVANS, M. K. (1969), *Macroeconomic Activity: Theory, Forecasting and Control, An Econometric Approach.* New York: Harper and Row.

EVANS, M. K., and L. KLEIN (1967), *The Wharton Econometric Forecasting Model.* Philadelphia: University of Pennsylvania.

EVANS, M. K., and L. KLEIN (1968), *The Wharton Econometric Forecasting Model* (rev. ed.), Philadelphia: University of Pennsylvania.

EVANS, G. B. A., and N. E. SAVIN (1982), "Conflict Among the Criteria Revisited, the W, LR and LM Tests", *Econometrica,* 50:737–748.

EVANS, M. K., L. KLEIN, and M. SAITO (1972), "Short Run Predictions and Long Run Simulations of Wharton Model", in B. G. HICKMAN, (ed.), *Econometric Models of Cyclical Behavior.* National Bureau of Economic Research, New York: Columbia University Press.

EZEKIEL, M., and K. FOX (1959). *Methods of Correlation and Regression Analysis.* New York: Wiley.

FAIR, R. (1971), *A Short-Run Forecasting Model of the United States Economy.* Lexington, MA: Heath Lexington Books.

FAIR, R. (1974), "An Evaluation of a Short-Run Forecasting Model", *International Economic Review,* 15:285–303.

FAIR, R. C., and D. M. JAFFEE (1972), "Methods of Estimation for Markets in Disequilibrium", *Econometrica,* 40:497–514.

FAIR, R. C., and H. H. KELEJIAN (1974), "Methods of Estimation for Markets in Disequilibrium: A Further Study", *Econometrica,* 42:177–190.

FAMA, E. (1976), "Forward Rates as Predictors of Future Spot Rates", *Journal of Financial Economics,* 3:361–377.

FAMA, E., and G. W. SCHWERT (1977), "Asset Returns and Inflation", *Journal of Financial Economics,* 5:115–146.

FARBER, S. (1981), "Buyer Market Structure and R and D Effort—A Simultaneous Equation Model", *Review of Economics and Statistics,* 58:336–345.

FAREBROTHER, R. W. (1980), "The Durbin-Watson Test for Serial Correlation when There is no Intercept in the Regression", *Econometrica,* 48:1553–1563.

FARRAR, D. E., and R. R. GLAUBER (1967), "Multicollinearity in Regression Analysis: The Problem Re-Visited", *Review of Economics and Statistics,* 49:92–107.

FEIGE, E. (1964), *The Demand for Liquid Assets: A Temporal Cross-Section Analysis.* Englewood Cliffs, NJ: Prentice-Hall.

FELDSTEIN, M. (1968), *Economic Analysis for Health Services Efficiency.* Amsterdam: North Holland.

FELDSTEIN, M. (1973), "Multicollinearity and Mean Squared Error of Alternative Estimators", *Econometrica,* 41:337–346.

FERGUSON, L. E. (1965), "Time-Series Production Functions and Technological Progress in American Manufacturing Industries", *Journal of Political Economy,* 73:135–147.

FIGLEWSKI, S., and P. WACHTEL (1981), "The Formation of Inflationary Expectations", *Review of Economics and Statistics,* 58:1–10.

FIJUMAGARI, D. K. (1986), "Small Sample Tests for Separate Regressions", unpublished, Queen's University, Kingston, Ontario.

FISHER, F. M. (1965), "Dynamic Structure and Estimation in Economy Wide Econometric Models", in J. DUESENBERRY, G. FROMM, L. R. KLEIN, and E. KUH (eds.), *The Brookings Quarterly Econometric Model of the United States.* Chicago: Rand McNally.

FISHER, F. M. (1966), *The Identification Problem of Econometrics.* New York: McGraw Hill.

FISHER, F. M. (1970), "Tests on Equality Between Sets of Coefficients in Two Linear Regressions: An Expository Note", *Econometrica,* 28:361–366.

FISHER, G. R. (1983), "Tests for Two Separate Regressions", *Journal of Econometrics,* 21:117–132.

FISHER, G. R., and M. MCALEER (1981), "Alternative Procedures and Associated Tests of Significance for Nonnested Hypotheses", *Journal of Econometrics,* 16:103–119.

FISHER, W. D., and W. J. WADYCKI (1971), "Estimating a Structural Equation in a Large System", *Econometrica,* 39:461–465.

FLAVIN, M. A. (1981), "The Adjustment of Consumption to Changing Expectations About Future Income", *Journal of Political Economy,* 89:974–1009.

FLEISHER, B. M., and G. H. RHODES (1976), "Unemployment and the Labor Force Participation of Married Men and Women: A Simultaneous Model", *Review of Economics and Statistics,* 58:398–406.

FOX, K. A. (1958), *Econometric Analysis for Public Policy.* Ames: Iowa State University Press.

FRENKEL, J. A. (1977), "The Forward Exchange Rate, Expectations and the Demand for Money, The German Hyper-Inflation", *American Economic Review,* 67:653–670.

FRIEDMAN, B. (1980), "Survey Evidence on the Rationality of Interest Rate Expectations", *Journal of Monetary Economics,* 6:453–465.

FRIEDMAN, M. (1957), *A Theory of the Consumption Function.* Princeton, NJ: Princeton University Press.

FROMM, G. (1969), "An Evaluation of Monetary Policy Instruments", in J. S. DUESENBERRY, G. FROMM, L. R. KLEIN, and E. KUH (eds.), *The Brookings Model: Some Further Results.* Chicago: Rand McNally.

FROMM, G. (ed.) (1971), *Tax Incentives and Capital Spending.* Amsterdam: North Holland.

FROMM, G., and L. KLEIN (eds.) (1975), *The Brookings Model, Perspective and Recent Developments*. Amsterdam: North Holland.

FROMM, G., and P. TAUBMAN (1968), *Policy Simulations With an Econometric Model*. Amsterdam: North Holland.

FUSS, M. A. (1977), "The Demand for Energy in Canadian Manufacturing", *Journal of Econometrics,* 5:89–116.

FUSS, M. A., and L. WAVERMAN (1975), "The Demand for Energy in Canada", Working Paper, Institute for Policy Analysis, University of Toronto.

GARCIA-FERRAR, A., R. A. HIGHFIELD, and A. ZELLNER (1987), "Macro-Economic Forecasting Using Pooled International Data", *Journal of the American Statistical Association, Journal of Business and Economic Statistics,* 5:53–67.

GHOSH, S. K. (1972), "Canonical Correlation and Extended Limited Information Methods Under General Linear Restrictions on Parameters", *International Economic Review,* 13:728–736.

GHOSH, S. K. (1976), "Estimating From a More General Time Series Cum Cross-Section Data Structure", *American Economist,* 20:15–21.

GHOSH, S. K. (1986), "A Stochastic Approximation Algorithm for a Class of Nonlinear Dynamical Econometric System", *Sankhya: Indian Journal of Statistics, Series B,* 78:401–426.

GHOSH, S. K. (1989), "Currency Substitution and Demand for Money in Canada, Further Evidence", *Journal of Macroeconomics,* 11:81–93.

GILES, D. E. A., and M. L. KING (1978), "Fourth Order Autocorrelation: Further Significance Points for the Wallis Test", *Journal of Econometrics,* 8:1023–1026.

GILLEN, W. J., and A. GUCCIONE (1970), "The Estimation of Postwar Regional Consumption Function in Canada", *Canadian Journal of Economics,* 13:276–290.

GLESJER, H. (1969), "A New Test for Heteroscedasticity", *Journal of the American Statistical Association,* 64:316–323.

GODFREY, L. G. (1978), "Testing Against General Autoregression and Moving Average Error Models Where the Regressors Include Lagged Dependent Variables", *Econometrica,* 46:1293–1302.

GODFREY, L. G., and M. H. PESARAN (1983), "Tests of Nonnested Regression Models: Small Sample Adjustments and Monte Carlo Evidence", *Journal of Econometrics,* 21:133–154.

GOLDBERG, I., and F. C. NOLD (1980), "Does Reporting Deter Burglars? An Empirical Analysis of Risk and Return in Crime", *Review of Economics and Statistics,* 52:424–431.

GOLDBERGER, A. S. (1959), *Impact Multipliers and Dynamic Properties of the Klein–Goldberger Model*. Amsterdam: North Holland.

GOLDBERGER, A. S. (1964), *Econometric Theory*. New York: Wiley.

GOLDBERGER, A. S. (1972), "Maximum Likelihood Estimation of Regressions Containing Unobservable Independent Variables", *International Economic Review,* 11:441–454.

GOLDBERGER, A. S., and T. GAMALETSOS (1970), "A Cross-country Comparison of Consumer Expenditure Patterns", *European Economic Review,* 1:357–400.

Goldfeld, S. M. (1976), "The Case of the Missing Money", *Brookings Papers on Economic Activity,* 3:638–730.

Goldfeld, S. M., and R. E. Quandt (1972), *Nonlinear Methods in Econometrics.* Amsterdam: North Holland.

Goldfeld, S. M., and R. E. Quandt (1975), "Estimation in a Disequilibrium Model and the Value of Information", *Journal of Econometrics,* 3:325–348.

Goldfeld, S. M., and R. Quandt (1976), *Studies in Nonlinear Estimation.* Cambridge, MA: Ballinger.

Goldsmith, R. W. (1955), *A Study of Savings in the U.S.* Princeton, NJ: Princeton University Press.

Goodnight, J., and T. D. Wallace (1972), "Operational Techniques and Tables for Making Weak MSE Tests for Restrictions in Regressions", *Econometrica,* 40:699–709.

Gordon, D. F., and A. Hynes (1970), "On the Theory of Price Dynamics", in E. Phelps (ed.), *Macro Economic Foundation of Employment and Inflation Theory.* New York: Norton.

Gordon, R. J. (1982), "Price Inertia and Policy Ineffectiveness in the U.S. 1890–1980", *Journal of Political Economy,* 90:1087–1117.

Granger, C. W. J. (1969), "Investigating Causal Relations By Econometric Models and Cross Spectral Methods", *Econometrica,* 37:424–438.

Granger, C., and P. Newbold (1974), "Spurious Regressions in Econometrics", *Journal of Econometrics,* 3:111–120.

Graybill, F. A. (1961), *An Introduction to Linear Statistical Models, Vol. 1.* New York: McGraw-Hill.

Greenwood, M. J. (1980), "Metropolitan Growth and the Intra-metropolitan Location of Employment, Housing and Labor Force", *Review of Economics and Statistics,* 52:491–501.

Griffin, J. M., and P. R. Gregory (1976), "An Intercountry Translog Model of Energy Substitution Responses", *American Economic Review,* 66:845–857.

Griliches, Z. (1961), "A Note on Serial Correlation Bias in Estimates of Distributed Lags", *Econometrica,* 29:65–73.

Griliches, Z. (1977), "Estimating the Returns to Schooling: Some Econometric Problems", *Econometrica,* 45:1–22.

Griliches, Z. (1980), "Schooling Interruption, Work While in School and the Returns From Schooling", *Scandinavian Journal of Economics,* 82:291–303.

Griliches, Z. (1986), "Productivity, Research and Development and Basic Research at the Firm Level in the 1970's", *American Economic Review,* 76:141–154.

Griliches, Z., and J. A. Hausman (1986), "Errors in Variables in Panel Data," *Journal of Econometrics,* 31:93–110.

Griliches, Z., and P. Rao (1969), "Small Sample Properties of Several Two Stage Regression Methods in the Context of Autocorrelated Errors," *Journal of the American Statistical Association,* 64:253–272.

Griliches, Z., and V. Ringstad (1971), *Economies of Scale and the Form of the Production Function.* Amsterdam: North Holland.

HADLEY, G. (1961), *Linear Algebra*. Reading, MA: Addison-Wesley.

HALL, R. (1978), "Stochastic Implications of the Life Cycle-Permanent Income Hypothesis: Theory and Evidence", *Journal of Political Economy,* 86:971–987.

HALL, R. E., and F. MISHKIN (1982), "The Sensitivity of Consumption to Transitory Income: Estimates from Panel Data on Households", *Econometrica,* 50:461–481.

HALTER, A. N., H. O. CARTER, and J. G. HOCKING (1957), "A Note on Transcendental Production Functions", *Journal of Farm Economics,* 39:966–974.

HALVORSEN, R. H. (1976), "Energy Substitution in the U.S. Manufacturing", University of Washington and National Bureau of Economic Research.

HALVORSEN, R. H., and J. FORD (1978), Substitution Among Energy, Capital and Labor Inputs in U.S. Manufacturing", in R. S. PINDYCK (ed.), *Advances in the Economics of Energy and Resources, Vol. 1*. Greenwich, CT: JAI Press.

HANNAN, E. J. (1967), "Canonical Correlation and Multiple Equation System in Economics", *Econometrica,* 35:123–138.

HART, B.I. (1942), "Significance Levels for the Ratio of the Mean Square Successive Difference to the Variance", *Annals of Mathematical Statistics,* 13:445–447.

HARTLEY, H. O. (1964), "Exact Confidence Regions for the Parameters in Non-Linear Regression Laws", *Biometrika,* 51:347–364.

HARVEY, A. C. (1981), *The Econometric Analysis of Time Series*. New York: Wiley.

HARVEY, A. C., and I. D. MCAVINCHEY (1979), "On the Relative Efficiency of Various Estimators of Regression Models With MA Disturbances", in E. G. CHARATSIS (ed.), *Proceedings of the Econometric Society European Meeting, Athens*. Amsterdam: North Holland.

HARVEY, A. C., and G. D. A. PHILLIPS (1973), "A Comparison of the Power of Some Tests for Heteroscedasticity in the General Linear Model", *Journal of Econometrics,* 2:312–316.

HARVEY, A. C., and G. D. A. PHILLIPS (1981), "Testing for Heteroscedasticity in Simultaneous Equation Models", *Journal of Econometrics,* 11:311–340.

HATANAKA, M. (1976), "Several Efficient Two Step Estimators for the Dynamic Simultaneous Equations Models with Autoregressive Disturbances", *Journal of Econometrics,* 4:189–204.

HAUGH, L. D., and G. E. P. BOX (1977), "Identification of Dynamic Regression (Distributed Lag) Models Connecting Two Time Series", *Journal of the American Statistical Association,* 72:121–130.

HAUSMAN J. (1978a), "A Conditional Probit Model for Qualitative Choice: Discrete Decisions Recognizing Interdependence and Heterogenous Preferences", *Econometrica,* 46:403–426.

HAUSMAN, J. (1978b), "Specification Tests in Econometrics", *Econometrica,* 46:1251–1271.

HAUSMAN, J. (1979), "Individual Discount Rates and the Purchase and Utilization of Energy-Using Durables", *Bell Journal of Economics,* 1:33–54.

HAUSMAN, J. (1980), "The Effect of Wages, Tax and Fixed Costs on Women's Labor Force Participation", *Journal of Public Economics,* 14:161–164.

HAUSMAN, J., and D. McFADDEN (1984), "Specification Tests for the Multinomial Logit Model", *Econometrica,* 52:1219–1240.

HAUSMAN, J., and D. WISE (1978), "A Conditional Probit Model for Quantitative Choice: Discrete Decisions Recognizing Interdependence and Heterogenous Preferences", *Econometrica,* 46:403–426.

HAYASHI, F. (1982), "The Permanent Income Hypothesis: Estimation and Testing by Instrumental Variables", *Journal of Political Economy,* 90:895–918.

HAYASHI, F. (1985a), "Permanent Income Hypothesis and Consumption Durability: Analysis Based on Japanese Panel Data", *Quarterly Journal of Economics,* 90:895–916.

HAYASHI, F. (1985b), *Tests for Liquidity Constraints: A Critical Survey.* National Bureau of Economic Research, Working Paper No. 1720.

HECKMAN, J. J. (1976), "The Common Structure of Statistical Models of Truncation, Sample Selection and Limited Dependent Variables and a Simple Estimator for Such Models", *Annals of Economic and Social Measurement,* 5:475–492.

HECKMAN, J. J. (1979), "Sample Selection Bias as a Specification Error", *Econometrica,* 47:153–161.

HELLIWELL, J. (1972), *The TRACE Econometric Model of the Canadian Economy* by N. K. CHOUDRY et al. Book Review, *Canadian Journal of Economics,* 5:461–463.

HELLIWELL, J. F., H. T. SHAPIRO, G. R. SPARKS, I. A. STEWART, F. W. GORBET, and D. R. STEPHENSON (1971), *The Structure of RDX2, Part 1.* Ottawa: Bank of Canada.

HENDRY, D. F. (1971), "Maximum Likelihood Estimation of Systems of Simultaneous Regression Equations with Errors Generated by a Vector Autoregressive Process", *International Economic Review,* 22:257–272.

HENDRY, D. F. (1979), "The Behavior of Inconsistent Instrumental Variables Estimators in Dynamic Systems with Autocorrelated Errors", *Journal of Econometrics,* 9:295–314.

HENDRY, D. F., and G. MIZON (1978), "Serial Correlation as a Convenient Simplification, Not a Nuisance", *Economic Journal,* 88:549–563.

HENDRY, D. F., and A. R. TREMAYNE (1976), "Estimating Systems of Dynamic Reduced Form Equations with Vector Autoregressive Errors", *International Economic Review,* 17:463–471.

HICKMAN, B. G. (1965), *Investment Demand and U.S. Economic Growth.* Washington, D.C.: The Brookings Institution.

HILDEBRAND, G. H., and T. C. LIU (1965), *Manufacturing Production Functions in the U.S., 1957.* Ithaca: New York State School of Industrial Relations.

HILDRETH, C., and J. P. HOUCK (1968), "Some Estimates for a Linear Model with Random Coefficients", *Journal of the American Statistical Association,* 63:584–595.

HILDRETH, C., and J. Y. LU (1960), "Demand Relations with Autocorrelated Disturbances", *Technical Bulletin 276,* Michigan State University.

HILL, M. A. (1983), "Female Labor Force Participation in Developing and Developed Countries—Considerations of the Informal Sector", *Review of Economics and Statistics,* 55:459–468.

HINES, A. G., and G. CATEPHORES (1970), "Investment in U.K. Manufacturing Industry", in K. HILTON and D. HEATHFIELD (eds.), *The Econometric Study of the U.K.* London: Macmillan.

HIRSCH, A. A. (1973), "The BEA Quarterly Model as a Forecasting Instrument", *Survey of Current Business,* 43:24–38.

HOCH, I. (1962), "Estimation of Production Function Parameters Combining Time-Series and Cross-Section Data", *Econometrica,* 30:34–53.

HOCKING, R. R. (1976), "The Analysis and Selection of Variables in Multiple Regression", *Biometrics,* 32:1–49.

HODGSON, J. S., and A. B. HOLMES (1977), "Structural Stability of International Capital Mobility: U.S.–Canadian Bank Claims", *Review of Economics and Statistics,* 49:465–473.

HOEL, P. G. (1962), *Introduction to Linear Statistical Models, third ed.* New York: Wiley.

HOERL, A. E., and R. W. KENNARD (1970a), "Ridge Regression: Biased Estimation for Non-Orthogonal Problems", *Technometrics,* 12:55–68.

HOERL, A. E., and R. W. KENNARD (1970b), "Ridge Regression: Applications to Non-Orthogonal Problems", *Technometrics,* 12:69–82.

HORST, T. (1972), "Firm and Industry Determinants to Invest Abroad: An Empirical Study", *Review of Economics and Statistics,* 44:258–266.

HUDSON, E. A., and D. W. JORGENSON (1974), "U.S. Energy Policy and Economic Growth", *Bell Journal of Economics,* 5:471–514.

JEONG, KI-JUN (1985), "A New Approximation of the Critical Point of the Durbin–Watson Test for Serial Correlation", *Econometrica,* 53:477–482.

JOHNSON, N. L., and S. KOTZ (1972), *Distributions in Statistics: Continuous Multivariate Distributions.* New York: Wiley.

JORESKOG, K. G., and A. S. GOLDBERGER (1975), "Estimation of a Model with Multiple Indicators and Multiple Causes of a Single Latent Variable", *Journal of the American Statistical Association,* 70:631–639.

JORESKOG, K. G., and D. SORBOM (1981), *LISREL V User's Guide.* Chicago: National Educational Resources.

JORGENSON, D. W. (1963), "Capital Theory and Investment Behavior", *American Economic Review, Papers and Proceedings,* 53:247–253.

JORGENSON, D. W. (1965), "Anticipations and Investment Behavior" in J. S. DUESENBERRY, G. FROMM, L. R. KLEIN and E. KUH (eds.), *The Brookings Quarterly Econometric Model of the United States.* Chicago: Rand McNally.

JORGENSON, D. W. (1967), "The Theory of Investment Behavior", in R. FARBER (ed.), *Determinants of Investment Behavior.* New York: National Bureau of Economic Research.

JORGENSON, D. W. (1971), "Econometric Studies of Investment Behavior: A Survey", *Journal of Economic Literature,* 9:1111–1147.

JORGENSON, D. W. (ed.) (1976), *Econometric Studies of the U.S. Energy Policy.* Amsterdam: North Holland.

JORGENSON, D. W., and J. LAFFONT (1974), "Efficient Estimation of Nonlinear Simultaneous Equations with Additive Disturbances", *Annals of Economic and Social Measurement,* 3:615–640.

JORGENSON, D. W., and C. B. SIEBERT (1968), "Comparison of Alternative Theories of Corporate Investment Behavior", *American Economic Review,* 58:681–712.

JORGENSON, D. W., and J. A. STEPHENSON (1967), "Investment Behavior in U.S. Manufacturing, 1947–60", *Econometrica,* 35:169–220.

JORGENSON, D. W., and J. A. STEPHENSON (1969), "Issues in the Development of the Neoclassical Theory of Investment Behavior", *Review of Economics and Statistics,* 51:346–353.

JORGENSON, D. W., J. HUNTER, and M. I. NADIRI (1970a), "A Comparison of Alternative Econometric Models of Quarterly Investment Behavior", *Econometrica,* 38:187–212.

JORGENSON, D. W., J. HUNTER, and M. I. NADIRI (1970b), "The Predictive Performance of Econometric Models of Quarterly Investment Behavior", *Econometrica,* 38:213–224.

KADANE, J. B. (1971), "Comparison of K-Class Estimators Where the Disturbances are Small", *Econometrica,* 39:723–737.

KADIYALA, K. R. (1968), "A Transformation Used to Circumvent the Problem of Autocorrelation", *Econometrica,* 36:93–96.

KALDOR, N. (1955–1956), "Model of Distribution", Chapter 3, in A. K. SEN (ed.) (1971), *Growth Economics Selected Readings.* Baltimore, MD: Penguin.

KELEJIAN, H. (1971), "Two Stage Least Squares and Econometric Models Linear in Parameters But Nonlinear in Endogenous Variables", *Journal of the American Statistical Association,* 65:373–374.

KENDALL, M. G., and A. STUART (1958), *The Advanced Theory of Statistics, Volume 1.* London: Charles Griffin.

KENDALL, M. G., and A. STUART (1961), *The Advanced Theory of Statistics, Volume 2.* London: Charles Griffin.

KINAL, T., and K. LAHIRI (1983), "Specification Error Analysis With Stochastic Regressors", *Econometrica,* 51:1209–1219.

KINAL, T., and K. LAHIRI (1984), "A Note on Selection of Regressors", *International Economic Review,* 25:625–629.

KING, M. A. (1986), "Capital Market "Imperfections" and the Consumption Function", *Scandinavian Journal of Economics, Conference Proceedings,* 88:59–84.

KING, M. L. (1981a), "The Alternative D–W Test: An Assessment of Durbin and Watson's Choice of Test Statistic", *Journal of Econometrics,* 9:51–66.

KING, M. L. (1981b), "D–W Test for Serial Correlation: Bounds for Regression with Trend and/or Seasonal Dummy Variables", *Econometrica,* 49:1571–1581.

KING, M. L., and D. E. A. GILES (1978), "A Note on Wallis' Test and Negative Correlation", *Econometrica,* 45:1023–1026.

KENKEL, J. L. (1974), "Some Small Sample Properties of Durbin's Test for Serial Correlation in Regression Models Containing Lagged Dependent Variables", *Econometrica,* 42:763–769.

KLEIN, L. R. (1950), *Economic Fluctuations in the United States, 1921–1941.* New York: Wiley.

KLEIN, L. R. (1969a), "Estimation of Interdependent Systems in Macroeconomics", *Econometrica,* 37:171–192.

KLEIN, L. (1969b), "An Econometric Analysis of the Tax Cut of 1964", in J. S. DUESENBERRY, G. FROMM, L. R. KLEIN, and E. KUH (eds.), *The Brookings Model: Some Further Results.* Chicago: Rand McNally.

KLEIN, L. (1971), "Forecasting and Policy Evaluation Using Large Scale Econometric Models: The State of the Art", in M. D. INTRILIGATOR (ed.), *Frontiers of Quantitative Economics*. Amsterdam: North Holland.

KLEIN, L., and A. S. GOLDBERGER (1955), *An Econometric Model of the United States, 1929–1952*. Amsterdam: North Holland.

KLOEK, T., and L. B. M. MENNES (1960), "Simultaneous Equation Estimation Based on Principal Components of Predetermined Variables", *Econometrica,* 28:45–61.

KMENTA, J., and R. F. GILBERT (1968), "Small Sample Properties of Alternative Estimators of Seemingly Unrelated Regressions", *Journal of the American Statistical Association,* 63:1180–1200.

KOOPMANS, T. C., and W. C. HOOD (eds.) (1953), *Studies in Econometric Methods*. Cowles Commission Monograph 14, New York: Wiley.

KOOPMANS, T. C., H. RUBIN, and R. B. LEIPNIK (1950), "Measuring the Equation Systems of Dynamic Economics", in T. C. KOOPMANS (ed.), *Statistical Inference in Dynamic Economic Models*. New York: Wiley.

KORMENDI, R. C., and P. G. MEGUIRE (1984), "The Real Output Effects of Monetary Shocks, Cross-country Tests of Rational Expectations Propositions", *Journal of Political Economy,* 92:875–908.

KOYCK, L. M. (1954), *Distributed Lags and Investment Analysis*. Amsterdam: North Holland.

KUZNETS, S. (1942), "Uses of National Income in Peace and War", Occasional Paper No. 6, National Bureau of Economic Research.

LAMOTTE, L. R., and A. MCWHORTER (1976), "A Test for the Presence of Random Coefficients in a Linear Regression Model", *Proceedings of the 1976 Annual Meeting,* Business and Economic Statistics Section, American Statistical Association:400–405.

LANCASTER, T. (1968), "Grouping Estimators on Heteroscedastic Data", *Journal of the American Statistical Association,* 63:191.

LATANE, H. H. (1954), "Cash Balances and the Interest Rate: A Pragmatic Approach", *Review of Economics and Statistics,* 42:445–449.

LAUMAS, G. S., and D. E. SPENCER (1980), "The Stability of the Demand for Money: Evidences from the Post-1973 Period", *Review of Economics and Statistics,* 52:456–459.

LEAMER, E. E. (1978), *Specification Searches—An Ad Hoc Inference with Non Experimental Data*. New York: Wiley.

LEAMER, E. E. (1981), "Is it a Demand Curve or is it a Supply Curve? Partial Identification Through Inequality Constraints", *Review of Economics and Statistics,* 53:319–327.

LEAMER, E. E. (1983), "Model Choice and Specification Analysis" in Z. GRILICHES and M. D. INTRILIGATOR (eds.), *Handbook of Econometrics, Vol. 1*. Amsterdam: North Holland.

LEE, Y., and L. B. FLETCHER (1968), "A Generalization of the CES Production Function", *Review of Economics and Statistics,* 40:449–452.

LEIDERMAN, L. (1980), "Macroeconomic Testing of the Rational Expectations and Structural Neutrality Hypothesis for the United States", *Journal of Monetary Economics,* 6:103–124.

LEONTIEF, W. W. (1951), *The Structure of the American Economy, 1919–1939, second ed.* New York: Oxford University Press.

LEVINE, P. B., and O. S. MITCHELL (1988), "The Baby Boom's Legacy, Relative Wages in the Twenty First Century", *American Economic Review, Papers and Proceedings of the One Hundredth Annual Meeting of the American Economic Association, December 28-30, 1987*:66–69.

LILIEN, D. M. (1982), "Sectoral shifts and Cyclical Unemployment", *Journal of Political Economy,* 90:777–793.

LIU, T. C. (1963), "An Exploratory Quarterly Econometric Model of Effective Demand in the Post-war U.S. Economy", *Econometrica,* 31:301–348.

LIU, T. C. (1969), "A Monthly Recursive Econometric Model of the United States, A Test of Feasibility", *Review of Economics and Statistics,* 41:1–13.

LIU, T. C., and E. C. HWA (1974), "Structure and Applications of a Monthly Econometric Model of the U.S. Economy", *International Economic Review,* 15:328–365.

LIVIATAN, N. (1963), "Consistent Estimation of Distributed Lags", *International Economic Review,* 4:44–52.

LOVELL, C. A. K. (1973), "Estimation and Prediction With CES and VES Production Functions", *International Economic Review,* 14:676–692.

LUCAS, R. E. JR. (1973), "Some International Evidence on Output–Inflation Trade-Offs", *American Economic Review,* 63:326–334.

LUCAS, R. E. JR. (1976), "Econometric Policy Evaluation: A Critique" in K. BRUNNER and A. H. MELTZER (eds.), *The Phillips Curve and Labor Market Vol. 1,* Carnegie-Rochester Conference on Public Policy. Amsterdam: North Holland.

MCALEER, M. (1985), "Specification Tests for Separate Models: A Survey", in M. L. KING and D. E. A. GILES (eds.), *Specification Analysis in the Linear Model.* London: Routledge and Kegan Paul.

MCALEER, M., G. FISHER, and P. VOLKER (1982), "Separate Misspecified Regressions and the U.S. Long Run Demand for Money Function", *Review of Economics and Statistics,* 64:572–583.

MACAVOY, P. W., and R. S. PINDYCK (1975), *The Economics of the Natural Gas Shortage (1960–1980).* Amsterdam: North Holland.

MCCALLUM, B. T. (1972), "Relative Asymptotic Bias from Errors of Omission and Measurement", *Econometrica,* 40:757–758.

MCCALLUM, B. T. (1977), "The Role of Speculation in Canadian Forward Exchange Market: Some Estimates Assuming Rational Expectation", *Review of Economics and Statistics,* 49:145–151.

MCCARTHY, M. D. (1972), *The Wharton Quarterly Econometric Forecasting Model, Mark III.* Philadelphia: University of Pennsylvania.

MCCURDY, T. E. (1986), "Modeling the Time Series Implications of Life Cycle Theory", Mimeo, Stanford University.

MCFADDEN, D. (1987), "Regression Based Specification Tests for the Multinomial Logit Model", *Journal of Econometrics,* 34:63–82.

MCELROY, M. B. (1985), "The Joint Determination of Household Membership and Market Work: The Case of Young Men", *The Journal of Labor Economics,* 3:293–316.

McElroy, M. B. (1987), "Additive General Error Models for Production, Cost and Derived Demand or Share Systems", *Journal of Political Economy*, 95:737–757.

McNown, R. F., and K. R. Hunter (1980), "A Test for Autocorrelation in Models with Lagged Dependent Variables", *Review of Economics and Statistics*, 52:313–317.

Maddala, G. S. (1971), "The Use of Variance Components Models in Pooling Cross-Section and Time Series Data", *Econometrica*, 39:341–358.

Maddala, G. S. (1974), "Some Small Sample Evidence on Tests of Significance in Simultaneous Equation Models", *Econometrica*, 42:841–852.

Maddala, G. S. (1977), *Econometrics*. New York: McGraw-Hill.

Maddala, G. S. (1983), *Limited Dependent and Qualitative Variables in Econometrics*. Cambridge, England: Cambridge University Press.

Maddala, G. S., and F. D. Nelson (1974), "Maximum Likelihood Methods for Models of Markets in Disequilibrium", *Econometrica*, 42:1013–1030.

Maddala, G. S., and A. S. Rao (1973), "Tests for Serial Correlation in Regression Models with Lagged Dependent Variables and Serially Correlated Errors", *Econometrica*, 41:761–774.

Maddala, G. S., and R. P. Trost (1982), "On Measuring Discrimination in Loan Markets", *Housing Finance Review*, 1:245–268.

Magnus, J. R. (1979), "Substitution Between Energy and Non-Energy Inputs in the Netherlands, 1956–1976", *International Economic Review*, 20:465–484.

Makin, J. H. (1982a), "Anticipated Money, Inflation Uncertainty, and Real Economic Activity", *Review of Economics and Statistics*, 54:126–134.

Makin, J. H. (1982b), "Real Interest, Money Surprises, Anticipated Inflation and Fiscal Deficits", *Review of Economics and Statistics*, 54:374–384.

Malinvaud, E. (1970), *Statistical Methods of Econometrics*. Amsterdam: North Holland.

Mallows, C. L. (1973), "Some Comments on C_p", *Technometrics*, 15:661–676.

Mann, H. B., and A. Wald (1943), "On the Statistical Treatment of Linear Stochastic Difference Equations", *Econometrica*, 11:173–220.

Manski, C. (1975), "Maximum Score Estimation of the Stochastic Utility Model of Choice", *Journal of Econometrics*, 3:205–228.

Manski, C. (1986), "Operational Characteristics of Maximum Score Estimation", *Journal of Econometrics*, 32:85–100.

Mariger, R. P. (1987a), *Consumer Behavior and the Effects of Government Fiscal Policies*. Cambridge, MA: Harvard University Press.

Mariger, R. P. (1987b), "A Life Cycle Consumption Model With Liquidity Constraints: Theory and Empirical Results", *Econometrica*, 55:533–558.

Marquardt, D. W. (1962), "On the Portrayal of Confidence Regions for Simultaneous Nonlinear Parameters", Monograph.

Marquardt, D. W. (1963), "An Algorithm for Least Squares Estimation of Nonlinear Parameters", *SIAM, Applied Mathematics*, 11:431–441.

Marriott, F. H. C., and J. A. Pope (1954), "Bias in the Estimation of Autocorrelations", *Biometrika*, 41:390–402.

Masson, R. T., and L. M. Debrock (1980), "Structural Effects of State Regulation of Retail Fluid Milk Prices", *Review of Economics and Statistics*, 52:254–262.

MAYES, D. G. (1981), *Application of Econometrics*. London: Prentice-Hall.

MEHTA, J. S., and P. A. V. B. SWAMY (1978), "The Existence of Moments of Some Simple Bayes Estimators of Coefficients in a Simultaneous Equation Model", *Journal of Econometrics,* 7:1–13.

MIKHAIL, W. M. (1975), "A Comparative Monte Carlo Study of the Properties of Econometric Estimators," *Journal of the American Statistical Association,* 70:94–104.

MILES, M. (1978), "Currency Substitution, Flexible Exchange Rates and Monetary Independence", *American Economic Review,* 68:428–436.

MINCER, J. (1974), *School, Experience and Earnings*. New York: Columbia University Press.

MISHKIN, F. (1982a), "Does Anticipated Monetary Policy Matter? An Economic Investigation", *Journal of Political Economy,* 90:22–50.

MISHKIN, F. (1982b), "Does Anticipated Aggregate Demand Policy Matter?", *American Economic Review,* 72:788–802.

MIZON, G. E., and J. F. RICHARD (1986), "The Encompassing Principle and Its Application to Testing Nonnested Hypotheses", *Econometrica,* 54:657–678.

MODIGLIANI, F., and R. E. BRUMBERG (1954), "Utility Analysis and the Consumption Function", in K. KURIHARA (ed.), *Post-Keynesian Economics*. New Jersey: Rutgers University Press.

MOOD, A. M., and F. A. GRAYBILL (1965), *Introduction to the Theory of Statistics*. New York: McGraw-Hill.

MORISHIMA, M., and M. SAITO (1977), "A Dynamic Analysis of the American Economy, 1902–1982", in MORISHIMA et al., *The Working of the Econometric Models*. New York: Cambridge University Press.

MUELBAUER, J., and O. BOVER (1986), "Liquidity Constraints and Aggregation in the Consumption Function Under Uncertainty", Discussion Paper No. 7: Oxford Institute of Economics and Statistics.

MUNDELL, R. A. (1968), *International Economics*. New York: MacMillan.

MUNDLAK, Y. (1963), "Estimation of Production and Behavioral Functions From a Combination of Cross-Section and Time-Series Data", in C. F. CHRIST (ed.), *Measurement in Economics*. Stanford: Stanford University Press.

MUNDLAK, Y. (1978), "On the Pooling of Time Series and Cross-Section Data", *Econometrica,* 46:69–86.

NAGAR, A. L. (1959), "The Bias and Moment Matrix of the General K-Class Estimators of the Parameters in Simultaneous Equations", *Econometrica,* 27:575–595.

NAGAR, A. L. (1962), "Double K-Class Estimators of Parameters in Simultaneous Equations and their Small Sample Properties", *International Economic Review,* 3:168–188.

NERLOVE, M. (1963), "Returns to Scale in Electricity Supply", in C. F. CHRIST, *Measurement in Econometrics*. Stanford: Stanford University Press.

NERLOVE, M., and K. F. WALLIS (1966), "Use of the D–W Statistics in Inappropriate Situations", *Econometrica,* 34:235–238.

NICHOLS, D. A. (1983), "Macro-Economic Determinants of Wage Determinants in White Collar Occupations", *Review of Economics and Statistics,* 55:203–213.

OHTANI, K. (1982), "Bayesian Estimation of the Switching Regression Model with Autocorrelated Errors", *Journal of Econometrics,* 18:251–261.

OHTANI, K. (1985), "A Note on the Use of a Proxy Variable In Testing Hypotheses", *Economics Letters,* 17:107–110.

PAGAN, A. (1982), "Econometric Issues in the Analysis of Regressions with Generated Regressions", *International Economic Review,* 21:221–247.

PAGAN, A. (1984), "Econometric Issues in the Analysis with Generated Regressors", *International Economic Review,* 25:221–247.

PARK, R. E., and B. M. MITCHELL (1980), "Estimating the Autocorrelated Error Model With Trended Data", *Journal of Econometrics,* 13:185–201.

PARK, S. B. (1982), "Some Sampling Properties of Minimum Expected Loss (MELO) Estimators of Structural Coefficients", *Journal of Econometrics,* 18:295–311.

PARKE, W. R. (1982), "An Algorithm for FIML and 3SLS Estimation of Large Nonlinear Models", *Econometrica,* 50:81–96.

PEARCE, D. K. (1979), "Comparing Survey and Rational Measures of Expected Inflation", *Journal of Money, Credit and Banking,* 11:447–456.

PESANDO, J. E. (1975), "A Note on the Rationality of the Livingston Price Expectations", *Journal of Political Economy,* 83:849–858.

PESARAN, M. H. (1974), "The General Problem of Model Selection", *Review of Economic Studies,* 41:153–171.

PESARAN, M. H. (1982), "A Critique of the Proposed Tests of the Natural Rate—Rational Expectations Hypothesis", *Economic Journal,* 92:529–554.

PESARAN, M. H., and A. S. DEATON (1978), "Testing Nonnested Nonlinear Regression Models", *Econometrica,* 46:677–694.

PHILLIPS, P. C. B. (1972), "The Estimation of Parameters in Systems of Stochastic Differential Equations", *Biometrika,* 46:67–76.

PHILLIPS, P. C. B. (1974), "The Estimation of Some Continuous Time Models", *Econometrica,* 42:803–833.

PHILLIPS, P. C. B. (1986), "Understanding Spurious Regressions in Econometrics", *Journal of Econometrics,* 33:311–340.

PIERCE, D. A. (1971), "Distribution of Residual Autocorrelation in the Regression Model with Autoregression—Moving Average Errors", *Journal of the Royal Statistical Society,* 33:140–146.

PIERCE, D. A. (1977), "Relationships—and the Lack Thereof—Between Economic Time Series, With Special Reference to Money and Interest Rates", *Journal of the American Statistical Association,* 72:11–22.

PINDYCK, R. S. (1979), "Interfuel Substitution and the Industrial Demand for Energy: An International Comparison", *Review of Economics and Statistics,* 51:169–179.

PLOSSER, C. I., G. W. SCHWERT, and H. WHITE (1982), "Differencing As a Test of Specification", *International Economic Review,* 23:535–552.

POIRIER, D. J. (1974), *The Econometrics of Structural Change.* Amsterdam: North Holland.

POIRIER, D. J., and S. G. GARBER (1974), "The Determinants of Aerospace Profit Rates 1951–71", *Southern Economic Journal,* 41:228–238.

POLACHEK, S. W. (1981), "Occupational Self Selection: A Human Capital Approach to

Sex Differences in Occupational Structure'', *Review of Economics and Statistics,* 53:60–69.

Pollak, R. A., R. C. Sickles, and T. J. Wales (1984), ''The CES–Translog Specification and Estimation of a New Cost Function'', *Review of Economics and Statistics,* 56:602–608.

Powell, M. J. D. (1964), ''An Efficient Method for Finding the Minimum of a Function of Several Variables Without Calculating Derivatives'', *Computer Journal,* 7:155–162.

Prais, S. J., and C. B. Winston (1954), ''Trend Estimators and Serial Correlation'', Cowles Commission Discussion Paper No. 383, Chicago.

Press, S. J., and R. B. Brooks (1969), ''Testing for Serial Correlation in Regression'', Report No. 6911, Centre for Mathematical Studies in Business and Economics, University of Chicago.

Preston, R. S. (1972), *The Wharton Annual and Industry Forecasting Model.* Philadelphia: University of Pennsylvania.

Preston, R. S. (1975), ''The Wharton Long Term Model: Input–Output Within the Context of a Macro Forecasting Model'', *International Economic Review,* 16:3–19.

Prucha, I. R., and H. Kelejian (1984), ''Structure of Simultaneous Equation Estimates: A Generalization Towards Non-Normal Disturbances'', *Econometrica,* 52:721–736.

Quandt, R. E. (1958), ''The Estimation of the Parameters of a Linear Regression System Obeying Two Separate Regimes'', *Journal of the American Statistical Association,* 53:873–880.

Quandt, R. E. (1982), ''Econometric Disequilibrium Models'', *Econometric Reviews,* 1:1–63.

Raj, B., and A. Ullah (1981), *Econometrics A Varying Coefficients Approach.* London: Croom Helm.

Rao, C. R. (1948), ''Large Sample Tests of Statistical Hypotheses Concerning Several Parameters with Applications to Problems of Estimation'', *Proceedings of the Cambridge Philosophical Society,* 44:50–57.

Rappoport, P. N., and N. J. Kniesner (1974), ''The Illusion of the Shifting Phillips Curve: A Model with Random Coefficients'', *Proceedings of the 1974 Annual Meeting,* Business and Economics Statistics Section, American Statistical Association: 535–539.

Rasche, R. H., and H. Shapiro (1968), ''The FRB–MIT Econometric Model: Its Special Features and Implications for Stabilization Policies'', *American Economic Review, Papers and Proceedings,* 58:123–149.

Rausser, G. C., and P. S. Laumas (1976), ''The Stability of Demand for Money in Canada'', *Journal of Monetary Economics,* 3:367–380.

Ravencraft, D. J. (1983), ''Structure–Profit Relationship at the Line of Business and Industry'', *Review of Economics and Statistics,* 55:22–31.

Reinhardt, U. (1972), ''A Production Function for Physician Services'', *Review of Economics and Statistics,* 42:55–66.

Revankar, N. S. (1971), ''A Class of Variable Elasticity of Substitution Production Functions'', *Econometrica,* 39:61–71.

Rhomberg, R. (1964), ''A Model of the Canadian Economy Under Fixed and Flexible Exchange Rates'', *Journal of Political Economy,* 64:1–31.

Richardson, D. H. (1968), "The Exact Distribution of a Structural Coefficient Estimator", *Journal of the American Statistical Association,* 63:1214–1226.

Riddell, W. C. (1980), "Estimating Switching Regressions: A Computational Note", *Journal of Computation and Simulation,* 10:95–101.

Riddell, W. C., and A. Buse (1980), "An Alternative Approach to Specification Errors", *Australian Economic Papers,* 19:211–214.

Riddell, W. C., and P. M. Smith (1982), "Expected Inflation and Wage Changes in Canada, 1967–81", *Canadian Journal of Economics,* 15:377–394.

Ringstad, V. (1967), "Econometric Analysis Based on a Production Function with Neutrally Variable Scale Elasticity", *Swedish Journal of Economics,* 69:115–133.

Robins, P. K., and R. W. West (1977), "Measurement Errors In the Estimation of Home Values", *Journal of the American Statistical Association,* 72:290–294.

Robinson, P. M. (1976a), "The Estimation of Linear Differential Equations with Constant Coefficients", *Econometrica,* 44:751–764.

Robinson, P. M. (1976b), "Instrumental Variables Estimation of Differential Equations", *Econometrica,* 44:756–776.

Rosen, S. (1974), "Hedonic Prices and Implicit Markets: Product Differentiation in Price Competition", *Journal of Political Economy,* 82:34–55.

Rosen, S. (1986), "Prizes and Incentives in Elimination Tournaments", *American Economic Review,* 76:701–715.

Rothenberg, T. J. (1980), "Comparing Alternative Asymptotically Equivalent Tests", Invited Paper Presented at the World Congress of the Econometric Society, Aix-en-Provence.

Rowley, J. C. R., and D. A. Wilton (1973), "Quarterly Models of Wage Determination: Some New Efficient Estimates", *American Economic Review,* 63:380–389.

Rowley, J. C. R., and D. A. Wilton (1974), "Empirical Foundations for Canadian Phillips Curve", *Canadian Journal of Economics,* 7:240–259.

Roy, E. J. (1981), "Tariff and Non-Tariff Barriers to Trade in the U.S. and Abroad", *Review of Economics and Statistics,* 53:161–168.

Rubinfeld, D. L. (1977), "Voting in a Local School Election—A Micro Analysis", *Review of Economics and Statistics,* 49:30–42.

Sadan, E., and Z. Tropp (1973), "Consumption Function Analysis in a Commercial Household: Cross Section and Time Series", *Review of Economics and Statistics,* 45:475–481.

Sargan, J. D. (1961), "The Maximum Likelihood Estimation of Economic Relationships with Autoregressive Residuals", *Econometrica,* 24:414–426.

Sargan, J. D. (1964), "Wages and Prices in the United Kingdom: A Study in Econometric Methodology", in P. E. Hart et al., *Econometric Analysis for Natural Economic Planning*. London: Butterworth.

Sargan, J. D. (1974), "Some Discrete Approximations to Continuous Time Stochastic Models", *Journal of the Royal Statistical Society,* Series B, 36:74–90.

Sargan, J. D., and F. Mehta (1983), "A Generalization of the Durbin Significance Test and Its Application to Dynamic Specification," *Econometrica,* 51:1551–1567.

Sargan, J. D., and W. M. Mikhail (1971), "A General Approximation to the Distribution of Instrumental Variable Estimates", *Econometrica,* 39:131–169.

SARGENT, T. (1978), "Rational Expectations, Econometric Exogeneity and Consumption", *Journal of Political Economy,* 86:673–700.

SATO, K., and R. F. HOFFMAN (1968), "Production Functions With Variable Elasticity of Factor Substitution: Some Analysis and Testing", *Review of Economics and Statistics,* 50:453–460.

SAUNDERS, R. S. (1982), "The Determinants of Interindustry Variation of Foreign Ownership in Canadian Manufacturing", *Canadian Journal of Economics,* 15:77–84.

SAVIN, N. E. (1976), "Conflicts Among Testing Procedures in a Linear Regression Model with Autoregressive Disturbances", *Econometrica,* 44:1303–1313.

SAVIN, N. E., and K. J. WHITE (1977), "The Durbin–Watson Test for Serial Correlation with Extreme Sample Sizes or Many Regressors", *Econometrica,* 45:1989–1996.

SCHEFFE, H. (1959), *The Analysis of Variance.* New York: Wiley.

SCHINK, G. R. (1975), "The Brookings Quarterly Model: As an Aid to Longer Term Economic Policy", *International Economic Review,* 16:39–53.

SCHMIDT, P. (1976), *Econometrics.* New York: Marcel Dekker.

SCHMIDT, P., and R. N. WAUD (1973), "Almon Lag Technique and the Monetary and Fiscal Policy Debate", *Journal of the American Statistical Association,* 68:11–19.

SCHULTZ, H. (1938), *The Theory and Measurement of Demand.* Chicago: University of Chicago Press.

SEWELL, W. P. (1969), "Least Squares, Conditional Predictions and Estimator Properties", *Econometrica,* 37:39–43.

SHERMAN, R., and R. TOLLISON (1971), "Advertising and Profitability", *Review of Economics and Statistics,* 53:397–407.

SIMS, C. (1972), "Money, Income, and Causality", *American Economic Review,* 62:540–552.

SIMS, C., J. H. STOCK, and M. W. WATSON (1986), "Inference in Linear Time Series Models with Some Unit Roots", manuscript, Stanford University.

SMITH, V. K. (1973), *Monte Carlo Methods.* Lexington: Lexington Books.

STOCK, J. H., and M. W. WATSON (1988), "Variable Trends in Economic Time Series", *Journal of Economic Perspectives,* 2:147–174.

STONE, R. (1954), *The Measurement of Consumer's Expenditure and Behavior in the United Kingdom, 1920–1938.* New York: Cambridge University Press.

SWAMY, P. A. V. B. (1970), "Efficient Inference in a Random Coefficient Regression Model", *Econometrica,* 38:311–323.

SWAMY, P. A. V. B. (1971), *Statistical Inference in Random Coefficient Regression Models.* New York: Springer-Verlag.

SWAMY, P. A. V. B. (1973), "Criteria, Constraints and Multicollinearity in Random Coefficient Regression Models", *Annals of Economic and Social Measurement,* 2:429–450.

SWAMY, P. A. V. B. (1974), "Linear Models with Random Coefficients", in P. ZAREMBKA (ed.), *Frontiers in Econometrics.* New York: Academic Press.

SWAMY, P. A. V. B., and P. N. RAPPOPORT (1975), "Relative Efficiencies of some Simple Bayes Estimators of Coefficients in a Dynamic Equation With Serially Correlated Error I", *Journal of Econometrics,* 3:273–296.

SWAMY, P. A. V. B., and P. N. RAPPOPORT (1978), "Relative Efficiencies and Some Simple Bayes Estimators of Coefficients in a Dynamic Equation with Serially Correlated Error II", *Journal of Econometrics,* 7:245–258.

THEIL, H. (1953), "Estimation and Simultaneous Correlation in Complete Equation Systems", The Hague Central Planbureau.

THEIL, H. (1961), *Economic Forecasts and Policy, second rev. ed.* Amsterdam: North Holland.

THEIL, H. (1966), *Applied Economic Forecasting.* Amsterdam: North Holland.

THEIL, H., and J. C. G. BOOT (1962), "The final form of Econometric Equation Systems", *Review of the International Statistical Institute,* 30:136–152.

THEIL, H., and A. L. NAGAR (1961), "Testing the Independence of Regression Disturbances", *Journal of the American Statistical Association,* 56:793–806.

TINTNER, G. (1952), *Econometrics.* New York: Wiley.

TOBIN, J. (1955), "The Application of Multivariate Probit Analysis to Economic Survey Data", Cowles Foundation Discussion Paper 1.

TOBIN, J. (1958), "Estimation of Relationships for Limited Dependent Variables", *Econometrica,* 50:24–36.

TORO-VIZCARRONDO, C. E., and T. D. WALLACE (1968), "A Test of the Mean Squared Error Criterion for Restrictions in Linear Regression", *Journal of the American Statistical Association,* 63:558–572.

TSURUMI, H. (1970), "Nonlinear 2SLS Estimations of CES Production Functions Applied to the Canadian Manufacturing Industries 1926–39, 46–67", *Review of Economics and Statistics,* 42:200–207.

TSURUMI, H., and T. SHIBA (1982), "A Bayesian Analysis of a Random Coefficient Model in a Simple Keynesian System", *Journal of Econometrics,* 18:239–249.

TURNOVSKY, S. J. (1980), "Some Empirical Evidence on the Formation of Price Expectations", *Journal of the American Statistical Association,* 65:39–63.

TYBOUT, J. R. (1983), "Credit Rationing and Investment Behavior in a Developing Country", *Review of Economics and Statistics,* 55:598–607.

UZAWA, H. (1962), "On a Two-Sector Model of Economic Growth", *Review of Economic Studies,* 29:40–47.

WALD, A. (1940), "The Fitting of Straight Lines if Both Variables are Subject to Error", *American Mathematical Statistics,* 11:284–300.

WALES, T. J., and A. D. WOODLAND (1977), "Estimation of the Allocation of Time for Work, Leisure and Housework", *Econometrica,* 45:111–132.

WALES, T. J., and A. D. WOODLAND (1980), "Sample Selectivity and the Estimation of Labor Supply Functions", *International Economic Review,* 21:437–468.

WALES, T. J., and A. D. WOODLAND (1983), "Estimation of Consumer Demand Systems with Binding Non-Negativity Constraints," *Journal of Econometrics,* 21:263–286.

WALLACE, T. D. (1972), "Weaker Criteria and Tests for Linear Restrictions in Regression," *Econometrica,* 40:689–698.

WALLACE, T. D., and A. HUSSAIN (1969), "The Use of Error Component Models in Combining Cross Section With Time-Series Data", *Econometrica,* 37:55–72.

WALLACE, T. D., and C. E. TORO-VIZCARRONDO (1969), "Tables for Mean Squared Error Test for Exact Linear Restrictions in Regression," *Journal of the American Statistical Association,* 64:1649–1663.

WALLIS, K. F. (1972), "Testing for Fourth Order Autocorrelation in Quarterly Regression Equations", *Econometrica,* 40:617–636.

WALSH, J. (ed.) (1966), *Numerical Analysis: An Introduction.* London: Academic Press.

WASSERFALLEN, W. (1986), "Nonstationarities in Macro-economic Time Series—Further Evidence and Implications", *Canadian Journal of Economics,* 19:498–510.

WEISS, L. (1974), "The Concentration-Profits Relationship and Anti Trust", in H. J. GOLDSCHMIDT, H. M. MANN, and J. F. WESTON (eds.), *Industrial Concentration: The New Learning.* Boston: Little, Brown & Co.

WHITE, H. (1980), "Heteroscedasticity-Consistent Covariance Matrix Estimator and Direct Test for Heteroscedasticity", *Econometrica,* 48:817–838.

WHITE, K. J. (1978), "A General Computer Program for Econometric Methods—SHAZAM", *Econometrica,* 46:239–240.

WHITE, J. S. (1961), "Asymptotic Expansions for the Mean and Variance of the Serial Correlation Coefficient," *Biometrika,* 48:85–94.

WICKENS, M. R. (1972), "A Note on the Use of Proxy Variables", *Econometrica,* 40:759–761.

WILKS, S. S. (1962), *Mathematical Statistics.* New York: Wiley.

WILTON, D. A. (1975), "Structural Shift with an Interstructural Transition Function", *Canadian Journal of Economics,* 8:423–432.

WINEGARDEN, C. (1984), "Women's Fertility, Market Work and Marital Status: A Test of New Household Economics with International Data", *Economica,* 51:447–456.

WOLD, H., and L. JUREEN (1953), *Demand Analysis.* New York: Wiley.

WYMER, C. R. (1972), "Econometric Estimation of Stochastic Differential Equation Systems", *Econometrica,* 40:565–577.

WYMER, C. R. (1973), "A Continuous Disequilibrium Model of United Kingdom Financial Markets", in A. A. POWELL and R. A. WILLIAMS (eds.), *Econometric Studies of Macro and Monetary Relations.* Amsterdam: North Holland.

ZELLNER, A. (1962), "An Efficient Method of Estimating Seemingly Unrelated Regressions and Tests for Aggregation Bias", *Journal of the American Statistical Association,* 57:348–368.

ZELLNER, A. (ed.) (1969), *Readings in Economic Statistics and Econometrics.* Boston: Little, Brown & Co.

ZELLNER, A. (1970), "Estimation of Regression Relationships Containing Unobservable Variables", *International Economic Review,* 11:441–454.

ZELLNER, A. (1971), *An Introduction to Bayesian Inference in Economics.* New York: Wiley.

ZELLNER, A. (1978), "Estimation of Functions of Population Means and Regression Coefficients Including Structural Coefficients A Minimum Expected Loss (MELO) Approach", *Journal of Econometrics,* 8:127–158.

ZELLNER, A. (1985), "Further Results on Bayesian Minimum Expected Loss (MELO)

Estimates and Posterior Distributions for Structural Coefficients'', in DANIEL SLOTTJE (ed.), *Innovations in Quantitative Economics: Essays in Honor of Robert L. Basmann.* Greenwich, CT: JAI Press.

ZELLNER, A. (1986), ''Bayesian Estimation and Prediction Using Asymmetric Loss Functions'', *Journal of the American Statistical Association,* 81:446–451.

ZELLNER, A. (1988), ''Bayesian Analysis in Econometrics'', *Journal of Econometrics,* 37:27–50.

ZELLNER, A., and M. S. GEISEL (1968), ''Analysis of Distributed Lag Models With Applications to Consumption Function Estimation'', Paper Presented to the European Meeting of Econometric Society.

ZELLNER, A., and C. HONG (1985), ''Bayesian Methods for Forecasting Turning Points in Economic Time Series: Sensitivity of Forecasts to Asymmetry of Loss Structures'', Mimeo, University of Chicago.

ZELLNER, A., C. HONG, and G. M. GULATI (1987), ''Turning Points in Economic Time Series, Loss Structures and Bayesian Forecasting'', Technical Report, H. G. B. Alexander Research Foundation, University of Chicago.

ZELLNER, A., and S. B. PARK (1979), ''Minimum Expected Loss (MELO) Estimators for Functions of Parameters and Structural Coefficients of Econometric Models'', *Journal of the American Statistical Association,* 74:185–193.

ZELLNER, A., and N. S. REVANKAR (1969), ''Generalized Production Functions'', *Review of Economics and Statistics,* 36:241–250.

ZELLNER, A., and P. ROSSI (1984), ''Bayesian Analysis of Dichotomous Quintal Response Models'', *Journal of Econometrics,* 25:365–393.

ZELLNER, A., and H. THEIL (1962), ''Three Stage Least Squares: Simultaneous Estimation of Simultaneous Equations'', *Econometrica,* 30:54–78.

Index

Accelerator models, 345
Adams, F. G., 466
Adaptive expectations, 273, 309, 502
Adelman, F. L., 464*n*
Adelman, I., 464*n*
Agarwala, R., 287
Aigner, D., 379*n*
Aitken's (generalized least squares) estimators, 229–30, 442
Akaike, H., 519*n*
Akaike's IC criterion, 517, 519, 541
Allen, R. G. D., 152, 335
Almon's lags, 280, 346–47, 364
Altonji, T. G., 321–22, 325
Amemiya, T., 243, 248, 325*n*, 394*n*, 518*n*, 519*n*
Amemiya's P_c criterion, 517, 519, 541
Analysis of Variance, 37–39, 140–42
Anderson, T. W., 129, 388, 440*n*, 452*n*
Ando, A., 211, 314, 363, 469*n*, 478*n*
A priori information, 401–6
ARCH process, 236
ARIMA (0,1,1), 533–34, 534*n*
Arrow, K. J., 327*n*, 328
Asymptotic
  distributions, 117–20, 262–63
  efficient, 455
  properties of estimators, 122–23
  standard errors, 276
  unbiasedness, 122–23, 262–63
  variance, 122–23
Attfield, C. L. F., 381*n*, 497, 498
Auld, D. A. L., 236*n*
Autocorrelated disturbances, 211, 216–26
  estimation with, 224–25
  fourth-order, 221
  tests for, 218–23
Autocorrelation coefficient, 216–17, 219
Autocovariance, 215, 216*n*, 291
Autogressive processes, 216, 291, 503
Autoregressive moving average (ARMA) process, 291, 292–93, 294

Balestra, P., 338
Baltagi, B. H., 338, 437*n*
Bank of Canada, 477
Barro, R. J., 497, 500, 503
Barten, A. P., 232
Bartlett, M. S., 213
Basmann, R. L., 452*n*, 453*n*, 466*n*
Bayes' factor, 521
Bayes' theorem, 401–6
Bayesian test, 407
Bays, C. W., 200
Beach, C. D., 227*n*
Bean, C. R., 344, 348
Beckman, M., 327, 339
Belsley, D. A., 167
Berham, J. R., 267
Berndt, E. R., 333*n*, 447
Bernoulli (binomial) distribution, 370
Best linear unbiased estimate (BLUE)
  definition, 140
  in generalized variance model, 546
  in homoscedastic error model, 140
Betancourt, B., 278
Binomial Distribution, 197
Blinder, A., 321
Blomqvist, A. G., 278
Boatwright, B. C., 344, 351, 355, 364
Bollerslev, T., 238
Boot, J. C. G., 413

Bordo, M., 164
Bover, O., 321
Bowley, A. L., 152
Box, G. E. P., 217*n*, 293, 297, 301, 303*n*, 532*n*
Breusch, T. S., 213, 223
Brookings model, 466–68
Brooks, R. B., 219*n*
Brown, R. L., 394
Brumberg, R. E., 314
Brundy, J. M., 439*n*
Burley, H. T., 197*n*, 327–28, 363
Buse, A., 196, 199*n*
Business Cycles, 505

Campbell, J. Y., 322
Canonical correlation, 440*n*
Cargill, T. F., 287
Carlson, J. A., 490
Carroll, R. J., 228*n*
Casuality analysis, 298, 311
Catephores, G., 346
Central limit theorem, 120–21
Characteristic
  equation, 77
  root, 77
  vector, 77
Chenery, H. B., 328
Chi-square distribution (χ^2), 115
Choudhry, E. U., 164, 166
Choudhry, N. K., 472
Chow, G. C., 182, 203–4, 440*n*
Christensen, L. R., 327, 332, 447*n*
Christofides, L. N., 236*n*, 287
Cobb-Douglas production function, 134–35, 174, 327, 330*n*, 331, 454, 475
Cochrane-Orcutt method, 224–25, 278
Co-integrated vector, 536–37
Comanor, W. S., 183–84
Concentration ratio, 183, 214
Conditional Omitted Variable, 171
Confidence interval
  in general linear model, 147
  in simple linear model, 35
Consistency, 263
Constant elasticity of substitution production function, 174–75, 267–68, 327, 331
Consumption function, 5, 312
Consumption pattern of Pakistan, 306
Convergence
  in distribution, 118–20
  in probability, 118–20
Cook, R. D., 523*n*
Cooley, T. F., 400
Copas, J. B., 274
CORC procedure, 256, 306
Correlation coefficient
  multiple (also coefficient of multiple determination), 142–43
  partial, 46–47
  simple, 22, 24
Correlogram, 258
Cost functions
  generalized Leontief, 232, 232*n*
  translog, 327, 333
Cost share equations, 333
Covariance, 95, 416–17
Cox, D. R., 512, 512*n*
Cragg, J., 452
Cramer-Rao inequality, 125
Cramer's rule, 75–76
Cross-section data, 383
Cross validation, 522

Darby, M., 438*n*
Daughety, A. F., 337*n*
Davidson, R., 513, 513*n*, 525, 525*n*
Day, E. E., 134
Deaton, A., 321
Degenerate distribution, 117
Degrees of freedom, 37, 141
DeLeeuw, F., 346, 469*n*, 478*n*
Demand for natural gas, 459–60
Demery, D., 497
Denney, M., 232
Derived demand, 447
Deseasonalizing mechanism, 526–29
Determinant
  cofactor, 68
  definition, 68
  minor, 68
  properties, 69
Detrending mechanism, 529
Development expenditure of India, 161
Dhrymes, P. J., 281, 328
Dickey, D. A., 534
Differencing test, 525
Disequilibrium models, 505–6
Distributed Lags, 308, 346
Disturbances, 8–10
Douglas, P. H., 134–35
Drinkwater, J., 287
Duck, N. W., 497–98
Duesenberry, J. S., 313, 363, 466*n*
Duggal, V. G., 465*n*, 466
Dummy variables, 184–85
Durbin, J., 220, 226, 267, 395
Durbin test with lagged dependent variable, 221
Durbin-Watson test, 211, 218–20
Dvoretzky, A., 450*n*

Eaton, J. R., 344, 351, 355, 364
Eckstein, O., 483
Edgerton, D. L., 437
Efficiency, 122
Eisner, R., 346, 354
Elasticity of
  demand, 14, 321
  substitution, 335, 335*n*, 337
Encompassing principle, 516
Endogenous variables, 411, 413
Engle, R., 236–37, 371*n*, 536, 543
Ergodic, 529
Error Components model, 385
Error correction models, 537
Error correction representation, 536
Error, mean squared, 471
Errors in variables, 265–67

Evans, G. B. A., 372
Evans, J. M., 364
Evans, M. K., 346, 464*n*, 473*n*
Exogenous variables, 3, 411, 413
Expectations, 101–5, 120, 323, 485
Ezekiel, M., 129

F distribution, 115
F test, 510–11
Factor demand equations estimation, 447–48
Fair, R., 394*n*, 507, 507*n*, 508, 509*n*
Fama, E., 360
Farber, S., 432–33
Farebrother, R. W., 220
Farrar, D. E., 166*n*
Federal Reserve Board FMP/MPS, 469, 478
Feige, E., 153
Feldstein, M., 171
Ferguson, L. E., 327
Figlewski, S., 490
Fiscal Policy, 468
Fisher, F. M., 183, 421, 439
Fisher, G. R., 514, 540
Fisher, Irving, 307
Fisher, W. D., 438
Flavin, M. A., 361
Fletcher, L. B., 332
Flexible accelerator, 310–11
Fliesher, B. M., 416*n*, 424*n*
Flow diagram, 473, 504
Ford, J., 333*n*
Forecast
  accuracy, 149–51, 476–77
  inequality coefficient, 149–51
Fox, K. A., 464*n*
Frenkel, J. A., 300–1, 311
Frequency distribution, 90–91
Friedman, B., 490
Friedman, M., 226*n*, 273*n*, 317, 485
Fromm, G., 466*n*, 468
Fuller, W. A., 534
Full information maximum likelihood (FIML), 427, 448, 461
Fuss, M. A., 333*n*, 337

Gamaletsos, T., 320, 363
Garber, S. G., 193–96
Gauss-Markov theorem, 140, 546
Generalized least squares, 229
Ghosh, S. K., 164, 388, 440, 450*n*
Giesel, M. S., 277
Gilbert, R. F., 231*n*
Giles, D. F. A., 221, 221*n*
Gillen, W. J., 233–35
Glauber, R. R., 166*n*
Glesjer, H., 214
Godfrey, L. G., 203, 224*n*, 514, 514*n*, 525, 525*n*
Goldberg, I., 250, 260
Goldberger, A. S., 320, 363, 380, 382, 409, 463, 464*n*, 502*n*
Goldfeld, S. M., 213, 226, 394*n*, 506*n*
Goldsmith, R. W., 319, 363
Goodnight, J., 173
Gorbet, F. W., 477
Gordon, R. J., 399, 408, 500
Gramlich, E. M., 469*n*, 478*n*
Granger, C., 311, 532, 534, 543
Granger, C. W. J., 299
Graybill, F. A., 129
GRE, 377
Greek data, 456–57
Greenwood, M. J., 444
Gregory, P. R., 333*n*, 337, 447*n*
Griffin, J. M., 333*n*, 337, 447*n*
Griliches, Z., 227, 269*n*, 277, 332, 356, 358, 364
Guatemala, 307
Guccione, A., 233
Gulati, G. M., 406

Hadley, G., 86
Haessel, W., 278
Hall, R. E., 322, 363
Halvorsen, R. H., 333*n*, 337
Hannan, E. J., 440*n*
Hart, B. I., 219*n*
Hartley, H. O., 438*n*
Harvey, A. C., 213*n*, 227*n*, 276*n*, 417*n*
Hatanaka, M., 226*n*
Haugh, L. D., 303*n*
Hausman, J., 251*n*, 269*n*, 355, 361, 524*n*
Hausman's test, 524
Hayashi, F., 321, 326
Heckman, J. J., 247, 375–76
Helliwell, J. F., 475*n*, 476*n*, 477
Hendrey, D. F., 265*n*, 347, 364, 554
Heteroscedasticity, 212–15
Hickman, B. G., 278, 351
Hildebrand, G. H., 332
Hildreth, C., 225, 256, 396
Hill, M. A., 250, 260
HILU–procedure, 225, 256
Hirsch, A. A., 472*n*
Hock, I., 389
Hocking, R. R., 519*n*
Hocking's S_p criterion, 517, 519, 541
Hodgson, J. S., 272*n*
Hoel, P. G., 129
Hoerl, A. E., 170*n*
Hoffman, R. F., 332
Holmes, A. B., 272*n*
Homethetic, 232*n*
Homogenous
  equations, 71–72
  production functions, 333*n*
Hong, C., 406*n*
Hood, W. C., 440*n*
Horst, T., 191–93
Houck, J. P., 396
Hsiao, C., 388
Hudson, E. A., 447*n*
Hunter, J., 350*n*
Hunter, K. R., 222
Hussain, A., 388–89
Hwa, E. C., 470
Hynes, A., 399, 408
Hypothesis testing, 143–46

Idempotent matrix, 64, 78

Identification by
  exclusion restrictions, 419–20
  general linear restrictions, 419
  just identified case, 424
  order conditions, 421
  overidentified case, 424
  rank conditions, 420
  restrictions on coefficients, 419–21, 425
  restrictions on variance-covariance matrix, 425
  zero restrictions, 419
Indirect least squares, 427–30, 457
Information matrix, 125, 276
Instrumental variable (IV)
  with errors in variables, 265–66
  estimation, 264
  with lagged dependent variable, 277
Integrated process (or variable), 532
Interval estimation (or confidence intervals), 35, 146

JA Test, 513, 516
J Test, 513, 516
Jaffee, D. M., 394*n*, 507, 507*n*, 508, 509*n*
Jenkins, G. M., 217*n*, 296, 532*n*
Jeong, K., 220
Johnson, N. L., 375
Joreskog, K. G., 382, 382*n*
Jorgenson, D. W., 344, 350, 350*n*, 353–354, 364, 439*n*, 447*n*, 449, 483
Jureen, L., 312
Just identified case, 424. *See also* Identification

K-class estimators, 427, 437*n*
Kadane, J. B., 452*n*
Kadiyala, K. R., 544
Kaldor, N., 169
Kelejian, H., 278, 394*n*, 433*n*, 437, 448*n*
Kendall, M. G., 129
Kenkel, J. L., 222*n*
Kennard, R. W., 170*n*
Kibbutz, 389–91, 408
Kinal, T., 198, 379*n*, 519*n*
King, M. A., 326
King, M. L., 219*n*, 221, 221*n*
Klein, L. R., 226, 439, 464, 464*n*, 466*n*, 468, 473*n*, 483
Klein-Goldberger model, 439, 463–64, 464*n*
Klein interwar model, 411, 455, 462
Kloek, T., 438
Kmenta, J., 231*n*
Kniesner, N. J., 400*n*
Koopmans, T. C., 440*n*, 448
Kormendi, R. C., 498
Kotowitz, Y., 472
Kotz, S., 375
Koyck, L. M., 268, 270–71, 310
Kronecker product, 68
Kuh, E., 466*n*
Kuznets, S., 363

Laffont, J., 449
Lagged dependent variables, 221, 272–74
Lagged variables
  adaptive expectation, 273–78
  institutional, 270
  mean lags, 270
  median lags, 271
  partial adjustment, 272, 274–78
  psychological, 269
  technical, 269
Lag operator, 289
Lagrangean multiplier test, 366, 368–70, 406
Lag structure, 3
Lahiri, K., 198, 379*n*, 519*n*
LaMotte, L. R., 401
Lancaster, T., 212
Latane, H. H., 153
Latent variables, 379–80
Lau, L. J., 447*n*
Laumas, P. S., 226, 401
Leamer, E. E., 406, 521*n*, 523*n*
Least squares
  asymptotic theory, 261–64
  estimation method, 18, 137–39, 275–76
  Gauss-Markov theorem, 140, 546
  generalized (GLS), 229, 277
  ordinary (OLS), 18, 137–39
  simple linear regression, 18–22
  three-stage, 427, 441–46, 456
  two-stage, 427, 430–32, 456
  under linear constraints, 179–81
  with lagged dependent variable among regressors, 221–22, 272–78
Lee, Y., 332
Leiderman, L., 497
Leipnik, R. B., 448
Levine, P. B., 362
Likelihood function, 106, 276
Likelihood ratio test, 366, 406
Lilien, D. M., 207
Limited information maximum likelihood (LIML), 427, 440*n*, 464
Limiting distribution, 120, 535. *See also* Convergence in distribution
Linear expenditure system, 319–20, 363
Linearity, transformations producing, 49–51, 262
Linear regression model
  Bayesian estimation, 401–6
  multiple, 43–48, 135–49, 371
  simple, 14–43
Linear restrictions, estimation subject to test of, 179–81
Liquidity preference function, 176
Liquidity trap, 176
LISREL, 382*n*
Liu, T. C., 470–71
Liviatan, N., 278*n*
Logistic curve, 4, 239*n*
Logit analysis, 239–42, 243–44
Log linear form, 51
Log normal distribution, 177–79
Lovell, C. A. K., 332
Lucas, R. E. Jr., 483, 497, 500

MacAvoy, P. W., 483
MacKinnon, J. G., 227*n*, 513, 513*n*, 525, 525*n*
Maddala, G. S., 222*n*, 251, 252*n*, 260, 388, 394*n*, 424*n*
Makin, J. H., 293*n*
Malinvaud, E., 275*n*

Mallows, C. L., 518, 518*n*
Mallows' C_p criterion, 517–19, 540
Mann, H. B., 275
Manski, C., 239*n*
Mariger, R. P., 321, 325
Marquardt, D. W., 438*n*
Marriott, F. H. C., 274*n*
Martens, A. P., 321
Matrix
  adjoint, 72
  characteristic equations, 77
  characteristic roots (latent roots), 77–79
  characteristic vectors, 77
  determinant of, 68
  diagonal, 71, 454
  diagonalization, 75
  differentiation, 81–83
  eigen values and eigen vectors, 76
  idempotent, 64, 78
  inversion (inverse), 72
  Kronecker product, 68
  multiplication, 62–63
  nonsingular, 69
  orthogonal, 74–75
  partitioned, 65, 67
  positive and semi-positive definite, 79–81
  rank, 70–71
  scalar, 61
  symmetric, 64
  trace, 64
  transposition, 63
  unit (identity), 63
Maximum Likelihood (ML)
  with autocorrelated disturbances, 227–28, 553–54
  equivalence to OLS, 127
  estimator, 123–24, 224, 276, 276*n*
  full information (FIML), 427, 448
  limited information (LIML), 427, 440*n*
  properties of, 124–25
  under errors in variables, 265–67
  variance of stochastic disturbance term, 128–29
Maximum score estimation, 239*n*
Mayes, D. G., 43
McAleer, M., 512*n*, 513, 540
MCAT, 377
McAvinchey, I. D., 227*n*
McCallum, B. T., 379*n*, 434, 434*n*
McCarthy, M. D., 465*n*
McCurdy, T. E., 321
McElroy, M. B., 253*n*, 339
McFadden, D., 250*n*
McNown, R. F., 222
McWhorter, A., 401
Mean squared error, 122, 471
MeGuire, P. G., 498
Mehta, F., 222*n*
Mehta, J. S., 406*n*
Mennes, L. B. M., 438
Meyer, R. A., 287
Mikhail, W. M., 452*n*
Miles, M., 164
Mincer, J., 357*n*
Minhas, B. S., 328
Minimum chi-square, 242
Minimum variance bound (MVB), 124
Mishkin, F., 322–23, 501
Mitchell, B. M., 228*n*
Mitchell, O. S., 362
Mizon, G. E., 347, 364, 516
Model
  income determination, 2
  reduced form, 3, 415–16, 428
  selection, 505, 510
  structural form, 415
Modigliani, F., 49, 211, 314, 363, 469*n*, 478*n*
Moments, 96–97
Monte Carlo experiments, 222, 227
Mood, A. M., 129
Morishima, M., 464*n*
Moving average (MA) processes, 217, 275
Muelbauer, J., 321
Multicollinearity
  definition, 164
  detection, 166
  effects of, 165–66
  remedies, 168–70
Multinomial logit, 244–45, 250, 260
Multinomial probits, 245–46
Multiple indicator, multiple cause (MIMIC) model, 381–82
Multipliers
  equilibrium, 414, 414*n*
  impact, 414
Mundell, R. A., 170
Mundlak, Y., 388

Nadiri, I., 350*n*, 354
Nagar, A. L., 452*n*
National logitudinal survey (NLS), 253*n*
Nelson, F. D., 337*n*, 394*n*
Nerlove, M., 220, 268, 327, 388
Nested models, 505, 510
Nichols, D. A., 236*n*
Nold, F. C., 250, 260
Non-nested models, 505, 512
Normal distribution
  bivariate, 112–13
  multivariate, 111–12
  univariate, 109–11
Normal equations
  in a general model, 137–38
  in a three-variable model, 44
  in a two-variable model, 19

Ohtani, K., 379*n*, 406*n*
Operational mean square error criterion, 511–12
Ordinary least squares (OLS), 18, 43, 137
Orthogonality, 74–75
Overidentified equations, 424

Pagan, A. R., 213, 381*n*, 502
Park, R. E., 228*n*
Park, S. B., 406*n*
Parke, W. R., 449
Partial adjustment, 272
Partial correlation coefficient, 46
Pearce, D. K., 490
Permanent income hypothesis, 313

Persons, W. M., 134*n*
Pesando, J. E., 490
Pesaran, M. H., 406*n*, 514, 514*n*
Phillips, G. D. A., 213*n*, 417*n*
Phillips, P. C. B., 450*n*, 534, 543
Pierce, D. A., 297, 303*n*, 349*n*
Pindyck, R. S., 327, 333, 337, 364, 483
Plim, 262. *See also* Probability limit
Plosser, C. I., 525, 525*n*
Poirier, D. J., 193–96
Polachek, S. W., 440–41
Policy evaluation, 483–85
Pollak, R. A., 327, 364
Pope, J. A., 274*n*
Posterior Odds Criterion, 520, 522
Powell, M. J. D., 554
Prais, S. J., 544
Predicted errors (residuals), 522–23
Prediction
  in general linear models, 147–49
  in two variable models, 39–43
Prescott, E. C., 400
Press, S. J., 219*n*
Preston, R. S., 466
Pre-whitening mechanism, 296, 311
Principal components, 437, 549–53
Probability distribution
  asymptotic, 117–20
  bivariate, 91, 98–99
  conditional, 92, 114
  continuous, 98
  cumulative, 97
  density function of, 98
  discrete, 97–98
  expectations logic, 101–5
  marginal, 113
  multivariate, 101–3, 111
  random variable (vector), 98–99, 101–2
  univariate, 97
Probability limit (plim), 118–19
Probit analysis, 242–44, 253
Proxy variables, 377, 408
Prucha, I. R., 448*n*
Public expenditures of Pakistan, 161

Quadratic form, in normally distributed variables, 115–17
Qualtitative dependent variable, 238–42
Quandt, R. E., 213, 394, 506, 506*n*, 509*n*
Quantity theory of money, 537

Raj, B., 400*n*
Random coefficient models, 394–99
Random matrix, 102, 105
Random sampling, 106–7
Random variables
  linearly independent, 106
  sequence of, 119*n*
Random vectors, sequence of, 123
Random walk with drift, 531
Rao, A. S., 222*n*
Rao, C. R., 369. *See also* Cramer-Rao inequality
Rao, P., 227
Rappoport, P. N., 400*n*
Rasche, R. H., 469*n*, 478*n*
Rational expectation hypothesis, 485–86, 488, 502–4
Rausser, G. C., 401
Ravencraft, D. J., 214
Ray-Chaudhuri, D. K., 440*n*
Reaction coefficient, 310
Recursive residuals, 424
Recursive systems, 424, 456. *See also* Simultaneous equation systems
Reduced form equations
  estimation of, 428
  identification of, 415–16, 419–20
  stochastic specification of, 416–17
Reinhardt, H., 327
Replicated observations, 240
Restricted Least squares, 179–81
Revankar, N. S., 327, 332
Rhodes, G. H., 416*n*, 424*n*
Rhomberg, R., 416*n*
Richard, J. F., 516*n*
Richardson, D. H., 452*n*
Riddell, W. C., 198, 393, 408
Ridge regression, 170
Ringstad, V., 327, 332
Robins, P. K., 382
Robinson, P. M., 450*n*
Rosen, S., 355
Rossi, P., 406*n*
Rothenberg, T. J., 372
Rowley, J. C. R., 210, 235–36
Roy, E. J., 253, 260
Rubin, H., 440*n*, 448
Rubinfeld, D. L., 248, 260
Ruppert, D., 228*n*
Rush, M., 497

Sadan, E., 389, 408
Saito, M., 464*n*
Sample selectivity bias, 373–74, 407
Sargan, J. D., 222*n*, 225*n*, 450*n*, 452*n*
Sargent, T., 362
SAT, 377
Sato, K., 327, 333, 339
Saunders, R. S., 434
Savin, N. E., 220, 372, 563–66
Savings ratios, 363
Sawa, T., 452*n*
Sawyer, J. A., 472
Scheffe, H., 129
Schink, G. R., 468
Schmidt, P., 171, 281*n*
Schultz, H., 151–52
Schwert, G. W., 525, 525*n*
Seasonal Swing, 526
Seemingly unrelated regression equations (SURE), 230, 260
Sewell, W. P., 119, 263*n*
Shapiro, H. T., 469*n*, 477, 478*n*
SHAZAM program, 228
Shephard's lemma, 334, 334*n*, 338
Sherman, R., 183
Shiba, T., 406*n*
Sickles, R. C., 327, 364
Siebert, C. B., 350*n*

Significance tests
  in a general linear model, 143–46
  in a two-variable linear model, 26–39
Sims, C., 299, 311, 536
Simultaneous equation systems
  examples of, 410–15
  full-information maximum likelihood (FIML), 427, 448
  identification problem, 418–27
  inconsistency of OLS, 410–11, 413
  indirect least squares (ILS), 427–30
  instrumental variable (IV) estimation, 427
  least variance ratio, 440*n*
  limited-information maximum likelihood (LIML), 427, 440*n*, 464
  recursive system, 424
  three-stage least squares (3SLS) estimation, 427, 430–32
  two-stage least squares
    (2SLS) estimation, 427, 430–43
    2SLSPC, 438*n*
  vector autoregressive residuals, 553–54
Siow, A., 321
'Six and Five Rule', 160
Smith, V. K., 452*n*
Solow, R. M., 328
Sorbom, D., 382*n*
Sparks, G. R., 477
Specification error, 11, 196–99
Spencer, D. E., 226
Spherical normal variables, 111
Spline functions, 193–96
Spurious regression, 505, 532
Stationary, 529
Stationary time series, 531
Stephenson, D. R., 477
Stephenson, J. A., 344, 350*n*, 353–54
Stewart, I. A., 360–477
Stochastic trend, 530
Stock, J. H., 536, 536*n*
Stone, R., 312
Structural change, tests of, 181–83
Structural equations, 415
Structural neutrality hypothesis, 504
Stuart, A., 129
Studentized errors (residuals), 522–23, 540
Student's *t* distribution, 33, 115
Sum of squares
  decomposition of
    in general linear models, 141
    in three-variable models, 45–46
    in two-variable models, 22–24
  error (residual), 23–24
  regression, 23–24
  total, 33
Swamy, P. A. V. B., 396–400, 406*n*
Swidinsky, R., 236*n*, 288
Switching regressions, 392. *See also* Variable-parameter models
Systems of demand equations, 319–20

Taubman, P., 468
Technical change, 339–44
Tests of equilibrium, 509
Theil, H., 149*n*, 413, 444
Theil and Nagar, modification of the D-W test, 220
Theil's R^2 criterion, 517, 540
Thomas, W., 134
Three-stage least squares, 427, 441–44
Time series and cross section methods, 383
Time series methods, 289
  casualty tests, 298–303
  double pre-whitening, 296, 300–2
  pre-whitening, 296
  stationarity, 290
  transfer function, 294
Tintner, G., 421
Tobin, J., 252, 325
Tobit analysis, 246–47, 252–53, 547
Tollison, R., 183
Toro-vizcarrondo, C., 173
Transcendental logarithmic (translog) functions, 333, 337, 447*n*
Tremayne, A. R., 554
Tropp, Z., 389, 408
Trost, R., 251, 260
Tsurumi, H., 406*n*, 438*n*
Turnovsky, S. J., 489
Two-stage least squares (2SLS) equivalent to instrumental variable (IV) estimator, 436–37
Two-step estimator, 247, 503
Tybout, J. R., 450

Ullah, A., 400*n*
Unit root models, 505, 526, 532
Unobservable variables, 377
Unreplicated observations, 240
Uzawa, H., 335

Variable elasticity of substitution (VES), 332
Variable-parameter models, 392
Vector, autoregressive residuals, 449*n*, 553–54
Vectors
  linear dependence and independence, 70–71
  orthogonal, 74–75
Volker, P., 514, 540
von Neumann ratio, 218*n*

Wachtel, P., 490
Wadycki, W. J., 438
Wagner's law, 162
Wald, A., 266–67, 275
Wald test, 366, 406
Wales, T. J., 325*n*, 327, 362, 377*n*
Wallace, T. D., 173, 388–89
Wallis, K. J., 220–21
Walsh, J., 554
Wasserfallen, W., 534
Watson, M. W., 536, 536*n*
Waud, R. N., 281*n*
Waverman, L., 333*n*, 337
Weisberg, S., 523*n*
Weiss, L., 154
West, R. W., 382
Wharton group of models, 464
White, H., 220, 525, 525*n*, 563–66
White, J. S., 274

White, K. J., 228
Wickens, M., 379*n*
Wilks, S. S., 119*n*, 120*n*
Wilson, T. A., 183
Wilton, D. A., 210, 235–36, 287
Winder, J. A. L., 472
Winegarden, C., 459
Winston, C. B., 227, 544
Wise, D., 361*n*
Wold, H., 312
Women, labor force participation rate of, 458
Wood, D. O., 333*n*, 447
Woodland, A. D., 325*n*, 362, 377*n*
Woolridge, J. M., 238
Wymer, C. R., 450*n*

Zellner, A., 230, 277, 327, 380, 405*n*, 406, 406*n*, 409, 444, 444*n*, 502*n*
Zero restrictions, 419